Handbook of
INDUSTRIAL, WORK
AND ORGANIZATIONAL
PSYCHOLOGY

Volume 2
Organizational Psychology

Handbook of
INDUSTRIAL, WORK AND ORGANIZATIONAL PSYCHOLOGY

Volume 2
Organizational Psychology

Edited by

NEIL ANDERSON
DENIZ S. ONES
HANDAN KEPIR SINANGIL
CHOCKALINGAM VISWESVARAN

SAGE Publications
London • Thousand Oaks • New Delhi

First published 2001

Apart from any fair dealing for the purposes of research or private study, or criticism or review, as permitted under the Copyright, Designs and Patents Act 1988, this publication may be reproduced, stored or transmitted in any form, or by any means, only with the prior permission in writing of the publishers, or in the case of reprographic reproduction, in accordance with the terms of licences issued by the Copyright Licensing Agency. Inquiries concerning reproduction outside those terms should be sent to the publishers.

 SAGE Publications Ltd
6 Bonhill Street
London EC2A 4PU

SAGE Publications Inc
2455 Teller Road
Thousand Oaks, California 91320

SAGE Publications India Pvt Ltd
32, M-Block Market
Greater Kailash – I
New Delhi 110 048

British Library Cataloguing in Publication data

A catalogue record for this book is available from the British Library

ISBN Volume 1 0 7619 6488 6
Volume 2 0 7619 6489 4

Library of Congress Control number available

Typeset by SIVA Math Setters, Chennai, India
Printed in Great Britain by The Cromwell Press Ltd., Trowbridge, Wiltshire

To Mavis Anderson, my mother, and George Anderson (deceased), my father, for teaching me the meaning of conscientiousness in life (NA)

To my parents Drs Saime Ülker Öneş and Somer Öneş for continuing to inspire me with their talent and achievements (DSO)

To my dear parents Sevinç and Mustafa Kepir for their everlasting love and support (HKS)

To Sankaravadivoo (deceased), my mother, and S. P. Chockalingam, my father, for their confidence in me and for all their encouragement (CV)

Contents of Volume 2

Contents of Volume 1

Biographic Profiles

Editors

Neil Anderson is Professor of Work Psychology at Goldsmiths College, University of London. He is Founding Editor of the *International Journal of Selection and Assessment*. His research interests include recruitment and selection, organizational and work group socialization, innovation at work, and organizational climate. He has co-authored and edited a number of books including the *International Handbook of Selection and Assessment*, and his work has appeared in several scholarly journals including *Journal of Applied Psychology*, *Human Relations*, *Journal of Organizational Behavior*, *Journal of Occupational and Organizational Psychology*, and the *International Journal of Selection and Assessment*. Neil has on-going research projects, either collaboratively or alone, into interviewer and applicant decision-making in assessment interviews, work group socialization of graduates, the structure and psychometric properties of popular 'Big Five' measures of personality, telephone-based interviewing procedures, and the practitioner–researcher divide in work and organizational psychology. Committed to an international perspective in work psychology, Neil has been Visiting Professor to the University of Minnesota (USA) and the Free University of Amsterdam (The Netherlands). Neil is a fellow of the British Psychological Society and the Society for Industrial and Organizational Psychology.

Deniz S. Ones is an international expert in personality and integrity testing for personnel selection and personality assessment for workplace applications. She received her PhD from the University of Iowa in 1993 and was previously a faculty member of the University of Houston. Currently, she is the holder of the Hellervik Endowed Professorship in Industrial and Organizational Psychology at the Department of Psychology of the University of Minnesota. Dr Ones is the author of over 60 articles and over 200 international/national conference papers and published abstracts on topics ranging from the reliability of performance ratings to influences of social desirability on personality test validity to discipline problems at work. Her research has appeared in the *Annual Review of Psychology, Journal of Applied Psychology*, *Personnel Psychology*, and *Psychological Bulletin*, among others. In 1994, Dr Ones received the Society of Industrial and Organizational Psychology's (Division 14 of the American Psychological Association) S. Rains Wallace Best Dissertation Award. In 1998, she received the Ernest J. McCormick Early Career Contributions Award from the Society for Industrial Organizational Psychology (Division 14 of the American Psychological Association), making her one of two people to ever receive both awards. Her current research and teaching interests include personality as it relates to job performance, integrity testing, and the application of meta-analytic techniques in the social sciences. Dr Ones is a Fellow of the American Psychological Association (Divisions 5 and 14) and the Society for Industrial and Organizational Psychology and serves on the editorial boards of *Personnel Psychology*, *International Journal of Selection and Assessment*, and *European Journal of Work and Organizational Psychology*. Recently, she has edited special issues for two prestigious journals (*Human Performance* on ability testing, and *International Journal of Selection Assessment* on counterproductive work behaviors).

Handan Kepir Sinangil is Professor of Work and Organizational Psychology at Marmara University, Organizational Behaviour Graduate Program, and Adjunct Professor at Bogazici University. She is the General Secretary of European Association of Work and Organizational Psychology (EAWOP) and a member of the American Psychological Association (APA), the Society for Industrial and Organizational Psychology (SIOP, APA Division 14), the International Association of Applied Psychology (IAAP), and the International Association of Cross-Cultural Psychology (IACCP). Dr Sinangil's international and national publications exceed 70 as book chapters and conference papers. She is also associate editor of *International Journal of Selection and Assessment* (*IJSA*). Her ongoing research projects, either with international collaboration or alone include expatriate management, organizational culture and change, performance appraisal and selection. Additionally, her current teaching interests include assessment, training and development, and psychology of management.

Chockalingam (Vish) Viswesvaran is an international expert in performance measurement, modeling performance determinants, personality and integrity testing, personnel selection and meta-analysis. He received his PhD from the University of Iowa in 1993. Currently, he is an Associate Professor at the Department of Psychology of the Florida International University. Dr Viswesvaran is the author of over 70 articles and over 200 international/national conference papers and published abstracts. His research has appeared in the *Journal of Applied Psychology*, *Personnel Psychology*, *Journal of Vocational Behavior* and *Educational and Psychological Measurement*, among others. In 1995, Viswesvaran received the Society of Industrial and Organizational Psychology's (Division 14 of the American Psychological Association) S. Rains Wallace Best Dissertation Award. In 1998, he received the Ernest J. McCormick Early Career Contributions Award from the Society for Industrial Organizational Psychology (Division 14 of the American Psychological Association), making him one of two people to ever receive both awards. His current research and teaching interests include job performance assessment, personality as it relates to job performance, integrity testing, and the application of meta-analytic techniques in the social sciences. Viswesvaran is a Fellow of the Society for Industrial and Organizational Psychology and serves on the editorial boards of *Personnel Psychology* and *Educational and Psychological Measurement*. Recently, Viswesvaran has edited a special issue for *Human Performance* on ability testing.

Authors

John Arnold is Professor of Organizational Behaviour at The Business School, Loughborough University, United Kingdom. He was previously a senior lecturer at the same institution; a lecturer and then senior lecturer at Manchester School of Management, UMIST, United Kingdom; and a Visiting Fellow at the University of New South Wales, Australia. He has published widely in the field of careers and career management, including many journal articles and the book *Managing Careers into the 21st Century* (1997, Paul Chapman/Sage). He is lead author of the successful textbook *Work Psychology*, now in its third edition (1998, FT/Pitman Publishing). He has conducted many funded research projects, including most recently graduates' psychological contracts in small companies and the career choices of potential nurses and professionals allied to medicine. He is a Chartered Psychologist registered with the British Psychological Society.

Neal Ashkanasy is a Professor of Management in the Graduate School of Management, The University of Queensland, Brisbane, Australia. He has a PhD in Psychology from the same university, and has research interests in emotions, organizational culture, leadership, and ethics. He is on the editorial boards of the *Academy of Management Journal* and the *Journal of Management*, and has published in journals such as *Organizational Behavior and Human Decision Processes*, the *Journal of Personality and Social Psychology*, and *Accounting, Organizations and Society*. He is also Program Chair of the Academy of Management Managerial and Organizational Cognitions Division. Neal is co-editor of the *Handbook of Organizational Culture and Climate* (Sage, 2000) and *Emotions in the Workplace* (Quorum, 2000). He is the founder and administrator of two international email discussion groups: 'Orgcult' (The Organizational Culture Caucus) and 'Emonet' (The Network for Emotions in Organizations).

Francesco Avallone (1943) is Professor of Work Psychology at 'La Sapienza' University of Rome. Fullbright scholar at Gonzaga University of Spokane, he attended the postgraduate School of Psychology at the University of Rome. He wrote about 100 printed works. He is editor of *Quaderni di Psicologia del Lavoro*, a series reviewing the growing research, theory, and practice in work and organizational psychology in Italy and in Europe. His current research topics concern complex thinking, organizational change, and psychological training. For 25 years, he has been also a practitioner.

Bob Cardy is a Professor of Management at Arizona State University. He received his doctorate from Virginia Tech in 1982 and has teaching and research interests in human resource management, particularly in the areas of performance appraisal and quality. His performance appraisal research has focused on cognitive processing issues and on the impact of affect on the appraisal process. His recent work on quality management focuses on merging human resource management practices with the contemporary organizational environment. He has co-edited books, authored a research-oriented book on performance appraisal, and authored numerous articles in journals, including *Journal of Applied Psychology*, *Organizational Behavior and*

Human Decision Processes, *Journal of Management*, *Management Communication Quarterly*, and *HR Magazine*. He is the co-author of a text on human resource management and is cofounder and editor of the *Journal of Quality Management*.

David Chan is an Associate Professor at the National University of Singapore and Scientific Advisor to the Centre for Testing and Assessment, Republic of Singapore. He received his PhD from Michigan State University. David's research interests include individual adaptation to changes, testing and measurement issues, and application of these areas to personnel selection and newcomer socialization. He is currently on the editorial boards of *Human Performance and Journal of Organizational Behavior*. David was the 1999 recipient of the William A. Owens Scholarly Achievement Award and the 1998 recipient of the Edwin E. Ghiselli Award for Research Design from the Society for Industrial and Organizational Psychology.

Amy Colbert is a doctoral student in the Department of Management and Organizations at the University of Iowa. She received an MS degree in decision sciences from Saint Louis University. Her research interests include personality, job attitudes, leadership, and group processes.

Cary L. Cooper, PhD, is the BUPA Professor of Organizational Psychology and Health in the Manchester School of Management, and Pro-Vice-Chancellor (External Activities) of the University of Manchester Institute of Science and Technology (UMIST). He is the author of over 80 books and has written over 300 scholarly articles for scientific journals, and is a frequent contributor to national newspapers, TV and radio. His current research interests are in the areas of occupational stress, women at work, and industrial and organizational psychology.

Deanne N. Den Hartog is Van der Leeuw Professor of Organizational Psychology at the Faculty of Economics of the Erasmus University in Rotterdam, the Netherlands. She received her PhD from the Free University in Amsterdam. Her research and writing has focused on (inspirational) leadership, organizational and national culture, commitment and trust, psychological contracts, HRM, team effectiveness and stress. Besides her Dutch and international journal articles, she is author of a Dutch book on leadership and coauthor of a Dutch book on human resource management. She is associate editor of *Leadership Quarterly* and *Gedrag and Organisatie*.

John J. Donovan is an Assistant Professor in Industrial/Organizational Psychology at the Department of Psychology, Virginia Polytechnic Institute and State University. He received his PhD in industrial/organizational psychology from the University at Albany, State University of New York. His current research focuses on the processes underlying dynamic self-regulation, including goal establishment, goal revision, and factors that influence reactions to goal–performance feedback.

Charles H. Fay is Professor of Human Resource Management and Director of Credit Programs in HRM in the School of Management and Labor Relations at

Rutgers University. His books include *Compensation Theory and Practice, The Compensation Sourcebook, The Performance Imperative, Rewarding Government Employees*, and the forthcoming *Executive Handbook on Compensation*. He was a Presidential appointee to the Federal Salary Commission. He served as Chair of the research committee of the ACA. He has testified before a Pay Equity Tribunal in Ontario as an expert witness in the area of job evaluation and pay-setting practices, and in other compensation-related cases.

Stephen Gilliland is an Associate Professor and the FINOVA Fellow of Management and Policy at the University of Arizona. He received his PhD from Michigan State University (1992) and was previously on faculty at Louisiana State University. Stephen's research interests include organizational justice, individual decision making, and the application of these areas to human resource policies and procedures. He is currently on the editorial boards of the *Journal of Applied Psychology* and *Personnel Psychology*, and previously served on the board of the *Academy of Management Journal*. Stephen was the 1997 recipient of the Ernest J. McCormick Award for Early Career Contributions from the Society for Industrial and Organizational Psychology.

Peter M. Hart, PhD, is the Director of Insight SRC Pty Ltd, an Australian-based organizational research firm, and is an Honorary Senior Fellow in the School of Behavioural Science at the University of Melbourne. He has played a key role in developing an organizational health framework and the associated measurement tools that are being used extensively within Australian organizations, and has published his work in books and scientific journals. His current research interests are in the areas of organizational health, stability, and change in work-related attitudes, and the use of employee opinion surveys.

Daniel Heller is a doctoral candidate in the Department of Management and Organizations at the Henry B. Tippie College of Business, University of Iowa. He received his Masters from the Hebrew University in Jerusalem. His research interests include individual differences, attitudes, and teams and leadership processes.

Rob Heneman is a Professor of Management and Human Resources and Director of graduate programs in labor and human resources in the Max M. Fisher College of Business at the Ohio State University. Rob has a PhD in labor and industrial relations from Michigan State University, an MA in labor and industrial relations from the University of Illinois at Urbana-Champaign, and a BA in economics and psychology from Lake Forest College. Prior to joining the Ohio State University, Rob worked as a human resource specialist for Pacific Gas and Electric Company. Rob's primary areas of research, teaching, and consulting are in performance management, compensation, staffing, and work design. He has over 50 publications. He has received over $1 million in funds for his research from the Work in America Institute, AT&T Foundation, Ford Motor Company, American Compensation Association, State of Ohio, Consortium for Alternative Rewards Strategies Research, Hay Group, and the Kauffman Center for Entrepreneurial Leadership. He is the founder and editor of the *International Journal of Human Resource*

Management Education. He is on the editorial boards of *Human Resource Management Journal*, *Human Resource Management Review*, *Human Resource Planning*, *Compensation and Benefits Review*, and *SAM Advanced Management Journal*. He has been awarded the Outstanding Teacher Award in the Masters in Labor and Human Resources Program numerous times by the students at Ohio State University. He has written five books including, *Merit Pay: Linking Pay Increases to Performance Ratings, Staffing Organizations* (3rd ed.), and *Business-Driven Compensation Policies: Integrating Compensation Systems With Corporate Business Strategies.* Currently, he is editing two new books: *Human Resource Management in Virtual Organizations* and *Strategic Issues in Compensation System Design, Implementation, and Evaluation.* He is also writing two new books: *Human Resource Strategies for High Growth Entrepreneurial Firms* and *Pay-for-Performance.* He has consulted with over 60 public and private sector organizations including IBM, Owens-Corning, BancOne, Time Warner, American Electric Power, Whirlpool, Quantum, AFL-CIO, Nationwide Insurance, The Limited, Borden, ABB, POSCO, US Government Office of Personnel Management, and the states of Ohio and Michigan. Rob is past Division Chair, Program Chair, and Executive Committee member for the Human Resources Division of the Academy of Management. He is also a member of the certification program faculty of the American Compensation Association (ACA) and has served on the research, education, and academic partnership network advisory boards of the ACA. He has made over 50 presentations to universities, professional associations, and civic organizations. He has worked with business organizations and universities in North America, Europe, Russia, Asia, and Africa. His work has been reported in the *Wall Street Journal*, *USA Today*, *Money Magazine*, *ABCNEWS.COM*, and he is listed in *Who's Who in the World*, *Who's Who in America*, *Who's Who in American Education*, and *Outstanding People in the 20th Century*.

Beryl Hesketh is Dean of the Faculty of Science and Professor at the University of Sydney, having previously taught organizational psychology at Macquarie University and the University of New South Wales. She has published widely internationally in many areas of organizational psychology, including selection, applied decision making, training, and career development. Her current research involves the development of adaptive expertise in fire fighters, and factors that affect speed and time perception in driving behavior. She received the Elton Mayo Award in 1997 in recognition of her significant contribution to industrial/organizational psychology in Australia and internationally, through her research and professional activities.

Scott Highhouse received his PhD in 1992 from the University of Missouri at Saint Louis. He is Associate Professor and Director of the Industrial-Organizational Area in the Department of Psychology, Bowling Green State University. He has conducted numerous studies on decision making in employment contexts. His research interests include organizational attraction and job choice, organizational staffing, management risk taking, influence and persuasion, and the history of applied psychology. Currently, he is associate editor of *Organizational Behavior and Human Decision Processes.*

Gerard P. Hodgkinson, BA (CNAA), MSc (Hull), PhD (Sheffield), CPsychol, AFBPsS, FRSA is Professor of Organizational Behaviour and Strategic Management at Leeds University Business School, The University of Leeds, UK. He has held previous appointments at the Universities of Manchester, Sheffield, Leeds and Exeter, and has worked as a psychologist in the Home Office Prison Department. His research interests focus on the psychology of strategic management and the evaluation of assessment and selection practices in organizations. His work has appeared in a wide range of scholarly journals including *Strategic Management Journal, Human Relations, International Journal of Selection and Assessment, Journal of Occupational and Organizational Psychology, and Journal of Management Studies*. Professor Hodgkinson is editor of the *British Journal of Management* and on the editorial board (a consulting editor) of the *Journal of Occupational and Organizational Psychology*. A practising chartered occupational psychologist, he has carried out numerous advisory and consultancy assignments across a range of organizations within the public and private sectors. His most recent consultancy work has involved designing and facilitating strategy process workshops for middle and senior managers in private sector organizations.

Remus Ilies is a PhD student in the Department of Management and Organizations at the University of Iowa. He received his MBA from Iowa State University. His research interests include personality, mood, motivation, job attitudes, and dynamic processes in industrial psychology.

Camille Jackson earned her Masters of Management at the University of Queensland in 2000, where she was a Tutorial Fellow and an associate lecturer in the Graduate School of Management. She was recently appointed lecturer at the University of Southern Queensland, Toowoomba, Australia. Camille worked as Administrative and Research Assistant with Professor Ashkanasy on the *Handbook of Organizational Culture and Climate* (Sage, 2000). Her principal research interests are in organisational change and leadership.

Susan E. Jackson, PhD, is a Professor of Human Resource Management in the School of Management and Labor Relations at Rutgers University, where she also serves as Graduate Director for the Doctoral Program in Industrial Relations and Human Resources. Her primary research interests include managing team effectiveness, workforce diversity, and the design of human resource management systems to support business imperatives. She has authored or co-authored over 100 articles on these and related topics. In addition, she has published several books, including *Managing Human Resources: A Partnership Perspective* (with Randall Schuler), *Management* (with Don Hellriegel and John Slocum) and *Diversity in the Workplace: Human Resource Initiatives*, a volume in the SIOP Practice Series. She is an active member of the Society for Industrial and Organizational Psychology, the Academy of Management and the International Association of Applied Psychology.

Gary Johns is a Professor of Management at Concordia University in Montreal. His research interests include absenteeism, job design, constraints on behavior, self-serving behavior, and methodology. He has published in *Journal of Applied Psychology, Academy of Management Journal, Academy of Management Review,*

Organizational Behavior and Human Decision Processes, Personnel Psychology, Journal of Management, Research in Organizational Behavior, Journal of Organizational Behavior, and *International Review of Industrial and Organizational Psychology,* and is a co-author of *Organizational Behavior: Understanding and Managing Life at Work* (5th ed., Addison-Wesley). He was the recipient of the Academy of Management OB Division's New Concept Award and SIOP's Edwin E. Ghiselli Research Design Award, and recently, Chair of the Canadian Society for Industrial and Organizational Psychology. He has served on the editorial boards of *Academy of Management Journal, Journal of Management, Occupational and Organizational Psychology, Canadian Journal of Administrative Sciences,* and *Personnel Psychology.* He is a consulting editor for *Journal of Organizational Behavior.*

Aparna Joshi is a doctoral candidate at the School of Management and Labor Relations, Rutgers University. Her dissertation research focuses on the process and performance outcomes of team diversity in the US workplace. She also conducts research in the area of international human resource management. In particular, she studies the individual and organizational factors associated with expatriate adjustment and the functioning of multicultural, geographically dispersed teams. Her work on these and related topics has appeared in the *Journal of Applied Psychology, the International Journal of Human Resource Management,* the *Indian Journal of Industrial Relations,* the *Indian Journal of Gender Studies.*

Timothy A. Judge is the Stanley M. Howe Professor in Leadership, Department of Management and Organizations, Henry B. Tippie College of Business, University of Iowa. Tim holds a Bachelor of Business Administration degree from the University of Iowa, and master's and doctoral degrees from the University of Illinois. Before joining the University of Iowa, Tim was an assistant and associate professor in the School of Industrial and Labor Relations, Cornell University. Tim's research interests are in the areas of personality and individual differences, leadership and influence behaviors, internal and external staffing, and job attitudes.

John Kammeyer-Mueller is a doctoral student in Human Resources and Industrial Relations at the University of Minnesota, where he teaches courses related to general HR management and training. He received his BA degree in Psychology in 1995 from the University of St. Thomas in St. Paul, Minnesota. His research interests include employee socialization and retention, evaluating the impact of structural changes on organizational behavior, and learning processes in organizational settings.

Paul Koopman is a Professor of the Psychology of Management and Organization at the Vrije Universiteit Amsterdam, the Netherlands. He studied different types of processes of management and decision making at the organizational level (industrial democracy, reorganization, turnaround management, privatization in Eastern Europe) and departmental level (leadership and motivation, works' consultation, quality circles, teamwork, automation, innovation management). For a few years he joined the Philips organization, where he was involved in complex reorganization processes. He is a visiting professor to Hangzhou University (People's Republic of

China), and an honorary associate of the Tavistock Institute (Centre for Decision Making Studies) in London. From 1995–1999 he was member of the executive committee of the European Association of Work and Organizational Psychology (EAWOP). At this moment, he is interested and actively involved in cross-cultural research, in particular in relation to issues of HRM, leadership and organizational culture. He is a coauthor of books on decision making, charismatic leadership, organizational culture, and human resource management.

Janice Langan-Fox spent 10 years in industry before becoming an academic in 1983. Janice has degrees from the Universities of East Anglia, Nottingham, and Melbourne, and worked at Monash, Deakin and RMIT Universities before coming to the University of Melbourne in 1991, where she is now a senior lecturer in the Department of Psychology. Her research interests are in the area of aptitude-treatment interactions (ATI) which centre on optimizing individual performance and work/learning conditions. Research areas include the acquisition of skill and mental models of tasks and systems, training, human motivation, multimedia treatments, and other areas important to ergonomics and human resource development.

Hüseyin Leblebici, a Professor of Organizational Behavior at University of Illinois, received his MBA and PhD in organizational behavior from University of Illinois at Urbana-Champaign. His research interests are in organizational sociology, organizational design, and interorganizational relations. He is currently working on studies of organizational forms–their creation and diffusion–in professional service organizations. He currently serves on the editorial boards of *Administrative Science Quarterly*, *Organization Science*, *Journal of Management*, and *Organization Studies*. He is also the director of the Office of Business Innovation and Entrepreneurship, which focuses on the role of venture capital and innovation in the development of high-growth firms.

Michelle A. Marks is an Assistant Professor of Psychology at Florida International University. She received her PhD in industrial/organizational psychology from George Mason University. Her primary research interests are in the areas of team training and processes and career development. She is a member of the Society of Industrial Organizational Psychology and the Academy of Management.

John E. Mathieu is a Professor of Management and Organization at the University of Connecticut. He received a PhD in industrial/organizational psychology from Old Dominion University in 1985. He has published over 50 articles and chapters on a variety of topics, mostly in the areas of micro- and meso-organizational behavior. He is a member of the Academy of Management and a Fellow of the Society of Industrial Organizational Psychology, and the American Psychological Association. His current research interests include models of training effectiveness, team and multiteam processes, and cross-level models of organizational behavior.

Andrew Neal received his PhD from the University of New South Wales in 1996, and is currently a senior lecturer in organizational psychology and human factors at the University of Queensland. His research focuses on the determinants and consequences of individual job performance at the individual, group, and organizational levels of analysis. His recent publications have examined a range of topics, including the relationship between safety climate and safety behavior; the relationship between contextual performance and effectiveness in air traffic control; and the effects of organizational climate and human resource management practices on organizational productivity and profitability.

Sharon K. Parker is at the Australian Graduate School of Management, The University of New South Wales. She obtained her PhD from the Institute of Work Psychology, University of Sheffield, UK. Her research interests include how work design initiatives such as job enrichment and autonomous group working affect employee job satisfaction, mental health, and learning. She is also interested in the effects on employees of other modern initiatives (e.g., downsizing, temporary contract employment, flexible technologies); particularly how the negative effects of these practices for employees can be minimized and the potential postive effects maximized. Her research has appeared in leading journals such as the *Journal of Applied Psychology* and the *Academy of Management Journal*. She is the co-author of a book entitled *Job and Work Design*: *Organizing Work to Promote Well-being and Effectiveness*.

Denise M. Rousseau is H.J. Heinz II Professor of Organizational Behavior and Public Policy at Carnegie Mellon University, jointly in the Heinz School of Public Policy and Management and in the Graduate School of Industrial Administration. A graduate of the University of California at Berkley, she has been a faculty member at Northwestern University, the University of Michigan, and the Naval Postgraduate School (Monterey) and visiting faculty at Renmin University (Beijing), Chulalongkorn University (Bangkok), and Nanyang Technological University (Singapore). Her research, which addresses the changing psychological contract at work, has appeared in academic journals such as *Journal of Applied Psychology*, *Academy of Management Review*, *Academy of Management Journal*, *Journal of Organizational Behavior*, and *Administrative Science Quarterly*. Her books include *Psychological Contracts in Employment: Cross-National Perspectives* with René Schalk; *Psychological Contracts in Organizations: Understanding Written and Unwritten Agreements*, which won the Academy of Management's best book award in 1996; the *Trends in Organizational Behavior Series* with Cary Cooper; *Developing an Interdisciplinary Science of Organizations* with Karlene Roberts and Charles Hulin; *The Boundaryless Career* with Michael Arthur; and *Relational Wealth* with Carrie Leana. She is a Fellow in the American Psychological Association, the Society for Industrial and Organizational Psychology, and the Academy of Management and is editor-in-chief of *Journal of Organizational Behavior*.

T.T. Selvarajan is a doctoral candidate at the Department of Management, College of Business, Arizona State University. His research interests are in the areas of performance appraisal and ethical performance appraisal. He has presented papers at the Academy of Management and the Western Academy of Management conferences.

René Schalk is currently Associate Professor in the Department of Policy and Organization Studies at Tilburg University in the Netherlands. He has also worked at Utrecht Business School, Tilburg Institute for Academic Studies (TIAS), and

Nijmegen University, from which he earned his PhD in Social and Organizational Psychology. His research focuses on the issues of organizational psychology, personnel assessment and selection, quality of work, stress and health, motivation and commitment, and employee–organization linkages, with a special focus on the psychological contract, international differences and (virtual) team work. He is a consulting editor for *Journal of Organizational Behavior*, and co-editor of the book *Psychological Contracts in Employment: Cross-National Perspectives*. His books (in Dutch) include *Determinants of Frequent Short-Term Absenteeism* and *Older Employees in a Changing World*. Among the English language journals in which he has published articles are *Journal of Organizational Behavior*, *International Journal of Selection and Assessment*, *Leadership and Organization Development Journal*, *Journal of Social Behavior and Personality*, and *European Journal of Work and Organizational Psychology*.

Kan Shi received his PhD in 1990 in Industrial/Organizational Psychology from the Chinese Academy of Sciences. He is Professor and Director of the Department of I/O Psychology in the Institute of Psychology, Chinese Academy of Sciences, where he teaches classes in the areas of human resources management, selection and training, organizational change, and employee development. Dr Shi was a visiting professor at Michigan Prevention Center, University of Michigan, in 1996–1997. His research has focused on issues such as organizational change, unemployment, job analysis, organizational justice, career development, competency analysis method, selection and training, cross-cultural research.

Behlül Üsdiken is a Professor at the Graduate School of Management, Sabanci University, Istanbul. He received his BA degree from Boǧaziçi University, Istanbul, MSc from The City University, London, and PhD from the University of Istanbul. He has taught at Boǧaziçi University and Koç University. His work has appeared, in addition to Turkish academic journals, in outlets like *Organization Studies*, *Strategic Management Journal*, *British Journal of Management*, *Scandinavian Journal of Management*, and *International Studies of Management and Organization*. He is currently a co-editor of *Organization Studies*. His research interests are in organization theory and history of management thought. He is currently working on the evolution of management thinking in Turkey and Turkish top management teams.

Connie Wanberg received her PhD in 1992 in Industrial/Organizational Psychology from Iowa State University. She is an Associate Professor at the University of Minnesota in the Department of Human Resources and Industrial Relations, where she teaches classes in the areas of staffing, training, and employee development. She was previously on the faculty at Kansas State University in the Department of Psychology. Her research has focused on issues such as unemployment, welfare-to-work, job-search behavior, career indecision, perceived justice of layoffs, organizational change, employee socialization, and mentoring.

Zhong-Ming Wang is Professor of Human Resource Management and Industrial/Organizational Psychology at the School of Management, Zhejiang University, in China. He received an MA in applied psychology from the Gothenburg University, Sweden (1985) and a PhD (1987) in industrial/organizational psychology from Hangzhou University, a joint program with Gothenburg University in Sweden. He is currently the Executive Dean of School of Management, Zhejiang University, and the Director of the Center for Human Resources and Strategic Development. He is also President of Chinese SIOP, Vice-President of Chinese Ergonomics Society, and the Vice-President of the Chinese Personnel Assessment Committee. Wang is the associate editor of both *Chinese Journal of Applied Psychology* and *Chinese Ergonomics*, and is on the editorial boards of *International Journal of Human Resource Management, International Journal of Selection and Assessment, Applied Psychology, Journal of Cross-Cultural Psychology, Journal of Organizational Behavior and Human Decision Process, International Journal of Management Review, Journal of Management Development, Journal of Managerial Psychology, Journal of World Business*, and *Journal of Organizational Behavior.* He has published several books and many articles at home and abroad. His main research areas include strategic human resource management, cross-cultural organizational behavior, personnel selection and assessment, performance appraisal, compensation and reward systems, organizational decision making, leadership teams, organizational culture, and organization development.

Michael West is a Professor of Organizational Psychology at the University of Aston, Business School. He has been Co-Director of the Corporate Performance Programme of the Centre for Economic Performance at the London School of Economics since 1991. He is a visiting professor at the University of North London, University of Eindhoven, and the University of Amsterdam. He is a member of the Council of the British Psychological Society, and Chair of the Society's Journal Committee. He was, until recently, Vice Chair of the UK Economic and Social Research Council's Research Grants Board. He has authored, edited or co-edited 12 books including, *Developing Creativity in Organizations* (1997, BPS) and the *Handbook of Workgroup Psychology* (1996, Wiley). He has also written more than 120 articles for scientific and practitioner publications, and chapters in scholarly books. He is a member of the editorial boards of several international journals, including *Applied Psychology: An International Review, Journal of Organizational Behavior*, and *the Canadian Journal of Administrative Science.* He is a past editor of the *Journal of Occupational and Organizational Psychology.*

He is a Fellow of the British Psychological Society, the American Psychological Association, the APA Society for Industrial and Organizational Psychology and the Royal Society for Arts, Manufactures and Commerce. His areas of research interest are team and organizational innovation and effectiveness, and the well-being of people at work.

Stephen J. Zaccaro is an Associate Professor of Psychology and Associate Director of the Center for Behavioral and Cognitive Studies at George Mason University. He received a PhD in social psychology from the University of Connecticut in 1981. He has published numerous articles, chapters, and books on work stress, leadership, group processes, and team effectiveness. He is a member of the Academy of Management, the Society of Industrial and Organizational Psychology, and the American Psychological Association. His current research interests include executive leadership, leader–team relationships, and the role of shared mental models in team effectiveness.

Preface
Toward a Global Science of IWO Psychology

From scientific management to human relations movement, from cottage industries to craft guilds, from the industrial age to the informational society, the issues that have dominated the field of Industrial, Work and Organizational (IWO) Psychology have changed over the years. In the 21st century, IWO Psychology is becoming a global science and an arena for professional practice. In editing these two volumes, our objectives were (1) to cover recent research on work and organizational psychology by leading experts around the globe and (2) to develop a psychology of work principles that are applicable across international boundaries.

Volume 1 primarily focuses on individuals in organizations and covers personnel psychology issues. Volume 2 primarily covers organizational psychology topics that have a greater emphasis on the group, inter-group, and organizational level analyses. Both volumes include chapters on topic areas stipulated in the SIOP (Society for Industrial and Organizational Psychology), EAWOP (European Association for Work and Organizational Psychology), and Australian I/O psychology teaching syllabi, as well as topics commonly laid down by national bodies and associations in IWO Psychology.

It was our intention, as editors of this Handbook, to produce a globally contributed, globally oriented, and globally relevant collection of chapters which comprehensively covered the major topics comprising our field into the 21st Century. Such lofty ideals may well occur to the reader as having a somewhat grandiose flavor to them, so much so that in reality it is impossible to produce a truly 'global' treatise given such manifest cross-cultural, socio-economic, and historical differences. We were indeed highly conscious that this aim set our sights high, but we were equally determined not to allow a drift downward into parochial, single nation, local issues and perspectives to dominate this Handbook. The very title *Handbook of Industrial, Work and Organizational Psychology* reflects these aspirations on the part of the editors. Credit is due to our esteemed colleague Paul Sackett who proposed this internationally encompassing title for our field as a combination of Industrial–Organizational (I/O) Psychology in the USA, and Work and Organizational (W/O) Psychology in Europe and other countries worldwide. It is our sincere hope that IWO Psychology becomes the embracing, internationally recognized title for our field as it develops into a global arena for science and practice into the next millennium.

One important question that arises immediately from this simple issue over our choice of a title for these volumes is, 'to what extent is IWO Psychology presently a global science and professional practice?'. As editors of this two-volume set, our view is that our field is fast becoming precisely this, a global science and practice. Let us consider the scientific and practitioner wings briefly in turn.

First, scientific findings in IWO Psychology generated predominantly in the USA have been increasingly subjected to validation in other countries around the world. No area has been more exposed to such a trend toward verification of the international validity generalization of American findings as that of recruitment and selection. Selection researchers in Europe, and elsewhere, have begun to suggest that results for certain effects found in the USA do indeed possess generalizability to other countries and cultures, countering earlier challenges that the science of IWO Psychology is merely an artifact of American culture rather than a truly global science.

Second, we have witnessed the emergence of an entirely new sub-discipline within IWO Psychology concerned exclusively with cross-national and international issues. The growth of international assignments, expatriate selection and management issues has further fueled this field, with organizations and scientists in IWO Psychology becoming concerned with cross-national moves, issues of leadership style, and re-acculturation in post-overseas assignment of personnel back into their countries of origin. These developments have shifted the perceptual, analytical, and disciplinary boundaries of IWO Psychology forever away from parochial, within-country studies; our zone of proximal development, so to speak, has been inexorably driven by these environmental changes toward international concerns and challenges.

With regard to the practice of IWO Psychology, alongside this diversification of scientific focus, simultaneous changes in the practice of organizational psychology have also taken on an increasingly multi-national shape and size. Several consultancies now boast a multi-national presence and practice with IWO Psychologists being moved between different country offices where and whenever appropriate. The largest consultancies, including Personnel Decisions International, SHL, SRA, Aon and Gallup have indeed possessed this global presence for some years now; the inevitable implication of which has been a move toward a more synonymous and standardized practice across rather than within countries. Whether there is yet a single, global market for IWO consultancy is a moot point; national and cultural differences clearly still play some part in the professional practice of our discipline. But what is inescapable is that the move toward global players on the practitioner wing of our discipline has resulted in significantly greater collaboration and sharing of expertise across countries in IWO Psychology.

In this two-volume series, we set out to summarize the major principles learnt over the years in IWO Psychology. The chapters are written by internationally eminent authors based in a variety of countries worldwide, including the USA, UK, Spain, Australia, Belgium, China, The Netherlands, Turkey, Italy, and Canada. This eclectic mix of countries of author origin was intentional on the part of the editors, in part to ensure a truly global set of contributions to this Handbook.

This is especially the case at the organizational level of analysis, where the globalization of international business and work organizations has created strikingly similar issues to come to the fore in many countries worldwide over more recent years. To neglect these inescapable inter-linkages would be to neglect the globalization of business markets, and it is therefore entirely appropriate that IWO psychology embraces these trends and insurgent patterns.

The chapters in both volumes are geared to consolidate the research and theory on topics that IWO psychologists study, drawing upon research and practice across the globe, to build theory. The ideas presented herein, hopefully, reflect and satisfy the demands of an increasingly global science and practice of IWO Psychology in the 21st century.

Handan Kepir Sinangil, Istanbul
Deniz S. Ones, Minneapolis
Chockalingam Viswesvaran, Miami
Neil Anderson, London/Amsterdam
March, 2001

Acknowledgments

Co-editing a major, globally relevant *Handbook of Industrial, Work and Organizational Psychology* required much collaboration and effort from all of us. We also experienced, first hand, what is possible in working with a team whose members were on different continents, and from varied cultural backgrounds. First, and foremost thanks are due to each other for making this a fun team to be part of. We have provided each other intellectual challenges and social support through the past three years. We have been good for each other, and hopefully good for these volumes. The order of authorship listed for the two volumes (Anderson, Ones, Sinangil, and Viswesvaran) is alphabetical. We truly shared the work equally.

For the actualization of the Handbook with 43 chapters across 2 volumes, our gratitude goes to the 79 eminent authors across 14 countries. They accepted our invitation with enthusiasm, and devoted considerable amount of effort to this project. Not only did they produce outstanding chapters, but also were timely with their revisions.

The volume of administrative work on this undertaking turned out to be much greater than anticipated. In hindsight, working with individuals across 14 different time zones is not an easy task. Our support staff at the University of Minnesota's Psychology Department, where our Administrative Headquarters was located, were more helpful and important for this project than they will ever realize. We would like to express our gratitude to Jocelyn Wilson and Jeanette Shelton, who were our chief editorial assistants during 2000–2001 and 1999–2000, respectively. Their efficiency, professionalism, and enthusiasm made our editorial work a little easier and a little less distressing. During especially hectic times, Barbara Hamilton, Rachel Gamm and Jennifer Benka also lent helping hands and we are thankful for that. Partial financial support for the Handbook editorial office was provided by the Department of Psychology of the University of Minnesota, as well as the Hellervik Chair endowment.

We also would like to extend our sincerest thanks to the original commissioning editor of these volumes, Naomi Meredith and the SAGE (publishing) team. During the various phases of the Handbook, we relied on opinions of many colleagues and students at the University of Minnesota, Marmara University, Goldsmiths College, and Florida International University. The intellectual stimulation and care that they so freely gave proved to be invaluable.

Those closest to us, perhaps gave the most and suffered the greatest during the completion of this project. To them, we offer genuine apologies for the neglect they had to endure and for the encouragement, they, nonetheless, provided, while we labored long hours during nights and weekends. For this, Deniz would like to thank Ates Haner (my dear husband, and an extraordinarily wonderful man), Handan would like to thank Sinan Sinangil (my good friend and husband), and Vish would like to thank Saraswathy Viswesvaran (my invaluable wife and best friend).

It is our sincere hope that these two volumes prove useful to the field of IWO Psychology.

Deniz S. Ones
Handan Kepir Sinangil
Neil Anderson
Chockalingam (Vish) Viswesvaran

INTRODUCTION TO
VOLUME 2 — ORGANIZATIONAL PSYCHOLOGY

Organizational Perspectives

HANDAN KEPIR SINANGIL,
CHOCKALINGAM VISWESVARAN,
DENIZ S. ONES, and NEIL ANDERSON

PREAMBLE TO VOLUME II

In this, the second volume of the *Handbook of Industrial, Work and Organizational Psychology*, the foci and level of analysis become more meso- and macro-analytical in order to consider aspects of organizational and managerial psychology associated with work groups, organizational systems and processes, organizational change, cross-cultural organizational psychology, and other aspects of Industrial, Work and Organizational (IWO) Psychology. The 21 chapters which make up this volume cover a diversity of topics including productivity, job satisfaction, stress, leadership, communication, teamwork, organizational development, organizational theory, culture and climate, and cognitive processes in strategic management, and several other topics.

The chapters are again written by authors based in a variety of countries worldwide, including the USA, UK, Australia, The Netherlands, Turkey, Italy, China and Canada. This eclectic mix of countries of author origin was intentional on the part of the editors, in part to ensure a truly global set of contributors to this Handbook. This is especially the case at the organizational level of analysis, where the globalization of international business and work organizations has caused strikingly similar issues to come to the fore in many countries worldwide over more recent years.

STRUCTURE OF THE VOLUME

In the first chapter of this volume, Neal and Hesketh consider the vexing issue of productivity in organizations. In common with several other chapters in this Handbook, problems present themselves to researchers active in this field from the outset, in that there exist on-going disagreements over precise definitions of the term 'productivity' in work organizations. The chapter begins with a valuable review of these conceptual differences of opinion, offering invaluable guidance to those new to this topic area on different conceptualizations of productivity and different operationalizations of the term by various researchers. Few would argue that productivity is not an important issue, regardless of the type of organization concerned; what is apparently more problematic is to specify with any degree of consensus exactly what is meant by the term. Nevertheless, Neal and Hesketh offer a useful guide through this debate and move on to consider productivity research at different levels of analysis and for different types of outcome variables. They consider the range of methods for measuring productivity (e.g., operational outcomes, profitability, market value, financial efficiency), all of which have predictable advantages and disadvantages it seems. Notwithstanding these issues of definitional and measurement difficulty, they provide a concise and thorough review of extant research into the determinants of productivity at the organizational and work group levels of analysis. Some overlaps are apparent here with the chapters in this volume by West (Chapter 14) and Mathieu, Marks, and Zaccaro (Chapter 15), but the distinguishing characteristic of the present chapter is its attention to productivity concerns at both of these levels of analysis.

In the following chapter, Judge, Parker, Colbert, Heller and Ilies review the mass of research conducted by IWO psychologists into job satisfaction.

This topic, it seems, has generated one of the most active areas for empirical study in our field over the last few decades. The authors point to a substantial growth in the number and range of empirical studies conducted by IWO psychologists over recent years, and in so doing they provide a timely summary and overview of this burgeoning area. Basing their review on differing theoretical approaches to job satisfaction (situational, dispositional, and interactive), Judge et al., identify over 10,000 individual studies into job satisfaction, which they persuasively claim makes this topic 'perhaps the most widely studied topic in all industrial/organizational psychology'. Since most of these studies took place in the USA, the authors rightly raise the question of the international generalizability of the American findings, an issue that they go on to review in some worthwhile detail. Countering previous meta-analytical findings of an apparent lack of relation between job analysis and job performance, the authors present compelling international evidence that the two are more closely associated than past research had supposed. This in itself warrants the attention of IWO researchers active in this area, and the findings of Judge et al., presented in this chapter may well prove in the future to be a turning point in the historical development of job satisfaction research in our discipline.

The third chapter in this volume is by Donovan and focuses exclusively upon work motivation. Donovan organizes this chapter by the major theories of work motivation prominent in our field: Equity Theory, Expectancy Theory, Cognitive Evaluation Theory, Goal Setting Theory, Control Theory, and Social Cognitive Theory. For each, he presents a cogent review of the theoretical precepts followed by a more detailed review of the empirical research conducted into work motivation, which has adopted this theoretical orientation. Interestingly, what becomes quickly apparent from the author's neat structuring of this massive area of research is that the voluminous number of research studies carried out by IWO psychologists have each adopted a favored theoretical orientation almost to the total exclusion of other potentially complementary stances. On the other hand, only a small minority of studies have attempted an integrative theoretical orientation, perhaps in part dissuaded by the sheer complexity of this very task. This has resulted in a large but fragmented field of research, with individual researchers favoring a particular theoretical approach and largely carrying out studies solely within this approach. Donovan concludes his laudable integrative review of this disparate field by arguing for integrative model building and encompassing frameworks as the over-riding concern for researchers active in this area into the foreseeable future.

Heneman, Fay, and Wang contribute the following chapter (Chapter 4). The authors, emanating from the USA and China, review research into compensation systems from an international perspective but with particular reference to China as a country that is becoming increasingly affected by questions of worker compensation and reward. Compensation is defined as 'pay, benefits, and other rewards with monetary value', and as the authors point out, employee compensation alone can represent substantial portions of an organization's entire turnover in any financial year. Yet, relative to other areas in IWO psychology, less research attention appears to have been devoted to this topic than would be ideal, and the precise effects of different compensation strategies upon individual and team performance remain shrouded in some doubt, not least by the contradictory findings of some existing research. Moving the concern to an international or cross-cultural stage, it is not surprising therefore that the picture becomes fundamentally more complex and multi-faceted. The authors review existing findings and place them in an international context with some aplomb, concluding that compensation systems unequivocally affect individual, group, and organizational performance, and that earlier studies that were confined to the US may well have international generalizability to China.

Occupational stress and strain is the topic reviewed in Chapter 5 by Hart and Cooper. As traditionally one of the most prolifically active areas of research in IWO psychology, the authors undertake the gargantuan task of reviewing the literature and applied findings in this area with genuine brevity. Moreover, they undertake a constructively critical overview of this topic area by suggesting, some might consider somewhat controversially, that the framework of occupational health provides a key integrative vantage point from which to view these important issues. Decrying the lack of generally accepted definitions of stress and strain in the workplace, Hart and Cooper's chapter represents nothing less than a masterclass in the intellectual construction of integrative review; most crucially much of the latter part of their chapter is dedicated to the development of a synergistic perspective – organizational health as the quintessential nodal link between stress, individual performance, and organizational performance. Far from merely reviewing the morass of individual studies into stress and strain, the authors put forward an integrative, future-oriented framework upon which occupational stress research can be based, and within which stress research can be inextricably linked to individual and organizational performance.

In Chapter 6, Arnold presents an outstanding review of careers theory and empirical research. The author presents a state-of-the-art overview of this changing field, alluding to the huge shifts in business and work organizations which have inescapably impacted upon career trajectories for individuals on the one side, and the increasingly problematic activity of career management by organizations on the other. Arnold describes irrefutable accumulated evidence that the 'traditional' within-function, upward spiralling career is today almost an historic relic. Rather, multi-skilled, multiple-function, and disparate career trajectories are becoming the norm with the individuals themselves responsible for their own career management strategy rather than this being the preserve of the organization's personnel department or HRM function. The knock-on challenges to IWO Psychologists from these changes in career paths and the displacement of career management onto the individual are particularly noteworthy. Yet, as a discipline, Arnold notes that much is left to be done in this regard and that we are in the very early days of being able to respond constructively to these environmental changes which are forcing a fundamental re-think over the whole notion of careers for both individuals and organizations alike.

In Chapter 7 Schalk and Rousseau address the emerging topic of psychological contracts in the employment relationship. They present a notably concise review of the growing body of empirical studies into the causes, effects, and modus operandi of the psychological contract, suggesting that contracts are continually evolving, open to negotiation, and may well be violated more often than might be expected at first glance. In keeping with the theme of globalized IWO psychology for this Handbook, the authors consider elemental changes in the psychological contract in several diverse countries in North America, Europe, and Austral-Asia.

Organizational justice theory, models, and research are the concern of Chapter 8 by Gilliland and Chan. In common with the preceding chapter, organizational justice has emerged as a topic area in IWO psychology relatively recently compared with topics such as stress, job satisfaction, and selection. Yet the growth of research interest into organizational justice has, as the authors vividly point out, been marked over the last two or three decades particularly. Why should justice be a pertinent concern in IWO psychology, some might ask? The authors present a cogent rationale for the importance of fully incorporating justice research into mainstream IWO psychology, and moreover, present indisputable evidence for where justice has already been a pertinent concern in other related research areas in our discipline including selection, appraisal, compensation, sexual harassment, and diversity management. If anything, on reading this chapter one is struck by the potential for justice approaches to span most if not all areas currently forming IWO psychology, and that this topic area presents a multitude of potential theoretical and empirical linkages across our field. Gilliland and Chan subdivide their chapter into two parts, theory and application. In the first they consider the theoretical underpinnings of the construct of organizational

justice; in the second they review extant research into this importantly emergent area. They conclude with a future conditional for justice research, highlight the main directions for future research, and point again to the potential this construct undoubtedly has for sedimentary dispersal into other perhaps more established areas of IWO psychology.

Two Dutch IWO psychologists, Den Hartog and Koopman have contributed Chapter 9. In contrast to the preceding two chapters, no one would describe leadership as being a recently emergent topic in our discipline. Rather, as the authors themselves point out, leadership as an area, and leadership research, has been a longstanding concern for IWO psychologists for at least the last 60 years and some would argue for considerably longer. Reviewing trait, style and contingency theoretical approaches initially, the authors present an easily accessible but comprehensive overview of these major alternative approaches to conceptualizing and researching leadership. Highlighting issues such as charismatic leadership, contingency styles, perceptions amongst subordinates of a need for leadership, attribution processes and biases, and transactional and transformational leadership, they lead the reader through the mass of published applied research in this area. They conclude by discussing approaches to, and existing research on, cross-cultural leadership and the challenges to leaders posed by the globalization of business, overseas leadership assignments, and expatriate managerial moves. Perhaps as an apt mantra for this Handbook, and even the whole field of IWO psychology in the future, the authors cite Shamir (1999): '... boundaryless, flattened, flexible, project-based and team-based organizations that employ temporary, externalized and remote workers, whose tasks are more intellectual and less routine and cannot be controlled and coordinated by structure or direct supervision, need mechanisms of coordination through shared meaning systems, a shared sense of purpose, and high member commitment to shared values'.

Communication in organizations is the subject area considered by Langan-Fox in Chapter 10. Needless to say, the changes wrought by new information technology, particularly electronic mail, together with flatter, more team-based methods of work organization, have transformed past methods and means of communication between members of almost all organizations in the modern commercial world. The author provides a timely and much-needed review of this perhaps slightly neglected area in IWO psychology, and indeed she argues that research has failed to keep up with these environmental changes to some extent. In this 'brave new world' of information technology-facilitated communication in work organizations, she points out several challenging areas where research is called for, wherein communication is a central determinant of organizational performance, not just a mediating variable between other more important cause–effect relations.

In Chapter 11 Jackson and Joshi consider how the increasing diversity of workforces, either at the domestic local level or at the national and international level, has forced organizations to confront and to grapple with issues of substantive inter-individual differences in their staff member groups. Not least in the USA where several aspects of organizational entry, treatment of employees, promotion and career opportunities, and other human resource management issues are governed by legal provisions, the specter of diversity has loomed large in the concerns of HR practitioners and IWO consultants in the field. The chapter covers five major themes: complying with the legal requirements, interpersonal dynamics and how they relate to group differences, single attribute versus attribute profile research, situational specificity in diversity research, and, training and OD interventions to facilitate organization change. The authors conclude their impressively comprehensive review of these issues inherently associated with diversity with suggested directions for future research both within the USA and internationally.

Excuses the editors have used (with greater or lesser degrees of success it has to be admitted) include mechanical breakdowns of the train/car/metro/plane/bicycle, illness of self/family members, dental or doctors appointments, urgent phone calls from abroad, and for the past four years having to work from home/entirely away from home on a major, two-volume Handbook for our field. We refer, of course, to our lateness and absenteeism from our respective employing academic departments (or our homes)! Lateness and absenteeism constitute two of the three phenomena ably reviewed by Johns in Chapter 12. Together with his third phenomenon, turnover, these psychological processes, the author argues, form a comprehensive model of 'organizational withdrawal' by employees. Johns engages the reader in a compelling all-stops-tour of the literature in each of these three areas, his intent and style being one of critically questioning and examining taken for granted assumptions for related events in these aspects of counterproductive behavior in the workplace. He contrasts the withdrawal model with the social and dispositional models as alternative theoretical frameworks for these behaviors, and concludes with potent suggestions for improvements to research in these areas for the immediate future.

Chapter 13 is, in common with many others in this Handbook, the result of an international collaboration between the authors, Wanberg and Kammeyer-Mueller in the USA and Kan Shi in China. Not surprisingly, they adopt a cross-cultural perspective towards the potentially psychologically charged issues of job loss and unemployment. Even a cursory review of their chapter by the reader will reveal that the deleterious effects of unemployment are not confined to western, post-industrial countries. Indeed, the authors highlight specifically the current predicament of China where unemployment has risen as a result of massive scale programs of economic reform. To those who are unfamiliar with China's recent history and changing economic aspirations, this chapter will likely make informative reading, sufficient to confront several naive stereotypes of this country's employment policies and the economic realities facing workers. And these realities unavoidably include the disconcerting possibility of job loss and unemployment for the average citizen. As importantly, this chapter provides a notable example of the globalization of research in IWO psychology, in that the effects of unemployment and job search behavior found in earlier studies carried out in North American and European countries have been largely generalized to the very different social context of China.

In Chapter 14 West contributes a topic area which has increasingly occupied IWO psychologists over more recent years – teamwork. As organizations have become more team-based in their work designs and as ad hoc and permanent teams have become the norm within organizations as ways to maximize human potential and performance, it is encouraging for us to stand witness to this exponential growth in research efforts into team effectiveness directly as a result of these changes in organizational structures and cultures. West, prominent amongst researchers in this area, links team processes to innovation and creativity, as potential synergistic outcomes from numbers of individuals working together as part of a team or work group. His chapter draws from the notion that for humans beings working alongside others as part of a team is congruent with basic human nature, emotions, attitudes, and psychological needs. He goes on to present more than ample evidence that such aspects of teamwork processes are associated with innovation and creativity as measurable outputs of work groups.

It is fitting that the chapter which follows West's chapter on teamwork addresses the emergent topic of multi-team systems theory. Its authors, Mathieu, Marks, and Zaccaro posit a theory and model of multiple teams working interdependently within organizations, as a form of organization structuring that has gained substantially in popularity over recent years. Their chapter confronts square-on the meso-analytical ground of inter-team interactions, functioning, and processual dynamics in modern-day organizational settings, and it highlights the inherent challenges in such structures for leadership, communication, information technology, and organizational learning. Their MultiTeam Systems (MTS) theory represents an innovative point of departure for IWO psychologists active in team level research or practice interventions; most valuably the authors develop and explicate their carefully crafted theory with genuine eloquence and concern for its practical implications in MTS workplaces. Together with the previous chapter by West, which focused upon intra-team issues, this contribution by Mathieu, Marks, and Zaccaro toward a general theory of inter-team processes represents landmark reviews of teamwork issues now facing many organizations in several countries. IWO psychologists clearly have a major contribution to make to understanding these issues in practice, and indeed, it is likely that both intra-team and inter-team processual dynamics will become increasingly important areas to which our field can make a unique contribution.

Highhouse's chapter on judgment and decision making (Chapter 16) reminds us as IWO psychologists that other related fields in psychology and management research often have much to offer for our understanding of phenomena in the world of work, and that we should guard against becoming too isolated in our ontological and empirical perspectives. Indeed, as the author vividly shows, the field of judgment and decision making (JDM) has benefited tangibly from its historical development as a multidisciplinary field, drawing as it does from social, clinical, and consumer psychology, as well as several sub-disciplines of the management and organization behavior sciences. Despite these apparent benefits, Highhouse quite rightly bemoans the reluctance of IWO psychology to embrace JDM research and he details unequivocal areas of overlap between the two where the disparate fields could clearly learn from each other. Have we as IWO psychologists been myopic to the point of being blinded to the wider approaches and perspectives offered by JDM research? Highhouse argues in both the affirmatory and to the contrary. He suggests that in certain areas the IWO literature has been at the forefront of adopting JDM approaches and synergizing from its research findings, while in others he laments the continued isolation of IWO research. As an important review of the field of JDM research as it applies to IWO psychology, Highhouse's chapter provides IWO psychologists with a single-source introduction of stature that deserves to be attended to by colleagues in our field.

In Chapter 17 Sinangil and Avallone present the broad topic of organization development and change. Their chapter provides a comprehensive overview of the predominant perspectives, models, and important empirical research in organization development (OD). The authors' review covers a four-decade period from 1960 up until 2000, and is therefore laudable in its aim of presenting an accessible overview of the mass of empirical studies into OD interventions published across several countries over this 40-year period. Their chronological structuring of this large body of material also provides an insight into the ways in which OD has itself developed over these years, in terms of definitional characteristics, methodological sophistication, levels of analysis, intervention orientations, and published studies in this field. Sinangil and Avallone move on to critically consider the empirical evidence in support of a range of OD techniques, and it is clear that this field, despite benefiting from numerous studies over this period, still has some way to go to generate compelling data to overcome doubts over the efficacy of some of the more faddish OD methods and techniques we have witnessed over these years.

The vexing issue of management interventions into organizational systems is addressed in some detail in Chapter 18 by Cardy and Selvarajan. Few would dispute that a key role of senior management is to attempt to maximize the on-going performance of their organization both in the short-term and over the longer-term. Over the years this imperative has generated a whole host of planned intervention programs, most of which produce simultaneously immediate recognition and not a little skepticism amongst IWO psychologists – management by objectives, quality circles, total quality management, business process re-engineering, to name only some of the more recent ones. The authors adopt a cautiously critical approach to reviewing the gamut of such interventions, and the reader will be relieved to hear, present evidence both for and fundamentally against the more faddish manifestations of planned change programs. As importantly, especially in the context of our Handbook, which as already stated is intended for a global audience, this chapter critically evaluates the international generalizability of different management interventions.

Chapter 19 is far from unrelated to the previous chapter. Usdiken and Leblebici provide an expansive review of recent trends and developments in organization theory. For a long time only a distant disciplinary cousin to IWO psychology, which has tended to be more empiricist in orientation, the current state-of-the-art in organization theory is here ably reviewed by the authors. A brief historical overview is presented initially, from which the reader will glean invaluable insights into why the present-day field of organization theory appears to be highly pluralistic, lacking in consensus, and replete with competing paradigms, perspectives, and empirical assumptions. This chapter will be especially useful for IWO psychologists who are less familiar with this area, for instance if they have specialized in more micro-analytic issues of personnel selection, performance appraisal, ergonomics, or individual stress and strain. Equally, however, the chapter will provide a useful update and state-of-the-science review for practitioners and academic researchers active in this area. The authors conclude their chapter with a futurological discussion of the likely directions for organization theory, including increased methodological rigor, multidisciplinary theorizing, and tensions between fragmentation versus integration in this area.

In the penultimate chapter of this volume, Ashkanasy and Jackson review a topic area which has witnessed an explosive growth in interest from IWO psychologists over the last twenty years or so – organization culture and climate. They argue that 'culture and climate are overlapping and complementary constructs, amenable to multi-method research that cuts across disciplinary boundaries'. Adopting a primarily psychological conceptualization of these constructs, the authors nevertheless point up overlaps with sociological and anthropological research traditions into particularly culture, in so doing making a worthwhile distinction between climate and culture as separate but overlapping constructs. Ashkanasy and Jackson consider different definitions of each, measurement approaches by researchers to each, and relationships found in the extant research to outcome variables with each. Their chapter covers an expansive amount of ground with considerable clarity in interpreting what at times is complex and contradictory material in the literature.

In the final chapter of this volume, and of the Handbook as a whole, Hodgkinson presents a cogently argued review of cognitive processes in strategic management. Selected intentionally by the editors as a more projective area within IWO psychology which is likely to emerge to the foreground of our discipline over the coming years, Hodgkinson's chapter provides a persuasive rationale as to why IWO psychologists should be seriously considering this area for greater research and practice attention. The formulation of strategy and policy by senior management teams in organizations has traditionally not been a pressing concern for IWO psychologists, yet a cursory reading of this chapter will leave many readers wondering why this has been the case. Hodgkinson examines aspects of judgment heuristics, information processing biases and errors, and cognitive process dynamics, found by the extant research in this area to be related to strategic policy formulation. He proceeds to examine the ways in which management team composition may impact upon these processes, then reverts to a more individual level of analysis finally to explicate the ways in which research has uncovered senior managers mental models of organizational environments. Hodgkinson concludes this fundamentally challenging chapter to fellow IWO psychologists with calls for future research directions, and for the incorporation of this sub-field into mainstream IWO psychology as a logical next step. It would be indeed a brave researcher or practitioner in our field who would disagree with him.

CONCLUDING THOUGHTS

An important, pervasive and irreversible development in the recent years has been the globalization of business. The research summaries and ideas contained in the chapters of this volume will hopefully facilitate the training of IWO psychology professionals, help practitioners meet emerging challenges and enable researchers to embrace a truly globalized field of organizational psychology. Several exciting turns are ahead and we hope this volume captures some of the excitement in our field, as well as highlighting many of the invaluable contributions that IWO psychology has to offer work organizations presently and into the future.

ACKNOWLEDGMENT

Thanks are due to the University of Amsterdam and the Free University of Amsterdam for their support and facilities to Neil Anderson whilst drafting sections of this editorial chapter.

1

Productivity in Organizations

ANDREW NEAL and BERYL HESKETH

Despite the unquestioned importance of productivity for organizations, there is considerable disagreement regarding its conceptualization and measurement. The current chapter reviews the various usages of the term, the different types of measures used, and the relationship between productivity and the related constructs of performance, effectiveness, and efficiency. The chapter then addresses a range of measurement issues associated with productivity, and reviews the types of factors that have been found to predict productivity at the organizational and group levels of analysis.

INTRODUCTION

Over the past 15 years, we have seen a dramatic growth in interest in the development of models of individual job performance. Surprisingly, however, relatively little attention has been paid to the development of models of productivity. The individual performance literature has focused on building models of performance that specify the different components of performance, and the factors that are responsible for individual differences on these components (e.g., Motowidlo, Borman & Schmit, 1997). This research is important because it has substantially improved our understanding of performance, and has facilitated the development of more effective management practices. Within the productivity literature, however, we do not have integrative models that specify the different components of productivity and identify the factors that differentially affect each of these factors. As a result, we understand relatively little about productivity, or the mechanisms by which different factors influence productivity at different levels. In this chapter we address this issue by considering firstly problems relating to the conceptualization and measurement of productivity, and then reviewing

the factors that influence productivity at the group and organizational levels of analysis.

CONCEPTUAL ISSUES

Defining Productivity

Most previous reviews of the productivity literature have commented on the difficulty of defining and measuring productivity (e.g., Campbell & Campbell, 1988; Pritchard, 1992). There is substantial disagreement within the literature regarding the use of the term productivity, and related constructs such as performance, effectiveness, and efficiency. Part of the difficulty with defining productivity is the absence of generally agreed definitions for performance and effectiveness. Performance, effectiveness, efficiency, and productivity are used by a number of different academic disciplines, and are used at different levels of analysis. Disciplines that use these terms include work and organizational psychology, organizational behavior, industrial engineering, strategic management, finance, accounting, marketing, and economics. Levels of analysis at which these terms have been used include the individual, group, divisional, organizational, and national levels. In the current section, we review the varying uses of these terms within the work and organizational psychology literature.

There is relatively widespread agreement regarding the use of terms at the individual level of analysis. The definitions that are commonly used today were developed by Campbell, Dunnette, Lawler and Weick (1970). The term 'performance' is used to refer to the proficiency with which individuals carry out behaviors or activities that are relevant to the organization (e.g., Motowidlo et al., 1997). A number of different components of individual performance have been identified within the literature. These include technical proficiency, job dedication, teamwork, and citizenship (Conway, 1999; Neal & Hesketh, 2000; Organ, 1990; Van Scotter & Motowidlo, 1996). Performance is differentiated from effectiveness, which refers to the outcomes that stem from those behaviors or activities. Effectiveness is typically expressed as a ratio, in which the observed level of output is compared to a standard or goal. Examples include the ratio of actual to target sales, or the number of publications that an academic produces, compared to an accepted benchmark. Efficiency is also expressed as a ratio, in which the observed level of output is compared to the resources required to produce it. Examples include sales compared with salary, promotion and travel costs, or number of publications compared with grant income. There is general agreement that terms such as performance, efficiency, and effectiveness can be used at an individual level. However, there is some disagreement over the appropriateness of using the term 'productivity' at the individual level. Pritchard (1992) argues that the term 'productivity' should be reserved to refer to the output of units at a higher level of analysis, such as groups or organizations.

When moving to the group or organizational level of analysis, there is less agreement regarding meaning and the use of terms. Efficiency is the only term that appears to have a meaning that is consistent with its use at the individual level. All other terms are used inconsistently. This may reflect the greater variety of discipline areas that address productivity at a group level (e.g., economics and sociology, as well as psychology). The individual level, by contrast, tends to be primarily the domain of psychology and human resource management.

The term 'performance' is sometimes used to refer to the proficiency with which groups or organizations carry out specific types of activities (e.g., Brodbeck, 1996). According to this definition, performance reflects the proficiency with which the group applies knowledge, skill, and effort to the task. This use of the term is equivalent to that at the individual level. Other authors use the term 'performance' to refer to output. For example, McGrath (1964) uses 'performance outcomes' as criteria for evaluating group effectiveness. At the organizational level, the term 'firm performance' is frequently used when referring to financial or operational measures of output (e.g., Ketchen, Thomas & McDaniel, 1996).

Uses of the term 'effectiveness' also vary widely at the group and organizational levels. Quinn and Rohrbaugh (1983) identified four competing models of organizational effectiveness that are commonly used within the literature. These are the Rational Goal, Open Systems, Human Relations, and Hierarchical models. The Rational Goal model assumes that the dominant coalition within the organization has a set of coherent goals (e.g., profit maximization), and that measures of organizational effectiveness should assess the extent to which the organization attains those goals (Barnard, 1938; Etzioni, 1964). The Open Systems model assumes that the primary organizational goal is growth and the acquisition of resources, and measures effectiveness in these terms (Shipper & White, 1983; Yuchtman & Seashore, 1967). The Human Relations model defines effectiveness in terms of social attributes, such as trust, participation, and openness (e.g., Likert, 1967). Finally, the Hierarchical model emphasizes the importance of criteria such as stability, control, and efficiency.

Differences in the uses of the terms 'performance' and 'effectiveness' at the group and organizational level have created problems for definitions of productivity. One of the major discrepancies concerns the relationship between productivity and effectiveness. One view holds that effectiveness should be used as an indicator of productivity (Pritchard, 1992). This approach adopts the same definitions of effectiveness and efficiency found at the individual level of analysis within the work and organizational psychology literature (e.g., Campbell et al., 1970) for use at higher levels. According to this view, measures of productivity should assess output. Output can be assessed in relation to a goal ('effectiveness'), or in relation to the resources required to produce that output ('efficiency'). Pritchard's (1992) approach has been developed explicitly within a Rational Goal approach to organizational analysis (see also Pritchard, Jones, Roth, Stuebing & Ekeberg, 1988).

An alternative view, which is adopted in the current chapter, holds that productivity should be regarded as an indicator of effectiveness. According to this view, productivity is simply one of many criteria that can be used for evaluating the effectiveness of groups and organizations. Each of the different approaches within the competing values model can be used to generate effectiveness criteria. Hackman (1987), for example, distinguishes between three criteria for evaluating group effectiveness: productivity, well-being, and viability. Productivity is defined as output, and is assessed in relation to the expectations of relevant stakeholders, such as clients and managers. Well-being reflects the extent to which the group meets the social and psychological needs of its members. Viability is defined as the capacity of the group to continue working together in the future. These criteria reflect the differing orientations inherent in the Rational Goal, Human Relations, and Open Systems approaches to organizational effectiveness.

In the current chapter, the term 'productivity' refers to any type of output that is valued within a Rational Goal approach. By adopting a Rational Goal orientation, we do not mean to downplay the importance of the other types of effectiveness criteria that are emphasized within the Human Relations and Open Systems approaches. Indeed, the potential links between productivity and these other classes of effectiveness criteria demonstrates the importance of integrating research conducted within these alternative perspectives. For example, within the psychology literature, studies have reported positive relationships between employee morale and indicators of productivity, such as customer satisfaction and production quality (e.g., Ostroff, 1992; Ryan, Schmit & Johnson, 1996; Schneider, 1991; Tornow & Wiley, 1991; Wiley, 1991). Furthermore, Bernhardt, Donthu and Kennett (2000) found that relationships between customer satisfaction and profitability emerged when these variables were tracked over time. Within the strategic management literature, a number of studies have examined the link between corporate social responsibility and productivity. Some studies have reported a positive relationship between corporate social responsibility and productivity (Cochran & Wood, 1984; McGuire, Sundgren & Schneeweis, 1988; Waddock & Graves, 1997), while others have not (Aupperle, Carroll & Hatfield, 1985; Shane & Spicer, 1983, and McWilliams & Siegel, 2000). In the current paper, however, we focus only on productivity, and do not deal with these other criteria.

Finally, following Pritchard (1992), we restrict the use of the term productivity to the group and organizational levels of analysis. As a result, we do not include literature that has examined goal attainment at the individual level of analysis.

Measuring Productivity

There is a wide variety of measures of productivity that are commonly used in research and practice. Measures of productivity can include the following:

measures of operational outcomes, such as customer satisfaction, production quantity, production quality and production efficiency (e.g., machine utilization and machine downtime);

measures of profitability (alternatively referred to as 'accounting' measures), such as net profit, profit margin (profit divided by total revenue), and return on capital employed (net profit divided by the capital obtained from shares, reserves, and loans);

measures of market value (alternatively referred to as 'financial' measures), such as earnings per share (net profit divided by number of shares), yield on shares (dividend per share divided by share price), the price-to-earnings ratio (share price divided by earnings per share), and Tobin's q (market value of the firm divided by the replacement cost of assets);

measures of financial efficiency and liquidity, such as the total asset turnover ratio (sales divided by total assets), turnover per employee (sales divided by the total number of employees: also termed 'partial labor productivity'), the stock turnover ratio (average holding of unsold stock divided by sales), the ratio of current assets to current liabilities, and the gearing ratio (external borrowing divided by total capital employed); and

measures of market position, such as market share and growth.

Relatively little research has examined the overall factor structure of these different types of measures. The majority of research that has examined interrelationships among different types of productivity measures has simply focused on measures of profitability and market value. A number of studies have shown that the correlation between measures of profitability and market value is positive, but small. For example, Jacobson (1987) found that the correlation between return on investment and stock return for 241 firms over the period from 1963 to 1982 was only 0.14. More importantly, a number of studies have found that measures of profitability and market value load onto separate factors, and that these factors tend to have relatively low intercorrelations (e.g., Dubofsky & Varadarajan, 1987; Gomez-Mejia, Tosi & Hinkin, 1987; Hoskisson, Hitt, Johnson & Moesel, 1993; Murray, 1989; Rowe & Morrow, 1999).

In many respects it is not surprising that profitability and market value are weakly related. Measures of profitability assess productivity in the short term, and are based on historical data (e.g., sales in the past year). Measures of market value reflect the present value of future income, and are dependent upon investors' perceptions of future productivity. While perceptions of future productivity may be influenced by current profitability, a range of other factors may come into play. For example, Fryxell and Barton (1990) demonstrated that the relationship between measures of profitability and market value varied over time, and across groupings of companies pursuing different competitive strategies. When market conditions were stable, overall financial performance (estimated as a single latent factor within a confirmatory factor analysis) was predominantly determined by profitability. When market conditions were unstable, the factor loadings for profitability measures declined, while the loadings for market measures increased. These findings demonstrate that the factor structure of productivity measures can be influenced by temporal and contextual variables.

Another point to note is that different types of measures tend to be used at different levels of analysis, by different stakeholders, for different purposes. For example, managers use productivity data for at least three different purposes: (a) for strategic planning and policy making; (b) controlling and coordinating parts of the organization; and (c) motivating employees (Pritchard, 1990). Managers may use measures of profitability, financial efficiency, and market success for strategic planning, while using operational measures, such as production quality, for controlling the operation of production systems and motivating employees. Investors, on the other hand, may use financial measures, such as the gearing ratio and the price-to-earnings ratio, in order to evaluate the risk of an investment. There is no single operationalization of productivity that can be used across all contexts.

A final point to note is the comparative neglect of the timing of the measurement of the indicators of productivity. The current economic cycle in most Western countries tends to favor indicators that relate to the short term, in order to demonstrate immediate returns to shareholders and other interested parties. However, as noted previously, profitability in the short term is only weakly related to market value in the long term. The quickest way to achieve cost savings is to reduce staff, or to outsource many activities. These short-term measures obscure the longer-term costs stemming from the loss of staff loyalty and commitment, and from potential long-term skill shortages. Classic examples have been found recently in several large public utilities supplying gas, water, and electricity, where downsizing has been initiated ahead of privatization, in order to maximize the perceived profitability of the organization. Large-scale disasters in the form of power blackouts, inadequate quality control testing of water supply, and inadequate attention to maintenance and safety have cost the companies large sums in the long term. In many instances these disasters arose because the skill base of the organization had been degraded, reducing the capacity to cope with emergency situations and ongoing preventative maintenance. Time- or delay-discounting (Hesketh, Watson-Brown & Whiteley, 1998; Kirby & Herrnstein, 1995) provides a basis for understanding the short-term productivity trap. It is advisable to include indicators of productivity over various time spans in order to retain adaptive and functional organizations.

MEASUREMENT ISSUES

In addition to the conceptual issues associated with defining productivity, there are also a number of measurement issues that need to be considered. These include (a) the problems of criterion contamination and deficiency; (b) the difficulties posed by the proliferation of weakly related measures; and (c) the effects of sampling decisions and measurement models. Each of these issues is reviewed below.

Criterion Contamination and Deficiency

Criterion contamination represents a major problem in productivity measurement. Criterion contamination occurs when the criterion measure is influenced by factors that are outside of the control of the group or organization being studied. For example, an organization's growth in sales might be contaminated by the overall level of activity within the economy. While, in principle, we know how to control for the effects of extraneous variables using multivariate data analytic techniques, this is frequently difficult in practice. In many cases, it is not possible to identify and measure all potential confounding factors and sources of contamination. Furthermore, it is often easier to control for the effects of confounding factors in research studies, where there are large samples, than in practice, where productivity measurement is generally confined to the one organization.

Criterion deficiency is another major problem for productivity measurement. A measure suffers from criterion deficiency when it fails to capture important elements of the underlying construct. For example, operational measures of productivity that are commonly used in hospitals, such as bed utilization and average length of stay, fail to capture factors such as the quality of patient care. For this reason, it is common practice to use a wide array of measures in order to try and capture the criterion domain as completely as possible. However, the variety of different measures that can be used also creates problems, as explained below.

Proliferation of Weakly Related Measures

Over the past 40 years, we have seen a proliferation of productivity measures (Meyer & Gupta, 1994). Accountancy measures, such as return on investment, were widely used as a standard measure of organizational productivity until the late 1960s. These were then supplemented by financial measures focusing on dividends and share prices (e.g., earnings per share and return on equity) in the 1970s, which were supplemented by other measures in the 1980s and 1990s.

Meyer and Gupta (1994) argue that the proliferation of productivity measures can be attributed to the limited life span of most measures. The decline in use of accounting measures, such as return on investment, is illustrative. These measures were used by 50% of US firms for evaluating capital expenditures in 1959. By 1988, only 12% of firms were using these measures (Meyer & Gupta, 1994). When a measure is used as a standard to compare and evaluate different groups or organizations, then those units will respond to the contingencies and learn how to score highly on the measure. Part of this learning is 'real,' in the sense that there is an improvement on the underlying construct. For example, the dramatic reduction in the incidence of major hull failures by commercial jet aircraft since the 1950s represents a genuine improvement in outcome. However, learning can also be 'spurious,' in the sense that managers and employees learn how to produce improvements in figures, without producing any improvement in the functioning of the group or organization. For example, if university funding is related to student evaluation of course experience, faculty may do all they can to enhance the positive appraisal of their programs. Some aspects of this may reflect a genuine improvement in the quality of learning, but efforts to achieve positive student appraisals may also result in the provision of less effortful and challenging programs.

The effects of learning are reinforced by selection, since groups or organizations that do not respond to the contingencies are eliminated or rendered less viable. For example, organizational takeovers in the USA in the late 1970s and early 1980s favored organizations that maximized short-term profitability, and resulted in the elimination of firms that scored poorly on these measures (Meyer & Gupta, 1994). The result of these changes is a decline in the variance of each measure over time. Once productivity measures lose their ability to discriminate between units they are then replaced with newer measures that can discriminate. These new measures are typically orthogonal to the old measures, as there is no value in replacing an old measure with a new one if they are highly correlated. The changing goalposts and use of multiple indicators does help maintain organizational diversity and adaptability, but it creates considerable difficulties in achieving coherent measures.

Technology is an additional factor that may be partly responsible for the wide variety of operational measures that are currently used. The introduction of computerized technology has seen an increased diversity of production systems within organizations, making it increasingly difficult to develop standardized measures of performance and productivity (Hesketh & Neal, 1999). For example, the introduction of advanced manufacturing technology has seen an increase in the diversity of production systems within that sector. As a result, the operational measures that these firms employ vary quite widely. This makes systematic comparisons across organizations within the same sector difficult.

Sampling Decisions and Measurement Models

A final concern relates to the sampling procedures and measurement models that are used to characterize the data. Sampling decisions that have to be made include the number and composition of indicators that are used to represent an underlying construct; the level of analysis at which the data is collected and analyzed; the number of cases that are included; and the number of time intervals at which the data will be collected. Each of these decisions affects the kinds of measurement models that can be constructed, and hence the conclusions that can be drawn from the data.

Dealing with Multiple Indicators

It is frequently desirable to combine a number of different productivity measures into a single index, in order to make meaningful comparisons with the data. This is particularly important when using a wide array of indicators to overcome problems of criterion contamination and deficiency. A single index has a number of advantages (Pritchard, 1990). A single index can provide a lot of information in a simple format that is easily understood. This allows it to be used as an aid for decision making, and for the diagnosis and evaluation of organizational interventions. A single index is also a powerful motivational tool. It can be fed back to employees, allowing them to learn how to improve their performance, and motivating them to try harder. The motivational properties of this feedback can be further enhanced by using it within a goal setting or incentive program (e.g., Pritchard et al., 1988).

Unfortunately, aggregating across indicators is frequently difficult, because productivity measures are often not on the same scale, they are often collected at different levels of analysis, they may be based on different sample sizes, and may have differing variances. Where ratios are established to compare a variety of indicators of productivity for different groups against a series of benchmarks or a goals, the size of the target unit, and the benchmark unit matters. Productivity measures tend to have a lower reliability where there are a small number of component parts. Regression to the mean when the productivity levels within a unit are divided by size presents another problem. For example, within universities, comparisons of research productivity among departments with very different sizes need careful consideration. A single small unit with one or two stars will inevitably come top of the merit table. However, the contribution of stars is reduced when using measures such as average productivity per staff member. It becomes very difficult for large and highly successful units to be ranked ahead of smaller departments because of regression to the mean. Furthermore, where there are different variances in measures, these will also influence the weighting of the indicators. Understanding statistical anomalies is critical to avoid spurious results.

Creating Composition Variables

It is frequently desirable to aggregate productivity data across a number of subunits. For example, assume that a manager wishes to measure the productivity of a business unit, which has a number of work teams in it. In this example, there is no overall measure of productivity available and the manager has to aggregate the output of the different teams to create it. The manager needs a theory of composition (Chan, 1998) to guide the aggregation process. The manager could base the overall measure on (a) the mean level of output produced by the work teams; (b) the variance in output produced by the work teams; (c) the output produced by a particular work team (e.g., the best or the worst team); or (d) a complex algorithm based on a model of the processes by which the units interact with each other.

The particular composition model should depend upon the nature of the production system. The mean output model is best chosen when the overall productivity of the business unit reflects an additive combination of the different teams. For example, this might occur when the teams are working independently on a product. Variability of output should be used when the key concern of the manager is consistency. In certain manufacturing settings, for example, the focus of quality control is on the variability of production, rather than the mean level of production (Demming, 1986). The output of a particular team should be chosen when the production system operates conjunctively or disjunctively (Steiner, 1972). In a conjunctive production system, productivity depends on the worst team. For example, in a manufacturing cell, a single work team can disrupt the operation of the entire cell by failing to perform its tasks properly. In a disjunctive production system, productivity depends on the best team. Product design teams, for example, may compete with each other to produce a design. The productivity of the unit as a whole is a function of the team that comes up with the best design, or the team that comes up with the design the quickest. A process model needs to be created when the productivity of the unit reflects interactions among the constituent teams. For example, improvements in the quality of work carried out by a manufacturing team that supplies semiprocessed products to other teams in the manufacturing cell may allow the other teams to improve the quality of their work as well. In this example, improvements in the performance of one team can enhance the effects of improvements in other teams.

Incorporating Time and Context

Productivity measures are frequently collected over time, or across contexts. This creates a number of problems for data analysis. One problem is that the observations are nested, and the error terms are not independent. If we measure the productivity of an organization over time, then these observations are nested within the organization. Similarly, if we measure the productivity of a number of organizations that operate under different environmental conditions, then the observations are nested within contexts. Commonly used analysis techniques, such as ordinary least squares (OLS) regression are not appropriate under these circumstances, because they require the error terms to be independent (Hofmann, Griffin & Gavin, 2000).

A second problem is that the relationships between dependent variables can vary over time and across contexts. As noted earlier, Fryxell and Barton (1990) demonstrated that the relationship between accounting and market-based measures changes over time. If the researcher or practitioner uses a measurement model that does not account for any changes in the factor structure of the dependent variables, then this can produce systematically misleading conclusions.

A third problem is that the time lag between independent and dependent variables can vary. The duration and interval of sampling is critical (Nesselroade, 1991). The researcher or practitioner needs to ensure that he or she obtains a representative sample of the time periods in which the independent and dependent variables are changing, in order to estimate these lags. Nesselroade (1991) distinguishes between two kinds of temporal variance: variability and change. Variability refers to short-term fluctuations, whereas change refers to longer-term trends. These two effects are frequently caused by differing underlying (latent) variables, but are reflected in the same set of observed (manifest) variables. Relatively sophisticated analytic techniques are needed in order to model these effects.

ANALYTIC TECHNIQUES

In the current section, we examine a range of analytic techniques that are used to help address a number of the measurement issues discussed above.

ProMES

The Productivity Measurement and Enhancement System (ProMES; Pritchard et al., 1988) was specifically designed to overcome problems associated with aggregation. ProMES can be used to measure the productivity of groups, divisions, or organizations. There are three major steps involved in the development of productivity measures within ProMES. First, the overall objectives of the work unit are identified. Second, the unit develops indicators to measure whether they are achieving those objectives. Finally, subjective assessments are made by the unit regarding the relationship, or contingency, between performance on each of these indicators and the overall 'effectiveness' of the unit. Effectiveness is measured on a scale from $+100$, which is the maximum possible level of effectiveness that the unit could achieve, to -100, which is the worst possible level of effectiveness that the unit could achieve. These contingencies can be nonlinear, allowing the system to capture changes in the marginal rate of return for improvements in different indicators. The overall effectiveness score for the work unit is calculated by summing the effectiveness scores for each indicator. Where there are a number of subunits within a broader unit (e.g., work teams within a division), the effectiveness of the unit as a whole can be calculated by scaling the relative importance of each subunit (work teams) and summing the rescaled effectiveness scores to produce an overall score for the broader unit (the division).

ProMES has a number of advantages as a productivity measurement system. These include the ability to incorporate nonlinear effects, and the provision of a common metric for measuring productivity, and aggregating across different classes of criteria and levels of analysis. Furthermore, the data can be fed back to workgroups, and used as a tool for enhancing motivation. ProMES has been used successfully for this purpose in a number of different settings, in different parts of the world. Some examples include manufacturing firms in the Netherlands (Janssen, van Berkel & Stolk, 1995), Germany (Przygodda, Kleinbeck, Schmidt & Beckmann, 1995), and the USA (Jones, 1995), and service firms in Australia (Bonic, 1995), and Germany (Schmidt, Przygodda & Kleinbeck, 1995).

The major limitations of ProMES in its current form are its reliance on an additive composition model to perform aggregation and its failure to adjust for the size of the subunit. As noted previously, additive models are not appropriate in all circumstances. It is possible to use alternative composition methods within ProMES, for example, by creating a model of the process where the contributions of different workgroups are combined, however, these have not been explored within the literature. The process of psychological scaling in ProMES, where performance is assessed against expectations, can help to overcome some of the problems associated with varying sizes of subunits if size is taken into account when setting expected levels of performance.

Hierarchical Linear Modeling (HLM)

HLM (Bryk & Raudenbush, 1991) is increasingly being used as a tool for analyzing multilevel data sets within the social sciences. HLM was designed to overcome the problems associated with time and context described previously. One of the key advantages of HLM is that, unlike OLS regression, it provides separate estimates of the error terms within and between cases, hence accounting for the interdependence of observations within cases or contexts (Hofmann et al., 2000). Growth curve models (Rogosa & Willet, 1985) are used to examine variation or change over time. Separate regression equations are first estimated to describe the relationship between time and productivity for each case. The parameters from these equations (typically the intercept and slope) are then used as dependent variables in a series of analyses examining the factors that predict differences between the cases. For example, if we wish to examine the effect of human resource management (HRM) practices on organizational productivity over time, then we would first construct a separate regression equation for each organization describing the change in productivity over time within that organization. We would then examine whether HRM practices predict organizational differences in mean productivity (using the intercept of the level 1 equations as the dependent variable), and whether HRM predicts organizational differences in productivity growth (using the slope of the level 1 equations as the dependent variable). HLM is also used to examine the effects of contextual factors, such as environmental uncertainty and hostility, in a similar manner (e.g., see Hofmann, 1997).

Structural Equation Modeling (SEM)

SEM is an effective technique for dealing with the problems posed by multiple indicators. SEM allows the user to specify a measurement model describing the hypothesized relationships between indicators (manifest variables) and underlying constructs (latent variables). Relatively sophisticated models can be constructed to describe change over time. For example, Muthen (1991) describes a structural model that accounts for the sources of change and stability in negative affect over time. Similar models can be used to analyze the sources of variance in productivity.

Time Series Methods

A number of time series methods have been developed within economics to deal with data sets where there is a small number of cases (e.g., $n = 1$), a large number of time intervals (frequently over 50), and a small number of indicators for underlying constructs. In many cases, productivity data is collected in a similar manner. Examples of techniques that can be used to analyze this kind of data include state transition analysis methods, spectral analysis methods, and vector autoregression moving average methods (Jones, 1991). These methods are rarely used within the work and organizational psychology literature.

DETERMINANTS OF PRODUCTIVITY

In the current section we examine the theoretical perspectives that have influenced productivity research, and review some of the key findings from this literature. Given the size of the literature involved, this review is necessarily selective. The review adopts a psychological framework, and focuses on factors that affect organizational and group productivity by influencing or constraining the behavior of individuals within organizations. Where possible, we attempt to identify the mechanisms responsible for the observed effects.

Organizational Productivity

Theoretical Perspectives

There are a range of theoretical perspectives that have influenced research examining the determinants of organizational productivity. Some of the more commonly cited perspectives are structural contingency theory (Burns & Stalker, 1961; Woodward, 1965; Lawrence & Lorsch, 1967; Van de Ven & Drazin, 1985), strategic choice (Hrebiniak & Joyce, 1985), population ecology (Aldrich, 1979; Hannan & Freeman, 1984), resource dependence theory (Barney, 1991; Pfeffer & Salancik, 1978), and sociotechnical systems theory (Katz & Kahn, 1978; Trist & Bamforth, 1951; Trist et al., 1993).

Structural contingency theory assumes that productivity is dependent upon a fit between the internal characteristics of the organization, and the

environment in which it competes. Most of the research stemming from this tradition has focused on the fit between factors such as environmental uncertainty, and organizational structure, strategy, and technology. The strategic choice and population ecology perspectives also emphasize the importance of fit, but differ with respect to the role of management. The strategic choice position assumes that managers can make sense of the environment in which they operate, and make choices accordingly. Research stemming from the strategic choice position has, therefore, tended to focus on productivity as a key dependent variable. The population ecology position, on the other hand, assumes that organizational characteristics are environmentally determined, and that managers have relatively little freedom of choice. If an organization does not have the characteristics that are required for it to compete within its environment, then according to this view, it will fail. As a result, a limited number of organizational types will come to dominate the general population. These types will have the structures, strategies, and technologies that are congruent with their environment. Most of the research stemming from the population ecology tradition has, therefore, focused on organizational survival, and has tended not to incorporate measures of productivity.

Resource dependence theory is closely related to population ecology, and emphasizes the importance of interactions between the organization and the environment. Productivity is argued to be dependent upon the acquisition and exploitation of scare and valued resources. Organizations are argued to be more likely to gain a sustained competitive advantage if they can obtain resources that are valuable, scarce, difficult to imitate, and hard to substitute for (Barney, 1991). One of the problems with this approach has been the difficulty of operationalizing the concept of resources (Bedeian, 1994). Recently, however, substantial progress has been made in the measurement of human resources, which has allowed an examination of the link between human resources and productivity.

Finally, sociotechnical systems theory emphasizes the importance of interactions between the social and technical subsystems within the organization. According to this approach, the technology adopted by an organization constrains the social system by shaping the behaviors of individuals working with the technology. The social system, on the other hand, also constrains the way that the technology operates. In order to maximize productivity, the organization has to 'jointly optimize' the two subsystems, and effectively manage the interactions between these systems and the external environment.

The following section reviews some of the key empirical findings regarding the determinants of productivity at the organizational level.

Structure, Strategy, and Technology

Research has shown that the fit between organizational characteristics and environmental conditions does predict productivity, although the effects are not strong (Pennings, 1992). In a classic study, Burns and Stalker (1961) examined British electronic firms in the postwar era. The markets that these firms were competing in were changing and becoming more complex. Firms that adopted an organic structure (e.g., by reducing centralization and increasing employee participation) had higher levels of productivity than firms that retained a mechanistic structure. Similar findings have been reported more recently, although the findings are not always consistent (Ketchen, Thomas & Snow, 1993, Ketchen et al., 1996).

More recently, research has used configural analyses to test these hypothesized relationships. Organizational configurations refer to 'any multidimensional constellation of conceptually distinct characteristics that commonly occur together' (Meyer, Tsui & Hinings, 1993: 1175). Configural theories assume that particular configurations of structure, technology, and strategy co-occur within organizations operating within similar environments, because these characteristics are interdependent and are subject to the same constraints. These theories assume that the effectiveness of different configurations depends on the environment, although a number of different configurations can be effective in any given environment. Miles and Snow (1978), for example, identified four types of organizations: prospectors, defenders, analyzers, and reactors. Prospectors are characterized by organic structures, high levels of interdependence between units, nonroutine technologies, low levels of specialization, and high levels of environmental scanning. Defenders are characterized by mechanistic structures, routine technologies, high levels of specialization, low interdependence, and long-term planning. Analyzers operate routinely and efficiently in stable markets, but watch competitors closely for promising ideas, which are adopted quickly when the market is turbulent. Reactors have no consistent strategy. Doty, Glick and Huber (1993) found that measures of fit between organizational characteristics and the ideal types derived from Miles and Snow's (1978) theory predicted a range of financial and operational outcomes. Ketchen, Combs, Russell and Shook (1997) conducted a meta-analysis of existing configural studies, and found that there was a small but significant relationship between measures of configural fit and productivity. One of the problems in this field is the reliance on empirical techniques to identify configurations of organizational attributes. The study by Doty et al. (1993) is one of the few studies to test theoretically derived configural models. Research in this field is essentially descriptive and there is a need to test tight theory-driven hypotheses.

The strategic decision-making literature has also examined a range of factors relating to decision process. Rational, analytic, and fast decision processes are positively associated with productivity, particularly in dynamic environments (Dean & Sharfman, 1996; Eisenhardt, 1989; Ketchen et al., 1996; Thomas, Clark & Gioia, 1993), whereas political behavior during strategic decision making is negatively associated with productivity (Dean & Sharfman, 1996; Eisenhardt & Bourgeois, 1988). Furthermore, there is also evidence that the fit between decision process and decision content predicts productivity. Ketchen et al. (1996) found that opportunistic strategies were associated with better financial outcomes when organizations used less information in the decision-making process. Defensive strategies were associated with better financial outcomes when organizations used more information in the decision-making process.

The mechanisms by which strategy, structure, and technology influence productivity are complex, and often explained using constructs that fall outside of the domain of work and organizational psychology. For example, the effects of strategies, such as cost leadership and differentiation, can be partially explained using concepts from economics, such as supply, demand, and product substitutability (Porter, 1980). However, the success of particular groupings of strategy, structure, and technology is also thought to depend on the HRM practices that the organization uses. For example, Jackson, Schuler and Rivero (1989) found an association between the technological and structural characteristics of organizations, and the types of HRM practices that they used. Organizations using advanced manufacturing technology were more likely to use financial incentives, link performance appraisals to pay and training needs analysis, and provide jobs with high skill variety, than organizations using mass production technology. Furthermore, theoretical and empirical analyses in Europe, Japan and the USA, suggest that the relationship between advanced manufacturing technology and productivity is either mediated or moderated by HRM practices (Lowe, Delbridge & Oliver, 1997; Taira, 1996; Wall, 1996; Wall, Corbett, Martin, Clegg & Jackson, 1990; Zammuto & O'Connor, 1992). In the following section we review the effects of HRM practices, and the psychological mechanisms underlying these effects.

Human Resource Management
Practices

A number of authors have emphasized the importance of 'high-involvement' or 'high-performance' management systems for contemporary organizations (Lawler, Mohrman & Ledford, 1995; Walton, 1985; Womack, Jones & Roos, 1990). Proponents of the resource-based view of the firm (Barney, 1991), for example, argue that traditional sources of competitive advantage, such as access to technology and capital, are becoming less effective as these assets become more widely imitated. Human resources, on the other hand, represent an asset that can provide a source of sustained competitive advantage, since they are often difficult to imitate.

A substantial body of research over the past ten years has examined the relationship between HRM practices and organizational productivity. Most of this research has been conducted in the USA, although a number of studies have been conducted in the UK (Guest & Hoque, 1994; Hoque, 1999; Neal, West & Patterson, 2000; Patterson, West, Lawthom & Nickell, 1997; Wood & de Menezes, 1998), Canada (Betcherman, McMullen, Leckie & Caron, 1994), France (d'Arcimoles, 1997), and other countries (MacDuffie, 1995). A range of practices have been found to enhance productivity, including personnel selection techniques, employee training, performance appraisal, nonmonetary benefits, financial incentives, job enrichment, teamworking, and participation in decision making (e.g., Arthur, 1994; Delery & Doty, 1996; Huselid, 1995; Patterson et al., 1997; Youndt, Snell, Dean & Lepak, 1996). These practices have been labeled as 'progressive' HRM practices, since they treat employees as an asset, rather than a cost (Wood, 1999). Progressive HRM techniques are frequently contrasted with traditional techniques, which involve minimizing expenditure on selection, training, performance management, and compensation, and using mechanistic approaches to job design. Furthermore, it appears that organizations frequently adopt 'bundles' of progressive or traditional practices, since any individual practice is likely to be more effective when used in conjunction with other related practices (e.g., Betcherman et al., 1994; MacDuffie, 1995).

There are at least two mechanisms by which HRM practices enhance productivity and profitability (Neal & Griffin, 1999). The first involves employee commitment, job satisfaction, and motivation. Practices such as job enrichment, teamworking, participation, performance appraisal, compensation, and incentives are argued to enhance commitment, satisfaction, and motivation (e.g., Patterson et al., 1997), which in turn, enhance task performance and citizenship, and reduce absenteeism and turnover. The second mechanism involves employee knowledge, skill, and ability. Practices such as selection and training are argued to enhance employee knowledge, skill, and ability (Huselid, 1995), which in turn enhance task performance. Increasing task performance and citizenship, and reducing absenteeism and turnover should enhance organizational productivity.

Much of the debate within the HRM literature has centered around the question of whether the effects of HRM practices are universal across organizations, or whether the effectiveness of HRM practices are contingent upon other factors. A number of factors have been proposed as moderators of the link between HRM practices and organizational effectiveness, including organizational strategy, quality management practices (e.g., total quality management, TQM), and culture or climate (Wood, 1999). Some studies have found evidence for fit between HRM practices and strategy (Delery & Doty, 1996; Guest & Hoque, 1994; Hoque, 1999; Youndt et al., 1996). A number of studies have found evidence for fit between HRM practices and quality management practices (Lawler et al., 1995, Lawler, Mohrman & Ledford, 1998; MacDuffie, 1995), while others have found minimal evidence of fit (Huselid, 1995).

One study has tested for interactions between HRM practices and different types of organizational climate (Neal et al., 2000). This study examined the effects of two types of climate: a human relations climate (emphasizing employee well-being) and a rational goal climate (emphasizing goal attainment). The relationship between HRM practices and productivity was stronger when there was a poor human relations climate, suggesting that progressive HRM practices can compensate for a poor human relations climate, and vice versa. This two-way interaction between HRM and human relations climate was strongest when there was a minimal emphasis on goal attainment within the workplace. When employees reported that there was a strong emphasis on goal attainment, HRM practices and human relations climate exerted additive effects on productivity.

Group Productivity

Theoretical Perspectives

Research into the determinants of group productivity has evolved within a number of different research traditions. Two of the most widely cited traditions within the work and organizational psychology literature are the sociotechnical systems approach (Trist & Bamforth, 1951), and the input–process–output approach (McGrath, 1964). The sociotechnical tradition has adopted an action research perspective, investigating the effectiveness of interventions, such as self-managing workteams. This research has been carried out across a number of different countries, including Britain, India, Norway, Australia, and the USA (e.g., Trist et al., 1993). A number of studies have found that the introduction of self-managed workteams does lead to improvements in productivity (e.g., Cohen & Ledford, 1994), although the effects are inconsistent, and relatively few studies have examined the mediating mechanisms (for an exception see Wall, Kemp, Jackson & Clegg, 1986).

Research conducted within the input–process–output tradition has focused on the mechanisms by which different factors influence productivity. Inputs examined include (a) individual factors, such as ability, personality and attitudes, (b) group factors, such as size, tenure, and goals, and (c) situational factors and task characteristics, such as complexity, time pressure, and autonomy. A common assumption within this literature is that internal group processes (teamwork) at least partially mediate the relationship between these inputs and productivity (Cohen & Bailey, 1997). This literature is reviewed below.

Teamwork

A substantial body of research has examined the link between teamwork and productivity at the group level of analysis. A variety of teamwork factors have been found to predict objective and subjective measures of productivity, including (a) task-related activities, such as communication, coordination, planning, and leadership activities (e.g., Campion, Medsker & Higgs, 1993; Erez, 1992; Stout, Salas & Carson, 1994; Weingart, 1992), (b) boundary management activities, such as external representation (Ancona, 1990; Ancona & Caldwell, 1992), and (c) maintenance activities, such as social support (Campion et al., 1993, Campion, Papper & Medsker, 1996).

Individual Factors

There is strong evidence to suggest that the attributes of individuals within groups influence group productivity. This research has mostly focused on the mean levels of particular attributes within groups, however, a range of other composition models have also been examined, including variance models and minimum attribute models. This literature is reviewed below.

Mean composition models have been used to examine the effects of a wide variety of attributes. The mean level of individual knowledge, skill, and ability within a group has consistently been shown to be a strong predictor of group productivity (e.g., Tannenbaum, Beard & Salas, 1992). A number of attitudinal variables have been found to predict productivity, including cohesion (Mullen & Copper, 1994), and potency (e.g., Campion et al., 1993, 1996). Most of the studies within this literature have used mean composition models. Recent research has demonstrated that the mean level of personality traits, such as conscientiousness, extraversion, and emotional stability can also influence group productivity (Barrick, Stewart, Neubert & Mount, 1998; Barry & Stewart, 1997).

A number of studies have examined the effect of variability of attributes across individuals in organizations. Variability of individual skills and attributes has been found to be a positive predictor of productivity (Goodman, 1986; Guzzo & Dickson, 1996). Groups that have a diverse range of attributes appear to perform better, because they can draw upon a wider range of resources when carrying out their task. Other research has demonstrated that variability can also be a negative predictor of productivity. Stout, Cannon-Bowers, Salas and Milanovich (1999) demonstrated that tactical teams who do not share common mental models or who do not develop shared situation awareness perform poorly under high workload conditions. However, it should be possible to have shared mental models which include optimum use of varied resources in the group.

The leadership literature has examined the effects of specific individuals on group productivity. This literature demonstrates that the attributes of the group leader influences group productivity (e.g., Eden, 1990; Kabanoff & O'Brien, 1979; Vecchio, 1990; Vogelaar & Kuipers, 1997). Other studies have demonstrated that the group member with the lowest level of ability, conscientiousness or agreeableness can influence the productivity of the group as a whole (Barrick et al., 1998; LePine, Hollenbeck, Ilgen & Hedlund, 1997). When groups are performing conjunctive tasks, a single individual who performs poorly appears to be able to disrupt the performance of the entire group. LePine et al. (1997) found that this effect was stronger when the group leader had high levels of ability and conscientiousness.

Group Factors

Factors such as size, tenure, and goals refer to attributes of the group itself, rather than the individuals within that group. Size does not appear to exert a consistent effect on productivity. Sometimes size appears to be positively related to productivity, and sometimes it is negatively related to productivity. Gooding and Wagner (1985), for example, conducted a meta-analysis of available studies, and found either no relationship between size and productivity, or a negative relationship, depending on the measure of productivity used. Tenure has been found to predict productivity. Newly formed groups tend to have lower levels of productivity than established groups, presumably because they have not developed the shared mental models that underlie effective teamwork (Guzzo & Dickson, 1996). Finally, there is strong evidence that group goal setting enhances productivity (e.g., Pritchard et al., 1988). This effect is typically assumed to be mediated by motivation.

Situational Factors
and Task Characteristics

Situational factors and task characteristics, such as complexity, time pressure, interdependence, autonomy, and significance, influence group productivity

(Salas, Bowers & Cannon-Bowers, 1995; Tannenbaum et al., 1992). Some of these effects are direct (e.g., Goodman, 1986), whereas others appear to be mediated by motivation. Group members often respond to situational constraints by increasing or decreasing effort (e.g., Weingart, 1992). Factors such as autonomy and task significance are thought to improve group productivity by improving individual motivation (e.g., Campion et al., 1993, 1996; Cohen & Ledford, 1994).

A Model of Group Productivity

The current section develops a model of group productivity that attempts to articulate at least some of the mechanisms responsible for the findings reviewed above. This model is shown in Figure 1.1. Following Neal and Griffin (1999), we assume that ability is a major antecedent of individual task performance, and that this relationship is mediated by knowledge and skill. We also assume that personality and attitudes are major antecedents of individual teamwork (a component of contextual performance), and that these relationships are mediated by motivation. Furthermore, we assume that knowledge and skill can influence teamwork, while motivation can influence task performance. There is strong evidence from the individual performance literature to support most components of this model (e.g., Borman, White, Pulakos & Oppler, 1991; McCloy, Campbell & Cudeck, 1994).

Many of the effects examined within the group productivity literature can be explained using this model. Group tenure is thought to enhance productivity by improving individual knowledge and skill. Leadership is thought to enhance individual knowledge and skill, as well as motivation. Task characteristics and group goals are thought to influence individual motivation, although task characteristics may also exert a direct effect on productivity. Coworker attitudes should also influence individual motivation, although this effect is probably mediated by individual attitudes. An individual's attitudes are likely to influence the attitudes of his or her coworkers. Coworker attitudes, in turn, are likely to affect the individual's attitudes.

Two additional factors are needed to explain the relationship between individual performance and group productivity. The first factor is the effect of individual teamwork on the behavior of other group members. Individuals who engage in teamwork activities can help their coworkers perform their tasks better, and can motivate their coworkers to devote more effort to the task, and engage in teamwork activities themselves. These linkages are reciprocally interdependent, since coworker teamwork, in turn, affects the individual's motivation to perform task and teamwork activities. Over time,

group members are likely to learn how much effort each other member devotes to task and teamwork activities, and will adjust their levels of effort accordingly. A single individual who devotes relatively little effort to task and teamwork activities can, therefore, cause a downward spiral, as other group members withdraw effort in response (an effect termed 'social loafing': Latane, Williams & Harkins, 1979).

The second factor is the interaction between the contributions of individuals, their coworkers, and leaders. Task characteristics influence the way in which the contributions of group members and leaders are combined (Steiner, 1972). We assume that teamwork does not have a direct effect on group productivity, and that the effects of teamwork are mediated by the task performance of individuals or their coworkers. Since additive tasks, by definition, involve an additive combination of individual inputs, there should be no interactions between performance of individuals, coworkers and leaders within groups performing these tasks. There should be no interactions for disjunctive tasks either. This is because group output simply reflects the performance of the best group member in disjunctive tasks. However, for conjunctive tasks, there should be an interaction. The relationship between the mean level of coworker task performance and group productivity should become weaker as the task performance of the worst group member (or leader) declines. We term this interaction a disruption effect, because this performance of this person disrupts the performance of the group, making the other members and the leader less effective.

Other types of interactions may also be possible. In some situations, the group may compensate for the performance of the worst group member. LePine et al. (1997) argue that this effect is likely to occur when group members attribute the poor performance of this person to a lack of ability, rather than a lack of motivation. In this case, the relationship between the mean level of coworker task performance and group productivity should increase as the task performance of the worst group member (or leader) declines. In other situations, the performance of the best group member or leader may moderate the relationship between the mean level of coworker performance and group productivity. This interaction could work in either direction. The relationship between coworker performance and productivity could become stronger as the performance of the best group member or leader increases (an enhancement effect), or could become weaker as the performance of the best group member or leader increases (a compensation effect). At present, we do not have sufficiently strong models of group task characteristics to predict, with confidence, the specific situations in which these types of effects may be observed.

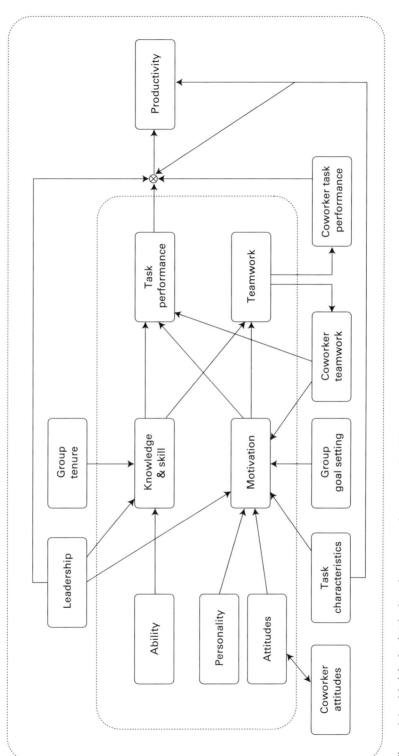

Figure 1.1 *Model of individual performance and group productivity*

CONCLUSION

The current chapter has examined some of the key conceptual and measurement issues associated with the assessment of productivity, and reviewed the types of factors that have been found to influence productivity at the organizational and group levels of analysis. Despite the confusion within the literature regarding the definition and measurement of productivity, it is possible to state some general conclusions regarding the field. At the organizational level, we know that HRM practices do have a substantial impact on productivity. Furthermore, it appears that the effects of other organizational characteristics, such as strategy and technology, may be at least partially mediated by HRM practices. At the group level, we know that the characteristics of the group as a whole, as well as the individuals within the group are critical. Ultimately, it is hoped that by identifying the full range of psychological factors that affect group and organizational productivity, multilevel models of productivity can be developed. These models would provide a coherent explanation of the mechanisms by which individual performance influences group productivity, and the mechanisms by which group productivity influences organizational productivity. It is hoped that the current chapter provides a further step towards the development of such models.

ACKNOWLEDGMENT

We wish to acknowledge the assistance of Barbara Griffin in the preparation of this manuscript.

REFERENCES

Aldrich, H. (1979). *Organizations and environments*. Englewood Cliffs, NJ: Prentice-Hall.

Ancona, D.G. (1990). Outward bound: Strategies for team survival in an organization. *Academy of Management Journal*, *33*(2), 334–365.

Ancona, D.G., & Caldwell, D.F. (1992). Bridging the boundary: External activity and performance in organizational teams. *Administrative Science Quarterly*, *37*(4), 634–665.

Arthur, J.B. (1994). Effects of human resource systems on manufacturing performance and turnover. *Academy of Management Journal*, *37*(3), 670–687.

Aupperle, K.E., Carroll, A.B., & Hatfield, J.D. (1985). An empirical examination of the relationship between corporate social responsibility and profitability. *Academy of Management Journal*, *28*(2), 446–463.

Barnard, C.I. (1938). *The functions of the executive*. Cambridge, MA: Harvard University Press.

Barney, J. (1991). Firm resources and sustained competitive advantages. *Journal of Management*, *17*, 99–120.

Barrick, M.R., Stewart, G.L., Neubert, M.J., & Mount, M.K. (1998). Relating member ability and personality to work-team processes and team effectiveness. *Journal of Applied Psychology*, *83*(3), 377–391.

Barry, B., & Stewart, G.L. (1997). Composition, process, and performance in self-managed groups: The role of personality. *Journal of Applied Psychology*, *82*(1), 62–78.

Bedeian, A.G. (1994). Organization theory: Current controversies, issues and directions. In C. Cooper, & I.T. Robertson (Eds.), *Key reviews in managerial psychology: Concepts and research for practice*. Chichester: John Wiley.

Bernhardt, K.L., Donthu, N., & Kennett, P.A. (2000). A longitudinal analysis of satisfaction and productivity. *Journal of Business Research*, *47*, 161–171.

Betcherman, G., McMullen, K., Leckie, N., & Caron, C. (1994). *The Canadian workplace in transition*. Kingston, Ontario: IRC Press.

Bonic, I. (1995). ProMES and computer service technicians: An Australian application. In R.D. Pritchard (Ed.), *Productivity measurement and improvement: Organizational case studies* (pp. 119–139) Westport, CT: Praeger Publishers.

Borman, W.C., White, L.A., Pulakos, E.D., & Oppler, S.H. (1991). Models of supervisory job performance ratings. *Journal of Applied Psychology*, *76*(6), 863–872.

Brodbeck, F.C. (1996). Criteria for the study of work group functioning. In M. West (Ed.), *Handbook of work group psychology*. (pp. 285–315). Chichester: John Wiley.

Bryk, A.S., & Raudenbush, S.W. (1991). *Hierachical linear models*. Newbury Park, CA: Sage.

Burns, T., & Stalker, G.M. (1961). *The management of innovation*. London: Tavistock Publications (reprinted Oxford: OUP, 1994).

Campbell, J.P., Dunnette, M.D., Lawler, E.E., & Weick, K.E. (1970). *Managerial behavior, performance, and effectiveness*. New York: McGraw-Hill.

Campbell, J.P., & Campbell, R.J. (1988). *Productivity in organizations: New perspectives from industrial and organizational psychology*. San Francisco, CA: Jossey-Bass.

Campion, M.A., Medsker, G.J., & Higgs, A. (1993). Relations between work group characteristics and effectiveness: Implications for designing effective work groups. *Personnel Psychology*, *46*(4), 823–850.

Campion, M.A., Papper, E.M., & Medsker, G.J. (1996). Relations between work group characteristics and effectiveness: A replication and extension. *Personnel Psychology*, *49*(2), 429–452.

Chan, D. (1998). Functional relations among constructs in the same content domain at different levels of analysis: A typology of composition models. *Journal of Applied Psychology*, *83*(2), 234–246.

Cochran, P.L., & Wood, R.A. (1984). Corporate social responsibility and financial performance. *Academy of Management Journal*, *27*, 42–56.

Cohen, S.G., & Bailey, D.E. (1997). What makes teams work: Group effectiveness research from the shop floor to the executive suite. *Journal of Management, 23*(3), 239–290.

Cohen, S.G., & Ledford, G.E. (1994). The effectiveness of self-managing teams: A quasi-experiment. *Human Relations, 47*(1), 13–43.

Conway, J.M. (1999). Distinguishing contextual performance from task performance for managerial jobs. *Journal of Applied Psychology, 84*(1), 3–13.

d'Arcimoles, C.H. (1997). Human resource policies and company performance: A quantitative approach using longitudinal data. *Organization Studies, 18*(5), 857–874.

Dean, J.W. Jr., & Sharfman, M.P. (1996). Does decision process matter? A study of strategic decision-making effectiveness. *Academy of Management Journal, 39*(2), 368–396.

Delery, J.E., & Doty, D.H. (1996). Modes of theorizing in strategic human resource management: Tests of universalistic, contingency and configurational performance predictions. *Academy of Management Journal, 39*(4), 802–835.

Demming, W.E. (1986). *Out of crisis: Quality, productivity and competitive position.* Cambridge: Cambridge University Press.

Doty, D.H., Glick, W.H., & Huber, G.P. (1993). Fit, equifinality, and organizational effectiveness: A test of two configurational theories. *Academy of Management Journal, 36*(6), 1196–1250.

Dubofsky, P., & Varadarajan P.R. (1987). Diversification and measures of performance: Additional empirical evidence. *Academy of Management Journal, 30*(3), 597–608.

Eden, D. (1990). Pygmalion without interpersonal contrast effects: Whole groups gain from raising manager expectations. *Journal of Applied Psychology, 75*(4), 394–398.

Eisenhardt, K.M. (1989). Making fast strategic decisions in high-velocity environments. *Academy of Management Journal, 32*(3), 543–576.

Eisenhardt, K.M., & Bourgeois, L.J. (1988). Politics of strategic decision making in high-velocity environments: Toward a midrange theory. *Academy of Management Journal, 31*(4), 737–770.

Erez, M. (1992). Interpersonal communication systems in organisations, and their relationships to cultural values, productivity and innovation: The case of Japanese corporations. *Applied Psychology: An International Review, 41*(1), 43–64.

Etzioni, A. (1964). *Modern organizations.* Englewood Cliffs, NJ: Prentice-Hall.

Fryxell, G.E., & Barton, S.L. (1990). Temporal and contextual change in the measurement structure of financial performance: Implications for strategy research. *Journal of Management, 16*(3), 553–569.

Gomez-Mejia, L.R., Tosi, H., & Hinkin, T. (1987). Managerial control, performance, and executive compensation. *Academy of Management Journal, 30*(1), 51–70.

Gooding, R.Z., & Wagner, J.A. (1985). A meta-analytic review of the relationship between size and performance: The productivity and efficiency of organizations and their subunits. *Administrative Science Quarterly, 30*(4), 462–481.

Goodman, P.S. (1986). The impact of task and technology on group performance. In P. Goodman (Ed.), *Designing effective workgroups.* (pp. 120–167). San Francisco: Jossey-Bass.

Guest, D., & Hoque, K. (1994). The good, the bad and the ugly: Employee relations in new non-union workplaces. *Human Resource Management Journal, 5*, 1–14.

Guzzo, RA., & Dickson, M.W. (1996). Teams in organizations: Recent research on performance and effectiveness. *Annual Review of Psychology, 47*, 307–338.

Hackman, J.R. (1987). The design of work teams. In J. Lorsch (Ed.), *Handbook of Organizational Behavior.* (pp. 315–342). Englewood Cliffs, NJ: Prentice-Hall.

Hannan, M.T., & Freeman, J. (1984). Structural inertia and organizational change. *American Sociological Review, 49*, 149–164.

Hesketh, B., & Neal, A. (1999). Technology and performance. In D.R. Ilgen, & E.D. Pukalos (Eds.), *The changing nature of work performance: Implications for staffing, motivation, and development* (pp. 21–55). San Francisco: Jossey Bass.

Hesketh, B., Watson-Brown, C., & Whiteley, S. (1998). Time-related discounting of value and decision-making about job options. *Journal of Vocational Behavior, 52*(1), 89–105.

Hofmann, D.A. (1997). An overview of the logic and rationale of hierachical linear models. *Journal of Management, 23*, 723–738.

Hofmann, D.A., Griffin, M.A., & Gavin, M. (2000). The application of Hiearchical Linear Modeling to management research. In K. Klein, & S. Kozlowski (Eds.), *Multilevel theory, research, and methods in organizations* (pp. 467–511). San Francisco: Jossey Bass.

Hoque, K. (1999). Human resource management and performance in the UK hotel industry. *British Journal of Industrial Relations, 37*, 419–443.

Hoskisson, R.E., Hitt, M.A., Johnson, R.A., & Moesel, D.D. (1993). Construct validity of an objective (entropy) categorical measure of diversification strategy. *Strategic Management Journal, 14*(3), 215–235.

Hrebiniak, L.G., & Joyce, W.F. (1985). Organizational adaptation: Strategic choice and environmental determinism. *Administrative Science Quarterly, 30*(3), 336–349.

Huselid, M.A. (1995). The impact of human resource management practices on turnover, productivity, and corporate financial performance *Academy of Management Journal, 38*(3), 635–672.

Jacobson, R. (1987). On the validity of ROI as a measure of business performance. *American Economic Review, 77*, 470–478.

Jackson, S.E., Schuler, R.S., & Rivero, J.C. (1989). Organizational characteristics as predictors of personnel practices. *Personnel Psychology, 42*(4), 727–786.

Janssen, P., van Berkel, A., & Stolk, J. (1995). ProMES as part of a new management strategy. In R.D. Pritchard (Ed.), *Productivity measurement and improvement:*

Organizational case studies. (pp. 43–61). Westport, CT: Praeger Publishers.

Jones, K. (1991). The application of time series methods to moderate span longitudinal data. In L. Collins, & J. Horn (Eds.), *Best methods for the analysis of change: Recent advances, unanswered questions, future directions.* (pp. 75–87). Washington, DC: American Psychological Association.

Jones, S.D. (1995). ProMES in a small manufacturing department: Results of feedback and user reactions. In R.D. Pritchard (Ed.), *Productivity measurement and improvement: Organizational case studies.* (pp. 81–93). Westport, CT: Praeger Publishers.

Kabanoff, B., & O'Brien, G.E. (1979). Cooperation structure and the relationship of leader and member ability to group performance. *Journal of Applied Psychology, 64*(5), 526–532.

Katz, D., & Kahn, R.L. (1978). *The social psychology of organizations.* (2nd Ed.). New York: John Wiley.

Ketchen, D.J. Jr., Combs, J.G., Russell, C.J., & Shook, C. (1997). Organizational configurations and performance: A meta-analysis. *Academy of Management Journal, 40*(1), 223–240.

Ketchen, D.J., Thomas, J.B., & McDaniel, R.R. (1996). Process, content and context: Synergistic effects on organizational performance. *Journal of Management, 22*(2), 231–257.

Ketchen, D.J., Thomas, J.B., & Snow, C.C. (1993). Organizational configurations and performance: A comparison of theoretical approaches. *Academy of Management Journal, 36*(6), 1278–1313.

Kirby, K.N., & Herrnstein, R.J. (1995). Preference reversals due to myopic discounting of delayed rewards. *Psychological Science, 6*(2), 83–89.

Latane, B., Williams, K., & Harkins, S. (1979). Many hands make light the work: The causes and consequences of social loafing. *Journal of Personality and Social Psychology, 37*(6), 822–832.

Lawler, E.E., Mohrman, S.A., & Ledford, G.E. (1995). *Creating high performance organizations.* San Francisco: Jossey-Bass.

Lawler, E.E., Mohrman, S.A., & Ledford, G.E. (1998). *Strategies for high performance organizations.* San Francisco: Jossey-Bass.

Lawrence, P.R., & Lorsch, J.W. (1967). *Organisation and environment.* Homewood, IL: Irwin.

LePine, J.A., Hollenbeck, J.R., Ilgen, D.R., & Hedlund, J. (1997). Effects of individual differences on the performance of hierarchical decision-making teams: Much more than g. *Journal of Applied Psychology, 82*(5), 803–811.

Likert, R. (1967). *The human organization.* New York: McGraw-Hill.

Lowe, J., Delbridge, R., & Oliver, N. (1997). High-performance manufacturing: Evidence from the automotive components industry. *Organization Studies, 18,* 783–798.

MacDuffie, J.P. (1995). Human resource bundles and manufacturing performance: Organizational logic and flexible production systems in the world auto industry. *Industrial and Labor Relations Review, 48,* 197–221.

McCloy, R.A., Campbell, J.P., & Cudeck, R. (1994). A confirmatory test of a model of performance determinants. *Journal of Applied Psychology, 79*(4), 493–503.

McGrath, J.E. (1964) *Social psychology: A brief introduction.* New York: Holt, Rinehart, & Winston.

McGuire, J.B., Sundgren, A., & Schneeweis, T. (1988). Corporate social responsibility and firm financial performance. *Academy of Management Journal, 31*(4), 854–872.

McWilliams, A., & Siegel, D. (2000). Corporate social responsibility and financial performance: Correlation or misspecification? *Strategic Management Journal, 21*(5), 603–609.

Meyer, A.D., Tsui, A.S., & Hinings, C.R. (1993). Configurational approaches to organizational analysis. *Academy of Management Journal, 36*(6), 1175–1195.

Meyer, M.W., & Gupta, V. (1994). The performance paradox. *Research in Organizational Behavior, 16,* 309–369.

Miles, R.E., & Snow, C.C. (1978). *Organizational strategy, structure, and process.* New York: McGraw-Hill.

Motowidlo, S.J., Borman, W.C., & Schmit, M.J. (1997). A theory of individual differences in task and contextual performance. *Human Performance, 10*(2), 71–83.

Mullen, B., & Copper, C. (1994). The relation between group cohesiveness and performance: An integration. *Psychological Bulletin, 115*(2), 210–227.

Murray, A.I. (1989). Top managerial heterogeneity and firm performance. *Strategic Management Journal, 10,* 125–141.

Muthen, B.O. (1991). Analysis of longitudinal data using latent variable models with varying parameters. In L. Collins, & J. Horn (Eds.), *Best methods for the analysis of change: Recent advances, unanswered questions, future directions.* (pp. 1–17). Washington, DC: American Psychological Association.

Neal, A., & Griffin, M.A. (1999). Developing a theory of performance for Human Resource Management. *Asia Pacific Journal of Human Resources, 37,* 44–59.

Neal, A., & Hesketh, B. (2000). *Productivity in organizations: A global perspective.* Paper presented at the 15th Annual Conference of the Society for Industrial and Organizational Psychology, New Orleans.

Neal, A., West, M.A., & Patterson, M. (2000). An examination of interactions between organizational climate and human resource management practices in manufacturing organizations. *Aston Business School Memo, No. RP 0003.*

Nesselroade, J.R. (1991). Interindividual differences in intraindividual change. In L. Collins, & J. Horn (Eds.), *Best methods for the analysis of change: Recent advances, unanswered questions, future directions* (pp. 92–105). Washington, DC: American Psychological Association.

Organ, D.W. (1990). The motivational basis of organizational citizenship behavior. *Research in Organizational Behavior, 12,* 43–72.

Ostroff, C. (1992). The relationship between satisfaction, attitudes, and performance: An organizational level analysis. *Journal of Applied Psychology, 77*, 963–974.

Patterson, M., West, M.A., Lawthom, R., & Nickell, S. (1997). Impact of people management practices on business performance. *Issues in people management, 22*. London: Institute of Personnel and Development.

Pennings, J.M. (1992). Structural contingency theory: A reappraisal. *Research in Organizational Behavior, 14*, 267–309.

Pfeffer, J., & Salancik, G.R. (1978). *The external control of organizations: A resource dependence perspective.* New York: Harper & Row.

Porter, M.E. (1980). *Competitive strategy.* New York: Free Press.

Pritchard, R., Jones, S., Roth, P., Stuebing, K., & Ekeberg, S. (1988). The effects of group feedback, goal setting and incentives on organizational productivity. *Journal of Applied Psychology [Monographs], 73*(2), 337–358.

Pritchard, R.D. (1990). *Measuring and improving organizational productivity: A practical guide.* New York: Praeger Publishers.

Pritchard, R.D. (1992). Organizational productivity. In M.D. Dunnette, & L.M. Hough (Eds.), *Handbook of industrial and organizational psychology*, Vol. 3 (2nd edn) (pp. 443–471). Palo Alto, CA: Consulting Psychologists Press.

Przygodda, M., Kleinbeck, U., Schmidt, K., & Beckmann, J. (1995). Productivity measurement and enhancement in advanced manufacturing systems. In R.D. Pritchard (Ed.), *Productivity measurement and improvement: Organizational case studies*, (pp. 62–80). Westport, CT: Praeger Publishers.

Quinn, R.E., & Rohrbaugh, J. (1983). A spatial model of effectiveness criteria: Towards a competing values approach to organizational analysis. *Management Science, 29*, 363–377.

Rogosa, D.R., & Willet, J.B. (1985). Understanding correlates of change by modeling individual differences in growth. *Psychometika, 50*(2), 203–228.

Rowe, W.G., & Morrow, J.L. (1999). A note on the dimensionality of the firm financial performance construct using accounting, market, and subjective measures. *Canadian Journal of Administrative Sciences, 16*(1), 58–70.

Ryan, A.M., Schmit, M.J., & Johnson, R. (1996). Attitudes and effectiveness: Examining relations at the organizational level. *Personnel Psychology, 49*, 853–882.

Salas, E., Bowers, C.A., & Cannon-Bowers, J.A. (1995). Military team research: 10 years of progress. *Military Psychology, 7*(2), 55–75.

Schmidt, K., Przygodda, M., and Kleinbeck, U. (1995). Development of a productivity measurement and feedback system in a firm of commercial painters. In R.D. Pritchard (Ed.), *Productivity measurement and improvement: Organizational case studies.* (pp. 243–264). Westport, CT: Praeger Publishers.

Schneider, B. (1991). Service quality and profits: Can you have your cake and eat it too? *Human Resource Planning, 14*, 151–157.

Shane, P.B., & Spicer, B.H. (1983). Market response to environmental information produced outside the firm. *Accounting Review, LVIII*(3), 521–536.

Shipper, F., & White, C.S. (1983). Linking organizational effectiveness and environmental change. *Long Range Planning, 16*, 99–106.

Steiner, I.D. (1972). *Group process and productivity.* New York: Academic Press.

Stout, R.J., Cannon-Bowers, J.A., Salas, E., & Milanovich, D.M. (1999). Planning, shared mental models, and coordinated performance: An empirical link is established. *Human Factors, 41*(1), 161–172.

Stout, R.J., Salas, E., & Carson, R. (1994). Individual task proficiency and team process behavior: What's important for team functioning? *Military Psychology, 6*(3), 177–192.

Taira, K. (1996). Compatibility of human resource management, industrial relations, and engineering under mass production and lean production: An exploration. *Applied Psychology: An International Review, 45*(2), 97–117.

Tannenbaum, S.I., Beard, R.L., & Salas, E. (1992). Team building and its influence on team effectiveness: An examination of conceptual and empirical developments. In K. Kelley (Ed.), *Issues, theory, and research in industrial/organizational psychology. Advances in psychology.* (pp. 117–153). Amsterdam, Netherlands: North-Holland.

Thomas, J.B., Clark, S.M., & Gioia, D.A. (1993). Strategic sensemaking and organizational performance: Linkages among scanning, interpretation, action, and outcomes. *Academy of Management Journal, 36*(2), 239–270.

Tornow, W.W., & Wiley, J.W. (1991). Service quality and management practices: A look at employee attitudes, customer satisfaction, and bottom line consequences. *Human Resource Planning, 14*, 105–116.

Trist, E.L., & Bamforth, K.W. (1951). Some social and psychological consequences of the Longwall method of coal-getting. *Human Relations, 4*, 3–38.

Trist, E.L., Murray, H., & Trist, B. (Eds.) (1993). *The social engagement of social science: A Tavistock anthology*, Vol. 2, *The socio-technical perspective.* Philadelphia: University of Pennsylvania Press.

Van de Ven, A., & Drazin, R. (1985). The concept of fit in contingency theory. In B.M. Staw, & L.L. Cummings (Eds.), *Research in organizational behavior*, Vol. 7 (pp. 333–365). Greenwich, CT: JAI Press.

Van Scotter, J.R., & Motowidlo, S.J. (1996). Interpersonal facilitation and job dedication as separate facets of contextual performance. *Journal of Applied Psychology, 81*(5), 525–531.

Vecchio, R.P. (1990). Theoretical and empirical examination of cognitive resource theory. *Journal of Applied Psychology, 75*(2), 141–147.

Vogelaar, A.L.W., & Kuipers, H. (1997). Reciprocal longitudinal relations between leader and follower effectiveness. *Military Psychology, 9*(3), 199–212.

Waddock, S.A., & Graves, S.B. (1997). The corporate social performance – Financial performance link. *Strategic Management Journal, 18*(4), 303–319.

Wall, T., Kemp, N., Jackson, P., & Clegg, C. (1986). Outcomes of autonomous work groups: A long-term field experiment. *Academy of Management Journal, 29*(2), 280–304.

Wall, T.D. (1996). Modern manufacturing and work organization: The value of a wider perspective. *Applied Psychology: An International Review, 45*(2), 123–126.

Wall, T.D., Corbett, J.M., Martin, R., Clegg, C.W., & Jackson, P.R. (1990). Advanced manufacturing technology, work design and performance: A change study. *Journal of Applied Psychology, 75*(6), 691–697.

Walton, R. (1985). From 'control' to 'commitment' in the workplace. *Harvard Business Review, 63*, 77–84.

Weingart, L.R. (1992). Impact of group goals, task component complexity, effort, and planning on group performance. *Journal of Applied Psychology, 77*(5), 682–693.

Wiley, W.W. (1991). Customer satisfaction and employee opinions: A supportive work environment and its financial cost. *Human Resource Planning, 14*, 117–128.

Womack, J., Jones, D.T., & Roos, D. (1990). *The machine that changed the world*. New York: Rawson Associates.

Wood, S. (1999). Getting the measure of the transformed high-performance organization. *British Journal of Industrial Relations, 37*, 391–417.

Wood, S., & de Menezes, L. (1998). High commitment management in the UK: Evidence from the workplace industrial relations survey, and employers' manpower and skills practices survey. *Human Relations, 51*(4), 485–515.

Woodward, J. (1965). *Industrial organization: Theory and practice*. London: Oxford University Press.

Youndt, M.A., Snell, S.A., Dean, J.W., & Lepak, D.P. (1996). Human resource management, manufacturing strategy, and firm performance. *Academy of Management Journal, 39*(4), 836–866.

Yuchtman, E., & Seashore, S.E. (1967). A systems resource approach to organizational effectiveness. *American Sociological Review, 32*, 891–903.

Zammuto, R.F., & O'Connor, E.J. (1992). Gaining advanced manufacturing technologies' benefits: The roles of organization design and culture. *Academy of Management Review, 17*(4), 701–728.

2

Job Satisfaction: A Cross-Cultural Review

TIMOTHY A. JUDGE, SHARON PARKER, AMY E. COLBERT, DANIEL HELLER and REMUS ILIES

This chapter considers research and theory concerning job satisfaction, perhaps the most widely studied concept in organizational psychology. The chapter begins with consideration of the concept of job satisfaction, and then reviews theories of job satisfaction that have attracted the most attention. These theories include situational theories, which argue that job satisfaction results from aspects of the job or work environment (Herzberg's two-factor theory, social information processing theory, job characteristics model), dispositional approaches, which assume that job satisfaction results from the personality of the individual, and interactive theories, which consider job satisfaction to be a function of situational influences and individual differences (Cornell integrative model, Locke's value-percept theory). After reviewing these theories, we conclude that the job characteristics model, dispositional approaches, and Locke's value-percept theory have garnered the most support. Next, several important areas are reviewed, including measures of job satisfaction, the relationship of job satisfaction to several critical outcomes, and how job satisfaction is treated in organizations. A major section of the study is devoted to comparing the previous research literature, largely conducted in the USA, to that in international contexts. In reviewing this literature, although the level of support and frequency of investigation has varied, most findings appear to generalize across international contexts. Finally, an agenda for future research investigating international aspects of job satisfaction is presented.

INTRODUCTION

There are few, if any, concepts more central to industrial/organizational psychology than job satisfaction. In this century, the advent of the human relations movement is credited with emphasizing the importance of workplace attitudes. Indeed, the pioneers of the movement – Likert (1967), Maslow (1965), McGregor (1966), and Roethlisberger and Dickson (1939) – are credited with raising the field's consciousness with respect to workplace morale. Hoppock's (1935) landmark book roughly coincided with the Hawthorne studies that were the origin of the human relations movement. Hoppock's opening to his book aptly describes the emphasis that scholars of the time placed on job satisfaction, 'Whether or not one finds his employment sufficiently satisfactory to continue in it … is a matter of the first importance to employer and employee' (p. 5).

From this auspicious beginning, the job satisfaction literature has had its ebbs and flows. In his influential review, Locke (1976) estimated that over 3300 studies on job satisfaction had been conducted up to 1973. Using the PsycINFO database, we were able to find references to another 7856 studies on job satisfaction published since 1973, making job satisfaction perhaps the most widely studied topic in all of industrial/organizational psychology. Yet, currently, research on job satisfaction appears to be on the decline. As Figure 2.1 reveals, across all journals in the PsycINFO database, the rate of publications on job satisfaction has declined since the nirvana of the 1980s. As Figure 2.2 shows, in the top industrial/organizational psychology journals, the rate of publications has declined precipitously since the 1970s. Whether this is a long-term trend of short-term fluctuation is a question this chapter cannot answer.[1] We review research on job satisfaction, despite this apparent decline in research interest, for four reasons: (1) job satisfaction may be the most widely researched topic in the history of industrial/organizational psychology; (2) even if research is declining in a relative sense, job satisfaction still is among the most frequently investigated constructs in industrial/organizational psychology; (3) job satisfaction occupies a central role in many theories and models of individual attitudes and behaviors; and (4) job satisfaction research has practical application for the enhancement of individual lives and organizational effectiveness.

The purpose of this chapter is to provide a review of job satisfaction research as it has been conducted in the USA and internationally. Specifically, we will describe what we know about the nature, causes, measurement, and consequences of job satisfaction based on previous, largely American-based, research. Then, we summarize cross-cultural and international job satisfaction research, paying particular attention to research conducted in the last 20 years. Finally, partly based on discrepancies between US and international research, we lay out an agenda for future research that would provide greater understanding of the international aspects of job satisfaction.

WHAT IS JOB SATISFACTION?

Locke (1976) defined job satisfaction as '... a pleasurable or positive emotional state resulting from the appraisal of one's job or job experiences' (p. 1304). It is important to note the use of both cognition (appraisal) and affect (emotional state) in Locke's definition. Thus, Locke assumes that job satisfaction results from the interplay of cognition and affect, or thoughts and feelings. Recently, some organizational scholars have questioned this view, arguing that typical measures of job satisfaction are more cognitive than affective in orientation (e.g., Organ & Near, 1985). Brief (1998) comments,

'... organizational scientists often have been tapping the cognitive dimension while slighting or even excluding the affective one' (p. 87). In support of this argument, Brief and Roberson (1989) found that a purported measure of work cognitions correlated more strongly with job satisfaction than did positive and negative affectivity (PA and NA). The limitation with this study exposes the problem with the argument – it seems likely that job beliefs (cognitions) are as influenced by affect as is job satisfaction itself. Indeed, Brief and Roberson's results show that PA correlated more strongly with their purported measure of cognitions than it did with job satisfaction itself! In this study, as well as others, *both* cognition and affect contribute to job satisfaction. A recent study (Weiss, Nicholas & Daus, 1999) revealed that when cognitions about the job and mood were used to predict job satisfaction in the same equation, both were strongly related to job satisfaction, and *the relative effects were exactly the same*.

Thus, in evaluating our jobs both cognition and affect appear to be involved. When we think about our jobs, we have feelings about what we think. When we have feelings while at work, we think about these feelings. Cognition and affect are thus closely related, in our psychology and even in our psychobiology. Evidence indicates that when individuals perform specific mental operations, a reciprocal relationship exists between cerebral areas specialized for processing emotions and those specific for cognitive processes (Drevets & Raichle, 1998). There are cognitive theories of emotion (Reisenzein & Schoenpflug, 1992), and emotional theories of cognition (Smith-Lovin, 1991).

Let us be clear here. We do not mean to suggest that researchers should not investigate the roles of affect and cognition in judgments of job satisfaction. We believe the Weiss et al. (1999) study, for example, has revealed important insights into the psychological processes underlying judgments of job satisfaction. On the other hand, we do not believe it is productive to classify or characterize measures of job satisfaction as either cognitive or affective. Nor do we believe there is a need to develop new, affectively laden measures of job satisfaction, or to replace measures of job satisfaction with 'work affect' measures. Cognition and affect can help us better understand the nature of job satisfaction, but we do not believe bifurcation in the measures of job satisfaction, after more than 70 years of research, will prove fruitful.

Most scholars recognize that job satisfaction is a global concept that also comprises various facets. The most typical categorization of facets (Smith, Kendall & Hulin, 1969) considers five: pay, promotions, coworkers, supervision, and the work itself. Locke (1976) adds a few other facets: recognition, working conditions, and company and management. It is common for researchers to separate

Number of studies including
job satisfaction in keywords

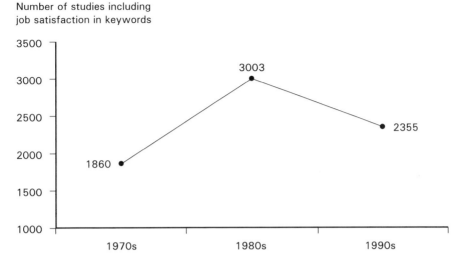

Figure 2.1   *Number of studies including 'job satisfaction' in keywords of PsycINFO database as a function of date of the study*

Number of studies including
job satisfaction in keywords

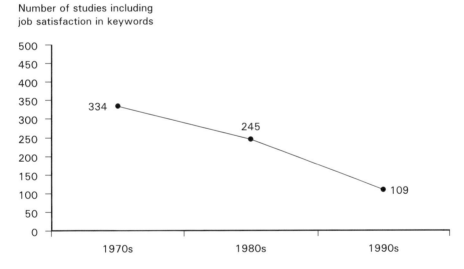

Figure 2.2   *Number of studies including 'job satisfaction' in keywords of PsycINFO database – top-tier industrial/organizational psychology and organizational behavior journals (Academy of Management Journal, Journal of Applied Psychology, Organizational Behavior and Human Decision Processes, Personnel Psychology)*

job satisfaction into intrinsic and extrinsic elements where pay and promotions are considered extrinsic factors and coworkers, supervision, and the work itself are considered intrinsic factors. Such an organizational structure is somewhat arbitrary; other structures were offered by Locke (1976), such as

events or conditions versus agents (where agents are supervisors, coworkers, and company or management), or work versus rewards versus context.

Another definitional issue is whether job satisfaction and dissatisfaction are polar opposites (exist on opposite ends of a bipolar continuum) or are separate concepts. The answer to this issue is closely bound up in Herzberg's two-factor theory, which will be reviewed shortly. Suffice it for now to conclude that satisfaction and dissatisfaction appear to lie at opposite ends of the same continuum and thus do not represent separate concepts (see Locke, 1976).

THEORIES OF JOB SATISFACTION ANTECEDENTS

Many theories concerning the causes of job satisfaction have been proposed. They can be loosely classified as falling into one of three categories: (1) situational theories, which hypothesize that job satisfaction results from the nature of one's job or other aspects of the environment; (2) dispositional approaches, which assume that job satisfaction is rooted in the personological make-up of the individual; and (3) interactive theories, which propose that job satisfaction results from the interplay of the situation and personality. To be sure, this is a gross categorization. For example, need theories could be argued to be situational or interactive (or perhaps even dispositional). However, since the main practical implications of need theories lie in changing the context of the job, we classify need theories as situational theories.

Situational Theories

Although many situational theories of job satisfaction have been proposed, we believe three stand out as most influential: (1) Herzberg's two-factor theory; (2) social information processing; (3) job characteristics model. Below we provide a review of each of these theories.

Two-Factor Theory

Herzberg (1967) argued that the factors that lead to satisfaction are often different from those that lead to dissatisfaction. This conclusion was based on a series of interviews of workers. When asked to consider factors connected to a time when they felt satisfied with their jobs, individuals generally talked about intrinsic factors such as the work itself, responsibilities, and achievements ('motivators'). Conversely, when workers were asked to consider factors that lead to dissatisfaction, most individuals discussed extrinsic factors such as company policies, working conditions, and pay ('hygiene factors'). Herzberg further found that intrinsic factors were more strongly correlated with satisfaction, while extrinsic factors were more strongly correlated with dissatisfaction. Based on these findings, Herzberg argued that elimination of hygiene factors from a job would only remove dissatisfaction, but not

bring satisfaction. To bring out job satisfaction, then, the organization must focus on motivator factors, such as making the work more interesting, challenging, and personally rewarding.

Despite its intuitive appeal, the two-factor theory has been roundly criticized by researchers. There are many logical problems with the theory, and many flaws in Herzberg's methodology (see Locke, 1969). One of the main problems is that most of the support of the theory comes from Herzberg's samples and methodology. Numerous empirical studies have attempted to replicate and test Herzberg's findings with independent data and methods, with little success (e.g., Hulin & Smith, 1967). Contrary to Herzberg's claim, research has consistently shown that intrinsic and extrinsic factors contribute to both satisfaction and dissatisfaction (Carroll, 1973; Wernimont, 1966). Thus, though the theory continues to be advocated by Herzberg and recommended for further study by others (Brief, 1998), these attempts at resurrecting the theory run against considerable scientific evidence. As Korman (1971) noted, disconfirming evidence has 'effectively laid the Herzberg theory to rest' (p. 179). Given the virtual absence of tests of the two-factor theory since 1971, we find Korman's comment a suitable epitaph.

Social Information Processing

Social information processing approaches to job attitudes argue that job satisfaction is a socially constructed reality (Salancik & Pfeffer, 1977, 1978). According to the theory, individuals do not really form judgments of job satisfaction until they are asked and, when they are asked, they rely on social sources of information such as interpretations of their own behaviors, cues by their coworkers, or even the way survey questions are posed. Substantively, the theory holds that individuals are apt to provide the responses they are expected to, and then seek to rationalize or justify their responses. As Hulin (1991) notes, one piece of evidence against the social information processing perspective is that the same job attributes appear to predict job satisfaction in different cultures, even though the social environments, values, and mores in these cultures often are quite different. Stone (1992) provides an in-depth, and fairly devastating, review and critique of the social information perspective. Although the theory continues to be brought up and occasionally endorsed, interest in it appears to have waned in the same way that exclusively situationalist explanations for attitudes and behaviors have declined.

Job Characteristics Model

The job characteristics model (JCM) argues that jobs which contain intrinsically motivating characteristics will lead to higher levels of job satisfaction, as well as other positive work outcomes, such as enhanced job performance and lower withdrawal. The model, introduced by Hackman and Oldham (1976), but derived from earlier work by Hackman and Lawler (1971), focuses on five core job characteristics:

Task identity – degree to which one can see one's work from beginning to end;

Task significance – degree to which one's work is seen as important and significant;

Skill variety – extent to which job allows employees to do different tasks;

Autonomy – degree to which employees have control and discretion for how to conduct their job;

Feedback – degree to which the work itself provides feedback for how the employee is performing the job.

According to the theory, jobs that are enriched to provide these core characteristics are likely to be more satisfying and motivating than jobs that do not provide these characteristics. More specifically, it is proposed that the core job characteristics lead to three critical psychological states – experienced meaningfulness of the work, responsibility for outcomes, and knowledge of results – which in turn lead to the outcomes.

There is both indirect and direct support for the validity of the model's basic proposition that core job characteristics lead to more satisfying work. In terms of indirect evidence, first, when individuals are asked to evaluate different facets of work such as pay, promotion opportunities, coworkers, and so forth, the nature of the work itself consistently emerges as the most important job facet (Jurgensen, 1978). Second, of the major job satisfaction facets – pay, promotion opportunities, coworkers, supervision, and the work itself – satisfaction with the work itself is almost always the facet most strongly correlated with overall job satisfaction (e.g., Rentsch & Steel, 1992). Thus, if we are interested in understanding what causes people to be satisfied with their jobs, the nature of the work (intrinsic job characteristics) is the first place to start.

Research directly testing the relationship between workers' reports of job characteristics and job satisfaction has produced consistently positive results. There have been several quantitative reviews of the literature indicating positive results (Fried & Ferris, 1987; Loher, Noe, Moeller & Fitzgerald, 1985). Recently, Frye (1996) provided an update and reports a true score correlation of .50 between job characteristics and job satisfaction. This provides strong support for the validity of the job characteristics model.

Although the model did not explicitly acknowledge individual differences in receptiveness to job characteristics in its original formulation, early on the model was modified from a purely situational model to more of an interactional model. According to Hackman and Oldham (1976), the relationship between intrinsic job characteristics and job satisfaction depends on employees' Growth Need Strength (GNS), which is employees' desire for personal development, especially as it applies to work. High-GNS employees want their jobs to contribute to their personal growth, and derive satisfaction from performing challenging and personally rewarding activities. According to the model, intrinsic job characteristics are especially satisfying for individuals who score high on GNS. In fact, research supports this aspect of the theory. Across the 10 studies that have investigated the role of GNS in the relationship between intrinsic job characteristics and job satisfaction, the relationship tends to be stronger for employees with high GNS (average $r = .68$) than for those with low GNS (average $r = .38$) (Frye, 1996). However, it is important to note that intrinsic job characteristics are related to job satisfaction even for those who score low on GNS.

There are some limitations to the theory. First, most of the studies have used self-reports of job characteristics, which has garnered its share of criticisms (Roberts & Glick, 1981). It is true that subjective reports of job characteristics correlate more strongly with job satisfaction than do objective reports. However, objective reports, even with all of their measurement imperfections, still show consistently positive correlations with job satisfaction (Glick, Jenkins & Gupta, 1986). Second, the relationship between perceptions of job characteristics and job satisfaction appears to be bidirectional (James & Jones, 1980; James & Tetrick, 1986). Thus, it cannot be assumed that any association between job characteristics and job satisfaction demonstrates a causal effect of job characteristics on job satisfaction. Third, there is little evidence that the critical psychological states mediate the relationship between job characteristics and outcomes as proposed. Finally, the formulaic combination of the five core characteristics has not been supported. Research indicates that simply adding the dimensions works better (Arnold & House, 1980). This limitation does not seem to be a serious problem with the theory, as whether an additive or multiplicative combination of job dimensions works best does not undermine the potential usefulness of the theory.

Dispositional Approaches

Of the three principal approaches to studying job satisfaction, the dispositional approach to job satisfaction is the most recently evolved and, perhaps as a result, the most poorly developed.

However, there has been recognition of individual differences in job satisfaction for as long as the topic of job satisfaction has been studied. For example, Hoppock (1935) found that workers satisfied with their jobs were better adjusted emotionally than dissatisfied workers. It was 50 years later, though, beginning with the publication of two influential studies by Staw and colleagues (Staw & Ross, 1985; Staw, Bell & Clausen, 1986), that the dispositional source of job satisfaction came into its own as a research area. Indeed, since the Staw studies, it has become one of the most popular areas of inquiry in the job satisfaction literature. Although, early on, this literature had its critics (Cropanzano & James, 1990; Davis-Blake & Pfeffer, 1989; Gerhart, 1987; Gutek & Winter, 1992), these criticisms have waned. Few scholars would dispute the contention that job satisfaction is, to a significant degree, rooted in individuals' personalities.

In reflecting on this literature, it appears there are two broad categories of studies. The first group, which we will call *indirect studies*, seek to demonstrate a dispositional basis to job satisfaction by inference. Typically, in such studies, disposition or personality is not measured, but is inferred to exist from a process of logical deduction or induction. Staw and Ross (1985), for example, inferred a dispositional source of satisfaction by observing that measures of job satisfaction were reasonably stable over a two-year ($r = .42$, $p < .01$), three-year ($r = .32$, $p < .01$), and five-year ($r = .29$, $p < .01$) period of time. Staw and Ross further discovered that job satisfaction showed significant stability under situational change – even when individuals changed both employers and occupation over a five-year period of time ($r = .19$, $p < .01$), though this stability is much less than for individuals who changed neither occupation nor employer ($r = .37$, $p < .01$). Another indirect, albeit provocative study, was authored by Arvey, Bouchard, Segal and Abraham (1989), who found significant similarity in the job satisfaction levels of 34 pairs of monozygotic (identical) twins reared apart from early childhood.

Though this series of indirect studies can be credited for establishing interest in the dispositional perspective, they have an obvious limitation – they cannot demonstrate a dispositional source of job satisfaction. For example, stability in job satisfaction over time can be due to many factors, only one of which is due to the personality of the individual (Gerhart, 1987; Gutek & Winter, 1992). Similarly, since babies have no jobs they cannot be born with job satisfaction. Thus, evidence showing similarity in twins' job satisfaction levels is indirect evidence, since the similarity must be due to other factors (i.e., personality).

The other group of studies, which we will term *direct studies*, relate a direct measure of a construct purported to assess a personality trait to job satisfaction. The specific traits that have been investigated have varied widely across studies. Staw et al. (1986), for example, utilized clinical ratings of children with respect to a number of adjectives assumed to assess affective disposition ('cheerful,' 'warm,' and 'negative'). Judge and Hulin (1993) and Judge and Locke (1993) used a measure, adapted from Weitz (1952), assessing employees' reactions to neutral objects common to everyday life. Despite the predictive validity of these measures for job satisfaction, most research has focused on other measures. These are reviewed below. Before proceeding, we should note that Ganzach (1998) has related general mental ability or intelligence to job satisfaction. However, this research is not reviewed beyond here because intelligence is not a personality trait and, further, the two concepts were virtually uncorrelated, $r = -.02$.

One group of studies has focused on positive and negative affectivity (PA and NA). According to Watson, Clark and colleagues, PA is characterized by high energy, enthusiasm, and pleasurable engagement, whereas NA is characterized by distress, unpleasurable engagement, and nervousness (Watson, Clark & Tellegen, 1988). An interesting finding in the literature supporting the distinction between PA and NA is that they appear to display different patterns of relationships with other variables (Watson, 2000). The general trend seems to be that PA more strongly relates to positive outcomes whereas NA is more strongly associated with negative outcomes. Several studies have related both PA and NA to job satisfaction (Agho, Mueller & Price, 1993; Brief, Butcher & Roberson, 1995; Brief, Burke, George, Robinson & Webster, 1988; Levin & Stokes, 1989; Necowitz & Roznowski, 1994; Watson & Slack, 1993). Thoresen and Judge (1997) reviewed the 29 studies that have investigated the PA-job satisfaction relationship and the 41 studies that have investigated the NA-job satisfaction relationship and found true score correlations of .52 and −.40, respectively. Thus, it appears that both PA and NA are generally related to job satisfaction.

Recently, Judge, Locke and Durham (1997), drawing from several different literatures, introduced the construct of core self-evaluations. According to Judge et al. (1997), core self-evaluations are fundamental premises that individuals hold about themselves and their functioning in the world. Judge et al., argued that core self-evaluation is a broad personality construct comprising several more specific traits: (1) self-esteem; (2) generalized self-efficacy; (3) locus of control; (4) neuroticism or emotional stability. Two primary studies have related core self-evaluations to job satisfaction. Judge, Locke, Durham and Kluger (1998), analyzing data across three samples, found that core self-evaluations had a 'true score' total effect of .48 on job satisfaction when both constructs were self-reported by employees and .37 when core self-evaluations were measured independently (by a significant other). Judge, Bono and Locke (2000) found that core self-evaluations correlated .41 ($p < .01$) with job satisfaction when both constructs were self-reported and .19 ($p < .05$) when core self-evaluations were reported by significant others. Judge and Bono (2001) have completed a meta-analysis of 169 independent correlations (combined $N = 59,871$) on the relationship between each of the four core traits and job satisfaction. When the four meta-analyses where combined into a single composite measure, the overall core trait correlated .37 with job satisfaction.

Although research on the dispositional source of job satisfaction has made enormous strides, considerable room for further development exists. Early in this research stream, Davis-Blake and Pfeffer (1989) criticized dispositional research for its failure to clearly define or carefully measure affective disposition. To some extent, this criticism is still relevant. As the above review attests, even those that have directly measured affective disposition have done so with fundamentally different measures. What traits and measures are best suited to predicting job satisfaction? Despite many studies on job satisfaction, there have been very few efforts to compare, contrast, and integrate these different conceptualizations and measures of affective disposition. Brief, George, and colleagues focus on mood at work and have used positive and negative affectivity as dispositional constructs. Weiss, Cropanzano and colleagues emphasize affective events at work and the emotions and cognitions these events produce. Judge, Locke, Erez and colleagues focus on core self-evaluations. The differences in these approaches are important. However, we should not assume that they are oriented toward different objectives – all seek to better understand the dispositional source of job attitudes. The approaches may not even be competitors. We view these different approaches as signs of a healthy area of scientific inquiry.

An equally important research need is to uncover the processes by which personality influences job satisfaction. This need has been voiced repeatedly in the literature (Brief, 1998; House, Shane & Herold, 1996; Judge, 1992; Judge et al., 1997; Spector, 1997). Given these repeated calls, it is amazing how little progress has been made in understanding psychological processes underlying the dispositional source of job satisfaction. Although the exceptions are noteworthy (Brief, 1998; Motowidlo, 1996; Weiss & Cropanzano, 1996), it remains a relatively atheoretical area of research.

Interactive Theories

Interactive theories of job satisfaction are those that consider both person and situation variables.

Though there are many such theories, we will focus on two: the Cornell integrative model and Locke's value-percept theory.

Cornell Model

Hulin, Roznowski and Hachiya (1985), subsequently elaborated upon by Hulin (1991), proposed a model of job satisfaction that attempted to integrate previous theories of attitude formation. According to the model, job satisfaction is a function of the balance between role inputs, what the individual puts into the work role (e.g., training, experience, time, and effort), and role outcomes, what is received (pay, status, working conditions, and intrinsic factors). The more outcomes received relative to inputs invested, the higher work role satisfaction will be, all else equal. According to the Cornell model, the individual's opportunity costs affect the value individuals place on inputs. In periods of labor oversupply (i.e., high unemployment), the individual will perceive their inputs as less valuable due to the high competition for few alternative positions, and the opportunity cost of their work role declines (i.e., work role membership is less costly relative to other opportunities). Therefore, as unemployment (particularly in one's local or occupational labor market) rises, the subjective utility of inputs falls – making perceived value of inputs less relative to outcomes – thus increasing satisfaction. Finally, the model proposes that an individual's frames of reference, which represent past experience with outcomes, influence how individuals perceive current outcomes received. The fewer, or less valued, the outcomes received in the past and as current employment opportunities erode, the same outcomes per inputs will increase job satisfaction (i.e., more was received than had been in the past). Again, the reverse scenario is also true. Although the breadth and integration of the Hulin model is impressive, direct tests of the model are lacking. One partial test (Judge, 1990) of the model was not particularly supportive. More research on it is needed.

Value-Percept Theory

Following his definition of values as that which one desires or considers important, Locke (1976) argued that individuals' values would determine what satisfied them on the job. Only the unfulfilled job values that were valued by the individual would be dissatisfying. Accordingly, Locke's value-percept theory expresses job satisfaction as follows:

$$S = (V_c - P) \times V_i \quad \text{or}$$
$$\text{Satisfaction} = (\text{want} - \text{have}) \times \text{importance}$$

Where S is satisfaction, V_c is value content (amount wanted), P is the perceived amount of the value provided by the job, and V_i is the importance of the value to the individual. Thus, value-percept theory predicts that discrepancies between what is desired and received are dissatisfying only if the job facet is important to the individual. Individuals consider multiple facets when evaluating their job satisfaction, so the satisfaction calculus is repeated for each job facet.

One potential problem with the value-percept theory is that what one desires (V_c or want) and what one considers important (V_i or importance) are likely to be highly correlated. Though in theory these concepts are separable, in practice many people will find it difficult to distinguish the two. For example, why should I desire a great deal of pay if pay is not important to me? Indeed, one study dropped the discrepancy, simply investigating the moderating effect of facet importance on the relationship between facet amount and satisfaction. Despite this limitation, research on Locke's theory has been supportive (Rice, Phillips & McFarlin, 1990). Rice, Gentile and McFarlin (1991) found that facet importance moderated the relationship between facet amount and facet satisfaction, but it did not moderate the relationship between facet satisfaction and overall job satisfaction. This is exactly what Locke predicted in his theory, as he argued that facet satisfactions should additively predict overall satisfaction because facet importance was already reflected in each facet satisfaction score.

Summary and Integration

Of the job satisfaction theories that have been put forth, it appears that three have garnered the most research support: Locke's value-percept theory, the job characteristics model, and the dispositional approach. It is interesting to note that one of these theories is, essentially, a situational theory (job characteristics model), another is a person theory (dispositional approach), and another is a person–situation interactional theory (value-percept model). Although this may lead one to assume that these theories are competing or incompatible explanations of job satisfaction, this is not the case. Judge et al. (1997), in seeking to explain how core self-evaluations would be related to job satisfaction, proposed that intrinsic job characteristics would mediate the relationship. Indeed, Judge et al. (1998) showed that individuals with positive core self-evaluations perceived more intrinsic value in their work. Judge et al. (2000) showed that the link between core self-evaluations and intrinsic job characteristics was not solely a perceptual process – core self-evaluations was related to the actual attainment of complex jobs. Since job complexity is synonymous with intrinsic job characteristics, this shows that part of the reason individuals with positive core self-evaluations perceived more challenging jobs and report higher levels of job satisfaction is that they actually have obtained more complex (and thus challenging and intrinsically enriching)

jobs. The work of Judge and colleagues thus shows that dispositional approaches and the job characteristics model are quite compatible with one another.

What about the relationship between the job characteristics model and value-percept theory? If most individuals value the nature of the work itself more than other job facets, and evidence indicates that they do (Jurgensen, 1978), then Locke's theory would predict that increasing the level of intrinsic job characteristics (thus reducing the have–want discrepancy with respect to intrinsic characteristics) would be the most effective means of raising employees' job satisfaction. Thus, although the job characteristics model and Locke's value-percept model present different perspectives on job satisfaction, their implications may be the same – as long as employees value intrinsic job characteristics (which they appear to), both would suggest, for most people, the most effective way to increase job satisfaction would be to increase intrinsic job characteristics.

MEASUREMENT OF JOB SATISFACTION

Perhaps the two most extensively validated measures are the Job Descriptive Index (JDI; Smith et al., 1969) and the Minnesota Satisfaction Questionnaire (MSQ; Weiss, Dawis, England & Lofquist, 1967). The JDI assesses satisfaction with five different job facets: pay, promotion, coworkers, supervision, and the work itself. The JDI is reliable and has an impressive array of validation evidence behind it. The MSQ has the advantage of versatility – long and short forms are available, and faceted and overall measures are available. There are additional measures that have been widely used in research, though these measures do not carry with them validation evidence as impressive as the JDI or MSQ. Another good measure is the Brayfield and Rothe (1951) job satisfaction measure, an 18-item measure of overall job satisfaction. In some of our research (e.g., Judge et al., 2000), we have used a reliable (i.e., internal consistencies [α] at .80 or above) five-item version of this scale. The five items are:

I feel fairly satisfied with my present job.
Most days I am enthusiastic about my work.
Each day at work seems like it will never end.
I find real enjoyment in my work.
I consider my job to be rather unpleasant.

There are two additional relevant issues. First, some measures of job satisfaction, such as the JDI, are faceted, while others are global. If a measure is facet-based, overall job satisfaction is typically defined as a sum of the facets. Scarpello and Campbell (1983) found that individual questions about various aspects of the job did not correlate well with a global measure of overall job satisfaction. Based on these results, the authors argued that faceted and global measures do not measure the same construct. In other words, the whole is not the same as the sum of the parts. Scarpello and Campbell conclude, 'The results of the present study argue against the common practice of using the sum of facet satisfaction as the measure of overall job satisfaction' (p. 595). This conclusion is probably premature. Individual items generally do not correlate highly with independent measures of the same construct. If one uses job satisfaction *facets* (as opposed to individual job satisfaction *items*) to predict an independent measure of overall job satisfaction, the correlation is considerably higher. For example, using data one of the authors has collected, if one uses the JDI facets to predict a measure of overall job satisfaction, the combined multiple correlation is $R = .87$. If this correlation were corrected for unreliability, it would be very close to unity. As has been noted elsewhere (e.g., Judge & Hulin, 1993), the job satisfaction facets are highly enough correlated to suggest that they indicate a common construct. Thus, there may be little difference between measuring general job satisfaction with an overall measure and measuring it by summing facet scores.

Second, while most job satisfaction researchers have assumed that single-item measures are unreliable and therefore should not be used, this view has not gone unchallenged. Wanous, Reichers and Hudy (1997) found that the reliability of single-item measures of job satisfaction is .67. For the G.M. Faces scale, another single item measure of job satisfaction that asks individuals to check one of five facets that best describes their overall satisfaction (Kunin, 1955), the reliability was estimated to be .66. Though these are respectable levels of reliability, it is important to keep in mind that these levels are lower than most multiple-item measures of job satisfaction. For example, Judge, Boudreau and Bretz (1994) used a three-item measure of job satisfaction that was reliable ($\alpha = .85$). The items in this measure were:

1. All things considered, are you satisfied with your present job (circle one)? YES NO

2. How satisfied are you with your job in general (circle one)?

1	2	3	4	5
Very Dissatisfied	Somewhat Dissatisfied	Neutral	Somewhat Satisfied	Very Satisfied

3. Below, please write down your best estimates on the percent time your feel satisfied, dissatisfied, and neutral about your present job on average. The three figures should add-up to equal 100%. ON THE AVERAGE:

The percent of time I feel satisfied with my present job (*note*: only this response is scored) ____%

The percent of time I feel dissatisfied with my present job ____%

The percent of time I feel neutral about my present job ____%

TOTAL ____%

When used in practice, these items need to be standardized before summing. Although this measure is no substitute for the richness of detail provided in a faceted measure of job satisfaction, we do believe it is a reasonably valid measure of overall job satisfaction, and more reliable than a single-item measure.

OUTCOMES OF JOB SATISFACTION

Given the centrality of the construct to industrial/organizational psychology, job satisfaction has been correlated with many outcome variables. The relationship of job satisfaction to the most frequently investigated and important outcome variables is reviewed below.

Life Satisfaction

Researchers have speculated that there are three possible forms of the relationship between job and life satisfaction: (1) spillover, where job experiences spill over onto life, and vice versa; (2) segmentation, where job and life experiences are balkanized and have little to do with one another; (3) compensation, where an individual seeks to compensate for a dissatisfying job by seeking fulfillment and happiness in his or her nonwork life, and vice versa. Judge and Watanabe (1994) argued that these different models may exist for different individuals and that individuals can be classified into the three groups. On the basis of a national stratified random sample of workers, they found that 68% of workers could be classified as falling into the spillover group, 20% of individuals fell into the segmentation group, and 12% fell into the compensation group. Thus, the spillover model appears to characterize most individuals.

Consistent with the spillover model, a quantitative review of the literature indicated that job and life satisfaction are moderately strongly correlated – a meta-analysis revealed the average 'true score' correlation of $+ .44$ (Tait, Padgett & Baldwin, 1989). Since the job is a significant part of life, the correlation between job and life satisfaction makes sense – one's job experiences spill over onto life. However, it also seems possible the causality could go the other way – a happy nonwork life spills over onto job experiences and evaluations. In fact, research suggests that the relationship between job and life satisfaction is reciprocal – job satisfaction does affect life satisfaction, but life satisfaction also affects job satisfaction (Judge & Watanabe, 1993).

Job Performance

The relationship between job satisfaction and performance has an interesting history. The Hawthorne studies are credited with making researchers aware of the effect of attitudes on performance. Shortly after the Hawthorne studies, researchers began taking a critical look at the hypothesis that a happy worker is a productive one. Most of the qualitative reviews of the literature suggested a weak, positive, and somewhat inconsistent relationship among the constructs. In 1985, a quantitative review of the literature suggested that the true correlation between job satisfaction and performance was .17 (Iaffaldano & Muchinsky, 1985). These authors concluded that the presumed relationship among the constructs was a 'management fad' and that the correlation was 'illusory.' This study has had an important impact on researchers. Most industrial organizational psychologists who write on the topic conclude that the relationship among the constructs is trivial. Relying on Iaffaldano and Muchinsky, the satisfaction–performance relationship has been described as 'meager' (Brief, 1998: 42), 'negligible' (Weiss & Cropanzano, 1996: 51), and 'bordering on the trivial' (Landy, 1989: 481).

Not everyone agrees with this conclusion. Organ (1988) suggests that the failure to find a relationship between job satisfaction and performance is due to the narrow means that is often used to define job performance. Organ argued that when performance is construed to include many constructive behaviors not generally reflected in a performance appraisal instrument, such as organizational citizenship behaviors, its correlation with job satisfaction will improve. Research tends to support Organ's proposition in that job satisfaction correlates reliably with organizational citizenship behaviors (Organ & Ryan, 1995).

There is another perspective. Perhaps researchers have been wrong to dismiss the relationship between job satisfaction and performance. We have completed a study that represents a much more comprehensive review of the literature than has been the case in previous research, identifying 311 independent correlations (Judge, Thoresen, Bono & Patton, in press). When the correlations are corrected for the effects of sampling error and measurement error (based on interrater reliability for job performance and composite reliability for job satisfaction), the average true score correlation between overall job satisfaction and job performance is .30. This value is considerably higher than Iaffaldano and Muchinsky's (1985) estimate because these authors

inappropriately corrected estimates based on internal consistency, rather than interrater, estimates of reliability, and because they mostly analyzed correlations at the facet (as opposed to overall) satisfaction level. (The average uncorrected correlation was .18; the corrected correlation is much higher because performance ratings are notoriously unreliable. See Viswesvaran, Ones & Schmidt, 1996.) The correlation between job satisfaction and performance was considerably higher for complex jobs than for less complex jobs, indicating that complex jobs may afford greater autonomy, thus giving individuals greater latitude to act on their satisfaction (or dissatisfaction). Thus, contrary to previous reviews, it does appear that job satisfaction is moderately correlated with performance. It also appears that the relationship between satisfaction and performance generalizes to the organizational level of analysis (Harter & Creglow, 1998). Although the correlation between overall job satisfaction and overall job performance could be argued to mask potential relations with dimensions of job performance, this is not a serious issue as performance dimensions tend to be strongly intercorrelated and, furthermore, Judge et al. (in press) note that correlating overall job satisfaction with facets of job performance would violate the principle of correspondence as the concepts would no longer be matched in terms of their generality.

Withdrawal Behaviors

Job satisfaction displays relatively consistent, negative, and weak correlations with absenteeism and turnover. The average correlation is generally in the −.25 range. Job satisfaction also appears to display weak, negative – but significant – correlations with other specific withdrawal behaviors, including unionization, lateness, drug abuse, and retirement. Hulin et al. (1985) have argued that these individual behaviors are manifestations of the underlying construct of job adaptation. Hulin et al., proposed that these individual behaviors can be grouped together as manifestations of job adaptive proclivities. Because the base rate of occurrence of most single withdrawal behaviors is quite low, aggregating across a variety of adaptive behaviors, as Hulin (1991) demonstrated, improves both the distribution and the theoretical basis of the withdrawal construct. Rather than predicting isolated behaviors, withdrawal research would do better, as this model suggests, to consider individual behaviors as manifestations of an underlying adaptive construct. Several studies have been supportive of Hulin's approach, finding that isolated withdrawal behaviors can be grouped into one or more behavioral families, and job satisfaction better predicts these behavioral families than the individual behaviors constituting these families.

HOW JOB SATISFACTION IS VIEWED AND TREATED IN ORGANIZATIONS

Assuming correlations in the area of .30 are important (if such correlations are not important, the field of industrial/organizational psychology is dominated by unimportant correlations), the correlations of job satisfaction with behaviors such as job performance and withdrawal are not to be dismissed. Accordingly, one would expect that job satisfaction is in the forefront of employers' minds. Interestingly enough, however, the extent to which organizations have adopted the term and institutionalized interventions based on job-satisfaction-related theory and research is mixed at best. Job satisfaction, for example, is rarely included as part of an organization's key values, basic beliefs, core competencies, or guiding principles, nor is the topic given much direct exposure in popular business books. Judge and Church (2000) conducted a survey of practitioners (most of whom were employed in the human resource area) regarding their organization's general perception of job satisfaction, its relative importance, and the use of the term in their organizations. Roughly half of the practitioners indicated that job satisfaction as a term and singular construct was rarely if ever mentioned or considered in their organizations. When asked next about the utilization of current theory and research on job satisfaction, the results were even less optimistic. Most practitioners indicated that research was rarely, if ever, consulted or valued in their organizations.

To some degree, this appears to be skepticism about the value of the research process, but also about the importance and relevance of the construct itself. For example, some of the practitioner comments included:

'There is some questioning of whether job satisfaction is desirable anyway.'

'Many feel that there are more serious, real issues to address.'

'Our employees are very busy, we have grown considerably during the last few years and have a relatively inexperienced workforce, our organization is quite decentralized, and there can be a lack of resources. All of these make it difficult to address job satisfaction issues as extensively as we would like to.'

'Timeframes – no CEO here dares to initiate a project with a 2–3 year or longer return on investment time frame.'

As one can see from these statements and the prior review of the literature, there is a real gap between how important job satisfaction is viewed by researchers and organizations. As was noted earlier, job satisfaction may be the most widely studied topic in industrial/organizational psychology, with important implications for job performance, yet organizations do not seem to place much credence in the construct. We are uncertain how this research–practice gap can or should be resolved. We would think it healthy for researchers to become more familiar with how job satisfaction is viewed and treated in organizations, and for managers to better acquaint themselves with research findings. In our view, the research–practice gap has less to do with job satisfaction research *per se* than with the broader issue of why research findings in many areas of industrial/organizational psychology fail to be adopted by organizations (see Church, 1997). Thus, resolution of the issue is beyond the scope of this chapter, but we would be remiss to fail to acknowledge the issue.

INTERNATIONAL JOB SATISFACTION RESEARCH

Most (though certainly not all) of the research studies that provided the foundation for the foregoing review were carried out by American researchers studying American workers. In order to determine whether this research literature generalizes to a global context, we conducted a literature review. In the first step of the literature review, we used the PsycINFO database (1980–present) to search for studies with 'job satisfaction' as a keyword and one of the following keywords: various country names (e.g., 'Israel,' 'China'), nationalities (e.g., 'French,' 'Korean'), or 'international.' Second, we manually searched the following journals for articles on job satisfaction that either were completed by international (non-US) researchers, or were based on international (non-US) samples: *Academy of Management Journal*, *Applied Psychology: An International Review*, *Journal of Applied Psychology*, *Journal of Management*, *Journal of Occupational and Organizational Psychology*, *Journal of Organizational Behavior*, *Organizational Behavior and Human Decision Processes*, and *Personnel Psychology*. Once we had obtained the articles produced by these searches, we classified them according to our previous review. Thus, below we provide a review of this research, organized in the same manner as our previous review.

There are limitations to this review. In cases where we located no international research (e.g., social information processing models), no review is provided. By the same token, international research that focused on isolated variables not considered in this review (e.g., age and job satisfaction; Clark, Oswald & Warr, 1996) is not reviewed. The latter exclusionary criteria omits numerous studies. For instance, some studies have compared the effect of socio-demographic variables on job satisfaction, such as social mobility and status inconsistency, across countries or between subpopulations based on nationality (Hawkes, Gaugnano, Acredolo & Helmick, 1984; Marshal & Firth, 1999). Other research has investigated the effects of organizational climate variables (e.g., leadership style, innovation and change, etc.) on job satisfaction across countries (Krishnan & Krishnan, 1984).[2] Most of these studies are unique in the sense that one set of results is rarely subsequently replicated in another study, nor is there a theoretical framework that would integrate them. Thus, because it is virtually impossible to assimilate these results, they are not reviewed here. However, it should be recognized that many international studies on job satisfaction fall into this broad category.

Theories of Job Satisfaction

Two-Factor Theory

Studies testing Herzberg's two-factor theory using international samples have been no more supportive of the theory than studies conducted in the USA (Hines, 1973). Critiques of Herzberg's theory have proposed alternative explanations for his findings. According to Schneider and Locke (1971) and Locke (1973), intrinsic factors are related to job satisfaction and extrinsic factors are related to job dissatisfaction because employees see themselves as responsible for their satisfaction and blame others for their dissatisfaction. Adler (1980) found support for this explanation using an Israeli sample. Adler asked subjects to recall both a satisfying and a dissatisfying incident and to evaluate the importance of various agents in causing each incident. Subjects saw external agents as more responsible for dissatisfying incidents than for satisfying incidents.

Adigun and Stephenson (1992) compared critical incidents related to job satisfaction/dissatisfaction reported by small samples of British and Nigerians ($N = 31$ and $N = 42$, respectively) living in England. The authors concluded that the responses of the British sample were more in accordance with predictions from Herzberg's theory than were the responses of the Nigerian sample. That is, the British sample was more prone than the Nigerian sample to identify content (intrinsic) and context (extrinsic) factors with satisfaction and dissatisfaction, respectively.

Job Characteristics Model

Based on research conducted in the USA, intrinsic job characteristics have emerged as the most consistent situational predictor of job satisfaction. The relationship between intrinsic job characteristics and job satisfaction has been supported in international samples as well. The majority of the research used the job characteristics model (JCM; Hackman & Oldham, 1976) as a framework. In addition to examining the validity of the JCM outside the USA, these studies also suggested additional intrinsic job characteristics that may be related to job satisfaction, examined the dimensionality of a common measure of the core job characteristics, and examined the form of the relationship between job satisfaction and job characteristics.

Research examining the validity of the JCM using international samples has generally found support for the relationships tested. Using an Israeli sample, Fox and Feldman (1988) found that, with the exception of task identity, the core job characteristics (skill variety, task significance, autonomy, and feedback) were significantly correlated with job satisfaction. However, the mediating properties of the three critical psychological states were not supported. The relationships specified by the JCM were also tested in a study of Canadian schoolteachers (Barnabé & Burns, 1994). In this study, support was found for the proposed relationships between the five core job characteristics and the psychological states and between the psychological states and job satisfaction. The mediating properties of the psychological states were also supported. In a study of Chinese employees, Xie (1996) found that high job autonomy and high demands were associated with job satisfaction.

Although studies using Israeli and Canadian samples generally supported the JCM, similar results were not found in a study of the nursing staff at a Malaysian hospital (Pearson & Chong, 1997). For this sample, the core job characteristics were not significantly related to job satisfaction; however, feedback from others, an interpersonal dimension of social information, was significantly related to job satisfaction. According to Pearson and Chong (1997), these results were expected based on the Malaysian culture. The Malaysian culture has a tradition of role compliance which results in lower initiative, discretion, and self-actualization among the workforce; therefore, the core job characteristics identified in the JCM are less likely to increase job satisfaction in this culture. In a study of black South Africans, Orpen (1983) directly tested the moderating effects of the degree of Westernization on the job characteristics–job satisfaction relationship. For subjects with a low degree of Westernization, skill variety, task identity, autonomy, and feedback had nonsignificant relationships with job satisfaction; however, for subjects with a high degree of Westernization, both autonomy and task identity were significantly related to job satisfaction.

In addition to testing the relationships proposed by the JCM, several studies have suggested additional intrinsic job characteristics that may be related to job satisfaction. Jans and McMahon (1989) included a self-expression scale as a measure of person–task fit in their study of Australian public sector employees. The scale measured the degree to which the job allowed learning, the extent to which previous learning was used, and the degree to which tasks performed were interesting. Self-expression made a unique contribution to the variance explained in job satisfaction beyond that explained by the five core job characteristics in one of the two samples surveyed. Baba and Jamal (1991) conceptualized the five core job characteristics as nonroutine job content. Employee participation in routine or nonroutine work shifts was included as a measure of routinization of job context. In a sample of Canadian nurses, higher job satisfaction was found when job content was nonroutine and when job context was routine.

Kiggundu (1983) proposed including initiated and received task interdependence as core job characteristics. Initiated task interdependence was defined as the degree to which other positions relied on work performed by the employee and was expected to be positively related to job satisfaction, while received task interdependence was defined as the extent to which the employee was reliant on work inflows from other positions and was expected to be negatively related to job satisfaction. In a study of the Canadian life insurance industry, a positive relationship was found between initiated task interdependence and job satisfaction; however, the relationship between received task interdependence and job satisfaction was near zero. Corbett, Martin, Wall and Clegg (1989) found that technological coupling, or the degree of integration between advanced manufacturing technology (AMT) applications, had a significant negative relationship with job satisfaction controlling for the five core job characteristics for employees at a computer manufacturing company in the United Kingdom.

Two studies of Australian workers found that employees in autonomous or self-managing workgroups had higher levels of job satisfaction than those in traditionally designed jobs (Cordery, Mueller & Smith, 1991; Wright & Cordery, 1999). Significantly, Wright and Cordery (1999) further showed that this relationship was moderated by production uncertainty such that the relationship was positive at high levels of uncertainty and negative at low levels of uncertainty. In a study designed to determine the relative effects of objective monotony (measured as repetitive work and work underload) and subjective monotony on job satisfaction for a sample of blue collar workers in Israel, Melamed, Ben-Avi, Luz and Green (1995) found that subjective monotony partially mediated the relationship between objective monotony and job satisfaction.

Two other studies have also found relationships between a number of intrinsic job characteristics and job satisfaction similar to those found in US samples. For army officers in Sweden, leader support, coworker support, job characteristics (autonomy and variation), workload, role explicitness, human resource management, and career possibilities were found to be positively related to job satisfaction, while role conflict, mental fatigue, and psychosomatic symptoms were found to be negatively related to job satisfaction (Nystedt, Sjöberg &

Hägglund, 1999). Similarly, the job satisfaction of nurses in the Netherlands was shown to be correlated with job complexity and difficulty, feedback and clarity, work pressure, autonomy, promotional and group opportunities, patient attending and caring, social leadership, and the nursing care system structure (Landeweerd & Boumans, 1994).

Several studies using international samples have examined the form of the relationship between job characteristics and job satisfaction. Using a sample of employees in Hong Kong, Wong, Hui and Law (1998) examined the causal direction between perceptions of job characteristics and job satisfaction. This study found that overall and intrinsic job satisfaction are reciprocally related to perceptions of job characteristics. Extrinsic job satisfaction had causal effects on the perception of job characteristics; however, the reciprocal relationship was not supported. In a second study of the relationship between job characteristics and job satisfaction, De Jonge and Schaufeli (1998) tested Warr's (1987) vitamin model, which proposes nonlinear relationships between job characteristics and job satisfaction. In a sample of Dutch health care workers, both job demands and job autonomy were linearly related to job satisfaction, while social support had a nonlinear relationship. When considering the effects of all three variables on emotional exhaustion, anxiety, and job satisfaction, a nonlinear model provided a better fit than the linear model.

Overall, the results of research examining the relationship between intrinsic job characteristics and job satisfaction in international samples are similar to those found in US samples. It is important to note, however, some divergent results and that many of the samples in these studies come from cultures that are similar to the USA. More research on samples whose culture is more divergent from the USA is needed.

Dispositional Approaches

Most of the international research on the dispositional source of job satisfaction that we located comprised direct studies. These studies investigated a large variety of specific traits (e.g., individualism–collectivism, core self-evaluation construct and components, human needs). In fact, we were able to locate only two indirect studies (Hershberger, Lichtenstein & Knox, 1994; Newton & Keenan, 1991). Newton and Keenan (1991) investigated the stability of job satisfaction among young British engineers experiencing situational change (from university studies to full-time employment, change of employer). They found evidence for job satisfaction instability (based on mean differences rather than retest correlations), some evidence for stability in job satisfaction relative rankings, and general support for the importance of situational changes, lending support to the interactional rather than dispositional approach. Hershberger et al. (1994)

examined the genetic influences on job satisfaction using a four-group twin design. These researchers failed to replicate Arvey et al.'s (1989) findings; they did not find significant genetic influences on job satisfaction. Yet, since the more compelling support for the dispositional approach comes from the direct studies, these two studies do not pose too much of a threat to the approach. Our review of international research on direct studies is organized around the traits that have been investigated in these studies.

Individualism and collectivism   Recently, interest in the relationship between the individualism–collectivism construct and job satisfaction has emerged (e.g., Chiu & Kosinski, 1999; Hui & Yee, 1999; Hui, Yee & Eastman, 1995). This is a uni-dimensional, bipolar construct, with the collectivistic pole representing people who attribute high value to in-group solidarity, while the individualistic pole represents people who prefer 'to do their own thing.' This construct can be used both at an individual and cultural level. Consequently, the aforementioned relationship has been studied both at the national level and individual level, yielding conflicting results.

Some studies suggest a positive link between individualism and job satisfaction. For example, workers in countries classified as lower on individualism appeared to be less satisfied than their counterparts in more individualistic countries. In a 1978 poll, De Boer found that Sweden had the highest percentage of satisfied workers at 63%, followed by the UK (54%), Brazil (53%), and Japan (20%) (see also Griffith & Hom, 1987; Lincoln & Kalleberg, 1985). Hui et al. (1995) using international survey research data, found a nonsignificant relationship between overall job satisfaction and the individualism index, but found a negative relationship for individualism with interpersonal relationships at work. A recent study by Chiu and Kosinski (1999), based on 626 registered nurses from two western-individualistic countries (Australia and United States) and two Asian-collectivistic countries (Hong Kong and Singapore), found that individualistic employees had higher scores on job satisfaction than nonindividualistic employees.

However, other studies found a positive relationship between collectivism and job satisfaction. Hui et al. (1995) examined the relationship between collectivism and job satisfaction in two samples of employees in a Hong Kong department store. They found that collectivism was related to higher job satisfaction ($r = .25$ and $r = .18$). Hui and Yee (1999) replicated this relationship between collectivism and job satisfaction ($r = .17$), in two additional groups of employees in Hong Kong: salespersons of a department store chain and customer-service operators in a public utility company.

In trying to explain these conflicting results, we observed that studies comparing countries or samples

of workers *across* countries found individualism to have a positive link with job satisfaction, while studies *within* a country found collectivism to have a positive relationship with job satisfaction. Hui and Yee's (1999) moderator – workgroup atmosphere – of the individualism–collectivism and job satisfaction relationship seems to fit nicely with our observation. They showed that in 'warm' workgroups (i.e., groups wherein colleagues readily help each other) the collectivism–satisfaction link is stronger than in 'cold' workgroups (groups wherein mutual support and collaboration are lacking or not expected). Extrapolating this finding to the country level, we think that within the Asian 'warm' collectivistic countries (the 'within' country studies) collectivism is positively linked to job satisfaction, but at the between country level (including both individualistic and collectivistic countries, cold and warm, respectively) the individualistic–job satisfaction positive link holds. Clearly, more research is needed to resolve this issue, and to assess the accuracy of the latter explanation.

Locus of control, self-esteem, and neuroticism   Several studies investigated the relationship between locus of control and job satisfaction (Judge et al., 1998; Judge, Thoresen, Pucik & Welbourne, 1999; Kirkcaldy & Cooper, 1992; Nelson & Cooper, 1995; Sharma & Chaudhury, 1980; Sui & Cooper, 1998). Data from various sources (Israeli sample, a multinational sample, British and German samples) all point to a positive and significant relationship between an internal locus of control and overall job satisfaction ($r = .22$, $r = .32$, $r = .37$, $r = .33$, respectively). However, in one study, Sui and Cooper (1998) produced a different set of results. Using a sample of employees working in Hong Kong, they found that locus of control was not significantly correlated with overall job satisfaction ($r = .18$), was correlated with satisfaction with the job itself ($r = .29$), and was not related to satisfaction with the organization. Three studies investigated the relationship between self-esteem and job satisfaction and found low positive relationships. Brook (1991), based on 81 employees in New Zealand and a complex measure of self-esteem (actual-self/ideal-self discrepancy in a repertory grid approach), found a positive but not significant relationship. The second study (Judge et al., 1998), based on an Israeli sample, reported a .16 uncorrected correlation between self-esteem and job satisfaction. The last study (Judge et al., 1999), based on a heterogeneous sample (employees from Australia, Britain, Korea, Scandinavia and America), reported a .31 uncorrected correlation. Finally, two studies examined the relationship between neuroticism and job satisfaction. In an Israeli sample, Judge et al. (1998) found a modest correlation of $r = -.07$. Moyle (1995) found a stronger relationship ($r = -.20$), in a British sample.[3]

Other traits   Cawsey, Reed and Reddon (1982) in an explorative study examined the relationship between human needs, as measured by the Personality Research Form, and job satisfaction (total JDI), controlling for social desirability. Two groups of Canadian managers for a national consumer lending company were used, one consisting of English-speaking individuals and the other consisting of French-speaking individuals. Needs predictive of job satisfaction in the *English* sample were: achievement, autonomy, affiliation, and abasement (multiple $R = .41$). Needs predictive of job satisfaction in the *French* sample were: autonomy, nurturance, and cognitive structure (multiple $R = .37$).

The research described above was mostly atheoretical, and did not help uncover the processes by which personality influences job satisfaction. In the international research literature, there are a few exceptions. Judge et al. (1999) showed that the relationship of positive self-concept (similar to core self-evaluations) and risk tolerance with job satisfaction was roughly half-mediated by coping with organizational change. Moyle (1995) showed that neuroticism (measured with negative affectivity) affected job satisfaction as mediated through perceptions of control opportunities (decision latitude). Sui and Cooper (1998) examined the moderating effects of locus of control on stressors–job satisfaction relationship. The moderating ('buffering') effect of locus on the relationship stressors–job satisfaction was only marginal (for similar weak results see also Kirkcaldy & Cooper, 1992).

Value-Percept Model

Three international studies used various aspects of Locke's (1976) value-percept theory as a framework for the study of job satisfaction. In a comparative study of the job satisfaction of teachers at technological institutions in England and India, subjects provided an evaluative judgment of the difference between the desired and current amounts of various job content and context factors (Indiresan, 1981). These judgments were used to predict job satisfaction. In general, context factors (e.g., boss, salary, prestige) were more highly related to job satisfaction for Indian teachers, while content factors (e.g., achievement, recognition) were more highly related to job satisfaction for English teachers. The impact of importance on these relationships cannot be determined because a measure of importance was not included in this study.

Research incorporating Locke's (1976) value-percept theory has also examined the relationship between importance and satisfaction. In a study of the European electronics industry, Borg (1991) proposed that the form of this relationship would differ based on the job factor under consideration. For factors such as the company itself, Borg hypothesized a positive correlation such that satisfactory aspects of the job are rated as more important. For factors such as pay, promotions, or one's supervisor, Borg hypothesized a V-shaped relationship such that both satisfying and dissatisfying factors are judged as more important than those that are moderately satisfying. In general, Borg proposed that the relationship 'should be less V-shaped the more an individual is able to reduce his or her dissatisfaction by intrapsychic means rather than by changing the real world' (p. 84). The results generally supported Borg's hypotheses.

In a third study, Staples and Higgins (1998) used a Canadian sample to test Locke's (1976) theory that facet satisfaction reflects both the value-percept discrepancy and the importance of the facet. Based on this, weighting ratings of facet satisfaction by importance of the facet should not increase the percentage of variance explained in overall job satisfaction. Staples and Higgins' results supported Locke's theory. When unweighted facet satisfaction ratings were used, 55% of the variance in overall job satisfaction was explained. The percentage of variance explained dropped to 47% when the facet satisfaction ratings were weighted by the importance of the facet.

Measurement of Job Satisfaction in an International Context

In a global business environment that is characterized by increasing mobility across national borders, it has become particularly important to understand job attitudes in a cross-cultural framework. When looking at the concept of job satisfaction from a cross-cultural perspective, in order to make meaningful inferences, researchers need to use standard measures and methods (Ryan, Chan, Ployhart & Slade, 1999). Even though it might not be the most desirable theoretical approach, the typical way researchers study job satisfaction across cultures is an *imposed-etic* approach (Hulin, 1987; Ryan et al., 1999), in which instruments developed in one culture (usually the USA) are used (eventually translated) to capture job satisfaction in other cultures. We will not address here the theoretical issue of psychometric equivalence of job satisfaction instruments (for an in-depth discussion see Hulin, 1987); instead we will look at empirical evidence related to the scale translation process.

The Job Descriptive Index (JDI; Smith, Kendall & Hulin, 1969), in addition to being the most widely used measure in the USA, is the instrument that has been the subject of most equivalence and translation investigations. We found that research results point towards some degree of cross-cultural nonequivalence in most studies. For example, Hulin and Mayer (1986) found that one-third of the JDI items were noninvariant across languages and subpopulations, and Ryan et al.'s (1999) results suggested differential reliability of measurement for a four-factor structure that included a job satisfaction dimension. Other research also supports some cross-cultural differences in the measurement of job satisfaction. Simonetti and Weitz (1972) found that job facets contributed differently to overall job satisfaction across three countries, suggesting that the nature of the latent construct may differ across countries. Spector and Wimalasiri (1986) found different factor structures of the job satisfaction survey in two samples of American and Singaporean employees. A more recent analysis of job satisfaction structure in an Indian industrial setting (Takalkar & Coovert, 1994), employing a confirmatory factor analytic approach, found support for the generalizability of the job satisfaction dimensions developed in the USA (for similar results see also Sekaran, 1981).

Thus, the measurement properties of job satisfaction surveys appear to vary across cultures. One could conclude from the evidence that job satisfaction measures do not generalize across cultures. However, we do not agree with such an interpretation. That measures fail to achieve perfect instrument invariance across cultures does not mean the measures do not generalize. A lack of invariance across translations at the item level or even slightly different factor structures in different cultures may still allow the instrument to display generalizable characteristics as a whole. For example, Ryan et al. (1999) concluded that, even though 'we found several instances of a lack of invariance' (p. 50), the differences would not warrant the modification of their multinational employee opinion survey, given that their 'proposed model fit well in all four countries' (p. 50). McCabe, Dalessio, Briga and Sasaki (1980) concluded, for example, that the JDI and the Index of Organizational Reactions (IOR; Smith, 1976) English forms were successfully translated into Spanish, based on 'high convergent and discriminant validities, along with greater convergence across the same instrument than across the same language' (p. 785).

Cross-Cultural Perspectives on the Outcomes of Job Satisfaction

International research on the outcomes of job satisfaction has been focused on many of the same of variables as has American research, though perhaps with a slightly different emphasis. Whereas both American and international scholars have studied life satisfaction, job performance, and adaptive behaviors as broad categories of job satisfaction outcomes, American researchers have been somewhat more concerned with the relationship between job satisfaction and job performance, whereas international research has been more likely to investigate the relationship of job satisfaction to nonwork

attitudes (e.g., see Warr, 1999). With respect to the other major outcome variable – adaptive behaviors – it seems that international research has adopted a dual focus on both withdrawal and citizenship behaviors, while American research has devoted relatively more attention to withdrawal behaviors. This differential focusing approach is consistent with Erez's (1994) findings that performance appraisal was a central focus of American and Israeli research but not of Scandinavian, German, Japanese, or Indian research, which focused more on employee well-being and satisfaction.

In the review of studies that investigated relationships between job satisfaction and its possible outcomes we did not find direct tests of an eventual moderating effect that culture might have on the strength or direction of the job satisfaction–outcome relationships. With few exceptions, international research has focused on studying those relationships from the same perspective as American research, implying that much international research has sought to generalize the results of American research rather than looking for cultural differences. We believe that there is a need for studies that explicitly incorporate cultural variables as possible moderators of the relationships of job satisfaction and its hypothesized outcomes. International research on job satisfaction's relationships with the three principal categories of outcomes is reviewed in the following sections.

Life Satisfaction

International research has focused on the same three mechanisms (segmentation, spillover, and compensation) that offer competing explanations for the relationship between job and life satisfaction as has American research.[4] While all studies that we reviewed found significant relationships between job satisfaction and life satisfaction (reported correlations ranged from .19 to .49), support for the prevalence of a specific mechanism was mixed. Hart (1999), analyzing structural equations models of three waves of data obtained from 479 Australian police officers found support for the segregation (more commonly known as segmentation) model, rather than the spillover model. Shamir and Ruskin (1983), in a study that matched a sample of kibbutz residents with town and city residents, obtained results that suggest that 'strong compensatory mechanisms between life spheres can operate only in highly segregated communities' (p. 219). A possible integration of the segregation and spillover frameworks is offered by Steiner and Truxillo (1987). The data from this study, which included a combined French and American sample, supported the segregation hypothesis for the intrinsic component of job satisfaction, while it suggested that the spillover model applies to extrinsic job satisfaction. In a study that compared survey responses from 10 Western European countries in order to compare predictors of life satisfaction, Near and Rechner (1993) did not find a substantial variation in the relationships between job satisfaction and life satisfaction across those 10 countries (correlation coefficients varied from .41 to .54), suggesting a spillover effect.

A line of research related to the study of the life-satisfaction–job-satisfaction relationship that has developed outside the segmentation–spillover–compensation framework is the investigation of the meaning of working across cultures. England (1990) extended the research from a comprehensive Meaning of Working (MOW) study, which was first reported in the scientific literature in 1981 followed by detailed international comparative results in 1987 (MOW International Research Team, 1987). In his 1990 article, England compared data for representative labor force samples from Germany, Japan, and the United States. Although no national-specific consistent patterns for the meaning of work were observed, the data showed that there is a strong contingency between work-meaning pattern membership (England proposed eight distinct work-meaning patterns and investigated people's pattern membership across countries) of the individual and levels of outcome realization (outcomes such as income, quality of work, occupational satisfaction, and job satisfaction).

Job Performance

Although fewer international than American studies have investigated the relationship between job satisfaction and job performance, we located 20 satisfaction–performance correlations contained in 16 studies (three studies contained multiple samples). These correlations are provided in Table 2.1. As is shown in the table, these studies are fairly diverse in nationality and occupation. The average unweighted uncorrected satisfaction–performance correlation is .20 and, as the table shows, only one of the correlations is negative. If this correlation were corrected for unreliability in satisfaction and performance, it would be greater than .30. These results are quite similar to, and even slightly higher than, the overall uncorrected correlation of .18 (.30 corrected) reported in Judge et al.'s (in press) review of mostly American studies. Thus, it appears that the satisfaction–performance relationship in international contexts is similar to that in the USA. However, it is important to note that, unlike the USA where many studies investigate different models of the satisfaction–performance relationship, almost none of the international studies in Table 2.1 focused on the satisfaction–performance relationship *per se* (Orpen, 1978, is an exception). Rather, in the typical study, a satisfaction–performance correlation was reported, but the purpose of the study was otherwise (e.g., Saks & Ashforth, 1996, studied the relationship of socialization to various outcomes, including satisfaction and performance). Thus, while

we can conclude the satisfaction–performance relationship at a bivariate level generalizes cross-culturally, little is known about the causal relationship among the constructs in a cross-cultural context.

Withdrawal Behaviors

Mirroring American research, international research also found relatively weak, but consistently negative, correlations between job satisfaction and withdrawal behaviors (Adler & Golan, 1981; Arnold & Feldman, 1982; Jamal, 1999; Koslowsky, 1991; Lum, Kervin, Clark, Reid & Sirola, 1998). An exception is a study by Iverson and Roy (1994), who found a moderately strong association ($r = .48$) between job satisfaction and intention to stay in the organization, but in this case the self-report nature of the criterion may explain the relatively strong correlation. Regarding the relationships among withdrawal behaviors, Clegg (1983) reported partial support for a progressive withdrawal model, while Adler and Golan (1981) found the relationship between lateness and absenteeism not to be progressive in nature. Future research on models of withdrawal is needed in general, but especially in international contexts where different cultural norms for absence, lateness, mobility, and other forms of withdrawal might affect the relations among these behaviors.

A separate line of research includes studies that propose job satisfaction to be a consequence of withdrawal behaviors such as lateness and absenteeism. From those studies, we found particularly interesting the research efforts that directly tested the causality of the relationship between job satisfaction and lateness or absenteeism. Clegg (1983), using a sample of British workers, employed a time-lagged design and gave simultaneous analytic consideration to three possible hypotheses of causality (X influences Y, or Y influences X, or X and Y display an association due to a third variable influencing both X and Y) in an attempt to capture the direction flow of the associations between job satisfaction and absence and lateness. Clegg found no evidence that affect (job satisfaction and organizational commitment) influences absence but found some support for the hypothesis that affect influences turnover. Clegg's results rather suggested that the reverse hypothesis might be true (the data supported the hypothesis that absence predicts job satisfaction). Using a similar design on a sample of Australian workers, Tharenou (1993) also found that 'uncertified absence is more likely to influence job dissatisfaction, than the reverse' (p. 282).

Organizational Citizenship Behaviors

The Organizational Citizenship Behavior (OCB) construct can be considered to be part of the same broader construct of adaptive behaviors, but having an opposite orientation when compared to withdrawal

Table 2.1 *International Studies of the Correlation Between Job Satisfaction and Job Performance*

R	Sig.	N	Country	Sample	Study
.26	—	116	India	Dairy institute researchers	Anand & Sohal (1981)
.25	—	24	India	Dairy institute teachers	Anand & Sohal (1981)
.28	—	22	India	Dairy institute extension workers	Anand & Sohal (1981)
.05	*ns*	107	Poland	Shipping supervisors	Borucki (1987)
.31	p < .01	159	Australia	Bank personnel	Hesketh, McLachan & Gardner (1992)
.59	p < .01	100	Bangladesh	Industrial workers	Khaleque, Hossain & Hoque (1992)
.03	*ns*	117	Canada	Prison custodians	Maillet (1984)
.12	p < .05	338	Israel	High technology employees	Mannheim, Baruch & Tal (1997)
-.07	*ns*	61	Canada	Food service managers	Meyer, Paunonen, Gellatly, Goffin & Jackson (1989)
.23	*ns*	80	Canada	Teacher interns	Nhundu (1992)
.03	*ns*	80	South Africa	Gold mine supervisors	Orpen & Bernath (1987)
.45	p < .05	47	South Africa	Urban factory supervisors	Orpen (1978)
.02	*ns*	54	South Africa	Rural (tribal) factory supervisors	Orpen (1978)
.24	p < .05	183	South Africa	Clerks	Orpen (1982)
.23	p < .05	346	South Africa	Managers	Orpen (1985)
.13	*ns*	98	South Africa	Electronics firm employees	Orpen (1986)
.25	p < .05	99	Australia	Nurses	Randall & Scott (1988)
.14	p < .05	163	Australia	Nurses	Randall & Scott (1988)
.28	p < .01	153	Canada	Accountants	Saks & Ashforth (1996)
.19	p < .05	200	Australia	Electrician apprentices	Tharenou (1993)

Note: Sig. = Significance level (significance levels not reported for Anand & Sohal [1981] because the correlations were averaged across performance criteria).

behaviors. In a study of African workers, Munene (1995) found that job satisfaction was correlated with OCBs (OCBs were rated by supervisors in this study) but its impact was not as strong as those of job involvement and attitudinal commitment. Farh, Podsakoff, and Organ (1990), in a study of Taiwanese workers, proposed that job satisfaction would be a mediator for the relationship between leader fairness and task scope and OCBs, rather than an antecedent of OCBs. Contrary to their hypothesis, the results suggested a model in which job satisfaction and OCBs were both consequences of leader fairness and job scope. Although we have not seen research that has attempted to integrate withdrawal behaviors and OCBs, and eventually relate job satisfaction to the broad construct of adaptive behaviors proposed by Hulin (1991), we believe that our understanding of the mechanisms through which job satisfaction relates to behavior would be enriched by such an attempt.

SUMMARY AND RECOMMENDATIONS FOR FUTURE RESEARCH

Our cross-cultural review of the job satisfaction literature highlights two key points. First, research on non-US samples has often replicated findings from US samples, demonstrating the generalizability of some core principles concerning the concept. Second, international research enriches the topic by addressing new questions, adopting distinct approaches, and highlighting cultural influences. In this final section, we recap the core findings for which there is a high convergence, and point to future research areas suggested by our comparison of US and international studies. The antecedents, measurement, and outcomes of job satisfaction are discussed in turn.

Antecedents of Job Satisfaction

Across cultures, the nature of work people do, their individual personality, and the interaction between these two aspects, all influence job satisfaction. Most research attention has focused on the effect of work content on job satisfaction. Of the various situational theories put forward, the one that has had the most consistent support is the JCM. Findings from US and international studies are largely supportive of this model's core proposition that intrinsic job characteristics such as autonomy and variety promote job satisfaction, especially for individuals with high growth and development orientations. Personality research is somewhat confused by the use of a wide range of concepts and measures. However, studies from around the world that directly investigated the link between personality and job satisfaction have mostly shown that personality

traits influence satisfaction. For example, individuals with high positive affectivity, low negative affectivity, and positive core self-evaluations are more likely to be satisfied with their jobs. Finally, a small set of US and international studies support value-percept theory, such that an individual's values about each job aspect influence their satisfaction.

Incorporating an international dimension offers more than increased confidence in US findings, and would offer new insights into these literatures that would increase understanding of job satisfaction in the US and abroad. It would also hold the promise of opening up entirely new areas of inquiry. Our cross-cultural review highlights three key research needs to enhance understanding about job satisfaction antecedents. The first concerns expanding the range of antecedents. The JCM has been criticized for its focus on a rather narrow range of 'core' job characteristics (Parker & Wall, 1998). International studies have shown that additional intrinsic job characteristics (e.g., interdependence, self-expressions, work load/pressure), as well as group-level job characteristics (e.g., self-managing teams), affect job satisfaction. Some of these job characteristics are more salient now compared to when the JCM was developed because of the changes occurring in the workplace. For example, with the extensive downsizing taking place in many organizations, excessive workload is likely to be an important job feature, and the current emphasis on teamwork highlights the need to consider group-level job characteristics. Thus, we may need to include additional intrinsic characteristics if we are to understand the full potential of situational factors in promoting satisfaction.

At this point, it is important to observe that we do not make the same recommendation in relation to dispositional antecedents. Although there are advantages in including new personality variables if they have particular cultural salience (see later), the main problem characterizing this research is the diverse set of measures and concepts used. To prevent further fragmentation, and to facilitate theoretical development, there is a need to integrate the diffuse set of dispositional concepts and measures that have been linked to job satisfaction.

A second research need identified from our review relates to cultural influences on the antecedents. Findings from some international studies (e.g., Pearson & Chong's, 1997, study of Malaysian nurses) have shown that the widely accepted core job characteristics for promoting job satisfaction, such as job autonomy, are not necessarily the most important job aspects in non-US samples. There is some evidence that the less Westernized the sample is, the less likely that the core job characteristics will be the most salient aspects for job satisfaction. We call for research that examines the importance of various job characteristics within less Westernized cultures. This research need is not unrelated to that described above, since the breadth of job characteristics will probably need to be widened to include all those that are important within the culture. One study, for example, suggested a greater emphasis on extrinsic job factors such as salary than is typical in US studies (Indiresan, 1981).

Dispositions might also have different consequences for job satisfaction according to the culture. Only a few of the international studies we reviewed suggested this explicitly (Cawsey et al., 1982), although our analysis of the research on individualism–collectivism led us to predict that the influence of this variable will differ in collectivist cultures such as Asia (collectivism will be positively related to job satisfaction) compared to individualist cultures such as the USA (individualism will be positively related to job satisfaction). One might also hypothesize that core self-evaluations as assessed in US-based studies will less important for job satisfaction in cultures that emphasize the 'interdependent self' rather than the 'independent self' (Markus & Kitayama, 1991). We recommend international comparative studies investigating dispositional antecedents of job satisfaction, and suggest that these should draw on the extensive (and growing) literature on cross-cultural aspects of personality.

The third research need is to gain a better understanding of the nature of the relationship between antecedents and job satisfaction. This includes investigating: contingency factors; nonlinear relationships; mediational processes; non-recursive processes; and processes at different levels of analysis. Individual growth need strength is the most clearly established contingency, although international research has highlighted other potential individual-level moderators (e.g., locus of control) and, as described above, the potential moderating influence of culture. Also significant is the international research showing that job characteristics were more strongly linked to job satisfaction in highly uncertain contexts. There has been surprisingly little attention given to the moderating effect of work context, despite the fact that later variants of the JCM proposed context satisfaction as a moderator (Oldham, 1996). The moderating influence of context is especially important to investigate in modern organizations in which many employees are facing downsizing and career uncertainty. More broadly, identifying contingencies will ensure greater consistency in research findings, and enable more precise predictions about when changing job content will enhance job satisfaction.

Most US research has assumed a linear form of relationship between intrinsic job characteristics and job satisfaction, or 'more is better.' A contribution from international research is the demonstration of curvilinear relationships; that too little and too much of a job feature can be detrimental to job satisfaction (De Jonge & Schaufeli, 1998). Such findings are important because their practical implication is that

work redesign may be bounded. We recommend that researchers consider nonlinear relationships when investigating the link between job characteristics and job satisfaction. Ganzach's (1998) study of the interactive effects of intelligence and job complexity on job satisfaction is a good exemplar here.

The mediational processes underlying the link between antecedents and job satisfaction have not received much attention in either US or international research. In terms of work content, it is typically assumed that the job characteristics are satisfying because they fulfill individual needs. However, other mechanisms are plausible. For example, evidence suggests that job autonomy enhances employees' ability to cope with stressful demands (Parker & Sprigg, 1999), and more effective coping could lead to job satisfaction. There have also been only a handful of US studies investigating the processes by which personality influences job satisfaction. From these, an interesting avenue of inquiry is the idea that dispositions (i.e., core self-evaluations) lead to the attainment of more complex jobs (Judge et al., 2000). This attempt to link situational and dispositional approaches is supported by the international evidence showing that dispositions can affect job satisfaction via their effect on the way employees interact with the situation (i.e., more effective coping with organizational change), or by their effect on employees' perceptions of the situation (e.g., perceiving more job autonomy).

It is also valuable to investigate nonrecursive processes. As demonstrated in both US and international studies, satisfaction can also affect perceptions of work content. It is typically assumed that positive affect leads to a more favorable evaluation of job content, but higher satisfaction could also lead to changed job content via other mechanisms. For example, job satisfaction has been shown to enhance OCBs and job performance, which in turn could result in individuals being assigned, or seeking out, more autonomous work. These types of processes have received little research attention. The same argument for investigating nonrecursive processes can be applied to personality research. That is, it is possible that, as well as dispositions influencing situations, situations might affect individuals, particularly over the long term. For example, if an individual works in a narrow and simplified job for many years, it is possible that such job experience might lead to less positive core self-evaluations.

A final way to further investigate the nature of the relationship between antecedents and job satisfaction is to consider these associations at different levels of analysis. With the exception of a few studies investigating the effect of autonomous workgroups on individual job satisfaction, most of the research we reviewed has focused on individual-level antecedents and their effect on individual job satisfaction. However, affective reactions have been meaningfully conceptualized at the group level ('group affective tone'), and evidence suggests that aggregated group personality can be an important determinant of a group's affect (George, 1990). A recent Australian study (Griffin & Hart, 1998) took this idea one step further, showing that dispositions have differential effects on group-level satisfaction compared to individual job satisfaction. Our understanding of job satisfaction processes will be advanced by considering job satisfaction, and the job and dispositional antecedents, at the group level. Such group-level analyses might be especially relevant within collectivist cultures such as Asia, where one might expect, for example, group-level job autonomy (such as in autonomous workgroups) to be more important than individual job autonomy.

Measurement

Good measures of job satisfaction exist, although there are two outstanding research issues. The first is the question of whether the sum of individual items, or facets, of job satisfaction equate with global indices. This issue is not yet resolved, although we believe for the most part global measures and summed-facet measures will yield equivalent results. The second issue concerns the generalizability of measures across cultures. The applicability of US-developed measures (particularly the JDI) in non-US samples has been examined in several studies. It is encouraging that there have been studies showing cross-cultural equivalence, but there have also been studies demonstrating a lack of invariance across items or factors. We believe that the advantages gained by using standardized measures in comparative studies probably outweigh small differences in item or factor structure, and that the latter do not necessarily mean the scale as a whole is not generalizable. However, more studies of cross-cultural measurement equivalence are required, including studies that systematically examine factors that might influence the degree of cross-cultural equivalence, such as the culture of the sample, the quality of item translation, and the measure of job satisfaction used. For example, are global job satisfaction measures more generalizable than measures that sum up individual items or facets? Furthermore, where applicable, it is important that studies distinguish the effects of language from nationality (e.g., Hispanics in the USA).

Outcomes of Job Satisfaction

Finally, we turned to the consequences of job satisfaction. The US and international research we reviewed was quite consistent in the size and direction of the association between job satisfaction and the outcomes of life satisfaction, job performance,

and withdrawal behaviors. For life satisfaction, there have also been consistencies in the approach taken. Both US and international studies have aimed to identify how job satisfaction and life satisfaction relate to each other. Most research has shown a moderate positive correlation between job satisfaction and life satisfaction, suggesting that job experiences 'spillover' and affect life satisfaction (and/or vice versa). The correlation is not perfect, which is consistent with the idea that segmentation or compensation occur for at least some individuals. However, it is quite impossible to tease out potential cultural influences on how job satisfaction affects life satisfaction from the studies reviewed. One large cross-cultural study showed that countries did not significantly vary in the meaning they attached to work, which suggests that cultural differences in the link between job and life satisfaction might not be so great. On the other hand, a large-scale cross-cultural study on life satisfaction showed different life satisfaction determinants across nations (Oishi, Diener, Lucas & Suh, 1999), although this study did not include job satisfaction as one of the determinants. We need to investigate whether different links between job and life satisfaction occur as a function of individual differences (such as values and dispositions), occupations, circumstances, culture, or, as one international study showed, the type of job satisfaction assessed.

Finding a link between job satisfaction and job performance has been a particular preoccupation in US job satisfaction research, although confidence in the idea diminished considerably after the Iaffaldano and Muchinsky (1985) meta-analysis. A more recent and comprehensive US meta-review, our analysis of international studies, and organizational-level research suggests a stronger relationship between job satisfaction and performance than hitherto accepted as the case. The causal association between job satisfaction and performance, however, has mostly been investigated in US samples. International studies lag behind in this respect, and non-US studies are needed that test explicitly whether job satisfaction causes improved job performance.

It is cause for optimism that researchers are beginning to investigate contingencies that affect the satisfaction–performance relationship, such as job complexity (Judge et al., in press). Results will be inconsistent within cultures, let alone across cultures, as long as important individual and situational contingencies are not taken into account. Given that discretionary aspects of behavior rather than prescribed aspects are most likely to be affected by individuals' satisfaction, a further positive development is the inclusion of discretionary behaviors such as OCBs into assessments of performance. Indeed, linking this idea with the contingency of job complexity, one could speculate that it is in more complex jobs that discretionary aspects are especially important for performance, and therefore that job satisfaction will be an especially strong predictor of broadly assessed performance within complex jobs.

Finally, both US and international studies show weak, but consistently negative, associations between job satisfaction and employee withdrawal behaviors, such as lateness and absenteeism. An advance within US research has been to conceptualize withdrawal as a set of adaptive behaviors. Adopting this approach has been shown to result in stronger and more consistent links between job satisfaction and withdrawal. Extending the set of adaptive behaviors to include OCBs (or, more accurately, a lack of OCBs) will further enhance our understanding. International research appears to have taken a different direction. A few studies have investigated whether withdrawal behaviors progressively relate to each other, with only partial support for this idea; and some have examined reverse causal associations between job dissatisfaction and withdrawal, with some evidence suggesting that absence leads to dissatisfaction. The combination of US and international developments has much potential to improve within-culture studies. However, cross-cultural studies are also relevant because there are likely to be cultural differences in norms for absence and other such behaviors. Johns and Xie (1998), for example, found cross-cultural differences in the reasons given for absence for Canadian managers (less likely to endorse domestic reasons) compared to Chinese managers (less likely to endorse illness, stress, and depression).

How Job Satisfaction is Viewed and Treated

A final point to make is that job satisfaction is an applied research topic. Some would go as far as to argue there is little point continuing the research if the findings are not applied in practice. It is disturbing that there appears so little interest in the concept from US practitioners. We do not have the data to make international comparisons on this dimension, but it is likely that the different social policies, economics, and other such factors will affect the practical salience of the concept across different countries. For example, in Sweden, the amended Work Environment Act specifies how work should be designed according to the various human relations criteria, such as giving employees the opportunity to participate in work decisions (Kompier, 1996). We suspect that, as a consequence, job satisfaction is of much more interest to Swedish practitioners. In this article we have focused on research across the globe. However, there is probably also a great deal to be gained by comparing international *practice* relating to job satisfaction. Perhaps such research will reveal ways to reduce the practice–research gap.

CONCLUSION

The business environment is increasingly a global one. As such, we need to integrate and develop international understanding about fundamental work attitudes such as job satisfaction. Our review of US and international studies has revealed much consistency in findings across cultures. It has also highlighted ways in which incorporating international studies enriches the US approach, and has revealed important gaps in our understanding about job satisfaction in cultures distinct to the USA.

ACKNOWLEDGMENT

Small portions of this chapter are from Judge, T.A. & Church, A.H. (2000). Job satisfaction: research and practice. In C.L. Cooper & E.A. Locke (Eds.), *Industrial/organizational psychology: Linking theory with practice* (pp. 166–198). Oxford, UK: Blackwell.

NOTES

1 Though we cannot explain the apparent declining interest in job satisfaction, some speculation can be offered. First, the term used to describe the construct of job satisfaction continues to evolve. Researchers in the 1930s and 1940s generally used the term morale. Beginning in the 1950s, the term 'job satisfaction' began to supplant 'morale.' Today, other work attitudes (e.g., organizational commitment, mood at work) have become more common, perhaps at the expense of job satisfaction. Second, it is possible that organizations care less about job satisfaction than has been the case in the past, and therefore researchers' interest has waned as well. Finally, it is possible that because, increasingly, the concept of a job is being supplanted by more flexible work roles, some may see the concept of job satisfaction as somewhat archaic (though we would note that most questions on a job satisfaction survey seem as applicable today as ever).

2 It is important to acknowledge that several explicitly cross-cultural studies have been completed in the job satisfaction area, typically comparing job satisfaction in one country to that in the USA (e.g., Krishnan & Krishnan, 1984; Roberts, Glick & Rotchford, 1982; Slocum, 1971; Spector & Wimalasiri, 1986). Although these studies clearly are cross-cultural in orientation, typically they focused on isolated aspects of job satisfaction.

3 As was noted earlier, Judge and colleagues argue that self-esteem, locus of control, and neuroticism are subsumed under the core self-evaluations construct (Judge et al., 1998; Judge et al., 1999). Indeed, the relative consistency of the results reported above ($M_r = .25$, $SD_r = .09$) supports the validity of the construct (the three traits appear to have indistinct relations with job satisfaction) and suggests that the results generalize cross-culturally.

4 Given the international origins of much of the work in this area, it might be more appropriate to comment that American researchers have focused on the same functional forms of the relationship as has international research.

REFERENCES

Adigun, I.O., & Stephenson, G.M. (1992). Sources of job motivation and satisfaction among British and Nigerian samples. *Journal of Social Psychology*, *132*, 369–376.

Adler, S. (1980). Self-esteem and causal attributions for job satisfaction and dissatisfaction. *Journal of Applied Psychology*, *65*, 327–332.

Adler, S., & Golan, J. (1981). Lateness as a withdrawal behavior. *Journal of Applied Psychology*, *66*, 544–554.

Agho, A.O., Mueller, C.W., & Price, J.L. (1993). Determinants of employee job satisfaction: An empirical test of a causal model. *Human Relations*, *46*, 1007–1027.

Anand, U., & Sohal, T.S. (1981). Relationship between some personality traits, job satisfaction, and job performance of employees. *Indian Journal of Applied Psychology*, *18*, 11–15.

Arnold, H.J., & Feldman, D.C. (1982). A multivariate analysis of the determinants of job turnover. *Journal of Applied Psychology*, *67*, 350–360.

Arnold, H.J., & House, R.J. (1980). Methodological and substantive extensions to the job characteristics model of motivation. *Organizational Behavior and Human Decision Processes*, *25*, 161–183.

Arvey, R.D., Bouchard, T.J., Segal, N.L., & Abraham, L.M. (1989). Job satisfaction: Environmental and genetic components. *Journal of Applied Psychology*, *74*, 187–192.

Baba, V.V., & Jamal, M. (1991). Routinization of job context and job content as related to employees' quality of working life: A study of Canadian nurses. *Journal of Organizational Behavior*, *12*, 379–386.

Barnabé, C., & Burns, M. (1994). Teachers' job characteristics and motivation. *Educational Research Volume*, *36*, 171–185.

Borg, I. (1991). On the relationship between importance and satisfaction ratings on job aspects. *Applied Psychology: An International Review*, *40*, 81–92.

Borucki, Z. (1987). Perceived organizational stress, emotions, and negative consequences of stress: Global self-esteem and sense of interpersonal competence as moderator variables. *Polish Psychological Bulletin*, *18*, 139–148.

Brayfield, A.H., & Rothe, H.F. (1951). An index of job satisfaction. *Journal of Applied Psychology*, *35*, 307–311.

Brief, A.P. (1998). *Attitudes in and around organizations*. Thousand Oaks, CA: Sage.

Brief, A.P., Burke, M.J., George, J.M., Robinson, B.S., & Webster, J. (1988). Should negative affectivity remain an unmeasured variable in the study of job stress? *Journal of Applied Psychology*, *73*, 193–198.

Brief, A.P., Butcher, A., & Roberson, L. (1995). Cookies, disposition, and job attitudes: The effects of positive mood inducing events and negative affectivity on job satisfaction in a field experiment. *Organizational Behavior and Human Decision Processes*, *62*, 55–62.

Brief, A.P., & Roberson, L. (1989). Job attitude organization: An exploratory study. *Journal of Applied Social Psychology*, *19*, 717–727.

Brook, J.A. (1991). The link between self-esteem and work/nonwork perceptions and attitudes. *Applied Psychology: An International Review*, *40*, 269–28.

Carroll, B. (1973). *Job satisfaction: A review of the literature*. Ithaca, NY: New York State School of Industrial and Labor Relations, Cornell University.

Cawsey, T.F., Reed, P.L., & Reddon, J.R. (1982). Human needs and job satisfaction: A multidimensional approach. *Human Relations*, *35*, 703–715.

Chiu, R.K., & Kosinski, F.A. (1999). The role of affective dispositions in job satisfaction: Comparing collectivist and individualist societies. *International Journal of Psychology*, *34*, 19–28.

Church, A.H. (1997). From both sides now: The impact of I/O psychology. *Industrial/Organizational Psychologist*, *35*, 103–113.

Clark, A., Oswald, A., & Warr, P. (1996). Is job satisfaction U shaped in age? *Journal of Occupational and Organizational Psychology*, *69*, 57–81.

Clegg, C.W. (1983). Psychology of employee lateness, absence, and turnover: A methodological critique and an empirical study. *Journal of Applied Psychology*, *68*, 88–101.

Corbett, J.M., Martin, R., Wall, T.D., & Clegg, C.W. (1989). Technological coupling as a predictor of intrinsic job satisfaction: A replication study. *Journal of Organizational Behavior*, *10*, 91–95.

Cordery, J.L., Mueller, W.S., & Smith, L.M. (1991). Attitudinal and behavioral effects of autonomous group working: A longitudinal field study. *Academy of Management Journal*, *34*, 464–476.

Cropanzano, R., & James, K. (1990). Some methodological considerations for the behavior genetic analysis of work attitudes. *Journal of Applied Psychology*, *75*, 433–439.

Davis-Blake, A., & Pfeffer, J. (1989). Just a mirage: The search for dispositional effects in organizational research. *Academy of Management Review*, *14*, 385–400.

De Boer, C. (1978). The polls: Attitudes toward work. *Public Opinion Quarterly*, *42*, 414–423.

De Jonge, J., & Schaufeli, W.B. (1998). Job characteristics and employee well-being: A test of Warr's vitamin model in health care workers using structural equation modeling. *Journal of Organizational Behavior*, *19*, 387–407.

Drevets, W.C., & Raichle, M.E. (1998). Reciprocal suppression of regional cerebral blood flow during emotional versus higher cognitive processes: Implications for interactions between emotion and cognition. *Cognition & Emotion*, *12*, 353–385.

England, G.W. (1990). The patterning of work meanings which are coterminous with work outcome levels for individuals in Japan, Germany and the USA. *Applied Psychology: An International Review*, *39*, 29–45.

Erez, M. (1994). Toward a model of cross-cultural industrial and organizational psychology. In H.C. Triandis, M.D. Dunnette, & L.M. Hough (Eds.), *Handbook of Industrial and Organizational Psychology* (2nd ed., Vol. 4, pp. 559–607). Palo Alto, CA: Consulting Psychologists Press.

Farh, J.L., Podsakoff, P.M., & Organ, D.W. (1990). Accounting for organizational citizenship behavior: Leader fairness and task scope versus satisfaction. *Journal of Management*, *16*, 705–721.

Fox, S., & Feldman, G. (1988). Attention state and critical psychological states as mediators between job dimensions and job outcomes. *Human Relations*, *41*, 229–245.

Fried, Y., & Ferris, G.R. (1987). The validity of the job characteristics model: A review and meta-analysis. *Personnel Psychology*, *40*, 287–322.

Frye, C.M. (1996). *New evidence for the job characteristics model: A meta-analysis of the job characteristics-job satisfaction relationship using composite correlations.* Paper presented at the Eleventh Annual Meeting of the Society for Industrial and Organizational Psychology, San Diego, CA.

Ganzach, Y. (1998). Intelligence and job satisfaction. *Academy of Management Journal*, *41*, 526–539.

George, J.M. (1990). Personality, affect, and behavior in groups. *Journal of Applied Psychology*, *75*, 107–116.

Gerhart, B. (1987). How important are dispositional factors as determinants of job satisfaction? Implications for job design and other personnel programs. *Journal of Applied Psychology*, *72*, 366–373.

Glick, W.H., Jenkins, G.D., & Gupta, N. (1986). Method versus substance: How strong are underlying relationships between job characteristics and attitudinal outcomes? *Academy of Management Journal*, *29*, 441–464.

Griffin, M.A., & Hart, P.M. (1998). *Individual dispositions and reactions to work: Differences across work groups.* Paper presented at the 13th Annual conference of the Society for Industrial Psychology, Dallas, Texas, April.

Griffith, R.W., & Hom, P.W. (1987). Some multivariate comparisons of multinational managers. *Multivariate Behavioral Research*, *22*, 173–191.

Gutek, B.A., & Winter, S.J. (1992). Consistency of job satisfaction across situations: Fact or framing artifact? *Journal of Vocational Behavior*, *41*, 61–78.

Hackman, J.R., & Lawler, E.E. (1971). Employee reactions to job characteristics. *Journal of Applied Psychology*, *55*, 259–286.

Hackman, J.R., & Oldham, G.R. (1976). Motivation through the design of work: Test of a theory. *Organizational Behavior and Human Performance*, *16*, 250–279.

Hart, P.M. (1999). Predicting employee life satisfaction: A coherent model of personality, work, and nonwork experiences, and domain satisfactions. *Journal of Applied Psychology*, *84*, 564–584.

Harter, J.K., & Creglow, A. (1998). *A meta-analysis and utility analysis of the relationship between core GWA employee perceptions and business outcomes*. Working paper 2.0, The Gallup Organization.

Hawkes, G.R., Gaugnano, G.A., Acredolo, C., & Helmick, S.A. (1984). Status inconsistency and job satisfaction: General population and Mexican-American sub-population analyses. *Sociology and Social Research*, *68*, 378–389.

Hershberger, S.L., Lichtenstein, P., & Knox, S.S. (1994). Genetic and environmental influences on perceptions of organizational climate. *Journal of Applied Psychology*, *79*, 24–33.

Herzberg, F. (1967). *Work and the nature of man*. Cleveland, OH: World Book.

Hesketh, B., McLachan, K., & Gardner, D. (1992). Work adjustment theory: An empirical test using a fuzzy rating scale. *Journal of Vocational Behavior*, *40*, 318–337.

Hines, G.H. (1973). Cross-cultural differences in two-factor motivation theory. *Journal of Applied Psychology*, *58*, 375–377.

Hoppock, R. (1935). *Job satisfaction*. New York: Harper.

House, R.J., Shane, S.A., & Herold, D.M. (1996). Rumors of the death of dispositional research are vastly exaggerated. *Academy of Management Review*, *21*, 203–224.

Hui, C.H., & Yee, C. (1999). The impact of psychological collectivism and workgroup atmosphere on Chinese employees' job satisfaction. *Applied Psychology: An International Review*, *48*, 175–185.

Hui, C.H., Yee, C., & Eastman, K.L. (1995). The relationship between individualism-collectivism and job satisfaction. *Applied Psychology: An International Review*, *44*, 276–282.

Hulin, C.L. (1987). A psychometric theory of evaluations of item and scale translations: Fidelity across languages. *Journal of Cross Cultural Psychology*, *18*, 115–142.

Hulin, C.L. (1991). Adaptation, persistence, and commitment in organizations. In M.D. Dunnette, & L.M. Hough (Eds.), *Handbook of industrial and organizational psychology* (Vol. 2, pp. 445–505). Palo Alto, CA: Consulting Psychologists Press.

Hulin, C.L., & Mayer, L.J. (1986). Psychometric equivalence of a translation of the Job Descriptive Index into Hebrew. *Journal of Applied Psychology*, *71*, 83–94.

Hulin, C.L., Roznowski, M., & Hachiya, D. (1985). Alternative opportunities and withdrawal decisions: Empirical and theoretical discrepancies and an integration. *Psychological Bulletin*, *97*, 233–250.

Hulin, C.L., & Smith, P.C. (1967). An empirical investigation of two implications of the two factor theory of job satisfaction. *Journal of Applied Psychology*, *51*, 396–402.

Iaffaldano, M.R., & Muchinsky, P.M. (1985). Job satisfaction and job performance: A meta-analysis. *Psychological Bulletin*, *97*, 251–273.

Indiresan, J. (1981). Job satisfaction of engineering teachers: A cross-cultural study. *Indian Journal of Applied Psychology*, *18*, 16–26.

Iverson, R.D., & Roy, P. (1994). A causal model of behavioral commitment: Evidence from a study of Australian blue-collar employees. *Journal of Management, 20,* 15–41.

Jamal, M. (1999). Job stress, Type-A behavior, and well-being: A cross-cultural examination. *International Journal of Stress Management, 6,* 57–67.

James, L.R., & Jones, A.P. (1980). Perceived job characteristics and job satisfaction: An examination of reciprocal causation. *Personnel Psychology, 33,* 97–135.

James, J.R., & Tetrick, L.E. (1986). Confirmatory analytic tests of three causal models relating job perceptions to job satisfaction. *Journal of Applied Psychology, 71,* 77–82.

Jans, N.A., & McMahon, A. (1989). The comprehensiveness of the job characteristics model. *Australian Journal of Psychology, 41,* 303–314.

Johns, G., & Xie, J.L. (1998). Perceptions of absence from work: People's Republic of China versus Canada. *Journal of Applied Psychology, 83,* 515–530.

Judge, T.A. (1990). *Job satisfaction as a reflection of disposition: Investigating the relationship and its effects on employee adaptive behaviors.* Unpublished doctoral dissertation, University of Illinois.

Judge, T.A. (1992). The dispositional perspective in human resources research. *Research in Personnel and Human Resources Management, 10,* 31–72.

Judge, T.A., & Bono, J.E. (2001). Relationship of core self-evaluations traits – self-esteem, generalized self-efficacy, locus of control, and emotional stability – with job satisfaction and job performance: A meta-analysis. *Journal of Applied Psychology, 86,* 80–92.

Judge, T.A., Bono, J.E., & Locke, E.A. (2000). Personality and job satisfaction: The mediating role of job characteristics. *Journal of Applied Psychology, 85,* 237–249.

Judge, T.A., Boudreau, J.W., & Bretz, R.D. (1994). Job and life attitudes of male executives. *Journal of Applied Psychology, 79,* 767–782.

Judge, T.A., & Church, A.H. (2000). Job satisfaction: Research and practice. In C.L. Cooper, & E.A. Locke (Eds.), *Industrial and organizational psychology: Linking theory with practice* (pp. 166–198). Oxford, UK: Blackwell.

Judge, T.A., & Hulin, C.L. (1993). Job satisfaction as a reflection of disposition: A multiple-source causal analysis. *Organizational Behavior and Human Decision Processes, 56,* 388–421.

Judge, T.A., & Locke, E.A. (1993). Effect of dysfunctional thought processes on subjective well-being and job satisfaction. *Journal of Applied Psychology, 78,* 475–490.

Judge, T.A., Locke, E.A., & Durham, C.C. (1997). The dispositional causes of job satisfaction: A core evaluations approach. *Research in Organizational Behavior, 19,* 151–188.

Judge, T.A., Locke, E.A., Durham, C.C., & Kluger, A.N. (1998). Dispositional effects on job and life satisfaction: The role of core evaluations. *Journal of Applied Psychology, 83,* 17–34.

Judge, T.A., Thoresen, C.J., Bono, J.E., & Patton, G.K. (in press). The job satisfaction–job performance relationship: A qualitative and quantitative review. *Psychological Bulletin.*

Judge, T.A., Thoresen, C.J., Pucik, V., & Welbourne, T.M. (1999). Managerial coping with organizational change: A dispositional perspective. *Journal of Applied Psychology, 84,* 107–122.

Judge, T.A., & Watanabe, S. (1993). Another look at the job satisfaction-life satisfaction relationship. *Journal of Applied Psychology, 78,* 939–948.

Judge, T.A., & Watanabe, S. (1994). Individual differences in the nature of the relationship between job and life satisfaction. *Journal of Occupational and Organizational Psychology, 67,* 101–107.

Jurgensen, C.E. (1978). Job preferences (What makes a job good or bad?). *Journal of Applied Psychology, 50,* 479–487.

Khaleque, A., Hossain, M.M., & Hoque, M.E. (1992). Job satisfaction, mental health, fatigue and performance of industrial workers. *Psychological Studies, 37,* 136–141.

Kiggundu, M.N. (1983). Task interdependence and job design: Test of a theory. *Organizational Behavior and Human Performance, 31,* 145–172.

Kirkcaldy, B.D., & Cooper, C.L. (1992). Cross-cultural differences in occupational stress among British and German managers. *Work & Stress, 6,* 177–190.

Kompier, M.A.J. (1996). Job design and well-being. In M.J. Schabracq, J.A.M. Winnubst, & C.L. Cooper (Eds.), *Handbook of work and health psychology* (pp. 349–368). New York: Wiley.

Korman, A.K. (1971). *Industrial and organizational psychology.* Englewood Cliffs, NJ: Prentice Hall.

Koslowsky, M. (1991). A longitudinal analysis of job satisfaction, commitment, and intention to leave. *Applied Psychology: An International Review, 40,* 405–415.

Krıshnan, A., & Krishnan, R. (1984). Organizational variables and job satisfaction. *Psychological Research Journal, 8,* 1–11.

Kunin, T. (1955). The construction of a new type of attitude measure. *Personnel Psychology, 8,* 65–77.

Landeweerd, J.A., & Boumans, N.P.G. (1994). The effect of work dimensions and need for autonomy on nurses' work satisfaction and health. *Journal of Occupational and Organizational Psychology, 67,* 207–217.

Landy, F.J. (1989). *Psychology of work behavior.* Pacific Grove, CA: Brooks/Cole.

Levin, I., & Stokes, J.P. (1989). Dispositional approach to job satisfaction: Role of negative affectivity. *Journal of Applied Psychology, 74,* 752–758.

Likert, R. (1967). *The human organization.* New York: McGraw-Hill.

Lincoln, J.R., & Kalleberg, A.L. (1985). Work organization and workforce commitment: A study of plants and employees in the U.S. and Japan. *American Sociological Review, 50,* 738–760.

Locke, E.A. (1969). What is job satisfaction? *Organizational Behavior and Human Performance, 4,* 309–336.

Locke, E.A. (1973). Satisfiers and dissatisfiers among white-collar and blue-collar employees. *Journal of Applied Psychology, 58,* 67–76.

Locke, E.A. (1976). The nature and causes of job satisfaction. In M.D. Dunnette (Ed.), *Handbook of industrial and organizational psychology* (pp. 1297–1343). Chicago: Rand McNally.

Loher, B.T., Noe, R.A., Moeller, N.L., & Fitzgerald, M.P. (1985). A meta-analysis of the relation of job characteristics to job satisfaction. *Journal of Applied Psychology*, 70, 280–289.

Lum, L., Kervin, J., Clark, K., Reid, F., & Sirola, W. (1998). Explaining nursing turnover intent: Job satisfaction, pay satisfaction, or organizational commitment? *Journal of Organizational Behavior*, 19, 305–320.

Maillet, L.J. (1984). Influence of perceived job enrichment and goal characteristics on employee's satisfaction, motivation, and performance. *Psychological Reports*, 54, 131–137.

Mannheim, B., Baruch, Y., & Tal, J. (1997). Alternative models for antecedents and outcomes of work centrality and job satisfaction of high-tech personnel. *Human Relations*, 50, 1537–1562.

Markus, H.R., & Kitayama, S. (1991). Culture and the self: Implications for cognition, emotion and motivation. *Psychological Review*, 98, 224–253.

Marshal, G., & Firth, D. (1999). Social mobility and personal satisfaction: Evidence from ten countries. *British Journal of Sociology*, 50, 28–48.

Maslow, A.H. (1965). *Eupsychian management.* Homewood, IL: Irwin.

McCabe, D.J., Dalessio, A., Briga, J., & Sasaki, J. (1980). The convergent and discriminant validities between the IOR and the JDI: English and Spanish forms. *Academy of Management Journal*, 23, 778–786.

McGregor, D.M. (1966). *Leadership and motivation.* Cambridge, MA: MIT Press.

Melamed, S., Ben-Avi, I., Luz, J., & Green, M.S. (1995). Objective and subjective work monotony: Effects on job satisfaction, psychological distress, and absenteeism in blue-collar workers. *Journal of Applied Psychology*, 80, 29–42.

Meyer, J.P., Paunonen, S.V., Gellatly, I.R., Goffin, R.D., & Jackson, D.N. (1989). Organizational commitment and job performance: It's the nature of the commitment that counts. *Journal of Applied Psychology*, 74, 152–156.

Motowidlo, S.J. (1996). Orientation toward the job and organization: A theory of individual differences in job satisfaction. In K.R. Murphy (Ed.), *Individual differences and behavior in organizations* (pp. 175–208). San Francisco: Jossey-Bass.

MOW International Research Team. (1987). *The meaning of working.* London: Academic Press.

Moyle, P. (1995). The role of negative affectivity in the stress process: Tests of alternative models. *Journal of Organizational Behavior*, 16, 647–668.

Munene, J.C. (1995). 'Not-on-seat': An investigation of some correlates of organisational citizenship behaviour in Nigeria. *Applied Psychology: An International Review*, 44, 111–122.

Near, J.P., & Rechner, P.L. (1993). Cross-cultural variations in predictors of life satisfaction: An historical view of differences among West European countries. *Social Indicators Research*, 29, 109–121.

Necowitz, L.B., & Roznowski, M. (1994). Negative affectivity and job satisfaction: Cognitive processes underlying the relationship and effects on employee behaviors. *Journal of Vocational Behavior*, 45, 270–294.

Nelson, A., & Cooper, C.L. (1995). Uncertainty amidst change: The impact of privatization on employee job satisfaction and well-being. *Journal of Occupational and Organizational Psychology*, 68, 57–71.

Newton, T., & Keenan, T. (1991). Further analyses of the dispositional argument in organizational behavior. *Journal of Applied Psychology*, 76, 781–787.

Nhundu, T.J. (1992). Job performance, role clarity, and satisfaction among teacher interns in the Edmonton public school system. *Alberta Journal of Educational Research*, 38, 335–354.

Nystedt, L., Sjöberg, A., & Hägglund, G. (1999). Discriminant validation of measures of organizational commitment, job involvement, and job satisfaction among Swedish army officers. *Scandinavian Journal of Psychology*, 40, 49–55.

Oishi, S., Diener, E.F., Lucas, R.E., & Suh, E.M. (1999). Cross-cultural variations in predictors of life satisfaction: Perspectives from needs and values. *Personality and Social Psychology Bulletin*, 25, 980–990.

Oldham, G.R. (1996). Job design. In C.L. Cooper, & I.T. Robertson (Eds.), *International Review of Industrial and Organizational Psychology* (Vol. 11, pp. 33–60). New York: Wiley.

Organ, D.W. (1988). A restatement of the satisfaction-performance hypothesis. *Journal of Management*, 14, 547–557.

Organ, D.W., & Near, J.P. (1985). Cognition vs. affect in measures of job satisfaction. *International Journal of Psychology*, 20, 241–253.

Organ, D.W., & Ryan, K. (1995). A meta-analytic review of attitudinal and dispositional predictors of organizational citizenship behavior. *Personnel Psychology*, 48, 775–802.

Orpen, C. (1978). Relationship between job satisfaction and job performance among western and tribal black employees. *Journal of Applied Psychology*, 63, 263–265.

Orpen, C. (1982). The effects of social support on reactions to role ambiguity and conflict. *Journal of Cross Cultural Psychology*, 13, 375–384.

Orpen, C. (1983). Westernization as a moderator of the effect of job attributes on employee satisfaction and performance. *Humanitas: Journal for Research in the Human Sciences*, 9, 275–279.

Orpen, C. (1985). The effects of need for achievement and need for independence on the relationship between perceived job attributes and managerial satisfaction and performance. *International Journal of Psychology*, 20, 207–219.

Orpen, C. (1986). The effect of job performance on the relationship between job satisfaction and turnover. *Journal of Social Psychology*, 126, 277–278.

Orpen, C., & Bernath, J. (1987). The effect of role conflict and role ambiguity on employee satisfaction and performance. *Psychological Studies*, *32*, 25–28.

Parker, S.K., & Sprigg, C.A. (1999). Minimizing strain and maximizing learning: The role of job demands, job control, and proactive personality. *Journal of Applied Psychology*, *84*, 925–939.

Parker, S.K., & Wall, T.D. (1998). *Job and work design: Organizing work to promote well-being and effectiveness*. Thousand Oaks, CA: Sage.

Pearson, C.A.L., & Chong, J. (1997). Contributions of job content and social information on organizational commitment and job satisfaction: An exploration in a Malaysian nursing context. *Journal of Occupational and Organizational Psychology*, *70*, 357–374.

Randall, M., & Scott, W.A. (1988). Burnout, job satisfaction, and job performance. *Australian Psychologist*, *23*, 335–347.

Reisenzein, R., & Schoenpflug, W. (1992). Stumpf's cognitive-evaluative theory of emotion. *American Psychologist*, *47*, 34–45.

Rentsch, J.R., & Steel, R.P. (1992). Construct and concurrent validation of the Andrews and Withey job satisfaction questionnaire. *Educational and Psychological Measurement*, *52*, 357–367.

Rice, R.W., Gentile, D.A., & McFarlin, D.B. (1991). Facet importance and job satisfaction. *Journal of Applied Psychology*, *76*, 31–39.

Rice, R.W., Phillips, S.M., & McFarlin, D.B. (1990). Multiple discrepancies and pay satisfaction. *Journal of Applied Psychology*, *75*, 386–393.

Roberts, K.H., & Glick, W. (1981). The job characteristics approach to task design: A critical review. *Journal of Applied Psychology*, *66*, 193–217.

Roberts, K.H., Glick, W.H., & Rotchford, N.L. (1982). A frame of reference approach to investigating part and full time workers across cultures. *International Review of Applied Psychology*, *31*, 327–343.

Roethlisberger, F.J., & Dickson, W.J. (1939). *Management and the worker*. New York: Wiley.

Ryan, A.M., Chan, D., Ployhart, R.E., & Slade, L.A. (1999). Employee attitude surveys in a multinational organization: Considering language and culture in assessing measurement equivalence. *Personnel Psychology*, *52*, 37–58.

Saks, A.M., & Ashforth, B.E. (1996). Proactive socialization and behavioral self-management. *Journal of Vocational Behavior*, *48*, 301–323.

Salancik, G.R., & Pfeffer, J. (1977). An examination of need-satisfaction models of job attitudes. *Administrative Science Quarterly*, *22*, 427–456.

Salancik, G.R., & Pfeffer, J. (1978). A social information processing approach to job attitudes and task design. *Administrative Science Quarterly*, *23*, 224–253.

Scarpello, V., & Campbell, J.P. (1983). Job satisfaction: Are all the parts there? *Personnel Psychology*, *36*, 577–600.

Schneider, J., & Locke, E.A. (1971). A critique of Herzberg's incident classification system and a suggested revision. *Organizational Behavior and Human Performance*, *6*, 441–457.

Sekaran, U. (1981). Are U.S. organizational concepts and measures transferable to another culture? An empirical investigation. *Academy of Management Journal*, *24*, 409–417.

Shamir, B., & Ruskin, H. (1983). Type of community as a moderator of work-leisure relationships: A comparative study of kibbutz residents and urban residents. *Journal of Occupational Behaviour*, *4*, 209–221.

Sharma, U., & Chaudhury, P.N. (1980). Locus of control and job satisfaction among engineers. *Psychological Studies*, *25*, 126–128.

Simonetti, S. H., & Weitz, J. (1972). Job satisfaction: Cross cultural effects. *Personnel Psychology*, *25*, 107–118.

Slocum, J.W. (1971). A comparative study of the satisfaction of American and Mexican operatives. *Academy of Management Journal*, *14*, 89–97.

Smith, F.J. (1976). The index of organizational reactions (IOR). *Catalog of Selected Documents in Psychology*, *6*, 54–55.

Smith, P.C., Kendall, L.M., & Hulin, C.L. (1969). *The measurement of satisfaction in work and retirement*. Chicago: Rand McNally.

Smith-Lovin, L. (1991). An affect control view of cognition and emotion. In J.A. Howard, & P.L. Callero (Eds.), *The self-society dynamic: Cognition, emotion, and action* (pp. 143–169). New York: Cambridge University Press.

Spector, P.E. (1997). *Job satisfaction*. Thousand Oaks, CA: Sage.

Spector, P.E., & Wimalasiri, J. (1986). A cross cultural comparison of job satisfaction dimensions in the United States and Singapore. *International Review of Applied Psychology*, *35*, 147–158.

Staples, D.S., & Higgins, C.A. (1998). A study of the impact of factor importance weightings on job satisfaction measures. *Journal of Business and Psychology*, *13*, 211–232.

Staw, B.M., Bell, N.E., & Clausen, J.A. (1986). The dispositional approach to job attitudes: A lifetime longitudinal test. *Administrative Science Quarterly*, *31*, 437–453.

Staw, B.M., & Ross, J. (1985). Stability in the midst of change: A dispositional approach to job attitudes. *Journal of Applied Psychology*, *70*, 469–480.

Steiner, D.D., & Truxillo, D.M. (1987). Another look at the job satisfaction-life satisfaction relationship: A test of the disaggregation hypothesis. *Journal of Occupational Behaviour*, *8*, 71–77.

Stone, E.F. (1992). A critical analysis of social information processing models of job perceptions and job attitudes. In J. Cranny, P. Smith, & E.F. Stone (Eds.), *Job satisfaction: How people feel about their jobs and how it affects their performance* (pp. 165–194). New York: Lexington Books.

Sui, O.L., & Cooper, C.L. (1998). A study of occupational stress, job satisfaction and quitting intention in Hong Kong firms: The role of locus of control and organizational commitment. *Stress Medicine*, *14*, 55–66.

Tait, M., Padgett, M.Y., & Baldwin, T.T. (1989). Job and life satisfaction: A reevaluation of the strength of the relationship and gender effects as a function of the date of the study. *Journal of Applied Psychology, 74*, 502–507.

Takalkar, P., & Coovert, M.D. (1994). The dimensionality of job satisfaction in India. *Applied Psychology: An International Review, 43*, 415–426.

Tharenou, P. (1993). A test of reciprocal causality for absenteeism. *Journal of Organizational Behavior, 14*, 269–287.

Thoresen, C.J., & Judge, T.A. (1997). *Trait affectivity and work-related attitudes and behaviors: A meta-analysis*. Paper presentation at the annual convention of the American Psychological Association, Chicago, IL.

Viswesvaran, C., Ones, D.S., & Schmidt, F.L. (1996). Comparative analysis of the reliability of job performance ratings. *Journal of Applied Psychology, 81*, 557–574.

Wanous, J.P., Reichers, A.E., & Hudy, M.J. (1997). Overall job satisfaction: How good are single-item measures? *Journal of Applied Psychology, 82*, 247–252.

Warr, P. (1987). *Work, unemployment, and mental health*. Oxford: Clarendon Press.

Warr, P. (1999). Well-being and the workplace. In D. Kahneman, E. Diener, & N. Schwarz (Eds.), *Well-being: The foundations of hedonic psychology* (pp. 392–412). New York: Russell Sage Foundation.

Watson, D. (2000). *Mood and temperament*. New York: Guilford.

Watson, D., Clark, L.A., & Tellegen, A. (1988). Development and validation of brief measures of positive and negative affect: The PANAS Scales. *Journal of Personality and Social Psychology, 54*, 1063–1070.

Watson, D., & Slack, A.K. (1993). General factors of affective temperament and their relation to job satisfaction over time. *Organizational Behavior and Human Decision Processes, 54*, 181–202.

Weiss, H.M., & Cropanzano, R. (1996). Affective events theory: A theoretical discussion of the structure, causes, and consequences of affective experiences at work. *Research in Organizational Behavior, 18*, 1–74.

Weiss, D.J., Dawis, R.V., England, G.W., &. Lofquist, L.H. (1967). *Manual for the Minnesota Satisfaction Questionnaire*. Minneapolis: Industrial Relations Center, University of Minnesota.

Weiss, H.M., Nicholas, J.P., & Daus, C.S. (1999). An examination of the joint effects of affective experiences and job beliefs on job satisfaction and variations in affective experiences over time. *Organizational Behavior and Human Decision Processes, 78*, 1–24.

Weitz, J. (1952). A neglected concept in the study of job satisfaction. *Personnel Psychology, 5*, 201–205.

Wernimont, P.F. (1966). Intrinsic and extrinsic factors in job satisfaction. *Journal of Applied Psychology, 50*, 41–50.

Wong, C., Hui, C., & Law, K.S. (1998). A longitudinal study of the job perception-job satisfaction relationship: A test of the three alternative specifications. *Journal of Occupational and Organizational Psychology, 71*, 127–146.

Wright, B.M., & Cordery, J.L. (1999). Production uncertainty as a contextual moderator of employee reactions to job design. *Journal of Applied Psychology, 84*, 456–463.

Xie, J.L. (1996). Karasek's model in the People's Republic of China: Effects of job demands, control, and individual differences. *Academy of Management Journal, 39*, 1549–1618.

3

Work Motivation

JOHN J. DONOVAN

The present chapter provides a review of six of the more dominant theories of work motivation; Equity Theory, Expectancy Theory, Cognitive Evaluation Theory, Goal-Setting Theory, Control Theory, and Social Cognitive Theory. For each of these theories, the central tenets of the model are presented, followed by a summary of the research support that has been obtained for these theoretical propositions and a critical evaluation of the theory as a model of work motivation. Following this discussion, the chapter is concluded with several broad theoretical and methodological suggestions for improving the quality of future research in the field of work motivation.

INTRODUCTION

Since the formal inception of the field of work motivation during the 1930s, numerous theoretical models have been forwarded to both explain and predict motivated behavior in organizational settings. Although no clear consensus exists as to the 'proper' definition, work motivation can be generally defined as 'a set of energetic forces that originates both within as well as beyond an individual's being, to initiate work-related behavior, and to determine its form, direction, intensity & duration' (Pinder, 1998: 11). In perhaps the earliest formulation of a theory of work motivation intended to describe these 'energetic forces', Lewin (1938) developed an expectancy-based model (termed 'resultant valence' theory), which emphasized the role of subjective perceptions in determining worker behavior. In the time since this initial effort, subsequent theoretical models have proposed a widely divergent set of factors to be responsible for motivated behavior. For example, three of the earliest theories of work motivation all focused on different determinants of behavior: while drive theories (e.g., Hull, 1943) emphasized the role of physiological need deprivation, and reinforcement theories (e.g., Skinner, 1953) asserted that the primary determinants of behavior

were the consequences and/or rewards associated with past behavior, need theories (e.g., McClelland, 1961) focused on the role of psychological needs or values in motivation. Although these particular theories have since fallen out of favor with the work motivation research community (Kanfer, 1990), the diversity in assumptions represented by these theories remains in today's literature. Modern explanations for motivated behavior range from the principles of hedonism (e.g., Vroom, 1964), to the principles of equity (e.g., Adams, 1963), to the concept of dynamic homeostasis (e.g., Campion & Lord, 1982).

In light of this diversity in current explanations for motivated behavior in organizations, the purpose of the present chapter is to provide an overview and critical evaluation of the major theories of motivation present in the organizational behavior research literature: Equity Theory, Expectancy Theory, Cognitive Evaluation Theory, Goal-Setting Theory, Control Theory, and Social Cognitive Theory. Although a number of other theories of work motivation exist, an exhaustive review of these theories is beyond the scope of this chapter (for such a review, see Kanfer, 1990). Instead, this chapter focuses on the theories that have garnered the most theoretical and empirical interest in the work motivation literature during the past several decades.

In addition to this review of the major theoretical studies in the field of work motivation, a somewhat secondary purpose of this chapter is to provide recommendations for future research to facilitate the development of more comprehensive and integrated models of work motivation.

THEORIES OF WORK MOTIVATION

Equity Theory

Overview of Theory

According to Adams's (1963, 1965) equity theory, workers perceive their work-related participation in an organization as an exchange process where they provide inputs to the organization (e.g., experience, effort, education) in return for valued outcomes (e.g., pay, promotions, recognition). The central tenet of this theory is that individuals are motivated to attain fairness or equity within this exchange process in terms of the outcomes they receive relative to the inputs that they provide. Individuals evaluate the fairness of this exchange through a social comparison process in which they compare the ratio of their perceived outcomes to their perceived inputs (termed an equity ratio) to the equity ratio of a 'referent other,' which may be a coworker, the individual in a previous situation (e.g., at a previous job), a hypothetical 'ideal other,' or a system referent (Goodman, 1974). Adams (1963) posited that when these two equity ratios are judged to be approximately equal to one another, workers perceive their exchange with the organization to be equitable or fair, resulting in feelings of satisfaction. Conversely, when workers determine that there is a discrepancy between these two ratios, the resulting perceptions of inequity (either underpayment or overpayment) produce an aversive state of tension within the individual in proportion to the magnitude of the inequity. This tension state is thought to motivate individuals to engage in various cognitive or behavioral measures designed to reduce inequity, including: altering their own inputs or outcomes, altering the inputs or outcomes of their referent other, changing their referent other, cognitively reevaluating their own inputs and outcomes or those of the referent other, or leaving the field (Adams, 1963). According to equity theory, individuals will actively engage in such discrepancy reduction activities until perceptions of equity are restored and the accompanying inequity tension is eliminated.

Research Evidence

In the years following the formulation of equity theory, numerous laboratory studies were conducted to examine the effects of perceptions of inequity on productivity (Mowday, 1991). Adams (1963) predicted that underpayment should reduce the quantity and/or quality of production under an hourly payment plan, but increase production quantity under a piece rate payment plan in an attempt to restore equity. Conversely, it was predicted that overpayment should reduce production quantity (while increasing quality) in a piece rate payment plan, and increase production quantity and/or quality under an hourly payment plan. Although the general findings from these early studies showed strong support for the predicted reactions to underpayment, support for the proposed reactions to overpayment was inconsistent (Greenberg, 1982). While some studies obtained support for the effects of overpayment (e.g., Adams & Jacobsen, 1964), other studies found either no effects (e.g., Valenzi & Andrews, 1971) or effects that quickly disappeared (e.g., Lawler, Koplin, Young & Fadem, 1968). Subsequent laboratory research on this topic has generally confirmed these results (Mowday, 1991), leading researchers to conclude that individuals are likely to be more tolerant of overpayment than underpayment, and therefore less likely to engage in behaviors designed to reduce overreward inequity.

Although an impressive amount of research was generated during this time to test equity theory predictions, these early laboratory studies were subject to a number of criticisms. First, the generalizability of these studies to actual organizational settings was questioned by a number of researchers (e.g., Greenberg, 1982). It was argued that the experimental settings typically used in these studies were likely to constrain an individual's choice of equity restoration behaviors (e.g., it is typically not possible to alter the referent other's outcomes/inputs or leave the field), and therefore the responses to equity violations observed in such settings may be much different than those that occur in the workplace. Second, virtually all of these early studies failed to measure key variables in the motivational processes described by equity theory, including perceptions of inputs and outcomes, choice of a referent other, and perceptions of equity (Goodman & Friedman, 1971). As a result, these studies are unable to provide any definitive evidence about the validity of equity theory, or rule out alternative explanations for results that appear to support equity theory (Mowday, 1991).

In an attempt to partially address such criticisms, Greenberg (1988, 1989, 1990) conducted a series of field studies examining the effects of perceived inequity in actual organizations. The findings from these studies provided further evidence that workers may lower productivity in response to a reduction in outcomes received (Greenberg, 1988), engage in cognitive reevaluation as a means of equity restoration (Greenberg, 1989), and seek to increase nonpay outcomes to offset reductions in pay (Greenberg, 1990). Although Greenberg's research appears promising for equity theory predictions of behavior, subsequent field research has yielded inconsistent results. For example, although Sheehan (1993) found that perceptions of inequity led to a decrease in worker performance, Summers and Hendrix (1991) concluded that inequity perceptions did not have an impact on performance. Similarly, although Moorman (1991) found that perceptions of outcome equity (i.e., distributive justice) were unrelated to the occurrence of organizational citizenship behaviors (OCBs), Lee (1995) found a negative relationship between these perceptions and OCBs.

Other than this handful of recent studies, it appears that there is little research currently being directed towards tests of equity theory predictions of worker behavior (Ambrose & Kulik, 1999). While this disinterest may be partially due to the inconsistent findings obtained by recent research, it is more likely that this disinterest stems from the substantial number of theoretical criticisms that have been leveled against equity theory. Although an exhaustive discussion of these criticisms is beyond the scope of the present chapter (see Leventhal, 1980; Mowday, 1991), three of the more common criticisms will be summarized to provide a sense of their scope and magnitude.

Issues with Equity Theory

Limited predictive utility Perhaps the strongest criticism of equity theory is that it is unable to generate specific predictions about the behaviors that individuals are likely to utilize when attempting to restore perceptions of equity. Although researchers have proposed a number of factors that may influence the method of equity restoration chosen, little has been done to systematically test these assertions (Mowday, 1991). As a result, we know little about the mechanisms that lead to the choice of one method of equity restoration over other alternative methods. This not only severely limits the utility of equity theory as an explanation of behavior in organizations, but also hinders our ability to conduct a definitive test of the validity of this theory and its predictions.

Neglect of individual difference variables Despite the statement by Adams (1963) that 'there are probably individual differences in tolerance [for inequity] and flexibility [of reactions to inequity]' (p. 428), the role of such differences in equity theory has been largely ignored by researchers. While some research has examined the impact of variables such as moral maturity (Vecchio, 1981), and self-esteem (Brockner, 1985), this body of work is largely atheoretical and unsystematic, contributing little to our understanding of how individual differences are likely to influence the processes specified by equity theory (for an exception, see the work on equity sensitivity by Huseman, Hatfield & Miles, 1985;

King & Miles, 1994; King, Miles & Day, 1993). A number of researchers (e.g., Mowday, 1991) have pointed out that this failure to incorporate individual differences into equity theory has led to an overly simplistic view of motivation, and ignored the potential such variables hold for improving the accuracy of equity theory predictions.

Ambiguity concerning the referent other Although Adams (1963) assigns a key role to the referent other in worker motivation, there are two problems inherent in equity theory's treatment of this referent other. First, equity theory fails to clearly specify how individuals are likely to go about choosing a referent for evaluating their work situation, and subsequent researchers have failed to empirically examine this process (for two notable exceptions, see Goodman, 1974; Summers & DeNisi, 1990). Second, equity theory appears to implicitly assume that individuals utilize only one referent other when evaluating their exchange with the organization. As such, this theory offers no predictions as to how individuals are likely to utilize information from multiple referents. However, research by Goodman (1974) and Summers and DeNisi (1990) has demonstrated that multiple referent others are often used during this process, indicating that equity theory's focus on a single referent other represents a restricted and potentially unrealistic perspective on the social comparison process.

Evaluation of Equity Theory

Although initial evaluations of equity theory were highly positive (e.g., Weick, 1966), more recent evaluations have tended to be less optimistic (e.g., Miner, 1984; Pinder, 1998) for several reasons. First, despite the relatively strong evidence for negative responses to underpayment inequity, inconsistencies in the results regarding overpayment, as well as difficulties inherent in interpretation of empirical tests of this theory, make it difficult to conclude that there is consistent research support for equity theory. Moreover, a number of researchers (e.g., Lawler, 1973) have demonstrated that the findings of equity theory can easily be accounted for by other theories of motivation, such as expectancy theory. Second, the inability of this theory to make concrete predictions about worker responses to inequity severely limits the applicability of this theory to actual organizational settings as a means of either explaining or modifying behavior (Goodman & Friedman, 1971). Finally, while equity theory provides a relatively parsimonious approach to explaining motivation, it appears that such parsimony comes at the expense of explanatory power. By focusing on inequity as the sole force behind worker behavior, this theory oversimplifies the process of motivation and presents a limited perspective on the factors that motivate worker behavior. In line with these problems, it appears that the value of equity theory as an explanatory or predictive model of work motivation is questionable at best.

Beyond Equity Perceptions: Recent Conceptualization of Justice in Organizations

Although equity theory is of questionable utility as a theory of work motivation, many current researchers acknowledge that perceptions of justice act as powerful motivators of human action. Recent work on organizational justice has examined an expanded view of fairness in organizations that incorporates the concept of procedural justice.

Procedural justice As research on equity theory progressed throughout the 1970s, there was a growing recognition on the part of researchers that individuals assess their exchange relationship with an organization not only it terms of the fairness of outcomes received (i.e., distributive justice), but also in terms of the fairness of the procedures used to distribute those outcomes (i.e., procedural justice; Thibaut & Walker, 1975; Leventhal, 1980). While initial work in this area focused on identifying factors related to perceptions of procedural justice (e.g., Landy, Barnes & Murphy, 1978), subsequent research has focused on how procedural and distributive justice perceptions interact to determine employees' evaluations of their exchange with the organization. Perhaps the most interesting finding from this body of research is the 'fair process effect' (Folger, Rosenfeld, Grove & Corkran, 1979), which refers to situations in which the typically negative reactions associated with an unfair outcome are reduced or eliminated by perceptions that fair procedures were used to distribute the outcomes. To illustrate, Greenberg (1990) found that employee theft in response to a pay cut was reduced when individuals were given an adequate explanation for the pay cut. Providing an explanation for reduced outcomes increased perceptions of procedural justice, presumably reducing the motivation to regain lost outcomes through theft. Similarly, Brockner et al. (1994) found that employees reported less negative feelings in response to being downsized when perceptions of procedural justice were high, while Skarlicki and Folger (1997) found that retaliatory behaviors (e.g., theft or sabotage) were less likely to occur in response to negative outcomes when perceptions of procedural justice were high. In general, there appears to be consistent research support for the fair process effect (Cropanzano & Folger, 1991), indicating that perceptions of procedural and distributive justice are likely to interact with one another to influence employee responses to organizational exchange processes.

Although the addition of procedural justice provides a broader perspective on the factors that influence perceptions of fairness, it is important to realize that the addition of procedural justice is not a remedy for the problems inherent in equity theory. For example, although we have evidence that the impact of distributive inequity on subsequent worker reactions is likely to be influenced by perceptions of procedural justice, we are still unable to generate clear predictions about the behaviors that will be enacted by individuals in response to injustice. Thus, despite the value added by procedural justice, we are still left with a motivational theory that does not allow us to predict employee behavior in organizational settings.

Conclusions and Future Directions

At present, given the numerous problems inherent in equity theory, this model appears to hold little value for the field of work motivation. However, the concept of organizational justice derived from equity theory may hold some value for future research as a model of job attitudes. More specifically, although the integration of procedural justice theories with equity (distributive justice) theory is inadequate as a means of predicting worker behaviors, this integration may be useful in the identification of work situations that are likely to lead to worker dissatisfaction (Mowday, 1991).

Expectancy Theory

Overview

Based upon the early work of Tolman (1932), the central assumption made by expectancy theory is that human behavior is the result of conscious choices made by individuals among alternative courses of action. According to this theory, such choices are made by the individuals with the goal of maximizing the pleasure and minimize the pain that results from their choice. In his Valence–Instrumentality–Expectancy (VIE) model, Vroom (1964) argued that individuals accomplish this goal by utilizing three perceptions in the decision making process: expectancy, instrumentality, and valence. Expectancy refers to the perceived likelihood that engaging in a given act or behavior will lead to a particular set of outcomes (termed first level outcomes). Instrumentality represents perceptions of the strength and nature of the relationship between attainment of these first level outcomes and subsequent attainment of a given set of second level outcomes. Valence represents the affective orientation that individuals hold towards these second level outcomes. Positively valent outcomes are perceived as attractive or desirable by the individual, while negatively valent outcomes are perceived as undesirable. Vroom (1964) proposes that these three perceptions combine to produce a motivational 'force' on the individual. Mathematically, Vroom (1964) states this as:

$$V_j = f\left[\sum_{j=1}^{n} I_{jk} V_k\right] \quad \text{and} \quad F_i = f\sum_{i=1}^{n} (E_{ij} V_j)$$

where

V_j = the valence of outcome j
I_{jk} = the instrumentality of outcome j in attaining second level outcome k
V_k = the valence of second level outcome k
F_i = the psychological force acting on the individual to perform act i
E_{ij} = the strength of the expectancy that act i will be followed by outcome j

According to this model,[1] individuals choose the course of action that exerts the largest amount of positive force (or the weakest negative force) on them in a particular situation. Thus, individuals will engage in behaviors that are likely to lead to valued outcomes, provided they perceive that they can successfully produce such behaviors. Although a number of different forms of expectancy theory have appeared since Vroom's initial formulation of the model (e.g., Fishbein & Azjen, 1975; Porter & Lawler, 1968), the VIE model remains the most widely accepted and researched version of expectancy theory in the field of work motivation (Pinder, 1998).

Research Evidence

The introduction of the VIE model into the work motivation literature stimulated a substantial amount of research during the years following its inception. Although the results of this early research showed some level of support for Vroom's (1964) model, the magnitude of this support was less than impressive (Campbell & Pritchard, 1976; Pinder, 1987), leading researchers to conclude that that the validity of this theory was, at best, moderate. However, at the same time that such conclusions were being drawn, there was a growing realization on the part of researchers that much of the research being conducted to test this model contained serious methodological flaws. Although a complete listing of these flaws has been presented in numerous other reviews (e.g., Campbell & Pritchard, 1976), three of these flaws merit brief discussion: the use of between-subjects designs, the use of the force model to predict performance, and the measurement of the VIE elements.

Use of between-subjects designs In his original formulation of his force model, Vroom (1964) explicitly states that this model was intended to predict an individual's choice among his/her various behavioral alternatives (i.e., within-individual choice). However, the vast majority of the research

that has been conducted to test this model has been between-subjects in nature (Mitchell, 1974; Pinder, 1987). Clearly, such an approach is at odds with Vroom's conceptualizations, and suffers from a number of serious methodological problems (e.g., failing to take into account individual differences). In addition, several studies (e.g., Kennedy, Fossum & White, 1983) have demonstrated that the results obtained using a between-subjects design (as opposed to a within-subjects design) are likely to underestimate the true predictive validity of the VIE model. In light of the prevalence of this approach in the expectancy theory literature, it appears that the vast majority of expectancy theory research holds little value for assessing the validity of this model.

Job performance as a criterion In its original form, expectancy theory was explicitly designed to predict three variables: an individual's choice, intention, or level of effort. Contrary to popular belief, this model was not designed to predict job performance because, as stated by Vroom (1964), performance is likely to be influenced by many factors other than those considered by expectancy theory (e.g., ability, environmental constraints, role clarity). Despite this fact, a large number of studies have drawn conclusions about the validity of Vroom's model based upon its ability to predict job performance. As noted by Campbell and Pritchard (1976), the use of this model to predict job performance is not only inappropriate, but also likely to underestimate the true predictive validity of this theory.

Measurement of VIE elements Several researchers have pointed out that many of the empirical tests of the multiplicative relationships implied by the VIE model are problematic due to the methods commonly used to assess the components of this model (Campbell & Pritchard, 1976; Pinder, 1987). For example, deLeo and Pritchard (1974) noted that the low reliabilities typically observed with commonly used measures of valence, instrumentality, and expectancy may cause researchers to underestimate the true validity of the VIE model in predicting various criteria. Similarly, Schmidt (1973) pointed out that the common practice of measuring the elements of VIE theory using interval level scales makes the formation of the model's product terms (e.g., $E \times V$) inappropriate, since the multiplication of scales is only logically meaningful if the elements are measured on a true ratio scale (Lord & Novick, 1968). Further, Schmidt (1973) demonstrated that the use of interval level scales and transformations of those scales could substantially distort the correlation between the product terms generated by Vroom's (1964) model and a criterion variable.

In acknowledgment of these and other methodological issues present in the expectancy theory research literature, many researchers have concluded that these early studies hold little value in establishing the validity of the force model in predicting human behavior (Arnold, 1981; Campbell & Pritchard, 1976). As noted by Pinder (1987), 'In spite of the numerous studies conducted since 1964 that have ostensibly sought to test versions of the theory, very little is known about this theory's validity' (p. 144). Unfortunately, despite these repeated admonitions by researchers concerning the methodological flaws present in many tests of expectancy theory (e.g., Arnold, 1981; Mitchell, 1974; Pinder, 1987), research testing this model of motivation continues to suffer from these same flaws, utilizing between-subjects designs (e.g., Brooks & Betz, 1990), and performance as a criterion (e.g., Harder, 1991).

In light of this lack of clear evidence concerning the validity of Vroom's model, Van Eerde and Thierry (1996) attempted to provide some clarity by conducting a meta-analysis testing the efficacy of this model in predicting a number of criteria (performance, effort, intentions, preference, and choice). Based on the results obtained in this meta-analysis, these authors concluded that there appears to be little support for the propositions of Vroom's (1964) VIE theory. However, approximately 75% of the effect sizes examined in this meta-analysis were obtained from studies that either utilized a between-subjects design, or utilized job performance as a criterion. Given the fact that such studies are likely to provide inaccurate estimates concerning the true predictive validity of the VIE model (Campbell & Pritchard, 1976; Kennedy et al., 1983), conclusions concerning the validity of this theory based on these results seem unwise and potentially misleading. To illustrate, an examination of the meta-analytic results obtained for studies utilizing both a within-subjects design and an appropriate criterion variable (effort, intention, or choice) indicates that the VIE model demonstrated substantial correlations with intentions ($r = .49$), and effort ($r = .57$). However, in light of the small number of effect sizes available for these analyses, it appears that, rather than providing conclusive evidence as to the validity of Vroom's VIE model, this meta-analysis instead simply reinforces the point that we still have yet to conduct an adequate number of methodologically sound tests of this model, despite over 30 years of research on this topic.

In recent years, research interest in Vroom's formulation of expectancy seems to have declined, perhaps due to the perception of researchers that many of the central questions concerning the validity of this theory have been answered (Ambrose & Kulik, 1999). Most of the recent research on this theory has moved away from direct tests of this model, focusing instead on how one or more of the individual elements of expectancy theory relate to organizational behavior (e.g., Wood, Atkins & Bright, 1999), or simply utilizing expectancy theory as a general framework (e.g., Harrison, 1995). Of the little research that has been conducted to directly test expectancy theory, the results of these studies have tended to show moderate levels of support for the predictive capabilities of this model (e.g., Snead & Harrell, 1994).

Issues with Expectancy Theory

Although a sizable number of theoretical criticisms have been directed towards expectancy theory, two of the more significant criticisms concern the theory's emphasis on the 'economic man,' and the theory's assumption of a multiplicative nature among its elements in determining choice.

Emphasis on the 'economic man'　Throughout Vroom's (1964) original formulations, the assumption is made that individuals are fully cognizant of all alternative courses of action, as well as the outcomes associated with these actions. It is also assumed that individuals will go through an exhaustive series of computations designed to determine the optimal course of behavior that should be taken. However, it is likely that this representation of human behavior is unrealistic for three reasons (Lawler, 1973). First, due to limited cognitive resources, most individuals do not have complete knowledge of all possible courses of action or a full understanding of the outcomes that may result from those behaviors. Also, individuals may attend to only a select number of outcomes when making decisions, rather than considering all possible outcomes that may result from a given behavior (Wanous, Keon & Latack, 1983). Second, there is evidence to suggest that individuals do not always utilize the principles of optimization when choosing among behavioral alternatives (e.g., Feldman, Reitz & Hilterman, 1976). In certain situations, individuals may engage in nonoptimal information processing strategies (e.g., Bowen & Qiu, 1992; Petty & Cacioppo, 1986; Whan, 1978), and may simply choose a course of behavior that is 'good enough' (Simon, 1957), rather than going through a lengthy series of computations in search of the optimal choice. Finally, there is also evidence indicating that individuals do not typically attempt to evaluate all possible alternative behavioral choices in a given situation. Instead, individuals appear to search for behavioral alternatives until they either identify an alternative that is 'good enough,' or until the perceived benefit of searching for additional behavioral alternatives is outweighed by the costs associated with this search (Janis & Mann, 1997). In light of these issues, researchers have questioned the accuracy of this model's depiction of the individual as an 'economic man.'

Multiplicative nature of the model　Vroom's (1964) force model presents an individual's choice as a multiplicative function of his or her perceptions of valence and expectancy. Inherent in this approach is the assumption that a value of zero for either of these elements results in zero motivational force on the individual to engage in a given behavior. However, research has indicated that individuals may utilize an additive, rather than multiplicative, integration of these elements in making choices among alternative behaviors (e.g., Stahl & Harrell, 1981; Harrell & Stahl, 1986). This research also suggests that a value of zero for any of the elements does not preclude the presence of motivational force. Taken together, these findings question the appropriateness of a universal multiplicative model of choice, and suggest that there may be individual differences in preferences for combining the information multiplicatively or additively (Stahl & Harrell, 1981).

Evaluation of Expectancy Theory

Past reviews of the work motivation literature have varied widely in their evaluations of the validity of expectancy theory, perhaps due to the difficulties inherent in evaluating a theory based on a research literature that suffers from many problems. Although several researchers have noted the relative validity of this model (Pinder, 1987), the most recent evaluation of the VIE model was much less optimistic (Van Eerde & Thierry, 1996). However, negative evaluations such as these appear to be unwarranted for several reasons. First, what little research has been done correctly appears to provide strong support for this model as predictor of intentions and effort, and marginal support for this model as a predictor of choice. Second, in contrast to the difficulties encountered in attempts to apply models such as Adams's (1963) equity theory to actual organizational settings, a number of researchers have demonstrated that expectancy theory is well suited to the prediction and modification of behavior in actual organizational settings (Lawler, 1973; Pinder, 1987). In fact, the principles of Vroom's (1964) model are often utilized as the basis for systems of organizational compensation (Pinder, 1987). Finally, while this model is clearly not the most parsimonious model of motivation (due to the numerous formulas and mathematical computations involved), it does provide a clear and coherent model of the processes that individuals engage in when making choices in organizational settings. Based upon these pieces of evidence, it appears that expectancy theory represents a potentially valid and useful model of work motivation.

Conclusions and Future Directions

Although many researchers and theorists argue that there appears to be no need for further research conducted to test the main assertions of Vroom's model (Ambrose & Kulik, 1999), such suggestions may be premature given that the vast majority of the studies conducted to date to test this theory have been methodologically flawed. As noted in the prior discussion of Van Eerde and Thierry's (1996) meta-analysis, over 75% of the studies conducted so far have utilized inappropriate research designs in their tests of Vroom's model, limiting the utility of these studies in testing the validity of this theory. Thus, despite the large number of studies that have set out to assess the validity of this theory, we are still left with very few studies that actually test this theory in an appropriate manner. As such, it appears that we have yet to convincingly answer some of the basic questions concerning the accuracy of this model, suggesting that this research area would benefit greatly from additional, quality research assessing the validity of this model.

In addition, the integration of expectancy theory with other models of motivation (e.g., goal setting theory) appears to be a fruitful direction for future research. Such integrations have already been developed (e.g., Klein, 1991a) and appear to hold promise for the field of motivation. Such integrations should continue to be pursued in the hope of utilizing the knowledge gained through expectancy theory and these other theories to move towards a more unified model of work motivation.

Cognitive Evaluation Theory

The introduction of expectancy models of work motivation in the mid-1960s spurred a growth in the popularity of organizational systems seeking to enhance worker motivation by associating high levels of performance with valued, externally mediated outcomes (e.g., pay, promotions). While the popularity of such approaches continued to increase during the early 1970s (e.g., Lawler, 1973), a number of studies conducted during this period observed that the use of such reward systems may have detrimental effects on a worker's intrinsic motivation, generally defined as the propensity to perform a given behavior in the absence of external rewards or reinforcement (Deci, 1971, 1972; Lepper, Greene & Nisbett, 1973). To explain this finding, Deci and colleagues (Deci, 1971, 1972; Deci & Ryan, 1985) formulated Cognitive Evaluation Theory (CET).

Overview of CET

According to early formulations of CET (Deci, 1972), rewards exert their influence on intrinsic motivation through their ability to satisfy or frustrate two innate, higher-order needs in individuals: the need for competence (White, 1959) and the need for self-determination (deCharms, 1968). As used here, competence refers to an individual's capacity for effective interactions with their environment, while self-determination refers to an individual's freedom to initiate their own behavioral courses of action (Deci & Ryan, 1985). Deci proposed that rewards that increase the individual's perceptions of competence or self-determination will increase subsequent intrinsic motivation, whereas factors that lower such perceptions are likely to decrease intrinsic motivation. Although initial versions of CET focused on the specific impact of rewards on intrinsic motivation, more recent conceptualizations of this theory have broadened their focus to include an examination of other environmental factors that may influence intrinsic motivation through their impact on feelings of self-determination and competence, such as performance feedback, and recognition (Deci & Ryan, 1985). At present, this theoretical work has identified a large list of factors proposed to decrease intrinsic motivation, including performance-contingent rewards, negative feedback, threats, deadlines, directives, and competition, as well as a number of factors that are likely to enhance intrinsic motivation, including positive performance feedback, choice, and self-direction (Ryan & Deci, 2000).

Research Evidence

Initial research provided strong support for the propositions of CET concerning the proposed effects of rewards on intrinsic motivation (e.g., Deci, 1971, 1972; Lepper et al., 1973; Ross, 1975). However, subsequent research has obtained less consistent results. For example, while Harackiewicz (1979) and Harackiewicz, Manderlink and Sansone (1984) demonstrated that performance-contingent rewards may lower intrinsic motivation, Karniol and Ross (1977) found that the presence of performance-contingent rewards actually increased intrinsic motivation. Similarly, whereas Harackiewicz (1979) and Ryan, Mims and Koestner (1983) found that positive feedback was likely to increase intrinsic motivation, Dollinger and Thelen (1978) found no support for this proposition. As a result of these inconsistencies, the conclusions drawn by researchers in the field of work motivation concerning the validity of this model have varied greatly. In addition, the presence of a number of methodological problems with CET research has further complicated the evaluation of this model (Bandura, 1986; Eisenberger & Cameron, 1996). For example, the typical research paradigm utilized in CET research (see Deci, 1972) involves examining the impact of rewards on intrinsic motivation *after* the reward is removed, rather than examining the impact of extrinsic rewards on intrinsic motivation while the rewards are still present (Dickinson, 1989; Eisenberger & Cameron, 1996). As such, these studies are unable to truly determine if the presence of rewards decreases intrinsic motivation. In addition, many of the studies conducted to test CET have operationalized intrinsic motivation as the amount of time individuals spend engaging in the focal task during a period of free choice in which they are no longer rewarded for performing the task (e.g., Deci, 1971, 1972). Although some have argued for the superiority of this approach over other methods of measurement (e.g., Deci, Koestner & Ryan, 1999), such an operationalization is problematic because the amount of free time spent on the focal task is likely to be influenced by a number of factors other than intrinsic motivation, including satiation and the availability of attractive alternative tasks (Bandura, 1986; Eisenberger & Cameron, 1996).

Despite the presence of these inconsistencies and problems in much of the research conducted to test CET, the notion that rewards can negatively impact intrinsic motivation has become well accepted in the popular literature on organizational behavior during the last decade (e.g., Kohn, 1993). This increase in popularity, however, has been accompanied by a dramatic decline in the amount of original research conducted to test these very assertions. It appears that, rather than attempting to refine past empirical attempts to establish the validity of CET, researchers have instead focused their efforts on utilizing meta-analytic techniques as a means of either verifying or refuting the assertions of this theory (Cameron & Pierce, 1994; Deci et al., 1999; Eisenberger & Cameron, 1996; Eisenberger, Pierce & Cameron, 1999; Tang & Hall, 1995; Wiersma, 1992). Unfortunately, the conclusions drawn from these quantitative reviews appear to be no more consistent than the research literature upon which they are based. For example, while Eisenberger and Cameron (1996) found little support for CET propositions concerning the negative effects of rewards on intrinsic motivation, other reviews have concluded that there is either strong support (Deci et al., 1999), or moderate support for this model (Wiersma, 1992). Despite these apparent inconsistencies, however, a closer inspection of the results of two of the more recent meta-analyses reveals a certain level of agreement among these reviews with respect to the effects of rewards on intrinsic motivation. To illustrate, Eisenberger and Cameron (1996) found no evidence to suggest that tangible rewards had any harmful effects on self-reports of intrinsic motivation, while Deci et al. (1999) concluded that certain types of tangible rewards have a detrimental effect on intrinsic motivation. However, an examination of the results obtained by Deci et al. (1999) reveals that the effect sizes associated with this decrease in intrinsic motivation were very weak in magnitude, ranging from $-.17$ to $-.07$. Thus, despite the disparity in the conclusions drawn by these reviewers, both sets of analyses appear to indicate that tangible rewards appear to have little or no practical impact on intrinsic motivation as measured through self-report,[2] and as such, demonstrate little support for the propositions of CET.

Issues with CET

In addition to the empirical criticism that has been directed towards CET, this model has also been the subject of a number of theoretical criticisms concerning the applicability of this theory to actual organizational settings, the ambiguity surrounding the mediating variables proposed by CET, and the frequent modifications made to this model.

Applicability of CET to the workplace The applicability of this theory of intrinsic motivation to the workplace has been frequently questioned (e.g., Locke & Latham, 1990) for several reasons. First, as noted by Deci et al. (1999) and Ryan and Deci (2000), the propositions of CET only apply to situations where initial intrinsic interest in the task is high (i.e., the task is perceived as novel, challenging, or aesthetically valuable). Given that many of the activities required as a daily part of one's job may not meet this criterion (i.e., parts of the job are seen as repetitive or boring), the applicability of this theory to the prediction of worker behavior is somewhat limited. Second, many of the factors proposed to decrease intrinsic motivation (Deci & Ryan, 1985) are often integral and necessary parts of the workplace, including salient performance incentives, deadlines, performance appraisals, and negative feedback (Locke & Latham, 1990). Finally, as noted by Deci and Ryan (1985), the decrease in intrinsic motivation that is proposed to result from the presence of contingent rewards is likely to be accompanied by an increase in extrinsic motivation. Given that this increase in extrinsic motivation is likely to exert a positive influence on performance, coupled with the fact that evidence for the harmful effects of rewards on intrinsic motivation is inconsistent (Eisenberger & Cameron, 1996), we are left wondering how, and if, the principles of CET should be incorporated into the workplace.

Ambiguity concerning mediating variables Despite the long history of CET research, few studies have attempted to verify the accuracy of CET's depiction of feelings of competence and self-determination as the key mediating variables in the relationship between rewards and intrinsic motivation. In addition, evidence presented by Eisenberger et al. (1999) suggests that the rewards posited by CET to decrease perceptions of self-determination may actually increase such perceptions. Although these findings are based on a small number of studies, they nonetheless bring into question CET's primary assertions that rewards negatively affect intrinsic motivation by reducing feelings of self-determination.

Frequent model modifications Since the inception of this model, proponents of CET have argued that the occasional failure to find support for the propositions of this theory does not render the theory invalid, but instead simply points to additional contextual factors that moderate the impact of rewards on intrinsic motivation. As such, these researchers often use such findings as support for new conceptualizations of the CET model that take into account these additional contextual factors. Although the continuous modification of CET to account for such seemingly contradictory findings may be beneficial from a theory-building perspective, such modification has also made it extremely difficult to conduct a definitive test of CET as a model of motivation, given that virtually any obtained results can be cited as support for CET.

Conclusions and Future Directions

Although the research evidence gathered to date does not appear to support CET propositions concerning work motivation, the theory may still be able to contribute to the future of work motivation through its theoretical and empirical work on the concept of intrinsic motivation. However, such a contribution is contingent upon the ability of future research to correct the methodological issues present in previous research, and construct a stronger theoretical statement of the propositions of CET. In addition, it would appear that progress in determining the validity of this model and resolving the conflicting conclusions surrounding this theory might best be achieved through collaboration between the two dominant groups of researchers in this area (Deci et al., 1999; Eisenberger et al., 1999). Rather than focusing on the development of replies, rebuttals, and reanalyses, perhaps researchers in this area should follow the model set forth by Latham, Erez and Locke (1988) which illustrates how the use of collaboration can serve to resolve research conflicts with the field of work motivation.

In conclusion, while the concept of intrinsic motivation is intuitively appealing to many, researchers in this area need to find more appropriate ways to study and measure this phenomenon before CET can significantly contribute to the field of work motivation.

Goal-Setting Theory

The notion that goals or intentions represent one of the primary initiators and regulators of behavior has a long history in the field of work motivation (Austin & Vancouver, 1996). Starting with early work of Ach (1935, as cited in Locke and Latham, 1990) on 'determining tendencies', and continuing with Lewin's work on level of aspirations (Lewin, 1961; Lewin Dembo, Festinger & Sears, 1944) and Ryan's (1958, 1970) work on intentions, goals have played a central role in many theories of human motivation. One of the more popular goal-based theories of motivation is Goal Setting Theory (Locke, 1968; Locke & Latham, 1990).

Overview

In contrast to other goal-based theories of motivation that attempt to predict a wide variety of behaviors (e.g., Campbell, Dunnette, Lawler & Weick, 1970), Goal-Setting Theory (GST; Locke, 1968; Locke & Latham, 1990) takes a much narrower approach, focusing on the impact of performance goals on task performance. Based upon the early findings of Locke (1966, 1967, 1968), the central proposition of GST states that the performance goals that people hold for a particular task are likely to determine how well they perform the task. More specifically, GST argues that differences in the content of performance goals (i.e., goal difficulty and specificity) held by individuals are related to differences in task performance such that specific, difficult goals result in higher levels of performance than vague, easy, or do-your-best goals (Locke & Latham, 1990). According to GST, specific, difficult goals enhance performance because such goals clearly define acceptable levels of performance, increase the amount of effort an individual exerts, increase task persistence, lead to more extensive strategy development and planning, and orient individuals towards goal-related knowledge and activities (Locke & Latham, 1990).

Although GST argues that the positive effect of specific, difficult goals on performance is likely to generalize across tasks and individuals, this theory also acknowledges that there are several variables that are likely to moderate the impact of such goals on performance. More specifically, GST proposes that the following conditions must be satisfied in order for goals to enhance performance: individuals must accept and be committed to the goal, performance relevant feedback must be present, and individuals must also have the requisite levels of task-relevant ability. According to GST, the absence of any of these three factors is likely to preclude or substantially reduce the positive impact of goals on task performance (Locke & Latham, 1990).

In addition to these assertions, more recent conceptualizations of GST (e.g., Locke & Latham, 1990) have extended the scope of this theory to include propositions concerning the factors that are likely to influence an individual's goal choice. Locke and Latham (1990) suggest that the level of an individual's performance goal is likely to be positively related to their ability, past performance levels, and the individual's self-efficacy (Bandura, 1977).

Research Evidence

Locke and Latham's (1990) extensive review of the research literature examining the goal-setting model of task performance clearly indicates that specific, difficult goals lead to higher levels of performance than vague, easy, or do-your-best goals across a wide variety of settings and task types. In addition, meta-analytic reviews by Tubbs (1986), Wood,

Mento and Locke (1987), and Mento, Steel and Karren (1987) have all found that on average, individuals assigned specific, difficult performance goals substantially outperform individuals given easy goals, do-your-best goals, or no goals. Taken together, these findings provide strong support for the impact of specific, difficult goals, and have led to the general conclusion among researchers that this effect represents one of the more robust findings within the field of work motivation (Kanfer, 1990; Locke & Latham, 1990; Pinder, 1998).

In addition to the research supporting GST's main propositions concerning goal specificity/difficulty, a substantial number of studies have also confirmed Locke and Latham's (1990) propositions concerning the mechanisms by which goals impact performance. Research in this area has clearly demonstrated that specific difficult goals lead to higher levels of effort (e.g., Bandura & Cervone, 1983; Bryan & Locke, 1967), lead to greater task persistence (e.g., Bavelas & Lee, 1978; Hall, Weinberg & Jackson, 1987), direct individuals towards goal-relevant activities and knowledge (e.g., Locke & Bryan, 1969; Terborg, 1976), lead to the development of task strategies (e.g., Latham & Saari, 1982; Klein, Whitener & Ilgen, 1990), and stimulate planning on the part of the individual (e.g., Earley, Wojnaroski & Prest, 1987; Smith, Locke & Barry, 1990).

Moderators of the goal–performance relationship
As noted previously, GST proposes that several factors may limit the impact of goals on performance, including the individual's ability level, performance feedback, and goal commitment. Research has demonstrated that the impact of goals on performance is likely to be limited by the individual's task-relevant ability, such that the relationship between goals and performance is likely to become weaker or disappear as performance goals move beyond the individual's task capabilities (e.g., Kanfer & Ackerman, 1989; Locke, Frederick, Buckner & Bobko, 1984). A number of studies have also observed that task-relevant feedback moderates the relationship between goals and performance such that goals are likely to have little or no impact on performance when feedback is not present (e.g., Erez, 1977; Frost & Mahoney, 1976). In contrast to the evidence for these two moderators, the empirical support for the moderating effects of goal commitment has been much less consistent. A meta-analytic review of this moderating effect by Donovan and Radosevich (1998) indicated that, across studies, the average magnitude of this effect was weak and that there was considerable variability in the support obtained in these studies for the moderating role of goal commitment. As such, the existence or impact of the moderating role of goal commitment remains unclear at the present time. In addition to these three moderators, several studies (e.g., Earley, Connolly & Ekegren, 1989; Gist,

Stevens & Bavetta, 1991), as well as meta-analytic work by Wood et al. (1987), have demonstrated that task complexity also moderates the impact of goals on performance, such that the impact of specific, difficult goals on performance decreases in magnitude as the complexity of the task increases.

Determinants of self-set goals A review of the goal-setting literature also provides clear support for GST propositions concerning the factors that determine goal choice. Numerous studies have observed that an individual's goal choice is likely to be influenced by past performance levels (e.g., Locke et al., 1984; Williams, Donovan & Dodge, 2000), ability (e.g., Campion & Lord, 1982; Vance & Colella, 1990), and self-efficacy (e.g., Bandura & Cervone, 1986; Locke et al., 1984). In addition, recent empirical work has uncovered several other factors that are likely to influence an individual's goal choice, including: goal orientation (e.g., Phillips & Gully, 1997; Vande Walle, Brown, Cron & Slocum, 1999), conscientiousness (e.g., Barrick, Mount & Strauss, 1993; Gellatly, 1996), need for achievement (e.g., Phillips & Gully, 1997; Hollenbeck, Williams & Klein, 1989), goal instrumentality (e.g., Mento, Locke & Klein, 1992), and mood (e.g., Brown, Cron & Slocum, 1997; Hom & Arbuckle, 1988).

Criticisms of GST research In contrast to the numerous problems encountered in the research literature for equity theory, cognitive evaluation theory, and expectancy theory, research conducted to test GST has suffered from relatively few methodological problems (Pinder, 1998). Although early GST research was often criticized for its focus on the effects of assigned, rather than self-set, goals, and its reliance upon relatively simple tasks in demonstrating the impact of goals, more recent research has begun to answer such criticisms (Ambrose & Kulik, 1999) through its examination of the determinants and impact of self-set goals (e.g., Phillips & Gully, 1997; Williams et al., 2000), and through its utilization of more complex tasks (e.g., Gilliland & Landis, 1992; Kanfer, Ackerman, Murtha, Dugdale & Nelson, 1994). One issue that remains problematic in this research literature, however, is the widely divergent operationalizations of goal difficulty utilized by researchers. Although Locke and colleagues (e.g., Locke, 1991a; Locke & Latham, 1990) have offered several suggestions, no clear consensus exists as to how goal difficulty should be operationalized. Given the centrality of this construct to GST research, and that the various operationalizations are likely to result in substantially divergent results (Wright, 1990), one must be cautious when evaluating the impact of 'difficult' goals on performance across studies utilizing distinct operationalizations of goal difficulty.

Issues with GST

Although GST has generally been well accepted by the field of work motivation, two concerns have been raised about this theory as a model of work motivation: GST's focus on task performance, and GST's static approach to motivation.

Focus on task performance Although Locke and Latham (1990) argue that GST's limited focus on task performance is actually an asset of the theory, a number of other researchers have criticized this model for its inability to predict or explain worker behaviors other than task performance (e.g., Austin & Bobko, 1985). In addition, GST has also received criticism for its failure to incorporate goals other than quantity performance goals. As noted by Austin and Bobko (1985), GST has generally neglected to address issues such as the impact of conflicting quality and quantity goals on performance, and the impact of multiple task goals on performance (for an exception see Locke, Smith, Erez, Chah & Schaffer, 1994), thus providing only a limited perspective on how goals may operate in organizational settings.

Static view of motivation GST has also been criticized for its emphasis on the motivational processes that occur within a single performance episode, rather than the motivational processes that occur over the course of multiple performance episodes. That is, much of GST focuses on the impact of performance goals on immediate task performance with little regard for how such goals are likely to be maintained or revised in response to goal-relevant performance feedback. Given that most instances of goal setting in the workplace are likely to involve multiple instances of goal setting and subsequent goal revision, it has been argued that GST's focus on a single performance episode provides an incomplete and moderately unrealistic perspective on worker motivation (Campion & Lord, 1982).

Conclusions and Future Directions

As present, GST is one of the more popular and well-accepted theories of work motivation (Pinder, 1998). Proponents of this model have pointed out that, in addition to the considerable research support that exists for this model, GST represents a parsimonious yet accurate depiction of the impact of performance goals on task performance that is directly applicable to organizational settings (Frayne & Latham, 1987; Latham & Yukl, 1975; Locke & Latham, 1990; Rodgers & Hunter, 1991). However, for GST to continue to contribute to the field of work motivation, future work on this model should seek to expand the relatively limited focus of this theory. For example, studies should explore the effectiveness of performance goals in more complex environments (e.g., environments with multiple goals or conflicting goals) to provide a more realistic model of task performance as it is likely to occur in organizational settings. Additionally, given the increased importance of self-set goals in organizations, future research should expand its search for factors that are likely to influence goal choice. Finally, future GST research should focus on an exploration of the process by which individuals revise their performance goals in response to performance feedback (i.e., the process of goal revision). Although recent research has begun to examine the processes involved in goal revision (e.g., Phillips, Hollenbeck & Ilgen, 1996; Williams et al., 2000), further study of this process is clearly warranted.

Control Theory

Although the popularity of Goal-Setting Theory (GST) increased rapidly during the decade following its introduction, early formulations of GST were criticized for their failure to address issues such as the origin of self-set or personal goals, the processes by which individual utilize goals over time (i.e., dynamic self-regulation), and how individuals are likely to react to multiple goals in complex performance environments (Campion & Lord, 1982). In an attempt to address these issues and develop a more complete motivational framework, researchers turned to the principles of cybernetic control systems (Miller, Galanter & Pribrum, 1960; Powers, 1973; Wiener, 1948), developing what is commonly referred to as Control Theory (Carver & Scheier, 1981; Campion & Lord, 1982).

Overview

Although theoretical and empirical work in the field of motivation often refers to Control Theory (CT) as if it were a single, unified model of motivation, CT actually represents a broad category of models that includes two distinct forms of CT: early cybernetic CT models (e.g., Miller et al., 1960; Powers, 1973, 1978), and subsequent rational CT models (e.g., Campion & Lord, 1982; Kernan & Lord, 1990; Klein, 1989). Although both approaches focus on how individuals gather and evaluate environmental feedback to regulate behavior, there are a number of critical differences between these two models.

Cybernetic control theory models   According to Cybernetic Control Theory (CCT) models, individuals monitor their behavioral outputs through an environmental sensor that allows them to make comparisons between their current behavior and their behavioral referent (i.e., their goal or standard). If this comparison does not detect any goal–behavior discrepancies, the individual simply maintains their current behavior(s). However, the detection of any goal–behavior discrepancy creates a self-correcting motivational tendency that leads the individual to engage in either cognitive (e.g., altering the referent) or behavioral measures (e.g., increasing effort) designed to reduce this discrepancy. Following this, a subsequent goal–behavior comparison is performed to determine if additional corrective actions are needed to bring behavior in line with the individual's referent or goal. In line with terminology of cybernetic control systems, this continuous monitoring/adjustment process is referred to as a negative feedback loop. According to CCT models, these negative feedback loops are arranged in complex hierarchies that span from higher-order or superordinate goals (e.g., self-actualization) to lower level or subordinate goals (e.g., specific task behaviors). These hierarchies operate such that superordinate goals dictate the referent levels utilized for subordinate goals, while subordinate goal–behavior discrepancy information provides input to the negative feedback loops regulating superordinate goals (Powers, 1973). It is important to note that these cybernetic perspectives argue that individuals seek to avoid all goal–behavior discrepancies (both positive and negative). That is, behaviors that surpass one's goal (positive goal–behavior discrepancies) are just as troubling to individuals as behaviors that fail to reach their desired referent or standard (negative goal–behavior discrepancy; Miller et al., 1960; Powers, 1973, 1978). As such, these positive goal–behavior discrepancies initiate the same cognitive/behavioral discrepancy reduction mechanisms invoked by negative discrepancies.

Rational control theory models   While early CCT models provided a useful heuristic framework for understanding how goals and feedback are utilized in self-regulatory processes, a growing number of researchers began to recognize that human motivation cannot be adequately modeled using a mechanical systems approach (e.g., Campion & Lord, 1982; Lord & Hanges, 1987). As such, subsequent conceptualizations of CT moved towards a more rational (and less mechanistic) formulation of CT. While these Rational Control Theory (RCT) formulations continued to utilize the concept of a feedback loop as the primary framework for understanding motivation, these models (e.g., Campion & Lord, 1982; Klein, 1989; Lord & Hanges, 1987) made a number of substantial modifications to the original CCT framework. Although a complete discussion of these modifications is beyond the scope of this chapter (for such a review see Klein, 1989), four of the more significant modifications merit brief discussion. First, RCT models have recognized that the presence of a goal–behavior discrepancy does not automatically trigger the self-correcting process implied by CCT models, arguing that individuals are likely to be tolerant of small goal–behavior discrepancies (Campion & Lord, 1982). Additionally, recent RCT models have argued that in order for goal–behavior discrepancies to trigger either behavioral or cognitive reactions, individuals must be aware of the discrepancy (i.e., focus their attention inward; Carver & Scheier, 1981, 1998), and the goal must be seen as important to the individual (Klein, 1989). Second, in contrast to CCT's focus on discrepancy reduction as the primary process underlying motivation, RCT models recognize that individuals are also likely to engage in discrepancy production behaviors (e.g., setting goals above past performance levels) when setting initial goals for a given behavior or following goal attainment (Campion & Lord, 1982). Third, while early CCT models proposed that goal choice was dictated by superordinate goals, these models offered no clear predictions as to the origin of these superordinate goals. More recent RCT models have avoided this issue by arguing that goal choice is primarily a function of the individual's past performance levels and perceptions of ability (Campion & Lord, 1982; Klein, 1989). Finally, while initial CCT models did not clearly specify the factors that are likely to influence an individual's choice among cognitive and behavioral mechanisms of discrepancy reduction, recent conceptualizations of RCT have identified a number of such factors, including the magnitude of the discrepancy, the individual's expectancy for future success in reducing this discrepancy, and the individual's past success or failure in reducing such discrepancies. According to RCT, individuals are likely to engage in cognitive discrepancy reduction measures when they experience very large goal–behavior discrepancies, have low expectancies for future success, and experience repeated failures in attempting to reduce goal–behavior discrepancies (Campion & Lord, 1982; Kernan & Lord, 1990).

In light of these modifications, it is clear that although both RCT and CCT models utilize the concept of feedback loops, there are relatively few additional similarities between these two classes of models. In light of the numerous problems that have been identified with CCT approaches to motivation (Bandura, 1986; Klein, 1989; Locke, 1991b; Locke & Latham, 1990), the remainder of this section will focus on the more recent RCT models.

Research Evidence

Although RCT models of motivation have been in existence for quite some time, there has been remarkably little research conducted to test these theories as a means of explaining and predicting worker behavior (Bandura, 1991; Locke, 1991b). In fact, it appears that the majority of the work on RCT has been theoretical (rather than empirical) in nature as evidenced by the large number of theoretical publications on the tenets of various RCT models (e.g., Klein, 1989; Lord & Hanges, 1987; Lord & Kernan, 1989). However, there is a small body of research that provides tentative evidence of the validity of this model of motivation. Several studies

have demonstrated that large goal–behavior discrepancies are associated with higher levels of effort (e.g., Campion & Lord, 1982; Matsui, Okada & Inoshita, 1983), and that in order for goal–behavior discrepancies to activate self-regulatory mechanisms, individuals must be actively focusing their attention inward toward their goals or standards (e.g., Carver, Blaney & Scheier, 1979; Kernis, Zuckerman, Cohen & Spadafora, 1982) and the goals must be seen as important (e.g., Hollenbeck & Williams, 1987; Kernan & Lord, 1990). Research has also shown that individuals are likely to be tolerant of small goal–behavior discrepancies (e.g., Williams et al., 2000) and that individuals may raise their goals or standards following goal attainment (e.g., Phillips et al., 1996) and lower their goals following repeated failures (e.g., Campion & Lord, 1982). Finally, although far from conclusive, there is research that suggests that expectancies for future success at reducing goal–behavior discrepancies are likely to impact an individual's choice among cognitive and behavioral means of discrepancy reduction (e.g., Williams et al., 2000; Carver et al., 1979). In addition, although not specifically conducted to test CT predictions, many of the research findings from the literature on Goal-Setting Theory, as well as Social Cognitive Theory (Bandura, 1986), are consistent with CT's propositions concerning the determinants of goal choice (Locke & Latham, 1990), the interdependent effects of feedback and goals on self-regulation (e.g., Erez, 1977), and the impact of large goal–behavior discrepancies on subsequent behavior (e.g., Bandura & Cervone, 1986; Cervone, Jiwani & Wood, 1991).

Although this body of literature provides some initial support for RCT predictions, it is important to realize that virtually no research has been conducted to test the more complex and large-scale assertions of RCT concerning the dynamic operation of multiple, complex goal hierarchies as regulators of behavior (Vancouver & Putka, 2000). Instead, the empirical research conducted to test RCT has focused on testing specific components of this model (Locke, 1991b). As such, it remains unclear whether RCT's perspective on such motivational processes represents a valid and coherent explanation of these processes.

Issues with Control Theory

While numerous criticisms have been leveled against CT models of motivation (e.g., Bandura, 1986; Locke, 1991b), many of these criticisms appear to be largely directed at initial cybernetic versions of control theory, rather than at more recent RCT models (Klein, 1991b). Given the substantial differences between current RCT models and these early cybernetic models, such criticisms hold little value for evaluating the validity of RCT. However, in addition to these criticisms directed at early CCT models, researchers have also directed a number of criticisms at more recent RCT models, including RCT's unclear model specification, and RCT's poor 'testability.'

Unclear model specification   Despite nearly two decades of theoretical and empirical work on RCT models of motivation, several aspects of RCT's explanation of behavior remain unclear, hindering the ability of this theory to explain or predict motivated behavior. For example, although the concept of goal hierarchies is central to current RCT models, relatively little theoretical work has been done to clearly delineate the specific processes that operate within these goal hierarchies (e.g., how attention is redirected among specific levels of the hierarchy). Further, while one of the stated advantages of RCT is its ability to address the presence of multiple, simultaneous goals, theoretical formulations of RCT offer only vague propositions as to how individuals are likely to manage such goals and their associated hierarchies (for an exception, see Kernan & Lord, 1990; Vancouver & Putka, 2000). Finally, recent RCT models of motivation are not all entirely consistent with one another with respect to their predictions of worker behaviors (e.g., reactions to goal–behavior discrepancies; see Klein, 1989, for a review of these differences). In light of these ambiguities and inconsistencies, a number of researchers have concluded that control theory is too diverse in meaning, as well as inconsistent in content to serve as an appropriate framework for understanding work motivation (e.g., Locke, 1994; Vancouver, 1996).

Poor 'testability'   Following directly from criticisms concerning RCT's problems with model specification, a number of researchers (e.g., Bandura, 1991) have characterized the RCT framework as inherently 'untestable.' That is, due to the ambiguities present in several of the model's components, as well as the inherent complexity that would be involved in testing this model's propositions concerning the dynamic processes underlying self-regulation, it is extremely difficult to conduct a definitive test of this framework. As such, research testing RCT appears to be relegated to an examination of one or more of the specific components in isolation, and therefore is unable to provide strong evidence of the validity or accuracy of many of this framework's assertions (e.g., how attention shifts up and down levels of a single goal hierarchy and across multiple goal hierarchies).

Evaluation of Control Theory

In light of the relatively sparse research literature conducted to test RCT, as well as the criticisms of this model, several proponents of CT have acknowledged that, in its current state, CT is not truly a fully developed theoretical model, but rather a heuristic framework of work motivation (e.g., Lord & Hanges, 1987: 163). Nonetheless, this heuristic framework represents a relatively parsimonious and flexible description of how individuals are likely to utilize goals or standards to regulate their behavior over time. In addition, RCT clearly extends the limited scope of GS Theory to produce a more realistic and potentially useful motivational framework. As such, this model holds great applied and theoretical potential for the future of work motivation, assuming that future work on RCT can move towards the development of a more complete specification of motivational processes.

Conclusions and Future Directions

Although proponents of other theories of motivation (particularly GST and SCT) have often been extremely critical of CT as a model of motivation (e.g., Locke, 1991b), it is important to realize that the differences between these theories and the most recent versions of CT (i.e., the noncybernetic approaches) are actually very minor. Clearly these approaches are compatible, and should not be viewed as opposing (and contradictory) explanations for motivation. As such, the most fruitful direction for future research on CT appears to be a move toward unification with other goal-based theories. Klein's (1989) integrated CT model of motivation represents an admirable first step in this process, and future research should continue this process in the hope of developing a more fully specified theory of work motivation.

Social Cognitive Theory

Bandura's original theoretical formulations on the concept of human motivation (e.g., Bandura, 1977) were largely derived from a dissatisfaction with the principles of strict behaviorism. In contrast to these principles, Bandura's Social Learning Theory (Bandura, 1977) emphasized the role of human cognitions and environmental influences in governing the processes involved in motivation. While the most recent version of Social Learning Theory has maintained this emphasis on cognitive and environmental influences on motivation, this approach has also taken a more explicitly goal-based approach to motivation, arguing that the goal's held by individuals are one of the primary determinants of motivated behavior.[3] Bandura has termed this approach Social Cognitive Theory (SCT; Bandura, 1986, 1997).

Overview

According to SCT (Bandura, 1986), the self-regulation of behavior entails four interrelated processes: goal establishment, self-observation, self-evaluation, and self-reaction.

Goal establishment is the process by which individuals set goals or standards that represent desired behavioral states. These goals are a function of the individual's past behavior and self-efficacy, defined as the 'self-belief in one's capabilities to exercise control over events to accomplish desired goals' (Wood & Bandura, 1989: 364). According to SCT, the goals held by individuals are arranged in complex hierarchies consisting of proximal (short-term) and distal (long-term) goals. However, in contrast to Control Theory propositions, SCT states that proximal goals are not simply subordinate goals whose sole purpose is to serve as a means of obtaining superordinate goals. Rather, proximal goals act as a source of self-satisfaction, increasing feelings of personal mastery and self-efficacy and helping to sustain interest in the task while also facilitating progress towards distal goal attainment.

Following goal establishment, individuals engage in a period of self-observation where they monitor their behavior or performance with respect to a given task. Although this process is common, Bandura (1986) argues that individuals do not automatically engage in self-observation for all behaviors, but rather they focus on behaviors that are perceived as being important and/or related to the attainment of valued internal goals. After a period of self-observation, individuals engage in self-evaluation by utilizing the information gathered during self-monitoring to make comparisons between their current behavior and their behavioral goals. The results of this comparison lead to affective and cognitive self-reactions such that performance that meets or exceeds one's goal (i.e., a positive goal–behavior discrepancy) leads to satisfaction and an increase in self-efficacy, while performance below one's goal (i.e., a negative goal–behavior discrepancy) leads to dissatisfaction and a decrease in self-efficacy. Following a negative discrepancy, the dissatisfaction experienced by the individual exerts a motivational force to engage in cognitive and/or behavioral measures designed to reduce the magnitude of this discrepancy (i.e., discrepancy reduction processes). This may entail increasing effort, changing task strategies, lowering one's goal, or abandoning the activity if the goal–behavior discrepancy is sufficiently large (Bandura, 1986, 1989). According to SCT, the choice among these alternatives is likely to be influenced by the individual's self-efficacy and his or her beliefs concerning the causes of their performance (i.e., causal attributions). Following a positive discrepancy, individuals are proposed to set higher standards for themselves (i.e., discrepancy production processes), although Bandura (1986) acknowledges that this tendency is likely to depend on the individual's self-efficacy beliefs, his or her ability level, and the perceived importance of the behavior. It is important to note that these discrepancy production and reduction tendencies are not automatic; individuals may respond differently to discrepancy feedback due to dispositional, affective, cognitive, and contextual factors which influence perceptions of goal–performance discrepancies (Bandura, 1986, 1989).

Taken together, these two mechanisms – discrepancy production and discrepancy reduction – are thought to regulate performance such that effective self-regulation is generally characterized by alternating cycles of discrepancy production and discrepancy reduction; individuals set challenging goals for themselves creating a goal–behavior discrepancy, work towards reducing this discrepancy, and following discrepancy reduction, set new challenging goals for themselves (Bandura, 1986).

Research Evidence

Much of the research conducted to test the validity of SCT has focused on two areas: the impact of self-efficacy on goal establishment and subsequent performance, and the impact of goal–behavior discrepancies on subsequent motivational processes.

Impact of self-efficacy The construct of self-efficacy has received perhaps the most attention out of all of the components of SCT. Numerous studies have demonstrated the positive impact of self-efficacy perceptions on goal establishment processes (for a review see Locke & Latham, 1990), as well as performance on both simple and complex tasks (Stajkovic & Luthans, 1998). Further, self-efficacy has also been associated with increases in strategy development (e.g., Bandura & Wood, 1989), and planning activities (e.g., Earley, Connolly & Lee, 1989). In addition, the importance of the self-efficacy construct has also been demonstrated in a number of studies conducted in organizational settings (e.g., Harrison, Rainer, Hochwarter & Thompson, 1997; Martocchio, 1994; Morin & Latham, 2000), providing evidence of the applicability of this construct to issues of work motivation. Taken as a whole, this body of work provides clear support of the role of self-efficacy in the self-regulatory processes specified by SCT.

Impact of goal–behavior discrepancies Research has also demonstrated the motivational impact of goal–behavior discrepancies on subsequent affective, cognitive, and behavioral reactions. A number of empirical studies have observed that negative discrepancies are associated with decreases in self-efficacy (e.g., Thomas & Mathieu, 1994), and increases in self-dissatisfaction (e.g., Bandura & Cervone, 1983; Roney & Sorrentino, 1995). Such discrepancies have also been shown to be related to behaviors focused on discrepancy reduction, including increases in effort (e.g., Bandura & Cervone, 1983, 1986), and subsequent downward goal revision (e.g., Donovan, 1998; Williams et al., 2000). Similarly, positive discrepancies have been found to be associated with discrepancy production tendencies including upward goal revision (e.g., Lewin et al., 1944; Phillips et al., 1996; Williams et al., 2000) and subsequent increases in self-efficacy (e.g., Mathieu & Button, 1992;

Thomas & Mathieu, 1994). Further, although not conducted from a SCT perspective, the findings from several studies testing Control Theory predictions are consistent with SCT predictions concerning reactions to negative goal–behavior discrepancies (e.g., Campion & Lord, 1982; Kernan & Lord, 1990).

Several studies have also supported Bandura's (1986, 1989) propositions concerning potential variability in individual reactions to goal–behavior discrepancies based upon cognitive, dispositional, contextual, and affective factors. Recent research has indicated that an individual's cognitive and behavioral reactions to goal–behavior discrepancies are likely to be moderated by a number of factors, including both stability and controllability causal attributions (e.g., Mone & Baker, 1992; Thomas & Mathieu, 1994; Williams et al., 2000), time deadlines (e.g., Donovan, 1998; Williams et al., 2000), an individual's goal orientation (e.g., Donovan, 1998) and need for achievement (e.g., Phillips et al., 1996), and goal-related affect (e.g., Brown et al., 1997). Taken together with the findings presented above, this body of empirical work lends strong support to SCT assertions regarding the effects of goal–behavior discrepancies on subsequent self-regulatory processes.

In addition to the work conducted on self-efficacy and goal–behavior discrepancies, there is also some evidence to support SCT's assertion that proximal goals serve a self-satisfying function and lead to increases in feelings of efficacy and task interest when utilized as a means of facilitating attainment of long-term or distal goals (e.g., Bandura & Schunk, 1981; Bandura & Simon, 1977). However, relatively little work has been conducted to further explore SCT's notion of goal hierarchies, and as such, these findings must be interpreted as only initial support for such propositions.

Issues with Social Cognitive Theory

In contrast to the previously discussed theories of work motivation, SCT has received relatively few criticisms as a theory of work motivation. However, one specific aspect of this theory has received a considerable amount of critical attention: SCT's assumptions about the prevalence of discrepancy production.

Prevalence of discrepancy production SCT proposes that individuals attaining a goal will generally set a more challenging goal for themselves for future performance episodes (e.g., Bandura, 1989: 38). However, a number of researchers have argued that this process of discrepancy production is a relatively rare occurrence. For example, Klein (1991b) argues that, 'The continuous creation of discrepancies is also at variance with the way people usually act … people frequently say 'good enough' and focus their attention on other concerns' (p. 35). Similar concerns have been voiced by a

number of other control theorists, including Powers (1978) and Carver and Scheier (1981), who argue that discrepancy production is likely to be the exception in human self-regulation, rather than the rule. Although a recent laboratory study by Phillips et al. (1996) found some evidence to refute such claims, control theorists have argued that since this study utilized college students performing relatively simple verbal and mathematical tasks, it is unclear whether the results found in this study are likely to generalize to an organizational settings using actual workers in substantially more complex environments.

Evaluation of Social Cognitive Theory

In light of the generally supportive research evidence obtained from tests of SCT, it appears that this model provides a useful framework for understanding the processes underlying self-regulation, as well as identifying factors that are likely to influence such processes (e.g., self-efficacy beliefs, causal attributions). Although Control Theory models also offer a useful framework for examining self-regulation, SCT more clearly articulates the specific factors that are likely to be involved in the utilization of feedback to regulate behavior. In addition to its value as a theoretical framework, the propositions of SCT are also clearly and directly related to important motivational issues in the workplace, given the increased use of dynamic, self-determined goals in interventions utilized in organizational settings (Parker, 2000). Finally, although SCT presents a relatively complex model of motivation that contains several processes and boundary conditions affecting self-regulation, this model nonetheless represents a relatively straightforward and comprehensive means of explaining these processes. However, it is still important to realize that there has yet to be any grand-scale test of SCT propositions concerning self-regulation over a substantial period of time in actual organizational settings. As such, it is unclear whether the support found for this model in a laboratory setting will generalize to the more complex environment that is characteristic of many organizations.

Conclusions and Future Directions

Despite the assertions of several researchers to the contrary (e.g., Locke, 1991b), an SCT approach to work motivation is clearly compatible with (and highly similar to) Rational Control Theory models of motivation (e.g., Campion & Lord, 1982; Kernan & Lord, 1990). Although some differences between these approaches do exist (cf. Williams et al., 2000), both models are in agreement that self-regulation involves goal establishment, monitoring of performance, evaluation of performance relative to the goal, and subsequent cognitive and/or behavioral reactions. Given such a high degree of similarity, both Control Theory and SCT would benefit from an integration of their various components to form a more comprehensive and accurate model of self-regulation, especially given that the current debates centered around the superiority of one theory over another (e.g., Locke, 1991b) have accomplished little in terms of furthering our understanding of the processes underlying self-regulation.

In addition to this move towards an integrative framework, recent research also points to the value of future research designed to examine distinct components or facets of self-efficacy as predicting motivational processes. For example, Wood, Atkins and Tabernero (2000) suggest that the separate examination of two facets of self-efficacy (i.e., search efficacy, processing efficacy) may enhance our understanding of the effects of self-efficacy on self-regulatory processes such as task strategy search and development. Similarly, Parker (2000) suggests that a role-breadth facet of the broad self-efficacy construct (role-breadth self-efficacy) may hold value for organizational interventions designed at facilitating self-management among employees. Although such research is clearly in its initial stages, this direction appears to hold some promise for future research on SCT.

SUMMARY AND RECOMMENDATIONS FOR FUTURE RESEARCH

Looking back across the various theoretical models reviewed in this chapter, one can observe that although early theoretical models of motivation were quite diverse in their propositions concerning the determinants of motivated behavior, more recent models have demonstrated a greater degree of consistency. More specifically, these recent theories all share a common emphasis on the importance of goals in self-regulatory processes; Goal-Setting Theory, Control Theory, and Social Cognitive Theory all agree that goals represent one of the primary determinants of motivated behavior. Given the strong support for the propositions of these theories concerning the impact of goals on behavior as well as the mechanisms by which feedback and goals are utilized to regulate behavior, this goal-based approach appears to hold considerable promise for the advancement of the field of work motivation. However, in order to fully realize the potential of these models, several theoretical and methodological recommendations should be incorporated into future research efforts.

Theoretical Recommendations

Although several directions for future research have been suggested in previous sections of this chapter, three particular recommendations merit additional discussion: model integration, increased examination of dispositional influences on motivation, and increased attention to variable interactions.

Model integration Given the high degree of similarity among Goal-Setting Theory, Control Theory, and Social Cognitive Theory, one important recommendation for future efforts is that, rather than debating the merits of each approach and formulating criticisms of opposing models, future work should move towards the development and validation of an integrated, goal-based model of self-regulation that incorporates the important components of these various theories. Although Klein's (1989) integrative Control Theory model represents an important initial effort at developing such a model, we have yet to see a substantial amount of research activity directed at testing the assertions of this model. In addition, very few attempts have been made to theoretically clarify some of the more ambiguous components of this model, including the situational characteristics and individual difference variables that are likely to influence the process of self-regulation. As such, rather than representing a complete theoretical framework, this model represents a valuable initial foundation upon which future integrative efforts should be built. Although the development of this integrative framework should be largely based upon the well-supported theoretical propositions of the self-regulation models, several key components from other models of motivation discussed within this chapter may also benefit the development of such a model. For example, several of the components of expectancy theory appear to play important roles in goal-related processes such as goal establishment (Klein, 1991a), goal commitment (Hollenbeck & Klein, 1987), and reactions to goal–behavior discrepancies (e.g., Kernan & Lord, 1990). Similarly, although Equity Theory's propositions concerning the impact of inequity on subsequent behavior have received inconsistent support, it is clear that perceptions of fairness may exert a strong influence on the goal pursuit processes that individuals engage in following goal establishment (e.g., how much effort individuals are willing to exert towards goal attainment). In light of these potential contributions, efforts at future model development should recognize that a movement towards a goal-based integrative model would clearly benefit from an incorporation of a number of components derived from other theoretical perspectives.

Increased examination of dispositional influences on motivation Although past research in the field of human motivation has demonstrated the potential role of stable dispositional traits in various motivational and cognitive processes, very few modern theories of work motivation have attempted to fully integrate the findings from this body of research into their theoretical formulations (Austin & Klein,

1996; Kanfer, 1990; Kanfer & Ackerman, 2000). For example, although it is clear that McClelland's (1961) concept of achievement motivation is likely to impact numerous motivational processes including behavioral intentions, choice, goal establishment, and reactions to goal failure (Kanfer & Heggestad, 1997), many of the models reviewed in the present chapter have failed to formally acknowledge the role of this dispositional factor. Given that recent research in the field of work motivation has demonstrated that achievement motivation, along with other dispositional factors such as conscientiousness (e.g., Barrick et al., 1993) and goal orientation (e.g., Phillips & Gully, 1997; Vande Walle et al., 1999), influences the process of goal establishment (Phillips & Gully, 1997; Phillips et al., 1996), it would seem clear that such variables should be given a greater role in future conceptualizations of both the antecedents and consequences of the processes involved in work motivation.

Increased recognition of variable interactions
Although the impact of individual differences and situational characteristics on the process of self-regulation has received some recent attention, there has been little research examining how such variables are likely to interact with one another to influence self-regulation. For example, although a number of studies have demonstrated the impact of causal attributions on reactions to goal–behavior discrepancies (e.g., Mone & Baker, 1992; Thomas & Mathieu, 1994; Williams et al., 2000), there has been virtually no work conducted to examine how such causal attributions are likely to interact with other individual differences (e.g., goal orientation) and/or situational characteristics (e.g., time deadlines) to influence such reactions. Given that such variables are likely to exert a simultaneous impact on self-regulation, a focus on these variables in isolation from one another presents an overly restrictive, and potentially misleading depiction of the processes underlying self-regulation. Therefore, future research efforts would benefit greatly from a more complex, interaction-based analysis of the impact of such variables.

Methodological Recommendations

In addition to these theoretical recommendations, a consideration of the methodology typically utilized in the study of work motivation suggests two other avenues for improving future research: the use of more appropriate tasks, and the use of more complex research designs.

Use of more appropriate tasks Much of our knowledge of the processes involved in work motivation has been derived from studies utilizing relatively simple experimental tasks. Although such studies have clearly advanced our basic knowledge

about motivation, it is important to realize that many of these tasks are likely to hold little or no personal meaning for study participants (i.e., there are typically no positive or negative consequences associated with task performance). As noted by both Control Theory and Social Cognitive Theory, individuals are unlikely to engage in active self-regulation of task behavior for tasks that are seen as unimportant or unrewarding (Bandura, 1986; Klein, 1989). As such, conclusions drawn about work motivation based on studies utilizing such tasks may present a restricted perspective on the processes underlying self-regulation. Therefore, it is clear that future research in this area should move towards the use of more interesting and ego-involving tasks to provide a more accurate depiction of how these processes are likely to operate.

Use of more complex research designs
Although self-regulation is, by definition, a process that occurs over time, relatively few studies have taken a longitudinal approach to the examination of this process. Instead, most studies have relied on an assessment of behavior within a single behavioral episode or behavior across a few closely spaced episodes. Given that there is evidence to suggest that temporal factors are likely to play an important role in self-regulatory processes (e.g., Donovan, 1998; Williams et al., 2000) and that self-regulation in organizational settings is likely to involve behaviors and processes that are enacted over time, this approach is clearly inadequate for describing and evaluating the processes involved in dynamic self-regulation. As such, future research would benefit greatly from a move toward a more longitudinal approach to the study of motivation.

In addition, although both Social Cognitive Theory and Control Theory make propositions concerning the effects of nonperformance goals (e.g., quantity goals), as well as the presence of multiple, potentially conflicting goals, little research has been conducted to examine how such goals are likely to impact an individual's behavior. Because workers in a typical organizational setting are likely to hold multiple goals and/or nonperformance goals, future research should begin to focus on the impact of such goals in order to provide us with a more comprehensive understanding of the impact of diverse types of goals on behavior.

CONCLUSION

Although great strides have been made in our understanding of work motivation over the past four decades, it is evident from the present review of this literature that we are far from a clear and precise understanding of the processes that determine motivated behavior in organizational settings. It is the hope of this author that the information and recommendations provided in this chapter will facilitate our journey towards a better understanding of these processes.

NOTES

1 In actuality, Vroom's (1964) VIE theory comprises two models. The first equation represents what is referred to as the 'valence model,' while the second equation is termed the 'force model.' Although Vroom (1964) presents the valence model as an independent model designed to predict the anticipated satisfaction associated with a given outcome, he also states that this model may serve as an input into the force model. The present chapter will focus on the valence model as in input to force-model predictions of behavior, rather than on the valence model as a predictor of outcome attractiveness.

2 Although these reviews also examined the effects of rewards on 'free-time spent' measures of intrinsic motivation, these results are not discussed due to the problems inherent in such measures of intrinsic motivation (Bandura, 1986; Eisenberger & Cameron, 1996).

3 Although Social Cognitive Theory actually encompasses a broad array of important psychological processes (e.g., vicarious learning, modeling), this section will focus on the component of this theory that is most applicable to the study of work motivation, the process of self-regulation.

REFERENCES

Adams, J.S. (1963). Towards an understanding of inequity. *Journal of Abnormal and Social Psychology, 67*, 422–436.

Adams, J.S. (1965). Inequity in social exchange. In L. Berkowtiz (Ed.), *Advances in experimental social psychology* (Vol. 2, pp. 267–299). New York: Academic Press.

Adams, J.S., & Jacobsen, P.R. (1964). Effects of wage inequities on work quality. *Journal of Applied Psychology, 69*, 19–25.

Ambrose, M.L., & Kulik, C.T. (1999). Old friends, new faces: Motivation research in the 1990s. *Journal of Management, 25*, 231–292.

Arnold, H.J. (1981). A test of the validity of the multiplicative hypothesis of expectancy-valence theories of work motivation. *Academy of Management Journal, 24*, 128–141.

Austin, J.T., & Bobko, P. (1985). Goal setting theory: Unexplored areas and future research needs. *Journal of Occupational Psychology, 58*, 289–308.

Austin, J.T., & Klein, H.J. (1996). Work motivation and goal striving. In K.R. Murphy (Ed.), *Individual Differences and Behavior in Organizations* (pp. 209–257). San Francisco; Jossey-Bass.

Austin, J.T., & Vancouver, J.B. (1996). Goal constructs in psychology: Structure, process, and content. *Psychological Bulletin, 120*, 338–375.

Bandura, A. (1977). *Social learning theory*. Englewood Cliffs, NJ: Prentice-Hall.

Bandura, A. (1986). *Social foundations of thought and action: A social cognitive theory*. Englewood Cliffs, NJ: Prentice-Hall.

Bandura, A. (1989). Self-regulation of motivation and action through internal standards and goal systems. In L.A. Pervin (Ed.), *Goal concepts in personality and social psychology* (pp. 19–85). Hillsdale, NJ: Lawrence Erlbaum Associates.

Bandura, A. (1997). *Self-efficacy: The exercise of control*. New York: Freeman.

Bandura, A. (1991). Human agency: The rhetoric and the reality. *American Psychologist, 46*, 157–162.

Bandura, A., & Cervone, D. (1983). Self-evaluative and self-efficacy mechanisms governing the motivational effects of goal systems. *Journal of Personality and Social Psychology, 45*, 1017–1028.

Bandura, A., & Cervone, D. (1986). Differential engagement of self-reactive influences in cognitive motivation. *Organizational Behavior and Human Decision Processes, 38*, 92–113.

Bandura, A., & Schunk, D.H. (1981). Cultivating competence, self-efficacy, and intrinsic interest through proximal self-motivation. *Journal of Personality and Social Psychology, 41*, 586–598.

Bandura, A., & Simon, K.M. (1977). The role of proximal intentions in self-regulation of refractory behavior. *Cognitive Therapy and Research, 1*, 177–193.

Bandura, A, & Wood, R.E. (1989). Effect of perceived controllability and performance standards on self-regulation of complex decision making. *Journal of Personality and Social Psychology, 56*, 805–814.

Barrick, M.R., Mount, M.K., & Strauss, J.P. (1993). Conscientiousness and performance of sales representatives: Test of the mediating effects of goal setting. *Journal of Applied Psychology, 78*, 715–722.

Bavelas, J.B., & Lee, E.S. (1978). Effects of goal level on performance: A trade off of quantity and quality. *Canadian Journal of Psychology, 32*, 219–240.

Bowen, J., & Qiu, Z. (1992). Satisficing when buying information. *Organizational Behavior and Human Decision Processes, 51*, 471–481.

Brockner, J. (1985). The relation of trait self-esteem and positive inequity to productivity. *Journal of Personality, 53*, 517–529.

Brockner, J., Konovsky, M., Cooper-Schneider, R., Folger, R., Martin, C., & Bies, R. J. (1994). Interactive effects of procedural justice and outcome negativity on victims and survivors of job loss. *Academy of Management Journal, 37*, 397–409.

Brooks, L., & Betz, N.E. (1990). Utility of expectancy theory in predicting occupational choices among college students. *Journal of Counseling Psychology, 37*, 57–64.

Brown, S.P., Cron, W.J., & Slocum, J.W. (1997). Effects of goal directed emotions on salesperson volitions, behavior, and performance: A longitudinal study. *Journal of Marketing, 61*, 39–50.

Bryan, J.F., & Locke, E.A. (1967). Goal setting as a means of increasing motivation. *Journal of Applied Psychology*, *51*, 274–277.

Cameron, J., & Pierce, W.D. (1994). Reinforcement, reward, and intrinsic motivation: A meta-analysis. *Review of Educational Research*, *64*, 363–423.

Campbell, J.P., Dunnette, M.D., Lawler, E.W., & Weick, K.E. (1970). *Managerial behavior, performance, and effectiveness*. New York: McGraw-Hill.

Campbell, J.P., & Pritchard, R.D. (1976). Motivation theory in industrial and organizational psychology. In M.D. Dunnette (Ed.), *Handbook of industrial and organizational psychology* (pp. 63–130). Chicago: Rand-McNally.

Campion, M.A., & Lord, R.G. (1982). A control systems conceptualization of the goal setting and changing process. *Organizational Behavior and Human Performance*, *30*, 265–287.

Carver, C.S., & Blaney, P.H., & Scheier, M.F. (1979). Reassertion and giving up: The interactive role of self-directed attention and outcome expectancy. *Journal of Personality and Social Psychology*, *37*, 1859–1870.

Carver, C.S., & Scheier, M.F. (1981). *Attention and self-regulation: A control theory approach to human behavior*. New York: Springer-Verlag.

Carver, C.S., & Scheier, M.F. (1998). *On the self-regulation of behavior*. New York: Cambridge University Press.

Cervone, D., Jiwani, N., & Wood, R. (1991). Goal setting and the differential influence of self-regulatory processes on complex, decision-making performance. *Journal of Personality and Social Psychology*, *61*, 257–266.

Cropanzano, R., & Folger, R. (1989). Referent cognitions and task decision autonomy: Beyond equity theory. *Journal of Applied Psychology*, *74*, 293–299.

Cropanzano, R., & Folger, R. (1991). Procedural justices and worker motivation. In R.M. Steers, & L.W. Porter (Eds.), *Motivation and work behavior* (pp. 131–143). New York: McGraw-Hill.

deCharms, R. (1968). *Personal causation: The internal affective determinants of behavior*. New York: Academic Press.

Deci, E.L. (1971). Effects of externally mediated rewards on intrinsic motivation. *Journal of Personality and Social Psychology*, *18*, 105–115.

Deci, E.L. (1972). The effects of contingent and noncontingent rewards and controls on intrinsic motivation. *Organizational Behavior and Human Performance*, *8*, 217–229.

Deci, E.L., Koestner, R., & Ryan, R.M. (1999). A meta-analytic review of experiments examining the effects of extrinsic rewards on intrinsic motivation. *Psychological Bulletin*, *125*, 627–668.

Deci, E.L., & Ryan, R.M. (1985). *Intrinsic motivation and self-determination in human behavior*. New York: Plenum Press.

deLeo, P.J., & Pritchard, R.D. (1974). An-examination of some methodological problems in testing expectancy-valence models with survey techniques. *Organizational Behavior and Human Performance*, *12*, 143–148.

Dickinson, A.M. (1989). The detrimental effects of extrinsic reinforcement on 'intrinsic motivation'. *The Behavior Analyst*, *12*, 1–15.

Dollinger, S.J., & Thelen, M.H. (1978). Overjustification and children's intrinsic motivation: Comparative effects of four rewards. *Journal of Personality and Social Psychology*, *36*, 1259–1269.

Donovan, J.J. (1998). *Affective, contextual, dispositional, and cognitive influences on goal revision*. Unpublished doctoral dissertation, University at Albany, State University of New York.

Donovan, J.J., & Radosevich, D.R. (1998). The moderating role of goal commitment on the goal difficulty-performance relationship: A meta-analytic review and critical re-analysis. *Journal of Applied Psychology*, *83*, 308–315.

Earley, P.C., Connolly, T., & Ekegren, G. (1989). Goals, strategy, and task performance: Some limits on the efficacy of goal setting. *Journal of Applied Psychology*, *74*, 24–33.

Earley, P.C., Connolly, T., & Lee, C. (1989). Task strategy interventions in goal setting: The importance of search in strategy development. *Journal of Management*, *15*, 589–602.

Earley, P.C., Wojnaroski, P., & Prest, W. (1987). Task planning and energy expended: Exploration of how goals influence performance. *Journal of Applied Psychology*, *72*, 107–114.

Eisenberger, R., & Cameron, J. (1996). Detrimental effects of reward: Reality or myth? *American Psychologist*, *51*, 1153–1166.

Eisenberger, R., Pierce, W.D., & Cameron, J. (1999). Effects of reward on intrinsic motivation–negative, neutral, and positive: Comment on Deci, Koestner, & Ryan (1999). *Psychological Bulletin*, *125*, 677–691.

Erez, M. (1977). Feedback: A necessary condition for goal setting/performance relationship. *Journal of Applied Psychology*, *62*, 624–627.

Feldman, J.M., Reitz, H.J., & Hilterman, R.J. (1976). Alternatives to optimization in expectancy theory. *Journal of Applied Psychology*, *61*, 712–720.

Fishbein, M., & Azjen, I. (1975). *Belief, attitude, intention, and behavior: An introduction to theory and research*. Reading, MA: Addison-Wesley.

Folger, R., Rosenfeld, D., Grove, J., & Corkran, L. (1979). Effects of 'voice' and peer opinions on responses to inequity. *Journal of Personality and Social Psychology*, *37*, 2253–2261.

Frayne, C.A., & Latham, G.P. (1987). Application of social learning theory to employee self-management of attendance. *Journal of Applied Psychology*, *72*, 387–392.

Frost, P.J., & Mahoney, T.A. (1976). Goal setting and the task process: An interactive influence on individual performance. *Organizational Behavior and Human Performance*, *17*, 328–350.

Gellatly, I.R. (1996). Conscientiousness and task performance: Test of a cognitive process model. *Journal of Applied Psychology*, *81*, 474–482.

Gilliland, S.W., & Landis, R.S. (1992). Quality and quantity goals in a complex decision task: Strategies and outcomes. *Journal of Applied Psychology, 77,* 672–681.

Gist, M.E., Stevens, C.K., & Bavetta, A.G. (1991). Effects of self-efficacy and post-training intervention on the acquisition and maintenance of complex interpersonal skills. *Personnel Psychology, 44,* 837–861.

Goodman, P.S. (1974). An examination of the referents used in the evaluation of pay. *Organizational Behavior and Human Performance, 12,* 170–195.

Goodman, P.S., & Friedman, A. (1971). An examination of Adams' equity theory of inequity. *Administrative Science Quarterly, 16,* 271–288.

Greenberg, J. (1982). Approaching equity and avoiding inequity in groups and organizations. In J. Greenberg, & R.L. Cohen (Eds.), *Equity and justice in social behavior* (pp. 389–346). New York: Academic Press.

Greenberg, J. (1988). Equity and workplace status: A field experiment. *Journal of Applied Psychology, 73,* 606–613.

Greenberg, J. (1989). Cognitive reevaluation of outcomes in response to underpayment inequity. *Academy of Management Journal, 32,* 174–184.

Greenberg, J. (1990). Employee theft as a reaction to underpayment inequity: The hidden cost of pay cuts. *Journal of Applied Psychology, 75,* 561–568.

Hall, H.K., Weinberg, R.S., & Jackson, A. (1987). Effects of goal specificity, goal difficulty, and information feedback on endurance performance. *Journal of Sport Psychology, 9,* 43–54.

Harackiewicz, J.M. (1979). The effects of reward contingency and performance feedback on intrinsic motivation. *Journal of Personality and Social Psychology, 37,* 1352–1363.

Harackiewicz, J.M., Manderlink, G., & Sansone, C. (1984). Rewarding pinball wizardry: Effects of evaluation and cue value on intrinsic interest. *Journal of Personality and Social Psychology, 47,* 287–300.

Harder, J.W. (1991). Equity theory versus expectancy theory: The case of major league baseball free agents. *Journal of Applied Psychology, 76,* 458–464.

Harrell, A. & Stahl, M. (1986). Additive information processing and the relationship between expectancy of success and motivational force. *Academy of Management Journal, 29,* 424–433.

Harrison, A.W., Rainer, R.K., Hochwarter, W.A., & Thompson, K.R. (1997). Testing the self-efficacy-performance linkage of social-cognitive theory. *Journal of Social Psychology, 137,* 79–87.

Harrison, D.A. (1995). Volunteer motivation and attendance decisions: Competitive theory testing in multiple samples from a homeless shelter. *Journal of Applied Psychology, 80,* 371–385.

Hollenbeck, J., & Klein, H. (1987). Goal commitment and the goal-setting process: Problems, prospects, and proposals for future research. *Journal of Applied Psychology, 72,* 212–220.

Hollenbeck, J.R., & Williams, C.R. (1987). Goal importance, self-focus, and the goal setting process. *Journal of Applied Psychology, 72,* 204–211.

Hollenbeck, J.R., Williams, C.R., & Klein, H.J. (1989). An empirical examination of antecedents of commitment to difficult goals. *Journal of Applied Psychology, 74,* 18–23.

Hom, H.L. & Arbuckle, B. (1988). Mood induction effects upon goal setting and performance in young children. *Motivation and Emotion, 12,* 113–122.

Hull, C.L. (1943). *Principles of behavior.* New York: Appleton-Century-Crofts.

Huseman, R.C., Hatfield, J.D., & Miles, E.W. (1985). Test for individual perceptions of job equity: Some preliminary findings. *Perceptual and Motor Skills, 61,* 1055–1064.

Janis, I.L., & Mann, L. (1997). Satisficing. In J. Billsberry (Ed.), *The effective manager: Perspectives and illustrations.* London: Open University Press.

Kanfer, R. (1990). Motivation theory and industrial and organizational psychology. In M.D. Dunnette, & L.M. Hough (Eds.), *Handbook of industrial and organizational psychology* (2nd ed.; pp. 75–170). Palo Alto, CA: Consulting Psychologists Press.

Kanfer, R., & Ackerman, P.L. (1989). Motivation and cognitive abilities: An integrative aptitude/treatment interaction approach to skill acquisition. *Journal of Applied Psychology, 74,* 657–690.

Kanfer, R., & Ackerman, P.L. (2000). Individual differences in work motivation: Further explorations of a trait framework. *Applied Psychology: An International Review, 49,* 470–482.

Kanfer, R., Ackerman, P.L., Murtha, T.C., Dugdale, B., & Nelson, L. (1994). Goal setting, conditions of practice, and task performance: A resource allocation perspective. *Journal of Applied Psychology, 79,* 826–835.

Kanfer, R., & Heggestad, E.D. (1997). Motivational traits and skills: A person-centered approach to work motivation. In L.L. Cummings, & B.M. Staw (Eds.), *Research in Organizational Behavior* (Vol. 19, pp. 1–56). Greenwich, CT: JAI Press.

Karniol, R., & Ross, M. (1977). The effect of performance-relevant and performance-irrelevant rewards on children's intrinsic motivation. *Child Development, 48,* 482–487.

Kennedy, C.W., Fossum, J.A., & White, B.J. (1983). An empirical comparison of within-subjects and between-subjects expectancy theory models. *Organizational Behavior and Human Performance, 32,* 124–143.

Kernan, M.C., & Lord, R.G. (1990). Effects of valence, expectancies, and goal-performance discrepancies in single and multiple goal environments. *Journal of Applied Psychology, 75,* 194–203.

Kernis, M.H., Zuckerman, M., Cohen, A., & Spadafora, S. (1982). Persistence following failure: The interactive roles of self-awareness and the attributional basis for negative expectancies. *Journal of Personality and Social Psychology, 43,* 1184–1191.

King, W.C., & Miles, E.W. (1994). The measurement of equity sensitivity. *Journal of Occupational and Organizational Psychology, 67,* 133–142.

King, W.C., Miles, E.W., & Day, D.D. (1993). A test and refinement of the equity sensitivity construct. *Journal of Organizational Behavior, 14*, 301–317.

Klein, H.J. (1989). An integrated control theory model of work motivation. *Academy of Management Journal, 14*, 150–172.

Klein, H.J. (1991a). Further evidence on the relationship between goal setting and expectancy theories. *Organizational Behavior and Human Decision Processes, 49*, 230–257.

Klein, H.J. (1991b). Control theory and understanding motivated behavior. *Motivation and Emotion, 15*, 29–44.

Klein, H.J., Whitener, E.M., & Ilgen, D.R. (1990). The role of goal specificity in the goal setting process. *Motivation and Emotion, 14*, 179–193.

Kohn, A. (1993). *Punished by rewards*. Boston: Houghton-Mifflin.

Landy, F.J., Barnes, J.L., & Murphy, K.R. (1978). Correlates of perceived fairness and accuracy of performance evaluation. *Journal of Applied Psychology, 63*, 751–754.

Latham, G.P., Erez, M., & Locke, E.A. (1988). Resolving scientific dispute by the joint design of crucial experiments by the antagonists: Application to the Erez–Latham dispute regarding participation in goal setting. *Journal of Applied Psychology, 73*, 753–772.

Latham, G.P., & Saari, L.M. (1982). The importance of union acceptance for productivity improvement through goal setting. *Personnel Psychology, 35*, 781–787.

Latham, G.P. & Yukl, G. (1975). A review of research on the application of goal setting in organizations. *Academy of Management Journal, 18*, 824–845.

Lawler, E.E. (1973). *Motivation in work organizations*. Belmont, CA: Brooks/Cole.

Lawler, E.E., Koplin, C.A., Young, T.F., & Fadem, J.A. (1968). Inequity reduction over time in an induced overpayment situation. *Organizational Behavior and Human Performance, 3*, 253–268.

Lee, C. (1995). Prosocial organizational behaviors: The roles of workplace justice, achievement striving, and pay satisfaction. *Journal of Business and Psychology, 10*, 197–206.

Lepper, M.R., Greene, D., & Nisbett, R.E. (1973). Undermining children's intrinsic interest with extrinsic rewards: A test of the overjustification hypothesis. *Journal of Personality and Social Psychology, 28*, 129–137.

Leventhal, G.S. (1980). What should be done with equity theory? In K.J. Gergen, M.S. Greenberg, & R.H. Willis (Eds.), *Social exchange: Advances in theory and research* (pp. 27–55). New York: Plenum.

Lewin, K. (1938). *The conceptual representation and the measurement of psychological forces*. Durham, NC: Duke University Press.

Lewin, K. (1961). Intention, will, and need. Reprinted in T. Shipley (Ed.), *Classics in psychology*. New York: Philosophical Library.

Lewin, K., Dembo, T., Festinger, L., & Sears, P.S. (1944). Level of aspiration. In J. Hunt (Ed.), *Personality and behavior disorders*. New York: Ronald Press.

Locke, E.A. (1966). The relationship of intentions to levels of performance. *Journal of Applied Psychology, 50*, 60–66.

Locke, E.A. (1967). Motivational effects of knowledge of results: Knowledge or goal setting? *Journal of Applied Psychology, 51*, 324–329.

Locke, E.A. (1968). Toward a theory of task motivation and incentives. *Organizational Behavior and Human Performance, 3*, 157–189.

Locke, E.A. (1991a). Problems with goal setting research in sports – and their solution. *Journal of Sport and Exercise Psychology, 8*, 311–316.

Locke, E.A. (1991b). Goal theory vs. control theory: Contrasting approaches to understanding work motivation. *Motivation and Emotion, 15*, 9–28.

Locke, E.A. (1994). The emperor is naked. *Applied Psychology: An International Review, 43*, 367–370.

Locke, E.A., & Bryan, J.F. (1969). The directing function of goals in task performance. *Organizational Behavior and Human Performance, 4*, 35–42.

Locke, E.A., Frederick, E., Buckner, E., & Bobko, P. (1984). Effect of previously assigned goals on self-set goals and performance. *Journal of Applied Psychology, 69*, 694–699.

Locke, E.A., & Latham, G.P. (1990). *A theory of goal setting and task performance*. Englewood Cliffs, NJ: Prentice-Hall.

Locke, E.A., Smith, K.G., Erez, M., Chah, D.O., & Schaffer, A. (1994). The effects of intra-individual goal conflict on performance. *Journal of Management, 20*, 67–91.

Lord, F.M., & Novick, M.R. (1968). *Statistical theories of mental test scores*. Reading, MA: Addison-Wesley.

Lord, R.G., & Hanges, P.J. (1987). A control systems model of organizational motivation: Theoretical development and applied implications. *Behavioral Science, 32*, 161–178.

Lord, R.G., & Kernan, M.C. (1989). Application of control theory to work settings. In W.A. Hershberger (Ed.), *Volitional action: Conation and control* (pp. 493–514). New York: Elsevier.

Martocchio, J.J. (1994). Effects of conceptions of ability on anxiety, self-efficacy, and learning in training. *Journal of Applied Psychology, 79*, 819–825.

Mathieu, J.E., & Button, S.B. (1992). An examination of the relative impact of normative information and self-efficacy on personal goals and performance over time. *Journal of Applied Social Psychology, 22*, 1758–1775.

Matsui, T., Okada, A., & Inoshita, O. (1983). Mechanisms of feedback affecting task performance. *Organizational Behavior and Human Performance, 31*, 114–122.

McClelland, D.C. (1961). *The achieving society*. Princeton: Van Nostrand Reinhold.

Mento, A.J., Locke, E.A., & Klein, H.J. (1992). Relationship of goal level to valence and instrumentality. *Journal of Applied Psychology, 77*, 395–405.

Mento, A.J., Steel, R.P., & Karren, R.J. (1987). A meta-analytic study of the effects of goal setting on task performance: 1966–1984. *Organizational Behavior and Human Decision Processes, 39*, 52–83.

Miller, G.A., Galanter, E., & Pribrum, K.H. (1960). *Plans and the structure of behavior*. New York: Holt, Rinehart, and Winston.

Miner, J.B. (1984). The validity and usefulness of theories in an emerging organizational science. *Academy of Management Review*, 9, 296–306.

Mitchell, T.R. (1974). Expectancy models of job satisfaction, occupational preference, and effort: A theoretical, methodological, and empirical appraisal. *Psychological Bulletin*, 81, 1053–1077.

Mone, M.A., & Baker, D.D. (1992). A social-cognitive, attributional model of personal goals: An empirical evaluation. *Motivation and Emotion*, 16, 297–321.

Moorman, R.H. (1991). Relationship between organizational justice and organizational citizenship behaviors: Do fairness perceptions influence employee citizenship? *Journal of Applied Psychology*, 76, 845–855.

Morin, L., & Latham, G.P. (2000). The effect of mental practice and goal setting as a transfer of training intervention on supervisors' self-efficacy and communication skills. *Applied Psychology: An International Review*, 49, 566–578.

Mowday, R.T. (1991). Equity theory predictions of behavior in organizations. In R.M. Steers, & L.W. Porter (Eds.), *Motivation and work behavior* (5th ed., pp. 111–131). New York: McGraw-Hill.

Parker, S.K. (2000). From passive to proactive motivation: The importance of flexible role orientations and role breadth self-efficacy. *Applied Psychology: An International Review*, 49, 447–469.

Petty, R.E., & Cacioppo, J.T. (1986). *Communication and persuasion: Central and peripheral routes to attitude change*. New York: Springer-Verlag.

Phillips, J.M., & Gully, S.M. (1997). Role of goal orientation, ability, need for achievement and locus of control in the self-efficacy and goal setting process. *Journal of Applied Psychology*, 792–802.

Phillips, J.M., Hollenbeck, J.R., & Ilgen, D.R. (1996). The prevalence and prediction of positive discrepancy creation: Examining a discrepancy between two self-regulation theories. *Journal of Applied Psychology*, 81, 498–511.

Pinder, C.C. (1987). Valence-instrumentality-expectancy theory. In R.M. Steers, & L.W. Porter (Eds.), *Motivation and work behavior* (4th ed., pp. 144–164). New York: McGraw-Hill.

Pinder, C.C. (1998). *Work motivation in organizational behavior*. Englewood Cliffs, NJ: Prentice-Hall.

Porter, L.W., & Lawler, E.E. (1968). *Managerial attitudes and performance*. Homewood, IL: Dorsey Press.

Powers, W.T. (1973). Feedback: Beyond behaviorism. *Science*, 179, 351–356.

Powers, W.T. (1978). *Behavior: The control of perception*. Chicago: Aldine.

Rodgers, R., & Hunter, J.E. (1991). Impact of management by objectives on organizational productivity. *Journal of Applied Psychology*, 76, 322–336.

Roney, C.J.R., & Sorrentino, R.M. (1995). Reducing self-discrepancies or maintaining self-congruence? Uncertainty orientation, self-regulation, and performance.

Journal of Personality and Social Psychology, 68, 485–497.

Ross, M. (1975). Salience of reward and intrinsic motivation. *Journal of Personality and Social Psychology*, 32, 245–254.

Ryan, R.M., & Deci, E.L. (2000). Intrinsic and extrinsic motivations: Classic definitions and new directions. *Contemporary Educational Psychology*, 25, 54–67.

Ryan, R.M., Mims, V., & Koestner, R. (1983). Relation of reward contingency and interpersonal context to intrinsic motivation: A review and test using cognitive evaluation theory. *Journal of Personality and Social Psychology*, 45, 736–750.

Ryan, T.A. (1958). Drives, tasks, and the initiation of behavior. *American Journal of Psychology*, 71, 74–93.

Ryan, T.A. (1970). *Intentional behavior*. New York: Ronald Press.

Schmidt, F.L. (1973). Implications of a measurement problem for expectancy theory research. *Organizational Behavior and Human Performance*, 10, 243–251.

Sheehan, E.P. (1993). The effects of turnover on the productivity of those who stay. *The Journal of Social Psychology*, 133, 699–706.

Simon, H.A. (1957). *Administrative behavior* (2nd ed.). New York: MacMillan.

Skarlicki, D.P., & Folger, R. (1997). Retaliation in the workplace: The roles of distributive, procedural, and interactional justice. *Journal of Applied Psychology*, 82, 434–443.

Skinner, B.F. (1953). *Science and human behavior*. New York: Free Press.

Smith, K.G., Locke, E.A., & Barry, D. (1990). Goal setting, planning, and organizational performance. *Organizational Behavior and Human Decision Processes*, 46, 118–134.

Snead, K.C., & Harrell, A.M. (1994). An application of expectancy theory to explain a manager's intentions to use a decision support system. *Decision Sciences*, 25, 499–513.

Stahl, M., & Harrell, A. (1981). Modeling effort decisions with behavioral decision theory: Toward an individual differences model of expectancy theory. *Organizational Behavior and Human Performance*, 27, 303–325.

Stajkovic, A.D., & Luthans, F. (1998). Self-efficacy and work related performance: A meta-analysis. *Psychological Bulletin*, 124, 240–261.

Summers, T.P., & DeNisi, A.S. (1990). In search of Adams' other: Reexamination of referents used in the evaluation of pay. *Human Relations*, 43, 497–511.

Summers, T.P., & Hendrix, W.H. (1991). Modeling the role of pay equity perceptions: A field study. *Journal of Occupational Psychology*, 64, 145–157.

Tang, S.H., & Hall, V.C. (1995). The overjustification effect: A meta-analysis. *Applied Cognitive Psychology*, 9, 365–404.

Terborg, J.R. (1976). The motivational components of goal setting. *Journal of Applied Psychology*, 61, 613–621.

Thibaut, J. & Walker, L. (1975). *Procedural justice: A psychological analysis*. Hillsdale, NJ: Erlbaum.

Thomas, K.M., & Mathieu, J.E. (1994). Role of causal attributions in dynamic self-regulation and goal processes. *Journal of Applied Psychology, 79*, 812–818.

Tolman, E.C. (1932). *Purposive behavior in animals and men*. New York: Century.

Tubbs, M.E. (1986). Goal setting: A meta-analytic examination of the empirical evidence. *Journal of Applied Psychology, 71*, 474–483.

Valenzi, E.R., & Andrews, I.R. (1971). Effect of hourly overpay and underpay inequity when tested with a new induction procedure. *Journal of Applied Psychology, 55*, 22–27.

Vance, R.J., & Colella, A. (1990). Effects of two types of feedback on goal acceptance and personal goals. *Journal of Applied Psychology, 75*, 68–76.

Vancouver, J.B. (1996). Living systems theory as a paradigm for organizational behavior: Understanding humans, organizations, and social processes. *Behavioral Science, 41*, 165–204.

Vancouver, J.B., & Putka, D.J. (2000). Analyzing goal-striving processes and a test of the generalizability of perceptual control theory. *Organizational Behavior and Human Decision Processes, 82*, 334–362.

Vande Walle, D., Brown, S.P., Cron, W.L., & Slocum, J.W. (1999). The influence of goal orientation and self-regulation tactics on sales performance: A longitudinal field test. *Journal of Applied Psychology, 84*(2), 249–259.

Van Eerde, W., & Thierry, H. (1996). Vroom's expectancy models and work-related criteria: A meta-analysis. *Journal of Applied Psychology, 81*, 575–586.

Vecchio, R.P. (1981). An individual-differences interpretation of the conflicting predictions generated by equity theory and expectancy theory. *Journal of Applied Psychology, 66*, 470–481.

Vroom, V.H. (1964). *Work and motivation*. New York: Wiley.

Wanous, J.P., Keon, T.L., & Latack, J.C. (1983). Expectancy theory and occupational/organizational choices: A review and test. *Organizational Behavior and Human Performance, 32*, 66–86.

Weick, K.E. (1966). The concept of equity in the perception of pay. *Administrative Science Quarterly, 11*, 414–439.

Whan, P.C. (1978). A seven point scale and a decision maker's simplifying choice strategy: An operationalized satisficing-plus model. *Organizational Behavior and Human Performance, 21*, 252–271.

White, R.W. (1959). Motivation reconsidered: The concept of competence. *Psychological Review, 66*, 297–333.

Wiener, N. (1948). *Cybernetics: control and communication in the animal and the machine*. Cambridge: MIT Press.

Wiersma, U.J. (1992). The effects of extrinsic rewards intrinsic motivation: A meta-analysis. *Journal of Occupational and Organizational Psychology, 65*, 101–114.

Williams, K.J., Donovan, J.J., & Dodge, T.L. (2000). Self-regulation of performance: Goal establishment and goal revision processes in athletes. *Human Performance, 13*, 159–180.

Wood, R.E., Atkins, P.B., & Bright, J.E.H. (1999). Bonuses, goals, and instrumentality effects. *Journal of Applied Psychology, 84*, 703–720.

Wood, R.E., Atkins, T.B., & Tabernero, C. (2000). Self-efficacy and strategy on complex tasks. *Applied Psychology: An International Review, 49*, 430–446.

Wood, R.E., & Bandura, A. (1989). Social-cognitive theory of organizational management. *Academy of Management Review, 14*, 361–384.

Wood, R.E., Mento, A.J., & Locke, E.A. (1987). Task complexity as a moderator of goal effects: A meta-analysis. *Journal of Applied Psychology, 72*, 416–425.

Wright, P.M. (1990). Operationalization of goal difficulty as a moderator of the goal difficulty-performance relationship. *Journal of Applied Psychology, 75*, 227–234.

4

Compensation Systems in the Global Context

ROBERT L. HENEMAN, CHARLES H. FAY
and ZHONG-MING WANG

A selective review of the compensation literature was conducted. Compensation is a multidimensional concept and topics covered include base pay, variable pay, individual incentives, ownership, and benefits. A history of compensation, a summary of the current state of knowledge, and directions for future theory, research, and practice are provided. Throughout the chapter global issues are discussed. Our goal for the chapter is to continue to invigorate compensation as an area of study in work psychology.

INTRODUCTION

Compensation (defined here as pay, benefits, and other rewards with monetary value) is by far the most costly human resource intervention in organizations. Compensation budgets of over $1 billion are not uncommon in Fortune 50 companies. As much as 80% of total budgets in service sector organizations are made up of compensation costs (Milkovich & Newman, 1999). Given the huge costs associated with compensation, it is surprising the small amount of attention devoted to compensation issues in the industrial psychology literature relative to other human resource interventions such as staffing and training and development. The purpose of this chapter is to selectively review the history of the study of compensation in industrial psychology, to summarize the current state of knowledge, and to offer directions for future theory, research, and practice. Throughout the chapter we will cover global issues, especially as they relate to recent developments in China. Our ultimate aim is to help to continue to invigorate compensation as an area of study in work psychology.

HISTORY OF WORK PSYCHOLOGY CONTRIBUTIONS TO COMPENSATION

There has never been a steady stream of research with a direct focus on compensation issues from work psychology. Contributions to the compensation literature from work psychologists have been indirect rather than direct and have been sporadic rather than regular. Although indirect and sporadic, the contributions made by work psychologists have been very influential. Indirectly, the field of compensation has benefited greatly from the efforts of work psychologists in areas such as motivation (e.g., Campbell, 1976) and criterion issues (Smith, 1976). Interestingly, the first edition of the *Handbook of Industrial and Organizational Psychology* (Dunnette, 1976) did not have a chapter on compensation. However, the chapters on motivation and criterion issues just mentioned were on the 'must-read' list of compensation scholars. Motivation theory provides analysis of the processes whereby compensation decisions affect the attitudes and behaviors of employees, while the criterion problem plagues pay-for-performance plans.

Historically, the most influential work psychologist who has directly addressed compensation is Lawler. His first major work on compensation, *Pay and Organizational Effectiveness* (1971) was a major review of the micro research literature. More importantly he placed it in the context of organizational effectiveness theory showing the practical importance of compensation to organizations. While the importance of selection decisions had been pointed out in the industrial and organizational (I/O) literature (e.g., Cronbach & Gleser, 1965), Lawler provided the first major statement of the importance of compensation to organizational effectiveness.

Another major contribution of Lawler was his little known, yet highly important book *Pay and Organizational Development* (1981). This book was some 10 years ahead of the field in terms of both research and practice. In this book Lawler clearly framed the need to understand the organizational psychology of compensation decision making. That is, compensation was viewed as a powerful organizational development intervention in organizations. As such, he required that the organizational processes to deliver pay were as important or more important than the amount of pay.

Lawler was again years ahead of practice and research with his book *Strategic Pay* (1990). Influenced by the business policy literature, Lawler recognized that compensation systems not only could be integrated with the business strategies and processes in the organization, but that they should be integrated in order for organizations to have competitive advantage relative to their competitors in product and labor markets. Hence, pay systems not only needed to be framed in terms of process to be effective, but so too must they be framed in the context of the specific goals of the organization.

In his latest book, Lawler again pushes the frontier of our knowledge about compensation systems (Dawler, 2000). He argues that job-based pay systems that rely upon job descriptions and job evaluation systems are not flexible enough to adapt to the changing nature of work. Instead, pay systems should be based on people rather than jobs where people are defined by their competencies (i.e., KSAOs). It remains to be seen whether organizations will replace job-based pay systems with person-based pay systems.

In recent years, compensation has begun to receive more direct and consistent attention in the work psychology literature. The second edition of the *Handbook of Industrial and Organizational Psychology* (Dunnette & Hough, 1992) contained two chapters on compensation: one by Gerhart and Milkovich (1992) and one by Lawler and Jenkins (1992). The Frontier Series of the Society for Industrial and Organizational Psychology published an entire book on compensation topics entitled: *Compensation: Progress and Prospects* (Rynes & Gerhart, 2000). Both of these events are symbolic of the importance now being placed on compensation decision making by work psychologists.

Work psychology is not the only scholarly field investigating compensation. Economists, and particularly labor economists, have studied compensation (generally focusing on wage levels) for a much longer period than have work psychologists (e.g., Hicks, 1934; Cartter, 1959). Labor economists have developed a rich theory base to speak to some of the same issues of interest to work psychologists (e.g., criterion measurement, motivation) and others which could be, but so far have not been addressed in depth by work psychologists (e.g., perceived value of jobs, tradeoffs between different forms of compensation). Similarly, sociologists such as Treiman have considered bias and reliability problems in job analysis and job evaluation processes (Treiman, 1979; Treiman & Hartman, 1981). While work from the three fields is not integrated, work psychologists should be aware of the literature on compensation of both labor economics and sociology and make use of it in the development of psychological theory that focuses on compensation. An excellent example from work psychology where all of these fields are drawn upon is Viswesvaran and Barrick (1992).

As a result of historical developments within the field (and the influence of the literatures of labor economics, sociology, and business policy), compensation is now viewed by work psychologists as a system within the organization rather than a set of techniques. The focus has shifted away from the psychometric properties of compensation techniques to the integration of the compensation system with other organizational systems in order to achieve organizational effectiveness. It is our belief that this more macro focus to the study of compensation is going to continue, especially in light of the ongoing globalization of business practices. The next big challenge to be faced by compensation researchers and practitioners alike is how to best pay people in a global business environment.

THE CURRENT STATE OF AFFAIRS

Our focus in this chapter is the total cash compensation system in the organization as shown in Figure 4.1. Elements of this system include base pay (wages and salaries), variable pay, individual incentives, ownership, and benefits. Each of these elements has cash value to the employee and organization. All need to be integrated with the compensation strategy and with one another. The compensation strategy in concert with the total cash compensation system yields outcomes related to the effectiveness of the organization, including productivity, innovation, higher quality, and customer satisfaction.

We will first focus on issues that arise in the formulation and execution of compensation strategy.

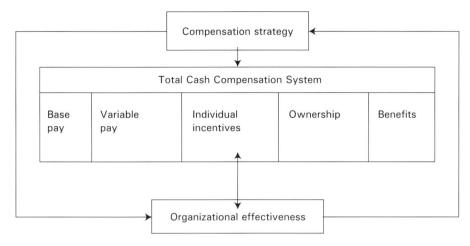

Figure 4.1 *Chapter framework*

Next we will review the issues that arise with each element of total cash compensation. Lastly, we will review the relationship between each element of total cash compensation and organizational effectiveness criteria.

Compensation Strategy

The most important stream of research that has been developed in compensation the past 15 years is the study of pay from a strategic perspective. With this approach, the organization is the unit of analysis rather than individuals in the organization (Lawler & Jenkins, 1992). Compensation is studied from the perspective of how compensation can be used by organizations to adapt to a rapidly changing business environment (Gomez-Mejia & Balkin, 1992).

At the most general level, two steps are undertaken to make compensation systems strategic (Wright, Dyer, Boudreau & Milkovich, 1999). First, the compensation system is aligned with the goals of the organization. Second, the compensation system is fully integrated with other human systems in the organization. Operationally, the first step is carried out by aligning each element of the compensation system with the vision and mission of the organization. The second step is achieved by integrating elements of the compensation system with the human resource goals of the organization (Heneman, 2001).

The strategic compensation process is depicted in Figure 4.2. As can be seen, the ultimate goal of strategic compensation decision making is to achieve a 'fit' between organizational goals, compensation systems, and human resource goals. A consistent finding in the literature is that a strategic approach to compensation is associated with enhanced business performance by the organization (Becker & Gerhart, 1992).

Interestingly, it appears that of the two-stage strategic process just described, the most important step is the alignment of compensation with the business strategy rather than the integration of compensation with other human resource goals. Main effects for compensation are usually significant, while interaction effects between compensation and other human resource systems are usually nonsignificant (Gerhart, Trevor & Graham, 1996). There are several possible interpretations to this repeated finding. First, it may be that compensation systems are so powerful that they overwhelm the effects of other human resource systems. Second, it may be the case that there has not been enough careful theoretical development regarding the interaction of compensation with other human resource systems (Heneman, 2000). Third, there may be multicollinearity in the data due to strong correlation between the main effect for compensation and the interaction effects for compensation and other human resource system variables.

It should also be noted that business strategy sometimes has an indirect as well as direct effect on compensation decisions. Tullar (1998) conducted a study in a food and beverage distribution center where he found that the compensation strategy impacted the design of work and in turn the design of work impacted job evaluation point level assignments. In particular, business process reengineering was associated with a significant increase in Hay System job evaluation points.

Government Reform and Compensation Strategy

Compensation systems reform often has a fundamental impact on compensation strategy. In China, for example, compensation was for a long time

Figure 4.2   *Strategic compensation process*

under a centralized national system with a more institutional basic time-pay with eight levels of skills or positions. During the period between the first pay systems reform in 1956 and the nationwide readjustment in 1976, the characteristics of compensation system were universal salary grades, centralized salary operations, fixed basic wages, and equalitarian wage distribution. In the governmental and administrative departments, the pay system was reformed, changing from a wage grade system started in 1956 to a structured wage system in 1985, consisting of basic wage, position pay, tenure wage, and reward wage.

In 1983, two measures were taken to adjust the pay systems among industrial organizations in China: (1) linking pay with the firms' economic performance; (2) adopting a performance appraisal system for promotion of pay. By 1995, more than 40,000 enterprises implemented the 'Position and Skill Pay' on the basis of work evaluation and actual performance. Therefore, we see a clear move from the egalitarian wage-payment system with a flat reward structure towards performance-based pay system (Wang & Feng, 2000).

When China started its economic reform in 1978, one of the important strategies in managing State enterprises was to restore the bonus system that was abolished in 1966, and to develop more effective compensation systems. The bonus systems were regarded as a supplementary gain to the basic wage and closely based on actual performance. This became the first active area in industrial and organizational psychology in China in the early and mid-1980s. Field studies on work motivation and compensation systems design were conducted in various enterprises.

Individual Differences and Compensation Strategies

In a field study, Wang (1994) found significant age differences and organizational position differences in employees' needs for the types of compensations. Intrinsic needs for technical training and satisfactory jobs were most preferred by young employees, while a bonus was more important to the middle-aged. Among the elder employees, social rewards such as an excellent worker title appeared to be more important. A more flexible and comprehensive multiple compensation structure combining social rewards with material incentives should be used in order to motivate the workforce. A field experiment was then implemented using a flexible multireward system in some departments of a steel file company. Employees who completed their production targets could choose an incentive among five alternatives: bonus, technical training, flexible working time, group vocation, and excellent worker title. Compared with the control group, the experimental group under the multicompensation system resulted in significant higher motivation and doubled productivity.

In examining the relative importance of the compensation components in recruiting, motivating and retaining local Chinese employees, Luk and Chiu (1998) found that base salary, merit pay and year-end bonus were the three most significant items among 37 components, perceived by employers, for all three levels of employees (managers, supervisors, and workers) in all three functions (attraction, motivation, and retention). Generally speaking, the fourth and fifth places were occupied by housing provision, annual leave, cash allowance, and individual bonus interchangeably.

Organizational Structure and Compensation Strategies

In a recent study on comparisons among compensation systems in administrative bureaus versus industrial organizations, Wang and Chen (2000) emphasized the structural effects of compensation management in administrative bureaus and enterprises on work motivation and performance. More than 490 management staff from 18 enterprises and 16 administrative bureaus participated in this study. The main results showed: (1) different ownership systems (state-owned enterprises, international joint ventures, township companies, and governmental offices) had different effects on compensation management, particularly human resources management practices, organizational cultures, satisfaction, and performance; (2) organizational culture had influences on the implementation of compensation systems; (3) human resource management patterns can affect compensation management systems; (4) the position levels had influences on compensation management, employees' satisfaction, and performance. In terms of compensation management, employees from enterprises showed higher pay satisfaction and compensation justice than that of governmental staff though the latter had higher organizational performance than the former. As to the cross-ownership comparison, employees from township companies showed the highest compensation satisfaction, state-enterprise employees second, and joint venture employees third.

Base Pay

The process used to establish base wages and salaries in organizations is shown in Figure 4.3. The results of a job analysis are used in the job evaluation and market survey process. Job evaluation is a process whereby standards are developed to assess the value of the job to the organization. Each job description is graded using a predefined set of standards. Market surveys are conducted to assess the value of the job external to the organization. Job descriptions are used to ensure that the jobs being compared are comparable to one another. The results of the job evaluation and market survey processes are merged together to form a pay structure. The pay structure sets forth the parameter of pay levels possible for each job in the organization. The process just described has been researched over the years and several important themes emerge from this research that will now be covered.

Job Evaluation

The research over the years consistently shows that different job evaluation systems lead to different results (Treiman, 1979, Madigan, 1985; Collins & Muchinsky, 1993). That is, the rank order of jobs and subsequent pay varies as a function of the job evaluation method. The important implication here is that great care must be taken in selecting or developing a job evaluation system. Attention needs to be paid to both the reliability and validity of the system. Reliability, of course, serves as the upper bound to validity. It can be strengthened by carefully defining the job evaluation standards. However, even with a job evaluation system reliability of .9, Treiman (1979, p. 41) demonstrates that job assignment in an 18-grade pay structure will have an error of as much as ± 2.75 grades. Validity can be enhanced by carefully matching the standards to the goals of the organization (Heneman, 2001).

While the labor economics literature reports many different models that speak to job value (Wallace & Fay, 1988); work psychology has not developed extensive theory in this area. Yet, to a

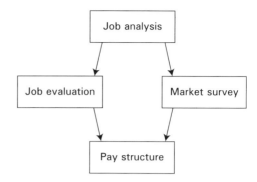

Figure 4.3   *Process followed to develop base pay*

great extent, job value is a function of individual and group perceptions. Neither economic nor sociological theory speaks specifically to affect issues surrounding perceptions of job value.

Market Surveys

In creating a pay structure, a decision must be made as to how much weight to place on the value of the job as established internally by a job evaluation system and as established by the market value of jobs. Research indicates that greater weight is usually placed on the market value (Weber & Rynes, 1991). Increasingly, a job evaluation approach known as market pricing is being used by organizations where the sole determinant of base pay is the market value. While the heavy weighting of market survey results may seem like a good solution to the problems with job evaluation, it is not. Market surveys are plagued by measurement error and sampling error (Rynes & Milkovich, 1986). Shoddy craftsmanship of surveys results in dubious market data. For example, job titles are often used rather than job analysis to define jobs. Job titles are notoriously misleading and may create measurement error. Convenience samples are often used in selecting companies to survey leading to sampling error. In order to generate meaningful market data, careful attention needs to be given to measurement theory in designing the surveys and to sampling theory in selecting companies to survey (Heneman & Dixon, 1998).

Even when many different survey sources are used, it is unlikely that market matches will be found for all jobs in an organization. Johnson and Johnson, for example, which practices pure market pricing (i.e., no job evaluation is done) can get market rates for only about 85% of their jobs. Statistical models (usually multiple linear regression) utilizing job attributes are developed to estimate wages of jobs for which no market rates are available.

Pay Structures

The administrative tool used by most organizations to link market data and job evaluation judgments is the salary structure. Traditionally the typical organization had one salary structure for every broad job family (e.g., blue collar, clerical, technical, administrative). Each structure had anywhere from two to four grades for every layer of organizational hierarchy among the jobs covered.

Increasingly, organizations are reducing the number of pay grades in the organization and increasing the width of the remaining pay grades. Usually, this is done in response to changes in the business strategy where the organization needs to be made more flexible in order to more rapidly adapt to the changing business environment. By reducing the number of pay grades, employees and pay become more flexible to be in alignment with the strategy. Employee job duties are more broadly defined under this approach and base pay dispersion is more marked than under a system with many pay bands. Also, consistent with a business strategy of cost reduction, broadbanding may lead to a reduction in labor costs as fewer people are needed because employees can perform multiple duties.

Unfortunately, no analytical research has been conducted on broadbanding. The data collected to date are only descriptive in nature. The best descriptive survey to date was conducted by Abosch and Hand (1998). Their data indicate that when asked to evaluate the effectiveness of broadbanding, 70% of managers, 85% of human resource professionals, and 56% of employees in organizations with broadbanding rated it as effective or very effective. Broadbanding is typically used for exempt rather than nonexempt employees. There has been a considerable expansion of broadbanding to international company locations. Broadbanding is used relatively more often in Latin America than in Europe or Asia and broadbanding is expected to grow rapidly in Europe, Asia, and Latin America (Abosch & Hmurovic, 1998).

Although these initial results are promising, care must be taken in using broadbanding. Initially, broadbanding may lead to increased rather than decreased costs. Because pay grade widths are broader, the maximum amount of pay available increases and unless control points are used in the bands, usually based on market values, broadbanding can lead to runaway labor costs. As a result, there also needs to be a sound method of assessing employee contributions to the organization. A well-developed performance appraisal or competency assessment is needed to ensure that progression within pay grades is based upon 'true' performance rather than error-filled ratings.

Person-Based Pay

Again, due to the need to create more flexible organizations, organizations have enacted person-based pay systems to allow employees to be more flexible in the duties they perform. Ultimately, the hope with these systems is to decrease headcount and labor costs as employees will have multiple skills and be able to perform multiple tasks. The primary theory base for person-based pay is human capital theory (Becker, 1975), which posits that most individuals decide to pursue formal education (and make other human capital investments in knowledge, skills or abilities) based on expected career returns. Conversely, job value is affected by the degree of formal education and other human capital investment required.

Skill-based pay systems are usually used for lower-level employees and provide pay increases or bonuses for mastering new skills to be used at work. Competency-based pay is usually used for professional and managerial positions. Pay is provided for competency development where competencies are defined as knowledge, skills, abilities, and other factors (e.g., personality) related to effective performance.

Both descriptive and analytical studies have been conducted on skill-based pay and the results are encouraging. Jenkins, Ledford, Gupta and Doty (1987) reported that at least 80% of organizations with skill-based pay reported that their skill-based pay was at least moderately successful. An excellent study was conducted by Murray and Gerhart (1998) using a time series design. When a plant using skill-based pay was compared to a comparable plant without skill-based pay, the results indicated that the skill-based pay plant had 58% greater productivity, 16% less labor costs, and favorable quality outcomes relative to the comparison plant without skill-based pay. It should be noted that cost reductions should be expected in the long run, but not in the short run with skill-based pay. The direct and indirect start-up costs are high. Indirect costs include large training and certification expenses. Direct costs are the result of higher wages with skill-based pay.

A descriptive study of competency-based pay was conducted by the American Compensation Association (1996). The interesting finding reported here was that while competencies were being extensively used for staffing and development purposes, they are seldom being used for compensation purposes. Preliminary results of an analytical study of competencies for a large multinational food company show a relationship between competencies and business results (Heneman, Ledford & Gresham, 2000).

Merit Pay

The links of pay increases in base salary to performance ratings continues to be a controversial issue. Although confidence in merit pay as an effective reward system has waned, it continues to be frequently used (Eskew & Heneman, 1996). For example, many companies in Japan are using merit pay to replace seniority-based systems. The major problem with merit pay seems to be that it is used as a stand-alone reward program meant to reward all aspects of performance in the organization. In order to overcome this problem, two steps need to be taken (Heneman, in press). First, generic performance standards should not be used to assess performance. Instead, performance standards should be directly tied to the business strategy of the organization. Second, merit pay plans should be used in conjunction with other reward plans such as variable pay. For example, Heneman, Eskew and Fox (1998) document the effective use of profit sharing and merit pay in concert with one another. In the flight simulator company examined, merit pay was used as the funding gate for employees to receive a differential share of the profits.

Variable Pay

The use of variable pay plans continues to increase (Lawler, Mohrman & Ledford, 1998). Common features to these plans include a pay-for-performance component, performance measured at the team, business unit, or organizational level, and pay in the form of a cash bonus rather than an increase to base pay (Miceli & Heneman, in press). Typical types of variable pay plans include gain sharing, goal sharing, team pay, and profit sharing (Heneman, Ledford & Gresham, 2000). Gain sharing plans usually measure performance at the business unit level and pay for cost reductions. Goal sharing plans also usually measure performance at the business unit level and pay for cost reductions and revenue generation activities (e.g., customer service). Team pay is used for small, intact work groups (e.g., self-directed work teams). Profit-sharing measures performance at the organizational level.

Variable pay is held in high regard by management relative to base pay increases for three major reasons. First, variable pay plans are self-funding; e.g., no profit share payout is made unless there is a profit. Second, variable pay is seen to reduce the entitlement psychology inherent with increases to base pay. Pay is tied to the results of the business rather than to market or cost of living conditions. Third, pay is viewed as less of an annuity. With pay increases due to merit, for example, the merit increase is permanently built into base pay and compounds itself over time. Variable pay must be re-earned every year (or every other pay period).

A major drawback to variable pay plans is the concept of line of sight (Heneman, Ledford & Gresham, 2000). Fashioned loosely on expectancy theory (Vroom, 1964), line of sight refers to the perceived influence that employees have over the outcomes that must be impacted to achieve a cash bonus. Profit as a performance measure, for example, has a very long line of sight that diminishes the motivational value of the reward. By contrast, measures at the individual level have a less lengthy line of sight.

Recent research has also begun to examine variable pay in international environments such as China. In China there was a long tradition of egalitarianism and the 'iron rice bowl' (i.e., guaranteed employment and guaranteed pay irrespective of performance) during the 1950s through 1970s. In the early 1980s, as a reaction to the 'iron rice bowl' problem in pay distribution, an individualistic piece-rate bonus system emphasizing individual performance became popular in some Chinese industries. This practice discouraged collective responsibility and weakened team effectiveness (Wang, 1990). Thus, studies of industrial/organizational psychology were carried out to compare work efficiencies between individual and group compensation systems and to provide systematic evidence for improving the structure of compensation systems in Chinese enterprises. A series of field experiments were carried out to find out the effects of workers' attributions upon performance under individual versus team reward systems in Chinese enterprises. The results showed that under the group compensation system, employees tended to attribute their performance to the team cooperation and collective efforts which may maintain or enhance work motivation, and under the individual compensation system, they more frequently attributed their performance to personal factors or task difficulty which may reduce their work motivation. An implication of this study was that a team-oriented compensation system with clear responsibility structure would be more effective in facilitating morale, cooperation, and productivity in Chinese enterprises (Wang, 1994).

Individual Incentives

Individual incentive plans also link pay to performance in the form of a cash bonus. Unlike variable pay plans, however, pay is linked to individual performance rather than to group measures of performance (e.g., piece rate, sales). As a result of using individual rather than group measures of performance, the line of sight is probably shorter for individual incentive plans than for variable pay plans. In support of the line of sight advantage of individual incentives, the research clearly shows that they have the largest impact on employee performance (Heneman et al., 1998).

A distinct disadvantage to individual incentives is that they may detract from team performance (Wageman, 1995). It is sometimes possible to overcome this disadvantage, however, when incentive pay is coupled with variable pay (Crown & Rosse, 1995) especially in those business environments where both individual and organizational business goals are emphasized (Heneman et al., 1998).

Individual incentives for CEOs have recently been an active area of study in the global context. Wang and Feng (2000), for example, completed a study recently concerning the relationship among the compensation program dimensions, compensation perception, and performance among 251 managers in Chinese companies, and attempted to build up an assessment model of compensation program characteristics for managers. The results indicated that: (1) compensation program dimensions included need dimension, goal dimension, motivation dimension, and performance regulation dimension; (2) distributive justice was more related to the goal dimension and organizational systems and procedural justice was more dependent upon the need dimension and organizational level features of compensation programs, while both kinds of justice were closely related with performance regulation dimension. Compensation perception affected managerial performance. Managers' achievement motive affected level of effort and also affected indicators of company performance directly.

Ownership

At the other end of the spectrum from individual incentives in terms of line of sight are ownership plans where employees are made stockholders. The performance measure to be influenced by employees for a reward is the value of company stock. Many factors exogenous to the company (e.g., economy), yet alone to the employee, have an impact on the value of stock. Even with the long sight of sight, there has been an explosion in the use of ownership plans in recent years (Capell, 1996).

One interesting variation on stock ownership plans is 'phantom stock' used in privately held companies. Under this approach, internal stock is issued that serves as a proxy for public stock. The 'stock' is based on the book value of the company rather than the market value of the stock (Tully, 1998). Although no empirical comparison has been made between phantom and regular stock ownership plans, one would expect that the line of sight would be shorter with phantom stock because it is less at the mercy of the economic market. Book value reflects indices more under the control of employees, such as cost (Heneman, Ledford & Gresham, 2000).

Benefits

Benefits, once considered a 'fringe' element in total cash compensation now constitute the second largest component (26.5%) of total cash compensation (US Bureau of Labor Statistics, 1999). Unfortunately, while the amount spent on benefits has increased, there has not been a great deal of benefits research by psychologists. Some current issues in the benefits arena follow.

Flexible Benefit Plans

It used to be the case that most employees in one company all received the same benefits. While easy to administer, standard benefit plans often fail to provide meaningful benefits to employees, who have varying ages, needs, and lifestyles. In response to this situation, many organizations now provide choice in benefits selection by employees. That is, employees are given the opportunity to choose the benefits that best suit their needs at various stages in their lives. From a motivational point of view, flexible benefits are advantageous because they allow employees to select from a 'cafeteria' of benefits plans those benefits which have positive valence for them. In turn, these benefits with positive valence are likely to be motivational (Vroom, 1964). Another advantage with flexible benefits is that they allow the company to control costs by no longer providing all benefits to all employees even if all employees didn't need certain benefits. They also enable cost control through the introduction of cost sharing with employees, either through coinsurance (e.g., increased deductibles, exclusions) or shared premium payments.

One disadvantage to flexible benefits is that employees may fail to select certain benefits critical to their well-being. As a result, most flexible benefits plans require a core set of benefits to be selected by all employees (e.g., health-care insurance). Another disadvantage of cafeteria-style plans is the huge number of benefit options that may confront the employees. For example, at one company employees were overwhelmed with over 16,000 possible benefit choices! In response, the company developed an expert system to aid employee decision making. An expert system was created to show the employees the most logical options for them to select depending upon their demographic characteristics (Bloom & Milkovich, 1999).

Cash Balance Pension Plans

Given the large costs associated with employee pension plans, many large organizations are converting their existing defined benefit pension plans to 'cash balance' or 'pension equity plans.' As with traditional pension plans, these plans are funded by the employer, guarantee a retirement benefit that has little or no risk to the employee and are governed by the same provisions of ERISA that govern traditional defined benefit pension plans. But unlike traditional plans, the amount available upon retirement is based on earnings in a hypothetical individual account rather than on the basis of years of service. Each year an employee's cash balance account grows by (usually) some percentage of annual salary. The account also increases in value through accrued interest or in line with some index such as the CPI. Thus, cash balance plans grow over the entire career of the employee; a career average pay plan rather than a final average pay plan that is characteristic of the traditional pension (Quick, 1999) As a result, cash balance plans are advantageous to those employees that are mobile in their careers, while traditional benefit plans are advantageous to those that remain for a long period of time with an employer. More money is available to employees sooner in their careers with a cash balance plan (McNamee, 1999). The shift from traditional pension plans to cost balance pension plans by many employers may fundamentally alter the nature of the employment relationships from long-term duration to short-term duration with a corresponding decrease in employee commitment and turnover (Tsui, Pearce, Porter & Tripoli, 1997). More research is needed on this important topic.

Employer-Based Rehabilitation

As a result of sky rocketing costs associated with workers compensation laws and the Americans with Disabilities Act, some employers are now developing early return-to-work programs. These programs help get injured employees back on the job who might otherwise be at home to recover. In essence, these programs make it possible to return to work earlier than normal to perform modified work duties while they are recovering (Growick, 1998). As such, they are more cost effective than time off for recovery because under modified work duties, the employee is able to provide some services to the company while recovering.

ORGANIZATIONAL EFFECTIVENESS

Both narrative and meta-analytical reviews of the research literature clearly show that cash compensation is correlated with individual performance (e.g., Gupta & Mitra, 1998) and organizational effectiveness (Heneman et al., 1998). In light of this convincing data, it is amazing how the 'does money matter' argument continues to be advanced every decade or so. The latest iteration of this argument, the belief that money has a negative influence on behavior in work organizations, is in a book titled *Punished by Rewards* (Kohn, 1993).

While it has been clearly shown that pay does have an impact on organizational effectiveness, several themes must be kept in mind in interpreting evaluative studies associated with pay systems. First, the level of pay system effectiveness varies by measure of organizational effectiveness. For example, self-report data using rating scales of company performance completed by human resource professionals tend to report a larger impact on organizational effectiveness than do studies with 'hard,' archival measures of performance such as productivity and profit. Second, some pay plans are clearly more effective than others. Regardless of the

measures of organizational effectiveness used, individual incentive plans have the largest impact on organizational effectiveness (Heneman et al., 2000).

Third, causality is an issue seldom addressed. In terms of compensation evaluation studies, the vast bulk of studies are correlational in nature rather than experimental. Well-designed studies like Murray and Gerhart (1998) and Petty, Singleton and Connell (1992) are difficult to find in the literature. As a result, causality is an issue. The central question is whether highly effective organizations have the capabilities to use certain monetary reward systems or if certain monetary reward systems result in improved organizational performance.

Fourth, the research literature clearly shows that the effectiveness of pay plans varies as a function of the pay plan design features and implementation strategies (McAdams & Hawk, 1995). Psychometric properties of pay plan measures appear to be only one of many design and implementation issues that must be accounted for if a pay plan, regardless of type, is to be effective. Fifth, the evaluation studies to date are culture bound. The vast majority of studies have been conducted in the United States. The evaluation of pay plans in other countries is relatively new.

Given these caveats, Table 4.1 shows our collective best judgments of the impact of varying forms of total cash compensation on organizational performance. Satisfaction refers to satisfaction with the job and satisfaction with pay. These satisfaction measures are correlated with one another and are also correlated with absenteeism, turnover, and union vote (Heneman, 1985).

NEW DIRECTIONS

The field of compensation has always followed the scientist-practitioner model of industrial/organizational psychology. Science and practice are intertwined in compensation decision making. Consequently, we will structure our recommendations for future directions around theory, research, and practice. Given the global context to this chapter, we have also included a separate section on global compensation.

Theory

As indicated in the historical section of this chapter, we are very pleased at the shift in the unit of analysis in the study of compensation decision making from a focus on the individual to a focus on the organization. While being pleased with this shift in the unit of analysis, much theory building needs to be undertaken with the organization as the unit of analysis. While theory building is highly advanced at the individual level in compensation

Table 4.1   *Compensation plan effectiveness*

Plan	Organizational productivity	Employee satisfaction
Broadbanding	?	?
Person-based pay	Moderate	High
Market-based pay	?	?
Merit pay	Low	Moderate
Variable pay	Moderate	Moderate
Individual incentives	High	Low
Ownership	Low	Moderate
Flexible benefits	?	High

Sources: Barber, Dunham & Formisano (1992); Welbourne & Gomez-Mejia (1995); Jenkins, Mitra, Gupta & Shaw (1998); Kruse (1993); Blinder (1990); McAdams & Hawk (1995); Heneman (1992); Lawler, Mohrman & Ledford (1998); Blasi, Conte & Kruse (1996); Gerhart & Milkovich (1992); Lawler & Jenkins (1992); Jenkins, Ledford, Gupta & Doty (1987); Schuster (1989); Peck (1984, 1989, 1991); O'Dell (1987); Abosch & Hand (1998).

(e.g., expectancy theory), theory building is at a more basic level when the unit of analysis is the organization. In building theory at the organizational level, we believe that several steps need to be taken.

A major theoretical issue is the choice of dependent variable(s). Just as the 'criterion problem' has plagued theory building at the individual level, so too will the criterion problem nag at theory building at the organizational level. Clearly, organizational performance is multidimensional (Whetten & Cameron, 1994) and the task for those building organizational-level compensation models will be to carefully match the independent variables to the appropriate measures of organizational performance. The appropriate measures are likely to vary as a function of the goals of the organization (Rogers & Wright, 1998) and the goals of the compensation plan (Heneman, Ledford & Gresham, 2000). The nomological net between the goals of the organization, goals of the compensation plan, and organizational effectiveness will need to be clearly explicated by our theories. If not, a 'shotgun' empiricism approach may prevail with significant findings being a function of chance or convenience of measures available, rather than being grounded in a well-conceived nomological net.

Another major issue in theory development is the need to move away from only focusing on the outcome of the compensation plan. In order to understand the well-documented impact of compensation, focus needs to be on developing models of the underlying process whereby compensation decisions at the organizational level are translated into impacts on organizational effectiveness. In order to achieve this end, compensation should not be treated as a homogeneous construct due to the common denominator of money across all pay plan types. Instead, midrange theories need to be developed that explicate the different processes involved with different types of pay systems. By doing so, we are more likely to be able to know which measures of organizational effectiveness are likely to be impacted by each pay plan type and also be able to explain the

differential effects of different pay plan types on the same measures of organizational effectiveness. Heneman (in press) suggests that new midrange theories will need to be created for this purpose to supplement grand compensation theories such as agency theory.

Research

A rich irony in the study of compensation is the increased need for the study of compensation and the reluctance of organizations to allow their compensation systems to be studied. In terms of need, many new populations (e.g., public sector, non-profits, small companies) are using new forms of pay for the first time ever. At the same time, however, organizations are very reluctant to show their 'dirty laundry' (i.e., poor-performing compensation system) in public. Ultimately, the choice not to study one's compensation system is a poor strategic choice. The state of Kentucky, for example, has forced, by law, school districts to use financial incentives (Odden & Kelley, 1997). One can envision other organizations, even in the private sector, where such legislation could be forthcoming. For example, health care would be a likely candidate. Gain-sharing plans could logically be mandated to save on escalating health-care costs. Although this example is speculative, the point is that organizations may need to be more open in sharing pay intervention data if they wish to retain control of the pay plan interventions that they prefer to implement.

While there has been a noticeable increase in the study of new forms of pay, there is also a need for the study of pay in new environments. Systematic data collected from the public sector, small companies, and nonprofits are almost nonexistent. Because this is a new area of study, especially for new pay systems, a qualitative case-study approach would be helpful to identify the facilitating factors and restraints faced by these special sectors of our economy.

Lastly, in terms of research, more longitudinal research is needed. The benefits as well as costs associated with various pay plans sometimes do not emerge when viewed within the context of cross-sectional data. For example, skill-based pay has high upfront costs in the form of both direct (pay increases) and indirect costs (training and adminis-tration). If evaluated only from a short-term per-spective, the fact may be overlooked that these short-term costs for skill-based pay are overcome by increased organizational effectiveness over the long term (Murray & Gerhart, 1998).

Practice

Several recent trends in practice need to be carefully scrutinized. These trends include the broadbanding of pay ranges, the increasing emphasis on market value over job evaluation, and the use of classifica-tion systems of job evaluation to replace point-factor systems. In particular, the relationship between broadbanding and organizational effectiveness has not been documented with anything other than self-report data. Employee reactions to market pricing have never been investigated. The psychometric properties of classification systems, as opposed to point-factor systems, are not well established.

Unlike the selection area, the dollar value impact of compensation decisions has not been well docu-mented. Utility analysis needs to be extended from staffing decision making to compensation decision making. An excellent first step has been taken in this direction by Klaas and McClendon (1996) who looked at the financial impact of competitive pay level policies for organizations. Similarly, Bloom (1999) has provided an initial study on the impact of pay dispersion on individual and group perfor-mance. Unfortunately, the setting (major league baseball) focuses on organizations that are very different from the typical work organization.

Similar studies are needed in other areas related to total compensation practice. Little is known, for example, about the attractiveness to potential employees of different mixes of components of the total compensation package, or the individual differ-ences that might be associated with such prefer-ences. It is likely, for example, that a compensation package with a large component of individual incen-tive pay would be more appealing to an applicant who believes herself to be a high performer and who has low risk aversion than a package of equal expected value consisting mostly of base pay and benefits.

Global Compensation

Changes in pay systems at the international level have tremendous implications for practice. Sweeping generalizations about the effectiveness of pay using broad measures of culture (e.g., Hofstede, 1980) have not been particularly useful. It has been shown that very specific attitudes (e.g., entitlement) rather than general cultural attitudes (e.g., power distance) are more predictive of the receptivity of different cultures to compensation plans (Mueller & Clark, 1998). Moreover, it has been argued that corporate business strategy and local labor market conditions are more likely to impact the effectiveness of pay plans than are culture-based attitudes (Milkovich & Bloom, 1998, Bloom & Milkovich, 1999).

This is not to say that significant differences in pay practices do not exist. Pay data from national surveys (including both local national and multinational firms) conducted by HayGroup, for example, indi-cate different pay relationships between different job levels. The Hay job evaluation system is used in each country to provide a common metric of internal job value. Market rates for different jobs are col-lected in each country and pay lines are constructed. Table 4.2 shows that wage dispersions across job varies greatly from country to country. The ratio of market rates for jobs valued at 600 Hay points to those for jobs valued at 300 Hay points ranges from 1.7 to 3.1; the ratio of market rates valued at 1000 Hay points to those for jobs valued at 300 Hay points ranges from 2.2 to 6.6 (HayGroup, 1999).

However, it is possible that other approaches to defining culture (e.g., Hampden-Turner & Trompenaars, 1993; Trompenaars, 1993) may be of more use in differentiating the impact of culture on compensation systems. Trompenaars (1993), for example, notes differences in achievement- and ascription-oriented organization cultures and the impact on performance-based pay systems. This framework can be used to explain the finding of Mueller and Clark (1998) where entitlement atti-tudes were found to be much more pervasive among business school students in the former Communist countries of central and eastern Europe than among similar students in the United States. In contrast, a study of Russian and US managers and student (Giacobbe-Miller, Miller & Victorov, 1998) found equity/performance equally important in attitudes about pay determination except when individual need was a factor.

Cultural influence on reward allocation has been a crucial topic in understanding of fairness and global compensation. In his review chapter on negotiation and reward allocations across cultures, Leung (1997) noticed the effects of individualism–collectivism framework on distributive behavior and proposed a contextual model which assumes that culture interacts with a number of situational variables to determine the allocation rule used. Leung, Smith and Wang (1996) studied joint-venture hotels in the Hangzhou and Shanghai areas in China. A total of 137 Chinese managerial staff from 42 joint-venture hotels participated in the study. Procedural justice and performance-based distributive justice

Table 4.2   *Comparison of market rates for jobs of different value*

Country	Market rate ratio of jobs valued at 600 to jobs valued at 300 Hay points	Market rate ratio of jobs valued at 1000 to jobs valued at 300 Hay points
Argentina	2.83	5.46
Australia	1.70	2.79
Brazil	2.74	5.53
Canada	1.64	2.54
China	2.49	6.16
Columbia	2.78	6.29
France	1.90	2.97
Germany	1.85	3.22
Hong Kong	2.45	5.18
Indonesia	3.02	5.73
Japan	1.87	2.77
Malaysia	2.81	5.21
Mexico	2.88	5.96
Norway	1.53	2.17
Poland	2.57	5.38
Singapore	2.36	4.34
South Korea	2.15	3.83
Sweden	1.67	2.94
United Arab Emirates	2.38	4.32
United Kingdom	1.78	3.02
United States	1.81	3.12
Venezuela	2.96	6.58

Source: Computed from HayGroup's PayNet© Services, Country Guides, *http://www.haypaynet.com*
Representative job titles at 300 Hay points include entry-level college graduate, foreman, and sales representative. Representative job titles at 600 Hay points include senior engineer, sales manager, and experienced professional staff. Representative job titles at 1000 Hay points include plant manager (small plant), middle/senior management, and functional directors.

were found to be predictive of job satisfaction. However, unlike American results, interactional justice was not related to job satisfaction in joint ventures in China. It is possible that because of the higher acceptance of hierarchy and authority figures in Chinese organizations, the level of interactional justice required by Chinese employees from their superiors may be lower. This finding makes it clear that justice theories developed and confirmed in the United States should not be automatically assumed to be valid in different cultures. As predicted, the comparison with expatriate staff did not account for additional variance in the prediction of job satisfaction. Clearly, local staff did not regard them as a meaningful referent group for social comparison in the perception of distributive justice. In contrast, the comparison with other local staff was able to add to the prediction of job satisfaction. This finding highlights the importance of social comparison in fairness judgments of compensation systems in joint ventures. The conceptualization of distributive justice as a comparison between performance inputs and salaries is too narrow in joint ventures and needs to be broadened to include social comparison processes.

Also, senior managers showed the lowest level of perceived procedural and interaction justice. This pattern of results suggests that senior staff probably expected decision-making processes to be fairer, and interpersonal treatment received from expatriate staff more positive.

Contrary to expectation, rank did not show any effect on performance-based distributive justice. This recent finding probably reflects the fact that all levels of staff in these jointventures are paid at a comparable level based on their performance inputs. It is interesting to note that the only significant effect involves the comparison with local employees in state-owned hotels. Middle managers reported the highest level of perceived justice, whereas senior managers and supervisors regarded their pay as less fair in comparison with local staff in other state-owned hotels.

Legal and regulatory systems differ considerably across countries in way that impact at least the benefits segment of the total compensation program. In the United States, Japan, and parts of Western Europe, for example, company pension plans account for a significant portion of typical retirement income. In Singapore, most of Latin America, France and Italy, the typical retiree receives little or no retirement income from a company pension plan, but instead relies on government programs (Towers Perrin, 1999) and private savings. The use

Table 4.3   *Comparison of legal holidays and mandated minimum vacation time*

Country	Official holidays (days)	Legally mandated vacation (days)
Argentina	10	14
Australia	10	20
Brazil	10	30
Canada	9	10
China	7	0
Columbia	15	18
France	11	25
Germany	7–10	20
Hong Kong	17	7
Indonesia	13	12
Japan	14	10
Malaysia	14	8–16
Mexico	7	6
Norway	10	21
Poland	12	18
Russia	10	20
Singapore	11	11
South Korea	18	10 + 1/yr
Sweden	11	25
United Arab Emirates	9	30
United Kingdom	8	15
United States	10	0*
Venezuela	13	15

Source: HayGroup's PayNet© Services, Country Guides, *http://www.haypaynet.com*
* No legally mandated vacation time; 10 days plus additional days based on length of service is customary.

of perquisites varies widely from country to country and is usually driven by tax law (Moorman-Scrivener & Terry, 1996). Labor law and practice differs widely across countries and differences in governance approaches (e.g., works councils in Germany, codetermination in Sweden, joint consultation systems in Japan) and these differences impact many aspects of the rewards system. (Begin, 1997; Heneman, von Hippel, Eskew & Greenberger, 1997).

An indication of some specific differences driven by law and culture is provided in Table 4.3. This table shows the differences in official holidays and minimum mandated vacation days in selected countries. While companies may choose to provide more paid time off, the number of legal holidays varies from 7 to 18 days in the countries studied, and mandated minimum vacation time ranges from 0 to 30 days.

Also for practice, there appears to be a convergence of pay plan types across countries (Gross & Wingerup, 1999). This convergence movement appears to run counter to popular opinion that pay plans must vary by country in order to be effective. For example, Milliman, Nason, Lowe, Nam-Hyeon and Huo (1995) found a similar factor structure for performance appraisal practices across Japan, Korea, Taiwan, and the United States. Similarly, Japanese companies operating in the United States have shifted US subsidiary compensation practices to conform more closely to those of their US competitors, and to a lesser extent have shifted practices in

the Japanese parent (Mukuda, 1999). In contrast, another survey found executive pay practices in US subsidiaries of foreign firms shifted to meet US standards with little or no impact on executive pay practices in the parent firm (Graskamp, 1999).

Hence, while local conditions must be recognized, core components of the compensation plan such as performance appraisal may be common across countries. As such, multinational organizations may be able to adapt a 'mass-customization' strategy (LeBlanc, 1997) whereby there is a common core of compensation techniques with some alterations to the plan to meet local circumstances. That is, there is a common compensation platform across countries with some, but not total accommodations to meet local conditions.

CONCLUSION

As indicated in this selective review, large changes are taking place in the manner in which employees are compensated in organizations. Emphasis across all areas of pay is on rewarding contribution to the organization rather than membership in the organization. This focus on performance-based pay systems is gaining attention in all areas of the world, not just the United States. Given the evaluation studies conducted to date, there is reason for optimism about the results of efforts by companies to shift from a focus on membership to performance. These new pay plans do seem to have positive outcomes. Missing, however, is a fundamental understanding of why these pay systems work and under what circumstances they work. There is a large need for more and better theory development and research as to the processes whereby these pay programs work. Work psychologists can have a marked impact in developing this new body of theory and research.

REFERENCES

Abosch, K.S., & Hand, J.S. (1998). *Life with broadbands*. Scottsdale, AZ: American Compensation Association.

Abosch, K.S., & Hmurovic (1998). A traveler's guide to global broadbanding. *ACA Journal*, Summer, 38–46.

American Compensation Association (1996). *Raising the bar: Using competencies to enhance employee performance*. Scottsdale, AZ: Author.

Barber, A.E., Dunham, R.B., & Formisano, R.A. (1992). The impact of employee benefits on employee satisfaction: A field study. *Personnel Psychology*, *45*, 55–75.

Becker, B., & Gerhart, B. (1992). Special research forum: Human resource management and organizational performance. *Academy of Management Journal*, *39*(4), entire issue.

Becker, G.S. (1975). *Human capital: A theoretical and empirical analysis, with special reference to education* (2nd ed.). New York: Columbia University Press.

Begin, J.P. (1997). *Dynamic human resource systems: Cross-national comparisons*. New York: Walter de Gruyter.

Blasi, J., Conte, M., & Kruse, D. (1996). Employee stock ownership and corporate performance among public companies. *Industrial and Labor Relations Review*, *50*, 60–79.

Blinder, A.S. (Ed.). (1990). *Paying for productivity: A look at the evidence*. Washington, DC: Brookings Institution.

Bloom, M. (1999). The performance effects of pay dispersion on individuals and organizations. *Academy of Management Journal*, *42*(1), 25–40.

Bloom, M., & Milkovich, G.T. (1999). A SHRM perspective on international compensation and reward systems. *Research in personnel and human resources management* (Supplement 4) Greenwich, CT: JAI Press, 283–303.

Campbell, J.P. (1976). Motivation theory in industrial and organizational psychology. In M.D. Dunnette (Ed.), *Handbook of industrial and organizational psychology* (pp. 63–130). New York: John Wiley.

Capell, K. (1996). Owens Corning plays share the wealth. *Business Week*, July 22, 82–83.

Cartter, A.M. (1959). *Theory of wages and employment*. Homewood, IL: Richard D. Irwin.

Collins, J.M., & Muchinsky, P.M. (1993). An assessment of the construct validity of three job evaluation methods. *Academy of Management Journal*, *36*, 895–901.

Cronbach, L.J., & Gleser, G.C. (1965). *Psychological tests and personnel decisions*. Urbana, IL: University of Illinois Press.

Crown, D.F., & Rosse, J.G. (1995). Yours, mine, and ours: Facilitating group productivity through the integration of individual and group goals. *Organizational Behavior and Human Decision Processes*, *64*, 138–150.

Dunnette, M.D. (Ed., 1976). *Handbook of industrial and organizational psychology*. Chicago: Rand-McNally.

Dunnette, M.D., & Hough, L.M. (1992). *Handbook of industrial and organizational psychology*, Vol. 3 (*2nd ed.*). Palo Alto, CA: Consulting Psychologists Press.

Eskew, D., & Heneman, R.L. (1996). A survey of merit pay plan effectiveness: End of the line for merit pay or hope for improvement? *Human Resource Planning Journal*, *19*(2), 12–19.

Gerhart, B., & Milkovich, G.T. (1992). Employee compensation: Research and practice. In M.D. Dunnette, & L.M. Hough (Eds.), *Handbook of industrial and organizational psychology*, Vol. 3 (2nd ed., pp. 1009–1055), Palo Alto, CA: Consulting Psychologists Press.

Gerhart, B., Trevor, C.D., & Graham, M.E. (1996). New directions in compensation research: Synergies, risk, and survival. In G. Ferris (Ed.), *Research in personnel and human resources management* (pp. 143–203). Greenwich, CT: JAI Press.

Giacobbe-Miller, J.K., Miller, D.J., & Victorov, V.I. (1998). A comparison of Russian and U.S. pay allocation decisions, distribution judgments, and productivity under different payment conditions. *Personnel Psychology*, *51*(1), 137–163.

Gomez-Mejia, L.R., & Balkin, D.B. (1992). *Compensation, organizational strategy, and firm performance*. Cincinnati, OH: South-Western.

Graskamp. E. (1999). How foreign companies use U.S. incentive pay practices in the United States. *Compensation and Benefits Management*, *15*(3), 60–63.

Gross, S.E., & Wingerup, P.L. (1999). Global pay? Maybe not yet! *Compensation and Benefits Review*, July/August, 25–34.

Growick, B.S. (1998). Employer-based rehab: Wave of the future. *Workers Compensation Cost Control*, *7*(4), 1–3.

Gupta, N., & Mitra, A. (1998). The value of financial incentives: Myths and empirical realities. *ACA Journal*, Autumn, 58–66.

Hampden-Turner, C., & Trompenaars, A. (1993). *The seven cultures of capitalism*. New York: Doubleday.

Heneman, H.G. III (1985). Pay satisfaction. In K.N. Rowland, & G.R. Ferris (Eds.), *Research in personnel and human resources management*, Vol. 3 (pp. 115–139). Greenwich, CT: JAI Press.

Heneman, R.L. (1992). *Merit pay: Linking pay increases to performance ratings*. Reading, MA: Addison-Wesley-Longman.

Heneman, R.L. (2000). The changing nature of pay systems and the need for new midrange theories of pay. *Human Resource Management Review*, *10*, 245–247.

Heneman, R.L. (2001). *Business-driven compensation policies: Integrating compensation systems with corporate strategies*. New York: AMACOM.

Heneman, R.L. (in press). Merit pay. In C. Fay (Ed.), *The Executive Handbook of Compensation*. New York: Free Press.

Heneman, R.L., Eskew, D., & Fox, J. (1998). Using employee attitudes to evaluate a new incentive program. *Compensation and Benefits Review, 28*(1), 40–44.

Heneman, R.L., & Dixon, K. (1998). How to find, select, and evaluate market surveys to meet your organizations needs. In R. Platt (Ed.), *Salary survey guidebook* (pp. 1–5). New York: AMACOM.

Heneman, R.L., Ledford, G.E., & Gresham, M. (2000). The changing nature of work and its effects on compensation design and delivery. In S. Rynes & B. Gerhart *Compensation in Organizations: Current Research and Practice* (Society for Industrial and Organizational Psychology Frontiers of Industrial and Organizational Psychology Series) pp. 195–240. San Francisco: Jossey-Bass.

Heneman, R.L., von Hippel, C., Eskew, D.E., & Greenberger, D.B. (1997). Alternative rewards in unionized environments. *ACA Journal*, Summer, 42–55.

Hicks, R. (1934). *Theory of wages*. New York: McMillan.

Hofstede, G. (1980). *Cultures consequences*. Newbury Park, CA: Sage.

Jenkins, D.G., Jr., Ledford, G.E., Jr., Gupta, N., & Doty, D.H. (1987). Skill-based pay: Practices, payoffs, pitfalls, and prescriptions. Scottsdale, AZ: American Compensation Association.

Jenkins, G.D., Jr., Mitra, A., Gupta, N., & Shaw, J.D. (1998). Are financial incentives related to performance? A meta-analysis review of empirical research. *Journal of Applied Psychology, 83*, 777–787.

Klaas, B.S., & McClendon, J.A. (1996). To lead, lag, or match: Estimating the financial impact of pay level policies. *Personnel Psychology, 49*, 121–135.

Kohn, A. (1993). *Punished by rewards*. Boston: Houghton-Mifflin.

Kruse, D.L. (1993). *Profit sharing: Does it make a difference*? Kalamazoo, MI: Upjohn Institute.

Lawler, E.E., III (1971). *Pay and organizational effectiveness*. New York: McGraw-Hill.

Lawler, E.E., III (1981). *Pay and organizational development*. Reading, MA: Addison-Wesley.

Lawler, E.E., III (1990). *Strategic pay*. San Francisco: Jossey-Bass.

Lawler, E.E., III (2000). *Rewarding excellence: Pay strategies for the new economy*. San Francisco: Jossey-Bass.

Lawler, E.E., III, & Jenkins, G.D., Jr. (1992). Strategic reward systems. In M.D. Dunnette, & L.M. Hough (Eds.), *Handbook of industrial and organizational psychology*, Vol. 3 (2nd ed., pp. 1009–1055). Palo Alto, CA: Consulting Psychologists Press.

Lawler, E.E. III, Mohrman, S.A., & Ledford, G.E. (1998). *Strategies for high performance organizations*. San Francisco: Jossey-Bass.

LeBlanc, P. (1997). Mass customization. *ACA Journal*, Spring, 16–31.

Leung, K. (1997). Negotiation and reward allocation across cultures, In P.C. Earley, & M. Erez (Eds.), *New Perspectives on International Industrial/Organizational Psychology*. San Francisco: The New Lexington Press.

Leung, K., Smith, P.B., & Wang, Z.M. (1996). Job satisfaction in joint venture hotels in China: An organizational justice analysis, *Journal of International Business Studies, 27*(5), 947–962.

Luk, V.W.M., & Chiu, R.K. (1998). Reward systems for local staff in China. In J. Selmer, (Ed.), *International Management in China: Cross-Cultural Issues* Chapter 10. London: Routledge.

Madigan, R.M. (1985). Comparable worth judgments: A measurement properties analysis. *Journal of Applied Psychology, 70*, 137–147.

McAdams, J.L., & Hawk, E.J. (1995). *Organizational performance and rewards*. Scottsdale, AZ: American Compensation Association.

McNamee, M. (1999). Good pensions, bad sales pitch. *Business Week*, October 4, 44.

Miceli, M., & Heneman, R.L. (in press). Contextual determinants of variable pay plan design: A proposed research framework. *Human Resource Management Review*.

Milkovich, G.T., & Bloom, M. (1998). Rethinking international compensation. *Compensation and Benefits Review, 30*(1), 15–23.

Milkovich, G.T., & Newman, J.M. (1999). *Compensation*, Vol. 3. (6th ed. pp. 481–570). Palo Alto, CA: Consulting Psychologists Press.

Milliman, J.F., Nason, S., Lowe, K., Nam-Hyeon, K., & Huo, P. (1995). An empirical study of performance appraisal practices in Japan, Korea, Taiwan, and the US. *Academy of Management Best Paper Proceedings*, 182–186.

Moorman-Scrivener, S., & Terry, J., (Eds.) (1996). *International benefit guidelines 1996*. New York: William M. Mercer.

Mueller, S.L., & Clark, L.D. (1998). Political-economic context and sensitivity to equity: Differences between the United States and the transition economics of central and eastern Europe. *Academy of Management Journal, 41*, 319–329.

Mukuda, M.K. (1999). Compensation and HR practices: Global challenges of Japanese companies. *ACA Journal, 8*(3), 61–66.

Murray, B., & Gerhart, B. (1998). An empirical analysis of a skill-based pay program and plant performance outcomes. *Academy of Management Journal, 41*, 68–78.

Odden, A., & Kelley, C. (1997). *Paying teachers for what they know and do: New and smarter compensation strategies to improve schools*. Thousand Oaks, CA: Corwin Press.

O'Dell, C.O. (1987). *Major findings from people, performance, and pay*. Scottsdale, AZ: American Compensation Association.

Peck, C. (1984). *Pay and performance: The interaction of compensation and performance appraisal*. Research Bulletin No. 155. New York: Conference Board.

Peck, C. (1989). *Variable pay: New performance rewards*. Research Bulletin No. 246. New York: Conference Board.

Peck, C. (1991). *Gainsharing for productivity.* Report No. 967. New York: Conference Board.

Petty, M.M., Singleton, B., & Connell, D.W. (1992). An experimental evaluation of an incentive plan in the electric utility industry. *Journal of Applied Psychology, 77,* 427–436.

Quick, C. (1999). An overview of cash balance plans. *Employee Benefit Research Institute Notes, 20*(7), 1–8.

Rogers, E.W., & Wright, P.M. (1998). *Measuring organizational performance in strategic human resource management: problems and prospects.* (Working Paper 98–09). School of Industrial and Labor Relations, Cornell University.

Rynes, S., & Gerhart, B. (Eds.) (2000). *Compensation in organizations: progress and prospects.* San Francisco: New Lexington Press.

Rynes, S.L., & Milkovich, G.T. (1986). Wage surveys: Dispelling some myths about the market wage! *Personnel Psychology, 34,* 71–90.

Schuster, J.R. (1989). Improving productivity through gainsharing: Can the means be justified in the end? *Compensation and Benefits Management, 5,* 207–210.

Smith, P.C. (1976). Behaviors, results, and organizational effectiveness: The problem of criteria. In M.D. Dunnette (Ed.), *Handbook of industrial and organizational psychology* (pp. 745–776). New York: John Wiley.

Towers Perrin. (1999). *Worldwide total rewards 1998.* New York: Towers Perrin Global Resource Group.

Treiman, D.J. (1979). *Job evaluation: An analytic review.* Washington DC: National Academy Press.

Treiman, D.J., & Hartman, H.I. (Eds.) (1981). *Women, work and wages: Equal pay for jobs of equal value.* Washington, DC: National Academy Press.

Trompenaars, A. (1993). *Riding the waves of culture: Understanding cultural diversity in business.* London: Nicholas Brealey.

Tsui, A.S., Pearce, J.L., Porter, L.W., & Tripoli, A.M. (1997). Alternative approaches to the employee-organization relationship: Does investment in employees pay off? *Academy of Management Journal, 40,* 1089–1121.

Tullar, W.L. (1998). Compensation consequences of reengineering. *Journal of Applied Psychology, 83,* 975–980.

Tully, S. (1998). A better taskmaster than the market? *Fortune,* October 26, 277–286.

US Bureau of Labor Statistics (1999). *Employer costs for employee compensation – March 1999.*

USDL: 99–173. Washington, DC: US Department of Labor.

Viswesvaran, C., & Barrick, M.R. (1992). Decision-making effects on compensation surveys: Implications for market wages. *Journal of Applied Psychology, 77,* 588–597.

Vroom, V. (1964). *Work and motivation.* New York: Wiley.

Wageman, R. (1995). Interdependence and group effectiveness. *Administrative Science Quarterly, 40,* 145–180.

Wallace, M.J., Jr., & Fay, C.H. (1988). *Compensation: theory and practice* (2nd edn.). Boston: PWS-Kent.

Wang, Z.M. (1990). Human resource management in China: Recent trends. In R. Pieper (Ed.), *Human Resource Management: An International Comparison.* Berlin: Walter de Gruyter.

Wang, Z.M. (1994). Culture, economic reform, and the role of industrial and organizational psychology in China. In H.C. Triandis, M.D. Dunnette, & L.M. Hough, (Eds.), *Handbook of industrial and organizational psychology,* Vol. 4 (2nd ed., Chapter 14). Palo Alto, CA: Consulting Psychologist Press.

Wang, Z.M., & Chen, Z. (2000). Compensation systems structure, justice and impact of organizational systems. In Z.M. Wang et al. (Eds.), *Research advances in human resources and organizational behavior.* Beijing: China People's University Press (in press).

Wang, Z.M., & Feng, Z.Q. (2000). CEO compensation design and its motivational mechanism. In Z.M. Wang et al. (Eds.), *Research advances in human resources and organizational behavior.* Beijing: China People's University Press (in press).

Weber, C.L., & Rynes, S.L. (1991). Effects of compensation strategy on job pay decisions. *Academy of Management Journal, 34,* 86–109.

Welbourne, T., & Gomez-Mejia, L.R. (1995). Gainsharing: A critical review and a future research agenda. *Journal of Management, 21,* 559–609.

Whetten, D.A., & Cameron, K.S. (1994). Organizational effectiveness: Old models and new constructs. In J. Greenberg (Ed.), *Organizational behavior: The state of the science* (pp. 135–154). Hillsdale, NJ: Lawrence Erlbaum Associates.

Wright, P.M., Dyer, L.D., Boudreau, J.W., & Milkovich, G.T. (1999). Strategic human resources management in the twenty-first century. *Research in personnel and human resources management,* supplement 4. Stamford, CT: JAI Press.

5

Occupational Stress: Toward a More Integrated Framework

PETER M. HART and CARY L. COOPER

Although the stressors and strain approach has become the dominant theme in the occupational stress literature, a growing body of empirical evidence has called this approach into question. Additionally, limitations with many of the process theories of occupational stress prevent them from being fully integrated into the mainstream literature on work and organizational psychology. In this chapter we argue that these limitations can be addressed by adopting an organizational health framework. According to this framework, it is important to focus simultaneously on employee well-being *and* organizational performance. It is argued that these are determined by a combination of individual (e.g., personality and coping) and organizational (e.g., organizational climate and work experiences) characteristics. We outline a research agenda for the organizational health framework and demonstrate how it can be used to provide a stronger link between occupational stress and other areas of work and organizational psychology. We believe this approach will help to improve the relevance of occupational stress to work organizations.

INTRODUCTION

Occupational stress is a growing problem that results in substantial cost to individual employees and work organizations around the globe. The changing nature of work has placed unprecedented demands on employees, and fuelled concerns about the effect this change is having on the well-being and health of employees and their work organizations. In many large organizations, for example, the 1990s were a period of dramatic downsizing, outsourcing, and globalization. Although these changes have led to greater mobility and more flexible work arrangements for some employees, for others they have raised concerns about employment security, increased work demands, and the loss of 'connectedness' that can result from the move toward less secure forms of employment (e.g., part-time and short-term contract work). In many organizations, these changes have also been coupled with

rapid technological change, and a strong push for greater efficiency, increased competitiveness, and improved customer service. Conventional wisdom suggests that it is this climate of continual change that is placing many employees under pressure and creating the types of work organizations that will produce high levels of occupational stress. This places a premium on being able to understand the causes and consequences of occupational stress, so that appropriate policies and practices can be developed to ameliorate these concerns.

In this chapter, we review the traditional approach to occupational stress that has been adopted in both research and applied settings, and call into question the core assumptions that have underpinned this approach. In particular, we believe that it is necessary to develop stronger links between the occupational stress literature and other areas of work psychology (Wright & Croponzano, 2000a), in order to broaden our understanding of occupational stress and demonstrate that employee well-being is central to the ongoing viability and success of work organizations.

DEFINITIONS OF OCCUPATIONAL STRESS

The starting point in this chapter should be to provide a clear, coherent and precise definition of occupational stress. Unfortunately, this is not straightforward. Despite the key words 'occupational stress,' 'work stress,' and 'job stress' being used in 2,768 scientific articles published during the 1990s, the scientific community has still not reached an agreed position on the meaning and definition of occupational stress. There has been considerable debate, for example, about whether occupational stress should be defined in terms of the person, the environment, or both (e.g., Cooper, 1998; Cotton, 1995; Quick, Murphy & Hurrell, 1992a). This lack of coherence has led to a degree of fragmentation in the occupational stress literature, and may explain, in part, why during the 1990s only 8% of the research articles related to occupational stress were published in the leading applied psychology and management journals (see Table 5.1 for details).

The Stressors and Strain Approach to Occupational Stress

The ongoing debate about the meaning and definition of occupational stress has allowed the stressors and strain approach to become the dominant theme in the occupational stress literature (e.g., Spector & Jex, 1998). The stressors and strain approach is based on a relatively simplistic theory that views stress as occurring when work characteristics contribute to poor psychological or physical health (Beehr, 1995). According to this approach, *stressors* refer to the work-related characteristics, events or situations that give rise to stress, and *strain* refers to an employee's physiological or psychological response to stress (Hurrell, Nelson & Simmons, 1998). The main interest, however, is on the presumed causal relationship between stressors and strain. Cox (1978) has likened this approach to an engineering model in which environmental demands may put people under pressure, and the strain created by this pressure may place people at risk of experiencing physiological and psychological harm.

The stressors and strain approach is at the core of most recent research into occupational stress. This research has concentrated on identifying the occupational and organizational sources of strain that are related to various indices of strain (e.g., job dissatisfaction, psychological distress, burnout, and sickness absence) and, in some instances, has focused on identifying the individual (e.g, perceived control) and organizational (e.g., decision-latitude) factors that moderate the stressor–strain relationship (e.g., Quick et al., 1992a; Sauter & Murphy, 1995). However, despite the volume of research into the stressors and strain approach, we believe that our understanding of occupational stress has not progressed that far over the past decade. Moreover, the implications stemming from this volume of research have not been fully integrated into an appropriate theoretical framework that enables us to build a strong bridge between the occupational stress literature and other areas in the management science and work psychology literatures.

Four Assumptions Underpinning the Stressors and Strain Approach

In order to put much of the recent occupational stress research into its proper perspective, it is important to understand the assumptions that have tended to underpin the stressors and strain approach. We believe that four basic assumptions characterize the stressors and strain approach, and these assumptions continue to influence most research into occupational stress. These assumptions have generally been accepted as 'givens' in the occupational stress literature and, despite contrary evidence being found in other areas of psychology, occupational stress researchers have rarely challenged or empirically tested these assumptions.

Occupational Stress Is Associated with Unpleasant Emotions

First, it is generally believed that occupational stress is associated with the aversive or unpleasant emotional states that people experience as a consequence of their work. For example, Kyriacou and Sutcliffe (1978) defined occupational stress as the experience of unpleasant emotions, such as tension, frustration, anxiety, anger, and depression. This definition has been used extensively in the occupational stress literature (e.g., Newton, 1989), and is similar to definitions of psychological distress (Headey & Wearing, 1992) and negative affect (Watson, 1988). Several influential theories have also reinforced this view by emphasizing the link between occupational stress and psychological strain (e.g., Beehr & Newman, 1978; French, Caplan & Harrison, 1982; cf. Cooper, 1998). Although some researchers draw a distinction between stress and psychological distress (e.g., Quick, Murphy & Hurrell, 1992b), this distinction is seldom made by the lay community where occupational stress is typically associated with the negative feelings that employees have about their work (Jex, Beehr & Roberts, 1992).

Table 5.1   *Articles published since 1990 using the key words of 'occupational stress,'*
'work stress,' or 'job stress'

Journal	Published articles
Academy of Management Journal	14
Academy of Management Review	3
Journal of Applied Psychology	22
Journal of Occupational and Organizational Psychology	70
Journal of Occupational Health Psychology	49
Journal of Organizational Behavior	32
Journal of Personality and Social Psychology	1
Journal of Vocational Behavior	24
Personnel Psychology	1
Psychological Bulletin	0
All other journals	2,552
Total	2,768

Note: The literature search was conducted on PsychLit and identified all listed articles published from 1 January 1990 to November 1999.

Positive and Negative Reactions
Are Inversely Related

The second assumption is that people experience feelings of stress at the expense of more pleasurable emotions, such as those typically associated with positive affect, psychological morale, and a sense of overall well-being (cf. Hart, 1994; Headey & Wearing, 1992; Lazarus & Folkman, 1984). This assumption implies, for example, that stress and morale are at the opposite ends of an occupational well-being continuum, where one rises as the other falls. This may explain why occupational well-being indices, such as morale, have received little theoretical and empirical attention in recent times (Organ, 1997). Moreover, this assumption is consistent with the fact that none of the 23 articles in an edited publication entitled *Stress and Well-Being at Work* (Quick et al., 1992a) defined the nature of the relationship between stress and well-being. It was merely assumed that stress resulted in an absence of well-being.

Stress Can Be Measured by
a Single Variable

The third assumption is that stress can be expressed as a single variable. In other words, many researchers have assumed, at an operational level, that a single measure can be used to capture the concept of 'stress.' There is some debate, however, as to whether this measure should assess the objective characteristics of the environment, an individual's subjective interpretation of the environment, or an individual's psychological response to the environment. Newton (1989) has observed, for example, that response-based measures, such as those focusing on anxiety, depression, job satisfaction, or psychophysiological symptoms, are often used to assess stress in occupational settings. This approach has persisted throughout the 1990s, with

many studies still using single measures, such as the Minnesota Satisfaction Questionnaire (Weiss, Dawis, England & Lofquist, 1967) or the General Health Questionnaire (Goldberg, 1978), to assess occupational stress. To a lesser extent, other approaches have included the use of work-related event inventories (Sewell, 1983), similar to those used in the life events literature of the 1970s (e.g., Holmes & Rahe, 1967), and the use of stressor scales to identify the stress caused by work-related factors (e.g., Hurrell et al., 1998).

Stress Is Caused Primarily
by Adverse Work Experiences

The fourth assumption is that adverse work experiences (i.e., adverse characteristics, events or situations in the work environment) contribute to the personal (e.g., poor quality of work life, low job satisfaction, burnout, and lack of motivation) and organizational (e.g., increased sickness absence, stress related workers' compensation claims, poor productivity, and high turnover) outcomes normally attributed to occupational stress (e.g., Quick et al., 1992a; Sauter & Murphy, 1995). This may explain why many occupational stress researchers focus almost exclusively on the relationship between negative work experiences (stressors) and employees' psychological outcomes, but say little, if anything, about the role played by positive experiences.

Calling the Stressors and Strain
Assumptions into Question

Although these four assumptions permeate much of the occupational stress literature, they have been called into question by a growing body of empirical evidence in the work psychology (e.g., Hart, 1999), health psychology (e.g., Lazarus & Folkman, 1984), and perceived quality of life (e.g., Headey &

Wearing, 1992) literatures. For example, many of the theoretical developments in recent years suggest that stress cannot be located in any single variable (Lazarus, 1990), but instead, results from the interplay between a broad system of variables (e.g., Cooper, 1998).

These developments highlight that one of the major limitations of the stressors and strain approach is that it is not driven by a strong coherent theory. Instead, researchers merely attempt to identify the stressors experienced by different workgroups and then attempt to relate these to indices of strain and psychological distress (e.g., Sauter & Murphy, 1995). Unfortunately, the mere identification of the stressors that affect employees' psychological outcomes will not help to accumulate knowledge about the causes and consequences of occupational stress. This will require a much stronger commitment to theory-based research.

Moreover, the 'field' nature of most occupational stress studies means that the role of theory becomes even more crucial when trying to establish causation. In a field study, the variables of interest can rarely be manipulated experimentally. Instead, the naturally occurring covariation between these variables must be carefully examined. This requires a clearly articulated theory that describes the relationships within the system of variables under investigation. Only then will it be possible to use appropriate measures and analytic techniques to examine the adequacy of the theory within a traditional hypothesis-testing framework. As noted by Hobfoll (1989: 513), 'without a clear theoretical backdrop, it is difficult to create a true body of knowledge because there are no defined borders of theory to be challenged.' The absence of a strong theoretical framework has meant that many occupational stress studies have adopted an exploratory analytic approach, rather than a hypothesis-testing framework that allows for an empirical assessment of competing hypotheses and theoretical positions.

PROCESS THEORIES OF OCCUPATIONAL STRESS

Despite the fact that a large volume of research has focused on linking stressors to strain, a growing number of process theories have been developed to provide a more coherent framework for understanding occupational stress (Cooper, 1998). Some of these theories have a strong occupational orientation (e.g., Edwards, 1992), whereas others can be readily applied to other domains of an employee's life (e.g., Hart, 1999). One thing that most process theories have in common, however, is that they are based on the transactional approach to stress.

The transactional approach treats stress as a dynamic process operating between a person and his or her environment. Although the term 'transaction' is used to emphasize the fact that stress results from the conjunction between personal and environmental variables (Cox, 1978; Lazarus & Folkman, 1984), it is the dynamic, reciprocal nature of the relationships between these variables that distinguishes transactional models from other more static, or unidirectional theories. For example, the traditional stressors and strain approach assumes that stressors cause strain. There is no allowance for the fact that a reciprocal causal relationship may exist between stressors and strain, or that employees' levels of strain may actually cause them to experience stressors. Moreover, the reciprocity or mutual determinism that is an integral part of transactional theories serves to create a self-regulating system that is constantly striving to maintain a state of homeostasis or equilibrium (Edwards, 1992; Hart, 1999; Headey & Wearing, 1989). This means that in order to understand occupational stress, it is necessary to understand how a system of variables relate to one another over time. Unfortunately, little is known about how occupational stress variables actually relate to one another over time, because the vast majority of occupational stress studies have been cross-sectional, rather than longitudinal in nature.

The transactional approach has led to the development of specific occupational stress theories, such as French et al.'s (1982) person–environment fit theory, which suggests that a misfit between the characteristics of an individual (e.g., abilities and goals) and his or her work environment (e.g., work demands and organizational climate) will result in psychological, physiological, and behavioral strain. Although such theories have been discussed widely in the occupational stress literature (Edwards, 1992), their specific occupational nature does not easily facilitate a more systemic view that integrates the various domains of employees' lives. More importantly, however, the theoretical emphasis placed on strain does not adequately account for the fact that people's psychological responses to their environment include both positive (e.g., well-being, positive affect, morale) and negative (e.g., ill-being, negative affect, psychological distress) dimensions (Agho, Price & Mueller, 1992; Bradburn, 1969; Diener & Emmons, 1985; Watson & Tellegen, 1985), each potentially having their own unique set of causes and consequences (e.g., Costa & McCrae, 1980; Hart, 1994; Hart, Wearing & Headey, 1994; Headey, Glowacki, Holmstrom & Wearing, 1985; Headey & Wearing, 1992).

The Cognitive-Relational Approach

The cognitive-relational theory developed by Lazarus and his colleagues (e.g., DeLongis, Folkman & Lazarus, 1988; Lazarus & Folkman, 1984) is a transactional theory that can be applied to all domains of a person's life, and can be used to explain the positive and negative responses that people have to their environment. Based on this approach, stress has been variously defined as a multivariate process (Lazarus, 1990) or term for an area of study (Lazarus, DeLongis, Folkman & Gruen, 1985). However, these definitions have been criticized for being too vague and, in themselves, provide no information about the sorts of variables or relationships that should be considered important. This definitional approach contrasts with other transactional theorists, like Cox (1978) and McGrath (1970), who have defined stress as the imbalance between people's perceived environmental demands and their perceived ability to cope with these demands. Although this definition is more precise, it still fails to convey the true dynamic nature of stress.

The major contribution of the cognitive-relational theory is not the way in which it defines stress, but its introduction of the notion that the interdependent processes of *appraisal* and *coping* mediate the relationship between a person's environment and his or her adaptational outcomes. Adaptation refers to the continual interplay between appraisal and coping, and is the process through which people manage their environment to maintain an optimum level of physical, psychological and social well-being. The outcomes of this process have been operationally defined as positive and negative affect (Kanner, Coyne, Schaefer & Lazarus, 1981), as well as anxiety, depression, perceived social competence, and general self-worth (Kanner, Feldman, Weinberger & Ford, 1991), but may also include other indicators of psychological well-being, somatic health, and social functioning (Lazarus, 1990; Lazarus et al., 1985).

According to the cognitive-relational approach, people's experience of their environment is mediated through appraisal. Appraisal is a cognitive process through which people constantly monitor the conditions in their environment to determine whether these conditions are likely to have consequences for their well-being (referred to as *primary appraisal*), and if so, what can be done about it (referred to as *secondary appraisal*). When environmental conditions are appraised as being potentially harmful, beneficial, threatening, or challenging, people will interpret the conditions as having consequences for their well-being and, therefore, this will result in the use of coping processes (Folkman & Lazarus, 1988).

Coping processes refer to the cognitive or behavioral efforts that people bring into play in an attempt to alter their environment (e.g., problem-focused coping) or manage their emotions (e.g., emotion-focused coping). This definition of coping has been widely accepted (Latack & Havlovic, 1992), and emphasizes the importance of what people actually *do* to cope or deal with a stressful situation, whether it is effective or not. In other words, there is a recognition that people sometimes engage in coping strategies that may actually make matters worse.

For example, when people are confronted with a situation that is potentially harmful or threatening to their well-being they may engage in a range of coping strategies, such as logically analyzing the problem, planning what to do, and doing things that will actually address or remove the problem. These types of strategies all have a focus on dealing with the problem or situation at hand. Additionally, people may also engage in coping strategies such as denying the seriousness of the situation, trying to convince themselves that the problem will go away of its own accord, using relaxation techniques to reduce anxiety or tension, or turning to alcohol, tobacco and other substances to help manage their emotional response. Although, in some circumstances, these strategies may be beneficial in helping people to manage their emotions, they do not manage or deal with the stressful situation. Consequently, when people adopt coping strategies that focus almost exclusively on managing their emotions, the initial problem will not be addressed and may sometimes become worse.

Focusing on what people actual *do* when they attempt to cope or deal with a stressful situation is quite different from the focus that is sometimes placed on the availability of coping resources. Coping resources can be defined as any characteristic of the person or the environment that can be *used* during the coping process. For example, people's levels of self-esteem and their social support networks are resources that could be drawn upon to help them manage or deal with stressful situations (see Kahn & Byosiere, 1992, for a review of the relationship between self-esteem, social support, and occupational stress). In some circumstances, however, people may have access to coping resources that they choose not to use. This highlights the distinguishing feature between coping processes and coping resources. Coping processes refer to what people actually do, rather than the resources that may be available to them. To further emphasize this distinction, it is sometimes helpful to use the term 'coping strategies' instead of coping processes.

The notion that people use a broad range of coping strategies when faced with stressful situations is widely accepted (further information on the types of different coping strategies can be found in Carpenter, 1992; Carver, Scheier & Weintraub, 1989; Zeidner & Endler, 1996). Some research suggests, however, that the extent to which one strategy is used over another varies across situations (e.g., Folkman, Lazarus, Gruen & DeLongis, 1986), and that different types of strategies might be effective as different stages of the stressful situation unfold (e.g., Folkman & Lazarus, 1985). This is consistent with the view that emotion-focused strategies are effective when people have little control over the situation, particularly during the early stages of a stressful situation, and that problem-focused strategies are effective when the situation is amenable to change (Auerbach, 1989). Nevertheless, this view has not always been supported (e.g., Conway & Terry, 1992). Others suggest that the effects of different coping strategies remain much the same, irrespective of the situation. Several studies have found, for example, that the use of problem-focused strategies tends to be adaptive or beneficial to well-being, whilst the use of emotion-focused strategies tends to be maladaptive or harmful to well-being, when used to deal with a broad range of stressful situations (e.g., Headey & Wearing, 1990; Holahan & Moos, 1986). Again, these findings have not always been replicated (e.g., Bolger, 1990).

These apparent discrepancies may well demonstrate the complexity of the coping process, as well as the infancy of the coping literature (Folkman, 1992). For example, there are problems associated with the conceptualization and measurement of coping (Stone, Kennedy-Moore, Newman, Greenberg & Neale, 1992; Zeidner & Endler, 1996), as well as an ongoing debate regarding the extent to which coping is either a trait or a state (e.g., Bolger, 1990; McCrae & Costa, 1986; Terry, 1994). Moreover, occupational stress research has tended to focus on coping strategies that were initially identified through studies in the areas of clinical and health psychology (e.g., avoidance, denial, logical analysis, wishful thinking). It is possible, however, that in the area of occupational stress, it would be more appropriate to take a broader approach, and include job skills, training, and knowledge as part of the coping repertoire that employees can draw upon when dealing with stressful situations. Notwithstanding the need to resolve these issues, it is clear that when faced with a stressful situation, the outcome of the coping process will influence people's subsequent appraisal (referred to as *reappraisal*) of their environmental conditions (Lazarus, 1990) and, ultimately, their adaptational outcomes (Bolger, 1990). Since the effects of coping are always mediated through appraisal, however, cognition is considered the linchpin that 'actively negotiates' between a person and his or her experience of the environment (Lazarus, 1993, p. 6).

The Dynamic Equilibrium Theory of Stress

Although the cognitive-relational approach has been one of the dominant theories of stress since the early 1980s, it has been called into question for discounting the role that enduring personality characteristics (Costa & McCrae, 1990) and emotions

(Worrall & May, 1989) play in the stress process (cf. Lazarus, 1993). The dynamic equilibrium theory of stress proposed by Hart et al. (1993, 1994; cf. Headey & Wearing, 1989) deals with these concerns by integrating the perceived quality-of-life literature (e.g., Headey & Wearing, 1992) with the cognitive-relational approach. According to the dynamic equilibrium theory, stress results from a broad system of variables that include personality (e.g., Costa & McCrae, 1980) and environmental (Michela, Lukaszewski & Allegrante, 1995) characteristics, coping processes (e.g., Bolger, 1990), positive and negative experiences (e.g., Hart, 1994; Kanner et al., 1981), and various indices of psychological well-being (e.g., Diener, 2000; George, 1996). As noted by Lazarus (1990), stress cannot be located in any one of these variables. Rather, stress occurs when a state of disequilibrium exists within the system of variables relating people to their environments, and only when this state of disequilibrium brings about change in people's normal (i.e., equilibrium) levels of psychological well-being. This suggests that stress is a relatively abstract construct that cannot be assessed directly. Instead, stress can only be understood by assessing a complex system of variables, and establishing how these variables relate to one another over time.

Drawing on a considerable body of empirical evidence, it is argued that separate positive and negative affectivity paths underpin the relations that link the stable (trait) and situational (state) components of these variables (Hart et al., 1995; cf. George, 1996). The terms positive and negative affectivity refer to the general emotional orientation that appears to underpin these variables. It has been shown, for example, that the enduring personality constructs of neuroticism and extraversion are related to life experiences (Headey & Wearing, 1989; Magnus, Diener, Fujita & Pavot, 1993), coping processes (Bolger, 1990; McCrae & Costa, 1986), and perceived quality-of-life indices (Costa & McCrae, 1980). Different patterns of association often emerge, with neuroticism correlating more strongly with negative life experiences, emotion-focused coping, and indices of psychological distress (e.g., negative affect), while extraversion correlates more strongly with positive experiences, problem-focused coping, and indices of well-being (e.g., positive affect).

These findings demonstrate that neuroticism and extraversion are more than a mere methodological nuisance (Spector, Fox & Van Katwyk, 1999; Williams, Gavin & Williams, 1996). They are an informative and important part of the process that enables people to interpret and respond to their environment. Since neuroticism and extraversion are almost completely stable over long periods of time (Costa & McCrae, 1989), it follows, as a logical consequence of their links with life experiences, coping processes, and indices of psychological well-being, that these constructs must also exhibit a degree of temporal stability that can be predicted on the basis of a person's personality characteristics (Hart, 1999; Headey & Wearing, 1989; Staw & Ross, 1985). This implies that each of these constructs has a stable (equilibrium) and situational (change from equilibrium) component.

Moreover, enduring personality characteristics determine, in part, the psychological meaning that a person may ascribe to an event (Brief, Butcher, George & Link, 1993). This does not mean that people's subjective experience of their environments and their coping processes are necessarily benign or mere reflections of personality. Several studies have shown that coping processes (e.g., Bolger, 1990), life experiences (e.g., Headey & Wearing, 1989), and daily work and nonwork experiences (e.g., Hart, 1999) make additional contributions to psychological well-being.

The dynamic equilibrium theory has important implications for the way in which occupational stress is viewed. For example, it is commonly believed, by researchers and the lay community alike, that police are among the most stressed of all occupational groups (e.g., Gaines & Jermier, 1983); a view that is intuitively appealing given the dangerous and unsavory aspects of police work that are portrayed in the media. According to the dynamic equilibrium theory, however, a police officer may dislike some aspects of their work, such as attending a fatal road accident or dealing with traumatized victims, but this does not necessarily mean that the tasks are, in themselves, stressful. When confronted with these 'unsavory' aspects of police work, an officer may report feeling anxious or find it difficult to cope with the experience. Given that stress is sometimes viewed as an imbalance between perceived demands and the ability to cope with those demands (Cox, 1978; Lazarus, 1990; McGrath, 1970), and often assessed in occupational settings with anxiety or other psychological distress measures (Newton, 1989), these experiences would generally be considered stressful. The dynamic equilibrium theory of stress suggests, however, that these scenarios cannot be construed as 'stressful' unless the experiences represent a deviation from the officer's normal pattern of experiences *and* they bring about change in his or her equilibrium levels of psychological well-being. It is a reasonable and normal reaction for police, as with any other occupational group, to report feeling uncomfortable or express difficulty with some aspects of their work. This, in itself, however, is not sufficient to infer that a police officer is experiencing stress or that police work is necessarily stressful. In fact, there is some evidence to suggest that the levels of psychological well-being among police officers are generally more favorable than those reported for other occupational groups (Hart et al., 1995) and, like many other occupational groups, police officers' levels of psychological well-being are determined more by nonwork, rather than the work domains of their lives (Hart, 1999).

TOWARD AN ORGANIZATIONAL HEALTH FRAMEWORK

One of the key strengths of the dynamic equilibrium theory of stress is that it can be applied to all domains of an employee's life. This has considerable benefit, for example, in helping to guide research into the relationship between the work and nonwork domains of employees' lives (e.g., Hart, 1999). However, one of the main limitations of an occupational stress theory that applies to all domains of an employee's life, is that it can become incidental to the mainstream work psychology literature. In other words, it may lead to occupational stress being viewed as a topic that is primarily concerned with general health issues, rather than a topic that is integrally linked to the ongoing viability and profitability of work organizations. This is a serious problem facing many of the approaches to occupational stress, and we believe that one of the ways to address this problem is to focus more attention on the concept of organizational health.

The concept of organizational health differs from many of the traditional approaches to occupational stress in two important ways. First, it emphasizes the need to simultaneously focus on employee well-being and an organization's 'bottom-line' (Cox, 1992; Griffin, Hart & Wilson-Evered, 2000). By 'bottom-line' we mean the performance of an organization in terms of its financial, social, and environmental responsibilities. Ultimately, its performance in these areas will affect its ongoing health and viability as a business or work organization. A fundamental requirement for most organizations that wish to improve their 'bottom-line,' however, is the need to develop appropriate structures and processes that will reduce occupational stress and, at the same time, enhance employee satisfaction and performance. From this viewpoint, the organizational health perspective recognizes the fact that having happy and satisfied employees is of little value to an organization unless employees are also performing efficiently and productively. Likewise, having an efficient and productive organization is of little value if this is achieved at the expense of employee well-being. Although this view is intuitively appealing, research and practice in the area of occupational stress has rarely focused simultaneously on employee well-being *and* organizational performance (cf. Wright & Cropanzano, 2000b).

Second, the organizational health perspective recognizes that employee well-being and organizational performance are both influenced by a

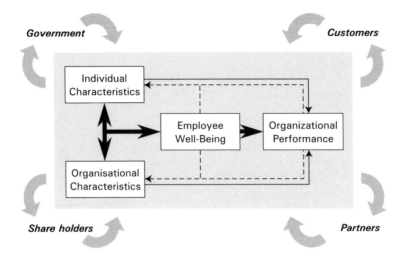

Figure 5.1   *A heuristic model of organizational health*

combination of individual and organizational characteristics. This view is consistent with a range of studies that have linked personality (e.g., Barrick & Mount, 1991), coping processes (e.g., Judge, Thoresen, Pucik & Welbourne, 1999), organizational climate (Michela et al., 1995), and work experiences (e.g., Hart et al., 1995), to various indices of psychological well-being and performance. In fact, a range of different individual and organizational characteristics has been included in the major process theories of occupational stress (e.g., Cooper, 1998). The emphasis placed on organizational characteristics, however, means that the organizational health perspective requires the development of multilevel approaches to occupational stress. This is an important departure from traditional approaches to occupational stress, given that it is typically conceptualized at the individual level of analysis.

The organizational health approach to occupational stress is shown diagrammatically in Figure 5.1. As indicated by this diagram, we believe that individual and organizational factors contribute to employee well-being, which in turn, contributes to organizational performance. Individual and organizational characteristics also have a direct link to organizational performance. The model also allows for a number of reciprocal relationships or feedback loops. For example, there is a reciprocal relationship between individual and organizational characteristics. By 'organizational characteristics' we mean both the objective aspects of an organization's environment (e.g., resources and structure), as well as employees' subjective experience of that environment (e.g., organizational climate and work experiences). By 'individual characteristics' we mean those factors that are typically associated with

individual differences among employees, such as their personalities and coping processes, as well as their individual attitudes and behaviors. Given these broad definitions, it is reasonable to assume that there would be some reciprocity in the relationship between individual and organizational characteristics (e.g., Headey et al., 1985).

It is also necessary to include feedback loops from employee well-being and organizational performance to individual and organizational characteristics. For example, the cognitive-relational theory of stress uses the concepts of primary, secondary, and reappraisal to explain the continual interplay between how a person might feel at any given point in time, and the way in which they will perceive and respond to their environment (Lazarus & Folkman, 1984). Moreover, it is quite feasible that an organization's performance will influence the quality of its work environment, as well as the attitudes and behaviors of its employees.

The organizational health model shown in Figure 5.1 also shows that the relationship between individual and organizational characteristics on the one hand, and employee well-being and performance on the other, operates in a broader context. The nature of this broader context varies, depending on the level of analysis that is applied to the core elements of the model. For example, if the core elements of the model were applied to a particular work team, then the policies and practices of the wider organization will form part of the context in which the work team must operate. If the core elements of the model were applied to the organization as a whole, however, then other factors, such as government policies, regulatory authorities, and the marketplace, will make up the broader context in which the organization operates. At another level again, if the core elements of the model were applied to a series of organizations or occupational groups in a particular country, then factors, such as ethnicity, culture, and globalization, become an important part of the context in which these organizations or occupational groups operate.

One of the pitfalls with the model shown in Figure 5.1 is that it can be seen as providing an overly simplistic view of occupational stress. However, we believe that it is important to distinguish between macro and micro approaches to the study of occupational stress. The main strength of the organizational health model shown in Figure 5.1 is that it provides a broad (i.e., macro) theoretical framework that can be used to guide research and practice in the area of occupational stress. For example, this model has been used extensively over the past decade to guide the development of policies and programs aimed at reducing occupational stress and improving performance in a wide variety of Australian private and public sector organizations (e.g., Griffin et al., 2000; Hart, Griffin, Wearing & Cooper, 1996). Similar work has also occurred in other countries and cultural settings (Murphy & Cooper, 2000; Williams & Cooper, 1994).

Moreover, the organizational health framework can be used to guide theory-driven research that (a) helps to unify the different, and often competing, approaches to the study of occupational stress, (b) encourages the development of stronger links between the study of occupational stress and other areas of work psychology, and (c) leads to occupational stress research that demonstrates a clear link to 'bottom-line' performance and, therefore, has greater relevance to work organizations. This framework also enables research to be conducted at a very broad (i.e., macro) or relatively specific (i.e., micro) level. For example, it is possible to address broad research questions about the relationships among the four core elements shown diagrammatically in Figure 5.1, or to focus on any one of these elements and address questions such as the one recently posed by Kasl (1998) about the need to develop a taxonomy of relevant organizational characteristics.

Although the organizational health approach to occupational stress was first introduced during the late 1980s (Cox, 1988), the concept has received relatively little empirical attention. For example, a search of the PsychLit database showed that only 48 scientific articles have been published during the 1990s and indexed with the term 'organizational health.' There have also been relatively few books published on the topic (cf. Cooper & Williams, 1994; Murphy & Cooper, 2000). Nevertheless, there has been considerable research in the occupational stress, quality of life, and broader work psychology literatures that can be used to inform our current understanding of the organizational health model, and identify the key issues that need to be addressed in future research.

Structure of Employee Well-Being

One of the first issues that must be addressed in order to understand the organizational health framework is to develop a coherent model that defines the components and structure of employee well-being. It is necessary, for example, to develop a model that includes cognitive and affective components, positive and negative components, as well as individual and group components. By understanding how each of these components relates to the broader construct of employee well-being, we will be in a much better position to develop and test theories about the causes and consequences of organizational health.

With some notable exceptions (e.g., Burke, Brief, George, Roberson & Webster, 1989), the structure of employee well-being has received little empirical attention in the occupational stress and work psychology literatures. Quality-of-life researchers, however, have long been interested in the structure of psychological well-being (e.g., Diener, 2000), and their efforts can be used to inform our understanding of employee well-being. In the quality-of-life literature, for example, it is generally accepted that psychological well-being includes both affective and cognitive components. The affective component is often characterized by the two broad dimensions of positive and negative affect (Watson, 1988), whereas the cognitive component is associated with life satisfaction and satisfaction with various life domains (Pavot & Diener, 1993).

Since the early work of Bradburn (1969), perceived quality-of-life researchers have made a distinction between the positive and negative dimensions of psychological well-being. Strong empirical support has been found for the notion that a person's emotional experience can be explained by the two conceptually independent dimensions of positive and negative affect (Agho et al., 1992; Diener & Emmons, 1985; Headey & Wearing, 1992; Watson & Tellegen, 1985). Positive affect is a pleasurable emotional state characterized by terms such as enthusiasm, energy, mental alertness, and determination, whereas negative affect refers to the subjective experience of distress and includes emotional states such as anger, anxiety, fear, guilt, and nervousness (Watson, 1988).

Although job satisfaction has sometimes been equated with positive affect (e.g., Edwards, 1992), a growing number of work-related studies have called this view into question and support the quality-of-life literature. For example, Agho et al. (1992) found that job satisfaction was distinct from dispositional measures of positive and negative affect. Brief and Roberson (1989) investigated the extent to which three different measures of job satisfaction were affectively or cognitively laden, and found that one of the most commonly used job satisfaction questionnaires, the Minnesota

Satisfaction Questionnaire (Weiss et al., 1967), was predominantly cognitive in nature. More recently, Hart (1994, 1999) found empirical support for the notion that people make a judgment about their overall levels of job satisfaction by weighing up their good and bad experiences. These findings are consistent with the fact that job satisfaction is typically measured on scales that range from 'extremely dissatisfied' to 'extremely satisfied', and as such, embrace both positive and negative dimensions.

The tendency for people to respond more toward the positive end of job satisfaction scales may have tempted some researchers to equate job satisfaction with positive affect (e.g., Edwards, 1992). Job satisfaction, however, is actually an umbrella construct that refers to the summary judgments that employees make about how satisfied they are with their positive and negative experiences. Given that job satisfaction differs conceptually and empirically from positive affect, it is not appropriate to distinguish between psychological distress and job satisfaction when investigating the positive and negative dimensions of employees' well-being. The bipolar nature of job satisfaction means that it will be confounded to some extent with measures of psychological distress, rather than forming an independent positive dimension. A more appropriate distinction can be made between psychological distress and morale.

Smith (1966) has referred to morale as a group phenomenon that exists when there is persistence and energy, enthusiastic striving, cohesion, and cooperation. Although morale is often viewed as a group phenomenon, a growing number of researchers recognize that the individual experience of morale is psychologically more meaningful (Doherty, 1988; Evans, 1992; Lazarus & Folkman, 1984). Taking this phenomenological approach, Hart, Wearing, Conn, Carter & Dingle (2000) defined morale as the energy, enthusiasm, team spirit, and pride that employees experience as a result of their work. These adjectives mirror Smith's description of morale, and are similar to those used by Watson (1988) in defining positive affect. In terms of our understanding about the structure of employee well-being, the concepts of psychological distress and morale can be considered analogous to positive and negative affect, in that they represent the aversive and pleasurable emotional states that people experience as a result of their work (Hart, 1994). Accordingly, we believe that the concepts of job satisfaction, psychological distress, and morale form a three-dimensional model of employee well-being that is consistent with the views held in the quality-of-life literature.

In terms of developing a coherent model of employee well-being, however, it is important to focus attention on the appropriate level of analysis. For example, George (1990) introduced the concept

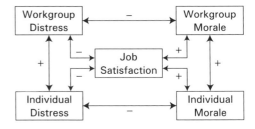

Figure 5.2   *A model of employee well-being ('+' indicates a positive relationship; '−' indicates a negative relationship)*

of group affective tone. This was based on the premise that between-group differences could be found in employees' aggregate levels of affect. However, George's approach to group affective tone was largely a methodological one, in which individual affect scores were aggregated to provide a group level variable. This means that group affective tone was merely an aggregation of how the individual employees in a workgroup actually felt.

At a conceptual level, however, we believe that it is the experience of group affective tone that is more meaningful to employees. In other words, rather than merely aggregating the way in which individual employees feel in themselves, group affective tone should be conceptualized as an employee's experience of the emotional tone of his or her particular workgroup. As demonstrated by Griffin et al. (2000), for example, it is meaningful to distinguish between the levels of energy and enthusiasm that individual employees actually feel in themselves, and the extent to which they believe there is a sense of energy and enthusiasm among their workgroup. Although this means that employees in the same workgroup could experience group affective tone differently, we expect that it would operate much more like a group level variable (i.e., greater between-group variance) than would a simple aggregation of individual employees' levels of affect. From this perspective, it is possible to conceive of psychological distress and morale as operating at two levels of analysis (e.g., Hart et al., 1996). This is shown diagrammatically in Figure 5.2.

As shown in Figure 5.2, we believe that occupational well-being has five core components. First, there are individual morale and individual distress, which operate at the individual level of analysis, and are akin to definitions of positive and negative affect. Second, there are workgroup morale and workgroup distress, which operate more at the group level of analysis, and refer to employees' experience of the workgroup's positive and negative emotional tone. Although these are not entirely group-level variables, we would expect to find considerably more between-group variation in workgroup distress and workgroup morale, than we would in individual distress and individual morale (cf. Van Yperen & Snijders, 2000). Moreover, we would expect the individual and workgroup variables to have different causes and consequences. For example, we would expect team- and workgroup-oriented variables (e.g., organizational climate) to have a stronger influence on workgroup distress and morale, but individual difference variables (e.g., personality) to have a stronger influence on individual distress and morale. Third, job satisfaction is a cognitively oriented variable that reflects employees' judgments about how satisfied they are with their current work situation. This component of employee well-being is viewed as a summary judgment that results from the positive and negative emotional experiences associated with an employees work. It also reflects employees' individual experiences and their experience of the workgroup's emotional tone.

Organizational Characteristics

The distinctions we have made in our proposed model of employee well-being between the cognitive and emotionally laden variables, the positive and negative emotionally oriented variables, as well as between the individual and group-level variables, can also be applied to the way in which we think about organizational characteristics. For example, a long-standing criticism of the occupational stress literature is that there has been a reliance on emotionally laden constructs when investigating the relationship between organizational stressors and psychological distress (Brief, Burke, George, Robinson & Webster, 1988; Kasl & Rapp, 1991). This criticism could, in part, be dealt with by focusing on the cognitively oriented construct of organizational climate (Schneider, 1990). This raises questions, however, about the nature of the relationship between organizational climate and organizational stressors.

Turning first to the concept of *stressors*, this is an emotionally laden concept that reflects the attributions employees make about the source of their distress. Stressors can refer to a wide variety of environmental conditions or situations that affect the well-being of employees (Hurrell et al., 1998). When completing a stressors scale, for example, employees are typically asked to consider a number of organizational or job characteristics and to rate the level of distress that has been associated with each characteristic (e.g., Karasek, Brisson, Kawakami, Houtman, Bongers & Amick, 1998; Williams & Cooper, 1998). The vast majority of occupational stress studies have focused on chronic

stressors. These can be defined as the sources of distress that persist over long periods of time (e.g., problematic leadership styles, communication difficulties, conflict with coworkers, and difficulties balancing home and work life). Although the concept of daily hassles has typically been viewed differently (Wheaton, 1994), recent evidence suggests that daily work hassles also tend to be enduring over time and, therefore, operate much like chronic stressors (Hart, 1999). Other common approaches to the concept of stressors have included a focus on acute, critical or traumatic events (e.g., Anshel, Robertson & Caputi, 1997; Sewell, 1983), and an emphasis on concepts such as role ambiguity, role conflict, and role overload (e.g., Beehr, 1995; Jackson & Schuler, 1985). Moreover, a distinction has often been made between the generic stressors that are relevant to most occupational groups and the stressors that are peculiar to the occupational group under investigation (Hart et al., 1994).

The different approaches to the conceptualization of stressors share one thing in common. They all focus on the negative work experiences that are believed to influence employee well-being. This common theme fails to recognize, however, that positive experiences also play a role. According to the cognitive-relational theory of stress, for example, employees can appraise their environmental conditions or situations in either positive (i.e., potentially beneficial to well-being) or negative (i.e., potentially harmful to well-being) terms (DeLongis et al., 1988; Lazarus & Folkman, 1984). This view is consistent with several studies in the quality-of-life literature showing that positive and negative life events make independent contributions to people's overall levels of psychological well-being (e.g., Headey & Wearing, 1989).

The role of positive work experiences has received little empirical attention in the occupational stress literature. Nevertheless, there is some evidence to suggest that positive and negative work experiences are largely uncorrelated, and contribute differently to employee well-being. It has been found, for example, that negative work experiences tend to contribute to indices of psychological distress, but not to morale, whereas positive work experiences tend to contribute to morale, but not to psychological distress (Hart, 1994; Hart et al., 1995). It has also been found that positive and negative work experiences contribute independently, and sometimes equally, to employees' levels of job satisfaction (Hart, 1999). These results demonstrate the importance of taking into account both positive and negative experiences when investigating the determinants of employee well-being.

Another theme that is common to the different conceptualizations of stressors, is that an emphasis has often been placed on organizational experiences (e.g., Hurrell et al., 1998; Sauter & Murphy, 1995). This may reflect the fact that general organizational experiences, such as those associated with leadership, coworker relations, decision making, and goal setting, are relevant to employees in most work organizations. It may also reflect the view, however, that organizational experiences influence employee well-being much more than stressors that are peculiar to the job or occupational group under investigation. This view has even been supported in reputedly high-stress occupations such as police work (e.g., Hart et al., 1995) and teaching (e.g., Borg, 1990), which highlights the central role of organizational climate (e.g., Griffin et al., 2000; Hemingway & Smith, 1999; Michela et al., 1995).

Organizational climate refers to the perceptions that employees have about the way in which their organization functions (James & McIntyre, 1996). As noted by Griffin et al. (2000), this means that organizational climate has two components. It involves the organizational structures and processes that are part of everyday organizational activity, as well as individual employees' perceptions of these activities. We believe that one of the key differences between organizational climate and organizational stressors, however, is that perceptions of organizational climate do not have an emotional overtone. In other words, organizational climate is not related to how people feel about their organizational experiences. It is merely a judgment or description about what is happening in the organization (Hart et al., 2000). This is why we believe that organizational climate is a cognitively, rather than emotionally oriented variable.

Moreover, organizational climate can be used at the individual and group levels of analysis (Schneider, 1990). It is reasonable to expect that the focus on organizational structures and processes will mean that organizational climate has clear between group differences. This is consistent with the view that individual difference variables, such as personality, will have a stronger influence on organizational stressors than on perceptions of organizational climate. This is largely due to the fact that the concept of organizational stressors has a strong emotional overtone, and considerable evidence suggests that this emotional component is influenced, to a large extent, by personality characteristics, such as neuroticism (e.g., Costa & McCrae, 1990).

Given that there are meaningful differences between organizational climate and organizational stressors, we believe that it is important to include both in the study of occupational stress (e.g., Hemingway & Smith, 1999). It is also important, however, to focus on employees' positive *and* negative emotionally laden experiences. Accordingly, we believe that there are three core components that underpin employees' organizational experiences, and that each of these components will relate differently to indices of employee well-being. Although there has been substantial research into the role of negative emotionally laden experiences (i.e., stressors), relatively little research has been conducted into the role of positive emotionally laden experiences and organizational climate. Moreover, little has been done to establish a taxonomy of the types of organizational experiences that should be included as part of these three core constructs (Kasl, 1998).

Personal Characteristics

There are a number of different personal characteristics that are relevant to the organizational health model shown in Figure 5.1. For example, a large volume of literature exists about the direct, indirect, and moderating effects that coping (e.g., Cartwright & Cooper, 1996; De Rijk, Le Blanc, Schaufeli & de Jonge, 1998), locus of control (e.g., Spector, 1998), hardiness (Cox & Ferguson, 1991), Type A Behavior (e.g., Ganster, 1987; Lee, Ashford & Jamieson, 1993), and self-esteem (Jex & Elacqua, 1999) have on the stressors and strain relationship (Kahn & Byosiere, 1992). One area that has received little empirical attention, however, is the role of the Big Five personality characteristics (Costa & McCrae, 1989). The Big Five has become a dominant theme in the personality literature, and provides an integrated framework that can be used to examine the role that dispositional factors play in determining organizational health. The Big Five refers to the personality characteristics of neuroticism, extraversion, openness, agreeableness, and conscientiousness. In the occupational stress literature, there has been considerable interest in the role of neuroticism (also known as dispositional negative affectivity, Costa & McCrae, 1990) and, to a lesser extent, extraversion, but there has been very little interest in the role of openness, agreeableness, and conscientiousness.

Neuroticism refers to a person's tendency to focus on the negative aspects of themselves and his or her environment (Costa & McCrae, 1989). It has also been referred to as a mood-dispositional dimension that reflects a person's tendency to experience negative emotions (Watson, 1988). It is not surprising, therefore, that strong relationships have been found between neuroticism and other variables, such as coping, negative work experiences (i.e., stressors), and various indices of psychological distress (e.g., Hart et al., 1995; Moyle, 1995). The strength of these relationships has raised concerns about whether neuroticism is merely a methodological nuisance or really has substantive effects (Burke et al., 1993; Spector et al., 1999; Williams et al., 1996). This is a difficult question that is still yet to be resolved. Nevertheless, it is important to control for neuroticism in any studies that are concerned with establishing the relationships between negative emotionally laden variables (Brief et al., 1989; Costa & McCrae, 1990). This is necessary to ensure that reported relationships do in fact exist, and are not merely a methodological or substantive artefact of neuroticism or dispositional negative affectivity.

Extraversion refers to a person's tendency to be active, talkative, person-oriented, optimistic, fun-loving, and affectionate (Costa & McCrae, 1989). In general terms, it can be characterized by three related, but separate components. These include the extent to which a person prefers to engage in social interaction (e.g., gregariousness), the extent to which a person is predisposed to display interpersonal warmth (e.g., empathy), as well as the extent to which a person tends to have a positive outlook and experience positive emotions (e.g., positive affectivity). This does not mean, however, that extraversion and dispositional positive affectivity are the same constructs. Although positive affectivity is a component of extraversion, extraversion is considered to be a much broader construct that includes aspects of gregariousness and interpersonal warmth.

As noted earlier in this chapter, a considerable body of research in the quality-of-life literature has shown that extraversion is related to problem-focused coping, positive life experiences, and indices of psychological well-being (e.g., Headey & Wearing, 1989; Magnus et al., 1993). Similar results have also been found in occupational stress studies (Hart, 1999; Hart et al., 1995; cf. George, 1996). Overall, this body of evidence suggests that extraversion should be included as a matter of routine in occupational stress studies that are concerned with establishing the relationships between positive emotionally laden variables. As with the negative affectivity literature, however, a question remains as to whether the influence of extraversion is methodological or substantive in nature.

The role of agreeableness, openness, and conscientiousness in determining employee well-being is less clear. It is possible to theorize about potential relationships, but the paucity of empirical evidence means that it is difficult to argue a firm position. For example, agreeableness refers to a person's predisposition to be compliant and cooperative, as well as being someone who is easy to get along with (Costa & McCrae, 1989). Accordingly, people who tend to be more agreeable may experience less conflict with their supervisors and coworkers. If this were the case, it is likely that they would experience a more positive organizational climate, fewer interpersonal stressors and, ultimately, better levels of well-being (Michela et al., 1995).

Employees who are high on openness tend to be open to new ideas and experiences (Costa & McCrae, 1989). This may predispose them to participate in meetings or volunteer to serve on committees. However, employees who are high on openness also tend to be dreamy and artistic. In some contexts, these attributes may not be valued or may even be actively discouraged. In these circumstances, employees who exhibit more openness behaviors may feel uncomfortable and withdraw from work situations that involve meetings or committees. This may result in less favorable views about organizational climate and, subsequently, poorer levels of well-being.

There is some evidence to suggest that conscientiousness is more likely to be related to performance than to employee well-being (Barrick & Mount, 1991; Miller, Griffin & Hart, 1999). However, this could be due to the fact that employee well-being has generally been equated with job satisfaction and psychological distress. By including the concept of morale in definitions of employee well-being, it may be possible to find stronger links with conscientiousness. Employees' enthusiasm for their work is one of the key components of morale (Hart et al., 2000; Organ, 1997). Moreover, conscientiousness refers to a predisposition to be dutiful, dedicated, thorough, and persistent (Costa & McCrae, 1989). It is possible that employees who display these characteristics are more likely to be enthusiastically engaged in their work.

It is apparent that the Big Five personality characteristics are likely to play an important role in the organizational health framework shown in Figure 5.1. Some characteristics, such as neuroticism and extraversion, are more likely to influence employee well-being, whereas other characteristics, such as conscientiousness, are more likely to contribute to organizational performance. Nevertheless, there is relatively little empirical evidence in the occupational stress literature about the role of the Big Five personality characteristics. Moreover, it is not known whether the Big Five personality characteristics provide additional predictive power, or merely account for the effects of other personality constructs such as Type A Behavior, locus of control, and self-esteem, in determining employee well-being.

Organizational Performance

In terms of the organizational health framework, the notion of organizational performance should be considered quite broadly. Relatively few occupational stress theories have explicitly addressed the relationship between employee well-being and performance, with most theories focusing on ill-health as the ultimate outcome (e.g., Cooper, 1998). It is generally assumed, however, that ill-health results in substantial cost to work organizations through sickness absence, medical expenses, and lost productivity. These potential outcomes of occupational stress are highly relevant to the organizational health framework, because they can have a substantial affect on an organization's 'bottom-line.' Human resources often account for a large part of an organization's cost structure in delivering its products and services, and any substantial increase in these costs can adversely affect the ongoing viability and profitability of the organization. Unfortunately, there is relatively little empirical evidence in the occupational stress literature to demonstrate a causal relationship between employee well-being and the types of outcomes that affect the 'bottom-line' of work organizations.

A promising area of research that may help to provide a stronger link between employee well-being and performance is the work currently being undertaken in the area of contextual performance. Contextual performance refers to the discretionary behaviors that are not formally required of employees, but are necessary for the overall success of the organization (e.g., Motowidlo & Van Scotter, 1994). These behaviors are related to the concepts of prosocial organizational behavior (Brief & Motowidlo, 1986) extra-role behavior (Katz & Kahn, 1978), and organizational citizenship behavior (Bateman & Organ, 1983), and include activities such as volunteering to carry out tasks, cooperating with coworkers, exerting effort, and promoting the organization to others. These behaviors are under the volitional control of employees, and are likely to be influenced by employees' levels of morale (George & Brief, 1992). This suggests that rather than trying to establish a link between psychological distress and performance, it will be more fruitful to explore the link between performance and morale.

Accordingly, by integrating the concepts of psychological distress, job satisfaction, and morale into a broader model of employee well-being, it may be possible for occupational stress researchers and practitioners to demonstrate a strong link between employees' levels of well-being and organizational performance (cf. Wright & Cropanzano, 2000b). This link may best be achieved, however, by focusing on a broad range of organizational performance indicators, including discretionary behaviors such as contextual performance, as well as behaviors that are directly related to the cost of human resources (e.g., sickness absence, turnover, medical expenses, and legal compensation claims for stress-related injury). In this way, researchers and practitioners will be better placed to demonstrate that occupational stress plays an important role in determining the overall success of work organizations.

TESTING THE ORGANIZATIONAL HEALTH FRAMEWORK

There are many different ways in which research into the organizational health framework can be carried forward. One possible way is through the research model shown in Figure 5.3. Although this model integrates many of the key variables that have been discussed throughout this chapter, it is not meant to represent an exhaustive list of occupational stress variables, nor do we intend it to reflect all of the variables that are considered central to the organizational health framework. Its main purpose is to serve as a heuristic model that illustrates how we can generate and test competing hypotheses about organizational health.

The model draws on the cognitive-relational (e.g., Lazarus & Folkman, 1984) and dynamic equilibrium (e.g., Hart, 1999) theories of stress, as well as our earlier discussion about the structure of employee well-being and organizational experiences. The traditional stressors and strain approach is also embedded within this model, but in its most elementary form, can be explained by just two of the 16 variables (i.e., negative work experiences and distress). This demonstrates how limiting the stressors and strain approach has become in helping us to understand the causes and consequences of occupational stress.

The model suggests that organizational climate plays a central role in determining employee well-being (Griffin et al., 2000; Michela et al., 1995). This reflects the view that employees will engage in coping processes when exposed to the conditions and situations in their organizational environments. Moreover, the organizational environment and employees' coping processes will influence the way in which employees appraise their work experiences in positive or negative terms (Hart et al., 1995). This is consistent with Lazarus's (1990) view that coping processes influence people's reappraisal of their environmental conditions, and that measures of positive and negative experiences (e.g., hassles and uplifts; Hart, 1999) reflect these reappraisals, rather than the initial conditions or situations that triggered the coping response. It is the organizational environment, as well as employees' positive and negative experiences associated with this environment that, ultimately, influences employee well-being (Hemingway & Smith, 1999). The model also reflects the positive and negative affectivity paths that are typically thought to underpin the relationships between neuroticism, emotion-focused coping, negative work experiences, and distress, on the one hand, and extraversion, problem-focused coping, positive work experiences, and morale, on the other (e.g., Costa & McCrae, 1980; Hart, 1999; Headey & Wearing, 1992; cf. George, 1996). Although no specific links

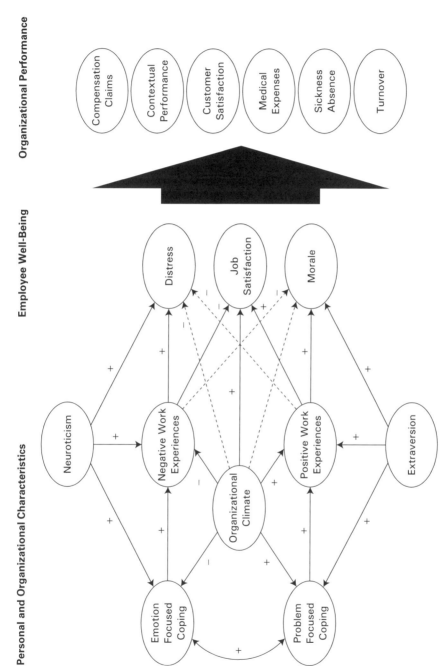

Figure 5.3   *Example of an organizational health research model ('+' indicates a positive relationship; '−'indicates a negative relationship. Dotted lines indicate possible relationships that are expected to be comparatively weak.)*

to organizational performance have been specified, the model allows for this possibility. Based on our discussions throughout this chapter, the following propositions can be made about this model.

P1:   Employee well-being includes both cognitive and emotional components, with the emotional component being further divided into separate positive and negative dimensions.

P2:   The emotional component of employee well-being operates at the individual and workgroup levels of analysis.

P3:   Employee well-being influences organizational performance.

P4:   Positive and negative work experiences operate independently to determine employees' levels of well-being, with negative work experiences having a stronger influence on distress and positive work experiences having a stronger influence on morale.

P5:   Positive and negative work experiences contribute equally to job satisfaction.

P6:   Organizational climate contributes equally to employees' positive and negative work experiences.

P7:   Organizational climate operates at the individual and workgroup levels of analysis.

P8:   Coping processes partially mediate the relationship between organizational climate and employee's positive and negative work experiences.

P9:   Emotion-focused coping contributes to negative work experiences and problem-focused coping contributes to positive work experiences.

P10:   Employees will engage in both emotion-focused and problem-focused coping processes to manage or deal with the conditions and situations in their organizational environment.

P11:   Neuroticism contributes to emotion-focused coping, negative work experiences, and distress, whereas extraversion contributes to problem-focused coping, positive work experiences and morale.

P12:   Neuroticism, extraversion, and organizational climate will exhibit more temporal stability than coping processes, positive and negative work experiences, and indices of employee well-being.

P13:   Employee well-being, positive and negative work experiences, and coping processes will have both stable (i.e., equilibrium) and situational (i.e., deviations from equilibrium) components.

P14:   Employees' equilibrium levels of well-being can be explained by enduring personality characteristics, such as neuroticism and extraversion, and enduring characteristics of the organizational environment, as well as

by their equilibrium patterns of work experiences and coping processes.

P15:   Employees' normal (i.e., equilibrium) levels of well-being can change, either positively or negatively, if a change occurs in their normal patterns of work experiences and coping processes.

P16:   Stress occurs when there is a state of disequilibrium between employee well-being, work experiences, coping processes, and enduring personal and organizational characteristics, provided that this state of disequilibrium brings about change, either positively or negatively, in the employee's normal levels of well-being.

P17:   Stress cannot be expressed as a single variable.

P18:   It is a normal and inevitable part of daily work life for employees to experience some degree of distress, and to dislike certain conditions and situations in their environment, but this does not necessarily mean that they are experiencing stress.

P19:   Day-to-day fluctuations in employee well-being, work experiences, and coping processes are a normal part of day-to-day work life, and do not, in themselves, imply that an employee is stressed.

These propositions reflect a particular theoretical position that has been taken in relation to the model shown in Figure 5.3. We acknowledge, however, that in many cases alternate viewpoints can be argued. Also, we have not referred to other variables that we believe are important in helping us to understand occupational stress, nor have we addressed the potential moderating and interaction effects that may apply to this system of variables. It is our intention, however, that these propositions illustrate one potential starting point for theory-driven research that lends itself to a traditional hypothesis-testing approach. Moreover, these propositions highlight a number of methodological issues that have often been raised in relation to the study of occupational stress.

Methodological Considerations

First, the heuristic model shown in Figure 5.3 highlights the need for more large-scale studies in the area of occupational stress. The number of variables included in this model means that it could only be investigated with relatively large samples. Although it would be possible to examine different sections of the model in isolation, this would raise the possibility of a major limitation. One of the major concerns with nonexperimental methodologies is that it is often difficult, even with longitudinal data, to establish what is a causal, rather than spurious, relationship (Kessler & Greenberg, 1981). This is particularly true when self-report measures are used to investigate variables that have some degree of conceptual overlap. In part, this is the problem that has underpinned much of the concern that has been raised about the negative affectivity bias in occupational stress research (e.g., Brief et al., 1988). Although not completely eliminating the problem, by including all relevant variables in a given study it is possible to minimize this limitation.

Second, in addition to using large samples of employees, consideration must be given to the hierarchical structure of the sample. A number of propositions refer to the possibility of considering variables at different levels of analysis. In order to investigate these propositions, it is necessary to sample sufficient workgroups to provide the necessary power for the planned analyses, as well as sampling sufficient employees within each workgroup to provide accurate estimates of the workgroup variables. This often involves the use of cluster sampling designs (e.g., Van Yperen & Snijders, 2000), which is an approach not often used in the occupational stress literature. The lack of cluster sampling designs is probably due to the fact that the vast majority of occupational stress studies have focused on the individual level of analysis. Moreover, analyzing data at different levels of analysis will require occupational stress researchers to make more use of hierarchical linear modeling techniques (e.g., Klein & Kozlowski, 2000).

Third, many of the propositions about the heuristic model cannot be investigated with cross-sectional data. Some propositions imply causal relations among the variables shown in the model, whereas other propositions refer to issues of stability and change. These propositions can only be investigated with longitudinal data that is obtained from the same employees at different points in time (e.g., Hart, 1999; Kessler & Greenberg, 1981; Schaubroeck, Ganster & Kemmerer, 1996). Moreover, the analysis of longitudinal data, particularly when a large system of nonexperimental variables is involved, ideally requires the use of mathematical modeling procedures, such as structural equation analysis (e.g., Byrne, 1998).

Fourth, the model shown in Figure 5.3 is concerned with the relations among a large system of variables. Accordingly, the proper investigation of these relations will require the use of regression-based statistical procedures, such as multiple regression analysis (e.g., Cohen & Cohen, 1983), structural equation analysis (e.g., Byrne, 1998), and hierarchical linear modeling analysis (e.g., Klein & Kozlowski, 2000). These techniques will provide much greater insight into the nature of a relationship than can typically be obtained from procedures such as the analysis of variance. The value in using regression-based techniques also applies to the investigation of any moderating and interaction effects that may exist among the variables shown

in Figure 5.3. Analysis of variance often requires the variables under investigation to be collapsed (e.g., dichotomized), and this can result in the loss of valuable information. Accordingly, it is often best to use the full range of information available on a set of variables, and to focus on reporting the strength of relationships and the amounts of variance explained by different effects, rather than reporting the results of significance tests that merely show whether or not an effect is present.

Fifth, an investigation of the model shown in Figure 5.3 requires that careful attention be paid to the issue of construct validity. There is a degree of conceptual overlap among many of the variables shown in the model. This type of conceptual confounding has been a source of much criticism in the occupational stress literature (e.g., Burke et al., 1993), and has led some methodologists to call for the use of more 'objective' measures (e.g., Kasl, 1987). It is hard to avoid the fact, however, that occupational stress resides largely in the subjective experience of employees. Nevertheless, the differences among some of the variables shown in Figure 5.3 are based on subtleties in the way they operate over time or across levels of analysis.

For example, neuroticism and distress are both concerned with negative affectivity. The difference between these variables, however, lies in the fact that neuroticism refers to dispositional negative affectivity, whereas distress refers to situational negative affectivity. From an empirical point of view, this can be demonstrated by showing that other situational variables contribute to distress, once the effects of neuroticism have been taken into account, and that neuroticism and distress differ in terms of the temporal stability that can be observed in these variables over time. Likewise, organizational climate and organizational work experiences have a degree of conceptual overlap and, therefore, should be moderately correlated. The key differences between these variables, however, are the extent to which one is more cognitively, rather than emotionally laden, and the extent to which they operate at the individual or workgroup levels of analyses. These differences can be empirically tested. Although we acknowledge the difficulties that these subtle differences may pose in selecting or developing appropriate measures, it is important for occupational stress researchers to pay greater attention to construct validity in order to avoid the methodological criticisms that have often been targeted at the occupational stress literature.

CONCLUDING REMARKS

The organizational health framework provides considerable flexibility and scope for developing our understanding of occupational stress. Moreover, it provides a broad theoretical framework that can be used to integrate the different approaches to occupational stress, and emphasizes the need for occupational stress research to become more aligned with the wider work psychology literature. As suggested by the organizational health framework, it is also important for occupational stress researchers and practitioners to adopt a much broader perspective than the traditional stressors and strain approach, and to demonstrate that a link exists between occupational stress and an organization's 'bottom-line' performance. By adopting this broader approach, it will be possible to develop and test more coherent theories that enable us to understand the complex dynamics that underpin occupational stress. Ultimately, we believe that sustained improvements can only be brought about by using this broader approach to develop effective strategies and policies for managing stress in work organizations.

REFERENCES

Agho, A.O., Price, J.L., & Mueller, C.W. (1992). Discriminant validity of measures of job satisfaction, positive affectivity and negative affectivity. *Journal of Occupational and Organizational Psychology*, 65, 185–196.

Anshel, M.H., Robertson, M., & Caputi, P. (1997). Sources of acute stress and their appraisals and reappraisals among Australian police as a function of previous experience. *Journal of Occupational and Organizational Psychology*, 70, 337–356.

Auerbach, S.M. (1989). Stress management and coping research in the health care setting: An overview and methodological commentary. *Journal of Consulting and Clinical Psychology*, 57, 388–395.

Barrick, M.R., & Mount, M.K. (1991). The Big Five Personality Dimensions and job performance: A meta-analysis. *Personnel Psychology*, 44, 1–25.

Bateman, T.S., & Organ, D.W. (1983). Job satisfaction and the good soldier: The relationship between affect and employee 'citizenship'. *Academy of Management Journal*, 26, 587–595.

Beehr, T.A. (1995). *Psychological stress in the workplace*. London: Routledge.

Beehr, T.A., & Newman, J.E. (1978). Job stress, employee health, and organizational effectiveness: A facet analysis, model, and literature review. *Personnel Psychology*, 31, 665–699.

Bolger, N. (1990). Coping as a personality process: A prospective study. *Journal of Personality and Social Psychology*, 59, 525–537.

Borg, M.G. (1990). Occupational stress in British educational settings: A review. *Educational Psychology*, 10, 103–126.

Bradburn, N.M. (1969). *The structure of psychological well-being*. Chicago: Aldine.

Brief, A.P., Burke, M.J., George, J.M., Robinson, B.S., & Webster, J. (1988). Should negative affectivity remain an unmeasured variable in the study of job stress? *Journal of Applied Psychology*, 73, 193–198.

Brief, A.P., Butcher, A.H., George, J.M., & Link, K.E. (1993). Integrating bottom-up and top-down theories of subjective well-being: The case of health. *Journal of Personality and Social Psychology*, 64, 646–653.

Brief, A.P., & Motowidlo, S.J. (1986). Prosocial organizational behaviors. *Academy of Management Review*, 11, 710–725.

Brief, A.P., & Roberson, L. (1989). Job attitude organization: An exploratory study. *Journal of Applied Social Psychology*, 19, 717–727.

Burke, M.J., Brief, A.P., & George, J.M. (1993). The role of negative affectivity in understanding relations between self-reports of stressors and strains: A comment on the applied psychology literature. *Journal of Applied Psychology*, 78, 402–412.

Burke, M.J., Brief, A.P., George, J.M., Roberson, L., & Webster, J. (1989). Measuring affect at work: Confirmatory analyses of competing mood structures with conceptual linkage to cortical regulatory systems. *Journal of Personality and Social Psychology*, 57, 1091–1102.

Byrne, B.M. (1998). *Structural equation modeling with LISREL, PRELIS, and SIMPLIS*. Mahwah, NJ: Lawrence Erlbaum.

Carpenter, B.N. (Ed.) (1992). *Personal coping: Theory, research, and application*. Wesport, CT: Praeger.

Cartwright, S., & Cooper, C.L. (1996). Coping in occupational settings. In M. Zeidner, & N.S. Endler (Eds.), *Handbook of coping: Theory, research, applications* (pp. 202–220). New York: John Wiley.

Carver, C.S., Scheier, M.F., & Weintraub, J.K. (1989). Assessing coping strategies: A theoretically based approach. *Journal of Personality and Social Psychology*, 56, 267–283.

Cohen, J., & Cohen, P. (1983). *Applied multiple regression/correlation analysis for the behavioral sciences* (2nd ed.). Hillsdale, New Jersey: Lawrence Erlbaum.

Conway, V.J., & Terry, D.J. (1992). Appraised controllability as a moderator of the effectiveness of different coping strategies: A test of the goodness of fit hypothesis. *Australia Journal of Psychology*, 44, 1–7.

Cooper, C.L. (Ed.). (1998). *Theories of organizational stress*. New York: Oxford.

Cooper, C.L., & Williams, S. (Eds.) (1994). *Creating healthy work organizations*. Chichester: John Wiley.

Costa, P.T. Jr., & McCrae, R.R. (1980). Influence of extraversion and neuroticism on subjective well-being. *Journal of Personality and Social Psychology*, 38, 668–678.

Costa, P.T., Jr., & McCrae, R.R. (1989). *NEO PI/FFI Manual Supplement*. Odessa, FL: Psychological Assessment Resources.

Costa, P.T. Jr., & McCrae, R.R. (1990). Personality: Another 'hidden factor' in stress research. *Psychological Inquiry*, 1, 22–24.

Cotton, P. (1995). *Psychological health in the workplace: Understanding and managing occupational stress.* Carlton, Australia: The Australian Psychological Society.

Cox, T. (1978). *Stress.* London: Macmillan.

Cox, T. (1988). Organizational health. *Work and Stress, 2,* 1–2.

Cox, T. (1992). Occupational health: Past, present, and future. *Work and Stress, 6,* 99–102.

Cox, T., & Ferguson, E. (1991). Individual differences, stress and coping. In C.L. Cooper, & R. Payne (Eds.), *Personality and stress: Individual differences in the stress process.* New York: John Wiley.

DeLongis, A., Folkman, S., & Lazarus, R.S. (1988). The impact of daily stress on health and mood: Psychological and social resources as mediators. *Journal of Personality and Social Psychology, 54,* 486–495.

De Rijk, A.E., Le Blanc, P.M., Schaeufeli, W.B., & de Jonge, J. (1998). Active coping and the need for control as moderators of the job demand-control model: Effects on burnout. *Journal of Occupational and Organizational Psychology, 71,* 1–18.

Diener, E. (2000). Subjective well-being: The science of happiness and a proposal for a national index. *American Psychologist, 55,* 34–43.

Diener, E., & Emmons, R.A. (1985). The independence of positive and negative affect. *Journal of Personality and Social Psychology, 47,* 1105–1117.

Doherty, J. (1988). Psychological morale: Its conceptualisation and measurement. The Doherty Inventory of Psychological Morale (DIPM). *Educational Studies, 14,* 65–75.

Edwards, J.R. (1992). A cybernetic theory of stress, coping and well-being in organizations. *Academy of Management Review, 17,* 238–274.

Evans, L. (1992). Teacher morale: An individual perspective. *Educational Studies, 18,* 161–171.

Folkman, S. (1992). Making a case for coping. In B.N. Carpenter (Ed.), *Personal coping: Theory, research, and applications* (pp. 31–46). Westport, CT: Praeger.

Folkman, S., & Lazarus, R.S. (1985). If it changes it must be a process: Study of emotion and coping during three stages of a college examination. *Journal of Personality and Social Psychology, 48,* 150–170.

Folkman, S., & Lazarus, R.S. (1988). The relationship between coping and emotion: Implications for theory and research. *Social Science & Medicine, 26,* 309–317.

Folkman, S., Lazarus, R.S., Gruen, R.J., & DeLongis, A. (1986). Appraisal, coping, health status, and psychological symptoms. *Journal of Personality and Social Psychology, 50,* 571–579.

French, J.R.P., Jr., Caplan, R.D., & Harrison, R.V. (1982). *The mechanisms of job stress and strain.* London: John Wiley.

Gaines, J., & Jermier, J.M. (1983). Emotional exhaustion in a high stress organization. *Academy of Management Journal, 26,* 567–586.

Ganster, D.C. (1987). Type A behavior and occupational stress. In J.M. Ivancevich, & D.C. Ganster (Eds.), *Job stress: From theory to suggestion* (pp. 61–84). New York: Haworth Press.

George, J.M. (1990). Personality, affect, and behavior in groups. *Journal of Applied Psychology, 75,* 107–116.

George, J.M. (1996). Trait and state affect. In K.R. Murphy (Ed.), *Individual differences and behavior in organizations* (pp. 145–171). San Francisco: Jossey-Bass.

George, J.M., & Brief, A.P. (1992). Feeling good–doing good: A conceptual analysis of the mood at work-organizational spontaneity relationship. *Psychological Bulletin, 112,* 310–329.

Goldberg, D. (1978). *Manual for the general health questionnaire.* Windsor: National Foundation for Educational Research.

Griffin, M.A., Hart, P.M., & Wilson-Evered, E. (2000). Using employee opinion surveys to improve organizational health. In L.R. Murphy, & C.L. Cooper (Eds.), *Health and productive work: An international perspective* (pp. 15–36). London: Taylor & Francis.

Hart, P.M. (1994). Teacher quality of work life: Integrating work experiences, psychological distress and morale. *Journal of Occupational and Organizational Psychology, 67,* 109–132.

Hart, P.M. (1999). Predicting employee life satisfaction: A coherent model of personality, work and nonwork experiences, and domain satisfactions. *Journal of Applied Psychology, 84,* 564–584.

Hart, P.M., Griffin, M.A., Wearing, A.J., & Cooper, C.L. (1996). *Manual for the QPASS survey.* Brisbane: Public Sector Management Commission.

Hart, P.M., Wearing, A.J., Conn, M., Carter, N.L., & Dingle, R.K. (2000). Development of the School Organizational Health Questionnaire: A measure for assessing teacher morale and school organizational climate. *British Journal of Educational Psychology, 70,* 211–228.

Hart, P.M., Wearing, A.J., & Headey, B. (1993). Assessing police work experiences: Development of the Police Daily Hassles and Uplifts Scales. *Journal of Criminal Justice, 21,* 553–572.

Hart, P.M., Wearing, A.J., & Headey, B. (1994). Perceived quality of life, personality and work experiences: Construct validation of the Police Daily Hassles and Uplifts Scales. *Journal of Criminal Justice and Behavior, 21,* 283–311.

Hart, P.M., Wearing, A.J., & Headey, B. (1995). Police stress and well-being: Integrating personality, coping and daily work experiences. *Journal of Occupational and Organizational Psychology, 68,* 133–156.

Headey, B., Glowacki, T., Holmstrom, E., & Wearing, A.J. (1985). Modelling change in perceived quality of life. *Social Indicators Research, 17,* 267–298.

Headey, B., & Wearing, A.J. (1989). Personality, life events, and subjective well-being: Toward a dynamic equilibrium model. *Journal of Personality and Social Psychology, 57,* 731–739.

Headey, B., & Wearing, A.J. (1990). Subjective well-being and coping with adversity. *Social Indicators Research, 22*, 327–349.

Headey, B., & Wearing, A.J. (1992). *Understanding happiness: A theory of subjective well-being.* Melbourne: Longman Cheshire.

Hemingway, M.A., & Smith, C.S. (1999). Organizational climate and occupational stressors as predictors of withdrawal behaviours and injuries in nurses. *Journal of Occupational and Organizational Psychology, 72,* 285–299.

Hobfoll, S.E. (1989). Conservation of resources, a new attempt at conceptualizing stress. *American Psychologist, 44*, 513–524.

Holahan, C.J., & Moos, R.H. (1986). Personality, coping and family resources in stress resistance: A longitudinal analysis. *Journal of Personality and Social Psychology, 51*, 389–395.

Holmes, J.H., & Rahe, R.H. (1967). The Social Readjustment Rating Scale. *Journal of Psychosomatic Research, 5*, 335–357.

Hurrell, J.J., Jr., Nelson, D.L., & Simmons, B.L. (1998). Measuring job stressors and strains: Where we have been, where we are, and where we need to go. *Journal of Occupational Health Psychology, 3,* 368–389.

Jackson, S.E., & Schuler, R.S. (1985). A meta-analysis and conceptual critique of research on role ambiguity and role conflict in work settings. *Organizational Behavior and Human Decision Processes, 36,* 16–78.

James, L.R., & McIntyre, M.D. (1996). Perceptions of organisational climate. In K. Murphy (Ed.), *Individual differences and behavior in organisations* (pp. 416–450). San Francisco: Jossey-Bass.

Jex, S.M., Beehr, T.A., & Roberts, C.K. (1992). The meaning of occupational stress items to survey respondents. *Journal of Applied Psychology, 77,* 623–628.

Jex, S.M., & Elacqua, T.C. (1999). Self-esteem as a moderator: A comparison of global and organization-based measures. *Journal of Occupational and Organizational Psychology, 72*, 71–81.

Judge, T.A., Thoresen, C.J., Pucik, V., & Welbourne, T.M. (1999). Managerial coping with organizational change. *Journal of Applied Psychology, 84*, 107–122.

Kahn, R.L., & Byosiere (1992). Stress in organizations. In M.D. Dunnette, & L.M. Hough (Eds.), *Handbook of industrial and organizational psychology* (2nd ed., Vol. 3, pp. 571–650). Palo Alto, CA: Consulting Psychologists Press.

Kanner, A.D., Coyne, J.C., Schaefer, C., & Lazarus, R.S. (1981). Comparison of two modes of stress measurement: Daily hassles and uplifts versus major life events. *Journal of Behavioural Medicine, 4*, 1–39.

Kanner, A.D., Feldman, S.S., Weinerger, D.A., & Ford, M.E. (1991). Upflits, hassles, and adaptional outcomes in early adolescents. In A. Monat, & R.S. Lazarus (Eds.), *Stress and coping: An anthology* (pp. 158–181). New York: Columbia.

Karasek, R., Brisson, C., Kawakami, N., Houtman, I., Bongers, P., & Amick, B. (1998). The Job Content Questionnaire (JCQ): An instrument for internationally comparative assessments of psychosocial job characteristics. *Journal of Occupational Health Psychology, 3*, 322–355.

Kasl, S.V. (1987). Methodologies in stress and health: Past difficulties, present dilemmas, future directions. In S.V. Kasl, & C.L. Cooper (Eds.), *Stress and health issues in research methodology* (pp. 307–318). New York: Wiley.

Kasl, S.V. (1998). Measuring job stressors and studying the health impact of the work environment: An epidemiologic commentary. *Journal of Occupational Health Psychology, 3*, 390–401.

Kasl, S.V., & Rapp, S.R. (1991). Stress, health and well-being: The role of individual differences. In C.L. Cooper, & R. Payne (Eds.), *Personality and stress: Individual differences in the stress process* (pp. 269–284). Chichester: Wiley.

Katz, D., & Kahn, R.L. (1978). *The social psychology of organizations* (2nd ed.). New York: Wiley.

Kessler, R.C., & Greenberg, D.F. (1981). *Linear panel analysis: Models of quantitative change.* New York: Academic Press.

Klein, K.J., & Kozlowski, S.W.J. (Eds.) (2000). *Multilevel theory, research, and methods in organizations: Foundations, extensions, and new directions.* San Francisco: Jossey-Bass.

Kyriacou, C., & Sutcliffe, J. (1978). A model of teacher stress. *Education Studies, 4*, 1–6.

Latack, J.C., & Havlovic, S.J. (1992). Coping with job stress: A conceptual evaluation framework for coping measures. *Journal of Organizational Behavior, 13*, 479–508.

Lazarus, R.S. (1990). Theory-based stress measurement. *Psychological Inquiry, 1*, 3–13.

Lazarus, R.S. (1993). From psychological stress to the emotions: A history of changing outlooks. *Annual Review of Psychology, 44*, 1–21.

Lazarus, R.S., DeLongis, A., Folkman, S., & Gruen, R. (1985). Stress and adaptational outcomes, the problem of confounded measures. *American Psychologist, 40*, 770–779.

Lazarus, R.S., & Folkman, S. (1984). *Stress, appraisal, and coping.* New York: Springer.

Lee, C., Ashford, S.J., & Jamieson, L.F. (1993). The effects of Type A behavior dimensions and optimism on coping strategy, health, and performance. *Journal of Organizational Behavior, 14*, 143–157.

Magnus, K., Diener, E., Fujita, F., & Pavot, W. (1993). Extraversion and neuroticism as predictors of objective life events: A longitudinal analysis. *Journal of Personality and Social Psychology, 65*, 1046–1043.

McCrae, R.R., & Costa, P.T., Jr. (1986). Personality, coping, and coping effectiveness in an adult sample. *Journal of Personality, 54*, 385–405.

McGrath, J.E. (Ed.) (1970). *Social and psychological factors in stress.* New York: Holt, Rinehart and Winston.

Michela, J.L., Lukaszewski, M.P., & Allegrante, J.P. (1995). Organizational climate and work stress: A general framework applied to inner-city schoolteachers. In S.L. Sauter, & L.R. Murphy (Eds.), *Organizational risk factors for job stress* (pp. 61–80). Washington, DC: American Psychological Association.

Miller, R., Griffin, M.A., & Hart, P.M. (1999). Personality and organizational health: The role of conscientiousness. *Work and Stress, 13*, 7–19.

Moran, E.T., & Volkwein, J.F. (1992). The cultural approach to the formation of organizational climate. *Human Relations, 45*, 19–47.

Motowidlo, S.J., & Van Scotter, J.R. (1994). Evidence that task performance should be distinguished from contextual performance. *Journal of Applied Psychology, 79*, 475–480.

Moyle, P. (1995). The role of negative affectivity in the stress process: Tests of alternative models. *Journal of Organizational Behavior, 16*, 647–670.

Murphy, L.J., & Cooper, C.L. (Eds.) (2000). *Health and productive work: An international perspective*. London: Taylor & Francis.

Newton, T.J. (1989). Occupational stress and coping with stress: A critique. *Human Relations, 42*, 441–461.

Organ, D.W. (1997). Toward an explication of 'morale': In search of the m factor. In C.L. Cooper, & S.E. Jackson (Eds.), *Creating tomorrow's organizations: A handbook for future research in organizational behavior* (pp. 493–504). Chichester: John Wiley.

Pavot, W., & Diener, E. (1993). Review of the Satisfaction With Life Scale. *Psychological Assessment, 2*, 164–172.

Quick, J.C., Murphy, L.R., & Hurrell, J.J., Jr. (1992a). *Stress and well-being at work: Assessments and interventions for occupational mental health*. Washington, DC: American Psychological Association.

Quick, J.C., Murphy, L.R., & Hurrell, J.J., Jr. (1992b). Preface. In J.C. Quick, L.R. Murphy, & J.J. Hurrell, Jr. (Eds.), *Stress and well-being at work: Assessments and interventions for occupational mental health* (pp. ix–x). Washington, DC: American Psychological Association.

Sauter, S.L., & Murphy, L.R. (1995). *Organizational risk factors for job stress*. Washington, DC: American Psychological Association.

Schaubroeck, J., Ganster, D.C., & Kemmerer, B. (1996). Does trait affect promote job attitude stability? *Journal of Organizational Behavior, 17*, 191–196.

Schneider, B. (Ed.) (1990). *Organizational climate and culture*. San Francisco: Jossey-Bass.

Sewell, J.D. (1983). The development of a critical life events scale for law enforcement. *Journal of Police Science and Administration, 11*, 109–119.

Smith, K.R. (1966). A proposed model for the investigation of teacher morale. *Journal of Educational Administration, 4*, 143–148.

Spector, P.E. (1998). A control theory of the job stress process. In Cooper, C.L. (Ed.), *Theories of organizational stress* (pp. 153–169). New York: Oxford.

Spector, P.E., Fox, S., & Van Katwyk, P.T. (1999). The role of negative affectivity in employee reactions to job characteristics: Bias effect or substantive effect? *Journal of Occupational and Organizational Psychology, 72*, 205–218.

Spector, P.E., & Jex, S.M. (1998). Development of four self-report measures of job stressors and strain: Interpersonal Conflict at Work Scale, Organizational Constraints Scale, Quantitative Workload Inventory, and Physical Symptoms Inventory. *Journal of Occupational Health Psychology, 3*, 356–367.

Staw, B.M., & Ross, J. (1985). Stability in the midst of change: A dispositional approach to job attitudes. *Journal of Applied Psychology, 70*, 469–480.

Stone, A.A., Kennedy-Moore, E., Newman, M.G., Greenberg, M., & Neale, J.M. (1992). Conceptual and methodological issues in current coping assessments. In B.N. Carpenter (Ed.), *Personal coping: Theory, research, and applications* (pp. 15–30). Westport, CT: Praeger.

Terry, D.J. (1994). Determinants of coping: The role of stable and situational factors. *Journal of Personality and Social Psychology, 66*, 895–910.

Van Yperen, N.W., & Snijders, T.A.B. (2000). A multilevel analysis of the demands-control model: Is stress at work determined by factors at the group level or the individual level? *Journal of Occupational Health Psychology, 5*, 182–190.

Watson, D. (1988). Intraindividual and interindividual analyses of positive and negative affect: Their relation to health complaints, perceived stress, and daily activities. *Journal of Personality and Social Psychology, 54*, 1020–1030.

Watson, D., & Tellegen, A. (1985). Toward a consensual structure of mood. *Psychological Bulletin, 98*, 219–235.

Weiss, D.J., Dawis, R.V., England, G.W., & Lofquist, L.H. (1967). *Manual for the Minnesota Satisfaction Questionnaire*. Minneapolis: University of Minnesota.

Wheaton, B. (1994). Sampling the stress universe. In W.R. Avison, & I.H. Gotlib (Eds.), *Stress and mental health: Contemporary issues and prospects for the future* (pp. 77–114). New York: Plenum.

Williams, S., & Cooper, C.L. (Eds.) (1994). *Creating healthy work organizations*. Chichester: John Wiley.

Williams, S., & Cooper, C.L. (1998). Measuring occupational stress: Development of the Pressure Management Indicator. *Journal of Occupational Health Psychology, 3*, 306–321.

Williams, L.J., Gavin, M.B., & Williams, M.L. (1996). Measurement and nonmeasurement processes with negative affectivity and employee attitudes. *Journal of Applied Psychology, 81*, 88–101.

Worrall, N., & May, D. (1989). Towards a person-in-situation model of teacher stress. British *Journal of Educational Psychology, 59*, 174–186.

Wright, T.A., & Cropanzano, R. (2000a). The role of organizational behavior in occupational health psychology: A view as we approach the new millennium. *Journal of Occupational Health Psychology, 5*, 5–10.

Wright, T.A., & Cropanzano, R. (2000b). Psychological well-being and job satisfaction as predictors of job performance. *Journal of Occupational Health Psychology, 5*, 84–94.

Zeidner, M., & Endler, N.S. (1996). *Handbook of coping.* New York: John Wiley.

6

Careers and Career Management

JOHN ARNOLD

Careers are, for many people, less predictable and more varied than they once were. Work organizations are compelled (and sometimes choose) to change form, strategy, and size in ways which affect the kinds of work roles and careers available. It can be argued that managing careers is difficult yet necessary for both individuals and organizations in these circumstances. Some argue that careers are now boundaryless, involving many more radical moves, improvisation and expression of personal values than was once the case. Yet at the same time there is a major risk that many people who lack key skills or resources will find themselves more constrained than ever before. Social cognitive psychological theories are being used to predict and explain how individuals handle the tasks of career management, which may well require quite high levels of self-awareness and 'advanced' patterns of thought. The career choices people make are more complex and varied than simply the type of work they wish to do, and yardsticks of career success are increasingly self-defined rather than by socially accepted norms. Many interventions are available to organizations for managing careers. Mentoring has received the most attention from both researchers and practitioners, and others that appear relatively regularly in the applied psychological literature include development centers, succession planning, and developmental work assignments. However, with the partial exception of mentoring, there is frustratingly little good evidence available concerning the efficacy of these techniques *per se*, nor about how to design them for maximum effect. In any case, it seems likely that the impact of interventions depends heavily on their integration with other organizational processes and their acceptance by key stakeholders.

INTRODUCTION

It is possible to take either of two general approaches to careers and career management. On the one hand, one might conclude that the world of work is now too fast-moving and too uncertain to justify using concepts like career which imply efforts to understand and manage the future. Opportunism and flexibility is all. Acceptance of that point of view would result in a very short chapter! The approach taken here is therefore that the world is indeed fast-moving and uncertain, but that this reality increases the salience of career issues. As Herriot, Hirsh and Reilly put it: 'Far, therefore, from careers and career management going out of the window along with jobs

for life, they are the most important personnel issue facing organizations today' (1998: 7). The fact that careers are more problematic than they were means that we should try all the harder to manage them, not give up. In any case, construing opportunism and flexibility as anathema to careers implies that careers are necessarily planned and inflexible. This is not accurate. The key questions for the purposes of this chapter are therefore how best to construe career, and how careers can be managed and by whom.

This chapter begins by defining career and briefly pointing out some of the trends that affected careers and their management during the last part of the 20th century. The concept of the boundaryless career is used as a vehicle to analyze the implications of those trends for people's career behaviors, thoughts, and feelings. Particular attention is paid to self and identity. Then some specific issues in career psychology are reviewed. These include the application to career of ideas on motivation and thinking; the structure and process of making career choices; making career transitions; and career success. Then some of the career management interventions that can be used in organizations are examined, considering first general issues and then (very briefly) specific techniques. Some issues in the evaluation of the impact of career management are then highlighted. The conclusion points out general lessons that can be learned, and issues that remain or will emerge in the future. Other reviews of some similar areas can be found in Arnold (1997a, b), Sullivan (1999), and Cohen (2000).

As we will see, career is potentially a very wide-ranging topic. Hence this chapter inevitably has many links with others in these volumes. Coverage is therefore selective in order to ensure a healthy synergy with, rather than wasteful duplication of, the chapters on performance appraisal, training and learning, individual development, withdrawal behaviors, socialization, psychological contracts, unemployment, and diversity. The fact that there remains plenty to cover illustrates well the wide scope of the career construct.

DEFINING CAREERS AND CAREER MANAGEMENT

There is a substantial element of arbitrariness about most definitions in the social sciences. A characteristically post-modern solution is to formulate definitions which have useful effects, though that begs questions of what useful means, and to whom. A definition of career is perhaps most useful if it links with (but does not merely duplicate) accepted definitions of related constructs, and if it embraces the actual or potential experiences of as many people as possible. In everyday language it is still quite common for careers to be construed approximately as described by Perlmutter and Hall (1992):

> Occupations that are characterized by inter-related training and work experiences, in which a person moves upward through a series of positions that require greater mastery and responsibility, and that provide increasing financial return.

This definition is inadequate when considered against the criteria outlined above. Careers are seen as occupations, and therefore 'out there' in the world rather than an aspect or attribute of a person. What's more, careers are confined to occupations of a certain type, requiring specific training and socialization experiences and predictable upward movement with more money. The following definition

(Arnold, 1997b) is preferred here. It is quite close to others offered towards the end of the 20th century (e.g., Arthur & Rousseau, 1996; Greenhaus & Callanan, 1994):

> A career is the sequence of employment-related positions, roles, activities and experiences encountered by a person.

This permits career to have both subjective and objective elements. It includes parts of a person's life which are outside employment, but which are related to it. Like most definitions of career, it encompasses the notion of sequence, or unfolding over time. There is no assumption that employment (which is defined here as any kind of money-earning work, including self-employment) will be in just one occupation or organization, nor that there will be increases in status or income, nor that there will be linked training and work experiences. One limitation of this definition might be that the word 'encountered' implies that the person passively stumbles across his or her experience. Alternative views could be that the experience is planned in advance, or conversely that it is constructed after the event in order to sustain a coherent identity and life history (Young & Collin, 1992).

A meaning of career management follows on from the above discussion. Career management concerns attempts to influence the career of one or more people. The person concerned might be oneself, or it might be others. Usually, those others will be located in the same employing organization as the person(s) attempting to do the influencing, but not necessarily. The influence may be over the objective elements of career (e.g., the posts a person fills), or it may be over the subjective elements (e.g., the connections a person sees between one job they have done and another they might do). It is likely to be future-oriented, but it could be retrospective – for example in encouraging a person to view his or her past achievements more favorably. The influencing could reflect the influencer's goals (e.g., succession planning), or it could be focused on the agenda of the person whose career is being influenced (e.g., career counseling).

Career management is usually defined by psychologists in very individualistic terms. Greenhaus and Callanan (1994) suggest that career management by individuals for themselves concerns the establishment of realistic career goals based on accurate information about self and work, and the monitoring of progress towards those goals. Noe (1996) more explicitly includes a person's behavioral strategies in his depiction of career management as a process by which individuals do three things. First, they collect information about values, interests, and skill strengths and weaknesses – often called career exploration. Second, they identify one or more career goals. Third, they engage in strategies that increase the probability that those career goals will be achieved. It is probably necessary to be flexible about what a career goal is (it could be short-term, specific, and modest), and to recognize that exploration refers to environment as well as self. Noe's definition of career management leaves suitably unspecified the sources from which a person might collect information about self and occupational environment, and the strategies a person might adopt to achieve a career goal. Those strategies might be, for example, social networking, identifying and seizing opportunities to develop valuable skills, exhibiting motivation, adaptability and resilience, and wise patterns of thinking. Some of these are examined in more detail later in this chapter.

Career management by organizational agents can involve a number of techniques, many of which are shown in Table 6.1. Some organizations have withdrawn from managing careers, favoring either an aggressive 'you're on your own' message to employees, or a more sympathetic but distinctly low-key support for employee self-development. Systematic evidence is hard to find concerning how many organizations use these techniques and how widespread that usage is within organizations. Terms like counseling and mentoring may well mean quite different things to different respondents in surveys about career management. Those respondents may also have an inaccurate impression of the usage of the various techniques in their organizations. It is, however, clear that all the interventions are used in some organizations, and some are quite prevalent (Gutteridge, Leibowitz & Shore, 1993; Iles & Mabey, 1993). Most of them can be used primarily in pursuit of organizational goals, or alternatively as a support to individuals' efforts at self-development. Internal job advertising and training are not surprisingly almost universal. Mentoring is common and on the rise. It is also much researched and written-about (e.g., Kram, 1985). Personal development plans appear to have enjoyed increasing usage but much less formal research analysis than mentoring. Some of the key issues and findings regarding the use of these techniques are discussed towards the end of this chapter.

CONCEPTUALIZING CAREERS AND CAREER MANAGEMENT

The Changing Context and Nature of Careers

The ways in which organizations and work have been changing were written about a great deal in the 1990s, though mainly from the perspective of western countries (see, e.g., Cascio, 1993; Howard, 1995). Large organizations shed layers and numbers of staff, and required more work and more flexibility from those who remained. Many outsourced non-core activities, and engaged in mergers, acquisitions

and joint ventures to preserve or enhance their market position. Recruitment is now based more on the consistency of a person's competencies and values with the overall thrust of the organization, than on his or her match with any particular job description (Lawler, 1994; Templer & Cawsey, 1999). Time-limited employment contracts, project-based multidisciplinary teams, performance-related pay, and part-time working have all become more common. Often there are many 'outsourced' people working on the premises of an organization who are not employed by it, with potential implications for staff commitment and relationships. Interestingly, though, it appears that temporary contract workers are often relatively contented with their lot and their attitudes are quite similar to those of organizational insiders (Pearce, 1993, Millward & Brewerton, 1999). Managers' predominantly negative reactions to organizational changes have been investigated by Goffee and Scase (1992) and Thomas and Dunkerley (1999) among others. Amabile and Conti (1999) have shown how the creativity of 'surviving' employees can be substantially damaged over a sustained period by downsizing, while Shah (2000) demonstrated that friendships lost through downsizing are difficult to replace and the loss leads to negative reactions among survivors.

Individuals are exhorted to update and expand their skills throughout their working lives. Some but not all analyses suggest that people are moving jobs with ever greater frequency, and that they feel a greater employment insecurity, even if economic data suggest that they have no particular need to (Hartley, Jacobson, Klandermans & Van Vuuren, 1991). An increasing proportion of the labor force is working in small organizations, an increasing proportion of it is female, and its average age is increasing. More people are working at or from home (Chapman, Sheehy, Heywood, Dooley & Collins, 1995).

These changes have had a major impact on the kinds of career some people experience and the skills required to manage them. The general, though not unanimous, opinion is that in many western countries careers have become less predictable, less structured, and less safe for many people. Promotions are more difficult to obtain, and may involve a bigger jump in status when they do happen. Downward and sideways moves are more common than they were (Inkson, 1995). What Kanter (1989) has described as professional and entrepreneurial career forms have become more the norm, at the expense of what she terms the bureaucratic career. There is a greater onus on individuals to manage their own careers rather than waiting for someone else to take an initiative on their behalf. This includes identifying their own characteristics, their development needs, and likely trends in future opportunities. It also means finding the development and other opportunities they feel they need, and making them

Table 6.1   *Career management interventions in organizations*

Internal vacancy notification. Information about jobs available in the organization, normally in advance of any external advertising, and with some details of preferred experience, qualifications, and a job description.

Career paths. Information about the sequences of jobs that a person can do, or competencies he or she can acquire, in the organization. This should include details of how high in the organization any path goes, the kinds of interdepartmental transfers that are possible, and perhaps the skills/experiences required to follow various paths.

Career workbooks. These consist of questions and exercises designed to guide individuals in determining their strengths and weaknesses, identifying job and career opportunities, and determining necessary steps for reaching their goals.

Career planning workshops. Cover some of the same ground as workbooks, but offer more chance for discussion, feedback from others, information about organization-specific opportunities and policies. May include psychometric testing.

Computer-assisted career management. Various packages exist for helping employees to assess their skills, interests, and values, and translate these into job options. Sometimes those options are customized to a particular organization. A few packages designed for personnel or manpower planning also include some career-relevant facilities.

Individual counseling. Can be done by specialists from inside or outside the organization, or by line managers who have received training. May include psychometric testing.

Training and educational opportunities. Information and financial support about, and possibly delivery of, courses in the organization or outside it. These can enable employees to update, retrain or deepen their knowledge in particular fields. In keeping with the notion of careers involving sequences, training in this context is not solely to improve performance in a person's present job.

Personal development plans (PDPs). These often arise from the appraisal process and other sources such as development centers. PDPs are statements of how a person's skill and knowledge might appropriately develop, and how this development could occur, on a given timescale.

Career action centers. Resources such as literature, videos, and CD-ROMS and perhaps more personal inputs such as counseling available to employees on a drop-in basis.

Development centers. Like assessment centers in that participants are assessed on the basis of their performance in a number of exercises and tests. However, development centers focus more on identifying a person's strengths, weaknesses, and styles for the purpose of development, not selection.

Mentoring programmes. Attaching employees to more senior ones who act as advisers, and perhaps also as advocates, protectors, and counselors.

Succession planning. The identification of individuals who are expected to occupy key posts in the future, and who are exposed to experiences which prepare them appropriately.

Job assignments/rotation. Careful use of work tasks can help a person stay employable for the future, and an organization to benefit from the adaptability of staff.

Outplacement. This may involve several interventions listed above. Its purpose is to support people who are leaving the organization to clarify and implement plans for the future.

happen. Many people are working harder and have less time to look ahead, but there is paradoxically a greater need to do so. It is said to be important to review one's career continuously. Waiting until things are starting to go wrong is leaving it too late (Handy, 1994). Social networks are increasingly important, and so are skills of entrepreneurship and personal financial management. There is often a greater need to understand the perspectives of people from different cultural and occupational backgrounds to one's own.

Some writers have asserted that careers have been completely transformed or even rendered obsolete (e.g., Bridges, 1995), whereas others have found that many elements of traditional careers are alive and reasonably well (Guest & Mackenzie Davey, 1996). Perhaps Hall & Mirvis (1995) reflect the most realistic balance between old and new when they suggest that 'people's careers will become increasingly a succession of mini-stages of exploration – trial – mastery – exit, as they move in and out of various product areas, technologies, functions, organizations,

and other work environments.' Some tensions are apparent, however one looks at it. Perhaps the most pervasive practical and ethical dilemmas arise from some senior managers' desire for a totally committed yet totally expendable workforce (Hirsh & Jackson, 1996). One practical problem is how people can be encouraged to feel loyalty to an organization that manifestly is not making any deep commitments to them. An ethical issue concerns the temptation for senior managers in organizations to conceal or lie about the extent and nature of their commitments to employees. Even less explicit in much career writing is the implication that those with limited skills will find work of any kind even more difficult to obtain and keep than hitherto. There is the danger, and perhaps reality, of an underclass of impoverished and angry people who have little chance to participate in careers of any kind (Hutton, 1995).

Some who are in work also feel aggrieved by changes in the last decade of the 20th century. They believe that their psychological contract with their employer has been broken. The psychological contract can be thought of as the agreement an employee believes exists with his or her employer about what each side should be giving to and receiving from the other (Rousseau, 1995). In the eyes of many employees, long-term relationships they once had with their employer based on unwritten understandings concerning mutual trust and loyalty have been unilaterally replaced by a much more short-term transactional 'deal' where they work hard for (sometimes) good pay, and if they are lucky they stay in work. Top management might argue that this is necessary in a climate of increasing competition, but that line of reasoning often does not impress those who feel they have given their all for their employer over many years (Herriot & Pemberton, 1995).

Herriot and Pemberton (1995) have argued that there can be no return to unwritten and perhaps unstated expectations of mutual trust. What each side expects of the other must be clearly negotiated, monitored and renegotiated – indeed, Herriot and Pemberton define career as this sequence of negotiations and renegotiations. So on this analysis, career management from both individual and organizational perspectives means being clear about your wants, what you are prepared to negotiate on, and what you can offer the other party. It also means both sides have to be open with each other, avoiding 'hype.' It means both sides must be well-informed about their present and short-term future needs, and have ways of verifying whether a deal, once struck, is being adhered to. It seems likely that the willingness of each side to engage in such negotiation will be influenced by both labor market conditions and the cultural context.

The nature and utility of the notion of the psychological contract can be debated (see Guest, 1998; Rousseau, 1998a), but there is an intuitive appeal about it, and about models of what is likely to happen when the agreement people thought they had with their employer is violated (Morrison & Robinson, 1997; Turnley & Feldman, 2000). Nevertheless, there is the danger of sloppy and inconsistent conceptualization and measurement as researchers jump upon the psychological contract bandwagon.

Boundaryless Careers and Their Implications

The professional and the entrepreneurial career forms are both consistent with a more general term that has become widely used – namely, the boundaryless career (Arthur, 1994; Arthur & Rousseau, 1996). Careers are boundaryless because they nowadays cross organizational boundaries based on function and hierarchy (where these still exist). They emphasize personal flexibility, so that there are no boundaries around a person's activities and skills – or at least no long-term ones. A person is

likely to be employed in several occupations during his or her working life. The notion of the boundaryless career also reminds us that there are no rigid barriers between work and nonwork. Family issues impact upon work and vice versa. People pursuing boundaryless careers draw upon information and support from professional and other networks outside an organization where they are currently employed. There is a general sense that individuals are transcending structures.

In fact the boundaryless career is not so very new. Saxenian (1996) describes the history of Silicon Valley, USA, and argues that many of the features of the boundaryless career were strongly in evidence as long ago as the 1950s. Moving between companies, setting up one's own company, establishing networks that transcended organizational boundaries, and repeatedly learning new skills were all commonplace there at that time. This was a contrast to the companies on the US eastern seaboard where structures were more rigid and procedures more formal.

Arthur, Inkson and Pringle (1999) liken the old career to a long-running theater production. All the action occurred at one place. Actors played the same role for a long time, working from a constant or nearly constant script. If an actor left the production, his or her role was filled by someone else and the production continued. Actors in such productions could stay in work for a long time. But they ran the risk of being identified with one part for too long too soon, and failing to expand their skills and experience. The boundaryless career on the other hand is more akin to street theater. Scripts and roles are much more fluid, and there is a lot of improvisation. It can be set up very quickly with minimal props, and does not need a constant venue. It is probably composed of short episodes and vignettes rather than long scenes and acts. There may not be a coherent plot which unfolds as the drama progresses. Actors need to be flexible and responsive to their audience. It is important to be mobile, to respond quickly to opportunity, to adjust what is offered to the wishes of those present, and to move on soon and with minimal disruption. For the manager (if there is one) of the street theater, it is important to allow actors space to craft their own roles, to manage through relationships rather than procedures, and to tolerate failures.

A related point can be drawn from social psychology's concept of strong versus weak situations (Mischel, 1968). Strong situations are those where there are clear guidelines and rules about how one should behave, whereas weak situations lack these features. Hence strong situations suppress individual differences because everyone knows the rules. There may also be strong sanctions against those who contravene them. In weak situations people are more likely to behave in line with their personality or inclinations because there are fewer indications of what is supposed to happen. Weick (1996) among others has pointed out that many situations at work are weaker than they once were because of the changes noted earlier, and perhaps because of the increased value placed on innovation (King & Anderson, 1995) and diversity (Jackson, 2001). This means there is more opportunity, indeed requirement, to choose how one will behave and the situations one will seek out.

This seems a plausible line of thinking but there are some caveats. In many organizations there are attempts to reinforce culture through shared values as guides to behavior (Smith & Peterson, 1988). Also, as Weick notes, most work situations aren't so very weak. There are still defined tasks to be carried out; goals to be accomplished. And in cultures high on power distance and collectivism it is probable that work situations remain strong for most of those at middle and lower levels of organizations (Hofstede, 1980; Trompenaars, 1993). Nevertheless, the point is taken that from an individual's point of view career management means deciding or finding out for oneself what it is best to do. A clear identity, or identities, will help here. So will good social networks and decision-making skills and probably a high anxiety threshold and tolerance of ambiguity. Career management from the organizational viewpoint perhaps means defining core values which act as boundaries but leaving much scope for individuals to choose their behavior (cf. Schein, 1971). It may also mean resisting the temptation to recruit and reward only certain kinds of people, such as those who are similar to senior management.

Another important issue concerns so-called feminization at work (Fondas, 1996). This concerns not only the increasing participation of women in the labor market, but also the role of stereotypically feminine characteristics and experiences at work. In some respects the reality of the boundaryless career reflects the experience of women over many years. Historically, women have probably been more accustomed than men to adjusting to different kinds of work, retraining, and balancing family and work demands. This is perhaps a rather reactive image compared with the proactive go-getter implied by some proponents of the boundaryless career, but it still involves making decisions and choices as well as handling flexibility and discontinuity. It can also be argued that work styles which emphasize the feminine characteristics of cooperation, empathy, and community are likely to be better adapted to the 21st century workplace than the masculine style of independent goal-directed action. The point is, however, arguable – the masculine style of independent action to achieve personal goals also has some fairly obvious resonances with features of the boundaryless career. It is also apparent that masculine values prevail in many organizations, with a corresponding devaluing of feminine ones (Marshall, 1989). Women's pay also tends to be lower than men's, even for the same kind of work (Davidson, 1996).

Section Summary

Careers present many challenges to individuals and to organizations. The pace of change, unpredictable futures, and intense competition mean that learning must be continuous, and that personal and organizational development must be flexible and speedy while high performance is maintained. Perhaps it was always thus, but now it is more so, or more obviously so, than during most of the 20th century. People change jobs and types of work quite frequently, and in a relatively unpredictable way governed both by the demands of the labor market and their own vocational and lifestyle aspirations. There may well be more room for individual self-expression and self-direction than there once was, though not everyone finds this pleasant, and not everyone even experiences it.

KEY ISSUES IN CAREERS AND CAREER MANAGEMENT

Self and Identity in Careers

Much theory and practice in careers is based on the assumption that people will be happy and productive in their work if there is a good match between their interests, skills, and values on the one hand and the requirements and opportunities of work, on the other. At one level this must necessarily be true up to a point, but in the 21st century this self-fulfillment based conception is perhaps too simplistic. Most of us could not easily work for long in an environment which was seriously contrary to elements of our core self. On the other hand, many would not want to perform work to which we were well-suited but which did not preserve our future employability. Some tradeoffs and strategic thinking are needed. Also, tensions are possible between a person's abilities, interests, and values. These can have serious consequences. For example, staff in some strongly values-based organizations such as charities or pressure groups are likely to be attracted by those values. But there is a danger that they will not think enough about whether they will find the day-to-day work interesting or challenging.

Most of the self-assessment and career choice literatures assume that there is a fairly stable and general sense of self waiting to be assessed and expressed in individual action. It is thought to be helpful for the individual if a person's self-concept is accurate in the sense of agreeing with psychometric test results (Schrader & Steiner, 1996), and the perceptions of others (Church, 1997), though often this agreement is elusive. This whole approach is a distinctly western point of view, and may not be reflected in cultures which emphasize collective affiliations, joint action, and work as a duty rather than an opportunity for self-expression. Even within western cultures, many people when they complete self-assessment instruments say something like 'well, I'm like this at work, but like that at home.' In other words, they are saying that while there may be some core aspects of self, some other significant aspects are salient only in certain contexts.

Many would argue that the economic and workplace changes briefly described earlier have served to fragment and confuse many people's sense of self. Blustein and Noumair (1996) say: 'Given the prevalence of such powerful changes, one may be tempted to ask if we can ever really know ourselves, or are we forever caught in a web of nothingness?' They answer their own question by asserting that the notion of identity is still very useful, but must be seen as embedded in a person's relationships as well as personal histories. Relationships presumably change when a person's job does. Perhaps identities can be maintained through continuity in nonwork relationships, and new communication technologies may help in this. Even so, Sennett (1998) has argued that when people move with their work, they tend to be treated by their new neighbors as if they are starting a new life. Hence there is little encouragement to maintain existing relationships.

Senior managers say they desire employee commitment to the values and culture of the organization while also referring to the need to keep staffing levels to a minimum and the labor force as flexible as possible. To the extent that we do have a core sense of self identity, the current workplace therefore presents some challenges to individuals regarding how much of that self to invest in work, or more specifically in the employing organization. Rousseau (1998b) has argued that we do still identify with the organizations in which we work. If this is so, then we are going to need to be flexible in modifying our self-concepts as we move between organizations or our organizations change form around us.

Theories of career development reflect to some extent the social cognitive revolution in psychology (e.g., Brown, Brooks & Associates, 1996). The self is seen as a cognitive construct which plays a regulatory role in behavior, attitudes, and feelings. The concept of self-efficacy enjoys prominence here, as it does within social cognition more generally. Self-efficacy is defined as a person's belief in his or her ability to perform the actions necessary to bring about defined ends, and is therefore best considered a task-related construct rather than a general personality characteristic (Bandura, 1986). Self-efficacy affects career management in a number of direct and indirect ways. People's progress in career decision making (see below) is affected by the extent to which they believe they are capable of tackling the career decision-making task (Lent, Brown &

Hackett, 1994). Their sense of efficacy across a range of career management activities is likely to affect how willing they are to tackle them, how much effort they put in, and the goals they set themselves (Sadri & Robertson, 1993). More generally, self-efficacy influences people's choice of activities, which in turn affects self-perceived interests and abilities, and thus the sort of work they wish to engage in (Lent, Brown & Hackett, 1996). Furthermore, a sense of self-efficacy appears to play a direct role over and above vocational interests in helping people attain occupations that satisfy them (Donnay & Borgen, 1999), and there seem to be opportunities to influence self-efficacy through career interventions (Betz & Schifano, 2000).

Motivation and Thinking in Career Management

London (1993) has developed a conceptualization and measure of career motivation with three components. First is *career resilience*, which is the ability to adapt to changing circumstances, to take risks, and to bounce back from setbacks. *Career insight* is the extent to which a person has realistic perceptions of self and occupational environment, and can use these to formulate realistic career goals. The third component is *career identity*, which is the degree to which people define themselves in terms of their work and (if appropriate) the organization they work in. London equates these respectively to the persistence, energy, and direction components of motivation. Grzeda and Prince (1997) have found some support for the construct validity of these concepts. Nevertheless, motivation may not be the most appropriate label for this collection of constructs. Motivation is normally construed as the force driving behavior, but some of London's conceptualization looks more like skills and personal resources.

Expectancy theory could be more useful in predicting when a person will engage in attempts to manage his or her career. In the language of expectancy theory, valence would concern the value a person placed on experiencing whatever rewards he or she thought might arise from attempts to manage his or her career. Instrumentality would reflect the extent to which a person believes that successfully engaging in career management will make a difference to outcomes he or she values. Expectancy would refer to whether the person believed that he or she had the skills required to engage in effective career management. As already noted, this last point has received some attention in the careers literature in the form of self-efficacy.

Other motivation theories may also be relevant to career management. Goal-setting theory would predict that people will be most inclined to engage in career management when they have set specific and difficult but not impossible career goals. In terms of self-regulation theory described by Kuhl (1992), when a person has clear intentions and there is a moderate discrepancy between his or her current and desired positions, then that person is likely to adopt an action orientation, where self-regulatory strategies such as selective attention and emotion control come into play to keep behavior directed towards the goal.

Some strands of theory on adult cognitive development are potentially relevant to career management, but the connections have not yet been explored fully. The first strand is post-formal logic (Commons, Sinnott, Richards & Armon, 1989). This adopts post-modern philosophies in treating knowledge as subjective rather than objective, filtered as it is through various viewpoints and derived from asking certain questions as opposed to others. So-called advanced thinkers recognize this. Such thinkers are also characterized by acceptance of contradictions and attempts to integrate them into a coherent picture based on their own values which they recognize may be different from those held by some other people (Kramer, 1989).

A second theoretical strand relates to what is often called wisdom. This has been defined in many different ways, usually involving some combination of amount of knowledge, depth of understanding, and wholesomeness – that is, knowing what is good for self or other. Smith and colleagues (e.g., Smith & Baltes, 1990) have defined it in fairly practical terms as 'a cognitive expertise in the domain of fundamental life pragmatics, visible in situations related to life planning, life management, and life review.' A wise person is characterized by five features: (1) rich factual knowledge; (2) a range of procedures for organizing and manipulating information; (3) an understanding that events are embedded in different cultural and historical contexts; (4) an understanding of differences between people; and (5) a knowledge of the relative indeterminacy and unpredictability of life.

These cognitive approaches suggest that a key feature of the thinking of skilled career managers will be recognizing apparently contradictory tendencies between their career-related values and their interests, or between thoughts and feelings, and finding ways of integrating them in new self-understandings (Arnold, 1997c). They will do this using an internal dialog in which the 'speakers' argue from substantially different positions. They will be open to the possibility of personal change, rather than seeing the self as a constant around which the world has to be arranged. They will be able to accept the idea that there is no sure-fire solution to career problems without going to the other extreme, sometimes called the post-formal pathology, that all solutions are equally good or bad.

This focus on thinking is consistent with the current dominance of social cognition in psychology. However, more attention in social and organizational psychology in general is now being paid to the role of emotion in behavior at work, and to how emotions such as moods interact with attitudes and values (Kidd, 1998). Emotion has not been explicitly analyzed much in career theory. It needs to receive more attention from psychologists, not least because people have strong feelings about their careers and events which affect them.

Career Choice

The terms choice and decision, although perhaps subtly different in meaning, will be used interchangeably here. Career choice has long been construed as deciding what field of work, or occupation, one intends to work in. The focus remains on choice of type of work even though such choices can no longer be expected to last a working lifetime. Careers counselors know that many other kinds of career decisions also arise, such as whether to accept a relocation, whether to re-enter the workforce, whether to try to switch from one workgroup to another, and so on. Academic approaches to career choice tend to have one of two foci. The first is the *content of choice* (that is, what type of work a person chooses or ought to choose), and the second is the *choice process* (that is, how do they go about making choices, or how should they). The latter originally stemmed partly from the pioneering work of Donald Super (e.g., Super, 1957, 1990), who mapped out stages and substages of career, and in particular developed the concepts of career maturity and readiness for decision making.

Let us consider content-based approaches first. A number of typologies of people and occupations have been offered over the years (e.g., Roe, 1956). Several approaches to psychometric testing for career decision making were also made, partially independently of the typologies (Strong, 1943). But for some time now the most influential content-based theory has been that of John Holland (see Holland, 1997, for his most recent version). Briefly, Holland argues on the basis of practical counseling experience and a lot of research data that there are six 'pure types' of vocational personality (Figure 6.1):

(1) *Realistic* people, who like practical and/ or physical activities requiring strength or co-ordination as opposed to abstract, theoretical thinking. They are not particularly interested in social interaction and may be resistant to expressing feelings.
(2) *Investigative* people, who are interested in concepts, logic, and abstract problem solving. They tend to be logical, critical, and cautious. They put a low emphasis on human relations and like to tackle problems in a rational, impersonal way.
(3) *Artistic* people, who like to use their imagination an self-expression. They enjoy

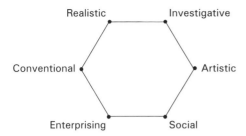

Figure 6.1　*John Holland's six types of vocational personality. (Source: Holland, 1997.)*

environments with few rules, where they can use their creativity and be in touch with their feelings. They tend to dislike rules and regulations.

(4) *Social* people, who tend to enjoy working together to help others and solve problems. They are often quite idealistic and altruistic. They usually come across to others as quite warm and caring.

(5) *Enterprising* people, who, like social ones, enjoy contact with people. But unlike social types, they are interested in managing, persuading, and getting their own way in an assertive manner. They enjoy action rather than thought and tend to seek leadership roles.

(6) *Conventional* people, who tend to emphasize organization and planning. They like structured environments such as administrative offices, and they value security and dependability. They enjoy clarity and being in control, but are less comfortable using their imagination.

The arrangement of the six types on a hexagon illustrates their degree of similarity with each other. Each person's personality resembles each of the six pure types to varying degrees. Occupational environments are transmitted largely through the people who inhabit them, and therefore occupations can be described using the same types as people. Other things being equal, effective career decisions are likely to be marked by congruence – that is, a good match between a person's personality and the occupational environment they have chosen. Holland has developed several self-report instruments to help people in the choice process. The most notable of these is the Self-Directed Search (SDS) (Holland, 1995), which is designed to be transparent and interpretable by the person who completed it without the help of an 'expert.'

Holland's theory has generated much research and debate. Some of this has concerned the hexagonal structure of types. There is reasonably supportive evidence that his concepts of personality link fairly well with others derived from the personality theory literature (e.g., Hogan & Blake,

1999). It also seems that the hexagonal structure is a reasonably accurate representation of the configuration of the types (Rounds & Tracey, 1993), though others have proposed alternatives based upon two axes (people vs. things and data vs. ideas – Prediger & Vansickle, 1992), and on a hierarchical structure (Gati, 1986). On the other hand, research on the benefits of congruence has not been so supportive. It seems that being in a congruent environment often does not lead to greater satisfaction (Young, Tokar & Subich, 1998). This could well be more a problem with research and measurement than with the theory itself (Chartrand & Walsh, 1999). It may be that jobs with the same or similar title vary a lot between organizational settings, and that assessment of the occupational environment needs to be more sensitive to individual circumstances than it currently is. Gottfredson (1999), among others, points out that developments along these lines are happening. Also, perhaps nowadays more diversity within occupations is tolerated or even welcomed than was once the case. Some research has tested the cross-cultural applicability of Holland's structure of vocational personalities, with moderately positive results (Farh, Leong & Law, 1998; Leong, Austin, Sekaran & Komaraju, 1998). The structure of interests seems to hold up quite well but is not necessarily the basis upon which people make career decisions.

Much attention has also been paid to the process of career decision making. This perhaps reflects the philosophy of many careers guidance practitioners that the key thing is to make decisions wisely rather than make wise decisions, though presumably the former tends to lead to the latter. As noted earlier, the concept of self-efficacy is important here because it dictates how, and how much, a person is able to approach career decision-making tasks. The assumption that being decided is necessarily a good thing is less prevalent than it was, and there is increasing interest in how apparently chance events in people's lives that lead to career decisions and success (such as being noticed by someone influential) are actually often a consequence of their skillful maneuvering into the right place at the right time (Mitchell, Levin & Krumboltz, 1999).

Krumboltz (1979) has made extensive use of social learning theory to explain career-related phenomena such as career decidedness and exploration, and to develop methods of 'treating' individuals with difficulties in these areas. Extensive work over the years has identified different reasons why a person might be undecided, and diagnostic tools have been developed to measure them (e.g., Gordon, 1998). One basic distinction which has major implications for choice of intervention is between being undecided and being habitually indecisive. Increasingly, the measures and interventions based upon them tend to focus on the dynamics of a person's thought processes as opposed to his or her static psychological state (e.g., the Career Beliefs Inventory, Krumboltz, 1991), with a particular focus on the metacognitions or frames of mind that people bring to career decisions. Decision-making methods and styles are also the subject of much research and practitioner attention. The focus is usually on rational emotion-free information processing techniques – for example, Gati's (1986) sequential elimination approach and Peterson, Sampson and Reardon's (1991) CASVE cycle.

Career Success

It is tempting to see the boundaryless career as liberating for individuals, and so indeed it is for some. However, there are casualties, particularly among those who lack marketable skills or who find it difficult to construe themselves as independent agents separable from their social context (Hirsch & Shanley, 1996). Those who are inclined to define career success in terms of organizational status may have a hard time, as status is more ambiguous than it was in many organizations, and as noted above, upward moves may be scarcer. The erosion of external signals of success also puts more of an onus on individuals to define their own success criteria. This in turn requires quite a deep self-understanding and perhaps closer attention to one's real values than was once needed. This can be difficult, but also offers the possibility of a greater sense of autonomy and individuality.

Of course, there has always been some variation in the criteria individuals use to evaluate their career. This is recognized to some extent in the literature on career success (e.g., Wayne, Liden, Kraimer & Graf, 1999). One general distinction is between objective and subjective success criteria. The former include salary, formal status in an organizational hierarchy, and (perhaps less obviously) avoiding involuntary unemployment. The latter include a sense of career or job satisfaction, feeling one has achieved what one wanted to, and believing that one has mastered the skills required in one's job. Sturges (1999) has argued that most managers do not spontaneously use the traditional career success criteria of status and salary when evaluating their own career, and that this may be a response to the advent of the boundaryless career. Personal achievement, accomplishment, enjoyment, recognition, and informal influence seem more salient, at least among managers. This may suggest that the erosion of external cues signaling success does not take away people's sense of 'psychological success' to the extent that is sometimes feared (Mirvis & Hall, 1996).

Another analysis of alternative conceptions of career success has been offered by Schein (1985), who developed the concept of career anchor. This refers to the set of interests, values, needs and skills a person develops through work experience, and which guides his or her career choices and criteria for evaluating career success. It is, as the word 'anchor' suggests, a stable point from which a person will not willingly drift very far. Schein has suggested on the basis of some empirical evidence from MIT graduates that there are nine distinct career anchors. Although there is not a large research literature on career anchors, the concept became more prominent at the end of the 20th century (e.g., Ettington, 1998). Schein (1996) has discussed how career anchors can be applied to 21st century careers. People who subscribe to the security/stability anchor may be most vulnerable, but there are tensions for most of us. For example, those with a technical/functional competence anchor can probably rest assured that experts will always be required, but then again the nature of their knowledge and skills tends to change rapidly, and they must keep up to date. Overall, it seems that career anchors are useful in helping both individuals and organizations define what they want and the issues that may arise in attaining their goals.

It is perhaps not surprising that many factors have been found to predict the extent to which a person experiences career success (Tharenou, 1997). Often it is easier to predict objective than subjective success. Much of the research has, however, involved managers in large organizations, so findings may not be easily generalizable to other settings, and may indeed reflect patterns of career that are becoming outdated. Individual and human capital variables such as ability, education, and length and type of work experience often have an impact on career success (e.g., Aryee, Chay & Tan, 1994). These may be outweighed by social psychological variables such as being sponsored or encouraged by a supervisor (Wayne et al., 1999), though this could depend a lot on the personnel decision-making processes an organization uses. It does seem that some significant influences on career success may be identifiable early in life. Long-term longitudinal data reported by Judge, Higgins, Thoresen and Barrick (1999) have shown that childhood personality (particularly conscientiousness) and mental ability substantially predict subjective and objective career success in middle adulthood.

Unfortunately, more obviously discriminatory factors such as gender, ethnicity, and age also play a role. Specifically regarding gender, there is clear evidence that even when other factors such as length of time in the labor market are controlled for, women managers still experience less objective success on average than men (Brett, Stroh & Reilly, 1992; Schneer & Reitman, 1995). These effects are less marked in environments where the proportion of women is higher. Women's investments in their development seem to bring less benefit than men's, but they do still help. Barriers to development experienced by women can be quite subtle (Ohlott, Ruderman & McCauley, 1994), and operate even when a woman has already attained quite high status (Lyness & Thompson, 1997).

Organizational factors such as recruitment and promotion policies and organizational structures can also make a difference. In larger organizations it has been argued that making a good start is crucial because the system operates rather like a knock-out tournament. Early 'wins' get a person noticed and greatly increase the probability that he or she is deemed worthy of subsequent advancement (Rosenbaum, 1989). Although this tournament model of careers sounds rather old-fashioned, elements of it are still visible in some organizations (Hurley & Sonnenfeld, 1998). Interpersonal factors and individual behavioral strategies tend to be difficult to disentangle in empirical research. For example, presumably work performance matters. Evaluations of performance may, however, be a product of other factors such as ability, the extent to which a person has been able to garner information and support from social networks and mentors, and the ways in which his or her behavior is interpreted and evaluated by the supervisor and other superiors (Greenhaus & Parasuraman, 1993).

Summary of Section

Vocational psychologists have made much progress in describing individuals' occupationally relevant identities and diagnosing their progress in various career-related tasks. However, perhaps some of the most salient issues in the early 21st century concern how much and what aspects of their identity individuals wish to express in the workplace. Other important questions concern the extent and nature of the cognitive skills, behavioral strategies and motivation individuals have at their disposal to engage in career management, and the processes involved in career management by individuals.

CAREER MANAGEMENT INTERVENTIONS IN ORGANIZATIONS

General Issues in the Provision of Interventions

The techniques for managing careers described in Table 6.1 vary a great deal in several respects. Some are formal occasions, such as development centers, career workshops, and some forms of counseling. Others can occur as part of a person's normal work. These include mentoring, personal development plans, career action centers and job assignments/rotation. Others again may happen 'behind closed doors' as far as those affected by them are concerned. Succession planning and the formation of career paths are examples. The various interventions also differ in terms of the amount of academic and practitioner literature devoted to them. Mentoring is

the clear leader here, with succession planning and development centers probably in a rather distant joint second place.

Perhaps more notable, however, is the variation that can occur between different manifestations of the same intervention. One choice is whether to focus on the person-at-work or on the whole person. Even an organizationally driven technique like succession planning can take into account a person's out-of-work commitments and interests, or alternatively just their work achievements and ambitions (Fletcher & Bailyn, 1996). Another issue is whether the intervention concerns principally the present and near future, or whether it encompasses the medium and long term. This may be a matter of organizational policy – for example, a personal development plan is often designed to focus on the present and near future (Tamkin, Barber & Hirsh, 1994). Alternatively, an intervention may be based on the needs and concerns of each individual, as is the case with counseling. A third issue is who owns the output of an intervention. A few organizations which use development centers simply hand the written feedback over to the person about whom it was written, for them to do with what they will. It is more common, however, for representatives of the organization to keep a copy and use it (often in collaboration with development center participants) for development, placement, and selection decisions (Jackson, 1993).

Decisions about these issues are, one suspects, often not thought through very carefully in the design of the intervention. Underlying them should be a clear sense of where responsibility for career management lies, the timescale upon which it can realistically be based, and what are the key goals it is designed to achieve. At least five possible purposes can be identified (Hirsh, Jackson & Jackson, 1995: 30). These are filling vacancies; *assessment* of potential, competencies, skills or interests; *development* of skills or competencies; identification of career or life options; and action to implement career or life plans. Note that all can be done with either organizational or individual needs top of the agenda.

It is not easy to ensure that interventions run smoothly, effectively, or indeed at all. Whatever goals are primary, everyone involved needs to see something worthwhile in it for them. Managers who feel they are operating in a culture which values short-term results above all else are unlikely to wish to allocate any of their own time or that of their teams to activities aimed at long-term planning. This is especially true if, as is increasingly the case, they have to find any costs from their own budgets. And insult is added to injury if there is the additional prospect of losing valued team members earmarked for promotion or developmental assignments, though managers may be able to see wider benefits beyond such local losses (Campion, Cheraskin & Stevens, 1994). A further hazard is that some influential people in an organization may see career management interventions as symptomatic of an overly paternalistic culture.

Thus these techniques do not automatically produce results. If the goals are not clear and/or not valued, if people do not feel competent to carry out the intervention, if there is no reward for doing so, and if the intervention is not tuned to individual needs, then there will be little motivation to do it, no matter what the potential organizational benefits. While oft-quoted factors like top management support can help, their impact is very limited unless they affect people's day-to-day experiences of using the intervention. As Hirsh and Jackson (1996) have said, it is better to do a small number of things thoroughly than a large number sketchily. This is especially true when senior management needs to reestablish its credibility in the organization, and show that its rhetoric has some link with reality as experienced by the rank and file (Herriot, Hirsh & Reilly, 1998).

Some Specific Interventions

Space does not permit an examination of the literatures on each individual organizational career management intervention. Some brief comments are nevertheless appropriate. The voluminous literature on *mentoring* includes theoretical analyses (e.g., Gibb, 1999), empirical tests (e.g., Arnold & Johnson, 1997), and case studies and advice about how to set up and run a mentoring scheme (e.g., Gray, 1989). Having received mentoring is often associated with greater career success as measured by traditional objective indices. Formal mentoring schemes are not always able to reproduce the benefits of informal mentoring relationships that spring up spontaneously, and in any case the research often does not show conclusively that mentoring itself was the cause of any outcomes observed. The possibilities and pitfalls of mentoring as a way of countering gender and ethnic disadvantage have been examined in some depth (e.g., Dreher & Dougherty, 1997). The focus has usually been on what happens to people on the receiving end of mentoring, but recently more attention has been paid to the mentor him- or herself (Allen, Poteet & Burroughs, 1997) and to the potentially harmful effects of mentoring that goes wrong (Scandura, 1998; Feldman, 1999).

Succession planning has diverse meanings. At the extremes, it can mean grooming one person for one post, or alternatively establishing a general staffing plan and implementing it (Hirsh, 1990). Research on succession planning has tended to focus on the impact upon company performance and strategy of chief executive officer (CEO) succession, particularly in terms of the functional specialization of the successor and whether he or she came from inside or outside the organization (Kesner & Sebora,

1994). Results have been somewhat inconclusive, though Lauterbach, Vu and Weisberg (1999) found that outsiders as opposed to insiders are more likely to take over as CEO when firm performance is poor, and that a firm's performance is more likely to improve with an external than an internal, even after one takes into account that a poor performing firm has more scope for improvement than an already successful one. Much of the research in this area also highlights the less than rational bases on which CEO selection decisions are often made.

Coverage of *development centers* (see Carrick & Williams, 1999, for a review) overlaps with that of assessment centers in its attention to the psychometric properties of assessors' ratings of candidates. There is some evidence that attending a development center influences a person's subsequent career behavior and success (e.g., Jones & Whitmore, 1995) but in general research on this is sparse even though Jackson (1993) pointed out that integrating development centers into organizational functioning is a much more problematic issue than running the center itself.

Regarding *development through work assignments*, McCauley, Ruderman, Ohlott and Morrow (1994) have identified 15 features of managerial jobs such as developing new directions and handling external pressure that can be regarded as developmental for the jobholder, though also potentially painful to live through. They have developed a questionnaire called the Developmental Challenge Profile (DCP) to assess these. What is developmental for one jobholder may not be for another, depending on his or her past experience, but the DCP may be a useful tool for placing managers appropriately. Campion et al. (1994) have suggested that using job rotation and placement on a large scale can bring net benefits, at least as seen through the eyes of those involved. The literature on *outplacement* is quite thin. There have been critiques of the conflicting roles and interests of those involved in outplacement provision (Miller & Robinson, 1994), and one relatively rigorous evaluation of outplacement provision has found that informal support was more helpful than outplacement in assisting people to find satisfactory new employment (Davy, Anderson & DiMarco, 1995).

Coverage of *personal development plans* has been mainly descriptive rather than evaluative, and has tended to show the limited scope of many PDPs (Tamkin et al., 1994). It is nevertheless clear that sometimes a PDP can require a more proactive approach to career development from individuals than they are accustomed to (Floodgate & Nixon, 1994). There is a huge literature on counseling in general, and some on *career counseling* specifically (e.g., Nathan & Hall, 1992). But there is little on how to implement career counseling in organizations. There is also little in the public domain on *career workshops* run in organizations.

Over the years there has been much concern about the high expectations of many new arrivals in organizations, and about the consequences for motivation, commitment, and voluntary turnover of those expectations being unmet. *Realistic job previews (RJPs)* are sometimes used to try to counter this (Wanous, 1989). As the name suggests, an RJP is designed to portray the job and organization as insiders really experience it rather than in 'hyped' terms designed to make the place sound as attractive as possible. Evidence suggests that the impact of RJPs is small but significant, and worth having at least for big organizations (Phillips, 1998). There is still some uncertainty about how RJPs work, when they do. Is it because they convey an air of honesty, because they encourage unsuitable people to drop out of the application process, or because they enable people to think in advance about how they will cope with the reality of the job? It is worth noting that RJPs put the onus to adjust on the individual, when perhaps representatives of the organization should instead be considering whether jobs could be made more palatable. There is also still a persistent fear that they may deter able applicants who would have been successful in the job (Bretz & Judge, 1998).

Evaluating the Impact of Career Management Activity

Considerable claims are made for the impact of career management interventions in organizations (e.g., London & Stumpf, 1982; Gutteridge et al., 1993). The claimed benefits seem best-suited to organizations with a high proportion of core employees who may expect, and be expected, to spend a long time in the organization. The benefits are said to include:

increasing employee commitment, satisfaction, and motivation
increasing productivity, performance, and person–job fit
identification of employees with most potential
identification of how well employees match organizational requirements
development of employees in line with organizational needs
socializing employees into the organizational culture

It has to be admitted that evaluations of the impact of career management by individuals for themselves, and by organizations for their members, are few and far between. Probably many reports of organizational evaluations are not released for public consumption. Outcome measures in published work often reflect traditional concepts of individuals' career success such as salary and promotion. Alternatively, some research has used either quite distal outcome measures such as organizational performance, or specific reaction-level ones in the form of 'happy sheets' where people indicate whether or not they liked what was offered. Intermediate measures seem less often to be used. This is in spite of the fact that they might match quite well the stated aims of the particular piece of career management concerned. Intermediate measures include recipients' career satisfaction, or the extent to which they feel clear about what they are trying to achieve and are empowered to achieve it, or the extent to which the skills of individuals match present and future organizational needs. Measures of constructs like career decidedness that are designed primarily for young people in education may also have some uses in organizational settings.

Evidence casting doubt on the value of individual career management has been presented by Noe (1996). Over a six-month period he examined the extent to which the reported use of career management by about 50 technical, clerical, and managerial employees predicted their willingness to engage in development activities, their development behavior (as rated by their bosses) and their job performance (again as rated by their bosses). He found almost no connections. On the other hand, Orpen (1994) reported more optimistic findings. He used self-report data from 129 supervisory and middle managers in various organizations, and found that the extent to which both the individuals and their organizations engaged in career management was correlated with objective measures of career success (salary growth and promotions received) and with subjective ones (self-rated career performance and career satisfaction). These evaluations are nevertheless limited in scope. They are relatively short-term and they focus on observable behaviors rather than patterns of thinking.

Although these words are often used, it is probably fair to say that more research really is required to evaluate the impact of career management activities. But of course thorough evaluations are long drawn out, not least because any fruits of career management might be expected to become apparent only after some time. Choice of time-lag is in fact quite difficult. It should be geared to the design and goals of the intervention being evaluated. There is also the difficulty that other events may serve to obscure or moderate the impact of what is being evaluated. Further, as noted earlier, evaluation criteria need to be more carefully chosen to match organizational and personal career priorities.

Section Summary

A wide variety of career management interventions is available in organizational settings, and many organizations use at least one or two of them. In many cases, though, one suspects that their efficacy is limited. Unclear goals, a lack of obvious benefits for one or more of the parties involved, poor design or implementation or poor integration with other organizational processes are the likely culprits. Research has been frustratingly sparse concerning the impact of interventions and which features of their design which can most enhance their impact. Both those who talk up career management as a vital tool and those who decry it as a waste of time should heed this lack of strong evidence.

CONCLUSIONS

There is little doubt that careers have become, on average, less predictable and in many ways more demanding for the individuals experiencing them and the organizations in which they work. It has been argued here that careers and career management need careful attention in these challenging circumstances. Among other things this means bringing to bear theory from psychology and a determination to examine the key issues from the perspectives of individual, employing organization, and wider society. It also means a greater attention to the evaluation of attempts to manage careers. Although difficult to achieve, more robust study designs with longer time-frames and well-chosen outcome measures are badly needed. Cross-cultural tests of key theories, techniques, and measures are beginning to be reported with more frequency (e.g., Chay & Aryee, 1999; Aryee, Fields & Luk, 1999) but many more are needed. Moreover, such tests normally concern the operation of western ideas in other cultural contexts. More efforts are needed to use ideas from, for example, Asian and Chinese cultural contexts in western contexts. The applicability and effectiveness of career management techniques in small organizations as opposed to large ones also requires further investigation.

A serious commitment at societal level to lifelong learning and career management requires investment in impartial careers guidance (Watts, 1996) and continuing education and training. In many countries this investment will probably come from government, if it comes at all. Nevertheless, individuals will continue to carry the major responsibility for managing their careers. A daunting range of skills and personal resources could be involved. These include: a variety of social skills; personal adaptability, insight, and resilience; effective thought patterns; up-to-date competencies and knowledge (including the use of information and communication technology); and the ability to identify future job and career management opportunities. No doubt this list could be extended. Organizations probably need to employ a limited range of career management interventions with adequate resourcing and clear goals that are consistent with their culture and which can be seen to benefit all parties involved. Or at least, that is how it seems at present. As implied above, research has yet to uncover what are the most important elements of career management, or even whether it is possible to speak of most important elements with any generality.

Work and organizational psychology will be enriched greatly by deeper understanding of a number of other career-related issues. Analysis of how people can deploy their identities and commitments to deal with the complex demands made by work and other arenas of life requires integration of several areas of applied and not-so-applied psychology. The development of theories and practical resources to help people with career decisions other than choice of field of work is needed, and so is a more refined understanding and/or measurement of the concept of congruence between person and career environment. Further objective data about the careers people follow in different cultures would aid our understanding of what is really happening as opposed to what is believed to be happening. More information about how people experience their careers and construct narratives to make sense of them in a world lacking readily available storylines would also be informative. Most, though not all of the psychological research on careers is quantitative and hypothesis testing, and more qualitative work that uses people's own stories would be helpful (Young & Borgen, 1990). The consequences of those narratives for how individuals tackle their futures might turn out to be one of the most important issues for careers research from a psychological perspective in the 21st century.

ACKNOWLEDGMENT

Thanks to Lisa Jones for her assistance in compiling the references and correcting stylistic errors and deficiencies.

REFERENCES

Allen, T.D., Poteet, M.L., & Burroughs, S.M. (1997). The mentor's perspective: A qualitative inquiry and future research agenda. *Journal of Vocational Behavior, 51,* 70–89.

Amabile, T.M., & Conti, R. (1999). Changes in the work environment for creativity during downsizing. *Academy of Management Journal, 42,* 630–640.

Arnold, J. (1997a). The Psychology of career in organizations. In C.L. Cooper, & I.T. Robertson (Eds.), *International review of industrial and organizational psychology,* Vol. 12. Chichester: Wiley.

Arnold, J. (1997b). *Managing careers into the 21st century*. London: Paul Chapman Publishing.

Arnold, J. (1997c). Nineteen propositions concerning the nature of effective thinking for career management in a turbulent world. *British Journal of Guidance and Counselling*, 25, 447–462.

Arnold, J., & Johnson, K. (1997). Mentoring in early career. *Human Resource Management Journal*, 7(4), 61–70.

Arthur, M.B. (1994). The boundaryless career: A new perspective for organizational enquiry. *Journal of Organizational Behavior*, 15, 295–306.

Arthur, M.B., Inkson, K., & Pringle, J. (1999). *The new careers*. London: Sage.

Arthur, M.B., & Rousseau, D.M. (Eds.) (1996). *The boundaryless career: A new employment principle for a new organizational era*. Oxford: Oxford University Press.

Aryee, S., Chay, Y.W., & Tan, H.H. (1994). An examination of the antecedents of subjective career success among a managerial sample in Singapore. *Human Relations*, 47, 487–509.

Aryee, S., Fields, D., & Luk, V. (1999). A cross-cultural test of a model of the work-family interface. *Journal of Management*, 25, 491–511.

Bandura, A. (1986). *Social foundations of thought and action: A social cognitive theory*. Englewood Cliffs, NJ: Prentice-Hall.

Betz, N.E., & Schifano, R.S. (2000). Evaluation of an intervention to increase Realistic self-efficacy and interests in college women. *Journal of Vocational Behavior*, 56, 35–52.

Blustein, D.L., & Noumair, D.A. (1996). Self identity in career development: Implications for theory and practice. *Journal of Counseling and Development*, 74, 433–441.

Brett, J.M., Stroh, L.K., & Reilly, A.H. (1992). Job transfer. In C.L. Cooper, & I.T. Robertson (Eds.), *International review of industrial and organizational psychology*. Vol. 7. Chichester: Wiley.

Bretz, R., & Judge, T. (1998). Realistic job previews: A test of the adverse self-selection hypothesis. *Journal of Applied Psychology*, 83, 330–337.

Bridges, W. (1995). *Jobshift: How to prosper in a workplace without jobs*. London: Nicholas Brealey.

Brown, D., Brooks, L., & Associates (1996). *Career choice and development* (3rd ed.). San Francisco: Jossey-Bass.

Campion, M.A., Cheraskin, L., & Stevens, M.J. (1994). Career-related antecedents and outcomes of job rotation. *Academy of Management Journal*, 37, 1518–1542.

Carrick, P., & Williams, R. (1999). Development centres – a review of assumptions. *Human Resource Management Journal*, 9, 77–92.

Cascio, W.F. (1993). Downsizing: What do we know? What have we learned? *Academy of Management Executive*, 7, 95–104.

Chapman, A.J., Sheehy, N.P., Heywood, S., Dooley, B., & Collins, S.C. (1995). The organizational implications of teleworking. In C.L. Cooper, & I.T. Robertson (Eds.), *International review of industrial and organizational psychology*, Vol. 10. Chichester: Wiley.

Chartrand, J., & Walsh, W.B. (1999). What should we expect from congruence? *Journal of Vocational Behavior*, 55, 136–146.

Chay, Y.-W., & Aryee, S. (1999). Potential moderating influence of career growth opportunities on careerist orientation and work attitudes: Evidence of the protean career era in Singapore. *Journal of Organizational Behavior*, 20, 613–623.

Church, A.H. (1997). Managerial self-awareness in high-performing individuals in organizations. *Journal of Applied Psychology*, 82, 281–292.

Cohen, L. (2000). Careers. In T. Redman, & A.J. Wilkinson (Eds.), *Human resource management: Theory and practice*. London: Addison-Wesley.

Commons, M.L., Sinnott, J.D., Richards, F.A., & Armon, C. (Eds.) (1989). *Adult development: Comparisons and applications of developmental models*. New York: Praeger.

Davidson, M.J. (1996). Women and employment. In P. Warr (Ed.), *Psychology at work* (4th ed.). London: Penguin.

Davy, J.A., Anderson, J.S., & DiMarco, N. (1995). Outcome comparisons of formal outplacement services and informal support. *Human Resource Development Quarterly*, 6, 275–288.

Donnay, D.A.C., & Borgen, F.H. (1999). The incremental validity of vocational self-efficacy: An examination of interest, self-efficacy, and occupation. *Journal of Counseling Psychology*, 46, 432–447.

Dreher, G.F., & Dougherty, T.W. (1997). Substitutes for career mentoring: Promoting equal opportunity through career management and assessment systems. *Journal of Vocational Behavior*, 51, 110–124.

Ettington, D. (1998). Successful career plateauing. *Journal of Vocational Behavior*, 52, 72–88.

Farh, J.-L., Leong, F., & Law, K.S. (1998). Cross-cultural validity of Holland's model in Hong Kong. *Journal of Vocational Behavior*, 55, 425–440.

Feldman, D.C. (1999). Toxic mentors or toxic proteges? A critical re-examination of dysfunctional mentoring. *Human Resource Management Review*, 9, 247–278.

Fletcher, J.K., & Bailyn, L. (1996). Challenging the last boundary: Reconnecting work and family. In M.B. Arthur, & D. Rousseau (Eds.), *The boundaryless career: A new employment principle for a new organizational era*. Oxford: Oxford University Press.

Floodgate, J.F., & Nixon, A.E. (1994). Personal development plans: The challenge of implementation – a case study. *Journal of European Industrial Training*, 18, 43–47.

Fondas, N. (1996). Feminization at work: Career implications. In M.B. Arthur, & D. Rousseau (Eds.), *The boundaryless career: A new employment principle for a new organizational era*. Oxford: Oxford University Press.

Gati, I. (1986). Making career decisions – a sequential elimination approach. *Journal of Counseling Psychology*, 33, 408–417.

Gibb, S. (1999). The usefulness of theory: A case study in evaluating formal mentoring schemes. *Human Relations*, *52*, 1055–1076.

Goffee, R., & Scase, R. (1992). Organizational change and the corporate career: The restructuring of managers' job aspirations. *Human Relations*, *45*, 363–385.

Gordon, V.N. (1998). Career decidedness types: A literature review. *Career Development Quarterly*, *46*, 386–403.

Gottfredson, G.D. (1999). John L. Holland's contributors to vocational psychology: A review and evaluation. *Journal of Vocational Behavior*, *55*, 15–40.

Gray, W.A. (1989). Situational mentoring: Custom designing planned mentoring programs. *Mentoring International*, *3*, 19–28.

Greenhaus, J.H., & Callanan, G.A. (1994). *Career management* (2nd ed.). London: Dryden Press.

Greenhaus, J.H., & Parasuraman, S. (1993). Job performance attributions and career advancement prospects: An examination of gender and race effects. *Organizational Behavior and ·Human Decision Processes*, *55*, 273–297.

Grzeda, M.M., & Prince, J.B. (1997). Career motivation measures: A test of convergent and discriminant validity. *The International Journal of Human Resource Management*, *8*, 172–196.

Guest, D. (1998). Is the psychological contract worth taking seriously? *Journal of Organizational Behavior*, *19*, 649–664.

Guest, D., & Mackenzie Davey, K. (1996) Don't write off the traditional career. *People Management*, 22 February, 22–25.

Gutteridge, T.G., Leibowitz, Z.B., & Shore, J.E. (1993). *Organizational career development*. San Francisco: Jossey-Bass.

Hall, D.T., & Mirvis, P.H. (1995). The new career contract: Developing the whole person at midlife and beyond. *Journal of Vocational Behavior*, *45*, 328–346.

Handy, C. (1994). *The empty raincoat*. London: Hutchinson.

Hartley, J., Jacobson, D., Klandermans, B., & Van Vuuren, T. (1991). *Job insecurity: Coping with jobs at risk*. London: Sage.

Herriot, P., Hirsh, W., & Reilly, P. (1998). *Trust and transition*. Chichester: Wiley.

Herriot, P., & Pemberton, C. (1995). *New deals*. Chichester: Wiley.

Hirsch, P.M., & Shanley, M. (1996). The rhetoric of boundaryless – or, how the newly empowered managerial class bought into its own marginalization. In M.B. Arthur, & D. Rousseau (Eds.), *The boundaryless career: A new employment principle for a new organizational era*. Oxford: Oxford University Press.

Hirsh, W. (1990). *Succession planning: Current practice and future issues*. Brighton: Institute of Manpower Studies.

Hirsh, W., & Jackson, C. (1996). *Strategies for career development: Promise, practice and pretence*. Brighton: Institute for Employment Studies.

Hirsh, W., Jackson, C., & Jackson, C. (1995). *Careers in organisations: Issues for the future*. Brighton: Institute for Employment Studies.

Hofstede, G. (1980). *Culture's consequences*. London: Sage.

Hogan, R., & Blake, R. (1999). John Holland's vocational typology and personality theory. *Journal of Vocational Behavior*, *55*, 41–56.

Holland, J.L. (1995). *Self-directed search (SDS) form R* (4th ed.). Odessa: Psychological Assessment Resources.

Holland, J.L. (1997). *Making vocational choices: A theory of vocational personalities and work environments*. (3rd ed.). Englewood Cliffs, NJ: Prentice-Hall.

Howard, A. (1995). A framework for work change. In A. Howard (Ed.), *The changing nature of work*. San Francisco: Jossey-Bass.

Hurley, A.E., & Sonnenfeld, J.A. (1998). The Effect of organizational experience on managerial career attainment in an internal labor market. *Journal of Vocational Behavior*, *52*, 172–190.

Hutton, W. (1995). *The state we're in*. London: Cape.

Iles, P., & Mabey, C. (1993). Managerial career development programmes: Effectiveness, availability and acceptability. *British Journal of Management*, *4*, 103–118.

Inkson, K. (1995). Effects of changing economic conditions on managerial job changes and careers. *British Journal of Management*, *6*, 183–194.

Jackson, C. (1993). *Development centres: Developing or assessing people?* Brighton: Institute of Manpower Studies.

Jackson, S. (2001). Diversity in organizations. In N. Anderson, D.S. Ones, H.K. Sinangil, & C. Viswesvaran (Eds.), *International handbook of work and organizational psycyhology*. London: Sage.

Jones, R.G., & Whitmore, M.D. (1995). Evaluating developmental assessment centers as interventions. *Personnel Psychology*, *48*, 377–388.

Judge, T.A., Higgins, C.A., Thoresen, C.J., & Barrick, M. (1999). The big five personality traits, general mental ability, and career success across the life span. *Personnel Psychology*, *52*, 621–652.

Kanter, R.M. (1989). *When giants learn to dance*. New York: Simon & Schuster.

Kesner, I.F., & Sebora, T.C. (1994). Executive succession: Past, present and future. *Journal of Management*, *20*, 327–372.

Kidd, J. (1998). Emotion: An absent presence in career theory. *Journal of Vocational Behavior*,

King, N., & Anderson, N. (1995). *Innovation and change in organizations*. London: Routledge.

Kram, K.E. (1985). *Mentoring at work: Developmental relationships in organizational life*. Glenview, IL: Scott, Foresman & Co.

Kramer, D.A. (1989). Development of an awareness of contradiction across the life span and the question of postformal operations. In M.L. Commons, J.D. Sinnott, F.F. Richards, & C. Armon (Eds.), *Adult development: Comparisons and applications of developmental models*. New York: Praeger.

Krumboltz, J.D. (1979). A social learning theory of career decision making. In A.M. Mitchell, G.B. Jones, & J.D. Krumboltz (Eds.), *Social learning and career decision making.* Cranston, RI: Caroll Press.

Krumboltz, J.D. (1991). *Manual for the career beliefs inventory.* Palo Alto, CA: Consulting Psychologists Press.

Kuhl, J. (1992). A theory of self-regulation: Action versus state orientation, self-discrimination and some applications. *Applied Psychology: an International Review, 41,* 97–129.

Lauterbach, B., Vu, J., & Weisberg, J. (1999). Internal vs. external successions and their effect on firm performance. *Human Relations, 52,* 1485–1504.

Lawler, E.E. III (1994). From job-based to competency-based organizations. *Journal of Organizational Behavior, 15,* 3–15.

Lent, R.W., Brown, S.D., & Hackett, G. (1994). Toward a unifying social cognitive theory of career and academic interest, choice and performance. *Journal of Vocational Behavior, 45,* 79–122.

Lent, R.W., Brown, S.D., & Hackett, G. (1996). Career development from a social cognitive perspective. In D. Brown, L. Brooks. *Career choice and development* (3rd ed.). San Francisco: Jossey-Bass.

Leong, F., Austin, J.T., Sekaran, U., & Komaraju, M. (1998). An evaluation of cross-cultural validity of Holland's theory: Career choices by workers in India. *Journal of Vocational Behavior, 55,* 441–455.

London, M. (1993). Relationships between career motivation, empowerment and support for career development. *Journal of Occupational and Organizational Psychology, 66,* 55–69.

London, M., & Stumpf, S. (1982). *Managing Careers.* Reading, MA: Addison-Wesley.

Lyness, K.S., & Thompson, D.E. (1997). Above the glass ceiling? A comparison of matched samples of female and male executives. *Journal of Applied Psychology, 82,* 359–375.

Marshall, J. (1989). Re-visioning career concepts: A feminist invitation. In M.B. Arthur, D.T. Hall, & B. Lawrence (Eds.), *Handbook of career theory.* New York: Cambridge University Press.

McCauley, C.D., Ruderman, M.N., Ohlott, P.J., & Morrow, J.E. (1994). Assessing the developmental components of managerial jobs. *Journal of Applied Psychology, 79,* 544–560.

Miller, M.V., & Robinson, C. (1994). Managing the disappointment of job termination: Outplacement as a cooling out device. *Journal of Applied Behavioral Science, 30,* 5–21.

Millward, L.J., & Brewerton, P.M. (1999). Contractors and their psychological contracts. *British Journal of Management, 10,* 253–274.

Mirvis, P.H., & Hall, D.T. (1996). Psychological success and the boundaryless career. In M.B. Arthur, & D. Rousseau (Eds.), *The boundaryless career: A new employment principle for a new organizational era.* Oxford: Oxford University Press.

Mischel, W. (1968). *Personality and assessment.* New York: Wiley.

Mitchell, K., Levin, A.S., & Krumboltz, J.D. (1999). Planned happenstance: Constructing unexpected career opportunities. *Journal of Counseling and Development, 77,* 115–124.

Morrison, E.W., & Robinson, S.L. (1997). When employees feel betrayed: A model of how psychological contract violation develops. *Academy of Management Review, 22,* 226–256.

Nathan, R., & Hill, L. (1992). *Career counselling.* London: Sage.

Noe, R.A. (1996). Is career management related to employee development and performance? *Journal of Organizational Behavior, 17,* 119–133.

Ohlott, P.J., Ruderman, M.N., & McCauley, C.D. (1994). Gender differences in managers' developmental job experiences. *Academy of Management Journal, 37,* 47–67.

Orpen, C. (1994). The effects of organizational and individual career management on career success. *International Journal of Manpower, 15,* 27–37.

Pearce, J.L. (1993). Toward an organizational behavior of contract laborers. *Academy of Management Journal, 36,* 1082–1096.

Perlmutter, M., & Hall, E. (1992). *Adult development and ageing* (2nd ed.). Chichester: Wiley.

Peterson, G.W., Sampson, J.P., & Reardon, R.C. (1991). *Career development and services: A cognitive approach.* Pacific Grove, CA: Brooks/Cole.

Phillips, J. (1998). Effects of realistic job previews on multiple organizational outcome: A meta-analysis. *Academy of Management Journal, 41,* 673–690.

Prediger, D.J., & Vansickle, T.R. (1992). Locating occupations on Holland's hexagon: Beyond RIASEC. *Journal of Vocational Behavior, 40,* 111–128.

Roe, A. (1956). *Psychology of occupations.* New York: Wiley.

Rosenbaum, J.E. (1989). Organization career systems and employee misperceptions. In M.B. Arthur, D.T. Hall, & B. Lawrence (Eds.), *Handbook of Career Theory.* New York: Cambridge University Press.

Rounds, J., & Tracey, T.J. (1993). 'Prediger's dimensional representation of Holland's RIASEC circumplex', *Journal of Applied Psychology, 78,* 875–890.

Rousseau, D.M. (1995). *Psychological contracts in organizations.* London: Sage.

Rousseau, D.M. (1998a). The 'problem' of the psychological contract reconsidered. *Journal of Organizational Behavior, 19,* 665–671.

Rousseau, D.M. (1998b). Why workers still identify with organizations. *Journal of Organizational Behavior, 19,* 217–233.

Sadri, G., & Robertson, I.T. (1993). Self-efficacy and work-related behaviour: A review and meta-analysis. *Applied Psychology: An International Review, 42,* 139–152.

Saxenian, A. (1996). Beyond boundaries: Open labour markets and learning in Silicon Valley. In M.B. Arthur, & D. Rousseau (Eds.), *The boundaryless career: A new employment principle for a new organizational era.* Oxford: Oxford University Press.

Scandura, T.A. (1998). Dysfunctional mentoring relationships and outcomes. *Journal of Management, 24,* 449–467.

Schein, E.H. (1971). The individual, the organization, and the career: A conceptual scheme. *Journal of Applied Behavioral Science, 7,* 401–426.

Schein, E.H. (1985). *Career anchors: Discovering your real values.* London: Pfeiffer and Co.

Schein, E.H. (1996). Career anchors revisited: Implications for career development in the 21st century. *Academy of Management Executive, 10,* 80–99.

Schneer, J.A., & Reitman, F. (1995). The impact of gender as managerial careers unfold. *Journal of Vocational Behavior, 47,* 290–315.

Schrader, B.W., & Steiner, D.D. (1996). Common comparison standards: An approach to improving agreement between self and supervisory performance ratings. *Journal of Applied Psychology, 81*(6), 813–820.

Sennett, R. (1998). *The corrosion of character: The personal consequences of work in the new capitalism.* Norton: New York.

Shah, P.P. (2000). Network destruction: The structural implications of downsizing. *Academy of Management Journal, 43,* 101–112.

Smith, J., & Baltes, P.B. (1990). A study of wisdom-related knowledge: Age/cohort differences in response to life planning problems. *Developmental Psychology, 26,* 494–505.

Smith, P.B., & Peterson, M.F. (1988). *Leadership, organizations and culture: An event management approach.* London: Sage.

Strong, E.K. (1943). *Vocational interests of men and women.* Stanford University Press, California.

Sturges, J. (1999). What it means to succeed: Personal conceptions of career success held by male and female managers at different ages. *British Journal of Management, 10,* 239–252.

Sullivan, S.E. (1999). The changing nature of careers: A review and research agenda. *Journal of Management, 25,* 457–484.

Super, D.E. (1957). *The psychology of careers.* New York: Harper & Row.

Super, D.E. (1990). Career and life development. In D. Brown, & L. Brooks (Eds.), *Career choice and development* (2nd ed.). San Francisco, Jossey-Bass.

Tamkin, P., Barber, L., & Hirsh, W. (1994). *Personal development plans: Case studies of practice.* Brighton: Institute for Employment Studies.

Templer, A.J., & Cawsey, T.F. (1999). Rethinking career development in an era of portfolio careers. *Career Development International, 4,* 70–76.

Tharenou, P. (1997). Managerial career advancement. In C.L. Cooper, & I.T. Robertson (Eds.), *International review of industrial and organizational psychology,* Vol. 12. Chichester: Wiley.

Thomas, R., & Dunkerley, D. (1999). Careering downwards? Middle managers' experiences in the downsized organization. *British Journal of Management, 10,* 157–170.

Trompenaars, F. (1993). *Riding the waves of culture.* London: Brealey.

Turnley, W.H., & Feldman, D.C. (2000) Re-examining the effects of psychological contract violations: Unmet expectations and job dissatisfaction as mediators. *Journal of Organizational Behavior, 21,* 25–42.

Wanous, J.P. (1989). Installing a realistic job preview: Ten tough choices. *Personnel Psychology, 42,* 117–133.

Watts, A.G. (1996). Toward a policy for lifelong career development: A transatlantic perspective. *Career development quarterly, 45,* 41–53.

Wayne, S.J., Liden, R.C., Kraimer, M.L., & Graf, I.K. (1999). The role of human capital, motivation and supervisor sponsorship in predicting career success. *Journal of Organizational Behavior, 20,* 577–595.

Weick, K.E. (1996). Enactment and the boundaryless career: Organizing as we work. In M.B. Arthur, & D. Rousseau (Eds.), *The boundaryless career: A new employment principle for a new organizational era.* Oxford: Oxford University Press.

Young, G., Tokar, D., & Subich, L. (1998). Congruence revisited: Do 11 indices differentially predict job satisfaction and is the relation moderated by person and situation variables? *Journal of Vocational Behavior, 52,* 208–223.

Young, R.A., & Borgen, F. (Eds.) (1990). *Methodological approaches to the study of career.* New York: Praeger.

Young, R.A., & Collin, A. (Eds.) (1992). *Interpreting career: Hermeneutical studies of lives in context.* Westport, CT: Praeger.

7

Psychological Contracts in Employment

RENÉ SCHALK and DENISE M. ROUSSEAU

Contemporary employment relationships are changing as a consequence of fundamental shifts in the nature of work. Changing the conditions under which firms are considered successful impacts on the critical features of the employment relationships that comprise them. In the context of the psychological contract, differences between workers relate to basic features in the negotiation of the employment relationship. The pressures for greater firm-level flexibility have led to significant changes in employment relations within firms. The degree to which these changes have occured, and the concomitant ease of their implementation, are linked to societal factors that dictate the zone of negotiability and shape the roles played by government and other parties to the employment relationship. The psychological contracts workers experience cross-nationally are becoming more diverse within firms, more idiosyncratic between people, and more directly shaped by market-related factors. The implications of these trends are that employers and workers are expected to bargain over a broader range of terms (including work/family balance, the worker's stake in the company, the employer's rights to worker knowledge and intellectual products, etc.). The parties to the psychological contract are expected to become even more diverse (and more differentiated between workers) as more firms and workers value and participate in inter-organizational relationships (clients, joints ventures, occupational groups, professions, start-up ventures, etc.). Firms and workers will strive to make their employment terms more explicit and to reduce miscommunication, particularly in arrangements that are short term or cross cultural boundaries. In the future, we can expect considerable innovation and experimentation in contracting. Critical questions will center on how to balance differentiation and fairness, especially in situations where employees are interdependent, and how to integrate groups and promote cooperation while keeping clear individual psychological contracts.

INTRODUCTION

Exchange relationships and the promises on which they are based are as old as mankind. Indeed, the first recorded psychological contract violation may well be the story of Adam and Eve. When they violated the agreement not to eat from the tree of knowledge, they began a long history of promise, commitment, violation, and renewed relationships.

This chapter includes insights gained from considering the nature of psychological contracts from a cross-national point of view. Employment relationships in today's global society are increasingly based upon mutually accepted, voluntarily exchanged promises between two or more parties, where each gains if the exchange agreement is fulfilled, and loses if it is not (Rousseau & Schalk, 2000). These relationships confront certain common forces the world over, promoting comparable

Table 7.1   *Past and emergent forms of employment relationships*

Characteristic	Past form	Emergent form
Focus	Security, continuity, loyalty	Exchange, future employability
Format	Structured, predictable, stable	Unstructured, flexible, open to (re)negotiation
Underlying basis	Tradition, fairness, social justice, socioeconomic class	Market forces, saleable abilities and skills, added value
Employer's responsibilities	Continuity, job security, training, career prospects	Equity (as perceived), reward for added value
Employee's responsibilities	Loyalty, attendance, satisfactory performance, compliance with authority	Entrepreneurship, innovation, enacting changes to improve performance, excellent performance
Contractual relations	Formalized, mostly via trade union or collective representation	Individual's responsibility to bargain for their services (internally or externally)
Career management	Organization's responsibility, internal careers planned and facilitated through personnel department input	Individual's responsibility, outspiraling careers by personal reskilling and retraining

developments. At the same time, psychological contracts, like the people who are party to them, are affected by the societies in which they are embedded. We first address common developments in employment across countries and then examine the cultural and institutional similarities and differences that persistently affect the formation of psychological contracts. The chapter concludes with the prospects for the future.

TRENDS IN EMPLOYMENT RELATIONSHIPS

Contemporary employment relationships are changing as a consequence of fundamental shifts in the nature of work. Breakthroughs in information systems, a rise in global competition, and escalating interdependence between organizations and people have created new fundamental 'rules' for organizations. Today, a firm's success is often gauged in terms of capacity for rapid change and its responsiveness to multiple constituencies, in an environment of telescoping time frames for performance and a need for greater internal and external cooperation. Changing the conditions under which firms are considered successful impacts the critical features of the employment relationships that constitute them (Anderson & Schalk, 1998). For many employees, the most important change has been the increasing pressure for greater flexibility on their part coupled with a loss of job security. Employers are demanding greater worker innovation and contribution at the same time they are assessing the demonstrable value each worker provides. Across nations, this has led to greater use of explicit performance requirements as conditions of employment. Indeed, traditional concepts such as organizational citizenship,

defined as extra-role behavior on behalf of the firm, may no longer carry the same meaning when very little behavior is considered 'extra role' and workers are expected to contribute to the organization above and beyond the letter of any formal job descriptions (Anderson & Schalk, 1998). Anderson and Schalk present an overview of past and emergent forms of the 'typical' working relationship, shown in Table 7.1.

As firms move towards the 'emergent' form, they do so in response to pressure for greater organizational flexibility. This increased flexibility is manifest in the diversity between workers in employment relationships and in the changes in each individual worker's duties and performance demands over the duration of the employment relationship. In the context of the psychological contract, differences between and within workers relate to two basic features in the negotiation of the employment relationship:

(1) the degree to which firms and workers are able to negotiate around a broad or narrow set of employment related terms, known as the 'zone of negotiability';
(2) the diversity of parties to the contract, which can include the firm, the workgroup, clients/customers, managers, the union, and the state.

The Zone of Negotiability

The 'zone of negotiability' refers to the terms and conditions of employment that society allows either the worker or the firm to negotiate. The vast majority of contracts in which the average person participates have terms that are imposed by society – for example, few homeowners have the ability to negotiate an individual price for electricity. Psychological contracts in employment follow a

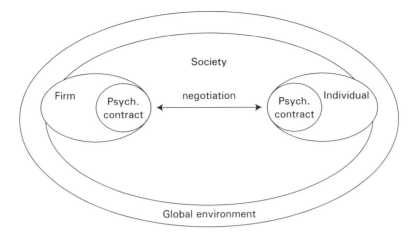

Figure 7.1   *Key contexts for psychological contracting*

similar pattern: all societies impose some limits on the bargaining power of employees and firms, and a worker cannot typically sign away the protections his or her country's labor laws provide. Negotiations about employment relationships take place within this context and vary with worker status, which differs for independent contractors, full-time workers, and part-time employees (see Figure 7.1).

The freedom to enter into exchange relationships is always a matter of degree; the very meaning of the word 'freedom' is the subject of an ongoing debate. The question is whether the absence of legal protections for workers promotes greater worker choice or greater inequality between the haves and have-nots. These issues mirror those discussed in economic sociology (e.g., Swedberg, 1993), but from the psychological contract perspective the debate raises a fundamental question about the consequences of psychological contracts for firms and workers and the consequences that stem from other forms of binding obligations, such as those imposed by law or civic duty (e.g., government-mandated pensions or health care benefits).

Societal and cultural beliefs influence the kinds of exchanges that are negotiable in an employment relationship. A manager in an American firm, for example, might eschew hiring close friends or family members due to fears over potential conflicts of interest, while a Mexican manager might believe that hiring a superior's *compadres* is appropriate and in the firm's best interest. Similarly, promising new hires that taking a job with the firm will ultimately help them be employable elsewhere may be attractive in a highly mobile society and a sign of employer unreliability in a less mobile one. Cultural factors can also constrain one's ability to enter into agreements in the first place, as with differing roles and responsibilities that make certain work conditions difficult or impossible to accept.

Whether fathers have access to and are willing to accept paternity leave varies in Sweden, Canada, and Singapore. Finally, workers and owners who are party to numerous interrelated obligations, as is often the case in societies where personal ties drive business opportunities, may be limited in the number of new agreements they can enter into without compromising their ability to fulfill their existing commitments.

The breadth of the zone of negotiability varies across countries. Legal requirements, customs, and other societal institutions define the conditions that can be (or, in some cases, must be) bargained for by employee and employer. Where these definitions are restrictive, there is a narrow zone of negotiability. As an example, laws mandating paid time off on certain national holidays are not subject to bargaining, except perhaps for the payment of overtime for people willing to work on those days. The same is true of government-mandated pension benefits for which workers and employers are required to pay. In some countries, workers who prefer to manage their own pension funds are constrained from doing so, as are firms that would prefer to base pension benefits on employee merit or firm performance. Workers and firms can still benefit from not having to negotiate every aspect of the employment relationship.

Workers who have a broad zone of negotiability face fewer constraints, but also have fewer institutional protections and guaranteed resources. In one sense, legal protections for workers and other constraints on firm behavior limit freedom (or, one might argue, the excesses of freedom). But legal protections can also offset imbalances in power between the parties, particularly where employers have greater financial resources than employees. How societies regard these power differences shapes the legal protections they enact for workers.

Typically, Britain and the United States have been less concerned with mitigating power differences between firm and worker than have France and Germany. This divergence gives rise to greater variability in individual-level employment relations in the former countries than the latter. This variability impacts the ease with which firms in those countries hire and fire workers and gives rise to the distinctive employment relationships enjoyed by high performers and other highly sought out participants in the British and American labor forces.

In sum, broad-scale societal institutions shape employment conditions and affect the degree of flexibility workers and firms have in deciding upon the terms of their employment arrangements. Given the power differences between workers and firms, societies still vary considerably in the value they place on employment flexibility versus workers protection. The balance between what is negotiable, what is guaranteed, and what is off the table is an important consideration in future research on employment relations, especially now that greater variability is occurring.

Who the Parties Are

A wide range of societal actors can be party to employment agreements. Rousseau and Schalk (2000) highlight the diversity of parties that might participate in an employment relationship, from the individual and firm to the union, workgroup, and even the state. Which parties are involved in an employment agreement varies with the level at which the exchange agreement is created: between the individual worker and the firm, between groups of workers and the firm, between groups of workers and groups of firms, or in a central agreement involving groups of workers, employers, and the state. The level at which the employment agreement arises is strongly related to the industrial relations system operating within a society. An industrial relation system involves three sets of actors (Dunlop, 1993): employers; workers, typically in groups within or between firms; and the government, through direct negotiation involving governmental officials, governmental mediation of employee–employer agreements, and the creation of laws and statutes specifying conditions of employment.

The status and esteem of government and the state differ considerably between countries, which contributes to the relative importance of the government as a party to the exchange relationship. Based on this, three general types of employment and industrial relations systems can be discerned:

Direct exchanges between firm and employee, which are more prevalent in countries such as Israel, New Zealand, Singapore, and the United States (except in the case of unionized firms, which represent a declining proportion of the workforce).

Central agreements between employer organizations and unions (or comparable parties), with possible segregation at different levels, such as regional or industry-specific agreements. These systems play an important role in Australia, Belgium, India, Mexico, the Netherlands, and Sweden.

Employment relationships anchored in the state and its institutions, where regulations and statutes dominate the construction of employer– employee exchanges, as in the case of France and Japan.

Other parties to the employment relationship influence whom workers look to for contract fulfillment and whom they are likely to blame for any violations that occur (Guest & Conway, 2000). 'The organization' cannot be considered a single party to the psychological contract, and it does not always speak with one voice. Recruiters, managers, personnel policies/handbooks, and colleagues may all send different messages to employees (Rousseau, 1995). Interdependencies differ across and with firms, which can lead to expectations that different parties are obligated to fulfill the contract employees have made with their employer. In Singapore, for example, employees often believe that their coworkers are obligated to fulfill commitments the employer has made, while American employees generally believe that their supervisors are obligated to do so (Rousseau, 2000).

Much work remains to be done examining the dynamics of psychological contracts across the array of societal actors who may be party to the employment relationship. One thing is certain: simplistic models of employment relations, as found in the stylized models of agency theory fail to represent the complex reality of multiple contract makers, an array of parties to the employment relationship of any given worker, and the dynamic characteristics of group-level normative contracts.

Although factors at several levels – individual, firm, and societal – shape psychological contracts, such contracts differ from related concepts such as general meta-obligations (e.g., honesty, acceptance of authority, and contribution to a social security fund, or socially derived duty). Meta-obligations stem from the broader social experience of individuals and are linked to societal norms and laws. Whether a society's predominant form of employment relationship is an individually negotiated employment agreement or a normative arrangement derived from a union contract or governmental statutes has a powerful impact on how that society's employment system responds to global economic change. The level at which the employment agreement arises reflects how societies view within-group variability in rewards. When a social unit (workgroup, union) forms the basis of the employment negotiation, we expect fewer contract differences within these groups when individuals bargain for themselves (Rousseau, in press).

Recent writings on psychological contracts indicate a variety of roles the parties to the contract can play. In a study conducted in the United Kingdom, Guest and Conway (2000) found that senior managers – though not their more junior counterparts – are seen as key agents of the firm and, in turn, see themselves as embodying the organization. Inhibiting a worker's ability to adhere to professional obligations can engender more negative consequences for a firm than failing to honor obligations more closely tied to the worker's self-interest (Bunderson, 2000, in a study of American medical professionals including nurses and physicians). The powerful role of one's immediate manager is underscored in a series of studies on workers in the United States that illustrate how the relationship can impact the experience of violation (Rousseau, 1995; Tekleab & Taylor, 2000).

Negotiability combined with diverse prospective parties to the employment relationship create some significant changes in employment worldwide. Where negotiability is broad and contracts generally exist at the individual level, as in the case of New Zealand, the United Kingdom, and the United States, we observe *increasingly idiosyncratic employment relations*, even for individuals within the same firm. The globalization of firms and the declining role of shared institutional or cultural infrastructures in multinationals give rise to a *preference for transparency* in promoting mutually understood employment relations. Finally, in response to market pressures on firms to be more flexible and responsive, we observe the *increasing salience of market-related factors* in shaping the psychological contract.

Idiosyncratic Individual Employment Arrangements

As economic development shifts from manufacturing to service-oriented and knowledge-based industries, the traditional labor laws of many nations have less influence on worker–firm employment relations. Declining unionization worldwide (e.g., Kabanoff, Jimmieson & Lewis, 2000; Sels, Janssens, Van den Brande & Overlaet, 2000) and increasing employment in sectors not covered by traditional labor statutes means fewer normative agreements constraining the kinds of employment arrangements individuals encounter. As these external controls diminish and the market power of knowledge workers increases at the same time, individual employment agreements begin to emerge – even within the same firm. People can and do bargain different employment terms; as a result, they participate in different psychological contracts in the workplace. For example, women in a largely male-oriented firm may be more successful at negotiating flexible work schedules than their male

colleagues. Cafeteria-style benefits plans and flexible reward systems have long characterized compensation plans aimed at meeting the needs of a diverse workforce. Coworkers need not necessarily participate in the same employment arrangement even when they perform the same job.

Variation in reward allocation is common in societies as different as Australia, the Netherlands, Singapore, and the United States. Firms often overpay low performers and underpay high performers, but give the latter public recognition and status in an effort to reward individual merit while sustaining a sense of shared organizational membership (Frank & Cook, 1995). Historically, people avoided calling attention to their differential outcomes, especially those earning more than their colleagues. A preference for apparent equality led workers to downplay differences, known as the 'tall poppy syndrome' in Australia and the desire to be 'normal' in the Netherlands. In the United States, there has historically been much greater acceptance of unequal outcomes, as long as a sense of equal opportunity also existed. American workers' psychological contracts are likely to combine individual and community-oriented elements (e.g., differential rewards based upon performance, some degree of attachment to the larger organization) along with idiosyncratic features negotiated by either the employer or the individual worker. Accepted variation at the individual level has been increasing as a function of fewer legal constraints on differential employment arrangements and a greater focus on rewarding highly skilled workers and high contributors. Accepted variations in employment arrangements also make it more likely that firms can combine full-time, part-time, contingent, and other employees under one roof with success.

Preference for Transparency

Increased globalization has created a more diverse workforce within firms. One consequence of diversity, particularly with respect to differences in experience and culture, is that coworkers from one background cannot readily interpret the subtle cues and tacit signals regarding roles, responsibilities, and performance requirements that are sent by others from a different background. Since reading subtle signals is difficult in a culturally heterogeneous society, direct and explicit communication becomes more valued and culturally accepted. Hall (1990) describes the US culture as 'low context,' where individual behaviors tend to be relatively interpretable by others without a lot of contextual clues, whereas Japan is characterized by Hall as a 'high-context' society.

Transparency in social relations refers to a well-specified, consistent set of structures and practices, involving direct and explicit communication that leaves little room for ambiguity. This preference for transparency in social interactions was supported in the early 20th century by the rise of scientific management, which criticized arbitrariness and 'unscientific' discretion on the part of employers (Guillen, 1998). More recently, the push for transparency has been supported by the scientific endeavors of industrial–organizational psychology and the efforts of multinational firms to create one-culture companies. Current trends in human resource practices lean toward a rational, scientific basis for hiring, firing, promotion, and incentivizings, explicit job performance criteria specified up-front; and two-way or even multiple (360° feedback) performance appraisals are consistent with a continued movement toward transparency in employment (Roe, Schalk & Van den Berg, 1999). While country-specific practices such as graphology (France) and apprenticeships (Germany) can serve as a basis for selecting employees, global firms are moving toward the use of criteria with cross-national meaning such as prior experience, formal credentials, and standardized testing (Moskos & Butler, 1996).

Multinational firms, including firms operating in the United States (where relatively few labor laws protect worker rights), tend to place a high value on within-firm procedural justice. To ensure due process in internal personnel decisions, firms must apply procedures consistently and impartially across workers while allowing affected parties to participate (Sitkin & Bies, 1993). Research indicates that, in firms as well as in government, procedural justice based upon transparent practices reinforces the public's perception that loyalty to its institutions is appropriate and justified even in the face of negative outcomes (e.g., Pearce, Bigley & Branyiczki, 1998; Tyler, 1990).

How easily transparent social relations can be achieved differs across nations. American firms tend to rely upon explicit communication of interests and performance expectations. Direct communication of worker and firm interests can be an important basis for the formation of an employment agreement and for the creation of mutually agreed upon psychological contracts. However, in some nations, high power differences and cultural norms discouraging confrontation make such direct communications difficult. Ang, Tan and Ng (2000) describe the Singaporean tendency to avoid direct requests, which leads many workers to impart their needs to managers after they are hired, rather than raise such issues during recruitment. Nonetheless, Singaporean society prizes merit over relationships and tends to downplay the traditional particularistic relations of Chinese society, making performance the basis for allocating organizational rewards. In contrast, Diaz-Saenz and Witherspoon (2000) suggest that power differences in Mexican society can lead to an emphasis on relational ties between worker and manager, and less reliance on direct communication of expectations, particularly on the

part of the worker. Thus, we would expect more explicit communication regarding employment conditions in firms primarily based within the United States and in other countries in which explicit communication is acceptable (Australia, The Netherlands, New Zealand, United Kingdom). Similarly, a preference toward transparency among multinational firms should manifest itself in their performance expectations, career advancement systems, and other signalling devices regarding the conditions of employment.

Expanding Market Mentality and Worker Access to Capital

Regardless of their rank within the firm (blue-collar worker, white-collar professional, executive, independent contractor), workers are increasingly aware of the functioning of economic markets and their effects both on the firm and upon them individually. The conflicts of interest characterizing owners and labor, from the industrial revolution to the mid-20th century, have to some extent been transformed in many countries by a shift toward employment relations based upon trust and partnership, such as high-involvement work systems (Miles & Creed, 1995). These partnerships can entail greater sharing of financial information with workers (i.e., 'open book management,' Ferrante & Rousseau, 2001), which makes external market issues more salient to employees than they traditionally have been. Partnerships and shared information reduce status differences between workers and managers and signal the community-oriented message that labor, management, and owners have common interests.

Concomitantly, greater risk-sharing between workers and owners is evident in the shift from fixed pay (salary) to variable pay (incentives) based upon firm performance (Rynes & Gephart, 2000). As a result, entrants to the American labor market as well as workers in high-technology sectors in countries as diverse as India, Israel, and New Zealand are more likely to expect an equity stake in the firm or some kind of profit-sharing scheme. This expectation arises both from the common inability of start-ups to pay market wages but also from the pressures felt by even more established firms to provide compensation similar to that offered by their competitors in the labor market. Thus, although we might expect divergent terms in the employment agreements of workers and managers, these differences are likely to be decreasing in firms shifting toward cooperation and mutuality.

The movement toward workers thinking more like owners, with the two groups sharing a focus on the market consequences of various firm-related decisions, is based on the presumption that workers and owners have common beliefs and expectations and the ability to interpret shared information about the business and make decisions accordingly (Rousseau & Shperling, 2000). Without these factors, effective collaboration, effectively shared risks, and well-articulated mutual interests are impossible.

As workers come to have a greater ownership stake in the firm, their expectations regarding participation in firm decisions influence the extent to which they actually participate and how satisfied they are with the results of their participation (Pierce, Rubenfeld & Morgan, 1991). Even when workers have an equity stake in the company, managers may not necessarily encourage their active participation in decision making, and employees may not expect to participate (Hammer & Stern, 1980). Rhodes and Steers (1981) report greater participative decision making in worker cooperatives than in conventionally owned firms, though workers' ownership of the firm does not automatically translate into greater participation (Hammer & Stern, 1980; Pierce, Rubenfeld & Morgan, 1991). Although participation is greater when financial information is shared with investors and workers (Bernstein, 1979), how much information is shared depends on the level of business literacy workers possess. When workers have little financial knowledge, they typically do not participate in firm decisions or are ineffective in their attempts to do so (Tannenbaum, Kavcic, Rosner, Vianello & Wieser, 1974).

In the case of employee owners, Klein and Hall (1988) report that the degree to which employee participation expectations are met significantly impacts employee satisfaction with the ownership arrangement. Interestingly, workers may not wish to participate in decisions that were previously the domain of managers. This reaction arises from concerns over an increased workload, a lack of skills to make such decisions, incompatible beliefs regarding terms of the psychological contract with the employer, and otherwise ineffective implementation (Rousseau & Tijoriwala, 1999; in this study, one participant likened the redistribution of decision making to workers as 'communism,' p. 524). In contrast, the worker-owned cooperative Fagor Group in Mondragon, Spain, requires its owner/members to attend meetings or risk a temporary loss of their voting rights (Greenwood & Gonzales Santos, 1992).

We note that participation can occur without any particular ties to equity stakes (Heller, Pusic, Strauss & Wilpert, 1998). In the case of Saturn Corporation, a division of General Motors, worker participation in production planning accompanies the sharing of financial information across all organizational levels, a set of practices referred to as 'ownership for all' (Bennett, 1999). Thus, the decoupling of equity stakes and participation can give rise to psychological ownership (Pierce et al., 1991) where participation becomes a form of quasi-ownership.

The significance of equity stakes is changing as less tangible, collective assets such as shared skills and knowledge become more economically valuable than physical assets (Rousseau & Shperling, 2000). Financial aspects of ownership, including risks, information, and decision making, are increasingly shared with both managers and workers as well as outside investors. However, because participation, information access, and profit sharing do not always operate in conjunction with one another, 'financial ownership' can take on a variety of meanings. Participation in decision making varies widely among investors, managers, and nonmanagerial workers in different firms and is linked to the opportunities these parties have to participate, their expectations regarding participation, their access to financial information, and their ability to interpret this information in order to make financial decisions.

In sum, the pressures for greater firm-level flexibility have led to significant changes in employment relations within firms. The degree to which these changes have occurred, and the concomitant ease of their implementation, are linked to societal factors that dictate the zone of negotiability and shape the roles played by government and other parties to the employment relationship. The psychological contracts workers experience cross-nationally are becoming more diverse within firms, more idiosyncratic between people, and more directly shaped by market-related factors. We next address the implications of these trends.

THE FUTURE

For the foreseeable future, the practices we describe above are likely to escalate. Employers and workers are expected to bargain over a broader range of terms (including work/family balance, the worker's stake in the company, the employer's rights to worker knowledge and intellectual products, etc.). The parties to the psychological contract are expected to become even more diverse (and more differentiated between workers) as more firms and workers value and participate in inter-organizational relationships (clients, joint ventures, occupational groups, professions, start-up ventures, etc.). Firms and workers will strive to make their employment terms more explicit and to reduce miscommunication, particularly in arrangements that are short-term or cross cultural boundaries. Highly marketable workers will become increasingly aware of their leverage in employment negotiations, and employers will find themselves pressured to offer them more valuable employment agreements than their less marketable or less mobile counterparts. Last but not least, the difference between labor and capital will blur for many workers as they expect – and accept – a greater portion of their pay in equity.

Having raised these issues throughout this chapter, it is necessary to acknowledge that the current trends create a number of dilemmas for firms and workers. Experience suggests that all societies struggle with the tension between the rights of individuals to act upon their personal values and the need for groups to promote commonality and cooperation. The history of employment relations has cycled between market forces promoting different outcomes for different firms and workers and the pressure to create harmony and downplay differences among the various societal actors (e.g., Barley & Kunda, 1992). The industrial relations systems of many societies have historically downplayed differences between workers by seeking to standardize the terms of employment, creating normative psychological contracts (Frank & Cook, 1995; Rousseau & Schalk, 2000). How will societies respond to the apparently competing goals of promoting flexibility and social harmony?

A shift in the cultural definitions and responsibilities of workers, managers, and owners is one possible response. The market mentality that once delineated the divergent interests of labor and capital has expanded to encompass a new conception of the roles played by labor and capital, along with the reallocation of business risks between owners/investors and workers. This blurring of the boundary between workers and owners is at odds with the traditional roles of capital and labor, upon which many societal practices and organizational theories are based.

But heterogeneity in employment relations underscores the point that 'separate but equal' almost never is. Employers' rising need for organizational flexibility is leading firms to establish diverse employment arrangements to cope with fluctuations in organizational production capacity. Some of the trends include using temporary workers, on-call contracts, and fixed-term contracts, as well as hiring workers through employment agencies. Flexibility also means a changing allocation of business risks as firms more often base pay on performance, give workers equity stakes in the company, and differentiate highly valued core workers from more peripheral contingent employees.

These trends have implications for the relative power of workers and employers. As the workforce places a greater emphasis on employability and employees become more responsible for their own career paths, both within and outside of organizations, some employers will become more powerful because they have more means to 'set the rules.' On the other hand, knowledge workers may be in a more powerful position when negotiating the terms of employment – they often find themselves in a seller's market where they have the upper hand. We expect that the intersection of the market mentality with greater market power for some workers will require firms to pay even closer attention to trends in the larger labor market in order to remain competitive for scarce, valuable workers.

This pattern may result in a greater variation in psychological contract terms, particularly as negotiated by workers in more valued sectors of the labor market.

Also in the future, we call for greater attention to the context shaping each individual psychological contract. Global changes and cross-national differences provide the general background for how psychological contracts are made, sustained, and ended. But within societies, specific circumstances (e.g., laws, alternative opportunities on the labor market), situational factors (personal power, relations with the supervisor and organization, mobility opportunities), and the type of job being entered into all make a difference in the features and terms of individual psychological contracts. How psychological contracts are created in each context depends on the fit between what an organization is willing to offer and what the individual demands.

In addition, while the societal context generally determines the zone of negotiability, large differences may exist within the same country. The availability of other employment opportunities on the labor market – that is, the labor-market power of employers and specific groups of employees (e.g., information technology specialists vs. low-skilled workers) determines which contract terms may be negotiated and what employers are prepared to offer in order to hire and retain employees. These differences are reflected in the type of employment contracts offered (e.g., short term or long term, flexible or fixed), and the terms offered (e.g., level of pay, attractiveness of tasks, opportunities for further development).

Related to this are differences in the focus of negotiation about the psychological contract. For example, working conditions and pay levels are less highly regulated for higher-level jobs (managerial, professional) than for lower-level jobs (white- or blue-collar). Negotiations may focus on pay and working circumstances, opportunities for development, additional benefits, job content, and so on. This has implications for the boundaries of what is considered acceptable within the agreement made. Breaches of the contract will have different meanings to employees in different positions, as a result of the generally different focus on terms of the exchange relationship. Next to this, there is another process involved: employers will accept more from, and be willing to offer more for, hard-to-get workers.

Employers recruiting in a difficult labor market may gain an advantage by communicating that they are willing to negotiate customized psychological contracts. But an employer who has 100 workers and 99 different deals may engender perceptions of unfair treatment when individuals compare their deals with those of their coworkers. Ferrante and Rousseau (2000) suggest that customized contracts are adopted by firms that lack systematic human resource practices, which can erode any sense of procedural justice even when distributive justice is high. The state of management practice is such that we do not know very much about how to offer idiosyncratic arrangements that are procedurally as well as distributively fair.

The features, content, and evaluation of a psychological contract are shaped by who is party to it. The participation of government and unions has served to promote a sense of procedural justice among workers while reducing the variability in their actual conditions of employment. Governmental regulations and union influence limit and shape the mix of employment types employers offer (e.g., with respect to the number of employees hired through employment agencies, specific regulations for employment agencies, and regulations for firing employees). These actors also try to influence the terms of employment, for example, by creating favorable conditions for companies for providing child care, early retirement, or employee ownership. The network of regulations aimed at protecting employees affects what is acceptable in employment arrangements, to both employers and employees. Much can be learned by cross-national comparison about the tradeoffs between distributive and procedural justice, and we may even identify ways in which they can intersect to produce both flexibility and societal equity.

Who the parties are to a psychological contract can also be viewed from a broader perspective, related to the issue of the distinction between employer and employee. Organizations serve multiple stakeholders – including the community, employees and their families, and other stakeholders – and the traditional owner/labor distinction continues to blur as more employees acquire ownership (stock) in the companies for which they work. This means that employees may gain more control over contract terms, not only if they increased market power (as is the case with knowledge workers), but also through the expansion of employee ownership. A fascinating question for future research is how employees who also hold equity stakes in the firm view their relationship with their employer. When employees are workers and owners, and engage in some degree of self-management, what are the various possible meanings of organizational commitment or organizational citizenship behaviors?

In the future, we can expect considerable innovation and experimentation in contracting. Critical questions will center on how to balance differentiation and fairness, especially in situations where employees are interdependent, and how to integrate groups and promote cooperation while keeping clear individual psychological contracts. A greater variety of contract types, including more 'individualized' results of contract negotiations, will

exist. Contracts made today are a way to both know and shape the future. The management of psychological contracts is a core task for firms that attempt to develop 'people-building' rather than 'people-using' organizations, in an organizational climate characterized by trust. Increasingly, managing the psychological contract is a core task for workers themselves, who seek to meet their own needs in active individual and group-level negotiations with their employer.

ACKNOWLEDGMENTS

This chapter builds on a recent special issue of the *Journal of Organizational Behavior*, edited by Neil Anderson and René Schalk, and on the insights developed by a multinational team from 13 countries that participated in the writing of *Psychological contracts in employment: cross-national perspectives*:

Australia: Boris Kabanoff, Nerina L. Jimmieson, Malcolm J. Lewis; Belgium: Luc Sels, Maddy Janssens, Inge Van den Brande, Bert Overlaet; France: Loïc Cadin; Hong Kong: Cynthia Lee, Catherine H. Tinsley, George Zhen Xiong Chen; India: Snehal Shah; Israel: Moshe Krausz; Japan: Motorhiro Morishima; Mexico: Hector R. Diaz-Saenz, Patricia D. Witherspoon; The Netherlands: Charissa Freese, René Schalk; New Zealand: Simon Peel, Kerr Inkson; Singapore: Soon Ang, Mei Ling Tan, Kok Yee Ng; United Kingdom: Lynne Millward, Peter Herriot; United States: Denise M. Rousseau.

This chapter synthesizes these works along with other recent trends in psychological contract change.

REFERENCES

Anderson, N., & Schalk, R. (1998). The psychological contract in retrospect and prospect. *Journal of Organizational Behavior*, *19*, 637–648.

Ang, S., Ling, T.M., & Yee Ng, K. (2000). Psychological contracts in Singapore. In D.M. Rousseau, & R. Schalk (Eds.), *Psychological contracts in employment: Cross-national perspectives*. (pp. 213–230). Thousand Oaks: Sage.

Barley, S.R., & Kunda, G. (1992). Design and devotion: Surges of rational and normative ideologies of control in managerial discourse. *Administrative Science Quarterly*, *37*, 363–399.

Bennett, W. (1999). *Innovation at Saturn*. Presentation at the *Journal of Organizational Behavior* meeting, November 15, Detroit, MI, USA.

Bernstein, P. (1979). *Workplace democratization: Its internal dynamics*. New Brunswick, NJ: Transaction Books.

Bunderson, J.S. (2000). *Perceived ideological divergence: Violating the psychological contracts of professional employees*. Working Paper. Olin School of Business, Washington University, St. Louis, MO.

Diaz-Saenz, H.R., & Witherspoon, P.D. (2000). Psychological contracts in Mexico. In D.M. Rousseau, & R. Schalk (Eds.), *Psychological contracts in employment: Cross-national perspectives* (pp. 158–175). Thousand Oaks: Sage.

Dunlop, J.T. (1993). *Industrial relations systems* (rev. ed.). Boston: Harvard Business School Press.

Ferrante, C.J., & Rousseau, D.M. (2000). *What is fair? A study of expatriate compensation systems*. Unpublished manuscript. Pittsburgh, PA: Carnegie Mellon University.

Ferrante, C.J., & Rousseau, D.M. (2001). Open book management. In C.L. Cooper, & D.M. Rousseau (Eds.), *Trends in organizational behavior*. (Vol. 8) pp. 97–116.

Frank, R.H., & Cook, P.J. (1995). *The winner-take-all society*. New York: Free Press.

Greenwood, D., & Gonzales Santos, J.L. (1992). *Industrial democracy as process: Participatory action research in the Fagor Cooperative Group of Mondragon*, Stockholm: Arbetslivscentrum.

Guest, D.E., & Conway, N.E. (2000). *Can an organization have a psychological contract? A conceptual and empirical analysis*. Paper presented at the Academy of Management meetings in Toronto, August.

Guillen, M.F. (1998). International management and the circulation of ideas. In C.L. Cooper, & D.M. Rousseau (Eds.), *Trends in organizational behavior* (Vol. 5), pp. 47–64. Chichester: Wiley.

Hall, E.T. (1990). *The hidden dimension*. New York: Anchor Books.

Hammer, T.H., & Stern, R.M. (1980). Employee ownership: Implications for the organizational distribution of power. *Academy of Management Journal*, 23, 78–100.

Heller, F., Pusic, E., Strauss, G., & Wilpert, B. (1998). *Organizational participation: Myths and reality*. New York: Oxford University Press.

Kabanoff, B., Jimmieson, N.L., & Lewis, M.J. (2000). Psychological contracts in Australia. In D.M. Rousseau, & R. Schalk (Eds.), *Psychological contracts in employment: Cross-national perspectives* (pp. 29–46). Thousand Oaks: Sage.

Klein, K., & Hall, R.J. (1988). Correlates of employee satisfaction with stock ownership: Who likes an ESOP most? *Journal of Applied Psychology*, 73, 630–638.

Miles, R.E., & Creed, W.E.D. (1995). Organizational forms and managerial philosophies: A descriptive and analytical review. In: L.L. Cummings, & B.M. Staw (Eds.), *Research in organizational behavior* (Vol. 17, Greenwich, CN: JAI Press, pp. 333–372).

Moskos, C.C., & Butler, J.S. (1996). *All we can be: Black leadership and racial integration in the Army way*. New York: Basic Books.

Pearce, J.L., Bigley, G.A., & Branyiczki, I. (1998). Procedural justice as modernism: Placing industrial/organizational psychology in context. *Applied Psychology: An International Review*, 47, 371–396.

Pierce, J.L., Rubenfeld, S.A., & Morgan, S. (1991). Employee ownership: A conceptual model of process and effects. *Academy of Management Review*, 16, 121–144.

Rhodes, S.R., & Steers, R.M. (1981). Conventional versus worker-owned organizations. *Human Relations*, 34, 1013–1035.

Roe, R.A., Schalk, M.J.D., & Van den Berg, P.T. (1999). *Selection in the new millennium*. Paper presented at SIOP, Atlanta.

Rousseau, D.M. (1995). *Psychological contracts in organizations. Understanding written and unwritten agreements*. Thousand Oaks: Sage.

Rousseau, D.M. (2000). *Psychological Contract Inventory Technical Report #3*. Pittsburgh, PA: Heinz School of Public Policy, Carnegie Mellon University.

Rousseau, D.M. (in press). Idiosyncratic deals. *Organizational Dynamics*.

Rousseau, D.M., & Schalk, R. (Eds.) (2000). *Psychological contracts in employment: Cross-national perspectives*. Thousand Oaks: Sage.

Rousseau, D.M., & Shperling, Z. (2000). *Pieces of the action: Ownership, psychological contracts, and power*. Paper presented at the Academy of Management meetings in Toronto, August.

Rousseau. D.M., & Tijoriwala, S.A. (1999). What's a good reason to change? Motivated reasoning and social accounts in promoting organizational change. *Journal of Applied Psychology*, 84, 514–528.

Rynes, S., & Gephart, B. (2000). *Compensation*. Frontiers in Industrial/Organizational Psychology series. San Francisco: Jossey-Bass.

Sels, L., Janssens, M., Van den Brande, I., & Overlaet, B. (2000). Belgium: A culture of compromise. In D.M. Rousseau, & R. Schalk, (Eds.), *Psychological contracts in employment: Cross-national perspectives* (pp. 47–66). Thousand Oaks: Sage.

Sitkin, S.B., & Bies, R.J. (1993). *The legalistic organization*. Newbury Park, CA: Sage.

Swedberg, R. (1993). *Explorations in Economic Sociology*. New York: Russell Sage Foundation.

Tannenbaum, A.S., Kavcic, B., Rosner, M., Vianello, M., & Wieser, G. (1974). *Hierarchy in organizations: An international comparison*. San Francisco: Jossey-Bass.

Tekleab, A.G., & Taylor, M.S. (2000). *Easing the pain: Determinants of psychological contract violations*. Paper presented at Academy of Management, Toronto, August.

Tyler, T.R. (1990). *Why people obey the law*. New Haven: Yale University Press.

8

Justice in Organizations: Theory, Methods, and Applications

STEPHEN W. GILLILAND and DAVID CHAN

Organizational justice has emerged as an important construct for understanding attitudes and behavior in work settings. We review and discuss organizational justice research from the perspectives of theories and applications. In the theories section, we define the major justice constructs and relate these constructs to employee attitudes and behaviors. We also review and critique the dominant theories and methods used to investigate justice constructs. In the applications section of this chapter, we review research that has applied organizational justice to performance evaluation, personnel selection, and diversity management. For each of these applications, we review the major findings, discuss the contributions that have been made to understanding organizational justice, and identify future research directions. We conclude this chapter with the assertion that solid theory development in the areas of why justice is important and how justice evaluations develop is lacking. For organizational justice research to make an enduring contribution to organizational psychology, comprehensive theories must be developed.

INTRODUCTION

One of the most central goals of organizational psychology is to develop an understanding of attitudes and behavior in work settings. In pursuit of this goal, researchers have studied work motivation, job satisfaction, and decision making in organizations (see the corresponding chapters in this volume for discussions of these topics). Through research in these different areas, organizational justice has emerged as an important determinant of attitudes, decisions, and behavior. Job satisfaction and organizational commitment are, in part, shaped by perceptions of just treatment by managers and organizations (Martin & Bennett, 1996). Compensation and other resource allocation decisions are guided by concerns for equity and justice (Scarpello & Jones, 1996). Finally, there is much evidence that voluntary behavior in organizations, both positive organizational citizenship behavior and negative antisocial acts, are substantially related to perceptions of justice and fairness (Greenberg, 1990; Moorman, 1991). Given the important role of justice in many areas of work and organizational psychology, there has been an explosion of research in the field of organizational psychology that has been labeled organizational justice.

Perhaps the greatest evidence of the proliferation of interest in organizational justice can be seen in the wide and varied areas of work and organizational psychology that have adopted concepts of organizational justice. Traditional areas of work psychology that have applied organizational justice include the following:

Selection and staffing (Gilliland, 1993),
Performance appraisal (Korsgaard & Roberson, 1995),
Compensation (Miceli, 1993),
Conflict resolution (Shapiro & Rosen, 1994),
Layoffs (Konovsky & Brockner 1993).

Beyond these traditional areas, justice concepts have recently been applied to a wide variety of organizational and managerial issues including the following:

Diversity management (Day, Cross, Ringseis & Williams, 1999),
Sexual harassment (Adams-Roy & Barling, 1998),
Discrimination claiming (Goldman, 1999),
Labor relations (Skarlicki & Latham, 1996),
Benefits (Tremblay, Bruno & Pelchat, 1998),
Human resource information systems (Eddy, Stone & Stone-Romero, 1999),
Entrepreneur–investor relations (Sapienza & Korsgaard, 1996).

Clearly, research is demonstrating that organizational justice is a central concept in the psychology of work and organizations.

Given the current enthusiasm for organizational justice, it is not surprising to see a number of recent reviews of this literature (Beugre, 1998; Cropanzano & Greenberg, 1997; Folger & Cropanzano, 1998; Greenberg & Lind, in press). These reviews can serve as valuable sources for readers interested in developing a broader understanding of this literature than that provided in our chapter. To provide a contribution that is unique from these other reviews, we have chosen to orient our chapter around four themes. First, we approach our review of the literature from a 'state-of-the-science' perspective. That is, in reviewing theories and research findings, we focus predominantly on recent research to tell us what we know and where gaps exist in our understanding. For a more exhaustive review of prior research, the reader is encouraged to consult Beugre (1998). Second, we provide a methodological critique of the research we review and the research methods that have been used to study organizational justice. Third, we discuss applications of justice to three specific areas of work psychology: personnel selection, performance evaluation, and diversity. These areas share a common perspective in that they all deal with individual differences and individual evaluation. For discussion of application of organizational justice to other areas, readers are encouraged to see Cropanzano and Greenberg (1997) and Folger and Cropanzano (1998). Finally, consistent with the international nature of this handbook, we emphasize international research where such research exists.

This chapter is divided into two main sections: theory and application. The theory section begins with a brief overview of the constructs that constitute organizational justice. In addition to differentiating the various 'types' of justice, we offer suggestions for integration and address the balance between specificity and parsimony. This discussion of justice constructs leads into a review of the relationship between justice and other constructs from organizational psychology. Specifically, we examine the relationships between justice and employee attitudes and behaviors. We then discuss and critique the major theories of organizational justice. We also point out the absence of theory in many investigations of organizational justice. Finally, we conclude the theory section with a critique of measurement issues.

The application section of the chapter addresses performance evaluation, personnel selection, and diversity management. In each of these areas of application, we provide a brief review of major findings and then discuss how the application has contributed to our understanding of organizational justice concepts. We also identify needed research within each of these areas of application. We conclude the chapter by reexamining the relationship between theory and application and discussing the vital link between theory and application. That is, theory is best developed and tested through application; and generalizable application can only come when that application is theory-based.

DEVELOPING ORGANIZATIONAL JUSTICE THEORIES

There is no organizational justice theory. Most clearly, there is a collection of constructs that are discussed under the heading of organizational justice. There are also a number of theories that attempt to link and relate these constructs. However, unlike many other areas of organizational psychology, the primary focus of researchers studying organizational justice has been on constructs and not theories. This has resulted in limitations in theory development and in the research methods used to study justice issues. To understand and substantiate these assertions, we begin with a discussion of organizational justice constructs.

Organizational Justice Constructs

Organizational justice research addresses perceptions of fairness in organizational decisions and decision-making procedures. Within this general domain of perceived fairness, considerable variation exists in the number, types, and labels for various organizational justice constructs. Most basically, organizational justice can be divided into fairness of outcomes (distributive justice) and fairness of processes (procedural justice). A third type of justice was added to these two in the late 1980s as researchers realized that people also consider interpersonal treatment to be a form of justice (interactional justice; Bies & Moag, 1986). Although many researchers continue to discuss three types of justice (distributive, procedural, and interactional; e.g., Beugre, 1998), recent reviewers have returned to the basic distinction between fairness of process and fairness of outcome and suggest that interactional justice is really a subcomponent of procedural justice (e.g., Cropanzano & Greenberg, 1997).

In this chapter, we opt for the more parsimonious duality of distributive and procedural justice. We believe this distinction also aligns more completely with the natural distinction between decision procedures and decision outcomes. We review these two central justice constructs and identify their various components or principles.

Distributive Justice

Long before the term 'organizational justice' was coined, researchers were investigating fairness of decision outcomes under the guise of equity theory (Adams, 1965). From this perspective, distributive justice can be seen as the fairness of a distribution relative to the distribution allocated to a comparison other. Unfortunately, there are many potential referent comparisons that can be used to judge equity in a given situation and predicting which referent people use in a giving situation has proved difficult (see Kulik & Ambrose, 1992, for a discussion of referent choice). Further complicating this issue is evidence that choice of referents varies over time, especially with respect to nonmonetary outcomes (Stepina & Perrewe, 1991). Beyond referents, Deutsch (1975) pointed out that equity is only one of a number of possible distribution rules that can be used to evaluate distributive justice. Equality, which suggests that a fair distribution is one in which all parties receive equal share, and need, which suggests fairness in allocations based on relative needs, are two of the most commonly studied alternatives to equity. After reviewing much equity research, Greenberg (1982) concluded that the equity norm tends to be the predominant distributive rule. However, cross-cultural differences are observed with greater preference for equality in collectivist cultures (Miles & Greenberg, 1993).

Some researchers have bypassed the issues of referent choice and distribution rules by conceptualizing distributive justice as a matching of expectations with outcomes. From this perspective, individuals can use any of a number of referents and distribution rules to arrive at an outcome expectation, which is then used to evaluate the justice of the outcome. Cherry, Ordonez and Gilliland (1999) studied distributive fairness perceptions among students receiving feedback regarding exam scores and found support for this expectation-matching proposition. Perceived fairness was greatest when exam scores match expected exam scores. Mueller, Iverson and Jo (1999) found similar results and extended this research cross-culturally by looking at the influence of societal values and expectation-matching of distributive justice evaluations. In a comparison of US and South Korean teachers, they found support for the hypothesis that met expectations about rewards that are highly valued in a society have the strongest impact on justice evaluations. Specifically, they found that met expectations regarding autonomy explained more variance in US justice evaluations, whereas met expectations regarding advancement opportunities explained more variance in South Korean justice evaluations.

Defining distributive justice in terms of met expectations demonstrates some clear utility. However, focusing on expectations may oversimplify and fail to capture the heart of distributive justice evaluations. For example, based on prior experience with my organization, I may expect to receive a poor pay raise. When my actual pay raise is given that meets this expectation, I am likely to perceive the raise as distributively unfair, even though it met my expectation. That is, the failure of the raise to meet a standard based on what I feel I *deserve* may be a stronger driver of distributive justice perceptions than the match with expectations. While in many cases perceived deserved outcome is the same as expected outcome, future research should attempt to more precisely define the nature of this comparison standard.

Another area where greater precision is needed in distributive justice research is with the constructs outcome favorability, outcome fairness, and outcome satisfaction. In many studies, these constructs are used interchangeably. Brockner and Wiesenfeld (1996) identify differences between outcome valence (the extent to which one benefits from the outcome) and outcome fairness (the legitimacy of the outcome) but choose not to distinguish between the two because of conceptual overlap and similar empirical findings regarding the two. They adopt the term outcome favorability to capture both valence and fairness. However, there are times when an outcome is unfavorable but fair (e.g., I did not get the job, but I realize the best person did). Similarly, an outcome can be favorable but unfair (e.g., I received a bigger raise than anyone else, not because of my performance, but because I am friends with my boss).

A conceptual overlap and yet distinction also exists between outcome fairness and outcome satisfaction. According to equity theory (Adams, 1965), both fairness and satisfaction are influenced by perceptions of equity in outcome distributions. Some researchers (e.g., Gilliland, 1994) have even included both satisfaction and fairness items in outcome 'fairness' scales. One the other hand, McFarlin and Sweeney (1992) distinguished fairness and satisfaction and found that fairness was predictive of satisfaction. Similarly, Cherry et al. (1999) found that expectation matching predicted fairness, whereas satisfaction was more strongly predicted by outcome valence. Given these subtle, but potentially important distinctions between valence (or favorability), fairness, and satisfaction, future researchers should be more precise when conceptualizing and assessing these constructs.

Procedural Justice

In the mid-1970s, researchers began to recognize that people are not only concerned about the fairness of outcomes, but are also concerned about the fairness of the process that leads to the outcomes. Thibaut and Walker (1975) identified process control or the ability to present one's arguments as an important determinant of procedural justice. This determinant was subsequently labeled 'voice' (Folger, 1977) and considerable research has demonstrated the importance of voice for procedural justice in many areas of organizational behavior and human resource management (see Folger & Cropanzano, 1998, for a review). Approaching procedural justice from a somewhat different, resource allocation perspective, Leventhal (1980) discussed procedural justice as arising from the satisfaction or violation of the following procedural justice principles: bias suppression, consistency, accuracy of information, correctability, representativeness, and ethicality. As with voice, research has offered support for many of these procedural justice principles (e.g., Greenberg, 1986a).

Procedural justice research initially focused on the structural elements of procedural justice identified by Thibaut and Walker (1975) and Leventhal (1980). However, Bies extended the concept of procedural justice by examining the interpersonal aspects of justice that he termed 'interactional' justice (Bies & Moag, 1986). Interactional justice includes explanations, honesty, and interpersonally sensitive treatment. Although many researchers continue to discuss the three 'types' of justice, recent writing has combined procedural and interactional and discussed three aspects of procedural justice: structural procedures, informational justification, and interpersonal sensitivity (Cropanzano & Greenberg, 1997; Gilliland, 1993).

Not all researchers agree with combining procedural and interactional justice. Arguing that procedural justice and interactional justice are distinct construct, Masterson, Lewis, Goldman and Taylor (2000) provide evidence that interactional justice perceptions are most strongly related to supervisor-related outcomes (e.g., job satisfaction) whereas procedural justice perceptions are most strongly related to organization-related outcomes (e.g., organizational commitment). On the other hand, Cropanzano, Byrne and Prehar (1999) argue that this distinction has less to do with different types of justice and rather reflects the focus of our typical measures of procedural and interactional justice. Procedural justice typically addresses formal company procedures, whereas interactional justice addresses manager communication and interpersonal style. Based on data, they suggest that more can be learned by addressing both procedural and interactional justice from a multifoci approach (e.g., supervisor and organization).

Just as distributive justice researchers have attempted to consolidate different justice principles and referents into the concept of expectation matching, Pearce, Bigley and Branyiczki (1998) provide a consolidation of procedural justice concepts. They argue that many of the principles of procedural justice can be found in organizations with meritocratic management practices. Further, in a study of Lithuanian and American engineers and managers, they found that political economy (i.e., country) was significantly related to perceived use of meritocratic practices and procedural justice and that use of meritocratic practices mediated the relationship between political economy and procedural justice. Although this study presents a useful first attempt to consolidate many principles of procedural justice, it is unclear how well the interpersonal and social principles of procedural justice are captured by meritocratic management practices.

One final extension to the procedural justice literature was offered by Mossholder, Bennett and Martin (1998). They proposed that procedural justice also exists at a work unit level and can be assessed by aggregating individual justice perceptions across members of the work unit. Using hierarchical linear modeling, they found that for satisfaction (but not commitment) unit level procedural justice explained variance beyond that accounted for by individual justice perceptions. Two cautions we note with regard to this direction are methodological and theoretical. Methodologically, it is important to determine whether aggregated perceptions actually represent a shared construct, rather than a simple statistical average. The organizational climate literature has developed statistical techniques for examining this issue (e.g., Kozlowski & Hattrup, 1992). Theoretically, the issue is more problematic, since justice has traditionally been considered an individual perception. When aggregated to a unit level it will be important to distinguish justice from climate and culture.

Justice/Injustice Asymmetry

One recent advance in the definition of organizational justice constructs has been the differentiation of justice and injustice. Specifically, some researchers have questioned whether justice and injustice represent symmetric end of a continuum. Gilliland, Benson and Schepers (1998) applied concepts from decision making's image theory (Beach, 1996) and suggested that instances of injustice would have a greater impact on subsequent actions that instances of justice. Specifically, they presented evidence for an injustice threshold, which once surpassed cannot be compensated by just treatment. Mikula (1993; Mikula, Petri & Tanzer, 1990) takes this one step further and propose a theoretical model of injustice. He suggests that injustice arises from perceived violations of entitlement and the attributions of responsibility and blame to someone else. They presented support for this model of injustice through a series of studies with Austrian samples.

Any study of the asymmetry between justice and injustice must be with respect to some outcome of interest – for example, perceived fairness, decisions to retaliate, decisions to engage in organizational citizenship behavior. It is possible that injustice is the strongest driver of decisions to retaliate or withhold effort, but that justice is a much stronger predictor of decisions to engage and offer additional effort. The first step in understanding these relationships is to systematically distinguish justice from injustice. Most current models and measures of organizational justice do not provide this distinction. Clearly, we believe this is an area in need of further theoretical and methodological development.

Having defined organizational justice constructs, in the following section we discuss relationships between justice and employee attitudes and behavior.

Outcomes of Justice

Organizational justice has emerged as an important focus of organizational research because it is predictive of many attitudes and behaviors of employees. A discussion of these outcomes of justice helps illustrate the centrality of justice constructs and also helps distinguish justice constructs from other organizational behavior constructs. In the following sections we present research on the relationships between organizational justice and employee attitudes and behaviors. Included with the discussion of employee attitudes is emotional responses, which although not strictly attitudes, are clearly linked to both justice and attitudinal reactions.

Justice and Employee Attitudes

Researchers have consistently demonstrated that perceptions of procedural and distributive justice are correlated with many employee attitudes. In a large survey of US government employees, Alexander and Ruderman (1987) found that both procedural and distributive justice perceptions were correlated with job satisfaction, evaluations of supervisors, trust in management, and intentions to turnover. Additionally, they found that for all but intentions to turnover, procedural justice was a stronger predictor of attitudes than distributive justice. In addition to demonstrating links between justice and attitudes, this research launched a long stream of studies examining the relative importance of different types of justice.

McFarlin and Sweeney (1992; Sweeney & McFarlin, 1993) tested a two-factor model

wherein procedural justice primarily predicts organization-oriented attitudes (e.g., organizational commitment) and distributive justice predicts personal attitudes (e.g., pay satisfaction). Support was found for this two-factor model. Martin and Bennett (1996) considered the two-factor model from another perspective and suggested that when justice perceptions are used to predict satisfaction and commitment, satisfaction and commitment are causally independent constructs. This line of research has been extended with differentiation between the structural and social (i.e., interactional) elements of procedural justice. For example, Masterson et al. (2000) demonstrated that structural elements of procedural justice predict organizational commitment, whereas the social elements of procedural justice predict job satisfaction. In non-US cultures, these relationships have not always held up. For example, Leung, Smith, Wang and Sun (1996) studied the relationships between justice and satisfaction among employees of joint venture hotels in China. Both distributive justice and structural procedural justice predicted satisfaction, but social procedural justice did not.

In addition to studying the relative effects of procedural and distributive justice on attitudes, McFarlin and Sweeney (1992) examined interactive effects. They found that organizational commitment was predicted by the interaction between procedural and distributive justice such that procedural justice had a strong effect on organizational commitment when distributive justice was low and distributive justice had a stronger effect on organizational commitment when procedural justice was low. Brockner and Wiesenfeld (1996) summarized 45 studies that examined this interactive relationship between procedures and outcomes on a variety of attitudinal outcomes and found that the basic interaction was quite robust. They presented various theoretical explanations for the interaction effect, but suggested that future research was needed to determine which explanations were more or less robust under different conditions. We discuss some of these theoretical explanations in a later section of this chapter.

Current research continues to examine relationships between justice and attitudes, but is looking at more complex mediating relationships. For example, Mossholder, Bennett, Kemery and Wesolowski (1998) examined whether procedural justice mediated the relationship between social power bases and work attitudes. Across two samples, support was found for a full mediation effect. Additionally, researchers have searched for mediators of the relationships between different types of justice and attitudes. Both perceived organizational support and leader–member exchange have demonstrated mediating roles (Masterson et al., 2000).

Our concern with much of the research on justice and attitudes is that it is driven more by boxes and arrows (and the associated statistical techniques) than by solid theory. Additionally, when all of these constructs are entered into a nomological network, considerable construct overlap can be seen. For example, perceived organizational support, which reflects the quality of the relationship between employee and organization, shares construct space with perceived structural elements of procedural justice. Similarly, leader–member exchange, which is defined as the quality of the relationship between employees and supervisors, shares construct space with perceived social elements of procedural justice. This concern with construct overlap is even more evident when various measures of these constructs are compared. As we discuss further in a later section of this chapter, part of the problem is the absence of solid organizational justice theory.

In addition to studying justice and employee attitudes, recent research has examined the influence of justice on emotions. In early work on equity theory, Adams (1965) discussed the role of inequity on emotions such as anger and guilt. Despite this early discussion, justice researchers have only recently began to examine the nature of discrete or differential emotional reactions and perceived injustice. Mikula, Scherer and Athenstaedt (1998) examined data from a large sample drawn from over 37 countries to determine which emotions were associated with perceived injustice. They found that anger, disgust, and sadness were emotions most commonly linked to events perceived to be unfair. Building on the work that demonstrates interactive effects of procedures and outcomes (see Brockner & Wiesenfeld, 1996), Weiss, Suckow & Cropanzano (1999) developed hypothesized emotional reactions to different forms of justice and injustice based on appraisal theories of emotions. Happiness appeared to be based purely on the outcome; people were happier with positive outcomes than negative, regardless of procedural justice or injustice. On the other hand, anger resulted from a combination of a negative outcome and a procedure that was unfavorably biased against the recipient. Guilt resulted from a favorable outcome based on a procedure that was biased in favor of the recipient. One of the strengths of this particular study was the success at linking theories of emotions with elements of justice.

Justice and Employee Behavior

Early research on equity theory examined influences of overcompensation and undercompensation inequity on quality and quantity of work performance (see Greenberg, 1982, for a review). More recently, researchers have examined the influence of perceived justice and injustice on discretionary employee behaviors – both positive (Moorman, 1991) and negative (Greenberg, 1993). Positive discretionary behaviors have been studied under the label of organizational citizenship behaviors (e.g., Moorman, 1991), whereas negative discretionary behaviors include both theft (Greenberg, 1990) and more broadly defined organizational retaliation behaviors (Skarlicki & Folger, 1997).

In one of the first studies of justice and organizational citizenship behaviors (OCB), Farh, Podsakoff and Organ (1990) found that Taiwanese perceptions of procedural justice were related to one dimension of OCB. Moorman (1991) extended this research by examining both structural and social dimensions of procedural justice as well as distributive justice and their influences on OCB. With two samples of US manufacturing employees, he found that the social elements of procedural justice predicted four of the five dimensions of OCB. In an interesting follow-up using Chinese samples, Farh, Earley and Lin (1997) found that the relationships between justice and OCB were moderated by cultural values.

Two recent studies have examined perceived organizational support as a mediator of the procedural justice – OCB relationships (Masterson, et al., 2000; Moorman, Blakely & Niehoff, 1998). Perceptions of justice are proposed to be one of the factors that influence the development of perceived organizational support. Based on a social exchange model, employees who perceive the organization as supporting them are more likely to reciprocate and support the organization through OCB. Both studies found support for this mediating role of perceived organizational support, although Masterson et al., found mediation only for the structural elements of procedural justice and not the social elements.

Just as perceived justice has been related to positive OCB, injustice has been related to theft and retaliation behavior. Greenberg (1990, 1993) demonstrated in field and laboratory experiments that the combination of distributive and procedural injustice can lead to increased employee theft. He also found that these theft rates can be mitigated by enhanced procedural justice. Further, both the informational and the interpersonal aspects of procedural justice contribute in an additive fashion to decreased theft rates (Greenberg, 1993). Skarlicki and Folger (1997) extended this research to broader organizational retaliation behavior including damaging equipment, calling in sick when not ill, and spreading rumors about coworkers. They found that a three-way interaction between distributive justice, and the structural and social elements of procedural justice predicted retaliation behavior. Specifically, distributive injustice had the greatest impact on retaliation behavior when the two elements of procedural justice were low. In a follow-up study, they found that personality also influence these relationships such that injustice had the greatest impact on retaliation for individuals low in agreeableness or high in negative affectivity (Skarlicki, Folger & Tesluk, 1999).

Conclusions

With regard to outcomes of justice, more than 15 years of research has consistently demonstrated the justice perceptions are predictive of employee attitudes, emotions, and behavior. The research on justice and employee behavior is particularly interesting in that current efforts are being developed around social exchange theories with clear differentiation between positive and negative discretionary behavior. It would be interesting for this research to take the next step and clearly differentiate between justice and injustice. In much of this research justice is assessed on a continuum so it is unclear the extent to which justice or injustice is the primary motivator of behavior. For example, do employees engage in OCB when they are not experiencing injustice or when they are experiencing particularly justice treatment?

Research on justice and employee attitudes is somewhat less clear in terms of theoretical conclusion. It is indisputable that justice perceptions correlate with satisfaction and commitment, but the theory behind these relationships is in need of further elaboration. Part of the problem in this domain is that the lack of longitudinal research hampers conclusions of causality. Some work by Chan and colleagues (e.g., Chan, Schmitt, Sacco & DeShon, 1998) on justice perceptions in personnel selection elaborated these issues of causality and shed some light on how justice perceptions develop over time. We will discuss these issues in the section on personnel selection. The problem of causality is also exacerbated by the conceptual overlap between justice perceptions and related perceptual constructs. Developing a solid theory of organizational justice would undoubtedly aid research on justice and attitudes. We now turn our attention to theories of organizational justice.

Theories of Organizational Justice

Organizational justice research grew out of a merging of Adams' (1965) equity theory with Thibaut and Walker's (1975) research on procedural justice. In spite of this early foundation in equity theory, a more comprehensive theory of organizational justice has not been developed. What have been developed are a number of frameworks that summarize organizational justice. For example, Greenberg (1987a) proposed a taxonomy of organizational justice theories that distinguished proactive from reactive approaches to studying justice and content versus process approaches. Similarly, researchers have developed frameworks for understanding and studying different dimensions or elements of justice in specific content domains such as performance appraisal (Greenberg, 1986a) and personnel selection (Gilliland, 1993). These frameworks have provided the foundation for considerable

empirical research, but none provide a theory of organizational justice.

That is not to say that attempts have not been made at theory development. Lind and Tyler (1988) differentiated a self-interest model of procedural justice from a group value model. Folger (1986) proposed referent cognitions theory (RCT) as an explanation for reactions to injustice. Unfortunately, for the most part these theories have been only loosely applied by organizational justice researchers; few organizational studies have actually attempted to test or extend these theories. Additionally, these theories do not adequately explain the range of findings that have been presented by organizational justice researchers. On the other hand, researchers in social psychology have given more attention to theory development and have made some interesting extensions to these theories.

Before presenting a review of recent theory development, it is useful to discuss the qualities or properties we believe should be inherent in a comprehensive theory of organizational justice. We then use these criteria for evaluating existing theories and suggesting directions for future theory development. First, a good theory of organizational justice should explain both *why* people are concerned about justice and *how* people react to just injust situations. For example, equity theory (Adams, 1965) proposed that people are motivated to maintain a balance in exchange relationships (why justice is important) and that they evaluate equity by comparing inputs to outcomes relative to comparison others. Inequity produces negative emotions, which people attempt to minimize by altering their inputs or outcomes. The comparison process and responses to inequity represent the 'how' aspect of the theory. In addition to explaining why and how, a theory of organizational justice should be testable by accounting for existing empirical findings and suggesting new hypotheses. Through empirical evaluation of these hypotheses, a good theory of organizational justice should be refutable. This was one of the chief limitations of equity theory. For any individual, there are so many possible inputs, outcomes, comparison others, and responses to inequity that it is virtually impossible to refute the basic equity propositions. Even when imposing the refutability requirement, we are not sure how many theories of organizational justice meet this criterion. Finally, for a theory to be embraced by organizational justice researchers, it needs to be parsimonious. Many comprehensive theories of work motivation were never fully embraced by organizational researchers because they were too complicated (e.g., Kanfer & Ackerman, 1989; Naylor, Pritchard & Ilgen, 1980).

The two main streams of theory development in organizational justice research are the self-interest versus group value models (Lind & Tyler, 1988) and referent cognitions theory (RCT – Folger, 1986).

The former initially approached theory development from a 'why' perspective, whereas the latter approached theory development from a 'how' perspective. We review each of these streams, including current theoretical developments.

Self-Interest Versus Group Value Models

The self-interest and group value models of justice originally emerged as models of procedural justice from the social psychology literature. The self-interest model (hypothesis) proposes that people are concerned about procedural justice to the extent that procedural justice leads to favorable outcomes (Thibaut & Walker, 1975). This is primarily an instrumental model and was proposed to address the desire by the recipient for input into or control over decision processes. Lind and Tyler (1988) proposed an alternate model (i.e., group value model) based on social relationships and the desire for membership within a social group. Group membership provides self-validation, and relational information about relative position within the group enhances self-perceptions. Procedural justice is valued in a group situation because it provides evidence of respect and long-term stability of social standing. Therefore, a primary distinction between the self-interest model and the group value model is that people desire procedural justice as a means to an end within the self-interest perspective, but they desire procedural justice as an end in itself from the group value perspective (Brockner & Wiesenfeld, 1996).

Rather than presenting these two models in competition, most researchers acknowledge value in both perspectives. Tyler (1994) proposed an integrated model of the two perspectives and suggested that the social exchange aspects of the self-interest model account primarily for variation in distributive justice, whereas the relational aspects of the group value model account for variation in both procedural and distributive justice. Survey data was presented that supported these distinctions. Tyler, Degoey and Smith (1996) provided additional evidence that group value concerns are directly related to group-oriented outcomes such as OCB and organizational commitment.

Although the self-interest and group value models provide two good explanations for why people value justice, they do not offer much insight into how justice is evaluated and how perceptions of justice impact attitudes and behavior. Lind, Kulik, Ambrose and de Vera Park (1993) proposed fairness heuristic theory as an integration of the group value model with heuristic notions of decision making. Basically, this theory assumes that people frequently feel uncertain about their relationship with authority in a group situation. Impressions regarding fair treatment are used to decide whether the authority is trustworthy and unbiased. Once established, this impression serves as a heuristic to guide interpretation of subsequent events. Based on

fairness heuristic theory, Van den Bos, Vermunt and Wilke (1997) proposed that early information regarding justice would have a greater impact on fairness perceptions than later information, because early information is used to form a fairness heuristic. Additionally, since people typically encounter procedures before outcomes, procedural justice tends to contribute more strongly to reactions than distributive justice. This would account for a common observation in the justice literature that procedural justice is more predictive of a variety attitudinal and behavioral outcomes than distributive justice. By manipulating the order in which people encountered information about the procedure and outcome, Van den Bos et al. (1997) demonstrated that what people judge to be fair is more strongly influenced by early information than by later information.

Fairness heuristic theory provides a valuable extension of the group value model. Thus far, however, most research on this theory has appeared in the social psychology literature rather than the organizational psychology literature. Additionally, the fairness heuristic does not include a self-interest motive regarding procedural justice and does not explicitly address differential effects of different forms of justice on attitudinal and behavioral outcomes. For example, it does not explain why satisfaction tends to be more strongly associated with distributive justice, while organizational commitment tends to be more strongly associated with procedural justice (Sweeney & McFarlin, 1993).

Referent Cognitions Theory

Folger (1986) approached justice theory more from the 'how' perspective than the 'why' in his development of referent cognitions theory (RCT). RCT proposes that negative or dissatisfying outcomes trigger the recollection of events that might have contributed to the outcome. If unjustified or illegitimate events contributed to the outcome and it is possible to imagine more justified events that would have led to a more favorable outcome, the outcome is perceived as unfair. Therefore, fairness perceptions arise from 'should/would' reasoning whereby the situation is most unfair if the person believes the decision agent should have acted differently and this would have resulted in a more favorable outcome. RCT is based on Kahneman and Tversky's (1982) research in decision making on the simulation heuristic, which suggests that dissatisfaction and regret arise from imagining counterfactual alternatives to the actual situation that would have changed the outcome.

RCT presents an interesting description of how unfairness perceptions arise. However, in terms of a general theory of justice, it has some problems. First, RCT has been most clearly articulated with regard to unfavorable outcomes. It is less clear how the theory applies to favorable outcomes.

Additionally, RCT does not directly address why people are motivated to pursue fairness. Finally, in its original version, RCT did not address the social aspects of procedural justice and how interpersonal sensitivity may limit counterfactual would/should reasoning. Recently, Folger and Cropanzano (1998) proposed fairness theory as an update to RCT that addresses some of these problems.

Under fairness theory, '*Would*' counterfactuals defined by RCT are expanded to include counterfactual reasoning in response to any negative event. Whereas RCT focuses on responses to negative outcomes, Folger and Cropanzano (1998) suggest that negative events related to procedural justice can also trigger counterfactual reasoning. Additionally, RCT suggested a deliberate process of creating alternate scenarios, whereas fairness theory suggests that these scenarios can be automatically or implicitly generated without conscious awareness. Once counterfactual alternatives are generated, people respond to the magnitude of the discrepancy between the negative experience and the alternate counterfactual. Beyond simply reacting to this discrepancy, people also generate 'COULD' counterfactuals and 'SHOULD' counterfactuals. A Could counterfactual addresses whether the negative event was under decision maker's discretionary control. We react more negatively or hold the decision maker more accountable if they had discretionary control than if they had no choice in the situation. Should counterfactuals address moral conduct and suggest that we also evaluate whether the decision maker acted in accordance with moral or ethical standards? These various counterfactuals combine in the following manner: people make an initial negative judgment by way of the Would counterfactual (imagining an alternative event that is less negative) and then evaluate whether sufficient Could and Should counterfactuals exist to make this judgment stick.

Given the expansion of would counterfactuals to include negative events and not just negative outcomes and given the inclusion of could and should counterfactuals, fairness theory includes many concepts from distributive and procedural justice. Additionally, fairness theory offers an explanation for the frequently observed interaction between procedures and outcomes (Brockner & Wiesenfeld, 1996). Fairness theory also demonstrates some interesting similarities to image theory of decision making (Beach, 1996). In that theory, Beach suggested that decisions are made through a process of matching alternatives with our images of who we are and where were are going rather than an analytic process of weighting and evaluating alternatives as is suggested by traditional decision theory. Gilliland (1996) extended image theory to justice evaluations and suggested this image-matching process may help explain the process of judging the fairness of events and outcomes. It is possible that applying some of the concepts from image theory may help to further develop fairness theory, given that image theory provides more detail and specific hypotheses than fairness theory on the process by which people match experiences with mental images.

Unfortunately, fairness theory does fall short on some of our suggested criteria for effective theory. First, although Folger and Cropanzano (1998) suggest that fairness theory can (in principle) be applied to positive events and not just negative events, their presentation focuses on negative events. Second, as with fairness heuristic theory, fairness theory does not effectively account for differential reactions to various attitudinal and behavioral outcomes. For example, some research has demonstrated that with outcomes that are self-evaluative in nature, it is sometimes better if a negative outcome is accompanied by an unfair procedure. For example, Gilliland (1994) found that self-efficacy was lower when a candidate was rejected by a job-related selection procedure (high procedural justice) than an unrelated selection procedure (low procedural justice). Van den Bos, Bruins, Wilke and Dronkert (1999) found a similar effect when the self-evaluative context was highly salient, but not when less salient. It is unclear how fairness theory would account for this apparent reversal in the 'fair process' effect under conditions of high self-evaluation.

A final problem with fairness theory that may limit the extent to which it is embraced by organizational justice researchers is that it is somewhat complicated. We began our discussion of theory by suggesting that one criterion for an effective justice theory is parsimony. We worry that in their attempt to account for various justice observations, Folger and Cropanzano (1998) may have developed a theory that is comprehensive but not parsimonious. Just as fairness heuristic theory has been adopted mainly by social psychologists, who are possibly more interested in theory development than practical applications, fairness theory may be neglected by organizational psychologists focusing on practical issues in organizations. We view this lack of emphasis on theory development as one of the fundamental challenges facing research in organizational justice. Additionally, we believe the impact of insufficient theory development is reflected in measurement issues characteristic of much organizational justice research. In the following section, we turn our attention to these measurement issues.

Measurement Issues

Rather than a comprehensive review of the wide variety of measurement issues, this section focuses on four specific issues that we think are particularly important to the advancement of justice research.

First, we discuss the issue of validity in the use of generic versus domain specific scales. Next, we turn our attention to the validity of inferences drawn from laboratory research versus field studies. Finally, we discuss levels of analysis issues relevant to the valid measurement of justice constructs and assessment of relationships between justice and other constructs of interest.

Generic Versus Domain-Specific Scales

Generic scales of justice constructs consist of general attitudinal items that are 'context-free.' These items require the respondents to indicate their fairness perceptions without providing them specific contexts or domains of interest. Example items are '*The rewards I receive from my job are fair*' (measuring distributive justice) and '*The procedures for determining rewards for employees here are fair*' (measuring procedural justice). On the other hand, domain specific scales, as the name suggests, consist of domain- or context-specific items such that they refer to some specific aspect of the work environment. These items require the respondents to indicate their fairness perceptions in a specific context or domain of interest. Example items are '*The salary I receive is a fair reward of what I do on the job*' (measuring distributive justice in the pay context) and '*When judging my job performance, my supervisor gives me a chance to express my views or explain what I have done*' (measuring procedural justice in the performance appraisal context).

Greenberg (1996) argued against investigating justice in a context-free manner and advocated studying justice issues as they apply to specific contexts such as performance appraisal and employee theft. He argued that, while studying general attitudes toward fairness (i.e., context free) is less informative, studying justice in context provides new insights that help increase our theoretical understanding and address practical concerns associated with organizational phenomena in the specific contexts. Domain-specific scales, rather than generic scales, direct the respondent's attention to a specific aspect of a situation about which he or she is likely to have focused justice attitudes. In addition, it is possible to develop domain-specific scales in a theory-driven manner so that the various facets of a theory of justice are operationalized and tested. For example, a theory of procedural justice may explicate 'voice in decision making' as one of the procedural rules that contribute to procedural justice perceptions. The use of domain specific scales containing items similar to '*When judging my job performance, my supervisor gives me a chance to express my views or explain what I have done*' would allow the researcher to directly investigate the role of voice in decision making.

We agree with Greenberg (1996) that it is important to study justice in specific contexts or domains because it allows measurement that is theory-driven and tailored to fit the specific setting. Generic items tend to be less informative, since they do not tell us the specific aspects of the work situation the respondents had in mind when reporting their fairness perceptions. If respondents have different contexts in mind when they answered generic items and fairness perceptions do indeed vary in important ways across contexts, then the fairness scores obtained from generic items could be misleading. On the other hand, we believe that the use of generic scales to measure overall fairness perceptions is appropriate for certain research questions. For example, a researcher may be interested in the relationship between overall fairness perceptions at work and organizational cynicism. When the concern is with global justice perceptions, then it is perfectly appropriate to use generic items such as '*The procedures for determining rewards for employees here are fair*.' The central measurement issues concerning the use of generic versus domain-specific scales are issues of validity. Because validity refers to the accuracy of inferences drawn from the scale scores rather than an inherent property of the scale, the choice between generic and domain specific scales should be driven by the nature of the research question and the justice construct of interest.

Another measurement issue concerning the use of generic versus domain-specific scales may be the extent to which justice perceptions contain a dispositional component. Although some researchers have examined individual differences in equity sensitivity (Huseman, Hatfield & Miles, 1987), we are not aware of research that systematically examines dispositional influences on justice perceptions. Notwithstanding methodological limitations, it is possible that twin studies may prove informative for investigating dispositional effects. Given that domain-specific scales anchor justice perceptions in a specific situation, we expect dispositional influences to have a greater influence on generic than domain-specific scales.

Laboratory Research Versus Field Studies

Laboratory research on organizational justice refers to studies conducted under controlled experimental conditions, in which the independent variables were manipulated. In these studies, the justice constructs are either the independent or dependent variables, depending on the hypotheses in question. For example, in an experimental study by Greenberg (1993) examining justice effects on theft, distributive justice was manipulated by paying participants equitably in one condition and not in the other condition. In another experimental study by Van den Bos et al. (1997), justice (fairness perceptions) was examined as a dependent variable, with the order in which participants encountered information about the procedure and outcome as the independent variable. In field studies of organizational justice, the independent (or more accurately, predictor) variables were typically measured rather than manipulated. For example, McFarlin and Sweeney (1992) administered a survey to a sample of bank employees, which included measures of fairness perceptions (distributive and procedural justice) and a measure of organizational commitment. The authors treated the justice variables as independent variables predicting organizational commitment.

The strengths and weaknesses of laboratory and field studies have been well discussed in organizational psychology and we do not intend to repeat them here. Much of the discussions can be summarized in the tension between internal and external validity. Specifically, laboratory studies often rely on college students in a contrived experimental setting that may offer little generalizability to work settings. On the other hand, field studies investigate realistic but uncontrolled situations, which prevents us from ruling out the multitude of alternative plausible explanations for results.

We think that a program of research that would truly advance the study of justice is one that employs both laboratory and field studies in a complementary fashion. As laboratory studies establish causal relationships, field studies generalize the laboratory findings to naturalistic settings. Field studies also help identify relevant variables to be included and generate causal hypotheses to be tested in laboratory studies. Together, laboratory and field studies ask converging questions of justice phenomena and their findings could provide convergent evidence. Greenberg's program of research on justice-based accounts of theft and performance appraisals exemplifies this integrative approach to laboratory and field studies. For example, he used a laboratory study (Greenberg, 1993) to follow up his field study (Greenberg, 1990) on theft because the former allowed him to control key variables that were impossible to control in the field. As another example, Greenberg used surveys in the field setting (Greenberg, 1986a) as well as laboratory experiments (Greenberg, 1987b) to obtain convergent evidence for his justice-based accounts of performance appraisals.

Before leaving this section on laboratory versus field studies, we want to caution against two confusions. The first is not to confuse the laboratory–field distinction with the experimental–correlational distinction. The laboratory-field distinction refers to study setting, whereas the experimental–correlational distinction refers to study design. The two distinctions are conceptually orthogonal, although most studies conducted in laboratory settings have employed experimental designs and most studies conducted in field settings have employed correlational designs. In fact, we believe there has been an over reliance on correlational

field studies to investigate justice phenomena. In part, this may have limited theory development, as was discussed earlier in this chapter. Additionally, it has limited the practical conclusions that can be drawn from justice research. Whereas correlational studies can lead to the conclusion that perceptions of justice are correlated with organizational commitment, they cannot lead to the recommendation that improving justice within an organization will improve employee commitment. This latter conclusion requires a field experiment. Field experiments, when adequately conducted, provide a promising way to study justice, since they have more realism over laboratory experiments (hence increasing external validity) and more control over correlational field studies (hence increasing internal validity). Unfortunately, only a few studies conducted in field settings have employed quasi-experimental or experimental designs to examine justice perceptions (e.g., Greenberg, 1990).

Levels of Analysis Issues

With the increased use of workteams to accomplish work, as well as the increased interest in multilevel research, there is an increased proliferation of new constructs at multiple levels (e.g., workgroup, organization). Each higher-level construct is composed from the established construct at the individual level (Chan, 1998). The justice construct, which is essentially an individual level construct insofar as it refers to an individual's perceptions, could be similarly composed to higher levels. Indeed, earlier in the chapter we mentioned that Mossholder et al. (1998) proposed that procedural justice also exists at the workgroup level. However, as we engage in higher-level or multilevel research, such as examining procedural justice at the workgroup level, we need to address levels of analysis issues. Many of these levels issues concern construct validity and measurement involved in proposing or 'composing' higher-level constructs from established lower-level constructs. The reader is referred to Chan (1998) for a summary of these issues and a proposed typology of composition models, which serves as a framework for organizing, evaluating, and developing constructs and theories in multilevel research.

In this section, we emphasize the need to specify adequate *composition models* when examining justice at higher levels of analysis. Composition models specify the functional relationships among constructs at different levels of analysis that reference essentially the same content but are qualitatively different at different levels of analysis (Rousseau, 1985). For example, a composition model of workgroup procedural justice would specify how the group-level construct of procedural justice is derived from the established individual-level construct of procedural justice perceptions and how this new group-level construct can be empirically validated.

Without adequate composition models, there is a danger that the increased interest in multilevel theorizing would lead to a multitude of higher-level justice labels, all of which purportedly refer to scientific constructs but in reality have no incremental explanatory value over the individual level justice construct. In Chan's (1998) typology there are five basic forms of composition, and each composition model is defined by a particular form of *functional relationship* specified between constructs at different levels. These composition models have direct implications for the manner in which we conceptualize and measure justice at a level higher than the individual (e.g., workgroup level).

Consider the construct of procedural justice at the individual and group levels. Should we adopt an *additive composition* (Chan, 1998) in which the individual group members' justice perception scores are simply summed or averaged to represent the group's score on procedural justice? Chan (1998) argued that whether or not the relationship between levels is additive (or some other composition form) depends on the definition of the higher-level construct, which is part of the composition theory explicitly specified by the researcher or, more often, implicit in the hypothesized relationships between focal constructs in the study. If by group procedural justice we mean the average justice perceptions of individual group members, then an additive composition form would be relevant. On the other hand, consider the case in which the researcher is interested in testing the hypothesis that *workgroup procedural justice is positively associated with group cohesion*. The researcher may base this hypothesis on the theory that the more similar the extent of procedural justice perceptions is among individual members of a group (i.e., smaller within-group variance regardless of group mean), the higher the extent of group cohesion. In this formulation, within-group consensus in justice perception scores is construed as the operationalization of the group-level construct (i.e., *dispersion composition* in Chan's typology). This dispersion measure, typically labeled *climate strength*, is then correlated with the measure of group cohesion to test the researcher's hypothesis, which is more accurately formulated as *workgroup procedural justice climate strength is positively associated with group cohesion*.

While the issues of generic versus domain specific scales and laboratory versus field studies are relatively well discussed in various areas of organizational research, researchers are only beginning to be introduced to conceptual and measurement issues concerning levels of analysis. We predict that levels of analysis issues will become more salient in future work on organizational justice, as in other areas of organizational research.

APPLICATIONS OF ORGANIZATIONAL JUSTICE

Organizational justice constructs and models have been applied to a wide variety of resource allocation and personnel decision situations. Rather than attempt to comprehensively review this wide body of literature, we have chosen to focus on three particular applications: performance evaluation, personnel selection, and diversity management. All of these applications focus on personnel decisions involving recognizing and evaluating individual differences. Additionally, these three areas can be seen as falling on continuum in terms of stages of development. Research on justice in performance evaluation began in the mid-1980s and is fairly well developed. More recently, research on justice in personnel selection began in the early 1990s and research on justice in diversity management is a very recent application of organizational justice principles.

Performance Evaluation

Researchers in the area of performance evaluation have long acknowledged that reactions of people being evaluated by an evaluation system are critical to the success of that system (Carroll & Schneier, 1982). Early research on reactions to performance evaluations demonstrated that aspects of the appraisal process had a greater influence on perceptions of fairness and accuracy than the actual ratings themselves (Landy, Barnes-Farrell & Cleveland, 1980). However, it was the work of Greenberg (1986a, b) that clearly applied organizational justice to the study of performance evaluation. Greenberg (1986b) argued that distributive justice in performance evaluation reflects both the accuracy of ratings based on performance and the linkage between evaluations and outcomes such as pay or promotion. Greenberg (1986a) expanded the application of organizational justice to performance evaluation by identifying procedural justice determinant of perceived fairness. Specifically, using an open-ended questionnaire, Q-sort techniques, and importance ratings, he identified the following five procedural factors: (1) soliciting and using input prior to evaluation; (2) two-way communication during the feedback interview; (3) ability to challenge evaluation; (4) rater familiarity with ratee's work; (5) consistent application of standards. Many of these factors are clearly related to Leventhal's (1980) dimensions of procedural justice in a resource allocation context.

Beyond identifying what aspects of the evaluation process and outcomes influence perceptions of organizational justice, researchers have examined the influence of perceptions of fairness on attitudinal and behavioral outcomes. For example, Folger and Konovsky (1989) collected perceptions of four dimensions of procedural justice (feedback, planning, recourse, and observation) as well as three aspects of distributive justice and examined the relationship between these perceptions and satisfaction with pay raise, organizational commitment, and trust in supervisor. They found that procedural justice (mainly feedback) was the primary predictor of organizational commitment and trust in supervisor, whereas both procedural justice and distributive justice predicted pay raise satisfaction.

Despite the identification of many components of procedural justice in performance evaluation, most attention has been direction toward employee participation or voice in the evaluation/feedback process. Korsgaard and Roberson (1995) examined the roles of instrumental and noninstrumental voice in predicting satisfaction with the review and trust in supervisor. Both types of voice were found to predict satisfaction, while only noninstrumental voice was found to predict trust in supervisor. After identifying 27 studies that examined the relationship between participation in the performance evaluation process and employee reactions, Cawley, Keeping and Levy (1998) a conducted meta-analysis and found an average effect size of $r = .61$. They found that participation had the greatest effects on satisfaction and perceived fairness and moderate effects on motivation to improve and perceived utility of the performance evaluation.

Current research on organizational justice and performance evaluation has adopted a broader performance management system approach. Gilliland and Langdon (1998) argued that the performance management process involves three interrelated processes: (1) system development, (2) appraisal processes, and (3) feedback processes, and that organizational justice is important in all three processes. Consistent with this suggestion, Giles, Findley and Field (1997) examined perceptions of the performance appraisal system, perceptions of the feedback session, and perceptions of supervisors actions outside the session. All three sets of perceptions were found to explain unique variance in evaluations of appraisal fairness. Cherry and Gilliland (1999) focused on the system development stage of the performance management process and found that input during system development, predicted reactions to performance appraisals and trust in supervisor 18 months after system development.

Perhaps some of the best research from a performance management system approach has been conducted by Taylor and colleagues (Taylor, Tracy, Renard, Harrison & Carroll, 1995; Taylor, Masterson, Renard & Tracy, 1998). Taylor et al. (1995) conducted a field experiment in which they implemented a due-process performance appraisal system (DPPS) in a government agency. The concept of a DPPS was discussed by Folger, Konovsky and Cropanzano (1992) and involves providing adequate notice (e.g., training for employees and managers to develop standards and training on giving and receiving feedback), fair hearing (e.g., self-appraisals and training on two-way communication), and judgment based on evidence (e.g., appraisals fitted to job and training on collecting and recording performance related information). In Taylor et al.'s (1995) study, reactions and attitudes were collected from employee and supervisors who experienced the new performance appraisal system and from those in a control group who continued to use the existing system. Compared to employees in the control group, the DPPS resulted greater perceived appraisal fairness and satisfaction with rating, more positive evaluations of supervisor, and stronger intentions to remain with the organization. For managers, the system resulted in decreased work problems and increased job satisfaction.

Clearly, application of organizational justice has resulted in greater understanding of the performance evaluation process. Prior to research oriented around organizational justice concerns, most research on performance evaluation focused on rater accuracy and rater errors (Murphy & Cleveland, 1995). Organization justice research has demonstrated that managing fairness perceptions is one of the keys to effective performance management (Gilliland & Langdon, 1998). Beyond the application of organizational justice to performance evaluation, it is interesting to ask: To what extent has performance evaluation research contributed to understanding of organizational justice? We now turn our attention to this question.

Contributions to Organizational Justice

One of the clearest contributions that performance evaluation research has made to understanding organizational justice is in the area of employee input or 'voice.' Through performance evaluation research, we have learned that voice can involve much more than simply asking for employee input. In their meta-analysis of the relationship between employee participation and reactions to performance evaluation, Cawley et al. (1998) distinguished value expressive voice, instrumental voice, completion of a self-appraisal, and simple time spent talking. Over a wide variety of studies, these four types of voice demonstrated substantial differences in their relationships with employee reactions. Value expressive and instrumental voice demonstrated the strongest relationships with reactions ($r = .47$ and $.42$ respectively), whereas self-appraisals and time spent talking demonstrated much weaker relationships with reactions ($r = .22$ and $.16$ respectively).

Dulebohn and Ferris (1999) expanded the notion of voice further by distinguishing informal voice mechanisms from the more commonly studied aspects of voice, such as those studied by Cawley et al. (1998). Informal voice includes supervisory-focused influence tactics, such as ingratiation tactics of flattery and doing favors, as well as job-focused influence tactics that include self-promotion activities. In a study of food service workers, procedural justice evaluations were found to be positively related to supervisory-focused influence tactics and negatively related to job-focused influence tactics. These effects were moderated by instrumental voice such that influence tactics had the greatest effect on procedural justice when instrumental voice was low. In addition to expanding our conceptions of voice, this study demonstrated some interesting interplay between different types of voice.

Another contribution to organizational justice from research in performance evaluation is the demonstration that justice is important to both the decision recipient and the decision maker. In their study of a DPPS, Taylor and colleagues (1995) demonstrated that procedural justice in the performance evaluation system has a positive impact on both employees' and supervisors' attitudes. A follow-up study (Taylor et al., 1998) demonstrated that for managers, the positive effect of the DPPS on their working relationship with their employees and the negative effect on tendencies to distort ratings were moderated by the perceived unfairness of managers' own performance evaluations. The effects of the DPPS were strongest for those managers who perceived greatest unfairness in their own evaluations. Both of these studies by Taylor and colleagues demonstrate that justice is important for decision maker as well as recipients. We know of no other research that examined the impact of justice on individuals responsible for allocating the outcome.

Future Research Directions

We believe that Taylor and colleagues (1995, 1998) have demonstrated some interesting effects of just performance evaluation on managers. Future research should extend this line of inquiry by examining how managers' own experiences influence their implementation of just performance evaluation. Taylor and colleagues (1998) suggested that the procedurally just DPPS had a greater impact on managers who perceived their evaluations to be unfair because these managers were sensitized to issues of mistreatment and bias and therefore they made greater efforts to avoid these biases. Unfortunately, they provided to data on actual manager behavior. Do managers treat employees differently during performance evaluations as a result of their own experiences of justice or injustice? More generally, do managers' experiences of justice impact their managerial behavior? We might expect that those managers who had themselves been laid off at some point would be more sensitive to just treatment when laying off their own employees. On the other hand, it is possible that prior injustice desensitizes managers in terms of their own

behavior. We believe that this is an interesting area for future research.

Another area in performance evaluation that may benefit from future research is an investigation of potential negative effects that result from implementing just performance evaluations. It is possible that employees who are sensitized to fair treatment through training associated with a procedurally just performance evaluation system may be more likely to complain when they are treated unfairly with that new system. Do complaints or challenges to performance evaluation increase with increased attention to procedural justice? This research question is similar to a sensitization to sexual harassment and increase in sexual harassment claims to the EEOC by more than 50% following the Clarence Thomas – Anita Hill hearings in 1991 (Bennett-Alexander & Pincus, 1998). More research is needed to identify whether negative outcomes increase as a result of sensitization to justice.

Personnel Selection

Traditionally, the discussion of fairness in personnel selection focuses on the psychometric properties of selection tests as they relate to concerns such as adverse impact and differential prediction across demographic groups. While research in this direction has continued (e.g., Arvey & Sackett, 1993; Bobko, Roth & Potosky, 1999; Sackett & Roth, 1996; Schmitt, Rogers, Chan, Sheppard & Jennings, 1997), there is a surge of recent interest in selection test fairness *perceptions* and other related test perceptions such as perceived job relevance (e.g., Arvey, Strickland, Drauden & Martin, 1990; Bauer, Maertz, Dolen & Campion, 1998; Chan, 1997; Chan & Schmitt, 1997; Chan, Schmitt, DeShon, Clause & Delbridge, 1997; Chan, Schmitt, Sacco et al., 1998; Gilliland, 1993; 1994; 1995; Smither, Millsap, Stoffey, Reilly & Pearlman, 1996). In this section, we review the applications of justice principles to personnel selection research, focusing on what aspects of the selection process are most important to the applicant, as well as highlight how these applications have in turn contributed to our understanding of organizational justice. For detailed reviews of the status of research on applicant reactions to selection tests, including test fairness perceptions, see Gilliland and Steiner (2001) and Schmitt and Chan (1999).

Initial models of applicants' reactions to personnel selection did not explicitly mention organizational justice. For example, Iles and Robertson (1989) discussed the psychological impact of selection on candidates and hypothesized that the features of selection methods, the nature of the decision, and the specificity of feedback would influence cognitive and affective reactions to selection. In turn, these reactions would influence work attitudes and performance. Similarly, Schuler (1993) suggested that the following four factors influenced the acceptability of selection situations: (a) the presence of job-relevant information, (b) participation or representation in the development of the selection process, (c) understanding the nature and relevance of the evaluation process, and (d) the content and form of feedback accompanying the decision. Both of these models clearly contain components that are related to structural and informational dimensions of procedural justice.

Organizational justice constructs and research were directly applied to personnel selection in the framework proposed by Gilliland (1993). Gilliland defined several procedural justice rules specifically for the selection context and classified these rules into three categories. *Formal rules*, such as job-relatedness of the test, opportunity to perform during the selection process, opportunity for reconsideration or review of test scores, and the consistency of test administration, are determined by the type and content of the selection specific tests or procedures. *Explanation rules*, such as feedback about test results and justifications regarding selection decisions, are concerned with the extent to which information derived from the selection process is made known and the selection decisions made are explained to applicants. *Interpersonal treatment rules* concern the actions of test administrators and other human resource personnel encountered by applicants during the selection process and they refer to the extent to which applicants perceive themselves as being treated fairly.

Gilliland argued that violations of these rules lead to perceptions of procedural injustice and negative applicant reactions. This argument has been largely supported by the empirical research on applicant test perceptions, both in laboratory (e.g., Gilliland, 1994; Smither et al., 1996) and field settings (e.g., Bauer et al., 1998; Chan, Schmitt, Jennings, Clause & Delbridge, 1998; Ryan & Chan, 1999). Among the selection procedural justice rules posited by Gilliland, the most robust finding is probably the importance of the job-relatedness rule in influencing test fairness perceptions, which has been documented by the majority of studies on test reactions (e.g., Kluger & Rothstein, 1993; Rynes & Connerley, 1993; Schmit, Ryan, Stierwalt & Powell, 1995). Job-relatedness refers to both the face validity and perceived predictive validity of the selection procedure (Chan, Schmitt, Jennings et al., 1998). Most simulations including assessment centers have this 'transparent' quality (Schuler, 1993), which explains the favorable fairness perceptions often engendered by these selection procedures (e.g., Macan, Avedon, Paese & Smith, 1994; Rynes & Connerley, 1993). The general consensus from the research findings is that selection procedures involving simulations elicit more favorable test fairness perceptions than those using paper-and-pencil measures (for review, see Schmitt & Chan, 1999).

The importance of the other procedural rules in influencing selection fairness perceptions has also been documented. The opportunity to perform rule, which is conceptually rooted in the procedural justice concept of voice (Thibaut & Walker, 1975), was demonstrated in studies which showed that unstructured interviews were perceived as fairer than structured interviews because applicants believed that they have more opportunity to demonstrate or describe their abilities (Latham & Finnegan, 1993; Schuler, 1993). The importance of the opportunity for reconsideration rule has also been documented by Murphy, Thornton and Reynolds (1990), who reported that applicants perceived the use of drug testing in selection as fairer if there was a provision for retesting.

Compared to the procedural justice aspects, the distributive justice aspects of Gilliland's (1993) model appears to have received less attention. Gilliland mentioned three distributive justice rules (equity, equality, need) but only equity concerns have been the major focus of selection fairness studies. Recall that equity refers to the notion that people should receive outcomes that are coincident with the inputs they provide. In the selection context, the inputs provided by the applicants are their job relevant experiences and skills, and their outcomes are judged relative to other job applicants with whom they are familiar. Outcomes are typically the hiring decisions.

A major reason for the interest in fairness perceptions in the selection context was the assumption that these perceptions had an impact on subsequent applicant attitudes and behaviors. There is now some evidence to support this assumption. Singer (1992, 1993) found that individuals who perceived unfairness in the staffing procedures were less likely to accept a job than those who perceived the procedures to be fair. Gilliland (1994) found that workers who perceived that they were selected by unfair means had poorer work attitudes and job performance than those who perceived that they were selected fairly. Bauer et al. (1998) examined the importance of procedural justice in the prediction of several outcomes before and after actual applicants for an office position received feedback about their performance on a paper-and-pencil ability test. After the test, but before the provision of outcome feedback, outcomes including applicants' perceptions of organizational attractiveness and their intentions about future involvement with the organization were related to the provision of information about the test and treatment at the test site. Bauer et al., also found that procedural justice contributed incrementally to the prediction of test fairness perceptions and test-taking self-efficacy, beyond the prediction afforded by knowledge of test pass/fail outcome. However, no similar incremental prediction was found when the outcome was organizational attractiveness or future organizational involvement intentions.

Earlier in the chapter, we noted that one frequently cited hypothesis in the organizational justice literature is that there is an interaction between distributive justice and procedural justice in predicting reactions and outcomes. In the selection context, Gilliland (1994) experimentally manipulated job relatedness and explanations offered for the tests (procedural justice) and hiring decisions (distributive justice) and found that job relatedness and hiring decision interacted to affect perceptions of outcome fairness. In addition, there was an explanation by decision interaction effect on recommendation intentions. The nature of the two interactions was such that the procedural rule mattered only to rejected applicants in that their outcome fairness perceptions were more positive when an explanation was offered or when the tests were considered more job-related.

We think that the procedural justice by distributive justice interaction in selection contexts, as well as the relative importance of procedural rule violations versus the selection outcome, should be researched further. It would be useful to collect data on the relative importance of the various procedural rules in the production of the procedural justice by distributive justice interaction. One practical objective of such studies would be to establish the most effective ways to reduce the negative perceptions that result from a rejection decision in the selection context.

Contributions to Justice Research

The applications of justice principles in personnel selection research contribute to research on organizational justice in several important ways. First, justice-based studies of the selection process together provide a good mix of approaches to increasing our understanding of justice. For example, researchers were able to obtain convergent evidence for procedural justice effects by conducting studies that employed simulations (e.g., Chan et al., 1997) and those that employed actual experiences of applicants (e.g., Chan, Schmitt, Jennings et al., 1998), studies that used experimental designs (e.g., Gilliland, 1994) and those that used correlational designs (e.g., Steiner & Gilliland, 1996), and studies in laboratory settings (e.g., Smither et al., 1996) and those in field settings (e.g., Smither, Reilly, Millsap, Pearlman & Stoffey, 1993). Justice-based personnel selection research represents a good example of how a variety of methodological approaches can be used in an integrative fashion to advance justice research, as we have recommended earlier in the chapter (see section on measurement issues).

A second contribution concerns the careful delineation of the specific justice rules involved in the notion of procedural justice violations. Explicating the procedural rules allows the researcher to formulate more theory-driven hypotheses and explanations of results. Procedural injustice effects are likely to vary in magnitude according to the specific rule violation in question. Also, as noted earlier, procedural rules are likely to vary in the likelihood to produce a procedural justice by distributive justice interaction, as well as the nature and strength of the interaction, if one exists. We believe that a major reason for the large amount of published works generated from Gilliland's (1993) model of selection fairness is that the model explicitly described a number of procedural justice rules that allowed a variety of specific hypotheses to be formulated and tested.

A third contribution of selection fairness perception research concerns the timing of the administration of procedural justice perception measures relative to distributive justice perceptions. Several selection or test fairness perception studies have shown that the level of procedural justice perceptions, as well as the effects of these perceptions, varied according to whether the data on procedural justice perceptions were collected before or after performance on the selection test, as well as before or after knowledge of selection/test outcome (e.g., Bauer et al., 1998; Ryan & Chan, 1999). The issue of the timing of procedural justice perception data is important for conceptual, methodological, and practical reasons (Chan, Schmitt, Sacco et al., 1998). Consider the issue of pretest versus posttest collection of procedural justice perception data. It is possible that relative to posttest justice perceptions, pretest justice perceptions are more influenced by applicants' general belief in testing and their past experiences with tests, and that posttest justice perceptions are influenced by performance on the test. Posttest procedural justice perceptions on the test may be self-serving in the sense that applicants who believe that they did poorly report that the test is unfair or irrelevant, whereas those who did well report favorable justice perceptions.

Conceptually, comparing procedural justice perceptions across pretest and posttest data collection could help clarify the nature of justice perceptions and the causal relationships between test performance and these perceptions. Methodologically, if justice perception data collected before and after test performance yield different response patterns and have differential associations with external variables (e.g., test performance, general belief in tests), then perception data across the two measurement occasions may not be equivalent or directly comparable. When justice perception data from pretest and posttest measurements are combined across studies in a meta-analysis, the results may not be meaningful and may even be misleading. Additionally, if pretest and posttest justice perceptions differ as a function of test performance, then inferences base on justice reactions to selection tests that underlie important practical recommendations and decisions may vary depending on when justice reactions data are collected.

Future Research Directions

Future studies examining procedural justice perceptions of selection procedures should assess distributive justice perceptions (Schmitt & Chan, 1998). Some studies have attempted to explain fairness perceptions of selection tests in terms of self-serving bias (e.g., Chan et al., 1997). The notion of self-serving bias is clearly related to notions of distribution justice insofar as both are concerned with attitudes towards desired outcomes. Combining accounts of test reactions based on applicant motivational and self-serving mechanisms with the justice accounts of test perceptions offered by Gilliland's (1993) model could provide a better explanation of applicant fairness perceptions in selection contexts (Chan, Schmitt, Jennings et al., 1998; Schmitt & Chan, 1998).

While there is some evidence to indicate that justice perceptions in selection matters, we think more research is needed concerning the practical consequences of justice perceptions. Most of the research on outcomes of selection fairness perceptions has been relatively contrived and conducted with college students. In addition, the outcome variables were often intentions rather than actual behaviors.

Another promising avenue of research concerns the way in which justice perceptions on a selection test can actually affect the intended test constructs. Some evidence regarding this possibility is provided by the research of Chan and colleagues (Chan & Schmitt, 1997; Chan et al., 1997; Chan, Schmitt, Sacco et al., 1998), which showed that a component of the systematic variance in ability test scores may reflect differences in test taker perceptions of the test rather than true differences in ability.

Because of obvious sociopolitical implications in the USA, a research-worthy issue concerns racial differences in justice perceptions of the selection process. Future research in this direction is likely to build on existing studies that have consistently found that African American test takers reported lower test fairness perceptions and other test-taking motivation (e.g., Chan et al., 1997; Schmit & Ryan, 1997), particularly when the selection tests were administered in a paper-and-pencil format (Chan & Schmitt, 1997). Issues of racial differences in justice perceptions are critical in diversity management in organizations, which is another area of application of organizational justice.

Diversity Management

Compared to research on justice in performance evaluation and personnel selection, research on justice in diversity management is a very recent application of organizational justice principles. In the United States, diversity management is becoming increasingly popular in management practices as organizations respond to demographic changes in the workforce and attempt to harness a strategic advantage from their demographically diverse pool of employees (Cox, 1991; Cox & Blake, 1991). However, as noted by Gilliland and Gilliland (2001), diversity management can sometimes be ineffective and can even lead to negative reactions and lawsuits. We discuss how organizational justice principles have been or can be applied to explain reactions to different types of diversity management programs. Specifically, we examine how different aspects of the diversity management process may violate or enhance justice perceptions, which could in turn affect other reactions and behaviors.

One of the first applications of organizational justice principles to diversity management was a study by Leck, Saunders and Charbonneau (1996), which examined the effects of employee fairness perceptions of affirmative action programs (AAPs) on employee attitudes and behaviors. Using Gilliland's (1993) model of fairness perceptions of selection systems and findings from research about AAPs, Leck et al. (1996) proposed a model of fairness perceptions of AAPs. In their model, justice (distributive and procedural) perceptions have effects on employee diversity attitudes (i.e., resistance to diversity integration) as well as behaviors that affect diversity integration. Using data from a sample of 1412 employees at a large printing and publishing company in Canada, the authors obtained results that were generally consistent with the model. Specifically, the results showed that when employees perceived the AAP to be distributively and procedurally fair, they were more likely to have positive attitudes towards working with women and minorities, as well as more likely to engage in diversity integration behaviors.

In terms of recipients of affirmative action, Chacko (1982) found that women who felt that they were holding token positions reported low job satisfaction and organizational commitment. Heilman, Kaplow, Amato and Stathatos (1993) found that women who perceived that gaining employment was due to their gender rather than qualifications reported lower self-perceptions of competence. Following up from these findings, Richard and Kirby (1998) argued that diversity programs that are perceived as procedurally unjust would result in negative beneficiary attitudes, regardless of a positive outcome produced. They found empirical support for the argument in an experimental, scenario-based study using a sample of 90 white women business students in a US midwestern university. Results indicated that when procedural justice was low, the women participants rated the decision to hire them as part of the diversity program more negatively, experienced more negative attitudes toward their own abilities, rated the diversity program more negatively, and rated coworker perceptions toward them more negatively.

A recent study by Day et al. (1999) examined the self-categorization of 254 library employees

(70% female; 87% white/non-Hispanic) by asking them if they consider themselves to be a member of an underrepresented group. Of those who considered themselves to be members of an underrepresented group, 15% were white majority group members. These nontraditional underrepresented group members reported more negative general attitudes toward diversity-related issues than employees classified as traditionally underrepresented or not underrepresented. Procedural justice perceptions toward diversity-related issues were found to completely mediate the relationship between nontraditional underrepresented group identity and attitudes toward diversity.

Contributions to Justice Research

Unlike performance evaluation and personnel selection research, the application of justice principles to diversity research is very recent and we feel that it is too early to evaluate the contributions that diversity research has made to understanding organizational justice. However, we speculate that a potential contribution of diversity research lies in the controversial nature of diversity issues.

In issues of performance evaluation and personnel selection (independent of diversity issues such as AAPs in selection), it is usually not difficult to find some relatively universal principles (at least within a culture) that are associated with fairness perceptions. For example, the principle of meritocracy is typically and easily associated with fairness perceptions of selection and evaluation decisions. This makes it easy to present a selection or evaluation situation that would predictably elicit fair (or unfair) perceptions. Diversity management decisions and programs, on the other hand, typically occur in controversial and complex contexts involving multiple principles (e.g., meritocracy, equal opportunity) and domains (e.g., legal, political, sociocultural). This makes it less easy to predict whether fair or unfair perceptions will be elicited by a diversity situation. Although we can make gross predictions that traditionally underrepresented group members (women and minorities) are more likely to perceive fairness in diversity programs than would non-underrepresented group members (white male), the studies we reviewed above indicate that more complex relationships exist. For example, as shown in Richard and Kirby (1998), even beneficiaries of a diversity program could perceive procedural unfairness and hold negative attitudes, regardless of a positive outcome produced.

We think that diversity management researchers who propose justice-based accounts will have a difficult and challenging task in delineating the justice principles involved and explicitly linking them to the constructs of interest. We actually view this difficulty as a potential contribution that diversity management research can make to understanding organizational justice. The complexities involved in understanding diversity attitudes and behaviors force the proposed justice-based accounts to be made explicit. Because of the complexities, the resulting justice-based model is likely to be more elaborate, forcing the serious researcher to expand the construct space and integrate multiple constructs and theories to better represent reality and explain the data, which in turn contributes to a better understanding of organizational justice. Simple bivariate associations are unlikely to provide satisfactory justice-based accounts of diversity attitudes and behaviors.

Future Research Directions

With globalization and demographic changes in the workforce, diversity management will become increasingly important. More research is needed to understand the basis of reactions to diversity management, especially the reasons for resistance to various diversity programs. We believe that justice-based accounts provide promising explanations and potential avenues for designing effective interventions to increase the effectiveness of diversity management.

Adequate justice-based accounts are those empirically supported by theory-driven research. One promising avenue of research is to explicate how specific aspects of procedural justice affect diversity attitudes and behaviors. For example, what is it about marketing arguments that make them elicit favorable justice perceptions about a hiring decision as part of a diversity management program? Since marketing arguments can vary greatly in terms of the extent to which they appeal to cost, creativity, problem solving, and other market considerations, it is important to identify the justice principles invoked in the marketing argument that elicited the fair or unfair perceptions.

Another promising avenue of research is to examine justice perceptions in the context of diversity training. Diversity training, probably the most common approach to diversity management (Cox, 1991), provides an excellent context to investigate several justice issues. For example, justice training is one context to compare the different distributive justice rules. Gilliland and Gilliland (2001) noted that distributive justice in training may be more strongly determined by equality and needs than equity because training outcomes are generally not allocated on a meritorious basis as are pay increases in performance evaluation or job offers in personnel selection. This is particularly true for diversity training because it is often provided to everyone in the unit (equality principle) or to those with special needs (need principle), rather than those most deserving based on inputs (equity principle). Diversity training also provides an excellent context to isolate the sources of differences in justice perceptions, and separate those attributable to stable individual differences from those attributable to malleable variables. In addition to increasing our understanding of justice effects, this variance partitioning is practically important because it helps identify causal variables that are malleable and hence inform the design of interventions to enhance justice perceptions in diversity management.

CONCLUSIONS

We started this chapter by highlighting a number of the areas of organizational and work psychology to which organizational justice concepts have been applied. This clearly demonstrates the widespread relevance of justice concepts to organizational management. The latter sections of this chapter also highlight the contributions of some application of justice research to theory development. Research on justice in performance evaluation has expanded our understanding of voice and the different ways in which employee input enhances procedural justice. Personnel selection research has expanded our conceptualization of specific procedural justice rules and the dynamic nature of justice perceptions across a decision-making process. Finally, although contributions of diversity management research have yet to be realized, the study of justice and diversity promises to expand our understanding of individual differences in justice perceptions. This reciprocal relationship between theory and application is one of the real strengths of organizational justice research.

Unfortunately, the push to apply justice constructs to new organizational issues has perhaps led to neglect in the area of theory development. As demonstrated earlier, most of the theory development in the area of justice has come from social psychology rather than organizational psychology. Although the exchange of ideas between these two disciplines is useful, we believe that organizational researchers have unique contributions to make to theory development. The study of individual differences in psychological phenomena has a much stronger history in organizational psychology than social psychology. Extending individual difference research to organizational justice theories may provide some important extensions to these theories. Additionally, issues of multiple levels of analysis are also most clearly articulated by organizational psychology researchers and may contribute to our development of organizational justice theories.

With the current popularity of organizational justice, we feel that the need for theory development is more critical than ever. If organizational justice theory remains at the stage of boxes and arrows, rather than articulating the more substantial issues of 'why' justice is important to people and 'how' justice evaluations develop, we do not believe that the current popularity of organizational justice will last. Attention will shift to the next constructs that become popular. For organizational justice to continue to make an enduring contribution to organizational psychology, comprehensive, generalizable, and parsimonious theories of organizational justice must the developed and adopted by organizational researchers.

REFERENCES

Adams, J.S. (1965). Inequity in social exchange. In L. Berkowitz (Ed.), *Advances in experimental social psychology* (Vol. 2, pp. 267–299). New York: Academic Press.

Adams-Roy, J., & Barling, J. (1988). Predicting the decision to confront or report sexual harassment. *Journal of Organizational Behavior*, 19, 329–336.

Alexander, S., & Ruderman, M. (1987). The role of procedural and distributive justice in organizational behavior. *Social Justice Research*, 1, 177–198.

Arvey, R.D., & Sackett, P.R. (1993). Fairness in selection: Current developments and perspectives. In N. Schmitt, & W. Borman (Eds.), *Personnel selection* (pp. 171–202). San Francisco: Jossey-Bass.

Arvey, R.D., Strickland, W., Drauden, G., & Martin, C. (1990). Motivational components of test taking. *Personnel Psychology*, 43, 695–716.

Bauer, T.N., Maertz, C.P. Jr., Dolen, M.R., & Campion, M.A. (1998). Longitudinal assessment of applicant reactions to employment testing and test outcome feedback. *Journal of Applied Psychology*, 83, 892–903.

Beach, L.R. (1996). *Decision making in the workplace: A unified perspective.* Mahwah, NJ: Lawrence Erlbaum.

Bennett-Alexander, D.D., & Pincus, L.B. (1998). *Employment law for business* (2nd ed.). Boston: Irwin/McGraw-Hill.

Beugre, C.D. (1998). *Managing fairness in organizations.* Westport, CN: Quorum.

Bies, R.J., & Moag, J.S. (1986). Interactional justice: Communication criteria for fairness. *Research on Negotiation in Organization*, 1, 43–55.

Bobko, P., Roth, P.L., & Potosky, D. (1999). Derivation and implications of a meta-analytic matrix incorporating cognitive ability, alternative predictors, and job performance. *Personnel Psychology*, 52, 561–590.

Brockner, J., & Wiesenfeld, B.M. (1996). An integrative framework for explaining reactions to decisions: Interactive effects of outcomes and procedures. *Psychological Bulletin*, 120, 189–208.

Carroll, S.J., & Schneier, C.E. (1982). *Performance appraisal and review systems: The identification, measurement, and development of performance management in organizations.* Glenview, IL: Scott Foresman.

Cawley, B.D., Keeping, L.M., & Levy, P.E. (1998). Participation in the performance appraisal process and employee reactions: A meta-analytic review of field investigations. *Journal of Applied Psychology*, 83, 615–633.

Chacko, T.L. (1982). Women and equal opportunity: Some unintended effects. *Journal of Applied Psychology*, *67*, 119–123.

Chan, D. (1997). Racial subgroup differences in predictive validity perceptions on personality and cognitive ability tests. *Journal of Applied Psychology*, *82*, 311–320.

Chan, D. (1998). Functional relations among constructs in the same content domain at different levels of analysis: A typology of composition models. *Journal of Applied Psychology*, *83*, 234–246.

Chan, D., & Schmitt, N. (1997). Video-based versus paper-and-pencil method of assessment in situational judgment tests: Subgroup differences in test performance and face validity perceptions. *Journal of Applied Psychology*, *82*, 143–159.

Chan, D., Schmitt, N., DeShon, R., Clause, C., & Delbridge, K. (1997). Reactions to cognitive ability tests: The relationships between race, test performance, face validity, and test-taking motivation. *Journal of Applied Psychology*, *82*, 300–310.

Chan, D., Schmitt, N., Jennings, D., Clause, C., & Delbridge, K. (1998). Applicant perceptions of test fairness: Integrating justice and self-serving bias perspectives. *International Journal of Selection and Assessment*, *6*, 232–239.

Chan, D., Schmitt, N., Sacco, J., & DeShon, R.P. (1998). Understanding pretest and posttest reactions to cognitive ability and personality tests. *Journal of Applied Psychology*, *83*, 471–485.

Cherry, B., & Gilliland, S.W. (1999). *Employee input in the development of performance appraisal systems*. Paper presented at the 59th Annual Meeting of The Academy of Management, Chicago, IL, August.

Cherry, B., Ordonez, L.D., & Gilliland, S.W. (1999). *Grade expectations: The effects of expectations on fairness and satisfaction perceptions*. Unpublished manuscript.

Cox, T. (1991). The multicultural organization. *Academy of Management Executive*, *5*, 34–47.

Cox, T.H., & Blake, S. (1991). Managing cultural diversity: Implications for organizational competitiveness. *Academy of Management Executive*, *5*, 45–56.

Cropanzano, R., Byrne, Z.S., & Prehar, C.A. (1999). *How workers manage relationships in a complex social world: A multi-foci approach to procedural and interactional justice*. Paper presented at the 1st International Round Table: Innovations in Organizational Justice. Nice, France, June.

Cropanzano, R., & Greenberg, J. (1997). Progress in organizational justice: Tunneling through the maze. In C.L. Cooper, & I.T. Robertson (Eds.), *International review of industrial and organizational psychology*, Vol. 12. Chichester, UK: Wiley.

Day, D.V., Cross, W.E., Ringseis, E.L., & Williams, T.L. (1999). Self-categorization and identity construction associated with managing diversity. *Journal of Vocational Behavior*, *54*, 188–195.

Deutsch, M. (1975). Equity, equality, and need: What determines which value will be used as the basis of distributive justice? *Journal of Social Issues*, *31*, 137–149.

Dulebohn, J.H., & Ferris, G.R. (1999). The role of influence tactics in perceptions of performance evaluations' fairness. *Academy of Management Journal*, *42*, 288–303.

Eddy, E.R., Stone, D.L., & Stone-Romero, E.F. (1999). The effects of information management policies on reactions to human resource information systems: An integration of privacy and procedural justice perspectives. *Personnel Psychology*, *52*, 335–358.

Farh, J., Earley, P.C., & Lin, S. (1997). Impetus for action: A cultural analysis of justice and organizational citizenship behavior in Chinese society. *Administrative Science Quarterly*, *42*, 421–444.

Farh, J., Podsakoff, P.M., & Organ, D.W. (1990). Accounting for organizational citizenship behavior: Leader fairness and task scope versus satisfaction. *Journal of Management*, *16*, 705–722.

Folger, R. (1977). Distributive and procedural justice: Combined impact of 'voice' and improvement on experienced inequity. *Journal of Personality and Social Psychology*, *35*, 108–119.

Folger, R. (1986). Rethinking equity theory: A referent cognitions model. In H.W. Bierhoff, R.L. Cohen, & J. Greenberg, (Eds.), *Justice in social relations* (pp. 145–162). New York: Plenum.

Folger, R., & Cropanzano, R. (1998). *Organizational justice and human resource management*. Thousand Oaks, CA: Sage.

Folger, R., & Konovsky, M.A. (1989). Effects of procedural and distributive justice on reactions to pay raise decisions. *Academy of Management Journal*, *32*, 115–130.

Folger, R., Konovsky, M.A., & Cropanzano, R. (1992). A due process metaphor for performance appraisal. *Research in Organizational Behavior*, *14*, 129–177.

Giles, W.F., Findley, H.M., & Field, H.S. (1997). Procedural fairness in performance appraisal: Beyond the review session. *Journal of Business and Psychology*, *11*, 493–506.

Gilliland, S.W. (1993). The perceived fairness of selection systems: An organizational justice perspective. *Academy of Management Review*, *18*, 694–734.

Gilliland, S.W. (1994). Effects of procedural and distributive justice on reactions to a selection system. *Journal of Applied Psychology*, *79*, 691–701.

Gilliland, S.W. (1995). Fairness from the applicant's perspective: Reactions to employee selection procedures. *International Journal of Selection and Assessment*, *3*, 11–19.

Gilliland, S.W. (1996). *Images of justice*. Paper presented at the 11th annual meeting of the Society for Industrial and Organizational Psychology, San Diego, CA, April.

Gilliland, S.W., Benson, L. III., & Schepers, D.H. (1998). A rejection threshold in justice evaluations: Effects on judgment and decision making. *Organizational Behavior and Human Decision Processes*, *76*, 113–131.

Gilliland, S.W., & Gilliland, C.K. (2001). An organizational justice analysis of diversity training. In S.W. Gilliland, D.D. Steiner, & D.P. Skarlicki (Eds.), *Research in social issues in management: Theoretical and cultural perspectives on organizational justice.* Greenwich, CT: Information Age Publishing.

Gilliland, S.W., & Langdon, J.C. (1998). Creating performance management systems that promote perceptions of fairness. In J.W. Smither (Ed.), *Performance appraisal: state of the art in practice.* San Francisco: Jossey-Bass.

Gilliland, S.W., & Steiner, D.D. (2001). Causes and consequences of applicant perceptions of unfairness. In R. Cropanzano (Ed.), *Justice in the workplace* (Vol. 2) pp. 175–195. Mahwah, NJ: Lawrence Erlbaum Associates.

Goldman, B.M. (1999). *Employment discrimination-claiming behavior: The effects of organizational justice, social guidance, and perceived discrimination.* Unpublished Manuscript.

Greenberg, J. (1982). Approaching equity and avoiding inequity in groups and organizations. In J. Greenberg, & R.L. Cohen (Eds.), *Equity and justice in social behavior*, pp. 389–435. New York: Academic Press.

Greenberg, J. (1986a). Determinants of perceived fairness of performance evaluations. *Journal of Applied Psychology, 71,* 340–342.

Greenberg, J. (1986b). The distributive justice of organizational performance evaluations. In H.W. Bierhoff, R.L. Cohen, & J. Greenberg, (Eds.), *Justice in social relations.* New York: Plenum Publications.

Greenberg, J. (1987a). A taxonomy of organizational justice theories. *Academy of Management Review, 12,* 9–22.

Greenberg, J. (1987b). Using diaries to promote procedural justice in performance appraisals. *Social Justice Research, 1,* 219–234.

Greenberg, J. (1990). Employee theft as a reaction to underpayment inequity: The hidden cost of pay cuts. *Journal of Applied Psychology, 75,* 561–568.

Greenberg, J. (1993). Stealing in the name of justice. *Organizational Behavior and Human Decision Processes, 54,* 81–103.

Greenberg, J. (1996). *The quest for justice on the job: Essays and experiments.* Thousand Oaks, CA: Sage.

Greenberg, J., & Lind, E.A. (in press). The pursuit of organizational justice: From conceptualization to implementation to application. In C.L. Cooper, & E.A. Locke (Eds.), *I/O psychology: What we know about theory and practice.* Oxford, UK: Blackwell.

Heilman, M.E., Kaplow, S.R., Amato, M.A.G., & Stathatos, P. (1993). When similarity is a liability: Effects of sex-based preferential selection on reactions to like-sex and different-sex others. *Journal of Applied Psychology, 78,* 917–927.

Huseman, R.C., Hatfield, J.D., & Miles, E.W. (1987). A new perspective on equity theory: The equity sensitivity construct. *Academy of Management Review, 12:* 222–234.

Iles, P.A., & Robertson, I.T. (1989). The impact of personnel selection procedures on candidates. In P. Herriot (Ed.), *Assessment and selection in organizations* (pp. 257–271). Chichester, UK: Wiley.

Kahneman, D., & Tversky, A. (1982). The simulation heuristic. In D. Kahneman, P. Slovic, & A. Tversky, (Eds.), *Judgment under uncertainty: Heuristics and biases* (pp. 201–208). New York: Cambridge University Press.

Kanfer, R., & Ackerman, P.L. (1989). Motivation and cognitive abilities: An integrative/aptitude-treatment interaction approach to skill acquisition. *Journal of Applied Psychology, 74,* 657–690.

Kluger, A.N., & Rothstein, H.R. (1993). The influence of selection test type on applicant reactions to employment testing. *Journal of Business and Psychology, 8,* 3–25.

Konovsky, M.A., & Brockner, J. (1993). Managing victim and survivor layoff reactions: A procedural justice perspective. In R. Cropanzano (Ed.) *Justice in the workplace: Approaching fairness in human resource management.* Hillsdale, NJ: Erlbaum.

Korsgaard, M.A., & Roberson, L. (1995). Procedural justice in performance evaluation: The role of instrumental and non-instrumental voice in performance appraisal discussions. *Journal of Management, 21,* 657–669.

Kozlowski, S.W.J., & Hattrup, K. (1992). A disagreement about within-group agreement: Disentangling issues of consistency versus consensus. *Journal of Applied Psychology, 77,* 161–167.

Kulik, C.T., & Ambrose, M.L. (1992). Personal and situational determinants of referent choice. *Academy of Management Review, 17,* 212–237.

Landy, F.J., Barnes-Farrell, J., & Cleveland, J.N. (1980). Perceived fairness and accuracy of performance evaluation: A follow-up. *Journal of Applied Psychology, 65,* 355–356.

Latham, G.P., & Finnegan, B.J. (1993). Perceived practicality of unstructured, patterned, and situational interviews. In H. Schuler, J.L., Farr, & M. Smith (Eds), *Personnel selection and assessment: Individual and organizational perspectives* (pp. 41–55). Hillsdale, NJ: Erlbaum.

Leck, J.D., Saunders, D.M., & Charbonneau, M. (1996). Affirmative action programs: An organizational justice perspective. *Journal of Organizational Behavior, 17,* 79–89.

Leung, K., Smith, P.B., Wang, Z., & Sun, H. (1996). Job satisfaction in joint venture hotels in China: An organizational justice analysis. *Journal of International Business Studies, 27,* 947–962.

Leventhal, G.S. (1980). What should be done with equity theory? New approaches to the study of fairness in social relationship. In K.J. Gergen, M.S. Greenberg, & R.H. Willis (Eds.), *Social exchange: Advances in theory and research* (pp. 27–55). New York: Plenum.

Lind, A.E., Kulik, C.T., Ambrose, M., & de Vera Park, M.W. (1993). Individual and corporate dispute resolution: Using procedural fairness as a decision heuristic. *Administrative Science Quarterly, 38,* 224–251.

Lind, A.E., & Tyler, T.R. (1988). *The social psychology of procedural justice.* New York: Plenum.

Macan, T.H., Avedon, M.J., Paese, M., & Smith, D.E. (1994). The effects of applicants' reactions to cognitive ability tests and an assessment center. *Personnel Psychology, 47,* 715–738.

Martin, C.L., & Bennett, N. (1996). The role of justice judgments in explaining the relationship between job satisfaction and organizational commitment. *Group and Organization Management, 21*, 84–104.

Masterson, S.S., Lewis, K., Goldman, B.M., & Taylor, M.S. (2000). Integrating justice and social exchange: The differing effects of fair procedures and treatment on work relationships. *Academy of Management Journal, 43*, 738–748.

McFarlin, D.B., & Sweeney, P.D. (1992). Distributive and procedural justice as predictors of satisfaction with personal and organizational outcomes. *Academy of Management Journal, 35*, 626–637.

Miceli, M.P. (1993). Justice and pay system satisfaction. In R. Cropanzano (Ed.), *Justice in the workplace: Approaching fairness in human resource management.* Hillsdale, NJ: Erlbaum.

Mikula, G. (1993). On the experience of injustice. *European Review of Social Psychology, 4*, 223–244.

Mikula, G., Petri, B., & Tanzer, N. (1990). What people regard as unjust: Types and structures of everyday experiences of injustice. *European Journal of Social Psychology, 20*, 133–149.

Mikula, G., Scherer, K.R., & Athenstaedt, U. (1998). The role of injustice in the elicitation of differential emotional reactions. *Personality and Social Psychology Bulletin, 24*, 769–783.

Miles, J.A., & Greenberg, J. (1993). Cross-national differences in preferences for distributive justice norms: The challenge of establishing fair resource allocations in the European Community. *Research in Personnel and Human Resource Management, 3*, 133–156.

Moorman, R.H. (1991). Relationship between organizational justice and organizational citizenship behaviors: Do fairness perceptions influence employee citizenship? *Journal of Applied Psychology, 76*, 845–855.

Moorman, R.H., Blakely, G.L., & Niehoff, B.P. (1998). Does perceived organizational support mediate the relationship between procedural justice and organizational citizenship behavior? *Academy of Management Journal, 41*, 351–357.

Mossholder, K.W., Bennett, N., Kemery, E.R., & Wesolowski, M.A. (1998). Relationships between bases of power and work reactions: The mediational role of procedural justice. *Journal of Management, 24*, 533–552.

Mossholder, K.W., Bennett, N., & Martin, C.L. (1998). A multilevel analysis of procedural justice context. *Journal of Organizational Behavior, 19*, 131–141.

Mueller, C.W., Iverson, R.D., & Jo, D. (1999). Distributive justice evaluations in two cultural contexts: A comparison of U.S. and South Korean teachers. *Human Relations, 52*, 869–893.

Murphy, K.R., & Cleveland, J.N. (1995). *Understanding performance appraisal: Social, organizational, and goal-based perspectives.* Thousand Oaks, CA: Sage.

Murphy, K.R., Thornton, G.C., III, & Reynolds, D.H. (1990). College students' attitudes toward employee drug testing programs. *Personnel Psychology, 43*, 615–631.

Naylor, J.C., Pritchard, R.D., & Ilgen, D.R. (1980). *A theory of behavior in organizations.* New York: Academic Press.

Pearce, J.L., Bigley, G.A., & Branyiczki, I. (1998). Procedural justice as modernism: Placing industrial/organizational psychology in context. *Applied Psychology: An International Review, 47*, 371–396.

Richard, O.C., & Kirby, S.L. (1998). Women recruits' perceptions of workforce diversity program selection decisions: A procedural justice examination. *Journal of Applied Social Psychology, 28*, 183–188.

Rousseau, D.M. (1985). Issues of level in organizational research: Multi-level and cross-level perspectives. In B.M. Staw, & L.L. Cummings (Eds.), *Research in organizational behavior* (pp. 1–37). Greenwich, CT: JAI Press.

Ryan, A.M., & Chan, D. (1999). Perceptions of the EPPP: How do licensure candidates view the process? *Professional Psychology: Research and Practice, 30*, 519–530.

Rynes, S.L., & Connerley, M.L. (1993). Applicant reactions to alternative selection procedures. *Journal of Business and Psychology, 4*, 261–277.

Sackett, P., & Roth, L. (1996). Multistage selection strategies: A Monte Carlo investigation of effects on performance and minority hiring. *Personnel Psychology, 49*, 1–18.

Sapienza, H.J., & Korsgaard, M.A. (1996). Procedural justice in entrepreneur-investor relations. *Academy of Management Journal, 39*, 544–574.

Scarpello, V., & Jones, F.F. (1996). Why justice matters in compensation decision making. *Journal of Organizational Behavior, 17*, 285–299.

Schmit, M.J., & Ryan, A.M. (1997). Applicant withdrawal: The role of test-taking attitudes and racial differences. *Personnel Psychology, 50*, 855–876.

Schmit, M.J., Ryan, A.M., Stierwalt, S.L., & Powell, A.B. (1995). Frame-of-reference effects on personality scale sores and criterion-related validity. *Journal of Applied Psychology, 80*, 607–620.

Schmitt, N., & Chan, D. (1998). *Personnel selection: A theoretical approach.* Thousand Oaks, CA: Sage.

Schmitt, N., & Chan, D. (1999). The status of research on applicant reactions to selection tests and its implications for managers. *International Journal of Management Reviews, 1*, 45–62.

Schmitt, N., Rogers, W., Chan, D., Sheppard, L., & Jennings, D. (1997). Adverse impact and predictive efficiency of various predictor combinations. *Journal of Applied Psychology, 82*, 717–730.

Schuler, H. (1993). Social validity of selection situations: A concept and some empirical results. In H. Schuler, J.L. Farr, & M. Smith (Eds.), *Personnel selection and assessment: Individual and organizational perspectives* (pp. 11–26). Hillsdale, NJ: Erlbaum.

Shapiro, D.L., & Rosen, B. (1994). An investigation of managerial interventions in employee disputes. *Employee Responsibilities and Rights Journal, 7*, 37–51.

Singer, M.S. (1992). Procedural justice in managerial selection: Identification of fairness determinants and associations of fairness perceptions. *Social Justice Research, 5*, 49–70.

Singer, M.S. (1993). *Fairness in personnel selection.* Aldershot, New Zealand: Avebury.

Skarlicki, D.P., & Folger, R. (1997). Retaliation in the workplace: The roles of distributive, procedural, and interactional justice. *Journal of Applied Psychology, 82,* 434–443.

Skarlicki, D.P., Folger, R., & Tesluk, P. (1999). Personality as a moderator in the relationship between fairness and retaliation. *Academy of Management Journal, 42,* 100–108.

Skarlicki, D.P., & Latham, G.P. (1996). Increasing citizenship behavior within a labor union: A test of organizational justice theory. *Journal of Applied Psychology, 81,* 161–169.

Smither, J.W., Millsap, R.E., Stoffey, R.W., Reilly, R.R., & Pearlman, K.E. (1996). An experimental test of the influence of selection procedures on fairness perceptions, attitudes about the organization, and job pursuit intentions. *Journal of Business and Psychology, 10,* 297–318.

Smither, J.W., Reilly, R.R., Millsap, R.E., Pearlman, K., & Stoffey, R.W. (1993). Applicant reactions to selection procedures. *Personnel Psychology, 46,* 49–76.

Steiner, D.D., & Gilliland, S.W. (1996). Fairness reactions to personnel selection techniques in France and the U.S. *Journal of Applied Psychology, 81,* 134–141.

Stepina, L.P., & Perrewe, P.L. (1991). The stability of comparative referent choice and feelings of inequity: A longitudinal field study. *Journal of Organizational Behavior, 12,* 185–200.

Sweeney, P.D., & McFarlin, D.B. (1993). Workers' evaluations of the 'ends' and the 'means': An examination of four models of distributive and procedural justice. *Organizational Behavior and Human Decision Processes, 55,* 23–40.

Taylor, M.S., Masterson, S.S., Renard, M.K., & Tracy, K.B. (1998). Managers' reactions to procedurally just performance management systems. *Academy of Management Journal, 41,* 568–579.

Taylor, M.S., Tracy, K.B., Renard, M.K., Harrison, J.K., & Carroll, S.J. (1995). Due process in performance appraisal: A quasi-experiment in procedural justice. *Administrative Science Quarterly, 40,* 495–523.

Thibaut, J., & Walker, L. (1975). *Procedural justice: A psychological analysis.* Hillsdale, NJ: Erlbaum.

Tremblay, M., Bruno, S., & Pelchat, A. (1998). A study of the determinants and of the impact of flexibility on employee benefit satisfaction. *Human Relations, 51,* 667–688.

Tyler, T. (1994). Psychological models of the justice motive: Antecedents of distributive and procedural justice. *Journal of Personality and Social Psychology, 67,* 850–863.

Tyler, T., Degoey, P., & Smith, H. (1996). Understanding why the justice of group procedures matters: A test of the psychological dynamics of the group-value model. *Journal of Personality and Social Psychology, 70,* 913–930.

Van den Bos, K., Bruins, J., Wilke, H.A.M., & Dronkert, E. (1999). Sometimes unfair procedures have nice aspects: On the psychology of the fair process effect. *Journal of Personality and Social Psychology, 77,* 324–336.

Van den Bos, K., Vermunt, R., & Wilke, H.A.M. (1997). Procedural and distributive justice: What is fair depends more on what comes first than on what comes next. *Journal of Personality and Social Psychology, 72,* 95–104.

Weiss, H.M., Suckow, K., & Cropanzano, R. (1999). Effects of justice conditions on discrete emotions. *Journal of Applied Psychology, 84,* 786–794.

9

Leadership in Organizations

DEANNE N. DEN HARTOG
and PAUL L. KOOPMAN

Leadership has always been an important topic in work and organizational psychology and much research has been devoted to the topic. This chapter describes the developments in this field over the last decades. Trait, style, and contingency theories of leadership in organizations are presented, as well as several alternative approaches to studying leadership. Special attention is also given to transformational/charismatic leadership. The growing importance of global and international world business creates a strong demand for managers who are sophisticated in international management and skilled at working with people from other countries. This has resulted in increased attention for cross-cultural perspectives the leadership field. Other currents of change, such as the developing information technology and the increased importance of teams and other lateral organizing mechanisms are influencing work and organizations in a pervasive manner. We conclude the chapter by presenting several possible ways in which these trends may change the role of leadership in future organizations.

INTRODUCTION

Legends and myths about what distinguishes 'great leaders' from 'commoners' seem to have always attracted people. Bass writes: 'The study of leadership rivals in age the emergence of civilization, which shaped its leaders as much as it was shaped by them. From its infancy, the study of history has been the study of leaders – what they did and why they did it' (1990a: 3). Leadership still fascinates scholars as well as the general public. However, the term 'leadership' means different things to different people. Definitions of leadership vary in terms of emphasis on leader abilities, personality traits, influence relationships, cognitive versus emotional orientation, individual versus group orientation, and appeal to self versus collective interests. Definitions also vary in whether they are primarily descriptive or normative in nature as well as in their relative emphasis on behavioral styles (Den Hartog, Koopman, Thierry, Wilderom, Maczynski &

Jarmuz, 1997). Leadership is sometimes distinguished from management (e.g., Kotter, 1990; Zaleznik, 1977) or seen as one of several managerial roles (e.g., Mintzberg, 1989). Bryman (1992) states that most definitions of leadership emphasize three main elements: *group*, *influence*, and *goal*. Table 9.1 provides several examples of definitions of leadership.

Another way to view leadership is in terms of the different *domains* leadership encompasses. Most approaches to leadership have been leader-centered. However, one can distinguish between the leader, follower, and relationship domain of leadership (Graen & Uhl-Bien, 1995). In all three domains different levels of analysis (i.e., individual, dyad, group or larger collectivities) can be the focus of investigation (e.g., Yammarino & Bass, 1991). According to Graen and Uhl-Bien (1995), leader behavior and characteristics and their effects are the primary issues of concern in the leader-based domain. A follower-based approach would lead to hypotheses focusing on follower issues such as follower characteristics, behaviors, and perceptions

Table 9.1   *Defining leadership*

Anglo-Saxon definitions of leadership
• Leadership is the influential increment over and above mechanical compliance with the routine directives of the organization (Katz & Kahn, 1978).
• Leadership is the process of influencing the activities of an organized group toward goal achievement (Rauch & Behling, 1984).
• Yukl (1998) broadly defines leadership as influence processes affecting the interpretation of events for followers, the choice of objectives for the group or organization, the organization of work activities to accomplish the objectives, the motivation of followers to achieve the objectives, the maintenance of cooperative relationships and teamwork, and the enlistment of support and cooperation from people outside the group or organization.
• Leadership is defined in terms of a process of social influence whereby a leader steers members of a group towards a goal (Bryman, 1992).
• Leadership is the ability of an individual to motivate others to forego self interest in the interest of a collective vision, and to contribute to the attainment of that vision and to the collective by making significant personal self-sacrifices over and above the call of duty, willingly (House & Shamir, 1993).

or topics such as empowerment (e.g., Hollander, 1992; Meindl, 1990). A relationship-based model takes the relationship between leader and follower as the starting point for research and theory building. Issues of concern are reciprocal influence and the development and maintenance of effective relationships (e.g., Bryman, 1992; Graen & Scandura, 1987). Graen and Uhl-Bien note that a multiple domain approach should be taken more often and that 'careful sampling from multiple domains within the same investigation should account for more of the potential leadership contribution, and thus increase the predictive validity and practical usefulness of our studies' (1995: 221).

As stated, most research in the leadership field so far has been done from a leader-centered point of view. The following section presents an overview of the major developments in leadership research and theory to date. This is followed by a more extensive treatment of the most recent trend in leadership research, which focuses on so-called charismatic, transformational, or inspirational leadership. The growing importance of global and international world business creates a strong demand for managers who are sophisticated in international management and skilled at working with people from other countries (Adler, 1991). This has led to increased attention for cross-cultural perspectives the leadership field. Therefore, the topic of international and cross-cultural research into leadership is also discussed. A discussion of the future of leadership and future leadership research concludes this chapter.

TRENDS AND DEVELOPMENTS IN LEADERSHIP RESEARCH

Leadership has been an important topic of investigation, especially in North America, for many decades. Several main trends can be distinguished

in the development of the study of (business) leadership. Prior to the 1980s the main approaches to leadership were the *trait, style,* and *contingency* approach. Table 9.2 presents a historical overview of the main trends in the leadership field. The dates in this table represent rough indications of the periods in which the emphasis was on that approach. A new stage did not necessarily mean the previous stage was completely abandoned; rather, a shift in emphasis occurred (Bass, 1990a; Bryman, 1992). Several alternative ways to conceptualize and study leadership have had a profound influence on the development of ideas about and research into leadership from the early 1980s onward. Below, the three aforementioned main trends and several of these alternative approaches to leadership will be described.

The Trait Approach

Early research into leadership can be characterized as a search for 'the great man.' Personal characteristics of leaders were emphasized and the implicit idea was that leaders are born rather than made. All leaders were supposed to have certain stable characteristics that made them into leaders. The focus was on identifying and measuring traits that distinguished leaders from nonleaders or effective from ineffective leaders (Hollander & Offermann, 1990). From these distinctions between leaders and nonleaders, a profile of an 'ideal' leader could be derived, which could serve as the basis for selection of future leaders.

Three main categories of personal characteristics were included in the search for the 'great man.' First, *physical* features, such as height, physique, appearance, and age. Second, *ability* characteristics such as intelligence, knowledge, and fluency of speech. And third, *personality* traits such as dominance, emotional control and expressiveness, and introversion–extraversion (Bryman, 1992).

Table 9.2   *Trends in leadership theory and research*

Period	Approach	Core theme
Up to late 1940s	Trait	Leaders are born; leadership as an innate ability
Late 1940s to late 1960s	Style	What do they do; effectiveness has to do with how the leader behaves
Late 1960s to early 1980s	Contingency	It all depends; effectiveness of leadership is affected by the situation/context
Since early 1980s	New leadership (including charismatic/ transformational leadership)	Leaders need vision and inspire loyalty and emotional attachment

Adapted from Bryman (1992: 1).

Research up to 1950 failed to yield a consistent picture of leader traits, therefore research into this area slowed. After about 25 years the interest in traits possessed by leaders revived. In 1974, after reviewing 163 studies that had been reported between 1949 and 1970, Stogdill showed that contrary to what had been concluded from earlier reviews, several universal personal traits and skills (such as vigor and persistence in the pursuit of goals, self-confidence and tolerance for uncertainty and frustration) were indeed associated with leadership (Bass, 1990a). Other studies have also shown that traits or personal characteristics do indeed play a more significant role in leadership than was concluded earlier (e.g., Kirkpatrick & Locke, 1991; Lord, De Vader & Allinger, 1986). Kirkpatrick and Locke's (1991) review suggests that drive, a desire to lead, honesty and integrity, self-confidence, cognitive ability, and knowledge of the business are personal characteristics that distinguish leaders from nonleaders. Other traits predicting effective leadership include: high energy level and stress tolerance, internal locus of control orientation, emotional maturity, socialized power motivation, moderate achievement motivation, and a low need for affiliation (Yukl, 1998).

The type of 'traits' under consideration in this 'reviving' trait approach are different form the early studies. Bryman (1992) warns that there is a danger that the term 'trait' becomes so stretched that it applies to any variable on which leaders and non-leaders differ, even certain behavioral patterns such as those discussed below. Thus, although there has been a resurgence of interest in the trait approach, the way in which traits are treated has changed. Also, traits are now considered along with other (situational and behavioral) variables.

Disillusionment followed the lack of empirical evidence for the existence of a 'leadership trait profile' in the early years of trait research. This led to a new emphasis in leadership research, the style approach.

Leadership Style

The second major trend in researching leadership emphasized *leader behavior*. The focus shifted from who leaders are (traits) to what leaders do (behavioral style). In this approach, effectiveness of leaders is dependent on the exerted leadership style. Whereas the trait approach focused on stable personal characteristics which were usually thought to be largely innate (implying selection of effective leaders rather than training), the style approach implied that leadership is a behavioral pattern, which can be learned. Thus, according to this approach, once one was able to discover the 'right' style, people could be trained to exhibit that behavior and become better leaders (Bass, 1990a; Bryman, 1992).

Most influential in this period was probably the series of questionnaire-based Ohio State studies. The Ohio State researchers concluded that leadership style could best be described as varying along two dimensions, i.e., '*consideration*' and '*initiating structure*' (e.g., Fleishman & Harris, 1962). A second major research program concerning leader behavior in this period was carried out at the University of Michigan. The results of these studies (summarized by Likert, 1961, 1967) show that they found three types of leader behavior differentiating between effective and ineffective managers: task-oriented behavior, relationship-oriented behavior, and participative leadership.

Some researchers proposed '*universal*' theories of effective leader behavior, stating that, for instance, effective leaders are both people- and task-oriented, so-called 'high–high' leaders. Blake and Mouton's (1982) managerial grid is an example of such a 'high–high' theory. Other prominent 'universal' theories were based on the idea that leaders who make extensive use of participative decision procedures are more effective than other leaders (e.g., Likert, 1967; McGregor, 1960).

Criticism of the Style Approach

There have been many criticisms of the style approach. Among the criticisms are the inconsistent findings and measurement problems, the problem of causality, the problem of the group, informal leadership, and, most pressing, the lack of situational analysis (Bryman, 1992). Korman (1966) showed that the magnitude and direction of correlations between leadership styles and outcomes were highly variable and divergent. Often, correlations were not statistically significant (see also Bass, 1990a). Identified measurement problems include response tendencies such as leniency effects and contamination by subordinate's implicit theories of leadership (implicit theories will be described in more detail below). Assumed causality was a problem in the early studies (this also goes for trait studies). These studies were usually cross-sectional, meaning that the notion that leadership style constitutes the independent rather than the dependent variable is an assumption in stead of a conclusion based on investigation of this view. Since then it has been shown that causality can run both ways (Bryman, 1992).

The problem of the group refers to the tendency in leadership research to focus on the group level rather than the individual or dyad levels of analysis. We will return to this below when briefly discussing the vertical dyad linkage (VDL) approach as an alternative way to study leadership. Most research described above was directed at formal, designated leaders who might behave different than informal leaders. Also, where designated leaders are not the actual group leaders the questions are probably not about the 'right' person (Bryman, 1992). Informal and emergent leadership are still rarely studied.

The failure of the style approach to pay attention to situational characteristics that act as possible moderators of the relationship between leadership and outcomes is probably its most serious problem. Possible moderators include task characteristics (e.g., complexity, interdependence) and subordinate characteristics (e.g., experience, motivation), but environmental factors or organizational culture could also influence the shape or form of the relationship between leadership style and outcomes. Attempts to address this situational issue led to the next main trend, contingency approaches to study leadership.

Contingency Approaches

As stated, many contingency approaches can be considered as an attempt to repair what researchers saw as the deficiencies of the aforementioned approaches (Smith & Peterson, 1988). The main proposition in contingency approaches is that the effectiveness of a given leadership style is *contingent on the situation*, implying that certain leader behaviors will be effective in some situations but not in others.

Fiedler's Model
The earliest contingency theory of leader effectiveness was the theory by Fiedler (1967). Fiedler is well-known and heavily criticized for his 'least-preferred-coworker' (LPC) measure. The

basic assumption is that a leader's description of the person with whom he has the greatest difficulty working reflects a basic leadership style. A second assumption is that which of the basic leadership styles contributes most to group performance varies with the 'situation favorability.' This favorability is determined by weighting and combining three aspects of the situation, namely leader–member relations, position power and task structure. For instance, a situation is least favorable for a leader when leader–member relations are poor, position power is low and the task is unstructured. The model predicts that when the situation is either highly favorable or very unfavorable, low LPC leaders are more effective than high LPC leaders. In intermediate situations, high LPC leaders should be more effective than low LPC leaders. Support for the model is at best weak. Also, the LPC measure and several of the assumptions made in the model (such as the weighting of situation aspects) are criticized for lacking a theoretical basis (Yukl, 1998).

More recently, Fiedler and Garcia (1987) developed a model that deals with the cognitive abilities of leaders (cognitive resources theory). According to this model, group performance depends on an interaction between two 'traits' (leader intelligence and experience), one type of leadership behavior (directive), and two aspects of the situation (interpersonal stress and the nature of the group task). So far, there is little empirical support for this model.

Situational Leadership Theory
Hersey and Blanchard's (1969, 1977) situational leadership theory (SLT) has been a popular basis for leadership training for many years. Originally SLT proposes that leaders should attune their behavior to fit with the 'maturity' or in later writings the 'development level' of the team as a whole as well as its individual members. Combining high or low task and relationship behavior creates four different leadership styles: telling (high task, low relations); selling (high, high); participating (low task, high relations); and delegating (low, low). These styles are more or less appropriate for different types of team members. For team members who are, for instance, low on willingness and ability a 'telling' style is appropriate. The empirical evidence for the theory is scant (Bass, 1990a; Yukl, 1998).

The Normative Decision-Making Model
Another widely known contingency theory focuses on criteria to determine whether or not a leader should involve subordinates in different kinds of decision making (Vroom & Yetton, 1973). The importance of using decision procedures that are appropriate for the situation has been recognized for some time (Heller, Pusic, Strauss & Wilpert, 1998; Yukl, 1998). For instance, Tannenbaum and Schmidt (1958) noted that a

leader's choice of decision procedures reflects forces in the leader, the subordinates and the situation. Also, Maier (1963) recognized the need for leaders to consider both the quality requirements of a decision and the likelihood of subordinate acceptance before choosing a decision procedure. Vroom and Yetton (1973) go beyond these approaches. In their model they try to indicate which decision procedure will be most effective in a specific situation. They distinguish five decision procedures, namely two types of autocratic decision (AI and AII), two types of consultative decision (CI and CII), and one joint decision by leader and group (GII). AI entails that a manager decides without asking others for input such as opinions or suggestions. In AII, a manager gathers the necessary information from subordinates (with or without explaining the problem at hand), then makes the decision. CI means sharing the problem with individual subordinates and considering their ideas and suggestions and CII involves getting them together as a group and sharing the problem. In both C cases, the manager still decides, and the decision may or may not reflect subordinates' opinions. Finally, GII implies sharing the problem with subordinates and that the solution should reflect agreement (consensus) of the group. The manager accepts and implements any decision the group reaches and does not have more influence over the final decision than others.

The Vroom and Yetton model predicts that the effectiveness of these decision procedures depends on several aspects of the situation, including the amount of relevant information held by leader and subordinates, the likelihood subordinates will accept an autocratic decision, and the extent to which the decision problem is unstructured. The model also provides a set of rules that help identify whether a decision procedure in a given situation is inappropriate (i.e., would it jeopardize decision quality and/ or acceptance?). For instance, when subordinates possess relevant information the leader does not have, an autocratic decision may not be appropriate because the leader would lack relevant information that needs to be considered. This model was updated and extended by Vroom and Jago (1988). Their revised version of the model takes some important aspects of the situation into account that the earlier model lacks (e.g., serious time constraints and geographical dispersion of subordinates). The model can be considered normative in the sense that it prescribes 'rules' for leaders to follow in order to make the best decisions under different circumstances. There is some empirical support for the model; however, it deals with a relatively small part of leadership and also has some conceptual weaknesses (see Yukl, 1998 for an overview).

Path–Goal Theory

The most influential and complete contingency theory to date is probably House's path–goal theory of leadership (House, 1971; House & Mitchell, 1974). This dyadic theory of supervision describes how formally appointed superiors affect the motivation and satisfaction of subordinates (House, 1996). House and Mitchell advanced two general propositions: (1) leader behavior is acceptable and satisfying to subordinates to the extent that subordinates see such behavior as either an immediate source of or instrumental to future satisfaction; (2) leader behavior is motivational (i.e., increases follower effort) to the extent that such behavior makes follower need satisfaction contingent on effective performance and to the extent that such behavior complements the environment of subordinates by providing guidance, support, and rewards necessary for effective performance (1974: 84). Leaders will be effective to the extent that they complement the environment in which their subordinates work by providing the necessary cognitive clarifications to ensure that subordinates expect they can attain work goals (i.e., path–goal clarifying behavior), and to the extent that subordinates experience intrinsic satisfaction and receive valent rewards as a direct result of attaining those work goals (i.e., behavior directed toward satisfying subordinate needs (House, 1996). House and Mitchell (1974) specify four types of leader behavior: directive path–goal clarifying behavior, supportive leader behavior, participative leader behavior, and achievement-oriented behavior. Proposed effects of leader behavior include subordinate motivation, satisfaction, and performance. Task and subordinate characteristics are treated as moderator variables.

Bryman (1992) describes several general problems with path–goal theory. Many of these problems are shared with the aforementioned Ohio tradition of investigating leadership style (e.g., inconsistent findings, problems associated with using group average methods of describing leaders, no attention for informal leadership, problems with causality and potential measurement problems). However, according to Evans (1996) the theory has not adequately been tested.

ALTERNATIVE APPROACHES TO STUDYING LEADERSHIP

The general dissatisfaction and pessimism that arose from the inconsistent research findings on the different contingency models stimulated several researchers to search for more or less radical 'remedies' to revive leadership theory. Smith and Peterson (1988) list five such remedies:

(1)   Replace leader style measures by measures of reward and punishment.
(2)   Differentiate between subordinates.

(3) Review the circumstances which call for leadership.
(4) Examine leaders' perceptions of subordinates.
(5) Reexamine the basis of subordinates' perceptions of leaders.

A sixth that can be added to these is focusing on the use of power and influence tactics rather than on 'leadership' (e.g., Yukl & Falbe, 1990). These 'remedies' reflect three broad developments. First, the tendency to relate the study of leadership to theoretical developments in other areas of social, cognitive, and organizational psychology as well as to those in other social sciences. Second, to pay more attention to the role of cognition and perceptions of those (both leaders and subordinates) under study. Third, to use greater control through more sophisticated statistical techniques and different methodologies, including experiments (Smith & Peterson, 1988).

Reward and Punishment

The first of the five remedies listed above focuses on leader reward and punishment. The analyses of leader's use of reward and punishment rather than leadership style developed from the application of conditioning and cognitive–behavioral models (see Podsakoff, 1982). Podsakoff, Todor and Skov (1982) found that leaders rewarding good performance had subordinates who performed better and were more satisfied than other subordinates. This did not hold for leaders rewarding regardless of performance or punishing leaders (see Smith & Peterson, 1988).

Differentiating Between Subordinates

The second remedy mentioned above focuses on differentiating between subordinates. Researchers in the leadership field tend to use group average scores rather than individual perceptions as indications for leadership style. This means treating individual followers and their relationship with the leader as interchangeable. The different exchange that leaders can develop with different individual subordinates is the focus of the work of Graen and colleagues (Graen & Cashman, 1975; Graen & Scandura, 1987; Graen & Uhl-Bien, 1995). Vertical Dyad Linkage and Leader–Member Exchange (LMX) focus on the dyadic exchange between leader and subordinate. The general point of the approach by Graen and colleagues is that leaders differentiate between subordinates and that group average perceptions are not necessarily the best reflection of leader behavior. So far, this work does not answer what the basis is for the differentiations leaders make. In their review of this approach, Graen and Uhl-Bien (1995) place the questions raised in the LMX tradition in the relation-based domain of leadership.

When Do We Need Leadership?

Reviewing the circumstances that do or do not call for leadership is the basis of the substitutes for leadership approach. This is the third remedy listed above. Essentially the substitutes for leadership model posits that there are a variety of situational variables that can substitute for, neutralize, or enhance the effects of leader behavior. Proposed variables include subordinate characteristics (e.g., experience, ability), task characteristics (e.g., a routine task, feedback provided by task) and organizational characteristics (e.g., a cohesive work group). Such variables can diminish or amplify the leader's ability to influence subordinates' attitudes, behavior, or performance (Howell, Dorfman & Kerr, 1986; Kerr & Jermier, 1978). The intuitive appeal of this approach is considerable and the model can nowadays be found in most textbooks on leadership and organizational behavior (e.g., Hughes, Ginnett & Curphy, 1999; Navahandi, 2000). However, the empirical support for the substitutes for leadership model (testing whether substitutes moderate relationships between leader behavior and subordinate outcome/criterion variables) has not been encouraging (e.g., Howell & Dorfman, 1981).

Podsakoff, MacKenzie and Bommer (1996) present a meta-analysis of the relationships between substitutes for leadership and employee attitudes, role perceptions, and performance. Their main effects test (i.e., not a moderator analysis) shows that the combination of substitutes and leader behavior accounted for the majority of variance in attitudes and role perceptions and for some of the variance in performance. The results indicate that in some cases the unique effects of the 'substitutes' on the outcomes are even stronger than the unique effects of the leadership behaviors. This implies that even though the model does not hold, the 'substitutes' themselves are important to consider in organizational research. More theoretical and empirical work on these issues is necessary.

De Vries, Roe and Taillieu (1999) focus on the 'need for leadership' as a characteristic of subordinates. As such they use a more follower-centered approach of leadership (see, e.g., Hollander & Offermann, 1990). The need for leadership reflects the extent to which an employee wishes the leader to facilitate the paths towards goals. De Vries et al. (1999) show that the need for leadership moderates the relationship between charismatic leadership and several outcomes.

The Role of Perception

The next two remedies focus on leader and subordinate perceptions. When researching how leaders perceive subordinates, leaders are seen as systems processing information about their subordinates.

On basis of that information, leaders then choose a strategy to influence a subordinate's behavior in the desired direction (Smith & Peterson, 1988). Attribution plays a major role. To what do leaders attribute the cause of subordinates' performance? Leaders can attribute performance (good or bad) either to subordinates themselves or to the circumstances. Bad performance could, for instance, be caused either by subordinates' incompetence or weak effort, or by unforeseen circumstances. Research shows that leaders tend to attribute failure to subordinates and success to themselves. Attributing failure to a subordinate is done most when the focal subordinate performs worse than others and when that subordinate has failed before on a similar task (Green & Mitchell, 1979). Below, subordinate perceptions of leaders will be described in more detail.

Leader Perception

Being perceived as a leader acts as a prerequisite for being able to go beyond a formal role in influencing others (Lord & Maher, 1991). Thus, perceptual processes on the part of followers play a crucial role in the leadership process as well as in researching leadership.

Most people are confronted with leadership almost daily, either in their job or through the media. As such, those people have (often implicit) ideas about what kind of characteristics leaders should have or should not have and what leaders should or should not do. An individual's implicit leadership theory refers to beliefs held about how leaders behave in general and what is expected of them (Eden & Leviatan, 1975). 'Implicit theories are cognitive frameworks or categorization systems that are in use during information processing to encode, process and recall specific events and behavior. An implicit theory can also be conceived as the personalized factor structure we use for information processing' (Bass, 1990a: 375–6). Implicit leadership theories (ILTs) are seen as personal constructs used to make judgments about leadership (Korukonda & Hunt, 1989). 'While leadership perceptions may not be reality, they are used by perceivers to evaluate and subsequently distinguish leaders from non-leaders. They also provide a basis for social power and influence' (Lord & Maher, 1991: 98). ILTs have been used in attempts to explain leadership attributions and perceptions (e.g., Lord, Foti & Phillips, 1982; Lord, Foti & De Vader, 1984; Offermann, Kennedy & Wirtz, 1994). Furthermore, ILTs have been shown to be a possible bias in the measurement of actual leader behavior (e.g., Gioia & Sims, 1985).

Leadership perceptions can, according to Lord and Maher (1991), be based on two alternative processes. First, leadership can be *recognized* based on the fit between an observed person's characteristics with the perceiver's implicit ideas of what 'leaders' are (ILTs). This type of process is tied closely to categorization theory (see Rosch, 1978). Lord and his

colleagues (1982, 1984) applied the principles of categorization to the field of leadership. They developed a theory on how leader perceptions are formed, focusing on the knowledge structures used to classify leaders and the actual information processes used in forming and evaluating leadership perceptions. Leadership perceptions are based on cognitive categorization processes in which perceivers match the perceived attributes of potential leaders they observe to an internal prototype of leadership categories (Foti & Luch, 1992). A prototype can be conceived as a collection of characteristic traits or attributes and the better the fit between the perceived individual and the leadership prototype, the more likely this person will be seen as a leader (Offermann et al., 1994; Foti & Luch, 1992).

Alternatively, leadership can be *inferred* from outcomes of salient events. Attribution processes are crucial in these inference-based processes (Lord & Maher, 1991). A successful business 'turnaround' is often quickly attributed to the high-quality 'leadership' of top executives or the CEO. Another example of such an inference-based process is that attributions of charisma to leaders are more likely when organizational performance is high (Shamir, 1992). In such cases charismatic leadership is inferred from business success. In Meindl's 'romance of leadership' approach, inference-based processes (leadership is inferred from good results) are central to the conception of leadership (Meindl, Ehrlich & Dukerich, 1985; Meindl, 1990).

Power and Influence

As Yukl (1998) notes, influence over followers is the essence of leadership. As such, the research by Yukl and associates on power and influence processes can be seen as an alternative way to study leadership.

Power can stem from different sources. In their well-known taxonomy, French and Raven (1959) describe five sources of power, namely reward power, coercive power, legitimate, referent, and expert power. However, these five are not complete, for instance, access to and control over information also acts as an important source of power (Pettigrew, 1972; Heller, Drenth, Koopman & Rus, 1988). Bass (1960) distinguishes between position power and personal power. Position power includes formal authority, control over punishments, rewards, and information, and ecological control. The latter refers to having control over the physical environment, technology, and organization of work. Personal power is derived from one's relationship to others rather than one's position in the hierarchy. Potential influence based on expertise, friendship, and loyalty can be seen as personal power. Research by Yukl and Falbe (1991) has shown these two types of power are relatively independent. Political processes in organizations involve members' efforts to increase or protect their power (Pfeffer, 1981). Contributing to such political power are: having control over key decisions, forming coalitions, cooptation, and institutionalization (Yukl, 1998).

Influence Tactics

Several studies have looked at influence tactics (e.g., Erez, Rim & Keider, 1986; Kipnis, Schmidt & Wilkinson, 1980; Yukl & Falbe, 1990; Yukl & Tracey, 1992). Yukl and his colleagues identified nine proactive influence tactics (see Yukl & Falbe, 1990; Yukl, 1998). The first is *pressure*. Threats, requests, persistent reminding or frequent checking are used to influence the target in the desired direction. The agent can also use *exchange*. This involves offering an exchange of goods/services, promises to return the favor later or promising the target a share in the benefits if the target complies with the request. When using *coalition tactics*, the agent enlists the aid of a third party to persuade the target to do something, or uses the support of others as a reason for the target to agree also. The agent can also resort to *legitimating tactics*. This involves trying to legitimate a request by claiming the authority or right to make it or by verifying and stressing that it is in accordance with organizational policies, rules, or traditions. Agents using *rational persuasion* use rational arguments and facts to convince the target that a request is reasonable and viable, and that it is likely to result in the attainment of the objectives. Another tactic is *inspirational appeals*: the agent makes a request or proposes something that arouses the target's interest and enthusiasm by appealing to his or her values, ideals, and aspirations or by increasing target self-confidence. The next tactic Yukl and associates distinguish is *consultation*. The agent asks the participation of the target in planning a strategy, activity, or change that requires target support and assistance, or is willing to modify a proposal to incorporate target suggestions. *Ingratiation* involves the agent using flattery, praise, or friendly behavior to get the target in a good mood or think favorably of the agent before making a request. Finally, agents can use *personal appeals* to the target's feelings of friendship and loyalty when asking for something.

The influence tactics are used in different directions, i.e., not only do managers try to influence subordinates, but these tactics are also used vice versa and to influence peers. Research shows that inspirational appeals, consultation, ingratiation, exchange, legitimating, and pressure are used more downward (i.e., to influence subordinates) than upward (i.e., to influence superiors) and that rational persuasion is used more upward than downward (Yukl & Falbe, 1990; Yukl, Falbe & Youn, 1993; Yukl & Tracey, 1992). There are also differences in sequencing of tactics within a prolonged influence attempt. 'Softer' tactics such as personal and inspirational appeals, rational persuasion, and consultation are used early on, and 'harder' tactics such

as pressure, exchange and coalitions are more likely to be used later (if the earlier tactics fail), as they involve greater costs and risks (Yukl et al., 1993; Yukl, 1998). Agents may also use a combination of tactics at the same time. Falbe and Yukl (1992) found that some combinations are more effective than others. For instance, combinations of soft tactics such as consultation, and inspirational and personal appeals, were usually more effective than using a single soft tactic. In contrast, combining soft tactics with a harder tactics such as pressure was usually less successful than using a soft tactic alone. Finally, the effectiveness of soft tactics was enhanced by combining them with rational persuasion.

THE 'NEW' LEADERSHIP

From the early 1980s onward a renewed interest in the concept of leadership itself arose in both scientific and professional fields. Meindl (1990) notes that this resurgence of interest appears to be accompanied by an acceptance of the distinction between transactional and transformational leadership, with an emphasis on the latter. Quinn (1988) compares transactional and transformational leadership with other differentiations in leadership such as relations-oriented–task-oriented leadership (Fiedler, 1967), consideration–initiating structure (Korman, 1966), and directive–participative or autocratic–democratic leadership (Heller & Yukl, 1969). However, Bass (1990b) claims that the transactional-transformational model is a new paradigm, neither replacing nor explained by other models such as the relations-oriented–task–oriented leadership model. Bryman (1992) refers to this new 'paradigm' as 'the new leadership' approach.[1]

Terms used to describe these 'new leaders' include: transformational, charismatic, 'leaders' (as opposed to managers), transforming, inspirational, visionary, or value-based. Despite the broad array of terms used by different authors within this approach, there seem to be more similarities than differences between these views of the phenomenon of leadership. In literature the terms 'transformational' and 'charismatic' leadership are the most often used terms to refer to this type of leadership (e.g., Hunt, 1999).

The theories attempt to explain how certain leaders are able to achieve extraordinary levels of follower motivation, admiration, commitment, respect, trust, dedication, loyalty, and performance. They also try to explain how some of these leaders succeed to lead their organizations or units to attain outstanding accomplishments, such as the founding and growing of successful entrepreneurial firms or corporate turnarounds (House, Delbecq & Taris, 1998). Comparing House's path–goal theory with his 1976 charismatic theory one could say that path–goal theory focuses on how follower needs and conditions determine leader behavior, whereas charismatic theory is about how leaders change people rather than respond to them (House, 1996). Another difference is that where in path–goal theory leaders are effective when they complement the environment, the new leadership focuses more on changing and creating the environment.

The Concept of Charisma

Most writers concerned with charisma begin their discussion with Max Weber's ideas. Charisma appears in his work on the origins of authority (Weber, 1947). Weber's charisma concept includes an exceptional leader, a (crisis) situation, the leader's vision or mission presenting a solution to the crisis, followers who are attracted to the leader and the vision, and validation of the charismatic qualities of the leader through repeated success (Trice & Beyer, 1986). These five components are present to some extent in almost all theories on charisma. The theories differ in how the components are operationalized and in which component is seen as the most important (Den Hartog, Koopman & Van Muijen, 1995).

Charisma as a Personal Attribute or a Social Relationship?

One of the most common views is that charisma is something that people 'have' or 'do not have,' a trait standpoint. There is an undeniable personal factor in the charismatic leadership. Such leaders are viewed by their followers as being special. Rather than treating charisma itself as a personality trait, most authors have attempted to distinguish personal factors associated with charismatic leadership. Examples of personal factors that have been named as potentially important in acquiring and maintaining charisma are: physical characteristics, such as a handsome appearance, piercing eyes, and distinct voice (Willner, 1984; Bryman, 1992). Psychological leader characteristics, such as high energy and self-confidence, dominance and a strong need for power, and a strong conviction in their own beliefs and ideals (e.g., House, 1977; House, Woycke & Fodor, 1988; House & Howell, 1992). Turner (1993) names audacity and determination as crucial personal qualities of leaders. Finally, ability characteristics, such as intelligence and inter-personal skills (Locke, 1991) as well as the leader's eloquence or rhetorical skills (e.g., Willner, 1984; Atkinson, 1984; Den Hartog & Verburg, 1997).

Exclusively defining charisma as a personal attribute or skill does not do justice to reciprocity of the relationship between leader and follower. Weber conceptualized charisma as a naturally fragile and unstable social relationship between leader and follower, in constant need of validation. Following

from Weber's writings, leader characteristics, behavior, and mission, followers' attribution of charisma, the situation, and the validation of charisma all play a role in a complex social relationship. This social relationship perspective does not imply that the idea of the leader as an exceptional person and the personal factors described above are not important; on the contrary, they are an important part of the relationship.

Although the emphasis is traditionally on the influence leaders have on followers, some authors emphasize that both followers and leaders are influenced by leadership processes. Burns (1978), for instance, conceptualizes transforming leadership as a two-way process; transforming leadership 'raises the level of human conduct and ethical aspiration of both the leader and the led, and thus it has a transforming effect on both' (p. 20).

Charismatic Leadership and Organizational Behavior

A first major application of charisma to the study of formal organizations can be found in House (1977), whose theory combines personal traits, leader behavior, and situational factors. According to House, four personal characteristics of the leader contribute to charismatic leadership: dominance, self-confidence, need for influence, and a strong conviction of the integrity of one's own beliefs. Charismatic leaders represent their values and beliefs through role modeling. To create a favorable perception with followers they can engage in image building and express ideological goals (a mission). They communicate high expectations of followers and show confidence in followers' ability to live up to those expectations. And, according to House, charismatic leaders are more likely than noncharismatic leaders to arouse motives (e.g., need for achievement) in followers that are relevant to attaining the mission. House assumes charismatic leadership is more likely to arise in stressful situations. A sense of crisis makes the attribution of charisma more likely. House (1977) specifies the following effects of such leadership: follower trust in the correctness of the leader's beliefs, similarity of followers' beliefs to those of the leader, unquestioning acceptance of and willing obedience to the leader, identification with and emulation of the leader, emotional involvement of the follower in the mission, heightened goals of the follower, and a feeling on the part of followers that they will be able to contribute to the accomplishment of the mission.

Charisma and Attribution

Several attribution-based explanations of charismatic leadership can be found in the literature. The most 'drastic' dismisses charisma as mere attribution, virtually unrelated to leader characteristics or behavior. Meindl (1990) speaks of charisma as a social contagion process. According to the social contagion view, charismatic elements of leader–follower relations are a function of processes occurring within the context of lateral relationships that develop among followers and subordinates themselves. The attribution and effects of charisma originate from the group, not from the leader and in that light, leaders are seen as largely interchangeable. The social contagion process is instigated by conditions causing stress or arousing excitement, which can be channeled and defined in terms of leadership and charisma and set in motion a social contagion process among followers.

A less radical example of an attribution-based explanation of charisma is the charismatic influence model developed by Conger and Kanungo (1987, 1988). In this model the basis for follower attributions of charisma is the leader's observed behavior, which can be interpreted as expressing charismatic qualities. According to Conger and Kanungo, charismatic leaders can be distinguished from non-charismatic leaders, by:

(1) their sensitivity to environmental constraints and follower needs and their ability to identify deficiencies in the status quo;
(2) their formulation of an idealized vision and extensive use of articulation and impression management skills;
(3) their use of innovative and unconventional means for achieving their vision and their use of personal power to influence followers.

Charismatic leadership is seen as (partly) attributional by most authors. Leaders must not only display certain characteristics, but must also be perceived as charismatic. According to Bass and Avolio (1990), transformational leaders (see below) are likely to become charismatic *in the eyes of their followers*. This seems to imply that charisma is not seen as a type of leader behavior, but as an attribution of followers, in other words a 'product' rather than a component of transformational leadership. Attributed charisma has been shown to be (in part) a function of the leader's prior success in reaching hard goals and accomplishing outstanding feats of performance. As stated, Shamir (1992) has shown that performance outcomes affect the attribution of influence and charisma to the leader.

Charisma and the Self-Concept

Rather than influencing by affecting the task environment of followers or using material incentives or threat of punishment, Shamir, House and Arthur (1993) state that charismatic leadership is seen as giving meaningfulness to work by infusing work and organizations with moral purpose and commitment. Their self-concept-based explanation of charisma proposes that 'charismatic leadership achieves its effects by implicating the self-concept

of followers and recruiting their self expressive motivation' (Shamir, 1991: 90–1). Thus, leader behavior is linked with follower effects through follower self-concepts.

The focus of this explanation of charisma is on the qualitative changes in follower's motivation that Burns (1978) and Bass (1985) describe, namely a strong internalization of the leader's values and goals, a strong personal or moral (as opposed to calculative) commitment to these values and goals and a tendency to transcend their own self-interests. Based on several assumptions about the self-concept, Shamir et al. (1993) describe several processes by which charismatic leaders have their transformational and motivational effect on followers. Leaders increase the intrinsic value of effort and goal accomplishment by linking them to valued aspects of the self-concept, thus harnessing the motivational forces of self-expression, self-consistency, specific mission-related self-efficacy, generalized self-esteem, and self-worth. Leaders also enhance self-efficacy, self-esteem, and collective efficacy through positive evaluations, expressions of confidence, higher expectations, and emphasizing the individual follower's ties to the collective. Thus the theory comprises four main parts: leader behaviors, effects on followers' self-concepts, further effects on followers, and the motivational processes by which the leader behaviors produce the charismatic effects.

Different Types of 'Charisma'?

The term *charismatic* has been applied to very diverse leaders in political arenas, religious spheres, social movements, and business organizations (Howell, 1988). A question raised by the widespread application of the term charisma is whether different types of charisma should be defined. Howell (1988), for example, differentiates between personalized and socialized charismatic leaders. Socialized charismatic leadership is based on egalitarian behavior, serves collective interests, and develops and empowers others. Personalized charismatic leadership is based on personal dominance, and narcissistic and authoritarian behavior, serves the leader's self-interest, and is exploitative of others. Similarly, Conger (1990) distinguishes negative from positive charismatic leaders. A different type of distinction is made by Etzioni (1961) and Hollander (1978). They hold that charisma can be a property of one's office (a position providing celebrity status) and/or of one's person.

A third way of distinguishing types of charisma has to do with the idea of social or psychological distance between leader and follower. Katz and Kahn (1978) state that charisma requires some psychological distance between leader and follower. The day-to-day intimacy of organization members and their immediate supervisors destroys the illusion needed in the charismatic relationship. They hold that charisma is only appropriate in the top echelon of the organization. A leader in the top echelon would be sufficiently distant from most organization members to make a simplified and almost magical image possible. Others (e.g., Bass, 1985; Conger & Kanungo, 1987) assume that charisma is common at all levels of the organization. A third position would be that charismatic leadership may be found at different levels, and in both a situation of close and distant leadership, but that relevant characteristics and behaviors as well as their effects are different for close and distant leaders. In other words, one can distinguish 'close' from 'distant' charismatic leadership (see Shamir, 1995).

Transactional and Transformational Leadership

Burns (1978) argues that transactional leadership entails an exchange between leader and follower. Followers receive certain valued outcomes (e.g., wages, prestige) when they act according to the leader's wishes. According to Burns the exchange can be economic, political, or psychological in nature. Bass (1985) notes that leadership in (organizational) research has generally been conceptualized as a cost–benefit exchange process. Such transactional leadership theories are founded on the idea that leader–follower relations are based on a series of exchanges or implicit bargains between leaders and followers. House et al. (1988) hold that the general notion in these theories is that when the job and the environment of the follower fail to provide the necessary motivation, direction, and satisfaction, the leader, through his or her behavior, will be effective by compensating for the deficiencies. The leader clarifies the performance criteria, in other words what he expects from subordinates, and what they receive in return. Several transactional theories have been tested extensively and some have received empirical support. Examples are the aforementioned path–goal theory and vertical dyad theory.

Transformational Leadership

Transformational leadership goes beyond the cost–benefit exchange of transactional leadership by motivating and inspiring followers to perform beyond expectations (Bass, 1985). Transformational leadership theories predict followers' emotional attachment to the organization and emotional and motivational arousal of followers as a consequence of the leader's behavior (House et al., 1988). Hater and Bass state: 'The dynamics of transformational leadership involve strong personal identification with the leader, joining in a shared vision of the future, or going beyond the self-interest exchange of rewards for compliance' (1988: 695). Transformational leaders broaden and elevate the interests of followers, generate awareness and acceptance among the followers of the purposes and mission of the group, and motivate followers to go beyond their self-interests for the good of the group. Tichy and Devanna (1990) highlight the transforming effect these leaders can have on organizations as well as on individuals. By defining the need for change, creating new visions, and mobilizing commitment to these visions, leaders can ultimately transform the organization. According to Bass (1985) such transformation of followers can be achieved by raising the awareness of the importance and value of designed outcomes, getting followers to transcend their own self-interests and altering or expanding followers' needs.

Contrasting transactional and transformational leadership does not mean the models are unrelated. Bass (1985) views these as separate dimensions, which would imply that a leader can be *both* transactional and transformational. He argues that transformational leadership builds on transactional leadership but not vice versa. Transformational leadership can be viewed as a special case of transactional leadership, in as much as both approaches are linked to the achievement of some goal or objective. The models differ on the *process* by which the leader motivates subordinates and the *types of goals* set (Hater & Bass, 1988).

Specific Behaviors

Bass (1985, 1997) defines both transactional and transformational leadership as comprising several dimensions. Transactional leadership has two dimensions. The first dimension is *contingent reward*. The leader rewards followers for attaining the specified performance levels. Reward is contingent on effort expended and performance level achieved. The second type of transactional leadership is *(active) management by exception*. When practicing *management by exception* a leader only takes action when things go wrong and standards are not met. Leaders avoid giving directions if the old ways work and allow followers to continue doing their jobs as always, as long as performance goals are met (e.g., Hater & Bass, 1988). A leader actively seeks deviations from standard procedures and takes action when irregularities occur.

Transformational leadership has four dimensions. The first dimension is *charisma*. The charismatic leader provides vision and a sense of mission, instills pride, gains respect and trust, and increases optimism (Bass, 1985). Charismatic leaders excite, arouse, and inspire their subordinates. According to Bass (1990a) attaining charisma in the eyes of one's employees is central to succeeding as a transformational leader. This dimension is sometimes referred to as *idealized influence*. The second dimension of transformational leadership is *inspiration*. Bass (1985) originally conceptualized inspiration as a subfactor within charisma. Inspiration describes a leader's capacity to act as a model for subordinates, the communication of a vision and the use of symbols to focus efforts. The third dimension is *individual consideration*. While a leader's charisma may attract subordinates to a vision or mission, the leader's use of individualized consideration also significantly contributes to a subordinate achieving his/her fullest potential (Yammarino & Bass, 1990). Individual consideration is in part coaching and mentoring, it provides for continuous feedback and links the individual's current needs to the organization's mission (Bass, 1985). Some feel that individualized consideration is similar to the Ohio State notion of consideration (Hunt, 1991; Bryman, 1992). Bass and Avolio, however, state that the two are related, but that individualized consideration builds on two aspects of behavior, i.e., individualization and development of followers, where as earlier scales measuring consideration were primarily concerned with whether a leader was seen a 'good guy or gal' or not (1993: 63). The last dimension of transformational leadership is *intellectual stimulation*. An intellectually stimulating leader provides subordinates with a flow of challenging new ideas to stimulate rethinking of old ways of doing things (Bass, 1985; Bass & Avolio, 1990). It arouses an awareness of problems, of subordinates' own thoughts and imagination, and a recognition of their beliefs and values. Intellectual stimulation is evidenced by subordinates' conceptualization, comprehension, and analysis of the problems they face and the solutions generated (Yammarino & Bass, 1990).

Other authors have included several other dimensions of this type of leadership, for instance, vision, demonstrating trust in subordinates, role modeling, and expressing high performance expectations (e.g., House, 1996; Podsakoff, MacKenzie, Moorman & Fetter, 1990).

Outcomes of Transformational/ Charismatic Leadership

Conger and Kanungo (1988) observe there is consensus among authors on the following effects of charismatic leaders on followers: high attachment to and trust in the leader, willing obedience to the leader, heightened performance and motivation, greater group cohesion in terms of shared beliefs and low intragroup conflict and a sense of empowerment. Other often-mentioned follower outcomes are commitment to the organization's goals, perceived leader effectiveness and follower's satisfaction with the leader (Den Hartog et al., 1995).

In general, charismatic/transformational leadership is expected to lead to more positive effects on subordinates than transactional leadership. Bass and associates find a consistent pattern of relationships between his leadership measures and the outcome and performance measures, with transformational leadership and the outcomes being highly positively

correlated and transactional leadership and the outcomes less so (Bass, 1997). Self-reports of extra effort, satisfaction with the leader, and perceived leader effectiveness were often used as dependent variables early on (e.g., Bass, Avolio & Atwater, 1996; Bryman, 1992). However, many other 'outcomes' have been studied, including: trust in the leader (e.g., Podsakoff et al., 1990; 1996); trust in management and colleagues (Den Hartog, 1997); organizational commitment (e.g., Den Hartog, 1997; Koh, Steers & Terborg, 1995; Podsakoff et al., 1996); leader performance (e.g., Yammarino, Spangler & Bass, 1993), business unit performance (e.g., Howell & Avolio, 1993); subordinate/work group performance (e.g., Howell & Frost, 1989); and organizational citizenship behaviors (Podsakoff et al., 1990; Koh et al., 1995).

The results of a comprehensive meta-analysis by Lowe, Kroeck & Sivasubramaniam (1996) indicate that transformational leadership scales reliably predict work unit effectiveness, both for subordinate perceptions (.80) and for (objective) organizational measures of effectiveness (.35). According to Lowe et al. (1996) subordinate ratings of effectiveness are probably inflated as raters would probably strive for consistency across independent and dependent variables. Again, logical distance is questionable. On the other hand, organizational measures are likely to be attenuated as they narrow the perspective of performance to a single measured criterion (financial indicators, percentage of goals met), rather than include the constellation of outcomes that would contribute to subordinate perceptions of leader effectiveness (e.g., individual development, organizational learning, more ethical principles). Lowe et al. (1996) found that transformational leadership consistently showed higher associations with effectiveness than transactional leadership. Against expectations, they also found that effect sizes were larger in public rather than private organizations and for lower- rather than higher-level leaders.

Possible Negative Effects

House and Singh (1987) conclude that charismatic and transformational leaders profoundly influence follower effort, performance and affective responses toward them. Thus, charismatic leaders can have a considerable influence on organizations; however, these consequences are not necessarily beneficial. The possible negative effects are sometimes referred to as 'the dark side of charisma.' Possible negative effects in organizations include poor interpersonal relationships, negative consequences of impulsive, unconventional behavior, negative consequences of impression management, poor administrative practices, negative consequences of self-confidence, and failure to plan for succession (Conger, 1990; Yukl, 1998). Charismatic leadership, by reducing in-group criticism and increasing unquestioning obedience could also have negative effects on group decision making (groupthink, Janis, 1982). Although transformational or socialized charismatic leaders are able to empower and develop followers, De Vries et al. (1999) find a positive relationship between charismatic leadership and the need for leadership. This suggests that subordinates are more rather than less 'dependent' when a charismatic leader is present. Such increased dependency on leaders may not always be beneficial to organizations.

CROSS-CULTURAL PERSPECTIVES: LEADERSHIP AROUND THE WORLD

Different cultural groups may have a different conception of what leadership should entail (Bass, 1990a; Hofstede, 1993). And, following from these different conceptions, the evaluation and meaning of many leader behaviors and characteristics may also strongly vary in different cultures. For instance, in a culture which endorses an authoritarian style, leader sensitivity might be interpreted as weak, whereas in cultures endorsing a more nurturing style, sensitivity is a prerequisite to be seen as a leader (Den Hartog et al., 1999).

Most research on leadership during the past half-century was conducted in the United States, Canada, and Western Europe. If research is conducted elsewhere, leadership theories and questionnaires developed in the USA are often translated and used abroad without much adaptation. An example is Bass and Avolio's (1990) Multifactor Leadership Questionnaire (MLQ). Besides in the USA and Canada, the MLQ is used in countries as diverse as Japan (Yokochi, 1989, reported in Bass, 1990a), New Zealand (Singer & Singer, 1990), Taiwan and Mexico (Dorfman & Howell, 1988), the Netherlands (Den Hartog, Van Muijen & Koopman, 1997), Austria (Geyer & Steyrer, 1998), and Belgium (Lievens, Van Geit & Coetsier, 1997).

However, the applicability of certain concepts and ways to measure these in a non-US context should not be taken for granted (e.g., Boyacigiller & Adler, 1991). Hofstede (1993: 81) states: 'In a Global perspective, US management theories contain a number of idiosyncrasies not necessarily shared by management elsewhere. Three such idiosyncrasies are mentioned: A stress on market processes, a stress on the individual and a focus on managers rather than workers.' Similarly, House (1995) notes that almost all prevailing theories of leadership and most empirical evidence is rather North American in character, that is, 'individualistic rather than collectivistic; emphasizing assumptions of rationality rather than ascetics, religion, or superstition; stated in terms of individual rather than group incentives, stressing follower responsibilities

rather than rights; assuming hedonistic rather than altruistic motivation and assuming centrality of work and democratic value orientation' (1995: 443). House also notes that much cross-cultural psychological, sociological, and anthropological research shows that there are many cultures that do not share these assumptions. 'As a result there is a growing awareness of need for a better understanding of the way in which leadership is enacted in various cultures and a need for an empirically grounded theory to explain differential leader behavior and effectiveness across cultures' (1995: 443–4, see also Boyacigiller & Adler, 1991; House et al., 1997). Kanungo and Mendonca (1996), for instance, describe how demands for leadership in developing countries differ from those placed on leaders in the USA. They examine the 'culture fit' of four distinct leader roles – task, social, participative and charismatic – relative to the sociocultural characteristics of developing countries and the internal work cultures of such countries. The impact of cultural contingencies on these four leader roles is described. Kanungo and Mendonca (1996) argue that organizational change is needed in such countries, rather than maintaining the status quo. As a result they see the charismatic leadership role as critical for organizations in developing countries. More theory development and testing is clearly needed in this area.

Studying Leadership Across Cultures

An increasing body of literature (including some of the aforementioned studies) deals with comparisons of leadership dimensions, behaviors or preferences across cultures (e.g., House et al., 1997; Peterson & Hunt, 1997; Dorfman, Howell, Hibino, Lee, Tate & Bautista, 1997). Still, much research to date has been limited in scope, usually comparing leaders and leader effectiveness in two or three countries. An interesting example of studying cross cultural aspects of leadership in a more elaborate project (involving over 25 countries) is found in the ongoing work on the event management model proposed by Smith and Peterson (1988). In this model 'leadership which contributes to effective event management can be defined '*as actions by a person which handle organizational problems as expressed in the events faced by others*' (Smith & Peterson, 1988: 80). The event management model presents an analysis of role relationships putting the role of leaders in the context of other sources of meaning. In handling events, managers can use different sources of information and meaning (e.g., rules, national norms, superiors, peers, subordinates). Smith, Peterson and Misumi (1994) show that managers in high power distance countries (i.e., countries where a high degree of inequality among people is considered normal by the population, cf. Hofstede, 1991) report more use of rules and procedures than do managers from low power distance countries.

Leader Prototypes

Several studies have focused on culture-based differences in leadership prototypes or implicit theories of leadership. As described above, implicit leadership theory (ILT) has been found to be a potent force in answering questions on leader behavior in the USA. Bryman (1987) conducted a study into the generalizability of implicit leadership theory and found strong support for the operation of implicit theories of leadership in Great Britain. Gerstner and Day (1994) performed a study focusing on a cross-cultural comparison of leadership prototypes. Respondents filled out a questionnaire (developed and tested only in the USA) which asks respondents to assign prototypicality ratings to 59 attributes relevant to (business) leadership. They compared these prototypicality ratings from a sample of American students ($n = 35$) to small samples ($n =$ between 10 and 22) of students from seven countries outside the United States (who on average had been living in the United States for 2.5 years). They found that the traits considered to be most (as well as moderately and least) characteristic of business leaders varied by respondents' country or culture of origin. This study has obvious limitations due to the small sample sizes, using only foreign students in the sample, and only an English-language trait-rating instrument, which has not been cross-culturally validated. However, the reliable differences found in leadership perceptions of members of various countries warrant further examination.

Another example of a study focusing on leadership preferences in different countries is the research by Singer and Singer (1990). Presuming subordinates' leadership preferences mediate the effectiveness of actual leader behavior, they conducted their study in New Zealand and Taiwan and found a common preference among their respondents for transformational leadership. This preference has also been found in the United States (Bass & Avolio, 1989). According to Bass (1997) such a preference for transformational leadership is found across a wide range of cultures.

The GLOBE Project

Increasing the understanding of culture-based differences in leadership perception is a key issue in the GLOBE research program. GLOBE is a long-term study directed toward the development of systematic knowledge concerning how societal and organizational cultures affect leadership and organizational practices (House et al., 1999). Approximately 60 countries from all major regions of the world participate in GLOBE, making it the most extensive investigation of cross-cultural

aspects of leadership to date. The project was originated by Robert House who has led 'the coordinating team' based in the United States. Besides the coordinating team, approximately 150 social scientists (Co-Country Investigators or CCIs) from around the world are responsible for managing the project and collecting data in their respective countries.

The main objectives of the GLOBE study are to answer questions such as: Are there leader behaviors that are universally accepted and effective across cultures and are there behaviors that are differentially accepted and effective across cultures? The overall hypotheses that are to be tested concern relationships between societal culture dimensions, organizational culture dimensions and CLTs (culturally endorsed implicit leadership theories) as well as relationships specified by structural contingency theory of organizations (e.g., Donaldson, 1995). The information ensuing from this project will be useful for understanding how leaders in various societal and organizational cultures can be effective and for identifying the constraints imposed on leaders by cultural norms, values, and beliefs (House et al., 1999).

The initial aim of the GLOBE project was to develop societal and organizational measures of culture and leadership attributes that are appropriate to use across cultures. This aim was accomplished in the first phase of the project. The results of two pilot studies support the reliability and construct validity of the questionnaire scales (Hanges et al., under review).

Data collection in the second (hypothesis testing) phase is now completed and the analyses to test the hypotheses are currently being conducted. Over 15,000 middle managers from approximately 800 organizations in the financial, food and/or telecommunications industries in 60 countries were asked to describe leader attributes and behavior that they perceived to enhance or impede outstanding leadership. Some first results of the GLOBE study report which leadership attributes are universally endorsed as contributing to outstanding leadership, which are universally seen as undesirable, and which are culturally contingent (Den Hartog et al., 1999).

Contributing to outstanding leadership in all cultures were several attributes reflecting integrity (being trustworthy, just, and honest) Also, an outstanding leader shows many attributes reflecting charismatic, inspirational, and visionary leadership (an outstanding leader is encouraging, positive, motivational, a confidence builder, dynamic, and has foresight). Team-oriented leadership is also universally seen as important (such a leader is effective in team building, communicating, and coordinating). Finally, other items that are universally endorsed include being excellence oriented, decisive, intelligent, and a win–win problem solver (Den Hartog et al., 1999: 240). The GLOBE study also shows that several attributes are universally viewed as ineffective or in other words as impediments to outstanding leadership. These include being a loner, being noncooperative, ruthless, nonexplicit, irritable, and dictatorial (Den Hartog et al., 1999: 240).

Finally, many leadership attributes were found to be culturally contingent, i.e., a high positive rating was obtained in some and a low or even negative rating in other cultures. For instance, country means for the attribute enthusiastic range from 3.72 to 6.44 on a seven point scale. Country means for risk taking range from 2.14 to 5.96, for sensitive from 1.96 to 6.35, for class-conscious from 2.53–6.09 and for autonomous from 1.63–5.17 (see Den Hartog et al., 1999: 241, for the complete list).

Regional Differences

Besides testing the overall 'global' hypotheses, the GLOBE data are also suited to look at regional differences. Studies by Brodbeck et al. (2000) and Koopman et al. (1999), for instance, focus on the European results, distinguishing different patterns of leadership and societal culture in Europe. Generally speaking, two broad clusters of cultures were distinguished in Europe, namely a north/western cluster and a south/eastern cluster. Concerning the culture dimensions, the north/west scored significantly higher on dimensions such as achievement orientation, future orientation, and uncertainty avoidance. In contrast, the south/east scored significantly higher on dimensions such as assertiveness and power distance. On gender egalitarianism the combination of the Nordic and the central/eastern European countries had a significantly higher score (indicating a more equal treatment of men and women) than the other European countries (e.g., Latin countries). On most culture dimensions there is considerable variance within Europe, in other words there is no typical 'European culture.'

Interesting differences between north/western Europe and the south/eastern Europe were also found on the leadership profiles. South/eastern Europe scores higher on administrative competence, being autocratic, a conflict inducer, diplomatic, face saving, nonparticipative, procedural, self-oriented, and status-conscious. In north/western Europe characteristics such as being inspiring and having integrity are seen as more important (Koopman et al., 1999). From the perspective of Bass's (1960) distinction between personal and position power, one might conclude that in the south/east of Europe the importance of position power is emphasized, whereas in the north/west the focus is on the (use of) personal power.

The GLOBE data can also be used for smaller scale in-depth comparisons between two (or more) countries. This allows for a focused comparison providing more detailed information than the general study that looks at differences at a global level, while being able to rely on the internationally developed and thoroughly tested questionnaires. An example of such a more focused comparison of national culture and leader attributes in the Netherlands and Poland, two of the European countries participating in the GLOBE study can be found in Den Hartog et al. (1997a). This study shows that Dutch respondents value attributes associated with integrity and inspirational leader behavior more strongly than Polish respondents. Visionary qualities score high in both countries. Diplomacy and administrative skills (being orderly, well-organized, and a good administrator) are considered more important in Poland. Polish respondents also have a less negative attitude towards autocratic leader behavior and status consciousness than the Dutch managers.

Enacting Leadership Behaviors

The GLOBE results show a 'universal' preference for certain leadership attributes. However, this does not mean such attributes will be enacted in the same manner across cultures. For example, Bass states that 'Indonesian inspirational leaders need to persuade their followers about the leaders' own competence, a behavior that would appear unseemly in Japan' (1997: 132). However, according to Bass, not withstanding the fact that it can be expressed in different ways, the concept of inspiration appears 'to be as universal as the concept of leadership itself' (1997: 132).

Similar examples of enacting positively valued attributes in a different manner in different countries ensue from the qualitative data that are also gathered in the GLOBE research (media analyses, interviews, and focus group meetings). For instance, Martinez and Dorfman (1998) gathered GLOBE data in Mexico. An example of behavior that was highly valued by the Mexicans, but might not be appropriate in other contexts was a high degree of involvement of a leader in the private lives of his employees. An example from their interviews is a leader calling the doctor when the husband of an employee was in hospital to make sure an operation was legitimate. However, such a behavior would be felt to be an invasion of privacy in other countries. Such examples clearly show that the behaviors indicative of consideration or compassion will differ strongly in different cultures even if the positive evaluation of the construct 'consideration' in itself is found across different cultures (see Den Hartog et al., 1999).

IS THERE A FUTURE FOR LEADERSHIP?

Currents of change such as the developing information technology and globalization are influencing work and organizations as we know them in a pervasive and long-lasting manner (e.g., Howard, 1995; Davis, 1995). Among the fundamental changes in organizations is the increasing use of teams to make decisions (Guzzo, 1995) and more generally the increased importance of teams and other lateral organizing mechanisms (Mohrman & Cohen, 1995).

Organizations are becoming more and more flexible. As Shamir (1999) puts it, an important characteristic of the new form of organization is 'the obliteration of boundaries within the organization and between the organization and elements in its external environment' (p. 52). Such 'boundaryless' organizations (Davis, 1995) to a large extent comprise temporary systems whose elements (people as well as technology) are assembled and disassembled according to the shifting needs of specific projects. As organizations can no longer rely on the traditional hierarchy, managing and coordinating the efforts of employees may become more difficult. In the flexible, boundaryless structures where people shift from team to team, leaders will not be able to rely on the same level of formal power they had in their position in the former hierarchies. Also, the content of work is changing. As House (1995) notes, much 21st century work will be intellectual rather than physical. Observing, monitoring, and controlling, in other words, direct supervision of such tasks, will be very difficult.

Such developments could lead to a less pronounced role for leaders in organizations. One could even suggest that the idea of a single person taking on the 'leadership role' may become obsolete in the future organization. Shamir (1999) describes several possible scenarios that imply a reduced importance of the role of leadership in the 21st century. One such scenario is 'disposable leadership.' As organizations increasingly rely on temporary arrangements (e.g., project teams), leadership itself will become such a temporary arrangement, and will as such be limited in scope and duration. The group member with the most relevant knowledge would then be leader regarding that specific task. A similar scenario is the idea of shared, distributed, peer, or collective leadership. As Shamir (1999) notes, the common element in these ideas is that leadership is not concentrated in the hands of one single 'heroic' leader or a limited group, but is divided and performed by many or all team members simultaneously or sequentially. Similarly, the idea behind 'self-managed teams' also implies a transfer of the leadership responsibility to the team as a whole (e.g., Barker, 1993; Manz & Sims, 1993).

A third scenario implying a reduction of the importance of leadership is what Shamir and Ben-Ari (1999) refer to as 'teleleadership.' As Shamir (1999) describes, the increasing use of computer-mediated technologies and group decision support systems may enhance the importance of leadership functions that relate to the transmission of information between leader and group members. It may also reduce the distance between the top and lower levels

in the organization and enable more effective communication between those parties. However, the role of leaders is obviously reduced to more cognitive elements (managing information flow) rather than the social, human, and emotional elements of leadership. Whether it is possible to identify with or trust leaders with whom one only communicates electronically is yet unclear (Shamir, 1999).

There are also other problems with these scenarios. Self-management does not always yield positive results. Also, identifying with a professional group, organization, or team increases commitment to that group and its goals and implies adherence to a pattern of values shared within such a group. Belonging to multiple groups with unclear boundaries may lead to identity problems (Emans, Koopman, Rutte & Steensma, 1996). House (1995) notes that the nonroutine tasks of the future will require problem solving, individual initiative, innovative behavior, and motivation, as well as a willingness to take on personal responsibility for getting the task done on the part of employees. Also, increased uncertainty and pace of change may be accompanied with increased feelings of uncertainty and anxiety on part of organization members. As West and Altink (1996) point out, a sense of psychological safety is essential for showing innovative behavior. Creating such a sense of safety and clarity and increasing motivation and commitment may still remain important leadership functions in tomorrow's organizations.

As Shamir summarizes, 'boundaryless, flattened, flexible, project-based and team-based organizations that employ temporary, externalized and remote workers, whose tasks are more intellectual and less routine and cannot be controlled and coordinated by structure or direct supervision, need mechanisms of coordination through shared meaning systems, a shared sense of purpose, and high member commitment to shared values' (1999: 59). Therefore, boundaryless organizations are likely to need strong leadership to perform integrative functions. Such integrative functions are less likely to be performed by movable or disposable leaders. Leaders have played an important role in promoting change and innovation and challenging the status quo in stable environments. In tomorrow's unstable environments the role of leaders is to balance an emphasis on change with providing (a sense of) stability and continuity, and to establish and maintain collective identities in the absence of traditional identity-forming boundaries (Shamir, 1999).

SOME SUGGESTIONS FOR FUTURE RESEARCH ON LEADERSHIP

The changing role of leadership in future organizations is an obvious and important topic for future research. As discussed above, the role of leaders in ever-changing organizations will be different from their traditional role in a more stable environment. An added problem in this respect is that leaders are often selected on a certain profile, relevant for a certain job or time period. Changes in the organization and environment may require new skills or characteristics that these managers were not selected on. As the pace of change increases, this problem may also increase. More research seems needed in this area.

Similarly, more theory development and research on the similarities as well as differences of leadership in different cultures around the world is clearly needed.

Also, in many studies on leadership in organizations the role of 'time' is not incorporated. It has often been noted that leadership is essentially a relational process unfolding over time. If leadership is supposed to contribute to the development of certain attitudes, emotional states, or self-efficacy, and increased performance, a longitudinal perspective is needed to capture some of this development. Examples of such longitudinal studies include Yammarino et al. (1993) and Howell and Avolio (1993). Not enough is known about leadership development over time. How leadership skills and perceptions develop, and which factors help or impede such development are interesting issues in need of further research. A possibility to study such topics would be to follow the development of attitudes and perceptions of both leaders and followers over time in groups in which new leaders start. Questions such as whether leaders can start out being 'inspirational' or do they first need to build 'idiosyncracy credit' (Hollander, 1978) and trust, and which leadership skills and behaviors can or cannot be learned are also interesting in this respect.

Another important way in which time exerts crucial influence is that people in organizations more often than not have a shared history and/or a shared future. Experiences from the past as well as expectations for the future shape both behavior and perceptions in ways which many studies are not designed or able to capture. The shared history implies that relationships have been shaped over time, and take place in a broader context which altered prior expectations. A shared future implies that some behaviors are less appropriate or effective than others. An example of the influence of shared history is that often, even after managers are trained to exert certain leader behaviors, and try to do so, they find that they are not perceived to be or behave any different. Also, circumstances and therefore the appropriateness of behavior may change over time. Becoming more experienced may influence followers' perception of leader behavior over time. For instance, depending on the need and stage of development of the follower, leader behaviors reflecting consideration can be interpreted

differently by the same people over time (Avolio, & Bass, 1995).

Although much can be done using questionnaires, leadership research would benefit from a multimethod approach. Yukl (1998) states that the field would benefit from descriptive research using observation and interviews to discover what leaders actually *do*. Using less traditional data sources, such as analyzing speeches (e.g., Den Hartog & Verburg, 1997; Shamir, Arthur & House, 1994) or doing historiometric studies (e.g., Deluga 1997; House, Spangler & Woyke, 1991) could also be used to triangulate self-report survey data. Insch, Moore and Murphy (1997) propose to use content analysis more often and give guidelines how to perform such analyses in this field. Increased use of (field) experiments is also important to gain more understanding of causal relationships and direction of causality of many relationships.

Another possibility for future research is to examine leadership in relation to topics stemming from other research fields: for example, expanding research into leadership and personality as well as followership and personality or incorporating recent trends from cognitive psychology. Examples in this direction are the development of the so-called leaderplex model (Hooijberg, Hunt & Dodge, 1997) as well as increased attention for perception and cognition (Lord & Maher, 1991). Relationships between leadership and leader as well as follower affect and emotions are also in need of more research.

In 1978, Burns stated that 'Leadership is one of the most observed and least understood phenomena on earth' (p. 2). Much has happened since: substitutes, LMX, globalization, and leadership perception are only some of the topics that have had a major impact. Also, the introduction of charisma and transformational leadership to the field of organizational leadership has inspired many to reexamine their ideas about the essence of leadership. These developments indeed seem to have enhanced the understanding of the phenomenon of leadership. However, the overview presented here shows that the quest is far from over.

NOTE

1 Not to be confused with Vroom and Jago's (1988) use of 'new leadership' as a term to describe a revised contingency approach to participation in decision-making (see paragraph 1.2.4).

REFERENCES

Adler, N.J. (1991). *International dimensions of organizational behavior* (2nd ed.). Belmont, CA: Wadsworth.

Atkinson, M. (1984). *Our masters' voices. The language and body language of politics*. London: Routledge.

Avolio, B.J., & Bass, B.M. (1995). Individual consideration viewed at multiple levels of analysis: A multi-level framework for examining the diffusion of transformational leadership. *Leadership Quarterly*, 6(2), 199–218.

Barker, J.R. (1993). Tightening the iron cage: Concertive control in self-managing teams. *Administrative Science Quarterly*, 38, 408–437.

Bass, B.M. (1960). *Leadership, psychology, and organizational behavior*. New York: Free Press.

Bass, B.M. (1985). *Leadership and performance beyond expectations*. New York: Free Press.

Bass, B.M. (1990a). *Bass and Stogdill's handbook of leadership: Theory, research and managerial applications* (3rd ed.) New York: Free Press.

Bass, B.M. (1990b). Editorial: Toward a meeting of minds. *Leadership Quarterly*, 1.

Bass, B.M. (1997). Does the transactional–transformational paradigm transcend organizational and national boundaries? *American Psychologist*, 52(2), 130–139.

Bass, B.M., & Avolio, B.J. (1989). Potential biases in leadership measures: How prototypes, leniency and general satisfaction relate to ratings and rankings of transformational and transactional leadership constructs. *Educational and Psychological Measurement*, 49, 509–527.

Bass, B.M., & Avolio, B.J. (1990). The implications of transactional and transformational leadership for individual, team, and organizational development. *Research in Organizational Change and Development*, 4, 231–272.

Bass, B.M., & Avolio, B.J. (1993). Transformational leadership a response to critiques. In M.M. Chemers, & R. Ayman (Eds.), *Leadership theory and research*. San Diego: Academic Press.

Bass, B.M., Avolio, B.J., & Atwater, L. (1996). The transformational and transactional leadership of men and women. *Applied Psychology: An international Review*, 45(1), 5–34.

Blake, R.R., & Mouton, J.S. (1982). Management by grid principles or situationalism: Which? *Group and Organization Studies*, 7, 207–210.

Boyacigiller, N., & Adler, N. (1991). The parochial dinosaur: Organizational science in a global context. *Academy of management Review*, 16, 262–290.

Brodbeck, F.C., Frese, M., & 44 coauthors (2000). Cultural variation of leadership prototypes across 22 European countries. *Journal of Occupational and Organizational Psychology*, in press.

Bryman, A. (1987). The generalizability of leadership theory. *Journal of Social Psychology*, 127, 129–141.

Bryman, A. (1992). *Charisma and leadership in organizations*. London: Sage.

Burns, J.M. (1978). *Leadership*. New York: Harper & Row.

Conger, J.A. (1990). The dark side of leadership. *Organizational Dynamics*, 1990, 44–55.

Conger, J.A., & Kanungo, R.N. (1987). Towards a behavioral theory of charismatic leadership in organizational settings. *Academy of Management Review*, 12, 637–647.

Conger, J.A., & Kanungo, R.N. (1988). Behavioral dimensions of charismatic leadership. In J.A. Conger, & R.N. Kanungo (Eds.), *Charismatic Leadership: The Elusive Factor in Organizational Effectiveness* (pp. 78–97). San Francisco: Jossey-Bass.

Davis, D.D. (1995). Form, function and strategy in boundaryless organizations. In A. Howard (Ed.), *The changing nature of work*. San Francisco: Jossey-Bass.

Deluga, R.J. (1997). Relationship among American presidential charismatic leadership, narcissism and rated performance. *Leadership Quarterly*, 8, 49–65.

Den Hartog, D.N. (1997). Inspirational leadership. VU doctoral dissertation. KLI-dissertation series, 1997-nr 2. Enschede: Ipskamp.

Den Hartog, D.N., House, R.J., Hanges, P., Dorfman, P., Ruiz-Quintanilla, A., & 159 coauthors (1999). Culture specific and cross-culturally endorsed implicit leadership theories: Are attributes of charismatic/transformational leadership universally endorsed? *Leadership Quarterly*, 10(2), 219–256.

Den Hartog, D.N., Koopman, P.L., Thierry, Hk., Wilderom, C.P.M., Maczynski, J., & Jarmuz, S. (1997a). Dutch and Polish perceptions of leadership and national culture: The GLOBE project. *European Journal of Work and Organizational Psychology*, 6(4), 389–415.

Den Hartog, D.N., Koopman, P.L., & Van Muijen, J.J. (1995). Charismatic leadership: A State of the Art. *The Journal of Leadership Studies*, 2(4), 35–50.

Den Hartog, D.N., Van Muijen, J.J., & Koopman, P.L. (1997). Transactional versus transformational leadership: An analysis of the MLQ. *Journal of Occupational and Organizational Psychology*, 70(1), 19–34.

Den Hartog D.N., & Verburg, R.M. (1997). Charisma and rhetoric: The communicative techniques of international business leaders. *Leadership Quarterly*, 8(4), 355–391.

De Vries, R.E., Roe, R.A., & Taillieu, T.C.B. (1999). On charisma and need for leadership. *European Journal of Work and Organizational Psychology*, 8(1), 109–127.

Donaldson, L. (1995). *American anti-management theories of organization*. Cambridge: Cambridge University Press.

Dorfman, P.W., & Howell, J.P. (1988). Dimensions of national culture and effective leadership patterns. *Advances in International Comparative Management*, 3, 127–150.

Dorfman, P.W., Howell, J.P., Hibino, S., Lee, J.K., Tate, U., & Bautista, A. (1997). Leadership in Western and Asian countries: Commonalities and differences in effective leadership processes across culture. *Leadership Quarterly*, 8(3), 233–274.

Eden, D., & Leviatan, U. (1975). Implicit leadership theory as a determinant of the factor structure underlying supervisory behavior scales. *Journal of Applied Psychology*, 60, 736–741.

Emans, B., Koopman, P.L., Rutte, C., & Steensma, H. (1996). Teams in organisaties: Interne on externe determinanten van resultaatgerichtheid. *Gedrag en Organisatie*, 9, 309–327.

Erez, M., Rim, Y., & Keider, I. (1986). The two sides of the tactics of influence: Agent vs. target. *Journal of Occupational Psychology*, 59, 25–39.

Etzioni, A. (1961). *A comparative analysis of complex organisations.* New York: Free Press.

Evans, M.G. (1996). R.J. House's A path–goal theory of leadership effectiveness. *Leadership Quarterly, 7,* 305–309.

Falbe, C.M., & Yukl, G. (1992). Consequences for managers of using single influence tactics and combinations of tactics. *Academy of Management Journal, 35,* 638–653.

Fiedler, F.E. (1967). *A contingency theory of leadership effectiveness.* New York: McGraw-Hill.

Fiedler, F.E., & Garcia, J.E. (1987). *New approaches to leadership: Cognitive resources and organizational performance.* New York: John Wiley.

Fleishman, E.A., & Harris, E.F. (1962). Patterns of leadership behavior related to emplyee grievances and turnover. *Personnel Psychology, 15,* 43–56.

Foti, R.J., & Luch, C.H. (1992). The influence of individual differences on the perception and categorization of leaders. *Leadership Quarterly, 3,* 55–66.

French, J., & Raven, B.H. (1959). The bases of social power. In D. Cartwright (Ed.), *Studies of social power.* Ann Arbor, MI: Institute for Social Research.

Gerstner, C.R., & Day, D.V. (1994). Cross-cultural comparison of leadership prototypes. *Leadership Quarterly, 5,* 121–134.

Geyer, A.L.J., & Steyrer, J.M. (1998). Transformational leadership and objective performance in banks. *Applied Psychology: An International Review, 47*(3), 397–420.

Gioia, D.A., & Sims, H.P. (1985). On avoiding the influence of implicit leadership theories in leader behavior descriptions. *Educational and Psychological Measurement, 45,* 217–243.

Graen, G.B., & Cashman, J.F. (1975). A role-making model of leadership in formal organizations: A developmental approach. In J.G. Hunt, & L.L. Larson (Eds.), *Leadership frontiers* (pp. 143–165). Kent, OH: Kent State University Press.

Graen, G.B., & Scandura, T. (1987). Toward a psychology of dyadic organizing. *Research in Organizational Behavior, 9,* 175–208.

Graen, G.B., & Uhl-Bien, M. (1995). Relationship-based approach to leadership: Development of leader-member exchange (LMX) theory of leadership over 25 years: applying a multi-level multi-domain perspective. *Leadership Quarterly, 6,* 219–247.

Green, S.G., & Mitchell, T.R. (1979). Attributional processes of leaders in leader member exchanges. *Organizational Behavior and Human Performance, 23,* 45–458.

Guzzo, R.A. (1995). Introduction: At the intersection of team effectiveness and decision making. In R.A. Guzzo, & E. Salas (Eds.), *Team effectiveness and decision making in organizations* (pp. 1–8). San Francisco: Jossey-Bass.

Hanges, P.J., House, R.J., Dickson, M.W., Dorfman, P.W., & 170 coauthors (in review). The development and validation of scales measuring societal culture and culturally shared implicit theories of leadership.

Hater, J.J., & Bass, B.M. (1988). Superiors' evaluations and subordinates' perceptions of transformational and transactional leadership. *Journal of Applied Psychology, 73,* 695–702.

Heller, F.A., Drenth, P.J.D., Koopman, P.L., & Rus, V. (1988). *Decisions in organisations: A three country comparative study.* London: Sage.

Heller, F., Pusic, E., Strauss, G., & Wilpert, B. (1998). *Organizational participation: Myth and reality.* Oxford: Oxford University Press.

Heller, F.A., & Yukl, G. (1969). Participation, managerial decisionmaking and situational variables. *Organizational Behavior and Human Performance, 4,* 227–241.

Hersey, P., & Blanchard, K.H. (1969). *The management of organizational behavior.* Englewood Cliffs, NJ: Prentice-Hall.

Hersey, P., & Blanchard, K.H. (1977). *Management of organizational behavior: Utilizing human resources* (4th ed.). Englewood Cliffs, NJ: Prentice-Hall.

Hofstede, G. (1991). *Cultures and organizations: Software of the mind.* London: MacGraw-Hill.

Hofstede G. (1993). Cultural constraints in management theories. *Academy of Management Executive, 7*(1), 81–94.

Hollander, E.P. (1978). *Leadership dynamics.* New York: Free Press.

Hollander, E.P. (1992). Leadership, followership, self, and others. *Leadership Quarterly, 3,* 43–54.

Hollander, E.P., & Offermann, L.R. (1990). Relational features of organizational leadership and followership. In K.E. Clark, & M.B. Clark (Eds.), *Measures of leadership* (pp. 83–98). West Orange, NJ: Leadership Library of America.

Hooijberg, R. Hunt, J.G., & Dodge, G.E. (1997). Leadership complexity and the development of the leaderplex model. *Journal of Management, 23,* 375–408.

House, R.J. (1971). Path-goal theory of leader effectiveness. *Administrative Science Quarterly, 16,* 321–338.

House, R.J. (1977). A 1976 theory of charismatic leadership. In J.G. Hunt, & L.L. Larson (Eds.), *Leadership: The cutting edge* (pp. 189–204). Carbondale, IL: Southern Illinois University Press.

House, R.J. (1995). Leadership in the 21st century: A speculative enquiry. In A. Howard (Ed.), *The changing nature of work.* San Francisco: Jossey-Bass.

House, R.J. (1996). Path-goal theory of leadership: Lessons, legacy and a reformulated theory. *Leadership Quarterly, 7*(3), 323–352.

House, R.J., Delbecq, A., & Taris, T.W. (1998). Value based leadership: An integrated theory and an empirical test. Internal publication.

House, R.J., Hanges, P.J., Ruiz-Quintanilla, S.A., Dorfman, P.W., Javidan, M., Dickson, M.W. et al. (1999). Cultural influences on leadership and organizations: Project GLOBE. In W.H. Mobley, M.J. Gessner, & V. Arnold (Eds.), *Advances in Global Leadership* (pp. 171–233). Stamford, CN: JAI Press.

House, R.J., & Howell, J.M. (1992). Personality and charismatic leadership. *Leadership Quarterly, 3*(2), 81–108.

House, R.J., & Mitchell, T.R. (1974). Path-goal theory of leadership. *Contemporary Business, 3,* 81–98.

House, R.J., & Shamir, B. (1993). Toward the integration of transformational, charismatic and visionary theories. In M.M. Chemers, & R. Ayman (Eds.), *Leadership theory and research: Perspectives and directions* (pp. 81–107).

House, R.J., & Singh, J.V. (1987). Organizational behavior: Some new directions for I/O psychology. *Annual Review of Psychology*, *38*, 669–718. New York: Academic Press.

House, R.J., Spangler, W.D., & Woyke, J. (1991). Personality and charisma in the US presidency: A psychological theory of leadership effectiveness. *Administrative Science Quarterly*, *36*, 364–396.

House, R.J., Woycke, J., & Fodor, E.M. (1988). Charismatic and noncharismatic leaders: Differences in behavior and effectiveness. In J.A. Conger, & R.N. Kanungo (Eds.), *Charismatic leadership: The elusive factor in organizational effectiveness* (pp. 98–121). San Francisco: Jossey-Bass.

House, R.J., Wright, N.S., & Aditya, R.N. (1997). Cross-cultural research on organizational leadership: A critical analysis and a proposed theory. In P.C. Early, & M. Erez (Eds.), *New perspectives on international industrial/organizational psychology*. San Francisco: The New Lexington Press.

Howard, A. (Ed.) (1995) *The changing nature of work*. San Francisco: Jossey-Bass.

Howell, J.M. (1988). Two faces of charisma: Socialized and personalized leadership in organizations. In J.A. Conger, & R.N. Kanungo (Eds.), *Charismatic leadership: The elusive factor in organizational effectiveness* (pp. 213–236). San Francisco: Jossey-Bass.

Howell, J.M., & Avolio B.J. (1993). Transformational leadership, transactional leadership, locus of control and support for innovation. *Journal of Applied Psychology*, *78*, 891–902.

Howell, J.M., & Frost, P.J. (1989). A laboratory study of charismatic leadership. *Organizational Behavior and Human Decision Processes*, *43*, 243-269.

Howell, J.P., & Dorfman, P.W. (1981). Substitutes for leadership: Test of a construct. *Academy of Management Journal*, *24*, 714–728.

Howell, J.P., Dorfman, P.W., & Kerr, S. (1986). Moderator variables in leadership research. *Academy of Management Review*, *11*, 88–102.

Hughes, R.L., Ginnett, R.C., & Curphy, G.J. (1999). *Leadership: Enhancing the lessons of experience* (3rd Ed.). Boston: Irwin/McGraw-Hill.

Hunt, J.G. (1991). *Leadership: A new synthesis*. Newbury park, CA: Sage.

Hunt, J.G. (1999). Transformational/charismatic leadership's transformation of the field: A historical essay. *Leadership Quarterly*, *10*(2), 129–144.

Insch, G.S., Moore, J.E., & Murphy, L.D. (1997). Content analysis in leadership research – example, procedures, and suggestions for future use. *Leadership Quarterly*, *8*, 1–25.

Janis, I.L. (1982). *Groupthink* (2nd ed.). Boston: Houghton-Mifflin.

Kanungo, R.N., & Mendonca, M. (1996). Cultural contingencies and leadership in developing countries. *Research in the Sociology of Organizations*, *14*, 263–295.

Katz, D., & Kahn, R.L. (1978). *The social psychology of organizations* (2nd ed.). New York: Wiley.

Kerr, S., & Jermier, J.M. (1978). Substitutes for leadership: Their meaning and measurement. *Organizational Behavior and Human Performance*, *22*, 375–403.

Kipnis, D., Schmidt, F.M., & Wilkinson, I. (1980). Intra-organizational influence tactics: Explorations in getting one's way. *Journal of Applied Psychology*, *65*, 440–452.

Kirkpatrick, S.A., & Locke, E.A. (1991). Leadership: Do traits matter? *Academy of Management Excecutive*, 5, 48–60.

Koh, W.L., Steers, R.M., & Terborg,. J.R. (1995). The effects of transformational leadership on teacher attitudes and student performance in Singapore. *Journal of Organizational Behavior*, *16*, 319–333.

Koopman, P.L., Den Hartog, D.N., Konrad, E., & 44 co-authors (1999). National culture and leadership profiles in Europe: Some results from the GLOBE study. *European Journal of Work and Organizational Psychology*, *8*, 503–520.

Korman, A.K. (1966). 'Consideration', 'initiating structure', and organizational criteria – a review. *Personnel Psychology*, *19*, 349–361.

Korukonda, A.R., & Hunt, J.G. (1989). Pat on the back vs. kick in the pants: An application of cognitive inference to the study of leader reward and punishment behaviors. *Group and Organization Studies*, *14*, 299–334.

Kotter, J.P. (1990). *A force for change: How leadership differs from management*. New York: Free Press.

Lievens, F., Van Geit, P., & Coetsier, P. (1997). Identification of transformational leadership qualities: An examination of potential biases. *European Journal of Work and Organizational Psychology*, *4*, 415–430.

Likert, R. (1961). *New patterns of management*. New York: McGraw-Hill.

Likert, R. (1967). *The human organization*. New York: McGraw-Hill.

Locke, E.A. (with Kirkpatrick, S.A., Wheeler, J.K., Schneider, J., Niles, K., Goldstein, H., Welsh, K., & D.O. Chah) (1991). *The essence of leadership*. New York: Lexington Books.

Lord, R.G., De Vader, C.L., & Allinger, G.M. (1986). A meta-analysis of the relationship between personality traits and leadership perceptions: An application of validity generalization procedures. *Journal of Applied Psychology*, *71*, 402–410.

Lord, R.G., Foti, R., & De Vader, C. (1984). A test of leadership categorization theory: Internal structure, information processing, and leadership perceptions. *Organizational Behavior and Human Performance*, *34*, 343–378.

Lord, R.G., Foti, R.J., & Phillips, J.S. (1982). A theory of leadership categorization. In J.G. Hunt, U. Sekaran, & C.A. Schriesheim (Eds.), *Leadership: Beyond establishment views* (pp. 104–121). Carbondale: Southern Illinois University Press.

Lord, R.G., & Maher, K.J. (1991). *Leadership and information processing*. London: Routledge.

Lowe, K.B., Kroeck, K.G., & Sivasubramaniam, N. (1996). Effectiveness correlates of transformational and trans- actional leadership: A meta-analytic review. *Leadership Quarterly, 7*, 385–425.

Maier, N.R.F. (1963). *Problem solving discussions and conferences*. New York: McGraw-Hill.

Manz, C.C., & Sims, H.P., jr. (1993). *Business without bosses: How self-managing teams are building high per- formance companies*. New York: Wiley.

Martinez, S., & Dorfman, P.W. (1998). The Mexican entrepreneur: An ethnographic study of the Mexican empressario. *International Studies of Management and Organizations, 28*, 97–123.

McGregor, D. (1960). *The human side of enterprise*. New York: McGraw-Hill.

Meindl, J.R. (1990). On leadership: An alternative to the conventional wisdom. In B.M. Staw, & L.L. Cummings (Eds.), *Research in organizational behavior, 12*, 159–203.

Meindl, J.R., Ehrlich, S.B., & Dukerich, J.M. (1985). The romance of leadership. *Administrative Science Quar- terly, 30*, 78–102.

Mintzberg, H. (1989). *Mintzberg on management*. New York: Free Press.

Mohrman, S.A., & Cohen, S.G. (1995). When people get out of the box: New relationships, new systems. In A. Howard (Ed.), *The changing nature of work*. San Francisco: Jossey-Bass.

Nahavandi, A. (2000). *The art and science of leadership* (2nd ed.). Upper Saddle River, NJ: Prentice-Hall.

Offermann, L.R., Kennedy, J.K., & Wirtz, P.W. (1994). Implicit leadership theories: Content structure, and generalizability. *Leadership Quarterly, 5*(1), 43–55.

Peterson, M.F., & Hunt, J.G. (1997). International pers- pectives on international leadership. *Leadership Quarterly, 8*(3), 203–231.

Pettigrew, A. (1972). Information control as a power resource. *Sociology, 6*, 187–204.

Pfeffer, J. (1981). Management as symbolic action: The creation and maintenance of organizational paradigms. *Research in Organizational Behavior, 3*, 1–52.

Podsakoff, P.M. (1982). Determinants of a supervisor's use of rewards and punishments: A literature review and suggestions for future research. *Organizational Behavior and Human Performance, 29*, 58–83.

Podsakoff, P.M., MacKenzie, S.B., & Bommer, W.H. (1996). Transformational leader behaviors and substi- tutes for leadership as determinants of employee satis- faction, commitment, trust and organizational citizenship behaviors. *Journal of Management, 22*, 259–298.

Podsakoff, P.M., MacKenzie, S.B., Moorman, R.H., & Fetter, R. (1990). Transformational leader behaviors and their effects on followers' trust in leader, satisfaction and organizational citizenship behaviors. *Leadership Quarterly, 1*(2), 107–142.

Podsakoff, P.M., Todor, W.D., & Skov, R. (1982). Effects of leader contingent and noncontingent reward, and punishment behaviors on subordinate performance and satisfaction. *Academy of Management Journal, 25*, 810–821.

Quinn, R.E. (1988). *Beyond rational management: Mastering the paradoxes and competing demands of high performance*. San Francisco, CA: Jossey-Bass.

Rauch, C.F., & Behling, O. (1984). Functionalism: Basis for an alternate approach to the study of leadership. In J.G. Hunt, D.M. Hosking, C.A. Schriesheim, & R. Stewart (Eds.), *Leaders and managers: International perspectives on managerial behavior and leadership*. Elmsford, NY: Pergamon Press.

Rosch, E. (1978). Principles of categorization. In E. Rosch, & B.B. Lloyd (Eds.), *Cognition and categoriza- tion*. Hillsdale, N.J.: Erlbaum.

Shamir, B. (1991). The charismatic relationship: Alterna- tive explanations and predictions. *Leadership Quarterly, 2*(2), 81–104.

Shamir, B. (1992). Attribution of charisma and influence to the leader: The romance of leadership revisited. *Journal of Applied Social Psychology, 22*(5), 386–407.

Shamir, B. (1995). Social distance and charisma: Theoretical notes and an exploratory study. *Leadership Quarterly, 6*(1), 19–47.

Shamir, B. (1999). Leadership in boundaryless organiza- tions: Disposable or indispensable? *European Journal of Work and Organizational Psychology, 8*(1), 49–71.

Shamir, B., Arthur, M.B., & House, R.J. (1994). The rhetoric of charismatic leadership: A theoretical exten- sion, a case study and implications for research. *Leadership Quarterly, 5*(1), 25–42.

Shamir, B., & Ben-Ari, E. (1999). Leadership in an open army? Civilian connections, interorganizational frame- works, and changes in military leadership. In J.G. Hunt, G.E. Dodge, & L.Wong (Eds.), *Out-of-the- box leader- ship: Transforming the 21st century army and other top performing organizations*. Stanford, CT: JAI Press.

Shamir, B., House, R.J., & Arthur, M.B. (1993). The moti- vational effects of charismatic leadership: A self- concept based theory. *Organization Science, 4*, 1–17.

Singer, M.S., & Singer, A.E. (1990). Situational constraints on transformational versus transactional leadership behavior, subordinates' leadership preference, and satis- faction. *Journal of Social psychology, 130*(3), 385–396.

Smith, P.B., & Peterson, M.F. (1988). *Leadership, organi- zations and culture*. London: Sage.

Smith, P.B., Peterson M.F., & Misumi, J. (1994). Event management and work team effectiveness in Japan, Britain and the USA. *Journal of Occupational and Organizational Psychology, 67*, 33–43.

Tannenbaum, R., & Schmidt, W.H. (1958). How to choose a leadership pattern. *Harvard Business Review, 36* (March-April), 95–101.

Tichy, N.M., & Devanna, M.A. (1990). *The transforma- tional leader* (2nd ed.). New York: Wiley.

Trice, H.M., & Beyer, J.M. (1986). Charisma and its routinization in two social movement organizations. *Research in Organizational Behavior, 8*, 113–164.

Turner, S. (1993). Charisma and obedience, a risk cogni- tion approach. *Leadership Quarterly, 4*, 235–256.

Vroom, V.H., & Jago, A.G. (1988). *The new leadership: Managing participation in organizations*. Englewood Cliffs, NJ: Prentice-Hall.

Vroom, V.H., & Yetton, P.W. (1973). *Leadership and decisionmaking.* Pittsburgh: University of Pittsburgh Press.

Weber, M. (1947). *The theory of social and economic organization* (A.N. Henderson, & T. Parsons, Eds., & trans.). Glencoe, IL: Free Press.

West, M.A., & Altink, W.M.M. (1996). Innovation at work: Individual, group, organizational, and socio-historical perspectives. *European Journal of Work and Organizational Psychology,* 5(1), 3–11.

Willner, A.R. (1984). *The spellbinders: Charismatic political leadership.* New Haven: Yale University Press.

Yammarino, F.J., & Bass, B.M. (1990). Long-term fore-casting of transformational leadership and its effects among naval officers: Some preliminary findings. In K.E. Clark, & M.B. Clark (Eds.), *Measures of leadership* (pp. 151–170). West Orange, NJ: Leadership Library of America.

Yammarino, F.J., & Bass, B.M. (1991). Person and situa-tion views of leadership: A multiple levels of analysis approach. *Leadership Quarterly,* 2, 121–139.

Yammarino, F.J., Spangler, W.D., & Bass, B.M. (1993). Transformational leadership and performance: A longitudinal investigation. *Leadership Quarterly,* 4(1), 81–102.

Yokochi, N. (1989). *Leadership styles of Japanese managers: Transformational and transactional.* Doctoral dissertation, United States International University, San Diego, CA.

Yukl, G. (1998). *Leadership in organizations* (4th ed.). Englewood Cliffs, NJ: Prentice-Hall.

Yukl, G., & Falbe, C.M. (1990). Influence tactics and objectives in upward, downward, and lateral influence attempts. *Journal of Applied Psychology,* 75(2), 132–140.

Yukl, G., & Falbe, C.M. (1991). The importance of dif-ferent power sources in downward and lateral relations. *Journal of Applied Psychology,* 76, 416–423.

Yukl, G., Falbe, C.M., & Youn, J.Y. (1993). Patterns of influence behavior for managers. *Group and Organi-zation Management,* 20, 272–296.

Yukl, G., & Tracey, B. (1992). Consequences of influence tactics used with subordinates, peers, and the boss. *Journal of Applied Psychology,* 77, 525–535.

Zaleznik, A. (1977). Managers and leaders: Are they different? *Harvard Business Review,* 15, 67–78.

10

Communication in Organizations: Speed, Diversity, Networks, and Influence on Organizational Effectiveness, Human Health, and Relationships

JANICE LANGAN-FOX

The way communication occurs in organizations has changed dramatically in the past 20 years, so much so, that research in industrial/organizational psychology seems to have failed to keep up with these changes. However in spite of this gap in research, an implicit assumption seems to be made in organizations and in the literature, that the more sophisticated the technology, the greater the efficiency gains. The present chapter reviews all the research which is pertinent to communication in organizations, for instance, formal and informal networks, technology and organizational structures, electronic communication types in organizations, emerging problems with communication technologies, and occupational health and technology. Various areas for future research are recommended in occupational health and technostress, computing technology skills and employment, efficiency gains from communication technologies, human relationships, and communications theory.

WORK AND COMMUNICATION-RICH ORGANIZATIONS: SOME QUESTIONS ABOUT THE 'BRAVE NEW WORLD'

In very recent times, technological innovations in computers and telecommunications have created a wide array of new communication media. For organizations, this represents opportunities to overcome communication problems associated with a geographically dispersed workforce and to enhance the productivity of organizational members. For instance, media such as teleconferencing and electronic mail provide communication capabilities to help improve the flow of information and facilitate the coordination of people not in the same location. It seems therefore, that the benefits of communication technologies appear to be substantial. However, Apgar (1998) has commented on issues he believes are emerging:

> We are moving from an era in which people seek connections with one another to an era where people will have to decide when and where to disconnect – both electronically and socially. (p. 121)

Several questions arise from his work: Is there any systematic monitoring of the effects of communication technologies on employees in different jobs and industries? Is there work or information overload, or, any psychological or physiological effect on workers as a consequence of the new technologies or the quickened pace of communication? Does the workforce have the appropriate skills to maximize opportunities in information technology and to control and regulate communication? Has the implicit assumption been confirmed ... namely that workers are more effective and productive in their jobs as a consequence of high-speed computing technologies?

This chapter reviews the literature on new communication technologies; dominant theoretical perspectives; informal and formal communication networks; the effects of new technologies and modes of communication on individuals, management and hierarchies; the intranet; workforce skills and skill upgrading; communication technology problems including controlling and regulating communication and innovation; and the effects of the new technologies on human health and relationships.

THEORIZING COMMUNICATION IN ORGANIZATIONS

As recently as the 1980s, we would have drawn a theory of organizational effectiveness such that communication was a mediating variable in our models. Now, we would place communication as a major causal variable determining many organizational outcomes influencing for example, strategy and an individual's organizational role (Rogers & Agarwala-Rogers, 1976).

A number of approaches exist in communication theory which parallel organizational theories. A 'mechanistic' perspective views communication as a transmission process by which a message physically travels across space through a channel, from one person to another, and assumes that the source governs what the receiver receives (Fisher, 1993). For example, Taylorism viewed communication as vertical (top-down), formal, and hierarchical, while Weberian 'bureaucracy' meant logic, order (command-and-control), and uniformity (Rogers & Agarwala-Rogers, 1976). Typically in the 'psychological' perspective, the receiver is the focus, with the assumption that individuals suffer information overload. From the 'interpretive-symbolic' perspective, behaviour creates and shapes the reality of the organization as well as its environment, the main emphasis being on shared meanings that form among people as they interact (Fisher, 1993). For instance, in the human relations school, information ascended from lower to upper levels of the organization, as well as flowing laterally. A 'systems' perspective focuses on people's external actions and sees communication as the whole being greater than the sum of parts (Rogers & Agarwala-Rogers, 1976). Correspondingly, integrated organizational

perspectives such as the sociotechnical model, suggest that communication depends on the organization and its situation (Fisher, 1993). 'Contemporary' perspectives prompt questions about how the organisation defines itself: the most organic views being the 'brain' metaphor (Morgan, 1986) which implies that organizations can learn, and the 'culture' metaphor which examines how people use language to express and form meanings (Fisher, 1993).

Modelling 'Effective' Communication

Communication can be defined as the process by which an idea is transferred from a source to a receiver, the intention being to change receiver behaviour. The main components in the process typically include source, message, channel, receiver, effect, and feedback (Rogers & Agarwala-Rogers, 1976). King and Cushman (1994) suggested that high-speed management reflects an 'effective' communication system employed by well-managed companies, who rapidly reorient the organisation to a changing environment to retain competitive advantage. A theory of communication then, should reflect 'effective' communication which follows a strategy of co-alignment of diverse interests, concerns, and contributions through the use of an open flexible communication system allowing for the co-alignment of both similarities and differences in an innovative, flexible, and rapid response system (Conrad, 1994). Thus, communication systems and organizational and cultural values should be interdependent. An example of this interdependence can be seen in a study by Erez (1992) who examined the patterns of communication in Japanese corporations in the light of antecedents (cultural values) and consequences (productivity and innovation). Based on 10 Japanese companies, findings showed that the interpersonal communication system was shaped by the cultural values in line with the traditional patterns of communication in Japanese society. This congruence intensified the smooth flow of communication with important consequences, (a) at the motivational level: the sharing of common values which made for better consensus and commitment to values; (b) at the cognitive level: the sharing of knowledge, ideas, and information which enhanced the level of productivity and innovation (see also the work of Gidden, 1984, on the 'duality of structure').

Communication in Organizations – a Theoretical Model

Despite the availability of communication models discussed earlier, it appears from a literature review that there is substantial theoretical work to be done to explain the complexity of communication in modern-day organizations. As a starting point for this work, it is suggested that a theoretical focus on communication as 'contextual' would be beneficial, in as much as it would include the cultural traditions (the past) of the organization but would also incorporate the 'new'. The 'newness' would include developments and shifts in communication styles, modes, and values which are common to organizational networks, cliques, liaisons, or groups, in all or parts of the organization. Such a model, simple as it is, could develop from Fisher's (1993) communication-in-context model which represents group characteristics, organization structure and culture, and task characteristics (Figure 10.1). Group characteristics include group norms; the organizational structure and culture includes the organization's design; and task characteristics include the nature of the work about which communication is taking place.

It is taken then, that an organization theoretically exists of a number of highly complex, interconnected contextualized relationships which could be represented as 'networks'. Such a perspective is difficult to analyse (see, e.g., Langan-Fox, Code & Langfield-Smith, 2000; Langan-Fox, Wirth, Code, Langfield-Smith & Wirth, in press), and may involve methodologies not common to psychology (see, e.g., Robins, Pattison & Langan-Fox, 1995). Thus, how would organizations be researched as contextual and networked? Below, the empirical work in these areas is examined to reveal some of the studies which relate to such a perspective.

THE ROLE OF NETWORKS IN ORGANIZATIONS

Formal Versus Informal Communication Networks

The formal network of an organization can typically be represented by the 'organizational chart' which reflects prescribed patterns for officially sanctioned messages. A network consists of interconnected individuals who are linked by patterned communication flows. Greenbaum (1974) identified four kinds of formal networks: the regulative (e.g., plans, regulations), the innovative (e.g., flexibility and change), the informative-instructive (e.g., productivity), and the integrative (e.g., maintenance of employee morale). Formal channels can be found to be an inefficient means of meeting unanticipated communication needs, for managing crises, or for dealing with complex or detailed problems (Conrad, 1994). On the other hand, the informal network comprises spontaneous, emergent patterns resulting from individual choices. Such networks: must regularly be used or they will disappear; are less structured; have less predictable communication flows than through formal networks; constantly change as

people's personal communication links change; may be more accurate than formal communication; have a shorter communication chain; are maintained through gossip; and allow people to temporarily ignore power and status differences. Informal networks help organizations by compensating for weaknesses in formal communication and fostering innovation.

In a large organization composed of thousands of individuals, many networks exist. Networks are much less structured than formal communication, occur more or less spontaneously, and are constantly changing (Rogers & Agarwala-Rogers, 1976). These elements of change can be seen in work by Weenig and Midden (1991) who studied communication network influences on the information diffusion process and the effects of two virtually identical communication programs. The results provided some insight into how people restrain each other from adoption and how this is related to the strength and number of communication ties.

Network laboratory experiments on small-group communication include the circle, the wheel, the chain, and all-channel design. Bavelas (1950) and Leavitt (1951) found that a centralized network (where one individual is central) had a communication flow which was faster and more accurate than a decentralized network. This was later found only to be true in the case of simple tasks – for complex tasks a decentralized network was more efficient. Stohl (1995) suggested that centralized networks are most efficient for simple problem solving and routine matters. When multiple operations have to be performed and adaptation and innovation is required, decentralized networks were most effective. Members of decentralized networks reported greater satisfaction with the group. Shaw (1954) studied the concept of independence, (or the degree of freedom with which an individual could function in a group), and found that independence was greater in decentralized networks like the circle, regardless of the type of task, and was positively related to individual satisfaction. Information overload or 'saturation' was highest for individuals in the wheel network.

Cliques and Liaisons
Networks are also made up of cliques usually containing 5 to 25 members. Such people communicate more often with one another than with other people in the organization, with some members becoming opinion leaders and informally influencing the attitudes and behaviours of other members. Other members are 'gatekeepers' which allows them to control the messages flowing through the network; boundary spanners; or 'cosmopolites' – people at the top or bottom of the organization's formal hierarchy who have a high degree of communication with the system's environment

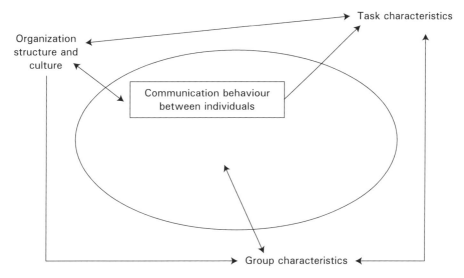

Figure 10.1   *From Fisher's (1993) communication-in-context model*

(Conrad, 1994). Different cliques are linked together by liaisons – people who connect two cliques but who are not members of either one and who are the 'cement' that holds the structural bricks of the organization together (Rogers & Agarwala-Rogers, 1976). For instance MacDonald (1970) used network analysis to investigate the cliques and liaisons among members of a federal agency in the Pentagon. Amend (1971) has argued that it is fruitful to conceive of every individual in a system as playing a liaison role, as liaisons are crucial for the effective operation of an organization's interpersonal network (Rogers & Agarwala-Rogers, 1976) while Tutzauer (1985) suggested that an organization is marked by an increasing number of cliques and factions as it dissolves.

The Grapevine and Rumours

A special type of informal network is the grapevine where there are several individuals who regularly function as liaisons and who often have higher unofficial status. The grapevine is a community phenomenon, crossing hierarchical levels, functional roles, and professional affiliations (Stohl, 1995). Rumours can be understood to be sets of messages which lack evidence as to their truth but explain confusing events and flourish in an atmosphere of secrecy and competition. Indeed their secrecy probably enhances the power of the message and increases their value! Messages on the grapevine travel swiftly (Stohl, 1995). Research has shown that grapevine information, which often travels in a 'cluster' (Fisher, 1993), is more than three-fourths accurate, while some organizational members might still mistrust such information (Walton, 1963). Crampton, Hodge & Mishra (1998) examined

managers' perceptions of the factors associated with grapevine activity and determined the extent of managers' positions affecting their perceptions of grapevine activity. The results demonstrated that 92.4% of companies surveyed had no policy to deal with the grapevine, and managers and organizations usually did not take an active role in managing/controlling informal communication networks. The results also indicated that the managers' level of knowledge about grapevine characteristics, causes, and outcomes was affected by organizational position.

Context and Culture

On a broader scale, some network researchers have examined communicative patterns in relation to the cultural and structural features of the organization. Marshall and Stohl (1993) used a network approach to study worker participation. Results indicated that the degree to which workers became involved in the communication system were differentially related to levels of workers' satisfaction and managerial assessments of worker performance.

With the development of theoretical models which suggest the interrelatedness of communication in organizations (Fisher, 1993), one research approach has been to analyse interpersonal communication patterns with network analysis procedures and then to compare these patterns with the formal communication patterns that would be expected on the basis of organizational structure and culture (Rogers & Agarwala-Rogers, 1976). For instance, Hall (1980) suggests that organizational cultures can be distinguished by the interconnectedness of communication networks and that context is the information that surrounds a message. Cultures with highly interconnected networks operate as high-context message producers, while cultures with segmented and compartmentalized networks operate as low-context message producers.

Other work on context, culture or environment can be seen in the work of Gladstein-Ancona and Caldwell (1987) who found that the network roles associated with effective product development teams were boundary-spanning roles. In several organizational studies, the most effective teams, as determined by external judges, were ones who had frequent contacts with the outside environment. It has been found that high-performing teams tend to be more highly linked with other groups in the organization than less effective groups (Tushman & Scanlan, 1981). On the other hand, the most cohesive and highly satisfied groups have been shown to interact infrequently with outside constituents (e.g., Ancona & Caldwell, 1988). In a study of how involvement in communication networks affects workers' commitment to an organization, Eisenberg, Monge and Miller (1983) found that highly connected employees who were not involved in their jobs were more committed to their jobs than those who had low job involvement and were not enmeshed within the system's work-related network. Kanungo (1998) investigated the influence of organizational culture on computer-mediated communication and information access (CMCIA) and found that while 'task-oriented' organizations had a positive relationship between user satisfaction and CMCIA, 'people-oriented' organizations had a negative relationship.

Role Awareness and Channelling Information Flows

There are a range of views on the relationship between interpersonal communication networks and informal social control. The relative merits of some of these viewpoints can be assessed by examining the distribution of interpersonal observability in communication networks. Friedkin (1983) examined communication networks and demonstrated that there was 'horizon to observability', a distance in a communication network beyond which persons are unlikely to be aware of other person's role performance. The number of contacts shared by two persons was a powerful predictor of the probability that one person was aware of the role performance of another (Friedkin, 1983).

Researchers have long been aware of the 'gap' in understanding among certain groups in organizations, for instance, between management and union members. Tompkins (1962) called this 'semantic information distance'. It needs to be remembered, however, that any formalization of information flows can actually intrude upon the natural development of personal communication networks when it is below top management, as was found by Marschan (1996). Thus, there is no rule of thumb about the

development of harmonious relationships when computer-mediated communication is implemented. Like any other innovation, the outcome is uncertain.

TECHNOLOGY AND ORGANIZATIONAL STRUCTURES

From the foregoing then, it can easily be established that communication networks have powerful influences on organizations. In the past, we would have safely assumed that once we knew about organizational structures, we would also know about communication structures. For instance, an hierarchical 'top-down' decision-making structure (typified by the 'pyramid') would strongly determine the way communication occurs in an organization. But changes in communication networks produced by the implementation of telematic services and other innovations may reveal that the reverse is now happening: *communication structure is determining organizational structure*. Information technology influences roles, power, and hierarchy so, for instance, a team-based, problem-focused group may emerge whose work centres around electronic communications, and business processes may be integrated across traditional functional, product, and geographical lines (Rice & Steinfield, 1994).

Hax (1989) pointed out that the new information technologies are beginning to replace the conventional managerial hierarchy and to contribute to the development of a 'network structure' in organizations. Digital technology has created links between telecommunications and computing technology, transforming the way information is exchanged and accessed.

Individuals, Management, and Hierarchies

Organizational researchers have long recognized that the power of individuals is largely a function of the extent to which they have access to information, people, and resources (Mechanic, 1962). Brass (1985) reported that an individual's position in the work flow was strongly related to influence. Although women were rated as less influential than men, both gender groups had similar performance evaluations. Women who were perceived as less influential were not well integrated into men's networks. Issues relevant to 'culture' also relate to gender differences. For instance, Amason and Allen (1997) investigated gender differences in the relationship between perceived organizational support and employee perceptions of their communication with top management, immediate supervisors, and coworkers in a university and in two engineering firms: males reported a positive coworker communication relationship indicating higher perceived organizational support, while this pattern did not emerge for females.

Weick (1987) argued that interpersonal communication is the essence of organizations because it creates structures which then affect what else gets said and done, and by whom. Structures form when communication uncovers shared occupational specialities or values that people want to preserve and expand. The structures themselves create hierarchical levels and communicative patterns observed at one level of the hierarchy which then shape configurations at other levels. Being in the middle often means having access to dominant coalitions and/or being on a critical path. However, message distortion may occur due to the number of people the message must pass through (Stohl, 1995) as well as the fact that hierarchical networks maximize the likelihood that messages could be intentionally distorted.

Cacioppe and Marshall (1989) surveyed communication between managers and their subordinates in public and private organizations and reported that managers and subordinates differed significantly in their communication perceptions in the following areas: defining goals and objectives of subordinates; personal lives; information about the job; and total communication as determined by an indicator which includes measures of standards of performance, personal life, work situation, organizational structure, and the environment. Contrary to previous research, there was no difference between the amount of communication between managers and subordinates in public or private sector organizations. Other research on organizational size by Smeltzer (1989), has shown that communication patterns do significantly differ in managers from large and small organizations, both in amount and type of medium. Differences have been found by occupational status: Sproull, Kiesler and McGuire (1986) state that email messages from managers tend to be longer, more focused, and have more negative-affect expressions than messages from professionals and other employees. It has been recommended that communication needs to vary by occupational status: Larkin and Larkin (1996) argued that executives who want people to change the way they do things, must also change the way they communicate. They suggest that because frontline supervisors are the real opinion leaders in any organization, senior managers must discuss any changes, face-to-face with supervisors, who will pass information along to their subordinates.

ELECTRONIC COMMUNICATION: FASTER, MORE SOPHISTICATED, MORE ACCESSIBLE ... AND IT'S HERE NOW

Communication behaviour between individuals (the centrepiece of Fisher's model described above), suggests that this element is crucial to organizational structure, the group, and the individual job. Thus, modes of communication which assist in this interdependent set of relationships will determine the nature of the individual behaviour, various outcomes such as productivity and any problems which emerge as a consequence of the communication mode. These modes are examined below, for their impact on individuals, groups and organizations.

Electronic Mail

Of all the communication media available, electronic mail (e-mail) has perhaps achieved the most widespread acceptance in organizations. At its simplest level, e-mail provides the capability to create a message on a computer, transmit it to one or more recipients, and store the message for subsequent display (Steinfield, 1990). Electronic mail does not provide the same richness as face-to-face conversation or even a telephone call, but there is an immediacy and informal flavour to e-mail which seems to lead many senders to construct idiosyncratic, shorthand messages. Consequently, e-mail messages can be ambiguous and subject to multiple interpretations. Each organizational setting appears to have different norms, policies, and cultures regarding the use of e-mail (Steinfield, 1990). It seems that there are individual differences in e-mail usage: Fuller (1996) investigated the use of social cognitions to assess the effectiveness of communication behavior and found that users of electronic media developed consistent misperceptions across several personality dimensions when judging individuals they communicate with, but with whom they have never met in person. This may have consequences for the work effectiveness of individuals in a 'virtual' team – individuals who communicate solely by e-mail.

Electronic mail may be more appropriate for simple and routine exchanges but it does allow 'news' to be disseminated rapidly and its interactivity enables a user to develop a more interpersonal relationship (Rice & Steinfield, 1994). The interactive nature of e-mail and organizational structural change was found in research by Danowski and Edison-Smith (1985) who examined change in computer-based communication structures in response to a crisis. All private email messages were 'captured' (users were unaware their messages were obtained) for one year. Monthly network analysis revealed that e-mail patterns changed with the development of the crisis.

Motivations to install e-mail systems originally focused on the productivity improvements that could be gained among managerial and professional staff. This followed studies of managers and professionals which estimated that 70–80% of the workday was spent on face-to-face meetings, telephone calls, reading and writing, and dialling a busy number. Searching for a mailing address could account for 30–60 minutes of every workday (Steinfield, 1990). Electronic mail eliminates many unnecessary functions and, in many cases, there are productivity benefits as a result of e-mail communication. A study at Xerox revealed that the majority of employees perceived that using e-mail improved their productivity, increasing the cohesiveness and coordination of work units, and increasing the connectedness with others in the company. However, problems with e-mail include the effect of the delayed response and the security of proprietary information (Steinfield, 1990). In a study by Lantz (1998) concerning how e-mail is used as a work tool for communication, managers seemed to have problems to a larger extent than members of other workgroups. Nonetheless, employees felt a shortage of time for handling e-mail and had difficulty organizing stored messages.

Electronic mail constitutes a new medium in organizational communication and has achieved considerable acceptance in organizations, including businesses, government agencies, and universities.

Telematics and Teleworking

Many jobs don't require a worker in a fixed location, especially 'information workers' (Kraut, 1987). Part of the 'alternative workplace' now includes 'remote work' or 'telecommuting' which involves the use of computers and telecommunications equipment to do office work away from a central location. Telework denotes a form of work organization, mediated by computers and telecommunications in which work is carried on outside a central office. Telematics (the integration of computer, telecommunication, and information technologies such as teleconferencing and teleworking) increase the number of messages exchanged (see, e.g., Fulk & Dutton, 1984; Rice, 1984a). It seems that even people not directly connected to the computer conferencing network experience a communication increment! Vertical information flows are also increased, especially upward communication (Hiltz, 1982). Workers may be more available as a result of telework, particularly those who need to mesh family and work obligations. Teleworkers reduce commuting time and incidental costs, and increase flexibility to coordinate work with personal schedules and responsibilities (Kraut, 1987). Telecommuting improves the quality of life away from work (Humble, Jacobs & Van Sell, 1995). At CSIRO, telecommuting facilitated business activities and the delivery of quality science (Knobel, 1993). Soares' (1992) investigations of telework experience in Brazil revealed that a shift towards decentralization was influenced by this form of communication.

As computing and communication technologies lead to more information-intensive work processes, the practice of telecommuting by white collar workers has increased. But still, the narrow bandwidth of telephone lines can be a technical hurdle preventing work at home. Often intranet access is blocked, and other psychological and sociological factors conflict with technological advances (Pliskin, 1998). The summarization of the benefits and negatives for employers and employees of telecommuting by Telework Analytics International (1999), indicates that careful consideration of a large range of factors is needed before telecommuting commences.

The potential of the phenomenon suggests a number of social and personal benefits. However, an assessment of the possible implications of work-at-home on the individual employee indicate that the burden may be greater than the benefits accrued (see, e.g., Salamon & Salamon, 1984). Similarly, research by Langan-Fox (1996) and Langan-Fox and Poole (1995), discusses social interaction at work and the advantages of separating home and work.

Videoconferencing

Videoconferencing permits live discussion between remote individuals and individuals/groups via satellite. The advent of videoconferencing eliminates the inconvenience of travel (e.g., time, cost, fatigue) and speeds up the communication process. Researchers concerned with the quality of outcome of different modes of communication, especially between groups of workers communicating via teleconferencing, have mainly focused on verbalization, linguistic activities, and the quantity of words or messages (Birrell & White, 1982). Such researchers have pointed out that teleconferencing (both audio and video), besides being more cost efficient, is more satisfactory to its users and more task-oriented than face-to-face interaction with the difference in efficiency and satisfaction being attributable to technical differences in the type of interaction (Rossetti & Surynt, 1985). For instance, Birrell and White (1982) have discussed difficulties that groups have when solving problems in a face-to-face interaction and reported on research that shows how an electronic alternative (e.g., videoconferencing) may be used to increase the decision-making effectiveness of the group. It is argued that the use of an electronic medium may be beneficial in decreasing some social psychological aspects of meetings (such as conformity, groupthink, enhancement of dominant attitudes, coalition formation) and in increasing task orientation. Rossetti and Surynt (1985) reported that the performance (problem-solving ability, measured by the correctness of the solution of each group) of videoconference groups was significantly higher than those that met face-to-face.

Further, research on electronic meetings where computer-supported electronic communication replaces verbal communication shows that larger groups generate more ideas of greater quality and member satisfaction than smaller groups (Dennis, Valacich & Nunamaker, 1990) In some cases, the quality of work in videoconferencing settings may be the same as 'face-to-face' as reported by Olson, Olson and Meader (1997), although remote groups spent more time managing their work and clarifying what they meant than face-to-face groups. Heath and Luff (1992) examined interpersonal communication in a sophisticated multimedia office environment and found that audiovisual technology introduces certain asymmetries into interpersonal communication which can transform the impact of visual and vocal conduct.

Other research focuses on the concept of 'presence' which is defined in terms of the user's perception of his or her environment. Williams, Rice and Dordick (1985) argued that videoconferencing is most effective for tasks which require exchange of information, a cooperative problem-solving situation or routine decision-making process, all of which are classified as low social presence tasks. Videoconferencing is not accepted as effective for high social presence tasks such as bargaining, negotiation, getting to know people, or tasks involving conflict.

Recently, Buxton, Sellen and Sheasby (1997) argued that conventional approaches to videoconferencing are generally limited in their support of the participants' ability to establish eye contact with other participants; to be visually aware of who is visually attending to them; to selectively listen to different, parallel conversations; to make side comments to other participants and hold parallel conversations; and to see co-participants in relation to work-related objects. Egido (1990) has reinforced the negatives associated with videoconferencing – that the use of videoconferencing ignores the informal interaction processes through which much of the communication in organizations takes place, but acknowledges that videoconferencing has been particularly useful for lecture style presentations in which structured, one-way communication with a large audience is desired. Similarly, O'Connail and Whittaker (1997) found that videoconferencing interactions include a more formal style of communication than face-to-face interactions. Speakers in videoconference interrupted less but were less likely to anticipate 'conversation endings' than were face-to-face speakers.

Straus (1997) examined the effect of communication media on group processes and the effect of processes on group cohesiveness, satisfaction, and productivity. Groups worked on idea generation, intellective, and judgment tasks in either computer-mediated (CM) or face-to-face (FTF) discussions. Findings showed that in comparison to FTF groups, CM groups were less productive across tasks and expressed lower satisfaction in the task and lower cohesiveness than did FTF groups. Analysis of communication processes among college students in three-person groups showed that CM groups had higher proportions of task communication and disagreement and greater equality of participation. In addition, CM groups did not engage in more attacking behaviour and exchanged higher rates of supportive communication than did FTF groups. Hearn (1992) examined a video cascade process within a large international airline of some 56,000 employees. The impact of cascade meetings was variable and depended on the interpersonal components of the cascade, the perceived relationship of the video to daily experiences, and the targetted group's attributional processes.

Video-based internal communication in large corporations is increasingly being used but has rarely been evaluated. Findings from research suggest that there are many facets of communication which remain unexamined, but which impact on performance.

The World Wide Web

The Web started with stand-alone systems, grew to small networks, and then to enterprise-wide networks (Cohen & Joseph, 1998). It is increasingly contributing to social and economic change (ABS, 1999b) dramatically influencing the way business is conducted, and how governments interact with business and society generally. Kelly (1996) reports that prior to the Web, many corporations were investing significant funds on connecting people to distributed information and that most of these companies were not satisfied with the results. Millions of end-users are entering the information market (Nicholas, Williams, Martin & Cole, 1998) with more that 40 million people becoming internet users in little more than four years, and the number of sites forecasted to exceed the population of the planet.

Malta, Switzerland, and Finland lead the rest of Europe in terms of internet and email use with 85% of large UK corporations having some form of internet access in 1997 (Nua Internet Surveys, 1997). The Australian Bureau of Statistics (ABS, 1999b) report that one in three businesses in Australia have used computers for at least five years or more. About 21% of all businesses had internet access at June 1997, though this varied by size of business: 85% of large businesses, 49% of medium-sized businesses, 19% of small businesses, and 17% of microbusinesses had internet access. The main uses of the internet were e-mail and information gathering. Only 1% of businesses used the internet for selling or purchasing goods or services. In March 1998, 52% of employed adults used computers at work and 17% of employed adults used the internet at work (ABS, 1999b).

Using global figures, men are the biggest users of the internet. Surveys conducted in 1994 and 1996, show that female use of the Web rose from just 5% in January 1994 to 31% in November 1996 (Pitkow & Kehoe, 1996). Women tend to use it for work purposes, while men often search for items of personal interest. The average age of Web users is increasing, reaching 34.9 years. Globally, the strongest growth is predicted for Africa/Middle East and Latin America (Paul Budde Communication, 1999). In Australia, reports by the Australian Bureau of Statistics show that men are more likely than women to engage in work-related activities on their home computer. In 1998, 73% of employed men aged 18 and over who frequently used a home computer used it for work-related activities compared to 60% of employed women. Male teleworkers (4%) outnumbered females (2%) (ABS, 1999a). In 1998, 2.3 million people reported using a home computer for work-related activities. This included employees taking work home, employees working from home ('teleworkers' or 'telecommuters') and the self-employed. Business users spend more than 50% of their time online for business matters, and primary business users outnumber primary home users (Emarketer, 1999).

Many Australian-based companies are providing company information online and are introducing the option of online job applications (Murry, 1997). Not surprisingly, Burrows (1994) predicted that companies which gather and use information effectively will in general have an advantage over their competitors.

ORGANIZATIONS KEEPING UP WITH TECHNOLOGY

Technology Uptake

Even when organizations have arranged their infrastructures to be conversant with the new communication technologies, successful implementation is not guaranteed. It is now apparent that high technology often means high risk, and that it is frequently the case that technology fails to live up to its original promise (Miniace & Falter, 1996) and often produces conflicting results: social isolation and increased connectedness; more complex socialization patterns and simpler socialization patterns (Salem, 1998). Salem (1998) concludes that the social impact of electronic communication technologies (ECT) is as varied as the initial conditions prior to their use where one type of social impact will exist along with an apparently opposite impact. The fault may lie in the failure to understand and manage the mutual influences of technology and the 'extended implementation process' (Walton, 1989). For instance a study demonstrating *successful* practice conducted by Miniace and Falter (1996) showed how top-down and bottom-up communication can be combined to encourage discussion of issues and

how the communication process effects strategy implementation.

AT&T is just one of the many organizations pioneering the 'alternative workplace' (AW) – the combination of nontraditional work practices, settings, and locations. The AW is changing the way people collaborate (Apgar, 1998). Nonetheless such programmes might not be adopted where there are ingrained behaviours and a person's ability to excel in an AW environment actually depends on an array of new skills in communication and leadership. Many features of the AW remain an innovation than well-accepted practice. 'Technology' *can* make communication more difficult, rather than improving it (More, 1989).

The Virtual Organization and Intranets

According to Dickerson (1998), 'virtual' organizations are those which attain maximum flexibility to respond to user needs by downsizing to core management activities and contracting out major manufacturing processes. But also, 'virtual' organizations are using the internet or intranets to provide and communicate information to their employees. Stevens (1998) argued that as more organizations reduce their human resources management (HRM) staff and look for ways for fewer employees to do more work, interest in developing electronic support for employees will increase. Ford has an intranet with over 80,000 employees using it daily. Hewlett Packard has about 200 Internal Web servers accessed by 10, 000 people in product divisions, field-sales offices, and corporate groups. Training departments in particular are using intranets for delivery of training and performance support (Smith, 1997).

Intranets are likely to be the key information technology revolution from the year 2000 (Barbera, 1996) although concerns have been expressed over security, manageability, and ongoing maintenance (Webmaster, 1999). Pincince (1998) suggested that the extranet – the use of the internet by a corporation's employees presents the opportunity for true, value-added services for network managers. Davis's survey (1997) of members of the Information Industry Association found that more than 90% of respondents used the internet and 50–90% used many other electronic communication systems. There has been a substantial increase in the use of the internet at work, while many people who use the internet at work also use it for personal and recreational purposes! When used correctly, it can enhance communication and collaboration, streamline procedures, and provide just-in-time information to a globally dispersed workforce. Cohen (1998) believes, however, that if misused, an intranet can intensify mistrust and increase misinformation. It seems that organizations are still struggling to learn the best ways to implement their intranets (Cohen, 1998).

Communication Technologies and Workforce Skills

Mingin (1984) discussed changes in the U.S. economy, which has moved from an emphasis on manufacturing to a rapid expansion of information-based technologies – a trend marked by labour that is less physically demanding. Thus, dramatic changes have occurred, and are occuring continuously, in needed workforce skills. During the 1980s, writers were already concerned about shortcomings in attitudes towards the impact of computers, and about skill shortages and skill upgrading. More than 15 years ago, Davie and Perry (1984) suggested that there should be an increased emphasis on continuing education. As early as 1982, warnings were expressed about the imperative of computer skill upgrading. For example, Lewis (1982) recommended that managers needed more skills in communication than did their predecessors. Similarly, Galati (1986) thought that as computer conferencing and electronic mail became routine, new skills, such as the ability to use equipment and to write concisely and quickly online, would be required. For many, but not all workers, participation in the workforce is now dominated by learning and information exchange. This trend will probably lead towards increased prevalence of abstraction skills necessary to process burgeoning mountains of information. Thus, now more than ever, at the turn of the century, calls continue to be made for the workforce to acquire skill diversity (see, e.g., Richardson, 1999).

Training professionals in the use of electronic communication must facilitate language change, the restructuring of jobs and acceptance from staff, especially at high management levels. Criticism has been levelled at managers for their apparent ineptitude and inaction. As Kiesler (1986) noted, managers either regard computers as a tool for storing and transmitting information or they fail to utilize high-technology innovations (Steinfield, 1990). In other ways, managers appear not to be completely informed about how their subordinates view communication in their organization. Surveys of Australian management styles, conducted through the 'Go BRW' online service found that 70% of respondents believed (surprisingly!) that they could do a better job than their boss. Lack of 'quality' communication was highlighted as the major cause of dissatisfaction among workers with respect to their leaders (James, 1996). Research into the relationship between communication satisfaction and other organizational variables by Ticehurst and Smith (1992), found that levels of communication satisfaction, organizational commitment, and job satisfaction were relatively low.

Companies operating at the frontiers of knowledge and technology in business need to be aware of the importance of employee perceptions and feelings as well as the value of their technological skills, and must develop innovative attitudes and strategies (Jacobs & Everett, 1988). Klobas (1996) described innovative uses of the internet by staff showing that the internet provided opportunities for communication among users, but posed challenges to the information systems professionals who supported them. Therefore, the characteristics of individual employees and the company culture are two factors which are crucial in determining organizational innovation.

Much of the dramatic change in skill and wage structure observed in recent years in the United States is believed to stem from the impact of new technology. Machin, Ryan and Van Reenan (1996) compared the changing skill structure of wages and employment in the USA with three other countries – the UK, Denmark, and Sweden. The authors investigated how far technical change could explain the growth in the importance of more highly skilled workers and found that growth of skilled workers had occurred in all countries. Nevertheless, findings by these authors suggested that technology only accounted for a relatively small part (about one quarter) of the changes in the skill structure in the Anglo-American nations.

The pace of technological change in ICT (information and communication technologies) has created the rise of 'techno-globalism' at a cross-organizational level by providing a new mode of diversification. As a result of increasing technological interrelatedness, specialization in a core pervasive technology develops tacit capabilities. As suggested by Penrose's 'theory of the growth of the firm' (Santangelo, 1998), an organization develops capabilities through an internal learning process and strengthens these capabilities into new activities and new geographical locations. In the current context, technology and innovative activity are also going through a globalization process. Three important factors were suggested by Janssens and Brett (1994) as impacting organizations' ability to coordinate activities: (1) electronic voice and data networks, (2) internal labor markets, and (3) a multicultural managerial workforce.

Other developments within organizations concern multimedia. Stewart and Williams (1998) suggest that multimedia technology is becoming ubiquitous in modern society and is having profound effects on institutions (see, e.g., Murray, 1999, on the impact of multimedia and Web technologies on educational institutions), although actual learning increments as a consequence of multimedia programs have yet to be reliably demonstrated (see, e.g., Langan-Fox, Waycott & Albert, 2000; Quealy & Langan-Fox, 1998).

Prediction about multimedia and communications technology needs to be informed, according to Stewart and Williams (1998), by a research framework that focuses attention on the key social, psychological, political, and economic influences on technology as well as the use of technology and the emergence of infrastructures, standards, training, and development.

EMERGING PROBLEMS WITH COMMUNICATION TECHNOLOGIES

Regulating and Controlling Communication

Information flows are changing political, economic, and cultural landscapes and are redefining work, education, and development. Communications is the fastest growing industry in the world due to the transformation of information flows caused by the convergence of telecommunications, information technology, and mass media (Ferguson, 1998). However, the telecommunications revolution is not happening at the same speed everywhere and some areas are gaining competitive advantage because they are quicker to exploit the opportunities (OECD, 1996). National governments and transnational organizations need to include area development in discussions about the future shape of universal service obligations given that these will now need to be applied on both an inter-operator and international basis. Without such policies the provision of advanced communication infrastructures is likely to reinforce existing territorial inequalities (OECD, 1996).

Rapalus (1997) reports that email addresses, internet access, and connectivity to the World Wide Web have added another level of 'threat' to already vulnerable organizations. Although organizations have experienced multiple attacks from both inside and outside, the greatest threat probably comes from inside. Rapalus (1997) recommends that policies and procedures need to be developed to protect information about the system and prevent liability from leaked information.

With today's technology and its associated telecommunications advances, 'knowledge management' (KM) can improve or expand human and technological networks which are capable of harnessing a company's collective expertise and experience. Knowledge management is a relatively new concept and refers to an organization that consciously and comprehensively gathers, organizes, shares, and analyses its knowledge to further its goals (Sunoo, 1999). KSE (knowledge-sharing environment) is a system of information agents for organizing, summarizing, and sharing knowledge from a number of sources: an organization's intranet. Users are organized into closed user groups or communities of interest with related or overlapping interests,

such as members of a project team (Martiny, 1998). The following aspects of KM will be important: retention and expansion of knowledge through sharing among departments; KM forms; and how human resource management can play a role in the use of KM (Greengard, 1998).

Innovation, Computer Networks, and Communication Interaction

Despite the importance of technological changes for corporate vitality, there are documented instances of corporations failing to capitalize on technological opportunities. Garud, Nayyar and Shapira (1997) suggest that innovation outcomes need to be driven by technology entrepreneurs and that organizational change is being carried by the technology. The restructured organization emphasizes the horizontal dimension of organizational communication, suggesting that decentralization can be achieved through the creation of semi-autonomous, specialized work teams that cooperate in interdependent decision making. Thus, networking can allow a large organization to retain characteristics of a small organization (Kovacic, 1994). But, the characteristics of a virtual organization can include employee loneliness, 'infocosms', remote control, and videoconferencing. Indeed, the kind of person who would fit well into the 'virtual' company may need to be specially profiled for selection purposes (Cohen, 1997).

An understanding of communication conflict is necessary if organizations are to run smoother (Benchmark, 1998). Communication media can increase the amount of communication employees receive, potentially reducing conflict and enhancing knowledge and commitment, but influencing perceptions of overload. Research by Kraut and Attewell (1997) suggests that electronic mail effectively spreads organizational information to peripheral employees while interrupting them less than other styles of communication. Using data from a US-based corporation to examine the effects of communication by electronic mail and other media, results showed that employees who used electronic mail extensively were better informed and were more committed to management goals. Electronic mail promoted 'information spillover', without subjecting marginal parties to interruption and information overload (Kraut & Attewell, 1997).

Management of new computer-mediated communication systems needs to avoid the tendency to consider new media only as essential substitutes for traditional communication channels. The new media may well significantly change how, and why, people in organizations communicate (Rice & Steinfield, 1994). For instance, research by Dean and Brass (1985) provided support for the idea that increased social interaction (communication) leads to a convergence of perceptions, such that perceptions are more similar to reality.

Networked computers eliminate the distance factor, which so often interferes with collaboration among workers. However, potential problems include electronic vandalism, fragile systems, and in many cases lack of technology for long-term care and storage of electronic information (Peterson, 1990).

OCCUPATIONAL HEALTH AND WORKING WITH COMMUNICATION TECHNOLOGIES

Work, Structures, and the Quality of Human Relationships

Alienation of humans in the information society can mean the impoverishment of natural communication as direct interpersonal contacts become rarer (Mayer, 1984). However, in other research, Sproull and Kiesler (1991a) demonstrated that although new problems can emerge with computer-based communication, it can create opportunities for new connections among people and stimulate new ways of thinking and working in a less structured environment. Marschan (1996) has suggested that less hierarchical structures encourage the development of personal and horizontal communication networks and that the decentralization process enhances personal communication networks among top managers.

There is encouraging evidence that information technology does positively impact human relationships. Rice and Case (1993) found that within five months of the installation of an integrated office system, 43% of managers reported exchanging messages with people they were previously not in touch with. Patterns of informal role taking can also change. For example, Hiltz and Turoff (1978) showed that participation rates become much more equal among those participating in computer teleconferencing sessions and that strong leaders are less likely to dominate electronic meetings than face-to-face groups. Electronic messaging also seems to make organization members more willing to initiate communication with bosses and their subordinates (Rice, 1984b).

Technostress

With the widespread use of the computer in the workplace, and the sureity that this will increase across all job types, there are problems emerging in occupational health which impact on employee performance and well-being. A growing number of studies conclude that there is 'technostress' related to human–computer interaction and that many stressors are similar to those experienced in blue-collar and automated jobs: high workload, work pressure, diminished job control, inadequate employee training, monotonous tasks, alienation, reduced job satisfaction, poor supervisory relations, job insecurity, lack of employee skill use, high job demands, technology breakdowns/slowdowns, and electronic performance monitoring. VDU problems are influenced by viewing distance, time on task, glare, and lighting. Bergqvist, Wolgast, Nilsson and Voss (1995) found that there were important factors influencing health of their sample of VDT workers who suffered musculoskeletal disorders: opportunities for flexible rest breaks, extreme peer contacts, task flexibility, and overtime, and ergonomic variables such as static work posture, hand position, use of lower arm support, repeated work movements, and keyboard or VDT vertical position. Physiological and psychological technostress includes increased physiological arousal; musculoskeletal system complaints, anxiety, stress perception resulting in increased metabolic activity, eye problems, and fatigue (Aaras, Horgen, Bjorset, Ro & Thoresen, 1998; Arnetz, 1997; Arora, 1994; Berg & Bengt, 1996; Dillon & Emurian, 1996; Hosokawa, Mikami & Saito, 1997; Lindstrom, Leino, Seitsamo & Torstila, 1997; Rechichi, De Mojoa & Scullica, 1996; Schleifer, Galinsky & Pan, 1996; Smith, 1997; Smith et al., 1998; Thomson, 1998; Waluyo, Ekberg & Eklund, 1996).

CONCLUSIONS AND DIRECTIONS FOR RESEARCH

Occupational Health and Technostress

Is there any systematic monitoring of the effects of communication technologies on employees in different jobs and industries? Is there work or information overload, or, any psychological or physiological effect on workers as a consequence of the new technologies or the quickened pace of communication?

There is an accumulating body of work which provides unequivocal evidence that such technologies have effects on employees, such as musculoskeletal disorders, eye strain, fatigue, and so on, and that VDT workers are especially at risk. The full impact of such effects has yet to be realized by organizations, but no doubt given research interest, reports will continue to grow and organizations will need to become more cognizent of such hazards, through education, counselling, prevention programmes, etc.

In times past, when large-scale mechanization of the workplace emerged as the dominant force for change, there was a profound effect on job content which resulted in worker alienation from techology-driven organizational change. We could be at the edge of experiencing similar types of problem in relation to the impact of communication technology. However, we should remember that as we approach the 'brave new world' of electronic communications, we are far more enlightened about the nature of work alienation than we were in those earlier times and the importance of 'factoring in' humanness and individuals into jobs to avoid job dissatisfaction, fatigue, boredom, occupational stress, and other alienating aspects of the workplace. This past work will help inform us about the burgeoning area of 'technostress'. Furthermore, the potential difficulty of recruiting and employing appropriately skilled employees may help to focus the minds of managers on the importance of job variety and interest.

Computing Technology Skills and Employment

Does the workforce have the appropriate skills to maximize opportunities in information technology and to control and regulate communication?

As the information age expands, and knowledge management (KM) is presumably achieved, the most acute problem will not be information overload, but the gap between those individuals who 'can' function in the information society and those who 'cannot' – those who fear to know, refuse to know, or do not have the ability to learn. The literature on computing technologies skills has often been referred to as belonging to younger, not older, segments of the working population who are thought to be highly employable in terms of commitment, work ethic, and job satisfaction but who are least likely to either have or be able to develop, computing skills. Yet, with workforce skill shortages in computing skills, it is anticipated that organizations may be 'forced' to employ older workers to make up skill shortfalls. Retraining and skill upgrading are vital for organizations to continue to be able to take up developments and innovations in the communication technologies. At the present time, reports suggest that the urgency of this need has yet to be grasped.

Knowledge management will remain an issue, as organizations continue to grapple with burgeoning mountains of information. A key issue in their success will be acquiring the skill and expertise to control and develop the intranet.

Efficiency Gains from Communication Technologies

Are workers more effective and productive in their jobs as a consequence of high-speed computing technologies? Insufficient research has been conducted to say with certainty that there are returns on productivity. Organizations have tended to accept as a 'given', productivity gains naturally occurring as a conseqence of new technologies. Most of the research available on this issue remains perceptual, but there is a small amount of research reported by organizations which shows actual productivity gains. Thus the signs of performance increments are there, with much more systematic research needed to establish the actual size, scope, and quality of such improvement. At the same time, there remain difficulties not sufficiently worked out by the organization prior to system implementation. The speed of organizational implementation often impacts on whether a proper evaluation is conducted on the productivity effects of new communication technologies. Such information is also highly sensitive, especially in regard to competitors, and may not be accessible to researchers.

One could hypothesize that the larger the organization, the more crucial is communication effectiveness, and one study reports differences in efficiencies based on organizational size. Like productivity gains, this issue remains to be investigated more thoroughly. It is likely that industry, and communication technology type (e.g., size of networks) will help to determine the importance of organizational size.

Human Relationships

Studies have shown that the great majority of computerization projects fail to meet their deadlines because human factors are not sufficiently taken into account during the planning and implementation phase of the project. The role of goals and values is central to effective interpersonal interactions, as is 'communicating' with computers, for greater accuracy of expression when describing computer activities. Also, the importance of person-to-person contact must be stressed.

Organizational networks are also the primary contextual determinants of conflict activity. When complexity increases, communication networks fragment and lead to different perspectives within units. If this condition is combined with high interdependence, conflict between units increases.

Theorizing Organizations

Weick (1996) sees the organization as an evolving system taking in equivocal information from the environment and using what has been learned. Research needs to investigate the ways in which 'deep structure' (including the 'informal' network), and 'surface structure' (including the 'formal' network) and levels of power and status, guide and constrain the actions and communication of employees. Theoretically, researchers could benefit from examining, in a qualitative sense, user interests, concerns, knowledge, skills, and ideas about productivity and effectiveness of the communication system as well as investigating the dominant cultural values of the organization, and make an assessment of how this corresponds to the existing and anticipated innovations within the system. Such qualitative material could form the basis of the development of a theory which is context and network-based, and which is innovative in its approach to methodology and measurement.

RESEARCHING COMMUNICATION IN ORGANIZATIONS: THE WAY AHEAD

If we look at the gargantuan changes that have occurred in communication in organizations over the past 20–30 years, we have to admit that in comparison, the amount of empirical research in the area is relatively small, especially in the area of industrial–organizational psychology. From a research perspective, the whole area of organizational communication is fraught with difficulty. A huge problem is the sheer pace of change in the technology and the ability of researchers to have knowledge of the anticipated changes, to negotiate and plan a research investigation, and to examine any 'before-and-after' effects. It seems that once one communication system is in place, another is planned and quickly implemented.

Thus, it is suggested that a principal way in which research will systematically occur is if the research is conducted in-house, most benefically together with university researchers. The in-house researcher, perhaps an industrial–organizational, ergonomist or human factor psychologist, could be located within the technical group, or within human resources. Whether such research would find its way into the scientific journals would probably depend on whether such research would contribute to a university credential of some sort. Thus, skill upgrading and credentialling-up is vital not only to individuals and organizations, but also to the body of knowledge existing in the scientific literature. Hopefully, universities will find ways of facilitating such skill upgrades and industry collaboration. If such strategies do not blossom, our understanding of communication in organizations could remain a rather limited one indeed.

ACKNOWLEDGMENTS

This chapter formed part of a larger project funded by Ericsson (Australia) Ltd. The author is indebted to Kathy Armstrong who assisted with literature reviews.

REFERENCES

Aaras, A., Horgen, G., Bjorset, H.H., Ro, O., & Thoresen, M. (1998). Effect of job demands and social support on worker stress: A study of VDT users. *Applied Ergonomics, 29*(5), 335–354.

ABS (1999a). *Australian social trends 1999 – catalogue no. 4102.0.* Canberra, ACT: Australian Bureau of Statistics.

ABS (1999b). *Year book Australia 1999 – catalogue no. 1301.0.* Canberra, ACT: Australian Bureau of Statistics.

Amason, P., & Allen, W.M. (1997). Intraorganizational communication, perceived organizational support, and gender. *Sex Roles, 37*(11–12), 955–977.

Amend, E.H. (1971). *Liaison communication roles of professionals in a research dissemination organisation.* Unpublished doctoral dissertation, Michigan State University, Michigan.

Ancona, D., & Caldwell, D. (1988). Beyond task and maintenance: Defining external functions in groups. *Group and Organisation Studies, 14*(4), 468–494.

Apgar, M. (1998). The alternative workplace: Changing where and how people work. *Harvard Business Review, May–June*, 121–136.

Arnetz, B.B. (1997). Technological stress: Psychophysiological aspects of working with modern information technology. *Scandinavian Journal of Work, Environment and Health, 23*, 97–103.

Arora, S. (1994). A comparative study of VDU-users and VDU-non users on stress, alienation and physical health. *Abhigyan, 84*, 39–44.

Barbera, J. (1996). The intranet: A new concept for corporate information handling. *Proceedings of the International Online Information Meeting.* London: Olympia.

Bavelas, A. (1950). Communication patterns in task-oriented groups. *Journal of Acoustical Society of America, 22*, 725–730.

Benchmark (1998). *Communication for results* [Video]. Aims Media.

Berg, M., & Bengt, A. (1996). An occupational study of employees with VDU-associated symptoms: The importance of stress. *Stress Medicine, 12*(1), 51–54.

Bergqvist, U., Wolgast, E., Nilsson, B., & Voss, M. (1995). The influence of VDT work on musculoskeletal disorders. *Ergonomics, 38*(4), 754–762.

Birrell, J.A., & White, P.N. (1982). Using technical intervention to behavioural advantage. *Behaviour and Information Technology 1*(3), 305–320.

Brass, D. (1985). Men and women's networks. *Academy of Management Journal, 2*, 327–343.

Burrows, B. (1994). The power of information: Developing the knowledge based organization. *Long Range Planning, 27*(1), 142–153.

Buxton, W., Sellen, A., & Sheasby, M. (1997). Interface for multiparty videoconferences. In K. Finn, J. Sellen, & S. Wilbur (Eds.), *Video-mediated communication.* Mahwah, NJ: Lawrence Erlbaum.

Cacioppe, R., & Marshall, V. (1989). Communication between managers and subordinates in the public. *Canberra Bulletin of Public Administration, 59*, 189.

Cohen, S. (1997). On becoming virtual. *Training and Development, 51*(5), 30–37.

Cohen, S. (1998). Knowledge management's killer app. *Training and Development, 52*(1), 50–57.

Cohen, S., & Joseph, D. (1998). *Human resources and the internet.* Ithaca, NY: State University of New York Press.

Conrad, C. (1994). *Strategic organisational communication – toward the twenty-first century.* Orlando, FL: Harcourt Brace.

Crampton, S.M., Hodge, J.W., & Mishra, J.M. (1998). The informal communication network: Factors influencing grapevine activity. *Public Personnel Management, 27*(4), 569–584.

Danowski, J.A., & Edison-Swift, P. (1985). Crisis effects on intraorganizational computer-based communication. *Communication Research, 12*(2), 251–270.

Davie, R.S., & Perry, J.H. (1984). The road to technological survival. *The Journal of the Institution of Engineers Australia, 56*(14), 34–36.

Davis, D.C. (1997). The internet and electronic communication systems in business and industry. *Business Education Forum, 51*(3), 11–14.

Dean, J.W., & Brass, D.J. (1985). Social interaction and the perception of job characteristics in an organization. *Human Relations, 38*(6), 571–582.

Dennis, A.R., Valacich, J.S., & Nunamaker, J.F. (1990). An experimental investigation of the effects of group size in an electronic meeting environment. *IEEE Transactions on Systems, Man, and Cybernetics, 20*(5), 1049–1057.

Dickerson, C.M. (1998). Virtual organizations: From dominance to opportunism. *New Zealand Journal of Industrial Relations, 23*(2), 35–46.

Dillon, T.W., & Emurian, H.H. (1996). Some factors affecting reports of visual fatigue resulting from use of a VDU. *Computers in Human Behaviour* (1), 49–59.

Egido, C. (1990). Teleconferencing as a technology to support cooperative work: Its possibilities and limitations. In J. Galegher, & R. Kraut (Eds.), *Intellectual teamwork: Social and technological foundations of cooperative work.* Hillsdale, NJ: Lawrence Erlbaum.

Eisenberg, E., Monger, P., & Miller, K. (1983). Involvement in communication networks as a predictor of organisational commitment. *Human Communication Research, 10*, 179–201.

Emarketer (1999). *EStats.* Online: http://www.emarketer.com/estats.

Erez, M. (1992). Interpersonal communication systems in organisations, and their relationships to cultural values, productivity and innovation: The case of Japanese corporations. *Applied Psychology: An International Review, 41*(1), 43–64.

Ferguson, K. (1998). World information flows and the impact of new technology: Is there a need for international communications policy and regulation? *Social Science Computer Review, 16*(3), 252–267.

Fisher, D. (1993). *Communication in organisations.* Minneapolis, MN: West.

Friedkin, N. (1983). Horizons of observability and limits of informal control in organizations. *Social-Forces, 62*(1), 54–77.

Fulk, J., & Dutton, W. (1984). Videoconferencing as an organisational information management system: Assessing the role of electronic meetings. *Systems, Objectives and Solutions, 4*, 105–118.

Fuller, R. (1996). Human-computer-human interaction: How computers affect interpersonal communication. In D.L. Day, & D.K. Kovacks (Eds.), *Computers, communication and mental models.* London: Taylor & Francis.

Galati, T. (1986). Electronic communication: Implications for training. *Training-and-Development Journal, 40*(10), 42–45.

Garud, R., Nayyar, P.R., & Shapira, Z.B. (Eds.) (1997). *Technological innovation: Oversights and foresights.* New York: Cambridge University Press.

Gidden, A. (1984). *The constitution of society.* Berkeley, CA: University of California Press.

Gladstein-Ancona, D., & Caldwell, D. (1987). Management issues facing new product teams in high technology companies. *Advances in Industrial and Labor Relations, 4*, 199–221.

Greenbaum, H.H. (1974). The audit of organizational communication. *Academy of Management Journal, 17*, 739–54.

Greengard, S. (1998). Storing, shaping and sharing collective wisdom. *Workforce, 77*(10), 82–84, 86–88.

Hall, E. (1980). *The silent language.* Westport, CT: Greenwood.

Hax, A.C. (1989). Building the firm of the future. *Sloan Management Review*, Spring, 75–82.

Hearn, G. (1992). Video magazine dissemination in large organisations: Why does the cascade freeze? *Australian Journal of Communication, 19*(2), 58–73.

Heath, C., & Luff, P. (1992). Media space and communicative asymmetries: Preliminary observations of video-mediated interaction. *Human Computer Interaction, 7*(3), 315–346.

Hiltz, S.R. (1982). The impact of a computerized conferencing system on the productivity of scientific research communities. *Behaviour and Information Technology, 1*, 185–195.

Hiltz, S.R., & Turoff, M. (1978). *The network nation: Human communication via computer.* Reading, MS: Addison-Wesley.

Hosokawa, T., Mikami, K., & Saito, K. (1997). Basic study of the portable fatigue meter: Effects of illumination, distance from eyes and age. *Ergonomics, 40*, 887–894.

Humble, J.E., Jacobs, S.M., & Van Sell, M. (1995). Benefits of telecommuting for engineers and other high-tech professionals. *Industrial Management, 37*(2), 15–19.

Jacobs, R.C., & Everett, J.G. (1988). The importance of team building in a high-tech environment. *Journal of European Industrial Training, 12*(4), 10–15.

James, D. (1996). Big-stick approaches get a caning from the floor. *Business Review Weekly, 18*(19), 164–165.

Janssens, M., & Brett, J.M. (1994). Coordinating global companies: The effects of electronic communication, organizational commitment, and a multi-cultural managerial workforce. In G. Cooper, L. Cary, & Rousseau, D.M. (Eds.), *Trends in organizational behavior* (pp. 31–46). Chichester, UK: John Wiley & Sons.

Kanungo, S. (1998). An empirical study of organizational culture and network-based computer use. *Computers in Human Behavior, 14*(1), 79–91.

Kelly, T. (1996). Forecasting the mobile communications market: A finger in the airwaves. *International Telecommunications Union*. Online: http://www.itu.int/ti/papers/hkmobile.htm.

Kiesler, S. (1986). The hidden messages in computer networks. *Harvard Business Review*, January–February, 46–60.

King, S., & Cushman, D. (1994). High-speed management as a theoretic principle for yielding significant organisational communication behaviours. In B. Kovacic, *New approaches to organisational communication*. Albany, NY: State University of New York Press.

Klobas, J.E. (1996). Networked information resources: Electronic opportunities for users and librarians. *Internet Research, 6*(4), 53–62.

Knobel, G. (1993). *Telecommuting – the CSIRO experience*. Paper presented at the Telecommunication Conference, Sydney, Australia.

Kovacic, B. (1994). *New Approaches to Organisational Communication*. Albany, NY: State University of New York Press.

Kraut, R.E. (1987). Predicting the use of technology: The case of telework. In R.E. Kraut (Ed.), *Technology and the transformation of white collar work*. Hillsdale, NJ: Lawrence Erlbaum.

Kraut, R.E., & Attewell, P. (1997). Media use in a global corporation: Electronic mail and organizational knowledge. In S. Kiesler (Ed.), *Culture of the Internet* (pp. 323–342). Mahwah, NJ: Lawrence Erlbaum.

Langan-Fox, J. (1996). Validity and reliability of measures of occupational and role stress using samples of Australian managers and professionals. *Stress Medicine, 12*(4), 211–225.

Langan-Fox, J., Code, S., & Langfield-Smith, K. (2000). Team mental models: Methods, techniques and applications. *Human Factors, 42*(2), 1–30.

Langan-Fox, J., & Poole, M.E. (1995). Occupational stress in managerial and professional women. *Stress Medicine, 11*, 113–122.

Langan-Fox, J., Waycott, J., & Albert, K. (2000). Text and graphic advance organizers: Properties and processing. *International Journal of Cognitive Ergonomics, 4*(1), 19–34.

Langan-Fox, J., Wirth, A., Code, S., Langfield-Smith, K., & Wirth, A. (in press). Analyzing shared and team mental models. *International Journal of Industrial Ergonomics*.

Lantz, A. (1998). Heavy users of electronic mail. *International Journal of Human Computer Interaction. 10*(4), 361–379.

Larkin, T.J., & Larkin, S. (1996). Reaching and changing frontline employees. *Harvard Business Review, 74*(3), 95–104.

Leavitt, H. (1951). Some effects of certain communication patterns on group performance. *Journal of Abnormal and Social Psychology, 46*, 38–50.

Lewis, A. (1982) Staff morale – part of every manager's job. *Rydge's October*, 137–138.

Lindstrom, K., Leino, T., Seitsamo, J., & Torstila, I. (1997). A longitudinal study of work characteristics and health complaints among insurance employees in VDT work. *International Journal of Human Computer Interaction, 9*(4), 343–368.

MacDonald, D. (1970). *Communication roles and communication contents in a bureaucratic setting*. Unpublished doctoral dissertation, Michigan State University, Michigan.

Machin, S., Ryan, A., & Van Reenen, J. (1996). *Technology and changes in skill structure: Evidence from an international panel of industries*. Discussion paper 297. London: London School of Economics and Political Science Centre for Economic Performance.

Marschan, R. (1996). New structural forms in multinationals: Decentralization at the expense of personal communication networks? *International Journal of Technology Management, 11*(1&2), 192–206.

Marshall, A., & Stohl, C. (1993). Participating as participation: A network approach. *Communication Monographs, 60*(2), 137–157.

Martiny, M. (1998). Knowledge management at HP consulting. *Organizational Dynamics, 27*(2), 71–77.

Mayer, J. (1984). Clovek 'na daljavo'? [Man 'from a distance'?] *Anthropos, 3*(6), 355–362.

Mechanic, D. (1962). Sources of power and lower participants in complex organisations. *Administrative Science Quarterly, 7*, 349–364.

Mingin, W. (1984–5). The trend toward being: What's after the information age? *Revision, 7*(2), 64–67.

Miniace, J.N., & Falter, E. (1996). Communication: A key factor in strategy implementation. *Planning Review, 24*(1), 26–30.

More, E. (1989). Research perspectives on organisations and new technology. *Australian Technology Review, 3*(5), 17–18.

Morgan, G. (1986). *Images of organisations*. Newbury Park, CA: Sage.

Murray, B. (1999). Technology invigorates teaching, but is the pizzazz worth the price? In *Monitor* (pp. 1, 36–37). Washington, DC: American Psychological Association.

Murry, J. (1997). Job applications using the internet. *Australian Journal of Career Development, 6*(3), 22–24.

Nicholas, D., Williams, P., Martin, H., & Cole, P. (1998). *The media and the internet*. London: Aslib.

Nua Internet Surveys (1997). Online: http://www.nua.ie.

O'Connail, B., & Whittaker, S. (1997). Characterizing, predicting, and measuring video-mediated communication: A conversational approach. In K. Finn, J. Sellen, & S. Wilbur (Eds.), *Video mediated communication*. Mahwah, NJ: Lawrence Erlbaum.

OECD (1996). *OECD workshop on information infrastructure and territorial development*. Organisation for Economic Co-operation and Development, Working paper *46*. Paris: OECD.

Olson, J., Olson, G., & Meader, D. (1997). Face-to-face group work compared to remote group work with and without video. In K. Finn, J. Sellen, & S. Wilbur (Eds.), *Video-mediated communication*. Mahwah, NJ: Lawrence Erlbaum.

Paul Budde Communication (1999). *Global internet market — demographics, revenues, statistics*. Online: http://www.budde.com.au.

Peterson, I. (1990). The electronic grapevine. *Science News*, *138*(6), 90–91.

Pincince, T. (1998). Extranets: Future trends and scenarios. *Telecommunications*, *32*(1), 61.

Pitkow, J., & Kehoe, C. (1996). *GVU (Graphic, Visualisation, and Usability Centre)'s 6th WWW user survey*. Online: http://www.gatech.edu/pitkow/survey/survey-1-1994/survey-paper.html.

Pliskin, N. (1998). Explaining the paradox of telecommuting. *Business Horizons*, *41*(2), 73–78.

Quealy, J., & Langan-Fox, J. (1998). Effectiveness of varying attributes in interactive multi-media in CAI. *Ergonomics*, *41*(3), 257–279.

Rapalus, P. (1997). Security measures for protecting confidential information on the Internet and Intranets. *Employment Relations Today*, *24*(3), 49–58.

Rechichi, C., De-Moja, C.A., & Scullica, L. (1996). Psychology of computer use: XXXVI. Visual discomfort and different types of work at videodisplay terminals. *Perceptual and Motor Skills*, *82*, 935–938.

Rice, R.E. (1984a). Evaluating new media systems. In J. Johnston (Ed.), *New direction for program evaluation* (pp. 53–71). San Francisco: Jossey-Bass.

Rice, R.E. (1984b). Mediated Group Communication. In R.E. Rice et al. (Eds.), *The new media: Communication, research and technology*. Newbury Park, CA: Sage.

Rice, R., & Case, D. (1983). Electronic message systems in the university. *Journal of Communication*, *33*, 131–52.

Rice, R.E., & Steinfield, C. (1994). Experiences with new forms of organisational communication via electronic mail and voice messaging. In J.H.E. Andriessen, & R.A. Roe (Eds.), *Telematics and work*. Hillsdale, NJ: Lawrence Erlbaum.

Richardson, J. (1999). Fear of technology stifles urge to learn. *The Australian* (newspaper), 17 November.

Robins, G., Pattison, P., & Langan-Fox, J. (1995). Group effectiveness: A comparative network analysis of interactional structure and performance in organizational workgroups. Presented at Social Networks Conference, London, July.

Rogers, E.M., & Agarwala-Rogers, R. (1976). *Communication in organisations*. London: Macmillan.

Rossetti, D.K., & Surynt, T.J. (1985). Video-teleconferencing and performance. *Journal of Business Communication*, *22*(4), 25–31.

Salamon, I., & Salamon, M. (1984). Telecommuting: The employee's perspective. *Technological Forecasting and Social Change*, *25*, 15–28.

Salem, P. (1998). *Paradoxical impacts of electronic communication technologies*. Paper presented at the International Communication Association/National Communication Association Conference, Rome, Italy.

Santangelo, G. (1998). *The impact of the information technology revolution on the internationalisation of corporate technology* Discussion papers in international investment and management, Department of Economics, University of Reading.

Schleifer, L.M., Galinsky, T.L., & Pan, C.S. (1996). Mood disturbances and musculoskeletal discomfort: Effects of electronic performance monitoring under different levels of VDT data-entry performance. *International Journal of Human Computer Interaction*, *8*(4), 369–384.

Shaw, M.E. (1954). Some effects of unequal distribution upon group performance in various communication nets. *Journal of Abnormal and Social Psychology*, *49*, 547–53.

Smeltzer, L.R. (1989). Comparison of managerial communication patterns in small, entrepreneurial organizations and large, mature organizations. *Group and Organization Studies*, *14*(2), 198–215.

Smith, M.J. (1997). Psychosocial aspects of working with video display terminals (VDTs) and employee physical and mental health. *Ergonomics*, *40*(10), 1002–1015.

Smith, M.J., Karsh, B.T., Conway, F.T., Cohen, W.J., James, C.A., Morgan, J.J., Sanmders, K., & Zehel, D.J. (1998). Effects of a split-keyboard design and wrist rest on performance, posture and comfort. *Human Factors*, *40*, 324–336.

Soares, A. (1992). Telework and communication in data processing centres in Brazil. In U.E. Gattiker, & R. Stollenmaier (Eds.), *Technology-mediated communication. Technological innovation and human resources* (Vol. 3, pp. 117–145). Berlin, Germany: Walter De Gruyter.

Sproull, L., & Kiesler, S. (1991a). Making connections: Computers can enhance employee commitment — at a cost. *Employment Relations Today*, Spring, 53–70.

Sproull, L., & Kiesler, S.B. (1991b). *Connections: New ways of working in the networked organization*. Cambridge, MA: The MIT Press.

Sproull, L. & Kiesler, S., & McGuire, T.W. (1986). Reducing social context cues! The case of electronic mail. *Management Science*, *32*, 1492–1512.

Steinfield, C.W. (1990). Computer-mediated communications in the organisation: Using electronic mail at Xerox. In B. Sypher (Ed.), *Case studies in organisational communication*. New York: Guilford.

Stevens, P. (1998). *Strategies for electronic career support to employees*. Sydney: Australia Centre for Worklife Counselling.

Stewart, J., & Williams, R. (1998). The coevolution of society and multimedia technology: Issues in predicting the future innovation and use of a ubiquitous technology. *Social Science Computer Review*, *16*(3), 268–282.

Stohl, C. (1995). *Organisational communication — connectedness in action*. London: Sage.

Straus, S.G. (1997). Technology, group process, and group outcomes: Testing the connections in computer-mediated and face-to-face groups. *Human-Computer Interaction*, *12*(3), 227–266.

Sunoo, B.P. (1999). Competitive advantage: How HR supports knowledge sharing. *Workforce*, *78*(3), 30–34.

Telework Analytics International (1999). *Pros and cons.* Online: http://www.teleworker.com.

Thomson, W.D. (1998). Eye problems and visual display terminals: The facts and the fallacies. *Opthalamic and Physiological Optics*, *18*, 111–119.

Ticehurst, B., & Smith, R. (1992). Communication satisfaction, commitment, and job satisfaction in Australian organisations. *Australian Journal of Communication*, *19*(1), 130–144.

Tompkins, P. (1962). *An analysis of communication between headquarters and selected units of a national labor union.* Unpublished doctoral dissertation, Purdue University, Lafeyette, IN.

Tushman, M., & Scanlan, T. (1981). Boundary spanning individuals: Their role in information transfer and their antecedents. *Academy of Management Journal*, *24*, 289–305.

Tutzauer, F. (1985). Toward a theory of disintegration in communication networks. *Social Networks*, *7*(3), 263–285.

Walton, E. (1963). A study of organizational communication systems. *Personnel Administration*, *26*, 46–49.

Walton, R.E. (1989). *Up and running: Integrating information technology and the organization.* Boston, MA: Harvard Business School Press.

Waluyo, L., Ekberg, K., & Eklund, J. (1996). Assembly work in Indonesia and in Sweden: Ergonomics, health and satisfaction. *Ergonomics*, *39*(4), 661–676.

Webmaster (1999). *Intranets – How the web is being used within business.* Online: http://www.cio.com/webmaster.

Weenig, M., & Midden, C.J.H. (1991). Communication network influences on information diffusion and persuasion. *Journal of Personality and Social Psychology*, *61*(5), 734–742.

Weick, K. (1987). Small wins: Redefining the scale of social problems. *American Psychologist*, *39*, 40–49.

Weick, K.E. (1996). *Sensemaking in organizations.* Newbury Park, CA: Sage.

Williams, F., Rice, R., & Dordick, H. (1985). Behavioural impacts in the information age. In B.D. Ruben, & D. Brent (Eds.), *Information and behaviour* (Vol. 1, pp. 161–182). New Brunswick, NJ: Transaction Publishers.

11

Research on Domestic and International Diversity in Organizations: A Merger that Works?

SUSAN E. JACKSON and APARNA JOSHI

This chapter describes five themes that summarize the evolution of diversity research during the past two decades. Research on diversity within a domestic context and research on international diversity are both considered. The chapter reveals the changing emphases in scholarly work over time, as well as differences in the approaches taken by scholars who study domestic and international diversity. The following contrasts are highlighted: concern about complying with laws versus improving organizational effectiveness; examining how members of groups differ versus understanding the interpersonal dynamics that unfold between members of different groups; studies of that focus on a single group attribute versus consideration of the attribute profiles that describe individuals; viewing the dynamics of diversity as generic versus examining how the social and organizational context shapes diversity dynamics; and, focusing on how to manage diversity through individual change versus managing diversity through organizational change. Opportunities for cross-fertilization in research on domestic and international diversity are highlighted.

INTRODUCTION

When studying organizational phenomena, many researchers implicitly assume that employees within an organization are homogeneous. They also assume that the phenomena being studied are unaffected by whether employees are different from each other. Diversity researchers reject both of these assumptions. Their work focuses on questions that arise when the workforce is acknowledged as a heterogeneous mix of people with different backgrounds, experiences, values, and identities. This chapter describes five themes that summarize the evolution of diversity research during the past two decades, as follows:

(I) from complying with laws to improving organizational effectiveness;

(II) from documenting group differences to understanding interpersonal dynamics;

(III) from focusing on single attributes to studying attribute profiles;

(IV) from viewing diversity as generic to understanding diversity in context;

(V) from changing individuals to changing organizations.

Included is research focused on domestic diversity and research focused on international diversity. *Domestic diversity* refers to diversity within a domestic workforce, excluding national differences. *International diversity* refers to diversity among the cultures of different countries.

Historically, research studies on domestic and international diversity evolved independently of each other, but in organizations, both types of diversity are increasingly important. Collaboration among researchers interested in domestic and international diversity is certainly desirable, and perhaps inevitable. An overarching goal of this chapter is to encourage such collaboration.

THEME I: FROM COMPLYING WITH LAWS TO IMPROVING ORGANIZATIONAL EFFECTIVENESS

In the United States, much of the early domestic diversity research grew out of concerns about employment discrimination and workplace fairness. During the past decade, however, a shift has occurred. Now, economic expansion and tight labor markets mean that finding a sufficient number of qualified employees is a major challenge for employers in both the United States and Europe (Chambers, Foulon, Handfield-Jones, Hankin & Michaels, 1998). Consequently, employers who once viewed diversity management activities as a legally driven bureaucratic cost are now seeking to create workplaces where employees from all backgrounds fully utilize their skills and feel personally comfortable.

Laws Stimulated Early Research on Domestic Diversity in the United States

Passage of the *US Civil Rights Act of 1964* made it illegal for US employers to make employment decisions based on information about a person's sex, race, color, religion, or national origin. Several other antidiscrimination laws prohibit the use of other personal characteristics (e.g., age, disability, pregnancy) when making employment decisions. In the United States, organizational research evolved when people believed that unfair discrimination in employment was common. Members of the demographic majority (e.g., men and whites) were assumed to be guilty of discriminating against members of demographic minorities, who in turn were cast into the role of victims. From this world view emerged diversity management practices aimed primarily at eliminating the discriminatory actions taken by members of the majority and, secondarily, developing the coping behaviors of members of the minority. Fear of legal penalties motivated employers to adopt such management practices.

The primary research objective during this period was helping employers develop nondiscriminatory personnel practices. This line of work defined nondiscrimination as basing personnel decisions on valid measures of a person's job qualifications. During the 1960s and well into the 1990s, organizational researchers helped employers develop legally defensible approaches to making personnel

decisions; at the same time, their work informed the development of governmental guidelines for how employers and the judicial system would evaluate evidence when judging whether illegal discrimination had occurred. Indeed, US-based research on diversity became so intertwined with legal concerns that reviews of recent court decisions appeared as research articles in leading psychology research publications (e.g., see Cascio & Bernardin, 1981; Malos, 1998; Varca & Pattison, 1993; Werner & Bolino, 1997). During this early era, little attention was paid to the question of whether these practices had positive consequences for members of the majority or for overall organizational effectiveness.

Improving Organizational Effectiveness is the Focus of Current Domestic Diversity Research

By the dawn of the 21st century, the US workforce had become substantially more diverse than it had been in the early 1960s, especially in terms of sex and ethnicity. Legislation aimed at creating equal employment opportunities was undoubtedly responsible for some of the changing workforce demographics, but so were changing immigration patterns, changing lifestyles, changing economic conditions, and changing business strategies. Furthermore, steady economic growth combined with slower growth in the size of the US labor force has created such a tight labor market that most employers cannot afford to reject job applicants based on irrelevant personal characteristics. Nor can they afford the high turnover costs that result when poorly managed diversity causes disgruntled employees from all backgrounds to leave the organization (e.g., see Morrison & Herlihy, 1992; Tsui, Egan & O'Reilly, 1992). Thus, irrespective of legal regulations, many US employers now view managing diversity as a business necessity (Jackson & Alvarez, 1992).

In fact, little empirical evidence is currently available to show that diversity or diversity management practices directly impact financial success (e.g., see Richard & Johnson, 1999). One exception is a study which found that firms with exemplary diversity programs (specifically, affirmative action programs) performed better as measured by stock prices, compared to firms that had paid legal damages to settle discrimination lawsuits (Wright, Ferris, Hiller & Kroll, 1995). More plentiful are studies that relate diversity to nonfinancial consequences that are believed to affect the bottom line. Two frequently studied intermediate consequences are cohesiveness and creative problem solving.

Cohesiveness

Cohesiveness refers to the degree of interpersonal attraction and liking among members of a group or organization. Under most circumstances, similarity leads to attraction. This is true for a variety of characteristics, including age, gender, race, education, prestige, social class, attitudes, and beliefs (e.g., Berscheid, 1985; Brass, 1984; Byrne, 1971; Cohen, 1977; Ibarra, 1992; Levine & Moreland, 1990; McPherson & Smith-Lovin, 1987; O'Reilly, Caldwell & Barnett, 1989; Riordan & Shore, 1997; Zander & Havelin, 1960).

Positive feelings such as attraction promote helping behavior and generosity, cooperation and a problem-solving orientation during negotiations (for a review, see Isen & Baron, 1991). Attraction may also translate into greater motivation to contribute fully and perform well as a means of gaining approval and recognition (Chattopadhyay, 1999; Festinger, Schachter & Back, 1950). Conversely, employees who believe their employer discriminates against people based on their ethnicity experience stress and low commitment (Sanchez & Brock, 1996).

Turnover

Dissimilarity often promotes conflict (Jehn, 1994; Knight et al., 1999; Pelled, Eisenhardt & Xin, 1999). Longer-term, the conflict associated with diversity may influence one's decision to maintain membership in a group or organization. This was illustrated in a study of 199 top management teams in US banks. During a four-year period, managers in more diverse teams were more likely to leave the team compared to managers in homogeneous teams. This was true regardless of the characteristics of the individual managers, and regardless of how similar a manager was to other members of the team. Simply being a member of a diverse management team increased the likelihood that a manager would leave (Jackson, Brett, Sessa, Cooper, Julin & Peyronnin, 1991). Presumably, more diverse teams experienced greater conflict and were less cohesive (cf. Wagner, Pfeffer & O'Reilly, 1984), creating feelings of dissatisfaction and perhaps increasing the perceived desirability of other job offers.

Several other studies have examined the relationship between team diversity and team turnover rates, and most results support the assertion that diversity is associated with higher turnover rates. In particular, several studies have shown that age and/or tenure diversity correlate with turnover (McCain, O'Reilly & Pfeffer, 1983; O'Reilly et al., 1989; Wagner et al., 1984). Some evidence indicates that the relationship between diversity and turnover holds in cultures as different from each other as the United States, Japan (Wiersema & Bird, 1993), and Mexico (Pelled & Xin, 1997). Not all types of diversity are associated with turnover, however, and even age and tenure diversity are not always correlated with turnover (Webber & Donahue, 1999).

The elevated turnover rates associated with diversity have usually been treated as negative. Under many circumstances, turnover can be disruptive. But turnover can also be beneficial. Over time, repeated exposure to the same people gradually results in the homogenization of attitudes, perspectives, and cognitive schemas; in the process, creative capacity diminishes. Thus, despite the disruption it can cause, turnover creates opportunities for renewal and the continual addition of fresh ideas.

Creative Problem Solving

Creative problem solving refers to activities that require formulating new solutions to a problem and/or resolving an issue for which there is no 'correct' answer. When teams are assigned tasks that require creative problem solving, diversity leads to better performance (Filley, House & Kerr, 1976; Hoffman, 1979; McGrath, 1984; Shaw, 1981). This effect has been found for diversity of many types, including personality (Hoffman & Maier, 1961), training background (Pelz, 1956), leadership abilities (Ghiselli & Lodahl, 1958), attitudes (Hoffman, Harburg & Maier, 1962; Triandis, Hall & Ewen, 1965; Willems & Clark, 1971) gender (Wood, 1987), occupational background (Bantel & Jackson, 1989), and education (Smith, Smith, Olian, Sims, O'Brannon & Scully, 1994).

Diverse perspectives seem to be beneficial on several counts. During the environmental scanning that occurs in the earliest phase of problem solving, people with diverse perspectives can provide a more comprehensive view of the possible issues that might be placed on the group's agenda. Subsequently, discussion among members with diverse perspectives can improve the group's ability to consider alternative interpretations and generate creative solutions that integrate their diverse perspectives. As alternative courses of action and solutions are considered, diverse perspectives can increase the group's ability to foresee all possible costs, benefits, and side-effects. Finally, diversity can enhance the group's credibility with external constituencies, which should improve their ability to implement their creative solutions (e.g., see Cowan, 1986; Hambrick, Cho & Chen, 1996; Jackson, 1992; McLeod & Lobel, 1992; McLeod, Lobel & Cox, 1996; Pearce & Ravlin, 1987; Porac & Howard, 1990; Simon, 1987; Triandis, Hall & Ewen, 1965; Watson, Kumar & Michaelson, 1993).

Legal Considerations and Organizational Effectiveness in International Diversity Research

The prominent role of legal considerations in early US research on domestic diversity contrasts sharply with the minor role of legal considerations in research on cross-cultural differences and international multiculturalism. Instead, due to the high cost of expatriate failure, the overriding focus has been on understanding the reasons for failure in international assignments (Black & Gregersen, 1990; Mendenhall & Oddou, 1986; Shaffer, Harrison & Gilley, 1999), with the hopes of reducing such failures. In the short run, conscientious employers can reduce the stress associated with expatriate assignments if they understand the personal characteristics and organizational conditions associated with such stress. In the long run, finding ways to increase cross-cultural adjustment among expatriates and their families should reduce premature termination of the assignment and thereby improve the organization's ability to achieve its goals (Black & Gregersen, 1990; Deshpande & Viswesvaran, 1992).

Because the costs associated with managing expatriates are both very high and easy to estimate, researchers have invested little effort in empirically documenting the relationship between the practices used to manage expatriates and organizational effectiveness. Nevertheless, some relevant evidence that focuses on the relationship between human resource management practices such as expatriate selection and training and premature expatriate return is beginning to accumulate (Tung, 1981; Teagarden & Gordon, 1995).

Opportunities for New Learning

With respect to the issue of legal compliance, we found few common threads running through the research literature on managing domestic and international diversity. On the other hand, the goal of improving individual and organizational performance is a unifying theme. Historically, this has been a dominant concern in the organizational research on intercultural adjustment and adaptation. More recently, research on domestic diversity has shifted to include this goal. Researchers in these two fields will have many opportunities to learn from each other. Here we suggest just a few areas for mutual exploration.

Managing Fairness in the Global Context
In an international setting, companies face the challenge of navigating through diverse legal systems and cultural milieus. Cultural values, embodied in customs and laws, dictate what is 'fair' and 'right' in the workplace (Schwartz, 1999). The magnitude of variation in what is considered fair is reflected in the differences in antidiscrimination laws worldwide. Corresponding to such differences in laws may be large differences in perceptions of fairness.

Recognizing cultural differences in perceptions of fairness is important because these are related

directly to outcomes such as employee satisfaction and turnover in the domestic context (Korsgaard, Schweiger & Sapienza, 1995). Cultural differences in perceptions of fairness among expatriates and host nationals may be manifested in expatriate managers' treatment of host national subordinates or vice versa, and have consequences for the success of the assignment.

Future organizational research could examine cultural antecedents of fairness perceptions. For instance, studies could address differences in perceptions of fairness among host country nationals and expatriates in relation to outcomes such as turnover among host nationals or premature expatriate return. Based on this research, organizational policies that account for cultural differences in perceptions of fairness and result in the fair treatment of employees in international settings can be formulated.

Managing Perceptions of Competence
Perceptions of competence also may affect success in international assignments. Research on bias and discrimination indicates that the negative outcomes experienced by minority group members often can be traced to majority members' negative beliefs about the competence of minority group members. In the case of expatriates, the minority group members of interest are the expatriates, and the majority group members are the local host-country employees. By extension, it is reasonable to expect that outcomes for expatriates could be improved by adopting management practices aimed at reducing bias and prejudice among the host-country nationals. Research on cross-cultural adjustment has identified host nationals' attitudes toward expatriates as a relevant predictor of expatriates' cross-cultural adjustment (Cox & Tung, 1997; Florkowski & Fogel, 1995; Caligiuri & Tung, 1999).

Majority group members show less bias against members of minority groups when they have information that validates the minority members' task-related competence. Conversely, minority group members show greater confidence in their ability to perform and succeed when they believe that task-related competencies were the primary consideration for selecting them to do the task (e.g., see Heilman, Lucas & Kaplow, 1990; Heilman, Rivero & Brett, 1991; Heilman, McCullough & Gilbert, 1996). Translating this to managing expatriates suggests that expatriates may be more likely to remain in and succeed at their international assignments to the extent that they believe they have the competencies required, and to the extent that host-country locals also believe the expatriate has the competencies required.

One way to establish confidence in an expatriate's competence may be by making the process of expatriate selection more transparent. Although employers usually give considerable attention to task-related competencies during the early phases of expatriate selection, expatriates and host-country employees may be completely unaware of the initial screening criteria. Consequently, host-country employees may assume that the expatriates' experience with the task in other locations is only marginally relevant to performing the task in their specific location.

Other organizational practices, such as career development programs for 'fast track' employees, may further erode the confidence that host-country employees have in the expatriates' abilities. Although career development and learning transfer are worthy objectives, in the minds of host nationals they take the focus away from the expatriate's competence. The unintended consequence may be that both expatriates and their host-country colleagues assume that the expatriate is less qualified than he or she is and should be.

Future research could help organizations develop practices to address the host nationals' attitudes towards expatriates. Such practices should include communications that ensure a clear understanding of the goals of the expatriate assignment among host national counterparts *prior* to the expatriate's arrival in order to reduce misconceptions about the purpose of the assignment and demonstrate alignment between the objectives of headquarters and the subsidiary.

THEME II: FROM DOCUMENTING GROUP DIFFERENCES TO UNDERSTANDING THE INTERPERSONAL DYNAMICS THAT CREATE GROUP DIFFERENCES

The topic of diversity is of interest in part because people believe that group memberships shape our everyday experiences in meaningful and important ways. Two types of differences that have been studied frequently are employment-related outcomes and psychological characteristics. Among the employment outcomes studied have been pay levels, educational attainment, performance, and rates of promotion. Psychological characteristics of interest include skills, abilities, values, personality, and behavioral styles (cf. McGrath, Berdahl & Arrow, 1995).

Documenting Domestic Group Differences in Employment-Related Outcomes

In the United States, documentation of differences in employment-related outcomes followed naturally from the focus on legal compliance, described above. For the US courts, group differences in employment-related outcomes are considered sufficient evidence to suggest that illegal discrimination may be operating. Conversely, if outcomes are similar for members of different demographic groups, fair and equal treatment is presumed. In this context, documenting between-group differences in employment outcomes is a necessary first step that establishes whether there is a phenomenon worthy of further investigation.

Research examining group-based differences in employment outcomes for US workers is vast and impossible to review thoroughly here, so we offer only a few examples to illustrate the general pattern of findings.

Performance

Measures of employee performance serve as the backbone of personnel systems. If group differences in measured performance exist, these effects can be expected to reverberate throughout the span of employees' careers.

Overall, group differences in subjective measures of performance appear to be small yet pervasive. Substantial evidence shows that the job performance of black employees is evaluated as slightly lower compared to white employees for both objective and subjective measures (Ford, Kraiger & Schechtman, 1986; Sackett & DuBois, 1991). Similar patterns have been found for other minority group members, including women and older employees.

Group differences in subjective ratings of performance are not fully explained by actual differences in performance (Arvey & Murphy, 1998). In a large study of military personnel, when peer ratings were used, women were rated lower than men, even when supervisors' ratings revealed no performance differences (Pulakos, Schmitt & Chan, 1996). Regarding age, older workers sometimes receive lower ratings from supervisors, but paradoxically, objective measures of performance indicate that older workers are more productive than their younger colleagues (Waldman & Avolio, 1986).

Career Outcomes

Whereas performance measures show relatively small group-based effects, indicators of career advancement and occupational success reveal larger differences in the outcomes experienced by various demographic of US employees. In general, women and members of most racial and ethnic minority groups advance more slowly in the organizational hierarchy and receive lower pay (Baron & Pfeffer, 1994; Morrison & Von Glinow, 1990; Powell & Butterfield, 1997; Ragins, Townsend & Mattis, 1998). An exception to the general pattern of lower attainment occurs for Asian Americans. For them, the picture is more complex. On the one hand, they generally attain higher levels of education and have higher incomes compared to European Americans and other racio-ethnic groups. On the other hand, compared to European Americans, Asian Americans receive lower returns on their educational attainments (Barringer, Takeuchi & Xenos, 1990; Duleep & Sanders, 1992; Friedman & Krackhardt, 1997; Tang, 1993), as do African American men (Kluegel, 1978; McGuire & Reskin, 1993; Smith, 1997).

For the few who make it to the top of the hierarchy, their experiences depend on who they are. For example, a study comparing men and women executives in comparable jobs within the same industry found that women had less authority, received fewer stock options, and had less international mobility (Lyness & Thompson, 1997). The routes that women take to get to the top may also differ from those of men, with successful women facing and overcoming more developmental barriers than successful men (Ibarra, 1997; Ohlott, Ruderman & McCauley, 1994).

Documenting Domestic Group Differences in Psychological Characteristics

Psychological differences refer to personal characteristics such as personalities, interests, values, and abilities. Certainly, there is evidence of group-based differences in these characteristics. Differences in achievement scores for members of various cultural groups (Ackerman & Humphreys, 1991), which are reflected in the stereotypes held by the American work force (Fernandez, 1988), have been a topic of much concern and debate. Gender and ethnic differences in verbal and nonverbal communication and interpersonal styles are also well documented (Cox, Lobel & McLeod, 1991; Glass, 1992; Tannen, 1990, 1995), as are gender differences in leadership style (Eagly & Johnson, 1990) and influenceability (Eagly, 1983; Eagly & Carli, 1981; Carli, 1989), and age and cohort differences in work attitudes and values (Elder, 1974; Rhodes, 1983; Thernstrom, 1973; Work Attitudes, 1986).

Such group differences may help explain some differences in work-related outcomes. To illustrate, a recent review of research on sex differences in self-esteem showed that men have somewhat higher self-esteem than women, and that this effect is particularly strong in late adolescence (Kling, Hyde, Showers & Buswell, 1999). Similarly, males tend to evaluate themselves more positively than females (Deaux, 1976). Perhaps for this reason they also have higher expectations for the levels of pay they deserve (Jackson, Gardner & Sullivan, 1992). Gender-based differences in pay expectations, in turn, may translate into actual differences in income attainment.

Group-based differences do in fact exist, but the mere existence of such differences is not sufficient reason to conclude that actual differences in psychological characteristics are the sole explanation for differences in work outcomes. For example, Eagly, Makhijani and Klonsky (1992) found that women leaders are evaluated more negatively than their male counterparts even when they have equivalent qualifications. And, whereas data from several million US students indicates that cognitive ability differences between males and females are negligible (Hyde, Fennema & Lamon, 1990; Hyde & Linn, 1988), males are generally perceived as more intelligent than females (Wallston & O'Leary, 1981). Similarly, the evidence indicates that the deteriorating effects of age have little impact on intellectual capacity until the seventh decade of one's life (Labouvie-Vief, 1989), yet managers appear to denigrate employees who are older than the norm for a particular job or position (Lawrence, 1988; see also Tsui, Xin & Egan, 1996) even if they are considerably younger than 70 years of age.

Toward Understanding the Causes of Differential Outcomes

Managers and researchers alike recognize that differences in the outcomes experienced by members of different groups can be created in different ways. Differences in outcomes may be due partly to differences in job qualifications and personal choices about work. But a full understanding of observed group-based differences in work outcomes requires understanding the interpersonal processes through which differential outcomes are created.

Jackson, May and Whitney (1995) developed a model that suggests more specifically how interpersonal processes may help explain the long-term consequences of diversity. As shown in Figure 11.1, Jackson et al.'s framework organizes constructs into four general categories that are linked as follows: aspects of diversity → mediating states and processes → short-term behavioral manifestations → longer-term consequences. They applied their model at three levels of analysis: individual, interpersonal, and team.

In Figure 11.1, short-term behavioral manifestations of diversity refer to observable phenomena, such as communications and the exercising of influence. Such behaviors are the most immediate determinants of longer-term consequences. Communications among team members are viewed as particularly important. Through their communications, employees manage information, tangible resources (e.g., equipment, tools, money), and human resources (e.g., skills, effort). To do so, they must exercise influence over each other. Influence communications, engaged in for the purpose of changing the attitudes, values, beliefs, and behaviors of others, are particularly potent, which is why they are highlighted in Jackson et al.'s model.

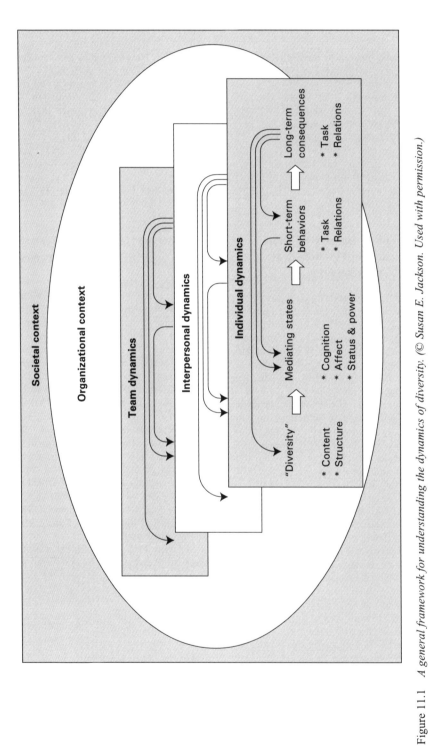

Figure 11.1 *A general framework for understanding the dynamics of diversity.* (© *Susan E. Jackson. Used with permission.*)

Observable behaviors are shaped by mediating states and processes, which describe the way people feel and think about themselves and each other. Included are feelings (e.g., attraction, discomfort, and admiration) as well as cognitive structures (e.g., mental models and stereotypes). Also included are social structures that reflect relationships between and among employees (e.g., status and power hierarchies).

The value of models such as the one shown in Figure 11.1 is that they suggest how the wide array of research findings related to diversity might be understood by focusing on a few fundamental phenomena. Here we attempt to illustrate this point by focusing on just three such phenomena: attraction, communication, and status.

Attraction

Regardless of the basis for identifying people as similar (members of an in-group) or dissimilar (members of an out-group), similarity and the attraction it creates shape how people behave toward each other. Loyalty and favoritism characterize interactions with similar, in-group members, while distrust and rivalry characterize interactions with dissimilar out-group members. The tendency to be attracted to and biased in favor of similar others is so pervasive that it operates even when people judge their similarity based on meaningless information (such as randomly determined group membership). Minimal and arbitrary categorizations lead people to rate members of their own group as more honest and cooperative. Not surprisingly, categorization as an in-group member also results in gaining more resources from other members of the group and in greater cooperation (Brewer; 1979; Kramer & Brewer, 1984; Tajfel, 1978).

A bias that favors similar others also appears to affect evaluations within organizations. Managers tend to rate subordinates who are the same gender more favorably and also report liking them more (Larwood & Blackmore, 1978; Tsui & O'Reilly, 1989). Similarity in age and job tenure also correlate with greater liking (Judge & Ferris, 1993).

Communication

Through communication behaviors, feelings can be translated into group-related differences in work outcomes. In general, communication networks are characterized by demographic homogeneity (Brass, 1984; Hoffman, 1985; Lincoln & Miller, 1979). For example, work-related communications between men and women are less frequent in units that are more diverse with respect to sex (South, Bonjean, Markham & Corder, 1982). Formal and informal meetings among peers and with immediate subordinates are lower in racially diverse groups (Hoffman, 1985). And age and tenure similarities between coworkers predicted levels of communication among project teams of engineers (Zenger & Lawrence, 1989).

Two categories of communication prevalent in organizations are task-related communication and relations-oriented communication.[1] Through task-related communication, members of an organization seek, offer, and negotiate for work-related information and resources (Jackson et al., 1995). Each person's access to information and resources, in turn, has important consequences for their performance as well as their ability to take advantage of personal and career-enhancing opportunities within the organization. Through relations-oriented communications, employees seek, offer, and receive social information and support. These in turn can facilitate (or hinder) a person's ability to form meaningful friendships and cope effectively with the challenges of organizational life coping.

Communication networks can be valuable resources for advancing a career. Employees who have contact with people in positions of power can gain power themselves and are more likely to be promoted (Brass, 1984). Communication networks that bridge a person to other firms and professional associations contribute to income attainment above and beyond the effects of other indicators of human capital (Boxman, De Graaf & Flap, 1991). People at the center of communication networks control more information and resources than do others, and also enjoy more career-related opportunities and benefits than others who are less centrally located (e.g., see Ibarra & Andrews, 1993; Rice, 1993).

Although research on networks is still in its infancy, it seems probable that differences in communication patterns and networks account for some of the differences in work-related outcomes experienced by members of different groups (see Ibarra & Smith-Lovin, 1997). Communication networks make it possible for employees to translate their human capital into positive work outcomes. When seeking new jobs or promotions, a wide range of network contacts can facilitate the process of locating desirable job openings. Communication networks also shape the amount and type of feedback and advice employees receive regarding their daily performance and career opportunities (cf. Friedman, 1996; Friedman & Krackhardt, 1997). The importance of communication networks partly explains why many employers have organized and supported employee networking or caucus groups targeted to specific employee populations, such as females, Hispanic Americans, and gays and lesbians (e.g., see Friedman, 1996; Friedman, Kane & Cornfield, 1998; Sessa, 1992).

Status

Even in the flattest organizations, some employees enjoy more status than others. Status, in turn, gives people power to wield influence and thereby determine resource allocation decisions. In the United States, decades of national opinion polls and psychological research on prejudice and discrimination show that the status attributed to individuals corresponds to their sex, age, and ethnicity (Jaffe, 1987; Johnston & Packer, 1987; Katz & Taylor, 1988; Kraly & Hirschman, 1990; *Chronicle of Higher Education*, 1992). Unfortunately, the workplace is not immune to these status attributions.

Status characteristics theory (SCT) specifies the processes through which evaluations of, and beliefs about the characteristics of team members become the basis of observable inequalities in face-to-face social interactions (Berger, Rosenholtz & Zelditch, 1980). Status characteristics can be specifically relevant to the task at hand (e.g., mathematical ability in a mathematical problem-solving group), or people may judge each other based on characteristics that have little to do with actual competence. According to SCT, differences in status characteristics create status hierarchies within groups. Sessa and Jackson (1995) referred to this as vertical differentiation. They argued that vertical differentiation helps explain why observed decision-making processes seldom fit an idealized, rational model. Due to status differences, available resources may not be identified and used during group decision making (Bottger & Yetton, 1988; Stasser & Titus, 1985).

The dysfunctional effects of status characteristics are likely to be greatest when low-status individuals have resources or expertise that the workgroup needs to perform their task, and high-status people do not. Compared to those with lower status, higher-status persons display more assertive nonverbal behaviors during communication: speak more often, criticize more, state more commands, and interrupt others more often; have more opportunity to exert influence, attempt to exert influence more, and actually are more influential (Levine & Moreland, 1990). Consequently, lower-status members participate less. Because the expertise of lower-status members is not fully used (Silver, Cohen & Crutchfield, 1994), status differences inhibit creativity and contribute to process losses (Steiner, 1972).

Status characteristics also create dissatisfaction and discomfort. Initially, group members behave more positively toward higher-status members (Ridgeway, 1982). Low-status team members often elicit negative responses from others and because of their low status they must absorb the negative reactions rather than respond and defend their positions (Ridgeway & Johnson, 1990).

In this section, we have provided a sampling of the research on three phenomena – attraction, communication, and status – that help explain some group-based differences in work outcomes for domestic US workers. Next we consider international differences and their consequences for interpersonal dynamics in organizations.

Documenting International Differences in Values

'Culture' has been defined as the 'human made part of the environment (that) includes both objective elements – tools, roads, appliances and subjective elements – categories, associations, beliefs, attitudes, norms, roles and values' (Triandis, 1993: 111). Differences in values have received the most attention. Hofstede (1980, 1982, 1991) developed the most extensively cited typology for describing value differences. Based on a survey of employees of a single organization across 60 countries in different time periods, Hofstede ranked countries according to their placement on the cultural dimensions of power distance, uncertainty avoidance, individualism, and masculinity. Subsequently, Hofstede's typology was extended to include a fifth dimension. Labeled Confucian dynamism, this dimension captures differences in the value attached to thrift, persistence, and a long-term time perspective (Hofstede & Bond, 1988). Research on international diversity has relied heavily on these rankings, which have since been validated in other organizational settings (Triandis, 1993).

More recently, using data from more than 40 countries, Schwartz (1999) identified seven cultural types by considering three value dimensions: conservatism versus autonomy, hierarchy versus egalitarianism, and harmony versus mastery over the environment. These dimensions relate to individuals' relationships to the group/community as well as individuals' relationships to the social context (Schwartz, 1999). A third conceptualization of cultural differences was proposed by Fiske (1992), who proposed four 'modes' of social relationships: communal sharing, authority ranking, equality matching, and market pricing. These four modes of social relationships influence individuals' values and are manifested in individuals' behaviors.

Research on international differences has shown that values predict behavioral outcomes such as communication, decision making, and leadership (Triandis, 1993). As in the domestic setting, however, the documentation of such international differences is of limited benefit to organizations. A deeper understanding of the interpersonal dynamics and behavioral outcomes affected by these differences is needed in order to develop organizational interventions that improve the outcomes of individual employees and those of the organization as a whole.

Toward Understanding the Consequences of International Differences in Values

In organizations that aim at expanding business globally, multinational teams are a necessity and their effective functioning is a primary concern (Snow, Davison, Snell & Hambrick, 1996). Thus, an understanding of how international diversity affects communication, decision making, and leadership dynamics in such teams should prove useful to global organizations.

Communication

In multicultural workgroups, knowledge transfer and information exchange are often key objectives, but cultural differences in communication behaviors can impede knowledge transfer. Cultural differences can arise in any of the five phases of communication: encoding, sending, receiving, decoding, and feedback (Gibson, 1999a; Triandis, 1989). For example, during encoding, cultural values (e.g., individualism or masculinity) may influence choices about the best source for a message, the message content, and the style of presentation. In cultures that emphasize collectivism rather than individualism, messages are more likely to refer to external sources of information, display empathy and emotions towards others in the group, and emphasize the collective entity rather than the individual (Hofstede, 1980; Gibson, 1999a). When received by colleagues whose values emphasize individualism, such messages may be less persuasive or have unintended consequences that create misunderstanding or inefficient knowledge transfer.

Team Decision-Making Processes

For teams involved in problem solving and decision making, international diversity creates challenges that are both similar to and distinct from those created by domestic diversity. Ilgen and his colleagues proposed that a team's cultural composition influences three aspects of decision making: the definition of the problem, the sharing of information, and conflict or consensus (Ilgen, LePine & Hollenbeck, 1999). Others have suggested that in-group–out-group identification based on nationality or culture may be related to conflict and formation of cliques, and ineffective information sharing (Armstrong & Cole, 1996). Earley and Mossakowski (2000) found that international diversity can be detrimental to team functioning early in the life of a team. However, given enough time, very diverse multinational teams in which there is no opportunity for nationality-based cliques to form can overcome these problems and outperform more homogeneous teams in the long run.

Leadership

Ultimately, the challenge of dealing with cultural differences in communication and decision making rests with leaders who manage and provide direction to groups characterized by international diversity. The GLOBE Project, a recent large-scale study of leadership, suggests that some attributes of effective leaders are culturally unique, while others are universal (Hartog, House, Hanges, Dorfman & Ruiz-Quintanilla, 2000). Research also indicates that the cultural orientations of followers can influence what effect a leadership style has on performance and motivation (Jung & Avolio, 1999). Thus, in culturally diverse groups, effective leadership is particularly challenging.

Studies such as those described above point to the salience of cultural differences as determinants of interpersonal dynamics within workgroups. Clearly, additional research could prove beneficial for improving our understanding of these processes and for suggesting organizational practices to enhance the effectiveness of culturally diverse workgroups.

THEME III: FROM FOCUSING ON A SINGLE ATTRIBUTE TO STUDYING ATTRIBUTE PROFILES

As already noted, early diversity research often focused on documenting differences between demographically defined groups. These early studies usually focused on only one attribute (e.g., men compared to women *or* African Americans compared to European Americans). Then came studies that examined subgroups created by considering two attributes at a time (e.g., African-American men compared to European-American men). Similarly, early cross-cultural studies generally focused on a single attribute–nationality. Recent work recognizes that identities are more complex. To fully describe a person requires assessing an entire profile of attributes.

The Content of Diversity

In everyday language, the term diversity is widely used within the United States, and increasingly within Europe, to refer to the gender, ethnic, and age composition of an organization's workforce. More recently, the meaning of diversity has broadened to include many other attributes. Because the term diversity can refer to so many different aspects of workforce composition, it is useful to organize the types of diversity found in organizations into the simple two-dimensional taxonomy shown in Table 11.1. In this taxonomy, the attributes that create diversity are categorized as *readily detected* or *underlying*, and as either *task-related* or *relationship-oriented* (Jackson et al., 1995).[2] Together, readily detected and underlying attributes contribute to the *total* diversity present in a team. To fully understand how diversity affects the functioning of organizations, the interpersonal dynamics associated with task-related diversity *and* relationship-oriented diversity must be considered.

Table 11.1   *A taxonomy for describing the content of diversity*

	Attributes that are more likely to be task-related	Attributes that are more likely to be relationship-oriented
Readily detected attributes	Department/unit membership Organizational tenure Formal credentials and titles Education level Memberships in professional associations	Sex Socioeconomic status Age Race Ethnicity Religion Political memberships Nationality Sexual orientation
Underlying attributes	Knowledge and expertise Cognitive skills and abilities Physical skills and abilities	Gender Class identity Attitudes Values Personality Sexual identity Racial identity Ethnic identity Other social identities

The examples shown are illustrative, not exhaustive. Adapted from Jackson et al. (1995), with permission.

Readily detected attributes can be determined quickly and consensually with only brief exposure to or a little knowledge about the person. Attributes that can be readily detected include organizational and team tenure, department or unit membership, formal credentials and education level, sex, race, ethnicity, and age. *Underlying attributes* are less obvious, more difficult to verify, and subject to more interpretation and construal. Furthermore, some attributes may be particularly relevant to work tasks, while others are important primarily because they affect the social relationships within an organization. Some attributes are more often task relevant than others. However, all attributes are *potentially* relevant to a specific task situation. Whether or not a particular attribute is *actually* relevant to the task at hand depends completely on the task.

Researchers have often assumed that readily detected attributes are associated with task-related underlying attributes (Hambrick & Mason, 1984; Lawrence, 1997). For example, an automotive design team that is occupationally diverse (e.g., it includes a purchasing manager, a market researcher, an R&D engineer and a foreman from the manufacturing plant) would be expected to make better design decisions than a more homogeneous team *because* of the diversity of task-relevant knowledge, skills, and abilities they presumably would bring to the task. Regarding relationship-oriented attributes, a common assumption is that readily-detected indicators of race (e.g., skin, hair, and facial features) are highly correlated with racial identities. Similarly, physical indicators of a person's sex are assumed to be highly correlated with gender identity. A more nuanced understanding recognizes that identities

are socially constructed and malleable (e.g., Frable, 1997; Nkomo, 1992, 1995; Helms, 1990; Hogg & Terry, 2000). Although some readily detected attributes are empirically correlated with some underlying attributes, the correlations are far less than one.

Managers often assume that task-related attributes are powerful determinants of behavior and outcomes in organizations and that relationship-oriented attributes play only a minor role. As described above, however, relationship-oriented attributes shape behavior even when they are not associated with task-related attributes. Relationship-oriented attributes trigger stereotypes that influence the way people think and feel about themselves and others, what information is attended to, who talks to whom, and who has the most influence in decision-making processes.

Whereas managers may tend to overestimate the importance of task-related attributes, organizational researchers may tend to overestimate the importance of underlying attributes. Many researchers have used readily detected attributes to assess diversity, but they do so with apologies, noting that convenience and economic considerations are the primary reasons for assessing these attributes rather than the underlying attributes with which they are presumably correlated (Hambrick & Mason, 1984). Consistent with the reasoning that underlying attributes are the more important determinants of behavior, Lawrence (1997) chastized organizational researchers for studying readily detected attributes and failing to assess underlying attributes. While this criticism is valid, it would be a mistake to assume that readily detected attributes are useful merely as convenient, imperfect indicators of underlying attributes. Rather, to fully understand diversity and its consequences, it may be necessary to assess and study all categories of attributes shown in Table 11.1.

Attribute Profiles

The need to assess more than one or two attributes in any particular study is widely recognized, and many studies of domestic diversity measure at least several readily detected attributes. However, when analyzing their data, researchers usually consider each attribute independently. For example, in a study of mentoring relationships, Ragins and Scandura (1997) measured several attributes, but they focused on the effects of gender alone; the other measured attributes were used as control variables.

Researchers seldom consider the consequences of different combinations of attributes. The one major exception to this generalization is research that considers the combined effects of race or ethnicity and sex. When race and sex are studied in combination, one of two approaches is typically used. One approach involves grouping the study participants into discrete categories (e.g., black men, white men, black women, and white women) and then studying each category separately. A second approach uses statistical procedures to test for significant race × sex interactions. A study that examined affirmative action attitudes illustrates the potential value of assessing several attribute dimensions and examining interactions among them (Thomas, Williams, Perkins & Barosso, 1997). In addition to self-reported race and gender, Thomas et al., measured ethnic identity. Their results revealed that ethnic identity moderated the relationship between race and affirmative action attitudes. Their results seemed to indicate that gender played no role in predicting affirmative action attitudes. A profile approach was also used by Friedman and Krackhardt (1997) in a study of career mobility among Asian Americans. Their results showed that profiles of ethnicity and education attributes (measured as interaction terms) predicted employees' locations within communication networks and their supervisors' ratings of career mobility. In another recent study, Jehn, Northcraft and Neale (1999) found that task-related diversity interacted with relations-oriented diversity to affect team performance and efficiency.

Surprisingly, however, in all of the studies just cited, the authors limited their analyses to two-way interactions rather than considering all possible profiles of attributes. There are two plausible explanations for the dearth of research using attribute profiles. An abundance of technical problems associated with data analysis and interpretation is one reason. A lack of adequate theory to guide the

research is another reason. Many of the technical problems that would arise if researchers used attribute profiles are due to problems of measurement and statistical power. These practical considerations are not trivial. However, given sufficiently interesting questions, resourceful researchers would undoubtedly find satisfactory ways to address such problems. We believe that lack of adequate theorizing has been the more significant barrier to more sophisticated profile analysis.

This state of affairs may change soon, due in part to a recent theoretical paper describing the potential importance of demographic 'faultlines.' Lau and Murnighan (1998) argue that the array of attributes across members of a group determine the strength of faultlines within the group. Strong faultlines occur when attributes are aligned in a way that creates natural coalitions. As an extreme example, a group would have a strong faultline if it were composed of two 50-year-old European-American salesmen and two 30-year-old Asian-American female marketeers. Faultlines would be much weaker if the attributes in the group were cross-cutting (see Brewer, 1995) so that task-related and relationship-oriented attributes were not aligned. Lau and Murnighan (1998) argue that faultlines affect groups in a variety of ways. For example, they may increase the probability that stable cliques or subgroups will form and become polarized. The presence of polarized subgroups, in turn, may shorten the sensemaking processes that groups engage in.

Attribute profiles have also been suggested as important determinants of employee stress. Sociologists have argued that stress is created by status inconsistencies across one's array of personal attributes (Bacharach & Bamberger, 1992). For example, Jackson (1962) found that stress symptoms were higher among people who were members of high-status (majority) racial groups but had low educational and occupational status. Due to the stress they create, status inconsistencies within one's attribute profile may also predict dissatisfaction, organizational withdrawal, and performance (Bacharach & Bamberger, 1992; Holmes & Butler, 1987).

Finally, recent research on the emergence of leaders points to the value of considering attribute profiles. Numerous studies of leadership behavior suggest that in mixed gender groups, men tend to emerge as leaders more often than women. Critics of this line of research note that the tasks used in leadership research often are relatively masculine. Thus, the typical research design inadvertently favored the males because, in effect, males were more likely to have the *task-related* knowledge and expertise needed to assume a leadership role. In an experiment designed to test this reasoning, Karakowsky and Siegel (1999) found support for the conclusion that leadership behaviors are best predicted by taking into account a person's profile of relationship-oriented (sex and gender) and task-related (knowledge) attributes.

From Single Attributes to Attribute Profiles in the International Context

Earlier in the chapter we summarized research on cross-national differences in employee values and behavior. Here we attempt to extend the theme of understanding attribute profiles to international diversity research. Because the existing research on international diversity seldom fits with this theme, we focus on outlining directions for future research.

The Content of International Diversity

As in the case of domestic diversity, international diversity may be viewed as encompassing both readily detected and underlying attributes. Nationality is readily detected, while cultural values represent underlying attributes. Researchers have often assumed that nationality is strongly correlated with cultural values (Gibson, 1999b; Jung & Avolio, 1999; Kirkman & Shapiro, 1997). This assumption is easily justified, given the results of past research by scholars such as Hofstede, Schwartz, and Fiske, which was summarized above. However, when nationality is treated as the attribute of interest, the complexity of national differences is often ignored. For example, consider a study designed to examine the role of individualism within groups. Because individualism is known to be lower in Asian countries and higher in the United States, the researchers compared Caucasian and Asian students. They interpreted their findings as supporting the important role of individualism. But the Caucasian and Asian students almost certainly differed on other values, other behavioral styles, and so on. Because nationality was the only attribute measured, however, the role of specific underlying attributes that tend to be related to nationality could not be assessed.

Attribute Profiles

Research using attribute profiles is rare in the domestic context, but it is virtually nonexistent in the international context. Yet, research on cultural differences makes it clear that nationality is only a weak indicator of underlying values. Furthermore, it is likely that other readily detected attributes, such as age and religion, combine with nationality in important ways to influence individual and group behavior. For example, in a multinational team, the experiences of lower-status Japanese females are likely to differ substantially from those of higher-status Japanese males. To assume that all Japanese team members have similar attitudes and engage in similar behaviors is too simplistic to enable a full appreciation of how intercultural diversity

will affect the workgroup. Indirect evidence for attribute profiles may be found in research on female expatriates that indicates that high-ranking married female expatriates may face fewer challenges in overseas locations (Caligiuri, Joshi & Lazarova, 1999).

Researchers who wish to consider attribute profiles in their studies of international diversity face challenges similar to those faced in domestic diversity research. Apart from methodological constraints (such as small sample sizes), the lack of adequate theory building is a theme that parallels research in a domestic context. Considerable effort and ingenuity will be needed to close these theoretical and methodological gaps.

THEME IV: FROM VIEWING DIVERSITY AS GENERIC TO STUDYING DIVERSITY IN CONTEXT

The proliferation of research on diversity in recent years has made one fact increasingly clear: the dynamics of diversity are difficult to specify. The observed effects sometimes vary markedly from one study to the next. Even where a general pattern of findings is established, studies that don't support that pattern usually can be found in the published literature. As a consequence of the great variation in effects found across studies, researchers cannot be certain that they understand phenomena well enough to justify making prescriptive statements about how to effectively manage diversity.

As research on diversity moved out of laboratory settings and into organizations, it became painfully obvious that diversity's consequences are shaped in part by subtle features of the task, the group or team context, by the larger organizational context, and even by the changing societal context. For example, after reviewing evidence regarding the relationship between group composition and performance, Jackson (1992b) concluded that diversity appears to be beneficial to performance on tasks that require creativity and judgment, but it was less clear that diversity is beneficial for routine tasks that required maximum speed. Several studies also suggest that team longevity plays an important role. For example, Harrison, Price, and Bell (1998) found that the effects of readily detected attributes (i.e., race, gender etc.) are 'neutralized' over a period of time. Pelled et al. (1999) also found that the effects of demographic attributes diminished over time as people worked together in a team. Many more years of research will be needed to achieve a good understanding of how context shapes diversity's consequences. The fastest progress is likely to occur regarding the group- or team-level effects, as this is already an active topic of research.

Groups and Teams as Context in Domestic Diversity Research

To this point, our discussion has focused on issues related to how people from different backgrounds respond to each other, and the consequences that such intergroup dynamics have for individuals and organizations. In much of this research, the social unit studied has been the dyad, such as a supervisor and subordinate or two peers. For dyads, similarities and differences appear to drive the dynamics of interaction (see Theme II). Somewhat surprisingly, however, perceptions of similarity and difference are not easy to predict. Similarity and difference are relative, not absolute, and their meaning is construed within a larger social context (Chatman, Polzer, Barsade & Neale, 1998; Ely, 1995).

Many different configurations of attributes can be present in a team, and demographic configurations can be powerful determinants of self and other perceptions, feelings about the group as well as communication and influence processes. The dynamics within a team that is completely homogeneous can be quite different from those within a team that is nearly homogeneous but includes a 'token' or 'solo' member (see Kanter, 1977). The experiences of a solo member can be quite different from the experiences of members of a small minority faction (i.e., two members who are similar to each other but distinctly different from the other members of a team). Finally, the members of a small faction will have different experiences than members of a faction within a completely bipolarized team made up of two equal-size coalitions.

The amount and nature of team diversity appear to be especially important to understanding conflict. Blalock (1967) argued that an increase in the proportionate size of a minority faction threatens the majority faction's power and access to scarce resources. The result is increased competition between the factions, and increased discrimination by the majority against the minority, at least up to a point. When the minority faction reaches a sufficient size, however, they are able to effectively combat such behavior, which lessens its effects (e.g., see Tolbert, Andrews & Simons, 1995).

Two widely recognized types of conflicts that arise in teams are relationship conflicts and task conflicts. Relationship conflicts can arise because team members have differing values (Jehn, 1994; Pelled, 1996) or simply because team members rely on readily detected attributes to define others as members of an in-group or out-group (cf. Pelled, 1996). Regardless of the source of relationship conflicts, they often result in negative outcomes such as absenteeism, turnover, low satisfaction and commitment, and poor performance (Baron, 1991; Jehn, 1995; Jehn, Chadwick & Thatcher, 1997; Thatcher, 1999).

Task conflict involves disagreements that are directly related to performing the task. Presumably, teams characterized by task-related diversity experience more task-related conflict (Pelled, 1996). Such conflict appears to improve performance when team members understand how to manage it effectively (Bottger & Yetton, 1988; Jehn, 1997). In a study of 57 top management teams, for example, task-related diversity was beneficial to company performance for teams that also engaged in vigorous debate, but diversity without debate was of little value (Simons, Pelled & Smith, 1999).

The evolving consensus among researchers who study conflict is that the types and amounts of diversity present in a team create a context within which conflict about relationships and the task unfold. Similar conclusions about diversity-as-context have been voiced by researchers studying other group phenomena. For example, a study of leadership behaviors in mixed gender groups found that being in the minority in terms of gender does not have the expected negative consequences for people who are in the majority in terms of task-related attributes (Karakowsky & Siegel, 1999). In other words, task-related diversity provides a context that shapes the effects of relations-oriented diversity. As another example, a study of social influence within top management teams suggests that the diversity context moderates the extent to which executives are likely to change each other's beliefs about the determinants of success in their business (Chattopadhyay, Glick, Miller & Huber, 1999).

The studies discussed so far in this section have focused on the relationship between diversity and teams' functioning from an internal perspective. An internal perspective implies that team characteristics (e.g., team composition, team task) are the major determinants of team experiences and outcomes. In contrast, an external perspective suggests that a team's relationships with other units within the organization are also significant predictors of team outcomes (Ancona & Caldwell, 1992). Teams that engage in effective boundary spanning behavior perform better and are viewed as more successful in the organization (Ancona & Caldwell, 1992; Gladstein, 1984). Ancona and Caldwell (1998) have argued that task-related diversity (i.e., tenure and function) influences team members' relationships outside the team. A similar argument may be made to incorporate relations-oriented diversity (i.e., race, age, gender). For example, Jackson (1992a) suggested that top management teams may be better able to persuade their constituents of the wisdom of their decisions if the team's demographic profile is similar to that of their constituents.

The Societal Context in Domestic Diversity Research

It is within the context of society that individuals are socialized to exhibit behaviors 'appropriate' to their membership in demographic groups, and it is within this context that individuals first learn to respond differentially to members of different demographic groups (see Maccoby & Jacklin, 1974; Jacklin, 1989). In addition, events in society – including new legislation, local politics, and nationally organized demonstrations – can stimulate changes in intergroup relations in the workplace (see Alderfer, 1992; Sessa, 1992).

The consequences of gradual societal changes can be profound. For example, the identity preferences of African-American children have changed substantially during the past several decades (Cross, 1991). During the 1940s and 1950s, African-American children generally showed a preference for a white identity. During the 1960s, social activists invested heavily in efforts to change the negative connotations of black identity, and these efforts proved to be effective. By the 1970s, African-American children showed a preference for a black identity. The children of the 1960s are the employees of the present, and the ethnic identities they developed as children are now shaping organizations in ways that contrast sharply with earlier generations. The historical shifts that occur within societies mean it can be risky to assume that results from the past generalize to the future.

Intergroup conflict and power struggles that occur at the societal level also shape the consequences of diversity within organizations. For example, in Northern Ireland and Quebec, opposing groups have been struggling for years over fundamental governance issues. These societal-level political struggles constrain the conversations and formation of relationships among neighbors and business partners alike (Pettigrew, 1998). To date, however, domestic diversity research has paid very little attention to the role that societal context plays in shaping the dynamics of diversity. The role of societal context has traditionally received greater attention in studies of international diversity. On the other hand, team contexts remain relatively ignored in this literature.

Groups and Teams as Context in International Diversity Research

With technological advances and organizational compulsions to deliver high-quality products within limited time frames, multinational, geographically dispersed team emerged (DeMeyer, 1991; Snow et al., 1996). How do multinational teams overcome linguistic, cultural, and often geographic barriers to form a team-level identity and function effectively? Armstrong and Cole (1996) found that in multinational dispersed teams, members tended to identify primarily with people who they met face to face and with whom they regularly communicated. Team members would not consider others located in remote sites, who they did not interact with regularly, as part of the same team. This led to strong subgroup identities and weak team-level identities. With regard to leadership, DeMeyer (1991) notes that, in an international context, team leaders must be able to integrate external information and translate it to the teams' needs. DeMeyer's (1991) research on international R&D labs indicates that the team leader may need to play the role of 'information gatekeeper' and monitor external information while facilitating information exchange within the team. These studies provide some indication of the challenges associated with a multinational team context.

Organizational Context

Approaches to globalization are dictated by the nature of the market, products and technology, and industry (Schuler, Dowling & DeCieri, 1993). In their efforts to exercise control over subsidiaries, ethnocentric companies rely on expatriates for staffing their operations overseas. In these companies international diversity in the subsidiary consists of two predominant national/cultural groups – the home-country nationals and the host-country nationals. As already explained, this bimodal distribution may set the stage for significant conflict to arise. By comparison, polycentric companies with decentralized worldwide operations may face relatively fewer challenges arising out of international diversity, because the workforces in its subsidiaries will be mostly host-country nationals. In geocentric companies, which employ the best talent available regardless of where it may be located, workgroups include home-country, host-country, and/or third-country nationals. Consistent with the findings of Earley and Mosakowski, the diversity found within these groups may be less likely to result in conflict and more likely to enhance performance. Thus, organizational approaches to globalization, reflected in staffing policies, are illustrative of the role that organizational context can play in shaping the consequences of international diversity.

Societal Context in International Diversity Research

Because societal context is so important for understanding international diversity, the question of whether research findings from one domestic setting (mostly US) generalize to other societal contexts must be raised (e.g., see Triandis, 1992). Undoubtedly, some findings generalize across cultures (the etic perspective) and other findings hold only within particular cultures (the emic perspective) (Pike, 1966; Brett, Tinsley, Janssens, Barsness & Lytle, 1999).

While researchers have argued over the relevance of each of these perspectives (etic versus emic) to international or cross-cultural research, recent advances in the field demonstrate a reconciliation between these two views (Triandis, 1993; Brett et al., 1999; Earley & Randel, 1996). For example, from the etic perspective, it may be possible to conclude that both task- and relationship-oriented diversity create conflict within teams. However, an emic perspective may be needed to predict which types of relationship-oriented diversity (e.g., ethnicity or religion or age) are more likely to provoke in-group–out-group dynamics.

THEME V: FROM OFFERING TRAINING TO CREATING ORGANIZATIONAL CHANGE

As US workplaces evolved from relatively homogeneous to more heterogeneous, managers paid little attention to the implications of increasing diversity. Affirmative action initiatives focused attention on bringing diversity into organizations but provided little guidance about how to manage more diverse organizations. Mergers, acquisitions, and the restructuring of work around teams also proceeded without much concern for how diversity impacts human relations in an organization. After 20 years of gradually increasing diversity, it is perhaps not surprising that during the 1990s the US saw explosive growth in the number of consultants offering assistance to organizations interested in 'managing diversity.'

Training for Diversity in a Domestic Context: Changing Attitudes and Behaviors

Many of the interventions offered by consultants and adopted by organizations focus on individual 'awareness' training. A typical program would be conducted over the course of one or two days. Among the activities would be information sharing intended to educate employees about the array of differences present in the workplace (e.g., see Alderfer, 1992). Some organizations supplemented formal training sessions with informal learning opportunities such as a Black History Month or a Gay and Lesbian Pride Week and using the time to focus on a group's history and cultural traditions. The hope was that raising awareness about differences would lead to attitudinal and behavior changes. Although there is scant research on the effectiveness of such awareness programs, the general consensus is that awareness programs *alone* do little to create positive change and may even lead to the deterioration of intergroup relations (Nemetz & Christensen, 1996).

Another approach to diversity training focuses more specifically on developing the behavioral competencies needed to work effectively in organizations characterized by diversity. Cox, for example, identified seven competencies that he felt were essential for anyone responsible for leading diverse groups (see Cox & Tung, 1997, for a description). Changing intergroup behaviors and developing interpersonal skills in general undoubtedly help to improve the climate within diverse workplaces (e.g., see Alderfer, 1992; Sessa, 1992). But, like awareness training, used alone such interventions can only begin to create fundamental changes in organizational systems and processes.

Towards an Organizational Change Perspective

For established organizations that evolved during an era when the workforce was relatively homogeneous, truly fundamental changes may be necessary to create an organization that effectively leverages the talents of a more diverse workforce. In his classic post World War II treatise, Allport (1954) hypothesized that the following conditions were necessary in order for intergroup contact to lead to reduced prejudice: equal group status within the situation (i.e., the work setting), active striving toward a common goal that requires interdependent cooperation, and explicit social sanctions supporting the development of intergroup relationships. When members of different social groups interact in settings that meet these conditions, attitudes toward outgroup members improve significantly (for a comprehensive review, see Pettigrew, 1998).

Allport's condition of a common goal that requires interdependent cooperation should be met in any organizational setting where people of different backgrounds work together toward shared objectives. This condition is met at least minimally by most organizations. Allport's other conditions for positive intergroup relations are less likely to be satisfied without intentional intervention. In organizational settings, efforts to create equal group status may include using group membership as a criterion when assigning people to powerful committees and taskforces. Following a merger, this tactic might be used to ensure that the two companies have equal representation in the new top management team (Schweiger, Ridley & Marini, 1992). When demographic differences are the concern, this tactic can be used to ensure that members of minority groups are included on advisory boards, as interviewers during the hiring process, and as members of committees involved in promotion and compensation decisions (e.g., see Alderfer, 1992).

The most problematic of Allport's conditions is the presence of social sanctions that support positive intergroup relations. Often, perhaps because diversity initiatives can be so threatening to members of a powerful majority, organizations create diversity programs but do not mandate full participation. According to a study involving several hundred organizations, the success of diversity interventions is greater when supporting sanctions are in place. Requiring managers to attend training programs and tying compensation and other rewards to success in meeting goals for recruiting, hiring, developing, and promoting people from diverse backgrounds is associated with greater success for diversity interventions (Rynes & Rosen, 1995).

Based on his review of research designed to test Allport's intergroup contact theory, Pettigrew concluded that intergroup contact improves attitudes to the extent that it engages four processes. One key process is *learning about the other group*. A variety of cognitive processes make inaccurate stereotypes resistant to change. Nevertheless, when people have sufficient disconfirming evidence, inaccurate stereotypes can be modified (Stephan & Stephan, 1984; Triandis, 1994). Learning about the other group is usually the objective of diversity awareness training. Thus, Pettigrew's analysis supports the use of awareness training. But it also makes clear that such training alone is not sufficient.

A second key process is *behavioral change*. Engaging repeatedly in a positive behavior with members of an out-group can lead to attitude change (Aronson & Patnoe, 1997). Structural interventions may be needed to encourage repeated positive interactions with members of another group. For example, if supervisors seem reluctant to hire people from particular backgrounds, the company might sponsor student internship programs that offer low-risk opportunities for employees and potential new hires from different backgrounds to interact. Pacific Bell used this approach to increase the proportion of Hispanic Americans in its workforce. Summer interns were considered a valuable resource for managers, so highly qualified Hispanic students were recruited for internship assignments. Managers were responsible for coaching and mentoring the interns, in addition to providing them with challenging work. Students evaluated their experiences at the end of the summer, and these evaluations were used in future years to determine which managers were assigned interns (Roberson & Gutierrez, 1992).

A third key process is *creating positive emotions associated with the out-group*. For example, the positive feelings associated with a close friendship with an individual member of an out-group are likely to generalize to the entire group (Pettigrew, 1997). The value of personal friendships may help explain why informal mentoring programs appear to be more effective than formal programs (Ragins & Cotton, 1991). Formal mentoring relationships may survive even if the parties involved never develop a close personal tie, but informal mentoring relationships depend on the development of a positive personal relationship to sustain them.

Finally, Pettigrew (1998) argues that change is facilitated when *people gain new insight about their own in-group* and come to understand that the in-group's norms and customs represent one of many possible approaches. At Digital, Core Groups provided opportunities for people to develop such insight. In Core Groups, people from different backgrounds discussed a wide range of issues related to intergroup relations. According to Walker and Hanson (1992), the true dialog that occurred in Core Group conversations helped people learn more about themselves as a natural part of learning about others.

Allport's early theorizing about conditions that support positive intergroup relations, and the subsequent research summarized by Pettigrew, provide several guiding principles to consider when designing diversity initiatives. Unfortunately, these principles have not, to date, been used as guidelines for designing organizational approaches to improving diversity management. To the extent an organization's management practices create all of the conditions required for positive intergroup relations to develop within a diverse organization, employee commitment to the organization and productivity should both be enhanced.

From Training to Organizational Change in the International Context

Training interventions for employees being sent abroad generally attempt to prepare the individual to adapt to a specific cultural context (Dowling, Welch & Schuler, 1999). However, as organizations have become increasingly diverse, some organizations have realized that internationalization exposes employees to the more complex challenge of working with a variety of cultures simultaneously. This challenge is faced by domestic managers and expatriates alike. Recognition of this challenge is manifested in organization-wide training initiatives that address the specific needs of everyone in the organization (Schneider & Barsoux, 1997).

Based on an extensive review, Dinges (1983) proposed a set of behavioral competencies needed for effective intercultural performance: information processes in cross-cultural situations, ability to learn in intercultural contexts, interpersonal communication styles, ability to tolerate stress, ability to maintain mutually rewarding relationships, motivation, positive reinforcements, and an emphasis of personal growth and development. More recently, Schneider and Barsoux (1997) compiled a similar

	Individual training	Team training
Single culture	Training regarding host country's culture, laws and language geared for specific overseas assignment I	Training modules that involve both parent country as well as host country nationals in mutual exploration of each other's culture, laws and language III
Multiple cultures	II Training programs aimed at developing global manager's generic intercultural competencies (e.g., interpersonal communication skills, ability to tolerate stress, emphasis on personal growth, sense of humor)	IV Training global, dispersed teams to develop common protocol for communication across distances using electronic mail, videoconferencing and voice messaging facilities Team-based training modules that are designed to facilitate face-to-face interaction among team members Socialization of new team members to multicultural context Long-term training aimed at developing team identity Leadership training designed specifically for multicultural context

Figure 11.2   *Approaches to training employees for work in international contexts*

list. Such competency models may serve as additional guidelines for design of training interventions within internationally diverse organizations.

Regardless of whether training addresses domestic or international diversity, organizations generally seem to favor individual training. But this approach may give too little weight to the powerful social dynamics that arise within natural work units, which increasingly emphasize teamwork. Future interventions might shift the focus of training to the team level. Training teams to manage and leverage their own diversity may prove more effective than training individuals. Similarly, training for the entire work unit that is affected by the arrival of an expatriate may prove more effective than individual training for the expatriate.

Four alternative approaches to training employees for work in international contexts are shown in Figure 11.2. Training interventions such as these may help the people involved meet short-term goals for successful intercultural contact. However, for an organization to develop a sustainable capability, large-scale organizational change and development efforts will be necessary.

For example, Fiat, an Italian automobile company, undertook organization-wide programs that included the reevaluation of international positions as well as organizational culture change. Their approach moved beyond the use of a single HR intervention – such as new staffing techniques or a training program – to include a systematic, large-scale change and development effort (Schneider & Barsoux, 1997). This more holistic approach is very similar to those now being used by US companies as they struggle to more effectively manage domestic diversity.

CONCLUSION

Within the United States, the topic of diversity is rooted in a long history of interest in workplace discrimination. From those roots has grown a large body of literature that informs our current understanding of how domestic diversity affects individual employees and how it affects their relationships with others in the organization. More recently, managers and researchers alike have begun asking whether there is any empirical link between domestic workforce diversity and organizational performance. At the same time that research on domestic diversity has been evolving, there has been a growing interest in understanding and managing international diversity. Historically, research in this field often focused on issues related to cross-cultural adaptation and adjustment among employees sent to foreign locations. As business globalization takes hold, however, both managers and researchers are beginning to see that the challenges of cross-cultural sojourning are no longer limited to addressing the needs of expatriates. Instead, globalization means that employees throughout the entire organization are working among a set of colleagues and customers who are internationally diverse. Thus, for organizations all around the world, it has become increasingly important to manage international diversity effectively.

Given the nature of modern organizations, the reality is that many employers will find it difficult and perhaps meaningless to separate the challenges of managing domestic diversity and managing international diversity. Both occur simultaneously, and both must be understood and effectively managed. In this chapter, we have attempted to illustrate how research studies in these two distinct literatures – one dealing with issues of domestic diversity, mostly within US organizations, and the other dealing with international diversity, mostly within the context of managing expatriates – can benefit from each other. There are some parallels in the types of research questions being asked within each literature, but there also are many differences. Just as differences between individual employees create opportunities for the development of new ideas and learning, we believe that the differences between these two streams of research create opportunities for innovation and the mutual advancement of work in both fields. We hope this chapter helps stimulate the cross-fertilization of ideas and the development of new collaborative projects.

NOTES

1 Elsewhere, a similar distinction has been referred to as instrumental and social exchanges (Elsass & Graves, 1997).

2 Other authors have suggested similar taxonomies. For comparisons, see Milliken and Martins (1996), Pelled (1996), Tsui and Gutek (1999).

REFERENCES

Ackerman, P.L., & Humphreys, L.G. (1991). Individual differences theory in industrial and organizational psychology. In M.D. Dunnette, & L.H. Hough (Eds.), *Handbook of Industrial and Organizational Psychology* (Vol. I, pp. 223–282). Palo Alto, CA: Consulting Psychologists Press.

Alderfer, C.P. (1992). Changing race relations embedded in organizations: Report on a long-term project with the XYZ Corporation. In S.E. Jackson (Ed.), *Diversity in the workplace: Human resource initiatives* (pp. 138–166). New York: Guilford Press.

Allport, G.W. (1954). *The nature of prejudice*. Reading, MA: Addison-Wesley.

Ancona, D.G., & Caldwell, D.F. (1992). Bridging the boundary: External activity and performance for organizational teams. *Administrative Science Quarterly, 37*, 634–665.

Ancona, D.G, & Caldwell, D.F. (1998). Rethinking team composition from the outside in. In D. Gruenfeld (Ed.), *Research on managing groups and teams*. Stamford, CT: JAI Press.

Armstrong, D., & Cole, P. (1996). Managing distances and differences in geographically distributed work groups. In S.E. Jackson, & M.N. Ruderman (Eds.), *Diversity in work teams: Research paradigms for a changing workplace* (pp. 187–215). Washington, DC: American Psychological Association.

Aronson, E., & Patnoe, S. (1997). *The jigsaw classroom*. New York: Longman.

Arvey, R.D., & Murphy, K.R. (1998). Performance evaluation in work settings: *Annual Review of Psychology, 49*, 141–168.

Bacharach, S.B., & Bamberger, P.A. (1992). Alternative approaches to the examination of demography in organizations. *Research in the Sociology of Organizations, 10*, 85–111.

Bantel, K.A., & Jackson, S.E. (1989). Top management and innovations in banking: Does the composition of the top team make a difference? *Strategic Management Journal, 10* (Special Issue), 107–124.

Baron, J., & Pfeffer, J. (1994). The social psychology of organizations and inequality. *Social Psychology Quarterly, 57*, 190–209.

Baron, R. (1991). Positive effects of conflict: A cognitive perspective. *Employees Responsibilities and Rights Journal, 4*, 25–36.

Barringer, I.R., Takeuchi, D.T., & Xenos, P. (1990). Education, occupational prestige, and income of Asian Americans. *Sociology of Education, 63*, 27–43.

Berger, J., Rosenholtz, S.J. & Zelditch, M., Jr. (1980). Status organizing processes. *Annual Review of Sociology, 6*, 479–508.

Berscheid, E. (1985). Interpersonal attraction. In G. Lindsey & E. Aronson (Eds.), *The handbook of social psychology* (Vol. 2, pp. 413–484). New York: Random House.

Black, J.S., & Gregersen, H.B., (1990). Expectations, satisfaction and intention to leave of American expatriate managers in Japan. *International Journal of Intercultural Relations, 14*, 485–506.

Blalock, H.M., Jr. (1967). *Toward a theory of minority group relations*. New York: Wiley.

Bottger, P.C., & Yetton, P.W. (1988). An integration of process and decision-scheme explanations of group problem-solving performance. *Organizational Behavior and Human Decision Processes, 42*, 234–249.

Boxman, E.A.W., De Graaf, P.A., & Flap, H.E. (1991). The impact of social and human capital on the income attainment of Dutch managers. *Social Networks, 13*, 51–73.

Brass, D.J. (1984). Being in the right place: A structural analysis of individual influence in organization. *Administrative Science Quarterly, 29*, 518–539.

Brett, J., Tinsley, C., Janssens, M., Barsness, Z., & Lytle, A.L. (1999). New approaches to the study of culture in industrial/organizational psychology. In P.C. Earley, & M. Erez (Eds.), *New approaches to intercultural and international industrial/organizational psychology* (pp. 75–129). The New Lexington Press: San Francisco.

Brewer, M.B. (1979). In-group bias in the minimal intergroup situation: A cognitive-motivational analysis. *Psychological Bulletin, 86*, 307–324.

Brewer, M.B. (1995). Managing diversity: The role of social identities. In S.E. Jackson, & M.N. Ruderman (Eds.), *Diversity in work teams: Research paradigms for a changing workplace* (pp. 47–68). Washington: American Psychological Association.

Byrne, D. (1971). *The attraction paradigm*. New York: Academic Press.

Caligiuri, P.M., Joshi, A., & Lazarova, M. (1999). Factors influencing the adjustment of women on global assignments. *The International Journal of Human Resource Management, 10*(2), 163–179.

Caligiuri, P.M., & Tung, R.L. (1999). Comparing the success of male and female expatriates from a US-based multinational company. *International Journal of Human Resource Management, 10*(5), 763–782.

Carli, L.L. (1989). Gender differences in interaction style and influence. *Journal of Personality and Social Psychology, 56*, 565–576.

Cascio, W.F., & Bernardin, H.J. (1981). Implications of performance appraisal litigation for personnel decisions. *Personnel Psychology, 34*, 211–226.

Chambers, E.G., Foulon, M., Handfield-Jones, H., Hankin, S.M., & Michaels, E.G. III (1998). The war for talent. *The McKinsey Quarterly, 3*, 44–57.

Chatman, J.A., Polzer, J.T., Barsade, S.G., & Neale, M.A. (1998). Being different yet feeling similar: The influence of demographic composition and organizational culture on work processes and outcomes. *Administrative Science Quarterly, 43*, 749–780.

Chattopadhyay, P. (1999). Beyond direct and symmetrical effects: The influence of demographic dissimilarity on organizational citizenship behavior. *Academy of Management Journal, 42*, 273–287.

Chattopadhyay, P., Glick, W.H., Miller, C.C., & Huber, G.P. (1999). Determinants of executive beliefs: Comparing functional conditioning and social influence. *Strategic Management Journal, 20*, 763–789.

Chronicle of Higher Education (1992). The *Chronicle of Higher Education* Almanac. *Chronicle of Higher Education, 39*, 15.

Cohen, J.M. (1977). Source of peer-group homogeneity. *Sociology of Education, 50*, 227–241.

Cowan, D.A. (1986). Developing a process model of problem recognition. *Academy of Management Review, 11*, 763–776.

Cox, T.H., Lobel, S.A., & McLeod, P.L. (1991). Effects of ethnic group cultural differences on cooperative versus competitive behavior on a group task. *Academy of Management Journal, 34*, 827–847.

Cox, T., & Tung, R.L. (1997). The multicultural organization revisited. In C.L. Cooper, & S.E. Jackson (Eds.), *Creating tomorrow's organizations: A handbook for future research in organizational behavior* (pp. 7–28). John Wiley.

Cross, W. (1991). *Shades of black: diversity in African-American identity*. Philadelphia: Temple University Press.

Deaux, K. (1976). Sex: A perspective on the attribution process. In J. Harvey, W. Ickes, & R. Kidd (Eds.), *New directions in attribution research* (pp. 335–352). Hillsdale, NJ: Erlbaum.

DeMeyer, A. (1991). Tech talk: How managers are stimulating global R&D communication. *Sloan Management Review, 32*, 49–58.

Deshpande, S.P., & Viswesvaran, C. (1992). Is cross-cultural training of expatriate managers effective: A meta-analysis. *International Journal of Intercultural Relations, 16*, 295–310.

Dinges, N. (1983). Intercultural competence'. In D. Landis, & R.W. Brislin (Eds.), *Handbook of intercultural competence* (Vol. 1, pp. 176–202). New York: Pergamon Press.

Dowling, P., Welch, D., & Schuler, R.S. (1999). *International human resource management: Managing people in a multinational context*. Cincinnati, OH: South-Western College Publishing.

Duleep, H.O., & Sanders, S. (1992). Discrimination at the top: American-born Asians and white men. *Industrial Relations, 31*, 416–432.

Eagly, A.H. (1983). Gender and social influence: A social psychological analysis. *American Psychologist, 38*, 971–981.

Eagly, A.H., & Carli, L.L. (1981). Sex of researchers and sex-typed communications as determinants of sex differences in influenceability: A meta-analysis of social influence studies. *Psychological Bulletin, 90*, 1–20.

Eagly, A.H., & Johnson, B.T. (1990). Gender and leadership style: A meta-analysis. *Psychological Bulletin, 108*, 223–256.

Eagly, A.H., Makhijani, M.G., & Klonsky, B.G. (1992). Gender and the evaluation of leaders: A meta-analysis. *Psychological Bulletin, 111*, 3–22.

Earley, P.C., & Mosakowski, E.M. (2000). Creating hybrid team cultures: An empirical test of international team functioning. *Academy of Management Journal, 43*, 26–49.

Earley, P.C., & Randel, A.E. (1997). Culture without borders: An individual-level approach to cross-cultural research in organizational behavior. In C.L. Cooper, & S.E. Jackson (Eds.), *Creating tomorrow's organizations: A handbook for future research organizational behavior* (pp. 59–73). John Wiley.

Elder, G.H., Jr. (1974). *Children of the great depression*. Chicago: Univesity of Illinois Press.

Elsass, P.M., & Graves, L.M. (1997). Demographic diversity in decision-making groups: The experiences of women and people of color. *Academy of Management Review, 22*(4), 946–973

Ely, R.J. (1995). The power in demography: Women's social constructions of gender identity at work. *Academy of Management Journal, 38*(3), 589–634.

Fernandez, J.P. (1988). New life for old stereotypes. *Across the Board* (July/August), 24–29.

Festinger, L., Schachter, S., & Back, K. (1950). *Social pressures in informal groups: A study of human factors in housing*. New York: HarperCollins.

Filley, A.C., House, R.J., & Kerr, S. (1976). *Managerial process and organizational behavior*. Glenview, IL: Scott, Foresman.

Fiske, A. (1992). The four elementary forms of sociability: Framework for a unified theory of social relations, *Psychological Review, 99*, 689–723.

Florkowski, G., & Fogel, D.S. (1995). *Perceived host ethnocentrism as a determinant of expatriate adjustment and organizational commitment.* Paper presented at the National Academy of Management Meetings, Vancouver, Canada.

Ford, J.K., Kraiger, K., & Schechtman, S.L. (1986). Study of race effects in objective indices and subjective evaluations of performance: A meta-analysis of performance criteria. *Psychology Bulletin, 99,* 330–337.

Frable, D.E.S. (1997). Gender, racial, ethnic, sexual, and class identities. *Annual Review of Psychology, 48,* 139–162.

Friedman, R. (1996). Defining the scope and logic of minority and female network groups: Can separation enhance integration? In G. Ferris (Ed.), *Research in personnel and human resource management* (pp. 307–349). Greenwich, CT: JAI.

Friedman, R., Kane, M., & Cornfield, D.B. (1998). Social support and career optimism: Examining the effectiveness of network groups among black managers. *Human Relations, 51*(9), 1155–1177.

Friedman, R.A., & Krackhardt, D. (1997). Social capital and career mobility: A structural theory of lower returns to education for Asian employees. *Journal of Applied Behavioral Science, 33*(3), 316–334.

Ghiselli, E.E., & Lodahl, T.M. (1958). Patterns of managerial traits and group effectiveness. *Journal of Abnormal and Social Psychology, 57,* 61–66.

Gibson, C. (1999a). Do you hear what I hear? A framework for reconciling intercultural communication difficulties arising from cognitive styles and cultural values. In P.C Earley, & M. Erez (Eds.), *New approaches to intercultural and international industrial/organizational psychology* (pp. 335–362). The New Lexington Press: San Francisco.

Gibson, C. (1999b). Do they do what they believe they can? Group efficacy and group effectiveness across tasks and cultures. *Academy of Management Journal, 42*(2), 138–152.

Gladstein, D. (1984). Groups in context: A model of task group effectiveness. *Administrative Science Quarterly, 29,* 499–517.

Glass, L.G. (1992). *He says, she says: Closing the communication gap between the sexes.* New York: G.P. Putnam's Sons.

Hambrick, D.C., Cho, T.S., & Chen, M. (1996). The influence of top management team heterogeneity on firms' competitive moves. *Administrative Science Quarterly, 41,* 659–684.

Hambrick, D.C., & Mason, P.A. (1984). Upper echelons: The organization as a reflection of its top managers. *Academy of Management Review, 9,* 193–206.

Harrison, D.A., Price, K.H., & Bell, M.P. (1998). Beyond relational demograohy: Time and the effects of surface – and deep-level diversity on work group cohesion. *Academy of Management Journal, 41*(1), 96–107.

Hartog, D., House, R., Hanges, P., Dorfman, P., & Ruiz-Quintanilla, S.A. (2000). Culture specific and cross-culturally generalizable implicit leadership theories: Are attributes of charismatic/transformational leadership universally endorsed? Unpublished manuscript, Wharton School of Management, University of Pennsylvania.

Heilman, M.E., Lucas, J.A., & Kaplow, S.R. (1990). Self derogating consequences of sex based preferential selection: The moderating role of initial self confidence. *Organizational Behavior and Human Decision Processes, 46,* 202–216.

Heilman, M.E., McCullough, W.F., & Gilbert, D. (1996). The other side of affirmative action: Reactions of non-beneficiaries to sex-based preferential selection. *Journal of Applied Psychology, 81,* 346–357.

Heilman, M.E., Rivero, J.C., & Brett, J.F. (1991). Skirting the competence issue: Effects of sex-based preferential selection on task choices of women and men. *Journal of Applied Psychology, 76,* 99–105.

Helms, J. (1990). An overview of racial identity theory. In J.E. Helms (Ed.), *Black and white racial identity: Theory, research, and practices* (pp. 67–80). Westport, CT: Greenwood.

Hoffman, E. (1979). Applying experiential research on group problem solving to organizations. *Journal of Applied Behavioral Science, 15,* 375–391.

Hoffman, E. (1985). The effect of race-ratio composition on the frequency of organizational communication. *Social Psychology Quarterly, 48,* 17–26.

Hoffman, L.R., Harburg, E., & Maier, N.R.F. (1962). Differences and disagreement as factors in creative group problem solving. *Journal of Abnormal and Social Psychology, 64,* 206–214.

Hoffman, L.R., & Maier, N.R.F. (1961). Quality and acceptance of problem solutions by members of homogeneous and heterogeneous groups. *Journal of Abnormal and Social Psychology, 62,* 401–407.

Hofstede, G. (1980). *Culture's consequences.* Beverly Hills, CA: Sage.

Hofstede, G. (1982). *Dimensions of national cultures in fifty countries and three regions.* Paper presented at the International Congress of Cross-cultural Psychology, Aberdeen, UK.

Hofstede, G. (1991). *Cultures and organizations.* London: McGraw-Hill.

Hofstede, G., & Bond, M.H. (1988). The Confucius connection: From cultural roots to economic growth. *Organizational Dynamics, 16,* 4–21.

Hogg, M.A., & Terry, D.J. (2000). Social identity and self-categorization processes in organizational contexts. *Academy of Management Review, 25,* 121–140.

Holmes, M., & Butler, J. (1987). Status inconsistency, racial separatism, and job satisfaction. *Sociological Perspectives, 30*(2), 201–224.

Hyde, J.S., Fennema, E., & Lamon, S.J. (1990). Gender differences in mathematics performance: A meta-analysis. *Psychological Bulletin, 107,* 139–155.

Hyde, J.S., & Linn, M.C. (1988). Gender differences in verbal ability: A meta-analysis. *Psychological Bulletin, 104,* 53–69.

Ibarra, H. (1992). Homophily and differential returns: Sex differences in network structure and access in an advertising firm. *Administrative Science Quarterly, 37,* 422–447.

Ibarra, H. (1997). Paving an alternative route: Gender differences in managerial networks for career development. *Social Psychology Quarterly, 60*, 91–102.

Ibarra, H., & Andrews, S.B. (1993). Power, social influence, and sense making: Effects of network centrality and proximity on employee perceptions. *Administrative Science Quarterly, 38*, 277–303.

Ibarra, H., & Smith-Lovin, L. (1997). New directions in social network research on gender and organizational careers. In C.L. Cooper, & S.E. Jackson (Eds.), *Creating tomorrow's organizations: A handbook for future research in organizational behavior* (pp. 359–384). New York: John Wiley.

Ilgen, D., LePine, J., & Hollenbeck, J. (1999). Effective decision making in multinational teams. In P.C. Earley, & M. Erez (Eds.), *New approaches to intercultural and international: Industrial/organizational psychology* (pp. 377–409). San Fransisco: The New Lexington Press.

Isen, A.M., & Baron, R.A. (1991). Positive affect as a factor in organizational behavior. In L.L. Cummings, & B.M. Staw (Eds.), *Research in organizational behavior*. Greenwich, CT: JAI Press.

Jacklin, C.N. (1989). Female and male: Issues of gender. *American Psychologist, 44*, 127–133.

Jackson, E. (1962). Status consistency and symptoms of stress. *American Sociological Review, 27*, 469–480.

Jackson, L.A., Gardner, P.D., & Sullivan, L.A. (1992). Explaining gender differences in self-pay expectations: Social comparison standards and perceptions of fair pay. *Journal of Applied Psychology, 77*, 651–663.

Jackson, S.E., (1992a). Consequences of group composition for the interpersonal dynamics of strategic issue processing. In P. Shrivastava, A. Huff, & J.E. Dutton (Eds.), *Advances in strategic management* (Vol. 8, pp. 345–382). Greenwich, CT.: JAI Press.

Jackson, S.E. (1992b). Team composition on organizational settings: Issues in managing an increasingly diverse work force. In S. Worchel, W. Wood, & J.A. Simpson (Eds.), *Group process and productivity*. Newbury Park: Sage Publications.

Jackson, S.E., & Alvarez, E.B. (1992). Working through diversity as a strategic imperative. In S.E. Jackson (Ed.), *Diversity in the workplace: human resources initiatives* (pp. 13–35). New York: The Guilford Press.

Jackson, S.E., Brett, J.F., Sessa, V.I., Cooper, D.M., Julin, J.A., & Peyronnin, K. (1991). Some differences make a difference: Individual dissimilarity and group heterogeneity as correlates of recruitment, promotions, and turnover. *Journal of Applied Psychology, 76*, 675–689.

Jackson, S.E, May K.E., & Whitney, K. (1995). Under the dynamics of diversity in decision-making teams. In R.A. Guzzo, & E. Salas (Eds.), *Team effectiveness and decision making in organizations* (pp. 204–261). San Francisco: Jossey-Bass.

Jaffe, M.P. (1987). Workforce 2000: Forecast of occupational change. In the technical appendix to W.B. Johnston, & A.E. Packer, *Workforce 2000: Work and workers for the 21st century* (p. 23). Washington, DC: US Department of Labor.

Jehn, K.A. (1994). Enhancing effectiveness: An investigation of advantages and disadvantages of value-based intragroup conflict. *International Journal of Conflict Management, 5*, 223–238.

Jehn, K.A. (1995). A multimethod examination of the benefits and detriments of intragroup conflict. *Administrative Science Quarterly, 40*, 256–282.

Jehn, K.A. (1997). A quantitative analysis of conflict types and dimensions in organizational groups. *Administrative Science Quarterly, 42*, 530–557.

Jehn, K.A., Chadwick, C., & Thatcher, S. (1997). To agree or not to agree: Diversity, conflict, and group outcomes. *International Journal of Conflict Management, 8*(4), 287–306.

Jehn, K.A., Northcraft, G.B., & Neale, M.A. (1999). Why differences make a difference: A field study in diversity, conflict, and performamnce in workgroups. *Administrative Science Quarterly, 44*, 741–763.

Johnston, W.B., & Packer, A.H. (1987). *Workforce 2000: Work and workers for the twenty-first century*. Indianapolis, IN: Hudson Institute.

Judge, T.A., & Ferris, G.R. (1993). Social context of performance evaluation decisions. *Academy of Management Journal, 36*, 80–105.

Jung, D., & Avolio, B. (1999). Effects of leadership style and followers cultural orientation on performance in group and individual task conditions. *Academy of Management Journal, 42*, 208–216.

Kanter, R.M. (1977). *Men and women of the corporation*. New York: Basic Books.

Karakowsky, L., & Siegel, J.P. (1999). The effects of proportional representation and gender orientation of the task of emergent leadership behavior in mixed-gender work groups. *Journal of Applied Psychology, 84*, 620–631.

Katz, P.A., & Taylor, D.A. (1988). *Eliminating racism: Profiles in controversy*. New York: Plenum Press.

Kirkman, B., & Shapiro, D. (1997). The impact of cultural values on employees resistance to teams: Toward a model of globalized self-managing self-managing work team effectiveness. *Academy of Management Review, 22*, 730–757.

Kling, K.C., Hyde, J.S., Showers, C.J., & Buswell, B. (1999). Gender differences in self-esteem: A meta-analysis. *Psychological Bulletin, 125*, 470–500.

Kluegel, J. (1978). The causes and cost of racial exclusion from job authority. *American Sociological Review, 43*, 285–301.

Knight, D., Pearce, C.L., Smith, K.G., Olian, J.D., Sims, H.P., Smith, K.A., & Flood, P. (1999). Top management team diversity, group process, and strategic consensus. *Strategic Management Journal, 20*, 445–465.

Korsgaard, A., Schweiger, D., & Sapienza, H. (1995). Building commitment, attachment, and trust in strategic decision making teams: The role of procedural justice. *Academy of Management Journal, 38*(1), 60–84.

Kraly, E.P., & Hirschman, C. (1990). Racial and ethnic inequality among children in the United States – 1940 and 1950. *Social Forces, 69*, 33–51.

Kramer, R.M., & Brewer, M.B. (1984). Effects on group identity on resource use in a simulated common dilemma. *Journal of Personality and Social Psychology, 46*, 1044–1057.

Labouvie-Vief, G. (1989). Intelligence and cognition. In J.E. Birren, & K.W. Schaie (Eds.), *Handbook of the psychology of aging* (2nd ed., pp. 500–530). New York: Van Nostrand Reinhold.

Larwood, L., & Blackmore, J. (1978). Sex discrimination in managerial selection: Testing predictions of the vertical dyad linkage model. *Sex Roles, 4*, 359–367.

Lau, D.C., & Murnighan, J.K. (1998). Demographic diversity and faultlines: The compositional dynamics of organizational groups. *Academy of Management Review, 23*, 325–340.

Lawrence, B.S. (1988). New wrinkles in a theory of age: Demography, norms, and performance ratings. *Academy of Management Journal, 31*, 309–337.

Lawrence, B.S. (1997). The black box of organizational demography. *Organizational Science, 8*. 1–22.

Levine, J.M., & Moreland, R.L. (1990). Progress in small group research. *Annual Review of Psychology, 41*, 585–634.

Lincoln, J.R., & Miller, J. (1979). Work and friendship ties in organizations: A comparative analysis of relational networks. *Administrative Science Quarterly, 24*, 181–199.

Lyness, K.S., & Thompson, D.E. (1997). Above the glass ceiling? A comparison of matched samples of female and male executives. *Journal of Applied Psychology, 82*, 359–375.

Maccoby, E.E., & Jacklin, C.N. (1974). *The psychology of sex differences*. Stanford, CA: Stanford University Press.

Malos, S.B. (1998). Current legal issues in performance appraisal. In J.W. Smither (Ed.), *Performance appraisal: State of the art of practice* (pp. 49–94). San Francisco: Jossey-Bass.

McCain, B.E., O'Reilly, C.A. III, & Pfeffer, J. (1983). The effects of departmental demography on turnover: The case of a university. *Academy of Management Journal, 26*, 626–641.

McGrath, J.E. (1984). *Groups: Interaction and performance*. Englewood Cliffs, NJ: Prentice-Hall.

McGrath, J.E., Berdahl, J.L., & Arrow, H. (1995). Traits, expectations, culture, and clout: The dynamics of diversity in work groups. In S.E. Jackson, & M.N. Ruderman (Eds.), *Diversity in work teams: Research paradigms for a changing workplace* (pp. 17–45). Washington: American Psychological Association.

McGuire, G., & Reskin, B. (1993). Authority hierarchies at work: The impacts of race and sex. *Gender and Society, 7*, 487–506.

McLeod, P.L., & Lobel, S.A. (1992). The effects of ethnic diversity on idea generation in small groups. *Academy of Management Best Paper Proceedings*, 227–231.

McLeod, P.L., Lobel, S.A., & Cox, T.H. (1996). Ethnic diversity and creativity in small groups. *Small Group Research, 27*, 248–264.

McPherson, J.M., & Smith-Lovin, L. (1987). Homophily in voluntary organizations: Status distance and the composition of face-to-face groups. *American Sociological Review, 52*, 370–379.

Mendenhall, M., & Oddou, G. (1986). Acculturation profiles of expatriate managers: Implications for cross-cultural training. *Columbia Journal of World Business, 21*(4), 73–79.

Miller, N., & Brewer, M. (Eds.) (1984). *Groups in contact: The psychology of desegregation*. Orlando, FL: Academic Press.

Milliken, F.J., & Martins, L.L. (1996). Searching for common threads: Understanding the multiple effects of diversity in organizational groups. *Academy of Management Review, 21*(2), 402–433.

Morrison, A.M., & Von Glinow, M.A. (1990). Women and minorities in management. *American Psychologist, 45*, 200–208.

Morrison, E.W., & Herlihy, J.M. (1992). Becoming the best place to work: Managing diversity at American Express travel related services. In S.E. Jackson (Ed.), *Diversity in the workplace: Human resource initiatives* (pp. 203–226). New York: The Guilford Press.

Nemetz, P.L., & Christensen, S.L. (1996). The challenge of cultural diversity: Harnessing adiversity of views to understand multiculturalism. *Academy of Management Review, 21*(2), 434–462.

Nkomo, S. (1992). The emperor has no clothes: Rewriting race in organizations. *Academy of Management Review, 17*, 487–513.

Nkomo, S. (1995). Identities and the complexity of diversity. In S.E. Jackson, & M.N. Ruderman (Eds.), *Diversity in work teams: Research paradigms for a changing workplace* (pp. 247–253). Washington, DC: American Psychological Association.

Ohlott, P.J., Ruderman, M.N., & McCauley, C.D. (1994). Gender differences in managers' developmental job experiences. *Academy of Management Journal, 37*, 46–67.

O'Reilly, C.A. III, Caldwell, D.F., & Barnett, W.P. (1989). Work group demography, social integration, and turnover. *Administrative Science Quarterly, 34*, 21–37.

Pearce, J.A., & Ravlin, E.C. (1987). The design and activation of self-regulating work groups. *Human Relations, 40*, 751–782.

Pelled, L.H. (1996). Demographic diversity, conflict, and work group outcomes: An intervening process theory. *Organization Science, 7*, 615–631.

Pelled, L.H., Eisenhardt, K.M., & Xin, K.R. (1999). Exploring the black box: An analysis of work group diversity, conflict, and performance. *Administrative Science Quarterly, 44*, 1–28.

Pelled, L.H., & Xin, K.R. (1997). Birds of a feather: Leader-member demographic similarity and organizational attachment in Mexico. *Leadership Quarterly, 8*, 433–450.

Pelz, D.C. (1956). Some social factors related to performance in a research organization. *Administrative Science Quarterly, 1*, 310–325.

Pettigrew, T.F. (1997). Generalized intergroup contact effects on prejudice. *Personality and Social Psychology Bulletin, 23*, 173–85.

Pettigrew, T.F. (1998). Intergroup contact theory. *Annual Review of Psychology, 49*, 65–85.

Pike, K.I. (1966). *Language in relation to a unified theory of structure of human behavior.* The Hague: Mouton.

Porac, J.F., & Howard, H. (1990). Taxonomic mental models in competitor definition. *Academy of Management Review, 2*, 224–240.

Powell, G.N., & Butterfield, D.A. (1997). Effect of race on promotions to top management in a federal department. *Academy of Management Journal, 40*, 112–128.

Pulakos, E.D., Schmitt, N., & Chan, D. (1996). Models of job performance ratings: An examination of rate, race, ratee gender, and rater level effects. *Human Performance, 9*, 103–119.

Ragins, B.R., & Cotton, J. (1991). Easier said than done: Gender differences in perceived barriers to gaining a mentor. *Academy of Management Journal, 34*, 939–951.

Ragins, B.R., & Scandura, T.A. (1997). The way we were: Gender and the termination of mentoring relationships. *Journal of Applied Psychology, 82*, 945–953.

Ragins, B.R., Townsend, B., & Mattis, M. (1998). Gender gap in the executive suite: CEOs and female executives report and breaking the glass ceiling. *Academy of Management Executive, 12*(1), 28–42.

Rhodes, S.R. (1983). Age-related differences in work attitudes and behavior. A review and conceptual analysis. *Psychological Bulletin, 93*, 328–367.

Rice, R.E. (1993). Using network concepts to clarify sources and mechanisms of social influence. In G. Barnett, & W. Richards Jr. (Eds.), *Advances in communication network analysis.* Norwood, NJ: Ablex.

Richard, O.C., & Johnson, N.B. (1999). Making the connection between formal human resource diversity practices and organizational effectiveness: Behind management fashion. *Performance Improvement Quarterly, 12*, 77–96.

Ridgeway, D.L. (1982). Status is groups: The importance of motivation. *American Sociological Review, 47*, 76–88.

Ridgeway, C., & Johnson, C. (1990). What is the relationship between socioemotional behavior and status in task groups? *American Journal of Sociology, 95*, 1189–1212.

Riordan, C., & Shore, L.M. (1997). Demographic diversity and employee attitudes: An empirical examination of relational demography within work units. *Journal of Applied Psychology, 82*, 342–358.

Roberson, L., & Gutierrez, N.C. (1992). Beyond good faith: Commitment to recruiting management diversity at Pacific Bell. In S.E. Jackson (Ed.), *Diversity in the Workplace: Human Resources Initiatives* (pp. 65–166). New York: The Guilford Press.

Rynes, S., & Rosen, B. (1995). A field survey of factors affecting the adoption and perceived success of diversity training. *Personnel Psychology, 48*, 247–270.

Sackett, P.R., & DuBois, C.L. (1991). Rater-ratee race effects on performance evaluation: Challenging meta-analytic conclusions. *Journal of Applied Psychology, 76*(6), 873–877.

Sanchez, J.I., & Brock, P. (1996). Outcomes of perceived discrimination among Hispanic employees: Is diversity management a luxury or a necessity? *Academy of Management Journal, 39*(3), 704–719.

Schneider, S., & Barsoux, J.L. (1997). *Managing across cultures.* London: Prentice Hall.

Schuler, R.S., Dowling, P.J., & DeCieri, H. (1993). *International dimensions in human resource management.* Boston: PWS Kent.

Schwartz, S.H. (1999). A theory of cultural values and some implications for work. *Applied Psychology: An International Review, 48*(1), 23–47.

Schweiger, D.M., Ridley, J.R. Jr., & Marini, D.M. (1992). Creating one from two: The merger between Harris Semiconductor and General Electric Solid State. In S.E. Jackson (Ed.), *Diversity in the workplace: Human resources initiatives* (pp. 167–201). New York: Guilford Press.

Sessa, V.I. (1992). Managing diversity at the Xerox Corporation: Balanced workforce goals and caucus groups. In S.E. Jackson (Ed.), *Diversity in the workplace: Human resources initiatives* (pp. 37–64). New York: Guilford Press.

Sessa, V.I., & Jackson, S.E. (1995). Diversity in decision-making teams: All differences are not created equal. In M.M. Chemers, S. Oskamp, & M.A. Costanzo (Eds.), *Diversity in organizations: New perspectives for a changing workplace* (pp. 133–156). Thousand Oaks, CA: Sage.

Shaffer, M.A., Harrison, D.A., & Gilley, K.M. (1999). Dimensions, determinants and differences in the expatriate adjustment process. *Journal of International Business Studies, 30*(3), 557–581.

Shaw, M.E. (1981). *Group dynamics: The psychology of small-group behavior.* New York: McGraw-Hill.

Silver, S.D., Cohen, B.P., & Crutchfield, J.H. (1994). Status differentiation and information exchange in face-to-face and computer-mediated idea generation. *Social Psychology Quarterly, 57*, 108–123.

Simon, H.A. (1987). Making management decisions: The role of intuition and emotion. *Academy of Management Executive* (February), 57–64.

Simons, T., Pelled, L.H., & Smith, K.A. (1999). Making use of differences: Diversity, debate, and decision comprehensiveness in top management teams. *Academy of Management Journal, 47*(6), 662–673.

Smith, K.G., Smith, K.A., Olian, J.D., Sims, H.P., Jr., O'Bannon, D.P., & Scully, J.A. (1994). Top management team demography and process: The role of social integration and communication. *Administrative Science Quarterly, 39*, 412–438.

Smith, R.A. (1997). Race, job authority, and income: A cross-temporal study of changes in the socioeconomic status of black and white men, 1972–1994. *Social Problems, 44*, 701–719.

Snow, C., Davison, S., Snell, S., & Hambrick, D. (1996). Use transnational teams to globalize your company. *Organizational Dynamics, 24*(4), 50–67.

South, S.J., Bonjean, C.M., Markham, W.T., & Corder, J. (1982). Social structure and intergroup interaction: Men and women of the federal bureaucracy. *American Sociological Review, 47*, 587–599.

Stasser, G., & Titus, W. (1985). Pooling of unshared information in group decision making: Biased information sampling during discussion. *Journal of Personality and Social Psychology, 48*, 1467–1478.

Steiner, I.D. (1972). *Group processes and productivity.* New York: Academic Press.

Stephan, W.G., & Stephan, C.W. (1984). The role of ignorance in intergroup relations. See Miller & Brewer 1984, pp. 229–256.

Tajfel, H. (1978). *Differentiation between social groups: Studies in the social psychology of intergroup relations.* San Diego, CA: Academic Press.

Tang, J. (1993). The career attainment of Caucasian and Asian engineers. *The Sociological Quarterly, 34*, 467–496.

Tannen, D. (1990). *You just don't understand: Men and women in conversation.* New York: Ballatine.

Tannen, D. (1995). *Talking from 9 to 5.* New York: Avon Books.

Teagarden, M., & Gordon, G. (1995). Corporate selection strategies and expatriate manager success. In J. Selmer (Ed.), *Expatriate management* (pp. 17–36). Westport, CT: Quorum Books.

Thatcher, S. (1999). The contextual importance of diversity: The impact of relational demography and team diversity on individual performance and satisfaction. *Performance Improvement Quarterly, 12*, 97–112.

Thernstrom, S. (1973). *The other Bostonians: Poverty and progress in the American metropolis, 1880–1970.* Cambridge, MA: Harvard University Press.

Thomas, K.M., Williams, K.L., Perkins, L.A., & Barroso, C. (1997). *Affirmative action attitudes: Looking beyond race and gender effects.* Paper presented at the annual meeting of the Society for Industrial and Organizational Psychology.

Tolbert, P.S., Andrews, A.O., & Simons, T. (1995). The effects of group proportions on group dynamics. In S.E. Jackson, & M.N. Ruderman (Eds.), *Diversity in work teams: Research paradigms for a changing workplace* (pp. 131–159). Washington: American Psychological Association.

Triandis, H. (1989). The self and social behavior in differing cultural contexts. *Psychological Review, 96*, 506–520.

Triandis, H.C. (1992). The importance of contexts in studies of diversity. In S.E. Jackson (Ed.), *Diversity in the workplace: Human resources initiatives* (pp. 225–233). New York: The Guilford Press.

Triandis, H.C. (1993). Cross-cultural industrial and organizational psychology. In H.C. Triandis, M.D. Dunnette, & L.M. Hough (Eds.), *Handbook of industrial and organizational psychology* (Vol 4, pp. 103–172). Palo Alto, CA: Consulting Psychologists Press.

Triandis, H.C. (1994). *Culture and social behavior,* (p. 330). New York: McGraw-Hill.

Triandis, H.C., Hall, E.R., & Ewen, R.B. (1965). Member heterogeneity and dyadic creativity. *Human Relations, 18*, 33–55.

Tsui, A.S., Egan, T.D., & O'Reilly, C.A., III. (1992). Being different: Relational demography and organizational attachment. *Administrative Science Quarterly, 37*, 549–579.

Tsui, A.S., & Gutek, B.A. (1999). *Demographic differences in organizations.* Lanham, MD: Lexington Books.

Tsui, A.S., & O'Reilly, C.A., III. (1989). Beyond simple demographic effects: The importance of relational demography in supervisor-subordinate dyads. *Academy of Management Journal, 32*, 402–423.

Tsui, A.S., Xin, K.R., & Egan, T.D. (1996). Relational demography: The missing link in vertical dyad linkage. In S.E. Jackson, & M.N. Ruderman (Eds.), *Diversity in work teams: Research paradigms for a changing workplace* (pp. 187–215). Washington, DC: American Psychological Association.

Tung, R.L. (1981). Selection and training for personnel for overseas assignments. *Columbia Journal of World Business,* (Spring), 21–25.

Varca, P.E., & Pattison, P. (1993). Evidentiary standards in employment discrimination: A view toward the future. *Personnel Psychology, 46*, 239–258.

Wagner, W.G., Pfeffer, J., & O'Reilly, C.A., III. (1984). Organizational demography and turnover in top-management groups. *Administrative Science Quarterly, 29*, 74–92.

Waldman, D.A., & Avolio, B.J. (1986). A meta-analysis of age differences in job performance. *Journal of Applied Psychology, 71*, 33–38.

Walker, B.A., & Hanson, W.C. (1992). Valuing differences at Digital Equipment Corporation. In S.E. Jackson (Ed.), *Diversity in the workplace: Human resources initiatives* (pp. 119–137). New York: Guilford Press.

Wallston, B.S., & O'Leary, V.E. (1981). Sex and gender make a difference: Differential perception of women and men. *Review of Personality and Social Psychology, 2*, 9.

Watson, W.E., Kumar, K., & Michaelson, L.K. (1993). Cultural diversity's impact on interaction process and performance: Comparing homogeneous and diverse task groups. *Academy of Management Journal, 36*, 590–602.

Webber, S.S., & Donahue, L.M. (1999). Examining the 'double-edged sword' of diversity in work groups: A meta-analysis. Unpublished manuscript.

Werner, J.M., & Bolino, M.C. (1997). Explaining U.S. courts of appeals decisions involving performance appraisal: accuracy, fairness, and validation. *Personnel Psychology*, *50*, 1–24.

Wiersema, M.F., & Bird, A. (1993). Organizational demography in Japanese firms: Group heterogeneity, industry dissimilarity, and top management team turnover. *Academy of Management Journal*, *36*, 996–1025.

Willems, E.P., & Clark, R.D., III. (1971). Shift toward risk and heterogeneity of groups. *Journal of Experimental and Social Psychology*, *7*, 302–312.

Wood, W. (1987). Meta-analytic review of sex differences in group performance. Psychological Bulletin, *102*, 53–71.

Work attitudes: Study reveals generation gap. *Bulletin to Management*, October 2, 1986, 326.

Wright, P., Ferris, S.P., Hiller, J.S., & Kroll, M. (1995). Competitiveness through management of diversity: Effects on stock price valuation. *Academy of Management Journal*, *38*, 272–287.

Zander, A., & Havelin, A. (1960). Social comparison and interpersonal attraction. *Human Relations*, *13*, 21–32.

Zenger, T.R., & Lawrence, B.S. (1989). Organizational demography: The differential effects of age and tenure distribution on technical communications. *Academy of Management Journal*, *32*, 353–376.

12

The Psychology of Lateness, Absenteeism, and Turnover

GARY JOHNS

Psychological processes underlying lateness, absenteeism, and turnover are reviewed. These processes have historically been dominated by a withdrawal model that assumes that the behaviors are the product of unfavorable job attitudes. It is argued that although the withdrawal model is useful for understanding the three behaviors, its dominance is something of an historical accident that is not well justified by contemporary meta-analytic evidence. Elaborations of the withdrawal model, including progression of withdrawal and the general withdrawal construct, are discussed. Alternatives to the withdrawal model include a social model and a dispositional model. The social model takes into account demography, social networks, and normative and cultural mechanisms. Dispositional perspectives center around personality and integrity constructs.

INTRODUCTION

The early days of work and organizational psychology were dominated by practical applications (Dunnette, 1976). Consequently, arriving at work late (Motley, 1926), being absent from work (Kornhauser & Sharp, 1932), and quitting work (Bezanson & Schoenfeld, 1925) were some of the first phenomena studied by work psychologists. Although these so-called work withdrawal behaviors have a long history of research prompted by their potential for cost and disruption, they have not until fairly recently profited from the kind of theoretical development that they deserve.

The labeling of lateness, absence, and turnover as withdrawal behaviors possibly originated with Hill and Trist's (1953, 1955) influential studies of accidents, absence, and turnover in a steel mill. The essential problem with the withdrawal label is that it connotes a single cause or motive to behaviors that are surely complexly determined. As such, the notion of withdrawal has exerted influence on research in this area well beyond its empirical basis.

Nevertheless, as a convention I will use the generic label *withdrawal behaviors* to refer to lateness, absence, and turnover and the term *withdrawal model* to refer to a model that posits attitudinal causes for the behaviors.

Given space restrictions, it is impossible to review the vast literature on withdrawal spanning antecedents, processes, outcomes, management, and methodology. Rather, I restrict myself to defining the behaviors, discussing their essential similarities, and reviewing three psychological models that pertain to the behaviors: the withdrawal (attitudinal) model, the social model, and the dispositional model. Although these models fit the purview of this handbook, it should be recognized that economists, sociologists, physicians, and epidemiologists have also had some useful things to say about withdrawal. The chapter concludes with ideas for improving research in the withdrawal domain.

Among the withdrawal behaviors, absence and turnover are covered most thoroughly because they have received the most research attention. However, lateness research has also contributed to our understanding of withdrawal, and it is incorporated as warranted in what follows.

DEFINITIONS AND OPERATIONALIZATIONS

Adler and Golan (1981: 544) define *lateness* as 'the tendency of an employee to arrive at work after the scheduled starting time.' Johns (1995: 1) defines *absenteeism* as 'the failure to report for scheduled work.' Martocchio and Harrison (1993: 263) define it as 'an individual's lack of physical presence at a given location and time when there is a social expectation for him or her to be there.' Thus, absence is the logical opposite of attendance. Price (1977: 4) defines *turnover* as 'the degree of individual movement across the membership boundary of a social system.' Lee (1997: 97) describes it as 'the termination of an individual's formal membership with an organization.' In any event, turnover is not the opposite of tenure, the amount of time a person has been employed by an organization.

These traditional definitions have in common physical removal from a particular workplace, either for part of a day, an entire day, or permanently. Thus, implicit in each is time allocation. Also, the unit of analysis in each case is the individual employee. Although lateness, absence, and turnover can all be expressed as rates of behavior that pertain to workgroups, departments, or organizations, such applications are less common in organizational psychology than might be imagined. The vast majority of research in psychology and management frames the withdrawal behaviors as dependent or criterion variables. Thus, the consequences of these behaviors have received much less theoretical and empirical scrutiny than their predictors (exceptions include Goodman & Atkin, 1984; Price, 1976, 1989; Staw, 1980; Tharenou, 1993). Finally, most research frames withdrawal behaviors as negative behaviors from the organization's point of view, presumably due to cost or disruption. This is so taken for granted that relevant underlying assumptions are seldom mentioned.

Most academic psychological research concerning lateness, absence, and turnover uses data from employee personnel files to measure the behaviors. Lateness is generally expressed as minutes late or the number of lateness incidents, both aggregated over some period of time ranging from several weeks to a year. There has been very little research on the psychometric properties of lateness data, although Blau (1994) presents a taxonomy of lateness (increasing chronic, stable periodic, unavoidable) based on patterns of frequency and duration.

Although there are many ways to count and aggregate absence data, many methods exhibit poor reliability and validity, especially in terms of presumptions about motivation and volition.

Contemporary research most often relies on total time lost (days) or frequency, the number of inceptions irrespective of duration. Typical aggregation periods range from 3 to 12 months. Chadwick-Jones, Nicholson and Brown (1982) and Hackett and Guion (1985) present evidence for the reliability and validity of these two measures. Johns (1994b) reviews the psychometric properties of a wide range of self-report measures of absence, the most salient of which is a marked tendency for underreporting.

Turnover is usually expressed as the occurrence of voluntary separation from an employer during some arbitrary time window ranging from a few months to well over a year. This arbitrary, cross-sectional treatment of time has been criticized by advocates of event history or survival analysis approaches (e.g., Somers & Birnbaum, 1999; Peters & Sheridan, 1988). Campion (1991) discusses the validity of the assumption of voluntariness and alternative conceptions of turnover, including that thought to be functional for the organization.

THE WITHDRAWAL MODEL

At its core, the withdrawal model assumes that withdrawal behaviors occur in response to unfavorable job or work attitudes. Prominent among these are job dissatisfaction and low organizational commitment. Hulin (1991) provides the most complete statement of this model, arguing that the various manifestations of withdrawal constitute means of *adapting* to unfavorable job attitudes. The meaning of adaptation is not very clear. On one hand, the idea of avoidance of or escape from negative work situations figures prominently in the notion of withdrawal. On the other hand, more proactive and restorative notions are also connoted by adaptation (Hackett & Bycio, 1996; Staw & Oldham, 1978). Hulin (1991) and Hanisch, Hulin and Rosnowski (1998) assert that exactly which withdrawal behavior is enacted in response to negative attitudes is partially a function of existing constraints on the other behaviors (cf. Johns, 1991).

Below it will be argued that:

1) the withdrawal model is useful in understanding lateness, absence, and turnover;
2) its usefulness is sometimes exaggerated at the expense of other models;
3) this perceived usefulness was something of an historical accident;
4) turnover research particularly suffered from the hegemony of the withdrawal model.

Some History

During the decade spanning 1955 to 1964 several key publications in work and organizational psychology appeared that would profoundly shape research concerning withdrawal behaviors for many years to come. Each of these publications summarized empirical evidence bearing on a key premise of the human relations movement, the belief that positive attitudes toward one's work and organization would result in a wide variety of favorable organizational outcomes, including enhanced productivity and reduced accidents, lateness, absence, and turnover. The felicity of these outcomes for the war effort provides a notable subtext to the earlier research (cf. Tansey & Hyman, 1992).

In their influential review of the attitude–work behavior literature, Brayfield and Crockett (1955: 408) concluded that there was little appreciable relationship between attitudes and performance, but that 'the data are suggestive mainly of a relationship between attitudes and two forms of withdrawal from the job [absence and turnover].' In an independent review conducted at the same time but published later in book form, Herzberg, Mausner, Peterson and Capwell (1957: 111) were more favorably inclined toward an attitude–performance connection. However, they also concluded that a stronger relationship existed for withdrawal, describing attitudes as 'unequivocally related' to both absence and turnover. Finally, Vroom (1964: 186) reported 'a consistent negative relationship' between job satisfaction and turnover, 'a less consistent negative relationship' between satisfaction and absenteeism, and 'no simple relationship' between satisfaction and performance.

A cogent argument can be made that the conclusions of the three reviews cited above established the status of a withdrawal-from-dissatisfaction model as appropriate for describing absence and turnover (and by extension, lateness) and did so by virtue of the presumed contrast to research on performance as much as any strong connection between satisfaction and absence or turnover. Subsequent qualitative reviews of the absenteeism and turnover literature (Muchinsky, 1977; Muchinsky & Tuttle, 1979; Nicholson, Brown & Chadwick-Jones, 1976; Porter & Steers, 1973; Price, 1977) indicated that the withdrawal model exerted something of a theoretical closed shop on withdrawal research, as other approaches to studying the behaviors simply tended to report atheoretical associations with demographic variables or organizational variables such as work unit size.

A Controversial Assertion

It is my contention that the closed shop that the withdrawal model exerted on absenteeism research began to falter in the early 1980s but that it persisted in turnover research, to its detriment. This course of events stemmed from a series of publications in the domain of absenteeism that unfroze researchers' attitudes about the behavior and a

parallel series of publications that solidified the extant turnover paradigm.

In 1976, Nicholson et al., published a qualitative review of the satisfaction–absence literature that included substantial original data. Going against the prevailing paradigm, they concluded that there was little if any connection between the two variables. Although the authors might have been overinfluenced by their own unoptimistic data (Hackett, 1989), this assault on the withdrawal model gained notice. It also corresponded to emerging research that work attitudes did little to supplement more distal influences on absence, such as demographics and job characteristics (Johns, 1978). At the same time, Steers and Rhodes (1978) presented the first version of their process model of attendance (Steers & Rhodes, 1978, 1984; Rhodes & Steers, 1990). Although this model incorporated job satisfaction, it rejected it as a principal cause and also considered pressure to attend (e.g., work ethic, workgroup norms, economic conditions, reward system) and ability to attend (e.g., sickness, family matters), factors that might run counter to work attitudes. Importantly, the model reminded researchers of the complexity of attendance behavior. Equally importantly, although its premises stimulated research (reviewed by Rhodes & Steers, 1990), the larger model itself did not become the focus of intensive, repeated testing.

Other publications contributed to the unfreezing of the withdrawal model's hold on absence research. Chadwick-Jones et al. (1982) presented theory and data that framed absenteeism as a product of social exchange. The same year, Johns and Nicholson (1982) urged researchers to look beyond the withdrawal model, recognize the social context of absenteeism, and incorporate a wider range of methodologies. The call for a more social, contextual, view of absence was perhaps the most notable contribution of these publications.

A final point that might be made concerning the work that emerged in the period under consideration has to do with research on technologies to manage or control absenteeism. In a word, this research can be described as *eclectic*, ranging from financial incentives (Schlotzhauer & Rosse, 1985), to self-management (Frayne & Latham, 1987), to alternative working schedules (Baltes, Briggs, Huff, Wright & Neuman, 1999). Importantly, this research was not grounded in a single theoretical model, such as the withdrawal model. Thus, the tendency for prevailing technology to calcify theory (cf. psychoanalysis and Freudian theory) was not a salient issue.

Recently, two comprehensive independent reviews of the absenteeism literature have appeared. Johns (1997) concluded that great strides had been made in absenteeism research in the preceding 15 years, citing advances in the understanding of absence cultures, how people view their own absence behavior, and other approaches that do not rely on withdrawal model dynamics. Examining roughly the same retrospective period, Harrison and Martocchio (1998: 342) described absence research as 'healthy, robust, cumulative' and having 'vigor, vitality, and variety.' Tellingly, Johns (1998a) recounted the wide variety of research methods that was used to achieve this state of affairs.

Following the three seminal reviews concerning withdrawal that were published between 1955 and 1964 the withdrawal model dominated turnover research into the 1990s (Hom & Griffeth, 1995). As will be seen shortly, this persistence is not well explained by the meta-analytic evidence concerning the relation between job satisfaction and turnover. What, then, does explain it?

During the 1955–1964 period, March and Simon (1958) published the immensely influential book *Organizations*. In this book, they developed a model designed to explain the motivation to 'participate' in organizations, a model that was meant to explain the quit–stay decision. Basically, turnover was framed as a function of two factors – the perceived desirability of movement from the organization (determined by job satisfaction) and the perceived ease of movement (determined by perceptions of alternative job prospects). For current purposes, this model had two crucial features. First, it reinforced the emerging notion that job satisfaction was a salient predictor of turnover. Next, it portrayed turnover as a calculated, rational process in which the calculus of desirability and ease of movement appeared absolute. This provision of a formal model of turnover had a tremendous impact on subsequent research, narrowing its focus to that prescribed by rational affect (Hom & Griffeth, 1995; Lee, 1997).

As disaffection with the withdrawal model was mounting among absence researchers, Mobley (1977) presented a model that elaborated the cognitive processes between job dissatisfaction and turnover, building on March and Simon (1958). The model proposed that people evaluate their existing job. If they are dissatisfied, in sequence, they think of quitting, evaluate the utility of job search and the costs of quitting, develop the intent to search for alternative jobs, make the search, evaluate the alternatives, compare the alternatives to the current job, intend to quit or stay, and act on their intentions.

The Mobley model had two noteworthy features. First, in proposing to measure variables psychologically closer to the actual act of turnover (such as intent to quit), it had the potential to account for increased variance in turnover. Although this criterion has been of particular interest to many turnover researchers, it is a dubious criterion by which to evaluate the validity of a within-person process model (Fichman, 1999; Mohr, 1982). Next, and more important, the Mobley model was decidedly cognitive, a characteristic that fit the *Zeitgeist* of the times, sandwiched temporally between the cognitive revolution in job interview research (Webster, 1964) and that in performance appraisal (Ilgen, Barnes-Farrell & McKellin, 1993). Mobley's model, confirmed in its broad brushstrokes and modified in its details, 'dominates all work on psychological approaches to turnover' (Hom & Griffeth, 1995: 57).

Mobley's (1977) contribution to the solidification of the withdrawal model as the cornerstone of turnover research was reinforced in the same period by a technology that came to dominate research on recruitment (Rynes, 1991) – realistic job previews. This technique, providing recruits with frank and realistic information about a prospective job and organization, is strongly oriented toward the containment of turnover. Although realistic previews have been argued to reduce turnover by several mechanisms, enhanced job satisfaction is thought to be a key component (Wanous, 1992). As Wanous explains, job satisfaction could theoretically be boosted by screening out those inclined to be dissatisfied or by reducing the documented unrealistic expectations of those who accept a job offer. Thus, unlike for absence research, the withdrawal model dominating turnover research found a corresponding technology in realistic job previews.

The contemporary paradigm, grounded in rational withdrawal from dissatisfaction, has gradually provoked a mounting degree of criticism as to its limitations. As Somers (1996: 315) explains, 'criticisms of the current turnover paradigm are harsh, to the point that we need new ways of thinking about the process of employee withdrawal.' Specific criticisms include a lack of cumulative knowledge (Somers, 1999), an excessively narrow and rational causal model (Lee & Mitchell, 1994; Lee, Mitchell, Wise & Fireman, 1996), and the use of 'research designs that are inherently flawed' (Peters & Sheridan, 1988: 232). Furthermore, Phillips's (1998) meta-analysis of realistic job preview outcomes for turnover reveals validity coefficients so low that they beg utility estimates to justify the practice, with mean rs in the $-.05$ to $-.09$ range depending on setting and turnover measure. The corresponding mean r for the relationship between exposure to realistic previews and job satisfaction was actually negative for lab studies, although it was positive (.10) for field studies. However, the met expectations hypothesis, which suggests that lowered expectations upon hiring will result in post-hire satisfaction and reduced turnover, has now been rather strongly refuted by empirical evidence. Although finding initial support (Wanous et al., 1992), the apparent role of met expectations has been shown to be a statistical artifact of the well-known problems of difference scores and residual difference scores (Hom, Griffeth, Palich & Bracker, 1999; Irving & Meyer, 1994, 1999).

Contemporary Evidence Concerning the Withdrawal Model

Job Satisfaction

Table 12.1 presents a summary of what I believe to be the best meta-analytic evidence concerning the relationship between job satisfaction and various work behaviors. Estimated population correlations are shown, all of which are corrected for sampling error. Iaffaldano and Muchinsky (1985) examined the relationship between satisfaction and job performance, correcting for unreliability in both variables. Hom and Griffeth (1995) summarized the connection between satisfaction and turnover, correcting for unreliability in satisfaction. Hackett and Guion (1985) estimated the correlation between satisfaction and time lost (total days absent) and frequency (number of absence incidents), correcting for unreliability in the absence measures. Hackett (1989) examined the relationship between satisfaction and absence, controlling for unreliability in both measures as well as refining the criterion to exclude frequency measures of excused absence and time lost measures of unexcused absence. Finally, Koslowsky, Sagie, Krausz and Singer (1997) summarized the relationship between satisfaction and lateness, controlling for unreliability in both variables.

A number of interesting points emerge from a perusal of Table 12.1. First, in contrast to the qualitative reviews of the 1955–1964 period, it is apparent that absenteeism and turnover are not more highly correlated with satisfaction than is job performance. In fact, a case might be made that the opposite is true. Second, there is little in the table to explain the continuing dominance of the withdrawal model in turnover research as compared to absenteeism research. Third, satisfaction with the work itself is the satisfaction facet that best predicts performance, turnover, and absenteeism. Fourth, there would appear to be some theoretical validity and practical utility for satisfaction in predicting all criteria, particularly since a linear combination of facets would likely exceed many of the values for individual facets given in the table.

The meta-analyses upon which Table 12.1 is based often reveal wide confidence intervals that signal the presence of moderators. Unfortunately, there has been relatively little examination of just when and how withdrawal processes might be more or less likely to apply, or to whom. This is curious, given the large literature concerning the sometimes elusive connection between attitudes and behavior (Ajzen & Fishbein, 1980; Deutscher, 1973). Absence, lateness, and turnover are often constrained by organizational policies and environmental factors (Johns, 1991), but these are seldom systematically investigated as a means of refining the withdrawal model. In fact, the study of withdrawal

behaviors has particularly suffered from the poor understanding of context that has generally characterized the field of work psychology (Cappelli & Sherer, 1991; Johns, 1993, 1998b; Mowday & Sutton, 1993). Nevertheless, it is probable that work attitudes interact with factors such as medical status to affect absenteeism (Johns, 1997). For instance, Webb, Redman, Hennrikus, Kelman, Gibberd and Sanson-Fisher (1994) found that job dissatisfaction and problem drinking had a compound effect on absences due to injury. More prosaically, Smith (1977) found that work attitudes predicted attendance on a very snowy day in Chicago but not on the same clear day in New York. Some people may be more inclined than others to withdraw in response to job dissatisfaction. Hackett (1989) found that the negative relationship between job satisfaction and absenteeism increased as the percentage of women in research samples increased.

In the domain of turnover, most research on moderators has centered around one issue – the potential for alternative employment or perceptions thereof to condition the impact of satisfaction on quitting. Such variables, of course, exemplify March and Simon's (1958) ease of movement construct. One of the great mysteries of organizational behavior research has been the frequent failure of perceived employment alternatives to predict turnover and their repeated failure to interact with job satisfaction to predict turnover (Griffeth & Hom, 1988). These failures are all the more striking when it is observed that aggregate turnover rates are highly correlated in the expected direction with unemployment rates and other economic conditions, both across time and industries (Hulin, Roznowski & Hachiya, 1985). Steel and Griffeth (1989) cited several possible reasons for a rather low ($r = .13$) population estimate of the relationship between perceived alternatives and turnover, and, by extension, their failure as a moderator. Single-item measures of alternatives may lack reliability and fail to capture both the quantity and quality aspects of perceived alternatives. Also, people who are not actively seeking jobs may have an uninformed view of the job market. Most importantly, however, individual-level studies of turnover have tended to use occupationally homogeneous, cross-sectional samples – people in one job in one organization experiencing one labor market at one time (Johns, 1991; Steel & Griffeth, 1989). This is hardly conducive to variation in perception of alternatives. Indeed, Carsten and Spector (1987) used meta-analysis to show that local unemployment rates, coded post hoc, moderated the relationship between job satisfaction and turnover as reported in a sample of individual-level studies. When unemployment was low, a more substantial connection between dissatisfaction and turnover was observed.

Table 12.1 *Meta-analytic corrected correlations between job satisfaction and work behaviors*

Satisfaction	Performance	Turnover	Absence (Time lost)	Absence (Frequency)	Absence (Time lost)	Absence (Frequency)	Lateness
Pay	.062 (25)	−.040 (16)	−.069 (41)	.000 (34)	−.070 (26)	−.080 (24)	−.220 (7)
Promotions	.145 (18)	−.140 (13)	−.071 (40)	−.066 (34)	−.070 (21)	−.090 (24)	−.280 (4)
Supervision	.186 (21)	−.100 (14)	−.055 (42)	−.107 (37)	−.080 (25)	−.130 (23)	—
Work	.207 (35)	−.190 (25)	−.068 (42)	−.162 (40)	−.140 (28)	−.210 (28)	—
Coworkers	.123 (20)	−.100 (11)	−.049 (41)	−.035 (34)	−.070 (22)	−.070 (23)	−.160 (7)
Overall[a]	.185 (54)	−.190 (78)	−.096 (22)	−.134 (33)	−.230 (8)	−.150 (17)	−.110 (15)
	.286 (9)						

Performance data from Iaffaldano and Muchinsky (1985); turnover data from Hom and Griffeth (1995); absence data from Hackett and Guion (1985, left two columns) and Hackett (1989, right two columns); lateness data from Koslowsky et al. (1997). Number of coefficients in parentheses. [a]For overall satisfaction, correlations with withdrawal behaviors include both sum-of-facets and global measures. For performance, .185 is global and .286 is sum-of-facets.

Decision Processes

The original Mobley (1977) intermediate linkages model of turnover and simplified versions of it have been exposed to repeated empirical tests, most having been cross-sectional, a curious strategy for testing a within-person process model. However, research by Hom, Griffeth, and colleagues (e.g., Hom & Griffeth, 1991; Hom, Caranikas-Walker, Prussia & Griffeth, 1992; Hom, Griffeth & Sellaro, 1984) has proven particularly cumulative and informative. Exploiting structural equation modeling, confirmatory factor analysis, meta-analysis, and longitudinality, these authors built upon previous research to devise the model shown in Figure 12.1. It shows that job satisfaction and organizational commitment influence both withdrawal cognitions and the expected utility of withdrawal. In turn, utility stimulates job search and the comparison of alternatives with the current job, a deciding factor for turnover.

This model is less serial than the original Mobley model, and it also involves fewer distinct variables; research has repeatedly had difficulty demonstrating the discriminability of all the constructs in the original model. It will also be noted that an explicit comparison of one's job with specific alternatives predicts turnover quite well in contrast to the vaguely held perceptions of alternative employment discussed earlier (Hom & Griffeth, 1995). An important innovation is the recognition of a direct link between withdrawal cognitions and turnover. This link allows for more impulsive, less calculated forms of withdrawal, as well as those that are calculated but do not involve alternative employment. Research supporting the unfolding model of turnover (Lee & Mitchell, 1994; Lee et al., 1996, Lee, Mitchell, Holtom, McDaniel & Hill, 1999) shows the advantages of this approach. Among other things, the model describes how 'shocks,' such as an unsolicited employment offer, might result in turnover irrespective of current satisfaction and without elaborate comparison processes. The

unfolding model provides a welcome contextual alternative to the intrapsychic emphasis of the Mobley model and its offspring.

An instance of turnover would usually represent a more important event for an employee than would a series of absence or lateness episodes. Thus, it is not obvious whether a rational decision model might apply to the latter behaviors. However, at least in the case of absence, such models do seem to apply, although the relevant research has not been framed as withdrawal-from-dissatisfaction research per se. At the most general level, event history models have shown that absence events unfold over a period of time in nonrandom and nonhabitual ways depending on evident degree of voluntariness, temporal trends, and previous absence behavior (Fichman, 1988, 1989; Harrison & Hulin, 1989). More specifically, there is good support for Martocchio and Harrison's (1993) decision theory of absence. This research shows that attitudes toward attendance, perceived norms to attend, and felt moral obligation to attend contribute to intention to attend work, which in turn is predictive of actual attendance (Harrison, 1995; Harrison & Bell, 1995; Martocchio, 1992). Unlike for turnover, this work complements, rather than dominates, other perspectives on withdrawal.

Organizational Commitment

Hom and Griffeth's (1995) inclusion of organizational commitment in the model shown in Figure 12.1 was done via meta-analytic inference, since most tests of the Mobley model and its variants did not include commitment. Using a clever combination of meta-analysis and path analysis, Tett and Meyer (1993) found that both satisfaction and commitment contributed independently to turnover intentions and cognitions, which in turn mediated almost all of their impact on turnover. Satisfaction was more highly correlated with intentions/cognitions than was commitment, while the reverse held true for actual turnover. They noted that their findings were somewhat clouded by the inclusion of withdrawal cognitions or

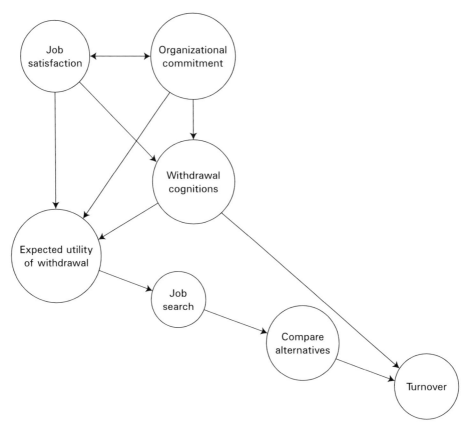

Figure 12.1   *The Hom and Griffeth integrative model of turnover. (Source: Employee Turnover, 1st edition, p. 108, by P. Hom and R. Griffeth © 1995. Reprinted with permission of a division of Thomson Learning.)*

intentions in some scales measuring both global satisfaction and organizational commitment.

As might be expected from the nature of the construct, organizational commitment has been shown to be a better predictor of turnover than absenteeism. Tett and Meyer (1993) reported a corrected population correlation of −.33 for turnover, while Mathieu and Zajac (1990) reported .10 for attendance, the logical inverse of absence. Isolating six studies that used a frequency measure of absence, Farrell and Stamm (1988) estimated a mean correlation of −.23 with commitment, a figure that approaches the highest correlations observed for job satisfaction reviewed in Table 12.1. All of this evidence pertains to affective commitment. Johns (1997) reviewed more contemporary research based on Meyer and Allen's (1991) tripartite theory of commitment. Although this research reaffirms the connection between affective commitment and absence, there is little evidence that implicates normative or continuance commitment. In particular, except for a study by Gellatly (1995), there is no support for the interesting prediction that continuance

commitment (being locked into an organization) might actually *stimulate* absenteeism. Meyer's (1997) review suggests that normative commitment (feeling an obligation to the organization) is consistently negatively related to turnover, while the connection with continuance commitment is inconsistent.

Social Exchange

The organization's commitment to its employees may be a better predictor of withdrawal than the employees' commitment toward the organization (cf. Shore & Wayne, 1993). In several samples, it has been shown that perceived organizational support is a particularly robust negative correlate of absenteeism (Eisenberger, Fasolo & Davis-LaMastro, 1990; Eisenberger, Huntington, Hutchison & Sowa, 1986). This research complements work showing that perceived inequity stimulates absenteeism (Geurts, Buunk & Schaufeli, 1994; van Dierendonck, Schaufeli & Buunk, 1998; Van Yperen, Hagedoorn & Geurts, 1996) as well as that revealing an increase in absenteeism following the failure to obtain a promotion (Schwarzwald,

Koslowsky & Shalit, 1992). These findings suggest that the rather passive view of withdrawal suggested by the withdrawal model needs to be supplemented with more proactive, equity-restoring motives (Johns & Nicholson, 1982). Even more generally, they suggest the value of incorporating a social exchange perspective into the withdrawal model. For example, Shore and Barksdale (1998) found that turnover intentions were lowest among employees who saw their obligations to the organization *and* the organization's obligations toward them as high.

Progression of Withdrawal

The connections among the various forms of work withdrawal have been of some interest to researchers. Theoretically, understanding such connections explicates more clearly exactly what is meant by *withdrawal*. Practically, such understanding may enable us to predict one form of withdrawal from the occurrence of another. Although relationships among lateness, absence, and turnover have been most studied, the withdrawal rubric might be extended to include psychological detachment, reduced in-role performance (Bycio, 1992; Bycio, Hackett & Alvares, 1990), reduced organizational citizenship (Chen, Hui & Sego, 1998; Mayer & Schoorman, 1992), choice of part-time work (Wise, 1993), or early retirement (Hanisch & Hulin, 1990).

Several plausible models might describe the connections between various withdrawal behaviors (Hulin, 1991; Rosse & Miller, 1984):

Independent forms. Despite some surface similarities, the behaviors have different causes and functions, and should thus be unrelated to each other.

Spillover. Withdrawal is nonspecific such that any given manifestation will be positively related to other manifestations.

Alternate forms. If the occurrence of one form of withdrawal is constrained, a substitute form will be manifested.

Compensatory forms. Similar functionality causes the specific forms of withdrawal to be negatively correlated.

Progression. Withdrawal will progress from minor, less salient acts, such as occasional lateness, to more salient acts, such as absence and, finally, turnover.

In the domain of lateness, absence, and turnover, the independent forms model can definitely be ruled out, as meta-analyses reveal common attitudinal correlates (Table 12.1) and substantial positive correlations between the various forms of withdrawal at the individual level (Hom & Griffeth, 1995; Koslowsky et al., 1997; Mitra, Jenkins & Gupta, 1992). The latter finding also speaks against

the generality of both the alternate and compensatory forms models, since both predict negative correlations. The difference between these two models is subtle. Alternative forms is based on the idea that the inability to react to dissatisfaction with one form of withdrawal will increase the occurrence of another form. Compensatory forms simply asserts that any act of withdrawal relieves dissatisfaction and thus reduces he probability of some other act. Isolated studies occasionally provide some support for one or the other of these formulations. Wise (1993) found that increased absenteeism was associated with a decrease in the adoption of part-time or casual work among nurses. Similarly, Dalton and Mesch (1992) determined that utility employees who requested a job transfer but had not received it experienced double the absence of those who had been given a transfer. Dalton and Todor (1993) speculated how absenteeism and the availability of internal transfers might affect subsequent turnover.

The strongest evidence appears to support the progression of withdrawal model. Longitudinal studies by Clegg (1983), Wolpin, Burke, Krausz and Freibach (1988), and Rosse (1988) found a lateness–absence progression, although Adler and Golan (1981) and Krausz, Koslowsky and Eiser (1998) did not. Blau (1994) found that a pattern of increasing chronic lateness was associated with elevated absence within the same 18-month period. Several studies reveal a progression from absence to turnover (Burke & Wilcox, 1972; Farrell & Peterson, 1984; Kanfer, Crosby & Brandt 1988; Krausz et al., 1998; Rosse, 1988; Sheridan, 1985; Waters & Roach, 1979), and Krausz et al. (1998) found that the progression was mediated by reduced job satisfaction.

If there is truly a progression from lateness to absence to turnover, we might expect that the two adjacent relationships in the progression would be stronger than the unadjacent relation between lateness and turnover. In fact, this appears to be the case when meta-analytic evidence is examined. Koslowsky et al. (1997) reported a corrected correlation of $r = .40$ between lateness and absence, and Mitra et al. (1992) reported a corrected correlation of .33 between absence and turnover. Koslowsky et al., estimated the mean correlation between lateness and actual turnover to be .07 and that between lateness and an apparent composite of actual turnover and turnover intentions to be .27.

Researchers have tended to look for linear progression. However, it is possible that nonlinearity may better capture the process. Using neural network and response surface methodologies, Somers (1999) found that turnover was invariant over a fairly wide range of attitudinal variation but increased dramatically with small changes above a certain threshold. Using catastrophe theory, Sheridan (1985) found a discontinuous, nonlinear increase in absenteeism in advance of turnover among nurses.

Is There a General Withdrawal Construct?

The positive relationship among the various behavioral manifestations of withdrawal has encouraged Hanisch, Hulin and Roznowski (e.g., Hanisch & Hulin, 1990, 1991; Hanisch et al., 1998) to posit the existence of a broad organizational withdrawal construct made up of job withdrawal (e.g., turnover and early retirement) and work withdrawal (e.g., lateness, absence, and escapist drinking). As implied, they favor the aggregation of 'specific withdrawal behaviors' (their term) into behavioral composites or aggregates, although most of the extant published research on the matter appears to use self-reported feelings, desires, expectations, and intentions to engage in the behaviors (Johns, 1998c). Although some psychometric gains are argued for the approach, its chief advantage would appear to be its capacity to accommodate the influence of various contextual constraints on the elicitation of a particular form of withdrawal. In other words, the approach allows for the idea that adaptation (see above) through withdrawal may vary in form according to organizational policies, legal sanctions, economic conditions, and so on. However, this accommodation seemingly occurs by treating context as useful noise rather than probing its intimate relationship with the various forms of withdrawal (Johns, 1998c).

Johns (1998c) opines that the broad withdrawal construct puts predictability above theoretical precision. It also overlooks theoretical successes achieved by *dis*aggregating various 'specific withdrawal behaviors,' such as that seen in the distinction between time lost and frequency of absence (Chadwick-Jones et al., 1982; Hackett & Guion, 1985) or between various patterns of lateness (Blau, 1994). Both Blau (1998) and Johns (1998c) worry that enthusiasm for a broad withdrawal construct has a tendency to beget a broad predictor construct that confounds attitudes, dispositions, and deviant tendencies. Adams and Beer (1998) found virtually no relationship between turnover intentions and retirement intentions. Nevertheless, the idea of a general withdrawal construct merits further research attention.

Conclusion

The withdrawal model, grounded in attitudes toward the job, gained prominence in part due to the assumption that attitudes predicted withdrawal better than they predicted performance. This assumption has been shown to be dubious. Nevertheless, the basic withdrawal model has demonstrated validity and the potential for development in the related domains of progression of withdrawal and a general withdrawal construct. However, researchers should also begin to pay greater attention to the neglected social and dispositional aspects of withdrawal.

THE SOCIAL CONTEXT OF WITHDRAWAL BEHAVIOR

As seen earlier, the withdrawal behaviors have literally been defined as pertaining to individual actors. Thus, it is not surprising that traditional absence and lateness research was dominated by individual attitudes and demographic factors, and that traditional turnover research was dominated by job attitudes and the intrapsychic machinations of the exit process. Despite this individual-level focus, there is considerable merit to considering the susceptibility of withdrawal to interpersonal influence. After all, timely and regular attendance is a *social* obligation to be at a particular place at a particular time (Martocchio & Harrison, 1993). Similarly, as Price (1977) reminds us, turnover represents movement between *social* systems.

Organizational Demography, Diversity, and Withdrawal

The impact of social context on turnover has been dominated by research on organizational demography. Originally conceived by Pfeffer (1983) to pertain to the distribution of the length of service of a workforce (tenure diversity), the term has been extended to the study of diversity in age, gender, race, ethnicity, and functional background. Pfeffer proposed that the distribution of tenure would affect the dynamics of power and control as well as cohort identity and conflict between cohorts. In turn, these social–contextual factors were expected to influence organizational performance and turnover patterns. A key prediction is that those who are most different from the dominant tenure cohort are likely to become turnover statistics.

Williams and O'Reilly (1998) sketch the theoretical underpinnings that predict the impact of demographic diversity on group processes and performance. Basically, they argue that theories of social identity and attraction predict that diversity will promote lower social integration and cohesion in groups, by extension increasing turnover. On the other hand, information-processing and decision-making theories point to the value of diversity for increasing the pool of available information and the variety of decision perspectives. In turn, this could enhance group performance. If the predominant negative relationship between individual performance and turnover (Bycio et al., 1990; Williams & Livingstone, 1994) also holds at the group level, some reduction in turnover might accrue.

Williams and O'Reilly (1998) conclude from their comprehensive review that both tenure and age diversity are associated with elevated group or organizational turnover. Although some of this research fails to measure group processes, O'Reilly,

Caldwell and Barnett (1989) found that social integration mediated the relationship between heterogeneity of group tenure and turnover. There is also a body of basic group research showing that tenure diversity has a negative impact on processes such as cohesion and communication, leading to dysfunctional turnover. This inference follows from the fact that those who are most different tend to leave and that there is no offsetting group performance improvement (Williams & O'Reilly, 1998).

Pelled (1996) presents a theory proposing that diversity of more visible demographic characteristics will promote turnover via affective conflict while diversity of job-related characteristics (e.g., functional specialty) will bolster task performance via task conflict. Unfortunately, there is little research that examines the impact of the distribution of visible characteristics such as gender, race, or ethnicity on turnover and virtually no such research on absence. Recently, Harrison, Johns and Martocchio (2000) explored how demography might influence absenteeism. For instance, it is well established that women exhibit higher absence rates than men (Côté & Haccoun, 1991) and that younger employees are absent more than older employees (Hackett, 1990). As gender or age diversity increases, it is likely that conflict concerning appropriate attendance norms would increase, especially under conditions of high task interdependence (cf. Barker, 1993). Harrison et al. (2000) also speculate that employees originating from more collective cultures might be more accepting of absence due to community or extended family concerns than those from individualistic cultures. In every case, diversity might affect both attributions concerning the legitimacy of certain causes of absence (cf. Addae & Johns, 1998; Johns & Xie, 1998) as well as expectations concerning what constitutes a reasonable level of absence.

Social Networks and Withdrawal

There has been a small but informative body of research concerning how location in social (i.e., communication) networks is related to employee turnover. This research has some conceptual ties to demography research in that communication patterns are logically linked to the concepts of identification, integration, and cohesion that are thought to underpin demographic effects.

Feeley and Barnett (1997) describe three models by which communication patterns might underlie employee turnover:

Structural equivalence. Turnover tends to occur among employees who communicate with identical others, whether or not they communicate directly with each other. That is, turnover follows patterns of informal role similarity.

Social influence. Turnover tends to occur along direct communication lines. That is, people who have direct links with leavers are likely to quit.

Erosion. Turnover tends to occur among those who lack strong communication links to others. That is, those least central to the communication network are prone to quit.

Both the structural equivalence and the social influence model allow for modeling and social information-processing mechanisms to influence turnover. However, structural equivalence would seem to load more on cognitive mechanisms (such as seeing the ease with which a structural counterpart found a new job), while social influence might impart both cognitive and affective information. Although the erosion model does not rule out modeling of turnover among the less attached, it differs conspicuously from the other two models in that it implicates a *lack* of communication in the turnover process. Thus, this model best represents the organizational demography prediction that those who are most different tend to leave.

All three models may be relevant to the turnover process. Krackhardt and Porter (1986) predicted and found structural equivalence among fast-food employees, describing the resulting turnover as a 'snowball effect.' Although they did not test the other two models, other analyses (Krackhardt & Porter, 1985) appear to run counter to the social influence model. However, Feeley and Barnett (1997) found support for all three models in a sample of supermarket employees. This is important, because it highlights the potential for multiple meanings of turnover in a single research site.

In some respects, network analysis treats turnover as an independent variable in that it is assumed (at least under structural equivalence and social influence) that turnover among some people causes turnover among others. Not nearly enough has been made of this perspective, in spite of the obvious impact that turnover might have on any well-defined social system. In other analyses of their fast-food data, Krackhardt and Porter (1985) examined the impact of turnover on the attitudes of friends who remained with the organization. Contrary to expectations, they found that friends became *more* satisfied and committed after the resignation of close counterparts. The authors attributed this effect to a reduction in negative cues from dissatisfied leavers. Similar insights might be had from research concerning the reactions of 'survivors' of corporate layoffs (e.g., Brockner & Wiesenfeld, 1993). Although this work is seldom identified as turnover research and does not employ network analysis, it indirectly concerns the impact of involuntary turnover on existing social networks.

Norms, Culture, and Withdrawal

Despite their insights, the demography and network approaches have some 'black box' qualities that limit their usefulness. However, there has been a growing body of research, mostly in the area of absenteeism, that looks more directly at the social correlates and causes of withdrawal.

Interest in the social causes of absenteeism began with the simple observation that there are differences in absence levels and patterns across social units such as workgroups within departments, departments within plants, and plants within companies, as well as between occupations, industries, and even nations (Chadwick-Jones et al., 1982; Johns, 1997). In many cases, these differences are of such a nature or magnitude that they are unlikely to stem from the simple distribution of individual characteristics such as ill health, work attitudes, or demographics. This logic, itself admittedly black box in nature, gave rise to the search for possible social correlates and causes of absence that would account for group differences. Rather peculiarly, differences in the base rate of *turnover* across samples have been portrayed as statistical artifacts (e.g., McEvoy & Cascio, 1987) that need to be corrected rather than sources of research inspiration.

It is now well established that perceived workplace norms play an important role in the occurrence of absenteeism. That is, people who tend to see their coworkers as exhibiting high absence tend to be absent more themselves. This finding applies to a wide variety of operationalizations of absence norms, including direct numerical estimates (e.g., Johns & Xie, 1998), ratings of peer absence (Baba & Harris, 1989), subjective norm estimates (e.g., Harrison, 1995), and return potential estimates (Gale, 1993). Gellatly (1995) found that perceived absence norms mediated the connection between workgroup absence frequency rates in one year and the absence exhibited by individual members the following year.

Why is absenteeism especially susceptible to social influence? Johns (1997) reviews considerable indirect evidence that both actors and observers tend to view absence as mildly deviant behavior. For example, people tend to underreport their own absence and see their attendance behavior as much better than that of their peers (Johns, 1994a, b; Johns & Xie, 1998). Despite such individual self-serving, attendance norms provide guidance regarding the vagaries of how much deviant behavior is considered legitimate in a given social setting (Gellatly & Luchak, 1998).

Gale (1993) found that cohesive workgroups and those operating under high task interdependence had the strongest norms against absence, and that such norms predicted time lost for both individuals and groups. Xie and Johns (2000) reported similar mediated results for cohesiveness among Chinese workgroups. In general, group cohesiveness is negatively associated with absenteeism, and both the task and social aspects of cohesion have been implicated (Johns, 1997). However, some interesting interactions have been observed, suggesting that the impact of cohesiveness is conditional. Drago and Wooden (1992) found cohesion resulted in high self-reported absence when job satisfaction was low and low absence when satisfaction was high. Xie and Johns (2000) determined that workgroup cohesiveness interacted with absence culture salience, the latter reflecting the group's attention to absenteeism and agreement about appropriate attendance levels. Although high cohesiveness was generally associated with low absence, the absence of cohesive groups also increased as cultural salience increased. The authors interpreted this as collusion in the most socially organized groups to take days off, reminiscent of Edwards and Scullion's (1982) case observation of posted 'absence schedules' in a well-organized metals plant.

The very best evidence concerning the impact of social influence on withdrawal comes from cross-level and multilevel studies that appear to illustrate the impact of work unit absence or lateness cultures (Chadwick-Jones et al., 1982; Johns & Nicholson, 1982; Nicholson & Johns, 1985) on individual behavior. Some of this research shows that absence or lateness aggregated at the work unit (usually workgroup) level accounts for variance in the withdrawal of individual work unit members (Blau, 1995; Gellatly & Luchak, 1988; Johns, 1994c; Markham & McKee, 1995; Mathieu & Kohler, 1990). This research variously implicates perceived absence norms, the salience of the absence culture, and supervisory expectations as explanatory mechanisms. Other research has shown that aggregate views about the likely consequences of absence (Martocchio, 1994) as well as those concerning cohesiveness and cultural salience (Xie & Johns, 2000) account for variance in individual absence. George (1990) found that the positive affective tone of workgroups was negatively correlated with group absence rates. Iverson, Buttigieg and Maguire (1999) determined that hospital wards with greater similarity in union membership status viewed absence as less legitimate when industrial relations climate was positive.

It must be emphasized that the findings supporting the existence of absence and lateness cultures are most impressive because virtually all of the research has controlled for relevant individual differences, especially in job satisfaction. This means that there is truly value added by the social approach to withdrawal.

As noted above, cross-site differences in turnover have been more often viewed as statistical nuisance rather than research opportunities. Nonetheless, some of the research on organizational culture and person–organization fit speaks indirectly to possible social influences on turnover. Sheridan (1992) found that differences in value profiles among six large accounting firms resulted in differential turnover rates. Measures of person–organization fit, whether based on value differences (e.g., O'Reilly, Chatman & Caldwell, 1991; Vandenberghe, 1999) or direct perceptions of fit (Saks & Ashforth, 1997) have been shown to predict subsequent turnover. Research bearing on Schneider's attraction–selection–attrition model suggests that the personality traits of organizational members may tend toward homogeneity over time, leading to attrition among those who fail to fit and thus creating distinctive climates or cultures for turnover (Schaubroeck, Ganster & James, 1998; Schneider, Goldstein & Smith, 1995).

Conclusion

One only has to examine the rather large differences in withdrawal behavior across various social units to see that what is considered normal is not an absolute matter and is unlikely to be a sole product of aggregate individual differences. This suggests that social and contextual influences on withdrawal deserve our attention. This may require a shift in level of analysis from the individual to the individual within a relevant social unit.

DISPOSITION AND WITHDRAWAL

Is there a dispositional substrate to some withdrawal behavior? That is, are some people prone to lateness, absence, or turnover by virtue of their personalities? Although the proneness concept has a history in the domain of withdrawal (Frogatt, 1970; Garrison & Muchinsky, 1977; Ghiselli, 1974), the history is checkered. This is due to concern that proneness is a hollow, circular construct, indiscriminable from the regularity of behavior that gives rise to its attribution (cf. Johns & Nicholson, 1982). Does the proneness concept have any scientific substance, or is it simply proof of people's tendency to attribute higher levels of what are normally low- base-rate behaviors to dispositional causes? A proneness explanation grounded in disposition suggests some stability of withdrawal behavior over time and especially across situations. The evidence of such stability is fairly well established for absenteeism. Farrell and Stamm's (1988) meta-analysis determined that absence history was correlated .65 with current absence frequency and .71 with time lost. Rentsch and Steel (1998) found that frequency of absence measured in 1983 was significantly correlated with frequency in five subsequent years, the consecutive rs being .74, .67, .56, .59, and .53. Regarding stability under situational change, Brenner (1968) reported that absence from high

school was positively correlated with absenteeism in subsequent employment. Similarly, Ivancevich (1985) found that past absence predicted subsequent absence even when substantial job design changes intervened.

There is very little evidence regarding the stability of turnover. However, Judge and Watanabe (1995) applied event history techniques to the turnover behavior of the US National Longitudinal Surveys Youth Cohort over a 10-year period. They determined that past quits were predictive of subsequent turnover, even controlling for other variables that have been shown to stimulate withdrawal.

In conclusion, the stability of absence and turnover appears conducive to a dispositional model. However, it does not rule out situational causes, such as the impact of chronic ill health on absence or the impact of structural opportunity (e.g., personal contacts gained through a series of past jobs) on turnover.

Over the years that the withdrawal model was dominant for all specific forms of withdrawal, occasional associations between personality and turnover were reported in the literature. Very little such research concerned absenteeism. Reviews did find evidence of associations between personality and turnover, particularly implicating 'extreme' values on personality dimensions (Muchinsky & Tuttle, 1979; Porter & Steers, 1973). However, as Muchinsky and Tuttle pointed out, reported significant associations were often drawn from a large pool of nonsignificant associations generated from the application of personality inventories and then seldom cross-validated. This tactic, typical of work-personality research of the era, was far from theory-driven.

Hough and Schneider (1996) recounted the advances in research that have rekindled interest in personality in organizations. Chief among these are the emergence of the the five-factor model of personality (the Big Five, Digman, 1990), the linking of specific traits to specific criteria, and the development of specialized work-related measures that draw on the Big Five, especially integrity tests. If personality influences withdrawal it would seem to operate through some combination of integrity, affect, or cognition.

Integrity

A potential link between disposition and withdrawal lies in the general (and somewhat vague) domain of undependability, irresponsibility, and low integrity. These traits signal deviance, and, as noted earlier, there is much evidence that people see absence as deviant behavior (Johns, 1997). Although such negative views of turnover are less documented and probably less intense, Ghiselli's (1974) portrayal of the 'hobo syndrome,' a form of irrational occupational wanderlust characterized by high mobility and low organizational commitment, is an example.

If these deviant attributions are smoke, do they signal fire, in the form of a deviant underpinning to some withdrawal activity? The best evidence comes from meta-analyses of integrity or honesty tests designed to predict theft and other counterproductive job behaviors. Overt integrity tests tap attitudes toward honesty and integrity and are generally designed to predict theft. Personality-based integrity tests (usually drawing from subtraits falling under the Big Five conscientiousness dimension) index integrity indirectly and are designed to predict broader counterproductivity. An extensive meta-analysis by Ones, Viswesvaran and Schmidt (1993) concluded that lateness, absence, and turnover were part of a broad composite of counterproductive behaviors predictable with both types of measures. However, more detailed analyses of these data are instructive. Ones, Viswesvaran and Schmidt (1992) found that the mean corrected correlation between personality-based tests and absenteeism was .33, while the corresponding figure for overt tests was .09. In another meta-analysis that did not differentiate test type, Viswesvaran, Ones and Schmidt (undated) reported an average corrected validity of .29 for the prediction of voluntary turnover and .34 for the prediction of involuntary turnover due to theft. These figures for dedicated integrity measures are much higher than the corrected correlations that Barrick and Mount (1991) reported between the Big Five dimensions and turnover, the highest of which was .09 for conscientiousness. Such meta-analytic treatment is unavailable for the relations between the basic Big Five dimensions and absenteeism. However, Judge, Martocchio and Thoresen (1997) found that time lost was negatively related to consciousness and positively related to extraversion. They also found that absence history partially mediated these associations, a finding that squares with a dispositional model. No association was observed for neuroticism. Conte and Jacobs (1999) reported a negative association between consciousness and frequency of absence, but not lateness.

Is it possible that the observed relationships between integrity and withdrawal actually signal the orthodox withdrawal model in disguise? That is, could satisfaction mediate between integrity and withdrawal? The answer is of some theoretical importance. As noted earlier, Blau (1998) and Johns (1998c) expressed concern that Hanisch et al.'s (1998) general withdrawal construct is confounded with deviance while being defined as a response to job dissatisfaction. Where does this leave the integrity construct? The answer to this question might be more apparent if job satisfaction and related attitudes were used as criteria in integrity research, which has evidently not been the case. Nevertheless, some speculation is possible. Both Ones, Schmidt and Viswesvaran (1994) and Hough (1992) address the validity of the integrity construct, agreeing that it is composed of conscientiousness and emotional stability but disagreeing on the agreeableness dimension. Thus, it appears that there is the *potential* for integrity to affect withdrawal independently of job satisfaction.

Affect and Cognition

Speculation that the integrity model can be separated from the conventional attitudinal withdrawal model does not in any way preclude dispositional influences on withdrawal behaviors via dissatisfaction. As Hough and Schneider (1996) remind us, personality is more than integrity. Indeed, there is growing evidence that there is a dispositional component to job satisfaction (Judge, Locke & Durham, 1997). Day, Bedeian and Conte (1998) found that job satisfaction mediated the relationship between the personality dimensions of self-control and extraversion and propensity to quit. Certainly, personality traits outside of the integrity nexus may be associated with withdrawal. For example, George (1989) found that positive affectivity was positively associated with being in a good mood at work, which in turn was negatively associated with absence. Iverson, Olekalns and Erwin (1998) reported somewhat analogous results, showing that positive affectivity stimulated feelings of personal work accomplishment, which in turn were associated with reduced absenteeism. The latter connection was not mediated by job satisfaction.

It is possible that personality might influence withdrawal via its impact on cognitions about the behaviors themselves rather than via affective mechanisms. For instance, personality might influence people's beliefs about the extent to which a given absence incident is viewed as legitimate or as voluntary. Seeing an absence as legitimate or as beyond one's control is likely to pose few barriers to engaging in the behavior. Judge and Martocchio (1995, 1996) studied the perceived degree of control that respondents believed they would have when faced with a variety of absence-inducing scenarios. They found clear evidence that personality affected these attributions. Individuals with external locus of control, low work ethic, a tendency to make excuses, or self-deceptive personalities were more prone to attribute absence events to external than internal causes. Similar effects might occur for turnover. Thus, we might expect chronic optimists to perceive more job alternatives and to view prospective job changes more favorably than pessimists.

Conclusion

As illustrated, there is developing evidence suggesting that personality may play a role in some withdrawal behavior. As indicated, it is still an open question to what extent such relationships are mediated by job satisfaction. Issues of moderation may be even more important and are conspicuously absent from the personality–withdrawal literature. Barrick and Mount (1993) found that personality was more strongly associated with performance when job autonomy was high. Perhaps the same is true for lateness and absence. More generally, personality may interact with other factors to affect withdrawal. For instance, Mowday, Stone and Porter (1979) found that needs for achievement and affiliation interacted with job scope to predict turnover. More theory-driven research in this domain is desirable.

IMPROVING WITHDRAWAL RESEARCH

A number of improvements can be suggested for withdrawal research that build upon past research. Although space does not permit detailed explication of these ideas, it should be emphasized that they are intended to be implemented in the context of full theoretical development and justification.

Withdrawal research would profit from more active integration with related literatures to which it has an obvious but unexploited affinity. Turnover research would particularly profit from greater linkages with areas that can highlight the *context* in which the behavior might occur, such as the work on careers (Ornstein & Isabella, 1993; Sullivan, 1999; Taylor & Giannantonio, 1993). Also, research on turnover could both contribute to and profit from linkage with the literature on expatriate adjustment (Shaffer & Harrison, 1998).

Withdrawal research needs to be less organization-centric, better incorporating how off-the-job factors affect withdrawal. Morgan and Herman (1976) showed how nonwork consequences influenced absenteeism more than organization-mediated consequences. Gignac, Kelloway and Gottlieb (1996) explored how eldercare responsibilities influenced absenteeism. We need to know much more about such matters, including how family situations affect turnover (cf. Cohen, 1997). In a related vein, we need more research on what people are doing when they are late or absent (Haccoun & Dupont, 1987) and where they are going when they quit (cf. Campion, 1991). Such knowledge will help us explain anomalous patterns of withdrawal.

Withdrawal research needs to better incorporate the role of time. Although the major forms of withdrawal can all be framed as problems concerning the allocation of time and place, and events that unfold over time, these facts of life have not made a strong impression on withdrawal theory or research. The problems of doing cross-sectional research on turnover have been recognized (Peters &

Sheridan, 1988), and event history methods have clarified the role of time in turnover (Dickter, Roznowski & Harrison, 1996; Somers, 1996; Somers & Birnbaum, 1999). What is needed, however, is stronger *theory* that can capitalize on event histories. The unfolding model of turnover (Lee & Mitchell, 1994) is one such theory. Harrison and Martocchio (1998) cleverly reviewed the absenteeism literature around the concept of time, discussing long-term (e.g., dispositional), mid-term (e.g., attitudinal), and short-term (e.g., acute stress-related) sources of variation in absence and the corresponding appropriateness of various absence aggregation periods.

Withdrawal research needs to be more focused on the changing world of work, recognizing the influence of new technology, teamwork, and revised psychological contracts. For example, it is not at all clear that the traditional rational affect paradigm for turnover speaks very well to the attraction and retention of high-tech talent, so-called knowledge workers. The unfolding model of turnover, which allows for a more contextualized range of paths to quitting, seems quite promising in this regard (Lee & Maurer, 1997). Harrison et al. (2000) discuss how information technology allows for work to be accomplished independent of the strictures of time, space, or direct social influence. In turn, they argue that the resulting 'weak situation' favors the stronger influence of individual attitudes and personality on absence, which they redefine as withdrawing from the task, a specific assignment or project. On the other hand, they submit that forces for increased teamwork will favor the increased impact of social control on absence, control that may be accompanied by workplace tension as teams face the realities of disciplining their own members.

We need to understand the cross-cultural similarities and differences in withdrawal behaviors and their determinants and consequences. Since the *act* of withdrawal can be measured in a culture-free way, the information gap in this area is surprising. Abrams, Ando and Hinkle (1998) determined that organizational identification predicted turnover intentions in both Britain and Japan, but that perceived social norms concerning turnover had less influence in Britain than in more collectivist Japan. Johns and Xie (1998) found that both Canadians and Chinese self-served, underreporting their own absenteeism and seeing their attendance records as superior to those of their peers. However, the Chinese also saw their workgroups' attendance as much superior to that of their occupation, thus exhibiting group serving. Both similarities and differences in the perceived legitimacy of various causes of absence were observed across the two cultures. Addae and Johns (1998) described a cross-cultural model of absence legitimacy based on locus of control, time urgency, social support, and gender-role differentiation. More work of this nature is warranted.

To conclude, withdrawal research has a venerable history that has not suffered from the faddishness and fashion of much construct-centered work. On the other hand, it has suffered from a lack of theoretical development both within and beyond the core tenets of the basic withdrawal model. Much remains to be done.

ACKNOWLEDGMENT

Preparation of this chapter was supported by grant 00-ER-0506 from Quebec's Fonds pour la Formation de Chercheurs et l'Aide à la Recherche and grant 410-99-1491 from the Social Sciences and Humanities Research Council of Canada.

REFERENCES

Abrams, D., Ando, K., & Hinkle, S. (1998). Psychological attachment to the group: Cross-cultural differences in organizational identification and subjective norms as predictors of workers' turnover intentions. *Personality and Social Psychology Bulletin, 24*, 1027–1039.

Adams, G.A., & Beer, T.A. (1998). Turnover and retirement: A comparison of their similarities and differences. *Personnel Psychology, 51*, 643–665.

Addae, H.M., & Johns, G. (1998). *National absence cultures: Dimensions and consequences.* Paper presented at the annual meeting of the Academy of Management, San Diego.

Adler, S., & Golan, J. (1981). Lateness as withdrawal behavior. *Journal of Applied Psychology, 66*, 544–554.

Ajzen, I., & Fishbein, M. (1980). *Understanding attitudes and predicting social behavior.* Englewood Cliffs, NJ: Prentice-Hall.

Baba, V.V., & Harris, M.J. (1989). Stress and absence: A cross-cultural perspective. *Research in Personnel and Human Resources Management, Suppl. 1,* 317–337.

Baltes, B.B., Briggs, T.E., Huff, J.W., Wright, J.A., & Neuman, G.A. (1999). Flexible and compressed workweek schedules: A meta-analysis of their effects on work-related criteria. *Journal of Applied Psychology, 84*, 496–513.

Barker, J.R. (1993). Tightening the iron cage: Concertive control in self-managing teams. *Administrative Science Quarterly, 38*, 408–437.

Barrick, M.R., & Mount, M.K. (1991). The big five personality dimensions and job performance: A meta-analysis. *Personnel Psychology, 44*, 1–26.

Barrick, M.R., & Mount, M.K. (1993). Autonomy as a moderator of the relationships between the big five personality dimensions and job performance. *Journal of Applied Psychology, 78*, 111–118.

Bezanson, A., & Schoenfeld, M. (1925). Labor turnover in the coal industry. *Journal of Personnel Research, 4*, 268–295.

Blau, G. (1994). Developing and testing a taxonomy of lateness behavior. *Journal of Applied Psychology, 79*, 959–970.

Blau, G. (1995). Influence of group lateness on individual lateness: A cross-level examination. *Academy of Management Journal, 38*, 1483–1496.

Blau, G. (1998). On the aggregation of individual withdrawal behaviors into larger multi-item constructs. *Journal of Organizational Behavior, 19*, 437–451.

Brayfield, A.H., & Crockett, W.H. (1955). Employee attitudes and employee performance. *Psychological Bulletin, 52*, 396–424.

Brenner, M.H. (1968). Use of high school data to predict work performance. *Journal of Applied Psychology, 52*, 29–30.

Brockner, J., & Wiesenfeld, B. (1993). Living on the edge (of social and organizational psychology): The effects of job layoffs on those who remain. In J.K. Murnighan (Ed.), *Social psychology in organizations: Advances in theory and research* (pp. 119–140). Englewood Cliffs, NJ: Prentice-Hall.

Burke, R.J., & Wilcox, D.S. (1972). Absenteeism and turnover among female telephone operators. *Personnel Psychology, 25*, 639–648.

Bycio, P. (1992). Job performance and absenteeism: A review and meta-analysis. *Human Relations, 45*, 193–220.

Bycio, P., Hackett, R.D., & Alvares, K.M. (1990). Job performance and turnover: A review and meta-analysis. *Applied Psychology: An International Review, 39*, 47–76.

Campion, M.A. (1991). Meaning and measurement of turnover: Comparison of alternative measures and recommendations for research. *Journal of Applied Psychology, 76*, 199–212.

Cappelli, P., & Sherer, P.D. (1991). The missing role of context in OB: The need for a meso-level approach. *Research in Organizational Behavior, 13*, 55–110.

Carsten, J.M., & Spector, P.E. (1987). Unemployment, job satisfaction, and employee turnover: A meta-analytic test of the Muchinsky model. *Journal of Applied Psychology, 72*, 374–381.

Chadwick-Jones, J.K., Nicholson, N., & Brown, C. (1982). *Social psychology of absenteeism.* New York: Prager.

Chen, X.P., Hui, C., & Sego, D.J. (1998). The role of organizational citizenship behavior in turnover: Conceptualization and preliminary tests of key hypotheses. *Journal of Applied Psychology, 83*, 922–931.

Clegg, C.W. (1983). Psychology of employee lateness, absence, and turnover: A methodological critique and an empirical study. *Journal of Applied Psychology, 68*, 88–101.

Cohen, A. (1997). Nonwork influences on withdrawal cognitions: An empirical examination of an overlooked issue. *Human Relations, 50*, 1511–1536.

Conte, J.M., & Jacobs, R.R. (1999). *Temporal and personality predictors of absence and lateness.* Paper presented at the annual convention of the Society for Industrial and Organizational Psychology, Atlanta.

Côté, D., & Haccoun, R.R. (1991). L'absentéisme des femmes et des hommes: Une méta-analyse. *Canadian Journal of Administrative Sciences, 8*, 130–139.

Dalton, D.R., & Mesch, D.J. (1992). The impact of employee-initiated transfer on absenteeism: A four-year cohort assessment. *Human Relations, 45*, 291–304.

Dalton, D.R., & Todor, W.D. (1993). Turnover, transfer, and absenteeism: An interdependent perspective. *Journal of Management, 19*, 193–219.

Day, D.V., Bedeian, A.G., & Conte, J.M. (1998). Personality as predictor of work-related outcomes: Test of a mediated latent structural model. *Journal of Applied Social Psychology, 28*, 2068–2088.

Deutscher, I. (1973). *What we say/what we do: Sentiments and acts.* Glenview, IL: Scott, Foresman.

Dickter, D.N., Roznowski, M., & Harrison, D.A. (1996). Temporal tempering: An event history analysis of the process of voluntary turnover. *Journal of Applied Psychology, 81*, 705–716.

Digman, J.M. (1990). Personality structure: Emergence of the five-factor model. *Annual Review of Psychology, 41*, 417–440.

Drago, R., & Wooden, M. (1992). The determinants of labor absence: Economic factors and workgroup norms across countries. *Industrial and Labor Relations Review, 45*, 764–778.

Dunnette, M.D. (1976). Toward fusion. In M.D. Dunnette (Ed.), *Handbook of industrial and organizational psychology* (pp. 1–12). Chicago: Rand McNally.

Edwards, P.K., & Scullion, H. (1982). *The social organization of industrial conflict: Control and resistance in the workplace.* Oxford: Blackwell.

Eisenberger, R., Fasolo, P., & Davis-LaMastro, V. (1990). Perceived organizational support and employee diligence, commitment, and innovation. *Journal of Applied Psychology, 75*, 51–59.

Eisenberger, R., Huntington, R., Hutchison, S., & Sowa, D. (1986). Perceived organizational support. *Journal of Applied Psychology, 71*, 500–507.

Farrell, D., & Peterson, J.C. (1984). Commitment, absenteeism, and turnover of new employees: A longitudinal study. *Human Relations, 37*, 681–692.

Farrell, D., & Stamm, C.L. (1988). Meta-analysis of the correlates of employee absence. *Human Relations, 41*, 211–227.

Feeley, T.H., & Barnett, G.A. (1997). Predicting employee turnover from communication networks. *Human Communication Research, 23*, 370–387.

Fichman, M. (1988). Motivational consequences of absence and attendance: Proportional hazard estimation of a dynamic motivation model. *Journal of Applied Psychology, 73*, 119–134.

Fichman, M. (1989). Attendance makes the heart grow fonder: A hazard rate approach to modeling attendance. *Journal of Applied Psychology, 74*, 325–335.

Fichman, M. (1999). Variance explained: When size does not (always) matter. *Research in Organizational Behavior, 21*, 295–331.

Frayne, C.A., & Latham, G.P. (1987). Application of social learning theory to employee self-management of attendance. *Journal of Applied Psychology, 72*, 387–392.

Frogatt, P. (1970). Short-term absence from industry. III. The inference of 'proneness' and a search for causes. *British Journal of Industrial Medicine, 27*, 297–312.

Gale, E.K. (1993). *Social influences on absenteeism.* Unpublished doctoral dissertation, Purdue University.

Garrison, K.R., & Muchinsky, P.M. (1977). Evaluating the concept of absentee-proneness with two measures of absence. *Personnel Psychology, 30*, 389–393.

Gellatly, I.R. (1995). Individual and group determinants of employee absenteeism: Test of a causal model. *Journal of Organizational Behavior, 16*, 469–485.

Gellatly, I.R., & Luchak, A.A. (1998). Personal and organizational determinants of perceived absence norms. *Human Relations, 51*, 1085–1102.

George, J.M. (1989). Mood and absence. *Journal of Applied Psychology, 74*, 317–324.

George, J.M. (1990). Personality, affect, and behavior in groups. *Journal of Applied Psychology, 75*, 107–116.

Geurts, S.A., Buunk, B.P., & Schaufeli, W.B. (1994). Social comparisons and absenteeism: A structural modeling approach. *Journal of Applied Social Psychology, 24*, 1871–1890.

Ghiselli, E.E. (1974). Some perspectives for industrial psychology. *American Psychologist, 29*, 80–87.

Gignac, M.A.M., Kelloway, E.K., & Gottlieb, B.H. (1996). The impact of caregiving on employment: A mediational model of work-family conflict. *Canadian Journal on Aging, 15*, 525–542.

Goodman, P.S., & Atkin, R.S. (1984). Effects of absenteeism on individuals and organizations. In P.S. Goodman, & R.S. Atkin (Eds.), *Absenteeism: New approaches to understanding, measuring, and managing employee absence* (pp. 276–321). San Francisco: Jossey-Bass.

Griffeth, R.W., & Hom, P.W. (1988). A comparison of different conceptualizations of perceived alternatives in turnover research. *Journal of Organizational Behavior, 9*, 103–111.

Haccoun, R.R., & Dupont, S. (1987). Absence research: A critique of previous approaches and an example for a new direction. *Canadian Journal of Administrative Sciences, 4*, 143–156.

Hackett, R.D. (1989). Work attitudes and employee absenteeism: A synthesis of the literature. *Journal of Occupational Psychology, 62*, 235–248.

Hackett, R.D. (1990). Age, tenure, and employee absenteeism. *Human Relations, 43*, 610–619.

Hackett, R.D., & Bycio, P. (1996). An evaluation of employee absenteeism as a coping mechanism among hospital nurses. *Journal of Occupational and Organizational Psychology, 69*, 327–338.

Hackett, R.D., & Guion, R.M. (1985). A reevaluation of the absenteeism-job satisfaction relationship. *Organizational Behavior and Human Decision Processes, 35*, 340–381.

Hanisch, K.A., & Hulin, C.L. (1990). Job attitudes and organizational withdrawal: An examination of retirement and other voluntary withdrawal behaviors. *Journal of Vocational Behavior*, 37, 60–78.

Hanisch, K.A., & Hulin, C.L. (1991). General attitudes and organizational withdrawal: An evaluation of a causal model. *Journal of Vocational Behavior*, 39, 110–128.

Hanisch, K.A., Hulin, C.L., & Roznowski, M. (1998). The importance of individuals' repertoires of behaviors: The scientific appropriateness of studying multiple behaviors and general attitudes. *Journal of Organizational Behavior*, 19, 463–480.

Harrison, D.A. (1995). Volunteer motivation and attendance decisions: Competitive theory testing in multiple samples from a homeless shelter. *Journal of Applied Psychology*, 80, 371–385.

Harrison, D.A., & Bell, M.P. (1995). *Social expectations and attendance decisions: Implications for absence control programs*. Paper presented at the annual meeting of the Academy of Management, Vancouver.

Harrison, D.A., & Hulin, C.L. (1989). Investigations of absenteeism: Using event history models to study the absence-taking process. *Journal of Applied Psychology*, 74, 300–316.

Harrison, D.A., Johns, G., & Martocchio, J.J. (2000). Changes in technology, teamwork, and diversity: New directions for a new century of absenteeism research. *Research in Personnel and Human Resources Management*, 18, 43–91.

Harrison, D.A., & Martocchio, J.J. (1998). A time for absenteeism: A 20-year review of origins, offshoots, and outcomes. *Journal of Management*, 24, 305–350.

Herzberg, F., Mausner, B., Peterson, R.O., & Capwell, D.F. (1957). *Job attitudes: Review of research and opinion*. Pittsburgh: Psychological Service of Pittsburgh.

Hill, J.M.M., & Trist, E.L. (1953). A consideration of industrial accidents as a means of withdrawal from the work situation. *Human Relations*, 6, 357–380.

Hill, J.M.M., & Trist, E.L. (1955). Changes in accidents and other absences with length of service. *Human Relations*, 8, 121–152.

Hom, P.W., Caranikas-Walker, F., Prussia, G.E., & Griffeth, R.W. (1992). A meta-analytical structural equations analysis of a model of employee turnover. *Journal of Applied Psychology*, 77, 890–909.

Hom, P.W., & Griffeth, R.W. (1991). Structural equations modeling test of a turnover theory. *Journal of Applied Psychology*, 76, 350–366.

Hom, P.W., & Griffeth, R.W. (1995). *Employee turnover*. Cincinnati, OH: South-Western.

Hom, P.W., Griffeth, R.W., Palich, L.L., & Bracker, J.S. (1999). Revisiting met expectations as a reason why realistic job previews work. *Personnel Psychology*, 52, 97–112.

Hom, P.W., Griffeth, R.W., & Sellaro, C.L. (1984). The validity of Mobley's 1977 model of employee turnover. *Organizational Behavior and Human Performance*, 34, 141–174.

Hough, L.M. (1992). The 'big five' personality variables – construct confusion: Description versus prediction. *Human Performance*, 5, 139–155.

Hough, L.M., & Schneider, R.J. (1996). Personality traits, taxonomies, and applications in organizations. In K.R. Murphy (Ed.), *Individual differences and behavior in organizations* (pp. 31–88). San Francisco: Jossey-Bass.

Hulin, C.L. (1991). Adaptation, persistence, and commitment in organizations. In M.D. Dunnette, & L.M. Hough (Eds.), *Handbook of industrial and organizational psychology* (2nd ed., Vol. 2, pp. 445–505). Palo Alto, CA: Consulting Psychologists Press.

Hulin, C.L., Roznowski, M., & Hachiya, D. (1985). Alternative opportunities and withdrawal decisions: Empirical and theoretical discrepancies and an integration. *Psychological Bulletin*, 97, 233–250.

Iaffaldano, M.T., & Muchinsky, P.M. (1985). Job satisfaction and job performance: A meta-analysis. *Psychological Bulletin*, 97, 251–273.

Ilgen, D.R., Barnes-Farrell, J.L., & McKellin, D.B. (1993). Performance appraisal process research in the 1980s: What has it contributed to appraisals in use? *Organizational Behavior and Human Decision Processes*, 54, 321–368.

Irving, P.G., & Meyer, J.P. (1994). Reexamination of the met-expectations hypothesis: A longitudinal analysis. *Journal of Applied Psychology*, 79, 937–949.

Irving, P.G., & Meyer, J.P. (1999). On using residual difference scores in the measurement of congruence: The case of met expectations research. *Personnel Psychology*, 52, 85–95.

Ivancevich, J.M. (1985). Predicting absenteeism from prior absence and work attitudes. *Academy of Management Journal*, 28, 219–228.

Iverson, R.D., Buttigieg, D.M., & Maguire, C. (1999). *Absence culture: The effects of union membership within work groups and industrial relations climate*. Paper presented at the annual meeting of the Academy of Management, Chicago.

Iverson, R.D., Olekalns, M., & Erwin, P.J. (1998). Affectivity, organizational stressors, and absenteeism: A causal model of burnout and its consequences. *Journal of Vocational Behavior*, 52, 1–23.

Johns, G. (1978). Attitudinal and nonattitudinal predictors of two forms of absence from work. *Organizational Behavior and Human Performance*, 22, 431–444.

Johns, G. (1991). Substantive and methodological constraints on behavior and attitudes in organizational research. *Organizational Behavior and Human Decision Processes*, 49, 80–104.

Johns, G. (1993). Constraints on the adoption of psychology-based personnel practices: lessons from organizational innovation. *Personnel Psychology*, 46, 569–592.

Johns, G. (1994a). Absenteeism estimates by employees and managers: Divergent perspectives and self-serving perceptions. *Journal of Applied Psychology*, 79, 229–239.

Johns, G. (1994b). How often were you absent? A review of the use of self-reported absence data. *Journal of Applied Psychology*, 79, 574–591.

Johns, G. (1994c). *Medical, ethical, and cultural constraints on work absence and attendance*. Presentation at the International Congress of Applied Psychology, Madrid.

Johns, G. (1995). Absenteeism. In N. Nicholson (Ed.), *The Blackwell encyclopedic dictionary of organizational behavior* (pp. 1–3). Oxford: Blackwell.

Johns, G. (1997). Contemporary research on absence from work: Correlates, causes and consequences. *International Review of Industrial and Organizational Psychology, 12*, 115–174.

Johns, G. (1998a). In praise of multiple methods: How methodological heterogeneity has improved our understanding of absence from work. In *Proceedings of the international work psychology conference*, Sheffield, UK.

Johns, G. (1998b). The nature of work, the context of organizational behaviour, and the application of industrial-organizational psychology. *Canadian Psychology, 39*, 149–157.

Johns, G. (1998c). Aggregation or aggravation? The relative merits of a broad withdrawal construct. *Journal of Organizational Behavior, 19*, 453–462.

Johns, G., & Nicholson, N. (1982). The meanings of absence: New strategies for theory and research. *Research in Organizational Behavior, 4*, 127–172.

Johns, G., & Xie, J.L. (1998). Perceptions of absence from work: People's Republic of China versus Canada. *Journal of Applied Psychology, 83*, 515–530.

Judge, T.A., Locke, E.A., & Durham, C.C. (1997). The dispositional causes of job satisfaction: A core evaluations approach. *Research in Organizational Behavior, 19*, 151–188.

Judge, T.A., & Martocchio, J.J. (1995). Attributions concerning absence from work: A dispositional perspective. In M.J. Martinko (Ed.), *Attribution theory: An organizational perspective*. Delray Beach, FL: St. Lucie Press.

Judge, T.A., & Martocchio, J.J. (1996). Dispositional influences on attributions concerning absenteeism. *Journal of Management, 22*, 837–861.

Judge, T.A., Martocchio, J.J., & Thoresen, C.J. (1997). Five-factor model of personality and employee absence. *Journal of Applied Psychology, 82*, 745–755.

Judge, T.A., & Watanabe, S. (1995). Is the past prologue? A test of Ghiselli's hobo syndrome. *Journal of Management, 21*, 211–229.

Kanfer, R., Crosby, J.V., & Brandt, D.M. (1988). Investigating behavioral antecedents of turnover at three job tenure levels. *Journal of Applied Psychology, 73*, 331–335.

Kornhauser, A., & Sharp, A. (1932). Employee attitudes: Suggestions from a study in a factory. *Personnel Journal, 10*, 393–401.

Koslowsky, M., Sagie, A., Krausz, M., & Singer, A.D. (1997). Correlates of employee lateness: Some theoretical considerations. *Journal of Applied Psychology, 82*, 79–88.

Krackhardt, D., & Porter, L.W. (1985). When friends leave: A structural analysis of the relationship between turnover and stayers' attitudes. *Administrative Science Quarterly, 30*, 242–261.

Krackhardt, D., & Porter, L.W. (1986). The snowball effect: Turnover embedded in communication networks. *Journal of Applied Psychology, 71*, 50–55.

Krausz, M., Koslowsky, M., & Eiser, A. (1998). Distal and proximal influences on turnover intentions and satisfaction: Support for a withdrawal progression theory. *Journal of Vocational Behavior, 52*, 59–71.

Lee, T.W. (1997). Employee turnover. In L.H. Peters, C.R. Greer, & S.A. Youngblood (Eds.), *The Blackwell encyclopedic dictionary of human resource management* (pp. 97–100). Oxford: Blackwell.

Lee, T.W., & Maurer, S.D. (1997). The retention of knowledge workers with the unfolding model of voluntary turnover. *Human Resource Management Review, 7*, 247–275.

Lee, T.W., & Mitchell, T.R. (1994). An alternative approach: The unfolding model of voluntary employee turnover. *Academy of Management Review, 19*, 51–89.

Lee, T.W., Mitchell, T.R., Holtom, B.C., McDaniel, L.S., & Hill, J.W. (1999). The unfolding model of employee turnover: A replication and extension. *Academy of Management Journal, 42*, 450–462.

Lee, T.W., Mitchell, T.R., Wise, L., & Fireman, S. (1996). An unfolding model of voluntary employee turnover. *Academy of Management Journal, 39*, 5–36.

March, J.G., & Simon, H.A. (1958). *Organizations*. New York: Wiley.

Markham, S.E., & McKee, G.H. (1995). Group absence behavior and standards: A multilevel analysis. *Academy of Management Journal, 38*, 1174–1190.

Martocchio, J.J. (1992). The financial cost of absence decisions. *Journal of Management, 18*, 133–152.

Martocchio, J.J. (1994). The effects of absence culture on individual absence. *Human Relations, 47*, 243–262.

Martocchio, J.J., & Harrison, D.A. (1993). To be there or not to be there? Questions, theories, and methods in absenteeism research. *Research in Personnel and Human Resources Management, 11*, 259–328.

Mathieu, J.E., & Kohler, S.S. (1990). A cross-level examination of group absence influences on individual absence. *Journal of Applied Psychology, 75*, 217–220.

Mathieu, J.E., & Zajac, D.M. (1990). A review and meta-analysis of the antecedents, correlates, and consequences of organizational commitment. *Psychological Bulletin, 108*, 171–194.

Mayer, R.C., & Schoorman, F.D. (1992). Predicting participation and production outcomes through a two-dimensional model of organizational commitment. *Academy of Management Journal, 35*, 671–684.

McEvoy, G.M., & Cascio, W.F. (1987). Do good or poor performers leave? A meta-analysis of the relationship between performance and turnover. *Academy of Management Journal, 30*, 744–762.

Meyer, J.P. (1997). Organizational commitment. *International Review of Industrial and Organizational Psychology, 12*, 175–228.

Meyer, J.P., & Allen, N.J. (1991). A three-component conceptualization of organizational commitment. *Human Resource Management Review, 1*, 61–98.

Mitra, A., Jenkins, G.D., Jr., & Gupta, N. (1992). A meta-analytic review of the relationship between absence and turnover. *Journal of Applied Psychology, 77*, 879–889.

Mobley, W.H. (1977). Intermediate linkages in the relationship between job satisfaction and employee turnover. *Journal of Applied Psychology, 62*, 237–240.

Mohr, L.B. (1982). *Explaining organizational behavior.* San Francisco: Jossey-Bass.

Morgan, L.G., & Herman, J.B. (1976). Perceived consequences of absenteeism. *Journal of Applied Psychology, 61*, 738–742.

Mowday, R.T., Stone, E.F., & Porter, L.W. (1979). The interaction of personality and job scope in predicting turnover. *Journal of Vocational Behavior, 15*, 78–89.

Mowday, R.T., & Sutton, R.I. (1993). Organizational behavior: Linking individuals and groups to organizational context. *Annual Review of Psychology, 44*, 195–229.

Motley, R. (1926). Lateness of plant employees: A study of causes and cures. *Journal of Personnel Research, 5*, 1–3.

Muchinsky, P.M. (1977). Employee absenteeism: A review of the literature. *Journal of Vocational Behavior, 10*, 316–340.

Muchinsky, P.M., & Tuttle, M.L. (1979). Employee turnover: An empirical and methodological assessment. *Journal of Vocational Behavior, 14*, 43–77.

Nicholson, N., Brown, C.A., & Chadwick-Jones, J.K. (1976). Absence from work and job satisfaction. *Journal of Applied Psychology, 61*, 728–737.

Nicholson, N., & Johns, G. (1985). The absence culture and the psychological contract – who's in control of absence? *Academy of Management Review, 10*, 397–407.

Ones, D.S., Schmidt, F.L., & Viswesvaran, C. (1994). *Do broader personality variables predict job performance with higher validity?* Presentation at the annual meeting of the Society for Industrial and Organizational Psychology, Nashville, TN.

Ones, D.S., Viswesvaran, C., & Schmidt, F.L. (1992). *Personality characteristics and absence taking behavior: The case of integrity.* Paper presented at the annual meeting of the Academy of Management, Las Vegas.

Ones, D.S., Viswesvaran, C., & Schmidt, F.L. (1993). Comprehensive meta-analysis of integrity test validities: Findings and implications for personnel selection and theories of job performance. *Journal of Applied Psychology, 78*, 679–703.

O'Reilly, C.A., III, Caldwell, D.F., & Barnett, W.P. (1989). Work group demography, social integration, and turnover. *Administrative Science Quarterly, 34*, 21–37.

O'Reilly, C.A., III, Chatman, J., & Caldwell, D.F. (1991). People and organizational culture: A profile comparison approach to assessing person-organization fit. *Academy of Management Journal, 34*, 487–516.

Ornstein, S., & Isabella, L.A. (1993). Making sense of careers: A review 1989–1992. *Journal of Management, 19*, 243–267.

Pelled, L.H. (1996). Demographic diversity, conflict, and work group outcomes: An intervening process theory. *Organization Science, 7*, 615–631.

Peters, L.H., & Sheridan, J.E. (1988). Turnover research methodology: A critique of traditional designs and a suggested survival model alternative. *Research in Personnel and Human Resources Management, 6*, 231–262.

Pfeffer, J. (1983). Organizational demography. *Research in Organizational Behavior, 5*, 299–357.

Phillips, J.M. (1998). Effects of realistic job previews on multiple organizational outcomes: A meta-analysis. *Academy of Management Journal, 41*, 673–690.

Porter, L.W., & Steers, R.M. (1973). Organizational, work, and personal factors in employee turnover and absenteeism. *Psychological Bulletin, 80*, 151–176.

Price, J.L. (1976). The effects of turnover on the organization. *Organization and Administrative Sciences, 7*, 61–88.

Price, J.L. (1977). *The study of turnover.* Ames, IA: Iowa State University Press.

Price, J.L. (1989). The impact of turnover on the organization. *Work and Occupations, 16*, 461–473.

Rentsch, J.R., & Steel, R.P. (1998). Testing the durability of job characteristics as predictors of absenteeism over a six-year period. *Personnel Psychology, 51*, 165–190.

Rhodes, S.R., & Steers, R.M. (1990). *Managing employee absenteeism.* Reading, MA: Addison-Wesley.

Rosse, J.G. (1988). Relations among lateness, absence, and turnover: Is there a progression of withdrawal? *Human Relations, 41*, 517–531.

Rosse, J.G., & Miller, H.E. (1984). Relationship between absenteeism and other employee behaviors. In P.S. Goodman & R.S. Atkin (Eds.), *Absenteeism: New approaches to understanding, measuring, and managing absence* (pp. 194–228). San Francisco: Jossey-Bass.

Rynes, S.L. (1991). Recruitment, job choice, and post-hire consequences: A call for new research directions. In M.D. Dunnette & L.M. Hough (Eds.), *Handbook of industrial and organizational psychology* (2nd ed., Vol. 2, pp. 399–444). Palo Alto: Consulting Psychologists Press.

Saks, A.M., & Ashforth, B.E. (1997). A longitudinal investigation of the relationship between job information sources, applicant perceptions of fit, and work outcomes. *Personnel Psychology, 50*, 395–426.

Schaubroeck, J., Ganster, D.C., & James, J.R. (1998). Organization and occupation influences in the attraction-selection-attrition process. *Journal of Applied Psychology, 50*, 869–891.

Schlotzhaur, D.L., & Rosse, J.G. (1985). A five-year study of a positive incentive absence control program. *Personnel Psychology, 38*, 575–585.

Schneider, B., Goldstein, H.W., & Smith, D.B. (1995). The ASA framework: An update. *Personnel Psychology, 48*, 747–773.

Schwarzwald, J., Koslowsky, M., & Shalit, B. (1992). A field study of employees' attitudes and behaviors after promotion decisions. *Journal of Applied Psychology, 77*, 511–514.

Shaffer, M.A., & Harrison, D.A. (1998). Expatriates' psychological withdrawal from international work assignments: Work, nonwork, and family influences. *Personnel Psychology, 51*, 87–118.

Sheridan, J.E. (1985). A catastrophe model of employee withdrawal leading to low job performance, high absenteeism, and job turnover during the first year of employment. *Academy of Management Journal, 28*, 88–109.

Sheridan, J.E. (1992). Organizational culture and employee retention. *Academy of Management Journal, 35*, 1036–1056.

Shore, L.M., & Barksdale, K. (1998). Examining degree of balance and level of obligation in the employment relationship: A social exchange approach. *Journal of Organizational Behavior, 19*, 731–744.

Shore, L.M., & Wayne, S.J. (1993). Commitment and employee behavior: Comparison of affective commitment and continuance commitment with perceived organizational support. *Journal of Applied Psychology, 78*, 774–780.

Somers, M.J. (1996). Modelling employee withdrawal behaviour over time: A study of turnover using survival analysis. *Journal of Occupational and Organizational Psychology, 69*, 315–326.

Somers, M.J. (1999). Application of two neural network paradigms to the study of voluntary employee turnover. *Journal of Applied Psychology, 84*, 177–185.

Somers, M.J., & Birnbaum, D. (1999). Survival versus traditional methodologies for studying employee turnover: differences, divergences and directions for future research. *Journal of Organizational Behavior, 20*, 273–284.

Smith, F.J. (1977). Work attitudes as predictors of attendance on a specific day. *Journal of Applied Psychology, 62*, 16–19.

Staw, B.M. (1980). The consequences of turnover. *Journal of Occupational Behaviour, 1*, 253–273.

Staw, B.M., & Oldham, G.R. (1978). Reconsidering our dependent variables: A critique and empirical study. *Academy of Management Journal, 21*, 539–559.

Steel, R.P., & Griffeth, R.W. (1989). The elusive relationship between perceived employment opportunity and turnover behavior: A methodological or conceptual artifact? *Journal of Applied Psychology, 74*, 846–854.

Steers, R.M., & Rhodes, S.R. (1978). Major influences on employee attendance: A process model. *Journal of Applied Psychology, 63*, 391–407.

Steers, R.M., & Rhodes, S.R. (1984). Knowledge and speculation about absenteeism. In P.S. Goodman & R.S. Atkin (Eds.), *Absenteeism: New approaches to understanding, measuring, and managing employee absence* (pp. 229–275). San Francisco: Jossey-Bass.

Sullivan, S.E. (1999). The changing nature of careers: A review and research agenda. *Journal of Management, 25*, 457–484.

Tansey, R.R., & Hyman, M.R. (1992). Public relations, advocacy ads, and the campaign against absenteeism during World War II. *Business and Professional Ethics Journal, 11*, 129–164.

Taylor, M.S., & Giannantonio, C.M. (1993). Forming, adapting, and terminating the employment relationship: A review of the literature from individual, organizational, and interactionist perspectives. *Journal of Management, 19*, 461–515.

Tett, R.P., & Meyer, J.P. (1993). Job satisfaction, organizational commitment, turnover intention, and turnover: Path analyses based on meta-analytic findings. *Personnel Psychology, 46*, 259–293.

Tharenou, P. (1993). A test of reciprocal causality for absenteeism. *Journal of Organizational Behavior, 14*, 269–290.

Vandenberghe, C. (1999). Organizational culture, person-culture fit, and turnover: A replication in the health care industry. *Journal of Organizational Behavior, 20*, 175–184.

van Dierendonck, D., Schaufeli, W.B., & Buunk, B.P. (1998). The evaluation of an individual burnout intervention program: The role of inequity and social support. *Journal of Applied Psychology, 83*, 392–407.

Van Yperen, N.W., Hagedoorn, M., & Geurts, S.A.E. (1996). Intent to leave and absenteeism as reactions to perceived inequity: The role of psychological and social constraints. *Journal of Occupational and Organizational Psychology, 69*, 367–372.

Viswesvaran, C., Ones, D.S., & Schmidt, F.L. (Undated) Predictability of turnover using integrity tests: A meta-analysis. Unpublished manuscript.

Vroom, V.H. (1964). *Work and motivation.* New York: Wiley.

Wanous, J.P. (1992). *Organizational entry: Recruitment, selection, orientation, and socialization of newcomers* (2nd ed.). Reading, MA: Addison-Wesley.

Wanous, J.P., Poland, T.D., Premack, S.L., & Davis, K.S. (1992). The effects of met expectations on newcomer attitudes and behaviors: A review and meta-analysis. *Journal of Applied Psychology, 77*, 288–297.

Waters, L.K., & Roach, D. (1979). Job satisfaction, behavioral intention, and absenteeism as predictors of turnover. *Personnel Psychology, 32*, 393–397.

Webb, G.R., Redman, S., Hennrikus, D.J., Kelman, G.R., Gibberd, R.W., & Sanson-Fisher, R.W. (1994). The relationships between high-risk and problem drinking and the occurrence of work injuries and related absences. *Journal of Studies on Alcohol, 55*, 434–446.

Webster, E.C. (1964). *Decision making in the employment interview.* Montreal: Applied Psychology Centre, McGill University.

Williams, C.R., & Livingstone, L.P. (1994). Another look at the relationship between performance and voluntary turnover. *Academy of Management Journal, 37*, 269–298.

Williams, K.Y., & O'Reilly, C.A., III (1998). Demography and diversity in organizations: A review of

40 years of research. *Research In Organizational Behavior, 20,* 77–140.

Wise, L.C. (1993). The erosion of nursing resources: Employee withdrawal behavior. *Research in Nursing and Health, 16,* 67–75.

Wolpin, J., Burke, R.J., Krausz, M., & Freibach, N. (1988). Lateness and absenteeism: An examination of the progression hypothesis. *Canadian Journal of Administrative Sciences, 5,* 49–54.

Xie, J.L., & Johns, G. (2000). Interactive effects of absence culture salience and group cohesiveness: A multi-level and cross-level analysis of work absenteeism in the Chinese context. *Journal of Occupational and Organizational Psychology, 73,* 31–52.

13

Job Loss and the Experience of Unemployment: International Research and Perspectives

CONNIE R. WANBERG,
JOHN D. KAMMEYER-MUELLER,
and KAN SHI

This chapter reviews major research and issues regarding the psychological experience of unemployment. Current evidence depicts unemployment as a predominantly stressful life experience. Factors shown to predict variations in the negativity of the unemployment experience include individuals' levels of financial hardship, commitment to employment, ability to structure time, social support, and coping. Research suggests job-search intensity and job-search interventions increase reemployment probability along with other critical factors such as the job seeker's occupational area, qualifications, demographic background, and level of unemployment insurance. The increasing prevalence of layoffs are discussed along with how layoff survivors are affected. The review is couched within an international context, highlighting research and policies around the world, with a special focus on China's current unemployment situation.

INTRODUCTION AND CROSS-CULTURAL NATURE OF THE TOPIC

The concept of unemployment is recognized by countries around the globe. In fact, unemployment has been identified as *the* major economic problem of the European Community in the 1990s (Smith, 1994). While some countries currently enjoy a low unemployment rate – e.g., Austria, Norway, and United States – others are experiencing high levels of unemployment – e.g., Australia, Finland, France, Germany, Italy, Spain (Organization for Economic Cooperation and Development, 1999), and China. Figure 13.1 provides standardized unemployment rates for seven leading industrial countries for a recent 13-year period.[1]

Research on the psychological experience of unemployment has been conducted in many countries, including, but not limited to, Australia (e.g., Feather & O'Brien, 1987), Canada (e.g., Lay & Brokenshire, 1997), Sweden (e.g., Hammarstroem & Janlert, 1997), The Netherlands (e.g., Schaufeli, 1997), Iceland (e.g., Smari, Arason, Hafsteinsson & Ingimarsson, 1997), India (e.g., Singh, Singh & Kumari, 1998), Ireland (e.g., Joseph, Weatherall & Stringer, 1997), Israel (e.g., Eden & Aviram, 1993), New Zealand (e.g., Cullen, Shouksmith & Habermann, 1997), the United Kingdom (e.g., Furnham & Rawles, 1996), and the United States (e.g., Caplan, Vinokur, Price & Van Ryn, 1989). Because this literature is very extensive, page limitations prohibit a comprehensive review. Instead, this chapter seeks to give an overview of

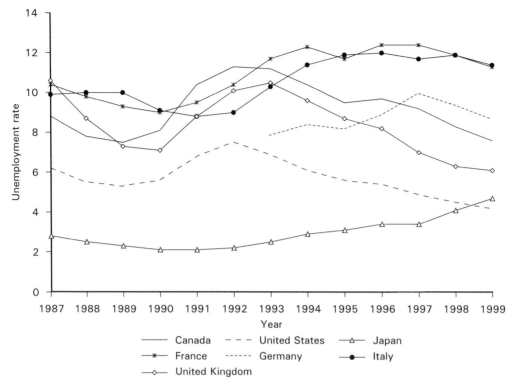

Figure 13.1   *Unemployment rates of the seven leading industrial nations. These rates represent figures standardized across Organization for Economic Cooperation and Development (OECD) countries (OECD 1999, OECD 2000). Unemployed individuals were defined as persons of working age who were without work, available to work, and who had taken steps to find employment. Data for unified Germany is not available prior to 1993.*

three important topics from the unemployment domain: (a) the stress-related impacts of unemployment, (b) successful job search and reemployment, and (c) layoff outcomes and best practices. While the chapter is based primarily on psychological issues related to job loss and reemployment, we have also sampled contributions from the economics and management literature.

At the end of the chapter we highlight one country's special encounter with issues related to job loss and unemployment. Specifically, China, due to extensive economic reform, is now facing new and serious issues related to unemployment. China is of special interest as this country has 25% of the world's population, and many of the world's largest industrial firms view China as an important target market (Si & Bruton, 1999).

IMPACT OF UNEMPLOYMENT

Average Impact of Unemployment

A popular research question on the topic of unemployment regards how the experience impacts

unemployed individuals' psychological and physical well-being, and the well-being of their families. A multitude of studies exist on this topic, first initiated in the 1930s during the time of the Great Depression (see, e.g., Bakke, 1933; Jahoda, Lazarsfeld & Zeisel, 1971; Eisenberg & Lazarsfeld, 1938). Researchers have assessed the impact of unemployment through a variety of methodologies, including case studies; cross-sectional surveys comparing unemployed and employed individuals; longitudinal surveys following individuals over time as they move from employment into unemployment, or from unemployment into employment; and aggregate studies correlating national or regional unemployment rates with indices such as mental hospital admissions and suicide rates. Overall, this research has produced fairly consistent findings across different countries, showing that on the average, unemployment is associated with diminished psychological well-being (e.g., higher levels of anxiety and depression) and diminished physical well-being (e.g., higher levels of stress-related symptoms such as headaches and stomach aches). Evidence also suggests that the emotional and financial stressors associated with unemployment may lead to other serious problems such as increased family conflict and even suicide. Several comprehensive reviews are available to outline these psychological and physical (cf. Fryer & Payne, 1986; Fryer, 1998; Kasl, Rodriguez & Lasch, 1998; O'Brien, 1986; Platt, 1984; Winefield, 1995), family (cf. Dew, Penkower & Bromet, 1991; Schliebner & Peregoy, 1994), and social (Ahlburg, 1986) related impacts of unemployment more specifically.

Despite the large number of narrative literature reviews that have addressed the impact of unemployment, only one meta-analysis to date has been published on this topic. The one identified meta-analytic study, completed by Murphy and Athanasou (1999), focused on longitudinal studies assessing mental health changes as individuals moved from employment into unemployment and/or from unemployment into employment. The authors limited their analysis to studies that were published between the years 1986 and 1996. The 16 longitudinal studies identified were from nine countries, including Australia, Britain, Denmark, Finland, Germany, Israel, The Netherlands, Norway, and the United States. In 14 of the 16 studies, individuals had significantly lower mental health scores while unemployed. Across the studies, a weighted effect size of .36 (standard error = .06) was calculated for mental health changes associated with moves from employment to unemployment, representing a decrease in mental health. A weighted effect size of .54 (standard error = .04) was calculated for moves from unemployment into employment, representing an increase in mental health.

The Murphy and Athanasou meta-analysis did not pay detailed attention to the personal and situational factors that might explain variations in the unemployment experience. For example, while the *average* experience of unemployment has been shown to be negative, not all individuals have a negative experience with their unemployment (cf. Hartley, 1980; Fineman, 1983). Several factors have been shown to explain variations in the unemployment experience. We now turn to a discussion of some of these factors.

Predictors of the Impact of Job Loss

Some of the more salient factors that have been shown to explain variations in the unemployment experience include (a) financial resources, (b) employment commitment, (c) the ability to structure one's time, (d) social support, and (e) coping strategies.

Economic Hardship

Individuals who are unemployed differ in the amount of economic hardship they experience. Some individuals have savings to rely on, or spouses that work. Others are able to pay for expenses by living on government-provided unemployment benefits. Several studies have shown that economic hardship is positively related to distress levels experienced by individuals and their families while unemployed (e.g., Payne & Hartley, 1987; Ullah, 1990; Yeung & Hofferth, 1998). In fact, studies in The Netherlands (Schaufeli & VanYperen, 1992), the United States (Kessler, Turner & House, 1987), and the United Kingdom (Rodgers, 1991) found that a large proportion of the impact of unemployment can be explained by financial hardship. It has also been suggested that levels of psychological distress due to unemployment may be lower in countries with high levels of government financial support for the unemployed (Schaufeli & VanYperen, 1992).

Employment Commitment

Employment commitment (or work role centrality) has been conceptualized as an aspect of work ethic that encompasses how important having a job and working are to a person (Warr, 1983). Several studies have shown that higher levels of employment commitment are related to higher levels of psychological distress during unemployment (Jackson, Stafford, Banks & Warr, 1983; Rowley & Feather, 1987; Stafford, Jackson & Banks, 1980; Ullah, Banks & Warr, 1985). In their longitudinal study of 16-year-old school leavers in England, Jackson et al. (1983) demonstrated that individuals who moved from employment into unemployment had a larger increase in psychological distress when they were high in employment commitment rather than low. On the other hand, when individuals high in employment commitment moved from unemployment into employment, they experienced a larger decrease in psychological distress than those who were low in employment commitment.

Time Structure

Another important factor that may influence reaction to unemployment is an individual's ability or inability to structure and plan his or her time during unemployment (DeFrank & Ivancevich, 1986; Jahoda, 1982). Most working individuals become adapted to a pattern of eating, working, sleeping, taking leisure time, and visiting with friends and family. The loss of a job affects this temporal pattern, and some people have great difficulty structuring their time after job loss. For example, in Fineman's (1983) interview study, some individuals remarked they were used to working and that it was hard to fill a day's time. Several studies have subsequently found that the ability or inability to keep busy and to structure one's day appears to be related to the psychological and physical health of unemployed individuals (Bond & Feather, 1988;

Brenner & Bartell, 1983; Feather & Bond, 1983; Hepworth, 1980; Kilpatrick & Trew, 1985; Swinburne, 1981; Wanberg, Griffiths & Gavin, 1997). Research has shown similar findings in the retirement literature (see, e.g., Talaga & Beehr, 1989).

Social Support

Similar to results showing the important benefits of social support during other stressful life events (cf. Kessler, Price & Wortman, 1985), research has shown that individuals who report higher levels of social support during unemployment exhibit higher psychological and physical health (Gore, 1978; Turner, Kessler & House, 1991; Ullah et al., 1985). In addition to finding support for the direct effects of social support on well-being, studies have suggested that social support may be particularly helpful for individuals who are experiencing the most stress during unemployment (e.g., supporting a buffering effect; Mallinckrodt & Bennett, 1992). Research further suggests that support from a significant other is associated with job seekers having positive attitudes toward the job search and exhibiting more job-search behaviors (Vinokur & Caplan, 1987; Wanberg, Watt & Rumsey, 1996). Unfortunately, it seems that stressful aspects of the unemployment experience provide an atmosphere that is not highly conducive to social support (Atkinson, Liem & Liem, 1986; Liem & Liem, 1990). For example, in a study of 815 recently unemployed job seekers and their spouses, Vinokur, Price and Caplan (1996) found that financial strain had significant effects on experienced depression. This depression was associated in turn with a decrease in social support and an increase in social undermining (e.g., criticism and displays of anger or dislike) of the spouse toward the job seeker.

Coping Techniques and Methods

Job loss creates a discrepancy between unemployed individuals' present and desired states. This imbalance leads individuals to engage in various coping strategies (Latack, Kinicki & Prussia, 1995). Coping strategies used by unemployed individuals might include proactive strategies, such as focusing time and energy on looking for a job (proactive search), keeping busy and working on ways to save money (nonwork organization), and thinking about one's skills and qualifications (positive self-assessment), and/or avoidance strategies, such as trying not to think about what happened (distancing from loss), or thinking that there are more important things in life than having a job (job devaluation) (Kinicki & Latack, 1990). Research in the United States and Hong Kong has suggested that use of nonwork organization, positive self-assessment, and distancing by individuals is associated with higher mental health during unemployment (Gowan, Riordan &

Gatewood, 1999; Lai & Wong, 1998; Wanberg, 1997). Wanberg (1997) reported that proactive search was negatively associated with mental health among individuals who perceived their chances of finding a job were low. Yet, higher proactive search was positively associated with finding a job. A further discussion of the role of coping in the unemployment experience can be found in Leana and Feldman (1990, 1992), Leana, Feldman and Tan (1998), and Smari et al. (1997).

Summary

Overall, unemployment has been shown to be a stressful life experience that is associated with lower levels of psychological and physical health, and increased marital conflict. Not all individuals experience unemployment in the same way, however. Unemployment seems to be especially difficult for individuals with higher financial strain and employment commitment, and lower time structure, social support, and coping. Fortunately, research has shown that individuals moving from unemployment into employment generally experience increased well-being. Given there are multiple interests (both individual and societal) in moving individuals back into work, the next section reviews research that has examined factors associated with successful reemployment.

JOB SEARCH AND REEMPLOYMENT

A growing amount of research has been devoted to understanding what variables are associated with successful reemployment. In this section we first describe the importance of job-search intensity and job-search methods to the reemployment process. Second, we discuss the relationship of occupational area, qualifications, and demographic variables to reemployment outcomes. We then address empirical work that has studied the relationship between levels of unemployment insurance and reemployment. Last, we address job-search skill interventions and their potential to aid the reemployment process.

Job-Search Intensity and Job-Search Methods

Extensive data indicate that higher job-search intensity (spending more time and effort on the job-search process) is related to faster reemployment. Barron and Mellow (1981) reported that a 10-hour increase per week in job search intensity increased the reemployment probability in the next month for the average unemployed individual in their sample by about 20%. Stumpf, Austin and Hartman (1984), in a longitudinal study of 78 graduate students in business, found that time spent thinking about career possibilities was positively related to whether a job offer was received. Saks and Ashforth (1999), in a study of university graduates, found that active job-search behavior (e.g., sending out résumés and having job interviews) predicted employment status at graduation, while preparatory job-search activities (e.g., analyzing self-interests and abilities and preparing a résumé) predicted employment status four months after graduation.

Evidence is less clear regarding whether higher job-search intensity pays off in terms of helping individuals find better jobs. Wanberg (1997) found that higher job-search intensity during unemployment was related to higher levels of job satisfaction once reemployed. Brasher and Chen (1999), however, reported no relationship between duration of job search, number of interviews, and number of offers with job/school match or starting salary. Because this study did not control for the qualifications of the job seekers, the authors noted that it is possible that job seekers with higher qualifications are able to acquire high quality jobs with fewer interviews.

Research has also examined the use and effectiveness of different job-search methods or techniques in relation to employment outcomes. This research highlights the importance of personal networks in the job-search process. For example, Reid (1972) reported that approximately 33% of 876 engineering and metal-trade workers in England found jobs through friends and family during the period between 1966 and 1968. More recently, Wanberg, Kanfer and Banas (2000) reported that 36.3% of job-seekers in a Midwestern state in the United States (representing a variety of industries and occupational levels) found jobs through either talking to friends, family, or previous coworkers or through 'networking.' This was in contrast to job seekers who found jobs through want ads/advertisements (30.8%), employment agencies (11.5%), job fairs (3.3%), the World Wide Web (2.2%), and other (16.5%). DeGraaf and Flap (1988) found social networks to play an important role in job acquisition in West Germany and the Netherlands, and Bian (1997) discusses personal networks in China. Despite the fact that jobs are often found through networking, data from Wanberg et al. (2000) suggest that individuals should use a variety of job-search methods in a job search and should not rely on networking alone.

While not a job-search method *per se*, Schmit, Amel and Ryan (1993) examined the relationship between 'assertive job-search behavior' and reemployment. Specifically, 202 job applicants were asked how likely it was that they would use assertive behaviors in their job search, such as asking an employer who did not have openings if he or she knew of other openings. For each of 25 different statements, the applicants responded on a scale

from (1) very unlikely to (6) very likely. Schmit et al.'s results showed that, after controlling for cognitive ability as measured by scores on the General Aptitude Test Battery, a one-point increase in assertive job-search behavior was associated with an 8% increase in probability of reemployment.

Given the demonstrated importance of job-search intensity and methods to the reemployment process, research has begun to examine individual difference predictors of job-search behavior. Several studies, for example, have now shown that job-search self-efficacy (or self-rated competence at job-search activities) is related to higher levels of job-search activity (e.g., Eden & Aviram, 1993; Ellis & Taylor, 1983; Kanfer & Hulin, 1985; Lay & Brokenshire, 1997; Saks & Ashforth, 1999; Wanberg, Kanfer & Rotundo, 1999b). Also important in motivating higher levels of search intensity are (a) the desire to work and earn money (Feather & O'Brien, 1987; Vinokur & Caplan, 1987; Wanberg et al., 1999b) and (b) the receipt of support for the job search from a significant other (Vinokur & Caplan, 1987; Wanberg et al., 1996). Finally, research has also shown that general characteristics of the person, such as levels of achievement motivation, conscientiousness, motivational control, extroversion, and self-esteem are related to higher levels of job-search intensity (e.g., Schmit et al., 1993; Sheppard & Belitsky, 1966; Wanberg et al., 1996; Wanberg et al., 2000; Wanberg et al., 1999b).

Fewer studies have examined what types of individuals gravitate to certain job-search methods. For example, do some individuals rely more heavily on techniques that require little human contact (e.g., sending out résumés and filling out applications) rather than those that involve more human contact (e.g., networking and contacting employers on the telephone)? Providing some answers to this question, Caldwell and Burger (1998) found that extroversion, along with openness to experience and conscientiousness to a lesser extent, was correlated with college students' use of social sources (e.g., talking to others) as a means of preparing for job interviews. Wanberg et al. (2000) found that extroversion and conscientiousness were associated with higher use of both networking and traditional job-search methods. Level of comfort with engaging in networking was, however, uniquely associated with networking intensity.

Occupation, Experience, and Demographic Variables

Research has further shown individuals' occupational area, qualifications, and demographic characteristics to be related to finding employment. First, some occupational areas are in higher demand than others. Individuals who are in occupations that are in low demand may have a difficult time finding a job. In both Europe and the United States, there is a high demand for workers with high levels of education and training, especially in professional and technical occupations that cannot be automated or computerized (Adnett, 1996; Silvestri, 1995). Some countries (e.g., United States and Australia) use occupation and industry data, along with other criteria, to 'target' or identify job seekers with a higher risk of long-term unemployment. Individuals identified as high risk may then be encouraged or required to participate in reemployment programs such as job-search workshops, or if appropriate, job retraining or self-employment assistance (Balducchi, Johnson & Gritz, 1997).

Individuals with more impressive qualifications also generally find jobs faster. For example, in a sample of college graduates, Marshall (1985) found that successful job seekers were those who had more impressive job references, higher GPAs (grade point average) in their fields, and were employed at least part time when the survey was taken. Overall GPA, volunteer experience, club memberships and leadership experiences, and number of paid jobs held that were related to career objectives did not differentiate the successful and unsuccessful job seekers. Steffy, Shaw and Noe (1989), in another study of college graduates, found that GPA was positively associated with number of interviews and negatively associated with search stress.

Finally, research has shown demographic variables are related to reemployment speed. For example, the literature in the United States has illustrated that women, minorities, older workers, and individuals with less education tend to experience longer unemployment durations (Fallick, 1996; Kletzer, 1998). The possible causal mechanisms (e.g., lower motivation to find a job, discrimination, inexperience with job-search techniques and methods) behind the associations between demographic variables and length of unemployment are clearly multifaceted and need further examination. For example, older individuals may take longer, on the average, to find work due to age discrimination, lower levels of education, obsolete skills, lower expectancies for finding work, or perhaps because their job-search or interview styles differ from younger individuals.

Levels of Unemployment Insurance

Several studies in the economic literature have examined the relationship between levels of unemployment insurance, job-search, and reemployment outcomes. Unemployment insurance (UI) refers to government-sponsored systems of financial benefits that eligible individuals receive while unemployed. In the United States, individuals are not eligible for UI when they have entered unemployment voluntarily, been fired for misconduct, or have

not made efforts to search for new employment (Atkinson & Micklewright, 1991). Eligibility criteria and the extent and duration of UI benefits differ widely from country to country (Atkinson & Micklewright, 1991; Storey & Niesner, 1997) so empirical results should be generalized across countries with caution.

A positive function of UI is that it provides unemployed individuals with at least some financial security during an unemployment spell, and it helps to retain purchasing power during an economic recession (Blaustein, O'Leary & Wandner, 1997). It has also been suggested that because UI reduces the financial urgency of becoming reemployed, individuals may be able to take the necessary time to find a job that will fit their skills and needs, rather than having to take the first job that they come by. A few studies are supportive of the notion that UI benefits may allow individuals to be more selective in their job search. In an analysis of 823 young males who experienced a permanent layoff in 1976 or 1977 in Canada, Belzil (1995) found that individuals who were further from exhausting their benefits desired a higher starting wage. Conversely, as individuals were closer to exhausting their unemployment benefits they were willing to accept a lower starting wage. Additionally, there is some evidence suggesting that UI benefits that come close to replacing all of a displaced worker's previous wages are associated with higher wages in subsequent employment (Ehrenberg & Oaxaca, 1976). Overall, however, it is surprising how little research has tried to examine the potentially positive consequences of UI provision. Blaustein et al. (1997) noted 'Attempts to measure the favorable job search effects of UI have been few and have not been regarded as satisfactory' (p. 26).

More research attention has been focused on the idea that UI may dull the incentive or urgency to find work. This research tends to show that the provision and level of UI is related to a decreased speed of reemployment (cf. Barron & Mellow, 1981). McCall (1997), in an analysis of data from Canada's 1986 Displaced Worker Survey, showed that the median jobless duration of female UI recipients was close to 47 weeks, while the median length of unemployment for female nonrecipients was 10 weeks. The median length of unemployment for male UI recipients was 34 weeks, versus six weeks for male nonrecipients. Several studies in the United States and Canada have also plotted reemployment frequencies by weeks on unemployment insurance. These studies show large spikes of reemployment at 26 weeks (United States) or 50 weeks (Canada), corresponding to the number of weeks that most individuals are eligible for unemployment insurance in that country (cf. Addison & Blackburn, 1997; Katz & Meyer, 1990). To some, this looks suspiciously like individuals wait to look for or to take jobs until their benefits are about to be terminated. Consistent with this explanation, it seems that individuals who have several weeks of unemployment insurance left do not look as hard for a job. Barron and Gilley (1979) reported that the number of weeks remaining to receive unemployment insurance benefits was related to the number of hours individuals report looking for a job each week. Specifically, an increase by one month in time left to receive unemployment insurance was associated with a reduction of job-search intensity of 6.5%. Although this might suggest that unemployment benefits should be reduced, Atkinson and Micklewright (1991) argue that only very large cuts in benefits would lead to substantial reductions in unemployment.

Job-Search Interventions

Job-search interventions have also been studied as a means of increasing both the speed and quality of reemployment. While a number of possible job-search interventions exist, we focus here on a successful large-scale project developed by researchers at the University of Michigan in the United States (Caplan et al., 1989). We choose this intervention as an example because the researchers carefully used the psychological literature to inform the design of a job-search skills training program (known as JOBS I) for recently unemployed individuals. According to Caplan et al. (1989) the eight-session program was designed to:

(1) establish trust between the participants and the workshop leaders;
(2) increase the motivation of workshop participants;
(3) build the skills necessary to conduct an effective job search;
(4) acquire the skills necessary to cope with rejection and setbacks, and
(5) build social support among participants.

Several articles have documented the success of the JOBS workshop (cf. Caplan et al., 1989; Price, Van Ryn & Vinokur, 1992; Van Ryn & Vinokur, 1992; Vinokur, Price & Caplan, 1991; Vinokur, Van Ryn, Gramlich & Price, 1991). In comparison to a randomly assigned control group, individuals who attended the JOBS I workshops were reemployed faster, reported a higher quality of working life, and were more likely to have found higher-paying jobs in their main occupation.

Vinokur, Price and Schul (1995) reported an extension and replication of JOBS I (known as JOBS II). Both short- and long-term follow-up studies supported consistent and significant beneficial effects of the workshop (Vinokur et al., 1995; Vinokur, Schul, Vuori & Price, in press). These studies also demonstrated that the JOBS II workshop was most useful for individuals defined

as at a higher risk for depressive symptoms and individuals with low levels of mastery (i.e., low job-search self-efficacy, low locus of control, and low self-esteem). Vinokur and Schul (1997) reported that the JOBS II intervention seemed to work by giving participants, especially those defined as high risk, a stronger sense of mastery. While the majority of the research on the JOBS program has been conducted in the United States, an effectiveness trial of the JOBS program is currently in progress in Finland and China, and beneficial results from similar job-search workshops have been reported in Israel (Eden & Aviram, 1993).

Summary

Several variables have been shown to be related to speed or probability of reemployment. Research has shown that job-search intensity, job-search method, occupational skill area, qualifications, demographics, and levels of unemployment insurance are all relevant to reemployment outcomes. Several additional variables (e.g., job-search self-efficacy) seem to be indirectly related to reemployment outcomes through their associations with job-search intensity. Finally, research regarding job-search skill interventions has shown that such interventions can increase the speed and quality of reemployment, especially for individuals with low levels of mastery or self-efficacy.

LAYOFFS: PREVALENCE, OUTCOMES, AND INTERNATIONAL VARIATIONS

Up to this point we have concentrated on the experience of not having a job and searching for work. It is also useful to directly discuss the increasing prevalence and scope of layoffs within the global economy, and the extent to which layoff procedures may have impacts on both survivors of the layoff and the individuals who are laid off. Finally, we discuss international variations in layoffs and job insecurity.

Layoffs: Increasing Prevalence and Scope

Layoffs refer to planned, permanent reductions in the number of individuals employed by an organization[2]. These planned reductions have been shown to be the consequence of factors such as loss of market share, changes in management structure, and low productivity (Budros, 1997). Layoffs have become more common in the United States, and increasingly, throughout the world (Cappelli, Bassi, Katz, Knoke, Osterman & Useem, 1997). Data shows a consistent, but mild, upward trend in involuntary job loss during the 1990s for the United States, even in the midst of a strong economic environment (Aaronson & Sullivan, 1998). Similarly, there was a dramatic reduction in manufacturing and mining sector jobs during the 1980s in the United Kingdom (Nolan, 1994). Even countries where downsizing is uncommon, such as Germany and Japan, have increasingly resorted to reduction in hours worked per employee and hiring freezes to adjust to market fluctuations (Usui & Colignon, 1996).

Besides increases in the numbers of layoffs, there has also been an increase in scope. In the 1960s and 1970s, layoffs mainly affected production workers and recent recruits, but management, professionals, and even those with high levels of seniority are increasingly targeted for reductions (Cappelli et al., 1997). Research has shown that downsizing during the late 1980s and early 1990s resulted in more layoffs for managers and supervisors than production and direct service workers (Cappelli, 1992). Other data shows that males and individuals with a college education are increasingly likely to be laid off (Schmidt & Svorny, 1998). This shift in the target of layoffs is socially significant because a segment of the workforce which considered its employment status secure must now face the possibility of job loss (Budros, 1997).

Reactions to Layoffs and Methods for Improving the Layoff Process

As a consequence of the increasing prevalence of layoffs, several studies have examined how layoff survivors (individuals who are not laid off) and layoff victims (individuals who are laid off) are affected by the layoff of others. First, the reactions of layoff survivors has been a topic of great concern. Often, there are increased job responsibilities thrust upon these employees at the same time that they may be most skeptical about their employer and anxious about their futures (Kozlowski, Chao, Smith & Hedlund, 1993). Considerable evidence shows that layoffs are associated with a fear of involuntary job loss, or perceived job insecurity, among those who remain (e.g., Roskies & Louis-Guerin, 1990). Individuals who believe their job status is highly insecure have been shown to have increased intentions to quit, increased somatic complaints, and decreased organizational commitment, trust, and job satisfaction (Ashford, Lee & Bobko, 1989; Roskies & Louis-Guerin, 1990).

Besides fear of losing a job, many of those who remain experience negative reactions toward the organization stemming from the manner in which layoffs were conducted. One important determinant of attitudes toward organizations is the degree to which consistent, equitable, and compassionate procedures are followed during layoffs (Brockner &

Greenberg, 1990). A lack of these characteristics is associated with a decrease in organizational commitment and increased intention to turnover among those who retain their jobs (Brockner, Wiesenfeld, Reed, Grover & Martin, 1993). Employees may fear that they will receive similar treatment if the company conducts more layoffs, or they may be angry about the treatment given to their former coworkers. When justifications for the layoff, such as technological change or economic necessity, are present, layoffs are seen as more fair (Rousseau & Anton, 1988).

As with survivors, those who are laid off react more positively to organizations which are seen as following fair procedures (Konovsky & Folger, 1991). In a study of individuals laid off from a variety of organizations, Wanberg, Bunce and Gavin (1999a) found that perceived fairness was highest among individuals who reported that their organizations had given them adequate levels of explanation about how and why termination decisions were made, and adequate opportunities to attempt to modify layoff procedures. The Wanberg et al., study demonstrated why it might be in an organization's interest to implement layoff procedures that will be seen as fair. In their study, perceived unfairness was associated with a lower willingness to endorse the terminating organization in the future, a higher desire to sue the terminating organization, and a lower willingness to be committed to future employers.

In response to the growing number of workforce reductions, a special panel of business and government leaders who had presided over layoffs was convened by the US government. The most consistent factor mentioned by all members of this group was the importance of communication during the transition period (Downsizing Study Team, 1997). The team emphasized that communication must (1) begin early in the process, (2) include ample opportunities for employees to voice their concerns so the organization can address them, and (3) continue in every stage of the downsizing process. Good communication was linked to the ability to assist those losing their jobs as well as maintaining morale among those who remained.

Other research speaks to the usefulness of employers giving advance notice of layoffs. Preliminary research on this topic suggests that advance notice of layoffs reduces the duration of unemployment following a layoff (Ehrenberg & Jakubson, 1988). Addison and Blackburn (1997) further demonstrated that advance notice has a small, but positive, effect on helping laid-off individuals avoid unemployment completely. Others have expressed reservations regarding advance notice based on the theory that workers will reduce effort, quit, or engage in sabotage following issuance of a plan to conduct layoffs. This is a difficult issue to resolve definitively. For example, while there is not a dramatic increase in quits and the most productive workers do not appear to be more likely to leave following announcements of layoff plans (Addison, 1989), this may be because employers are less likely to give advance notice to workers who are most likely to leave (Fallick, 1994). Research to estimate these effects in the future is somewhat complicated because legal changes mean there is no longer sufficient variability in provision of advanced notice to reliably estimate effects in cross-sectional data.

In sum, while research demonstrates that survivors and former employees experience negative reactions to layoffs, research has just as consistently demonstrated that organizations can take actions to increase perceptions of fairness. On a broader level, the research on justice theory suggests that even if people do not like the outcome of a situation, they will react less negatively if consistent, well-elaborated, and humane rules are followed (Brockner & Wiesenfeld, 1996). By extension, organizations conducting layoffs can improve their outcomes by acting in accord with these principles.

International Variations in Layoffs and Job Insecurity

There is wide variation in how nations respond to the possibility of layoffs. Here we compare government and corporate policy and their impact on job-loss experiences. While not explicitly discussed here, it is worth noting that labor unions play a major role in bargaining for and enforcing employment security provisions and in lobbying for greater government intervention (cf. Houseman & Abraham, 1995; Salvanes, 1997).

The United States and United Kingdom have generally allowed market forces to determine the optimal timing and level of job reductions. Businesses in these nations have great freedom to determine when and whether to reduce head count. This principle is codified in US case law as 'employment at will,' meaning that either employees or employers have the right to terminate the relationship at any time for any reason (Perritt, 1998). Free-market advocates point out that a flexible market is best able to adjust to changing conditions and improve transitions between firms and industries as needed; empirical research supports the proposition that less regulated labor markets are associated with lower unemployment (Lazear, 1990).

Western European countries have invoked strong legal regulations on layoffs. For example, German employers are prohibited from layoffs unless they can demonstrate that less drastic procedures like increasing part-time work or transfers cannot resolve their problems (Abraham & Houseman, 1995). The government will even make up for wages lost if hours per employee are cut, so the firm is able to lower labor costs without reducing head count, and workers are no worse off (Abraham & Houseman, 1995). Another example of European policy is mandatory severance benefits for those who have been laid off. At the extremes, Spain requires employers to provide almost 14 months of severance wages, Italy requires almost 16 months, and France requires approximately five months (Lazear, 1990). Severance packages both ease the strain of layoffs and induce employers to engage in layoffs only as a last resort.

Japan has taken a route quite different from either of the aforementioned. Rather than using government policy to secure employment security, Japan has developed a unique corporate structure that encourages long-term relationships. The system known as 'lifetime employment,' in which an employee enters a company at a young age and remains with this company until retirement exemplifies this tendency. Promotions are granted based on seniority (*nenko*), further encouraging long-term employee–employer bonds. It should be noted that this connection is not legally binding, but results from psychological and cultural expectations that have developed over the years (Billesbach & Rives, 1985). Japanese managers highlight the virtues of this strong commitment as a mechanism for both developing loyalty, as well as its usefulness in ensuring that management will be able to recoup its investments in training (Peterson & Sullivan, 1990). Large-scale research on work values found that Japanese workers are more likely than German or American workers to endorse work as a central life interest, and rate the economic returns from work as relatively unimportant (England & Quintanilla, 1989).

Unfortunately, this unique structure appears to be straining under its own weight. As the workforce ages, the *nenko* promotion system seems less tenable, because it tends to concentrate huge numbers of employees in the high-paying ranks of senior management, making it difficult to hire new applicants (Peterson & Sullivan, 1990). Some have suggested that not only are Japanese being forced to confront changes in lifetime employment due to changes in the economy, but that a change in attitudes is occurring. Schwind and Peterson (1985) conducted interviews with Japanese work trainees and found that younger Japanese valued individualistic goals more highly than their elders. In a cross-cultural study, Kawakubo (1987) actually found that Japanese workers reported lower commitment to their employer and believed that layoffs were more likely than their American counterparts. It appears that Japanese workers have begun to recognize the possibility that lifetime employment is eroding.

Summary

Layoffs appear to be related to negative reactions toward an employer, even among those who do not lose their jobs. However, actions taken to respond to the concerns of employees have been shown to reduce perceptions of unfairness. There are wide variations between nations in how layoffs are viewed and the legal regulation of workforce reductions. In general, research on policies shows a trade-off between efforts to reduce involuntary job loss and organizations' ability to adjust payrolls to correspond to market conditions.

UNEMPLOYMENT IN CHINA

In this section we describe China's efforts to move from a planned (government controlled) economy to a market economy, and the extent to which these changes have introduced serious unemployment issues. We discuss the actions the Chinese government has taken to help the unemployed, and we note the significant need for empirical research on the unemployment experience in this country.

Background and Current Situation

Before the policy of economic reform and opening was carried out during the late 1970s in China, state enterprises (SEs) were almost completely controlled by the government, under the policy of a planned economy. SEs did not compete with one another or with companies from other countries. They did not have to consider their economic efficiency, and SEs were never driven to adjust staffing levels to meet market requirements. Workers at SEs also enjoyed high social status. SEs provided almost all of their workers with lifetime jobs. These lifetime jobs were protected by law in China, unlike voluntary corporate protections in Japan. SEs were also responsible for much of their employees' welfare by providing food, clothing, housing, medical care, and retirement pensions. In spite of this, there was no central social welfare system in China. If a worker quit an SE, he or she would not receive any support directly from the government. Overall, in the prereform period SEs were not driven to improve and Chinese workers were tightly bound to the SEs they worked for.

When Chinese leader Deng Xiaoping began his policy of reforming and opening, which included the decisive step of transforming China's planned economy to a market economy, SEs began to assess how well their human resources policies satisfied market requirements. Competition, and the possibility of going out of business, urged SEs to seriously consider their economic performance. In previous periods there was government support for work stabilization and retention of surplus workers. In the mid-1990s, especially after Premier Zhu Rongji came into power, 'promoting economic benefits by downsizing,' was used as a political slogan to encourage greater flexibility in employment levels. The change in policy coupled with economic hardship drove SEs to begin mass layoffs. SEs laid off 6,340,000 workers in 1997 and 6,100,000 in 1998. SE layoffs were predicted to reach 6,000,000 in 1999 (Mo, 1999). Official statistics state that China's urban rate of unemployment in 1998 was at 3.1%, unchanged from the year before ('A million Chinese jobs to disappear,' 1999). However, experts widely agree that this is a gross underestimate of the true unemployment situation in China (see, e.g., Segal, 1999). The official tally is for urban workers only and reportedly leaves out (a) workers who still report to their work units even though there is no work for them to do, (b) individuals who have not registered with the employment bureau, and (c) thousands of individuals who are laid off but who believe they will be called back.

Main Measures of Chinese Government

To ensure social stability is maintained during this turbulent period, the government has established a series of policies and legislation to assist the unemployed including:

(1) a monthly payment based on what was established to be a minimal standard of living;
(2) a cost-sharing system between the government and the SEs (i.e., a social security system) to address retirement pensions and medical treatment;
(3) loans designed to assist small enterprises, so that they can create new jobs (Lin, 1999);
(4) free training to improve job skills;
(5) encouragement of academic discussion and studies on the methods and effects of training (The Beijing Labor and Social Insurance Bureau, 1999);
(6) requiring enterprises to form reemployment centers to provide information, registration, and compensation for laid-off workers. These centers are supplemented by separate government-sponsored reemployment centers.

Despite these measures, the layoff problem remains serious. First, the social security system for the unemployed is still in its early stages. Second, social services for reemployment are not achieving their goals. To date, they have not provided enough training in marketable job skills for laid-off workers. Third, in addition to SE layoffs, there are two other sources of labor with which laid-off workers must compete. First, the population level in China provides millions of newcomers to the labor market every year. The number of new entrants to the labor force has been estimated at 5,660,000 in 1999. The other source of surplus laborers consists of an estimated 107,810,000 peasants separated from the land during reform in rural areas in the 1970s and living in cities today. Many of these former peasants came to cities for employment (The National Developmental Program for Labor and Social Insurance, 1999). Many of those laid off in urban centers do not find work, while laborers from the countryside have been able to acquire jobs. For example, although 1,000,000 people from across the country came to Beijing and found jobs, over 100,000 Beijing natives remain unemployed. The combination of newcomers and former peasants makes openings available for laid-off workers even more scarce than they would be otherwise. It is estimated that the reemployment rate of SE layoffs was just 30% in 1999 (Mo, 1999).

Unemployment Research in China

Empirical research on the experience of unemployment is in its infancy in China. The Chinese government, however, has begun to support and encourage such research. A recent study by Shi (1999) studied attributions for layoffs among Chinese who had formerly worked for large SEs. This study assessed the extent to which respondents provided internal (lower education, not working hard, older, etc.) or external (government policy, SEs being irresponsible, leaders of SEs lacking ability, etc.) interpretations of their unemployment. This study showed that those who had lost jobs attributed their unemployment largely to external factors. While it is not unreasonable for Chinese to have external attributions for their unemployment, having such attributions may lead individuals to wait for the government to solve their unemployment problems. Even worse, many do not really think that they are laid off. On the contrary, they still consider themselves part of their former SEs, and believe they will return to the SEs some day.

Shi's (1999) investigation also found when a worker was laid off, emotions and behavior tended to change in a shock–optimistic–hopeless pattern. At first, because those who were laid off were not ready to be dismissed, they showed signs of shock. Then, when they began their job search, they tended to be blindly optimistic. However, because many were older, had few skills, and were short of experience in searching for jobs, they lost self-confidence as they failed again and again to find work, until at last they felt hopeless.

Research in China is also beginning to examine factors predictive of job-search intensity and reemployment. Song (1999) found significant relationships between job-seeking self-efficacy, motivation control, and job-seeking frequency among Chinese unemployed. Job-seeking frequency during unemployment also predicted higher job satisfaction among reemployed individuals. Song (1999) further showed that as individuals moved from

unemployment into reemployment, mental health increased. The mental health of continuously unemployed people deteriorated during the three-month period of the study. High-quality reemployment significantly improved mental health, but low-quality reemployment had no effect on mental health (Song, 1999). The results of this study closely resemble results found in the United States (cf. Wanberg 1995; Wanberg et al., 1999b).

Summary

Organizational downsizing is new to China, and its implementation has had a tremendous impact on the country. The unemployment situation in China is currently a serious one, and is receiving a great deal of attention. Our short 'spotlight' on China sought to provide information on some of the unemployment-related issues faced by this country as it grapples with economic reform.

FUTURE RESEARCH AND CONCLUSIONS

Studies of the stress-related impact of unemployment have been conducted in industrialized countries across the world. Across these countries, there is convergence in findings that unemployment is associated with psychological and physical distress. Given the many studies that have been conducted on this issue, additional effort should be taken to statistically analyze findings across studies. The only published meta-analysis to date in this area (Murphy & Athanasou, 1999) limited analysis of the relationship between unemployment and psychological health to longitudinal studies conducted between the years of 1986 and 1996. Future meta-analytic work on the health-related impact of unemployment should include (a) longitudinal studies conducted before 1986, (b) cross-sectional studies, (c) studies on physical health, and (d) a more extensive examination of moderators. Studies examining moderators of the unemployment experience across countries will also be valuable. One factor that differs across both individuals and cultures and is potentially important is *uncertainty avoidance* (Hofstede, 1980). Individuals and cultures that have a high need for certainty may have a more difficult time with unemployment. Levels of financial assistance provided to unemployed individuals and the extent to which unemployment is viewed as a social stigma in the different countries would clearly be important as well.

In comparison to the extensive research on the experience of unemployment, less research has focused on job search and how to facilitate reemployment. Research is needed to clearly delineate the predictors of job-search behavior and successful reemployment. This research should build upon literature from both psychology and economics

(McFadyen & Thomas, 1997). Relevant work regarding job choice (e.g., Schwab, Rynes & Aldag, 1987; Stevens & Beach, 1996) and applicant behavior in the employment interview (e.g., Paunonen, Jackson & Oberman, 1987; Tessler & Sushelsky, 1978) that has not thus far been effectively applied to the study of the job search and reemployment of unemployed adults should also be considered. Additionally, research is needed to examine the needs of job seekers in the job-search domain and to build existing knowledge into interventions. For example, what types of help might most benefit job seekers, and at what cost? Cross-cultural examinations of job-search activity and speed of reemployment might attend to cultural variables such as *activity orientation* (whether value is placed more on achievement and working or on enjoying life; Kluckhohn & Strodtbeck, 1961). Greater priority may be placed upon the job search in cultures that value achievement and working.

Another focus of our chapter was on the increasing prevalence of downsizing. While a growing amount of research has examined employees' attitudinal reactions to these cutbacks, several questions remain. For example, research has shown that layoff survivors who perceived the layoffs that occurred in their organizations as unfair are less satisfied with their jobs and report lower commitment to their employers. Yet, there have been almost no comparisons of attitudes between surviving employees in downsizing organizations and employees in nondownsizing organizations. In the search for moderators of reactions to layoffs main effects have been largely ignored or assumed to exist. Future research might additionally attend to behavioral and organizational outcomes. Topics which are beginning to receive more attention include violence following layoffs (Catalano, Novaco & McConnell, 1997) and overall profitability of layoffs (Palmon, Sun & Tang, 1997). Important questions remain regarding turnover rates among those who remain after layoffs and the impact of layoffs on actual work performance.

Cross-cultural research examinations of the outcomes associated with downsizing might benefit from the social comparison point of view offered by Brockner, Konovsky, Cooper-Schneider, Folger, Martin and Bies (1994). These authors suggest that national culture can have an important role in shaping employee perceptions of layoffs. For example, if downsizing is not used by other organizations in a culture, it may be seen especially negatively. Interviews with Japanese supervisors confirm that layoffs are often avoided because of the negative reaction it would generate among current employees and potential consumers (Usui & Colignon, 1996).

Our chapter took a brief look at the unemployment situation in China, where unemployment is a prominent issue. Research there on unemployment is in its infancy. Given the differences in culture, government, and the unique issues surrounding the emergence of unemployment in China, it is necessary to empirically assess the extent to which existing research generalizes to the Chinese situation. Also critical is research that sheds light on the reluctance of Chinese workers to take jobs that are not with large state enterprises. Examination of Chinese 'face-saving behavior' and its associations with reactions to unemployment would also be interesting. As the unemployment situation has evolved in China, employment counselors have found that face saving seems to prevent those who have been laid off from obtaining help. The face effect is so strong that married individuals in China may even hide the fact of being laid off from each other.

Overall, there is a wealth of information available on the experience of unemployment, and empirical research on this topic is being conducted in many countries. As with any other area of research, research in the area of unemployment has grown over the years in terms of its methodological sophistication. Future research in this area should continue to strive to meet high methodological standards. For example, the unemployment literature in the last 10 years has been increasingly characterized by longitudinal work. While this is a positive trend, most of the longitudinal studies in this area have included only two time waves of data. For many issues examined in the unemployment literature, the collection of additional points of data would be useful. For example, in the study of job-search behavior, many studies rely on one recall of search behavior in the last month. Surveys completed by the job seeker at multiple time points might allow for a closer approximation of the job seeker's actual job-search behavior (Barber, Daly, Giannantonio & Phillips, 1994).

In the pursuit of methodological sophistication, however, the value of interview and focus-group methodology should not be overlooked. While the literature on the impacts of unemployment on well-being includes what is perhaps a superfluous number of qualitative studies, the literature on job search and reemployment and perceived fairness of layoffs does not. Because the literature in these latter areas is not well developed, interviews and focus groups may help to advance the literature, develop theory, and stimulate research questions that can be pursued further through quantitative means.

NOTES

1 Because definitions of unemployment across countries differ in their level of inclusion, the Organization for Economic Cooperation and Development (OECD) provides unemployment rates standardized across countries, defining unemployed individuals as persons of

working age without work who have taken steps to find employment. For the purposes of this review, we define unemployment in a manner consistent with the OECD, recognizing that individual studies or countries may use more or less inclusive definitions of unemployment. For a discussion of how conceptualizations of unemployment vary across countries, we recommend Atkinson and Micklewright (1991).

2 While the term 'layoff' has been used to describe both permanent and temporary separations, in this chapter we use the term to describe only permanent separations.

REFERENCES

A million Chinese jobs to disappear (1999). *International Herald Tribune*, (May 28), 21.

Aaronson, D., & Sullivan, D.G. (1998). The decline of job security in the 1990s: Displacement, anxiety, and their effect on wage growth. *Economic Perspectives, 22,* 17–43.

Abraham, K.G., & Houseman, S.N. (1995). *Job security in America: Lessons from Germany*. Washington, D.C.: Brookings Institution.

Addison, J.T. (1989). The controversy over advance notice legislation in the United States. *British Journal of Industrial Relations, 27,* 235–263.

Addison, J.T., & Blackburn, M.L. (1997). A puzzling aspect of the effect of advance notice on unemployment. *Industrial and Labor Relations Review, 50,* 268–288.

Adnett, P. (1996). *European labor markets: Analysis and policy*. London: Longman.

Ahlburg, D.A. (1986). The social costs of unemployment. In R. Castle, D.E. Lewis, & J. Mangan (Eds.), *Work, leisure, and technology* (pp. 19–29). Melbourne, Australia: Longman Cheshire.

Ashford, S.J., Lee, C., & Bobko, P. (1989). Content, causes, and consequences of job insecurity: A theory-based measure and substantive test. *Academy of Management Journal, 32,* 803–829.

Atkinson, A.B., & Micklewright, J. (1991). Unemployment compensation and labor market transitions: A critical review. *Journal of Economic Literature, 29,* 1679–1727.

Atkinson, T.L., Liem, R., & Liem, J.H. (1986). The social costs of unemployment: Implications for social support. *Journal of Health and Social Behavior, 27,* 317–331.

Bakke, E.W. (1933). *The Unemployed Man*. London: Nisbett.

Balducchi, D.E., Johnson, T.R., & Gritz, R.M. (1997). The role of the employment service. In C.J. O'Leary, & S.A. Wander (Eds.), *Unemployment Insurance in the United States* (Vol. 1, pp. 457–504). Kalamazoo, MI: W.E. Upjohn Institute for Employment Research.

Barber, A.E., Daly, C.L., Giannantonio, C.M., & Phillips, J.M. (1994). Job search activities: An examination of changes over time. *Personnel Psychology, 47,* 739–766.

Barron, J.M., & Gilley, O.W. (1979). The effect of unemployment insurance on the search process. *Industrial and Labor Relations Review, 32,* 363–366.

Barron, J.M., & Mellow, W. (1981). Changes in the labor force status among the unemployed. *Journal of Human Resources, 16,* 427–441.

Belzil, C. (1995). Unemployment duration stigma and re-employment earnings. *Canadian Journal of Economics, 28,* 568–585.

Bian, Y. (1997). Bringing strong ties back in: Indirect ties, network bridges, and job searches in China. *American Sociological Review, 62,* 366–385.

Billesbach, T.J., & Rives, J.M. (1985). Lifetime employment: Future prospects for Japan and the U.S. *SAM Advanced Management Journal*, Autumn, 26–30, 46.

Blaustein, S.J. O'Leary, C.J., & Wandner, S.A. (1997). Policy issues. In C.J. O'Leary, & S.A. Wander (Eds.), *Unemployment Insurance in the United States* (Vol. 1, pp. 457–504). Kalamazoo, MI: W.E. Upjohn Institute for Employment Research.

Bond, M.J., & Feather, N.T. (1988). Some correlates of structure and purpose in the use of time. *Journal of Personality and Social Psychology, 55,* 321–329.

Brasher, E.E., & Chen, P.Y. (1999). Evaluation of success criteria in job search: A process perspective. *Journal of Occupational and Organizational Psychology, 72,* 57–70.

Brenner, S.O., & Bartell, R. (1983). The psychological impact of unemployment: A structural analysis of cross-sectional data. *Journal of Occupational Psychology, 56,* 129–136.

Brockner, J., & Greenberg, J. (1990). The impact of lay-offs on survivors: An organizational justice perspective. In J.S. Carroll (Ed.), *Applied social psychology and organizational settings* (pp. 45–75). Hillsdale, NJ: Erlbaum.

Brockner, J., Konovsky, M., Cooper-Schneider, R., Folger, R., Martin, C., & Bies, R.J. (1994). Interactive effects of procedural justice and outcome negativity on victims and survivors of job loss. *Academy of Management Journal, 37,* 397–409.

Brockner, J., & Wiesenfeld, B.M. (1996). An integrative framework for explaining reactions to decisions: Interactive effects of outcomes and procedures. *Psychological Bulletin, 120,* 189–208.

Brockner, J., Wiesenfeld, B.M., Reed, T., Grover, S., & Martin, C.M. (1993). Interactive effect of job content and context on the reactions of layoff survivors. *Journal of Personality and Social Psychology, 64,* 187–197.

Budros, A. (1997). The new capitalism and organizational rationality: The adoption of downsizing programs, 1979–1994. *Social Forces, 76,* 229–249.

Caldwell, D.F., & Burger, J.M. (1998). Personality characteristics of job applicants and success in screening interviews. *Personnel Psychology, 51,* 119–136.

Caplan, R.D., Vinokur, A.D., Price, R.H., & Van Ryn, M. (1989). Job seeking, reemployment, and mental health: A randomized field experiment in coping with job loss. *Journal of Applied Psychology, 74,* 759–769.

Cappelli, P. (1992). Examining managerial displacement. *Academy of Management Journal, 35,* 203–217.

Cappelli, P., Bassi, L., Katz, H., Knoke, D., Osterman, P., & Useem, M. (1997). *Change at work*. New York: Oxford University Press.

Catalano, R., Novaco, R., & McConnell, W. (1997). A model of the net effect of job loss on violence. *Journal of Personality and Social Psychology, 72*, 1440–1447.

Cullen, A.M., Shouksmith, G.A., & Habermann, G.M. (1997). Attitudes toward the unemployed in New Zealand as reflected in word associations. In G.M. Habermann (Ed.), *Looking back and moving forward: 50 years of New Zealand psychology* (pp. 22–34). Wellington, New Zealand: New Zealand Psychological Society.

DeFrank, R.S., & Ivancevich, J.M. (1986). Job loss: An individual level review and model. *Journal of Vocational Behavior, 28*, 1–20.

deGraaf, N.D., & Flap, H.D. (1988). 'With a little help from my friends': Social resources as an explanation of occupational status and income in West Germany, the Netherlands, and the United States. *Social Forces, 67*, 452–472.

Dew, M.A., Penkower, L., & Bromet, E.J. (1991). Effects of unemployment on mental health in the contemporary family. *Behavior Modification, 15*, 501–544.

Downsizing Study Team (1997). *Serving the American public: Best practices in downsizing*. http://www.npr.gov/cgi-bin/print_hit_bold.pl/library/ papers/benchmrk/ downsize.html?downsizing.

Eden, D., & Aviram, A. (1993). Self-efficacy training to speed reemployment: Helping people to help themselves. *Journal of Applied Psychology, 78*, 352–360.

Ehrenberg, R.G., & Jakubson, G. (1988). *Advance notice provisions in plant closing legislation*. Kalamazoo, MI: W.E. Upjohn Institute for Employment Research.

Ehrenberg, R.G., & Oaxaca, R.L. (1976). Unemployment insurance, duration of unemployment, and subsequent wage gain. *The American Economic Review, 66*, 754–766.

Eisenberg, P., & Lazarsfeld, P.F. (1938). The psychological effects of unemployment. *Psychological Bulletin, 35*, 358–390.

Ellis, R.A., & Taylor, M.S. (1983). Role of self-esteem within the job search process. *Journal of Applied Psychology, 68*, 632–640.

England, G.W., & Quintanilla, S.A.R. (1989). Major work meaning patterns in the national labor forces of Germany, Japan, and the United States. *Advances in international comparative management* (Vol. 4, pp. 77–94). Greenwich, CT: JAI Press.

Fallick, B.C. (1994). The endogeneity of advance notice and fear of destructive attrition. *Review of Economics and Statistics, 76*, 378–384.

Fallick, B.C. (1996). A review of the recent empirical literature on displaced workers. *Industrial and Labor Relations Review, 50*, 5–16.

Feather, N.T., & Bond, M.J. (1983). Time structure and purposeful activity among employed and unemployed university graduates. *Journal of Occupational Psychology, 56*, 241–254.

Feather, N.T., & O'Brien, G.E. (1987). Looking for employment: An expectancy-valence analysis of job-seeking behaviour among young people. *British Journal of Psychology, 78*, 251–272.

Fineman, S. (1983). *White collar unemployment: Impact and stress*. Chichester, UK: John Wiley.

Fryer, D. (1998). Labour market disadvantage, deprivation and mental health. In P.J.D. Drenth, & H. Thierry (Eds.), *Handbook of work and organizational psychology*, Vol. 2: *Work psychology* (2nd ed., pp. 215–227). Hove, UK: Psychology Press/Erlbaum.

Fryer, D., & Payne, R. (1986). Being unemployed: A review of the literature on the psychological experience of unemployment. In C.L. Cooper, & I. Robertson (Eds.), *International review of industrial and organizational psychology* (pp. 235–278). Chichester, UK: John Wiley.

Furnham, A., & Rawles, R. (1996). Job search strategies, attitudes to school and attributions about unemployment. *Journal of Adolescence, 19*, 355–369.

Gore, S. (1978). The effect of social support in moderating the health consequences of unemployment. *Journal of Health and Social Behavior, 19*, 157–165.

Gowan, M.A., Riordan, C.M., & Gatewood, R.D. (1999). Test of a model of coping with involuntary job loss following a company closing. *Journal of Applied Psychology, 84*, 74–86.

Hammarstroem, A., & Janlert, U. (1997). Nervous and depressive symptoms in a longitudinal study of youth unemployment-selection or exposure? *Journal of Adolescence, 20*, 293–305.

Hartley, J.F. (1980). The impact of unemployment upon the self-esteem of managers. *Journal of Occupational Psychology, 53*, 147–155.

Hepworth, S.J. (1980). Moderating factors of the psychological impact of unemployment. *Journal of Occupational Psychology, 53*, 139–146.

Hofstede, G.H. (1980). *Culture's consequences: International differences in work-related values*. Beverly Hills, CA: Sage Publications.

Houseman, S.N., & Abraham, K.G. (1995). Labor adjustment under different institutional structures. In F. Buttler (Ed.), *Institutional frameworks and labor market performance: Comparative views on the U.S. and German economies* (pp. 285–315). London, UK: Routledge.

Jackson, P.R., Stafford, E.M., Banks, M.H., & Warr, P.B. (1983). Unemployment and psychological distress in young people: The moderating role of employment commitment. *Journal of Applied Psychology, 68*, 525–535.

Jahoda, M. (1982). *Employment and unemployment: A social-psychological analysis*. New York: Cambridge University Press.

Jahoda, M., Lazarsfeld, P.F., & Zeisel, H. (1971). *Marienthal: The sociography of an unemployed community* (M. Jahoda, P.F. Lazarsfeld, H.J. Zeisel, J. Reginall, & T. Elsaesser, Trans.). Chicago, IL: Aldine Atherton (original work published 1933).

Joseph, S., Weatherall, K., & Stringer, M. (1997). Attributions for unemployment in Northern Ireland:

Does it make a difference what your name is? *Irish Journal of Psychology, 18,* 341–348.

Kanfer, R., & Hulin, C.L. (1985). Individual differences in successful job searches following lay-off. *Personnel Psychology, 38,* 835–847.

Kasl, S.V., Rodriguez, E., & Lasch, K.E. (1998). The impact of unemployment on health and well-being. In B.P. Dohrenwend (Ed.), *Adversity, stress, and psychopathology* (pp. 111–131). New York: Oxford University Press.

Katz, L.F., & Meyer, B.D. (1990). Unemployment insurance, recall expectations, and unemployment outcomes. *Quarterly Journal of Economics, 105,* 973–1002.

Kawakubo, M. (1987). Japanese style management is a myth. *Euro-Asia Business Review,* April, 34–36.

Kessler, R.C., Price, R.H., & Wortman, C.B. (1985). Social factors in psychopathology: Stress, social support, and coping processes. *Annual Review of Psychology, 36,* 531–572.

Kessler, R.C., Turner, J.B., & House, J.S. (1987). Intervening processes in the relationship between unemployment and health. *Psychological Medicine, 17,* 949–961.

Kilpatrick, R., & Trew, K. (1985). Life-styles and psychological well-being among unemployed men in Northern Ireland. *Journal of Occupational Psychology, 58,* 207–216.

Kinicki, A.J., & Latack, J.C. (1990). Explication of the construct of coping with involuntary job loss. *Journal of Vocational Behavior, 36,* 339–360.

Kletzer, L.G. (1998). Job displacement. *Journal of Economic Perspectives, 12,* 115–136.

Kluckhohn, F.R., & Strodtbeck, F.L. (1961). *Variations in value orientations.* Evanston, IL: Row Peterson.

Konovsky, M.A., & Folger, R. (1991). The effects of procedures, social accounts, and benefits level on victims' layoff reactions. *Journal of Applied Social Psychology, 21,* 630–650.

Kozlowski, S.W.J., Chao, G.T., Smith, E.M., & Hedlund, J. (1993). Organizational downsizing: Strategies, interventions, and research implications. In C.L. Cooper, & I.T. Robertson (Eds.), *International review of industrial and organizational psychology* (Vol. 8, pp. 263–332). Chichester, UK: John Wiley.

Lai, J.C.L., & Wong, W.S. (1998). Optimism and coping with unemployment among Hong Kong Chinese women. *Journal of Research in Personality, 32,* 454–479.

Latack, J.C., Kinicki, A.J., & Prussia, G.E. (1995). An integrative process model of coping with job loss. *Academy of Management Review, 20,* 311–342.

Lay, C.H., & Brokenshire, R. (1997). Conscientiousness, procrastination, and person-task characteristics in job searching by unemployed adults. *Current Psychology, 16,* 83–96.

Lazear, E.P. (1990). Job security provisions and employment. *The Quarterly Journal of Economics, 105,* 699–726.

Leana, C.R., & Feldman, D.C. (1990). Individual responses to job loss: Empirical findings from two field studies. *Human Relations, 43,* 1155–1181.

Leana, C.R., & Feldman, D.C. (1992). *Coping with job loss: How individuals, organizations, and communities respond to layoffs.* New York: Lexington Books.

Leana, C.R., Feldman, D.C., & Tan, G.Y. (1998). Predictors of coping behavior after a layoff. *Journal of Organizational Behavior, 19,* 85–97.

Liem, J.H., & Liem, G.R. (1990). Understanding the individual and family effects of unemployment. In J. Echenrode, & S. Gore (Eds.), *Stress between work and family* (pp. 175–204). New York: Plenum Press.

Lin, Y. (1999). The development of community service and small enterprise and reemployment of layoffs. *Training in China* (No. 6), 4.

Mallinckrodt, B., & Bennett, J. (1992). Social support and the impact of job loss in dislocated blue-collar workers. *Journal of Counseling Psychology, 39,* 482–489.

Marshall, A.E. (1985). Employment qualifications of college graduates: How important are they? *Employment Counseling, 22*(4), 136–143.

McCall, B.P. (1997). The determinants of full-time versus part-time reemployment following job displacement. *Journal of Labor Economics, 15,* 714–734.

McFadyen, R.G., & Thomas, J.P. (1997). Economic and psychological models of job search behavior of the unemployed. *Human Relations, 50,* 1461–1484.

Mo, R. (1999). The reemployment situation in China. *Training in China* (No. 5), 19.

Murphy, G.C., & Athanasou, J.A. (1999). The effect of unemployment on mental health. *Journal of Occupational and Organizational Psychology, 72,* 83–99.

Nolan, P. (1994). Labor market institutions, industrial restructuring, and unemployment in Europe. In J. Michie, & J.G. Smith (Eds.), *Unemployment in Europe* (pp. 61–71). London, UK: Academic Press.

O'Brien, G.E. (1986). *Psychology of work and unemployment.* Chichester, UK; New York: John Wiley.

Organization for Economic Cooperation and Development (1999). Standardised employment rates of selected OECD countries: annual data. *Quarterly Labor Force Statistics, 99*(1), 100.

Organization for Economic Cooperation and Development (2000). Standardised employment rates (May, retrieved June 12), http://www.oecd.org/news_and_events/new-numbers/sur/surlist.htm.

Palmon, O., Sun, H.L., & Tang, A.P. (1997). Layoff announcements: Stock price impact and financial performance. *Financial Management, 26,* 54–68.

Paunonen, S.V., Jackson, D.N., & Oberman, S.M. (1987). Personnel selection decisions: Effects of applicant personality and the letter of reference. *Organizational Behavior and Human Decision Processes, 40,* 96–114.

Payne, R., & Hartley, J. (1987). A test of a model for explaining the affective experience of unemployed men. *Journal of Occupational Psychology, 60,* 31–47.

Perritt, H.H. (1998). *Employee dismissal law and practice* (4th ed., Vol. 1) New York: Wiley Law Publications.

Peterson, R.B., & Sullivan, J. (1990). The Japanese lifetime employment system: Whither it goest? In S.B. Prasad (Ed.), *Advances in international comparative management* (Vol. 5, pp. 169–194) Greenwich, CT: JAI Press.

Platt, S.D. (1984). Unemployment and suicidal behaviour: A review of the literature. *Social Science and Medicine, 19*, 93–115.

Price, R.H., Van Ryn, M., & Vinokur, A.D. (1992). Impact of a preventive job search intervention on the likelihood of depression among the unemployed. *Journal of Health and Social Behavior, 33*, 158–167.

Reid, G.L. (1972). Job search and the effectiveness of job-finding methods. *Industrial and Labor Relations Review, 25*, 479–495.

Rodgers, B. (1991). Socio-economic status, employment and neurosis. *Social Psychiatry and Psychiatric Epidemiology, 26*, 104–114.

Roskies, E., & Louis-Guerin, C. (1990). Job insecurity in managers: Antecedents and consequences. *Journal of Organizational Behavior, 11*, 345–359.

Rousseau, D.M., & Anton, R.J. (1988). Fairness and implied contract obligations in termination: A policy capturing study. *Human Performance, 1*, 273–289.

Rowley, K.M., & Feather, N.T. (1987). The impact of unemployment in relation to age and length of unemployment. *Journal of Occupational Psychology, 60*, 323–332.

Saks, A.M., & Ashforth, B.E. (1999). Effects of individual differences and job search behaviors on the employment status of recent university graduates. *Journal of Vocational Behavior, 54*, 335–349.

Salvanes, K.G. (1997). Market rigidities and labour market flexibility: An international comparison. *Scandinavian Journal of Economics, 99*, 315–333.

Schaufeli, W.B. (1997). Youth unemployment and mental health: Some Dutch findings. *Journal of Adolescence, 20*, 281–292.

Schaufeli, W.B., & VanYperen, N.W. (1992). Unemployment and psychological distress among graduates: A longitudinal study. *Journal of Occupational and Organizational Psychology, 65*, 291–305.

Schliebner, C.T., & Peregoy, J.J. (1994). Unemployment effects on the family and the child: Interventions for counselors. *Journal of Counsåling and Development, 72*, 368–372.

Schmidt, S.R., & Svorny, S.V. (1998). Recent trends in job security and stability. *Journal of Labor Research, 19*, 647–668.

Schmit, M.J., Amel, E.L., & Ryan, A.M. (1993). Self-reported assertive job-seeking behaviors of minimally educated job hunters. *Personnel Psychology, 46*, 105–124.

Schwab, D.P., Rynes, S.L., & Aldag, R.J. (1987). Theories and research on job search and choice. *Research in Personnel and Human Resources Management, 5*, 129–166.

Schwind, H.F., & Peterson, R.B. (1985). Shifting personal values in the Japanese management system. *International Studies of Management and Organization, 15*, 60–74.

Segal, P. (1999). Chinese layoffs putting millions on the streets. *International Herald Tribune* (June 3), *1*, 18.

Sheppard, H.L., & Belitsky, A.H. (1966). *The Job Hunt*. Baltimore, MA: Johns Hopkins Press.

Shi, K. (1999). *Behavior research on laid-off (unemployed) job-seekers*. Beijing, China: Demarcate and Norm Publishing.

Si, S.X., & Bruton, G.D. (1999). Knowledge transfer in international joint ventures in transitional economies: The China experience. *Academy of Management Executive, 13*, 83–90.

Silvestri, G.T. (1995). Occupational employment to 2005. *Monthly Labor Review, 118*, 60–87.

Singh, L.B., Singh, P.P., & Kumari, M. (1998). Educated unemployed young men in India: An analysis of their level of development-orientation. *Applied Psychology: An International Review, 47*, 571–574.

Smari, J., Arason, E., Hafsteinsson, H., & Ingimarsson, S. (1997). Unemployment, coping and psychological distress. *Scandinavian Journal of Psychology, 38*, 151–156.

Smith, J.G. (1994). Policies to reduce European unemployment. In J. Michie, & J.G. Smith (Eds.), *Unemployment in Europe* (pp. 259–275). London: Harcourt Brace & Co.

Song, Z. (1999). *Predictors of reemployment among laid-off job-seekers in China*. Unpublished master's thesis, Institute of Psychology, Chinese Academy of Sciences, Beijing, China.

Stafford, E.M., Jackson, P.R., & Banks, M.H. (1980). Employment, work involvement and mental health in less qualified young people. *Journal of Occupational Psychology, 53*, 291–304.

Steffy, B.D., Shaw, K.N., & Noe, A.W. (1989). Antecedents and consequences of job search behaviors. *Journal of Vocational Behavior, 35*, 254–269.

Stevens, C.K., & Beach, L.R. (1996). Job search and job selection. In L.R. Beach (Ed.), *Decision making in the workplace: A unified perspective* (8th ed., pp. 33–47). Mahwah: Lawrence Erlbaum Associates.

Storey, J.R., & Niesner, J.A. (1997). Unemployment compensation in the group of seven nations. In C.J. O'Leary, & S.A. Wander (Eds.), *Unemployment insurance in the United States* (Vol. 1, pp. 599–668). Kalamazoo, MI: W.E. Upjohn Institute for Employment Research.

Stumpf, S.A., Austin, E.J., & Hartman, K. (1984). The impact of career exploration and interview readiness on interview performance and outcomes. *Journal of Vocational Behavior, 24*, 221–235.

Swinburne, P. (1981). The psychological impact of unemployment on managers and professional staff. *Journal of Occupational Psychology, 54*, 47–64.

Talaga, J., & Beehr, T.A. (1989). Retirement: A psychological perspective. In C.L. Cooper, & I. Robertson (Eds.), *International review of industrial and organizational psychology, 4*, 185–211. Chichester, UK: John Wiley.

Tessler, R., & Sushelsky, L. (1978). Effects of eye contact and social status on the perception of a job applicant in an employment interviewing situation. *Journal of Vocational Behavior, 13*, 338–347.

The Beijing Labor and Social Insurance Bureau (1999). A new way of vocational training. *Training in China* (No. 4), 7–10.

The National Developmental Program for Labor and Social Insurance (1999). *Training in China*, No. 7, p. 10.

Turner, J.B., Kessler, R.C., & House, J.S. (1991). Factors facilitating adjustment to unemployment: Implications for intervention. American *Journal of Community Psychology*, *19*, 521–542.

Ullah, P. (1990). The association between income, financial strain and psychological well-being among unemployed youths. *Journal of Occupational Psychology*, *63*, 317–330.

Ullah, P., Banks, M., & Warr, P. (1985). Social support, social pressures and psychological distress during unemployment. *Psychological Medicine*, *15*, 283–295.

Usui, C., & Colignon, R.A. (1996). Corporate restructuring: converging world pattern or societally specific embeddedness? *The Sociological Quarterly*, *37*, 551–578.

Van Ryn, M., & Vinokur, A.D. (1992). How did it work? An examination of the mechanisms through which an intervention for the unemployed promoted job-search behavior. *American Journal of Community Psychology*, *20*, 577–597.

Vinokur, A.D., & Caplan, R.D. (1987). Attitudes and social support: Determinants of job-seeking behavior and well-being among the unemployed. *Journal of Applied Social Psychology*, *17*, 1007–1024.

Vinokur, A.D., Price, R.H., & Caplan, R.D. (1991). From field experiments to program implementation: Assessing the potential outcomes of an experimental intervention program for unemployed persons. *American Journal of Community Psychology*, *19*, 543–562.

Vinokur, A.D., Price, R.H., & Caplan, R.D. (1996). Hard times and hurtful partners: How financial strain affects depression and relationship satisfaction of unemployed persons and their spouses. *Journal of Personality and Social Psychology*, *71*, 166–179.

Vinokur, A.D., Price, R.H., & Schul, Y. (1995). Impact of the JOBS intervention on unemployed workers varying in risk for depression. *American Journal of Community Psychology*, *23*, 39–74.

Vinokur, A.D., & Schul, Y. (1997). Mastery and inoculation against setbacks as active ingredients in the JOBS intervention for the unemployed. *Journal of Consulting and Clinical Psychology*, *65*, 867–877.

Vinokur, A.D., Schul, Y., Vuori, J., & Price, R.H. (in press). Two years after a job loss: Long term impact of the JOBS program on reemployment and mental health. *Journal of Occupational Health Psychology*.

Vinokur, A.D., Van Ryn, M., Gramlich, E.M., & Price, R.H. (1991). Long-term follow-up and benefit-cost analysis of the Jobs program: A preventive intervention for the unemployed. *Journal of Applied Psychology*, *76*, 213–219.

Wanberg, C.R. (1995). A longitudinal study of the effects of unemployment and quality of reemployment. *Journal of Vocational Behavior*, *46*, 40–54.

Wanberg, C.R. (1997). Antecedents and outcomes of coping behaviors among unemployed and reemployed individuals. *Journal of Applied Psychology*, *82*, 731–744.

Wanberg, C.R., Bunce, L.W., & Gavin, M.B. (1999a). Perceived fairness of layoffs among individuals who have been laid off: A longitudinal study. *Personnel Psychology*, *52*, 59–84.

Wanberg, C.R., Griffiths, R.F., & Gavin, M.B. (1997). Time structure and unemployment: A longitudinal investigation. *Journal of Occupational and Organizational Psychology*, *70*, 75–95.

Wanberg, C.R., Kanfer, R., & Banas, J. (2000). Predictors and outcomes of networking intensity among unemployed job-seekers. *Journal of Applied Psychology*, *85*, 491–503.

Wanberg, C.R., Kanfer, R., & Rotundo, M. (1999b). Unemployed individuals: Motives, job-search competencies, and job-search constraints as predictors of job seeking and reemployment. *Journal of Applied Psychology*, *84*, 897–910.

Wanberg, C.R., Watt, J.D., & Rumsey, D.J. (1996). Individuals without jobs: An empirical study of job-seeking behavior and reemployment. *Journal of Applied Psychology*, *81*, 76–87.

Warr, P. (1983). Work, jobs and unemployment. *Bulletin of the British Psychological Society*, *36*, 305–311.

Winefield, A.H. (1995). Unemployment: Its psychological costs. In C.L. Cooper, & I.T. Robertson (Eds.), *International Review of Industrial and Organizational Psychology* (Vol. 10, pp. 169–211). Chichester, UK: John Wiley.

Yeung, W.J.H., & Hofferth, S.L. (1998). Family adaptations to income and job loss in the U.S. *Journal of Family and Economic Issues*, *19*, 255–283.

14

The Human Team: Basic Motivations and Innovations

MICHAEL A. WEST

Human beings have always lived, loved, and worked in groups, and understanding the fundamental motivation to belong in groups, and associated emotions of people in groups, it is argued, is essential for understanding work teams in modern organizations. Structures, objectives, and processes are influenced by members' anxieties, guilts, jealousies, altruism, trust, and satisfaction. The link between these motivations and emotions and team exploration (creativity and innovation) is examined. Pressure to produce and a sense of internal group safety are major and positive influences on teams' capacity to innovate.

INTRODUCTION

He makes tools (and does so within more than one technical tradition), builds shelters, takes over natural refuges by exploiting fire, and sallies out of them to hunt and gather his food. He does this in groups with a discipline that can sustain complicated operations; he therefore has some ability to exchange ideas by speech. The basic biological units of his hunting groups probably prefigure the nuclear family of man, being founded on the institutions of the home base and a sexual differentiation of activity. There may even be some complexity of social organization in so far as fire-bearers and gatherers or old creatures whose memories made them the data banks of their 'societies' could be supported by the labour of others. There has to be some social organization to permit the sharing of co-operatively obtained food, too. There is nothing to be usefully added to an account such as this by pretending to say where exactly can be found a prehistoric point or dividing line at which such things had come to be, but subsequent human history is unimaginable without them. (Roberts, 1995: 18)

The activity of a group of people working cooperatively to achieve shared goals via differentiation of roles and using elaborate systems of communication is basic to our species. The current enthusiasm for team working in organizations reflects a deeper, perhaps unconscious, recognition that this way of working offers the promise of greater progress that can be achieved through individual endeavour or through mechanistic approaches to work. We begin this exploration of the role of groups or teams in work organizations from this basic perspective and consider why we are motivated to work in groups, and what are some of the *basic emotions and behaviours* that characterize human experience in groups. This is then linked to an examination of the workgroup conditions for *creativity and innovation*. Innovation is, after all, a fundamental reason for humans to work in groups. I suggest that creativity and innovation in groups emerges primarily when the group members' needs to belong are satisfied by group dynamics which create a sense of safety, shared intent, high levels of positive interaction, the effective management of conflict, and support for exploration.

The aim of this chapter is to consider basic, powerful, and often hidden influences on human workgroup functioning, rather than to duplicate the many excellent reviews of research on workgroups (see, e.g., Guzzo & Shea, 1992; Cohen & Bailey, 1997).

EMOTIONS IN TEAMS

The fundamental human drive and pervasive motivation to form and maintain lasting, positive, and significant relationships helps us to understand the functioning of teams at work, and in particular the emotions manifested in work groups. Satisfying this need to belong, according to Baumeister and Leary (1995), requires that our relationships are characterized by:

frequent interaction;
temporal stability and likely continuity;
mutual affective concern;
freedom from conflict.

Most current research and theories about the functioning of teams fail to take account of the solid evolutionary basis of our tendency to form strong attachments and by extension to live and work in groups. Human beings work and live in groups because groups enable survival and reproduction (Ainsworth, 1989; Axelrod & Hamilton, 1981; Barash, 1977; Bowlby, 1969; Buss, 1990a, b, 1991; Hogan, Jones & Cheek, 1985; Moreland, 1987). By living and working in groups early humans could share food, easily find mates, and care for infants. They could hunt more effectively and defend themselves against their enemies. Individuals who did not readily join groups would be disadvantaged in comparison with group members as a consequence. The need to belong, which is at the root of our tendency to live and work in groups, is manifested most profoundly in the behaviour of children and infants. Children who stuck close to adults were more likely to survive and be able to reproduce, because they would be protected from danger, cared for and provided with food. And we see across all societies that danger, illness, or the darkness of night causes people to have a desire to be with others, indicating the protection offered by group membership. Adults who formed attachments would be more likely to reproduce and adults who form long-term relationships would stand a greater chance of producing infants who would grow to reproductive age. 'Over the course of evolution, the small group became the survival strategy developed by the human species' (Barchas, 1986: 212).

This fundamental human motivation to belong therefore shapes much human behaviour and for our purposes helps to explain emotional reactions in teams. The absence of one or more characteristics of belongingness (frequent interaction, likely continuity and stability, mutual affective concern, and freedom from conflict and negative affect) will lead to conflict and disintegration within relationships and teams. Our tendency to concentrate on task characteristics and organizational context often blinds us to these fundamental socio-emotional requirements of team-based working. For the benefits of teamworking are not only improved task performance (West, 1996), but also intrapsychic and emotional benefits for team members (Carter & West, 1999; Patterson & West, 1999).

Early research in social psychology, such as the famous Robbers' Cave study, showed how psychological group identification occurs almost immediately when people are randomly assigned to groups, with dramatic behavioural consequences of strong loyalty and in-group favouritism (Sherif, Harvey, White, Hood & Sherif, 1961). People develop group identification with the most minimal social cues (Billig & Tajfel, 1973; Tajfel, 1970; Tajfel & Billig, 1974). The tendency of people to discriminate in favour of their own group and to discriminate against members of out-groups is pervasive (Turner, 1985). Moreover, this in-group favouritism occurs spontaneously and without obvious value to the individual. Research indicates that there is no need for material advantage to the self or inferred similarity to other group members for group identification to occur. However, there is evidence that external threats lead to the creation of firmer bonds within groups (Stein, 1976) while at the same time increasing the threat of rejection to deviants (Lauderdale, Smith-Cunnien, Parker & Inverarity, 1984). Groups clearly seek solidarity when confronted by external threat.

Early studies of organizational behaviour showed that workgroups profoundly influenced individual behaviour. In the 1920s and 1930s several studies were carried out at Western Electric's Hawthorne Works in Chicago, USA, to examine the effects of illumination in the plant on workers' performance in assembling and inspecting relays used in telephone equipment. The researchers varied the level of illumination and studied the effects on performance. They found that any variation in illumination (down to a level almost the equivalent of moonlight) was associated with improvements in performance. The results suggested that workers appreciated the attention and interest shown in their work by researchers and managers and this appreciation manifested in better performance. This effect has come to be known as the Hawthorn Effect and field studies that test methods of intervening in organizations have to demonstrate that positive effects are not simply due to the Hawthorn Effect. Further studies in the Hawthorn Works (the Relay Assembly test experiments) examined the effects of a variety of factors (such as number and length of rest periods and hours of work) upon the performance of a small group of female workers. The results suggested that the characteristics of the social setting or group in which behaviour takes place are at least as important as the technical aspects of the work in explaining performance. The Hawthorn studies (Roesthlisberger & Dixon, 1939) established how group influences have a major impact on workgroup behaviour.

By recognizing the influence of the need to belong upon the behaviour of individuals in teams we can come to understand something of the range and underlying causes of emotions in teams. Being accepted, included, and welcomed in the team will lead to feelings of happiness, elation, contentment, and calm. Being rejected, excluded, or ignored will lead to feelings of anxiety, depression, grief, jealousy, or loneliness. Team members' emotional reactions will be stimulated by real, potential, or imagined changes in their belongingness within their workteam. Real, potential, or imagined increases in belongingness will lead to an increase in positive individual- and team-level affect. Decreases in belongingness will be associated with threats to the individual and a sense of deprivation that will lead to negative affect.

Positive Emotions and Attitudes

When a new workteam is formed, team members tend to experience positive emotions and the creation of the team is often the cause for celebration. When new members join teams there tends to be an abundance of positive affect and warm expressions of welcome which are a consequence of the increase of the sense of belonging experienced by existing members and by the new member. Indeed this positive affect itself increases attraction and social bonding within the group (Moreland, 1987).

Satisfaction

One of the characteristics of a strong sense of belonging is the sense of mutuality in the relationship. So satisfaction in teams is also likely to be a consequence of both the costs as well as the rewards of team membership. People prefer relationships and teams within which all give and take. For example, Hays (1985) examined 'relationship satisfaction' from the perspective of behaviourism, assuming that rewards would determine people's satisfaction. He found instead that satisfaction was predicted by rewards plus costs, apparently because people prefer relationships and groups in which all both give and receive support and care. Baumeister, Wotman and Stillwell (1993) report that for both those who give love without receiving it, and those who receive love without giving it, the experience is aversive. Mutuality and reciprocity appear to be necessary for positive affect, and satisfaction will be highest when the sense of mutuality in teams is strong.

Satisfaction will also tend to be higher to the extent that the team members interact frequently, the tenure of the team is relatively enduring, there is a sense of mutual concern among team members, and there is not a high level of conflict. These propositions are, of course, easy to subject to empirical test.

Trust

Belonging implies a sense of mutual affective concern. When this shared affective concern is developed in teams it will lead to feelings of satisfaction among team members and particularly to trust. Holmes and Rempel (1989), reviewing the evidence on trust in relationships, concluded that trust depends on the mutual recognition of reciprocal concern and closeness. Trust will be most likely to develop in teams where there is a strong sense of reciprocal concern amongst team members.

Altruism

This mutual affective concern is also likely to translate into behaviour within the team and specifically to the expression of altruism. Much has been made in social psychology of the so-called 'bystander effect', where bystanders in the presence of others fail to take action to help someone in distress, apparently because of a sense of diffusion of responsibility and anxiety about the personal consequences of involvement. But what is less well known is the evidence that when bystanders are members of a cohesive group, the effect is nullified (Harkins & Petty, 1982). Moreover, members of large cohesive groups are more likely to help (whereas among strangers, larger numbers of bystanders lead to a lower likelihood of intervention). Social loafing (where group members exert less effort in task accomplishment in the presence of other group members) is not evident in cohesive groups where members have unique contributions, even when their contributions cannot be identified (Harkins & Petty, 1982).

Negative Emotions and Attitudes

The corollary is that the range of negative emotions manifested in teams at work is likely to be associated with threats to belongingness. The influence of the human need to belong is indicated by our strong tendency to respond with distress and protest to the end of relationships (Hazan & Shaver, 1994). For example, we see such phenomena even in training groups which come together for only a few days. Group members typically express some resistance to the notion that the group will dissolve. Members promise that they will stay in touch with each other and may even plan for reunions. More specific negative emotions manifested in teams as a consequence of threats to belonging include anxiety, depression, jealousy, loneliness, guilt, and grief. We briefly consider each of these below.

Anxiety

Human beings become anxious at the prospect of losing relationships and threats of social exclusion may be the most common cause of anxiety amongst workteam members. Indeed Horney

(1945) proposed that our basic anxiety resulted from a feeling of being isolated and helpless in a potentially hostile world. Team members may typically experience anxiety at the prospect of the break-up of the team, the impending close of a long-running team project, or their transfer to another team (Leary, 1990; Leary & Downs, 1995). Group instability (frequent member changes) and threatened dissolution of the team will also cause anxiety. High levels of conflict too will engender anxiety, since team members are likely to develop an anxious watchfulness in anticipation of conflict between team members.

Depression

Generally when we feel accepted or included this leads to feelings of happiness, whereas a sustained period of feeling isolated or excluded is associated with depression (Tambor & Leary, 1993). For example, Hoyle and Crawford (1994) found that depression and anxiety were significantly correlated (negatively) with students' sense of belonging to the university. We propose that similar emotional reactions will be associated with team membership and members' sense of belonging. Where team members feel excluded or isolated over a period of time, they are more likely to feel depressed. The team leaders may play a particularly important role in moderating this effect. In malfunctioning teams, members may deliberately make the leader a target of attempts to isolate or exclude, particularly where they perceive she or he has not enabled the team to feel a strong sense of belonging.

Jealousy

Pines and Aronson (1983) propose that jealousy is a consequence of the threat or experience of being excluded. Team members will be likely to experience jealousy when they feel that they are excluded by, or are less in the favour of, a particularly powerful or attractive team member. Jealousy may also manifest when team members feel that others are more accepted and included in the team than they themselves. Perceptions of inclusion or exclusion by the team leader are likely to be particularly important. Indeed, from a psychodynamic perspective it would be expected that a good inclusive relationship between team members and the team leader will reduce the likelihood of angry or defiant behaviour (Belsky, 1979; Miller, Cowan, Cowan, Hetherington & Clingempeel, 1993).

Loneliness

Human beings feel lonely when their needs to belong are insufficiently met. Jones (1981) has shown that this is not simply a result of lack of social contact. There are no differences in the level of social contact between those who are lonely and those who are not. The crucial factor appears to be spending time with people with whom one is close. It is social inclusion rather than the size of network that appears to influence loneliness, along with lack of intimate connections (Williams & Solano, 1983). Although people may work in teams, loneliness can still occur if there is no sense of closeness or relative intimacy of contact between team members. Those who work in multiple teams or short-lived project teams, and who thus have many social contacts, may feel loneliness nevertheless because they are prevented from developing close social contacts with other team members. Similar effects are likely to occur amongst team members who work in different locations and manage their interactions via technology-mediated communication such as video conferencing and e-mail. The relative impoverishment of these communication media will militate against the development of a strong sense of belonging in the team. Another cause of loneliness derived from the need to belong is when initial frequent contact between members of a strong team lapses. Members then have less contact over time so the establishment of an early sense of belonging is likely to be supplemented by loneliness. Where a team does not establish a sense of belonging early in its life (through the development of the four characteristics of belongingness) the change from frequent to infrequent contact is unlikely to lead to loneliness among team members.

Guilt

Guilt is induced in others to cause them to exert more effort to maintain the relationship by spending more time with or paying more attention to the partners in the relationship (Baumeister, Stillwell & Heatherton, 1994). Within a team, members may induce guilt in their colleagues when they feel they are spending inadequate time interacting interdependently with other team members, or if they feel they are showing inadequate concern for the well-being of their colleagues. Guilt-inducing signals are especially likely to be directed towards the team leader, since he or she carries a greater share of the responsibility for maintaining the sense of belonging in the team. Guilt induction can thus be seen as a response to disturbances or threats to attachments.

Grief

Grief occurs at the loss of relationships (Lofland, 1982). When couples divorce, even where they mutually agree on the desirability of the end of their relationships, they typically experience grief. In teams, the departure of members is also often an occasion where grief may be inexperienced. This is especially likely to be so when the individual is seen as having made a major contribution to the sense of belonging in the team, by contributing concern for the well-being of other team members, by interacting frequently, by enabling effectiveness or by ameliorating potential or actual conflicts. Such grief is a result of the threat to belongingness occasioned by the departure of the team member. More profound grief is likely to be felt by the departing individual, who loses a whole team (although here again, team members will often promise and even try to maintain contact with the departing team member via social events and through other forms of social contact).

Indirect Effects

Tesser (1991) has shown that, when a close relationship partner (or fellow team member) outperforms us on a performance dimension that is important to our self-definition, we tend to experience emotional distress or anger. If the performance of the team member is on a dimension that is unimportant to us, we tend to feel positive emotions as a result of what Tesser calls 'reflection'. We apparently believe that our identity is enhanced in the minds of others because of the good performance of strangers, which suggests that belongingness can have indirect effects on emotional reactions beyond the direct effects we have discussed above.

Our research evidence provides some support for the thesis we advance here. In a study of the mental health of health service workers, Carter and West (1999) compared those people who worked in teams, those who worked in pseudoteams and those not working in teams, in the United Kingdom National Health Service. Pseudoteam members were those who reported working in a team but indicated that there were not clear team objectives, or members who did not frequently work with other members of the team to achieve those objectives, or there were not separate roles, or the team was not recognized by others in the organization as a team. The sample of 2250 workers completed the General Health Questionnaire and individuals were categorized as 'cases' if their scores indicated that they would benefit from professional intervention, because of high stress levels (Hardy, Shapiro, Haynes & Rick, 1999). The results revealed that 35% of those that did not work in teams were cases; 30% of those who were in pseudoteams were cases; while only 21% of those who worked in real teams were cases. It appears from these data that working in teams is a significant buffer against the stresses between these teams. This could be attributed to the role of clarity experienced by team members, along with the high level of social support that they experienced. Moreover, working in teams appeared to ameliorate negative effects of organizational level difficulties. The findings extend to studies at the organisational level. Patterson and West (1999) showed that in 54 UK manufacturing organizations, the extent of teamworking was a predictor of the overall levels of mental health amongst employees.

But there is other evidence that simply not belonging may be damaging in itself, regardless of enacted support from those around. Cohen and Wills (1985) report that simply being a part of a supportive social network reduces stress even if those in the network do not provide emotional or practical assistance. Moreover, effects may translate from emotional reactions through to immunological and physiological functioning, particularly among those working in stressful environments, such as health care workers. Kiecolt-Glaser, Garner, Speicher, Penn, Holliday and Glaser (1984) found that loneliness was associated with a decrease in immunocompetence, particularly in relation to natural killer cell activity and elevations in levels of cortisol levels.

The thesis we have developed here should not be taken to imply that team membership is good in organizations come what may. Generalizing from evidence derived from research on social participation and bad marriages suggests that being in pathological teams may be worse than being in no team at all. Reis, Wheeler, Kernis, Spiegel and Nezlek (1985) report that quality of social relations (intimacy, pleasantness, satisfaction, mutual disclosure, initiation and influence) rather than quantity predicts health. Coyne and De Longis (1986) report that bad marriages are worse than being alone in terms of effects on happiness and health, while Kiecolt-Glaser, Fisher, Ogrocki, Stout, Speicher and Glaser (1987) found that immune function suffered among unhappily married women, and women who were separated from their husbands but still emotionally attached. Social undermining in the form of conflict, criticism, making life difficult, inducing feelings of being unwanted also have strong negative effects on mental health (Vinokur & van Ryn, 1993). Where these behaviours occur within teams they are likely to lead to a poor sense of belonging and to team member emotional damage.

Emotional responses in teams can be best understood from the perspective described above. Indeed, current approaches to understanding teams ignore fundamental human motivations (such as the need for control and the need to belong), and therefore provide inadequate explanations of the responses of people who work in teams. Here we have focused particularly on the motivation to belong, since much has been written about the need for control in the workplace and also about the materialistic drive.

Group Affective Tone

So far we have explored the role of the motivation to belong as an explanation and elucidation of the range and process of emotional reactions within the team at an individual level. Another important perspective, developed by George (1996), has been to consider the shared affect of teams at work and the implications for team performance. George (1996) uses the term 'group affective tone' to refer to 'consistent or homogenous affective reactions within a group'. If, for example, members of a team tend to be excited, energetic and enthusiastic, then the team itself can be described as being excited, energetic, and enthusiastic. As another example, if members of a team tend to be distressed, mistrustful, and nervous, then the team also can be described in these terms' (p. 78). George believes that a team's affective tone will determine how innovative and effective the team will be. Relevant to this belief is evidence that when individuals feel positive they tend to connect and integrate divergent stimulus materials – they are more creative (Isen & Daubman, 1984; Isen, Daubman & Nowicki, 1987; Isen, Johnson, Mertz & Robinson, 1985; Cummings, 1998); see interrelatedness among diverse stimuli; and use broader, inclusive categories (Isen & Daubman, 1984; Isen et al., 1987). How does this affect team or team behaviour? George suggests that if all or most individuals in a workteam tend to feel positive at work (the team has a 'high positive affective tone'), then their cognitive flexibility will be amplified as a result of social influence and other team processes. As a result of these individual and group level processes, the team will develop shared (and flexible) mental models. In effect, teams with a high positive affective tone will be creative.

Similarly, there is evidence that teams differ in the extent to which they create a climate of safety within which it is possible to engage in team learning. Edmondson (1996) demonstrated differences between teams in a study of hospital patient care, finding significant differences across workteams in their management of medication errors. In some teams, members openly acknowledged and discussed their medication errors (giving too much or too little of a drug, or administering the wrong drug) and discussed ways to avoid occurrence. In others, members kept information about errors to themselves. Learning about the causes of these errors as a team and devising innovations to prevent future errors were only possible in teams of the former type. Edmondson gives an example of how, in one learning-oriented team, discussion of a recent error led to innovation in equipment. A pump used to deliver intravenous medications was identified as a source of consistent errors, and so the nurses replaced it with a different type of pump. She also gives the example of how failure to discuss errors and generate innovations led to costly failure in the Hubble telescope development project (Capters & Lipton, 1993). In particular, Edmonson (1996) argues that learning and innovation will only take place where team members trust other members' intentions. This manifests in a group belief that well-intentioned action will not lead to punishment or rejection by the team, which Edmondson calls 'team safety':

The term is meant to suggest a realistic, learning oriented attitude about effort, error and change – not to imply a careless sense of permissiveness, nor an unrelentingly positive effect. Safety is not the same as comfort; in contrast, it is predicted to facilitate risk. (p. 14)

Edmondson proposes that perceptions of team safety will lead team members to engage in learning and risk-taking behaviour – that is, to innovation. Her research in 53 teams of a large manufacturer of office furniture showed that safety was the one consistent predictor of team learning, whether self- or observer-rated.

These two perspectives on emotions in teams, the need to belong and group affect, offer novel perspectives on understanding social interaction in the workplace and particularly emotional experience. Both also imply agendas for research and indications for practice. Emotional responses in teams, we believe, can best be understood from this perspective. Indeed, we argue that current approaches to understanding teams ignore fundamental human motivations (such as the need for control and the need to belong), and therefore provide inadequate explanations of the emotional responses of people who work in teams. Now we move on to consider the second major theme in the study of workteams; the reason we work in teams and groups is because they have enabled us (and continue to enable us) to develop huge improvements in the quality of our lives and the management of threat in our environments – teams are the seedbeds of creativity and the power sources for innovation. Yet that creativity is fundamentally dependent on the satisfaction of members' needs to belong within the group – manifested in safety, shared objectives, high levels of interaction, effective management of conflict, and support for exploration.

CREATIVITY AND INNOVATION IMPLEMENTATION IN TEAMS

Whether the context is producing TV programmes, training for war, managing health and illness in hospitals, developing new products in manufacturing organizations or providing financial services, the use of workgroup as a form of work organization is both ubiquitous and increasing (Guzzo, 1996). Researchers in applied psychology have responded by puzzling over the factors that influence the effectiveness of workgroups or teams, from the shopfloor through to top management teams (Cohen & Bailey, 1997; West, 1996).

Much less energy has been devoted to answering the question regarding what factors influence the extent to which teams generate and implement ideas for new and improved products, services and ways of doing things at work. This is not a trivial question. At the root of development of our species from our primitive beginnings to recent stunning advances in technology, communication, and social complexity, has been innovation – the development and implementation of improved processes, products, and procedures (Drazin & Schoonhoven, 1996; West & Atlink, 1996). Yet despite the fascination with individual creativity, innovation is not a solitary activity that results from the vigorous championing of an idea by one individual. It is more usually the result of concerted activities of groups of people developing and implementing their ideas over a period of time, and then diffusing successful innovations throughout organizations or societies.

I argue below that group innovation occurs when a group with requisite internal diversity experiences both high external demands and high levels of internal integration and psychosocial safety. Put succinctly, creativity requires safety, and innovation implementation requires high demands (whether in the form of threat or large reward). If creativity is the development of new ideas, innovation includes creativity as well as the process (and outcome) of putting creative ideas into practice – innovation implementation.

Groups will be creative primarily when their task is sufficiently interesting, motivating and challenging and when the group's internal environment or processes are experienced as safe. In general, creative cognitions occur when individuals are not pressured, feel safe, and feel positive (Claxton, 1997, 1998). The psychosocial safety of the group is one influence on group creativity (West, 1990, 1995), but another is the structure of the group – this must be appropriately integrated and have a requisite level and diversity of task-relevant knowledge, skills and abilities among group members.

Paradoxically, the requirement for innovation implementation is a demanding, uncertain or even threatening environment. In order to motivate a group to adapt itself or its environment, which requires sustained effort in the face of resistance, an external threat may be required. Or the environment must be experienced as aversively uncertain, stimulating innovation in the form of an uncertainty-reducing strategy. Equally of course a high reward for innovation will motivate the group to innovate.

At the same time, the team or group must be sufficiently integrated to enable coordinated effort to initiate and sustain the innovation implementation out there in the world. The essential elements are therefore:

appropriate task characteristics;
appropriate group structure including requisite diversity and integration;
psychosocial safety within the group;
high external demands (which will usually be much influenced by the organizational context).

Task Characteristics

The task a workgroup performs is a fundamental influence on the group, defining its structural, process, and functional requirements. Dimensions for classifying group task characteristics include task difficulty; solution multiplicity; intrinsic interest; cooperative requirements (Shaw, 1976); unitary versus divisible, conjunctive, disjunctive, and additive (Steiner, 1972); conflict versus cooperation; and conceptual versus behavioural (McGrath, 1984). These classification systems have been developed from within the experimental social psychology tradition and have not been adopted by researchers exploring group performance and innovation in organizational settings, probably because such goals as producing TV programmes, battleground training, health care, product development, and providing financial services cannot be neatly categorized into discrete tasks and subtasks. For example, primary health care teams which maintain and promote the health of people in local communities, have multiple stakeholders and a wide variety of tasks (Slater & West, 1999). Their team tasks are simple and difficult; unitary and divisible; involve conflict and cooperation; and demand both behavioural and conceptual responses.

Work and organizational researchers in Europe have been influenced by Action Theory (Frese & Zapf, 1994; Hacker, 1986; Volpert, 1984; Tschan & von Cranach, 1996), which describes tasks in relation to their hierarchical, sequential, and cyclical process requirements. Tschan and Cranach (1996) make the obvious but largely ignored point that in reality tasks in work situations are complex and varied. They argue that tasks should be deconstructed into their hierarchical requirements (goals and subgoals); their sequential demands (the restrictions that are imposed on the order in which subtasks are carried out (we have to break the eggs before we can cook the omelette, but whether we plan a structure for our poem at the beginning or halfway through may vary on our approach); and the cyclical nature of information processing (orienting, planning, executing, evaluating). Tschan and von Cranach also raise our awareness of the fact that the nature of communication will vary considerably according to whether the group task element is low level (relatively automated elements require little or no communication or creativity, such as monitoring materials flow in an assembly line team) or high level, requiring considerable communication, creativity, and innovation (planning a new research programme). However, Action Theory has not been used widely to inform studies of the effects of task characteristics on work group functioning.

One of the best-known models of group task classification is based on Job Design Theory (Hackman, 1990; Hackman & Lawler, 1971; Hackman &

Oldham, 1975), which identifies five characteristics of motivating tasks:

Autonomy: the freedom the group has to carry out the task in ways team members choose.
Task variety: the variation in the content of the work.
Task significance: the perceived important of the task to the organization or wider society.
Task identity: the extent to which the group's task represents a whole piece of work rather than (for example) one small element in an assembly line approach.
Relevant task feedback: the amount of information about the effectiveness with which the group carries out its task.

Variations in these characteristics have been related to job satisfaction (Drory & Shamir, 1988; Hackman & Lawler, 1971) and to workgroup effectiveness. Campion and colleagues (Campion, Medsker & Higgs, 1993; Campion, Papper & Medsker, 1996) studied employee and managerial workgroups in a financial sector organization and found that task design characteristics were relatively strong predictors of effectiveness. In particular, group autonomy was significantly correlated with measures of effectiveness. Theoretically, to the extent that a group's task is characterized by greater autonomy, variety, significance, identity and feedback, the more likely is the group to be innovative – a workgroup responsible for putting labels on supermarket products will have fewer opportunities for innovation than a primary health care team.

Integrated Group Structures

Group structures refer to the composition of the group – its size, tenure, the characteristics of members, and the status of the group and its members. To the extent that these elements are appropriately diverse and integrated the group will be creative.

Group Composition

Are those groups composed of a very different people (professional background, age, organizational tenure) more innovative than those whose members are similar? This research question is prompted by the notion that if people who work together in groups have different backgrounds, personalities, training, skills, experiences, and orientations, they will bring usefully differing perspectives on issues to the group. This divergence of views will create multiple perspectives, disagreements, and conflicts. If this informational conflict is processed in the interests of effective decision making and task performance rather than on the basis of egotistical motivation to win or prevail, or conflicts of interest,

this in turn will generate improved performance and more innovative actions will be the result (DeDreu, 1997; Hoffman & Maier, 1961; Pearce & Ravlin, 1987; Porac & Howard, 1990; Tjosvold, 1985, 1991, 1998).

In considering this question, researchers tend to differentiate between attributes that are directly related to work roles (such as organizational position or specialized technical knowledge), and those that are more enduringly characteristic of the person (such as age, gender, ethnicity, social status, and personality) (Maznevski, 1994). Jackson (1992, 1996), identifies a third dimension of diversity: readily detected or underlying, e.g., organizational position is a readily detected attribute, while specialized knowledge is an underlying task-related attribute. Readily detected person-centred attributes include age, gender, and ethnicity, but social status and personality would be classified as underlying relations-oriented attributes.

Jackson (1992) believes that the effects of diversity on team performance are complex; task-related and relations-oriented diversity have different effects which depend also on the team task. She rightly concludes that there is little clear evidence about the diversity effects of composition on team performance, with one exception. In relation to tasks requiring creativity and quality of decision making, Jackson says that 'for these types of tasks, the available evidence supports the conclusion that team diversity is associated with better quality team decision-making' (Jackson, 1996: 67), citing evidence provided by Filley, House and Kerr (1976), Hoffman (1979), McGrath (1984), and Shaw (1981). There is some evidence that heterogeneity in a number of domains is associated with group innovation, including heterogeneity in personality (Hoffman & Maier, 1961), training background (Pelz, 1956), leadership abilities (Ghiselli & Lodahl, 1958), attitudes (Hoffman, Harburg & Maier, 1962; Willems & Clark, 1971), gender (Wood, 1987), occupational background (Bantel & Jackson, 1989) and education (Smith, Smith, Olian, Sims, O'Brannon & Scully, 1994). However, we should be cautious about applying these findings to the experience of workgroups, since, although some of the research to date has been carried out in organizational settings (Pelz, 1956; Ghiselli & Lodahl, 1958; and the excellent work by Bantel & Jackson, 1989, and Smith, et al., 1994, with top management teams), most other research suggesting a positive effect of team diversity upon team creativity has been conducted only in laboratory settings.

Team members also differ in terms of their professional backgrounds and positions. Souder (1987) found that functionally diverse groups had difficulties in reaching agreements on implementing innovations, which is not surprising, given the different perspectives they hold. Zenger and Lawrence (1989) have suggested that functional diversity might influence workgroup performance as a result of the higher level of external communication which group members initiate, precisely because of their functional diversity. In related research, Ancona and Caldwell (1992) studied 45 new product teams in five high-technology companies and found that when a workgroup recruited a new member from a certain functional area in an organization, communication with that area went up dramatically. This in turn might favour innovation through the incorporation of diverse ideas and models gleaned from these different functional areas. Consistent with this, Ancona and Caldwell (1992) discovered that the greater the group's functional diversity, the more team members communicated outside the workgroup's boundaries and the higher the ratings of innovation they received.

The most significant study of innovation in teams to date is a UNESCO-sponsored international effort to determine the factors influencing the scientific performance of 1222 research teams (Andrews, 1979; see also Payne, 1990). Diversity was assessed in six areas: in projects; interdisciplinary orientations; in specialities; in funding resources; in R&D activities; and in professional functions. Overall, diversity accounted for 10% of the variance in scientific recognition, R&D effectiveness, and number of publications, suggesting that both flexibility of thought and organization, fostered by diversity, do influence team innovation. This landmark (and neglected) research also indicated that the extent of communication both within and between research teams had strong relationships with scientific recognition of their teams, R&D effectiveness, number of publications, and the applied value of their work.

Another consideration implied by these findings is the diversity consequent upon intergroup contacts. Mohrman, Cohen and Mohrman (1995) have pointed out that there are likely to be performance benefits of good linkages between groups and teams and across departments within organizations. The cross-disciplinarity, cross-functionality, or cross-team perspectives that such interactions can produce are likely to generate the kinds of dividends related to innovation that heterogeneity within teams can offer.

So does diversity predict group innovation? The research evidence indicates that, in some circumstances it does, but we do not know what types of diversity stimulate innovation and under what circumstances. I suggest that *requisite functional diversity* (the amount of functional diversity necessary for task performance and to create variety in, and flexibility of, cognitive responses and to encourage constructive controversy) will lead to innovation. Requisite diversity will increase the more complex is the group's task. However, when diversity begins to threaten the group's safety and integration then creativity and innovation implementation will suffer respectively. Where

diversity reduces group members' clarity about and commitment to group objectives, levels of participation (interaction, information-sharing and shared influence over decision making), task orientation (commitment to excellence of task performance), and support for new ideas, then innovation attempts will be resisted.

Group structures will themselves affect the level of safety. This is not to suggest that the less diverse a group is the safer it will be for its members. On the contrary, members will only discover safety through the effective management of diversity. Where the group is homogenous then there will be strong pressures for conformity. Where the group is heterogeneous there will be pressures to manage the centrifugal forces of diversity that could lead to the disintegration of the group and could also threaten individual members (others' differing perspectives threatening my own beliefs, for example). We only discover a solid sense of safety through the management of apparently threatening environments. The child who explores her environment is more confident than the child who never strays from her mother. In the latter case this may be because of anxious attachment that leads the child to relate in perpetually anxious ways to the world (Bowlby, 1988; Ainsworth, Blehar, Waters & Wall, 1978; Hazan & Shaver, 1987; Tidwell, Reis & Shaver, 1996).

Another potent influence on team innovation is the extent to which team members have the relevant knowledge, skills, and abilities to work effectively in groups – integration skills. Stevens and Campion (1994) believe that team members require appropriate team knowledge, skills, and abilities (KSAs) which for more effective communication of the ideas in this chapter I will call team integration skills. These are distinct from the technical KSAs which are relevant to task performance (such as medical skills for a physician). The team integration skills are individual, not team, attributes. Stevens and Campion identify two major domains – interpersonal and self-management integration skills. The former include conflict resolution integration skills, such as the skill to recognize and encourage desirable, but discourage undesirable conflict, and the skill to employ integrative (win–win) negotiation strategies. Collaborative problem-solving integration skills include the ability to identify situations requiring participative group problem solving; the skill to utilize decentralized communication networks to enhance communication; and the skill to communicate openly and supportively (to send messages which are behaviour-oriented, congruent and validating). Self-management integration skills include goal setting and performance management, such as the skill to monitor, evaluate, and provide feedback on both overall team performance, and individual team member performance; and the skill to coordinate and synchronize activities, information, and tasks between members.

Their work provides a powerful framework (and a well-constructed questionnaire) for assessing whether the individuals who make up a team possess the necessary KSAs to manage the complexities and challenges of working in a team effectively. The more of these integration skills team members have, the more likely it is that the benefits of team-working and team diversity will manifest, not just in terms of team performance, but also in innovation proposals and their successful implementation.

Status

The higher the status and the greater the power of the individuals who constitute the team, the more likely is innovation to occur. This proposition is relatively simple. The more power and higher status that individuals have within the organization, the more likely are they to be able to implement ideas for new and improved ways of doing things within organizations (West, 1987b). Moreover, high-status individuals who constitute a team can introduce more radical, novel, and major innovations than members of teams who have relatively low status or power within the organization (West & Anderson, 1996).

Status diversity is likely to threaten integration and safety in the group. The threat occasioned by disagreeing with high status members is likely to restrict public speculation by lower-status group members. Such status differentials, as much social psychological research has shown, will retard integration because of the barriers to cohesiveness and shared orientation they create (Brown, 1988). For example, De Dreu (1995) has shown that power and status asymmetries in groups produce hostile interaction patterns in contrast to groups in which there is power balance. Such hostility is clearly likely to inhibit creativity.

External Demands

A central contextual factor for workgroup innovation is reward for innovation implementation. Outcomes like money, fringe benefits, public recognition, and preferred work assignments are likely to lead to innovations being implemented. Abbey and Dickson (1983) in a study of 40 successful R&D teams in different companies found that reward systems had a strong positive relationship with R&D performance. Despite much popular belief to the contrary, there is evidence that extrinsic rewards encourage both creativity and innovation implementation. Rewards for team innovation in organizational settings *are* likely to produce the desired effects (Eisenberger & Cameron, 1996) and the higher the potential rewards, the greater the likelihood of innovation.

Previous writers have also suggested that resources available in organizations will determine the level of innovation (Rogers, 1983; Rogers & Agarwala-Rogers, 1976). In particular, the notion of slack resources is invoked to suggest that unused resources are likely to be used to invest in developing new and improved ways of doing things within organizations. However, there is one seam of evidence that suggests that resources are not related to levels of team innovation. For example, Payne (1990) in a review of the United Nations studies of research teams' effectiveness, concluded that there was no evidence from these studies that more resources and better facilities led necessarily to better scientific performance. In West and Anderson's (1996) study of top management teams in hospitals, the size of hospital budgets bore no relationship to the quantity or quality of innovation introduced by the teams.

Our research in manufacturing organizations (West, Patterson, Pillinger & Nickell, 1998) and in hospitals (West & Anderson, 1992) suggests that the environments within which organizations operate have a significant impact upon organizational innovation, and therefore will likely have an impact upon group innovation. The lower the market share of manufacturing organizations in relation to their primary products, the higher was the level of product innovation. It seems that the threat of being a small player in a competitive situation spurs innovation. The corollary is that market domination, at least in medium-sized enterprises (100–500 employees, with an average of 230), may inhibit innovation. Moreover, the extent of environmental uncertainty reported by senior managers in these organizations (in relation to suppliers, customers, market demands, and government legislation), was a strong predictor of the degree of innovation in organizational systems, i.e., in people management practices. Taken together, these findings suggest that if the environment of organizations is threatening and uncertain, the more likely it is that organizations will innovate in order to reduce the uncertainty or threat. This is likely also to impact upon the level of innovation of groups at work. The effort of initiating change in organizations, with all the attendant resistance, conflicts and experiences of failure is likely, in most instances, to elicit strong aversive reactions among group members. The impetus to maintain innovation attempts must be provided by an expectation of high rewards or by the perception of threat or uncertainty. Among individual health workers we have found in a number of studies that high work demands are significant predictors of individual innovation (Bunce & West, 1995, 1996; West, 1989). Indeed, our research on work role transitions has shown that changing role objectives, strategies, or relationships was a common response to the demands of new work environments (West, 1987a,b).

The external context of the group's work therefore, be it organizational climate, support systems, market environment, or environmental uncertainty, is likely to have a highly significant influence on its innovativeness. Yet too few cross-organizational studies of group innovation have been conducted to explore how such contextual demands or environmental threats affect groups' propensity to implement innovations.

Now, we turn to the task process and interpersonal streams which flow between team members and consider how these influence workgroup innovation.

Group Processes

Task characteristics, group structures, and external demands will all influence group processes such as the process of developing and redeveloping shared objectives, levels of participation, management of conflict, support for ideas to introduce new ways of doing things, and leadership (West, 1994, 1996). If these processes are sufficiently integrated (i.e., there are shared objectives, high levels of participation, constructive, cooperative conflict management, high support for innovation, and leadership which enables innovation), then creativity and innovation implementation will occur. Moreover, effective group processes will both be sustained by and increase the level of psychosocial safety in the group.

Developing Shared Objectives

In the context of group innovation, clarity of team objectives is likely to facilitate innovation by enabling focused development of new ideas, which can be filtered with greater precision than if team objectives are unclear. Theoretically, clear objectives will only facilitate innovation if team members are committed to the goals of the team, since strong goal commitment will be necessary to maintain group member persistence for implementation in the face of resistance among other organizational members.

However, there is little direct evidence relating clarity of team goals and member goal commitment to the innovativeness of teams. Pinto and Prescott (1987), in a study of 418 project teams, found that a clearly stated mission was the only factor which predicted success at all stages of the innovation process (conception, planning, execution, and termination). This is the only research directly relevant to the proposition, despite its face validity and importance. Where group members do not share a commitment to a set of objectives (or a vision of the goals of their work) the forces of disintegration created by disagreements (and lack of safety), diversity and the emotional demands of the innovation process are likely to inhibit innovation.

Participation in Decision Making

Research on participation in decision making has a long history in both social and industrial/organizational psychology, and suggests that participation fosters integration and commitment (Bowers & Seashore, 1966; Coch & French, 1948; Lawler & Hackman, 1969). There are obvious reasons for supposing that participation will be linked to team innovation. To the extent that information and influence over decision making are shared within teams, and there is a high level of interaction amongst team members, the cross-fertilization of perspectives which can spawn creativity and innovation (Cowan, 1986; Mumford & Gustafson, 1988; Pearce & Ravlin, 1987; Porac & Howard, 1990) is more likely to occur. More generally, high participation in decision making means less resistance to change and therefore greater likelihood of innovations being implemented. When people participate in decision making through having influence, interacting with those involved in the change process, and sharing information, they tend to invest in the outcomes of those decisions and to offer ideas for new and improved ways of working (Kanter, 1983; King, Anderson & West, 1992).

Conflict

Many scholars believe that the management of competing perspectives is fundamental to the generation of creativity and innovation (Mumford & Gustafson, 1988; Nemeth & Owens, 1996; Tjosvold, 1998). Such processes are characteristic of task-related or information conflict (as opposed to conflicts of interest, and emotional or interpersonal conflict; see De Dreu, 1997). They can arise from a common concern with quality of task performance in relation to shared objectives – what has been called 'task orientation' (West, 1990). Task orientation may be evidenced by appraisal of, and constructive challenges to, the group's processes and performance. In essence, team members are more committed to performing their work effectively and excellently than they are either to bland consensus or to personal victory in conflict with other team members over task performance strategies or decision options.

Dean Tjosvold and colleagues (Tjosvold, 1982; Tjosvold & Field, 1983; Tjosvold & Johnson, 1977; Tjosvold, Wedley & Field, 1986; Tjosvold, 1998) have presented cogent arguments and strong supportive evidence that such constructive (task-related) controversy in a cooperative group context, improves the quality of decision making and creativity (Tjosvold, 1991). Constructive controversy is characterized by full exploration of opposing opinions and frank analyses of task-related issues. It occurs when decision makers believe they are in a cooperative group context, where mutually beneficial goals are emphasized, rather than in a competitive context; where decision makers feel their personal competence is confirmed rather than questioned; and where they perceive processes of mutual influence rather than attempted dominance.

For example, the most effective self-managing teams in a manufacturing plant that Alper and Tjosvold (1993) studied were those which had compatible goals and promoted constructive controversy. The 544 employees who made up the 59 teams completed a questionnaire which probed for information about cooperation, competition, and conflict within the team. Teams were responsible for activities such as work scheduling, housekeeping, safety, purchasing, accident investigation, and quality. Members of teams which promoted interdependent conflict management (people cooperated to work through their differences), compared to teams with win/lose conflict (where team members tended to engage in a power struggle when they had different views and interests), felt confident that they could deal with differences. Such teams were rated as more productive and innovative by their managers. Apparently, because of this success, members of these teams were committed to working as a team. In a study which focused more directly on innovation (though not in teams), faculty members and employees of a large educational institution reported that when they discussed their opposing views openly, fully and forthrightly, they developed innovative solutions to problems. But when they discussed issues competitively, or from only one point of view, and were unable to integrate the differing views of colleagues, they were frustrated and developed poor-quality and low-novelty solutions (Tjosvold & McNeely, 1988).

Another perspective on conflict and innovation comes from minority influence theory. A number of researchers have shown that minority consistency of arguments over time is likely to lead to change in majority views in groups (Maass & Clark, 1984). Moreover, the experimental evidence suggests that while majorities bring about attitude change through public compliance prior to attitude change (i.e., that the individual may first publicly conform to the majority view prior to internalizing that view), minority influence works in the opposite direction. People exposed to a confident and consistent minority change their private views prior to expressing public agreement. Minority influence researchers have labelled this process as 'conversion'. Research on minority influence suggests that conversion is most likely to occur where the minority is consistent and confident in the presentation of arguments. Moreover, it is a behavioural style of persistence which is most likely to lead to attitude change and innovation.

In directly related work, Nemeth (Nemeth & Wachtler, 1983; Nemeth, 1986; Nemeth & Kwan, 1987; Nemeth & Chiles, 1988; Nemeth & Owens, 1996) suggests that minority influence leads to more independent, divergent, and creative thinking. In one study (Nemeth & Chiles, 1988) participants were exposed to a minority which consistently judged blue stimuli as green. When these participants were subsequently placed in a majority influence situation where the majority consistently incorrectly rated red stimuli as orange, they showed almost complete independence and did not differ significantly from control participants who made their judgements of the red stimuli alone. Those not exposed to minority dissent agreed on over 70% of trials with the majority's incorrect judgement of orange. In a study of originality (Nemeth & Kwan, 1987) participants were told that a majority or minority saw blue slides as green in previous studies. Each participant was subsequently exposed to a single subject who consistently rated blue slides as green. Finally, each participant was asked to respond seven times in a word association exercise to the words blue or green. Those exposed to a minority judgement gave more word associations and with a higher degree of originality (they were statistically less frequent according to normative data) than those exposed to a majority view. In reviewing this research Nemeth (1989) concludes that

> this work argues for the importance of minority dissent, even dissent that is wrong. Further, we assume that its import lies not in the truth of its position or even in the likelihood that it will prevail. Rather it appears to stimulate divergent thought. Issues and problems are considered from more perspectives and; on balance, (people) detect new solutions and find more correct answers. (p. 9)

Arguing from the perspective of social psychology, DeDreu and De Vries (1997) suggest that an homogenous workforce in which minority dissent is suppressed will reduce creativity, innovation, individuality and independence (DeDreu & De Vries, 1993; see also Nemeth & Staw, 1989). Disagreement about ideas within a group can be beneficial and some researchers even argue that team task or information-related conflict is valuable, whether or not it occurs in a collaborative context, since it can improve decision making and strategic planning (Cosier & Rose, 1977; Mitroff, Barabba & Kilmann, 1977; Schweiger, Sandberg & Rechner, 1989). This is because task-related conflict may lead team members to reevaluate the status quo and adapt their objectives, strategies, or processes more appropriately to their situation (Coser, 1970; Nemeth & Staw, 1989; Thomas, 1979; Roloff, 1987). From the perspective of systems theory , DeDreu invokes the concept of *requisite variety* to suggest that disagreement and variety are necessary for systems to adapt to their environment and perform well (Ashby, 1956).

Overall, therefore, task-related (as distinct from emotional or interpersonal) conflict and minority dissent will lead to innovation by encouraging debate (requisite diversity) and consideration of alternative interpretations of information available, leading to integrated and creative solutions. At the same time task orientation processes will encourage effective innovation since there will be a greater likelihood that ideas proposed will be carefully examined.

Support for Innovation

Innovation is more likely to occur in groups where there is support for innovation, and innovative attempts are rewarded rather than punished (Amabile, 1983; Kanter, 1983). Support for innovation is the expectation, approval, and practical support of attempts to introduce new and improved ways of doing things in the work environment (West, 1990). Within groups, new ideas may be routinely rejected or ignored, or attract verbal and practical support. Such group processes powerfully shape individual and group behaviour (for reviews see, e.g., Brown, 1988; Hackman, 1992) and those which support innovation will encourage team members to introduce innovations. In a longitudinal study of 27 hospital top management teams, Neil Anderson and I found that support for innovation was the most powerful predictor of team innovation of any of the group processes so far discussed (West & Anderson, 1996; Anderson & West, 1998).

Group Psychosocial Safety

Group psychosocial traits refer to shared understandings, unconscious group processes, group cognitive style, and group emotional tone (Cohen & Bailey, 1997). Examples include norms, cohesiveness, team mental models, and group affect. In groups with high levels of psychosocial safety there will be high creativity.

Creative ideas arise out of individual cognitive processes and, though group members may interact in ways which offer cognitive stimulation via diversity (cf. research on minority dissent described above – Nemeth & Owen, 1996), creative ideas are produced as a result of individual cognitions. A wealth of evidence suggests that, in general, creative cognitions occur when individuals are free from pressure, feel safe, and experience relatively positive affect (Claxton, 1997, 1998). For example, using the Luchins water jar problems (Rokeach, 1950), it is possible to demonstrate how time pressures inhibit creative problem solving. Moreover, psychological threats to face or identity are also associated with more rigid thinking (Cowen, 1952). Time pressure can also increase rigidity of thinking on work-related tasks such as selection decisions (Kruglansky & Freund, 1983). Another example of stress inhibiting the flexibility of responses (albeit a rather extreme one) is offered by Wright (1954) who asked people to respond to Rorschach inkblot tests. Half of the people were hospital patients awaiting an operation and half were 'controls'. The former gave more stereotyped responses, and were

less fluent and creative in completing similes (e.g., 'as interesting as …'), indicating the effects of stress or threat upon their capacity to generate creative responses.

Prince (1975) believes, on the basis of considerable applied work in organizations focused on increasing creativity, that speculation (a critical creative process) makes people in work settings feel vulnerable because we tend to experience our workplaces as unsafe (a finding also reported by Nicholson and West, 1986, in a study of the experience of work among UK managers). Questioning the person who comes up with an idea too closely, joking about the proposal (even in a light way), or simply ignoring the proposal can lead to the person feeling defensive, which tends to 'reduce not only his speculation but that of others in the group.' Prince goes on: 'The victim of the win–lose or competitive posture is always speculation, and therefore idea production and problem solving. When one speculates he becomes vulnerable. It is easy to make him look like a loser' (Prince, 1975).

A cooperative context will lead to a greater sense of integration and safety among the parties, consistent with what I propose in this chapter. Safety is the *consequence* of the management of diversity in views rather than the cause. If we operate in situations where there is no diversity or there is no conflict, we never have the opportunity to discover safety in our psychosocial environment. Certainly in our studies in service sectors (e.g., West & Wallace, 1991) we have found that cohesiveness in primary health care teams predicts levels of team innovation.

For creativity and innovation implementation to emerge from group functioning therefore, the context must be demanding but the supports for group integration must also be in place. These include a high proportion of innovators; members with the integration abilities to work effectively in teams; a challenging, varied task; an organizational climate supportive of innovation and the structural supports necessary for teamwork; and group leadership processes which nurture innovation, reflexivity, a positive psychosocial climate, and appropriate group processes (clarity of objectives, effective participation, constructive controversy, reflexivity, and support for innovation). Such conditions are likely to produce high levels of group innovation, but crucially too, the well-being which is a consequence of effective human interaction in challenging and supportive environments.

A more elaborated consideration of organizational context has been offered by Tannenbaum, Board and Salas (1992) who consider eight aspects of the organizational context: rewards systems (individual or team-based); resource scarcity; management control; level of stress in the organization; organizational climate; competition; intergroup relations within the organization; and environmental uncertainty. These factors have high face validity in models of workgroup functioning and effectiveness, but there is still little evidence about their influence on workgroup effectiveness.

Physical conditions are another situational constraint which can affect the relationship between performance dimensions and effectiveness. For example, a team whose members are dispersed across the countries of the European Union, will find decision making more difficult and ineffective than a team whose members share the same physical location.

CONCLUSIONS

We are captivated by the rhetoric of organizations in the 21st century, by emotive or media-inspired phrases like 'dotcom', 'high-involvement management', 'thinking outside the box', 'people management', and 'total quality management'. Teamwork itself is a word that seems redolent of the post-industrial, digital revolution, mass media culture. Yet humans have worked, lived, and loved in groups and teams throughout evolutionary history. There is little that is new within teamwork, despite the tsunami of books that press upon us the ways and advantages of working in teams. What is new is the complexity of the context within which humans now work in teams. The emotional stresses and benefits of teams are amplified by the complex organizational contexts within which they reside. Instead of communities of 80 to 120, we now have loose organizational communities of thousands with complex interconnections between them. There are strong internecine struggles (tribal divisions) within these organizations that nevertheless seek superordinate organizational loyalty from team members. The workload pressures on team members are also increasing, partly as a consequence of new and bizarre forms of organizing human work (such as lean production and repeated downsizing).

Teams now exist in more complex environments too, exacerbating the demands on team members, with consequent effects on emotional experience. Teams must scan the rapidly changing environments that they occupy (no longer the familiar savannah or craft workshop) and monitor changing customer demands, competitor actions, supplier behaviour, and new technology and very quickly adapt via innovation accordingly. Competitive pressures demand sophisticated management skills, innovation, and an agile organizational context. Of course, teams are the ideal form of organization to meet these changing circumstances, but their application also demands sophisticated and inclusive understanding of their functioning.

In this chapter I have proposed that, as a consequence of these new pressures, we must pay more, not less, attention to emotions and to the underlying basic motivations which influence individual and group behaviour in teams. We must also understand the processes by which teams generate creative ideas and effectively implement them in practice. Pressure to produce and neglect of people's deep needs for safety may produce quite the opposite to the desired effect at different stages of a team's work. We need to understand how basic psychological processes at individual and group levels influence behaviour and team outcomes.

REFERENCES

Abbey, A., & Dickson, J.W. (1983). R&D work climate and innovation in semi-conductors. *Academy of Management Journal, 25,* 62–368.

Agrell, A., & Gustafson, R. (1996). Innovation and creativity in work groups. In M.A. West (Ed.), *The handbook of work group psychology* (pp. 317–344). Chichester, UK: Wiley.

Ainsworth, M. (1989). Attachments beyond infancy. *American Psychologist, 44,* 709–716.

Ainsworth, M.D., Blehar, M.C., Waters, E., & Wall, S. (1978). *Patterns of attachment: A psychological study of the strange situation.* Hillsdale, NJ: Erlbaum.

Alper, S., & Tjosvold, D. (1993). *Co-operation theory and self-managing teams on the manufacturing floor.* Paper presented at the International Association for Conflict Management.

Amabile, T.M. (1983). The social psychology of creativity: A componential conceptualization. *Journal of Personality and Social Psychology, 4*(2), 357–376.

Ancona, D.F., & Caldwell, D.F. (1992). Bridging the boundary: External activity and performance in organizational teams. *Administrative Science Quarterly, 37,* 634–665.

Anderson, N., & West, M.A. (1998). Measuring climate for work group innovation: Development and validation of the team climate inventory. *Journal of Organizational Behavior, 19,* 235–258.

Andrews, F.M. (Ed.) (1979). *Scientific productivity.* Cambridge: Cambridge University Press.

Ashby, W.R. (1956). *An introduction to cybernetics.* London: Methuen.

Axelrod, R., & Hamilton, W.D. (1981). The evolution of cooperation. *Science, 211,* 1390–1396.

Bantel, K.A., & Jackson, S.E. (1989). Top management and innovations in banking: Does the demography of the top team make a difference? *Strategic Management Journal, 10,* 107–124.

Barash, D.P. (1977). *Sociobiology and behavior.* New York: Elsevier.

Barchas, P. (1986). A sociophysiological orientation to small groups. In E. Lawler (Ed.), *Advances in group processes* (Vol. 3, pp. 209–246). Greenwich, CT: JAI Press.

Baumeister, R.F., & Leary, M.R. (1995). The need to belong: Desire for interpersonal attachments as a fundamental human motivation. *Psychological Bulletin, 117*, 497–529.

Baumeister, R.F., Stillwell, A.M., & Heatherton, T.F. (1994). Guilt: An interpersonal approach. *Psychological Bulletin, 115*, 243–267.

Baumeister, R.F., Wotman, S.R., & Stillwell, A.M. (1993). Unrequited love: On heartbreak, anger, guilt, scriptlessness, and humiliation. *Journal of Personality and Social Psychology, 64*, 377–394.

Belsky, J. (1979). The interrelation of parental and spousal behavior during infancy in traditional nuclear families: An exploratory analysis. *Journal of Marriage and the Family, 41*, 749–755.

Billig, M., & Tajfel, H. (1973). Social categorization and similarity in intergroup behavior. *European Journal of Social Psychology, 3*, 27–52.

Bion, W.R. (1961). *Experiences in groups and other papers*. London: Tavistock.

Bowers, D.G., & Seashore, S.E. (1966). Predicting organizational effectiveness with a four-factor theory of leadership. *Administrative Science Quarterly, 11*, 238–263.

Bowlby, J. (1969). *Attachment and loss. Vol. I, Attachment*. London: Hogarth.

Bowlby, J. (1988). *A secure-base: Parent-child attachment and healthy human development*. New York: Basic Books.

Brown, R.J. (1988). *Group processes: Dynamics within and between groups*. London: Blackwell.

Bunce, D., & West, M.A. (1995). Changing work environments: Innovative coping responses to occupational stress. *Work and Stress, 8*, 319–331.

Bunce, D., & West, M.A. (1996). Stress management and innovation interventions at work. *Human Relations, 42*, 209–232.

Buss, D.M. (1990a). Toward a biologically informed psychology of personality. *Journal of Personality, 58*, 128.

Buss, D.M. (1990b). The evolution of anxiety and social exclusion. *Journal of Social and Clinical Psychology, 9*, 196–210.

Buss, D.M. (1991). Evolutionary personality psychology. *Annual Review of Psychology, 42*, 459–491.

Campion, M.A., Medsker, G.J., & Higgs, A.C. (1993). Relations between work group characteristics and effectiveness: Implications for designing effective work groups. *Personnel Psychology, 46*, 823–850.

Campion, M.A., Papper, E.M., & Medsker, G.J. (1996). Relations between work team characteristics and effectiveness: A replication and extension. *Personnel Psychology, 49*, 429–689.

Capters, R.S., & Lipton, E. (1993). Hubble error: Time, money and millionths of an inch. *The Academy of Management Executive, 4*, 41–56.

Carter, A.J., & West, M.A. (1999). Sharing the burden: Teamwork in healthcare settings. In J. Firth-Cozens, & R. Payne (Eds.). *Stress in health professionals: Psychological and organisational causes and interventions* (pp. 191–202). Chichester, UK: Wiley.

Carter, S.M., & West, M.A. (1998). Reflexivity, effectiveness and mental health in BBC TV production teams. *Small Group Research, 29*, 583–601.

Claxton, G.L. (1997). *Hare brain, tortoise mind: Why intelligence increases when you think less*. London: Fourth Estate.

Claxton, G.L. (1998). Knowing without knowing why: Investigating human intuition. *The Psychologist, 11*, 217–220.

Coch, L., & French, J.R. (1948). Overcoming resistance to change. *Human Relations, 1*, 512–532.

Cohen, S.G., & Bailey, D.E. (1997). What makes teams work: Group effectiveness research from the shop floor to the executive suite. *Journal of Management, 23*(3), 239–290.

Cohen, S., & Wills, T.A. (1985). Stress, social support, and the buffering hypothesis. *Psychological Bulletin, 98*, 310–357.

Coser, L.A. (1970). *Continuities in the study of social conflict*. New York: Free Press.

Cosier, R., & Rose, G. (1977). Cognitive conflict and goal conflict effects on task performance. *Organizational Behavior and Human Performance, 19*, 378–391.

Cowan, D.A. (1986). Developing a process model of problem recognition. *Academy of Management Review, 11*, 763–776.

Cowen, E.L. (1952). The influence of varying degrees of psychological stress on problem-solving rigidity. *Journal of Abnormal and Social Psychology, 1*, 420–424.

Coyne, J.C., & De Longis, A. (1986). Going beyond social support: The role of social relationships in adaptation. *Journal of Consulting and Clinical Psychology, 54*, 454–460.

Cummings, A. (1998). *Contextual characteristics and employee creativity: Affect at work*. Paper presented at 13th Annual Conference, Society for Industrial Organizational Psychology. Dallas, USA, April 1998.

DeDreu, C.K.W. (1995). Coercive power and concession making in bilateral negotiation. *Journal of Conflict Resolution, 39*, 646–670.

DeDreu, C.K.W. (1997). Productive conflict: The importance of conflict management and conflict issue. In C.K.W. DeDreu, & E. Van De Vliert (Eds.), *Using conflict in organisations* (pp. 9–22.). London: Sage.

DeDreu, C.K.W., & De Vries, N.K. (1993). Numerical support, information processing, and attitude change. *European Journal of Social Psychology, 23*, 647–662.

DeDreu, C.K.W., & De Vries, N.K. (1997). Minority dissent in organisations. In C.K.W. Drazin, R., & Schoonhoven, C.B. (1996). Community, population and organisation effects on innovation: A multilevel perspective. *Academy of Management Journal, 39*(5), 1065–1083.

Drazin, R., & Schoonhoven, C.B. (1996). Community, population and organization effects on innovation: A multilevel perspective. *Academy of Management Journal, 39*, 1065–1083.

Drory, A., & Shamir, B. (1988). Effects of organizational and life variables on job satisfaction and burnout. *Group and Organization Studies, 13*(4), 441–455.

Edmondson, A.C. (1996). Learning from mistakes is easier said than done: Group and organizational influences on the detection and correction of human error. *Journal of Applied Behavioral Science, 32*(1), 5–28.

Edmondson, A.C. (1999). Psychological safety and learning behavior in work teams. *Administrative Science Quarterly, 44*, 350–383.

Eisenberger, R., & Cameron, J. (1996). Detrimental effects of reward: Reality or myth? *American Psychologist, 51*(II), 1153–1166.

Filley, A.C., House, R.J., & Kerr, S. (1976). *Managerial process and organizational behaviour.* Glenview, IL: Scott Foresman.

Frese, M., & Zapf, D. (1994). Action as the core of work psychology: A German approach. In H.C. Triandis, M.D. Dunnette, & L.M. Hough (Eds.), *Handbook of industrial and organizational psychology* (2nd ed., Vol. 4, pp. 271–340). Palo Alto, CA: Consulting Psychologists Press.

George, J.M. (1996). Group affective tone. In M.A. West (Ed.), *Handbook of work group psychology* (pp. 77–94). Chichester, UK: John Wiley.

Ghiselli, E.E., & Lodahl, T.M. (1958). Patterns of managerial traits and group effectiveness. *Journal of Abnormal and Social Psychology, 57*, 61–66.

Guzzo, R.A. (1996). Fundamental considerations about work groups. In M.A. West (Ed.). *Handbook of work group psychology* (pp. 3–24). Chichester, UK: John Wiley.

Guzzo, R.A., & Shea, G.P. (1992). Group performance and intergroup relations in organizations. In M.D. Dunnette, & L.M. Hough (Eds.), *Handbook of industrial and organizational psychology* (Vol. 2, pp. 271–326). Palo Alto, CA: Consulting Psychologists Press.

Hacker, W. (1986). *Arbeitsychologie.* Bern: Huber.

Hackman, J.R. (Ed.) (1990). *Groups that work (and those that don't): Creating conditions for effective teamwork.* San Francisco, CA: Jossey-Bass.

Hackman, J.R. (1992). Group influences on individuals in organizations. In M.D. Dunnette, & L.M. Hough (Eds.), *Handbook of industrial and organizational psychology* (Vol. 3). Palo Alto, CA: Consulting Psychologists Press.

Hackman, J.R., & Lawler, E.E. (1971). Employee reactions to job characteristics. *Journal of Applied Psychology, 55*(3), 259–286.

Hackman, J.R., & Oldham, G. (1975). Development of the job diagnostic survey. *Journal of Applied Psychology, 60*, 159–170.

Hardy, G.E., Shapiro, D.A., Haynes, C.E., & Rick, J.K. (1999). Validation of the General Health Questionnaire using a sample of employees from the health care services. *Psychological Assessment, 11*, 1–7.

Harkins, S.G., & Petty, R.E. (1982). Effects of task difficulty and task uniqueness on social loafing. *Journal of Personality and Social Psychology, 43*(6), 1214–1229.

Hays, R.B. (1985). A longitudinal study of friendship development. *Journal of Personality and Social Psychology, 48*, 909–924.

Hazan, C., & Shaver, P. (1987). Romantic love conceptualised as an attachment process. *Journal of Personality and Social Psychology, 12*, 511–534.

Hazan, C., & Shaver, P.R. (1994). Attachment as an organizational framework for research on close relationships. *Psychological Inquiry, 5*, 1–22.

Hoffman, L.R. (1979). Applying experimental research on group problem solving to organizations. *Journal of Abnormal Social Psychology, 58*, 27–32.

Hoffman, L.R., Harburg, E., & Maier, N.R.F. (1962). Differences and disagreement as factors in creative group problem solving. *Journal of Abnormal and Social Psychology, 64*, 206–214.

Hoffman, L.R., & Maier, N.R.F. (1961). Sex differences, sex composition, and group problem-solving. *Journal of Abnormal and Social Psychology, 63*, 453–456.

Hogan, R., Jones, W., & Cheek, J. (1985). Socioanalytic theory: An alternative to armadillo psychology. In B.M. Schlenker (Ed.), *The self and social life* (pp. 175–198). New York: McGraw-Hill.

Holmes, J.G., & Rempel, J.K. (1989). Trust in close relationships. In M. Clark (Ed.), *Close relationships: Review of personality and social psychology* (Vol. 10, pp. 187–220). Newbury Park, CA: Sage.

Horney, K. (1945). *Our inner conflicts.* New York: Norton.

Hoyle, R.H., & Crawford, A.M. (1994). Use of individual level data to investigate group phenomena: issues and strategies. *Small Group Research, 25*(4), 464–485.

Isen, A.M., & Daubman, K.A. (1984). The influence of affect on categorization. *Journal of Personality and Social Psychology, 47*, 1206–1217.

Isen, A.M., Daubman, K.A., & Nowicki, G.P. (1987). Positive affect facilitates creative problem solving. *Journal of Personality and Social Psychology, 52*, 1122–1131.

Isen, A.M., Johnson, M.M.S., Mertz, E., & Robinson, G.F. (1985). The influence of positive affect on the unusualness of word association. *Journal of Personality and Social Psychology, 48*, 1413–1426.

Jackson, S.E. (1992). Consequences of group composition for the interpersonal dynamics of strategic issue processing. *Advances in Strategic Management, 8*, 345–382.

Jackson, S.E. (1996). The consequences of diversity in multidisciplinary work teams. In M.A. West (Ed.), *Handbook of work group psychology*, pp. 53–75. Chichester: John Wiley.

Jehn, K.A. (1995). A multimethod examination of the benefits and detriments of intragroup conflict. *Administrative Science Quarterly, 40*, 256–282.

Jones, W.H. (1981). Loneliness and social contact. *Journal of Social Psychology, 113*, 295–296.

Kanter, R.M. (1983). *The change masters: Corporate entrepreneurs at work.* New York: Simon & Schuster.

Kiecolt-Glaser, J.K., Fisher, L.D., Ogrocki, P., Stout, J.C., Speicher, C.E., & Glaser, R. (1987). Marital quality, marital disruption, and immune function. *Psychosomatic Medicine, 49*, 13–34.

Kiecolt-Glaser, J.K., Garner, W., Speicher, C., Penn, G.M., Holliday, J., & Glaser, R. (1984). Psychosocial modifiers of immunocompetence in medical students. *Psychosomatic Medicine, 46,* 7–14.

King, N., Anderson, N., & West, M.A. (1992). Organisational innovation: A case study of perceptions and processes. *Work and Stress, 5,* 331–339.

Kruglansky, A.W., & Freund, T. (1983). The freezing and unfreezing of lay influences: Effects on impressional primacy, ethnic stereotyping and numerical anchoring. *Journal of Experimental Social Psychology, 12,* 448–468.

Lauderdale, P. Smith-Cunnien, C., Parker, J., & Inverarity, J. (1984). External threat and the definition of deviance. *Journal of Personality and Social Psychology, 46*(5), 1058–1068.

Lawler, E.E. 3rd, & Hackman, J.R. (1969). Impact of employee participation in the development of pay incentive plans: A field experiment. *Journal of Applied Psychology, 53,* 467–471.

Leary, M.R. (1990). Impression management: A literature review and two component model. *Psychological Bulletin, 107,* 34–47.

Leary, M.R., & Downs, D.L. (1995). Interpersonal functions of the self-esteem motive: The self-esteem system as a sociometer. In M.H. Kernis (Ed.), *Efficacy, agency, and self-esteem* (pp.123–144). New York: Plenum.

Lofland, L.H. (1982). Loss and human connection: An exploration into the nature of the social bond. In W. Ickes, & E.S. Knowles (Eds.), *Personality, roles and social behaviour* (pp. 219–242). New York: Springer-Verlag.

Maass, A., & Clark, R.D. (1984). Hidden impacts of minorities: Fifty years of minority influence research. *Psychological Bulletin, 95*(3), 428–450.

Maznevski, M.L. (1994). Understanding our differences: Performance in decision-making groups with diverse members. *Human Relations, 47*(5), 531–552.

McGrath, J.E. (1984). *Groups, interaction and performance.* Englewood Cliffs, NJ: Prentice-Hall.

Menzies-Lyth, I. (1989). *The dynamics of the social.* London: Free Association Books.

Miller, N.B., Cowan, P.A., Cowan, C.P., Hetherington, E.M., & Clingempeel, W.G. (1993). Externalizing in preschoolers and early adolescents: A cross-study replication of a family model. *Developmental Psychology, 29*(1), 3–18.

Mitroff, J., Barabba, N., & Kilmann, R. (1977). The application of behaviour and philosophical technologies to strategic planning: A case study of a large federal agency. *Management Studies, 24,* 44–58.

Mohrman, S.A., Cohen, S.G., & Mohrman, A.M. (1995). *Designing team-based organizations New forms for knowledge work.* San Francisco: Jossey-Bass.

Moreland, J.P. (1987) *Scaling the secular city.* Grand Rapids: Baker Book House.

Mumford, M.D., & Gustafson, S.B. (1988). Creativity syndrome: Integration, application and innovation. *Psychological Bulletin, 103,* 27–43.

Nemeth, C. (1986). Differential contributions of majority and minority influence. *Psychological Review, 93,* 23–32.

Nemeth, C., & Chiles, C. (1988). Modelling courage: The role of dissent in fostering independence. *European Journal of Social Psychology, 18,* 275–280.

Nemeth, C., & Kwan, J. (1987). Minority influence, divergent thinking and the detection of correct solutions. *Journal of Applied Social Psychology, 9,* 788–799.

Nemeth, C., & Owens, P. (1996). Making work groups more effective: The value of minority dissent. In M.A. West (Ed.), *Handbook of work group psychology* (pp. 125–142). Chichester, UK: John Wiley.

Nemeth, C., & Staw, B.M. (1989). The trade offs of social control and innovation within groups and organizations. In L. Berkowitz (Ed.). *Advances in experimental social psychology* (Vol. 22, pp. 175–210). New York: Academic Press.

Nemeth, C.J., & Wachtler, J. (1983). Creative problem solving as a result of majority vs. minority influence. *European Journal of Social Psychology, 13,* 45–55.

Nicholson, N., & West, M.A. (1986). *Managerial job change: Men and women in transition.* Cambridge: Cambridge University Press.

Patterson, M.G., & West, M.A. (1999). Employee attitudes as predictors of organizational performance. Manuscript submitted for publication.

Payne, R.L. (1990). The effectiveness of research teams: A review. In M.A. West, & J.L. Farr (Eds.), *Innovation and creativity at work: Psychological and organisational strategies* (pp. 101–122). Chichester, UK: Wiley.

Pearce, J.A., & Ravlin, E.C. (1987). The design and activation of self-regulating work groups. *Human Relations, 40,* 751–782.

Pelz, D.C. (1956). Some social factors related to performance in a research organisation. *Administrative Science Quarterly, 1,* 310–325.

Pines, M., & Aronson, E. (1983). Antecedents, correlates, and consequences of sexual jealousy. *Journal of Personality, 51,* 108–135.

Pinto, J.K., & Prescott, J.E. (1987). Changes in critical success factor importance over the life of a project. *Academy of Management Proceedings,* New Orleans, pp. 328–332.

Porac, J.F., & Howard, H. (1990). Taxonomic mental models in competitor definition. *Academy of Management Review, 2,* 224–240.

Prince, G. (1975). Creativity, self and power. In I.A. Taylor, & J.W. Getzels (Eds.), *Perspectives in Creativity.* Chicago: Aldine.

Reis, H.T., Wheeler, L., Kernis, M.H., Spiegel, N., & Nezlek, J. (1985). On specificity in the impact of social participation on physical and psychological health. *Journal of Personality and Social Psychology, 48,* 456–471.

Roberts, J.M. (1995). *The history of the world.* Harmondsworth, UK: Penguin.

Roethlisberger, F.J., & Dixon, W.J. (1939). *Management and the worker.* Cambridge, MA: Harvard University Press.

Rogers, E.M. (1983). *Diffusion of innovations* (3rd ed.). New York: Free Press.

Rogers, E.M., & Agarwala-Rogers, R. (Eds.) (1976). *Communication in organizations.* New York: Free Press.

Rokeach, M. (1950). The effect of perception of time upon the rigidity and concreteness of thinking. *Journal of Experimental Psychology, 40*, 206–216.

Roloff, M.E. (1987). Communication and conflict. In C.R. Berger, & S.H. Chaffee (Eds.), *Handbook of communication science* (pp. 484–534). Newbury Park, CA: Sage.

Schweiger, D., Sandberg, W., & Rechner, P. (1989). Experimental effects of dialectical inquiry, devil's advocacy, and other consensus approaches to strategic decision making. *Academy of Management Journal, 32*, 745–772.

Shaw, M.E. (1976). *Group Dynamics: The psychology of small group behaviour*. New York: McGraw-Hill.

Sherif, M., Harvey, O.J., White, B.J., Hood, W.R., & Sherif, C.W. (1961). *Intergroup conflict and co-operation: The robbers cave experiment*. Norman, OK: Institute of Group Relations.

Slater, J.A., & West, M.A. (1999). Primary health care teams: United Kingdom National Health System. In J.J. Phillips, S.D. Jones, & M.M. Beyerlein (Eds), *Developing high performance work teams* (Vol. 2, pp. 199–214). Alexandria, VA: American Society for Training and Development.

Smith, K.G., Smith, K.A., Olian, J.D., Sims, H.P. Jr., O'Brannon, D.P., & Scully, J.A. (1994). Top management team demography and process. The role of social integration and communication. *Administrative Science Quarterly, 39*, 412–438.

Souder, W.E. (1987). Stimulating and managing ideas. *Research Management, 30*, 13–17.

Stein, A.A. (1976). Conflict and cohesion: A review of the literature. *Journal of Conflict Resolution, 20*, 143–172.

Stein, M. (1996). Unconscious phenomena in work groups. In M.A. West (Ed.), *Handbook of work group psychology* (pp. 143–158). Chichester, UK: John Wiley.

Steiner, I.D. (1972). *Group process and productivity*. New York: Academic Press.

Stevens, M.J., & Campion, M.A. (1994). *Staffing teams: Development and validation of the Teamwork-KSA test*. Paper presented at the 9th annual meeting of the Society of Industrial and Organisational Psychology, Nashville, TN.

Tajfel, H. (1970). Experiments in intergroup discrimination. *Scientific American, 223*(5), 96–102.

Tajfel, H., & Billig, M. (1974). Familiarity and categorization in intergroup behavior. *Journal of Experimental Social Psychology, 10*, 159–170.

Tannenbaum, S.I., Beard, R.L., & Salas, S.E. (1992). Team building and its influence on team effectiveness: An examination of conceptual and empirical developments. In K. Kelley (Ed.), *Issues, theory and research in industrial/organizational psychology*. Amsterdam: Elsevier Science.

Tesser, A. (1991). Emotion in social comparison and reflection processes. In J. Suls, & T.A. Wills (Eds.), *Social comparison: Contemporary theory and research* (pp. 117–148). Hillsdale, NJ: Erlbaum.

Thomas, K.W. (1979). Organizational conflict. In S. Kerr (Ed.), *Organizational behavior* (pp. 151–184). Columbus, OH: Grid Publishing.

Tidwell, M.O., Reis, H.T., & Shaver, P.R. (1996). Attachment, attractiveness, and social interaction: A diary study. *Journal of Personality and Social Psychology, 71*, 729–745.

Tjosvold, D. (1982). Effects of approach to controversy on superiors' incorporation of subordinates' information in decision making. *Journal of Applied Psychology, 67*, 189–193.

Tjosvold, D. (1985). Implications of controversy research for management. *Journal of Management, 11*, 21–37.

Tjosvold, D. (1991). *Team organization: an enduring competitive advantage*. Chichester, UK: John Wiley.

Tjosvold, D. (1998). Co-operative and competitive goal approaches to conflict: Accomplishments and challenges. *Applied Psychology: An International Review, 41*, 285–342.

Tjosvold, D., & Field, R.H.G. (1983). Effects of social context on consensus and majority vote decision making. *Academy of Management Journal, 26*, 500–506.

Tjosvold, D., & Johnson, D.W. (1977). The effects of controversy on cognitive perspective-taking. *Journal of Education Psychology, 69*, 679–685.

Tjosvold, D., & McNeely, L.T. (1988). Innovation through communication in an educational bureaucracy. *Communication Research, 15*, 568–581.

Tjosvold, D., Wedley, W.C., & Field, R.H.G. (1986). Constructive controversy, the Vroom–Yetton Model, and managerial decision-making. *Journal of Occupational Behaviour, 7*, 125–138.

Tschan, F., & Von Cranach, M. (1996). Group task structure, processes and outcome. In M.A. West (Ed.), *Handbook of Work Group Psychology* (pp. 95–121). Chichester, UK: John Wiley.

Turner, J.C. (1985). Social categorization and the self-concept: A social cognitive theory of group behavior. In E.J. Lawler (Ed.), *Advances in group processes: theory and research* (Vol. 2, pp. 77–122). Greenwich, CT: JAI Press.

Vinokur, A.D., & van Ryn, M. (1993). Social support and undermining in close relationships: Their independent effects on the mental health of unemployed persons. *Journal of Personality and Social Psychology, 65*(2), 350–335.

Volpert, W. (1984). *Handlungsstrukturanalyse als Beitrag zur Oualifikationsforschung*. Kon: Pahl Rugenstein.

West, M.A. (1987a). A measure of role innovation at work. *British Journal of Social Psychology, 26*, 83–85.

West, M.A. (1987b). Role innovation in the world of work. *British Journal of Social Psychology, 26*, 305–315.

West, M.A. (1989). Innovation among health care professionals. *Social Behaviour, 4*, 173–184.

West, M.A. (1990). The social psychology of innovation in groups. In M.A. West, & J.L. Farr (Eds.), *Innovation and creativity at work: Psychological and organisational strategies* (pp. 309–333). Chichester, UK: Wiley.

West, M.A. (1994). *Effective teamwork*. Leicester, UK: BPS Books.

West, M.A. (1995). Creative values and creative visions in teams at work. In C.M. Ford, & D.A. Gioia (Eds.), *Creative action in organizations: Ivory tower visions and real world voices* (pp. 71–77). London: Sage Publications.

West, M.A. (Ed.) (1996). *Handbook of workgroup psychology*. Chichester, UK: John Wiley.

West, M.A., & Altink, W.M.M. (1996). Innovation at work: Individual, group, organizational and socio-historical perspectives. *European Journal of Work and Organizational Psychology*, 2(1), 3–11.

West, M.A., & Anderson, N. (1992). Innovation, cultural values and the management of change in British hospitals. *Work and Stress*, 6, 293–310.

West, M.A., & Anderson, N. (1996). Innovation in top management teams. *Journal of Applied Psychology*, 81(6), 680–693.

West, M.A., Patterson, M., Pillinger, T., & Nickell, S. (1998). *Innovation and change in manufacturing.* Institute of Work Psychology, University of Sheffield, Sheffield, UK.

West, M.A., & Wallace, M. (1991). Innovation in health care teams. *European Journal of Social Psychology*, 21, 303–315.

Willems, E.P., & Clark, R.D. III (1971). Shift toward risk and heterogeneity of groups. *Journal of Experimental and Social Psychology*, 7, 302–312.

Williams, J.G., & Solano, C.H. (1983). The social reality of feeling lonely: Friendship and reciprocation. *Personality and Social Psychology Bulletin*, 9, 237–242.

Wood, W. (1987). Meta-analytic review of sex differences in group performance. *Psychological Bulletin*, 102, 53–71.

Wright, M. (1954). A study of anxiety in a general hospital setting. *Canadian Journal of Psychology*, 8, 195–203.

Zenger, T.R., & Lawrence, B.S. (1989). Organizational demography: The differential effects of age and tenure distributions on technical communication. *Academy of Management Journal*, 11, 353–376.

15

Multiteam Systems

JOHN E. MATHIEU, MICHELLE A. MARKS, and STEPHEN J. ZACCARO

We articulate a new 'teams-of-teams' organizational form that we refer to as multiteam systems (MTSs). We define MTSs as two or more teams that interface directly and interdependently in response to environmental contingencies toward the accomplishment of collective goals. MTS boundaries are defined by virtue of the fact that all teams within the system, while pursuing different proximal goals, share at least one common distal goal; and in doing so exhibit input, process, and outcome interdependence with at least one other team in the system. We describe MTSs in terms of their goal hierarchies, the nature of their operating environments, their component teams' interdependencies, and how they operate over time in an episodic framework. We further discuss how shared mental models, leadership, information technology, and reward systems operate as critical levers influencing the effectiveness of MTSs. We submit that focusing on MTS-related themes offers a new avenue for study of emerging organizational processes.

INTRODUCTION

Manufacturing units transform ideas into products at lightning speed. US Armed forces conduct multiservice coalitional operations ranging from war to humanitarian aid in a wide variety of settings. Emergency response teams interface with public safety teams and hospital teams to save lives every day. Extant theory tells us little about the functioning of collectives such as these because they are neither typically full-fledged organizations nor single teams operating in isolation. Instead, these collectives comprise multiple teams that form a tightly coupled system, operating in an environment that demands coordinated *interteam* as well as *intrateam* behaviors in order to succeed. Just as teams are often formed because each member contributes distinct skills and expertise to the tasks at hand, constellations of teams are formed or evolve because they possess specialized skills, capabilities, and functions that contribute to a collective objective. We refer to these networks of teams as *multiteam systems* (MTSs).

Our purpose in this chapter is to articulate a framework of multiteam effectiveness that we call multiteam systems (MTS). We define what MTSs are, distinguish them from other organizational collectives, discuss their core features, and argue that they represent a new meaningful level of inquiry for subsequent theoretical work and empirical research. We also model how multiple teams, tightly linked as part of a larger system, interact and integrate their efforts to achieve shared distal goals. In doing so, we borrow from team and organizational research to develop a framework specifically targeted at multiteam effectiveness. MTS are different from prior theories and models of system effectiveness (e.g., models found in organizational theory and strategic management literature), because previous conceptual frameworks have not attempted to explain the dynamics of how teams interact with each other to create an effective system. We conclude by elucidating four critical levers for enhancing the effectiveness of MTSs.

MULTITEAM SYSTEMS

The core elements of MTS are grounded in the notions of goal hierarchies, functional interteam interdependencies, performance episodes, and how work is coordinated both within and across teams. MTS are built on the foundation of a teams-of-teams concept. While a variety of definitions have been offered in the literature, for our purposes a *team* is considered to be 'any distinguishable set of two or more people who interact, dynamically, interdependently, and adaptively toward a common and valued goal/objective/mission, who have each been assigned specific roles or functions to perform, and who have a limited life-span of membership' (Salas, Dickinson, Converse & Tannenbaum, 1992: 4). Building on the notion of a single team, MTSs are defined as: *two or more teams that interface directly and interdependently in response to environmental contingencies toward the accomplishment of collective goals. MTS boundaries are defined by virtue of the fact that all teams within the system, while pursuing different proximal goals, share at least one common distal goal; and in doing so exhibit input, process, and outcome interdependence with at least one other team in the system.* In this sense, MTSs are larger entities than individual teams, although they are typically smaller than full-scale organizations. They are dynamic and open systems that are highly responsive to their environment. We argue that while not limited to such contexts, MTSs are usually formed or develop naturally to deal with highly turbulent environments that place a premium on the ability to transform work units and to respond rapidly to changing circumstances. In fact, MTSs are not necessarily restricted to within organizational boundaries and may include teams from public, private, and other types of organizations that must work together toward a shared ultimate goal. We should mention further that our concern is upon the MTS as a whole, rather than on its members, their individual attributes, or intrateam interpersonal dynamics (the last of which are well articulated by West, Chapter 14, this volume). Indeed, team membership is likely to be a constantly changing process in MTSs, and while important, is not our focus here.

Figure 15.1 presents an illustration of the functioning of an emergency response (ER) MTS comprising of four teams (fire fighters, emergency medical technicians (EMTs), an emergency room surgery team, and a recovery team) that collectively share the ultimate goal of saving victims' lives. In brief, numerous distinguishable teams would be activated in response to an accident reporting. These would include police, fire fighters, and EMTs who would be dispatched and routed to the accident scene by the dispatch center. Upon arrival, however, the fire fighters and EMT teams would work closely together to extract victims from the vehicles and to stabilize them. From there the EMTs would be directed by the dispatch center to transport the victims to a given hospital where they would receive care from an emergency room surgical team if their injuries were severe. Following surgery, patients would likely be admitted to an intensive care unit and attended to by a recovery team of doctors and nurses. Of course, this example is a simplified version of the complex network of teams involved in such situations and its specific configuration would likely differ from one community to another. But, it is useful for illustrative purposes. Further, this particular MTS crosses organizational boundaries and includes teams from county government and from a local hospital. It also illustrates how other teams in the environment may be associated with what we refer to as an MTS, yet not be members of it. We will make reference to this example throughout the remaining sections to highlight particular points of interest.

The goal hierarchy feature of MTSs that we mentioned highlights the fact that although individual teams within an MTS may pursue different individual goals, these goals must somehow come together and be intertwined at a higher level for an MTS system to exist. For example, the EMTs and surgical teams in our example perform markedly different tasks, yet their efforts are both ultimately directed toward saving patients' lives. Moreover, because the success of these teams is linked in terms of how badly the victims are hurt, how well and quickly they orchestrate patient transfers and information about their condition, and how well the victims ultimately fare, they share all three forms of interdependence noted above.

Another critical feature of MTSs is that they sequence activities both within and between teams. There is a growing awareness that performance unfolds over time or performance episodes, and that teams exhibit different performance trajectories (Marks, Mathieu & Zaccaro, In press). Mathieu and Button (1992) defined performance episodes as 'distinguishable periods of time over which performance accrues and is reviewed' (p. 1759). Adopting an episodic framework highlights the fact that traditional team and organizational input–process–output (IPO) models merely represent 'snapshots' of an ongoing stream of team behavior. We believe that outcomes of one episode may actually constitute inputs to later episodes. Furthermore, the performance of one team may act as the input to another team in the system. For example, to the extent that the fire fighters and EMTs can quickly extract victims from the accident scene and deliver them to the hospital, the patients are much more

Multiteam System
for handling severely injured accident victims

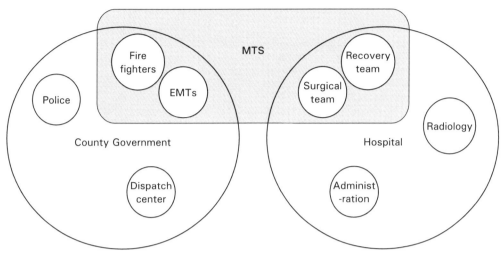

Figure 15.1 *Multiteam system for handling severely injured accident victims*

likely to survive surgical procedures than if they arrive later. While the pursuit of team-based proximal goals need not unfold over comparable episode durations, teams need to be synchronized in terms of how they collectively meet more distal system goals. Effectiveness of the MTS, then, is defined not only in terms of how well each team accomplishes its proximal goals, but more importantly on how well they collectively accomplish shared goals at the higher levels of the goal hierarchy.

CHARACTERISTICS OF MULTITEAM SYSTEMS

Defining the nature and boundaries of an organized collective is a difficult enterprise and subject to debate. Moreover, we acknowledge that demarcating where the boundaries are and rules for membership of a collective are somewhat arbitrary. These challenges, however, are no less true when researchers and scholars have sought to define what teams or organizations are. Our conception of MTSs as unique entities falls along five distinguishing characteristics:

(1) *MTSs are composed of two or more teams.* Minimally, MTSs are composed of two teams and maximally of *N* teams interacting with each other. Teams that compose MTSs, which we refer to as *component teams*, are nonreducible and distinguishable wholes with interdependent members and proximal goals.

(2) *MTSs are unique entities that are larger than teams yet typically smaller than the larger*

organization(s) within which they are embedded. Some MTSs, such as our ER example, may even cross traditional organizational boundaries. They differ from teams, organizations, and other collective forms such as departments and subsystems, in their architecture and functioning.

(3) *All component teams exhibit input, process, and outcome interdependence with at least one other team in the system.* This important concept is developed more fully below.

(4) MTSs *are open systems whose particular configuration stems from the performance requirements of environment that they confront and the technologies that they adopt.* The performance requirements, in turn, serve to articulate a goal hierarchy that guides MTS action.

(5) *Although MTS component teams may not share proximal goals, they share a common distal goal or set of goals. Further, MTSs have a single superordinate goal, for which all component teams have a vested interest* (in our example, saving victims' lives). This goal hierarchy feature is discussed in detail in a later section, along with a discussion of how MTSs exhibit goal-directed actions that unfold over time.

MTSs Are Unique Entities

MTSs are qualitatively different than other collective entities discussed in the literature. In the following sections we discuss similarities and differences between MTSs and other collective forms, including teams, organizations, subsystems, subassemblies, matrix organizations, and task forces.

MTSs Versus Teams

The distinction between teams and MTSs is fairly clear. MTSs are not teams themselves, but rather are composed of a minimum of two teams that work interdependently and are linked by shared superordinate goals. This makes the large body of team research relevant to MTSs in the sense that it describes the internal activity of component teams nested within the larger system. That literature is far less well suited for understanding a team's relationships with the surrounding environment and other teams. While a few researchers have examined team interaction with its surrounding environment (e.g., Ancona & Caldwell, 1992; Marks, Zaccaro & Mathieu, 2000; Tesluk & Mathieu, 1999), the extant team literature has not addressed how interdependent teams operate as a larger work unit. What we know about team effectiveness can be characterized largely as models of single team effectiveness. This is not sufficient for capturing the interdependencies across teams. Whereas several prominent theoretical frameworks (Gladstein, 1984; Guzzo & Shea, 1992; Hackman & Morris, 1975, Tannenbaum, Beard & Salas, 1992) feature the team's external environment as either an input or moderator for team functioning, the role of contextual influences on team effectiveness has not been articulated in depth. More specifically, the notion that other teams constitute important aspects of a team's performance environment has received scant attention in theory and empirical studies. We understand very little about the influence of teams on other teams, as well as how multiple teams coact in pursuit of common goals.

MTSs Versus Organizations

The organizational literature is also inadequate for learning about relationships among workteams. The vast array of meanings attached to the term 'organization' makes it challenging to distinguish an MTS from an organization because there is a lack of consensus on precisely what an organization is. However, most people agree that it is an organized collection of individuals with a semidefined hierarchy of roles in pursuit of shared goals. While an MTS could conceivably encompass an entire organization, more often they represent some subset of organizational teams. For example, MTSs are composed of multiple highly interdependent teams, whereas organizations often contain alternative structures that include more loosely coupled work units that do not share multiple forms of interdependence, as well as employees who do not work in team settings. Further, MTSs are not constrained to traditional organizational boundaries. As illustrated in Figure 15.1, the MTS contains teams from both county government and the hospital; yet not all teams from either setting are members of it. Finally, organizations often have several overall goals, whereas MTSs have a single superordinate goal that all component teams work toward.

MTSs Versus Similar Entities

The great majority of literature on collectives has focused on teams (groups) and organizations. We are proposing that MTSs are distinct entities that lie somewhere between the full-fledged organization and the individual team. Thus it is important to distinguish them from other collectives that have received attention in the literature. Subsystems, subassemblies, matrix systems, and task forces are all units that exist within organizations. Subsystems are the divisions of organizations featured prominently in open system theory (Katz & Kahn, 1978). They are formal structures within organizations that are defined by their function. For example, production and maintenance subsystems focus inward on operational issues within the organization, whereas adaptive and boundary subsystems interface with the surrounding environment. Subsystems are classified solely on their purpose in organizational effectiveness, and are not necessarily composed of interdependent teams that share a goal hierarchy. There are few boundaries on how subsystems can be incorporated into the larger organization, typically within functional departments, and sometimes by divisional or matrix departmentalization.

It is not uncommon to find a single MTS that performs production, maintenance, adaptive, and boundary-spanning functions in the pursuit of its objectives. MTSs differ from subsystems in that the former are composed of multiple interdependent teams, and the latter are functional groupings of individuals based on a purpose within the organization. Thus, MTSs could potentially occupy a subsystem of an organization, but only if that subsystem meets all five core characteristics.

Simon's (1962) notion of stable subassemblies is clearly akin to that of MTSs. *Subassemblies* are subsystems that retain a level of autonomy from the larger organization and function somewhat independently. Scott (1998) stated that 'When subsystems take the form of stable subassemblies, units capable of retaining their form without constant attention from superior units, then hierarchical forms have an important survival advantage over other systems. Many seemingly complex organizational systems are made up of, and depend for their stability on, units that are highly similar and capable of relatively autonomous functioning' (p. 91). Although subassemblies operate as autonomous units, like organizations themselves, they are not analogous to MTSs. Subassemblies, like subsystems, are structural arrangements designed to execute specified types of activities, whereas MTSs specify a collective of interdependent teams working towards a superordinate goal. However, neither subsystems or subassemblies specify the underlying nature of their interdependencies, nor thereby their working relationships across units as related to superordinate goal accomplishment.

MTSs also differ from *matrix organizations*. Matrix organizations have project teams, frequently referred to as cross-functional teams, composed of both functional and project specialists. Traditionally, organizations working in uncertain and dynamic environments have employed matrix systems to enhance flexibility and response efficiency. Cross-functional teams are essentially staffing arrangements, where individuals in different organizational roles serve on multiple teams. Like matrix systems, MTSs are designed to interact swiftly and effectively with the surrounding environment. However, rather than constituting new teams to meet an environmental demand, MTSs orchestrate the underlying nature of the interrelationships between existing teams to achieve shared goals. Our focus is on those relationships *per se*, not on the composition of the component teams. The point is that matrix staffing may occur within the confines of some MTSs, but it is a distinct concept. To the extent that individuals occupy roles on multiple interdependent teams, a matrix staffing arrangement could facilitate knowledge transfer and synchronization of efforts across teams.

In theory, *task forces* may be the most similar collective arrangement to our notion of an MTS. Task forces are composed of individuals that unite efforts to accomplish a particular objective or set of objectives handed down from a higher organizational level. Hackman (1990) refers to them as *ad hoc* groups that:

(1) do not work closely together in their permanent jobs;
(2) come together to perform a team task;
(3) perform a one-of-a-kind task or create a unique project;
(4) have an unusual amount of autonomy of operation;
(5) are dependent on external constraints that exist (e.g., clients);
(6) are temporary groups given a specific deadline for accomplishing their objectives.

Traditional taskforce designs have between four and twenty members, and are more commonly thought of as a particular type of team. MTSs share several elements of task forces while operating at the multiteam level. As with taskforces, MTSs are often formed in response to a unique organizational need that is best accomplished by a specialized network of teams working in close alignment. Also like taskforces, MTSs work as autonomous units within the context of their surrounding organizations and external environments and are typically assembled for a particular objective.

Although taskforces have many characteristics of MTSs, they have not been previously studied as a collection of teams and do not carry with them assumptions of interdependence. In fact, there has been very little research on taskforces as defined by Hackman (1990). Moreover, taskforces, unlike MTSs, are typically designed to deal with a particular need or project and then disbanded. MTSs usually have a much more permanent nature. In any case, the notion of a collective formed in response to a specific charge from a higher organizational level, and tasked with working autonomously to achieve their objectives provides an important basis for the existence of MTSs.

In sum, MTSs are not adequately represented in the literature by the previously studied concepts of organization, team, department, subsystem, subassembly, matrix arrangements, or taskforces. To date, no conceptualization has addressed a configuration of tightly coupled teams, contained either within a single organization or across organizations, working interdependently as a unique entity towards a single superordinate goal. We believe these types of work arrangements exist in many current venues and will likely increase in prominence in the future. The following section describes the nature of the interdependence that in large part delineates the network of teams that compose MTSs.

MTS Interdependence

Team researchers agree that an essential element of a team is the interdependence among its members (Campion, Medsker & Higgs, 1993; Fandt, Cady & Sparks, 1993; Saavedra, Early & Van Dyne, 1993; Salas et al., 1992; Wageman, 1995). The notion of interdependence at the organizational level refers to the sharing of information, resources, and strategies among organizations (Hitt, Keats & DeMarie, 1998). Multiteam interdependence is analogous to its meaning at both the team and organizational levels, except that it refers to the relationships among teams rather than among individuals or organizations.

A critical feature of MTSs is the functional interdependence that exists throughout the system. In a global economy, one could argue that all organizational entities are interdependent to some extent. Thus, we introduce the notion of *functional interdependence*, which stems directly from the activities that each of the component teams perform. Functional interdependence is *a state by which entities have mutual reliance, determination, influence, and shared vested interest in processes they use to accomplish work activities*. The purpose of this section is to illustrate the importance of functional interdependence to MTSs.

Following from the definition of teams that we adopted, all MTS component teams exhibit interdependence among their members (Salas et al., 1992; Sundstrom, DeMeuse & Futrell, 1990). Here, we focus our attention on the interdependence that exists *among* teams that compose MTSs. To do so, we have adopted a tripartite framework to explain the role of functional interdependence in MTSs. This framework depicts three forms of functional interdependence: inputs, processes, and outcomes associated with MTSs operations. Each team within the MTS is functionally interdependent (i.e., input, process, and outcome) with at least one other team. The rules for interdependence among teams within an MTS are delineated specifically because this serves as one way to elucidate the differences between MTSs and organizations. This also helps to articulate the boundaries of MTS membership.

Although many organizations have collective goals spread throughout their units, these units operate fairly independently in their attainment. In contrast, MTSs contain a network of functional interdependencies that evolve to realize a superordinate goal that requires the close collaboration of multiple workteams. If one were to draw an overlay of interteam network relations depicting input, process, and outcome dependencies, it might look like Figure 15.2. This figure illustrates two important points. First, MTS component teams must have all three types of interdependencies with at least one other team in the system. Note that teams such as the fire fighters and EMTs share all three forms of interdependence with each other, as do the surgical and recovery teams. Second, teams that do not meet this requirement are not considered part of the MTS. The figure illustrates that police and fire fighters share input and process interdependence with each other, but not outcome interdependence. Similarly, hospital administration shares only input interdependence with the EMTs and the recovery team. However, because police and hospital administration do not share all three forms of interdependence with any team in the system, they are not part of this MTS network.

Outcome interdependence is the extent to which personal benefits, rewards, costs, or other outcomes received by team members depend on the performance or successful goal attainment of others (Alpher, Tjosvold & Law, 1998; Guzzo & Shea, 1992; Wageman, 1995). Everyone in the MTS shares a vested interest in the accomplishment of the superordinate goal. However, by *functional outcome interdependence*, we are also describing the accomplishment of subgoals that require the joint activities of two or more teams. At least at the superordinate level, all teams are working towards a common objective requiring their synthesized efforts (e.g., saving lives). However, MTS functional outcome interdependence also resides at lower levels in the goal hierarchy, where component teams coordinate activities to achieve more proximal goals (e.g., fire fighters and EMTs working together to extract and to stabilize injured motorists). Superordinate goal accomplishment requires the compilation of different sets of functional activities, each with different sets of subgoals. Highly interdependent component teams share in more proximal outcomes that emerge from collective subgoal accomplishment, such as satisfaction, development, quality of work life, and perhaps financial benefits. Thus, functional outcome interdependence flows in large part from the collective goal hierarchy of the MTS.

Process interdependence is defined as the amount of *interteam* interaction required for goal accomplishment, and refers to the degree to which teams depend on each other to perform the tasks at hand. Process interdependence is similar to the concept of task interdependence in teams (Van de Ven & Ferry, 1980), yet we have chosen the term process interdependence because component teams are not simply working together on a single task, but rather on a collective mission. Teams work collaboratively to carry out processes such as boundary spanning, communication, and integration of actions, efforts, and timing.

The team literature has further depicted the nature of task interdependence by describing different forms of interdependent working arrangements, in order delineate more specifically the spectrum of teamwork arrangements (Saavedra et al., 1993; Tesluk, Mathieu, Zaccaro & Marks, 1997; Van de Ven & Ferry, 1980). These forms include pooled, sequential, reciprocal, and intensive interdependence, and are summarized in Tesluk et al. (1997). Goal hierarchies within MTSs give rise to multiple kinds of *functional process interdependencies* among component teams, including sequential, reciprocal, and intensive forms, which require teams to work interdependently while accomplishing goals. Although pooled interdependence can depict interteam relationships in organizations, the aggregation of multiple teams' efforts does not constitute MTS functional process interdependence because no workflow is required among component teams. Sequential (unidirectional workflow) and reciprocal interdependence (cyclical workflow) refer to patterns of work accomplishment that require one team to complete a task before another team can contribute. In our example, EMTs and emergency surgery teams have a sequentially interdependent working relationship; the EMT team's goal is to stabilize the accident victim until he or she is brought to the hospital and handed over to the surgery team for treatment. Intensive interdependence describes situations where teams must collaborate simultaneously and collectively. Fire fighters and EMTs work intensively to both stabilize victims and extract them from emergency conditions.

MTS Interdependence

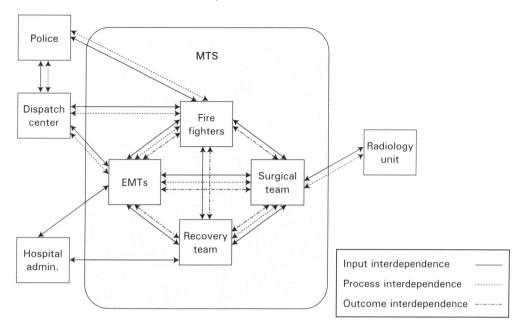

Figure 15.2   MTS interdependence

Input interdependence identifies the extent to which component teams must share inputs such as people, facilities, environmental constraints, equipment, and information related to collective goal accomplishment. By *functional input interdependence*, we mean that the inputs teams share are used for the attainment of more proximal goals. This notion is parallel to the concept of resource interdependence that has been defined at the team level (Wageman, 1995) as referring to members having joint use of resources such as a shared finances, equipment, or expertise. In the ER example, the fire fighters and EMTs share inputs such as rescue equipment and face common challenges at the accident scene. Elsewhere, the surgical and recovery teams share resources in terms of facilities, supplies, space, etc. at the hospital. The functioning of all component teams is driven at least in part by the severity of the injuries incurred.

In sum, functional interdependence is a defining characteristic of MTSs, whereby each component must have input, process, and output interdependence with at least one other component team. This yields a complex system of a tightly coupled network of teams bounded by their functional interdependencies. Whereas interdependent work arrangements can take different forms (e.g., sequential, reciprocal, intensive), our critical point is that no one individual team can single-handedly accomplish an MTS superordinate goal. This also means

that other teams that have limited interaction with component teams (e.g., the police or radiology teams in our example) would not fulfill MTS membership criteria. In the next section we describe how these tightly coupled MTSs interface with their environments.

The MTS Environment

The environment has received considerable attention in the literature for its influence on organizational structure, strategies, and survival (Hambrick, 1981; Jauch & Kraft, 1986; Katz & Kahn, 1978; Lawrence & Lorsch, 1967; Sastry, 1997; Sutcliffe, 1994). Hawley (1968) put forth a generic definition of an organizational environment as all phenomena that are external to and potentially or actually influence the organization. One point of consensus from this body of research is the critical role of the environment on organizational effectiveness: to the extent that environments are more dynamic and unpredictable, organizations must spend greater resources for monitoring external conditions and incorporating these conditions into subsequent planning, decisions, and action.

Unfortunately, the team literature is lagging considerably in its investigation of the relationship between teams and their performance environments. Several conceptual frameworks have delineated a generic 'team context' variable as an input or moderator of team effectiveness (Gladstein, 1984; Guzzo & Shea, 1992; Tannenbaum et al., 1992). However, at this point there is very limited research on how to conceptualize team relationships with their larger environment because most researchers have examined only the inner workings of teams as if they performed in a vacuum (for exceptions see Ancona & Caldwell, 1992; Marks et al., in press; Tesluk & Mathieu, 1999; Waller, 1999). In particular, to our knowledge there is no extant theory that considers the role of other interdependent teams as components of a given team's environment.

Like organizations, MTSs are open systems, interfacing fluidly with their surrounding environment (Katz & Kahn, 1978). As open systems, MTSs are characterized by the symbiosis of the parts in which they are composed, where the environment is viewed as a primary system component. Thus, understanding the environments in which MTSs perform is an essential element of this framework. Below we define the environments of MTSs, discuss the characteristics of typical MTS environments, and consider the structural arrangements of MTSs that arise in response to environmental demands.

MTSs have two types of environment: the embedding organization(s) and the external environment. The former consists of phenomena within the respective component teams' organizational boundary and includes characteristics such as the corporate culture, organizational norms and procedures, and human resource systems that impact MTS functioning. This would also include other (non-MTS) teams in the larger organization with whom MTS teams have to interface on some occasions. The external environment refers to the specific phenomena outside the surrounding organization(s) with which the MTS interfaces directly. These influences include actual units within the environment, such as customers, suppliers, news agencies, and lawmakers, as well as the characteristics of the environments, to be discussed in detail below.

Internal Versus Cross-Boundary MTSs

As mentioned earlier, one differentiating point between MTSs and organizations is that MTSs can cross-organizational boundaries to include component teams from the surrounding environment. There are two types of MTS with respect to their environment: those that are fully embedded within the organization (referred to as internal MTSs); and those that contain teams both within and external to the organization (referred to as cross-boundary MTSs). Cross-boundary MTSs exist when functional input, process, and outcome interdependence exists among teams from different organizations. For example, it is not unusual for teams within an organization to develop extremely close working relationships with sole source contractors, and

market outlets. In our example, two types of teams employed by the county government (fire fighters and EMTs) work across organizational boundaries with hospital teams (surgery and recovery) to accomplish the superordinate goal.

To the extent that MTSs are nested within a given organization, the larger system will serve more as a buffer of influences stemming from the external environment. For example, product development MTSs consisting of engineering and graphical design teams may be heavily influenced by aspects of its surrounding company, including the company's goals, culture, and reward systems. Both characteristics and entities of the larger organization, as well as those of the surrounding environment more directly influence cross-boundary MTSs (e.g., our emergency response MTS example) and internal MTSs that are situated close to organizational borders (e.g., those in the service industry).

Characteristics of the MTS Environment

A primary reason for the existence of MTSs is their responsiveness and adaptability to challenging performance environments. Environments that are challenging can have any combination of the following elements: (1) complexity; (2) dynamism; (3) novelty; and (4) uncertainty. Environmental complexity refers to the diversity of elements that must be dealt with by the MTS (Dess & Beard, 1984; Scott, 1998). Dynamism refers to the rate of variability, stability, and turbulence of the environment (Dess & Beard, 1984). Novelty means unfamiliar and unexpected performance situations that, while maintaining their primary mission and objectives for the team, differ in terms of their specific performance requirements and strategic approach (Marks et al., in press). Uncertainty indicates the unpredictability of the environment and the extent to which it is possible to forecast its behavior in advance (Sutcliffe, 1994; Waller, 1999). Collectively these four features combine to yield environments that could be scaled in terms of how challenging they are to operate in.

Complex, dynamic, novel, and uncertain environments are more difficult to work in because the performance challenges that arise are nonroutine (Dutton & Dukerich, 1994) and often require unique and system-wide responses in limited time periods. MTSs are particularly suited to work effectively within these types of challenging environments because they exhibit 'requisite variety' (Ashby, 1968), the ability to reconfigure themselves to best align with environmental demands. In this way, highly interdependent MTS component teams can change the nature of their interteam working relationships to best adapt to the particular environmental challenges or opportunities that arise. In our ER example, to the extent that there were more injured individuals than expected, effective fire fighters and EMTs would adjust their activities to secure all victims quickly, and then inform the surgery and recovery teams of the additional patients. Rapid coordination among teams allows the entire ER MTS to handle unexpected changes. As one portion of the system adapts to environmental pressures of one sort or another, the actions and processes of tightly coupled component teams must respond in a synchronous fashion if the MTS is to be effective.

Lawrence and Lorsch (1967) postulated that different subunits within organizations are confronted with unique environmental demands. They argued that the structure of subunits should be tailored to the particular environment within which they operate. Applying this notion to MTSs that resemble fairly autonomous and tightly coupled team-centered subunits, it is likely that different MTSs within the same organization face a unique set of environmental demands. For instance, an emergency room MTS in an inner-city location faces a more dynamic and unpredictable environment than a cancer unit in that same hospital, or a hospital emergency room in an affluent suburban community. This point further justifies the need to examine the MTS as a separate unit of analysis with respect to the external environment.

Structural Requirements for MTS Environmental Adaptation

As mentioned above, a key feature of MTSs is 'requisite variety' which provides them with the ability to adapt efficiently and effectively to challenging environments. This requires a structure that is capable of facilitating rapid coordination and information management processes in response to the environmental demands. Consistent with contingency theories that advocate that structural designs should be aligned with the nature of the environment and technology (Keller, 1994; Scott, 1987), MTSs occupy a variety of structures from steep hierarchies to decentralized sets of teams that share common goals. The nature of the work to be accomplished, coupled with the environment in which this work must be completed, drive the goal structures that direct MTS activity. In this sense, the goal hierarchies of MTSs are driven, at least in large part, by their environment (Lawrence & Lorsch, 1967) and the communication technologies that are present (Keller, 1994). Because most MTS environments are fairly challenging, their structures are designed for responsiveness and adaptation. Mechanisms that facilitate rapid, seamless interteam coordinated action enhance MTS responsiveness and effectiveness. For example, decentralized communication structures are characteristic of MTSs because they enable the free exchange of information as needed.

In sum, MTSs are open systems that operate interdependently with their surrounding environments. Their environments consist of both the larger embedding organization(s), as well as external forces that interact directly with the MTS. Organizations that contain MTSs entirely within their boundaries serve as a buffer between the MTS and the external environment, whereas cross-boundary MTSs interact much more closely with the surrounding environment. The complex and dynamic nature of the environment in which MTS goals must be accomplished requires efforts of multiple integrated teams working in close collaboration toward collective goals. The next section describes the goal structures that unite component teams and guide teams through interdependent task accomplishment.

MTS Goal Hierarchies and Performance Episodes

According to Locke and Latham (1990), goals are 'desired outcomes in terms of level of performance to be attained on a task' (p. 24). By their very nature, goals identify a quantity of work that must be accomplished by a certain time and within certain quality standards. A multitude of studies on goal setting have put forth abundant evidence for the favorable effects of goal setting on individual task performance. Goals influence performance through several motivational and cognitive mechanisms, including the mobilization of effort, the focus of attention in a particular direction, the encouragement of persistence and sustained effort over time (Locke, Shaw, Saari & Latham, 1981), and the regulation of effort expenditure (Locke, 1966). Goals also stimulate the development of task strategies (Bandura & Wood, 1989; Terborg, 1976). Specific and difficult goals direct attention towards a desired outcome, thus facilitating the evolution of particular task strategies by delineating aspects of the task that require attention (Early, Wojnaroski & Prest, 1987).

Researchers have also investigated the benefits of collective goals for group performance. A meta-analysis of the relationship between group goals and performance indicated that teams with specific, difficult yet attainable goals, performed approximately one standard deviation better than groups with 'do your best' goals (O'Leary-Kelly, Martocchio & Frink, 1994). In many ways, the mechanisms through which collective goals operate are analogous to those of individual goal setting: they direct attention, channel and sustain collaborative effort, and regulate group resource allocation. Yet collective goals have additional benefits: they energize team members, unify workers, reduce conflict among members, and facilitate a sense of unity and cohesion in the pursuit of a common goal (Sherif, 1966). Moreover, collective goals have been shown to enhance commitment to collective tasks, thereby decreasing performance decrements associated with social loafing (Hoffman, Kaplan & Metlay, 1994).

Collective goals facilitate two critical processes: the selection and generation of appropriate action plans or strategies, and collective coordination. Collective goals direct the team's attention and effort towards particular meaningful outcomes, thus enabling teams to develop strategies to reach those outcomes. Team strategies clarify the relationship between effort and performance, thereby increasing motivation. Team strategies also elucidate the roles and actions of members of the collective in reaching goals, which facilitates coordination among them. Research has shown that goals have their greatest impact on employees' behavior when they are set at difficult yet attainable levels, people are committed to accomplishing them, and progress feedback is provided (Locke & Latham, 1990). Feedback is important because it makes vivid the 'performance gap' that remains between how much a team has accomplished by any given point in time versus how much will ultimately be required (Kluger & DeNisi, 1996). These dynamics can only operate when goals are cast in some sort of time frame. These time frames constitute performance episodes. The following sections elaborate on this notion of performance episodes and how goals are linked both within and across component teams in an MTS. For simplicity's sake, we begin by explaining the role of temporal influences on the achievement of a single team goal. We then discuss the complexities teams face when managing the pursuit of multiple goals. Finally, we expand this thinking to include how multiple teams within an MTS simultaneously orchestrate the accomplishment of multiple goals over time.

Component Team Goals

In this section we describe the processes related to component team goal accomplishment. Our focus here is on team goal attainment, rather than phases of a team life cycle or single task accomplishment. We share McGrath's (1991) view that teams are typically engaged in the pursuit of multiple goals concurrently, thus several tasks are often being juggled at any one time. The pursuit of multiple goals simultaneously 'creates an environment where members are engaged in complex sequences of interdependent tasks that compose a larger project' (McGrath, 1991: 149). Whereas McGrath talks about time as an environmental driver, we add the notion that time is linked to goal accomplishment in an episodic framework (see Marks et al., in press, for more details). No theories have focused directly on explaining how time impacts team interaction processes for goal attainment.

Performance Episodes

The input–process–outcome (I-P-O) models explain team effectiveness as a function of inputs and processes. We believe this oversimplifies and distorts most teams' actual path to goal accomplishment, and that I-P-O models are more appropriately applied to smaller segments of team action. Team performance trajectories more commonly consist of several I-P-O type cycles that run sequentially and simultaneously (Marks et al., in press). Our theory is based on the idea that teams perform in temporal cycles of goal-directed activity called episodes. Episodes constitute the rhythms of task performance for teams. Episode durations stem, in large part, from the nature of the tasks that teams perform, as well as from the manner in which members choose to complete work. They are most easily identified by goals and by goal accomplishment periods.

Component teams have unique performance rhythms regulated by the task and temporal demands placed on proximal goal accomplishment. Performance rhythms refer to the interaction patterns that occur within episodes and the speed with which they occur, and are influenced by the environment and the nature of the performance requirements. Component teams may have different rhythms that would increase the challenge of interteam coordination. For example, the EMT and emergency surgical teams in our example have relatively short performance episodes, whereas the nursing crew and doctors responsible for patient recovery will likely segment time in much longer durations. For teams with high levels of task interdependence, their rhythms are necessarily yoked because of their mutual dependence on each other for shared knowledge or integration of actions. Again from our example, the fire fighters and EMT teams must closely synchronize their efforts in terms of quickly and safely extracting injured motorists from the crash scene. Teams with fewer interdependencies are concerned less with simultaneous action sequencing and more with the timing of information flow and knowledge transfer. The emergency room surgical team does not have to coordinate its' actions in real time with that of the EMT team. Their joint effectiveness, however, is tightly coupled in a sequential fashion and the extent to which patient status and other vital information is communicated effectively and remedial actions are passed from one team to the next will have substantial effects on the patients' likelihood of survival.

Performance episodes represent identifiable segments of an ongoing stream of behavior. Most teams, except for a few limited types such as taskforces, are responsible for accomplishing a number of activities over a fairly long period of time. The conclusion of one episode normally marks the initiation of another, whether these are work orders, quarterly sales profits, or halves of a sporting event (although there are variations on this pattern). Episodes may vary substantially in their duration. Moreover, longer-term episodes are often segmented into sections or subepisodes of more limited scope and duration that contribute to the larger effort. In this sense, performance episodes parallel recent thinking about the nature and structuring of goals (Austin & Vancouver, 1996; Bandura, 1991; Vallacher & Wagner, 1987). Thompson (1967) argued that breaking them down into their constituent parts, sequencing the requisite accomplishment of the parts, and then focusing attention on completing the subgoals accomplishes more distal goals. Some of these subgoals could be accomplished simultaneously, whereas other subgoals are dependent on others having been accomplished previously. Distilling them into more manageable subgoals and coordinating the requisite sequencing of proximal goal achievement accomplishes distal goals. This thinking can be applied equally to individual teams and MTSs as collectives.

The notion of breaking down distal goals into more proximal goals has been advanced in a wide variety of disciplines ranging from macro-organizational behavior (Carroll & Tosi, 1973), to team (Pritchard, Jones, Rother, Stuebing & Ekeberg, 1988) and individual behavior (Catrambone, 1996, 1998), to the nature of cognitive functioning (Ward & Allport, 1997). This raises the question of how one identifies the most salient 'chunking' or 'coarseness' of performance episodes. At one extreme, long-term organizational goals are too far removed in time, ambiguous, and dynamic to have any direct influence on the day-to-day activities of teams. On the other hand, once one starts breaking down distal goals to subgoals, an infinite regression begins and it is difficult to know when to stop dissecting the behavioral stream. For example, cognitive psychologists often break down subgoal routines to intervals lasting only seconds or less. This may be informative from a psychological perspective, but such a fine-grained analysis is of little value to researchers and practitioners wishing to influence team processes in macro-organizational settings.

We submit that salient team performance episodes are best identified by completing a thorough team task analysis to identify the most meaningful temporal segmenting of work (see Tesluk et al., 1997). Sometimes the nature of the work being performed has a natural rhythm. For example, the EMT team in our example would likely focus on how quickly and in what condition they delivered the patients to the hospital. Although they might also identify more specific subepisodes (e.g., getting to the accident scene, extracting the patients, stabilizing them, transporting patients to the hospital, and preparing to be available again), generally speaking 'the delivery of a stable patient' is what they focus on. In other instances, performance episodes are externally imposed and somewhat arbitrary. For instance, the radiology unit of the hospital in our example may concentrate on achieving quarterly goals related to efficiency and costs that have little

to do with the ebb and flow of patients through the emergency room. Furthermore, social–psychological factors such as the larger organizational culture, team histories, and even the personalities of team members may influence the establishment of particular episodes. Some teams seek feedback almost constantly and adopt very short episodes, whereas others performing the same task activity may go long periods of time before taking inventory.

Multitasking

Up to this point we have discussed performance episodes as though teams pursued simply one of them at a time. However, few real-world teams have the luxury of performing one task activity (McGrath, 1991). Virtually all present-day workteams have to multitask in order to manage a vector of performance episodes simultaneously. Teams often work in multiple performance episodes at a given point in time, each with its constituent subgoals and subepisodes along with its associated rhythms and sequence. Just as teams need to break down and sequence subepisode accomplishments, they must orchestrate multiple episode interfaces. Figure 15.3 illustrates team multitasking, where one team is concurrently working four tasks over a period of time. Tasks 1 and 2 are initiated first, while tasks 3 and 4 begin later on. The figure indicates that some subgoal episodes take longer to accomplish than others, and that I-P-O cycles occur within each subgoal episode of each task.

Moreover, the timing and duration of these episodes often differs markedly and may cause even greater coordination challenges. The primary challenge is for teams to develop and execute a multifaceted plan of work that simultaneously manages performance gaps in each of their important performance episodes. In so doing, teams may often neglect one or more particular tasks in order to close the gap on others. Alternatively, efforts might be diverted from shorter-term initiatives if a long-term project is at a critical juncture in its development. For example, the fire fighters in our example would not only have the responsibility to safely extract the crash victims from their automobiles, they would also be responsible for protecting the lives of others and minimizing further damage and loss of property. They would work with police officers to direct traffic and clear roadways, they might have to actively fight fires that resulted from the crash and/or spray fluids to prevent the onset of fire, and they would likely stay on the scene long after the immediate threats have subsided to ensure that no further fires developed. The array of activities described above stem merely from their presence at the crash scene. However, they are simultaneously responsible for several other activities with different time rhythms such as enhancing fire prevention and public awareness of hazardous situations.

MULTIPLE TASK Episode

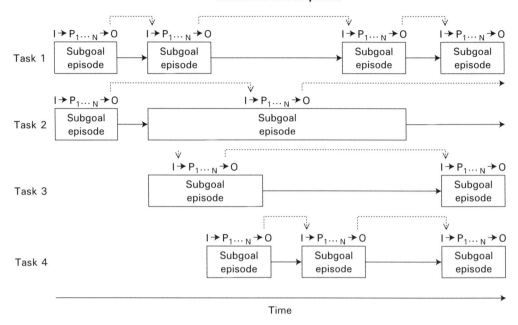

Figure 15.3 *Team multitasking*

Each goal and associated performance episode has a valence or relative importance attached to it that may heighten or weaken its salience to the team given the myriad of demands they face. Teams are constantly faced with a resource allocation challenge whereby they try to maximize their ultimate effectiveness by minimizing the magnitude of performance gaps of the most salient performance episodes. Complicating matters, the various episodes that teams are performing are not likely to be time synchronized, they have varying degrees of importance, and other unanticipated demands will likely be placed on the team. Additionally, these parameters are likely to change over time in unpredictable ways. The challenge then, is to devise strategies and to execute actions that enable the team to simultaneously work towards the accomplishment of multiple goals over time. These work processes need to be both concrete enough to guide specific behavioral requirements, yet flexible enough to be revised as circumstances warrant. Ultimately, team effectiveness, then, becomes a weighted product of the extent to which members maximize goal accomplishments over time. Having established this foundation of how individual component teams pursue their multiple-related proximal goals over time, we now turn to a consideration of MTS goal-related processes.

MTS Goal-Related Processes

Above we advanced the idea that MTS component teams are linked by virtue of functional interdependencies among their respective inputs, processes, and/or outcomes. Furthermore, we argued that component teams must manage the accomplishment of multiple proximal goals over time. Taken together, these processes combine to suggest that MTS component teams will exhibit a vast array of complex interdependencies with other teams over time, and that these relationships are embedded in an MTS goal hierarchy. Below we discuss the nature of such a hierarchy and its implications for MTS processes and functioning.

Goal Hierarchy

A central tenet of own MTS framework is that collective goals are nested hierarchically within the MTS. We define an MTS goal hierarchy as an interconnected network of collective goals, where the shortest term (proximal) goals are at the lowest levels of the hierarchy, longer-term goals (distal) are at higher levels, and superordinate distal goals that represent the MTS objectives are at the top of the hierarchy. Figure 15.4 illustrates a goal hierarchy consisting of four component teams and three goal levels in the context of our emergency response example. In this example, the fire-fighting and EMT teams must work very closely together to safely extract and stabilize the injured motorists. Doing so successfully would constitute accomplishing the first proximal goal (i.e., G1). The work of the two teams on G1 is best described as intensively linked. The joint efforts of the fire-fighter and EMT teams are then linked sequentially to those of the

MTS Goal Hierarchy

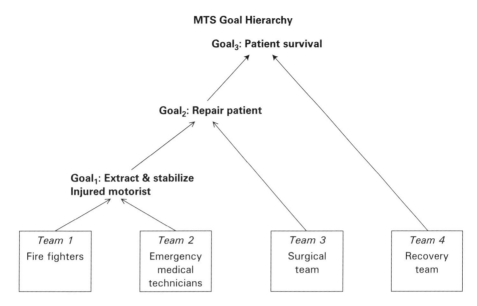

Figure 15.4   *MTS goal hierarchy*

emergency room surgical team, and finally to those of the recovery team. The work of each is influenced in large part by how well the preceding team(s) in the system performed their functions. For example, successful repair of the patient (G2) is predicated on how well G1 was accomplished and then how well the surgical team did its part. At this stage, the patients' status is a complex product of the coordinated efforts of three component teams. The ultimate effectiveness of the MTS is realized at G3 and reflects not only the combined efforts that lead to G2 accomplishment, but also the latter sequenced efforts of the long-term recovery team. The efforts of all component teams are necessary to reach superordinate goal attainment. Furthermore, the extent to which the efforts of the four teams are coordinated effectively plays a critical role in whether the superordinate MTS is realized.

The structure of a goal hierarchy is specific to each MTS, but some general statements can be made. All MTS goal hierarchies have at least two goal levels, but frequently more. Goal interdependence increases as one moves up the hierarchy as higher-level goal accomplishment depends, in part, on the accomplishment of lower-level goals. In other words, component teams may work independently towards lower-order goals, whereas higher-order goals require the coordinated efforts of multiple teams. The hierarchy apex represents the superordinate goal and rests on the accomplishment of all lower-order goals. More often than not, time will coincide with the level of the goal, such that larger tasks, and tasks that require the integrated actions of multiple teams, are more likely to be

longer-term goals. In addition, goal priority, the relative valence or importance assigned to goals in the system must be clarified. This is especially important within an MTS context because of its hierarchical goal structure. To complicate matters further, recall that all component teams are responsible for accomplishing multiple goals. Some of these may be linked with one set of teams in the hierarchy in a very short-term time frame and must be worked on in an intensive fashion, whereas other tasks may be liked sequentially with other teams' efforts and have a much longer time frame. Still other efforts may have to be directed toward activities that are outside the realm of a given MTS initiative but still must be performed in a timely and high-quality fashion (and may even be part of some other MTS).

Our notion of a goal hierarchy is not unique in organizational sciences. For example, March & Simon (1958) argued that general organizational goals serve as the starting point for the construction of means–ends chains that involve: '1) starting with the general goal to be achieved, 2) discovering a set of means, very generally specified, for accomplishing this goal, 3) taking each of these means, in turn, as a new subgoal and discovering a set of more detailed means for achieving it, etc.' (p. 191). Accordingly a hierarchy of goals is established whereby each level is '... considered as an end relative to levels below it and as a means relative to the levels above it. Through the hierarchy structure of ends, behavior attains integration and consistency, for each member [team] of a set of behavior alternatives is then weighted in terms of a comprehensive scale of values – the "ultimate" ends' (Simon, 1976: 63). In short, Collins (1975: 316) suggested that this organizational structure is best described 'as a nested set of plans for action.' This thinking is also embedded in the logic of management-by-objectives (MBO) schemes whereby top management first develops the goals for the company as a whole. These goals set the framework for the next layer of management, who define the goals for their divisions in support of the overall company goals. This goal-setting process cascades down the organization so that all managers work with their employees to create goals at every level of the organization in support of the overarching organizational goals. The goals link the layers of the organization together in an MBO system (Carroll & Tosi, 1973).

Embracing this hierarchical network of goals framework, the effectiveness of an MTS can be assessed on a macro level by superordinate goal accomplishment, as well as at more micro level by evaluating goal accomplishment rates of component teams and nestings of teams. Unlike the MBO system that requires challenging goals to be set with employee participation, MTS component team goals can be specified at any level (e.g., by executive teams or leaders, or more participatively by component team members) as long as there is goal acceptance at all levels (Locke & Latham, 1990).

Sources of Goal Hierarchies

So where does the underlying nature of a goal hierarchy come from? We submit that the predominant MTS technology drives the development and maintenance of a goal hierarchy. By technology we are referring to the more encompassing term employed in the organizational sciences literature rather than the more colloquial use of the term. More specifically, Hulin and Roznowski (1985: 47) define technology as 'the physical combined with the intellectual or knowledge processes by which materials in some form are transformed into outputs used by another organization or subsystem within the same organization.' In other words, we argue that the nature of how work gets accomplished within and between MTS teams articulates their operative goal hierarchy and should be revealed by a thorough team task analysis (see Tesluk et al., 1997). The interdependencies between teams may stem from an inherent demand for coordination from task requirements to simply routinized modes of informal communication. In any case, this hierarchy of goals drives the functioning of the MTS. We should add at this juncture a caveat in that our use of the term technology does not encompass the nature of how work flows within or between teams, which we see as a separate issue and discussed earlier in terms of alternative work processes (cf. Saavedra et al., 1993; Thompson, 1967; Van de Ven & Ferry, 1980).

Component teams operate in work settings where they are typically confronted with multiple and sometimes conflicting lower-order goals that must be managed for MTS goal attainment. MTS leadership is often tasked with developing a framework for goal prioritization in accordance with higher-order MTS goals and communicating this framework to component teams. MTSs place a premium on the mechanisms through which lower-order goals get aligned in consideration with superordinate goal attainment. One central role of leadership is to facilitate horizontal and vertical integration of MTS goals and related activities. In this manner, a collective process can evolve in an MTS via the goal hierarchy, even if component teams are oriented towards different proximal goals. This is not to say, however, that goals are derived strictly from top-down directives or emanate direct from the task environment. Teams may very well develop informal norms, working relationships, and other liaisons that take on the features of more formal prescribed goals and help to link activities and contribute to higher-order goal attainment.

Cooperative Goal Structure

A defining characteristic of nested goal hierarchies is that the interconnected network of team goals that support the larger MTS mission are cooperatively linked at a higher level in the network. In other words, component teams perceive that their goals are positively related, such that progress towards their proximal goal facilitates other teams' chances at reaching their goals, and vice versa. In Deutsch's (1983) theory of cooperation, he states that cooperative goal interdependence directly affects members' behaviors. Those with cooperative goals assist others in performing effectively to reach their goals, communicate more accurately and freely, and support each other, even if in so doing they must channel efforts away from accomplishment of their proximal goals. It is the realization that the individuals (or teams) are linked together in a larger system, and that the effectiveness of that larger system is of utmost importance, that enables individuals (and component teams in an MTS) to best allocate their resources.

Much of the empirical testing of cooperation theory is at the group level of analysis, yet Deutsch assumed that goal interdependence was just as important for intergroup relations because of the need for organizational groups to communicate, coordinate, exchange resources, reduce competition, and manage conflicts. Researchers have speculated that groups committed to their own (proximal) goals have trouble coordinating with others (Tjosvold, 1984), even when their goals are related. MTS goal relationships foster intergroup information exchange, interteam trust, support and reliance, and task commitment (Guzzo & Shea, 1992). One critical function of a cooperative goal structure is to synchronize interteam processes. The existence of superordinate goals integrates component team processes and outcomes by providing a direction and structure for collaboration. Organizations often expect individuals to work cooperatively, yet rewards are based on individual performance, thereby reinforcing competitive goals. Effective MTSs have component teams that not only work in a nested goal hierarchy, but also have awareness of the cooperative nature of proximal goals and avoid mixed messages (e.g., individual- or component-team-based pay incentive systems) that derail the cooperative goal structure.

In sum, MTSs use goal interdependence to generate cooperative cultures that enhance processes such as interteam coordination and communication. Superordinate goals give rise to the MTS processes that foster integration and coordination of the processes that occur in component teams. In turn, cooperation influences both MTS processes and outcomes.

MTS TIMING/PHASES OF PERFORMANCE

In this section we explain how temporal influences overlay MTS goal hierarchies and impact MTS level processes and goal attainment. Unlike our running example, many MTSs are subsumed within organizations and receive their superordinate goal from them. MTSs are created by organizations to handle time-sensitive demands imposed by a turbulent environment. Thus, their purpose is more proscribed than that of larger organizations, directing our focus to the effects of time on MTS goal attainment. Other MTSs, such as the ER example that we have elucidated, are formed to deal with more socially or community-based needs. Below, we discuss temporal patterns in goal-related MTS performance requirements to draw attention to the necessity of planning and pacing collective activities in order to accomplish goals. Recall that in our earlier discussion of goal hierarchies, we defined goals as specifying some amount of work to be completed within a given time frame and quality standards. The environments in which MTSs operate, along with the team interdependence requirements for goal attainment, impose temporal constraints on the goals and the larger goal hierarchy. A major challenge of the MTS is the temporal alignment of goal hierarchies with environmental pressures.

MTS component teams are interdependent and must integrate their efforts both within and across teams. Figure 15.5 depicts our example MTS component teams performing a sequence of interdependent goal-directed activities. Note that the fire-fighter and EMT teams work simultaneously and collaboratively initially, and the result of their joint efforts (i.e., the stabilized victim) becomes the starting point for the surgery and recovery teams. The heavy reliance on between team coordination in MTSs mandates that teams must synchronize their efforts in accordance with goal accomplishment. All goals have a temporal component in the form of an explicit or implicit time limitation or scope. The pace of performance is driven, at least in part, by the time demands conveyed by the goals (Latham & Locke, 1975). Thus, the rate and pattern of MTS coordination among component teams is driven in large part by the time constraints of the MTS goal structure. In turn, the hierarchical goal structure of the MTS drives the strategies, the between- and within-team interaction patterns, and performance over time. Teams must integrate their actions to meet the MTS coordination demands set by the overall MTS strategies for MTS goal accomplishment.

Critical Levers for MTS Effectiveness

Up to now we have defined MTSs, discussed their primary characteristics, including their interdependence requirements, the nature of their environments, and their goal hierarchies, and also discussed how they operate via a temporally based model of MTS effectiveness. However, there are a number of different processes that can exert influence on MTS effectiveness that have not yet been mentioned. In this section we discuss briefly four critical levers for MTS effectiveness: shared member mental models; leadership; information technology; and reward systems. These critical levers serve as intervening processes in the functioning of the MTS; effective implementation of each can facilitate overall system performance, and ineffective or the lack of implementation of each can detract significantly from an MTS's potential.

Shared Mental Models and MTS Effectiveness

The effectiveness of MTSs depends heavily upon how well the individual units coordinate their activities. An important determinant of such coordination is an understanding, held by the members of the MTS, of the MTS environment and the collective responses required by its contingencies. Several researchers have argued that, at the team level, effective coordination depends upon the emergence of a shared mental model, or common understanding among team members regarding expected collective behavior patterns during team action (Cannon-Bowers, Salas & Converse, 1993; Klimoski & Mohammed, 1994; Mathieu, Heffner, Goodwin, Salas & Cannon-Bowers, 2000). Well-developed mental models help individuals to process and classify information more efficiently,

MTS Sequence of Interdependent
Goal-directed Activities

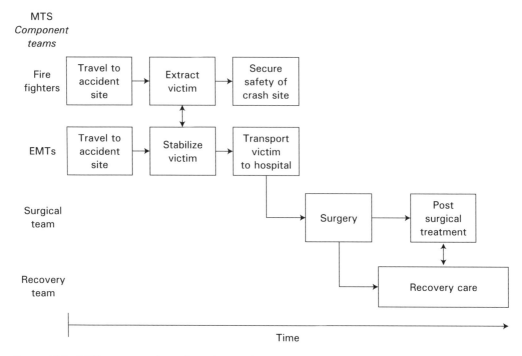

Figure 15.5   MTS sequence of interdependent goal-directed activities

and form more accurate expectations and predictions of task and system events (Cannon-Bowers et al., 1993; Rouse & Morris, 1986). When such models are shared among team members, they are better able to anticipate each other's actions and reduce the amount of processing and communication required during team performance. The result should be more effective team problem solving and performance (Klimoski & Mohammed, 1994).

The same effects apply at the MTS level; shared understanding among the teams in an MTS should promote more efficient collective information processing and coordinated actions. This raises an important question, though – what kinds of information must be shared in order to maximize effectiveness? Cannon-Bowers et al. (1993) suggested three kinds of knowledge structures in teams that we suggest have parallels at the MTS level. The first is a mental model that contains knowledge about the purpose of the team within the MTS and more specifically the task requirements related to this purpose (called a *task model*). This model includes task procedures, strategies, and information on how the task changes in response to environmental contingencies. In an MTS, each team is assigned a specific task in accordance with the functional interdependencies required by the larger

goal hierarchy. Team members need to have a common understanding of this task and how it fits within the larger goals of the MTS. Understanding this fit requires knowledge about the purposes and tasks of the other units in the MTS and how all of the different unit tasks are connected as part of a functional interdependency. Thus, in an ER MTS, the various teams each need to understand how their actions fit with those of the other units. They know, not only what they are to do, but also what other units are doing in anticipation of or in response to their own actions.

A second model represents knowledge about unit characteristics, including their task knowledge, abilities, skills, attitudes, preferences, and tendencies (called a *team model* by Cannon-Bowers et al., 1993). In planning their own activities, MTS units will make choices based on their understanding of the capabilities of their partnering units. If for example, there is a 'weak' unit, other units will have to compensate for this deficiency in their own actions. This kind of compensation requires a shared knowledge of each unit's resources that are brought to collective action. Indeed, Mathieu et al. (2000) demonstrated that to the extent that teammates shared both task and team mental models their team processes and ultimately team effectiveness were enhanced. A third model, and the one that is perhaps the most significant in terms of regulating collective action, encodes information with respect to the individual and collective requirements for successful interactions among team members. Cannon-Bowers et al. (1993) argued that to be effective, team members must understand their role in the task, which is their particular contribution, how they must interact with other team members, who require particular types of information, and so forth. Related to this, they must also know when to monitor their teammates' behavior, and when to step in, and help a fellow member who is over-loaded, and when to change his or her behavior in response to the needs of the team (p. 232).

When shared among team members, this model, called the *team interaction model*, is particularly crucial to effective *coordinated* action. Extrapolated to the MTS level, such interaction models define how individual units are to coordinate their responses with other units in the MTS. Thus, for example, in an ER MTS, each unit knows what it must do in relation to or interaction with the activities other units. Nurses and doctors wait for the actions of fire and EMT crews; the latter units complete their tasks at a trauma site, deliver patients to the ER, and then step aside. Doctors follow the activities of nurses, or vice versa. Members of each unit understand how and when the roles of their unit are coordinated with those of all other units. When this understanding is shared among MTS units, cross-team coordination and collective responses are more efficient and more adaptive.

These shared mental models, as we have described them, do not reflect specific situational contingencies. Converse and Kahler (1992) described another kind of shared knowledge structure, called a *strategic mental model* that connects unit capabilities and tasks with specific environmental requirements. They suggest that such mental models are 'comprised of information that is the basis of problem solving, such as actions to meet specific goals, knowledge of the context in which procedures should be implemented, actions to be taken if a proposed solution fails, and how to respond if necessary information is absent' (p. 6). These models are malleable, in that they are applied and modified in the context of dynamic environments.

In essence, strategic mental models are cue-contingency models operating at several levels. At a broad level, these models link MTS and unit missions with categories of collective responses. For example, in an ER MTS, the nursing unit has a certain mission that calls for sets of responses; the EMTs, having a different unit mission, has a separate set of responses. When the missions of these units change, their response sets change, accordingly. Thus, across an MTS, units share an understanding of their collective and singular missions, and how they are linked to specific environmental dynamics.

At a more specific task level, MTS units share strategic models that link specific environmental contingencies to specific MTS decision alternatives. In essence these can be described as 'if–then' representations, where MTS units understand that if a certain event or crisis occurs, each unit within the MTS needs to respond in certain ways, and in accordance with the actions of other MTS units. As such, these kinds of shared knowledge structures are crucial in promoting the ability of an MTS system to be effectively adaptive to the environment.

Cannon-Bowers et al. (1993) argued that shared mental models promote accurate expectations regarding the roles and behaviors of individual team members in concerted collective action. The same is true at the MTS level. Thus, the degree to which the team interaction and strategic mental models are (a) accurate and (b) shared among all MTS members should influence subsequent coordination of MTS units (Cannon-Bowers, et al., 1993; Klimoski & Mohammed, 1994). Also, if MTS members can make accurate predictions regarding subsequent collective actions, then team and MTS communication patterns should also be affected. That is, shared mental models promoted more efficient communication patterns and 'implicit coordination strategies' (Cannon-Bowers, et al., 1993) in MTS systems.

Leadership in MTSs

An important influence on the effectiveness of MTSs is the quality of leadership processes, both within and between teams. One perspective of leadership, the *functional leadership* approach, specifically addresses in broad terms the leader's relationship to the team (Fleishman, Mumford, Zaccaro, Levin, Korotkin & Hein, 1991; Hackman & Walton, 1986; Lord, 1977). This approach applies equally well to leadership in MTSs. As described succinctly by Hackman and Walton (1986, p. 75): 'The key assertion in the functional approach to leadership is that '[the leader's] main job is to do, or get done, whatever is not being adequately handled for group needs' (McGrath, 1962, p. 5). If a leader manages, by whatever means, to ensure that all functions critical to both task accomplishment and group maintenance are adequately taken care of, then the leader has done his or her job well.'

Broadly defined, this perspective suggests that individuals occupying leadership positions within and across an MTS are responsible for: (1) linking a team to the other units within the MTS; (2) linking the MTS as a whole to its external constituencies, stakeholders, and its larger external environment; (3) establishing strategic and operational directions for both team and MTS actions based on these linkages; and (4) facilitating within- and between-team operations to accomplish these directions. These activities suggest several critical distinctions regarding both team and MTS leadership. First, leadership includes boundary role activities linking: (1) teams to other teams within the MTS; and (2) the MTS as a whole to its broader environment (Katz & Kahn, 1978). For example, in an ER, the heads of the EMT teams and the emergency room teams are acutely attuned to the activities of their respective units and how they fit within the constellation of activities by other partnering units. They constantly monitor the environment of their respective units to know how to adapt the activities of their units accordingly.

Team and MTS leaders are typically responsible for learning developments and events within and outside of the MTS. Further, they are responsible for interpreting and defining environmental events. Zaccaro and Marks (1998) defined this as the leader's liaison role within teams. Because most team problems originate from their placement and role within the MTS, their diagnosis requires that leaders be attuned to developments and events within and outside of the MTS. Further, the team leader is responsible for interpreting tasks assigned to the team within the MTS, especially when such tasks change from routine practices as a function of changing environmental contingencies. While this role is important for team success (Ancona & Caldwell, 1988), it becomes absolutely critical within MTSs, as the tight linkages between teams require more extensive coordination. Accordingly, we would argue that communication among MTS unit leaders is more frequent and more closely linked than communications among unit leaders in more traditional organizational arrangements.

The second distinction is that leadership typically involves discretion and choice in what solutions would be appropriate in particular problem domains. MTS leadership is most necessary for problems in which multiple solutions are viable and/or requisite solutions need to be implemented in complex circumstances. Thus, when shifting environmental dynamics require nonroutine collective responses, MTS leaders set the directions for the MTS as a whole and for the each team within the MTS. The nature of these directions can be as broad as a 'vision' and as narrow as a task assignment. It can short-, medium-, or long-term in focus. Regardless of its scope, the direction established by the MTS leader provides the framework for the internal dynamics within the MTS. Further, effective MTS and unit leaders will establish directions for their units that keep them aligned with other units. Here, the liaison role becomes entwined with the direction-setting role leaders in an MTS. The understanding leaders have of the MTS's external context contributes to the goals and directions they establish for the MTS as a whole and for each team within it.

A major leadership requirement within MTSs is the careful coordination of activities both within and between teams. For example, within a team, leaders need to identify key individual resources, and to plan the correct timing, sequence, and level of individual actions based on these resources. They must carry out these activities in careful coordination with similar activities by leaders of other units within the MTS. Because of the intensity of connectiveness in an MTS, team leaders within an MTS probably spend a greater portion of their time on interteam coordination than team leaders in more traditional organizational arrangements.

Given these distinctions, we are suggesting that, more than in traditional organizational arrangements, the influence of leadership in MTSs needs to be considered at two levels – within each team, and across the MTS as a whole. As noted, the nature of an MTS and its integrative goal hierarchy places a premium on both team coordination and team boundary spanning activities. A goal hierarchy that specifies varying degrees of interdependence defines the relationships between teams in an MTS. The nature of the interdependence (sequential, reciprocal, intensive) determines precisely how each of the teams needs to coordinate with the others. These interdependencies also contribute significantly to the delineation of member roles within each team.

The team performance requirements that emerge from these interdependencies suggest a number of critical leadership influences on the development and maintenance of successful within team coordination that can be characterized in stages (Kozlowski, Gully, McHugh, Salas & Cannon-Bowers, 1996). First, leaders need to facilitate the identification and combinations of contributions from team members that are most likely to lead to task success. This means developing their own awareness of what resources are available to the team, and planning how best to effectively combine and integrate these resources. The second step is for leaders to provide training, instruction, and opportunities for team members to learn the roles and tasks that need to be integrated into effective teamwork. The focus is not as much on learning individual roles, but rather on developing the interaction patterns necessary for team success. Finally, the team leader needs to facilitate the development of mechanisms that regulate and standardize these patterns. Ideally, once these are established, they are reinforced by the team members themselves as they monitor their joint actions.

These steps produce regulated coordination patterns within the team. However, they do not necessarily foster team adaptation; indeed, they may cause the team to become more rigid in its responses within a dynamic environment, particularly if these patterns were successful on earlier tasks. This form of responding can be fatal to the success of an MTS that needs to change their actions quickly in the face of altering environmental contingencies. When team complexity increases to the point where established interaction patterns are not sufficient, the team leader needs to reconsider team resources, recombine them into more viable coordination patterns, and reorient team regulation mechanisms (Kozlowski et al., 1996). Also, to promote team adaptation, team leaders need to promote the display of flexibility and creativity among team members, albeit within the confines of MTS task requirements and environmental conditions.

Similar processes operate for the MTS as a whole. A fundamental leadership requirement at this level is to specify the appropriate functional interdependencies, given the goal structure dictated by environmental and strategic task demands. This requires knowing the functional capabilities and resources of all the teams within the MTS and assigning them accordingly to a place within the goal hierarchy. MTS leaders also need to facilitate both the emergence of regulatory mechanisms across the MTS so that interteam actions are well coordinated, and the creation of norms that promote MTS flexibility and adaptability. Because of the functional interdependencies within the MTS goal structure and the need for the MTS as a whole to be maximally adaptive, within-team leaders will need to focus more heavily on the development of coordinative regulatory mechanisms, while the MTS leadership team will typically need to devote more of their work time ensuring system flexibility.

The functional interdependencies within most MTSs require that within-team leaders maintain several alignments in order to ensure a coherence and integration of multiteam goals and directions. First, there needs to be a vertical alignment and integration, where goals established for teams at multiple levels are congruent with the operating strategies established for the MTS as a whole. Likewise, the alignment of goals of teams linked in sequential or reciprocal interdependence needs to be carefully established and maintained. While MTS leaders establish this alignment, within-team leaders carry the responsibility for maintaining vertical integration during action phases. Horizontal goal integration is just as important. MTSs will fail if different teams that are linked intensively are pulling in alternate directions. Thus, multiteam leaders need to align the goals of their intensively linked teams, while within-team leaders need to monitor and maintain these alignments.

In sum, the coordination and boundary spanning requirements for successful MTS functioning are enormous and typically the key responsibilities of MTS leadership teams. The importance of leadership increases as: (1) units operate in increasingly dynamic and fluid conditions; and (2) units within a system are tightly linked in some functional interdependence. Both are conditions that define MTS functioning, and point to the critical influence of leadership on MTS effectiveness.

INFORMATION TECHNOLOGY AND MTS PROCESSES

It is almost trite to say that information technology (IT) is changing the way in which work is accomplished. This is particularly true, however, in MTS systems. As the nature of modern work becomes more and more knowledge driven, digital means of communication and coordination take on even a larger role in present-day organizations (Bikson, Cohen & Mankin, 1999). Whereas the use of computer-aided work functions were previously viewed as a competitive advantage, they are now quickly becoming a technological imperative if organizations are to survive. These new technologies are not only enabling work to be done faster, but they are qualitatively changing the fundamental manner in which work gets accomplished, particularly in MTSs.

Bikson et al. (1999) advanced four generic avenues whereby information technology could enhance team functioning: internal communications; external communications; task information, applications, and analytic tools; and feedback purposes. We would argue that these same processes would apply even more acutely to MTSs. For example, Bikson et al. (1999) submitted that action team effectiveness during transition phases would be enhanced by the use of simulations and modeling for engagements as well as the use of sophisticated systems for tracking resources and other inputs. During engagements, Bikson et al., argued that information technology facilitated the communication among team members and between teams, as well as better coordinated the rapid deployment of resources when needed.

For example, Imperato (1999) describes how the introduction of computer-aided design (CAD), manufacturing (CAM), and engineering (CAE) changed the fundamental way that Ford's Product Development System (PDS – which we would characterize as an MTS) operated. In the previous design, the PDS would require over 200 custom-made prototypes to be constructed to test the impact of various design alternatives. The process was extremely expensive, took over 55 months to complete an average cycle, and stifled creativity. With the introduction of a sophisticated CAD/CAM/CAE system, design engineers from different functional areas could simultaneously introduce modifications to a master virtual (i.e., digital) prototype off-line, their contributions could be submitted and integrated digitally, and the average cycle time was reduced to approximately 24 months. What is important to note with this example is that the underlying nature of the functional interdependencies between units did not change (they were still highly process interdependent in terms of design modification implications). What the CAD/CAM/CAE system did, however, was to create slack time by disengaging design modification efforts from the design integration function, and then expediting the integration efforts when they did occur. This not only reduced cycle time and associated costs; it opened up avenues for engineers to try out innovative designs without imposing costly delay and testing repercussions. Kodak reaped similar benefits when they employed a CAD/CAM system to facilitate the coordination of an MTS created specifically to bring to market a disposable camera (Leonard-Barton, Bowen, Clark, Holloway & Wheelwright, 1998).

The need to rely on information technology is even more highly regarded when MTS teams never come face-to-face and must rely entirely on communicating technologies to coordinate their efforts (Mittleman & Briggs, 1999). Electronic collaboration tools such as audio and video conferencing, email, group decision support systems, group calendars and project management software can all help to minimize the coordination demands placed on MTSs. For example, real-time conferencing tools, whether they are audio, video, or simply an electronic chatrooms/whiteboards, enable more parties to be on-line and participating simultaneously. This is particularly beneficial during the critical transition phases. Real-time access to parts and/or service availability, instantaneous global communication systems, and on-line informative data streams have changed the nature of how MTSs get work accomplished during action phases. For example, a single military unit (tank, helicopter, or jet) equipped with the latest radar technology can travel slightly ahead of its peers, scan the battle space for enemy targets and literally assign dozens of targets to the internal weapons aiming systems on other allied vehicles, while being monitored simultaneously by a command-and-control team that has access to the same information. As a result, when the mass of allied units arrives on the scene, they can commence a simultaneously orchestrated attack on enemy positions that could never before have been realized using conventional fighting tactics and technology.

IT also enhances the role of feedback in MTS systems. Feedback is a multifaceted concept that not only includes knowledge of results that clarifies the magnitudes of performance gaps at any given point in time, but can also provide formative guidance and help to keep processes aligned. More so, feedback has a motivational component by virtue of its intrinsic value, and enables members to have more control over their environment (Kluger & Denisi, 1996). For example, Meyer (1998) submitted, 'The overarching purpose of a measurement system [which provides feedback] should be to help a team, rather than top managers, gauge its progress' (p. 52).' Sophisticated 911 tracking systems such as the one depicted in our emergency response example enable a communications specialist to track the positions of various emergency response vehicles along with knowledge of traffic congestion, hospital capabilities, and other needs. Consequently, the specialist can provide up to the moment briefs as to the best routes for the EMTs to take, or perhaps even divert them to a different hospital as circumstances change. Such feedback information would prove invaluable for realizing the MTS's ultimate goal, but should not necessarily be used as a performance index. Indeed, Meyer (1998) argued that 'many managers fail to realize that results measures like profits, market share, and costs, which may help them to keep score on the performance of their business, do not help a multi-functional team, or any organization [e.g., an MTS], monitor the activities or capabilities that enable it to perform a given process. Nor do such measures tell team members what they must do to improve their performance' (p. 57). Our point here, is that IT systems can enhance the feedback process and best enable component teams to perform their solo and joint activities, but that these systems should not be confused with those used to provide rewards. Rewarding MTS team members represents a different challenge to which we turn next.

MTSs and Reward Systems

MTSs present a unique challenge in terms of aligning rewards with performance. Several authors have submitted that in order to optimize overall effectiveness, human resource systems, and in particular compensation systems, must be aligned with organizational strategy and design (Gomez-Mejia & Balkin, 1989; Motemayor, 1996; Snell & Dean, 1994). Clearly one of the guiding principles for establishing such alignment is the extent to which work in the system is highly interdependent and the extent to which cooperation versus competition is valued (DeMatteo, Eby & Sundstrom, 1998). Previous research has found that team-based rewards positively influence performance when individuals' work is highly dependent on that of their teammates' (Saavedra, Earley & Van Dyne, 1993; Tjosvold, 1986; Wageman & Baker, 1997) and when the organizational culture values cooperation over competition among members (Kirkman & Shapiro, 1997; Morgenstern, 1995). However, DeMatteo et al. (1998: 161) submitted 'when work is designed so that teams must cooperate, rewards that reinforce individual team performance may increase competitive behavior across teams and decrease between-team cooperation.' In other words, team-based rewards my overly focus members' efforts on achieving proximal goals at the expense of the between-team cooperation that is critical for realizing superordinate goals (Gomez-Mejia & Balkin, 1989; Kay & Lerner, 1995). Because MTS designs place a premium on both within- and between-team cooperation, aligning formal reward systems becomes more complex.

It would appear as though the use of multitier and multifaceted compensation systems are most appropriate for MTSs. At a minimum, the alignment principle would likely suggest that MTS members' compensation should be based on a three-tier system that offers an individually linked base salary with incentives for both component team and MTS performance. Developing and managing such systems is difficult enough when all component teams are contained with the boundaries of a single organization, and even more challenging when they traverse such boundaries.

Most team-based compensation systems establish a portion of each member's compensation on the basis of individual attributes (Lawler, 1999). Traditionally this individual component has been based on factors such as member's educational background, the job he or she performs, tenure in the organization, and perhaps an individual incentive plans. However, recently there has been a call to shift the basis of this compensation facet to 'pay the person.' (Lawler, 1998). In other words, the individual component of an MTS compensation plan could be skill-based and reward individuals on the basis of how well prepared they are to operate in an MTS environment. Such emphases would go beyond traditional task-related knowledge, skills, and abilities, and include 'other characteristics' such as teamwork skills (cf. Stevens & Campion, 1994; Cannon-Bowers, Tannenbaum, Salas & Volpe, 1995).

Because MTSs are networks of interrelated team efforts, and both within and between team coordination and cooperation are essential, a delicate balance must be achieved if utilizing group-based rewards. On one hand, component team-based rewards must be salient enough to crystallize teamwork and to provide a direct 'line of sight' between members' actions and the rewards that they receive (Lawler, 1999). On the other hand, MTS members must not lose sight of the roles that their teams play in the larger system and should be compensated, at least in part, on how successfully the superordinate goal is realized. In other words, some portion of members' incentive compensation should be linked to how well they achieve proximal component team goals, whereas some portion should be linked to the success of the system. We submit that the relative apportion of the incentives should be guided by the nature of the MTS goal hierarchy. Specifically, to the extent that a component team has relatively few tight linkages with other teams in the system (i.e., is on the periphery of an MTS), their incentive pay should be weighted more heavily on the extent to which they meet their proximal goals. Conversely, to the extent that a component team is tightly intermeshed with others in the MTS, its incentive compensation should be weighted more heavily toward MTS bases. This could very well lead to different MTS component teams operating under differing

incentives ratios – each reflecting their relative role in the goal hierarchy.

While a multitier compensation program appears optimal for MTSs, we do not wish to imply that the nature of financial rewards must be uniform across the three bases. Indeed, we would anticipate that individually keyed compensation would be best administered in terms of salary bands commensurate with having developed various KSAOs (Knowledge, Skills, Abilities, and Other). Movement within such bands could be responsive to more traditional indices such as educational background and tenure with the organization. Team-level incentive compensation would likely be best awarded in terms of performance-based bonuses. Here performance would be evaluated in terms of proximal goal accomplishment as specified by previously agreed-upon performance standards. Notably, this would constitute *within-organizational* comparisons and be evaluated in an absolute sense (i.e., against performance standards rather than the performance of others). Finally, MTS-based performance incentives would likely come in the form of profit sharing, stock options, and other *externally* keyed indices.

Measures of performance(s) would also have to be scaled appropriately for such a multitiered system to be effective (Lawler, 1999). The skill-based individually keyed portion should have specified hurdles (e.g., having completed formalized or on-the-job training programs) and have performance evaluation systems that are both accurate and perceived to be fair (Lawler, 1999). Team-based evaluations could be tied to a variety of indices, but measures such as time to completion, performance levels, percentage of wasted materials, etc., could be employed depending on the nature of the workteam performed. 360 degree evaluation and feedback systems could also be utilized as long as care is taken to select raters who are familiar with each team's performance (the MTS goal hierarchy should provide a guide as to which teams are best positioned to evaluate the performances of which other teams). Because MTSs often operate in fluid and dynamic environments, customers and other sources of information outside of the MTS may offer unique perspectives and particularly sensitive sources of feedback.

Assessments of MTS-level performance will likely best employ external indices such as profits, return on investments, market share, and so forth. Benchmarking against previous MTS-level performance offers a useful ipsative measure for gauging continuous improvement efforts, and benchmarking against other similar MTSs (or other forms of collectives) provides a useful normative referent. Regardless of the specific algorithm and measures utilized to implement a multitiered system, however, two keys to its success will be the extent to which members are involved in the development of the system, and the extent to which the MTS maintains open communication about compensation elated matters. The participation feature helps to ensure that members are committed to the system, whereas the communication feature helps to minimize feelings of inequity that naturally arise in multitier systems.

Finally, we should note that reward issues become even more complicated when the MTS contains teams that come from different organizations. For example, the compensation programs of the police, fire fighter, EMT, 911 operators, and hospital-based teams are at best loosely coupled and at worst totally unrelated. Yet, rewarding teams for executing interfaces effectively is at a premium. We would suggest that members of component teams in such systems could still be rewarded in the context of two-tier systems that compensate individual skill development and team performance on proximal goals that are within their purview. We would then advocate that cross-organizational coalitions be formed that can develop and allocate rewards for effective MTS level performance. Such rewards would likely be in a form other than traditional bonuses or profit sharing, but may be valued by members nonetheless. 360 type feedback and evaluation systems could be employed to distinguish which teams of a certain 'type' contributed most effectively to overall MTS performance. For example, the 911-operators and hospital-based teams could perhaps vote on which fire-fighting and EMT units performed most effectively and delivered patients to the hospital in the most timely and stable conditions. If we can adapt an analogy from the world of sports to MTSs, professional athletes often claim that the most cherished awards that they receive are those that are voted on by opposing players. We would submit that component teams who feel recognized by their peers as among the best of 'their kind' would feel quite motivated regardless of whether the award constitutes a large financial windfall. Finally, cross-organizational MTSs may be able to benchmark their performance against other similarly structured MTSs. Towns and cities take great pride if their emergency response MTSs are recognized as among the best regionally or nationally. Here again, the recognition and intangible rewards are likely to be powerful additional motivational components if the remainder of the compensation systems is seen as equitable.

CONCLUSIONS

A primary goal of this chapter was to persuade readers that MTSs are important collectives that have yet to be formally recognized or studied in organizational sciences. Our intention was to spark interest and discussion about MTSs, so that researchers and practitioners will focus more on MTSs within and across organizations. Another important goal of this chapter was to set the theoretical stage for a program of empirical research on MTSs. One of the first directions for such an initiative would be to examine the underlying principles of MTSs, such as the impact of various forms of functional interdependencies on MTS processes and effectiveness. A related effort would be to create taxonomy of types of MTSs and how they operate. In a more applied vein, research could be directed toward illuminating which interventions (e.g., training, leadership, IT systems) best influence MTS processes and outcomes, and how such efforts combine with those of more traditional ones targeted at different levels (e.g., team training, organizational development). We believe that there is fertile ground to be mined, both in terms of theoretical richness and applied implications, by adopting this 'team-of-teams' approach and recasting our inquiry to focus on MTSs. In our personal observations of multiple interdependent teams working toward a shared objective, many if not most of the performance problems were due to between-team communication and coordination problems. We believe that focusing on MTS-related themes offers much value added beyond currently available approaches.

ACKNOWLEDGMENT

The preparation of this chapter was supported in part by the Air Force Office of Sponsored Research (AFOSR), Contract #F49620-98-1-0278). The opinions expressed herein, however, are strictly ours.

REFERENCES

Alper, S., Tjosvold, D., & Law, K.S. (1998). Interdependence and controversy in group decision making: Antecedents to effective self-managing teams. *Organizational Behavior and Human Decision Processes*, *74*, 33–52.

Ancona, D.G., & Caldwell, D.F. (1988). Beyond task and maintenance: Defining external functions in groups. *Group and Organizational Studies*, *13*, 468–494.

Ancona, D.G., & Caldwell, D.F. (1992). Bridging the boundary: External activity and performance in organizational teams. *Administrative Science Quarterly*, *37*, 634–665.

Ashby, W.R. (1968). Variety, constraint, and the law of requisite variety. In W. Buckley (Ed.), *Modern systems research for the behavioral sciences: A Sourcebook* (pp. 129–136). Chicago: Aldine.

Austin, J.T., & Vancouver, J.B. (1996). Goal constructs in psychology: Structure, process, and content. *Psychological Bulletin, 120*, 338–375.

Bandura, A. (1991). Social cognitive theory of self-regulation. *Organizational Behavior and Human Decision Processes*, *50*, 248–287.

Bandura, A., & Wood, R. (1989). Effect of perceived controllability and performance standards on self-regulation of complex decision-making. *Journal of Personality and Social Psychology*, *56*, 805–814.

Bikson, T.K., Cohen, S.G., & Mankin, D. (1999). Information technology and high-performance teams: Creating value through knowledge. In E. Sundstrom (Ed.), *Supporting work team effectiveness* (pp. 215–245). San Francisco: Jossey-Bass.

Campion, M.A., Medsker, G.J., & Higgs, A.C. (1993). Relations between work group characteristics and effectiveness: Implications for designing effective work groups. *Personnel Psychology*, *46*, 823–850.

Cannon-Bowers, J.A., Salas, E., & Converse, S.A. (1993). Shared mental models in expert team decision making. In N.J. Castellan, Jr. (Ed.), *Current issues in individual and group decision making*. Hillsdale, NJ: Erlbaum.

Cannon-Bowers, J.A., Tannenbaum, S.I., Salas, E. & Volpe, C.E. (1995). Defining competencies and establishing team training requirements. In R.A. Guzzo, E. Salas, & Associates (Eds.) *Team effectiveness and decision making in organizations* (pp. 333–380). San Francisco: Jossey-Bass.

Carroll, S.J., & Tosi, H.L. (1973). *Management by objectives: Applications and research*. New York: MacMillian.

Catrambone, R. (1996). Generalizing solution procedures learned from examples. *Journal of Experimental Psychology: Learning, Memory, and Cognition*, *22*, 1020–1031.

Catrambone, R. (1998). The subgoal learning model: Creating better examples so that students can solve novel problems. *Journal of Experimental Psychology: General*, *127*, 355–376.

Collins, R. (1975). *Conflict, Sociology: Toward an explanatory Science*. New York: Academic Press.

Converse, S.A., & Kahler, S.E. (1992). *Shared mental models, team performance, and knowledge acquisition*. Paper presented at the annual meeting of the American Psychological Association, Washington, DC.

DeMatteo, J.S., Eby, L.T., & Sundstrom, E. (1998). Team-based rewards: Current empirical evidence and directions for future research. *Research in Organizational Behavior*, *20*, 141–183.

Dess, G.G., & Beard, D.W. (1984). Dimensions of organizational task environment. *Administrative Science Quarterly*, *28*, 274–291.

Deutsch, M. (1983). Conflict resolution: Theory and practice. *Political Psychology*, *4*, 431–453.

Dutton, D.J., & Dukerich, D.M. (1994). Keeping an eye on the mirror: Image and identity in organizational adaptation. *Academy of Management Journal*, *34*, 517–554.

Early, P.C., Wojnaroski, P., & Prest, W. (1987). Task planning and energy expended: Exploration of how goals influence performance. *Journal of Applied Psychology Journal of Applied Psychology*, *72*, 107–114.

Fandt, P.M., Cady, S.H., & Sparks, M.R. (1993). The impact of reward interdependency on the synergogy model of cooperative performance: Designing an effective team environment. *Small Group Research*, *24*, 101–115.

Fleishman, E.A., Mumford, M.D., Zaccaro, S.J., & Levin, K.Y., Korotkin, A.L., & Hein, M.B. (1991). Taxonomic efforts in the description of leader behavior: A synthesis and functional interpretation. *Leadership Quarterly*, *2*, 245–287.

Gladstein, D. (1984). Groups in context: A model of task group effectiveness. *Administrative Sciences Quarterly*, *29*, 499–517.

Gomez-Mejia, L.R., & Balkin, D.B. (1989). Effectiveness of individual aggregate compensation strategies. *Industrial Relations*, *28*, 431–445.

Guzzo, R.A., & Shea, G.P. (1992). Group performance and intergroup relations in organizations. In M.D. Dunnette, & L.M. Hough (Eds.), *Handbook of industrial and organizational psychology* (2nd ed., Vol. 3, pp. 269–313). Palo Alto, CA: Consulting Psychologists Press.

Hackman, J.K., & Morris, C.G. (1975). Group tasks, group interaction processes, and group performance effectiveness: A review and proposed integration. In L. Berkowitz (Ed.), *Advances in experimental social psychology* (Vol. 8, pp. 45–99). New York: Academic Press.

Hackman, R. (1990). *Groups that work and those that don't*. San Francisco, CA: Jossey-Bass.

Hackman, J.R., & Walton, R.E. (1986). Leading groups in organizations. In P.S. Goodman, & Associates (Eds.), *Designing effective work groups*. San Francisco: Jossey-Bass.

Hambrick, D.C. (1981). Environment, strategy and power within top management teams. *Administrative Science Quarterly*, *26*, 253–276.

Hawley, A.H. (1968). Human ecology. In D.L. Sills (Ed.), *International encyclopedia of the social sciences*. New York: Macmillan.

Hitt, M.A., Keats, B.W., & DeMarie, S.M. (1998). Navigating in the new competitive landscape: Building strategic flexibility and competitive advantage in the 21st century. *Academy of Management Executive*, *12*, 22–42.

Hoffman, R.G., Kaplan, I.T., & Metlay, W. (1994). Effects of goal setting and feedback on social loafing. Paper presented at the Ninth Annual Conference of the Society for Industrial and Organizational Psychology, Nashville, Tennessee, April.

Hulin, C.L., & Roznowski, M. (1985). Organizational technologies: Effects on organizations' characteristics and individuals' responses. In L.L. Cummings, & B.M. Staw (Eds.), *Research in Organizational Behavior*, *7*, 39–85.

Imperato, G. (1999). SDRC wants you to go faster. *Fast Company*, 10 (October), 90–92.

Jauch, L.R., & Kraft, K.L. (1986). Strategic management of uncertainty. *Academy of Management Review*, *11*, 777–790.

Katz, D., & Kahn, R.L. (1978). *The social psychology of organizations* (2nd ed.). New York: John Wiley.

Kay, I.T., & Lerner, D. (1995). What's good for the parts may hurt the whole. *HR Magazine*, *40*(9), 71–77.

Keller, R.T. (1994). Technology-information processing fit and the performance of R&D project groups: A test of contingency theory. *Academy of Management Journal*, *37*, 167–179.

Kirkman, B.L., & Shapiro, D.L. (1997). The impact of cultural values on employee resistance to teams: Toward a model of globalized self-managing work team effectiveness. *Academy of Management Review*, *22*, 730–757.

Klimoski, R., & Mohammed, S. (1994). Team mental model: Construct or metaphor? *Journal of Management*, *20*, 403–437.

Kluger, A.N., & DeNisi, A. (1996). The effects of feedback interventions on performance: A historical review, a meta-analysis, and a preliminary feedback intervention theory. *Psychological Bulletin*, *119*, 254–284.

Kozlowski, S.W.J., Gully, S.M., McHugh, P.P., Salas, E., & Cannon-Bowers, J.A. (1996). A dynamic theory of leadership and team effectiveness: Developmental and task contingent leader roles. *Research in Personnel and Human Resources Management*, *14*, 253–305.

Latham, G.P., & Locke, E.A. (1975). Increasing productivity and decreasing time limits: A field replication of Parkinson's law. *Journal of Applied Psychology*, *60*, 524–526.

Lawler, E.E. (1998). *Strategies for high-performance organizations*. San Francisco: Jossey-Bass.

Lawler, E.E. (1999). Creating effective pay systems for teams. In E. Sundstrom (Ed.), *Supporting work team effectiveness* (pp. 188–214). San Francisco: Jossey-Bass.

Lawrence, P.R., & Lorsch, J.W. (1967). *Organization and environment*. Cambridge, MA: Harvard University Press.

Leonard-Barton, D., Bowen, H.K., Clark, K.B., Holloway, C.A., & Wheelwright, S.C. (1998). How to integrate work and deepen expertise. In J.R. Katenbach (Ed.), *The work of teams* (pp. 155–170). Boston, MA: Harvard Business School Publishing.

Locke, E.A. (1966). The relationship of intentions to level of performance. *Journal of Applied Psychology*, *50*, 60–66.

Locke, E.A., & Latham, G.P. (1990). *A theory of goal setting and task performance*. Englewood Cliffs, NJ: Prentice Hall.

Locke, E., Shaw, K.N., Saari, L.M., & Latham, G.P. (1981). Goal setting and task performance: 1969–1980. *Psychological Bulletin*, *90*, 125–152.

Lord, R.G. (1977). Functional leadership behavior: Measurement and relation to social power and leadership perceptions. *Administrative Science Quarterly*, *22*, 114–133.

March, J.G., & Simon, H.A. (1958). *Organizations*. New York: John Wiley.

Marks, M.A., Mathieu, J.E., & Zaccaro, S.J. (in press). A temporally-based framework and taxonomy of team processes. *Academy of Management Review*.

Marks, M.A., Zaccaro, S.J., & Mathieu, J.E. (2000). Performance implications of leader briefings and team interaction training for team adaptation to novel environments. *Journal of Applied Psychology*, *85*, 971–986.

Mathieu, J.E., & Button, S.B. (1992). An examination of the relative impact of normative information and self-efficacy on personal goals and performance over time. *Journal of Applied Social Psychology*, *22*, 1758–1775.

Mathieu, J.E., Heffner, T.S., Goodwin, G.F., Salas, E., & Cannon-Bowers, J.A. (2000). The influence of shared mental models on team processes and performance. *Journal of Applied Psychology*, *85*, 273–283.

McGrath, J.E. (1962). Leadership behavior: Some requirements for leadership training. Washington, DC: U.S. Civil Service Commission [Mimeographed].

McGrath, J.E. (1991). Time, interaction, and performance (TIP): A theory of groups. *Small Group Research*, *22*, 147–174.

Meyer, C. (1998). How the right measures help teams excel. In J.R. Katenbach (Ed.), *The work of teams* (pp. 51–64). Boston, MA: Harvard Business School Publishing.

Mittleman, D., & Briggs, R.O. (1999). Communication technologies for traditional and virtual teams. In J.R. Katenbach (Ed.), *The work of teams* (pp. 246–270). Boston, MA: Harvard Business School Publishing.

Montemayor, E.F. (1996). The evolution of strategic simplicity: Exploring two models of organizational adaptation. *Journal of Management*, *22*, 863–887.

Morgenstern, M.L. (1995). The board's perspective: Compensation and the new employment relationship. *Compensation and Benefits Review*, *27*, 37–44.

O'Leary-Kelly, A.M., Martocchio, J.J., & Frink, D.D. (1994). A review of the influence of group goals on group performance. *Academy of Management Journal*, *37*, 1285–1301.

Pritchard, R.D., Jones, S.D., Rother, P.L., Stuebing, K.K., & Ekeberg, S.E. (1988). Effects of group feedback, goal setting, and incentives on organizational productivity. *Journal of Applied Psychology*, *73*, 337–358.

Rouse, W.B., & Morris, N.M. (1986). On looking into the black box: Prospects and limits in the search for mental models. *Psychological Bulletin*, *100*, 349–363.

Saavedra, R., Earley, P.C., & Van Dyne, L. (1993). Complex interdependence in task-performing groups. *Journal of Applied Psychology*, *78*, 61–72.

Salas, E., Dickinson, T.L., Converse, S.A., & Tannenbaum, S.I. (1992). Toward an understanding of team performance and training. In R.W. Swezey, & E. Salas (Eds.), *Teams: Their training and performance* (pp. 3–29). Norwood, NJ: Ablex.

Sastry, M.A. (1997). Problems and paradoxes in a model of punctuated organizational change. *Administrative Science Quarterly*, *42*, 237–275.

Scott, W.R. (1987). The adolescence of institutional theory. *Administrative Science Quarterly*, *32*, 493–511.

Scott, W.R. (1998). *Organizations: Rational, natural, and open systems*. Saddle River, NJ: Prentice Hall.

Sherif, M. (1966). *In common predicament: Social psychology of intergroup conflict and cooperation*. Boston: Houghton Mifflin.

Simon, H.A. (1962). The architecture of complexity. *Proceedings of the American Philosophical Society, 106*, 467–482.

Simon, H.A. (1976). *Administrative behavior.* (3rd ed.). New York: Macmillan.

Snell, S.A., & Dean, J.W. (1994). Strategic compensation for integrated manufacturing: The moderating effects of jobs and organizational inertia. *Academy of Management Journal, 37*, 1109–1140.

Stevens, M.J., & Campion, M.A. (1994). The knowledge, skill, and ability requirements for teamwork: Implications for human resource management. *Journal of Management, 20*, 503–530.

Sundstrom, E., DeMeuse, K.P., & Futrell, D. (1990). Work teams: Applications and effectiveness. *American Psychologist, 45*, 120–133.

Sutcliffe, K.M. (1994). What executives notice: Accurate perceptions in top management teams. *Academy of Management Journal, 37*, 1360–1378.

Tannenbaum, S., Beard, R.L., & Salas, E. (1992). Team building and its influence on team effectiveness: An examination of conceptual and empirical developments. Issues, theory, and research in industrial/organizational psychology. In K. Kelley (Ed.), *Advances in Psychology, 82*, pp. 117–153.

Terborg, J.R. (1976). The motivational components of goal setting. *Journal of Applied Psychology, 61*, 613–321.

Tesluk, P.E., & Mathieu, J.E. (1999). Overcoming roadblocks to effectiveness: Incorporating management of performance barriers into models of work group effectiveness. *Journal of Applied Psychology, 84*, 200–217.

Tesluk, P., Mathieu, J.W., Zaccaro, S.J., & Marks, M.A. (1997). Task and aggregation issues in the analysis and assessment of team performance. In M.T. Brannick, E. Salas, & C. Prince (Eds.), *Team performance and measurement: Theory, methods, and applications.* Mahwah, NJ: Erlbaum.

Thompson, J.D. (1967). *Organizations in action.* New York: McGraw-Hill.

Tjosvold, D. (1984). Cooperation theory and organizations. *Human Relations, 37*, 743–767.

Tjosvold, D. (1986). The dynamics of interdependence in organizations. *Human Relations, 39*, 517–540.

Vallacher, R.R., & Wagner, D.M. (1987). What do people think they're actually doing? Action identification and human behavior. *Psychological Review, 94*, 3–15.

Van de Ven, A.H., & Ferry, D.L. (1980). *Measuring and assessing organizations.* New York: Wiley-Interscience.

Wageman, R. (1995). Interdependence and group effectiveness. *Administrative Science Quarterly, 40*, 145–180.

Wageman, R., & Baker, G. (1997). Incentives and cooperation: The joint effects of task and reward interdependence on group performance. *Journal of Organizational Behavior, 18*, 139–158.

Waller, M.J. (1999). The timing of adaptive group responses to nonroutine events. *Academy of Management Journal, 42*, 127–137.

Ward, G., & Allport, A. (1997). Planning and problem-solving using five-disc Tower of London task. *Quarterly Journal of Experimental Psychology: Human Experimental Psychology, 50*, 49–78.

Zaccaro, S.J., & Marks, M.A. (1998). Leader roles in organizational teams. In E. Sundstrom (Ed.), *Supporting work team effectiveness: Creating contexts for high performance.* San Francisco: Jossey-Bass.

16

Judgment and Decision-Making Research: Relevance to Industrial and Organizational Psychology

SCOTT HIGHHOUSE

Judgment and decision making is a highly interdisciplinary field that has flourished in recent years. This chapter was written with the objective of presenting an accessible treatment of modern judgment and decision making research, and stimulating ideas for decision research and application in the workplace. Special attention is given to topics that have historically been underrepresented in industrial and organizational psychology, including how people make risky decisions, when judgments and decisions are context-dependent, how feelings and emotions affect decisions, and how people make tradeoffs for tough choices. The chapter also presents a brief discussion of new methods for studying judgments and decision, and contrasts the behavioral decision making school with others schools such as naturalistic decision making and strategic decision making.

INTRODUCTION

I'm writing this manifesto to show that you can perform contrary actions at the same time, in one single, fresh breath. (Tristan Tzara, *Dada Manifesto of 1918*)

The last quarter of a century has witnessed an explosion of research on how people make decisions, and the study of Judgment and decision making (JDM) has emerged as a unique area of inquiry within psychology (Dawes, 1998). Modern JDM research has become well integrated into applied areas of psychology such as consumer, clinical, and forensic psychology, as well as other fields such as medicine, law, accounting, finance, and marketing. Industrial–organizational (I/O) psychology, however, has not been quick to embrace the findings from mainstream JDM. For example, even though one of the leading I/O psychology journals, *Organizational Behavior and Human Decision Processes*, is also one of the leading JDM journals,

the founding editor's hopes for cross-fertilization have never been fully realized (Naylor, 1984; Weber, 1998). Naylor commented,

I have been of the philosophical position that both constituencies (if I could get either to read the papers of the other) might indeed benefit! They have much to say to each other. I have even hoped that some sort of osmotic process of information exchange might take place, even if there was no intention to be exposed by either party. (1984: 2)

Indeed, a look at the directories for the Society for Judgment and Decision Making and the Society for Industrial and Organizational Psychologists reveals very little overlap in the memberships of the two organizations. This is despite the fact that there are a large number of topics in I/O that have strong judgment and decision-making components. For instance, I/O has been preoccupied throughout its history with the question of how best to assess and select employees who will be successful in the future, a seemingly natural fit with JDM's focus on making decisions under conditions of uncertainty. Other I/O topics with the potential for more JDM influence include job choice, performance evaluation and acceptance of feedback, organizational withdrawal and citizenship, compensation, strategic forecasting, and human resource planning.

I/O psychology, however, has gone its own way in studying how judgments and decisions are made in organizations. In some respects, I/O has been ahead of the pack. For example, advances in understanding judgment accuracy (see Sulsky & Balzer, 1988), along with contributions to the emerging area of naturalistic decision making (e.g., Cannon-Bowers & Salas, 1998; Hollenbeck, Ilgen, Tuttle & Sego, 1995), have made I/O an exception to the preoccupation with biases and errors that has historically characterized much of JDM research (see Funder, 1995, Orasanu & Connolly, 1993). On the other hand, I/O has clung tenaciously to the value-maximizing 'rational man' as a *descriptive* model of decision making, despite the beating this poor man has taken over the last 25 years. This is reflected in the continued widespread application of expected-value-based models, such as expectancy theory (Vroom, 1964) and image theory (Beach & Mitchell, 1990) to workplace issues (e.g., Harris & Greising, 1998; Klein, 1991; Lee, 1996; Stevens, 1998; Wanous & Colella, 1989).

Perhaps it is a difference in the dominant traditions of the two fields that has precluded more productive communication between them. I/O psychologists have traditionally concerned themselves with the things that make people different from one another. JDM's nomothetic approach, often favoring simple between-subjects experiments, may seem foreign or sterile to I/O researchers who prefer to use complex correlational procedures to examine data collected in organizations. Whatever the reason, there appears to be a gap between JDM and I/O research. One purpose of this chapter is to bridge this gap by providing an introduction to modern JDM research that is both accessible to and timely for I/O psychologists interested in decision making in organizations. I find JDM to be an enormously interesting and exciting field of study. It is composed of a wonderfully heterogeneous group of researchers, representing applied and basic interests from diverse fields. Because the area of JDM is so big, and the interests of its constituents are so varied, I have been highly selective (and not entirely representative) in my coverage of topics for this chapter (see Dawes, 1998, and Mellers, Schwartz & Cooke, 1998, for recent reviews). Special attention has been given to topics that I believe are relevant to I/O, but that have been underrepresented in the I/O literature.[1] I hope to stimulate ideas for decision-related research and application in the workplace. I seek most of all, however, to transmit a little of my excitement for JDM to the reader.

BACKGROUND

Many scholars of the history of decision-making research point to two papers published in the mid-1950s as marking the beginning of JDM as a field within psychology. The first was a review published in *Psychological Bulletin* by Edwards (1954) that exposed psychologists to important work on individual choice in economics and statistics (e.g., von Neumann & Morgenstern, 1944), showing its relevance to the psychology of choice. The second paper by Hammond (1955) was published in *Psychological Review* and showed how principles of perception (see Brunswick, 1956) were applicable to the study of judgment. Although one could point to other works at this time as being equally important and influential in the development of JDM (e.g., Luce & Raiffa, 1957; Meehl, 1954; Simon, 1955), the papers by Edwards (1954) and Hammond (1955) are notable for setting course two independent programs of research within JDM: *choice* and *judgment*.

Following the lead of Edwards (1954) and others working at the time on psychological perspectives on economic and statistical problems (see Thrall, Coombs & Davis, 1954), psychologists concerned with the choice program of research began studying how people make decisions involving uncertain probabilities. The gambling metaphor guided the thinking of these choice researchers, and behavior in the laboratory was compared to axioms of expected utility or models derived from psychophysics. Normative theories served as foils against which actual behavior could be compared. This provided choice researchers with a rich source of null hypotheses, and stimulated a lively program of research aimed at modeling decision-making behavior and cataloguing heuristics and biases (see Kahneman, 1991, for a review).

A second course was set by Hammond (1955) and others (e.g., Meehl, 1954) interested in how people transform information from the environment into judgments about the future. The gold standard for these researchers was not behavior prescribed by a normative theory, but the relationship between prediction and actual outcomes. Hammond (1955) showed how Brunswickian theory was relevant to the task of making inferences from incomplete and fallible cues in the environment. Whereas the gambling metaphor guided the thinking of choice researchers, the perception or 'lens' metaphor guided thinking in the judgment arena. According to this view, people are intuitive statisticians forced to make probabilistic judgments based on their perceptions of how environmental cues relate to one another. Studying judgment, therefore, required observing behavior in its natural environment, or in a laboratory situation that faithfully represents relevant aspects of the natural environment (Hammond, 1996).

Although ambitious attempts have been made to integrate choice and judgment research (e.g., Hammond, McClelland & Mumpower, 1980; Slovic & Lichtenstein, 1971), investigators in the two areas worked in relative isolation from one another for many years. This isolation probably stemmed partly from differences in methods of research, and also from fundamental differences in assumptions about human rationality (Jungermann, 1983). Whereas choice researchers have generally focused on deviations from rationality, judgment researchers have focused more on successful adaptation to the environment. This division is much less apparent in recent years, however, as many decision researchers have moved freely back and forth between choice and judgment. Goldstein and Hogarth commented on this present state of JDM research:

> JDM research is not 'paradigmatic.' There is no single, universally endorsed, overarching theoretical framework that researchers use to organize and guide their efforts. Rather, there are a number of schools of thought that identify different issues as interesting and deem different methods as appropriate. In addition, the situation is complicated by the fact that these schools overlap and interact. In fact, many researchers participate in several. (1997: 3)

In the following paragraphs, I review some of the major topics that have occupied JDM researchers in recent years. Along the way, I have also attempted to show how these topics relate to issues of concern for I/O psychologists. I begin by discussing one of the earliest concerns of JDM researchers – risky decision making.

DECISION MAKING UNDER RISK

Examining recent sales figures showing steady decreases in market share, the CEO of an historically dominant corporation believes the company has been relying on past successes for too long. Furthermore, he believes that the company needs to break out of old habits and start doing things differently, but wonders, 'Why won't people in this company take more risks?'

Cognitive Perspectives

Definitions of risk vary all the way from a focus on personal harm, found in medical and hazard research, to emphasis on possible opportunities, found in economic and business literatures. In JDM, the term 'risk' has often been used interchangeably with the term 'uncertainty.' Decision makers are said to be risk averse if they prefer a sure thing to an option whose outcome is uncertain (i.e., a risky option). Consider a newly hired sales employee,

named Susan; Susan is fresh out of college and is faced with a choice between a sure salary of $75,000 per year or a commission having 80% chance of earning $100,000 per year. If she is like most new college graduates, she will likely choose the sure salary. Susan would be considered risk averse with this choice, however, because the uncertain commission has a higher expected value (.80 × $100,000 = $80,000) than the sure salary of $75,000.

It has long been known that people do not operate on pure expected value. In fact, as early as 1738, Bernoulli noted that people use subjective utilities in place of dollars for these kinds of decision. Bernoulli's (1738/1954) hypothetical utility function proposes that subjective utilities are nonlinearly related to dollar amounts. For example, this decelerating utility function suggests that there is more psychological difference between $1000 and $2000 than between $10,000 and $11,000. This explains risk aversion such that, for instance, Susan will be willing to forgo the additional $25k offered with the commission in order to have the sure $75k salary. The incremental utility of going from $75k to $100k is no match for the excitement of going from $0 to $75k!

That people are generally risk averse is useful to know, but what may appear to present a problem for decision researchers is that people will occasionally exhibit risk-seeking behavior. People faced with options having negative consequences, for example, will often choose the riskiest option. Consider that irregularities were found in our friend Susan's tax statements. Her tax advisor gave her a choice between *paying* $7000 in taxes now, or trying a risky (albeit legal) alternative having an 80% chance of losing $10,000 and 20% chance of losing $0. In this situation, Susan chooses the risky option. Note, however, that this option has a more negative expected value (.80 × – $10,000 = – $8000) than the sure option (–$7000). Kahneman & Tversky (1979) would explain Susan's transformation from cautiousness to risk seeking as resulting from a tendency to evaluate outcomes differently whether one is looking to avert losses or add to gains. Figure 16.1 shows the hypothetical utility function proposed by Kahneman and Tversky's (1979) prospect theory.

Note that the upper right-hand (gain) quadrant is no different from the Bernoullian function, but that the lower-left (loss) quadrant reveals an accelerating utility function. People who have experienced gains are expected to view additional gains as having less incremental utility than people who have experienced losses. Thus, risk aversion is expected for gains, but risk seeking is expected for losses.

What does all of this have to do with decision making in organizations? For one, it suggests that organizational decision makers may take great risks to recoup real or perceived losses. Shefrin and Statman (1985) noted, for example, that financial

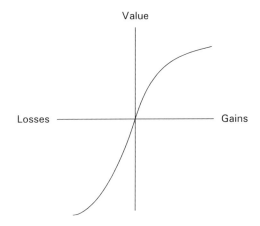

Figure 16.1   *A hypothetical value function in prospect theory. (Adapted from Kahneman & Tversky, 1979.)*

investors have a tendency to 'sell winners too early and ride losers too long.' In other words, when an investment has gained in value, investors often forgo future possible gains by getting out too quickly. Also, when an investment has fallen in value, investors will often hope for an upturn and risk further loss rather than accepting the certain loss (Moore, Kurtzberg, Fox & Bazerman, 1999). Returning to our example of the CEO who wonders why his employees avoid risk-taking behavior, prospect theory would suggest that employees of a company that has historically enjoyed a dominant market position would view risks from the perspective of a decision maker in the gain quadrant. Thus, these people would not be expected to view a change from the status quo as desirable.

The observed tendency to take unwarranted risks in order to recoup or avoid losses is related to the well-known sunk cost effect (Staw, Barsade & Koput, 1997). The sunk cost effect is a tendency to persist in an activity because of previously invested effort, time, or money. This violates the economically rational principle that people should ignore sunk costs and focus only on incremental costs when making future investment decisions. Staw (1981) argued that people fall prey to sunk costs in order to justify past decisions. Arkes (1996) suggested that another reason people fail to ignore sunk costs is that they overuse a 'don't waste' heuristic that serves them well in other life contexts. Arkes presented people with a vignette describing a company developing a material to be used in camping tents, only to find out that a competitor began marketing a superior product. People reported being willing to recommend abandoning the sunk cost in material development when they were told that the material could be sold to a roofer for $5000. People were not willing to recommend abandoning the

project, however, when the material was to be sold as scrap for $5000. In the latter instance, people preferred to honor the sunk cost rather than engage in a 'wasteful' act.

Whereas the sunk cost effect represents a tendency to persist in a state of action, a similar effect has been found to operate in cases of inaction. This phenomenon, labeled 'inaction inertia' (Tykocinski, Pittman & Tuttle, 1995), occurs when individuals fail to act on an opportunity after forgoing a more attractive opportunity earlier. For example, imagine decision makers in a corporation, considering acquiring a company when its stock price is low, deciding instead to wait. The next time the opportunity arises the company's stock price is higher, but the acquisition still makes economic sense. The decision makers decide, however, not to make the purchase. A series of studies have demonstrated this kind of behavior in a number of contexts (Butler & Highhouse, 2000; Hutzel & Arkes, 1997; Tykocinski et al., 1995). This research suggests that people view these (second) opportunities as losses, and forgo them in order to avoid experiencing regret.

Considerations of Motivation and Emotion

One notable feature of research on sunk costs and inaction inertia is the attention to the needs and desires of decision makers faced with risk. Lopes (1987) criticized traditional decision theoretic approaches to risk taking as being bereft of motivational and emotional concerns. According to Lopes:

> So it is with risky choice; after all the study and all the clever theorizing, we are left with a theory of risk taking that fails to mention risk. It also fails to consider (much less explain) the motivational and emotional factors that give risky choice its experiential texture: the hopes and fears that give us in due measure both purpose and pause. (1987: 263)

Drawing from work in achievement motivation, Lopes (1987) called for an understanding of risk taking that focuses on the approach/avoidance conflict inherent in risky decisions. She believed that risk taking could best be understood by considering the degree to which decision makers focus on the positive outcomes associated with risk (i.e., their hopes) versus the negative outcomes (i.e., their fears). Similar approaches to decision under risk have gained increasing attention in recent years (e.g., Dutton & Jackson, 1987; Higgins, 1997; Highhouse & Yüce, 1996; Kluger, Yaniv & Kühberger, 2000; March & Shapira, 1987, 1992), and have important implications for decision making in organizations. For example, March and Shapira (1987) interviewed executives about their approaches to risk taking for business decisions and found that the executives' decisions were influenced by the way their attention is focused on performance targets. According to the authors, 'For decision makers who are, or expect to be, below the performance target, the desire to reach the target focuses attention in a way that leads generally to risk taking. In this case, the opportunities for gain receive attention, rather than the dangers' (p. 1413). Highhouse and Yüce (1996) presented business students with a management in-basket exercise that emphasized either the opportunities or the threats associated with risk taking. The authors found significantly greater risk taking when the opportunities were emphasized than when the threats were emphasized, regardless of whether the cases involved recouping losses or adding to gains. These findings suggest that optimism and pessimism play important roles in the risk perception of organizational decision makers. Research is needed to investigate these effects on other risky decisions of interest to I/O psychologists, such as decision to leave an organization, or decision to engage in employee theft. Understanding the dispositions and organizational events that precipitate the viewing of risk taking as a threat versus an opportunity may allow us to better understand and predict risk-taking behavior.

INFORMATION PRESENTATION EFFECTS

The VP of human resources for a large corporation has instructed her staff to collect data on the impact of their training and staffing activities on organizational effectiveness. The staff collects various pieces of information intended to reflect intervention effect size (e.g., variance accounted for, bottom-line dollar estimates, subordinate perceptions, applicant pool growth, and user reactions). The VP wonders, 'How can I most effectively present this information to influence upper-management decision making?'

How information presentation influences decision making is a topic that has occupied social psychologists and human factors engineers for decades. More recently, a considerable body of research has emerged in JDM on information presentation effects on judgment and choice. One stream of research has been concerned with the *semantic framing* of options, while another stream has focused on the *display* of information in decision-making contexts. These are discussed in turn.

Semantic Framing

The way in which information is worded has long been known to influence people's perceptions. For example, Harris (1973) found that people asked 'How short was the basketball player?' estimated lower heights than people asked 'How tall was the basketball player?' Similarly, Loftus (1975) found that people asked 'Do you get headaches frequently?'

reported more headaches than people asked 'Do you get headaches occasionally?' More recently, researchers have identified numerous examples of how the wording of survey items can strongly impact self-reports of life satisfaction (Schwarz, 1999; Tversky & Griffin, 1991).

A special example of item-wording effects in decision making is research on framing effects. The term 'framing' has been most associated with tests of prospect theory by Tversky and Kahneman (1981). The framing of a dilemma as either a chance to recoup losses versus a chance to realize gains has been reliably demonstrated to influence people's risky choices (see Kühberger, 1998, and Levin, Schneider & Gaeth, 1998 for reviews). For example, when people are given a choice between a sure loss (e.g., eliminate 4000 of 6000 jobs) versus a small probability of no loss (e.g., 1/3 chance of keeping all 6000 jobs and 2/3 chance of eliminating all 6000), they tend to choose the long shot. However, when the same dilemma is framed as a choice between a sure partial gain (e.g., save 2000 jobs for sure) versus a small probability of a complete gain, people tend to opt for the conservative alternative (Bazerman, 1984; Zickar & Highhouse, 1998). This pattern of choice is predicted by prospect theory.[2] In addition to business settings, risky-choice framing has been demonstrated in educational (Fagley & Miller, 1987), financial (Highhouse & Paese, 1996), and health (Tversky & Kahneman, 1981) contexts.

Levin et al. (1998) noted that much confusion has been caused by researchers indiscriminately using the term 'framing' to describe very different types of semantic manipulations. Consider, for example, a study by Dunegan (1993) finding that members of an international company gave lower evaluations to a project team when it was described as having a 40% *failure* rate than when it was described as having a 60% *success* rate. Clearly, risk taking was not an issue in this study, and prospect theory sheds little light on the processes underlying this semantic manipulation effect. Levin et al. (1998) referred to this type of manipulation as *attribute framing*. This type of framing occurs when a single attribute within a given context is the subject of the framing manipulation. Examples of attribute framing in I/O contexts have included a study showing that layoff survivors evaluate companies more favorably when information emphasizes the criteria used to keep rather than dismiss employees (Brockner, Wiesenfeld & Martin, 1995), and a study showing that decision makers evaluate a placement program more favorably when its success rate is emphasized than when its failure rate is emphasized (Davis & Bobko, 1986).

Another type of framing effect identified by Levin et al. (1998) is *goal framing*. Goal-framing studies are commonly used in the persuasion literature, and involve the semantic manipulation of information to focus attention on obtaining a benefit or gain (positive frame) or on avoiding a harm or loss (negative frame). For example, Ganzach and Karsahi (1995) found that prospective credit card customers were influenced more by a message that emphasized losses from *not* using a card than by a message that emphasized the gains from using one. Note that both conditions promoted the same behavior in this study (i.e., using the credit card). Thus, the question in goal-framing studies is, which frame has the most persuasive impact for achieving the same end result? Although goal-framing studies have been rare in I/O psychology, Hazer and Highhouse (1997) found that some managers were more influenced by utility analysis information when the costs from not implementing a selection program (vs. the gains from implementing a selection program) were emphasized. Certainly this work could be extended to other I/O arenas concerned with influence and persuasion, such as leadership or recruitment.

Information Display

Aside from the effects of option wording on choice, there has been a recent flurry of activity in JDM on the effects of various physical information displays on decision making. This research is concerned with the format (e.g., frequencies vs. percentages; by attribute vs. by dimension) in which attribute information is presented to decision makers charged with making judgments and choices (e.g., Gigerenzer & Hoffrage, 1995; Kirkpatrick & Epstein, 1992; Klayman & Brown, 1994; Schkade & Kleinmuntz, 1994; Wells, 1992). Payne, Bettman and Johnson (1992) recommended that information display be used proactively to facilitate normatively appropriate decision making. This was the theme behind Russo's (1977) early work on consumer decision making in which he was able to induce supermarket customers to purchase products with lower prices by gathering unit price information and presenting it on a single list. Some recent work by Gigerenzer and Hoffrage (1995) suggested that people are capable of Bayesian reasoning when information is presented in frequency formats rather than probability statements. The authors asked a sample of experienced physicians to make inferences about the presence of a disease given a positive result for diagnostic tests. They found, for example, that physicians receiving mammography information in the probability format (e.g., probability of breast cancer is 1%) were much less likely to provide the estimate of cancer that is normatively appropriate than physicians receiving the information in the frequency format (e.g., 10 of every 1000 women have breast cancer).

Research along these lines may have important applications in I/O psychology. For instance, the practice of individual assessment usually involves having a third-party consultant collect and disseminate information about a job finalist. This information could include, for example, personality profiles, interview performance, and cognitive ability test results. How this information is reported back to the decision makers in the organization could have important effects on how the information is utilized by the client (see Highhouse, 1997). For example, Senter and Wedell (1999) presented information about apartments either by dimension (i.e., all apartments compared under one dimension) or by alternative (i.e., all dimensions compared under one apartment), and compared responses to a baseline of behavior under unconstrained search. Their results indicated that, when information was presented by dimension, the decision process was less effortful and closer to 'unconstrained' decisions than when information was presented by alternative. Additionally, Stone and Schkade (1991) found that presenting dimension values with words led to less compensatory processing than representing the values numerically, and Jarvenpaa (1990) found that information processing could be influenced by how graphic displays were organized (i.e., by dimension or by alternative). Research is needed to test the generalizability of these findings to organizational contexts, such as selection decision making or choosing among human-resource interventions.

Other lines of research on information display have focused on people's intuitive preferences for certain expressions of probability. For example, people have been found to strongly prefer to draw a bean from a bowl containing 10 winning beans and 90 losing beans than from a bowl containing 1 winning bean and 9 losing beans, even though they understand that the objective probability of winning is equal for the two bowls (Kirkpatrick & Epstein, 1992). A similar phenomenon was observed by Windschitl and Wells (1998) when people were faced with problems such as a raffle with 10 tickets:

Situation A: You hold 3 tickets and seven other people each hold 1.
Situation B: You hold 3 tickets and one other person holds 7.

In this case, Situation A would be preferred because you hold more tickets than any individual competitor (3-1-1-1-1-1-1-1). In Situation B you hold fewer tickets than your competitor (3-7). People faced with problems like this were much more likely to choose options in which they held the greatest number of chances for favorable outcomes compared to their individual competitors (i.e., Situation A). Research such as this suggests that people sometimes allow their intuitive preferences to override coldly rational information. A classic example of this was found by Ellsberg

(1961). Imagine a person is given a choice between two lotteries, each worth $100. To win either lottery, the person must choose a color (red or black) and draw one chip. The person wins if the chip matches the chosen color:

Lottery 1: 50 Red chips + 50 Black chips = 100 chips

Lottery 2: ?? Red chips + ?? Black chips = 100 chips

Given such a choice, people overwhelmingly favor Lottery 1 and will even pay to play the less ambiguous lottery – although people are indifferent to choosing red versus black chips in Lottery 2. This preference has been termed 'ambiguity aversion,' and has been demonstrated in cases where a person is faced with two options that appear to be equally probable, but differ on a second-order probability dimension such as reliability, degree of certainty, or information known (see Camerer & Weber, 1992).

Einhorn and Hogarth (1985) postulated that decision makers have a general tendency to be cautious when faced with ambiguity because they overweigh in their imaginations probabilities that are below some anchored value. Suppose, for example, a manager must decide between: (a) a quality management program that has been used extensively and has an error rate of 30%, and (b) a quality program that is new with an estimated error rate of 30%. According to Einhorn and Hogarth, decision makers will be more likely to imagine error rates above 30%, than below 30%, for the ambiguous program (option b). Thus, they prefer the quality management program with the known 30% error rate.[3] The authors recognize, however, that decision makers can come to live with ambiguity when contemplating loss. For example, a manager presented with a training program having a known 60% error rate might prefer a completely unknown error rate for an experimental program. Also, Highhouse (1994) found that people can be induced to seek ambiguity simply by making explicit a range of estimates around an anchor (e.g., the unknown error rate is estimated to be between 20% and 40%). Here, the decision maker is forced to consider probabilities *below* 30% along with probabilities above 30%, even though ambiguity remains constant across both examples. Kuhn (1997) found that such ambiguity seeking can be strengthened by framing the probability information differently. For example, the quality program could be presented in terms of success rates (70%) rather than error rates (30%).

That people have preferences for (or aversions to) some expressions of probability information may help us to understand reactions to information in other organizational contexts. For example, managers may devalue job candidates with missing application information, even when this information is beyond the candidate's control (see Highhouse & Hause, 1995). Job advertisements often use terms such as 'competitive salary' to indicate starting pay, but the ambiguity caused by this practice may lead to pessimistic inferences about starting pay (Yüce & Highhouse, 1998). Also, even though Cascio (1993) suggested that managerial decision makers will respond more favorably to utility analysis information presented in the form of confidence intervals, ambiguity research suggests that managers would prefer specific point estimates of utility. These competing predictions should be tested in the field.

DECISION MAKER HUBRIS

An organizational decision maker acquires a company that is on the verge of bankruptcy, believing that the company's problems were due to poor management. After successive years of investment without return, however, the decision maker decides to sell-off the unfortunate acquisition. The organizational decision maker wonders 'What was I thinking?'

Whereas ambiguity aversion is an example of a tendency toward pessimism in decision making, there are far more examples of a tendency toward unwarranted optimism (Taylor & Brown, 1988; Thompson, Armstrong & Thomas, 1998; Weinstein, 1980). People have been found to generally hold unrealistically positive views of themselves and their performance (Ashford, 1989; Greenwald, 1980). New entrepreneurs wildly overestimate the chances that their enterprises will succeed (Cooper, Woo & Dunkelberg, 1988), strategic planners grossly underestimate project completion times (Kahneman & Lovallo, 1993), and people generally believe that they will be happier, more confident, more hardworking, and less lonely in the future than their peers (Perloff, 1987).

Although there have been a number of explanatory mechanisms offered for decision maker hubris, including egocentric thinking and self-gratification (Perloff, 1987; Weinstein, 1980), one possible reason is that people desire personal control over their environment, and optimism implies a sense of control (Dutton, 1993; Thompson et al., 1998). Classic research by Langer (1975) showed that people act as if they can control outcomes in situations that are purely random. For example, people infer that they have greater control if they personally throw dice than if someone else does it for them. March and Shapira (1987) observed that this illusion of control may be especially strong among managers in organizations. The authors found that managers reject the notion of uncontrollable risk, preferring to view risk as a challenge to be overcome by skill and perseverance. Hayward and Hambrick (1997) suggested that this tendency is stronger for CEOs because they often receive credit for success even when such success could be objectively attributed to other sources.

Another form of decision maker hubris is *temporal discounting*. Research in behavioral decision making has suggested that decision makers consistently discount or devalue the significance of outcomes which are delayed, as opposed to outcomes that are close at hand (e.g., Kirby & Herrnstein, 1995; Loewenstein, 1988; Stevenson, 1986). Experimental evidence suggests that people discount both future losses and future gains. For example, Stevenson (1986) found that credit plans that demanded payment over a longer period of time were preferred over those that required payment over a shorter period of time, and Loewenstein (1988), found that people were indifferent between receiving $3000 today or receiving $4000 in one year. Recent evidence, however, suggests that losses lose their power to intimidate *faster* than gains lose their power to attract (Highhouse, Mohammed & Hoffman, in press; Shelley, 1994). Shelley found that a sample of MBA students became increasingly risk tolerant for lotteries as temporal distance of the outcomes increased, suggesting that decision makers choose to ignore the uncertainty inherent in opportunities but readily acknowledge the uncertainty inherent in threats. Such a tendency could dispose one to discount future negative events and engage in bold forecasting.

Certainly, human illusions of control and well-being may reflect a healthy adaptation to an uncertain world (Taylor & Brown, 1988). Unwarranted optimism, however, may keep people from taking appropriate measures toward defending against or preparing to cope with future negative events. An important agenda for I/O research, therefore, would seem to be to identify methods for tempering organizational hubris. Some recent research has suggested that people will abandon unrealistic optimism when self-relevant feedback is close at hand (Shepperd, Ouellette & Fernandez, 1996). In contrast, Byram (1997) found the tendency to underestimate task completion times (i.e., the planning fallacy) to be highly resistant to debiasing techniques.

THINKING AND DECIDING

An organization has two finalists for a plant manager position. The candidates have different strengths and weaknesses, but are overall quite comparable. The selection committee is split over which finalist should be made an offer, so it decides to continue searching. After the two finalists accept positions elsewhere, the committee wonders 'Why did we let them get away?'

Although thinking and deciding seem to be complementary activities, as the above situation illustrates, thinking over decisions can have its costs as well as its benefits. Below, I discuss research that has examined the sometimes paradoxical relation between thinking and deciding.

Thinking Too Little

Much of the decision-making literature over the years has focused on problems encountered by decision makers as a result of thinking too little about the problem at hand. Much of this research has been conducted under the 'heuristics and biases' rubric (Kahneman, Slovic & Tversky, 1982). A heuristic is a kind of cognitive shortcut that allows the decision maker to expend a small amount of effort to make otherwise taxing decisions. For example, the *representativeness* heuristic involves making judgments about likelihood based on the degree to which a situation resembles other situations ('this job candidate has a similar life history to mine and I am successful – so this person will also be successful'). Another heuristic, called *availability*, involves making estimates based on instances easily available in memory ('all of my friends want bigger cars, so I would estimate that most of the population would too'). Whereas heuristics typically lead to accurate judgments, along with conservation of effort, they can lead to systematic decision errors (Kahneman & Tversky, 1996).

Another area in which unsystematic thinking has been found to lead to decision errors is research on problem solving and reasoning (see Evans, 1989). A common paradigm used in this research is Wason's (1960) 2-4-6 task. Participants are presented with three numbers and asked to discover the rule behind the number string. In discovering the rule, however, the participant must generate three numbers, in response to which the experimenter indicates whether or not the participant-generated string is an instance of the rule. The participant is to stop the task when he or she believes that the rule has been discovered. Typically, the person generates exclusively confirmatory (rather than disconfirmatory) number sets and stops the task prematurely. A related phenomenon, termed 'pseudodiagnosticity' (Doherty, Mynatt, Tweney & Schiavo, 1979) involves failing to compare alternative hypotheses, instead comparing a single hypothesis against the evidence. For example, an organizational decision maker might observe that past managers hired without experience have been successful in the company. This could lead to the conclusion that experience is detrimental to successful leadership in that company. The problem with this reasoning is that lack of managerial experience is diagnostic of successful leadership only if the probability of successful leadership is higher for candidates with no experience than for candidates *with* managerial experience.

Heuristics and biases is one area of JDM that has received considerable interest from the I/O community. For example, Marlowe, Schneider and Nelson (1996) found evidence to suggest that use of the representativeness heuristic may be responsible for the infamous 'glass ceiling' between women and the executive suite. Also, evidence of confirmatory information search has been commonly found in the employment interview (see Dipboye, 1994). Hinsz, Kalnbach and Lorentz (1997) showed how the anchoring effect, a tendency to allow ostensibly irrelevant numerical anchors to bias judgments, could be used to establish challenging self-set goals. A line of research that is probably less familiar to I/O psychologists, however, is work showing that thinking too much can occasionally be harmful to decision making. This research is discussed next.

Thinking Too Much

Conventional wisdom suggests that good decisions are a product of careful and reasoned analysis. Indeed, decision researchers have commonly prescribed deliberate, objective reasoning for avoiding decision anomalies (e.g., Janis & Mann, 1977; Slovic, 1982). There is a growing body of literature, however, that suggests that thinking too hard about a judgment or choice can actually lead to poorer decision making (e.g., Dunning & Stern, 1994; Halberstadt & Levine, 1999; Shafir, Simonson & Tversky, 1993; Tetlock & Boettger, 1989; Wilson & Schooler, 1991). Wilson and Schooler (1991) noted that, just as automatic behavior can be disrupted when a person's attention is directed toward it, so can a decision be disrupted when a person is asked to reflect about the reasons for it. For example, Wilson and Schooler asked supermarket shoppers in one condition to analyze their reasons for liking different brands of strawberry jam. Shoppers in the other condition were simply asked to give their preferences without analyzing them. The authors found that shoppers asked to analyze their reasons expressed preferences that corresponded less well to those of experts (i.e., taste testers at *Consumer Reports*) than shoppers who did not analyze their reasons. Similarly, Halberstadt and Levine (1999) found that basketball experts asked to consider reasons why each team in a basketball tournament would do well or do poorly predicted fewer winners and predicted margins of victory that differed more from actual margins than experts explicitly told not to analyze their reasons. Dunning and Stern (1994) found that mock witnesses, presented with perpetrators from a photo lineup, were more accurate when judgments resulted from automatic recognition (e.g., 'his faced just "popped out" at me') than when judgments resulted from a process of elimination strategy. It seems that over-analyzing our decisions can be harmful when the

process of thinking interferes with our ability to focus on relevant information (Tordesillas & Chaiken, 1999). A natural extension of this research to the I/O area would be to investigate the effects of thinking too much on job choice. People searching for reasons to choose a job may give undue importance to job features that are unique to one job, rather than to features shared by the other job options (see, e.g., Dhar & Sherman, 1996).

Thinking too much has also been found to exacerbate errors such as dilution and decoy effects (Simonson, 1989; Tetlock & Boettger, 1989). Dilution occurs when people fail to ignore plainly nondiagnostic information in their judgments about others. For example, Nisbett, Zukier and Lemley (1981) found that decision makers, charged with making predictions about a student's grade point average (GPA), made strong predictions based on knowledge about the number of hours the student studied per week. However, these decision makers dramatically tempered their GPA predictions upon receiving information that was clearly nondiagnostic (e.g., the number of houseplants the student kept). Tetlock and Boettger (1989) found that dilution effects were magnified for people made accountable for their decisions, compared with people who did not have to justify their decisions. The authors argued that accountability causes decision makers to form more complex impressions of evidence, integrating irrelevant information into their cognitive representations of the problem.

Like the dilution effect, Simonson (1989) found that the decoy effect was even stronger for decision makers asked to justify their choices. Decoy effects occur when an inferior option (i.e., a decoy) influences preferences among superior options. Consider Table 16.1, from Highhouse (1996), using a simulated employee-selection scenario.

Participants in this study were presented with two comparable job finalists and one decoy candidate, along with work sample and promotability ratings. Participants receiving Decoy Candidate (a) along with the choice pair of Candidate 1 versus Candidate 2, preferred Candidate 1 by nearly a 3 to 1 ratio. In contrast, participants receiving Decoy Candidate (b) with the same choice pair preferred Candidate 2 in nearly the same proportion. Slaughter, Sinar and Highhouse (1999) found that this effect could occur even when decision makers are not given explicit numerical values for attributes, but are simply provided with visual performance information. Simonson suggested that the dominating relationship of the targeted option relative to the decoy provides accountable decision makers with a reason that can be used to justify their choices.

Thinking too much about reasons for choices has also been suggested as a reason for procrastination in decision making (e.g., Langer, 1994; Svenson, 1992; Tversky & Shafir, 1992). These authors have suggested that people faced with tough choices will

Table 16.1   *Ratings for candidate and decoys in Highhouse (1996)*

	Work sample rating	Promotability rating
Candidate 1	5	80
Candidate 2	7	66
Decoy candidate (a)	4	80
Decoy candidate (b)	7	54

avoid decision making unless they are able to make psychologically similar options look different in their minds. According to Langer (1994), decision makers faced with psychologically similar alternatives will gather information to differentiate the options until a 'reasonable' argument can be made for one of the options over the other. A proposition of this and similar models (e.g., Soelberg, 1967; Svenson, 1992) is that, failing to sufficiently differentiate options, people will avoid choice and continue to search for more options. This suggests that search may continue indefinitely, even when the choice set contains satisfactory alternatives. Some empirical support for this idea was found by Tversky and Shafir (1992). They found that, when decision makers are faced with choice options that have significant advantages and disadvantages, they are often compelled to delay choice and seek additional options. For example, imagine a job seeker considering two vacancies that differ on only two attributes:

	Advancement opportunities	Autonomy
Job A	High	Average
Job B	Average	High

In this example, one job is high in advancement opportunities but average in autonomy, whereas the other job is average in advancement opportunities but high in autonomy. Faced with this choice the job seeker decides to continue looking. Imagine instead that Job B was only average on *both* attributes. Under these circumstances, the job seeker discontinues search and chooses Job A. Thus, the hypothetical job seeker was willing to make a choice in the second circumstance but not the first, even though the overall quality of the choice set is higher in the first circumstance. Tversky and Shafir (1992) found repeated examples of people choosing to delay choice when conflict is high (i.e., options are psychologically similar), but not when one option clearly dominated the other. Moreover, this pattern persisted even when the search for additional options carried the risk of losing the original options. Research such as this has obvious implications for decision making in selection contexts, as shown in the hypothetical example at the beginning of this section. Most notably, continuing to search for job candidates when suitable minority candidates are available can constitute

prima facie evidence for disparate treatment (*McDonnell Douglas Corp. v. Green*, 1973).

FEELING AND DECIDING

A CEO directs: 'We want a leader who is people-oriented, but not too much of a people person. Our leader should also be bright, but intelligence is of no use if the person doesn't also have street smarts and an aggressive temperament. The only types who can be successful here are ones who had to fight their way to be where they are now.'

The CEO described above has developed a intuitive prototype of the effective leader for the organization. Such intuitions have strong face validity and are often jealously guarded by their champions. They can also, however, sometimes lead the decision maker astray. Below, I discuss research on judgment, prediction, and the role of intuition in decision making.

The tension between thinking too much and thinking too little, discussed in the previous section, seems to relate to a long-standing distinction in cognition between *analytical* and *intuitive* decisions. Analytical decisions are characterized by step-by-step logical processes, whereas intuitive decisions often produce choices without logically defensible methodical processes behind them. In his cognitive continuum theory, Hammond (1996) proposed that decision making is conducted on a continuum anchored by intuitive cognition at one pole and by analytical cognition at the other. Hammond argued that the most common mode of decision making is *quasirationality*, which includes elements of both intuition and analysis. Doherty and Kurz (1996) suggested that the process of selecting applicants for admission into graduate school is the classic example of Hammond's quasirationality. This task involves considering a number of attributes, some of which are objectively determined (e.g., standardized test scores) and some of which must be subjectively assessed (e.g., letters of recommendation); the nature of the criterion is fuzzy, no organizing principle is inherent in the task, and outcome knowledge is unavailable. Doherty and Kurz suggested that, under such conditions, the decision maker will slide between analysis and intuition. For example, a decision maker may try to intuitively balance glowing and mediocre letters, but also may try to analytically compare test scores to established norms, eventually settling on a decision about the candidate's suitability.

Many of the phenomena discussed in this chapter can be organized on Hammond's (1996) cognitive continuum. For example, decoy effects can be viewed as failures in analytical reasoning, whereas dilution can be viewed as a problem with intuition. Hammond, however, emphasized the adaptive quality of quasirationality. Hammond, Hamm, Grassia & Pearson (1987) found that highway engineers asked to make judgments about highway safety could, using intuition and analysis, make judgments that were more accurate than those produced using only formulas. Blattberg and Hoch (1990) compared formula-derived marketing judgments with managerial intuition *and* with a method that combines 50% formula and 50% intuition. The authors found that the combined model outperformed both the formula alone and intuition alone. Blattberg and Hoch suggested that combining intuition and statistical prediction works because, whereas formulas are immune to social pressures and biases, decision makers have the ability to recognize and interpret abnormal events that are diagnostic but too rare to incorporate into formulas (see also Whitecotton, Sanders & Norris, 1998). Ganzach, Kluger & Klayman (2000) similarly showed that expert 'fine-tuning' of mechanical combinations of employment interview scores resulted in more accurate predictions than when the mechanically combined scores were used alone.

Before we get too excited about the power of intuition, however, it is necessary to keep in mind that humans have a poor track record when it comes to making judgments from the gut (Meehl, 1986). Dawes (1994) provided many examples of instances in which 'expert' judgments have been made in light of statistical information only to result in poorer predictions than when the statistical information is used alone. Dawes cautioned that combining statistical and expert judgment only works when the expert judges have access to unique information not included in the statistical model, such as when some external condition prohibits the realization of the predicted outcome (commonly referred to as a 'broken-leg' cue).

One of the primary reasons that experts often underperform simple linear models is that people have a tendency to use configural rules in making predictions (Camerer & Johnson, 1997). With configural rules, like interaction effects in analysis of variance, the impact of one variable depends on the values of other variables. Configural rules are appealing because they typically offer compelling scenarios on which to base predictions. The compelling nature of them, however, is often what makes them less likely to occur. Consider, for example, the following two scenarios:

A. An all-out nuclear war between United States and Russia.
B. An all-out nuclear war between the United States and Russia in which neither country intends to use nuclear weapons, but both sides are drawn into the conflict by the actions of a country such as Iraq, Libya, Israel, or Pakistan.[4]

At first glance, B appears to be more likely to occur than A. However, B (i.e., only one way in which the countries could be led into war) is a subset of A (i.e., *any* of a number of ways in which countries could be led into war, including B). Decision researchers have found that decision makers are consistently seduced by highly detailed scenarios like this, causing them to violate simple rules of logic (e.g., Yates & Carlson, 1986). Configural rules are so attractive to decision makers, therefore, because they offer detailed and seemingly plausible causal explanations. Consider, for example, the hypothetical CEO specifying the characteristics of a successful leader. This executive has constructed from experience a profile of attributes that cannot be captured with simple linear (compensatory) models. Such 'folk theories' of performance are likely to be highly resistant to change, given the delay between prediction and feedback and the tendency to engage in confirmatory information search. Moreover, even when configural rules are found to be incorrect, they are often refined further rather than discarded or simplified (Camerer & Johnson, 1997). An important challenge for I/O psychologists is to understand how folk theories of performance develop (e.g., Borman, 1987), and how they can be modified to fit the existing scientific evidence (see e.g., Balzer, Doherty & O'Connor, 1989).

METHODS FOR STUDYING JUDGMENTS AND DECISIONS

Decision researchers have used a variety of techniques to make inferences about decision making. Techniques have differed by the degree to which the focus is on the content of decisions or the process of decision making. The simplest content approach has been to observe choice behavior in response to manipulations of the decision environment. Observation of preference reversals in response to attribute manipulations has taught us a great deal about how attribute importance is often unreliable, and how preferences are often constructed at the time of choice (Payne et al., 1992). Another approach to studying attribute importance is to model decisions by means of multiple linear regression analyses (Brunswick, 1956), although other approaches such as analysis of variance (Anderson, 1981) and nonlinear regression (Goldberg, 1971) have also been used. These 'policy capturing' approaches involve having people provide numerical evaluations of a large number of stimuli and fitting an algebraic model to the data. An implicit assumption common to both the preference-reversal and policy-capturing literatures is that people lack insight into the factors that determine their own decisions (cf. Reilly & Doherty, 1989).

Unlike content approaches that focus on the outcomes of decision processes, process-tracing approaches focus on the steps leading to a decision (see Ford, Schmitt, Schechtman, Hults & Doherty, 1989). The most common process-tracing approaches have been the use of verbal protocols and information boards. The verbal-protocol approach involves having decision makers think aloud as they work on a problem. These protocols are then transcribed and coded according to themes (e.g., Svenson, 1989). The information-board approach requires decision makers to uncover information arranged in an alternative-by-attribute matrix. Search patterns are then recorded and analyzed (e.g., Payne, 1976). The major finding from both process-tracing approaches has been that people use different strategies, depending on the stage of choice and the number of alternatives available. People generally use a noncompensatory approach early in the decision process, but switch to a compensatory approach when a smaller number of finalists survive initial screening (Ford et al., 1989).

Developments in computer-based applications have allowed researchers to gather more detailed information about search and decision behavior. For example, Wedell and Senter (1997) developed a computerized method for examining decision-maker looking behavior for attributes involved in a decision task. Participants are presented with unlabeled boxes on a computer screen; When the mouse enters the box, information is revealed and stays revealed until the mouse leaves the box. The method allows the researcher to record looking time and looking frequency for each piece of information. Another new development in process tracing is Levin and Jasper's (1995) phased-narrowing procedure. The phased-narrowing approach requires decision makers to use a series of discrete steps to narrow alternatives to a final choice. Decision makers are instructed to transition from an 'awareness set' to a 'consideration set,' and finally to a 'choice set.' The ultimate choice is made from this final choice set. One of the advantages of this technique is its ability to track changes in the relative impact of different attributes across successive decision stages. A computerized version is now available (Levin, Huneke & Jasper, 2000).

Kahneman (1999) has recommended that more researchers take 'bottom-up' approaches to analyzing people's reactions to information used in making judgments and decisions. Kahneman used the term 'instant utility' to refer to the strength of dispositions to continue or to interrupt experiences as they are occurring. Measuring instant utility requires techniques that assess on-line evaluations of information. This could take the form of verbal-protocol ratings, or continuous physical manipulation of a rating device. Such techniques are commonly used by political and consumer consultants to assess on-line reactions to speeches and commercials. For decisions that occur over a longer period of time, researchers could employ techniques such as diary keeping to examine how attribute evaluations evolve or change over extended periods. This would be particularly valuable for I/O psychologists interested in policy making, job search, or termination decisions.

CONCLUDING COMMENTS

My primary objective for this chapter was to provide an accessible treatment of modern JDM, and to show how this work is relevant to behavior in the workplace. The reference list has taken up a lot of the space in this chapter, but I am hoping that the chapter can serve as a rich reference source for I/O psychologists interested in workplace decision making. Had I more space to ramble on, I might have talked about research showing how negative information can have greater psychological impact than positive information of equal valence (Ito, Larsen, Smith & Cacioppo, 1998; Taylor, 1991). Certainly this work has relevance to research on the reactions of job candidates to realistic job previews (Bretz & Judge, 1998), and the selling of issues to top management (Dutton & Ashford, 1993). I might also have discussed work showing how simple context effects influence satisfaction with compensation (Bazerman, Schroth, Shah, Diekman & Tenbrunsel, 1994; Highhouse, Luong & Sarkar-Barney, 1999; Ordóñez, Connolly & Coughlan, 2000), or how work on omission/commission (Spranca, Minsk & Baron, 1991) and outcome biases (Tan & Lipe, 1997; Weber, 1996) relates to judgments of ethical or moral behavior in the workplace.

Another topic that did not receive coverage in this chapter is dynamic decision making, including the emergence of naturalistic decision making (NDM) as an alternative to or 'reinvention' of traditional decision research (Azar, 1999; Klein, 1998; Orasanu & Connolly, 1993). NDM focuses on expert or tactical decision making found in occupations such as fire fighting or tank commandeering. Decision making is not seen as an event, but as a series of events that occur under pressure and must be responded to quickly. Some researchers in NDM reject the laboratory approach, and even controlled measurement, preferring instead to qualitatively study events as they unfold in the natural environment (e.g., Orasanu & Fischer, 1997). Many I/O psychologists are already familiar with NDM, as much of the research has been conducted with workteams (e.g., Cannon-Bowers & Salas, 1998; Hollenbeck et al., 1995; Zsambok, 1997).

Also ignored in this chapter was strategic decision making (SDM). SDM is exclusively concerned with decisions made in organizations (Schwenk, 1995; Shapira, 1997) and has remained relatively independent from JDM. This is evidenced by the fact that separate chapters were devoted to JDM

(Stevenson, Busemeyer & Naylor, 1990) and SDM (Taylor, 1992) in the most recent edition of the *Handbook of Industrial and Organizational Psychology*. Despite its concern with organizations, however, SDM has had little impact on I/O psychology. One reason for this is that SDM is much more macro than micro in orientation, in that it borrows more from sociology, anthropology, and organization theory than from psychology. Another reason that SDM has failed to have more influence on applied fields, according to Bazerman (1999), is that it fails to provide falsifiable theory and refuses to acknowledge that some decisions are more rational than others. Schwenk (1995) has similarly argued that SDM needs to make more use of experimental research. Now seems to be an excellent time for I/O psychologists to bridge the gap between JDM and SDM.

I will conclude this chapter by suggesting that, even though I have argued throughout that JDM has much to offer to I/O psychology, I also believe that I/O psychology has much to offer JDM. First, I/O psychology's focus on criterion measurement could contribute much to the often ignored issues of reliability and validity in JDM research. For example, Harte and Koele (1997) discussed how classical test theory can be used as a framework for designing process-tracing studies, and Zickar and Highhouse (1998) showed how item-response theory may be used to more closely examine responses to common choice dilemmas. Second, attention to the use of individual differences to predict decision behavior is almost nil in the JDM literature (cf. Levin et al., 2000). This is an area where I/O could have much to contribute. For example, individual differences in need for security or achievement are likely to relate to preferences among job alternatives that vary on longevity or opportunities for promotion (Raghunathan & Pham, 1999). Finally, some of the obvious limitations to the generalizability of JDM research (e.g., lab studies, naïve subjects, decisions without consequences) could be addressed by I/O psychologists, using field studies in organizational contexts (e.g., Ganzach et al., 2000). Use of techniques such as diary keeping or web-based process tracing could shed much light on how people make high-stakes decisions in real-world contexts. Simply looking at JDM issues from the lens of a psychologist interested in workplace application can provide a unique perspective not enjoyed by basic theorists.

ACKNOWLEDGMENTS

I am grateful to Bill Balzer, Mike Doherty, Jody Hoffman, Jerel Slaughter, and Jeff Stanton for their helpful comments on earlier drafts of this manuscript. I am also grateful to Lilly Lin for her assistance in copy editing.

NOTES

1 I have consciously ignored other topics, such as negotiation, game theory, and group decision making, that are certainly relevant to organizations, but deserve a chapter of their own.

2 Whereas this semantic framing effect is similar to the 'Susan' example discussed in the section on risky choice, they are qualitatively different phenomena. The hypothetical Susan was risk averse for two objective gains, and risk seeking for two objective losses (i.e., a reflection effect). Risky-choice framing, however, involves taking the *same* objective outcomes and presenting them in terms of gains or losses (see Fagley, 1993, for a discussion of the difference between reflection effects and framing effects).

3 This example was an adaptation of an example presented by Keynes (1921) in which a patient must decide between a treatment with a known 50% success rate, and a treatment having physician-estimated 50% success rate.

4 This example was taken from Plous (1993).

REFERENCES

Anderson, N.H. (1981). *Foundations of information integration theory*. New York: Academic Press.

Arkes, H.R. (1996). The psychology of waste. *Journal of Behavioral Decision Making*, 9, 213–224.

Ashford, S.J. (1989). Self-assessments in organizations: A literature review and integrative model. *Research in Organizational Behavior*, *11*, 133–174.

Azar, B. (1999). Decision researchers split, but prolific. *APA Monitor*, May, 30.

Balzer, W.K., Doherty, M.E., & O'Connor, R. (1989). Effects of cognitive feedback on performance. *Psychological Bulletin*, *106*, 410–433.

Bazerman, M.H. (1984). The relevance of Kahneman and Tversky's concept of framing to organizational behavior. *Journal of Management*, *10*, 333–343.

Bazerman, M.H. (1999). [Review of the book *Organizational Decision Making*]. *Administrative Science Quarterly*, *44*, 176–179.

Bazerman, M.H., Schroth, H.A., Shah, P.P., Diekman, K.A., & Tenbrunsel, A.E. (1994). The inconsistent role of comparison others and procedural justice in reactions to hypothetical job descriptions: Implications for job acceptance decisions. *Organizational Behavior and Human Decision Processes*, *60*, 326–352.

Beach, L.R., & Mitchell, T.R. (1990). Image theory: A behavioral theory of decision making in organizations. *Research in Organizational Behavior*, *12*, 1–41.

Bernoulli, D. (1738/1954). Exposition of a new theory on the measurement of risk (L. Sommer, trans.), *Econometrica*, *22*, 22–36.

Blattberg, R.C., & Hoch, S.J. (1990). Database models and managerial intuition: 50% model + 50% intuition. *Managerial Science*, *36*, 887–899.

Borman, W.C. (1987). Personal constructs, performance schemata, and 'folk theories' of subordinate effectiveness: Explorations in an Army officer sample. *Organizational Behavior and Human Decision Processes, 40,* 307–322.

Bretz, R.D., & Judge, T.A. (1998). Realistic job previews: A test of the adverse self-selection hypothesis. *Journal of Applied Psychology, 83,* 330–337.

Brockner, J., Wiesenfeld, B.M., & Martin, C.L. (1995). Decision frame, procedural justice, and survivors' reactions to job layoffs. *Organizational Behavior and Human Decision Processes, 63,* 59–68.

Brunswick, E. (1956). *Perception and the representative design of psychological experiments.* Berkeley: University of California Press.

Butler, A., & Highhouse, S. (2000). Deciding to sell: Effects of prior inaction and offer source. *Journal of Economic Psychology, 21,* 223–232.

Byram, S.J. (1997). Cognitive and motivational factors influencing time prediction. *Journal of Experimental Psychology: Applied, 3,* 216–239.

Camerer, C., & Johnson, E.J. (1997). The process-performance paradox in expert judgment: How can experts know so much and predict so badly? In W.M. Goldstein, & R.M. Hogarth (Eds.), *Research on judgment and decision making: Currents, connections, and controversies* (pp. 343–364). Cambridge University Press.

Camerer, C., & Weber, M. (1992). Recent developments in modeling preferences: Uncertainty and ambiguity. *Journal of Risk and Uncertainty, 5,* 325–370.

Cannon-Bowers, J.A., & Salas, E. (1998). Team performance and training in complex environments: Recent findings from applied research. *Current Directions in Psychological Science, 7,* 83–87.

Cascio, W.F. (1993). Assessing the utility of selection decisions: Theoretical and practical considerations. In N. Schmitt, & W.C. Borman (Eds.), *Personnel selection in organizations.* San Francisco, CA: Jossey-Bass.

Cooper, A., Woo, C., & Dunkelberg, W. (1988). Entrepreneurs' perceived chances for success. *Journal of Business Venturing, 3,* 97–108.

Davis, M.A., & Bobko, P. (1986). Contextual effects on escalation processes in public sector decision making. *Organizational Behavior and Human Decision Processes, 37,* 121–138.

Dawes, R.M. (1994). *House of cards: Psychology and psychotherapy built on myth.* New York: The Free Press.

Dawes, R.M. (1998). Behavioral decision making and judgment. In D.T. Gilbert, S.T. Fiske, & G. Lindzey (Eds.), *The Handbook of Social Psychology* (pp. 497–548). Boston, MA: McGraw-Hill.

Dhar, R., & Sherman, S.J. (1996). The effect of common and unique features in consumer choice. *Journal of Consumer Research, 23,* 193–203.

Dipboye, R.L. (1994). Structured and unstructured selection interviews: Beyond the job-fit model. *Research in Personnel and Human Resources Management, 12,* 79–123.

Doherty, M.E., & Kurz, E. (1996). Social judgment theory. *Thinking and Reasoning, 2,* 109–140.

Doherty, M.E., Mynatt, C.R., Tweney, R.D., & Schiavo, M.D. (1979). Pseudodiagnosticity. *Acta Psychologica, 43,* 111–121.

Dunegan, K.J. (1993). Framing, cognitive modes, and image theory: Toward an understanding of a glass half full. *Journal of Applied Psychology, 78,* 491–503.

Dunning, D., & Stern, L.B. (1994). Distinguishing accurate from inaccurate eyewitness identifications via inquiries about decision processes. *Journal of Personality and Social Psychology, 67,* 818–835.

Dutton, J.E. (1993). The making of organizational opportunities: An interpretive pathway to organizational change. *Research in Organizational Behavior, 15,* 195–226.

Dutton, J.E., & Ashford, S.J. (1993). Selling issues to top management. *Academy of Management Review, 18,* 397–428.

Dutton, J.E., & Jackson, S.B. (1987). Categorizing strategic issues: Links to organizational action. *Academy of Management Review, 12,* 76–90.

Edwards, W. (1954). The theory of decision making. *Psychological Bulletin, 51,* 380–417.

Einhorn, H.J., & Hogarth, R.M. (1985). Ambiguity and uncertainty in probabilistic inference. *Psychological Review, 92,* 433–461.

Ellsberg, D. (1961). Risk, ambiguity, and the savage axioms. *Quarterly Journal of Economics,* 643–669.

Evans, J.St.B.T. (1989). *Bias in human reasoning: Causes and consequences.* London: Lawrence Erlbaum Associates.

Fagley, N.S. (1993). A note concerning reflection effects versus framing effects. *Psychological Bulletin, 113,* 451–452.

Fagley, N.S., & Miller, P.M. (1987). The effects of decision framing on choice of risky vs. certain options. *Organizational Behavior and Human Decision Processes, 39,* 264–277.

Ford, J.K., Schmitt, N., Schechtman, S.L., Hults, B.M., & Doherty, M.L. (1989). Process tracing methods: Contributions, problems, and neglected research questions. *Organizational Behavior and Human Decision Processes, 43,* 75–117.

Funder, D.C. (1995). On the accuracy of personality judgment: A realistic approach. *Psychological Review, 102,* 652–670.

Ganzach, Y., & Karsahi, N. (1995). Message framing and buying behavior: A field experiment. *Journal of Business Research, 32,* 11–17.

Ganzach, Y., Kluger, A.N., & Klayman, N. (2000). Making decisions from an interview: Expert measurement and mechanical combination. *Personnel Psychology, 53,* 1–20.

Gigerenzer, G., & Hoffrage, U. (1995). How to improve Bayesian reasoning without instruction: Frequency formats. *Psychological Review, 102,* 684–704.

Goldberg, L.R. (1971). Five models of clinical judgment: An empirical comparison between linear and nonlinear represenations of the human inference process. *Organizational Behavior and Human Performance, 6,* 458–479.

Goldstein, W.M., & Hogarth, R.M. (1997). Judgment and decision research: Some historical context. In W.M. Goldstein, & R.M. Hogarth (Eds.), *Research on judgment and decision making: Currents, connections, and controversies* (pp. 3–65). Cambridge University Press.

Greenwald, A.G. (1980). The totalitarian ego: Fabrication and revision of personal history. *American Psychologist, 35*, 603–618.

Halberstadt, J.B., & Levine, G.M. (1999). Effects of reasons analysis on the accuracy of predicting basketball games. *Journal of Applied Social Psychology, 29*, 517–530.

Hammond, K.R. (1955). Probabilistic functioning and the clinical method. *Psychological Review, 62*, 255–262.

Hammond, K.R. (1996). *Human judgment and social policy: Irreducible uncertainty, inevitable error, unavoidable injustice*. New York: Oxford University Press.

Hammond, K.R., Hamm, R.M., Grassia, J., & Pearson, T. (1987). Direct comparison of the efficacy of intuitive and analytical cognition in expert judgment. *IEEE Transactions on Systems, Man, and Cybernetics, SMC-17*, 753–770.

Hammond, K.R., McClelland, G.H., & Mumpower, J. (1980). *Human judgment and decision making: Theories, methods, and procedures*. New York: Praeger, Hemisphere.

Harris, M.M., & Greising, L.A. (1998). Alcohol and drug abuse as dysfunctional workplace behaviors. In R.W. Griffin, & A. O'Leary-Kelly (Eds.), *Dysfunctional behavior in organizations: Violent and deviant behavior* (pp. 21–48). Stamford, CT: JAI Press.

Harris, R.J. (1973). Answering questions containing marked and unmarked adjectives and adverbs. *Journal of Experimental Psychology, 97*, 399–401.

Harte, J.M., & Koele, P. (1997). Psychometric and methodological aspects of process tracing research. In R. Ranyard, W.R. Crozier, & O. Svenson (Eds.), *Decision making: Cognitive models and explanations*. New York: Routledge.

Hayward, M.L.A., & Hambrick, D.C. (1997). Explaining the premiums paid for large acquisitions: Evidence of CEO hubris. *Administrative Science Quarterly, 42*, 103–127.

Hazer, J.T., & Highhouse, S. (1997). Factors influencing managers' reactions to utility analysis: Effects of SDy method, information frame, and focal intervention. *Journal of Applied Psychology, 82*, 104–112.

Higgins, E.T. (1997). Beyond pleasure and pain. *American Psychologist, 52*, 1280–1300.

Highhouse, S. (1994). A verbal protocol analysis of choice under ambiguity. *Journal of Economic Psychology, 15*, 621–635.

Highhouse, S. (1996). Context-dependent selection: The effects of decoy and phantom job candidates. *Organizational Behavior and Human Decision Processes, 65*, 68–76.

Highhouse, S. (1997). Understanding and improving job-finalist choice: The relevance of behavioral decision

research. *Human Resource Management Review, 7*, 449–470.

Highhouse, S., & Hause, E. (1995). 'Missing information in selection: An application of the Einhorn-Hogarth ambiguity model'. *Journal of Applied Psychology, 80*, 86–93.

Highhouse, S., Luong, A., & Sarkar-Barney, S. (1999). Research design, measurement, and effects of attribute range on job choice: More than meets the eye. *Organizational Research Methods, 2*, 37–48.

Highhouse, S., Mohammed, S., & Hoffman, J.R. (in press). Temporal discounting of strategic issues: Bold forecasts for opportunities and threats. *Basic and Applied Social Psychology*.

Highhouse, S., & Paese, P.W. (1996). Problem domain and prospect frame: Choice under opportunity versus threat. *Personality and Social Psychology Bulletin, 22*, 124–132.

Highhouse, S., & Yüce, P. (1996). Perspectives, perceptions, and risk-taking behavior. *Organizational Behavior and Human Decision Processes, 65*, 159–167.

Hinsz, V.B., Kalnbach, L.R., & Lorentz, N.R. (1997). Using judgmental anchors to establish challenging self-set goals without jeopardizing commitment. *Organizational Behavior and Human Decision Processes, 71*, 287–308.

Hollenbeck, J.R., Ilgen, D.R., Tuttle, D.B., & Sego, D.J. (1995). Team performance on monitoring tasks: An examination of decision errors in contexts requiring sustained attention. *Journal of Applied Psychology, 80*, 685–696.

Hutzel, L., & Arkes, H.R. (1997). *Regret may be a fuel for inaction inertia*. Paper presented at the Annual Meeting of the Society for Judgment and Decision Making, Philadelphia, November.

Ito, T.A., Larsen, J.T., Smith, N.K., & Cacioppo, J.T. (1998). Negative information weighs more heavily on the brain: The negativity bias in evaluative categorizations. *Journal of Personality and Social Psychology, 75*, 887–900.

Janis, I.L., & Mann, L. (1977). *Decision making: A psychological analysis of conflict, choice, and commitment*. New York: Free Press.

Jarvenpaa, S.L. (1990). Graphic displays in decision making – the visual salience effect. *Journal of Behavioral Decision Making, 3*, 247–262.

Jungermann, H. (1983). The two camps on rationality In R.W. Scholz (Ed.), *Decision making under uncertainty: Cognitive decision research, social interaction, development and epistemology*. New York: North-Holland, Elsevier Science Publishers.

Kahneman, D. (1991). Judgment and decision making: A personal view. *Psychological Science, 2*, 142–145.

Kahneman, D. (1999). Objective happiness. In D. Kahneman, E. Diener, & N. Schwarz (Eds.), *Well-being: The foundations of hedonic psychology*. New York: Russell Sage Foundation.

Kahneman, D., & Lovallo, D. (1993). Timid choices and bold forecasts: A cognitive perspective on risk taking. *Management Science, 39*, 17–31.

Kahneman, D., Slovic, P., & Tversky, A. (1982). *Judgment under uncertainty: Heuristics and biases.* New York: Cambridge University Press.

Kahneman, D., & Tversky, A. (1979). Prospect theory: An analysis of decision under risk. *Econometrica, 47,* 263–291.

Kahneman, D., & Tversky, A. (1996) On the reality of cognitive illusions. *Psychological Review, 103,* 582–591.

Keynes, J.M. (1921). *A treatise on probability.* London: Macmillan Co.

Kirby, K.N., & Herrnstein, R.J. (1995). Preference reversals due to myopic discounting of delayed reward. *Psychological Science, 6,* 83–89.

Kirkpatrick, L.A., & Epstein, S. (1992). Cognitive-experiential self-theory and subjective probability: Further evidence for two conceptual systems. *Journal of Personality and Social Psychology, 63,* 534–544.

Klayman, J., & Brown, K. (1994). Debias the environment instead of the judge: An alternative approach to reducing error in diagnostic (and other) judgment. In P.N. Johnson, & E. Shafir (Eds.), *Reasoning and decision making.* Cambridge, MA: Blackwell.

Klein, G. (1998). *Sources of power.* Cambridge, MA: The MIT Press.

Klein, H.J. (1991). Further evidence on the relationship between goal setting and expectancy theories. *Organizational Behavior and Human Decision Processes, 49,* 230–257.

Kluger, A.N., Yaniv, I., & Kühberger, A. (2000). *Needs, self-regulation, and risk preference.* Paper presented at the 15th Annual Conference of the Society for Industrial and Organizational Psychology, New Orleans, LA, April.

Kühberger, A. (1998). The influence of framing on risky decisions. *Organizational Behavior and Human Decision Processes, 75,* 23–55.

Kuhn, K.M. (1997). Communicating uncertainty: Framing effects on responses to vague probabilities. *Organizational Behavior and Human Decision Processes, 71,* 55–83.

Langer, E.J. (1975). The illusion of control. *Journal of Personality and Social Psychology, 32,* 311–328.

Langer, E. (1994). The illusion of calculated decisions. In R.C. Schank, & E. Langer (Eds.), *Beliefs, reasoning, and decision making: Psycho-logic in honor of Bob Abelson.* Hillsdale, NJ: Lawrence Erlbaum Associates.

Lee, T.W. (1996). Why employees quit. In L.R. Beach (Ed.), *Decision making in the workplace: A unified perspective* (pp. 73–90). Mahwah, NJ: Lawrence Erlbaum Associates.

Levin, I., Huneke, M.E., & Jasper, J.D. (2000). Information processing at successive stages of decision making: Need for cognition and inclusion-exclusion effects. *Organizational Behavior and Human Decision Processes, 82,* 171–193.

Levin, I., & Jasper, J.D. (1995). Phased narrowing: A new process tracing method for decision making. *Organizational Behavior and Human Decision Processes, 64,* 1–8.

Levin, I.P., Schneider, S.L., & Gaeth, G.J. (1998). All frames are not created equal: A typology and critical analysis of framing effects. *Organizational Behavior and Human Decision Processes, 76,* 149–188.

Loewenstein, G.F. (1988). Frames of mind and intertemporal choice. *Management Science, 34,* 200–214.

Loftus, E.T. (1975). Leading questions and the eyewitness report. *Cognitive Psychology, 7,* 560–572.

Lopes, L.L. (1987). Between hope and fear: The psychology of risk. *Advances in Experimental Social Psychology, 20,* 255–295.

Luce, R.D., & Raiffa, H. (1957). *Games and Decisions.* New York: Wiley.

March, J.G., & Shapira, Z. (1987). Managerial perspectives on risk and risk taking. *Management Science, 33,* 1404–1418.

March, J., & Shapira, Z. (1992). Variable risk preferences and the focus of attention. *Psychological Review, 99,* 172–183.

Marlowe, C.M., Schneider, S.L., & Nelson, C.E. (1996). Gender and attractiveness biases in hiring decisions: Are more experienced managers less biased? *Journal of Applied Psychology, 81,* 11–21.

McDonnell Douglas Corp. v. Green, 5 FEP 732 (1973).

Meehl, P.E. (1954). *Clinical versus statistical prediction: A theoretical analysis and a review of the evidence.* Minneapolis: University of Minnesota Press.

Meehl, P.E. (1986). Causes and effects of my disturbing little book. *Journal of Personality Assessment, 50,* 370–375.

Mellers, B.A., Schwartz, A., & Cooke, A.D.J. (1998). Judgment and decision making. *Annual Review of Psychology, 49,* 447–477.

Moore, D.A., Kurtzberg, T.R., Fox, C.R., Bazerman, M.H. (1999). Positive illusions and forecasting errors in mutual fund investment decisions. *Organizational Behavior and Human Decision Processes, 79,* 95–114.

Naylor, J. (1984). Editorial: A time of transition. *Organizational Behavior and Human Performance, 34,* 1–4.

Nisbett, R.E., Zukier, H., & Lemley, R.E. (1981). The dilution effect: Nondiagnositc information weakens the implications of diagnostic information. *Cognitive Psychology, 13,* 248–277.

Orasanu, J., & Connolly, T. (1993). The reinvention of decision making. In G.A. Klein, J. Orasanu, R. Calderwood, & C.E. Zsambok (Eds.), *Decision making in action: Models and methods* (pp. 3–20). Norwood, NJ: Ablex.

Orasanu, J., & Fischer, U. (1997). Finding decisions in natural environments: The view from the cockpit. In C.E. Zsambok, & G. Klein (Eds.), *Naturalistic Decision Making* (pp. 343–358). Mahwah, NJ: Lawrence Erlbaum Associates.

Ordóñez, L.D., Connolly, T., & Coughlan, R. (2000). Multiple reference points in satisfaction and fairness assessment. *Journal of Behavioral Decision Making, 13,* 329–344.

Payne, J.W. (1976). Task complexity and contingent processing in decision making: An information search and protocol analysis. *Organizational Behavior and Human Performance*, *16*, 366–387.

Payne, J.W., Bettman, J.R., & Johnson, E.J. (1992). Behavioral decision research: A constructive processing perspective. *Annual Review of Psychology*, *43*, 87–132.

Perloff, L.S. (1987). Social comparison and illusions of invulnerability to negative life events, In C.R. Snyder, & C.E. Ford (Eds.), *Coping with negative life events: Clinical and social psychological perspectives* (pp. 217–242). New York: Plenum Press.

Plous, S. (1993). *The psychology of judgement and decision making*. New York: McGraw-Hill.

Raghunathan, R., & Pham, M.T. (1999). All negative moods are not equal: Motivational influences of anxiety and sadness on decision making. *Organizational Behavior and Human Decision Processes*, *79*, 56–77.

Reilly, B.A., & Doherty, M.E. (1989). A note on the assessment of self-insight in judgment research. *Organizational Behavior and Human Decision Processes*, *44*, 123–131.

Russo, J.E. (1977). The value of unit price information. *Journal of Marketing Research*, *14*, 193–201.

Schkade, D.A., & Kleinmuntz, D.N. (1994). Information displays and choice processes: Differential effects of organization, form, and sequence. *Organizational Behavior and Human Decision Processes*, *57*, 319–337.

Schwarz, N. (1999). Self-reports: How questions shape the answers. *American Psychologist*, *54*, 93–105.

Schwenk, C.R. (1995). Strategic decision making. *Journal of Management*, *21*, 471–493.

Senter, M., & Wedell, D.H. (1999). Information presentation constraints and the adaptive decision maker hypothesis. *Journal of Experimental Psychology: Learning, Memory, and Cognition*, *25*, 428–446.

Shafir, E., Simonson, I., & Tversky, A. (1993). Reason-based choice. *Cognition*, *49*, 11–36.

Shapira, Z. (1997). *Organizational decision making*. New York: Cambridge University Press.

Shefrin, H., & Statman, M. (1985). The disposition to sell winners too early and ride losers too long: Theory and evidence. *The Journal of Finance*, *50*, 777–791.

Shelley, M.K. (1994). Gain/loss asymmetry in risky intertemporal choice. *Organizational Behavior and Human Decision Processes*, *59*, 124–159.

Shepperd, J.A., Ouellette, J.A., & Fernandez, J.K. (1996). Abandoning unrealistic optimism: Performance estimates and the temporal proximity of self-relevant feedback. *Journal of Personality and Social Psychology*, *70*, 844–855.

Simon, H.A. (1955). A behavioral model of rational choice. *Quarterly Journal of Economics*, *69*, 99–118.

Simonson, I. (1989). Choice based on reasons: The case of attraction and compromise effects. *Journal of Consumer Research*, *16*, 158–174.

Slaughter, J.E., Sinar, E.F., & Highhouse, S. (1999). Decoy effects and attribute-level inferences. *Journal of Applied Psychology*, *84*, 823–828.

Slovic, P. (1982). Toward understanding and improving decisions. In W.C. Howell, & E.A. Fleishman (Eds.), *Information processing and decision making* (pp. 157–183). Hillsdale, NJ: Lawrence Erlbaum Associates.

Slovic, P., & Lichtenstein, S. (1971). Comparison of Bayesian and regression approaches to the study of information processing in judgment. *Organizational Behavior and Human Performance*, *6*, 649–744.

Soelberg, P.O. (1967). Unprogrammed decision making. *Industrial Management Review*, *8*, 19–29.

Spranca, M., Minsk, E., & Baron, J. (1991). Omission and commission in judgment and choice. *Organizational Behavior and Human Decision Processes*, *27*, 76–105.

Staw, B.M. (1981). The escalation of commitment to a course of action. *Academy of Management Review*, *6*, 577–587.

Staw, B.M., Barsade, S.G., & Koput, K.W. (1997). Escalation at the credit window: A longitudinal study of bank executives' recognition and write-off of problem loans. *Journal of Applied Psychology*, *82*, 130–142.

Stevens, C.K. (1998). Image theory and career-related decisions: Finding and selecting occupations and jobs. In L.R. Beach (Ed.), *Image theory: Theoretical and empirical foundations* (pp. 227–239). Mahwah, NJ: Lawrence Erlbaum Associates.

Stevenson, M.K. (1986). A discounting model for decisions with delayed positive and negative consequences. *Journal of Experimental Psychology: General*, *115*, 131–154.

Stevenson, M.K., Busemeyer, J.R., & Naylor, J.C. (1990). Judgment and decision-making theory. In M.D. Dunnette, & L.M. Hough (Eds.), *Handbook of industrial and organizational psychology* (Vol. 1, pp. 283–374). Palo Alto, CA: Consulting Psychologists Press.

Stone, D.N., & Schkade, D.A. (1991). Numeric and linguistic information representation in multiattribute choice. *Organizational Behavior and Human Decision Processes*, *49*, 42–59.

Sulsky, L.M., & Balzer, W.K. (1988). Meaning and measurement of performance rating accuracy: Some methodological and theoretical concerns. *Journal of Applied Psychology*, *73*, 497–506.

Svenson, O. (1989). Eliciting and analysing verbal protocols in process studies of judgement and decision making. In H. Montgomery, & O. Svenson (Eds.), *Process and structure in human decision making*. Chichester: Wiley.

Svenson, O. (1992). Differentiation and consolidation theory of human decision making: A frame of reference for the study of pre- and post-decision processes. *Acta Psychologica*, *80*, 143–168.

Tan, H.T., & Lipe, M.G. (1997). Outcome effects: The impact of decision process and outcome controllability. *Journal of Behavioral Decision Making*, *10*, 315–325.

Taylor, R.N. (1992). Strategic decision making. In M.D. Dunnette, & L.M. Hough (Eds.), *Handbook of industrial and organizational psychology* (Vol. 3, pp. 961–1007). Palo Alto, CA: Consulting Psychologists Press.

Taylor, S.E. (1991). Asymmetrical effects of positive and negative events: The mobilization–minimization hypothesis. *Psychological Bulletin*, *110*, 67–85.

Taylor, S.E., & Brown, J.D. (1988). Illusion and well-being: A social psychological perspective on mental health. *Psychological Bulletin, 103,* 193–210.

Tetlock, P.E., & Boettger, R. (1989). Accountability: A social magnifier of the dilution effect. *Journal of Personality and Social Psychology, 57,* 388–398.

Thompson, S.C., Armstrong, W., & Thomas, C. (1998). Illusions of control, underestimations, and accuracy: A control heuristic explanation. *Psychological Bulletin, 123,* 143–161.

Thrall, R.M., Coombs, C.H., & Davis, R.L. (Eds.) (1954). *Decision processes.* New York: Wiley.

Tordesillas, R.S., & Chaiken, S. (1999). Thinking too much or too little? The effects of introspection on the decision-making process. *Personality and Social Psychology Bulletin, 25,* 623–629.

Tversky, A., & Griffin, D. (1991). Endowment and contrast in judgments of well-being. In F. Strack, M. Argyle, & N. Schwarz (Eds.), *Subjective well-being: An interdisciplinary perspective* (pp. 101–118). Oxford: Pergamon Press.

Tversky, A., & Kahneman, D. (1981). The framing of decisions and the rationality of choice. *Science, 221,* 453–458.

Tversky, A., & Shafir, E. (1992). Choice under conflict: The dynamics of deferred decision. *Psychological Science, 3,* 358–361.

Tykocinski, O.E., Pittman, T.S., & Tuttle, E.E. (1995). Inaction inertia: Foregoing future benefits as a result of an initial failure to act. *Journal of Personality and Social Psychology, 68,* 793–803.

von Neumann, J., & Morgenstern, O. (1944). *Theory of games and economic behavior.* Princeton: Princeton University Press.

Vroom, V.H. (1964). *Work and motivation.* New York: Wiley.

Wanous, J.P., & Colella, A. (1989). Organizational entry research: Current status and future directions. *Research in Personnel and Human Resources Management, 7,* 59–120.

Wason, P.C. (1960). On the failure to eliminate hypotheses in a conceptual task. *Quarterly Journal of Experimental Psychology, 12,* 129–140.

Weber, E.U. (1998). From performance to decision processes in 33 years: A history of organizational behavior and human decision processes under James C. Naylor. *Organizational Behavior and Human Decision Processes, 76,* 209–222.

Weber, J. (1996). Influences upon managerial moral decision making: Nature of the harm and magnitude of the consequences. *Human Relations, 49,* 1–49.

Wedell, D.H., & Senter, S.M. (1997). Looking and weighting in judgment and choice. *Organizational Behavior and Human Decision Processes, 70,* 41–64.

Weinstein, N.D. (1980). Unrealistic optimism about future life events. *Journal of Personality and Social Psychology, 39,* 806–820.

Wells, G.L. (1992). Naked statistical evidence of liability: Is subjective probability enough? *Journal of Personality and Social Psychology, 62,* 739–752.

Whitecotton, S.M., Sanders, D.E., & Norris, K.B. (1998). Improving predictive accuracy with a combination of human intuition and mechanical decision aids. *Organizational Behavior and Human Decision Processes, 76,* 325–348.

Wilson, T.D., & Schooler, J.W. (1991). Thinking too much: Introspection can reduce the quality of preferences and decisions. *Journal of Personality and Social Psychology, 60,* 181–192.

Windschitl, P.D., & Wells, G.L. (1998). The alternative-outcomes effect. *Journal of Personality and Social Psychology, 75,* 1411–1423.

Yates, J.F., & Carlson, B.W. (1986). Conjunction errors: Evidence for multiple judgment procedures, including 'signed summation'. *Organizational Behavior and Human Decision Processes, 37,* 230–253.

Yüce, P., & Highhouse, S. (1998). The effects of attribute set-size and pay ambiguity on reactions to 'Help Wanted' advertisements. *Journal of Organizational Behavior, 19,* 337–352.

Zickar, M.J., & Highhouse, S. (1998). Looking closer at the effects of framing on risky choice: An item response theory analysis. *Organizational Behavior and Human Decision Processes, 75,* 75–91.

Zsambok, C.E. (1997). Naturalistic decision making research and improving team decision making. In C.E. Zsambok, & G. Klein (Eds.), *Naturalistic decision making* (pp. 111–120). Mahwah, NJ: Lawrence Erlbaum Associates.

17

Organizational Development and Change

HANDAN KEPIR SINANGIL
and FRANCESCO AVALLONE

The introduction concerns the historical evolution of theory, methods, and intervention techniques in organizational development (OD), considered as a part of those disciplines directed toward using behavioral science knowledge to assist organizations in dealing with the problems of change. On the basis of the fundamental questions that the researchers seek to answer from the early studies in 1960s up to 2000, the main findings on OD are presented starting from the traditional action research approach, which remains one of the common methods widely used in organizations research, to the learning organizations approach. The dimensions of organizational change (structures, processes, boundaries) are examined in the light of the most recent literature. An attempt to define future perspectives on OD research and intervention is finally proposed.

THE CONCEPT OF ORGANIZATIONAL DEVELOPMENT

In the last 40 years researchers as well as practitioners have been interested in organizational development (OD), considered as a response to accelerated changes in the technological, political, and institutional dimensions of our societies.

Although much discussion about the concept remains, OD has not disappeared from organizational literature and practice and it is still considered as a part of those disciplines directed toward using behavioral science knowledge to assist organizations in dealing with the problems of change. Organizational development and change, therefore, is a process by which behavioral science principles and practices are used, in an ongoing organization, in a planned and systematic way to attain such goals as developing greater organizational competence, improving the quality of work life, and organizational effectiveness (Huse & Cummings, 1985).

Systematic OD activities come from three main streams: the first two are the development of training groups (Lewin, 1947; Blake & Mouton, 1964) and the early work in survey research and feedback (Baumgartel, 1959; Marrow, 1969). In the development of both of these streams Lewin has been fundamental. The third stream is the sociotechnical approach originally developed by the Tavistock Institute of Human Relations in London (Jacques, 1951; Dicks, 1970). There is an approach the three streams have in common: the action research method, briefly described as 'a collaborative client-consultant inquiry consisting of preliminary diagnosis, data gathering from the client group, data feedback to the client group, data exploration and action planning by the client group, and action' (French & Bell, 1984: 35).

Because of its background, according to Bennis (1969), the modern concept of OD rests on three basic propositions: (1) each age adopts an organizational form which is most appropriate to that particular age and changes taking place in that age make it necessary to rethink our organizations; (2) the only real way to change organizations lies in changing the climate of the organization, its way of life made of beliefs and values that strongly contribute to regulating interactions; (3) people in organizations must develop a new sensibility toward social awareness.

According to the historic research by Clark and Krone (1972) the term organizational development was used for the first time in the 1960s, and in their article, the authors go over the main phases of the development of this discipline.

Bennis (1966: 82) describes planned change as involving a 'change-agent, who is typically a behavioral scientist brought in to help a client-system, which refers to the target of change. The change-agent, in collaboration with the client-system, attempts to apply valid knowledge to the client's problems.' Later, Bennis (1969: 2) defines OD as 'a response to change, a complex educational strategy intended to change the beliefs, attitudes, values and structure of organizations so they can better adapt.'

Beckhard (1969: 4) defines OD as 'an effort (1) planned, (2) organization-wide, and (3) managed from the top, to (4) increase organization effectiveness and health through (5) planned interventions in the organization's processes, using behavioral-science knowledge.'

Margulies and Raia (1978: ix) first described OD as 'a body of knowledge concerning the ways in which organizations can better adapt.' They later define it more specifically as a 'value based process of self-assessment and planned change, involving specific strategies and technology, aimed at improving the overall effectiveness of an organizational system' (Margulies & Raia, 1978: 24).

In 1974, the Annual Review of Psychology published the first article about OD (Friedlander & Brown, 1974). They describe the two main approaches that characterize the field: on one hand, the human-process approach, centered on the people in the organization as well as on all the organizational processes based on human behavior; while, on the other hand, the technostructural approach, focused mainly on the technological aspect of the organization, related to the many ways in which this influences and is influenced by organizational structure. This second approach stresses the importance of fulfilling organizational goals.

The key words most often used to define OD during the first years of its development are: change of beliefs, attitudes, and values; increase in organization effectiveness and health related to generic client's problems. We may follow the hypothesis according to which productive organizations,

especially big ones, have been forced – because of the technological innovations, the widening of their area of trade, and of the increasing complexity of the internal environment as well as of the cultural and social climate of the society the organization was living in – to rethink and reproject their own relation with the external environment, in order to find a new way to adapt to it as well as new techniques of intervention. The writings of the first scholars of OD seem to reveal an enthusiastic, almost mystic, idea of change, which is considered to be a value itself. The practitioner is defined with emphasis as a *change-agent*, who bears the techniques which should enable organizations to develop a better integration within the internal environment as well as to adapt more effectively to the outside world. Two different areas of organizational development are identified: the first one is related to organizational structure, the second one to its processes. There seems to be absolutely no reference to other kinds of organizations but firms.

It was not until the 1980s that the concept of OD found new and more articulated definitions. Beer (1980: 10) describes OD as 'a system-wide process of data collection, diagnosis, action planning, intervention and evaluation aimed at: (1) enhancing congruence between organizational structure, processes, strategy, people and culture; (2) developing new and creative organizational solutions; and (3) developing the organization's self-renewing capacity. It occurs through collaboration of organizational members working with a change agent using behavioral science theory, research, and technology.'

Burke (1982: 10) views OD as 'a planned process of change in an organization's culture through the utilization of behavioral science technology, research, and theory.'

Robey and Altman (1982: 1) define OD as 'a systematic process with an underlying value system which employs a variety of techniques introduced by a consultant to improve the effectiveness of complex organizations.'

French and Bell (1984: 17) describe OD as 'a top management-supported, long-range effort to improve an organization's problem-solving and renewal process, particularly through a more effective and collaborative diagnosis and management of organization culture – with special emphasis on formal work team, temporary team, and intergroup culture – with the assistance of a consultant-facilitator and the use of the theory and technology of applied behavioral science, including action research.'

Huse and Cummings (1985: 2) define OD as 'a system-wide application of behavioral science knowledge to the planned development and reinforcement of organizational strategies, structures, and processes for improving an organization's effectiveness.'

Beer and Walton suggest to enclose the discipline of OD in the wide area regarding human resource management, instead of defining it as a unique field of organizational research and practice. The article is important since it highlights the two main goals characterizing OD: the development of the organizational performance, and the improvement of the quality of work life within the organization (Beer & Walton, 1987).

Sashkin and Burke (1990) presented an accurate review of the literature concerning OD from the first years of its development until this past decade.

Some very interesting elements emerge from this study: it seems that the rapid development OD research had gone through in the 1960s and 1970s, almost stopped in the 1980s. Moreover, the review shows how the object of the studies of OD investigate, in the first place, the area of the research itself with particular concern for the problems that arise from it and for its methodologies; and secondly, various theories have been developed, though the literature regarding this area seems to be still suffering from a lack of contributions and an organized frame of reference.

Among the subjects most often mentioned there are 'team-building,' very popular in the 1980s, and the study of organizational culture and change. The latter is surprising, since that subject is almost never mentioned in the reviews of the 1970s, while it is the most popular theme in the second half of the 1980s (Sashkin & Burke, 1990).

In these years the action research approach was still very popular in the field, but new concepts were introduced: the need for coherence between organizational structure, processes, and culture; the need to find new creative organizational solutions; the development of organizational performance through the use of workteams; and the ability of organizations to self-regulate and self-renew.

During this time, organizations were not as worried by structural problems; social and trade-union problems became easier to deal with; operational matters were handled more quickly and with more effectiveness, thanks to technological progress and automatization; and the tendency arose to organize jobs in terms of goals instead of in terms of tasks. On the other hand, new problems concerning the economic aspect as well as a better use of the resources emerged, concerned with the ability of the organization to foresee, plan, develop programs, and to coordinate and control. Many new interventions were elaborated, and the emphasis shifted from a generic idea of change to more specific, goal-oriented changes; the change-agent became a consultant, whose work was aimed at improving the internal integration and opening the organization to the external environment. It was during this period in particular that organizations often became social laboratories where new forms

of aggregated life and of being in society were thought and experimented.

Lastly, in the 1990s new definitions of OD were proposed. Porras and Robertson (1992: 722) define OD as 'a set of behavioral science-based theories, values, strategies, and techniques aimed at the planned change of the organizational work setting for the purpose of enhancing individual development and improving organizational performance, through the alteration of organizational members' on-the-job behavior.'

Chesler (1994: 12–13) states that 'traditionally OD is a long range effort to introduce planned change; is based on a diagnosis that is shared by the members of an organization; involves the entire organization, or a significant subsystem; aims for increased organizational effectiveness and self-renewal; uses various strategies to intervene into ongoing activities to facilitate learning and choose alternative ways to proceed.'

With special regard to the multicultural aspect of OD, Sue (1995: 483) underlines that OD 'a) takes a social justice perspective …; b) believes that inequities that arise within organizations may be primarily due not to poor communication, lack of knowledge, poor management, person-organization fit problems, and so forth, but to monopolies of power; and c) assumes that conflict is inevitable and not necessarily unhealthy.'

Huffington, Cole and Brunning (1997: 20) define OD as 'a planned, organization-wide process of change, derived from behavioral science, to increase an organization's health and effectiveness through interventions in the organization's processes, usually involving a change agent, such that the organization actively anticipates and manages its own development and learning. The objective of OD is to integrate more fully the needs of individuals with the purpose or mission of their organization, such that there is better utilization of resources, notably human resources, and a consequent synergy of effort.'

As reported above, the definitions of the past decade represent the changes that occurred in the political, economical, cultural, and social climate. Organizations are asked to measure themselves by the globalization of the products, of capital and of jobs; moreover they are increasingly concerned with the quality of their products and services, since they need to confront new requests from within as well as from society. The development of new telecommunications and information technologies narrow space and time, and it becomes necessary to rethink the relation with the economical and multicultural context. Organizational development and change tend to refer to the whole organization, identifying higher levels of individual and organizational efficacy.

OD research becomes more aware of its possibilities but also of the limits, of the need to improve methods and intervention techniques, of the urgency to monitor and verify what professionals and scholars from different cultures do within their organizations.

Attention is still turned almost exclusively toward the Western countries, toward productive organizations, while a growing number of requests for OD research and intervention are coming from different areas of the world, starting now, with new awareness, to deal with the problem of organizational efficacy and effectiveness. These come from public organizations (governmental agencies, schools, hospitals, etc.) or from new organizational forms (nonprofit organizations) almost totally neglected from the present studies concerning OD.

THE FINDINGS ON ORGANIZATIONAL DEVELOPMENT AND CHANGE

'Organizational Development is still in its infancy and to date little research on its effectiveness exists' (Beer, 1976: 939). It has been more than two decades since this statement was made; researchers around the world are still seeking answers to the basic questions with empirical research at various organizations, developing theories and models.

Some of the fundamental questions that the researchers have sought to answer from the early studies in 1960s up to 2000 are (Beckhard, 1969; Bennis, 1969; Beer, 1976; French & Bell, 1973; Schein, 1990): Does OD work? Why does OD work? Does OD cause the desired effects? What is it about specific OD interventions that cause positive changes? What are the causal mechanisms occurring in OD programs that bring about desirable outcomes? If one observes the desired effects in an organization engaged in an OD program, can the effects be attributed to the OD program? To what extent can the OD methods be applied from laboratory training to learning organizations and new organizational forms?

Katz and Marshak (1996: 40–1) questioned the existing theories and practices and their core questions were:

How do Organizational Development (OD) assumptions about change, diagnosis and intervention developed in the 1940's, 1950's and 60's fit in today's Information Age? What is the role for OD "change" agents in organizations facing constant change? Do OD practitioners have the frameworks, capabilities and skills to diagnose and respond to issues in complex, multicultural global organizations? Does OD have the technology to work more rapidly with large complex systems and groups and still be effective? How well OD practitioners deal with the dynamic tension between the need to retool and feeling of confusion, ambiguity, loss of competence as they learn to work differently?

Will episodic or continuous change models and interventions be prominent in the near future (Weick & Quinn, 1999)?

Katz and Marshak (1996: 40) stated that not only the organizations but OD also has to reinvent itself. 'Just as the organizations are facing revolutionary changes to long established principles and practices, so too is Organization Development facing similar challenges to its established principles and practices. To remain effective and relevant OD must reinvent itself by developing more comprehensive theories, methods and practices.' They point out some of the emerging issues related to organizational change as: client definition; diagnostic methods; intervention approaches and practitioner work styles. These issues signal the need to reinvent OD strategies and interventions in order to continue to provide meaningful assistance to individuals, groups, and organizations.

At a glance through the methodology of OD, research methods and techniques widely used in recent years include: content analysis, interviews, questionnaires, participant observation, taskforce reports, case studies, archival research, oral histories, written documents, business histories, organization charts, organizational survey reports, survey methods, simulation techniques, action research, insider/outsider approach, daily/weekly journals of consultants, sense making/sense giving, and clinical inquiry techniques.

French and Bell (1984) referred to four main problems related to research in OD. They pointed out these as: problems with definitions and concepts, problems with internal validity, external validity, and problems with lack of a theory. It is still questionable whether we have valid answers to these problems today. However, Porras and Silvers (1991) in their review between 1985–1989 concluded that there was a shift in OD studies from social factors to organizational-level factors which led to an increased volume of work on organizational arrangements and organizational-level interventions. During this period, social factors research focused on a more innovative set of variables like managerial life cycles and organizational paradigms. Organizational vision, planned change, effects of new organizational forms, employee ownership, physical setting, effects of physical setting change, and organizational factors (like structure–culture) were expected to be the emerging topics for the 1990s. Another major conclusion of Porras and Silvers (1991) was to build theories that result in testable models.

Katz and Marshak (1996) argue that, if OD is to continue its function in the near future, it must create new methodologies while redefining, redesigning, and rethinking its role. Through this reinvention basic organization development dimensions should be considered. Theories, methods, and practices for change, clients, diagnostics, intervention, work styles, and other dimensions must be developed. 'Organization Development must develop mechanisms for diagnosis that are more holistic and extend beyond a rational linear approach. Diagnosis must take into account multidimensional data; the symbolic as well as the literal, the overt and the covert, the rational and the emotional. Diagnosis methods must provide information that encompasses the whole system and that integrate the rational, the emotional and psychological aspects of the system' (Katz and Marshak, 1996, 43–4).

Action research is one of the common methods widely used in organizations research after Lewin introduced in 1946. Yet it became more prominent in organization research to validate various research outputs. Eden and Huxham (1996: 526) point out that 'action research is better captured through an interlocking set of characteristics than definition.' They assert that 'action research involves the researcher in working with members of an organization over a matter which is of genuine concern to them and in which there is an intent by the organization members to take action based on the intervention' (Eden & Huxham, 1996: 527). They stated the 15 characteristics of action research (p. 539):

(1) Action research demands an integral involvement by the researcher in an intent to change the organization. This intent may not succeed, no change may take place as a result of the intervention, and the change may not be as intended.

(2) Action research must have some *implications beyond those required for action or generation of knowledge in the domain of the project.* It must be possible to envisage talking about the theories developed in relation to other situations. Thus it must be clear that the results *could* inform other contexts, at least in the sense of suggesting areas for consideration.

(3) As well as being usable in everyday life, action research demands *valuing theory*, with theory elaboration and development as an explicit concern of the research process.

(4) If the generality drawn out of the action research is to be expressed through the design of tools, techniques, models, and method, then this alone is not enough. The basis for their design must be explicit and shown to be related to the theories which inform the design and which, in turn, are supported through action research.

(5) Action research will be concerned with a system of *emergent theory*, in which the theory develops from a synthesis of the data and from the use in practice of the body of theory which informed the intervention and research intent.

(6) Theory building, as a result of action research, will be incremental, moving through a cycle of developing theory to action to reflection to

developing theory, from the particular to the general in small steps.

(7) What is important for action research is not a (false) dichotomy between prescription and description, but a recognition that description will be prescription, even if implicitly so. Thus presenters of action research should be clear about what they expect the consumer to take from it and present it with a form and style appropriate to this aim.

(8) For high-quality action research, a high degree of systematic method and orderliness is required in reflecting about, and holding on to, the research data and the emergent theoretical outcomes of each episode or cycle of involvement in the organization.

(9) For action research, the processes of exploration of the data – rather than collection of the data – in the detecting of emergent theories must either be replicable or, at least, capable of being explained to others.

(10) The full process of action research involves a series of interconnected cycles, where writing about research outcomes at the latter stages of an action research project is an important aspect of theory exploration and development, combining the processes of explicating preunderstanding and methodical reflection to explore and develop theory formally.

(11) Adhering to characteristics (1) to (10) is a necessary *but not sufficient* condition for the validity of action research.

(12) It is difficult to justify the use of action research when the same aims can be satisfied using approaches (such as controlled experimentation or surveys) that can demonstrate the link between data and outcomes more transparently. Thus in action research, the reflection and data collection process – and hence the emergent theories – are most valuably focused on the aspects that cannot be captured by other approaches.

(13) In action research, the opportunities for triangulation that do not offer themselves with other methods should be exploited fully and reported. They should be used as a dialectical device which powerfully facilitates the incremental development of theory.

(14) The history and context for the intervention must be taken as critical to the interpretation of the likely range of validity and applicability of the results of action research.

(15) The theory and context for the intervention must be taken as critical to the interpretation of the likely range of validity and applicability of the results of action research.

While conducting action research, taking these characteristics into consideration will lead to an increase in the rigor of the research. Consequently the researchers as well as practitioners will benefit more from the research. Another remarkable study was conducted by Beer and Eisenstat (1996) who focused on an action research project. The objective was to clearly define the technical specifications for an intervention process that develops an organization's capabilities to implement strategy and learn. The research techniques used were content analysis of taskforce reports, interviews, questionnaires, and participant observation. The main conclusions were that the process succeeded in the short term in all its intended objectives. It was possible to identify a number of elements of the intervention design that promote systematic change, increase organizational openness, and facilitate cross-level organizational partnership.

Laurila (1997) conducted a field study to elaborate the situational determinants which influence managerial choice between different types of technology. The study consisted of a retrospective analysis of the development of a paper industry and its paper mill. The instruments used were in-depth interviews (oral history) and archival data including internal memos, newsletters, production statistics, annual reports, business histories, organization charts, performance objectives for each division, consultant reports, and a questionnaire-based survey on organizational culture. The paper industry and mill as a case was examined in the survey. The conclusions demonstrated how advanced technology can be perceived as an opportunity or threat dependent of the available material resources and firms' competitive position.

Organizational learning or with a more populist approach 'learning organizations' has been a new approach for organization development researchers and practitioners in 1990s and considered 'having many virtues' (Levinthal, 1997: 167). One of the virtues is introduced as helping the organizations to develop the tendency to become more proficient at their current activities with experience. Another one is asserted by Senge (1990) as learning processes facilitate an organization's adaptation to changing circumstances in its competitive environment. Levinthal (1997) refers to these two facets of learning and adds another facet of learning. He indicates that 'the codifying of past experiences and responding to novel contexts are, in important respects, at odds. This inherent conflict poses another facet of learning. In stable words, we tend to view the codification of past experiences as wisdom. In changing environments, we tend to view this same phenomenon less favorably and term it inertia' (p. 167). He discusses the three facets of organizational learning processes and their interrelatedness.

Contrary to Levinthal and other 'believers' of organizational learning, Weick and Westley's (1996) perception and expression of 'organizational learning' is quite different than 'the believers and followers' of organizational learning. They express the differences and paradoxes of individual learning, organizations, and organizational learning. They indicate that current organizational-learning discussions, in particular related directly to information processing and indirectly to rational choice assumptions threaten to create once more an idealized sequence which in turn is not applied in organizations. They state that 'the experiential referent for the term organizational learning is elusive. This is so, for at least three reasons: imprecise referents for the word "organization", misinterpretations of achievement verb "learning" and debate about whether learning is an individual or organizational phenomenon' (p. 441).

The study of Whittington, Pettigrew, Peck, Fenton and Conyon (1999) summarize the literature on the three dimensions of change in Europe during the last decade.

Changing structures, which can be stated as delayering in organizations, especially removal of middle management, increasing operational and strategic decentralization with project based structures.

According to Whittington et al. (1999), *changing processes* in the organization's flexibility and knowledge has become of utmost importance in the new knowledge economy which demands vertical and horizontal interaction. New strategies and structures require new ways of managing and new kinds of managers. Human resources become central to making new forms of work/ organizations. The new HR practices should be concerned both with supporting horizontal networking and with maintaining organizational integration. Corporate mission building and high profile leadership is required for maintaining the 'sense of shared corporate identity on which exchange can be built' (Whittington et al., 1999: 587).

Changing boundaries: the importance of the concept of core competencies increases in relation to delivering, horizontal relationship, and competitive advantage.

Sakano and Lewin (1999) studied the impact of chief executive officer (CEO) succession on strategic and organizational changes. They investigated differences in Japan and the United States affecting succession consequences with a matched control group design. One of the findings was that the consequences of CEO succession in Japan were not observable in the first two years of a new CEO; however, in the United States these changes, related to strategic reorientation or organization restructuring, were observable in the first year. A remarkable finding due to the country/culture effects according to this study was that CEO succession in Japan did not have major impact on radical strategies and organizational changes (Sakano & Lewin, 1999).

Finally, as Weick and Quinn (1999) briefly state, 'change starts with failures to adapt and that change never starts because it never stops. Reconciliation of these disparate themes is a source of ongoing tension and energy in recent change research. Classic machine bureaucracies, with their reporting structures too rigid to adopt to faster-paced change, have to be unfrozen to be improved. Yet with differentiation of bureaucratic tasks comes more internal variation, more diverse views of distinctive competence, and more diverse initiatives. Thus, while some things may appear not to change, other things do' (p. 381). As Weick and Quinn (1999) state, to understand organizational change, one must go back and understand the organizational inertia's content, firmness, and interdependencies from the organizational point of view. Thus another fact, which must be taken into consideration, is that 'change is not an on-off phenomenon nor its effectiveness contingent on the degree to which it is planned and the trajectory of change is more often spiral or open ended than linear' (Weick & Quinn, 1999: 382). These statements once more acknowledge the dynamics of change and the concept of 'changing' reminds us and emphasizes that change is a continuous process.

According to the recent literature we can argue that change will continue interdependent of new technologies, new forms of organizations, innovations in research departments, downsizing and so on. At the intraorganization level, mergers/acquisitions, at the interorganizational level, joint ventures could be examples of continuous change due to the environmental changes in economy, social, political and cultural conditions in various regions (former Soviet Republics, the Far East, Korea, Japan, etc.).

OD consultants should have thorough knowledge of organizational development and change, Industrial Work and Organizational (IWO) Psychology, experience, vision, intuition, ethical standards, and be conscientious in their practices. They should have the perspective of the scientist–practitioner model, like IWO psychologists, not only providing success in their OD practices but should also help, support, and enhance the development of OD theory and methods. In other words they should work as researchers during their interventions and practices to disperse methodology in OD, and to lead progress in the area.

ORGANIZATIONAL DEVELOPMENT INTERVENTIONS

Different OD intervention definitions exist in the literature. Among these, French and Bell's (1984: 122) definition is an operational one: 'OD interventions are sets of structured activities in which selected organizational units (target groups or individuals) engage with a task or a sequence of tasks where the task goals are related directly or indirectly to organizational improvement.' Nine years later, Chell's (1993) definition is almost identical: 'OD interventions are sets of structured activities whereby groups or individuals engage in tasks whose goals are organizational improvement' (Chell, 1993, In C. Huffington, C.F. Cole & H. Brunning, 1997, p. 22).

The objective of OD is to provide organizational change to enhance improvement in organizations. Organizational development activities are designed to improve the organization's functioning through enabling organization members to manage their team and organizational culture effectively. A basic concept related to OD studies is the 'change-agent.' In every OD intervention a change-agent (internal or external) exists, who plans and carries out formal OD programs and interventions.

On the research about characteristics of effective change agents four groups of characteristics were found common (Porras & Robertson, 1992). The first group of characteristics is interpersonal competence (relational skills, ability to support and nurture others, awareness sensitivity, and ability to influence others). The second group includes theory-related problem-solving capacities (knowledge on theory and methods of change, the ability to link this knowledge with organizational realities, the ability to conceptualize and diagnose, to present options to the client).

The third group of characteristics is the change-agent's role as an educator (to be able to create learning experiences). The fourth group is self-awareness (the ability to have a clear understanding of one's own needs and motivation). Schein (1997) points to the relations of 'client' and the change-agent. He focuses on simplifying models that help the researchers understand types of clients and types of client relationships and on some general principles that apply to all of them.

From the 1960s OD researchers have been working on models and classifications of OD interventions. There are numerous ways of categorizing OD interventions. Glancing at the development of OD intervention typologies we come across Blake and Mouton's (1976) list of interventions according to their themes. These themes consisted of: discrepancy interventions, theory interventions, procedural interventions, relationship interventions, experimentation interventions, dilemma interventions, perspective interventions, organizational structure interventions, and cultural interventions. Blake and Mouton (1976) examined and refined the nature of interventions and proposed a theory and typology. Their 'consulcube' was built on three dimensions. The first one was related to what the consultant does, referring to the kind of intervention the consultant uses. They classified five basic types of interventions: acceptant (the consultant gives the client a sense of worth, value, acceptance, and support), catalytic (the consultant helps the client generate data and information to restructure the client's perceptions), confrontation (the consultant points out the value discrepancies in the client's beliefs and actions), prescription (the consultant tells the client what to do to solve the problem), theories and principles (the consultant teaches the client relevant behavioral science theory so that the client can learn to diagnose and solve his/her own problems).

The second dimension is the focal issues, categorized and identified as: power/authority, moral/cohesion, norms/standards of conduct, and goals/objective.

The third dimension of the cube – the units of change – are the target of the consultation. Five units are proposed: individual, group, intergroup, organization, and larger social systems such as community or even society. Blake and Mouton's "consulcube" represented a major contribution to the development of a theory of consultation and intervention. It is considered as a contribution that clarifies the role of organization development and the different interventions that make up the OD technology.

A similar approach was introduced by Schmuck and Miles (1971). They developed an OD cube based on three dimensions: the diagnosed problems, the focus of attention, and the mode of intervention. These typologies could be considered as the first road maps for OD interventions.

French and Bell (1984) stated that in order to gain a perspective of OD interventions, the typology of interventions should be based on questions like: Is the intervention directed primarily toward individual learning, insight, and skill building, or toward group learning? Does the intervention focus on task or process issues? However, they emphasize that interventions are not mutually exclusive; there is great overlap of emphasis and the activity will frequently focus on, for instance, task, at one time and process at a later time. Thus another way to view interventions is to see them as designed to improve the effectiveness of a given organizational unit.

French and Bell's (1984) typology or, as they call it, families of OD interventions, is grouped under 13 headings, including diagnostic activities, team-building activities, grid organization development activities, third-party peacemaking activities, coaching and counseling activities, life and career planning activities, planning and goal-setting activities, and strategic management activities.

Porras and Robertson (1992) developed a classification by deriving information from the earlier works of Beer (1980), Burke (1982), French and Bell (1984), Huse and Cummings (1985). Their classification of OD interventions is by organizational unit analysis and system variable impacted. Organizational units consist of individual, interpersonal, group, intergroup, organizational subheadings, and system variable impacted consists of organizing arrangements, social factors, technology, and the physical setting within which the various techniques and applications take place.

Porras and Robertson (1992) point out some recent developments in the early 1990s. An example is,

in the organizing arrangements category, 'circular organization,' which is a new structural form developed by Ackoff (1989). This form was designed to enhance organizational democracy, adaptability, and quality of working organizations. Another type of structural innovation that Porras and Robertson (1992) mentioned was developed by Alderfer and Tuckers in 1988, and called a 'race relations advisory group' (a group with balanced membership by gender with race representing a cross-section of hierarchical level and functional departments).

The outcomes of each type, dimension, or unit of interventions aim to help organizations to develop problem-solving skills and provide greater effectiveness and/or output and to offer a renewal process to organizations. It can be observed clearly that successful planned organizational change efforts lead to organizational members changing the way they behave on the job. Some examples may be changes in the decisions they make, the way they deal with tasks, the creativity they bring to the job, the initiatives they take, and the information they share (Porras & Robertson, 1992). Changes in the structure of the organization, machinery, job designs, responsibility, and budgeting system can only create long-term organizational change if the attitude and work-related behaviors of the organizational members change through OD interventions. In an interview with Wetlaufer (1999), the new CEO of Ford Motor, Nasser, states that the only way to change the individual's work-related behavior is through teaching. He indicates that in his company the mindsets had to change, the teachable point of view helped organizational members to become teachers of change. He concluded that 'people learned and the company turned around, we became leaders in quality' (Wetlaufer, 1999: 88).

Let us turn to the interaction between individual development and organizational performance outcomes. Organizational performance consists of a variety of outcomes generated by organizations. Such factors as revenues, costs, market share and market position can be considered as economic performance. Among the individual or human relations performance factors, turnover, absenteeism, and grievances could be mentioned. Numerous factors contribute to organizational performance, 'but perhaps the most important one is the behavior of individual organizational members' (Porras & Robertson, 1992: 737). However, as was believed in the 1960s, the changes in individual behavior or individual development alone cannot create the expected change on a large scale in organizations unless changes in organizational factors and/or technology, and physical environment occur.

The organizational culture concept seems to have high impact on organizational development. It has been classified as a social or organizational factor in OD interventions mainly because it involves values, management style, organizational communication patterns, and so on.

Schein (1996, 1997) states that one of the obstacles that organizations face, in the process of OD interventions is three different cultures existing in the same organization, unaware of each other's assumptions. He calls them 'operator culture,' 'engineering culture,' and 'executive culture' and indicates that they are often not aligned with each other, causing failures in organizational learning.

Schein (1999, 1987) proposes clinical inquiry/research to obtain in depth realities in OD interventions and argues that research in any form is an intervention itself.

Maes and Slagle (1994) refer to partnering as a process of organizational change and development with deep historical roots. They discuss partnering as a strategic management tool for change.

The last study is the story of the 1997 European Quality Award (EFQM) company: Beksa from Turkey (Savas, 1999).

Beksa is a 50/50 joint venture between Bekaert of Belgium and Sabanc Holding of Turkey. Of the shareholders, Bekaert, is the world's largest independent producer of steel wire. Founded in 1880 to produce barbed wire, the Bekaert Group now produces a wide range of steel cord and wire products. The 1996 sales turnover of Bekaert was 2.6 billion US dollars. It employs 16,000 people.

Sabanc Holding is the leading industrial conglomerate of Turkey. Founded in 1932, the Sabanc Group comprises many diverse sectors including banking, textiles, synthetic fibers, cement, automotive, tire and reinforcement materials, food, and others. The Group has joint ventures with global leaders such as Dupont, Bridgestone, Carrefour, Toyota, Dresdner Bank, etc. The 1999 sales turnover of Sabanc Holding was 11 billion US dollars. It employs 30,000 people.

Both Bekaert and Sabanci Groups found an excellent fit in forming Beksa in Turkey in 1987. To search for the roots of Beksa's quest for business excellence, we need to go back to early 1990s.

In Beksa, production started in 1988 with the imported half product. The initial investment and the integration of the processes were completed in 1990. Beksa was then ready to go, but couldn't. At that time, the market was depressed due to global recession; market growth was lower than expected. Sales could not support overhead and interests. To deteriorate the market situation further came the Gulf crisis and this was followed by the crisis in Bosnia-Herzegovina. The company was in trouble. The shareholders made an analysis to decide whether to support Beksa would be a right investment, and concluded that: 'Beksa is still a right investment, potential market is still there and it will pick up' (Savas, 1999).

A 'rescue' plan was drafted and executed together with the company management. The plan consisted of three major parts:

1. Restructuring of the organization; one-third of workforce was saved by job enrichment and elimination of non-value-added steps.
2. Structuring of a new working system based on total quality management.
3. Injection of money to minimize interest load; shareholders agreed to increase the capital of the company.

> Our quest for business excellence with the foundations of TQM started. We can now share our experience on how we changed, how we switched to a new working system based on TQM, what we have gained and what we have learned (Savas, 1999: 2).

In 1991, the management defined the TQM approach of Beksa through a 'Breakthrough Triangle'. Today, the 'business excellence triangle' considers all stakeholders who are customers, shareholders, people and in general our society (Savas, 1999).

The first steps were taken to structure a new working system based on TQM in Beksa. The management committee, with the assistance of consultants, developed clear TQM values for Beksa and defined the basics of the policy deployment model.

The new working system was based on two pillars: policy deployment system; and a new company culture.

The policy deployment model at Beksa had two main parts: 'What we will do?' and 'How will we do it?'

In formulating strategy, policies, and plans, they gathered information from different sources by utilizing various mechanisms and tools. All information first entered the related processes, then transferred to their system.

The strategic plan was based on the home-made business model *Beksa 2000* which is a set of linked computer programs combining relevant macroeconomic, market, financial, and technical information.

In 1991, with the assistance of consultants, the organization HR profile was subject to a survey. At the same time the management committee defined the target profile with the following qualifications: total quality oriented; high knowledge and skill; open minded to new developments; hard working; teamwork oriented; participatory; constructive; working priority for Beksa.

A consensus was reached on how to close the gap: intensive training, based on needs; effective communication, improvement on communication skills and determination of the communication needs; creative teamwork.

The lean organization had a significant positive effect on efficient top-down and bottom-up communication among the employees:

> Thanks to policy deployment, we could demolish the walls between the departments. Via interdepartmental team approach there are almost no boundaries among departments now.

At Beksa, we believe that it is the people that make the difference. Therefore it is vital for us to involve all employees in processes and to mobilize their creative talents. (Savas, 1999: 2)

What we have experienced during the past decade can be summarized in one word: change.

We believed we had to integrate our technology with the production, management and industrial relations; therefore we needed to change our structure and the way we used to do our work.

By changing our organizational structure, we needed to change our understanding, behavior and relations.

It was easy to remove functional boundaries in organizational structure on paper, but it took a longer time to remove them from each other's mind. After heavy training and other programs, we managed to minimize borders between departments and establish interdepartmental teams.

When we talk about "change" we can assure you on two things:

Change is painful

Change has to start at the top. (Savas, 1999: 2)

The management committee considered and reconsidered each requirement that would be needed to play the role of the leader and the coach for change in Beksa. It was top management's full commitment to change that brought the mobilization of others, that paved the way for the company from a crisis situation in 1990 to winning the European Quality Award in 1997.

Below are some quantitative results of their performance through their journey for business excellence.

50% increase in customer satisfaction;
60% increase in employee satisfaction;
73% increase in involvement;
67% decrease in work-related accidents;
57% decrease in scrap;
33% decrease in electricity consumption.

Finally, despite the extensive research data on OD interventions, some topics were neglected, like effects of organizational ownership and physical setting interventions, which will be the important topics in the new age of globalization.

Moreover, more integrative and collaborative approaches are needed for multidimensional dynamics in complex systems (Katz & Marshak, 1996).

FUTURE PERSPECTIVES

As far as the scientific aspect is concerned we must notice that some contributions tend to be superficial and fragile considering the methodological issues. Nevertheless we believe that research and research methodology in OD have been changing and improving, and therefore concepts belonging to organizational development and organizational change will always attract and interest researchers and practitioners.

We thereby propose a few conclusive considerations, to the attention of those who will engage in the area of study and intervention in organizations, briefly developed around 12 points.

(1) The process of organizational development and change is, from a psychological point of view, a knowledge production process. The practitioner, instead of offering pre-made solutions, as often done by many international consultancy companies, should aim at defining the relationship that individuals, groups, and organizations have established and consolidated with their external environment, in order to help them develop new knowledge concerning different and new ways to relate to the market, technology, and culture.

Bringing about research or interventions in the field of organizational development and change, therefore, means developing knowledge concerning the relation between people and the environment they live and work in. This very statement helps to avoid the risk that conclusions reached in a specific organization are improperly generalized to other organizations, or even that an easier way to suggest organizational solutions, often derived more from ideological than from scientific assumptions, is used instead of the hard process of new knowledge gaining.

Moreover, the previous statement enables psychology of work and organization to maintain a certain degree of peculiarity toward other approaches and disciplines which deal with the problem of change within organizations. Whoever deals with organizational change and development from a psychological point of view does not bring about a content, but a method which aims, as said, at developing new knowledge about external as well as internal ways to relate. The organizational development intervention is a technical procedure supported by theories of reference, aimed at reaching concrete and defined goals of knowledge production within individuals, groups, and organizations.

(2) The analysis of the relation between people and context, and the investigation of different ways to think about this relation are basically divided into four areas: (a) organizational structures, concerning the degree of division and differentiation of activities, the level of standardization of procedures and work, and the place where the authority takes decisions; (b) organizational processes involved in the operative system, in the information system, and in the management system; (c) the technology used, with reference both to hardware

and software; (d) organizational culture, which refers to shared values, norms and practices of behavior. These four areas, often treated separately, are strongly related. The relation between organization and its context will change if the ways of thinking and managing each of the four areas, or their relations, change profoundly. These named areas are the traditional field of intervention of OD and will continue to be relevant in future as well, even though the complexity of the change processes will need to be greater and more often involve a multidimensional intervention.

(3) Much of the literature of OD refers to profit organizations, but a wide area of research and intervention exists which does not concern this organizational type. Most public organizations (government agencies, regional and municipal offices, hospitals, schools, courts) and lots of private organizations (nonprofit organizations, unions, cultural foundations) are interested in giving opportunities to processes of organizational development and change. OD research studies and interventions in these areas are few. In many places in the world, not only in the so-called third world countries, the transformation of public organizations is the core of the development of democratic life, of the participation of citizens to social life, and it is a permanent instrument to increase life standards and styles.

(4) An additional area of research and intervention is concerned with small organizations. Most OD research and experience is concerned with large-scale organizations. This reason, too, contributes to the numerous problems still existing to verify the internal validity of OD, given the large number of variables interacting. Part of the world economy, though, is based on the work of managers in small organizations who, if they succeed, have to go through cultural difficulties more than economic ones in order to develop their organizations. Small enterprises, mainly if technologically advanced, are called to deal with problems concerning changing and developing processes: the transition from a family-based to an organization-based culture; from an industrial to a financial culture; from a local to a global culture. New economy enterprises as well, are going through change and development problems. It is nevertheless true that any work with small organizations requires personalized interventions, which are also hard to repeat, and it is not possible to apply experience deriving from multinational organizations, but the very process of knowledge development enables us to take into consideration these difficulties and to project targeted interventions.

(5) A field of interest which is gaining more and more interest concerns the transition from monocultural to multicultural organizations. Internationalization, globalization, etc., are words which the vocabulary of managers has recently acquired. Toward the mid-1980s the theme of globalization emerged to highlight the phase of change, of transition from management models linked to traditional multinational enterprises to new and yet completely defined models. Specifically, global means intercontextual: internationalized communication, which inserts into the net context of experience and direct contact with different contexts, which even if related remain different, has created a situation never seen before. Therefore, organizations living in a globalized world need to redefine their relation with the context, and this since they must not deal with an integrated and unified system of knowledge used around the world, but with a differentiated and widely spread system of competencies and information which are rooted in the intercontextual connection. Hence, we find two related aspects of globalization: interconnection, which transfers information from one place to another; and differentiation, which ties it to a specific place.

International organizations appear as networks, a horizontal configuration of resources and abilities distributed, differentiated, and interrelated. The importance of horizontal compared to vertical relations grows, as well as the need to rethink the relation between headquarters and subsidiary; the change processes of this organizational type do not occur based on decisions taken by the strategic top, but derive from actions of independent actors, according to a new approach based on the multiplication of decision-making subjects and on the broad level of intra-organization. International organizations could be, today, the main field in which to test new managerial abilities through the use of continuous learning processes on a worldwide level.

(6) The global society and the new economy are producing unified and unifying values and behavioral models. Organizations are not able to escape this tendency. The pressure toward homogeneity is growing stronger against the tendency to differentiate. Organizations have to deal with the problem of the relationship between homogeneity and difference. This problem exists because they often rely upon the same consultant companies, which seem to be the guardians of the prevalent ideology of organizational change and development.

The problem of keeping together lasting rules, precise procedures, and standards of performance with freedom and participation goes beyond organizations, which nevertheless can be a privileged laboratory in which to test human cohabitation styles and the paradigms which orient individuals and group life. An organization, therefore, becomes multicultural not only because it operates within different geographic contexts, but because it reflects the contributions of different cultural and social groups in their mission, operations, practices, products, and services. The problem, from the point of view of OD, is to promote new policies and practices that will support and advance cultural diversity.

(7) Organizational development and change, defined as a process which aims at producing knowledge concerning the relation between people and their environment, is not linear and static, but dynamic and circular. The past tendency, to perform psychologically reducing operations or the tendency, still present, to simplify reality in order to categorize facts into known schemes, must give way to exploration and of knowledge acquisition to be performed along with the actors of the process of change. OD is no longer a field in which to apply theories, methods and techniques created elsewhere, in order to reach contingent and practical goals only, but becomes, instead, a field from which a rigorous method can be developed, a privileged place of observation where research hypotheses and ideas regarding human behavior can be studied. If the complexity of reality is accepted, then oversimplified explanations of it can be avoided, which often go along with the proposal of final solutions, such as leadership, reengineering, total quality, customer focus, etc.

(8) There seems to be an ongoing challenge for OD researchers and especially consultants in the new decade. Given on the one hand, the problems of methodology in OD research and practice, the increasing complexity, multidimensionality in organizations, especially with globalization, on the other hand, will create constraints. Thus to be able to observe and analyze the core change requirements, they should be equipped not only with a thorough knowledge of organizational development and change but utilize scientist/practitioner model of work and organizational psychology methods in addition to experience, intuition, ethical standards, and conscientiousness in their practice. During OD interventions knowledge production is essential but also OD practitioners have to take a lead in knowledge management practices in organizations. Pfefer and Sutton (1999) claim that although extensive education training, management consulting and business research take place, what managers and organizations actually do has not changed at an extensive level. Thus, this can be considered as a need for further guidance and follow-up in organizations.

(9) The request of comprehension, of transparency, and of participation is growing in those who work inside the organization. This attitude is obviously present towards organizational change and development interventions as well. Literature has recognized long ago the importance of trust in the implementation of planned change. The prospect of organizational justice offers a way to apply within the area of interest of organizational change the concept of trust (Novelli, Kirkman & Shapiro, 1995). From this point of view, change depends on the creation of a feeling of justice in those who will experience the consequences of the change. To realize effective change it would not be enough to develop the view of the process altogether, or even the desire to reach the planned goals: it is necessary to focus on the different aspects of justice in organizational change: distributional justice (individual evaluation of the relation between efforts and results, compared to those of other significant people); procedural justice (perceived impartiality of methods and procedures used to determine who reaches the goals); interrelational justice (perceived honesty of the received interpersonal treatment within a decisional process). Justice problems management is, according to this perspective, the key element to successfully realize organizational changes and, at the same time, it explains why many OD interventions obtain only a formal consent from their addressees, because of the impossibility, real or perceived, to oppose by means of the power the innovation introduced.

(10) Methods problems in research and intervention remain crucial. Considering the past we may say that methodology is weak; blurry quantitative methods don't provide significant results. Field study is somewhat less problematic. Case studies are used widely, but they don't provide a common denominator. There are different streams of research, which mostly do not provide generalizations or even sometimes comparisons. Hence, methods problems concern both internal validity (the confidence that a given organizational change is in fact the cause of the observed effects) and external validity (the extent results from one study can be generalized to other organizations), but some reviews (Porras & Robertson, 1992) have given value and structure to main contributions and to theoretical and methodological evolution of this area of research and intervention. We may therefore share the statement made by Bandura (1986: xii) that 'theories are interpreted in different ways depending on the stage of development of the field of study. In advanced disciplines, theories integrate laws; in less advanced

fields, theories specify the determinants and mechanisms governing the phenomena of interest' but this does not exempt us from a specific commitment in the future.

(11)   Another item concerns the description of values of reference and of the idea of change that should go along every research or intervention of organizational development. Change is not a value in itself. The term development can be used in many different ways (e.g., economic-financial development, goods and services quality development, quality of work life development). Many OD experiences produced only a few results, since their underlying values were not explicit, hardening commitment and investment toward the planned change process.

In other situations a deep fracture developed, in terms of value, between those who propose the change process and those who have to manage it.

The theme of values underlying psychological research and intervention has become a problem: in recent years many privatizations have taken place, transformation of public enterprises sold to private owners so that they entered the free market of goods and services; many OD interventions considered, as a priority condition, a drastic staff reduction and the anticipated exclusion of skilled workers. Given the difficulties in obtaining consent, management used to introduce innovations, very far from participation and involvement; the logic of profit and free market, used in many OD interventions, seems not to have any kind of limit. Through development and change projects, a new organizational order is taking place, with evident consequences in the political and social balance of the world, as well as on the styles of human cohabitation.

(12)   Recent research indicates that there will be a growing need for OD research and practices in the new century. The study of Sinangil and Sanchez (2000) focused on important social and economic factors affecting the practice of industrial, work and organizational psychology, human resources, and management in the next five years. The sample consisted of subject matter experts (SMEs) from two continents, namely Europe and the United States. Respondents from both continents shared the impression that, the trend towards globalization will continue to put pressure on organizations; customer orientation will be greater by the growing of free markets; retention of key talent would be essential in addition to mergers, acquisitions and joint ventures, multiculturalism, and other diversity issues. Consequently, research and different studies project that organizational change will be

continuous in the next decade and there is a common ground for OD research methodology to progress and disseminate its findings.

REFERENCES

Ackoff, R.L. (1989). The circular organization: an update. *Academy of Management Executive, 3,* 11–16.

Alderfer, C.P., Tucker et al. (1988). The race relations advisory group: An inter-group intervention. In W.A. Pasmore, & R.W. Woodman (Eds.), *Research in organizational change and development* (Vol. 2). Greenwich, CT: JAI Press.

Bandura, A. (1986). *Social foundations of thought and action: a social-cognitive theory.* Englewood Cliffs, NJ: Prentice-Hall.

Baumgartel, H. (1959). Using employee questionnaire results for improving organizations: the survey (feedback) experiment. *Kansas Business Review, 12,* 2–6.

Beckhard, R. (1969). *Organization development: strategies and models.* Reading, MA: Addison-Wesley.

Beer, M. (1976). The technology of organizational development. In M.D. Dunnette (Ed.), *Handbook of industrial and organizational psychology* (pp. 939–984). Chicago: Rand-McNally.

Beer, M. (1980). *Organization change and development: a systems view.* Santa Monica, CA: Goodyear.

Beer, M., & Eisenstat R.A. (1996). Developing an organization capable of implementing strategy and learning. *Human Relations, 49*(5).

Beer, M., & Walton, A.E. (1987). Organization change and development. *Annual Review of Psychology, 38,* 339–367.

Bennis, W.G. (1966). *Changing organizations.* New York: McGraw-Hill.

Bennis, W.G. (1969). *Organization development: its nature, origins, and prospects.* Reading, MA: Addison-Wesley.

Blake, R.R., & Mouton, J.S. (1976). *Consultation,* Reading, MA: Addison-Wesley.

Blake, R.R., & Mouton, J.S. (1964) *The Managerial Grid,* Houston: Gulf.

Burke, W.W. (1982). *Organization development.* Boston, MA: Little, Brown.

Chell, E. (1993). The psychology of behaviour in organizations. In C. Huffington, C.F. Cole, & H. Brunning (Eds.), *A manual of organization development.* London: MacMillan.

Chesler, M.A. (1994). Strategies for multicultural organizational development. *The Diversity Factor,* Winter, 12–18.

Clark, J.V., & Krone C.G. (1972). Toward an overall view of organizational development in the early seventies. In J.M. Thomas, & W.G. Bennis (Eds.), *The management of change and conflict* (pp. 284–303). Middlesex, UK: Penguin.

Dicks, H.V. (1970). *Fifty years of the Tavistock Clinic.* London: Routledge and Kegan Paul.

Eden, C., & Huxham, C. (1996). Action research for the study of organizations. In S.R. Clegg,

C. Hardy, & W.R. Nord (Eds.), *Handbook of organization studies*. London: Sage.

French, W.L., & Bell, C.H. (1973). *Organization development*. Englewood Cliffs, NJ: Prentice-Hall.

French, W.L., & Bell, C.H. (1984). *Organization development: Behavioral science interventions for organization improvement* (3rd ed.). Englewood Cliffs, NJ: Prentice-Hall.

Friedlander, F., & Brown, L.D. (1974). Organization development. *Annual Review of Psychology*, 25, 313–341.

Huffington, C., & Cole, C.F., & Brunning, H. (1997). *A manual of organizational development: the psychology of change*. Madison, CT: Psychosocial Press/International Universities Press.

Huse, E.F., & Cummings, T.G. (1985). *Organization development and change* (3rd ed.). St. Paul, MN: West.

Jacques, E. (1951). *The changing culture of a factory*. London: Routledge and Kegan Paul.

Katz, J.H., & Marshak, R. (1996). Reinventing organization development theory and practice. *Organization Development Journal*, 14(1), 40–47.

Laurila, J. (1997). The thin line between advanced and conventional new technology: a case study on paper industry management. *Journal of Management Studies*, 34(2), 219–239.

Levinthal, D. (1997). Three faces of organizational learning: wisdom, inertia and discovery. In R. Garud, P.R. Nayyar, & Z.B. Shapira (Eds.), *Technological Innovation: versights and Foresights*. Cambridge: Cambridge University Press.

Lewin, K. (1947). Frontiers in group dynamics. II. Channels of group life; social planning and action research. *Human Relations*, 1, 143–153. (Reprinted in K. Lewin, *Field theory in social science*. New York: Harper, 1951, Chapter VIII.)

Maes, J., & Slagie, M. (1994). Partnering: a strategic management tool for change. *Organization Development Journal*, 12(3), 75–85.

Margulies, N., & Raia, A.P. (1978). *Conceptual foundations of organizational development*. New York: McGraw-Hill.

Marrow, A.J. (1969). *The practical theorist: the life and work of Kurt Lewin*. New York: Basic Books.

Massarik, F. (1990). The caos and change: examining the aesthetics of organization development. In F. Massarik (Ed.), *Advances in organization development* (Vol. 1, pp. 1–14). Norwood, NJ: Ablex.

Novelli, J.L., Kirkman, B.L., & Shapiro, D.L. (1995). Effective implementation of organizational change: An organizational justice perspective. In C.L. Cooper, & D.M. Rousseau (Eds.), *Trends in organizational behavior* (Vol. 2, pp. 15–36). Chichester, UK: John Wiley.

Pfeffer, J., & Sutton, R.I. (1999). Knowing 'what' to do is not enough: turning knowledge into action. *California Management Review*, 47(1), 83–108.

Porras, J.I., & Robertson, P.J. (1992). Organizational development: theory, practice and research. In M.L. Dunnette, & L.M. Hough (Eds.), *Handbook of industrial and organizational psychology* (2nd ed., Vol. 3). Palo Alto, CA: Consulting Psychologists Press.

Porras, J.I., & Silvers, R.C. (1991). Organization development and transformation. *Annual Review of Psychology*, 42, 51–78.

Robey, D., & Altman, S. (1982). *Organization development: progress and perspectives*. New York: Macmillan.

Sakano, T., & Lewin, A.Y. (1999). Impact of CEO succession in Japanese companies: a coevolutionary perspective. In *Organization Science*, 10(5), 654–671.

Sashkin, M., & Burke, W.W. (1990). Organization development in the 1980s. In F. Massarik (Ed.), *Advances in organization development* (Vol. 1, pp. 1–14). Norwood, NJ: Ablex.

Savas, B. (1999). 1997 *European Quality Award: Beksa Experience*, EFQM Conference Opening Speech.

Schein, E.H. (1987). *The clinical perspective in fieldwork*. Newbury Park, CA: Sage.

Schein, E.H. (1990). Innovative cultures and adaptive organizations. *SriLanka Journal of Development Administration*, 7(2), 9–39.

Schein, E.H. (1996). Three cultures of management: the key to organizational learning. *Sloan Management Review*, 38, 19–20.

Schein, E.H. (1997). The concept of 'Client' from a process consultation perspective: a guide for change agents. *Journal of Organizational Change Management*, 10(3), 202–216.

Schein, E.H. (1999). *Process consultation revisited*. Reading, Mass: Addison-Wesley.

Schmuck, R.A., & Miles, M.B. (Eds.) (1971). *OD in schools*. La Jolla: California University Associates.

Senge, P. (1990). *The fifth discipline: the art and practice of the learning organization*. New York: Doubleday.

Sinangil, H.K., & Sanchez, J. (2000). *Finding common ground for SIOP and EAWOP: convergence of work trends across the Atlantic Ocean*? Paper presented at SIOP 15 Annual Conference, New Orleans.

Sue, D.W. (1995). Multicultural organizational development: implications for the counseling profession. In J.G. Ponterotto, J.M. Casas et al. (Eds.), *Handbook of multicultural counseling*. Thousand Oaks, CA: Sage.

Weick, K.E., & Quinn, R.E. (1999). Organizational change and development. *Annual Review of Psychology*, 50, 361–386.

Weick, K.E., & Westley, F. (1996). Organizational learning: affirming an oxymoron. In S.R. Clegg, C. Hardy, & W.R. Nord (Eds.), *Handbook of organization studies*, London: Sage.

Wetlaufer, S. (1999). Driving change: an interview with Ford Motor Company's Jacques Nasser. *Harvard Business Review*, 77(2), 77–88.

Whittington, R., Pettigrew, A., Peck, S., Fenton, E., & Conyon, M. (1999). Change and complementaries in the new competitive landscape: a European panel study, 1992–1996. *Organization Science*, 10(5), 583–600.

18

Management Interventions

ROBERT L. CARDY and T.T. SELVARAJAN

Improving individual and organizational effectiveness has been a primary research focus for the management and organization theorists since the early part of this century. Starting with Taylor's scientific management approach, business organizations of this century have seen many management interventions aimed at improving their effectiveness. A partial list of such interventions include scientific management, participative management, quality of work life programs, Management by objectives (MBO), quality circles, total quality management (TQM), business process reengineering, and the balanced scored card approach, among others. A conceptual framework based on intervention criteria is presented in this chapter. Using this framework, this chapter will review and analyze the management interventions and the focus will be on selected important interventions such TQM, MBO, and participative management. Specifically, this chapter will address the history, development, and future of each of the management interventions. Since most of the management interventions were modeled for the American business organizations, there is a need to develop a model of management intervention that is applicable to the global workforce. Thus, this chapter attempts to integrate perspectives from various cultures so as to present a fuller spectrum of approaches that may be applicable around the globe.

INTRODUCTION

Management interventions can be viewed as planned changes in the work setting designed to change the behavior of organizational members and lead to desirable organizational outcomes (Porras & Silvers, 1991). Given this description, management intervention is a very broad topic area, even for purposes of a book, let alone a chapter. Virtually any systematic approach to improving performance effectiveness in organizations would qualify as a viable example of a management intervention. For purposes of this chapter, we focus on management interventions in the modern history of organizations since the industrial revolution. Further, we limit consideration here to interventions that are meant to influence performance effectiveness in organizations by working on or through the human resources in the organization. Finally, we have restricted coverage here to interventions that we view as being widely practiced or having had a major influence on management thinking and practice. This narrowing of the topic still leaves a wide variety of approaches and techniques to be considered. We hope that the level and breadth of consideration here is adequately balanced and sufficient to spark research development in this area.

The domain of management interventions is a rich and fruitful area for development of theory that bridges various types of interventions and for the conduct of empirical investigation into the effectiveness of interventions. We begin consideration of the topic of management interventions by first presenting a broad model of the intervention process. We then briefly review conceptual frameworks for analyzing management interventions before addressing specific intervention.

A general model of the management intervention process is presented in Figure 18.1. The model

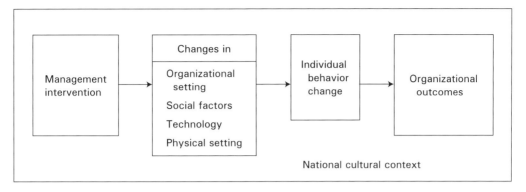

Figure 18.1   *Management intervention in a multicultural context*

Table 18.1   *Workplace characteristics and focus of intervention*

Workplace characteristics	Example of focus of intervention
Organizing arrangements	Goals, strategies, formal structures, administrative policies and procedures, formal reward systems, and ownership
Social factors	Culture, interactive processes at the level of individual, group, and intergroup, individual attributes such as motivations, behaviors, and attitudes
Technological factors	Work flow process, job design, and technical systems
Physical setting	Space configuration, physical ambiance, interior design, and architectural design

Source: Porras and Robertson (1992)

presents interventions as potentially producing changes in a variety of workplace characteristics (Porras & Robertson, 1992). A description of possible foci of intervention that seem most aligned with each of these categories of workplace characteristics is presented in Table 18.1.

Management interventions may involve changes to more than one of the four work settings identified in the model in Table 18.1. For example, Taylor's scientific management approach involved making changes to organizational arrangements, technology, and the physical setting (Taylor, 1911). The total quality management (TQM) intervention may involve changes to the organizational setting (e.g., management policy), social factors (e.g., teamwork), technology (e.g., job redesign), and the physical setting (e.g., physical ambience).

The central assumption in this model is that changing the work setting is the most potent tool for

changing individual behavior. The perspective that altering the work setting can introduce changes in individual behavior is based on cognitive models of behavior which postulate that an individual's environment is an important source of information about appropriate behaviors (Porter & Lawler, 1968; Vroom, 1964; Hackman, 1981). The ultimate goal is not just change in individual behavior but improved organizational outcomes. Therefore, another central assumption in this model is that changes in individual behavior will result in corresponding changes in organizational outcomes.

The intervention process model also explicitly recognizes the cultural context within which management interventions take place. Based on research in cross-cultural psychology (e.g., Triandis, 1980), we view culture as a dynamic phenomenon that changes with time and space. Many organizational scientists (e.g., Hofstede, 1980, 1991; Child , 1981; Boyacigiller & Adler, 1991; Tayeb, 1994) have asserted that unique historical and social conditions associated with each country will shape country-specific approaches to management.

Our objective in this chapter is to review the literature and cover the salient issues for some of the most popular management interventions. Conceptual frameworks for exploring management interventions will be considered. The remainder of the chapter will focus on management interventions. There have been numerous management interventions and covering each of these interventions in great detail is beyond the scope of a book chapter. Hence this chapter will focus on some of the most popular management interventions such as participative management, management by objectives (MBO), and total quality management (TQM). For each of the above management interventions, we consider the historical development, salient features, and where the approach seems to be headed in the next millennium. This chapter will integrate theoretical perspectives from different national

Table 18.2 *A framework for analyzing management interventions*

Intervention (Focal criterion)	Org setting	Social factors	Technology	Physical setting
Scientific management (outcome) Improving production process by efficient design of human–machine interfaces			×	×
Bureaucracy (outcome) A theory of organization built around specialization of labor, hierarchy, and rules and regulations	×			
Functional management (outcome) Views management as a process of performing general functions such as planning, organizing, controlling, and decision making	×			
Human relations (social) Orientation to management concerning individual differences, interpersonal relations, and participative practices		×		
MBO/goal setting (outcome) Management approach designed to involve individuals in defining and setting goals	×			
Behaviorism (social) A school of thought placing primary attention on individual and group processes in organizations		×		
Participative management (outcome and social) A management technique that requires involvement of workers in the decision-making process	×	×		
Sociotechnical system (outcome and social) A management system that aims at joint optimization of social (human) and technological systems	×	×	×	
Quality of work life (social) Promoting a favorable work environment that results in employee well-being and satisfaction		×		
Job redesign (outcome and social) Designing jobs that are more meaningful and provide more autonomy to workers	×	×	×	
Matrix organization (outcome) An organizational concept that displays two dimensional flow of authority. The vertical dimension is hierarchical in nature and horizontal dimension relates to project	×			
Pay for performance plans (outcome) Compensation systems that promote individual performance	×			
Gainsharing plans (outcome) Systems for compensating group/plant level performance	×			
Zero-based budgeting (outcome) A budgeting technique that begins with a new 'zero' base each year and focuses on the justification of all program elements	×			
Strategic planning (outcome) A management technique for deciding the basic direction an organization should take to meet future challenges	×			
Theory Z (outcome) An organizational form that combines Japanese and American management systems	×			
Total quality management (outcome) An organization-wide approach for managing quality that involves customer focus, continuous improvement, and teamwork	×	×		
Diversity management (social) Management technique for productively engaging and reducing conflict in an ethnically diverse workforce	×	×		

(Contd.)

Table 18.2   *(Contd.)*

Intervention (Focal criterion)	Org setting	Social factors	Technology	Physical setting
Workteams/autonomous workgroups (outcome and social)	×	×	×	
Organizing work around groups that have wide range of autonomy				
Downsizing/rightsizing (outcome)	×			
Structural change to an organization that results in reduction of number of employees				
Intrapreneuring (outcome)	×			
A process for recognizing and using entrepreneurship within the organization that results in quicker innovation				
360 degree appraisal (outcome)	×			
A performance appraisal system where an individual is appraised by self, peer, supervisor, subordinate, and customers				
Core competencies (outcome)	×			
Focusing and building on areas where a company can provide world class performance on a sustainable basis				
Business process reengineering (outcome)	×			
Redesigning business processes for reducing cost and improving productivity				
Balanced score card	×			
A performance management system that goes beyond financial performance indicators and include other performance metrices like innovation, quality, customer satisfaction, human resources, etc.				

cultures and draw implications for a globally integrated workforce for research and practice.

A CONCEPTUAL FRAMEWORK FOR ANALYZING MANAGEMENT INTERVENTIONS

Management interventions have been analyzed in many ways. A typical approach for analyzing management interventions has been to simply view them on a timescale. This approach provides a snapshot view of various management theories and can be seen in various management texts. However, such an approach does not provide an adequately rich conceptual/theoretical framework for meaningful insight into the subject matter. Another popular approach has been the development of taxonomies of management interventions based on the organization elements targeted for change. This approach has been utilized by researchers in organization theory/design. Organization design theorists analyze organizational change interventions in terms of changes to structure, technology, and people (e.g., Galbraith, 1973; Pugh & Hickson, 1993). This approach provides a rich conceptual framework grounded in organization theory/design. According to organization design theorists, organizations consist of various elements such as technology, structure, systems, and processes. Thus, a management intervention can be categorized

in terms of the organizational element that is the target of the intervention. Management intervention can comprise more than one organizational element. For example, a job design intervention can be categorized as an intervention affecting both technology and human resource systems.

One other possible dimension for analyzing management interventions would be in terms of criteria. Management interventions are generally introduced for arriving at some desired results/ goals. Some of the common criteria for management interventions are individual/organizational performance, job satisfaction, commitment, interpersonal relations and so on. These goals can be categorized as outcome criteria or social criteria. The outcome criterion includes measures such as job performance, absenteeism, turnover, accident rates, and so on. The social criterion can include measures such as satisfaction, commitment, resistance to change, and group cooperation.

A classification scheme based on the two dimensions organizational elements and criteria is presented in Table 18.2. The criteria can be categorized as representing either the outcome criterion or the social criterion. The organizational elements include organizational setting, social factors, technology, and physical setting. The table lists the interventions in a historical time line. The focal or dominant criterion for an intervention is given in parentheses after each intervention. A brief definition of each of these interventions is also presented next to the intervention. A given management intervention can influence one or more organizational elements. In addition, an intervention can be implemented with the intention to achieve social or outcome criteria or both. A taxonomy of management interventions based on criteria has not been, to our knowledge, developed before and such a framework may provide interesting insights into management intervention literature.

Table 18.2 lists some of the common management interventions. There are some interventions designed to improve outcomes. For example, Taylor's scientific management technique was aimed at improving individual employee productivity by building efficient technological systems and physical settings. In contrast, the human relations theorists were concerned with improving the psychological well-being of individual employees. Thus a human relations intervention can be categorized as an intervention aimed at social factors. As mentioned above, some interventions were designed to impact both outcomes and the social criterion. For example, participative management is often introduced to enhance both performance and satisfaction. This is evidenced by the fact that research on the effectiveness of participative management includes both satisfaction and performance as dependent variables.

It is also possible to classify management interventions according to the extent to which an intervention aims at reducing performance variance due to system factors. A classification scheme based on performance variance due to person and system factors is presented in Table 18.3. Some interventions are aimed at reducing variance due to the human factor by specifying system details. For example, interventions such as scientific management and TQM try to improve organizational performance by specifying system standards, and organizational members are required to maintain these standards. On the other hand, interventions such as diversity management and participative management aim at improving performance by enhancing variance due to person factors.

In the next section, we present a detailed discussion of some of the most important interventions listed in Table 18.2.

SCIENTIFIC MANAGEMENT

Frederick Taylor, often considered the father of modern management, was a trained industrial engineer. His concern was to improve production operations by carefully designing human–machine interfaces. He pioneered the time and motion studies which formed the basis for the scientific management theory (Taylor, 1911). The technique used by Taylor included (a) identifying a job, (b) calling

attention to wasteful motions, (c) timing the job and workers to achieve better performance, and (d) incentive plans to motivate workers to perform. Taylor approached management from an engineering perspective; that is, the work should be specialized, standardized, and simplified. Authority and decision making were supposed to be the job of managers at the top and workers at the lower level were asked to do and not think. In Taylor's scheme of management there was no room for considering psychological well-being of the individual.

In addition to Taylor, there were a few other scientists who made important contributions to scientific management. Frank Gilbreth developed the motion study which focused on the actual motions involved in a job and sought to minimize fatigue by developing the one best way to do the work (Gilbreth, 1911). Lillian Gilbreth focused on the psychological, rather than the physiological effects of fatigue (Gilbreth, 1914). Gantt, an associate of Taylor, developed the Gantt chart, and task and bonus system. The Gantt chart was used to plan production in terms of time rather than quantity and to sequence project activities to ensure the scheduled completion date was met (Gantt, 1919).

The scientific management technique was widely embraced by organizations well into 1950s and 1960s. Scientific management was integrated with assembly-line work by companies like Ford Motor Company with spectacular results in productivity gains. American Companies would come to dominate the world market with scientific management techniques. American managers thought they had discovered the ultimate approach to management (Lawler, 1986).

The scientific management technique, however, has been widely criticized. The classic Hawthorne experiments demonstrated that sociopsychological aspects of work could influence productivity. Human relations theorists such as McGregor and Maslow argued that scientific management ignored basic psychological needs of individuals at work. The basic criticism was that the standardized and narrow jobs created by scientific management would demotivate people at work. Sociologists like Blauner (1964) wrote about the alienating influence of technological processes envisaged by the scientific management techniques. During the same period, contingency organization theorists such as Woodward (1965) argued that there is no one best way to organize and manage things. Scientific management was hugely successful because of the unique socioeconomic environment that existed in the post world war era. There was a heavy post war demand and the scientific management's efficient assembly-line production process produced wonderful results. Practicing managers during that time did not see any need to change management processes despite the severe criticism from various quarters.

Table 18.3   *Management intervention as a function of criterion variance due to person factors*

Intervention (Focal criterion)	Range of variance due to human factor	
	High	Low
Scientific management (outcome)		x
Bureaucracy (outcome)		x
Classical organization theory (outcome)	x	
Human relations (social)	x	
MBO/goal setting (outcome)		x
Behaviorism (social)	x	
Participative management (outcome and social)	x	
Sociotechnical system (outcome and social)	x	
Quality of work life (social)	x	
Job design (outcome and social)	x	
Pay for performance plans (outcome)	x	
Gainsharing plans (outcome)		x
Quality circles (outcome)		x
Total quality management (outcome)		x
Diversity management (social)	x	
Workteams/autonomous workgroups (outcome and social)	x	

In spite of all the criticism of scientific management, it is the one intervention that had profound influence on the American economy. Out of Taylor's work was born a new field called industrial engineering. This field, along with ergonomics, made significant contributions to improving the physical work environment by designing more efficient human–machine interfaces. In addition, creating efficient production systems is important for removing system bottlenecks in the production process, which is an important component of the quality management system (Deming, 1986). Thus, in spite of the widespread criticism of scientific management, we see that practicing managers have not thrown out the baby with the bath water. In the 21st century, we expect that scientific management principles will be applied in the fields of industrial engineering and quality management for making continuous improvements in the physical work environment.

MANAGEMENT BY OBJECTIVES (MBO)

MBO was first introduced to organizations in the 1950s by Drucker (1954) and McGregor (1960). MBO is a procedure in which managers meet with workers to set realistic goals. This simple process developed into one of the most widely used management interventions during the 1960s and 1970s. Key components of the MBO model are generally thought to be: (1) objective or goal setting, (2) subordinate participation, (3) implementation, and (4) review and feedback.

The principle behind the MBO intervention was that an organization would be more successful if employees' efforts pull together in the same direction as that of the organization's and their contributions fit together to produce a whole, without gaps, without friction, and without unnecessary duplication of effort (Odiorne, 1978). It was thought that this focus on goal alignment as a way to improve organizational performance provides the best path to increased profitability.

The MBO model represented a shift in managerial thinking that existed during the 1950s (Quinn, 1996). At that time there existed two predominant schools of thought: scientific management and human relations. The scientific management model was a rational-goal model based on strict command and control and had little concern for workers' participation in management. The human relations model, on the other hand, focused on employee empowerment and collaboration but had no concern for organizational goals. The MBO model combined the elements of the scientific and human relations models. That is, MBO emphasized organizational goals (an element of the scientific management) but also postulated that workers should participate in setting objectives (an element of the participatory human relations model). Thus, MBO can be viewed as an attempt to merge two contrasting management models.

The MBO model was successfully applied at General Mills during the 1950s. Following its success, MBO systems became increasingly common in organizations during the 1960s and 1970s. A set of MBO implementation steps was also developed to allow consistent application of MBO across organizations (Odiorne, 1978). The steps are: (1) identification of organizational strategy, (2) collaborative goal setting, (3) rewards linked to goals, (4) development of action plans,

(5) cumulative periodic review of subordinate results against targets, and (6) review of organizational performance.

The effect of MBO interventions on organizational effectiveness has been well documented (e.g., Raia, 1974; Ivancevich, 1976; Wickens, 1968; Rodgers & Hunter, 1991, 1994; Guzzo, Jette & Katzell, 1985). These studies found supporting evidence for the hypothesis that goal setting within the MBO context resulted in higher levels of performance. Guzzo et al. (1985) conducted a meta-analytic study to find the effects of psychologically based intervention programs on worker productivity and concluded that MBO improved productivity. In a relatively recent meta-analytic study, Rodgers and Hunter (1992) found that all the 30 MBO studies included in their meta-analysis reported productivity gain. The authors also conducted a moderator analysis to delineate contextual factors that may influence success of MBO intervention. They found that the top management commitment is a crucial factor that moderates the influence of an MBO intervention and increase in productivity. When commitment was low the productivity increase was just 3%, but, when commitment was high, the productivity increase was 54%. Thus, they conclude that the failure of MBO in some organizations has nothing to do with the principles of MBO but is due to process issues involved in implementation.

Interestingly, although the MBO intervention is generally aimed at the productivity criterion, studies have found the intervention to also have a positive influence on the social criterion (e.g., Neumann, Edwards & Raju, 1989; McConkie, 1979). In a review of the impact of MBO, McConkie (1979) found that MBO had positively influenced social criteria such as motivation, job satisfaction, and interpersonal relations.

Despite the initial success of MBO and in spite of the fact that MBO was based on sound principles, the use of this intervention declined during the 1980s. MBO's widespread decline can be attributed to several factors (McConkie, 1979; Dinesh & Palmer, 1998):

(1) partial implementation of the system as an individual performance appraisal system rather than an overall goal congruence system;
(2) a lack of true employee participation in goal-setting efforts;
(3) programs tend to lose their appeal when another new program is introduced;
(4) lack of top management commitment;
(5) lack of a supportive culture and a structure that prevents participative culture.

Despite the decreasing importance given by scholarly researchers as well as practitioners, we believe that MBO is not dead. As observed by some scholars (e.g., Rodgers & Hunter, 1992;

McConkie, 1979) management interventions tend to become a fad after a period of time. This is partly because one intervention is supplanted by a newer and more appealing management intervention. In the case of MBO, it may have been replaced by an emphasis on quality circles and TQM in organizations. There are a number of elements common to MBO and TQM. For example, just as in MBO, TQM emphasizes participative management, goal setting, and feedback. Thus, the principles of MBO continue to exist in organizations in the form of other management interventions. The theoretical principles underlying MBO, namely, participative management, goal setting, and feedback are robust and based on years of research in industrial psychology and these principles will continue to be valid in the future. Thus, in the 21st century, we believe that the principles underpinning MBO interventions will continue to be applied in organizations even if the term itself becomes a thing of the past.

PARTICIPATIVE MANAGEMENT

Participative management is one of the earliest management interventions as well as one of the most researched topics in management. There have been many reviews of participative management since the landmark review by Locke and Schweiger (1979) and these reviews have generated considerable interest and debate. In this section, first, a historical perspective of this intervention will be reviewed. Second, the effect of participative management on various outcome measures will be discussed. Third, the impact of participative management across various national cultures will be reviewed. Finally, the usefulness of this intervention for organizations of the 21st century will be presented.

History of Participative Management

In this section, we present a historical overview of participation research and also review highlights of major reviews conducted in participative management.

The earliest proponent of participative management was Hugo Munsterberg (1913). He suggested that productivity could be improved by collaboration and joint participation between management and workers. Participative management was a topic of research in the Hawthorne studies (Mayo, 1933; Roethlisberger & Dickson, 1939) and the experiments conducted by Lewin and colleagues (Lewin, Lippit & White, 1939). The Hawthorne experiments studied the influence of supervisory style on worker productivity. The results of this work indicated that worker productivity increased when the supervisor's leadership style was more participative.

However, the Hawthorne studies have been criticized for methodological flaws (e.g., Sykes, 1965). Lewin et al. (1939) conducted a series of experiments to determine the influence of leadership styles on performance. They found that performance of groups led by autocratic leader was better than a group led by democratic leader when the leader was present, but the performance of the group led by democratic leader was better when the leader was absent. In a follow-up study, Lewin (1952) reported that the participatory approach was more effective than the lecture method in a study of getting housewives to serve different types of food.

Participative management became an area of management research with the seminal work of Coch and French (1948). In their study of a pajama factory, the authors conducted an experiment varying the level of participation. Specifically, there were three experimental groups: no participation, direct participation, and indirect participation. In the indirect participation group, workers elected representatives who participated in decision making, and in the direct participation group, workers directly participated in the decision-making process. The authors reported that productivity improvements were highest for the direct participation group. In addition, this study indicated that resistance to change was the least and satisfaction was the highest when workers participated directly in decision making.

During 1950s and 1960s scholars such as Argyris, McGregor, Likert, and Herzberg argued for a human relations approach to management. They advocated a more participatory style of management where workers had a role in decision making in their work environments. Herzberg's (1966) job enrichment envisaged vertical expansion of jobs that would give individuals greater opportunity to make decisions in their jobs. Job enrichment programs were implemented in organizations such as AT & T, US Air Force, Prudential, and Motorola. Herzberg's program was particularly influential in AT & T where more than 100,000 jobs were enriched (Lawler, 1986). Motorola claimed significant improvement in performance due to job enrichment and has since been a leading practitioner of participative management (Lawler, 1986).

During the same time, the sociotechnical system was introduced in Europe by the Tavistock Institute (Trist & Bamforth, 1951; Emery & Trist, 1969). The sociotechnical approach emphasized a fit between social and technical systems. The proponents of the sociotechnical system advocated a participative management approach and this system was successfully introduced in organizations in England and Norway.

Quality of work life (QWL) programs were introduced during the 1970s. Several companies such as General Motors, Proctor & Gamble, and General Foods initiated new approaches to organization design that incorporated principles of participative management (Lawler, 1986). The new plant design was based on the sociotechnical system developed in Europe. The pioneer of the new plant revolution was Proctor & Gamble, which introduced participative management in many of its manufacturing plants during the 1970s. Other organizations such as General Foods and General Motors started their own program based on Proctor & Gamble's participative management (Lawler, 1986). In the new plant design, workers often participated in decision making in areas which used to be an exclusive management prerogative. For example, workers in the new design plants had a say in policies involving employee selection, plant layout, the pay system, and job design. These organizations also often deemphasized a hierarchical approach and introduced a flatter organizational structure. Impressive outcomes in terms of lower absenteeism, lower turnover, lower costs, higher quality, and higher employee satisfaction due to participative management were reported by these organizations (Lawler, 1986).

American organizations faced a serious challenge from Japanese companies during 1980s. The success of Japanese organizations was attributed to a quality management system that involved employee participation in decision making. For example, Japanese organizations made use of employee problem-solving groups called quality circles to improve productivity and quality. A large number of American companies introduced quality circles in late 1970s and 1980s to improve quality and productivity. Ouchi introduced the Theory Z concept for the American companies to meet the Japanese challenge. Ouchi (1981) contrasted the Japanese method to the American method and formulated a modification which may be applicable to the United States. The Theory Z organization retains the Japanese commitments to long-term employment, consensual decision making, and a holistic concern for the employee, but adapts itself to the American value by employing monetary incentives, greater individual responsibility, and relatively more specialized careers. Ouchi points to companies that have incorporated Theory Z, such as Eli Lilly, as major success stories.

The 1990s saw an emergence of semi-/fully autonomous workteams. The team-based approach gave considerable opportunity for workers to participate in the decision making process. In the self-managing workgroups, the team members made decisions virtually in all management areas including hiring, fixing pay rates, specifying standards, and purchasing, among others.

In summary, the history of participative management indicates that few organizations employed this intervention until the mid-1970s. Although researchers have been advocating a more participative approach to management since the 1950s, it was not until the early 1980s that it became widespread. Many organizations have introduced quality management programs and workteams that infuse worker participation into the decision making.

The first major review of participative management was done by Locke and Schweiger (1979). They divided past research on participation into three groups: laboratory experiments, correlational field studies, and field experiments. Locke and Schweiger conducted a box score analysis of the three groups to summarize the results of research on participation. The results of their review indicate that participative management did not have any effect on performance. However, their review concluded that participative management did have a positive impact on satisfaction.

Miller and Monge (1986) conducted a meta-analysis of 47 studies on participation. The authors concluded that participation influenced both performance and satisfaction but the effect of participation on performance is small. The authors also observed that the effect of participation on performance is large for laboratory studies and studies that used perceptual measures.

The next major review was conducted by Wagner and Gooding (1987) who also employed the meta-analysis technique. Their review included 79 studies on participative management and reached conclusions similar to that of Miller and Monge (1986). The authors further analyzed the sample by controlling for the effect of common method bias and found that studies that used single-source, perceptual measures reported much higher correlation between participation and performance than the studies that employed multisource measures. Thus, the authors concluded that a higher participation – performance correlation is a method artifact.

Cotton, Vollrath, Froggart, Lengnick-Hall and Jennings (1988) conducted a major review of participation studies that included 91 articles published between 1978 and 1983. Based on the review they argued that participation is a multidimensional construct and offered a classification scheme for categorizing different forms of participation. Their classification scheme included the following forms of participation:

permanent form, in which workers have a formal, direct role in decision making;
consultative participation, in which worker's are encouraged to make suggestions (e.g., quality circles, gainsharing plans);
short-term participation, in which workers are consulted at an informal level;
employee ownership, in which workers are part owners and thus have a role in decision making;
representative participation, in which workers' representatives are elected as board members.
Cotton et al., compared the efficacy of different forms of participation and concluded that some

forms of participation are more capable of influencing performance and satisfaction. Specifically, they found that direct participation and employee ownership enhanced performance and informal participation and employee ownership increased satisfaction.

Wagner (1994) followed up with a major review of all the reviews conducted on participative management. The author controlled for the effect of single source bias and found that participation had a positive effect on performance but concluded that the effect size was small and practically insignificant.

The Impact of Participation on Outcomes

In this section, we discuss the impact of participative management on various outcome measures as well as review the research on contextual factors that may influence the participation – outcome relationship.

Performance and satisfaction are the two most important dependent variables considered in participation research (Wagner, 1994; Cotton et al., 1988; Wagner & Gooding, 1987; Ledford & Lawler, 1994; Miller & Monge, 1986; Locke & Schweiger, 1979). There are two camps of researchers who hold divergent views on the influence of participative management on outcomes. On the one hand, researchers such as Wagner (e.g., Wagner, 1994, 1995) argued that participative management had very little impact on performance improvements. The other camp of researchers (e.g., Cotton et al., 1988) are of the view that participative management is a multidimensional construct and that certain forms of participation can have a positive influence on job performance. A basic reason for this divergent view is that researchers employ different conceptualizations of the participation construct. Researchers such as Locke and Wagner (e.g., Locke & Schweiger, 1979; Wagner, 1994; Locke, Alavi & Wagner, 1997) view participation in narrow terms and define participation as joint decision making shared between subordinates and superiors. In their view, participation is just 'a process in which influence is shared among individuals who are otherwise hierarchical unequals, balancing the involvement of managers and their subordinates in decision making and problem solving activities' (Locke et al. 1997: 328). They also differentiate between participation and related constructs such as empowerment and involvement. Wagner (1995) argued that participation and empowerment are different constructs, since the latter involves delegation and distribution of authority, while participation does not involve any delegation. Leana (1987) differentiated delegation and participation with the former involving more personal autonomy and less social interaction than the latter. Wagner (1995) also argued that involvement is a much broader construct that includes changes in job design, goal setting, and rewards.

In contrast to this narrow view, Cotton et al. (1988) argued that participative management is a multidimensional construct. Based on a literature review, Black and Gregersen (1997) identified the following dimensions of participative management:

(1) Rationale, whether humanistic or pragmatic (e.g., Dachler & Wilpert, 1978);
(2) Structure, ranging from formal to informal (e.g., Cotton et al., 1988; Dachler & Wilpert, 1978);
(3) Form, ranging from direct to indirect (e.g., Cotton et al., 1988; Dachler & Wilpert, 1978);
(4) Decision issues, ranging from suggestion schemes for making small improvements to decision making in areas such as strategy and capital distribution;
(5) Degree of involvement, ranging from eliciting employee opinion to vesting complete ownership of the decision-making process.

Given the complex nature of participative management, Cotton et al. argue that there is no simplistic answer to the effect of participative management. In an empirical assessment in a multinational manufacturing firm in the United States, Black and Gregersen (1997) found that participation's effect on performance and satisfaction was contingent upon the degree of involvement. Lawler is also of the view that participation is a complex construct which may involve people at different levels ranging from a few individuals to the whole organization (e.g., Lawler, 1986; Ledford & Lawler, 1994). Lawler argued that 'participation is not something that organizations either have or do not have – it comes in many forms and can be brought about in many ways' (1986: 22). Lawler defines participation in terms of four dimensions: power, information, knowledge, and rewards. The degree of participation varies based on the extent to which power, information, knowledge, and rewards are shared by employees at lower levels of the organization. Lawler described three levels of participative management based on the degree of participation: parallel suggestion involvement, which includes interventions such as survey feedback and quality circles; job involvement, which includes job design and workteams; and high-involvement intervention, which is plant-wide or organization-wide participation intervention. Clearly, participation, to this group of researchers, is a complex, multivariate construct that has the potential to influence individual and organizational performance.

The theoretical rationale for the influence of participation on performance is given by Vroom (1964).

People are motivated to perform when they perceive that they will achieve the goals they desire. Participation affects employee perception of whether goals are achievable. In addition, when people participate in decisions regarding their performance objectives, it affects their commitment to achieve these objectives. However, Wagner (1994) argued that participation has very little influence on performance. Based on a review of all major reviews on participation, the author found that there is a mean correlation of 0.08 to 0.25 between participation and performance. But Wagner concluded that the effect size is very small, which raises questions about the practical significance of participative management. However, in our view, it is inconceivable that participation will have a large effect, especially when it is defined in narrow terms. As argued by Ledford and Lawler (1994), there is no theoretical reason to believe that participation as defined by Wagner will contribute to a sizable effect on performance. Ledford and Lawler further argue that studying participation in isolation is a futile exercise, since any participatory intervention that is not reinforced by appropriate rewards, communication, training etc. is not likely to have major effect on performance. This notion was supported in a study of the influence of participation and human resource practices on performance (Wright, McCormick, Sherman & McMahan, 1999). In this study of petrochemical refineries in the USA, it was found that effectiveness was greatest when companies invested in both participation and proactive human resource practices and effectiveness was least when the companies invested in only one of the two interventions. Lawler's definition of participation includes employee involvement in different forms and at various levels. Based on a survey of Fortune 1000 firms, Lawler reported that the vast majority of firms use some form of employee participation practices and that most companies reported that their practices are successful (Lawler, 1986).

The influence of participation on satisfaction is more positive than the impact of participation on performance. The mean correlation between participation and satisfaction was 0.44 (Wagner, 1994). Almost all the reviews have concluded that participation positively affects satisfaction. In addition to performance and satisfaction, other dependent variables such as absenteeism (e.g., Lawler & Hackman, 1969), turnover (e.g., Macy, 1982), commitment (Spector, 1986), accident and injury rates (Macy & Mirvis, 1982), and resistance to change (Coch & French, 1948) have been considered and the relationship between participation and these variables have been generally found to be favorable.

Several researchers have suggested that the reason for an inconsistent relationship between participation and performance may be due to situational factors (Lawler, 1986; Glew, O'Leary-Kelly,

Griffin & Van Fleet, 1995; Locke & Schweiger, 1979; Miller & Monge, 1986). That is, the relationship between participation and performance may be moderated by several contextual factors. These researchers identified several individual and organizational factors that may influence the participation–performance relationship. Individual contextual factors include personality, demographic factors, motivation, and manager attitudes toward participation. Some of the personality factors that may moderate the effect of participation are: need for autonomy (Vroom, 1959), locus of control (Kren, 1992), and self-efficacy (Bandura, 1986). Individuals with a high need for autonomy prefer participative management, and individuals with a low need for autonomy prefer structured leadership to participatory management (Hogan, 1991). Kren (1992) found that employees with an internal locus of control performed better under participative management. Thus, the effect of participation may be limited for individuals with an external locus of control.

Organizational factors that may influence the participation–performance relationship include organization size, culture, organization structure, nature of the task, and technology. In addition, Vroom and Yetton (1973) and Vroom and Jago (1974) suggested a decision tree in which several situational factors were identified as influencing the effectiveness of participatory decision making. Contingent factors identified in the Vroom–Yetton–Jago model include: locus of relevant knowledge, importance of decision quality, amount of time available to make the decision, whether subordinate commitment to the decision is important, and decision costs.

Organization size (Child, 1977) may influence the effectiveness of participation interventions (Connor, 1992). It is quite likely that it is easier to implement participation in relatively smaller organizations. Organizational structure is an important factor for the success of participatory approach. A mechanistic organization (Burns & Stalker, 1961) which emphasizes rules, hierarchy, and centralization of authority may not be conducive for implementing participatory management. Neumann (1989) suggested that hierarchical arrangements inhibit participation, since it emphasizes rank and status rather than competence. Employees may not be willing to participate and the intervention will be met with resistance from the managers who may fear loss of control and authority. Any attempt to introduce participatory management in such an environment is likely to produce unsatisfactory results. On the other hand, participatory management is likely to succeed in organizations with organic structure where employees may be more willing to participate and managers may not resist participatory roles for their subordinates.

The nature of the task is another important organizational factor that may moderate the effectiveness of participatory management (Lawler, 1986).

For simple and repetitive tasks, participative management may not be critical for successful performance. On the other hand, more complex tasks require participation and information sharing among all the employees in the task group (Locke et al., 1997). For example, a complex task like new product development requires a participatory management approach that may involve all the members of the new product development team.

Organizational culture is an important factor that may facilitate/inhibit participatory management (Miller, 1988). In organizations where hierarchy and status differences are valued, implementation of a participatory culture would certainly be a difficult prospect. On the other hand, a participatory management intervention could easily be integrated into an organization with an egalitarian culture. In an empirical study, Parnell, Bell, and Taylor (1992) reported that managers' propensity for participation is a function of managers' perceptions of organizational culture and managers' beliefs that participatory management may improve or impede managerial effectiveness.

Technology can be an important factor that may influence the effectiveness of participatory management. Even if the organization structure and culture are conducive of a participatory approach, it may not be a feasible implementation option for large, geographically diverse organizations. Before the advent of computers and networking, it was difficult for large organizations to collaborate efforts across multiple units. Rapid changes in computing and networking technology have facilitated successful implementation of participatory management. For example, Alavi and Keen (1989) reported that an advanced computer network infrastructure in a large firm facilitated effective participation and information exchange. There are many modern tools such as videoconferencing, computer mediated meeting systems, intranet discussion boards and email that may facilitate real-time participation among diverse groups of people spread across the globe. A taxonomy of groupware systems based on space and time dimensions was presented by Johansen (1989). A four-category groupware system was suggested by Johansen based on the fact that groups may require meeting at the same time and same place, same time and different place, different time and same place, and different time. Locke et al. (1997) report that multimedia companies have developed groupware to meet the requirements of all the four categories. They also reviewed the effectiveness of groupware for facilitating participative management and concluded that groupware improved decision quality measured in both objective and self-reported perceptual terms.

In addition to the individual and organizational factors mentioned above, attributes of a nation's culture may influence participatory management in organizations (Hofstede, 1980). In the next section, we discuss the influence of national cultures on the effectiveness of participatory management intervention.

National Culture and Participative Management

As mentioned earlier, several researchers have questioned the relevance of management interventions developed in the USA for other countries (Hoefstede, 1980, 1991; Triandis, 1994). In this section we review participation management studies conducted in various countries.

The theoretical rationale for differences in attitudes toward participative management across cultures is provided by Hofstede (1980). In his study of 64 nations, Hofstede identified four cultural dimensions along which nation's culture may be differentiated. The four dimensions are: individualism/collectivism, power distance, masculinity/femininity, and uncertainty avoidance. The dimension 'power distance' may explain differences in attitudes toward participative management. Hofstede defined power distance as the degree of inequality among people which the population of a country considers as normal. Power distance may range from relatively equal (that is, small power distance) to extremely unequal (large power distance). According to Hofstede's survey, western countries like the USA, Britain, etc., are low in power distance and developing countries in Asia are high in power distance. Based on Hofstede's work, it may be expected that participatory management can be easily implemented in cultures with low power distance because participation tends to reduce the power distance. In countries with high power distance, participatory management may be resisted by managers because it may go against the cultural norm of maintaining power inequality.

One of the first studies of participative management in an international context was conducted by Haire, Ghiselli and Porter (1966). They developed a questionnaire that measured attitudes toward participative management along four dimensions: capacity of people for leadership, propensity for sharing information, manager's belief in subordinates' ability to make decisions, and locus of control. Haire et al. (1966) conducted their study across a sample of 14 countries and found five clusters of countries: Nordic-European (Norway, Sweden, Denmark, Germany); Latin-European (France, Spain, Italy, Belgium); Anglo-American (Britain and United States); and developing countries (Argentina, India). Haire et al. (1966) found that national culture is an important differentiator that influences attitudes and beliefs of people toward management principles. Specifically, they found that for developing countries people scored lower on information sharing, internal locus of control,

and subordinate role for participative management. Their interpretation of the pattern of findings was that people in industrialized countries tend to practice a more democratic style of leadership than in developing countries which tend to favor paternalism and discourage participation among lower-level employees.

Haire et al.'s (1966) study has been supported by a number of studies in countries such as Australia (Clark & McCabe, 1970), Greece (Cummings & Schmidt, 1972), Israel (Vardi, Shirom & Jacobson, 1980), and Arabian states (Badawy, 1980).

A study conducted by Welsh, Luthans, and Sommer (1993) further adds support to the national culture hypothesis proposed by Haire et al. (1966) and Hofstede (1980). In a study of Russian factory workers, Welsh et al. (1993) found that participation resulted in a decrease in performance. The researchers concluded that participative management may be inappropriate for certain cultures and suggested that organizations need to take into account historical and cultural factors at a national level before implementing participative management. The results of Welsh et al.'s (1993) study are consistent with Hofstede's (1980) model. Russia is relatively high in power distance and thus, it can be expected that people will be reluctant to equalize power by participatory structures. Welsh et al. (1993) note that Russian workers have strong communal feelings and are very cautious about sharing information and expressing opinions. In addition, these workers respect authority and are loyal to their bosses. All of these factors inhibit a participatory management approach.

Differences in participatory management practices between Britain and France were examined in a study by Ryan (1999). This study compared the attitudes toward participation of British and French managers. The results of the study indicate that both cultures approved participatory management. However, the study found that British managers were more forthcoming in information sharing with subordinates compared to their French counterparts. This difference was explained by the fact that Britain had less power distance and thus there was a greater acceptance of a subordinate's right to be informed. The difference in participation between Britain and France is consistent with Hofstede's (1980) model.

The notion that national culture is an important differentiator that influences attitudes and beliefs of people toward management principles has been criticized (England & Negandhi 1979). In a critique of Haire et al.'s (1966) study, England and Negandhi argued that Haire et al., exaggerated differences among countries and that sources of differences in manager's beliefs and attitudes toward participative management are primarily occupational and individual.

In support of England and Negandhi's views, Banai and Katsounotos (1993) reported that managerial attitudes toward participative management are more influenced by management exposure to modern management theories than exposure to culture. They found that people who are more educated, and thus who are more exposed to modern management concepts, view participative management more favorably. Their study compared the attitudes of high-school managers and elementary-school managers in Cyprus. University education is a requirement for high-school managers and not for primary-school managers in Cyprus. Since high-school managers had longer years of education, the expectation was that they would be more favorably inclined to participative management. They found that high-school managers scored significantly higher than elementary-school managers in their attitude favoring participative management. They also compared locus of control, a trait not influenced by education, among elementary- and high-school managers and found that the two groups did not significantly differ in terms of locus of control. This further adds weight to their hypothesis that attitude toward participation is more a function of education than national culture. Taken together, the results of Banai and Katsounotos' study indicate that factors such as education can have favorable influences on attitude toward participation that may override national cultural factors.

McFarlin, Sweeney and Cotton (1992) compared attitude toward participation among managers from the United States, Britain, The Netherlands, and Spain. The results of the study showed that US managers viewed participation as a means to improve performance and British managers viewed it as a threat to their authority and control. Dutch managers had difficulty in understanding the need for formal participation structures since participation is part of societal obligation in the Netherlands.

Coopman, Drenth, Heller and Rus (1993) compared participative management in Britain, Netherlands and Yugoslavia. They found that British companies had the lowest level of participation and the Yugoslavian companies had the highest level of participation. The Dutch companies had participation levels between those of British and Yugoslavian. The authors in this study note that their results did not follow the cultural pattern claimed by Hofstede (1980). According to Hofstede's (1980) study, Britain had the lowest power distance and Yugoslavia had the highest power distance. Thus, one would expect that participation levels would be highest in Britain and lowest in Yugoslavia. Clearly, Coopman et al.'s (1993) study resulted in pattern of results contradicting Hofstede's model. The authors critique the idea of explaining differences based on national cultures and argue that the most important finding that can be usefully explained relates to differences between organizations or within organizations.

Huang (1997) examined the participatory management practices in a survey of 308 firms in Taiwan and found that the two most popular forms of participative management are employee stock ownership plans and employee suggestion schemes. Huang reported that participative management resulted in improved financial performance. Thus, Taiwan, a high power distance society, does seem to have strong participative management programs in their organizations.

In a study of 54 maquiladoras, or foreign-owned production plants, in northern Mexico, Pelled and Hill (1997) found that workers in Mexico responded favorably to participative management in spite of the fact that Mexico is a paternalistic, high power distance culture. The authors suggest that the participative management approach may be insensitive to cultural differences.

Mankidy (1995) studied participative management programs in the banking industry in India. The author reported that there is a growing trend toward participatory management in India. The findings of Mankidy's study is surprising because India is considered a high power distance country (Hofstede, 1980). One reason why India may have a higher degree of participation is that managers in India are increasingly exposed to western modern concepts through their education system. The earlier generation of entrepreneurs had very little formal business education and often practiced a paternalistic style of management. The newer generation of entrepreneurs and managers often have a business degree and this education and exposure may be changing the attitude of managers toward a participative approach.

In a study of participative decision making in Australia, Davis and Lansbury (1996) reported that organizations in Australia had few participatory intervention programs before the 1990s. The economic turbulence due to the increasing global competition provided a backdrop for adopting a participatory style of management to improve performance and remain competitive. Thus, Australia, a low power distance country (Hofstede, 1980) did not move toward a participative management until the economic conditions forced organizations to implement a participatory approach.

Holden (1999) compared the perception gap in employee participation between Sweden and Britain. In a study comparing the banking sector firms in these two countries, Holden found that Swedish firms had a higher degree of participation than the British firms. The author attributes the higher participation in Sweden to the presence of trade unions and work councils. These channels of participation are required by Swedish laws, thus making participation more formal and structured. In Britain, participatory efforts are voluntary in nature and organizations do not introduce new interventions unless there is a compelling business need.

In summary, research in participative management in an international context indicates mixed results in support of and against including national culture as a contextual factor. Researchers like Haire (e.g., Haire et.al., 1966) and Hofstede (e.g., Hofstede, 1980) argue for including national cultural differences while implementing management interventions such as participative management across different societies. Several research studies have supported the idea that participatory management may not be successful in cultures where power distance is high. However, as mentioned above, there is also research evidence that contradicts Haire et al.'s (1966) and Hofstede's (1980) propositions. One explanation for this discrepancy may be that culture is dynamic and continuously evolving, and research conducted across two time periods may result in different outcomes. It is also possible that, while culture is important in considering participative management, there could be other overriding factors that can neutralize the effect of culture on participative management. For example, in the USA, a low power distance culture, participative management was not widespread until the 1980s when forces of global competition forced American organizations to take a more participatory approach. As mentioned above, a similar experience was reported in Australia, another low power distance country. The existence of formal legal structures in the form of worker councils may also contribute to participatory management independent of any inhibiting cultural influences, as evidenced in the studies of participation in Sweden and Yugoslavia. These countries reportedly have higher degrees of participation than Britain, a relatively low power distance country, because of the existence of formal legal structures that support participation in Sweden and Yugoslavia. Education and exposure to modern management concepts could be another countervailing factor, as evidenced from research in India and Cyprus. Research in these countries has shown that managers who are exposed to modern management concepts are willing to implement a participatory approach and override cultural factors that may inhibit participatory management.

Future of Participative Management

Based on a review of all major reviews, Wagner (1994) concludes that 'research has provided evidence of statistically significant but small relationships between participation and performance or satisfaction and that it has failed to verify the presence of strong, large relationships ... [T]he conclusions of this article give cause to question the practical significance of participation as a means of influencing performance or satisfaction at work' (p. 319). Locke et al. (1997) also endorse the view that 50 years of participation research has shown that it is not an effective mechanism for improving

organizational outcomes. However, Locke et.al. (1997) are not pessimistic about the future of participatory management and suggest that participatory management research needs to move in new directions. Ledford and Lawler (1994) argued for the need to go beyond the limited definition of participation and to view participation within a broader organizational context. In their dialog, they conclude that 'limited participation has limited effects. Let us move on to more interesting research questions about participation' (p. 635).

We believe that participatory management will continue to be an important topic for the following reasons:

(1) The principles of the participative approach have been successfully integrated into other interventions such as quality management and workteams which will continue to be critical for the success of organizations in the next millennium. Locke et al. (1997) argue that 'participation has grown in incidence and importance as a result, and can be expected to continue to do so as innovations in computerized manufacturing, employee empowerment, concurrent engineering, high involvement management, corporate reengineering, and quality management reshape business conditions' (p. 307). The contribution of participatory management to the success of other interventions such as TQM has been supported empirically. In an analysis of 20 case studies of TQM, Harris and Purdy (1998) found that participatory management techniques contributed to the success of TQM programs by facilitating teamwork.

(2) As organizations become increasingly complex with hyper competition, rapid changes in technology, reduction in product life cycles, more demanding customers etc., the task environment in the future will continue to be more complex. As mentioned earlier, a complex task environment requires a more participative approach for organizations to survive. Organizations need to respond fast to survive in a fast changing environment and this requires that companies adopt a flatter structure and participation of employees at all levels so that they can be responsive.

(3) The world is moving toward democratic governance – this decade has seen many nations move toward democracy and this trend will likely continue in the next millennium. As societies become democracies, organizations within these societies will increasingly endorse a participative approach.

(4) Rapid changes in computer and communication technologies have made it easier to implement participation. As the world is getting increasingly wired with internet and other

technologies, the cost of participation will continue to decrease. Thus, organizations may find it easier and more profitable to implement participation.

For the future we suggest the following areas for research in participation:

(1) Future research needs to focus on the influence of various organizational factors on the success of participative management. As mentioned earlier, several organizational factors may moderate the success of participative management. Specifically, future research may focus on how organization size, organization culture, organization structure, nature of the task environment (e.g., service versus manufacturing), and presence of organized labor influence the effectiveness of participative management.

(2) Linkages between participative management and other management interventions need to be examined. As mentioned earlier, participative management is an important component of other management tools like quality management and workteams. It would be interesting to examine how participative management facilitates the success of other interventions which have participative components.

(3) As mentioned earlier, participative management may gain in importance as a society becomes increasingly democratized. It would be interesting to study the relationship between the changes in political structure from an autocratic to democratic setup and participative management in organizations.

(4) The influence of technology on participation is another interesting topic that needs to be further explored. As mentioned earlier, developments in technology have made it attractive for organizations to implement participatory management. In their review of participation research, Locke et al. (1997) suggest that researchers need to focus on the influence of information technology on participation endeavors. Their idea for future participation research is to recast participation as a process of knowledge transfer and information exchange. They argue that such a perspective would facilitate researchers to move away from the traditional mold of viewing participating as influencing motivation and commitment and study participation as a process of communication and coordination.

Technology has the potential to be the great equalizer. It facilitates participation by making information available to employees at all levels, thereby increasing the ability of employees to participate, and by eliminating social inhibitions of the unassertive. The interface between technology and the participative decision-making process offers opportunities for future research. Locke et al. (1997) proposed that the amount of support from information technology for the participative management process can be included as an independent variable. In addition, they suggest several mediating variables such as degree of knowledge acquisition (amount of growth in individual participant's knowledge) and information saturation (the extent of equalization of information among participants).

(5) Finally, more research needs to be done to understand the linkages between dimensions of participatory management identified by Black and Gregersen (1997) as well as linkages between these dimensions and outcome measures. There is very little understanding as to how the various dimensions such as rationale, form, structure, and degree of involvement relate to each other.

TOTAL QUALITY MANAGEMENT

More organizations may have implemented quality management than any other management intervention. Some scholars (e.g., Hackman & Wageman, 1995) have identified total quality management (TQM) as a social movement due to its pervasive influence on organizations that cut across industry, national, and cultural boundaries. According to one survey, 93% of manufacturing firms and 69% of service firms implemented some form of quality management practices (Conference Board, 1991). Another estimate indicates that more than 75% of US and British firms implemented some form of TQM (*Economist*, 1992). Although the management of quality as an intervention received considerable attention in practitioner circles during the past decade, only recently has it attracted the scholarly attention of academic research.

In this section, we first provide a historical perspective of the practice of quality management. Second, we review the salient features of quality management. Third, we review studies that examined the effectiveness of the TQM intervention. Fourth, we present an overview of quality management practices across various national cultures to examine the applicability of quality management practice in an international context. Fifth, we discuss the present status of quality management and the future of quality management in the 21st century.

A Historical Perspective on Quality Management

Concern for the quality of products has existed throughout the history of society. As early as

1700 BC, King Hammurabi of Babylon decreed rules for product quality for the home-building industry by declaring that 'if a building falls into pieces and the owner is killed then the builder shall also be put to death. If the owner's children are killed then the builders' children shall also be put to death' (Kehoe, 1994). During the Middle Ages, guilds of craftsman ensured standards for product quality, and during the industrial revolution, technological advances were made possible by standardization of components such as screw threads, nuts, and bolts. In this century, mass production required that quality standards be more systematically included in the production process. Garvin (1988) identified four eras of quality management in this century. The first era, which included the 1940s, emphasized inspection and rejection after the production process was completed. The responsibility for inspection and rejection rested with the production personnel who often let faulty goods pass through due to tight production targets and deadlines.

The second quality era introduced statistical control wherein statistics were used to control quality. In this approach, inspection was based on a random sample of finished products. The concept of acceptable quality levels (AQL) was introduced wherein it was acceptable for a percentage of a lot, say, 5%, to fall below the specified quality level. This resulted in customers receiving defective products since a certain percentage of products would not be in conformance with the quality standards. The first two eras treated quality as conformance to specifications. The assumption here is that the specification itself was correct and that products made to the specification would satisfy the needs of the customer. Clearly, this was not always a correct assumption, since the design of products was producer driven rather than customer driven. Customers were given what the producers thought was best for them, not necessarily what customers actually wanted (Pike & Barnes, 1996).

The third phase involved quality assurance in which quality systems were established encompassing many management functions and requiring longer implementation timescales. Gryna (1988) defines quality assurance as the activity of providing the evidence needed to establish confidence, among all concerned, that the quality function is being effectively performed. To assure that quality is maintained, organizations often designed and implemented systems in accordance with globally accepted standards such as ISO 9000 standards. Organizations certified as ISO 9000 companies often used it as a marketing tool to sell their products and services. Achieving ISO 9000 indicates to potential customers that the company has taken steps to get its systems and procedure in order. Thus the customer should be assured that the organization will deliver quality products and services. The quality assurance era is a step forward from the earlier inspection and rejection era, since quality assurance systems protect against quality problems that may arise and provide customers with confidence that things are being done properly.

A related innovation to improve quality was the introduction of quality circles in Japan during the 1960s. Quality circles are a bottom-up approach to quality improvement in which individual employees volunteer to form an informal improvement group and this group identifies improvement objectives on an ongoing basis. Based on the success of Japanese organizations, quality circles became very popular and spread to many countries throughout the world. At one time there were estimated to be more than one million quality circles in operation that involved more than 12 million employees (Barra, 1989). It was claimed by Barra that quality circles have both direct and indirect benefits: the direct benefit is improvement in quality as a result of ideas generated by the quality circle groups. The indirect benefit arises from the process of participation in problem solving; employees who are involved in problem solving may feel more valued and thus may have a greater sense of belonging to the organization (Barra, 1989). In spite of its popularity and initial success, quality circles were often found to be ineffective due to at least two reasons (Pike & Barnes, 1996): quality circle groups were often formed out of single departments; but problem solving in a competitive, fast-paced environment often requires cross-functional teams, rendering quality circles as an ineffective tool for problem solving. Another criticism of quality circles is that they are voluntary and thus may exclude people with expertise. Despite the potential problems, quality circles played an important role in creating widespread awareness toward quality management among management and employees across a large number of organizations.

In the fourth era, beginning in the 1980s, a total quality approach was defined in which everyone in the organization is involved in developing continuous improvement and a customer orientation through teamwork. One of the earliest proponents of the 'total' approach was Fiegenbaum (1983): 'Total quality control's organization-wide impact involves the managerial and technical implementation of customer-oriented quality activities as a primary responsibility of general management and of the main-line operations of marketing, engineering, production, industrial relations, finance, and service as well as of the quality control function itself' (p. 13). TQM offers a comprehensive approach impacting all elements of an organization: people (including employees, customers, and suppliers), systems, and techniques. TQM has been described as new way of managing organizations transcending the traditional view of quality as something confined to products or services (Chorn, 1991). The popularity of TQM can be gauged by the fact that it has been implemented across various industries ranging from traditional manufacturing to service organizations, public institutions, nonprofit organizations, and educational institutions (Hackman & Wageman, 1995). Continuous quality improvement (CQI), which is part of TQM, was also popular during this era. CQI, a production improvement process, is primarily achieved through the effective functioning of a variety of teams, including functionally oriented quality improvement teams (Banker, Potter & Schroeder, 1993). TQM also came to be associated with learning organizations (Senge, 1990). Organizational learning is viewed as a collective phenomenon, one in which organizations put in place new approaches such as TQM that enable them to perform more effectively and improve performance over time. Research in quality of service delivery attracted attention during this era (e.g., Schneider & Bowen, 1985). Schneider and Bowen empirically examined the relationship between service orientation and customer's service quality experienced by customers. The authors found that managerial practices like soliciting and being responsive to customer input, and having the necessary logistics and systems support contributed to service quality.

In summary, the history of quality management suggests that quality management has evolved from inspection and detection during the first half of this century to a more preventive quality assurance era during 1960s and 1970s. Since the 1980s quality management has taken a 'total' approach and is viewed as an organization-wide intervention. The elements of the total quality approach significantly differ from the quality management approaches of earlier eras. In the next section, we explore the elements of the TQM intervention.

Elements of TQM

One of the major difficulties in defining TQM is the way quality is defined (Forker, 1991). Garvin (1988) notes that quality is an unusually slippery concept, easy to visualize and yet exasperatingly difficult to define. It remains a source of great confusion to managers. Scholars and practitioners from different areas defined quality in different terms. Table 18.4 summarizes some of the common definitions of quality. Garvin (1988) identified five definitions of quality: transcendental, product based, user based, manufacturer based, and value based. Garvin explains how individuals from different departments within an organization may define quality; for example, marketing personnel may view quality as user based, while engineering personnel may use a manufacturer-based definition of quality. Garvin further described quality by identifying eight dimensions of quality: performance, features, reliability, conformance, durability, serviceability, aesthetics, and perceived quality.

Table 18.4 *Definitions of quality*

Authors	Definition of quality
Deming (1986)	Three categories of quality: Quality of design Quality of conformance Quality of performance
Crosby (1979)	Conformance to requirements Zero defects
Juran (1992)	Fitness for use
Garvin (1988)	Eight dimensions of quality: Performance Features Reliability Conformance Durability Serviceability Aesthetics Perceived quality
Cameron and Whetten (1996)	Seven dimensions of quality: User based Transcendental Product based Manufacturer based Value based Philosophical System based
Parasuraman, Zeithaml and Berry (1985)	Quality for service industries: Tangibles Reliability Responsiveness Assurance Empathy
Stone-Romero, Stone and Grewal (1997)	Four dimensions of quality: Flawlessness Appearance Durability Distinctiveness
Taguchi and Clausing (1990)	Loss product caused to society after product is shipped

Cameron & Whetten (1996) identified seven definitions of quality:

(1) Transcendent: according to Prisig (1974), 'quality is neither mind nor matter, but a third entity independent of the two ... even though quality cannot be defined, you know what it is.'

(2) Product based: Leffler (1982) defined quality in terms of amounts of the unpriced attributes contained in each unit of the priced attribute.

(3) User based: advocates of the user-based approach include Juran (1992) and Edwards (1968). Juran defined quality as 'fitness for use' from the viewpoint of customers. Edwards defined quality as an attribute that satisfies customers' wants.

(4) Manufacturing based: Crosby (1979) provided a manufacture-based definition in terms of conformance to requirements and specifications.

(5) Value based: this approach defines quality as a measure of excellence and worth at affordable price (Figenbaum, 1983).

(6) System based: according to Japanese Industrial Standards Committee (1981), quality is defined as a system of means to economically produce goods or services which satisfy customer's requirements.

(7) Philosophical: Sashkin and Kiser (1993) define quality in terms of an organization culture that supports constant attainment of customer satisfaction through an integrated system of tools, techniques and training.

Stone-Romero et al. (1997) identified four dimensions of quality: flawlessness, appearance, durability, and distinctiveness. They further categorized these dimensions into intrinsic and extrinsic cues: intrinsic cues refer to a product's inherent characteristics and extrinsic cues refer to nonphysical product characteristics that can be changed without altering the fundamental nature of the product.

Garvin's definition of quality is related to the manufacturing sector and this approach may be not applicable to the service sector. Parasuraman et al. (1985) identified different set of dimensions relevant for the service industries. These dimensions include tangibles, reliability, responsiveness, assurance, and empathy.

The pioneers of the quality management movement also defined quality in different terms. Deming (1986), generally considered a key pioneer of quality management, defined quality in terms of how well a product or service meets the user's needs. A product or service that most successfully satisfies customer needs is considered to have the highest quality.

In the mind of a production worker, he produces quality if he can take pride in his work. Poor quality to him is loss of business, and perhaps of his job. Good quality, he thinks, will keep the company in business. All this is true in the service industries as it is in manufacturing .... Quality to plant manager means to get the numbers out and to meet specifications. His job also, whether he knows it or not, continual improvement of processes and continual improvement of leadership .... The difficulty in defining quality is to translate future needs of the user into measurable characteristics so that a product can be designed and turned out to give satisfaction at a price that the user will pay. (Deming, 1986: 168–9)

Deming mentions three separate categories of quality: (1) Quality of design/redesign: how well a product design created with information from consumer research, sales analysis and service call analysis meets customers' needs. (2) Quality of

conformance: how well a company and its suppliers met the design specifications required to satisfy customer's needs. (3) Quality of performance: how well the company's products or services actually perform in the marketplace. Deming emphasized the use of statistics, control charts, and reduction of the supply base to achieve desired quality levels. The costs of quality can then be measured by finding how well a product is designed to achieve the purpose, how well a product manufactured meets the design standards, and how well the products perform in the hands of consumers.

Crosby (1979, 1984) another pioneer of quality management defined quality in terms of conformance to requirements. In the words of Crosby: 'The first erroneous assumption is that quality means goodness, or luxury, or shininess, or weight. The word "quality" is used to signify the relative worth of things in such phrases as "good quality", "bad quality" ...' (1984: 17). Crosby argued that there is ambiguity in the way people define quality because 'each listener assumes that the speaker means exactly what he or she, the listener, means by the phrase. It is a situation in which individuals talk dreamily about something without even bothering to define it .... That is precisely the reason we must define quality as 'conformance to requirements' if we are going to manage it .... Requirements must be clearly stated so that they cannot be misunderstood. Measurements are then taken continually to determine conformance to those requirements. The nonconformance detected is the absence of quality. Quality problems became non conformance problems, and quality became definable' (1984: 17). Crosby argued that quality can be measured exactly and products can be made error free with 'zero defects.'

Juran (1992), another quality guru, defined quality as 'fitness for use.' Juran observes that this short definition does not provide managers with courses of action and suggests two dimensions of this definition: (1) product features that meet customer needs and (2) freedom from defects. Thus, fitness for use is the extent to which products or services are designed to meet customer requirements and are actually made to match those standards.

Taguchi and Clausing (1990) measure quality as the loss a product caused to society after the product is shipped other than any losses caused by its intrinsic functions. This loss can be caused either by variability in the product's function or by adverse side effects. A high-quality product, therefore, functions in a manner that it was intended to without any variability and without causing any harm to the customer.

In sum, the above discussion indicates that quality is a multidimensional construct that can mean different things depending on the perspective and the situation. Quality leaders have provided a broad-based definition (e.g., fitness for use, conformance to standards) but they may not be useful for scholarly research purposes. What is needed is a contingency-based definition of quality that includes situational factors such as the nature of product, the industry, the customer, and culture.

As with the general concept of quality, the elements of TQM have been defined and categorized in various ways (Masterson & Taylor, 1996; Anderson, Rungtusanatham & Schroeder, 1994; Waldman, 1994; Dean & Bowen, 1994; Hackman & Wageman, 1995). A summary of major elements of TQM identified by researchers and pioneers of quality management is presented in Table 18.5.

Deming identified 14 points that constitute elements of quality management. He viewed these 14 points as 'principles of transformation' to be embraced by the top management in its efforts to continually change and enhance an organization's ability to survive (Deming, 1986). Deming's 14 points include certain obligations for top management (point 1 – create a vision for quality management; point 6 – institutionalize training; point 14 – develop an action plan to implement 14 points), behavioral practices aimed at changing organization's infrastructure and cultural system (points 8 and 9 that aim at fostering an open and cooperative culture), and methodological practices for implementing quality (point 3 – eliminate the need for inspection), improving production systems (point 5), and managing suppliers (point 4). In a review of Deming's management method, Anderson et al. (1994) suggest that Deming's 14 points allude to different management concepts already in existence. They argue that Deming's method represents 'a complex, prescriptive set of interrelated rules of inter and intraorganizational behavior, codified, and communicated in the linguistic form of commands' (1994: 476). Deming's approach to quality management requires top management to balance the needs of employees, customers, suppliers, communities, and investors in the long run.

Juran (1992) suggested a 'quality trilogy' for quality management. Juran's trilogy is based on three management processes: quality planning, quality control, and quality improvement. Quality planning is used to develop the goods and services desired by consumers. Quality control ensures that goals of planning phase are successfully achieved. Quality improvement aims to achieve even higher levels of quality than those already reached or planned. Quality improvement leads to new standards for quality control and future production.

Crosby (1984) advocated a zero-defects-based approach and recommended the following steps for implementing quality: (1) defining standards and communicating these standards to employees; (2) supplying tools, education, and training to employees to meet the requirements; (3) encouraging and motivating employees to meet the quality requirements. Crosby called for an approach to do things right the first time, every time.

Table 18.5 *Dimensions of total quality management*

Authors	Elements of quality management
Deming (1986)	14 points for implementing quality
Juran (1992)	Quality trilogy (quality planning, quality control, and quality improvement)
Crosby (1984)	Define standards
	Supply tools
	Motivate employees to meet quality requirements
Dean and Bowen (1994)	Continuous improvement
	Customer focus
	Teamwork
Waldman (1994)	Top management commitment
	A broad-based definition of quality
	Leadership
	Develop a quality culture
	Employee participation
	Scientific problem-solving techniques
Spencer (1994)	Quality goals
	Customer oriented definition of quality
	Role/nature of environment
	Role of management
	Role of employees
	Structural rationality
	Philosophy toward change
Anderson et al. (1994)	Visionary leadership
	Internal and external cooperation
	Learning
	Process of management
	Continuous improvement
	Employee fulfillment
	Customer satisfaction
Hackman and Wageman (1995)	Explicit identification of customer requirements
	Creation of supplier parternship
	Use of cross-functional teams
	Use of scientific method to monitor performance
	Use of process management heuristics to enhance team effectiveness
Masterson and Taylor (1996)	HR development and management
	Executive leadership
	Customer focus/satisfaction
	Information and analysis
	Management of process quality
	Role of management/supervisor
	Strategic planning

Dean and Bowen (1994) in their review of quality management identified three principles of TQM: customer focus, continuous improvement, and teamwork. Customer focus as a driving force behind work processes is a fundamental characteristic of the

TQM approach. The internal or external customer of the product or service becomes the focus for determining standards and for measuring performance. A top-down flowchart with vertical reporting relationships is the traditional view of the work structure, while lateral flows culminating in providing products or services to internal/external customers represent the TQM perspective (Cardy & Dobbins, 1996). The TQM focus is on the input, throughput, and outcomes in relation to customer needs and expectations, rather than on hierarchical reporting and power relationships. Organizational practices for implementing a customer focus include direct customer contact, collecting customer information through surveys, and using information from customer contact/surveys in the design and delivery of products and services (Dean & Bowen, 1994). Continuous improvement is another important characteristic of quality management environment. Rather than being fairly fixed or static situations, TQM organizations are dynamic and constantly trying to improve; processes in a TQM environment are fluid and always subject to change (Cardy & Dobbins, 1996). Continuous improvement can be implemented by using process analysis, reengineering, and problem-solving approaches. Teamwork is the third major component of TQM. Customer focus and continuous improvement are best achieved by collaboration throughout the organization as well as with customers and suppliers. Techniques for developing teamwork include the nominal group technique, group skills training, role clarification and group feedback (Dean & Bowen, 1994).

Waldman (1994) identified six dimensions of TQM based on the quality approaches of Deming (1986), Juran (1988), Crosby (1984), and Taguchi and Clausing (1990):

(1) top management commitment to quality as a top priority;
(2) a broad-based definition of quality as meeting customers' expectations at the least cost, which encompasses all phases of the design, production, and delivery of a product/service;
(3) institution of leadership practices oriented toward TQM values and vision;
(4) development of a quality culture;
(5) involvement and empowerment of all organizational members in cooperative efforts to achieve quality improvements;
(6) an orientation toward managing by facts, including the prolific use of scientific and problem-solving techniques such as statistical process control.

Clearly, top management commitment, broad-based definition, leadership, and statistical process control are part of Deming's 14 points for quality management. A broad-based definition of quality is

also part of Juran's and Taguchi's framework for quality improvement. Leadership and cultural change are part of Crosby's approach to quality management.

Spencer (1994) reviewed the literature on quality and organizations and summarized the major components of TQM in terms of the following elements (p. 447):

(1) Goal: TQM establishes quality enhancement as top priority and one that is vital for long-term effectiveness and survival; increase in quality also facilitates other goals (e.g., decrease in costs).
(2) Definition of quality: quality is satisfying or delighting the customer. All quality improvement initiatives must begin with an understanding of customer perceptions and needs.
(3) Role/nature of the environment: TQM blurs the boundaries between organization and environment; entities previously regarded as outsiders (e.g., suppliers, customers) are now considered part of organizational processes.
(4) Role of management: management's role is to create constancy of purpose for improvement of product and service and to create a system that can produce quality outcomes. Management and the system, and not workers, are held responsible for poor quality.
(5) Role of employees: employees are empowered to make decisions, build relationships, and take steps needed to improve quality within the system designed by management. Additional training and educational opportunities provide necessary skills for this broader role.
(6) Structural rationality: the organization is reconfigured as a set of horizontal processes that begin with the supplier and end with the customer. Teams are organized around processes to facilitate task accomplishment.
(7) Philosophy toward change: change, continuous improvement, and learning are encouraged. Ideally, all organizational members are motivated to improve the status quo.

Anderson et al. (1994) examined the management theory underlying Deming's method and identified the following characteristics of quality management:

(1) Visionary leadership: the ability of the management to establish, practice, and lead a long-term vision for organization driven by customer requirements.
(2) Internal and external cooperation: the propensity of the organization to engage in noncompetitive activities internally among employees and externally with respect to suppliers.
(3) Learning: the organizational capability to recognize and nurture the development of its skills, abilities, and knowledge base.

(4) Process management: the set of methodological and behavioral practices emphasizing the management of process, or means of actions, rather than results.

(5) Continuous improvement: the propensity of the organization to pursue incremental and innovative improvements of processes, products and services.

(6) Employee fulfillment: the degree to which employees of an organization feel that the organization continually satisfies their need.

(7) Customer satisfaction: the degree to which an organization's customers continually perceive that their needs are being met by the organization's products and services.

Anderson et al., offered the following statement that summarizes the quality management approach: 'The effectiveness of the Deming management method arises from leadership efforts toward the simultaneous creation of a cooperative and learning organization to facilitate the implementation of process management practices, which, when implemented, support customer satisfaction and organizational survival through sustained employee fulfillment and continuous improvement of processes, products and services' (1994: 479–80).

Hackman and Wageman (1995) conducted a comprehensive review of quality management practices and identified five elements of TQM:

(1) Explicit identification and measurement of customer requirements: with customer in a TQM context, including both external and internal customers.

(2) Creation of supplier partnership: organizations should choose vendors based on quality rather than on price.

(3) Use of cross-functional teams to identify and solve quality problems: the main purpose of these teams is to identify and analyze the vital or critical problems of the organization.

(4) Use of the scientific method to monitor performance and to identify points of high leverage for performance improvement: use of statistical tools such as control charts, Pareto analysis, and cost of quality analysis to monitor quality efforts.

(5) Use of process management heuristics to enhance team effectiveness: the three most commonly used techniques to improve effectiveness of quality teams are flowcharts, brainstorming, and cause-and-effect diagrams.

Hackeman and Wageman (1995) claim that these five dimensions provide the core of quality management. Knowledge of customer requirements provides a test for considering and evaluating process changes. Supplier partnerships ensure that materials entering the organization are of acceptable quality. Cross-functional teams bring the full spectrum of relevant information and expertise to bear on decisions about organization-wide problems. Scientific methods and statistical analysis provide teams with trustworthy data to use in their decision making. And process management heuristics can improve the quality of the decision-making process itself.

Masterson and Taylor (1996) used the Malcolm Baldridge criteria to summarize the elements of total quality management. The authors argue that Malcolm Baldridge criteria integrate different perspectives on quality management. The elements of TQM according to these criteria include:

(1) HR development and management: includes employee empowerment and participation in the pursuit of quality.

(2) Executive leadership: organizational leadership responsible for providing a vision encompassing organization's goals, and systems.

(3) Customer focus/satisfaction: quality defined in terms of meeting/exceeding customer expectations.

(4) Information and analysis: decision making is based on hard facts about quality obtained from various sources throughout the organization.

(5) Management of process quality: the primary focus is on systems of production and service as the key area where quality can be achieved.

(6) Role of management or supervisor: the role should be to help people and systems do a better job through a new management style.

(7) Strategic planning: all levels in the organization are linked and treated as interdependent in the pursuit of the strategy of continuous improvement.

In summary, this review of research on the elements of TQM indicates that there are certain common elements identified by all researchers and practitioners. Individual researchers/practitioners often use different terms to describe the same element/process.

Effectiveness of the TQM Intervention

The impact of TQM on organizational effectiveness is a controversial topic with evidence indicating both positive and negative results. The practitioner literature has plenty of anecdotes about companies achieving spectacular results due to TQM initiatives (e.g., Port, Carey, Kelly & Forest, 1992). For example, it was reported that the use of TQM resulted in a 38% decrease in customer complaints at Xerox, an 80% reduction in reduction in defects at Motorola, decreased turnaround times for refunds in the State of Wisconsin, substantial cost savings at the University of Michigan hospital, and reduced purchasing costs in the US Navy (Goal/QPC, 1992).

Several surveys conducted to assess the effectiveness of TQM have also reported positive results.

The US General Accounting Office (1991) conducted a survey of organizations that had implemented quality processes to a significant extent. The objective of this survey was to investigate the relationships between quality processes and desirable outcomes. The firms investigated in this survey were finalists in the Malcolm Baldrige competition. Four categories of outcomes were considered as dependent variables: (1) employee-related indicators including employee satisfaction, turnover, attendance, and safety; (2) reliability including on-time delivery, errors, product lead time, inventory turnover, and costs of quality; (3) customer satisfaction indicators including overall customer satisfaction, customer complaints, and customer retention; (4) financial performance indicators including market share, sales per employee, return on assets, and return on sales. The survey reported annual percentage improvement in all four outcome categories. The report also mentioned that these firms had outcomes that exceeded industry averages in each of the four outcome categories. Druckman, Singer and Van Cott (1997) observed that the results of this survey need to be interpreted with caution, since no causal relationships were examined in this survey and it is not clear whether quality management efforts improved organizational effectiveness or successful firms tend to implement quality management efforts.

The National Institute of Standards and Technology (NIST, 1996) of the Department of Commerce conducted a survey comparing the financial stock performance of Baldrige quality award winners with the Standard & Poor (S & P) 500 index. Results of the survey indicate that, for the period between 1988 and 1994, quality award winners had a 250% return compared to a 55% return for the S & P 500. In a survey of 123 firms, Snell and Dean (1992) examined the relationship between TQM and a variety of human resource management practices. The results of this survey indicate that the impact of TQM on performance was mixed. In another empirical study, Dean and Snell (1996) studied the effect of TQM on performance in a survey of 160 firms. The results of their survey indicate that firms implementing TQM improved their performance relative to the industry.

Ittner (1992) found that quality improvement efforts resulted in decreased costs and increased productivity. Ansari (1984, cited in Druckman et al., 1997) studied 150 firms and found that just in time practices led to improvement in productivity. More recently, Lemak, Reed and Satish (1997) surveyed a sample of 60 firms and found that firms that demonstrated a commitment to TQM for a period of at least five years reported a superior stockmarket performance (on a market and risk-adjusted basis) and improved profit margins. In a

study of four firms that implemented customer satisfaction practices, Griffin, Gleason, Preiss and Shevenaugh (1995) found that these firms outperformed the industry in asset utilization and profitability after adopting these practices. Cameron (1991, 1995) studied the relationship between the quality culture and effectiveness among automotive, electronics, and educational organizations. The results of their study suggest that organizations with advanced quality cultures had higher levels of organizational effectiveness than organizations with less advanced quality cultures. Hendricks and Singhal (1997) in a study of Baldrige-award-winning companies reported that strong relationship exists between quality efforts and financial performance. Benson, Saraph and Schroeder (1991) reported a strong relationship between quality improvement and performance. Adam (1994), in a study of 187 US business firms, found that quality improvement approach is strongly related to performance quality. Several field studies in manufacturing (e.g., Ittner, 1992; Garvin, 1988) found that quality practices are associated with higher productivity. In addition, several marketing studies reported positive relationship between customer service orientation and performance (e.g., Fornell & Johnson, 1993; Philips, Chang & Buzzell, 1983).

In contrast to the above studies, results of several other surveys indicate negative or limited influence of TQM on performance. A survey of 580 organizations conducted by Ernst and Young and the American Quality Foundation (1992) suggest that TQM provides the greatest benefits for firms that are already performing well and adoption of the strategy by poorly performing firms can result in poorer performance. A survey of McKinsey and Company of US and European firms found that 67% of the TQM programs that were more than two years old died for lack of results (Druckman et al., 1997). A Rath and Strong survey of Fortune 500 companies also found that only 20% reported having achieved their quality objects and that over 40% indicated that their quality initiatives were a complete flop (Druckman et al., 1997). The American Electronics Association survey from 1994 showed that TQM implementation dropped from 86% to 63% and that TQM did not result in a decrease in defect rates (Dooley & Floor, 1998). In addition, the Baldrige quality award winner People's Express went bankrupt within a year of winning the award (Cardy & Dobbins, 1994). Wallace corporation went out of business within an year of winning the Baldrige award (Ross, 1993) and AT & T announced that its plant, which won the Baldrige award in 1992, was laying off 1000 workers (Rogers, 1993). Marsh (1994) reports that there is a diminishing interest in quality evidenced by the fact that the number of applicants for the Baldrige award continues to decrease.

There may be several reasons for the mixed influence of TQM on organizational effectiveness:

(1) organizational readiness to implement TQM; (2) individual and organizational situational factors that may constrain/enable implementation of TQM; (3) methodological problems associated with TQM research. Each of these possibilities are considered below.

(1) *Organizational readiness*: Cardy and Dobbins (1996) argue that implementing total quality management requires movement from a traditional organization to a total quality (TQ) organization which can require considerable effort and time. Cardy and Dobbins identify several distinctions between traditional and TQ organizations and Table 18.6 summarizes these differences. Traditional and TQ organizations differ both in terms of process and content. The traditional organization emphasizes traditional authority and vertical flows of communication. Unilateral decision making and centralization are characteristics consistent with this type of environment. In contrast, the customer focus of a TQM environment would require an organization that is more consultative and decentralized. Traditional organizations emphasize a conventional detection approach to quality and this leads to a more administrative role for the organizations. In contrast, TQM emphasizes a prevention approach and continuous improvement, and this requires organizations to focus on continuous employee development rather than employee maintenance. Traditional organizations emphasize extrinsic motivational techniques. Training, rewards, recognition etc., are often offered to motivate or pull an employee toward better performance. In TQ organizations, the key to higher performance is viewed as releasing employee potential rather than pulling employees along to a higher level of job performance. The assumption here is that employees are intrinsically motivated and organizational arrangements (e.g., job redesign, teams) have to be made to emphasize intrinsic motivation. As can be seen from Table 18.6, there are five differences in the content characteristic of traditional and TQ organizations. Specifically, the hierarchical and functional separation typical of traditional organizations lead to a nomothetic approach, that is, one best or preferred way of doing things. For example, traditional organizations often emphasize quantitative performance indicators and excludes all other criteria. In contrast, the TQ organization, with an emphasis on customer satisfaction (both internal and external customers) and maintaining supplier relationships, requires a more pluralistic approach to satisfy the expectations of various stakeholders/constituencies. For example, performance criteria for employees in TQ organizations often includes interpersonal/ teamwork skills, problem-solving skills, prosocial behaviors, etc., in addition to traditional performance measures.

The more static nature of the traditional organization leads to an approach that is compartmentalized

Table 18.6 *Difference between traditional and TQ organizations*

	Traditional organizations	TQ organizations
Process characteristics	Unilateral role	Consulting role
	Centralization	Decentralization
	Pull	Release
	Administrative	Development
Content characteristics	Nomothetic	Pluralistic
	Compartmentalized	Holistic
	Worker oriented	System oriented
	Performance measures	Satisfaction measures
	Job based	Person based

Source: Cardy and Dobbins (1996).

and job based. In contrast, the more fluid and continuous improvement nature of TQ organizations should lead to an approach that is more holistic and person based. Identifiable jobs may not exist in a TQM organization where teams may be the norm and duties may rotate over time and across projects. Given this situation, a TQ organization must look beyond the traditional job-based framework and identify person characteristics important for success in the organization.

In a traditional organization the emphasis is on individual employees and systems, such as performance appraisals, are designed to focus on individual differences. In contrast, TQ organization focuses on removing system barriers to improving performance. Rather than focusing on individual performance, the TQ approach calls for improving organizational systems.

Given the fundamental differences between traditional and TQ organizations, implementation of TQM requires large scale and comprehensive changes to organizational structure, culture, and human resource management policies.

However, organizations, like physical entities, have inertia (Reger, Gustafson, DeMarie & Mullane, 1994) and it requires consistent application of forces (e.g., top management commitment) over a long period of time to move an organization from a traditional to a TQ orientation.

(2) *Situational factors*: there are several organizational and individual factors that may moderate the influence of TQM on performance (Shea & Howell, 1998; Stone & Eddy, 1996). Stone and Eddy (1996) suggest that organizations should develop at least four internal mechanisms to successfully implement TQM: a team based structure, job redesign, organizational policies, human relations systems. In a conceptual consideration, Waldman (1994) suggested that person and system factors influence performance and that job autonomy and hierarchy moderate the influence of person/ system factors. Specifically, Waldman proposed that system factors influence performance at lower

levels of hierarchy and in jobs lacking autonomy, and person factors (e.g., ability, motivation) affect job performance at higher levels of hierarchy and in jobs characterized by autonomy. The research by Lemak et al. (1997) indicates that a long term commitment is essential for TQM success. Stone and Eddy also identify individual factors such as ability, motivation, and values that may moderate the success of TQM efforts. For example, it will be difficult for organizations to implement TQM in an environment where individual employees do not value team work, cooperative/prosocial behaviors, and a customer orientation.

(3) *Methodological problems*: another reason for the mixed results of TQM intervention effectiveness is that there are serious methodological problems associated with many studies of the influence of TQM on performance (Hackman & Wageman, 1995). Most of the literature is based on single company case studies which do not use reliable and valid instruments for measuring quality and effectiveness. The primary issue is to establish whether it is TQM that is being implemented and not a subset of TQM or some related intervention. There are also problems associated with measuring organizational performance and effectiveness with standard measures of performance such as market share, profitability and stock price (Brief, 1984; Kaplan & Norton, 1992). The relationship between TQM and performance may be confounded by environmental factors (e.g., industrial and market factors) that may influence performance independent of the influence of TQM. Time is another dimension that may influence the effectiveness of TQM intervention. It is not clear as to how long after TQM interventions are implemented one can expect their influence on organizational effectiveness. Given these problems, it is difficult to statistically detect the direct effect of TQM on organizational performance. In the light of these constraints, studies that claim positive results as well as studies that claim negative results for TQM should be viewed with caution.

In summary, research suggests that the influence of TQM on performance is sometimes positive and sometimes negative. This ambiguous result may be explained by factors such as individual and organizational moderators, organizational readiness to move toward Total Quality organization, and methodological problems associated with TQM research.

TQM in an International Context

Quality management is mainly an American innovation (Williamson, 1993). It was Deming, Juran, and Crosby who introduced major quality principles and practices. The Japanese also played a major role in developing several quality improvement techniques (e.g., Ishikawa, 1985). There are opposing views regarding the transferability of quality management practices between various cultures. The culture specific view (e.g., Hofstede, 1991; Beechler & Yang, 1993) suggests that management concepts cannot be blindly imported across nations without taking into account the idiosyncrasies of national cultures. Punnett and Shenkar (1994) and Redding (1994) argue that management principles and methods must be compatible with the culture of each country.

Several studies have been conducted to examine the differences in quality management practices between US and Japan (e.g., Ford & Honeycutt, 1992; Ohmae, 1982; Yoshida, 1992; Morris & Pavett, 1992; Fram & Ajami, 1994; Yavas, 1995). A major finding from these studies is that US managers tend to believe that costs increase with quality, while the Japanese tend to believe that quality can bring down costs. Reitsperger and Daniel (1990) suggested that quality control practices in the US are characterized by the 'static optimization principle.' This principle suggests that there is a tradeoff between costs and quality. This principle recommends a cost minimizing quality level as a result of balancing costs that incur in improving quality with costs of having a certain amount of defective products.

The Japanese, in contrast seem to adopt a zero defect strategy that pursues zero defects regardless of the costs. Yoshida (1989) suggests that differences in culture and other social factors between these two countries can explain differences in perception toward quality and cost. To explain the difference, Yoshida distinguishes between acceptability and desirability. The Japanese, because of their unified value system, tend first to establish what is desirable and gravitate toward that goal. The process is analogous to defining a center of a wide area. Americans, on the other hand, because of their wide variety of value systems, tend to first specify the perimeter or boundary for what is acceptable. It is more difficult to define the exact boundary than to locate the center. Once rigid boundaries are set people naturally tend to gravitate toward meeting the lower requirements of acceptability rather than striving to achieve the more exacting ones of desirability (Yoshida, 1989).

In contrast to the culture specific view of quality management interventions, the opposing view is that there is much in common between Japanese and US quality management practices (Fram & Ajami, 1994). Japanese companies successfully implemented quality improvement techniques formulated by Deming, and Japan even instituted the Deming prize, its top quality award. Deming inspired quality improvement efforts transformed Japan from a low-quality producer to a world leader in producing high-quality products. Ironically, US organizations ignored these experts until Japanese competition forced these organizations to adopt quality improvement. Things came to a full circle when American organizations imported Japanese management concepts such as Kaizan, Kanban, Theory Z, and JIT. The Baldridge Quality award was an American answer to Japan's Deming prize. Quality improvement efforts in the US automobile industry were largely influenced by Japanese quality management practices. The successful turnaround of the US automobile industry, in part, can be attributed to these quality improvement efforts. Clearly, this illustrates that there is nothing culturally specific about quality management principles. The US and Japanese cultures not only traded their goods and services but their quality management concepts as well. Recent empirical evidence suggests that the US automobile industry has moved in the direction of Japanese management, while the Japanese have imported some American ways of doing business (Fram & Ajami, 1994). According to this study, closer interaction, technology, and competition appear to be helping to reduce cross-national managerial differences.

Although US society is characterized by individualism (Hofstede, 1980), US organizations seem to have successfully adopted teamwork, which is an essential ingredient of quality management. Likewise, although Japanese society is characterized by certain degree of vagueness in their approach to management and decision making, Japanese organizations have successfully adopted Deming's approach which requires precise measurement and control using statistical techniques. Several studies point to emerging similarities between the attitudes of US and Japanese managers with respect to issues such as top management involvement and quality–cost tradeoff (e.g., Yavas & Burrows, 1994; Yavas, 1995; Daniel & Reitsperger, 1994; Reitsperger & Daniel, 1990). More recently, Yavas and Marcoulides (1996) conducted a cross-cultural study to examine whether American and Japanese organizations differ on major components of quality. They examined the differences based on six quality components: communication, quality execution, commitment, control/responsibility, current status of quality and measurement. The statistical results of this survey indicate that, for the quality dimension, the two countries have similar number of factors, factor structure and correlation between factors. The authors conclude that there is much common ground with respect to quality management practices between Japan and the United States.

Rao, Raghunathan and Solis (1997) conducted a survey of quality management practices across China, India, and Mexico and used the Malcolm Baldrige award criteria as a framework for comparing quality practices. The results of their survey suggest that: (1) there was no significant difference among the three countries on all the seven Baldridge criteria; (2) organizations in all these countries scored high on all the seven Malcolm Baldrige criteria. Top management support is a significant factor

influencing strategic quality planning and quality improvement practices for all the three countries.

Jenner, Hebert, Appell and Baack (1998) examined the quality management practices in a Chinese cultural context. In their case study involving 10 US Chinese joint ventures, they found that Confucian/Mao culture permeates these organizations. Managers of 9 of the 10 organizations made no significant attempt to implement quality management practices because of their belief that these techniques would not be accepted by Chinese workers for cultural reasons. However, one organization succeeded in the attempt to introduce TQM because of continued top management support and by changing employee attitudes through extensive training and communication.

A number of other studies examined the TQM intervention in other countries. For example, Zink (1998), in a book on quality management practices in Europe, documents case studies of several successful quality management efforts in organizations across Western Europe. In a study of 184 manufacturing firms in New Zealand, Sluti (1992) found that quality management efforts had significant positive impact on performance measures such as process utilization, process output, production process, inventory and on time delivery. Azarang, Gonzales and Reavill (1998) examined quality improvement practices in 122 large manufacturing plants in Mexico. The findings indicate that qualitative improvement efforts significantly influenced productivity, quality, customer satisfaction, and employee morale.

In summary, the review of quality management practices in an international context indicates that TQM appears to be a sound management practice and a strategic management tool for achieving business objectives. TQM is based on management techniques such as teamwork and employee participation/empowerment. Based on Hofstede's (1980) work, one would expect that TQM techniques would fail in many cultural situations. Specifically, in Western cultures, which score high on individualism (Hofstede, 1980), there would be resistance to teamwork, an essential ingredient of TQM. Likewise, in Eastern cultures and developing nations, which score high on power distance (Hofstede, 1980), there would be resistance to introduce employee empowerment techniques, another essential element of TQM. However, the above review indicates that TQM has been successfully implemented in Western cultures such as the United States and European countries as well as Eastern cultures such as Japan, India, China, and Korea. A fundamental reason for this broad effectiveness of TQM could be that global business competition has forced organizations to adopt quality management. Organizations across the world may be willing to experiment with management interventions that make sound business sense irrespective of the national origin of the interventions.

Future of TQM

As mentioned earlier, the McKinsey survey and the Rath and Strong survey of Fortune 500 firms indicate that there is a declining interest in TQM (Druckman et al., 1997). Marsh's (1994) report points that the number of Baldrige award applicants continues to decline. There is disenchantment being voiced that TQM is just another management fad (Cardy, 1996).

Despite the pessimism, we believe that quality will remain a primary concern in organizations across the world for many years to come. While labels and programs may change, the management fundamentals underlying quality approaches will remain largely unchanged. For example, over a decade ago, quality circles seemed to be the key to sagging productivity in Western organizations. During the past decade, TQM was considered the right answer for achieving competitive advantage. Now, other systems such as business process reengineering may come to replace TQM. The characteristics underlying these quality interventions, such as teamwork and empowerment, will remain across various incarnations of quality improvement programs.

There are several areas that need to be considered for future research on TQM:

(1) There is a need to develop reliable and valid instruments for measuring TQM construct. The issue of construct validity is of primary concern because a large number of studies claim to cover TQM when they actually concern only a subset of TQM or a related concept (Hackman & Wageman, 1995).
(2) The influence of person and system factors influencing TQM efforts needs be examined. Although theoretical models that examined the person–system influences exist (e.g., Cardy & Dobbins, 1994; Stone & Eddy, 1996), there is a need to conduct empirical research to validate these models.
(3) Although researchers have identified the key dimensions of TQM, the interrelationship between the dimensions has not been given much attention. For example, it may be interesting to examine the relative importance of the key dimensions for achieving effectiveness.
(4) Research needs to focus on the influence of temporal dimension. It is not clear how much time it takes for organizations to successfully implement TQM.
(5) Hackman and Wageman (1995) point out that academics have not conducted much serious work on TQM. Most of the work has been conducted by practitioners who often do not pay attention to rigors of scientific methodology. Clearly, understanding of TQM can be facilitated by rigorous scientific research by academic scholars.

CONCLUSION

The objective of this chapter was to review the literature and cover the salient issues for some of the most popular management interventions. For the purpose of this chapter, we focused on interventions that are meant to influence performance effectiveness in organizations by working through human resource systems. Specifically, we focused on three popular interventions, namely MBO, participative management, and TQM. For each of these interventions, we traced its history and development, reviewed its salient features as enunciated by leading scholars in these areas, and examined the influence of the intervention on organizational effectiveness. We also reviewed the applicability of these interventions in a multicultural/international context by examining literature on the effectiveness of these interventions across various national cultures. We concluded the review of these interventions by discussing where these interventions are headed as we enter a new millennium.

In broad strokes, this review suggests that these management interventions appear to have gone through the lifecycle of a typical management fad (Campbell, 1971). That is, a new management intervention appears on the horizon and develops a large stable of advocates who first describe its successful use in a number of situations. A few empirical studies are carried out to demonstrate that the method works. Slowly, a few vocal opponents begin to criticize the usefulness of the technique, often without any supporting data. Around the same time, another new intervention appears on the horizon which grabs the attention of practitioners and managers, and the older intervention fades into oblivion, and this cycle repeats itself. More often, the new intervention is not entirely new; like the proverbial old wine in the new bottle, some of the salient features of the new intervention are drawn from the techniques of an earlier intervention. Thus, the introduction of a new intervention represents elements of continuity and change. The elements of continuity are often those management principles and techniques that have withstood the rigors of empirical scientific research. This review of management interventions indicated that certain management principles such as employee participation, collaborative work, and goal setting have found a home in one intervention after another because these principles are based on sound management theory and empirical research evidence. Management fads may come and go; what is enduring is this set of time-tested management principles.

This review suggests that these principles not only withstood the rigors of time but the space dimension too. While national culture exerts an important influence in shaping individual attitudes, the evidence reviewed in this chapter indicates that managers and employees are willing to adapt to management principles, although they may not be well aligned with their national cultural values. For example, we found that companies across the world have implemented total quality management, which has teamwork and employee participation as its constituent elements. This was the case despite Western cultures being more individualistic than team oriented and Asian cultures being more hierarchical than decentralized and empowered.

Finally, we suggested areas of research that need to be focused on for the future. We hope this review and discussion will generate further research in this area.

REFERENCES

Adam, E.E. (1994). Alternative quality improvement practices and organizational performance. *Journal of Operations Management, 12*, 27–44

Alavi, M., & Keen, P.G.W. (1989). Business teams in the information age. *The Information Society, 6*, 179–195.

Anderson, J.C., Rungtusanatham, M., & Schroeder, R.G. (1994). A theory of quality management underlying the Deming management method. *Academy of Management Review, 19*, 472–508.

Ansari, A. (1984). *An empirical investigation of the implementation of Japanese just in time purchasing practices and its impact on product quality and productivity in US firms.* Doctoral dissertation, University of Nebraska.

Azarang, M.R., Gonzales, G., & Reavill, L. (1998). An empirical investigation of the relationship between quality improvement techniques and performance – a Mexican case. *Journal of Quality Management, 3*(2), 265–292.

Badawy, M.K. (1980). Styles of mid-eastern managers. *California Management Review, 22*(3), 293–297.

Banai, B., & Katsounotos, P. (1993). Participative management in Cyprus. *International Studies of Management and Organization, 23*(3), 19–34.

Bandura, A. (1986). *Social foundations of thought and action: A social cognitive theory.* Englewood Cliffs, NJ: Prentice-Hall.

Banker, R., Potter, G., & Schroeder, R. (1993). Manufacturing performance reporting for continuous quality improvement. *Management International Review, 33*(2), 70–86.

Barra, R.J. (1989). *Putting quality circles to work.* New York: McGraw-Hill.

Beechler, S., & Yang, J.Z. (1993). The transfer of Japanese management to American subsidiaries: Contingencies, constraints, and competencies. *Journal of International Business Studies, 25*, 467–491.

Benson, P.G., Saraph, J.V., & Schroeder, R.G. (1991). The effect of organizational context on quality management: An empirical investigation. *Management Science, 37*(9), 1107–1124.

Black, J.S., & Gregersen, H.B. (1997). Participative decision making: An integration of multiple dimensions. *Human Relations, 50*(7), 859–878.

Blauner, R. (1964). *Alienation and freedom: The factory worker and his productivity.* Chicago: University of Chicago Press.

Boyacigiller, N.A., & Adler, N.J. (1991). The parochial dinosaur: Organizational science in a global context. *Academy of Management Review, 16*(2), 262–290.

Brief, A.P. (1984). *Productivity research in the behavioral and social sciences.* New York: Praeger.

Burns, T., & Stalker, G.M. (1961). *The management of innovation.* London: Tavistock Publications.

Cameron, K.S. (1991). Best practices in white collar downsizing: Managing contradiction. *Academy of Management Executive, 5*, 57–73.

Cameron, K.S. (1995). Downsizing, quality and performance. In R.E. Cole (Ed.), *The fall and rise of American quality movement.* New York: Oxford University Press.

Cameron, K.W., & Whetten, D.A. (1996). Organizational effectiveness and quality: The second generation. In J.R. Smart (Ed.), *Higher education: Handbook of theory and research.* New York: Agathon.

Campbell, J.P. (1971). Personnel training and development. *Annual Review of Psychology, 22*, 565–602.

Cardy, R.L. (1996). Editor's note. *Journal of Quality Management, 1*(1), 1–4.

Cardy, R.L., & Dobbins, G.H. (1994). *Performance appraisal: Alternative perspectives.* Cincinnati, OH: Southwestern.

Cardy, R.L., & Dobbins, G.H. (1996). Human resource management in a total quality environment: Moving from a traditional to TQHRM approach. *Journal of Quality Management, 1*(1), 5–20.

Child, J. (1977). *Organizations: A guide to problems and practice.* London: Harper & Row.

Child, J. (1981). Culture, contingency and capitalism in the cross national study of organizations. In L.L. Cummings, & B.M. Staw (Eds.), *Research in Organizational Behavior* (Vol. 3, pp. 303–356), Greenwich, CN: JAI Press..

Chorn, N.H. (1991). Total quality management: Panacea or pitfall? *International Journal of Physical Distribution and Logistics Management, 21*(8), 31–35.

Clark, W.A., & McCabe, W.S. (1970). Leadership beliefs of Australian managers. *Journal of Applied Psychology, 54*, 1–6.

Coch, L., & French, J.R.P. (1948). Overcoming resistance to change. *Human Relations, 1*, 512–532.

Conference Board (1991). *Employee buy-in to total quality.* New York: Conference Board.

Connor, P.E. (1992). Decision making patterns: The role of organizational context. *Academy of Management Journal, 35*(1), 218–231.

Coopman, P.L., Drenth, P.J., Heller, F.A., & Rus, V. (1993). Participation in complex organizational decisions: A comparative study of the United Kingdom, The Netherlands, and Yugoslavia. In W.M. Lafferty, & E. Rosenstein (Eds.), *International handbook of participation in organizations*. Oxford: Oxford University Press.

Cotton, J.L., Vollrath, D.A., Lengnick-Hall, M.L., & Jennings, K.R. (1988). Employee participation: Diverse forms and different outcomes. *Academy of Management Review, 13*, 8–22.

Crosby, P.B. (1979). *Quality is free: The art of making certain*. New York: McGraw-Hill.

Crosby, P.B. (1984). *Quality without tears: The art of hassle free management*. Milwaukee, WI: Quality Press.

Cummings, L.L., & Schmidt, S.M. (1972). Managerial attitudes of Greeks: The roles of culture and industrialization. *Administrative Science Quarterly, 17*, 265–272.

Dachler, H.P., & Wilpert, B. (1978). Conceptual dimensions and boundaries of participation in organizations: A critical evaluation. *Administrative Science Quarterly, 23*, 1–34.

Daniel, S.J., & Reitsperger, W.D. (1994). Strategic control systems for quality: An empirical comparison of the Japanese and US electronics industry. *Journal of International Business Studies, 25*, 275–294.

Davis, M., & Lansbury, R.D. (1996). Employee involvement and industrial reform: Reviewing a decade of experience in Australia. *Employee Relations, 18*(5), 5–25.

Dean, J.W., & Bowen, D.E. (1994). Management theory and total quality: Improving research and practice through theory development. *Academy of Management Review, 19*, 392–418.

Dean, J.W., & Snell, S.A. (1996). The strategic use of quality management: An empirical examination. *MDBR Strategic Management Journal, 17*, 459–480.

Deming, E.W. (1986). *Out of the crisis*. Cambridge: MA: MIT center for advanced engineering study.

Dinesh, D., & Palmer, E. (1998). Management by objectives and balanced score card. Will Rome fall again? *Management decision, 5*, 363–370.

Dooley, K., & Floor, R.F. (1998). Perceptions of success and failure in TQM initiatives. *Journal of Quality Management, 3*(2), 157–174.

Drucker, P.F. (1954). *The practice of management*. New York: Harper.

Druckman, D., Singer, J.E., & Van Cott, H. (1997). *Enhancing organizational Performance*. Washington, DC: National Academy Press.

Economist (1992). Cracks in quality. *The Economist* (April 18), 67–68.

Edwards, C.D. (1968). The meaning of quality. *Quality progress* (October), 37.

Emery, F.E., & Trist, E.L. (1969). Sociotechnical systems. In F.E. Emery (Ed.), *Systems thinking*. London: Penguin.

England, G.W., & Negandhi, A.R. (1979). National context and technology as determinants of employees' perceptions. In G.W. England, A.R., Negandhi, & B. Wilpert (Eds.), *Organizational functioning in a cross cultural perspective*. Kent, OH: Kent State University Press.

Ernst, & Young, & American Quality Foundation (1992). *International quality study: The definitive guide to best international quality management practices*, Cleveland: Thought Leadership Studies.

Fiegenbaum, A.V. (1983). *Total quality control*. New York: McGraw-Hill.

Ford, B.J., & Honeycutt, E.D. (1992). Japanese national culture as a basis for understanding Japanese business practices. *Business Horizons, 35*, 27–34.

Forker, L.B. (1991). Quality: American, Japanese, and Soviet perspectives. *Academy of Management Executive, 5*(4), 63–74.

Fornell, C., & Johnson, M.D. (1993). Differentiation as a basis for explaining customer satisfaction across industries. *Journal of Economic Psychology, 14*, 681–696.

Fram, E.H., & Ajami, R. (1994). Globalization of markets and shopping stress: Cross country comparisons. *Business Horizons, 37*, 17–23.

Galbraith, J.R. (1973). *Designing complex organizations*. Reading, MA: Addison-Wesley Publishing Company.

Gantt, H.L. (1919). *Organizing for work*. New York: Harcourt, Brace, and Howe.

Garvin, D.A. (1988). *Managing quality: Strategic and competitive edge*. New York: Free Press.

Gilbreth, F.B. (1911). *Motion study*. New York: Van Nostrand.

Gilbreth, L.M. (1914). *The psychology of management*. New York: Sturgis and Walton Company.

Glew, D.J., O'Leary-Kelly, A.M., Griffin, R.W., & Van Fleet, D.D. (1995). Participation in organizations: A preview of issues and proposed framework for future analysis. *Journal of Management, 21*(3), 395–421.

Goal/QPC (1992). *Total quality management: implementation manual*. Methuen, MA: Author.

Griffin, A., Gleason, C., Preiss, R., & Shevenaugh, D. (1995). Best practice for customer satisfaction in manufacturing firms. *Sloan Management Review, 36*, 87–98.

Gryna, F.M. (1988) Quality assurance. In A.J.M. Juran, & F.M. Gryna (Eds.), *Quality control handbook* (Section 9.2). New York: McGraw-Hill.

Guzzo, R.A., Jette, R.D., & Katzell, R.A. (1985). The effects of psychologically based intervention programs on worker productivity: A meta analysis. *Personnel Psychology, 38*, 275–291.

Hackman, J.R. (1981). Sociotechnical systems theory: A commentary. In A.H. van de Ven, & W.F. Joyce (Eds.), *Perspectives in organization design and behavior*. New York: Wiley.

Hackman, R.J., & Wageman, R. (1995). Total quality management: Empirical, conceptual, and practical issues. *Administrative Science Quarterly, 40*, 309–342.

Haire, M., Ghiselli, E.E., & Porter, L.W. (1966). *Managerial thinking: An international study*. New York: Wiley.

Harris, C.R., & Purdy, R.L. (1998). The role of participation in the implementation of total quality management programs. *International Journal of Technology Management, 16*, 466–480.

Hendricks, K., & Singhal, V. (1997). Does implementing an effective TQM program actually improve operating performance? Empirical evidence from firms that have won quality awards. *Management Science, 43*(9), 1258–1274.

Herzberg, F. (1966). *Work and nature of man.* Cleveland, OH: World Publishing.

Hofstede, G. (1980). *Culture's consequences: International differences in work-related values.* Beverly Hills, CA: Sage Publications.

Hofstede, G. (1991). *Culture and organizations: Software of the mind.* London: McGraw-Hill.

Hogan, R.T. (1991). Personality and personality measurement. In M.D. Dunnette, & L.M. Hough (Ed.), *Handbook of industrial and organizational psychology.* Palo Alto, CA: Consulting Psychologists Press.

Holden, L. (1999). The perception gap in employee empowerment: A comparative study of banks in Sweden and Britain. *Personnel Review, 28*(3), 222–241.

Huang, T.C. (1997). The effect of participatory management on organizational performance: The case of Taiwan. *International Journal of Human Resource Management, 8*(5), 677–689.

Ishikawa, K. (1985). *What is total quality control? The Japanese way.* Englewood Cliffs, NJ: Prentice-Hall.

Ittner, C. (1992). *The economics and management of quality costs.* Cambridge, MA: Harvard University School of Business Admin.

Ivancevich, J.M. (1976). Effects of goal setting on performance and satisfaction. *Journal of Applied Psychology, 61*, 605–612.

Japanese Industrial Standards Committee (1981). *Industrial standardization in Japan: Agency of industrial science and technology.* Ministry of International Trade and Industry.

Jenner, R.A., Hebert, L., Appell, E., & Baack, J. (1998). Using quality management for cultural transformation of Chinese state enterprises: A case study. *Journal of Quality Management, 3*(2), 193–211.

Johansen, R. (1989). *Groupware: computer support for business teams.* New York: Free Press.

Juran, J.M. (1988). *Juran on planning for quality.* New York: Free Press.

Juran, J.M. (1992). *Juran on quality by design.* New York: Free Press.

Kaplan, R.S., & Norton, D.P. (1992). The balanced scorecard measures that drive performance. *Harvard Business Review, 70*(1), 71–79.

Kehoe, D.F. (1994). *Fundamentals of quality management.* London: Chapman & Hall.

Kren, L. (1992). The moderating effects of locus of control on performance incentives and participation. *Human Relations, 45*(9), 991–1012.

Lawler, E.E. III (1986). *High involvement management.* San Francisco: Jossey-Bass.

Lawler, E.E., & Hackman, J.R. (1969). Impact of employee participation in the development of pay incentive plans. *Journal of Applied Psychology, 61*(2), 166–171.

Leana, C.R. (1987). Power relinquishment versus power sharing. Theoretical clarification and empirical comparison of delegation and participation. *Journal of Applied Psychology, 72*, 228–233.

Ledford, G.E., & Lawler, E.E. (1994). Research on employee participation: Beating a dead horse? *Academy of Management Review, 19*(4), 633–636.

Leffler, K.B. (1982). Ambiguous changes in product quality. *American Economic Review* (December), 956.

Lemak, D.J., Reed, R., & Satish, P.K. (1997). Commitment to total quality management: Is there a relationship with firm performance? *Journal of Quality Management, 2*(1), 67–86.

Lewin, K. (1952). Group decision and social change. In T. Newcomb, & E. Hartley (Eds.), *Readings in Social Psychology.* New York: Holt, Rinehart and Winston.

Lewin, K., Lippitt, R., & White, R.K. (1939). Patterns of aggressive behavior in experimentally created social climates. *Journal of Social Psychology, 10*, 271–299.

Locke, E.A., Alavi, M., & Wagner, J.A. (1997). Participation in decision making: An information exchange perspective. *Research in Personnel and Human Resources Management, 15*, 293–331.

Locke, E.A., & Schweiger, D.M. (1979). Participation in decision making: One more look. In Staw, B.M. (Ed.), *Research in Organizational Behavior* (Vol. 1, pp. 265–339), Greenwich, CN: JAI Press.

Macy, B.A. (1982). The Bolivar quality of work program. Success or failure? In Zagar, R., & Row, M.P. (Eds.), *The innovative organization: productivity programs in action.* New York: Pergamon.

Macy, B.A., & Mirvis, P.H. (1982). Organizational change efforts: Methodology for considering organizational effectiveness and program cost and benefits. *Evaluation Review, 6*(3), 301–372.

Mankidy, J. (1995). Changing perspective of worker participation in India with particular reference to the banking industry. *British Journal of Industrial Relations, 33*(3), 443–459.

Marsh, B. (1994). Baldridge award gets fewer applicants from small business. *The Wall Street Journal* (October 13), A2.

Masterson, S.S., & Taylor, S.M. (1996). Total quality management and performance appraisal: An integrative perspective. *Journal of Quality Management, 1*(1), 67–89.

Mayo, E. (1933). *The problems of an industrial civilization.* New York: Macmillan.

McConkie, M.L. (1979). Classifying and reviewing the empirical work on MBO: Some implications. *Group and Organization Studies, 4*, 461–475.

McFarlin, D.B., Sweeney, P.D., & Cotton, J.L. (1992). Attitudes toward employee participation in decision making. A comparison of European and American managers in an United States multinational company. *Human Resource Management, 31*(4), 363–383.

McGregor, D. (1960). *The human side of enterprise.* New York: McGraw-Hill.

Miller, K.I. (1988). Culture and role based predictors of organizational participation and allocation preference. *Communication Research, 15*(6), 699–725.

Miller, K.L., & Monge, P.R. (1986). Participation, satisfaction, and productivity. A meta analytic review. *Academy of management journal, 29*, 727–753.

Morris, T., & Pavett, R. (1992). Management style and productivity in two cultures. *Journal of International Business Studies, 23,* 180–196.

Munsterberg, H. (1913). *Psychology and industrial efficiency.* Boston: Houghton Mifflin.

Neumann, J.E. (1989). Why people do not participate in organization change. In R. Woodman, & W. Pasmore, (Eds.), *Research in Organizational Change and Development, 3,* 181–212.

Neumann, G.A., Edwards, J.E., & Raju, N.S. (1989). Organizational development interventions: A meta analysis of their effects on satisfaction and other attitudes. *Personnel Psychology, 42,* 461–489.

NIST Update (1996). Study finds quality stocks yield big pay offs. *National Institute of Standards and Technology, U.S. Department of Commerce,* February 5th.

Odiorne, G.E. (1978). MBO: A backward glance. *Business Horizons* (October), 14–24.

Ohmae, K. (1982). *The mind of the strategist.* London: Penguin.

Ouchi, W.G. (1981). *Theory Z: How can American companies meet the Japanese challenge.* Reading, MA: Addison-Wesley.

Parasuraman, A., Zeithaml, V.A., & Berry, L.L. (1985). A conceptual model of service quality and its implications for future research. *Journal of Marketing, 49,* 41–50.

Parnell, J.A., Bell, E.D., & Taylor, R. (1992). The propensity for participative management: A conceptual and empirical analysis. *Mid Atlantic Journal of Business, 28*(1), 31–43.

Pelled, L.H., & Hill, K.D. (1997). Participative management in Northern Mexico: A study of Maquiladoras. *International Journal of Human Resource Management, 8*(7), 197–212.

Philips, L., Chang, D., & Buzzell, R. (1983). Product quality, cost position and business performance. *Journal of Marketing, 47,* 26–43.

Pike, J., & Barnes, R. (1996). *TQM in Action.* London: Chapman & Hall.

Porras, J.I., & Robertson, P.J. (1992). Organizational development: Theory, practice, and research. In Dunnette, & L. Hough (Eds.), *Handbook of industrial and organizational psychology.* Palo Alto, CA: Consulting Psychologists Press.

Porras, J.I., & Silvers, R.C. (1991). Organization development and transformation. *Annual review of psychology, 42,* 51–78.

Port, O., Carey, J., Kelly, K., & Forest, S. (1992). Quality: small and midsize companies seize the challenge – not a moment so soon. *Business Week,* (November 30), 67–74.

Porter, L.W., & Lawler, E.E. (1968). *Managerial attitudes and performance.* Homewood, IL: Irwin.

Prisig, R. (1974). *Zen and the art of motorcycle maintenance.* New York: Bantam.

Pugh, D.S., & Hickson, D.J. (1993). *Writers on organizations: The omnibus edition.* Brookfield, VT: Dartmouth.

Punnett, B.J., & Shenkar, O. (1994). International management research: Toward a contingency approach. *Advances in International Comparative Management, 9,* 39–55.

Quinn, R.E. (1996). *Deep change.* San Francisco: Jossey-Bass.

Raia, A.P. (1974). *Management by objectives.* New York: McGraw-Hill.

Rao, S.S., Raghunathan, T.S., & Solis, L.E. (1997). A comparative study of quality practices and results in India, China, and Mexico. *Journal of Quality Management, 2*(2), 235–250.

Redding, G.S. (1994). Comparative management theory: Jungle, zoo, or fossil bed? *Organization Studies, 15*(3), 323–359.

Reger, R.K., Gustafson, L.T., DeMarie, S.M., & Mullane, J.V. (1994). Reframing the organization: Why implementing total quality is easier said than done. *Academy of Management Review, 19,* 565–584.

Reitsperger, W.D., & Daniel, S.J. (1990). Japan v. Silicon Valley: Quality-cost trade-off philosophies. *Journal of International Business Studies, 21,* 298–300.

Rodgers, R., & Hunter, J.E. (1991). Impact of management by objectives on organizational, productivity. *Journal of Applied Psychology, 76,* 322–336.

Rodgers, R., & Hunter, J.E. (1992). A foundation of good management practice in government: Management by objectives. *Public Administration Review, 52,* 27–39.

Rodgers, R., & Hunter, J.E. (1994). Discard of study evidence by literature reviews. *Journal of Applied Behavioral Science, 30*(3), 329–345.

Roethlisberger, F.J., & Dickson, W.J. (1939). *Management and the worker.* Cambridge, MA: Harvard University Press.

Rogers, T. (1993). Award winning AT & T plant lays off 1000. *Lansing State Journal,* May 15, p. 1D.

Ross, J.E. (1993). *Total quality management.* Delray Beach, FL: St. Lucie Press.

Ryan, M. (1999). The role of social process in participative decision making in an international context. *Participation and Empowerment: An International Journal, 7*(2), 33–42.

Sashkin, M. & Kiser, K.J. (1993). *Putting total quality management to work.* San Francisco: Barrett-Koehler.

Schneider, B., & Bowen, D. (1985). Employee and customer perception of service in banks: Replication and extension. *Journal of Applied Psychology, 70*(3), 423–433.

Senge, P. (1990). *The fifth discipline: The art and practice of the learning organization.* New York: Doubleday.

Shea, C.M., & Howell, J.M. (1998). Organizational antecedents to the successful implementation of total quality management: a social cognitive perspective. *Journal of Quality Management, 3*(1), 3–24.

Sluti, D.G. (1992). *Linking process quality with performance: An empirical study of New Zealand manufacturing plants. PhD Dissertation.* University of Auckland.

Snell, S.A., & Dean, J.W. (1992). Integrated manufacturing and human resource management: A human capital perspective. *Academy of Management Journal, 35,* 467–504.

Spector, P.E. (1986). Perceived control by employees: A meta analysis of studies concerning autonomy and participation at work. *Human Relations, 39,* 1005–1016.

Spencer, B.A. (1994). Models of organization and total quality management: A comparison and critical evaluation. *Academy of Management Review, 19,* 446–471.

Stone, D.L., & Eddy, E.R. (1996). A model of individual and organizational factors affecting quality related outcomes. *Journal of Quality Management, 1*(1), 21–48.

Stone-Romero, E.F., Stone, D.L., & Grewal, D. (1997). Development of a multidimensional measure of perceived product quality. *Journal of Quality Management, 2*(1), 87–111.

Sykes, A.J.M. (1965). Economic interests and Hawthorne researchers. *Human Relations, 18,* 253–263.

Taguchi, G. & Clausing, D. (1990). Robust quality. *Harvard Business Review, 68*(1), 65–75.

Tayeb, M. (1994). Organizations and national culture: Methodology considered. *Organization Studies, 15*(3), 429–446.

Taylor, F.W. (1911). *The principles of scientific management.* New York: Harper Brothers.

Triandis, H.C. (1980). Introduction to cross cultural psychology. In H.C. Triandis, & W.W. Lambert (Eds.), *Handbook of cross cultural psychology,* Vol. I. Boston: Allyn & Bacon.

Triandis, H.C. (1994). Cross cultural industrial and organizational psychology. In H.C. Triandis, & M.D. Dunnette (Eds.), *Handbook of industrial and organizational psychology.* Palo Alto, CA: Consulting Psychology Press.

Trist, E., & Bamforth, K.W. (1951). Some social and psychological consequences of the longwall method of coal-getting. *Human Relations, 4,* 3–38.

U.S. General Accounting Office (1991). *Management practices: U.S. companies improve performance through quality efforts.* Washington, DC: U.S. Government Printing Press.

Vardi, Y., Shirom, A., & Jacobson, D. (1980). A study of leadership of Israeli managers. *Academy of Management Journal, 23*(2), 367–374.

Vroom, V.H. (1959). Some personality determinants of the effects of participation. *Journal of Abnormal Social Psychology, 56,* 322–327.

Vroom, V. (1964). *Work and motivation.* New York: Wiley.

Vroom, V.H., & Jago, P.W. (1974). Decision making as a social process: Normative and descriptive models of leader behavior. *Decision Sciences, 5,* 743–770.

Vroom, V.H., & Yetton, P.W. (1973). *Leadership and decision making.* Pittsburgh: University of Pittsburgh Press.

Wagner, J.A. (1994). Participation's effects on performance and satisfaction: A reconsideration of the research evidence. *Academy of Management Review, 19,* 300–312.

Wagner, J.A. (1995). On beating dead horses, reconsidering reconsiderations, and ending disputes: Further thoughts about a recent study of research on participation. *Academy of Management Review, 20,* 506–509.

Wagner, J.A., & Gooding, R.Z. (1987). Shared influence and organizational behavior: A meta analysis of situational variables expected to moderate participation-outcome relationship. *Academy of Management Journal, 30,* 524–541.

Waldman, D.A. (1994). The contributions of total quality management to a theory of work performance. *Academy of Management Review, 19,* 510–536.

Welsh, D.H.B., Luthans, F., & Sommer, S.M. (1993). Managing Russian factory workers: The impact of U.S. based behavioral and participative techniques. *Academy of Management Journal, 36*(1), 58–79.

Wickens, J.D. (1968). Management by objectives: An appraisal. *Journal of Management Studies, 5,* 365–379.

Williamson, A.D. (1993). *Business terms.* Boston, MA: Harvard Business School Press.

Woodward, J. (1965). *Industrial organization: Theory and practice.* New York: Oxford University Press.

Wright, P.M., McCormick, B., Sherman, S.W., & McMahan, G.C. (1999). The role of human resource practices in petro chemical refinery performance. *International Journal of Human Resource Management, 10,* 551–554.

Yavas, B.F. (1995). A comparison of the quality perceptions of U.S. and Asian firms in the electronics industry. *Management International Review, 35*(2), 171–188.

Yavas, B.F., & Burrows, T. (1994). A comparative study of attitudes of U.S. and Asian managers toward product quality. *Quality Management Journal, 2,* 41–56.

Yavas, B.F., & Marcoulides, G.A. (1996). An examination of cross-cultural quality management practices in American and Asian Firms. *Advances in International Comparative Management, 11,* 51–67.

Yoshida, K. (1989). Deming management philosophy: Does it work in the U.S. as well as in Japan. *The Columbia Journal of World Business,* 10–17.

Yoshida, K. (1992). New economic principles in America – competition cooperation. *The Columbia Journal of World Business, 27,* 30–34.

Zink, K.J. (1998). *Total quality management as a holistic management concept. The European model of business excellence.* Berlin: Springer-Verlag.

19

Organization Theory

BEHLÜL ÜSDİKEN and HÜSEYİN LEBLEBİCİ

Organization theory has been a low-consensus field, a feature that became ever more pronounced in the late twentieth century. This chapter traces developments in organization theory over the last 50 years that have culminated in present-day fragmentation in theoretical and epistemological positions. Institutionalization as a separate field dates back to the rapprochement in the 1970s among concerns of earlier practitioner-theorists and sociologically orientated work and the ensuing divide between organization theory and organizational behaviour. The chapter reviews how what appeared like emerging consensus at the time was soon to break down with the advent in North America of influential research programmes rooted in sociology as well as economics. The last two decades also witnessed, primarily in Europe, the increasing popularity of alternative perspectives that challenged one or both of the scientistic and managerialist footings in the field. The chapter concludes by discussing the present state of pluralism in theoretical agendas and offering conjectures for possible futures of the discipline.

CHARACTERIZING ORGANIZATIONAL THEORIZING

The study of organization now has a history of around a hundred years. Although there has been some degree of continuity in central interests and approaches taken to address them, a lot has also changed over this period. What now passes as organizational theorizing (or for that matter, as organization science, organizational analysis, or organization studies) is in many ways different from the concerns and modes of investigating organization and organizations in the former part of the 20th century.

The study of organization went through a major transformation or, to put it perhaps more mildly, took a new direction around the mid-20th century. The redirection took place as a part of the broader move unfolding in American business schools towards bringing science into business studies and education (Locke, 1996). Although pioneering steps in this new direction date back to earlier years,

the more wholesale shift came after the late 1950s as a response to dissatisfactions about the state of business education in the USA at the time (Whitley, 1988; Miner, 1997). Broadly put, the turn involved the aspiration to draw upon science and the scientific method in dealing with managerial and business problems. The outcome was the injection of quantitative methods and behavioural sciences into business curricula coupled with an influx of faculty members trained in these fields who brought with them the inclinations and competencies for scientific research (Miner, 1997).

Scientization brought a shift from the experience-based claims and writings of earlier practitioner-theorists (Thompson & McHugh, 1995) on management and organization towards approaches grounded in the scientific method. The way of addressing managerial issues was changing, promising, and bringing, as in other areas of business studies, reputability and power to the field. However, the central concern, that of finding ways of solving problems of organizational functioning efficiently and effectively, by and large remained the same. In a sense, it was a happy marriage at the outset and served to shape the two central footings of the discipline that was emerging in the USA, namely *scientism* and *managerialism*.

For organization theory the merging of science and practical problems of management was character forming in a number of important ways, shaping features and strains that have since come to characterize the field, perhaps more so than other areas of business studies. The move towards the natural science model although integrative in one sense, ironically, was potentially divisive in two ways. For one, what scientization did was to distance those who studied managerial problems and those who practised management. Acceptance of ideas and principles put forward by practitioner-theorists had not been without problems either, due both to their universality claims and to interference with managerial prerogatives. With scientization the problem began to aggravate. As in any field that claims to be an applied science the problem of relating to practitioners or the strain between rigour and relevance set in to stay as a major source of concern and debate. Beyond the issue of translation to practice, differing degrees of allegiances were to take hold among those in the academia to the concerns emanating from the two footings of the field, science and the practical problems of management. Secondly, the infusion of science involved turning to other disciplines like psychology, social psychology, and sociology to borrow frameworks, concepts, and methods, as well as importing researchers trained in these areas. It also meant building upon and extending earlier work carried out on organizations within such disciplines. Not only was this reliance on a variety of social sciences character defining, in the sense of organizational theorizing becoming multidiscipline based (March, 1996), but also in breeding substantive dissension emanating from allegiances to different disciplinary traditions.

A tension of this kind emerged as the orientation towards the natural science model paved the way for the institutionalization of 'organization theory' as a separate field of study in US business schools (Hinings, 1988) with a redefined narrower domain. The gaining of a separate identity went through a number of stages within the broader tendency, spurred by the scientist reorientation, towards greater specialization in business studies. Initially, 'management' and 'administrative sciences' served as umbrella definitions for delimiting boundaries as seen, for example, in the emergence in late 1950s of what were later to become the leading American journals of the field, namely the *Administrative Science Quarterly* and the *Journal of the Academy of Management*. The 1960s and 1970s brought in the USA a split between 'organizational behaviour' and 'organization theory' or between the 'micro' and the 'macro' in organizational analysis. The advent of the contingency perspective was instrumental

in this process of separation as it triggered quantitatively based 'comparative' studies of internal design problems, building on the sociological tradition in the field and thus balancing the behavioural orientation that had come to dominate research.

Distancing from the focus on behavioural phenomena within organizations and the resultant confinement to organizational level issues served to narrow down the disciplinary basis of organization theory largely to sociology cast onto the administrative tradition of the earlier practitioner-theorists. Coupled with the increasing influence of the contingency perspective, it also offered towards the latter part of the 1970s the prospect of what may be called a paradigmatic consensus, which could even extend beyond the USA to include research at the time in Europe. The promise was very short lived, however; indeed it was breaking down when some were thinking that it was emerging. Theorizing on organizations was again displaying its low-consensus character, increasingly so after the early 1980s, leading to divisions that have now become much more fundamental.

Proliferation of epistemological and theoretical positions has had to do not only with the relatively more recent developments in the USA but also with increasing scholarly input from other parts of the world. The scientist revolution had occurred at a time when the USA was emerging as a super power and assuming a leadership role in the West and was looked up to as the epitome of business practice and education. The USA thus became, more so than in the former part of the century, a centre of attraction for learning about business and management leading to the dissemination of US-based institutions, ideas, and practices (Locke, 1996). Although American domination of the field still persists and the flow of theoretical perspectives is to a large degree one-way (Engwall, 1996; Hickson, 1996), there has been greater participation by scholars from other countries accompanied by an increasing number of research outlets with institutional bases outside North America. Greater international input into the field has contributed to the emergence of domain definitions and approaches different from those prevalent in the USA (Üsdiken & Pasadeos, 1995; Collin, Johansson, Svensson & Ulvenblad 1996).

Within the present state of theoretical pluralism in the field the search for and the hope of integration continues, an aspiration on which some believe that there is consensus (e.g., Elsbach, Sutton & Whetten, 1999). The current situation is regarded as a continuing pre-paradigmatic state (e.g., McKinley, Mone & Moon, 1999). For some others, on the other hand, it reflects an inevitable multiparadigmatic condition for the field (e.g., Kaghan & Phillips, 1998). Yet another view is that the present state is nothing but a prerevolutionary crisis (e.g., Hatchuel, 1999). The impending revolution is to eradicate what have been identified above as the two footings of organization theory (scientism and managerialism) as it became institutionalized in the USA as a separate discipline. The aspiration is for a 'new' theory of organization that is to be nonpositivist and nonmanagerialist (Watson, 1994).

The present chapter traces the journey of organizational theorizing from the mid-century scientistic turn in the USA to the present day. The next section extends the discussion of the move from earlier dispersed roots towards institutionalization as a separate field in USA in the 1970s. The section to follow considers chronologically parallel developments, primarily in Europe, challenging what was regarded as emerging orthodoxy in the field and paving the way for fundamental divisions that were to strengthen over time. The fourth to the sixth sections review the influential theoretical perspectives that have evolved in the last quarter of the century, that have undoubtedly served to enrich as well as extend the boundaries of the field, but also engendered new and a wider range of allegiances. The final section builds on this review to provide an assessment of the field at the end of the century, to be joined by speculations on what the foreseeable future may hold.

FROM DISPERSED ROOTS TO INSTITUTIONALIZATION

The Three Roots: Administrative, Sociological, and Psychological

By the late 1950s there were three strands of work emanating from different concerns and ways of thinking and that made reference to 'organization'. For one, there was the stream of contributions by practitioner-theorists from both North America (e.g., Mooney & Reiley, 1939) and Europe (e.g., Fayol, 1949; Urwick, 1944) who, broadly put, sought ways of formalizing the design of organizations and developing guidelines for effective managerial action in government and business. Work of this kind, in its own way, not only described the problem of organizing as an element of administration but also laid the foundations of the concern with the structural analysis of organized activity (Guillén, 1994). They did become subject to criticism, however, as the call for a science-based approach to internal design problems began to mount (e.g., Simon, 1947), questioning not only the adequacy of the evidence but also the extent to which they were able to provide practical guidance to managers.

Practitioner-theorists were joined in the 1940s and 1950s by sociologists, mostly from North America, in the structural analysis of organizations. Weber (1947) was brought into organizational analysis both for theory development on formal organizations and empirical investigation of the functioning of bureaucracies. Pioneering case study investigations (Selznick, 1949; Gouldner, 1954; Blau, 1955) evolved in the 1960s into comparative studies which were aimed at contrasting larger numbers of organizations with a view to understanding what shaped their features (Blau, 1974). Complementing these contributions was work that was geared to developing a conception of organizations as social systems. They were extensions of the concerns of another practitioner-theorist, Barnard (1938), with organizations as cooperative systems. Based on systems thinking, a central theme in these analyses was that organizations need to be treated as sociotechnical systems, faced with the problem of adapting to external and internal changes that required integration of the imperatives of technology and social relationships (e.g., Trist & Bamforth, 1951).

Systems thinking was also integrationist in the sense of relating to and serving as a bridge among sociological analyses and the third tradition, concerned primarily with the human element, which had developed from a base in psychology. The birth of industrial psychology was coterminous with scientific management, to be followed by the emergence of the human relations movement in the 1920s, which over the next three decades spurred empirical investigations of various kinds into individual and group behaviour in organizations as well as issues of leadership. Although geared primarily to such concerns, the human relations perspective and the ensuing behaviourist tradition also spoke to issues related to the way organizations were structured. Less hierarchy, participation in decision making, and teamwork were favoured structural arrangements (e.g., Likert, 1961).

Organizational Theorizing from the 1960s in North America and Europe

By the 1960s organization theory in the USA encompassed all these three traditions and was increasingly leaning towards a scientistic orientation, with behaviourist approaches in the forefront drawing upon a longer history of scientific research (Daft, 1980; Porter, 1996). The preoccupation initially was more with 'management' as the umbrella term that specified the domain for which there was a search for a general theory. Given the multiplicity of roots and traditions, strains had begun to emerge and concerns were expressed about the possibility of a unified theory (Koontz, 1961). Tensions were apparent, for example, between those that were sceptical about a 'theory' of management foreseeing development in the extension of the 'best practice' tradition and those that were inclined towards building a body of knowledge that would serve to identify general principles (Whitley, 1988). The latter were also challenged by those who were inclined to see unification coming through science-based approaches and under the framework of systems theory (Wren, 1994). There were also engagements by the more psychologically oriented with the structural-functionalism of the day for their neglect of human actors (e.g., Homans, 1964). Even then 'the field of "organization theory" appear(ed) so ununified and disorderly' (Rubenstein & Haberstroh, 1966: 3). (See also Hirsch & Levin, 1999.)

Taking place concurrently was the passage from considering organizing as a subset of managerial functions to a redefinition, as seen in the preceding quotation, by reference to organizations and organization theory, though employed interchangeably with the notion of 'organizational behaviour' and still with the explicit concern of 'helping' managers. Although there was reference to structural issues, the behaviourist slant was evident, leading, for example, Kassem (1976: 14) to characterize organization theory of the time in the USA as microscopic in approach, organizational psychology based, people and process focused, ideologically conservative, and geared towards practical theories. Kassem's (1976) intent in this characterization was to provide a contrast with what he observed as the predominant features of organizational theorizing in Europe at the time. For Kassem (1976: 14), European organization theory was macroscopic, drew upon sociology, focused on the organization as a whole, was conflict based, and orientated towards abstract theories. The organizational sociology of Europe was also characterized by diversity (Hofstede & Kassem, 1976) and some of what was produced found resonance in North America because their problematizations and methodologies fitted well with the scientistic tendencies in the latter.

The Micro–Macro Separation and Convergence Around the Contingency Framework

Indeed some of these contributions served as pioneers for later strands of theorizing that were to develop in North America. Notable in this respect is the work of Woodward (1958), Burns and Stalker (1961), and the Aston group (e.g., Hickson, Pugh & Pheysey, 1969) as early exemplars of structural-contingency theory and that of Crozier (1964) and Hickson, Hinings, Lee, Schneck and Pennings (1971) on structural analysis of power within organizations. The work of European researchers was accompanied by comparative studies of bureaucracy (e.g., Hall, 1962) and of business firms (e.g., Lawrence & Lorsch, 1967), as well as theoretical treatments (e.g., Thompson, 1967; Perrow, 1970) by American authors, that also portrayed organizational structures as contingent upon factors like size, technology or the external environment. The structural-contingency framework to emerge from these studies, buttressed as it was by systems theory, constituted a sociological open-systems perspective as a companion to the psychological one that had come earlier (Miner, 1990).

The contingency view of organization structure was based on two central themes. One argument was that there was no single best way of organization design. Organizations operated in different kinds of environment and employed different types of technology in carrying out their tasks. Environments varied in the degree of uncertainty and diversity, calling for different internal structural arrangements. So did the nature of tasks or technologies, notably with respect to routineness and interdependence (Perrow, 1970; Thompson, 1967). Organization structures were thus responses to information-processing demands emanating from external and internal conditions. Stable and simpler environments as well as routine technologies led to mechanistic structures characterized by formalization and hierarchy (Burns & Stalker, 1961). Dynamic environments and nonroutine tasks, on the other hand, called for more organic forms, structures that had less formal definitions and relied more on lateral rather than vertical relations. The second central theme of the contingency view complemented its deterministic flavour. Positive contribution of structural arrangements to organizational effectiveness and efficiency depended upon congruence, namely, the fit between conditions and design. Structural-contingency theory was very much in line with the times and owed its label to similar ideas that were being developed in relation to issues like leadership and decision making (Fiedler, 1967; Vroom & Yetton, 1973). Even a broader consensus appeared to be emerging around a contingency view of management (e.g., Kast & Rosenzweig, 1974).

The framework and the puzzles that contingency theory provided spurred in the 1970s larger-scale comparative studies of organization structure that helped to match the methodological orientations and advances of the behaviourist tradition. Coupled with new research agendas that were emerging, like interorganizational relations and power issues in organizations, the divorce from behavioural concerns was becoming clearer and organization theory was gaining, at least in the USA, a new and narrower definition. The central concerns of this redefined area of specialization were the determinants and outcomes of intra- and interorganizational design. The managerialist orientation was still there, as was the claim of being science based. The separation was based on disciplinary roots and, thus, on the level of analysis. The search, or hope, that dated back to 1950s, for gaining a separate identity through the fusion between sociology and the earlier practitioner-theorist tradition (Stern & Barley, 1996) was coming true. Not only was there now a new field with redefined boundaries but it would also appear that a consensus was emerging around a dominant paradigm provided by open-systems and contingency thinking. As this was happening, however, the seeds of new tensions and, indeed, fundamental divisions around the purpose and the ways of doing organizational analysis were being thrown mainly on the other side of the Atlantic.

CREEPING TENSIONS

The Early Attacks

Scholarly work in Europe on organizations, with the diversity it contained, produced not only studies in the genre of the Aston group (e.g., Hickson et al., 1969) that served as an important contribution to what was to follow under the label of contingency theory. It was also the source of views that were to challenge the boundaries and building blocks of organization theory, as it was understood in North America.

An early reaction came from Silverman (1970), regarded as seminal, primarily in the north of the English Channel, in what it brought up (Hassard & Parker, 1994). Silverman's book was a reaction to systems theory and proposed instead an 'action frame of reference' that located individual and group action at the centre of organizational analysis. Although Silverman (1970) had more sympathy towards later versions of the human relations perspective and the sociotechnical tradition, he was emphasizing the distinction between action and behaviour, in that the former embodied intentionality and the attachment of subjective meanings. The focus was thus on interactions among people and their everyday experiences in organizations. Silverman was not only critical of the systems approach because it helped to frame organizational issues in managerial terms but his position also involved a rejection of attempts to study causation in social phenomena. Of the central propositions that emanated from a social action perspective the first had to do with the 'fatal defect' (Silverman, 1970: 127) of not recognizing that the phenomena social and natural sciences dealt with were fundamentally different. The book engaged with both footings of organization theory, but involved a stronger challenge to its realist basis and, in turn, served as a stimulus for ethnomethodological research to follow.

Yet another 'critical' position against what was then becoming to be called 'mainstream' or 'orthodox' organization theory came from authors who were inspired by Marxian writings. Influential in this respect was Braverman's book (1974) and his focus on the 'labour process', the use of human labour in transforming raw materials into products and services. Organizations were considered as being located in a broader political economy and as instruments for managements to effect the control of labour (Clegg & Dunkerley, 1980).

In Europe the Paradigm Debate Begins

That there were by the end of 1970s at least traces of widely divergent views on organizations and the purpose and ways of theorizing them became strongly registered with the publication of Burrell and Morgan's (1979) book. With Burrell and Morgan the notion of paradigms and what was later to be called paradigm mentality (Willmott, 1993) entered into organizational analysis. Working from social theory, Burrell and Morgan (1979) specified two dimensions that they defined as 'sociology of regulation versus change' and 'objective versus subjective views of society'. The sociology of regulation was concerned with order, integration, and consensus, whereas that of change dealt with conflict, contradiction, and domination. An objectivist view of society was characterized by ontological and epistemological assumptions that treated the social world very much like natural phenomena. Subjectivism, on the other hand, reflected an opposing tradition in that the social could only be understood in terms of the subjective meanings attached by those involved. By juxtaposing these two dimensions, four 'paradigms' of social theorizing were identified, namely, functionalist, interpretive, radical humanist, and radical structuralist, that in turn informed organizational analyses. Functionalism, with its concern for regulation and objectivist basis, was thought to provide the dominant framework, the orthodoxy, for organization theorizing. The other three were challengers and differed from functionalism either due to emphasis on change (radical structuralism) or assumptions about social science (interpretive sociology) or in terms of both dimensions (radical humanism). Not only did Burrell and Morgan (1979) attempt to portray differences by articulating on the different traditions and their extensions in organization theory but also argued powerfully against the possibility of synthesis, as each of the paradigms derived from disparate metatheoretical bases.

These works heralded what was to follow in the next two decades, to a large degree outside the USA, primarily in the UK, some other parts of Europe, and other English speaking countries like Australia and Canada. Political and military language began to set into debates. So as early as the late 1970s Clegg and Dunkerley (1977) were talking about the '... style of research whose hegemony is maintained by the pages of the "*Administrative Science Quarterly*" (p. 2) and proposing 'to overcome existing organization theory' (p. 3). Not only were the managerialist and scientific footings of organization theory being challenged but indeed its identity as a separate discipline. As Hinings (1988: 2) put it, organizational theorizing was 'reclaimed for sociology'; a convention of labelling the field that still prevails in Europe (Hassard & Parker, 1994; Thoenig, 1998). The criticisms that were raised and the new agendas that were proposed were, and to a large degree continued to be, confined largely to the geographical space delineated above, often being targeted at the work of the Aston group and Donaldson's (1985) 'defence' of the contingency perspective. Despite attempts to expose North America to these ideas (Morgan, 1980; Clegg, 1981), the USA, in particular, remained largely unaffected (Aldrich, 1988; Üsdiken & Pasadeos, 1995) and had only a few alternative offerings of its own (e.g., Weick, 1969; Benson, 1977). The rather quiet separation between organization behaviour and organization theory occurring in the USA at roughly the same time and the resultant confinement of the field to claims to sociological and administrative roots was also serving as a seedbed for diversity, but of a different kind.

AMERICAN ADVANCES IN THE SOCIOLOGICAL APPROACH TO ORGANIZATIONAL ANALYSIS

The latter part of the 1970s marked the emergence in the USA too of new ways of thinking about organizations. Landmark contributions for what were later to become four influential research programmes (resource dependence, institutional theory, population ecology, and transaction cost theory) appeared in this period, leading a prominent author associated with one of these perspectives to proclaim, towards the end of 1980s, contingency theory dead (Carroll, 1988). This judgement has indeed received empirical support (Üsdiken & Pasadeos, 1999). More importantly, these developments have opened up a whole new range of tensions in the relatively tranquil setting in North America, the extent of which, after two decades, has come to be regarded as a threat to the identity of the discipline (Pffefer, 1993, 1997).

With the advent of these newer perspectives, problems, concepts, themes, units of analysis, and methods previously not within the purview of organization theory began to emerge. Even by the early 1980s these novel views were considered as divergent enough to generate discussions on 'central debates' (e.g., Astley & Van de Ven, 1983; Hrebiniak & Joyce, 1985) that, incidentally, incorporated only a limited selection of the issues fervently raised in the critical literature reviewed in the previous section. The debates that were engendered by the emergence of the newer perspectives emanated from different positions with regard to

the extent of free choice versus determinism in organizational action and the appropriate level of analysis for studying organizations (Astley & Van de Ven, 1983).

The Resource Dependence and External Control Views

The resource dependence perspective (Pfeffer & Salancik, 1978), preliminary versions of which had begun to emerge in the early 1970s built on the external environmental focus in contingency theory, but also drew upon earlier coalitional views (Cyert & March, 1963) and work on intraorganizational power (Hickson et al., 1971). Whilst structural-contingency theory emphasized the consequences of information-processing demands faced by organizations, the resource dependence perspective focused on problems of resource acquisition and the interdependencies that they generated. Organizations confronted not only the problem of adapting to environmental changes but also that of dealing with external demands. Need for resources controlled by external parties generated problems of dependence, outside influence, and threats to autonomy. Organizational action was motivated by finding ways of avoiding, reducing, or altering asymmetric dependencies and developing countervailing power, through, for example, interorganizational linkages. Another way of dealing with external dependence was through compliance and internal arrangements to better handle environmental contingencies. So what happened and what was or was not done in organizations had to do with external resource exchanges. Power was not only a currency, however, in environmental interactions but also within organizations. Indeed one mechanism through which the external environment impacted organizations was through its effects on the internal distribution of power.

The resource dependence perspective brought fresh ideas and a reworking of some themes that had been around for some time, which in their totality were both a contribution to the separation from organizational behaviour and, at the same time, served as an important challenge to views that had culminated around the structural-contingency approach. It was distinct from organizational behaviour approaches in that it stressed the structural or the context both in terms of external influences and internal phenomena. According to Pfeffer and Salancik (1978), behavioural change, for example, was more likely to be obtained not by individually orientated approaches typically advocated by the organizational behaviour literature but by the redesign of the context. The challenges that it offered to established ways of thinking within the structural-contingency tradition were also significant in various ways, though only tangentially related to the more critical stance emerging at the time to a large degree in Europe.

Perhaps of foremost significance in Pfeffer and Salancik's (1978) formulation was their extension of the boundaries of organization theory beyond conceptions that were limited to internal problems of structural design. This extension was not entirely new in that it had an affinity with some of the theoretical and empirical work of the 1960s and 1970s that focused on interorganizational relations with a specific interest in social service delivery systems in the USA (e.g., Van de Ven, 1976; Schmidt & Kochan, 1977). Pfeffer and Salancik's (1978) resource dependence perspective not only extended these issues to the world of business organizations but also involved conceptualizing the design of external linkages as a central problem and thus a significant matter for organizational analysis. Issues like cooptation, interlocking directorships, interfirm associations, vertical integration, diversification, joint ventures, and mergers were, thus, central concerns, leading critics like Donaldson (1995: 133) to claim still that the resource dependence perspective is 'strategy theory' rather than organization theory. Nevertheless, these issues did become important items in the agenda of organization theory, indeed increasingly so over the last decade with greater interest in network forms of organization (Üsdiken & Pasadeos, 1999).

A second important contribution of the resource dependence perspective, again not completely novel in that it drew upon earlier ideas of organizations as coalitions (Cyert & March, 1963), was the framing of a political view. Such a framing served as another challenge to technicist-rationalist and unitary conceptions of organization. Interests and power were at play not only in external linkages but within organizations as well. Although there have been claims that the resource dependence perspective is an offshoot of the antibusiness sentiments of the 1960s (Donaldson, 1995), power and politics are essentially treated as inevitable, indeed as 'functional' phenomena, that could serve as mechanisms for facilitating organizational adaptation to environmental conditions. Such a conception did also generate however concerns about how organizations, especially those that are large and powerful, were to be controlled.

With its focus on external constraints and control, the resource dependence perspective also problematized organizational autonomy and discretion, and the role of managements in affecting organizational outcomes. Its primary challenge was to heroic conceptions of management, claiming instead that organizational and managerial discretion was variable. In that sense, the resource dependence perspective was offering a bridge between the determinism of the structural-contingency view of the time and a critical position coming originally from Europe, the notion that there is 'strategic

choice' (Child, 1972). The structural-contingency theory had a smaller part for managers compared to the earlier views of practitioner-theorists and essentially described a reactive role (Astley & Van de Ven, 1983). Good management was about good diagnostics of the situation and the capability to install and implement structural arrangements that would be appropriate. The strategic choice view, on the other hand, allowed more room for managements as preferences or political considerations were likely to enter into design decisions (Child, 1972). The resource dependence perspective considered a broader spectrum, ranging from very little managerial effects to the discretionary role envisaged by the strategic choice view. Overall, however, according to Pfeffer and Salancik (1978), the possibilities for a discretionary role was limited to managers in relatively few organizations and that, in any case, performance and survival depended largely on the actions of others.

To recapitulate, the resource dependence perspective indeed mounted important challenges to the practitioner-theorist and the scienticized versions of organization theory and served to open up new avenues, but in essence did not diverge from the tenets of the latter version. Pffefer and Salancik (1978) were interested in developing explanatory models of organizational structures and actions, but they were equally concerned with their models serving as prescriptions for managers. Likewise, although there was reference to, for example, enactment processes within organizations, little was attributed to individual differences; the premise being that organizations were confronting an 'objective reality' that needed to be interpreted correctly. The managerialist and scientist orientations of organization theory remained intact.

The New Institutionalism in Organizational Analysis

Although the resource dependence perspective also considered social norms and governmental regulation as environmental factors that needed managing, it was neoinstitutionalist views that brought into organizational analysis the notions of institutional environments and institutionalization with important implications for the causes and consequences of organization structures and actions. Beginning with Meyer and Rowan's (1977) landmark article the infiltration of institutionalist ideas into organizational analysis, perhaps most significantly, involved a departure from both efficiency-based accounts of contingency theory and power-based explanations of the resource dependence perspective. Put broadly, the institutionalist perspective was built on an ideational view of organizations as opposed to the more materialist conceptions inherent in contingency and resource dependence theories. Organizations were thus viewed not as instruments for achieving ends or for wielding power but as 'institutions'. The notion of institution refers to 'structures and activities that provide stability and meaning to social behaviour' (Scott, 1995: 33) and as Zucker (1977: 728) has pointed out, in a widely quoted statement, 'institutionalization is both a process and a property variable'. Organizations, according to institutional theory, are located in institutional environments defined as the social and cultural context and themselves produce, embody and can become institutions.

The institutional environment is set conceptually apart from the notion of the technical environment that carries informational and material resources but, very much like the latter, is a source of powerful influence upon organizations. As such the institutionalist view becomes at one with contingency and resource dependence perspectives in ascribing primacy to the external context and portraying a passive image of organizations, though the accent on what matters is different. Formal rules, social norms, and cultural values surrounding organizations serve as influences that generate homogenization, more specifically, within what institutional theorists call 'organizational fields' (DiMaggio & Powell, 1983) or 'societal sectors' (Scott & Meyer, 1992). The notion of organizational field is central to institutional theory and refers not only to organizations that produce similar products or services but also others that they regularly interact with and that can have impact upon their performance (DiMaggio & Powell, 1983; Scott, 1995). Three sets of mechanisms can be in operation within organizational fields that produce homogenization or, in the language of institutional theory, isomorphism, namely, coercive, normative, and mimetic processes (DiMaggio & Powell, 1983). Coercive isomorphism refers to formal or informal pressures that organizations tend to comply with to avoid legal or social sanctions. The state, in particular, and other regulatory bodies are prime sources of coercive pressures. Organizations respond by conforming to such rules but may also be giving appearances of conformity. Normative pressures derive from norms, values, and beliefs that may have professional or broader societal bases. They may involve either external influence or internalization as ways of producing conformity. Finally, mimetism refers to imitation among organizations within a field, importing practices from others, especially in conditions of uncertainty.

These three ways of conceptualizing institutional effects on organizations constitute, according to Scott (1995), the three pillars of institutional thinking, which he labels as regulative, normative, and cognitive. The three pillars are a source of differentiation within institutional theory but they all refer to processes that can take place without recourse to efficiency considerations. Actually, the regulative

can be conceived as involving calculation and thus constituting a theme where institutionalist thinking comes closest to the resource dependence perspective (Scott, 1995; Tolbert & Zucker, 1996). Otherwise, organizational action is not driven by calculation but by concerns for gaining legitimacy and obtaining the support of external parties (Meyer & Rowan, 1977). Indeed, organizations tend to decouple their administrative structure from operational work, the former creating some kind of a facade with features that appear appropriate in view of social and cultural expectations (Meyer & Rowan, 1977). Likewise, structures and practices within organizations could also be decoupled from functional considerations, as they become normatively valued or taken for granted, thus gaining a symbolic and unquestioned character. These arguments have been tempered, however, by distinguishing between organizations that operate under stronger institutional environments as opposed to those where technical and market pressures are more pronounced. This distinction has been accompanied by the claim that institutionalist accounts are likely to be more relevant in contexts where evaluations of organizational effectiveness are more difficult (e.g., Meyer, Scott & Deal, 1992).

Despite such concessions, in substantive terms, institutional theory developed as a challenge to both functionalist and interest-based explanations of organizational phenomena. It also involved some degree of, or perhaps held potential for, deviation from the two central footings of organization theory. The passive view of organizations and the accompanying implicit image of managers as constrained in their reactions were not radically different from the picture offered by the resource dependence or the contingency perspective. However, the institutionalist approach, notably in its earlier stages of development, had a different tenor in that its central concerns were not framed in managerialist terms. Institutionalist work displayed little in the way of offering models that would also serve to help managers in solving problems, except perhaps indirectly by heightening awareness of institutional effects. However, more recent turns towards challenging the passivity of organizations in institutionalist thinking and attempting to accommodate strategic actions against institutional pressures (Oliver, 1991) or exploring diversity and its links to performance (Kondra & Hinings, 1998) may be setting the basis for developing the managerialist potential of the approach (e.g., McKinley, Sanchez & Schick, 1995). Moreover, although not in deed, but rather in promise, neoinstitutionalism in organizational analysis also holds potential for sway towards subjectivism. Indeed, realist and constructivist ontologies have been noted as constituting one of the major fault lines in present-day institutionalist theorizing (Scott, 1995), although more of the research to date has pursued the former line of reasoning and assumptions (Donaldson, 1995). Greater interest more recently in studying the role of human agency in responses to institutional pressures and the construction of institutions (Scott, 1995) is accompanied by calls for employing a broader variety of methodologies without relinquishing the use of more conventional methods (Tolbert & Zucker, 1996). In terms of research practice, institutionalist theory and empirical inquiry continues to remain broadly within the traditional model of science.

Organizational Ecology

An important distinctive feature of the neoinstitutionalist perspective compared to resource dependence and contingency theories has been to extend analysis beyond organizations to a higher level by introducing the notion of organizational field. Population ecology, the third influential research programme emanating in North America in the latter part of the 1970s, has done the same but by focusing on another unit of analysis, namely, populations of organizations. Like contingency, resource dependence and institutionalist views, the population ecology (or as it is often labelled more lately, the organizational ecology) perspective also attributes primacy to environmental factors. In doing so, however, it differs in two key and interrelated respects. First, the population ecology perspective begins with the question, 'Why are there so many kinds of organizations?' (Hannan & Freeman, 1977: 936) and proceeds to suggest that diversity portrays itself as the existence of different organizational forms or as the biological analogy would have it, different species. Organizations of the same form at points in time and circumscribed by social or political boundaries (nations, for example) constitute populations. Organizations possessing the same form and thus operating in similar environmental conditions are subject to common forces shaping their shared destiny. Thus there is the need to focus on the population rather than the organization level of analysis. Secondly, change, according to population ecology, occurs not as a result of attempts on the part of individual organizations to adapt but rather through processes of environmental selection operating upon populations.

The central notions and themes of the population ecology perspective derive from these fundamental tenets. Populations are considered as made up of organizations of the same form, in other words, organizations that have similar activities and recourse to similar resources, thus sharing the same portion of the environment or niche. In relatively more specific terms, organizational form refers to the core features of organizations that include mission, forms of authority, basic technology, and marketing strategy (Hannan & Freeman, 1989).

Very much like animal and plant life, survival of a particular organizational form or population depends on the availability of resources in the environment. Moreover, populations do not exist in isolation and can have overlapping niches leading to interpopulation competition. So both resource availability and variability and competition can serve as a source of organizational change. Those forms or populations that are fit survive and prosper, while those that are not disappear.

What happens within populations also matters, however, the key elements being density (the number of organizations in a population) and the carrying capacity (the level of resources in the environmental niche), both at particular moments in time. These states are postulated to affect vital rates in populations, namely, the rates of organizational births and deaths, a major preoccupation of empirical work in the population ecology tradition. Research on a variety of business and nonbusiness populations has provided evidence in support of the density-dependence argument in explaining the evolution of populations over time. Density has been argued to affect the processes of legitimation, referring to the acceptance of a particular form without much questioning, and competition for resources, which in turn determine founding and mortality rates. The relationship of population density to both rates is curvilinear but takes different forms. Increasing density leads to higher founding rates due to greater legitimacy that follows but then begins to fall with greater competition induced by higher levels of density and reduced legitimation effects of higher numbers of the same form. Mortality rates follow a U-shaped curve in that they are high in the early stages of population growth due to resource acquisition problems arising from a lack of legitimacy and tend to fall as the form gains increasing legitimation to rise again as intensified competition overrides decreasing legitimacy effects.

Incorporating organizational level variables into the analysis of organizational failures has extended the confinement of the density dependence argument to population level phenomena. Distinction is introduced between organizations with specialist (targeting a narrow range of clientele) and generalist (middle of the road) strategies. Likewise, organizational environments are distinguished in terms of the levels of uncertainty and whether they are fine grained (with smaller scale but frequent variations) or coarse grained (with larger but less frequent variability) (Hannan & Freeman, 1977). These distinctions have brought population ecology nearer to and into a confrontation with the structural contingency theory. Organizational age and size are also considered, leading to claims about the liability (higher degree of vulnerability) due to newness and smallness. Empirical evidence on age and size dependence is sketchy and has led to alternative formulations like liability of adolescence (Bruderl &

Schussler, 1990) and obsolescence (Barron, West & Hannan, 1994). They are, however, key ideas for the population ecology perspective, as they are related to the central assumptions of reliability and accountability as guarantors of organizational existence and survival. Reliability refers to consistency in performance and accountability to the capacity of organizations to produce rational justifications for their actions. Age and size are reliability and accountability enhancing and therefore contribute positively to survival chances.

Age and size also enhance structural inertia, the tendency to stay away from or the incapacity to change. The structural inertia theme leads to another set of central claims of the population ecology perspective, that organizations cannot easily engage in adaptive change, and that change, especially in core features, may be survival threatening. Thus, changes at the organizational level have less impact on the organizational panorama than do population level changes through births and deaths (Hannan & Freeman, 1984). Organizations have inertial tendencies because reliability and accountability require stability, repetitiveness and standardization. The structural inertia argument also draws upon other organizational theories, activating power and institutionalization themes. That is also why older and larger organizations are likely to be more inert. There are also differences, the argument goes, between core and peripheral characteristics, the former being essentially resistant to change. Indeed, it is when core features are altered that change may become hazardous, as accrued advantages are being given up and the vulnerability arising from newness sets in again. Thus, although the intentions may be there on the part of managers, change becomes difficult both because of internal and external constraints and because those organizations that do attempt core change may disappear on the way. Therefore significant change at the more aggregate levels comes about from replacement of forms and the emergence of new ones rather than the transformation of individual organizations. These ideas have been most controversial not only because they favour a selection as opposed to the much more common adaptive view of organizational change, but also because they allow little room for purposeful managerial action for creating change of any significance that could improve survival chances of organizations. The empirical evidence behind the structural inertia argument is much less robust than that on the density dependence theme and there are now calls for reconciling selection and adaptation views (Baum, 1996).

In the terms of the two footings of post-1960 organization theory, science and managerialism, the population ecology perspective proved to be the zenith of the scientist orientation both in its strive for generality and methodological sophistication. Although there have been criticisms of ambiguities in some of the central concepts like organizational form (e.g., Donaldson, 1995), the perspective has moved along a normal science route with repetitive tests of the same theoretical arguments and dealing with new puzzles that arose during the process (Pfeffer, 1993). The thrust, however, has been theoretical. Not only has the perspective been labelled 'antimanagement' because of its incapacitated image of managers (Donaldson, 1995), but there has also been little explicit concern during its evolution with the help it can provide to management, other than perhaps sensitizing them to constraints and extraneous influences on their actions. Only more recently can one observe a managerialist turn in attempts to make the perspective more accessible to nontechnical readers (e.g., Carroll & Hannan, 1995) and possibly a concomitant orientation towards further consideration of adaptive possibilities within a selection framework.

The latter part of the 1970s did not only bring the sociologically orientated advances and the accompanying strains that have been reviewed. It also brought at roughly the same time the beginnings of the challenge from an economistic view of organizations. Indeed, as it picked up, the economistic perspective was not only proving to be a challenge to the dominant sociological approach, but began to be perceived as a threat to the identity of the discipline (Pfeffer, 1993, 1997). The discipline was being claimed, this time, for economics.

ECONOMICS TURNS TO STUDYING ORGANIZATIONS

The economistic view of organizations, or 'organizational economics' (the oft-used label nowadays), claims an intellectual heritage that goes back to Coase's (1937) famous question, 'Why do firms exist?', which problematized why not all economic transactions take place within markets and that some are managed within firms. In contrast to conventional neoclassical economics that essentially neglected firms and what happened within them, the neoinstitutional economics which was to develop in the footsteps of Coase involved a turn towards the assumption that the way firms were designed mattered for economic analysis and prediction. This turn was soon to make a powerful impact on both organization theory and strategic management. Of the variety of economics-based perspectives that have been considered under the rubric of 'organizational economics' (Barney & Hesterly, 1996), the infiltration of neo-institutionalist economics into organization theory has occurred essentially through two theoretical streams, namely, transaction cost economics and agency theory.

The Transaction Cost Framework

Transaction cost theory, as formalized by Williamson (1975), was built on Coase's (1937) insightful question but also drew upon behavioural theories of the firm (Simon, 1947; Cyert & March, 1963). The central problem for transaction cost theory is how economic exchanges are governed. The unit of analysis therefore is the transaction, the nature of which and thus the costs that it generates shape the governance mechanism through which it is managed. Markets and hierarchies (or firms) are the two fundamental alternative mechanisms of governance, where the former refers to exchanges taking place among independent actors in the market and the latter to the internalization of the exchange within firm boundaries. Choice of governance mechanism depends on which of the two forms minimize transaction costs incurred to initiate, conclude, and monitor the exchange. Transaction costs exist in the first place because of two essential characteristics of human beings, their bounded rationality and opportunism. With these two assumptions transaction cost theorizing departs from standard neoclassical economic analysis. Humans are not treated as perfectly rational, but only limitedly so because of their information-processing capabilities. The notion of opportunism, on the other hand, goes beyond interest maximization to include malfeasance, not a characteristic attributed to all humans but to some, some of the time, sufficient threat, however, to take safeguarding measures in carrying out exchanges. In combination with these features two sets of conditions, the uncertainty surrounding the exchange (both environmental and behavioural) and the degree of exchange specific investments determine the level of transactions costs. Based on these fundamental ideas, the transaction cost perspective has been employed to address organizational issues like boundary problems and hybrid forms of exchange (e.g., strategic alliances, joint ventures, vertical integration) and internal design (e.g., the multidivisional firm).

Agency Theory

The companion agency theory has been concerned primarily with problems of monitoring within organizations and their relationships with external stakeholders. The central problem of agency theory emanates from the relationship or 'contract' between a 'principal' who delegates an activity to an 'agent' (Jensen & Meckling, 1976). Agency theory essentially shares with the transaction cost perspective the same assumptions about human beings and adds risk aversion as another central human feature. Given these assumptions the potential problems in an agency relationship are twofold. One of these refers to the possibility of divergence between the goals or interests of the principal and the agent and the second to differences in risk preferences (Eisenhardt, 1989). The problem is compounded by information asymmetry in that the principal may have limited information on how the agent is performing and obtaining information to that effect involves costs. To ensure that the interests of principals are served solutions need to be devised to deal with these agency problems. The key concern then is finding the most efficient form of governing the principal – agent relationship. Essentially, the mechanisms available to principals are monitoring and bonding arrangements (Barney & Hesterly, 1996). Monitoring refers to the surveillance of agents and can take the form of behavioural or output control. Bonding, on the other hand, involves incentive arrangements rewarding work in line with the interests of the principal.

As the unit of analysis is the relationship or the contract, agency theory is considered as applicable to a wide range of intra- and interorganizational phenomena that approximates the situation where one party acts on behalf of another. Indeed, agency theory leads to a conceptualization of organizations not as entities but as a 'nexus ... of contracting relationships' (Jensen & Meckling, 1976: 310). Although initial work in the agency theory stream began by a focus on the relationships between stockholders and managers (Jensen & Meckling, 1976), over time it has extended to a wider range of phenomena like managerial compensation, board structures, diversification, acquisitions, and vertical integration (Eisenhardt, 1989).

Reactions to the Economistic Intrusion

The penetration of economistic approaches to organizational analysis has met with mixed reactions. Their presentation to and promotion within the field has been accompanied by the emphasis on their revolutionary potential in providing a new and rich theoretical foundation that has been lacking (e.g., Jensen & Meckling, 1976). Positive reactions have noted the new ways of thinking and understanding that have been brought in (e.g., Hesterly, Liebeskind & Zenger, 1990; Eisenhardt, 1989; Carroll, Spiller & Teece, 1999) and the potential for cross-fertilization (Barney & Hesterly, 1996) and complementarity with sociologically orientated perspectives in organization theory (Eisenhardt, 1989; Carroll et al., 1999). Others, however, have found the encroachment of economics troublesome, indeed as flawed (Donaldson, 1995; Ghoshal & Moran, 1996) and even dangerous for the field (Perrow, 1986; Pffefer, 1997). Supporting these concerns, Üsdiken and Pasadeos (1999) have found that in the post-1980 period, empirical work published in two leading US-based journals

(*Administrative Science Quarterly* (*ASQ*) and *Academy of Management Journal* (*AMJ*)) was increasingly informed by theories based on economistic thinking. Indeed, the infusion of economics and the increasing popularity that it appears to enjoy, leading to the kind of predictions that '… the end result will be a coalescing of economics and organization theory' (Hesterly et al., 1990: 416) constitutes now another major strain that revolves around the character and identity that the field has gained, notably in the USA, as it developed, after the settlement in the 1970s, on its sociological and practical roots.

The arguments for distancing from economics rest on a number of premises. For one, there is disenchantment with the degree to which treating organizations as markets (indeed as 'simply legal fictions' – Jensen & Meckling, 1976: 310), and action as rationally driven and guided by the criterion of economic efficiency offers an adequate basis for understanding and explaining organizational phenomena. Secondly, there have been concerns, albeit in opposing ways, about the managerialism of organizational economics. On the one hand, attention has been drawn to the inherently conservative and one-sided nature of economistic thinking brought into organizational analysis (Perrow, 1986) as well as its conformity with neoliberal ideologies currently in vogue in the international scene (Buğra & Üsdiken, 1997). Alternatively, there have been strong doubts about the usefulness of transaction cost and agency theories as guides to practice (Ghoshal & Moran, 1996; Nilakant & Rao, 1994). Finally, fears have been expressed because of the 'imperialistic' (Hirshleifer, 1986) tendencies of economics and the threat of invasion as it were, especially given the present fragmented state of organization theory (Pfeffer, 1993, 1997).

In a sense the entry of economics can be considered as a further step in the scientization project of organization theory, formal modelling supplementing or replacing 'informal theories' in investigating at least some aspects of organizational life (Gibbons, 1999). In a different sense, the strain that has emerged is similar to the tension of some 30 years ago between organizational behaviour and organization theory, drawing, as they did, on psychologically as opposed to sociologically informed views. It is similar as it has to do with disciplinary bases, but also because it has to do with the problem of unit of analysis or the value of studying organizations in their totality (Freeman, 1999). Important as it is, economics has not been the only challenger to more conventional predominantly US-based visions of organization theory as it has developed over the last two decades. Divergence that was even more fundamental was also developing not primarily on home ground but further afield, proliferating by building and adding on or opposing the 'unorthodox' or 'critical' views of the 1970s.

ADVANCES IN NONPOSITIVIST AND NONMANAGERIALIST DIRECTIONS

As were the newer sociological and economics-orientated approaches influential in shaping the course of organization theory in and dissipating from the USA, so was Burrell and Morgan's (1979) introduction of the notion of paradigm and their cataloguing of different ways of studying organizations, but much more so outside the USA. Burrell and Morgan (1979) not only provided a framework for locating work that was already emerging and stood in some kind of opposition to what was being shaped at the time as organization theory, but also offered a background for debating paradigms and the possibility of interparadigm dialogue. Together with changes in this period in the international sociopolitical and economic scene and emerging intellectual currents, this was to make theorizing on organizations take, from early 1980s onwards, a very different turn, albeit limited largely to the UK, parts of Europe, and other English-speaking regions.

The Interpretive and Radical Positions

As observed by Willmott (1990) post-Burrell and Morgan (1979) impetus moved initially in two main directions, namely, the 'interpretive' and the 'radical'. Of these the former strand diverged, extending Silverman's (1970) action frame of reference, in opposing positivist methodology and took the direction of being driven by ethnomethodology and phenomenology. These currents are characterized first by a denial of the existence of organizations as a concrete object, problematizing therefore notions like structure which are typically dealt within organization theory (Burrell & Morgan, 1979; Hassard, 1990). The concern is not with generating generalized theory but ideographic accounts that are geared towards depicting everyday life from the perspective of those who are involved rather than that of an outside observer. The subjectivism of the interpretive approach leads to the focus on the sensuality of and meanings attached to actions and their interpretation by actors. So organizations are conceived not as, or having structures, but rather as processes continuously made or remade by the practices and social constructions of individuals. What their study can offer, through fieldwork, is not theories or explanations but descriptions of ordinary interpretations. Accumulating knowledge would be possible by insights that can be gained through comparisons (Deetz, 1996). Moving beyond earlier 'landmark' studies (Hassard, 1990: 101), interpretive work was fuelled with the expanding attention in the 1980s to organizational culture both in more popular managerialist writings and in academic circles (Deetz, 1996). The culturist movement as developed by both these groups involved a shift away from the focus and/or the expectation of effective solutions from the technical and rational towards the symbolic in organizational life. Treatments of culture differed (Smirchich, 1983) and for the interpretively inclined, culture served as a root metaphor; studying culture involved investigating meanings and interpretations that dominated or diverged across the organization (Turner, 1990). Although work in the interpretive tradition has been, for example, in opposition to instrumentalist or harmony-based views of culture found in popular management texts, there has not necessarily been an explicit antimanagerialist position or denial of managerial relevance. What the interpretive approaches essentially took issue with were the realist ontological assumptions and quantitative methodologies prevalent in studies that adhered to the natural science model.

The 'radical' in organization studies that was making itself apparent in the 1970s, involved two strands, what Burrell and Morgan (1979) labelled as the 'structuralist' and 'humanist' versions, though it was the former that was more pronounced in the 1970s and 1980s, as was the distinction. The structuralist critique was essentially based on Marxian thinking, though approaches characterized as radical Weberianism have also constituted a variant (Burrell & Morgan, 1979). Both lines of thinking have been concerned with unravelling managerial strategies of control over productive activity, located as they are within broader structures of power within societies. The radical Weberian variant has focussed on the bureaucratic form of organization as an instrument of domination, the issue of power being a central concern (e.g., Perrow, 1986). The Marxian tradition can be distinguished by a more specific concern with the labour process within capitalist societies and an explicit political agenda. A central premise has been that within the labour process there is a fundamental conflict of interest between management (and owners) and workers. The focus of theorizing and empirical work has therefore been on management control and forms of worker resistance. Earlier formulations have envisaged increasingly tighter control over employees, while later work has been more sensitive to the portfolio of control strategies available to managements and the variations at the organizational level distinguishing, for example, between direct control and commitment generating mechanisms granting more autonomy to workers (Reed, 1992). The labour process theory has also been more lately criticized for being overly rational and formalistic and therefore not being able to accommodate contradictions and choice (Reed, 1990). In any case, radical structuralism, especially its Marxian variant, engaged primarily with what had come to be regarded as the inherent managerialism of organization theory. The latter tended to frame problems and define issues within managerialist terms, whereas the structuralist critique and the knowledge produced thereof was arguably geared towards those that were disadvantaged in organizational relations.

The Marxian approach began to lose its impetus in the 1990s, due both, it would seem, to economic developments in advanced capitalist societies like the retreat of the working class and to the transformation of political and economic orders in Eastern Europe. The humanist version, on the other hand, considered nascent at the time by Burrell and Morgan (1979) has now become the critical voice, the more dominant of the radical positions (Deetz, 1996). For Burrell and Morgan (1979), radical humanism was the most antithetical approach to the functionalism of organization theory, as it stood opposed to both concerns with regulation and objectivism in social science. It was essentially 'anti-organization' theory (Burrell & Morgan, 1979: 310). The work representing this line of thinking, now considered under the umbrella term critical, does have affinity to radical structuralism in that its primary engagement is with domination in organizations and society at large. It is, however, distinct in a number of important ways (Alvesson and Deetz, 1996). First, the emphasis is on social constructions, on how they become naturalized and serve to prevent other constructions from being considered. Secondly, addressing the issue of domination and control and critiques of ideology do not only relate to class differences but involve all groups of employees within organizations. Third, as Alvesson and Deetz (1996: 198) put it '… critical theory, compared to Marxism, is not anti-management per se' (emphasis omitted) and can produce managerially useful knowledge. It can do so because, although management is considered as an institutionalized form of domination, a critical view can be sensitizing to the 'dark' side of organizational and managerial action. More is on offer, of course, for those who have been 'objectified' and who consent by being subjected to constructions favouring certain interests and to distorted communications. In that sense, critical approaches also have a political agenda, indeed very strong in moral and ethical terms, but represent a reformist stance (Deetz, 1996).

The Postmodern Turn

Towards the end of 1980s, the organization literature began to see early examples of the encounter with postmodernism (e.g., Cooper & Burrell, 1988), as yet another way of approaching managerial and organizational phenomena. The primary engagement of the postmodern is with modernity, its ways of organizing and ways of knowing. Modernity as an epoch involved the transition from traditional and preindustrial society to industrial capitalism, generating new institutions and transforming the nature of social relations. With its roots in the Enlightenment, modernism privileged reason and science as the only legitimate and valid means of knowledge production. For the postmodernist, not only has the modernist project, despite significant material advances in developed industrial societies, failed but it has been the source of many ills as it ran its course (Marsden & Townley, 1996). The notion of 'post-modern' (with a hyphen; Parker, 1992) has been employed to denote a new epoch, a fundamentally different set of conditions characterized by, for example, globalization, faster change in (particularly information) technology, and increasing differentiation of markets (Hatch, 1997). Postmodernism, however, owes its influence as an approach or philosophy, rather than as a characterization of a new epoch succeeding modernity. As a view (or rather a set of views), it sets itself apart by being against any kind of grand theory (including for example, Marxism), indeed any kind of general theory. Knowing is local and specific, as is knowledge about organizations (Marsden & Townley, 1996). Knowledge and expertise are treated not as neutral, the argument being that claims to expertise serve as tools of domination. Like critical perspectives there is an overall engagement with domination and power differentials and the fundamental premise is again that social reality is a construction. Postmodernism goes beyond critical approaches by turning attention to the role of discourse and language in the social construction process (Deetz, 1996). The postmodern also denies any essential features to humans, claiming that it is the discursive context that shapes identities. As humans are subject to a variety of discourses, especially in contexts where there are, as in present-day conditions, high levels of ambiguity, identities are more likely to be fragmented (Alvesson & Deetz, 1996). Individuals are thus denied the sovereignty and autonomy granted to them in modernist thinking (Willmott, 1994). A relativist position accompanies, in that according to postmodernists there can be no basis for claims to truth or universal criteria for comparing or judging the worth of different knowledge claims (Jackson & Carter, 1991). As the world, and for that matter the world of organizations is seen as text, then there is not much that social science can do and research can only usefully draw upon modes like discourse and rhetorical analysis and literary criticism. Postmodernism also differs from critical perspectives in that there is no political agenda, other than representing the voice of the marginal and the suppressed, and can in its writing become satiric and puzzling (e.g., Alvesson, 1995; Burrell, 1997).

The Search for a 'New' Theory of Organization

The views and themes reviewed in this section stand in different ways in stark contrast to those discussed in the previous two. The suggestion is not

that they present a uniform picture as they are also divided by many differences. Very much like the perspectives that have come to be regarded from the outside as more conventional, the 'contra' views (Marsden & Townley, 1996) have also experienced change as some have lost ground and newer positions have emerged. This becomes apparent, for example, in Deetz's (1996) revision of the Burrell and Morgan (1979) typology, where Marxian approaches become relegated to a subset of the critical position while space is opened as a new box for the postmodern. What all these, albeit different, views do share, however, is the orientation towards a 'new' approach to organization theory (Willmott, 1995; Hassard & Parker, 1994). Although there are different versions of what the 'new' can be, very broadly it entails a position that goes against both footings of more conventional US-led organization theorizing, an aspiration for a field of study that can be characterized as nonpositivist and nonmanagerialist (Watson, 1994). Again views vary but there is a largely shared scepticism about the traditional model of science, its claims to universality and value-free analysis as well as its preoccupations with causality, prediction, model testing, and quantitative methodologies. There is also the aspiration to redeem the study of organizational phenomena from narrower managerialist concerns by turning it into a scholarly or rather, an intellectual enterprise that engages with the human, the ethical, the aesthetic, and the spiritual in organizations (e.g., Zald, 1993; Strati, 1999; Tsoukas & Cummings, 1997). There are now claims to a rich and voluminous literature (Alvesson & Deetz, 1996) and to a momentum in these directions that cannot be ignored (Clegg & Hardy, 1996). However, as some proponents would also acknowledge (e.g., Burrell, 1996; Chia, 1995), recent penetration of these ideas and agendas into the core still appears to be not all that different (Üsdiken & Pasadeos, 1999) from what Aldrich (1988) observed over 10 years ago. There does appear to be a sizeably larger group of adherents (Astley, 1985), however, to justify the claim at the beginning of the chapter that these projects represent significant and fundamental divisions on the purpose and conduct of organization studies.

ORGANIZATION THEORY: ITS PRESENT AND POSSIBLE FUTURES

As the review and the discussion in this chapter must have shown, if there would be one point of agreement among organization scholars of different persuasions it would be around the observation that organization theory is currently in a state of fragmentation, although there would still be disagreement in the way extant pluralism is described let alone how it can be accounted for and what needs to be done about it. This chapter has argued that the divisions at one level are of a more fundamental nature going to the heart of the matter as it were, the identity of the field and what it can (and should) hope to achieve. There are then divergences among neighbouring views within similar orientations, some of which, however, go beyond friendly critiques.

Searching for Ways of Living or Dealing with Pluralism in Organization Theorizing

The reaction to growing pluralism in organization theory over the last two decades was based on two different interpretations and descriptions of what was taking place. On the one hand, there was the description prevalent in Europe, inspired very much by Burrell and Morgan's (1979) book, recognizing the 'alternatives' to what was labelled as functionalist scientistic orthodoxy and identifying the metatheoretical assumptions on how they differed from the latter and from one another. The emphasis on alternatives widened the range of views that were considered as party to fragmentation in the field. What it also did was to encourage questions related to the fundamentals of what was being examined, namely management and organizations, thus contributing to the extension of the boundaries of the field, drawing in and attempting to establish links with social theory and philosophy. The central debate it engendered revolved around the issue of paradigm commensurability. Burrell and Morgan (1979) had offered a strong urge for paradigm closure, the argument being that in order to make their voices heard and establish their legitimacy each programme needed to develop in its own terms. The paradigm closure argument was also based on the premise that the different paradigms relied on different metatheoretical assumptions which made dialogue impossible and precluded the possibility of overarching criteria for assessing relative merits (Astley, 1985; Jackson & Carter, 1991). This argument was later complemented by another version of the multiparadigmatic position suggesting that different paradigms offered a portfolio of partial views and could be used to provide different perspectives on the same organizational phenomena (e.g., Morgan, 1986; Hassard, 1991). Such an approach, however, elicited reactions to the ease it foresaw for researchers in transgressing paradigmatic boundaries. Others (e.g., Willmott, 1990) drew attention to what they saw as contradictions in Burrell and Morgan's (1979) demarcations and the presence of extant forms of social analysis which were geared explicitly to overcoming dualisms. Indeed, paradigm closure was criticized for allowing 'oppressive' organization theory and practice to continue (Willmott, 1990: 60). More lately, milder or middle-of-the road versions of the multiparadigmatic position have also emerged referring to orientations or discourses rather than paradigms (Deetz, 1996; Kaghan & Phillips, 1998). The argument is again that demarcations are likely to be fraught with contradictions and to ignore debates and contentions within similar ways of thinking. Moreover, although rejecting the facility of moving across orientations, there is the claim that organizational analysts often draw upon the resources that are provided by more than one 'discourse'. There have also been, even within the search for a 'new' theory of organization, arguments that there is now a need to move on to a postparadigmatic stage, a call, in fact, for rediscovering organizations after the preoccupation with theory and philosophy in the 1980s (Ackroyd, 1994).

Although there were early and more confined attempts towards classification of organizational perspectives (e.g., Astley & Van de Ven, 1983), it took more than a decade for the kind of debates reviewed above to reach the USA (e.g., Pfeffer, 1993; Canella & Paetzold, 1994; Van Maanen, 1995; Deetz, 1996; Eastman & Bailey, 1998). In parts of these debates and indeed more generally, the reaction in the USA to fragmentation revolved around the question of integration, the typical premise being that organization theory was showing the signs of being in a preparadigmatic stage. Unity was sought, based on the claim that fragmentation would be detrimental to the status of the discipline as well as disadvantaging the field in resource allocations and making it vulnerable to invasion by other more basic disciplines (Pfeffer, 1993). It would also limit the credibility and the capability of the discipline to offer advice to managerial audiences (McKinley & Mone, 1998). Moreover, again typically in the USA the issue of pluralism and debates around differences were confined to contingency, resource dependence, institutional, population ecology, and economistic perspectives (e.g., Carroll et al., 1999; McKinley & Mone, 1998). Debates around other perspectives which pervaded the European, primarily the UK scene, were either ignored or treated as marginal (McKinley et al., 1999). The most heated debates involved the strain between sociologically based post-1970s research programmes and the economistic intrusion (e.g., Barney, 1990; Donaldson, 1990; Gibbons, 1999; Freeman, 1999), especially in view of increasing penetration of latter approaches to organization studies (Üsdiken & Pasadeos, 1999). Otherwise the repeated desire and aspiration was and is towards paradigmatic unity either through a perspective superseding others or through more elitist (Pfeffer, 1993) or 'democratic' (McKinley & Mone, 1998) mechanisms of intervention. The more competitive spirit is evident in some of the ecological (e.g., Carroll, 1988) and organizational economics literature (Hesterly et al., 1990).

Attempts to synthesize different perspectives have also increasingly become popular as in the case of new labels like institutional ecology to bridge ecological and institutionalist thinking (e.g., Baum & Oliver, 1992). Other examples of searching for areas of compatibility are between institutionalist and transaction cost theories (e.g., Martinez & Dacin, 1999), institutionalism and resource dependence (e.g., Oliver, 1991), and transaction cost theory and all others (Carroll et al., 1999). Üsdiken and Pasadeos' (1999) have provided evidence supporting these tendencies, showing that empirical papers in *ASQ* and *AMJ* in the 1990s compared to the 1980s were more likely to be based on multiple theoretical perspectives. More recently however, a more European-like debate about the purpose and ways of doing organization studies has been gaining currency in the USA too, as seen in the calls for greater tolerance to diversity of views (Van Maanen, 1995) and to normative positions (Wicks & Freeman, 1998; Eastman & Bailey, 1998).

The Relevance Issue

Both of these sets of reactions have also had to contend with the issue of relevance, a concern lurking behind academic studies of organizations since the scientization shift around the 1950s and 1960s in the USA. The last two decades have seen concerns mount with greater market pressures (Van de Ven, 1999) and the expanding competition from alternative producers of knowledge like consultants and consultancies (Abrahamson, 1996). Given the footings of the discipline alluded to since the beginning of the chapter and its location, in particular in the USA, in business schools, has led to couching the issue of relevance in managerialist terms. On the other hand, the theoretical advances made in the interim and the legitimacy that organizational studies has gained over time as a science-based endeavour call for framing research concerns in a theory-driven rather than a problem-centred fashion. Üsdiken and Pasadeos' (1999) study does corroborate the tension in that the topics investigated in the 1990s show a greater proportion of present-day managerial concerns (like strategic alliances, joint ventures), while there are also indications that more lately there have been increases in studies justified primarily in theoretical terms.

The aspiration for building a 'new' theory of organization have not been immune to concerns with or pressures towards relevance either, perhaps with the exception of those with a postmodernist bent. Within the endeavours towards developing 'new' theory however, the notion of relevance gains a broader meaning. It may first have to do with going beyond the bounds of philosophizing and conceptual discussion to testing ideas empirically, a call lately made to critical theorists (Thompson & McHugh, 1995) and even those with a postmodernist

inclination (Alvesson & Deetz, 1996). Beyond that, especially for the critically minded theorist the audience is the managed, the oppressed in organizations. Those that are more inclined to portray an aspiration for the 'new' theory to penetrate into and perhaps replace present-day mainstream, do not eschew managerial relevance, criticizing purist critical theorists for ignoring managers (Clegg & Hardy, 1996). In fact, one criticism that such a programme would make of the more dominant orientations is that given their scientist aspirations, they have failed to be managerially relevant.

Relevance for managers of the 'new' theory could take one or more of a number of forms. It may be more inclined to inform managers who are more on the oppressed side, the emphasis here being more on managerial resistance and choice in view of totalizing tendencies of organizations (Alvesson & Deetz, 1996). It may also have a broader appeal to all kinds of managers the argument goes, by sensitizing them to experiences of others and to ethical and environmental issues.

Looking to the Future: Organization Theorizing in the Early 21st Century

Given this fragmented state, both in a more fundamental sense and lesser differences within broader metatheoretical orientations, what does then the future hold for organization theory? Two broad conjectures will be offered. One of these concerns what in this chapter have been considered as the two footings of organization theory. As broad tendencies, organization theory is likely to move in the direction of attempting to be managerially more relevant and concurrently there will be some further degree of retreat from the traditional model of science as the way of investigating organizations. This is not to suggest that theory-driven research and empirical work geared towards hypothesis testing will quickly erode. Indeed, Üsdiken and Pasadeos (1999) have shown that the trend identified by Daft (1980) towards greater methodological rigour and sophistication in the 1960s and 1970s in US-based organizational research has continued in the 1980s and 1990s. Theoretical framing supported by hypothesis-testing empirical research now has a strong institutional basis, especially in the USA and in some other countries where it has penetrated and is not likely to give way easily to alternative orientations. There are enough signs, however, that there will be increased institutional and competitive pressures towards being more relevant, coupled with and legitimized by intellectual currents that impute new demands due to changes in ways of organizing and the context in which they are taking place (Van de Ven, 1999). Supporting these conjectures, Üsdiken and Pasadeos (1999) found that in the

1990s work published even in the *Administrative Science Quarterly*, the major US-based scholarly journal and the bastion, according to some, of positivist organization theory was showing signs of increasingly justified in managerialist terms. Again even in US-based work there are not only calls for drawing upon a richer base like ethics, humanities, arts and music (Wicks & Freeman, 1998; Zald, 1993; Hassard & Holliday, 1998; Meyer, Frost & Weick, 1998), but also indications, as in the invitation in the call for the Academy of Management meeting in the year 2000 for submissions in the form of art and poetry, that alternative forms of presentation are likely to gain increasing legitimacy.

The second conjecture relates to the way present-day fragmentation may unfold given these broad tendencies. The central premise advanced here is that in line with the times and times that lie ahead in the foreseeable future there will be more integration and disintegration occurring at the same time. Integration can be expected along a number of realms and directions. Advances are likely to be made in bridging and building on the complementarities of now competing perspectives within broadly similar orientations and indeed to some degree perhaps across more fundamental divisions. Now important debates around, for example, adaptation versus selection, efficiency versus power, resources versus institutions, agency versus structure would be attracting more research attention and would be prone to new advances. Stronger alliances are likely to foster across regions, primarily between the USA and Europe, now considerably underpinning the fundamental divisions in the field. This is likely to occur as exporting of traditions from the latter to the former increases pace and offers possibilities for expanding partnerships. These alliances would be expected to build upon paradigmatic allegiances and lead over time to more balanced representations in now the more active research producing parts of the world, disseminating in time to other parts. This will serve, on the other hand, to maintain fundamental differences essentially around the way of doing organizational analysis. Indeed, one could also predict that the conduct of organizational analysis would be opening up new tensions as, for example, the formalism of economics increasingly penetrates the field. It is even foreseeable that, like the separation that occurred between organizational behaviour and organization theory some 30 or so years ago, a demarcation between organizational economics and organizational sociology or the subdivisions of the latter may become stronger. It may then, dare one say, become more difficult for 'organization theory' to claim a separate identity, apart from a part in management textbooks that continues to include the output of structural contingency theory. It is also foreseeable that a looser 'integration', or 'confederation' rather, under the rubric of 'organization studies' (some may still hope 'organization science') can emerge, accompanied by the recognition and the establishment of distinct traditions and disciplinary bases. What this may also bring is, akin to economics and to some degree to organization behaviour, a new division of labour among approaches with respect to their 'comparative advantage' to address certain sets of questions. Such a domain allocation does not appear to be in sight, but may well be the only way for a more tranquil coexistence among different viewpoints, at least among those that share metatheoretical assumptions.

REFERENCES

Abrahamson, E. (1996). Management fashion. *Academy of Management Review*, *21*(1), 254–285.

Ackroyd, S. (1994). Recreating common ground: elements for post-paradigmatic theories of organization. In J. Hassard, & M. Parker (Eds.), *Towards a new theory of organizations* (pp. 269–297). London: Routledge.

Aldrich, H. (1988). Paradigm warriors: Donaldson versus the critics of organization theory. *Organization Studies*, *9*(1), 19–25.

Alvesson, M. (1995). The meaning and meaninglessness of postmodernism: Some ironic remarks. *Organization Studies*, *16*(6), 1047–1075.

Alvesson, M., & Deetz, S. (1996). Critical theory and postmodernism approaches to organizational studies. In S.R. Clegg, C. Hardy, & W.R. Nord (Eds.), *Handbook of organization studies* (pp. 191–217). London: Sage.

Astley, W.G. (1985). Administrative science as socially constructed truth. *Administrative Science Quarterly*, *30*(4), 497–513.

Astley, W.G., & Van de Ven, A.H. (1983). Central perspectives and debates in organization theory. *Administrative Science Quarterly*, *28*(2), 245–273.

Barnard, C.I. (1938). *The functions of the executive*. Cambridge, MA: Harvard University Press.

Barney, J.B. (1990). The debate between traditional management theory and organizational economics: Substantive differences or intergroup conflict. *Academy of Management Review*, *15*(3), 382–393.

Barney, J.B., & Hesterly, W. (1996). Organizational economics: Understanding the relationship between organizations and economic analysis. In S.R. Clegg, C. Hardy, & W.R. Nord (Eds.), *Handbook of organization studies* (pp. 115–147). London: Sage.

Barron, D.N., West, E., & Hannan, M.T. (1994). A time to grow and a time to die: Growth and mortality of credit unions in New York City, 1914–1990. *American Journal of Sociology*, *100*(2), 381–421.

Baum, J.A.C. (1996). Organizational ecology. In S.R. Clegg, C. Hardy, & W.R. Nord (Eds.), *Handbook of organization studies* (pp. 77–114). London: Sage.

Baum, J.A.C., & Oliver, C. (1992). Institutional embeddedness and the dynamics of organizational populations. *American Sociological Review*, *57*(4), 540–559.

Benson, J.K. (1977). Organizations: A dialectical view. *Administrative Science Quarterly*, *22*(1), 1–21.

Blau, P.M. (1955). *The dynamics of bureaucracy*. Chicago: University of Chicago Press.

Blau, P.M. (1974). *On the nature of organizations*. New York: Wiley.

Braverman, H. (1974). *Labor and monopoly capital*. New York: Monthly Review Press.

Bruderl, J., & Schussler, R. (1990). Organizational mortality: The liabilities of newness and adolescence. *Administrative Science Quarterly*, *35*(3), 530–547.

Buğra, A., & Üsdiken, B. (1997). Introduction: State, market and organizational form. In A. Buğra, & B. Üsdiken (Eds.), *State, market and organizational form* (pp. 1–14) Berlin: Walter de Gruyter.

Burns, T., & Stalker, G.M. (1961). *The management of innovation*. London: Tavistock.

Burrell, G. (1996). Normal science, paradigms, metaphors, discourses and genealogies of analysis. In S.R. Clegg, C. Hardy, & W.R. Nord (Eds.), *Handbook of organization studies* (pp. 642–658). London: Sage.

Burrell, G. (1997). *Pandemonium*. London: Sage.

Burrell, G., & Morgan, G. (1979). *Sociological paradigms and organizational analysis*. London: Heinemann.

Canella, A.A., & Paetzold, R.L. (1994). Pffefer's barriers to the advance of organizational science: A rejoinder. *Academy of Management Review*, *19*(2), 331–341.

Carroll, G.R. (1988). Organizational ecology in theoretical perspective. In G.R. Carroll (Ed.), *Ecological models of organizations* (pp. 1–6). Cambridge, MA: Ballinger.

Carroll, G.R., & Hannan, M.T. (Eds.) (1995). *Organizations in industry*. New York: Oxford University Press.

Carroll, G.R., Spiller, P.T., & Teece, D.J. (1999). Transaction cost economics: Its influences on organizational theory, strategic management, and political economy. In G.R. Carroll, & D.J. Teece (Eds.), *Firms, markets and hierarchies* (pp. 60–88) New York: Oxford University Press.

Chia, R. (1995). From modern to postmodern organizational analysis. *Organization Studies*, *16*(4), 579–604.

Child, J. (1972). Organizational structure, environment and performance: The role of strategic choice. *Sociology*, *6*(1), 2–22.

Clegg, S.R. (1981). Organization and control. *Administrative Science Quarterly*, *26*(4), 545–562.

Clegg, S., & Dunkerley, D. (1977). Introduction: Critical issues in organizations. In S. Clegg, & D. Dunkerley (Eds.), *Critical issues in organizations* (pp. 1–6) London: Routledge and Kegan Paul.

Clegg, S., & Dunkerley, D. (1980). *Organization, class and control*. London: Routledge and Kegan Paul.

Clegg, S.R., & Hardy, C. (1996). Conclusion: Representations. In S.R. Clegg, C. Hardy, & W.R. Nord (Eds.), *Handbook of organization studies* (pp. 676–708) London: Sage.

Coase, R.H. (1937). The nature of the firm. *Economica*, *4*, 386–405.

Collin, S.-O., Johansson, U., Svensson, K., & Ulvenblad, P.-O. (1996). 'Market segmentation in scientific publications: Research patterns in American vs European management journals', *British Journal of Management*, *7*(2), 141–154.

Cooper, R., & Burrell, G. (1988). Modernism, postmodernism and organizational analysis. *Organization Studies*, *9*(1), 91–112.

Crozier, M. (1964). *The bureaucratic phenomenon*. Chicago: University of Chicago Press.

Cyert, R.M., & J.G. March (1963). *A behavioural theory of the firm*. Englewood Cliffs, NJ: Prentice-Hall.

Daft, R.L. (1980). The evolution of organizational analysis in A.S.Q., 1959–1979. *Administrative Science Quarterly*, *25*(4), 623–636.

Deetz, S. (1996). 'Describing differences in approaches to organization science: Rethinking Burrell, & Morgan and their legacy'. *Organization Science*, *7*(2), 191–207.

DiMaggio, P.J., & Powell, W.W. (1983). The iron cage revisited: Institutional isomorphism and collective rationality in organizational fields. *American Sociological Review*, *48*(2), 147–160.

Donaldson, L. (1985). *In defence of organization theory*. Cambridge: Cambridge University Press.

Donaldson, L. (1990). The ethereal hand: Organizational economics and management theory. *Academy of Management Review*, *15*(3), 369–381.

Donaldson, L. (1995). *American anti-management theories of organization*. Cambridge: Cambridge University Press.

Eastman, W., & Bailey, J.R. (1998). Mediating the fact-value antinomy: Patterns in managerial and legal rhetoric, 1890–1990. *Organization Science*, *9*(2), 232–245.

Eisenhardt, K. (1989). Agency theory: An assessment and review. *Academy of Management Review*, *14*(1), 57–74.

Elsbach, K.D., Sutton, R.I., & Whetten, D.A. (1999). Perspectives on developing management theory, circa 1999: Moving from shrill monologues to (relatively) tame dialogues. *Academy of Management Review*, *40*(4), 627–633.

Engwall, L. (1996). The Vikings vs the world: An examination of Nordic business research. *Scandinavian Journal of Management*, *12*(4), 425–436.

Fayol, H. (1949). *General and industrial management* (Trans. C. Storrs). London: Pitman (original version published in 1916).

Fiedler, F.E. (1967). *A theory of leadership effectiveness*. New York: McGraw-Hill.

Freeman, J. (1999). Efficiency and rationality in organizations. *Administrative Science Quarterly*, *44*(1), 163–175.

Ghoshal, S., & Moran, P. (1996). Bad for practice: A critique of transaction cost theory. *Academy of Management Review*, *21*(1), 13–47.

Gibbons, R. (1999). Taking Coase seriously. *Administrative Science Quarterly*, *44*(1), 145–157.

Gouldner, A.W. (1954). *Patterns of industrial bureaucracy.* New York: Free Press.

Guillén, M.F. (1994). *Models of management.* Chicago: University of Chicago Press.

Hall, R.H. (1962). Intraorganizational structural variation: application of the bureaucratic model. *Administrative Science Quarterly*, 7(3), 295–308.

Hannan, M.T., & Freeman, J. (1977). The population ecology of organizations. *American Journal of Sociology*, 82(5), 929–964.

Hannan, M.T., & Freeman, J. (1984). Structural inertia and organizational change. *American Sociological Review*, 49(2), 149–164.

Hannan, M.T., & Freeman, J. (1989). *Organizational ecology.* Cambridge, MA: Harvard University Press.

Hassard, J. (1990). Ethnomethodology and organizational research: An introduction. In J. Hassard, & D. Pym (Eds.), *The theory and philosophy of organizations* (pp. 97–108) London: Routledge.

Hassard, J. (1991). Multiple paradigms and organizational analysis. *Organization Studies*, 12(2), 275–299.

Hassard, J., & Holliday, R. (Eds.) (1998). *Organization-representation.* London: Sage.

Hassard, J., & Parker, M. (Eds.) (1994). *Towards a new theory of organizations.* London: Routledge.

Hatch, M.J. (1997). *Organization theory.* Oxford: Oxford University Press.

Hatchuel, A. (1999). The Foucauldian detour: A rebirth for organization theory? *Human Relations*, 52(4), 507–519.

Hesterly, W.S., Liebeskind, J., & Zenger, T.R. (1990). Organizational economics: An impending revolution in organization theory. *Academy of Management Review*, 15(3), 402–420.

Hickson, D.J. (1996). The *ASQ* years then and now through the eyes of a Euro-Brit. *Administrative Science Quarterly*, 41(2), 217–228.

Hickson, D.J., Hinings, C.R., Lee, C.A., Schneck, R.E., & Pennings, J.M. (1971). A strategic contingencies theory of intraorganizational power. *Administrative Science Quarterly*, 16(2), 216–229.

Hickson, D.J., Pugh, D.S., & Pheysey, D.C. (1969). Operations technology and organizational structures: An empirical reappraisal. *Administrative Science Quarterly*, 14(3), 378–397.

Hinings, C.R. (1988). Defending organization theory: A British view from North America. *Organization Studies*, 9(1), 2–7.

Hirsch, P., & Levin, D.Z. (1999). Umbrella advocates versus validity police: A life-cycle model. *Organization Science*, 10(2), 199–212.

Hirshleifer, J. (1986). Economics from a biological point of view. In J.B. Barney, & W.G. Ouchi (Eds.), *Organizational economics* (pp. 319–317). San Francisco: Jossey-Bass.

Hofstede, G., & Kassem, M.S. (Eds.) (1976). *European contributions to organization theory.* Assen: Van Gorcum.

Homans, G.C. (1964). Bringing men back in. *American Sociological Review*, 20, 809–818.

Hrebiniak, L.G., & Joyce, W.F. (1985). Organizational adaptation: Strategic choice and environmental determinism. *Administrative Science Quarterly*, 30(3), 336–349.

Jackson, N., & Carter, P. (1991). In defence of paradigm incommensurability. *Organization Studies*, 12(1), 109–127.

Jensen, M., & Meckling, W. (1976). Theory of the firm: Managerial behavior, agency costs, and ownership structure. *Journal of Financial Economics*, 3, 305–360.

Kaghan, W., & Phillips, N. (1998). Building the Tower of Babel: Communities of practice and paradigmatic pluralism in organization studies. *Organization*, 5(2), 191–215.

Kassem, M.S. (1976). Introduction: European versus American organization theories'. In G. Hofstede, & M. S. Kassem (Eds.), *European contributions to organization theory* (pp. 1–17). Assen: Van Gorcum.

Kast, F.E., & Rosenzweig, J.E. (1974). *Organization and management: A systems and contingency approach* (2nd ed). New York: McGraw-Hill (1st ed., 1970).

Kondra, A.Z., & Hinings, C.R. (1998). Organizational diversity and change in institutional theory. *Organization studies*, 19(5), 743–767.

Koontz, H. (1961). The management theory jungle. *Academy of Management Journal*, 4(3), 182–186.

Lawrence, P.R., & Lorsch, J.W. (1967). *Organization and environment.* Boston: Harvard University.

Likert, R. (1961). *New patterns of management.* New York: McGraw-Hill.

Locke, R.R. (1996). *The collapse of the American management mystique.* Oxford: Oxford University Press.

March, J.G. (1996). Continuity and change in theories of organizational action. *Administrative Science Quarterly*, 41(2), 278–287.

Marsden, R., & Townley, B. (1996). The owl of Minerva: Reflections on theory in practice. In S.R. Clegg, C. Hardy, & W.R. Nord (Eds.), *Handbook of organization studies* (pp. 659–675) London: Sage.

Martinez, R.J., & Dacin, M.T. (1999). Efficiency motives and normative forces: Combining transactions costs and institutional logic. *Journal of Management*, 25(1), 75–96.

McKinley, W., & Mone, M.A. (1998). The re-construction of organization studies: Wrestling with incommensurability. *Organization*, 5(2), 169–189.

McKinley, W., Mone, M.A., & Moon, G. (1999). Determinants and development of schools in organization theory. *Academy of Management Review*, 24(4), 634–648.

McKinley, W., Sanchez, C.M., & Schick, A.G. (1995). Organizational downsizing: Constraining, cloning, learning. *Academy of Management Executive* 9(3), 32–42.

Meyer, A., Frost, P.J., & Weick, K.E. (1998). The *Organization Science* jazz festival: Improvisation as a metaphor for organizing – overture. *Organization Science*, 9(5), 540–542.

Meyer, J.W., & Rowan, B. (1977). Institutionalized organizations: Formal structure as myth and ceremony. *American Journal of Sociology, 83*(2), 340–363.

Meyer, J.W., Scott, W.R., & Deal, T.E. (1992). Institutional and technical sources of organizational structure: Explaining the structure of educational organizations. In J.W. Meyer, & W.R. Scott, *Organizational environments*. (Updated ed., pp. 45–67) Beverly Hills, CA: Sage. (1st ed., 1983).

Miner, J.B. (1990). The role of values in defining the 'goodness' of theories in organizational science. *Organization Studies, 11*(2), 161–178.

Miner, J.B. (1997). Participating in profound change. *Academy of Management Journal, 40*(6), 1420–1428.

Mooney, J.D., & Reiley, A.C. (1939). *The principles of organization*. (2nd ed.). New York: Harper & Row (1st ed., 1931).

Morgan, G. (1980). Paradigms, metaphors and puzzle-solving in organization theory. *Administrative Science Quarterly, 25*(4), 605–622.

Morgan, G. (1986). *Images of Organization*. Beverly Hills, CA: Sage.

Nilakant, V., & Rao, H. (1994). Agency theory and uncertainty in organizations. *Organization Studies, 15*(2), 649–672.

Oliver, C. (1991). Strategic responses to institutional processes. *Academy of Management Review, 16*(1), 145–179.

Parker, M. (1992). Post-modern organizations or post-modern organization theory? *Organization Studies, 13*(1), 1–17.

Perrow, C. (1970). *Organizational analysis*. Belmont, CA: Wadsworth.

Perrow, C. (1986). *Complex organizations: A critical essay* (3rd ed.). New York: Random House (1st ed., 1972).

Pfeffer, J. (1993). Barriers to the advance of organizational science: Paradigm development as a dependent variable. *Academy of Management Review, 18*(4), 599–620.

Pfeffer, J. (1997). *New directions for organization theory*. Oxford: Oxford University Press.

Pfeffer, J., & Salancik, G.R. (1978). *The external control of organizations*. New York: Harper & Row.

Porter, L.W. (1996). Forty years of organization studies: Reflections from a micro perspective. *Administrative Science Quarterly, 41*(2), 262–269.

Reed, M. (1990). The labour process perspective on management organization: A critique and reformulation. In J. Hassard, & D. Pym (Eds.), *The theory and philosophy of organizations*. (pp. 63–82). London: Routledge.

Reed, M. (1992). *The Sociology of Organizations*. Hemel Hempstead: Harvester.

Rubenstein, A.H., & Haberstroh, C.J. (1966). The nature of organization theory. In A.H. Rubenstein, & C.J. Haberstroh (Eds.), *Some theories of organization*. (2nd ed.). Homewood, IL: Irwin-Dorsey (1st ed., 1960).

Schmidt, S.M., & T.A. Kochan (1977). Interorganizational relationships: Patterns and motivations. *Administrative Science Quarterly, 22*(2), 220–234.

Scott, W.R. (1995). *Institutions and organizations*. London: Sage.

Scott, W.R., & Meyer, J.W. (1992). The organization of societal sectors. In J.W. Meyer, & W.R. Scott, *Organizational Environments*. (Updated ed.). pp. 129–153). Beverly Hills, CA: Sage (1st ed., 1983).

Selznick, P. (1949). *TVA and the grass roots*. Berkeley: University of California Press.

Silverman, D. (1970). *The theory of organizations*. London: Heinemann.

Simon, H.A. (1947). *Administrative behavior*. New York: Macmillan.

Smirchich, L. (1983). Concepts of culture and organizational analysis. *Administrative Science Quarterly, 28*(3), 339–358.

Stern, R.N., & Barley, S.R. (1996). Organizations and social systems: Organization theory's neglected mandate. *Administrative Science Quarterly, 41*(1), 146–162.

Strati, A. (1999). *Organization and aesthetics*. London: Sage.

Thoenig, J-C. (1998). How far is a sociology of organizations still needed? *Organization Studies, 19*(2), 307–320.

Thompson, J.D. (1967). *Organizations in action*. New York: McGraw-Hill.

Thompson, P., & McHugh, D. (1995). *Work organizations* (2nd ed.). London: Macmillan (1st ed., 1990).

Tolbert, P.S., & Zucker, L.G. (1996). The institutionalization of institutional theory. In S.R. Clegg, C. Hardy, & W.R. Nord (Eds.), *Handbook of Organization Studies* (pp. 175–190). London: Sage.

Trist, E.L., & Bamforth, K.W. (1951). Some social and technical consequences of the longwall method of coal-getting. *Human Relations, 4*(1), 6–38.

Tsoukas, H., & Cummings, S. (1997). Marginalization and recovery: The emergence of Aristotelian themes in organization studies. *Organization Studies, 18*(4), 655–683.

Turner, B. (1990). The rise of organizational symbolism. In J. Hassard, & D. Pym (Eds.), *The theory and philosophy of organizations* (pp. 83–96). London: Routledge.

Urwick, L. (1944). *The elements of administration*. New York: Harper & Row.

Üsdiken, B., & Pasadeos, Y. (1995). Organizational analysis in North America and Europe: A comparison of co-citation networks. *Organization Studies, 16*(3), 503–526.

Üsdiken, B., & Pasadeos, Y. (1999). *Organization theory 'Made in USA': What has been changing lately in the produce of the world's largest manufacturer*. Paper presented at the 15th European Group for Organizational Studies Colloquium, Coventry, UK.

Van de Ven, A.H. (1976). On the nature, formation and maintenance of relations among organizations. *Academy of Management Review, 1*(4), 24–36.

Van de Ven, A.H. (1999). The buzzing, blooming, confusing world of organization and management theory: A view from Lake Wobegon University. *Journal of Management Inquiry, 8*(2), 118–126.

Van Maanen, J. (1995). Style as theory. *Organization Science*, 6(1), 133–143.

Vroom, V.H., & P.W. Yetton (1973). *Leadership and decision-making*. Pittsburgh, PA: University of Pittsburgh Press.

Watson, T. (1994). Towards a managerially relevant but non-managerialist organization theory. J. Hassard, & M. Parker (Eds.), *Towards a new theory of organizations* (pp. 209–224) London: Routledge.

Weber, M. (1947). *The theory of social and economic organization* (Trans. A.M. Henderson, & T. Parsons). New York: Free Press (original version published 1924).

Weick, K. (1969). *The social psychology of organizing*. Reading, MA: Addison-Wesley.

Whitley, R. (1988). The management sciences and managerial skills. *Organization Studies*, 9(1), 47–68.

Wicks, A.C., & Freeman, R.E. (1998). Organization studies and the new pragmatism: Positivism, antipositivism, and the search for ethics. *Organization Science*, 9(2), 123–140.

Williamson, O.E. (1975). *Markets and hierarchies*. New York: Free Press.

Willmott, H. (1990). Beyond paradigmatic closure in organizational enquiry. In J. Hassard, & D. Pym (Eds.), *The theory and philosophy of organizations* (pp. 44–60) London: Routledge.

Willmott, H. (1993). Breaking the paradigm mentality. *Organization Studies*, 14(5), 681–719.

Willmott, H. (1994). Bringing agency (back) into organizational analysis: Responding to the crisis of (post)modernity. In J. Hassard, & M. Parker (Eds.), *Towards a new theory of organizations* (pp. 87–130) London: Routledge.

Willmott, H. (1995). What has been happening in organization theory and does it matter? *Personnel Review*, 24(8), 33–53.

Woodward, J. (1958). *Management and technology*. London: HMSO.

Wren, D.A. (1994). *The evolution of management thought* (4th ed.). New York: Wiley.

Zald, M.N. (1993). Organization studies as a scientific and humanistic enterprise: Toward a reconceptualization of the foundations of the field. *Organization Science*, 4(4), 513–528.

Zucker, L.G. (1977). The role of institutionalization in cultural persistence. *American Sociological Review*, 42(5), 726–743.

20

Organizational Culture and Climate

NEAL M. ASHKANASY
and CAMILLE R.A. JACKSON

Based largely on the recently published *Handbook of Organizational Culture and Climate*, we address the topic of this chapter in five sections: (1) An overview of the different paradigms and constructs in the field; (2) discussion of measures of culture and climate, including their relationship with performance; (3) a treatise on the dynamic nature of culture and climate; (4) discussion of HRM aspects of culture and climate; and (5) perspectives on international dimensions of culture and climate. We conclude that research into organizational culture and climate continues to be robust and dynamic, with new horizons opening up at every turn. The chapter takes an essentially psychological approach, with a positivist epistemology, and an ontological perspective rooted in scientific realism, but strays nonetheless into areas of sociology and anthropology consistent with the traditional view of culture. This is, we feel, an inevitable consequence of the convergence of the constructs of climate and culture. We conclude that culture and climate are overlapping and complementary constructs, amenable to multimethod research that cuts across disciplinary boundaries.

INTRODUCTION

Organizational culture and climate comprise cognate sets of attitudes, values, and practices that characterize the members of a particular organization. As such, these constructs have occupied an important place in the industrial and organizational psychology literature in one form or another since the pioneering work of Lewin (1948, 1951). In this chapter, we will present a review of these constructs, largely based upon the contents of the *Handbook of organizational culture and climate (HOCC)*, a compendium of contemporary articles on this topic edited by Ashkanasy, Wilderom and Peterson (2000a). The *HOCC* presents a variety of contemporary views on organizational climate and culture, but takes a largely psychological point-of-view, rather than the more traditional sociological and anthropological perspectives, although these not ignored. Our view is also ostensibly distinct from the more postmodern perspective as represented, for example, in the *Handbook of Organization Studies* (Clegg, Hardy & Nord, 1996).

Of course, one of the distinguishing features of organizational culture and climate is the way that these constructs encompass a diversity of scholarly traditions, including anthropology, sociology, psychology, and management science. In the introduction to the *HOCC*, Ashkanasy, Wilderom and Peterson (2000b) make the point that each of these disciplines has brought its own paradigms and perspectives to bear on what is intrinsically a complex and ambiguous topic (see also Meyerson, 1991). In the end, however, organizational culture and climate provide windows on organizational life that transcend any one discipline or any particular organization. In this sense, constructs like shared attitudes, values, and meanings enable us to present a more encompassing picture than can be represented by transactions and behaviors alone.

Before proceeding further, it is important to note that the terms 'culture' and 'climate' are frequently and erroneously used interchangeably in the organizational literature. Denison (1996), however, has pointed out that they represent distinguishable perspectives, and that they are derived from different ontological traditions. He differentiated the two concepts by noting that culture refers to deeply embedded values and assumptions, while climate refers to consciously perceived environmental factors subject to organizational control. In this chapter, we recognize the differentiation between culture and climate, but nonetheless conclude that the two constructs are overlapping and complementary.

We begin our review with a look at the historical development of organizational climate and culture, rooted in the fields of the psychology and sociology of attitudes, and the anthropology of societies. The construct of organizational climate historically predated organizational culture by some 25 years, and is a derivative of Lewin's (1948, 1951) field theory. As such, organizational climate is linked to the Gestalt psychology of perception. Lewin and his colleagues were interested in the elements of field theory and roles in social processes. In this respect, field theory was limited to aspects of an organization that most needed to understand a particular individual or group phenomenon within a given organizational context. Thus, Lewin and his colleagues (Lewin, Lippitt & White, 1939) coined the term 'climate' to describe the attitudes, feelings, and social processes of organizations. Climate in this view fell into three major and well-known categories: autocratic, democratic, and *laissez-faire*.

Rensis Likert inherited Lewin's legacy, inventing the Likert scale for measuring attitudes and developing the *System 4* view of effective management (Likert, 1961). In this respect, Likert's intention was to develop measures to enable the study of a concept of organizational climate that could neither be known personally nor created artificially. Largely as a result of his advocacy, the use of surveys was the dominant way in which students of organizational climate in the 1960s and 70s described social processes within organizations.

Although James and McIntyre (1996) argue for a general factor of climate, Schneider (1975) has promulgated the view that a focus on a single climate, usually relating to social or employee well-being, has limited the potential of the construct. Schneider posits that organizations simultaneously maintain numerous climates. In the *HOCC*, Schneider and his colleagues (Schneider, Bowen, Ehrhart & Holcombe, 2000) deal specifically with the phenomenon of 'climate for service' but argue more generally that the principles they develop serve as a model for other applications of the organizational climate perspective. In particular, climate is presented as

shared subjective experiences of organizational members that have important consequences for organizational functioning and effectiveness.

By the 1970s, however, many in the field felt that the organizational context within which managers take specific actions is at best only roughly approximated by what the culture construct and its associated surveys can represent (see Reichers & Schneider, 1990). As a result, organizational culture came into prominence. Culture had traditionally been in the domain of anthropology. Thus, the new emphasis on culture brought into organization studies ways of thinking holistically about systems of meaning, values, and actions derived from anthropology. The early organizational culture researchers advocated working from direct experience within an organization and relied largely on inductive intuition to describe an organization's culture. As such, this tradition drew heavily on the ethnographic tradition in cultural anthropology (e.g., see Schein, 1992).

The Ashkanasy et al. (2000b) review of the anthropology literature on culture revealed three classes of climate and culture definitions, reflecting different ontologies. The first, and most common, is a structural realist ontology. In this view, organizations exist as structures that have climate and a culture. The second is based on social constructionist ontology, and places emphasis on the varying regularity in events that happen in organizations. This approach gives observers room to select which sets of events to group together into a culture, and reflects regularities they called work-related events. Finally, in the third view, organizations and culture are treated as linguistic conveniences.

Definitions of climate and culture also reflect three epistemological approaches. The first of these is the deductive approach, which emphasizes broadly applicable cultural dimensions or analytic categories. Knowledge comes from constructing these dimensions, looking to see where organizations fall, and then revising the dimensions when previously overlooked phenomena are noticed. In the second category are inductive approaches that recognize the presence of tacit elements. These tacit elements can sometimes be made explicit, but always shape the experience of specified constructs. Finally, radical approaches view the observer as not so much dispassionately interested in accuracy, but in producing constructions that reflect their own interests and experiences.

The interplay between the different paradigms (Schultz & Hatch, 1996) has been a feature of research into organizational culture and climate and will continue to be so. Thus, while many scholars argue that an ontology, epistemology, and methodology appropriate for studying whole cultures is best provided by the interpretive traditions within anthropology, others argue that the constructs can be examined within the more traditional frameworks of psychology, based on the use of surveys and of a positivist epistemology. In this chapter, we will review a variety of approaches from the different paradigms, with a view to enlightening readers about the ongoing controversies and flow of ideas in this exciting field. Our coverage is based in a selection of the chapters in the *HOCC* and, following the structure of the *HOCC*, is presented in five sections. The first deals with the understanding of the constructs in their different forms. The second examines survey measures of culture and climate, and the nexus between culture, climate, and performance. In the third section, we look at some of the dynamic aspects of culture and climate, moving on in the fourth section to consideration of how culture and climate contribute to socialization, commitment, and careers. In the final section, we consider some of the international dimensions of culture and climate.

PERSPECTIVES ON ORGANIZATIONAL CULTURE AND CLIMATE

In this section, we deal with some of the basic perspectives on organizational culture, and consider how values and meanings are represented and communicated in organizational settings. In particular, perspectives based on meanings and values are often seen as competing approaches. Value perspectives are normally associated with a functional view of society, based on the assumption that values can be characterized by dimensions that appeal to distinct cultures, organizations, and societies. Meaning perspectives, on the other hand, do not imply the existence of value dimensions at all, and are based on an interpretive paradigm. From this perspective, value dimensions serve only to constrain artificially our understanding of cultures. While these views are ostensibly contradictory, we argue in this chapter that the two views are reconcilable and that, by viewing them as complementary, rather than as competing, we can gain a richer understanding of culture and climate in organizations.

Stackman, Pinder and Connor (2000) have provided a succinct coverage of the values perspective, and take the position that work values are a special case of personal values in general. As such, values of organizational members govern key personal decisions, especially when these decisions involve ethical issues. In this case, as Stackman and his colleagues argue, values in the workplace embody the essence of work attitudes, and therefore lie at the heart of organizational behavior. Their starting point is Rokeach's (1968, 1973) definition of a personal value system as an 'organization of principles and rules to help one choose between alternatives,

resolve conflicts and make decisions' (Rokeach, 1968: 160). This indicates that values are intrinsically hierarchical, so that a personal value system is conceptualized as consisting of a rank-ordering of individual values. An individual's value system may be described as comprising a number of levels, ranging from the most explicit to the most basic. Further, Chusmir and Parker (1991) have shown that individuals have two different hierarchies of values: one for personal/family life and another for work. In this sense, values ought to be considered in *sets*; where particular sets of values become more or less important in guiding a person's attitude and behavior, depending on the context. As a corollary of this, it would seem that values are malleable to the extent that the context can be changed. There is also evidence (see Rokeach & Grube, 1979) that behavioral change can be brought about by focusing on and attempting to alter an individual's value system rather than the behavior itself. This is important, because the potential flexibility of values implies that the employer can manipulate values and behavior in ways that will increase employee uniformity and predictability, and ultimately, managerial control. This constitutes an ethical issue, because of the often widely held assumption on the part of employers that they have a right as part of the employment contract to attempt to influence the values of employees.

The propensity of management to attempt to manipulate members' values is exacerbated when the organization's culture is strong. In this respect, Meglino, Ravlin and Adkins (1989, 1991) define a strong organizational culture as the extent to which there is a high degree of consistency among organizational members in terms of their shared belief structures, values, and norms. Meglino and his colleagues argue that this aggregate homogeneity among the value structure of organizational actors is a source of job satisfaction, commitment, job proficiency, and long tenure of employees. A problem arises, however, when, in an attempt to engender a homogeneous workforce, employment selection choices are based on demographic characteristics such as sex, race, and age. In the latter instance, of course, such practices are unethical and, in many Western industrialized economies, unlawful.

In contrast to the values/functionalist perspective, Helms Mills and Mills (2000) take an interpretive view and apply it particularly to gendering of organizations. In this respect, they adopt Oakley's (1972) distinction between sex (as the basic physiological differences between men and women) and gender (as culturally specific patterns of behavior that may be attached to the sexes), and argue that gender in particular has served as a basis for discrimination. Helms Mills and Mills adopt a rules- or practice-based framework that is intrinsically different from the values perspective we described above. The rules framework offers an explanation of common action without implying a unity or pattern of beliefs, values, and learned ways of coping with experience. Rules simultaneously serve to contain differences of opinion, beliefs, and values while resulting in practices that give the appearance of unity of purpose.

Against this background, Helms Mills and Mills (2000) see culture as a heuristic to highlight holism, interconnectedness, and context for the focal issue of gendering. In particular, the distinction between sex and gender (Oakley, 1972), although not uncontested, represents a holistic approach to gender in that notions of womanhood and manhood are outcomes of a multitude of factors. These include language, attitudes, patterns of behavior, value systems, stories, rites, rituals, ceremonies, and physical artifacts. Further, this distinction has generated numerous feminist studies of the relationship between cultural milieu and gendered outcomes (e.g., Ginsberg & Tsing, 1990). Thus, through power dynamics within organizations, rules come to be established that shape meanings. Rules thus create coherence in organizational practices, regardless of variability in values or attitudes.

The rules framework proposed by Helms Mills and Mills is still a structured perspective, however. Theorists who take a symbolic or intepretivist view depart much further from the functionalist view. Rafaeli and Worline (2000) present a theme of symbols that is illustrative of interpretive theories of culture. They argue, consistent with Schein (1990), that symbols are not simple by-products of organizations, but rather that they are elements that structure members' active construction of sense, knowledge, and behavior. In this sense, symbols are visible, physical manifestations of organizations and indicators of organizational life, sensed through sight, sound, touch, and smell; and able to be experienced and used by organizational members to make meaning of their surroundings. Thus, meaning is conceptualized as a product of both internal associations and the matching of internal and external cues.

Rafaeli and Worline (2000) argue further that recognizing objects involves a process that draws on both affective and cognitive processes and is thus central to human evolution and survival. They thus construe organizational culture as a network of meanings or shared experiences and interpretations that provides members with a shared and accepted reality. Symbols provide a tangible expression of this shared reality. Therefore symbols are a bridge between organizational members and emotional and cognitive reactions. But symbols are more than this, they:

spark feelings and help make those feelings comprehensible;
are directly experienced and give a concrete form to what would otherwise be abstract meanings;

reflect organizational culture, and trigger internalized values;
provide a shared frame of reference and integrate systems of meaning throughout an organization.

Thus, as Schein (1990) also argues, symbols have a consensus-making function that allows people to make sense of the organization and to find their place within it. The symbols integrate multiple competing and potentially even conflicting systems of meaning in an organization. Symbols thus become physical manifestations of organizational life, essential for organizational members and observers to integrate their experiences into coherent systems of meaning.

In summary, the rules and symbolic perspectives described above are examples of semiotic analysis, and provide an interpretive framework. The implication here is that, in order to study an organization's culture fully, the relevant symbols, the content conveyed by the symbols, and the rules that bind them must be uncovered, without any reference to functionalism per se. Further, the rules and symbolic perspectives imply some form of a structural or physical manifestation.

Tyrrell (2000) offers an interesting, but radically different view. He emphasizes the intepretivist perspective inherent in anthropology, but draws as well from functional views that have been the source of cultural analyses of values, based upon elements of social and evolutionary psychology. He reconsiders the concept of culture as a holistic way of understanding communities, applying a culture perspective to 'cyber communities.' In so doing, he considers the nature of social institutions, how they are bounded, and how they change.

In particular, Tyrrell (2000) identifies four problems in reformulating the concept of culture:

The concept of culture. Culture has two separate and distinct meanings – at an organizational wide level and at levels within an organization (Trice & Beyer, 1993; Jordan, 1994).

The conceptualization of institutions. Institutions can be viewed from one of two perspectives. The first is that they may only operate in specific perceptually defined territories. The second is that they are shaped by the nature of the relationship between the institutions and general community (Malinowski, 1960).

The definition of community. Community is the relationship between individuals, their mutual expectations, obligations, rights, and responsibilities. Communities are thus a part of a large web of social relations that define any particular society and the relationship of one society to another (Turner, 1982).

Territories and sites. Territories contain the locations or sites in which and through which institutions, organizations, and communities operate.

Communities in this sense comprise communicative networks, and are broadly characterized along their communication lines: oral cultures, literate cultures, and digital cultures.

Based on this broad framework, Tyrrell (2000) introduces the idea of 'culture in cyberspace.' Cyberspace is defined in terms of dimensions of time (asynchronous vs. synchronous) and events (noninteractive vs. fully interactive), that provide a flow of experience and act as a shared basis for occupational, departmental, and work team subcultures. This flow of experience, in turn, provides the subjective, experiential basis for individual attachment to particular organizations and organizational units. These then allow for the continuing production of organization cultures. Within this context, communities supply their members with the rules to one or more games and the potential opportunity to engage in these. Communities by their very placement within larger environments will inevitably adapt culturally to their local conditions.

The final perspective that we canvass is that elucidated by Peterson and Smith (2000). Their approach offers a way out of the conflict implicit in the functional versus interpretivist division. Peterson and Smith base their conceptualization on the concept of *events*. They identify events as the object of the interpretation processes that occur within cultures and identify sources of meaning that can aid analysis of the way events are interpreted. Consistent with Trice and Beyer (1993), they posit that different sources of meaning can offer meanings associated with different values and, in the process of doing so, add a political element to the creation of meaning.

As an example, Peterson and Smith advance role theory (Kahn, Wolfe, Quinn, Snoek & Rosenthal, 1964; Merton, 1957) as one way at looking at meaning within the events context. In this view, role theory gives power to meanings through teleology. Thus, different role senders can take different ideological perspectives or apply the same perspective in different ways when seeking to influence the use a receiver makes of a perspective. In this sense, roles are charged with expectations, and so shape the future. Through interplay between what is actually occurring and characteristics of social actors, attention is selectively given to some events. Construction of meaning thus proceeds by linking events to existing interpretive structures. The process reaches closure as social actions modify or add to their interpretive structures and sometimes generate actions, choices, or intentions.

In this view, making a decision or taking an action is only one way to resolve an interpretive process. More often, interpretation is resolved by more subtle changes in interpretive structures. A person's thinking or an organization's culture may occasionally change radically but is *always* changing incrementally.

In summary of this section, we have presented a variety of views of organizational culture, including a values-oriented functionalist perspective, and several intepretivist perspectives, including rules-based, symbolic, anthropologic, and events-based frameworks. It is clear from this discussion that organizational culture is too complex a phenomenon to be adequately represented using only one perspective. Organizational cultures and climates encompass a complex interaction of personal and cognitive factors that require an eclectic, multi-disciplinary approach to understand even a little bit. In the following sections we deal with organizational culture and climate from a principally functionalist perspective but, as will become evident, this view is tempered with a good dose of interpretivism.

MEASUREMENT AND OUTCOMES OF CULTURE AND CLIMATE

A recurrent theme throughout this chapter is that organizational culture and climate, while distinguishable, are not as distinct from each other as is commonly believed. This is especially true when it comes to measurement of the constructs. In this respect, we must show our hands as lying within the paradigmatic perspective of scientific realism and its associated objective epistemology (Lincoln & Guba, 1989). In this section, therefore, we discuss approaches to measuring culture and climate as if they are objective phenomena, subject to quantification, and associated with distinctive and measurable outcomes.

In the first instance, it is important to reiterate our earlier point that culture and climate, although theoretically distinct, overlap from a phenomenological perspective. Payne (2000) addresses directly the overlap between measures of organizational culture and climate. In particular, he shows how a questionnaire measure of 'cultural intensity' can be used with the collaboration of organizational members to reflect cultural integration, diversification, and fragmentation (see Martin, 1995). Payne argues further that integration and fragmentation can be described in terms of dimensions of pervasiveness, intensity, and cultural context that are unique to each organization. Measurement of culture and climate in this instance is often achieved through the use of proprietary culture surveys that make use of the company's own history, language, myths, ceremonies, and systems.

As we noted earlier, surveys have been widely used in respect of culture and, more recently, to measure dimensions of culture. Two problems with this approach, however, are (1) the issue of levels of analysis and (2) the indeterminate structure of the constructs themselves.

In respect of level of analysis, Rousseau (1985) has identified four biases and misconceptions:

Misspecification. This occurs when an observed relationship is attributed to a level other than the actual organizational level where the observations were made. For example, observations based on individual organizational members' responses do not necessarily correspond to organizational level responses (see Hofstede, Bond & Luk, 1993).

Aggregation bias. This represents the extent to which aggregation of responses artificially induces an observed outcome. For example, relationships based on aggregated responses in homogeneous groups are mathematically higher than correlations based on individual responses (Hammond, 1973).

Cross-level fallacy. This occurs then relationships at one level are inappropriately assumed to hold at other levels.

Contextual fallacies. This is a failure to take into account the effect of contextual factors on observed relationships.

Taken together, these four problems represent a central threat to the validity of survey-based measures of culture and climate. Hofstede et al. (1993), in particular, have argued that incorrect appreciation of level is a pervasive issue in survey-based research. Indeed, most of the measures outlined in this chapter are applied using simple aggregation of individual responses, although some cross-cultural authors (e.g., House et al., 1999) have developed their measures by aggregation at societal levels using the r_{wg} technique advocated by James, DeMaree and Wolf (1984). Unfortunately, however, as Hofstede and his colleagues note, the issue of choosing the proper level of analysis is too often neglected.

Turning now to the dimensional structure of climate and culture measures, we find that the literature is replete with all sorts of dimensions and variants, many with unreported or doubtful psychometric properties (see Rousseau, 1990). More recently, Ashkanasy, Broadfoot and Falkus (2000) found a similar lack of consistency and rigor among extant measures. They identified two broad classification of culture measure, however: typing and profile measures. Typing measures (e.g., Cooke & Rousseau, 1988) are used to categorize organizations into specific culture 'types.' Profiling measures, on the other hand, provide a more detailed description of culture in terms of discrete dimensions. Ashkanasy et al., further dissect profiling surveys into three groups: effectiveness surveys, descriptive surveys, and fit profiles. Effectiveness surveys (e.g., Woodcock, 1989), attempt to identify the cultural dimensions most associated with high performance, and are the prevalent type. Descriptive instruments (e.g., Hofstede, 1980) do not attempt to evaluate the organization's effectiveness, but still measure values. Finally, fit profiles (e.g., O'Reilly,

Chatman & Caldwell, 1991) attempt to measure the level of congruence between individual and the organizational values.

Ashkanasy et al. (2000) illustrate and discuss the difficulties that they encountered in putting together a multidimensional culture measure. In their work, they assembled a multidimensional descriptive profile measure that they called the Organizational Culture Profile (OCP). The OCP encompasses 10 dimensions of culture, derived from a broad review of existing culture measures. In practice, however, Ashkanasy and his colleagues were only able to identify two factors, labeled 'Instrumental' and 'Expressive.' They discuss their findings by noting that multidimensional survey measures are most likely valuable when there is a focus on specific areas such as communications, but that broad dimensions have greater cross-situational validity.

A more widely known multi-dimensional measure of organizational culture is the Organizational Culture Inventory (OCI: Cooke & Rousseau, 1988; Cooke & Lafferty, 1994). Cooke and Szumal (2000) review the use of this instrument as a multidimensional typing tool, and conclude that it has potential to provide useful insights into key facets of organizational functioning. The OCI is used to assess 12 sets of norms that describe the thinking and behavioral styles that might be implicitly or explicitly required for people to 'fit in' and to 'meet expectations' in an organizational or subunit. The three types identified in the OCI are 'constructive,' 'passive/defensive,' and 'aggressive/defensive' cultures (see also Roberts, Rousseau & La Porte, 1994). Cooke and Szumal conclude that, while culture most likely impacts effectiveness, the success of an organization can also create inconsistencies between the different levels of culture and between cultures and outcomes by affecting variables such as resources and demands.

Cooke and Szumal (2000) also identify 'culture bypass' as an alternate dynamic that accounts for inconsistencies between values and philosophy, operating cultures, and organizational effectiveness. Culture bypass is evident when organizations adopt strategies for their operating units that produce negative cultures but are nevertheless successful. These strategies typically revolve around special resources, proprietary technologies, or standardized products that provide the organization with some type of competitive advantage. The technologies implemented and the structure and systems put into place to support them are implicitly designed to 'bypass' culture or its impact by directly controlling members' behavior.

Within scientific realism, there is an assumption that constructs are not only objectively measurable, but that their effects are also measurable. In organization science, the oft-asked question is 'Does culture or climate have measurable effects on organizational performance?' To answer this question, Wiley and Brooks (2000) argue that measures of organizational climate themselves provide important insights into high-performing organizations. They describe the linkage research model (Wiley, 1996) and, based on this model, extensively review published accounts linking culture measures to indicators of organizational effectiveness and performance. The linkage research model is based on employees' descriptions of their work environment and their relative performance success, taking into account the particular characteristics of the environment, including climate and culture.

The Wiley and Brooks (2000) model is consistent with findings by Johnson (1996), who conducted a study evaluating components of climate for service against a criterion of customer satisfaction. These results showed that climate for service was significantly related to at least one facet of customer satisfaction. The most significant findings in linkage research, however, are evident in longitudinal studies. Here the linkage research model implies that leadership practices precede employee results; these precede customer results that, in turn, lead to business performance.

The question of nexus between culture and organizational performance, however, is still unresolved. Although researchers such as Denison (1990) and Kotter and Heskett (1992) have conducted extensive studies, and have claimed that there is evidence for a culture–performance link, there are still many questions unresolved. Wilderom, Glunk and Maslowski (2000), in an extensive and critical review of the evidence, conclude that problems of inconsistent and often unreliable measurement continue to cloud the picture in this important area of research. Wilderom and her colleagues argue that the inconclusiveness of the data in this respect is as much a function of the inadequacy of performance measures, than any fault with the culture measures. No one seems to argue, however, that organizational performance is not itself an abstract construct, and cannot be assessed objectively. It seems incongruent to us, therefore, that critics of organizational culture often apply just this argument to objective measures of culture. Even well-known proponents of culture, such as Deal and Kennedy (1982) and Ouchi and Jaeger (1978), equivocate on this point.

LEADERSHIP AND THE DYNAMICS OF ORGANIZATIONAL CULTURE CHANGE

Despite the elusiveness of identifiable effects of culture on organizational performance, few would find it difficult to understand the key role that culture plays in organizational transformation. In particular, organizational culture is often seen as the cause of organizational dissolution or other dramatic organizational changes such downsizing, merger, or acquisition (Cartwright & Cooper, 1996). We argue that different types of organizational change respond differentially to different aspects of organizational culture. This clearly has important consequences for management of culture change in general, and leadership in particular.

Perhaps the most obvious and dramatic example of culture change occurs in mergers and acquisitions (M&As). Yaakov Weber (2000) deals with this from the point of view of top management teams. He argues that the interaction between politics and culture change is a major determinant of the success of M&As. In a field study, he found that turnover of managers of acquired firms was significantly greater when the cultural differences between the management team of the acquired versus acquirer was large. The 'culture clash' that occurs in M&As has implications for stress, attitudes, behavior, and turnover, especially of the managers and employees of the acquired company. Culture clash influences the effectiveness of postmerger integration processes, the integration of information systems, and the financial performance and shareholder value of the acquiring company (see also Ashkanasy & Holmes, 1995). Weber found also that predicted relationships between cultural fit and financial performance and turnover were moderated by the degree of 'cultural tolerance.'

Weber's (2000) findings appear to carry over to culture change in single organizations. In this regard, Michela and Burke (2000) argue that the success of organizational culture change depends on the degree of sophistication that top-management teams display in managing change. In particular, Michela and Burke posit that leaders need to understand the nature and management of culture and climate if they are to accomplish organizational changes associated with quality and innovation. This is based on Woods' (1997) identification of appropriate organizational culture as a necessary precursor of quality and innovation in organizations.

According to Michela and Burke (2000), there are two forms of culture and quality. The first type they describe as *traditional management*: employees have job descriptions that specify their tasks explicitly. The second type, *value-based management*, starts with analysis of the larger processes within which work activities are embedded, such as values and norms, and relies on concepts of leadership (see Schein, 1992). Values, Michela and Burke argue, influence a wide variety of specific behaviors and, as we have noted earlier in this chapter, are central to many definitions of organizational culture (e.g., see de Geus, 1997; Hurst, 1995; Stackman et al., 2000). Under value-based management, employees are given direction not in literal terms, but in terms of objectives, goals, or desired end states. Associated with values are norms: what organizational members do, and their shared understanding about what they are supposed to do.

Michela and Burke (2000) therefore argue that culture change within this model must be leader-driven, and that the leader must deal with the cognitive aspects of culture change, such as beliefs about the right way to go about doing things. These beliefs or schemata constitute mental frameworks or structures for identifying or understanding things, actors, events, and situations. In this respect, schemata constitute important elements of motivation and understanding culture specifically because they bind elements such as values and needs to action.

Zammuto, Gifford and Goodman (2000) argue more specifically that organizations are characterized by control-oriented managerial ideologies that are ill equipped for culture change. Ideology in this respect is defined by Beyer (1981) as a 'relatively coherent set of beliefs that bind some people together and that explain their worlds in terms of cause and effect relations' (pp. 166–167).

Taking this perspective, and based on the Quinn and Rohrbaugh (1983) competing values model, Zammuto and his associates argue that four content types of managerial ideologies are embedded within the larger social system, and that these ideologies constitute key elements in determining if change is to be successful. In particular, the ideological underpinnings of an organization's culture are a major determinant of innovation outcomes. In this view, organizational ideologies that emphasize externalized coordination and control mechanisms are likely to fail at implementing such innovations (or gain efficiency benefits only). Organizational ideologies that emphasize commitment-based coordination and control mechanisms, on the other hand, are more likely to avoid implementation failure and to gain both the efficiency and flexibility benefits such innovations offer.

Hatch (2000) goes even further. She proposes a broad-based model of the dynamics of organizational culture change. Within this framework, leaders play a role in initiating change, but the role of leadership in the change process itself is less important. Hatch makes the point that organizational members throughout the organization continually remake culture on a daily basis. Thus, dependence on leadership as the only crucial factor in culture change represents an oversimplification. Hatch compares her model with the work of Weber (1947) and the theory of routinization of charisma (see also Schroder, 1992). In this theory, culture change originates in the introduction of new ideas by a charismatic leader figure, but change at the level of everyday life follows the path of routinization of this charismatic influence.

Hatch's (2000) model integrates three levels of conceptual models: artifacts, values, and assumptions, with the concept of symbols. She identifies four processes linking these phenomena: manifestation, realization, symbolization, and interpretation (see also Schein, 1990; Ortner, 1973; Salancik & Pfeffer, 1978).

Manifestation occurs whenever specific values or behavioral norms are evoked perceptually, cognitively, or emotionally.

Realization follows manifestation only when such evocations find their expressions in outcomes or acts. Cultural values and norms then become realized in the products of culturally influenced action called artifacts.

Symbolization is the cultural process that links the meanings of artifacts through the recognition of personal and social significance, and is reflected in objects, acts, feelings, cognitions, or aesthetic responses.

Interpretation specifies meaning by locating the immediate experience associated with a symbol within the broader context of the history of cultural meanings and the geography of cultural artifacts.

Within Hatch's (2000) model, charismatic leaders themselves become artifacts. Their importance lies in their potency relative to the artifacts that they deliberately introduce in order to alter the culture they represent and enact with their person. In this case, when looking at leadership and cultural change, leaders can encourage symbolizing activity through their own example. Thus, the symbolic perception of leaders by organizational members constructs a meaningful reality of the organization and thereby influences the course of cultural change.

An important dimension of organizational change is whether it is an ongoing process of incremental change or a single major transformation. This issue is addressed by Sathe and Davidson (2000). They point out that the transformation model is the one most commonly referred to in the change literature. Sathe and Davidson also buy into the leadership model of effective organizational culture change, and discuss the type of motivators that are needed for change to succeed, noting that cultural change is often brought about by environmental changes such as global competition.

Sathe and Davidson (2000) discuss two further issues: (1) Is there a 'best culture' that is associated with optimum performance and survival? (2) What are the consequences for culture change? In respect of best culture, they refer to Kotter and Heskett's (1992) comprehensive study of this question. Kotter and Heskett concluded that strong cultures perform better financially, but only when there is an appropriate culture fit. Sathe (1985) argues in particular that stronger cultures are characterized by important assumptions that are widely shared throughout the organization, and are clearly prioritized.

In answer to the second question, Sathe and Davidson (2000) argue that the greater the strength of the culture and the larger the magnitude of the proposed change, the greater the resistance to change. In this respect, Kotter (1995) reported that, on most of the attempts at organizational change, failures were due to skipping or making mistakes at one of eight key steps:

establishing a sense of urgency;
forming a powerful guiding coalition;
creating a vision;
communicating the vision;
empowering others to act on the vision;
planning for and creating short-term wins;
consolidating improvements and producing more change;
institutionalizing new approaches.

In addition to describing phases of organizational change, it is possible to view culture change as a long-term evolutionary process. Harrison (1995) believes that there is a hierarchy of organization cultures, and that organizations gradually evolve up the levels of survival $\rightarrow$ defense $\rightarrow$ security $\rightarrow$ self-expression $\rightarrow$ transcendence. He argues further that organizations at the survival and defense levels are not amenable to culture change, since they need first to solve their operational problems.

Clearly, a key feature of adaptable organization forms is their ability to learn (Senge, 1993). One key feature of learning cultures is their tolerance for mistakes. Lawler (1996) speaks of creating a climate of continuous change through organizational experimentation and openness to learning about the positive and negative effects of particular practices. In this respect, Hurst (1995) argues further that organizations frequently mistakenly use financial indications as measures of success. Hurst points out that financial indications make people look backwards, rather than considering indicators of future success such as employee attitudes and customer satisfaction.

Finally, dealing with continuous change, Markus (2000) refers to what he calls 'reproduction of organizational culture.' In this scenario, the role of leaders is less pronounced than it is in the traditional model of transformational culture change. Markus concludes in particular that more knowledge on the dynamics of organizational culture provides a key to the tricky issue of culture's persistence. Cultures are aggregates of individual beliefs, values, and assumptions that are held in common within the social unit. Individual beliefs, values, and assumptions thus become culture by being shared. Culture is reinforced through the practice of the culture itself: day-to-day interactions between organization members sharing in the culture.

In conclusion of this section, it is clear that the dynamics of culture change are complex and situationally variable. Among the literature we have discussed there is, however, general agreement on two key points. The first of these is that appropriate organizational culture is a critical element of organizational change, no matter what type of change is taking place. Thus, organizational culture plays a role in sudden change such as occurs in M&As, in rapid transformational change, and in continuous change associated with learning organizations. The second is that cultures need to be adaptable, although there is still controversy surrounding the issue of culture strength.

The role of leadership in organizational and culture change is an area that continues to be contentious. In particular, the view that cultures are somehow the creation of leadership as espoused by Schein (1992) appears to be breaking down. In this sense, there are clearly exciting prospects for future research.

ORGANIZATIONAL CULTURE AND ITS EFFECTS ON HUMAN RESOURCE MANAGEMENT

In this section, we relate organizational culture and climate to four human resource management (HRM) issues: attachment, commitment, socialization, and careers. The focus of this discussion is essentially on the role of individuals in organizations; how they make their way in organizations, and how they identify with and become loyal to their organizations. These are topics that are not normally dealt with in the organizational culture literature, but that we feel should be. It would seem to go without saying that HRM outcomes and processes are inextricably linked with culture, especially if culture is to have relevance for practicing managers who deal with these issues on a day-to-day basis.

Culture, Climate, and Organizational Attachment and commitment

Dealing first with the broad topic of organizational culture and attachment, Beyer, Hannah and Milton (2000) have identified categories of social process that contribute to attachment, such as social interaction, affective and cognitive processes, symbolic beliefs, and behavior. These categories in turn are derived from three different traditions: sociology, anthropology, and psychology.

Within the sociological domain, authors such as Homans (1950) have theorized about the influences that cause people to form and to stay in communities. In this instance, there are three possible causes. The first of these is mechanical solidarity. This effect serves to reflect community bonds based on common beliefs, participation in collective action, and a common sense of identity and organic solidarity. These in turn reflect a form of material interdependence based on a division of labor. Homans argues that the ensuing social interaction, shared activities, and shared sentiments lead to social cohesion, a prototype of culture.

Geertz (1964), the doyen of anthropological and archaeological theories of culture, pursued a different line: ideology is a response to the inevitable and insoluble strains, conflicts, and contradictions in social life. He sees communal ideology as promoting social solidarity and knitting social groups together to create a sense of community. Anderson (1983), another anthropologist, believes that people can be tied together in an 'imagined community' where people never meet each other, but they share an image of their communion in their minds (see also Tyrrell, 2000).

Finally, Kelman (1958) is a representative of the psychological view. He explains social ties among individuals on three levels: (1) compliance, derived from contingent rewards; (2) identification, coming from a valued identity; and (3) internalization, based in attitude agreement. Together, these three forms of social cohesion create a degree of social exchange and attachment. Another psychological theory is that social groups are formed on the basis of intergroup attitudes, self-categorization, and identification processes (Tajfel, 1982).

According to Beyer et al. (2000), concepts underlying the study of attachment include involvement and commitment. Commitment, in particular is closely associated with organizational culture. Becker (1960) has postulated the 'side-bet theory of commitment,' whereby organizational members link their extraneous interests with a consistent line of activity associated with their employment. More specifically, Porter, Steers, Mowday and Boulian (1974) define that commitment as embodying three components: (1) a belief and acceptance of the values and goals of the organization, (2) willingness to exert effort on behalf of the organization to achieve organizational goals, and (3) a strong desire to maintain organization membership. Recently, Allen and Meyer (1991) have distinguished three types of commitment: affective, continuance, and normative.

Social identity theory (SIT) goes a step further than commitment. In this instance, identification with an organization results from individuals categorizing themselves as members of organizations or of organizational subgroups, and internalizing these social categories or memberships (Ashforth & Mael, 1989). Psychological contracts (see Rousseau, 1989) constitute another form of organizational attachment. The psychological contract arises out of the notion that employees perceive mutual obligations between themselves and their employing organization (see also Schein, 1992), including both relational and transactional obligations. The final commitment is citizenship behavior (Guzzo, Noonan & Elron, 1994; Robinson, 1996; Robinson & Rousseau, 1994), where individuals' willingness to engage in contextual behaviors is likely to vary to the extent they are attached to a social system. Thus, when organizational members are strongly attached, they may be more likely to engage in behaviors that further the interests of the organization (or organizational subgroup) to which they belong.

Within this framework, organizational culture is linked to attachment through ideologies that include the beliefs, values, and norms that an organizational members hold, together with the extent to which members interact repeatedly so that they learn the norms of the organization. In this sense, Beyer et al. (2000) assert that cultural forms foster attachment because of the need to communicate shared meanings and to encourage behavioral interaction among members of a group. These meanings, in turn, are expressed through symbols, scripted behavior, language, narratives, and practices.

Virtanen (2000) focuses more specifically on organizational commitment, but does so from an interesting perspective that sheds new light on the culture–climate debate. Virtanen asserts, consistent with Beyer at al. (2000), that commitments are *instruments* of climate, but posits further that commitments are the *constituents* of culture. He goes on to describe a model where culture is associated with emotionally driven desires, while climate is associated with utilitarian strategies.

Virtanen's (2000) case is based on the idea that the social nature of commitment includes issues such as consistent human behavior, loyalty, and observable behavioral acts, together with perspectives of ideology, conviction, and value systems associated with commitment (see Meyer & Allen, 1997). Thus, the strength of the commitment of an organizational member is a function of norms, strategies, and desires that determine interactively the role of obligations, utilities, and emotions in each situation the member is living in. Virtanen argues, consistent with Denison (1996), that climate is more controllable than culture, while culture is more constitutive of organizations than climate. Consequently, he views the relationship of climate and commitment to be external, and the relationship of culture and commitment to be internal. Therefore, since organizational climate can be understood to cover strategies, norms, and desires of members (Allen & Meyer, 1990), commitments are instruments of climate. Organizational culture, on the other hand, derives from social identity and normality (Tajfel, 1982), so that commitments constitute culture.

Socialization and Careers

We continue our discussion of the role of culture and climate in HRM with specific focus on socialization and careers. Major (2000) argues in particular that organizational socialization contributes to the maintenance of culture in high-performing organizations. She posits that high-performing cultures require new ways of socializing newcomers to the organization, utilizing relational processes that result in mutual growth of both newcomers and existing members. Organizational socialization practices thus can be critical for both transmitting and perpetuating organizational culture. In this sense, she defines socialization as a learning activity, where organizational newcomers learn about the organization's culture as they make the transition from outsiders to insiders.

Major (2000), however, takes her argument a step further. She contends that, because continuous change becomes the norm (e.g., see Lawler, 1992), the rigidity of the traditional job description is becoming increasingly inconsistent with the fluidity of modern-day work. The traditional employment arrangement in which employers offer a lifetime career in the same organization in exchange for continued loyal service is essentially nonexistent today (Kanter, 1983). The new employment contract is characterized by a recognition that the employment relationship is likely to be transitory, so that both the employer and employee share responsibility for maintaining the relationship as long as it is mutually beneficial.

Socialization in this sense goes beyond the established models (e.g., Van Maanen, 1975), and takes the form of a reciprocal process that facilitates the growth of both newcomers and insiders. An especially important aspect of socialization is relational socialization, based on an interactionist view of the organization (Chatman, 1991). The relational view requires conceptualizing socialization as an individual growth process that occurs through experiences and connections with others. Therefore, relational socialization recognizes that such interaction has important ramifications in addition to newcomer learning. In this sense, the high-performing organization is able to maintain the high level of flexibility needed to meet the demands of today's rapidly changing economic and social environment.

Gunz (2000) moves this line of reasoning one step further, and considers the relationship between culture, climate, and organizational members' career development. He deals with this topic from an interesting and original perspective, but arrives at conclusions essentially similar to those reached by Major. In particular, he demonstrates convincingly that careers both affect and are affected by culture. Focusing on the phenomenon of 'managerial rationality,' he presents a model of careers based on a mutually reinforcing cycle, and argues that maintenance of the cycle reinforces and builds organizational cultures, while disruption of the cycle can lead to sudden and unexpected changes in culture.

Gunz (2000) notes that, to the layperson, a career implies a biography, or a life history. He argues, however, that a career in this sense is embedded within the concept of managerial rationality, the set of assumptions and beliefs that renders certain actions and possibilities sensible and rational, while others are ignored or considered 'unrealistic.' Managerial rationality is thus used to explain why different organizations in similar situations make strategic decisions distinctive of those organizations. These rationalities thus become the shared, taken-for-granted assumptions of managers who are involved in decisions of any consequence to the organization (see also Schein, 1985). In essence, they become a reflection of the organization's culture as we have defined the concept earlier in this chapter.

Within this framework, Gunz (2000) defines 'career streams' and 'career logic.' Career streams are the pattern in the flow of people through and between organizations. The analytical framework for linking career streams to organizational cultures is the 'organizational career logic' (OCL). An OCL is defined as the logic an observer infers to lie behind the pattern of moves he or she sees managers making in a given organization. OCLs are thus a manifestation of the shared beliefs and practices in the organization and are closely linked to the organization's culture.

In summary of this section, we have discussed four aspects of the relationship between organizational culture and climate and human resource management. We believe, however, that this topic is much wider than we have presented in this brief overview. Clearly, organizational culture and climate have important ramifications across the whole spectrum of HRM. Indeed, we are concerned at the apparent neglect of HRM topics in the organizational culture and climate literature. We feel that this whole area presents another challenging but nonetheless potentially fruitful area for research in future years.

INTERNATIONAL DIMENSIONS OF ORGANIZATIONAL CULTURE AND CLIMATE

Arguably, one of the more active areas of research in organizational culture over the past 20 years has been in respect of international dimensions. In particular, one of the core choices in multinational corporate strategy is determination of how the parent company and offshore subsidiaries reconcile differing cultural orientations (Lemark & Bracker, 1988). In this respect, Perlmutter (1984) has argued that multinationals can adopt one of four 'EPRG profiles.' These are (see also Chakravarthy & Perlmutter, 1985: 5):

Ethnocentrism, where the values of the parent company predominate;
Polycentrism, where the cultural values of the local subsidiary country are adopted;
Regiocentrism, where the cultural orientation of the parent organization is blended with regional values;
Geocentrism, where local subsidiaries are integrated through a 'global systems approach'

Clearly, a central consideration in this choice is our understanding of the substantive dimensions of organizational culture in the context of national culture. Indeed, little was known of these dimensions until publication of Hofstede's (1980) *Culture's Consequences*, based on data collected in the IBM Corporation in the 1970s. Hofstede's ideas as presented in this volume remain the basis of our understanding of the international dimensions of culture, although recent work by House and his colleagues (see House et al., 1999) holds the potential to refine Hofstede's work considerably in the immediate future. In this section, we review a variety of approaches to studying the international dimensions of organizational culture and climate, based largely on the contributions to the *HOCC*.

The wide dissemination of Hofstede's (1980) work has led to a proliferation of diverse views and opinions on his work, many of which are critical. Hofstede, however, argues that much of the criticism of his work is based on misunderstandings, and has recently sought to clarify some of these issues (Hofstede & Peterson, 2000). Hofstede and Peterson note in particular instances where culture dimensions are overused in international research. They point out that national culture and organizational culture are fundamentally different – the former is about values and the latter is about practices. Their point is that this has tended to obscure the benefits of understanding national culture effects on organizations.

They point out further that culture is a collective programming of the mind, and is manifested in four basic ways: (1) symbols, which carry a particular meaning for culture members; (2) heroes, culture's role models; (3) rituals, technically superfluous but socially necessary for a culture; and (4) values, feelings reflecting preferences for certain states of affairs over others (see Hofstede, 1997).

Thus, having come to use the idea of culture, analysts face questions of how to divide a historically and contemporaneously integrated world into parts, from mankind in general into cultural pluralism. In this respect, culture is not specific to management – it belongs to the total society of which management is a part. In this respect, based on Inkeles and Levinson (1969), Hofstede (1980) postulated that culture can be represented in terms of four key dimensions (later amended to include a fifth dimension):

Power distance. The extent to which the less powerful members of organizations and institutions accept and expect that power is distributed unequally.
Individualism vs. collectivism. The extent to which individuals are integrated into groups.
Masculinity vs. femininity. This dimension contrasts assertive and competitive values and practices with modest and caring values and practices.
Uncertainty avoidance. Intolerance for uncertainty and ambiguity.
Long-term vs. short-term orientation (introduced in Bond and 'The Chinese Culture Connection,' 1987). The contrast between thrift and perseverance (long term) vs. respect for tradition, fulfillment of social obligations, and protection of 'face' (short term).

The principal, and controversial, point that Peterson and Hofstede (2000) make is that organizational and national cultures differ markedly in many central features, and should not be considered to decompose into the same dimensional categories. Thus, specific cultural constructs meaningful for nations are likely to be less meaningful for organizations and vice versa. In this case, the cultural dimensions developed for understanding nations simply do not work when applied to organizations. Thus, based on Hofstede, Neuijen, Ohayv and Sanders (1990), they argue that dimensions such as process oriented vs. results oriented, job oriented vs. employee-oriented, professional vs. parochial, open systems vs. closed systems, tightly controlled vs. loosely controlled, and pragmatic vs. normative are the distinguishing features of organizational cultures.

This is not a view shared by House and his colleagues (1999), however. In a major cross-national study of organizational culture, the Global Leadership and Organizational Behavior Effectiveness (GLOBE) project, that House claims is the most extensive and definitive international organizational research project to date, culture is measured in organizations and in society-at-large using the same constructs, but in two forms: 'should be' (values) and 'as is' (practices). Dickson, Aditya and Chhokar (2000), in an overview of the project, show how culture, represented in Hofstede-like dimensions at both the societal and organizational level of analysis is internally consistent. Further, an important outcome of the GLOBE study is the presence of marked differences between responses on practice and value items of the organizational culture measures.

The debate about the nexus of national and organizational culture and values is also evident in the work of Shalom Schwartz and his colleagues (see Sagiv & Schwartz, 2000). Based on the Rokeach Value Survey, Sagiv and Schwartz present national value data from key socializing agents in society – schoolteachers and their students. They demonstrate the relationship of values to national differences in role stress and manager values. Unlike Hofstede (1980), but consistent with GLOBE, these authors agree with Hampden-Turner and Trompenaars' (1993) argument that national culture directly affects organizational culture and individual behavior. In this respect, Schwartz and his associate identify dimensions of (a) analyzing vs. integrating, (b) work vs. family size in setting pay, and (c) organization vs. friend as the key dimensions of organizational culture based on personal values.

Finally, we review two markedly different approaches to the study of international dimensions of organizational culture, based on the traditional paradigmatic differences reflected in the body of this chapter. In this respect, we look in particular at organizational and national culture in two East-Asian countries, Japan and China.

From an economic standpoint, one of the most fascinating contrasts in organizational culture has been between Japanese and American societal culture (Ouchi, 1981). Japan's rapid recovery after the Second World War and its consequent emergence as a world industrial power sparked keen interest in Japanese management practices. Depending on local political and economic climates, Japan has been viewed as exemplar, potential market, competitor, or strategic ally. In this respect, Brannen and Kleinberg (2000) review and critique the stimulus that analyses of Japanese national and organizational culture provided for North American organizational culture theory. They describe ways in which anthropological analysis can add needed complexity and dynamism to overly simple models and provide a base for analyzing intercultural dynamics.

Brannen and Kleinberg (2000) argue that the early literature on Japanese management is divided into roughly two distinct views of culture process: the culturalist and the convergence perspectives. The *culturalist* perspective stems from work that is primarily comparative, seeking to understand differences between Japanese and US organizations and management primarily within the context of the two distinct social realities. The *convergence* perspective downplays the 'culture-bound' or conservative effect of societal culture in favor of what might be termed a more or less 'culture-free' view. This view generally has it that, rather than societal culture, the limitations of technology and economic efficiency circumscribe the industrial forms that a society can adopt.

Brannen and Kleinberg (2000) argue further that, although the culturalist and convergence perspectives offer possible explanations for cultural differences, neither offers much theoretical substance for understanding cultural dynamics. In particular, these views imply a parochial view of culture where culture is seen as static, and no allowance is made

for the possibility that cultures are reinterpreted of over time. As an alternative, Brannen and Kleinberg offer a 'negotiated culture perspective,' based on an anthropological, ethnographic approach.

In particular the anthropological approach to studying the linkages between national culture and behavior in organizations offers critical insights based on complex societal factors that are not always amenable to other approaches. For example, in the Japanese context, account needs to be taken of the emphasis on conforming through *taido* (attitude), *kangaekata* (way of thinking), and *ishiki* (spirit). This also holds true at the individual level of analysis, where ethnographic research highlights the tension between conceptualizing culture as a group-level phenomenon and recognizing that, within any cultural grouping, a range of individual interpretations is expressed. In society, we are able to reproduce familiar social structures only because individual social actors have both discursive knowledge and tacit or practical knowledge. Brannen (1994) has conceptualized this as a three-zone continuum of culturally 'hypernormal,' 'normal' or 'marginally normal' individuals. In summary, Brannen and Kleinberg bring the anthropological and ethnographic perspectives to bear in the domain of cross-cultural dimensions of organizational culture, arguing that the richness of culture cannot be understood without deep appreciation of the underlying society and the individuals who live in it.

By contrast, Granrose, Huang and Reigadas (2000) ask whether the study of organizational culture has been too much shaped by issues in the Japan – US relationship that stimulated it. As a consequence, Granrose and her associates argue that attempts to understand organizations in other countries have been neglected, or even impeded. As an example, they analyze the cultural dynamics surrounding leadership in China based in the traditional dynamic between the more active Confucian and more passive Taoist approaches to proactive leadership, and including the more recent influence of Maoist and post-Maoist political systems. Granrose and her colleagues maintain that, while the basic idea and theories of organizational culture make sense in the China context, we should expect some quite substantial amendments to these ideas when they are applied in new locales.

Granrose et al. (2000) also point out that different organizational cultures arise from different ideologies of entrepreneurial founders, from industrial constraints, and from societal differences. Thus, as Trice and Beyer (1993) have asserted, ideologies have a cathartic function, legitimizing tension through moral claims and creation of group solidarity. In the context of China, industrial differences have been strongly constrained by national political ideology, leaving organizational differences in culture to reside primarily in differentiated emphasis of national cultural values, and in different adaptations to market principles. This is reflected in particular in the central principle of Confucian thought: the primacy of hierarchical interpersonal relationships of obligation of the superior to protect, to sustain, and to guide the subordinate in exchange for loyalty and obedience. According to Confucianism, therefore, change occurs through moral and educational actions of rulers and elite leaders and is implemented by loyal followers. These conditions have held true even during the upheavals of communism, the Great Leap Forward, the Cultural Revolution, and, more recently, the move to a Chinese market economy.

In particular, interpretation and pseudosymbols in Chinese organizational culture act to preserve face or appearance of status, so that formal positions are honored in official public interaction. These represent pseudosymbols to members of the organization (Trice & Beyer, 1993). Further, the power of real leaders in an organization rests primarily in the network of relationships they each possess as a result of their access to organizational and nonorganizational resources.

As a result, real symbols of leadership as interpreted in the entire cultural context reveal a mixture of a few symbols of communist egalitarianism and Chinese patriotism, together with many symbols of Taoist harmony and Confucian hierarchy. In China, the government has made many plans for economic change and these changes have created an ongoing series of critical incidents and external circumstances that require Chinese organizations to change. But organizational leaders have limited autonomy in how to enact the organizational change needed to bring the organization into line with national policies, and few norms or models that might cause them to act in transformational leadership ways. Ultimately, the organizational cultural change required in China today demands moving from the socialist way of thinking to the market way of thinking.

Granrose et al. (2000) conclude that the image of Chinese leaders they describe does not fit the traditional view of transformational leaders and is more likely to fit the view of institutional and transactional leaders used for consolidating existing cultures. Only a few Chinese market organization leaders initiate novelty in their organizations, and these individuals still have obligations to do so within the political framework set out by higher government officials and by obligations to their own *guanxi* (family) networks. Clearly, understanding organizational culture in this context, as is the case in Japan, requires new and innovative approaches that depart from the traditional paradigms of research that we are used to in Western cultures.

In conclusion of this section dealing with the international dimensions of organizational culture, it is clear that we know a great deal more than we did 25 years ago about differences in organizational culture across national boundaries. Nevertheless,

there is still a very long way to go. Hofstede's pioneering work, and the more recent GLOBE project give us only the faintest outline of how organizational cultures vary. Qualitative studies based on principles of anthropology also contribute to our knowledge in this respect, but the results often raise as many questions as they answer. Interestingly, the GLOBE study also incorporated in-depth qualitative studies of selected nations (see House et al., 1999), although these are yet to be published. Sample chapters available from the GLOBE website (http://mgmt3.ucalgary.ca/web/globe.nsf/index) provide some interesting and tantalizing insights into the complexity and wondrous diversity of organizational culture in different national cultural settings.

CONCLUSION

In this chapter, we have provided a somewhat unconventional review of contemporary developments in the field of organizational culture and climate. Our review has relied extensively on the *HOCC*, for which the first author was the lead editor and the second author worked in an administrative assistant. As was done in the handbook, this chapter has considered the topic from five perspectives: (a) consideration of the different paradigms and constructs in the field, (b) measures of culture and climate, and their relationship with performance, (c) the dynamic nature of culture and climate, (d) HRM aspects of culture and climate, and, finally, (e) international dimensions of culture and climate.

The overwhelming impression that emerges from our review is the robust and dynamic nature of the field. The progression from Lewin's pioneering work on climate, to Likert, and then to Pettigrew, to Schein and, more recently, to Schneider, the field is continually developing, with new research horizons opening up at every turn. Our discussion of the HRM implications of culture and climate, for instance, is a clear example of a field ripe for further research and development. Similarly, our brief coverage of some of the international dimensions of, and approaches to organizational culture and climate give a sense only of the multifarious possibilities that future research will need to deal with.

We made it clear at the outset that our review places us within the psychological domain, with a positivist epistemology, and an ontological perspective rooted in scientific realism. Nonetheless, it is apparent that our discussion in many places strays into areas of sociology and anthropology more consistent with the traditional view of culture. This is, we feel, an inevitable consequence of the convergence of the very concepts of climate and culture. Consistent with Denison (1990, 1996) and Payne (2000), we are firmly of the view that culture and climate are overlapping and complementary constructs. As such both are amenable to multimethods that cut across narrow disciplinary boundaries.

REFERENCES

Allen, N.J., & Meyer, J.P. (1990). The measurement and antecedents of affective, continuance, and normative commitment to the organization. *Journal of Occupational Psychology, 63,* 1–18.

Anderson, B. (1983). *Imagined communities: Reflections on the origin and spread of nationalism.* London: Verso Editions and NLB.

Ashforth, B., & Mael, F. (1989). Social identity theory and the organization. *Academy of Management Review, 14,* 20–39.

Ashkanasy, N.M., Broadfoot, L., & Falkus, S. (2000). Questionnaire measures of organizational culture. In N.M. Ashkanasy, C.P.M. Wilderom, & M.F. Peterson (Eds.), *Handbook of organizational culture and climate* (pp. 131–146). Thousand Oaks, CA: Sage.

Ashkanasy, N.M., & Holmes, S. (1995). Perceptions of organizational ideology following merger: A longitudinal study of merging accounting firms. *Accounting, Organizations, and Society, 20,* 19–34.

Ashkanasy, N.M., Wilderom, C.P.M., & Peterson, M.F. (Eds.) (2000a). *Handbook of organizational culture and climate.* Thousand Oaks, CA: Sage.

Ashkanasy, N.M., Wilderom, C.P.M., & Peterson, M.F. (2000b). Introduction. In N.M. Ashkanasy, C.P.M. Wilderom, & M.F. Peterson (Eds.), *Handbook of organizational culture and climate* (pp. 1–18). Thousand Oaks, CA: Sage.

Becker, H.S. (1960). Notes on the concept of commitment. *American Journal of Sociology, 66,* 32–40.

Beyer, J.M. (1981). Ideologies, values, and decision making in organizations. In P.C. Nystrom, & W.H. Starbuck (Eds.), *Handbook of organizational design* (Vol. 2, pp. 166–202). New York: Oxford University Press.

Beyer, J.M., Hannah, D.R., & Milton, L.P. (2000). Ties that bind: Culture and attachments in organizations. In N.M. Ashkanasy, C.P.M. Wilderom, & M.F. Peterson (Eds.), *Handbook of organizational culture and climate* (pp. 323–338). Thousand Oaks, CA: Sage.

Bond, M.H., & 23 coresearchers ('Chinese Culture Connection'). (1987). Chinese values and the search for culture-free dimensions of culture. *Journal of Cross-Cultural Psychology, 18,* 143–164.

Brannen, M.Y. (1994). *Your next boss is Japanese: Negotiating cultural change at a Western Massachusetts paper plant.* Unpublished doctoral dissertation, University of Massachusetts, Amherst.

Brannen, M.Y., & Kleinberg, J. (2000). Images of Japanese management and the development of organizational culture theory. In N.M. Ashkanasy, C.P.M. Wilderom, & M.F. Peterson (Eds.), *Handbook of organizational culture and climate* (pp. 387–400). Thousand Oaks, CA: Sage.

Cartwright, S. & Cooper, C.L. (1996). Managing mergers, acquisitions and strategic alliances: Integrating people and cultures. Oxford, UK: Butterworth-Heinemann.

Chakravarthy, B.S., & Perlmutter, H.V. (1985). Strategic planning for a global business. *Columbia Journal of World Business, 20,* 3–10.

Chatman, J.A. (1991). Matching people and organizations: Selection and socialization in public accounting firms. *Administrative Science Quarterly, 36,* 459–484.

Chusmir, L.H., & Parker, B. (1991). Gender and situational differences in managers' values: A look at work and home lives. *Journal of Business Research, 23,* 325–335.

Clegg, S.R., Hardy, C., & Nord, W.R. (Eds.) (1996). *Handbook of organization studies.* Thousand Oaks, CA: Sage.

Cooke, R.A., & Lafferty, J.C. (1994). *Organizational Culture Inventory – Ideal.* Prymouth, MI: Human Synergistics.

Cooke, R.A., & Rousseau, D.M. (1988). Behavioral norms and expectations: A quantitative approach to the assessment of organizational culture. *Group and Organization Studies, 13,* 245–273.

Cooke, R.A., & Szumal, J.L. (2000). Using the organizational culture inventory to understand the operating cultures of organizations. In N.M. Ashkanasy, C.P.M. Wilderom, & M.F. Peterson (Eds.), *Handbook of organizational culture and climate* (pp. 147–162). Thousand Oaks, CA: Sage.

Deal, T.E., & Kennedy, A.A. (1982). *Corporate cultures: The rites and rituals of corporate life.* Reading, MA: Addison-Wesley.

de Geus, A. (1997). *The living company.* Boston, MA: Harvard Business School Press.

Denison, D.R. (1990). *Corporate culture and organizational effectiveness.* New York: Wiley.

Denison, D.R. (1996). What is the difference between organizational culture and organizational climate? A native's point of view on a decade of paradigm wars. *Academy of Management Review, 21,* 619–654.

Dickson, M.W., Aditya, R.M., & Chhokar, J.S. (2000). Definition and interpretation in cross-cultural organizational culture research: Some pointers from the GLOBE research program. In N.M. Ashkanasy, C.P.M. Wilderom, & M.F. Peterson (Eds.), *Handbook of organizational culture and climate* (pp. 447–464). Thousand Oaks, CA: Sage.

Geertz, C. (1964). *Ideology as a cultural system.* In D.E. Apter (Ed.), *Ideology and discontent* (pp. 47–76). London: The Free Press of Glencoe.

Ginsberg, F., & Tsing, A.L. (Eds.) (1990). *Uncertain terms: Negotiating gender in American culture.* Boston: Beacon.

Granrose, C.S., Huang, Q., & Reigadas, E. (2000). Changing organizational cultures in Chinese firms. In N.M. Ashkanasy, C.P.M. Wilderom, & M.F. Peterson (Eds.), *Handbook of organizational culture and climate* (pp. 483–496). Thousand Oaks, CA: Sage.

Gunz, H. (2000). Organizational cultures and careers. In N.M. Ashkanasy, C.P.M. Wilderom, & M.F. Peterson (Eds.), *Handbook of organizational culture and climate* (pp. 369–384). Thousand Oaks, CA: Sage.

Guzzo, R.A., Noonan, K.A., & Elron, E. (1994). Expatriate managers and the psychological contract. *Journal of Applied Psychology, 79*, 617–626.

Hammond, J.H. (1973). Two sources of error in ecological correlations. *American Sociological Review, 38*, 764–777.

Hampden-Turner, C., & Trompenaars, A. (1993). *The seven cultures of capitalism*. Garden City, NY: Doubleday.

Harrison, R. (1995). *The collected papers of Roger Harrison*. San Francisco, CA: Jossey-Bass.

Hatch, M.J. (2000). The cultural dynamics of organizing and change. In N.M. Ashkanasy, C.P.M. Wilderom, & M.F. Peterson (Eds.), *Handbook of organizational culture and climate* (pp. 245–260). Thousand Oaks, CA: Sage.

Helms Mills, J.C.H., & Mills, A.J. (2000). Rules, sense-making, formative contexts, and discourse in the gendering of organizational culture. In N.M. Ashkanasy, C.P.M. Wilderom, & M.F. Peterson (Eds.), *Handbook of organizational culture and climate* (pp. 55–70). Thousand Oaks, CA: Sage.

Hofstede, G. (1980). *Culture's consequences: International differences in work-related values*. Beverly Hills, CA: Sage.

Hofstede, G. (1997). *Cultures and organizations: Software of the mind* (Rev. Ed.). New York: McGraw-Hill.

Hofstede, G., Bond, M.H., & Luk, C. (1993). Individual perceptions of organizational cultures. A methodological treatise on level of analysis. *Organizational Studies, 14*, 483–503.

Hofstede, G., Neuijen, B., Ohayv, D.D., & Sanders, G. (1990). *Administrative Science Quarterly, 35*, 286–316.

Hofstede, G., & Peterson, M.F. (2000). Culture: National values and organizational practices. In N.M. Ashkanasy, C.P.M. Wilderom, & M.F. Peterson (Eds.), *Handbook of organizational culture and climate* (pp. 401–416). Thousand Oaks, CA: Sage.

Homans, G.C. (1950). *The human group*. New York: Harcourt, Brace.

House, R.J., Hanges, P.J., Ruiz-Quintanilla, S.A., Dorfman, P.W., Javidan, M. Dickson, M., Gupta, V., & 170 country coinvestigators (1999). Cultural influences on leadership and organizations: Project GLOBE. In W. Mobley, J. Gessner, & V. Arnold (Eds.), *Advances in global leadership* (Vol. 1, pp. 171–234). Stamford, CN: JAI Press.

Hurst, D.K. (1995). *Crisis and renewal: Meeting the challenge of organizational change*. Boston, MA: Harvard Business School Press.

Inkeles, A. & Levinson, D.J. (1969). National character: the study of modal personality and socio-cultural systems. In G. Lindzey, & E. Aronson (Eds.), *The handbook of social psychology* (2nd ed., pp. 418–506). Reading, MA: Addison-Wesley.

James, L.R., DeMaree, R.G., & Wolf, G. (1984). Estimating within-group inter-rater reliability with and without response bias. *Journal of Applied Psychology, 69*, 85–90.

James, L.R., & McIntyre, M.D. (1996). Perceptions of organizational climate. In K.R. Murphy (Ed.), *Individual differences and behavior in organizations* (pp. 416–450). San Francisco: Jossey-Bass.

Johnson, J.W. (1996). Linking employee perceptions of service climate to customer satisfaction. *Personnel Psychology, 49*, 831–851.

Jordan, A.T. (1994). Organizational culture: The anthropological approach. In A.T. Jordan (Ed.), *Practicing anthropology in corporate America: Consulting on organizational culture* (pp. 3–16). Arlington, VA: American Anthropological Association.

Kahn, R.L., Wolfe, D.M., Quinn, R.P., Snoek, J.D., & Rosenthal, R.A. (1964). *Organizational stress: studies in role conflict and ambiguity*. New York: Wiley.

Kanter, R.M. (1983). *The change masters: Innovations and entrepreneurship in the American corporation*. New York: Simon & Schuster.

Kelman, H.C. (1958). Compliance, identification, and internalization: Three processes of attitude change. *Journal of Conflict Resolution, 2*, 51–60.

Kotter, J.P. (1995). Leading change: Why transformation efforts fail. *Harvard Business Review* (March-April). 59–67.

Kotter, J.P., & Heskett, J.L. (1992). *Corporate culture and performance*. New York: The Free Press.

Lawler, E.E. (1992). *The ultimate advantage: Creating the high-involvement organization*. San Francisco: Jossey-Bass.

Lawler, E.E. (1996). *From the ground up: Six principles for building the new logic corporation*. San Francisco: Jossey-Bass.

Lemak, D.J., & Bracker, J.S. (1988). A strategic contingency model of multinational corporate structure. *Strategic Management Journal, 9*, 521–526.

Lewin, K. (1948). *Resolving social conflicts*. New York: Harper.

Lewin, K. (1951). *Field theory in social psychology*. New York: Harper.

Lewin, K., Lippitt, R., & White, R.K. (1939). Patterns of aggressive behavior in experimentally created climates. *Journal of Social Psychology, 10*, 271–299.

Likert, R. (1961). *New patterns of management*. New York: McGraw-Hill.

Lincoln, Y.S., & Guba, E.G. (1989). *Naturalistic inquiry*. Beverley Hills, CA: Sage.

Major, D.A. (2000). Effective newcomer socialization into high performance organizational cultures. In N.M. Ashkanasy, C.P.M. Wilderom, & M.F. Peterson (Eds.), *Handbook of organizational culture and climate* (pp. 355–368). Thousand Oaks, CA: Sage.

Malinowski, B. (1960). *A scientific theory of culture*. New York: Oxford University Press. (Original work published in 1944.)

Markus, K.A. (2000). Twelve testable assertions about cultural dynamics and the reproduction of organizational change. In N.M. Ashkanasy, C.P.M. Wilderom, & M.F. Peterson (Eds.), *Handbook of organizational culture and climate* (pp. 297–308). Thousand Oaks, CA: Sage.

Martin, J. (1995). Organizational culture. In N. Nicholson, (Ed.), *Encyclopedic dictionary of organizational behaviour* (pp. 376–382). Oxford: Blackwell.

Meglino, B.M., Ravlin, E.C., & Adkins, C.L. (1989). A work values approach to organizational culture: A field test of the value congruence process and its relationship to individual outcomes. *Journal of Applied Psychology, 74,* 424–432.

Meglino, B.M., Ravlin, C.E., & Adkins, C.L. (1991). Value congruence and satisfaction with a leader: An examination of the role of interaction. *Human Relations, 44,* 481–495.

Merton, R. (1957). The role-set. *British Journal of Sociology, 8,* 106–120.

Meyer, A.D., & Allen, N.J. (1997). *Commitment in the workplace: Theory, research, and application.* Thousand Oaks, CA: Sage.

Meyerson, D. (1991). Acknowledging and uncovering ambiguities. In P. Frost, L. Moore, M. Louis, C. Lundberg, & J. Martin (Eds.), *Reframing organizational culture* (pp. 131–144). Beverly Hills, CA: Sage.

Michela, J.L., & Burke, W.W. (2000). Organizational culture and climate in transformations for quality and innovation. In N.M. Ashkanasy, C.P.M. Wilderom, & M.F. Peterson (Eds.), *Handbook of organizational culture and climate* (pp. 225–244). Thousand Oaks, CA: Sage.

Oakley, A. (1972). *Sex, gender and society.* London: Temple Smith.

O'Reilly, C.A., Chatman, J.A., & Caldwell, D. (1991). People and organizational culture: A profile comparison approach to assessing person-organization fit. *Academy of Management Journal, 34,* 487–516.

Ortner, S.B. (1973). On key symbols. *American Anthropologist, 75,* 1338–1346.

Ouchi, W.G. (1981). *Theory Z: How American business can meet the Japanese challenge.* Reading, MA: Addison-Wesley.

Ouchi, W.G., & Jaeger, A.M. (1978). Type Z organizations: Stability in the midst of mobility. *Academy of Management Review, 3,* 305–314.

Payne, R.L. (2000). Climate and culture: How close can they get? In N.M. Ashkanasy, C.P.M. Wilderom, & M.F. Peterson (Eds.), *Handbook of organizational culture and climate* (pp. 163–176). Thousand Oaks, CA: Sage.

Perlmutter, H.V. (1984). Building the symbiotic social enterprise: A social architecture for the future. *World Futures, 19*(3/4), 271–284.

Peterson, M.F., & Hofstede, G. (2000). Culture: National values and organizational practices. In N.M. Ashkanasy, C.P.M. Wilderom, & M.F. Peterson (Eds.), *Handbook of organizational culture and climate* (pp. 401–416). Thousand Oaks, CA: Sage.

Peterson, M.F., & Smith, P. (2000). Sources of meaning, organizations, and culture: Making sense of organizational events. In N.M. Ashkanasy, C.P.M. Wilderom, & M.F. Peterson (Eds.), *Handbook of organizational culture and climate* (pp. 101–116). Thousand Oaks, CA: Sage.

Porter, L.W., Steers, R.M., Mowday, R.T., & Boulian, P.V. (1974). Organizational commitment, job satisfaction, and turnover among psychiatric technicians. *Journal of Applied Psychology, 59,* 603–609.

Quinn, R.E., & Rohrbaugh, J. (1983). A spatial model of effectiveness criteria: Toward a competing values approach to organizational analysis. *Management Science, 29,* 363–377.

Rafaeli, A., & Worline, M. (2000). Symbols in organizational culture. In N.M. Ashkanasy, C.P.M. Wilderom, & M.F. Peterson (Eds.), *Handbook of organizational culture and climate* (pp. 71–84). Thousand Oaks, CA: Sage.

Reichers, A.E., & Schneider, B. (1990). Climate and culture: An evolution of constructs. In B. Schneider (Ed.), *Organizational climate and culture* (pp. 5–39). San Francisco: Jossey-Bass.

Roberts, K.H., Rousseau, D.M., & La Porte, T.R. (1994). The culture of high reliability: Quantitative and qualitative assessment aboard nuclear aircraft carriers. *Journal of High Technology Management Research, 5,* 141–161.

Robinson, S.L. (1996). Trust and breach of the psychological contract. *Administrative Science Quarterly, 41,* 574–599.

Robinson, S.L., & Rousseau, D.M. (1994). Violating the psychological contract: Not the exception but the norm. *Journal of Organizational Behavior, 15,* 245–259.

Rokeach, M. (1968). *Beliefs, attitudes and values: A theory of organization and change.* San Francisco: Jossey-Bass.

Rokeach, M. (1973). *The nature of human values.* New York: Free Press.

Rokeach, M., & Grube, J.W. (1979). Can values be manipulated arbitrarily? In M. Rokeach (Ed.), *Understanding human values: Individual and societal* (pp. 241–256). New York: Free Press.

Rousseau, D.M. (1985). Issues of level in organizational research: Multi-level and cross-level perspectives. In L.L. Cummings, & B.M. Staw (Eds.), *Research in organizational behavior* (Vol. 7, pp. 1–38). Greenwich, CN: JAI Press.

Rousseau, D.M. (1989). Psychological and implied contracts in organizations. *Employee Responsibilities and Rights Journal, 2,* 121–139.

Rousseau, D.M. (1990). Assessing organizational culture: The case for multiple methods. In B. Schneider (Ed.), *Organizational climate and culture* (pp. 153–192). San Francisco: Jossey-Bass.

Sagiv, L., & Schwartz, S.H. (2000). A new look at national culture: Illustrative applications to role stress and managerial behavior. In N.M. Ashkanasy, C.P.M. Wilderom, & M.F. Peterson (Eds.), *Handbook of organizational culture and climate* (pp. 417–436). Thousand Oaks, CA: Sage.

Salancik, G.R., & Pfeffer, J. (1978). A social information processing approach to job attitudes and task design. *Administrative Science Quarterly, 23,* 224–253.

Sathe, V. (1985). *Culture and related corporate realities.* Homewood, IL: Irwin.

Sathe, V., & Davidson, E.J. (2000). Toward a new conceptualization of culture change. In N.M. Ashkanasy, C.P.M. Wilderom, & M.F. Peterson (Eds.), *Handbook of organizational culture and climate* (pp. 279–296). Thousand Oaks, CA: Sage.

Schein, E.H. (1985). *Organizational culture and leadership*. San Francisco: Jossey-Bass.

Schein, E.H. (1990). Organizational culture. *American Psychologist, 45*, 109–119.

Schein, E.H. (1992). *Organizational culture and leadership* (2nd ed.). San Francisco: Jossey-Bass.

Schneider, B. (1975). Organizational climates: An essay. *Personnel Psychology, 28*, 447–479.

Schneider, B., Bowen, D.E., Ehrhart, M.G., & Holcombe, K.M. (2000). The climate for service. In N.M. Ashkanasy, C.P.M. Wilderom, & M.F. Peterson (Eds.), *Handbook of organizational culture and climate* (pp. 21–36). Thousand Oaks, CA: Sage.

Schroder, R. (1992). *Max Weber and the sociology of culture*. London: Sage.

Schultz M., & Hatch M.J. (1996). Living with multiple paradigms: The case of paradigm interplay in organizational culture studies. *Academy of Management, Review, 21*, 529–557.

Senge, P.M. (1993). *The fifth discipline: The art and practice of the learning organization*. London: Century Books.

Stackman, R.W., Pinder, C.C., & Connor, P.E. (2000). Values lost: Redirecting research on values in the workplace. In N.M. Ashkanasy, C.P.M. Wilderom, & M.F. Peterson (Eds.), *Handbook of organizational culture and climate* (pp. 37–54). Thousand Oaks, CA: Sage.

Tajfel, H. (1982). Social psychology of intergroup relations. *Annual Review of Psychology, 33*, 1–39.

Trice, H.M., & Beyer, J.M. (1993). *The culture of work organizations*. Englewood Cliffs, NJ: Prentice-Hall.

Turner, V. (1982). *From ritual to theatre: The human seriousness of play*. New York: PAJ.

Tyrrell, M.W.D. (2000). Hunting and gathering in the early silicon age: Cyberspace, jobs, and the reformulation of organizational culture. In N.M. Ashkanasy, C.P.M. Wilderom, & M.F. Peterson (Eds.), *Handbook of organizational culture and climate* (pp. 85–100). Thousand Oaks, CA: Sage.

Van Maanen, J. (1975). Police socialization: A longitudinal examination of job attitudes in an urban police department. *Administrative Science Quarterly, 20*, 207–228.

Virtanen, T. (2000). Commitment and the study of organizational climate and culture. In N.M. Ashkanasy, C.P.M. Wilderom, & M.F. Peterson (Eds.), *Handbook of organizational culture and climate* (pp. 339–354). Thousand Oaks, CA: Sage.

Weber, M. (1947). *The theory of social and economic organization* (A.R. Henderson, & T. Parsons, Eds.). New York: Oxford University Press.

Weber, Y. (2000). Measuring cultural fit in mergers and acquisitions. In N.M. Ashkanasy, C.P.M. Wilderom, & M.F. Peterson (Eds.), *Handbook of organizational culture and climate* (pp. 309–320). Thousand Oaks, CA: Sage.

Wilderom, C.P.M., Glunk, U., & Maslowski, R. (2000). Organizational culture as a predictor of organizational performance. In N.M. Ashkanasy, C.P.M. Wilderom, & M.F. Peterson (Eds.), *Handbook of organizational culture and climate* (pp. 193–210). Thousand Oaks, CA: Sage.

Wiley, J.W. (1996). Linking survey results to customer satisfaction and business performance. In A.I. Kraut (Ed.), *Organizational surveys* (pp. 330–359). San Francisco: Jossey-Bass.

Wiley, J.W., & Brooks, S. (2000). The high performance organizational climate: How workers describe top performing units. In N.M. Ashkanasy, C.P.M. Wilderom, & M.F. Peterson (Eds.), *Handbook of organizational culture and climate* (pp. 177–192). Thousand Oaks, CA: Sage.

Woodcock, M. (1989). *Clarifying organizational values*. Brookfield, VT: Gower Publishing.

Woods, J.A. (1997). The six values of a quality culture. *National Productivity Review, 16*(2), 49–55.

Zammuto, R.F., Gifford, B., & Goodman, E. (2000). Managerial ideologies, organization culture and the outcomes of innovation: A competing values perspective. In N.M. Ashkanasy, C.P.M. Wilderom, & M.F. Peterson (Eds.), *Handbook of organizational culture and climate* (pp. 261–278). Thousand Oaks, CA: Sage.

21

Cognitive Processes in Strategic Management: Some Emerging Trends and Future Directions

GERARD P. HODGKINSON

Over the last two decades or so, there has been an explosion of scholarly interest in the application of psychological concepts, theories, and techniques in an attempt to better understand processes of strategy formulation and implementation in organizations, and as a basis for intervening within these processes. In this chapter three interrelated areas of theory and research from within this highly exciting and rapidly developing specialty are critically evaluated: (1) the nature and significance of judgemental heuristics and cognitive biases in strategic decision making; (2) top team composition, executive cognition and organizational outcomes; and (3) the analysis of mental representations of competitive environments. A number of methodological limitations common to each area are identified and various directions for future studies delineated.

INTRODUCTION

The psychology of strategic management is an emergent subfield situated at the interface between industrial, work and organizational psychology and several interrelated areas of management inquiry, especially strategy and marketing. The purpose of this chapter is to survey a number of key developments that are currently taking place within this highly exciting and rapidly developing specialty with a view to identifying some of the more salient issues worthy of research attention by industrial, work and organizational psychologists.

Arguably, strategic management is one of the most important but also one of the least understood areas of organizational life (Mintzberg, Ahlstrand & Lampel, 1998). Whereas other areas of management deal with routinized, operationally specific issues and problems of a short-term nature, strategic management addresses organization-wide issues

and problems of a fundamental nature. Strategic issues and problems, by definition, tend to be relatively ambiguous, complex, and surrounded by risk and uncertainty:

> Strategy is the direction and scope of an organization over the long term, which achieves advantage for the organization through its configuration of resources within a changing environment, to meet the needs of markets and to fulfil stakeholders' expectations. (Johnson & Scholes, 1999: 10)

Such is the complex nature of strategy and strategic management that no one single base discipline of the social sciences can adequately address the problems that fall within its domain. Within this field, researchers and practitioners alike must be able and willing to gain insights from a range of disciplines, in much the same way that the medical sciences draw upon biology, chemistry, physics, and so on, in order to refine theoretical and practical understanding. Consequently, isolating psychological contributions within the strategy field is potentially problematic. Ultimately, a broad range of social, economic, political, technical, and financial factors determine the success or failure of an organization's strategy and, accordingly, a range of cross-disciplinary perspectives are required in order to make sense of this phenomenon (see, e.g., Langley, Mintzberg, Pitcher, Posada & Saint-Macary, 1995; Mintzberg et al., 1998). However, the discipline of psychology potentially has much to contribute to this vitally important, multidisciplinary endeavour and a sufficient volume of work has now accumulated to warrant the status of an emergent subfield: the psychology of strategic management (Hodgkinson, 2001; Sparrow, 1994).

As we shall see, some of the most interesting developments are presently occurring as a result of scholars employing psychological theory and research in areas that have traditionally been the preserve of industrial organization economists and organizational sociologists. At the heart of these developments has been a fundamental shift away from a preoccupation with traditional 'content' issues in strategic management, for example, questions about the merits of various strategies such as organic growth versus mergers and acquisitions, related versus unrelated diversification, and so on. Concern is now much more with 'process' issues, regarding *how* particular strategies come to be formulated and implemented within organizations. Over the last two decades or so, there has been an explosion of scholarly interest in the application of psychological concepts, theories, and techniques in an attempt to better understand, and as a basis for intervening within, these processes (see, e.g., Eden & Ackermann, 1998; Eden & Spender, 1998; Finkelstein & Hambrick, 1996; Flood, Dromgoole, Carroll & Gorman, 2000; Hodgkinson & Thomas, 1997; Huff, 1990; Huff & Jenkins, in press; Porac & Thomas, 1989; Walsh, 1995).

The range of issues that can be legitimately addressed from a psychological perspective is potentially as broad as the entire field of strategic management itself, covering all aspects of strategy formulation, choice, and implementation. In recent years, researchers have investigated topics as varied as the psychological impact of mergers and acquisitions (Cartwright & Cooper, 1990, 1993; Hogan & Overmyer-Day, 1994), cognitive processes in the boardroom (Forbes & Milliken, 1999), strategic issue processing, image, and organizational identity (Dutton & Dukerich, 1991; Dutton & Jackson, 1987; Gioia & Thomas, 1996; Jackson, 1992; Jackson & Dutton, 1988), the nature and impact of the personality characteristics (especially locus of control beliefs) of the CEO (and other organization members) on organizational structure, strategy, and performance (Boone & De Brabander, 1993, 1997; Boone, De Brabander & van Witteloostuijn, 1996;

Hodgkinson, 1992, 1993; Miller, 1983; Miller, Kets De Vries & Toulouse, 1982; Miller & Toulouse, 1986), and psychological processes of strategic renewal (Barr, 1998; Barr & Huff, 1997; Barr, Stimpert & Huff, 1992; Floyd & Lane, 2000; Huff, Huff & Thomas, 1992; Lant, Milliken & Batra, 1992). Inevitably, therefore, the present chapter must be selective in its coverage. Here, attention is confined to a consideration of three interrelated areas of theory and research that have each, in differing ways and across varying levels of analysis, addressed key problems in strategic management from a cognitive perspective: (1) the nature and significance of judgemental heuristics and cognitive biases in strategic decision making; (2) cognitive processes in executive teams; and (3) the analysis of mental representations of competitive environments. Systematically bringing together theory and research from each of these key areas, within a unified review, enables the following sorts of question to be addressed:

How do the information-processing limitations of individual decision makers impact upon their understanding of strategic issues and problems and what practical steps can be taken to overcome these limitations?

What are the determinants that shape senior managers' and other stakeholders' mental representations of strategic issues and problems?

How do these mental representations impact upon key decision processes and individual and organizational outcomes?

By what processes and mechanisms do industry and market boundaries and competitive practices evolve and change?

A considerable volume of research has amassed over recent years which has been directed towards these sorts of questions. Drawing on the fields of cognitive and organizational psychology, Sparrow (2000) has argued that the many changes currently taking place within the world of work are placing unprecedented informational burdens upon those responsible for strategy formulation and implementation. Unfortunately, however, as much of the work reviewed in the remaining sections of this chapter demonstrates, information processing is not something that strategists do particularly well. A number of cognitive limitations have been identified which potentially might undermine the process of strategizing. Rather than simply viewing these limitations as a source of error, however, as Sparrow (2000) has observed, it is more fruitful to consider them as yet another strategic risk that has to be managed. Potentially, there are a number of useful insights that can be gained from the theory and research reviewed in this chapter to assist the reflective practitioner with this task.

HEURISTICS AND BIASES IN STRATEGIC DECISION MAKING

By their very nature, strategic decisions involve risk and uncertainty. Although there has been much discussion of risk and uncertainty within the field of strategic management, until relatively recently, most of this work has been informed by a neoclassical economics perspective, developed from the premise that decision makers and those concerned with the implementation of strategy are inherently rational actors. This perspective contrasts sharply with the predominant view held by members of the behavioural decision research (BDR) community.

Starting from the basic premise that, due to fundamental information-processing limitations, individuals are characterized by 'bounded rationality' (Simon, 1955, 1956), behavioural decision researchers (e.g., Kahneman, Slovic & Tversky, 1982; Tversky & Kahneman, 1974) have amassed a considerable volume of evidence that suggests that in order to render the world manageable, decision makers employ a variety of heuristics (or 'rules-of-thumb'). Whilst these heuristics enable decision makers to cope with a complex and uncertain world by making a number of simplifying assumptions that reduce the burden of information processing that would otherwise ensue, an unfortunate, latent consequence is that they can give rise to a variety of cognitive biases which in turn may result in inappropriate/suboptimal decisions (Bazerman, 1998; Goodwin & Wright, 1998). Potentially, this body of theory and research may provide some interesting and challenging insights into the processes of strategy making and implementation. Accordingly, over the past two decades or so there has been a growing interest in the application of BDR concepts, theories, and techniques within the field of strategic management, in an effort to better understand the nature and significance of the human information-processing limitations that characterize the individual decision maker. In so doing, however, strategy researchers have fully recognized that strategies are ultimately the product of a negotiated order (Walsh & Fahay, 1986) and that strategic decisions take place within the context of a wider sociopolitical arena (Johnson, 1987; Mintzberg, 1983; Pettigrew, 1973, 1985), the consequence of which is that the conflicting cognitions of differing stakeholders and stakeholder groups must some how be reconciled (see, e.g., Schwenk, 1989, 1995). Rarely do individuals take such decisions in isolation. Nevertheless, by focusing on the judgement processes that individual decision makers bring to bear upon particular problems within the wider sociopolitical arena of the organization, potentially BDR has much to contribute to our understanding of strategy formulation and implementation, not only in terms of theory building and theory testing, but also from a practical, interventionist standpoint.

The implications of BDR for understanding and potentially improving strategic decision making have been recognized for some time by researchers in strategic management. Schwenk (1984), for example, identified three different phases of the strategic decision process ('goal formulation and problem identification', 'alternative generation and evaluation', and 'selection') and systematically considered the possibility that senior managers may deploy particular heuristics (with the consequent danger that attendant biases may also accrue) during each phase of the process (see also Barnes, 1984; Das & Teng, 1999; Schwenk, 1995). Schwenk (1984) identified a set of heuristics and biases, then amassed supporting evidence for their presence in organizations by analysing accounts of how actual strategic decisions were taken in practice. He argued that the processes outlined in these descriptions match the processes thought to underpin particular heuristics and biases. He also illustrated how attendant biases arising from the deployment of these heuristics may have led to important errors of judgement, thereby reducing the overall quality of strategic decisions. For example, he describes a situation in which the head of an American retail organization held a very strong belief that there would be a depression at the end of the Second World War. This belief was based on the knowledge that a similar depression had occurred at the end of the First World War. So strongly held was this belief, that the individual concerned decided not to expand his business following increased competition induced by a major rival, a decision which led to a permanent loss of market share. Schwenk argued that this executive's erroneous belief about an impending depression, the primary reason for his poor decision, can be explained as a dysfunctional consequence of deploying the representativeness heuristic.

The representativeness heuristic involves judging the likelihood of an event based on the similarity between that event and existing knowledge about similar occurrences. Individuals who base their judgements solely on this heuristic often neglect other vitally important information that should be taken into account, as illustrated by the following problem – taken from Bazerman (1998: 19):

> *Mark is finishing his MBA at a prestigious university. He is very interested in arts and at one time considered a career as a musician. Is he more likely to take a job (a) in the management of the arts, or (b) with a management consulting firm?*

Most people opt for (a) because the description of Mark matches well, or is highly representative of that career path. In reality (b) is more likely. In point of fact, there is a larger absolute number of management consultants fitting Mark's description.

Whilst there are many MBAs in management consulting, there are relatively few in arts jobs, due to the fact that there are so few of the latter jobs available. By basing the judgement solely on representativeness, the actual frequencies of occurrence of the two types of job, called the base rate information, is overlooked.

Table 21.1 presents a selective summary of some of the many other heuristics and biases identified by behavioural decision researchers which Schwenk (1988) has argued are of potential key significance in the context of strategic decision making (see also Das & Teng, 1999; Schwenk, 1995). To the extent that this is the case, intervention techniques are required that will enable strategists to question their underlying assumptions with a view to debiasing their judgements.

In recent years there has been a steady accumulation of evidence both within laboratory and field settings (reviewed in Das & Teng, 1999, and Schwenk, 1995) which suggests that many of the phenomena initially identified by the BDR community are indeed highly applicable in the context of strategic decision making. Two trends are evident within this stream of research: the first has continued the line of inquiry established by Schwenk (1984), using documentary sources and anecdotal evidence in an attempt to identify the occurrence of particular heuristics and biases in the context of organizational strategic decision making; the second has employed experimental techniques, in an attempt to replicate and extend BDR findings, using relatively complex decision scenarios of direct relevance to this domain, and has employed a mixture of experienced and inexperienced research participants.

Evidence from Documentary Sources

Given the obvious difficulties of gaining organizational access to study ongoing strategic decisions, the vast majority of work in this area has utilized documentary sources in an attempt to identify whether or not particular heuristics and biases are evident within this context (for representative examples, see Barnes, 1984; Duhaime & Schwenk, 1985; Huff & Schwenk, 1990; Lyles & Thomas, 1988; Zajac & Bazerman, 1991). Like Schwenk (1984), many of these authors have also considered the need to debias managers' judgements, in an attempt improve the quality of strategic decision processes. Whilst the numerous examples of heuristics and biases identified by this group of researchers often appear quite compelling, in the absence of further supporting evidence, there are some obvious methodological limitations that preclude a wholesale acceptance of the findings. A major drawback of using documentary sources in strategic management research is that these documents are prepared

for particular audiences. Consequently, it is difficult to ascertain the extent to which the biases observed are genuinely a product of executives' sensemaking processes and/or a deliberate attempt to influence the perceptions of the stakeholders to whom the various documentary sources were initially directed. Clearly, therefore, we need to search for additional methods that will enable researchers to scrutinize these findings with greater rigour. One possibility in this respect, as advocated by Schwenk (1982, 1995), is laboratory research, suitably adapted in order to test directly whether or not the heuristics and biases identified by the BDR community, largely on the basis of undergraduate students performing much simpler, experimental tasks, readily generalize to the strategy arena.

Evidence from Experimental Research

As noted by Schwenk (1982), suitably adapted, the experimental method provides a useful means for ensuring that research is *both* rigorous *and* of relevance to practitioners, an essential requirement within the applied field of strategic management. Unfortunately, however, despite the obvious advantages of laboratory research in this particular context, the experimental method has been greatly underutilized (Hodgkinson & Maule, in press; Schwenk, 1995). Nevertheless, sufficient evidence has accumulated in order to demonstrate the value of this approach, as illustrated by recent research into the framing bias.

The framing bias arises when trivial changes to the way in which a decision problem is presented or 'framed', emphasizing either the potential gains or the potential losses, lead to reversals of preference, with decision makers being risk averse when gains are highlighted and risk seeking when losses are highlighted (Kahneman & Tversky, 1979, 1984; Tversky & Kahneman, 1981). In a pair of laboratory experiments, designed to explore 'the psychological context of strategic decision making', Bateman and Zeithaml (1989) investigated the impact of decisional frame (positive versus negative future outlook), together with feedback on a past decision (success versus failure) and perceived organizational slack (high versus low) on a reinvestment decision. In the first experiment, involving undergraduate students, all three variables were found to have main and interactive effects on the dependent variable (the amount in U.S. dollars that participants were prepared to reinvest). The second experiment, involving business executives, combined the decision feedback and organizational slack variables (i.e., failure feedback/low slack versus success feedback/high slack) and investigated the impact of this combined variable and decisional frame on the amount that participants were prepared

Table 21.1   *An evaluation of selected heuristics and biases in terms of their effects on strategic decision making*

Heuristic/bias	Effects
1. Availability	Judgements of the probability of easily recalled events are distorted
2. Selective perception	Expectations may bias observations of variables relevant to strategy
3. Illusory correlation	Encourages the belief that unrelated variables are correlated
4. Conservatism	Failure to revise sufficiently forecasts based on new information
5. Law of *small* numbers	Overestimation of the degree to which small samples are representative of populations
6. Regression bias	Failure to allow for regression to the mean
7. Wishful thinking	Probabilities of desired outcomes are judged to be inappropriately high
8. Illusion of control	Overestimation of personal control over outcomes
9. Logical reconstruction	'Logical' reconstruction of events which cannot be accurately recalled.
10. Hindsight bias	Overestimation of predictability of past events

Source: adapted from C.R. Schwenk (1988). The cognitive perspective on strategic decision making. *Journal of Management Studies*, 25, 41–55. © Blackwell Publishers Limited. Reproduced by kind permission of the publisher.

to reinvest. A significant main effect was obtained for decisional frame, together with a significant interaction effect between decisional frame and the combined feedback and organizational slack variable. Although in the predicted direction, the main effect for the combined feedback and organizational slack variable was found to be nonsignificant. Whilst the findings of these studies suggest that the way in which information concerning strategic decisions is framed can have an impact on the choice preferences of individuals, as noted by Hodgkinson and Maule (in press), merely demonstrating that this phenomenon occurs in the context of laboratory studies involving strategic decision scenarios does not enable us to answer two vital questions: (1) what is the precise cognitive mechanism underpinning this phenomenon? (2) What steps might be taken to minimize its effects?

Recent experimental research conducted by the present author and several of his colleagues (Hodgkinson, Bown, Maule, Glaister & Pearman, 1999; Hodgkinson & Maule, in press) has begun investigating these issues directly. Our own experimental studies, also using a combination of inexperienced participants (undergraduates) and senior managers (within a financial services organization) have uncovered evidence for the framing bias, supporting the contention that, left unchecked, this particular bias is likely to undermine the quality of strategic decision making in organizational field settings. In addition, we have investigated whether the framing biases induced by virtue of our experimental manipulations could be eliminated, using structured decision aids. One technique in particular, causal cognitive mapping (Axelrod, 1976; Huff, 1990), has been examined, on the basis of a growing body of evidence suggesting that more effortful thought prior to making decision choices can eliminate the framing bias (e.g., Maule, 1995; Sieck & Yates, 1997).

Causal mapping techniques fall within a general class of cognitive mapping procedures that Huff

(1990: 16) has categorized as methods for revealing understanding of 'influence, causality and system dynamics'. In their most basic form, causal maps can be depicted graphically, using the medium of the influence diagram (Diffenbach, 1982). Using this approach, variables are depicted as nodes in a network, interconnected by a series of arrow-headed pathways, terminating in each case on the dependent variable(s). The simplest forms of the technique are restricted to a consideration of positive (increases in one variable cause corresponding increases in one or more other variables), negative (increases in one variable cause corresponding decreases in one or more other variables), and neutral (no causality implied) relationships. More sophisticated variants of the technique enable these relationships to be differentially weighted, on the basis of the participant's belief strength, for example, as illustrated in Figure 21.1, or on the degree of certainty/uncertainty surrounding each particular causal assertion.

Our findings have confirmed our predictions in relation to both our student and managerial samples. In both cases, the application of causal mapping prior to choice eliminated the framing bias, providing supporting evidence for its efficacy as an intervention technique for use in practical settings. At the time of writing this chapter, ongoing work is exploring the structure and content of the participants' cognitive maps with a view to better understanding the ways in which the framing bias impacts on individuals' mental representations of strategic issues and problems and the means by which causal mapping techniques attenuate this bias.

Summary and Implications

In summary, the work reviewed in this section has illustrated some of the ways in which BDR has

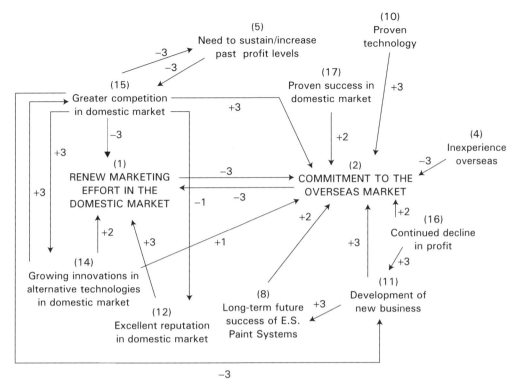

Figure 21.1 *Example of a causal cognitive map elicited from a participant in study 1 of the framing experiments conducted by Hodgkinson et al. (1999). (Source: G.P. Hodgkinson, & A.J. Maule [in press]. The individual in the strategy process: insights from behavioural decision research and cognitive mapping. In A.S. Huff, & M. Jenkins [Eds.],* Mapping Strategic Knowledge. *London: Sage.)*

contributed to our understanding of organizational strategic decision making by identifying and explaining various fundamental limitations inherent within the thinking and reasoning of the individual decision maker. Taken together, the findings of the various lines of inquiry reviewed in this section provide compelling evidence that BDR has much to contribute to the field of strategic management, not only in terms of enriching our understanding of the nature of strategic decision making, but also the development and evaluation of procedures for facilitating this vitally important activity.

The total body of evidence presented points overwhelmingly to the conclusion that a number of the heuristics and biases identified in the laboratory by the BDR community, using relatively simple decision tasks and inexperienced participants, are equally applicable in the comparatively complex situations that confront the senior executive. The accumulated findings also illustrate the value of combining a variety of methodological approaches in conducting applied research of this nature. The various attempts to match documentary descriptions

of actual strategic decisions to heuristics and biases previously identified in the laboratory are highly commendable in so far as this line of inquiry has enabled researchers to assess the relevance of this earlier work in this particular context. However, the documentary approach clearly lacks the rigour of the laboratory and, as noted earlier, we must be mindful of the fact that this approach relies heavily on the researcher's *post hoc* interpretation of data that was originally prepared for other purposes. On the other hand, while the laboratory ensures greater control, and thus has the potential to enable the researcher to disentangle the myriad cause-and-effect relationships underpinning real-life strategic decision episodes, no matter how experienced the participants and regardless of how detailed the case materials employed, the situation is always artificial, i.e., lacking ecological validity. Ultimately, if BDR is to realize its potential within the strategy field, both approaches are required, so as to ensure that findings continue to accumulate which are both well-grounded methodologically and of relevance to this particular focal domain (cf. Schwenk, 1995: 487).

TOP TEAM COMPOSITION, EXECUTIVE COGNITION AND ORGANIZATIONAL OUTCOMES

The Upper Echelons Perspective

For much of the past two decades the 'upper echelons' perspective, originated by Hambrick and Mason (1984), has dominated the literature on top management teams (TMTs). According to Hambrick and Mason (1984: 193) it is the values and 'cognitive base' of 'the dominant coalition,' the group of powerful actors at the very top of the organization, that ultimately determine its direction and outcomes. A diagrammatic representation of their model, recently revised and updated by Finkelstein and Hambrick (1996), which seeks to capture the cognitive processes underpinning strategic choice in executive teams, is shown in Figure 21.2.

As can be seen in Figure 21.2, Hambrick and Mason posit a three-stage filtration process comprising: (1) a limited field of vision; (2) selective perception; and (3) interpretation, which they argue underpins the tendency for executives to perceive only a limited portion of all potentially relevant information in the internal and external environment, often deriving idiosyncratic interpretations of reality and assigning differential weights to the various potential outcomes. The first stage of this filtration process, limited field of vision, arises from the fact that decision makers are exposed to a limited subset of the available stimuli, while the second stage, selective perception, occurs due to the fact that only a portion of the stimulus information within their limited field of vision is actually attended to. The third stage, interpretation, entails the attachment of meaning to stimuli. Starbuck and Milliken (1988) employ the term 'sensemaking' to describe this stage (see also Weick, 1995, 2001).

Until very recently, researchers investigating cognitive processes in top management teams have tended to utilize indirect methods of assessment, for much the same reason as researchers studying heuristics and biases in strategic decision making at the individual level of analysis: problems of gaining access. Drawing on a range of psychological and sociological studies, Hambrick and Mason argued that a variety of observable managerial characteristics such as age, socioeconomic roots, functional background, executive tenure, and education shape the values and beliefs of the individual manager, and in view of the obvious practical difficulties associated with attempting to study directly the psychological characteristics of senior executives, they advocated the use of these external characteristics as indicators of the givens that members of the TMT bring to bear on their administrative situation (Hambrick & Mason, 1984: 196).

Empirical Tests and Conceptual Refinements

Numerous studies exploring the correlates of top team demography in an attempt to empirically validate this model have subsequently been reported. Outcomes as varied as innovation (Bantel & Jackson, 1989), firm performance (Norburn & Birley, 1988), the nature and extent of strategic change (Wiersema & Bantel, 1992), bankruptcy (D'Avini, 1990), and, more recently, corporate illegal activity (Daboub, Rasheed, Priem & Gray, 1995; Williams, Barrett & Brabston, 2000), firms' competitive moves (Hambrick, Cho & Chen, 1996) and levels of international involvement in diversification strategies (Sambharya, 1996) have been investigated, a variety of indicators designed to capture the demographic composition (homogeneity vs. heterogeneity) of TMTs (reviewed in Tsui & Gutek, 1999) having been employed as predictor variables. In general, these studies (reviewed in Finkelstein, & Hambrick, 1996; Lau & Murnighan, 1998; Milliken & Martins, 1996; Pelled, 1996; Pettigrew, 1992; and Williams & O'Reilly, 1998) have yielded mixed findings, and, in an attempt to increase the predictive efficacy of top team demography, in recent years researchers have utilized increasingly sophisticated research designs, incorporating the use of control variables and contingency factors such as environmental turbulence (Haleblain & Finkelstein, 1993; Keck, 1997) and strategy process variables such as communication and social integration (e.g., Smith, Smith, Olian, Sims, O'Bannon & Scully, 1994) and decision comprehensiveness and debate (Simons, Pelled & Smith, 1999). Several other methodological enhancements, such as the use of longitudinal research designs in conjunction with time series data (e.g., Keck & Tushman, 1993) have also been introduced in an effort to strengthen results.

A number of researchers have begun to develop new theoretical constructs, in an effort to refine understanding of the linkages between team composition on the one hand, and team processes and outcomes on the other. The notion of 'demographic faultlines' (Lau & Murnighan, 1998), for example, is one such development, introduced as an explanation for subgroup processes of conflict. Demographic faultlines are hypothetical dividing lines, the effect of which is to split groups into subgroups on the basis of one or more key attributes, such as age or educational experience. According to Lau and Murnighan, the formation of conflicting subgroups becomes much more likely when the demographic characteristics within a group form a faultline and are related to the group's task.

In a second development, Pelled (1996) has introduced the notions of 'visibility' (the extent to which the demographic variables in question are observable

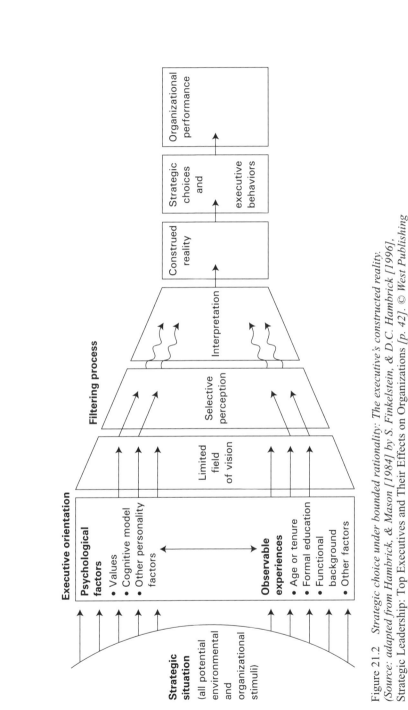

Figure 21.2 *Strategic choice under bounded rationality: The executive's constructed reality.*
(Source: adapted from Hambrick, & Mason [1984] by S. Finkelstein, & D.C. Hambrick [1996],
Strategic Leadership: Top Executives and Their Effects on Organizations [p. 42]. © West Publishing
Company. Reproduced by kind permission of the publisher.)

by group members) and 'job relatedness' (the extent to which the variables in question shape perspectives and skills directly related to tasks) in an attempt to account for the mixed effects of diversity on performance observed in previous studies. According to Pelled, affective conflict within the team is primarily a function of 'high visibility variables', such as age gender and race, while substantive (task) conflict is influenced by a variety of 'job relatedness variables' (e.g., organizational tenure, educational and functional background). Both of these relationships are mediated by group longevity, and turnover in the team is determined by affective conflict, whereas cognitive task performance is jointly influenced by substantive and affective conflict.

Recent Challenges to the Upper Echelons Perspective

Whilst these recent conceptual and empirical developments have undoubtedly extended and, to a certain extent, redirected the demographic approach to the analysis of TMTs, suggesting new hypotheses that may account for several of the discrepancies observed in traditional upper echelons research, other researchers have called into question fundamentally the adequacy of this whole approach as a basis for understanding the nature and significance of organizational processes (Lawrence, 1997; Pettigrew, 1992). Ultimately, the various conceptual refinements and empirical studies outlined above fail to address a philosophical issue which strikes at the very heart of the upper echelons tradition, and which calls into question the use of demography in the organizational sciences more generally, namely, the extent to which the external, background characteristics of the executive are adequate proxy variables for the assessment of perceptions and beliefs and other key intervening variables (cf. Pfeffer, 1983).

Relatively few studies have directly tested the assumed relationship between individual external characteristics and cognition and those that have, have yielded inconsistent and contradictory findings. Several recent studies (e.g., Beyer, Chattopadhyay, George, Glick, ogilvie & Pugliese, 1997; Walsh, 1988) investigating the relationship between functional background and executive beliefs, for example, have failed to replicate the findings of earlier work by Dearborn and Simon (1958) (upon which Hambrick & Mason, 1984, partially derived their original theoretical formulation) which had suggested that managers' views are biased by virtue of their functional positions. Other studies, however, such as that recently reported by Bowman and Daniels (1995), which revisited Dearborn and Simon's work on methodological grounds, have confirmed their original claim (but see also Waller, Huber & Glick, 1995).

As part of a wider multicultural study of managers employed by Hungarian companies which had recently come under foreign ownership, Markoczy (1997) investigated the relationships between functional background, age, hierarchical position, and national culture, on the one hand, and actors' causal belief systems with respect to organizational success, on the other, arguing that these particular characteristics have received the strongest support on the basis of previous theory and research within the Hambrick and Mason tradition. The findings of this study serve to reinforce the doubts and concerns raised by Hambrick and Mason's philosophical and theoretical detractors.

Employing a systematic method for eliciting and comparing causal maps devised by Markoczy and Goldberg (1995), partial relationships were observed between three of the four background characteristics investigated (output functional background, age, and non-Hungarian nationality) and the measured causal beliefs. The combination of these three factors accounted for just 17.2% of the variance (change in adjusted R^2) of the similarity to one of two empirically derived clusters formed on the basis of the participants' causal maps.[1] Given these findings, Markoczy concluded that researchers should abandon the use of external characteristics as substitutes for the direct measurement of executive perceptions and beliefs. In keeping with this prescriptive advice, a growing number of researchers have begun to employ direct measures of perceptions and beliefs in their studies, in an attempt to refine understanding of the nature and significance of executive cognition in strategic decision processes. It is to this research that we now turn, albeit briefly.

The Correlates of Executive Cognition

A great many factors must ultimately condition executive perceptions and beliefs, in a complex, dynamic interplay. In an attempt to capture this complexity, several recent studies exploring the correlates of executive cognition have incorporated a number of contextual and control variables. For example, in a study designed to investigate the relative explanatory power of two rival theoretical models, a 'functional conditioning model' and a 'social influence model', for predicting executives' beliefs concerning the efficacy of a broad set of business strategies and goals in achieving long-term profitability, Chattopadhyay, Glick, Miller and Huber (1999) controlled for 'environmental turbulence' and 'environmental munificence', 'degree of SBU autonomy from the parent organization', 'the extent to which the participating organizations were functionally or divisionally structured', 'organization size', and 'organizational effectiveness'. Other researchers have incorporated various team process

variables, previously identified as potential mediators and moderators of executive perceptions and
beliefs in the traditional upper echelons literature.
Knight et al. (1999), for example, incorporated
measures of 'agreement seeking' and 'interpersonal
conflict' in a LISREL analysis (Joreskog &
Sorbom, 1993) which competitively tested four
rival theoretical models seeking to explicate the
relationships between demographic diversity, team
processes, and strategic consensus, while Miller,
Burke and Glick (1998) incorporated measures of
'decision comprehensiveness' and 'extensiveness'
in three separate studies into the effects of cognitive
diversity on profitability.

Studies such as these are clearly beginning to
reshape the agenda of upper echelons research,
potentially opening up the black box of organizational demography. However, researchers have
barely scratched the surface in the quest to understand the causal antecedents and consequences of
executive cognition. Whilst these studies represent
a useful beginning, future research should extend
this embryonic line of inquiry by considering additional contextual and process variables that have
previously been explored as potential mediators and
moderators in traditional research investigating
linkages between TMT demographic composition
and organizational outcomes, including, for example, measures of 'communication' (e.g., Smith et al.,
1994; Pelled, Eisenhardt & Xin, 1999) and
'debate' (Simons et al., 1999). Future studies might
also extend this line of inquiry by exploring the
linkage between executive cognition and the
various outcome variables incorporated in previous
studies of TMT composition, such as innovation
(e.g., Bantel & Jackson, 1989), the nature and
extent of strategic change (Wiersema & Bantel,
1992), and firm performance (Norburn & Birley,
1988). The extent to which these hypothesized outcome variables impact on executive cognition, both
at the level of the focal executive and on the TMT
as a whole, might also be fruitfully investigated in
future work.

Without exception, all of these recent studies
investigating the correlates of executive cognition
have employed cross-sectional research designs,
albeit of relatively high levels of sophistication in
comparison to conventional (within the demographic tradition) investigations of upper echelon
teams, thus limiting the extent to which causal
inferences can be drawn in respect of the findings.
A major priority for future research, therefore, is to
extend this line of inquiry still further, through the
use of longitudinal designs.

It is also noteworthy that very few of these recent
studies have considered the correlates of executive
cognition beyond the individual level of analysis.
Two notable exceptions in this respect are the
studies by Chattopadhyay et al. (1999) and Knight
et al. (1999). The Chattopadhyay et al., study is
particularly commendable for its consideration of
individual- and group-level effects on the perceptions and beliefs of the individual executive.
Further multilevel studies of this nature are now
urgently required.

Finally, the vast majority of these studies
have employed simple summated rating scales for
the assessment of actors' beliefs (see, e.g.,
Chattopadhyay et al., 1999; Knight et al., 1999;
Miller et al., 1998; Sutcliffe, 1994; Sutcliffe &
Huber, 1998). Although relatively convenient to
administer, score, and interpret, as Sutcliffe (1994)
has observed, a key limitation of this type of
measure when used in this context is that the scales
employed may not be meaningful to senior managers, being too abstract in nature. Accordingly,
Sutcliffe (1994) and Wells and Bantel (2000) have
called for studies that utilize richer perceptual measures, specifically, causal cognitive mapping techniques. The primary strength of causal mapping lies
in its ability to capture the dynamics of strategic
thought. Causal mapping techniques are action oriented, as observed by Huff (1990: 16), not only
requiring individuals to reflect on events occurring
prior to the current situation, in an effort to derive
plausible explanations, but also to anticipate future
changes. With the notable exception of the aforementioned Markoczy (1997) study, however, very
few studies of executive perceptions and beliefs
have progressed beyond summated rating scales.

One technique that has been successfully
employed in several studies of organizational decision processes (e.g., Hitt & Middlemist, 1979;
Hitt & Tyler, 1991) and that lends itself to the
modelling of executive cognition in a form which is
considerably richer than the mere use of summated
rating scales is the method known as 'policy capturing' (Slovic & Lichtenstein, 1971). Using this
technique, participants are required to evaluate a
variety of scenarios by means of a wide range of
criteria, which a priori are likely to form the basis
of their decisions. Separate multiple regression
analyses are performed in turn on the judgements
elicited from each participant in order to identify
those criteria which are actually the most influential
in their decision making. As noted by Tyler and
Steensma (1998), policy capturing is advantageous
for two reasons. First, unlike many other methods
of cognitive assessment, by requiring participants
to evaluate scenarios within the context of their
own organization, as a basis for identifying the
influential criteria underpinning their decisions, it
enables the researcher to access their actual
'theories in use', as distinct from their 'espoused
theories in action' (Argyris & Schon, 1974).
Second, the stepwise regression technique used to
identify the influential criteria provides an in-built
check on the internal consistency of participants'
judgements in the derivation of their individual
models.[2]

Recently, Tyler and Steensma (1998) adopted this procedure in a study of executives' mental representations of technological alliance opportunities (see also Tyler & Steensma, 1995). The purpose of this study was to investigate the cognitive orientations executives use when they individually make assessments which they bring with them into the wider decisional arena. Assessment of alliance opportunities was modelled as a function of three major sets of factors: (1) executives' perceptions of their companies' emphasis on technology and risk and their perceptions of past successes and failure in alliances, (2) various alliance attributes specific to the technology, the firm, the partner and the relationship, and (3) executive experience (age cohort, educational orientation, and work experience). The policy-capturing exercise was based on some 30 scenarios and 17 predictor variables. *Inter alia*, it was hypothesized that older executives would have simpler mental models compared to their younger counterparts and that education, training, and functional background would, in differing ways, influence the assessment of potential alliances as depicted in the various scenarios. Education, for example, is likely to engender differing problem-solving skills and mental models, whilst individuals from technical as opposed to nontechnical backgrounds are likely to differ in terms of the extent to which they are proactive or reactive in their stance towards alliance formation. Risk judgements are also likely to vary as a function of education, training and functional background, nontechnical individuals being more risk averse in their assessments of potential technical alliances, in comparison to their technically educated, trained and/or experienced counterparts. The findings of this study offered support for several of these predictions. Technically educated executives were found to place greater weight on the opportunities provided by alliances, relative to those with other types of education, and those who perceived their firms to have a technological emphasis and past success in technical alliances were found to focus more on the opportunities of alliances and less on the risks involved, in comparison to those not sharing such perceptions.

Summary and Implications

Notwithstanding the obvious practical difficulties of negotiating access in order to study executives' perceptions and beliefs, the work reviewed in this section demonstrates unequivocally the vital importance of using direct methods of assessment. Researchers are now beginning to develop a number of highly innovative techniques for the investigation of actors' mental representations of strategic issues and problems, in an attempt to redress the limitations of the demographic approach that so dominated research into TMTs for much of the 1980s and early to mid-1990s. Two techniques in particular (causal mapping and policy capturing) have been highlighted, which appear to be particularly promising as a basis for exploring the antecedents and consequences of executive cognition.

As noted above, thus far, very few studies of executive cognition have gone beyond the individual level of analysis. To the extent that executives' individual perceptions and beliefs actually form a key element of the management decision process at the team level, it makes sense to continue exploring the determinants of strategic cognition at the individual level of analysis, along the lines of the studies recently reported by Miller et al. (1998), Sutcliffe (1994), and Sutcliffe and Huber (1998), amongst others. Ultimately, however, we need to better understand the ways in which the various factors influencing and affected by executive cognition interact with one another in the shaping of individual, team and organizational behaviour and outcomes. Such multilevel processes are likely to operate in very subtle ways, as illustrated by the Chattopadhyay et al. (1999) study. This conclusion is also borne out by a rapidly developing body of theory and research specifically devoted to the analysis of actors' mental representations of competitive environments, as reviewed in the following section.

COMPETITOR COGNITION

Competitive analysis, the identification of competitors, and the bases on which they compete with one another, is a fundamental issue in strategic management, the importance of which is reflected by its widespread prominence in the standard textbooks on the subject (see, e.g., Grant, 1998; Greenley, 1989; Hitt, Ireland & Hoskisson, 1996; Johnson & Scholes, 1999; Luffman, Sanderson, Lea & Kenney, 1987; Oster, 1990). Much of the literature on competitive analysis has been dominated by the notion of strategic groups, allied closely to the field of industrial organization economics (for reviews see McGee & Thomas, 1986; Thomas & Venkatraman, 1988). The commonly accepted definition of strategic groups is that provided by Porter:

> A strategic group is the group of firms in an industry following the same or a similar strategy along the strategic dimensions. An industry could have only one strategic group if all the firms followed essentially the same strategy. At the other extreme, each firm could be a different strategic group. Usually, however, there are a small number of strategic groups which capture the essential strategic differences among firms in the industry. (Porter, 1980: 129)

The strategic groups notion was initially developed by Hunt (1972) in a study which examined the differential performance of firms in the American home appliance industry (so-called 'white goods') in the 1960s, the ultimate goal being to account for intra-industry variations in the competitive behaviour and performance of firms. The theory predicts that intergroup differences in strategy and profitability arise for two main reasons, namely, differential entry barriers and, more generally, the presence of mobility barriers (Caves & Porter, 1977). Entry barriers constitute the various (largely economic) factors that prevent would-be players from entering a particular industry or market. Their effect is not uniform, however, with some strategic groups being afforded better protection than others. The concept of mobility barriers is a generalization of the concept of entry barriers, which seeks to explain the strategic behaviour of firms already operating within an industry. Mobility barriers are the various factors that prevent members of particular strategic groups from transferring or extending their membership to other groups.

Over recent years, there has been a growing recognition that this predominantly economic approach is limited fundamentally in terms of its ability to explain how or why competitive structures in industries and markets come to develop, and on what basis particular strategies are chosen. Increasingly, researchers have turned to psychological and sociological theory and research in an attempt to redress this criticism and refine understanding of the dynamics of competition.

The Evolution of Competitive Industry Structures: a Sociocognitive Analysis

Over the past 10 to 15 years, a number of researchers have advanced 'sociocognitive' (Lant & Phelps, 1999) or 'social constructionist' (Hodgkinson, 1997a) explanations for the emergence of competitive structures in industries and markets. The key elements of this emerging body of theory are summarized in Table 21.2.

Competitor Categorization Processes

As can be seen in Table 21.2, the basic starting point within this emerging body of theory is the premise that strategists do not attend equally to all potential competitors. Rather, for much the same reason that heuristics are deployed in judgement and decision making, firms are categorized and ordered within hierarchical taxonomic cognitive structures.

A great volume of work has accumulated within the cognitive sciences (for details see Lakeoff, 1987; Rosch, 1978) which suggests that categorical knowledge in general is organized in a hierarchical fashion. It has been shown that knowledge represented hierarchically is easier to process, since features which distinguish cognitive subcategories are stored at relatively high levels of abstraction, thus reducing the burden of information processing. Rosch and her associates (e.g., Rosch, Mervis, Gray, Johnson & Boyes–Braem, 1976) have shown that these hierarchically organized categories are characterized by indefinite boundary structures and that category exemplars vary in terms of their representativeness. Certain stimuli are considered to be more prototypical and these prototypes act as the 'cognitive reference points' against which other stimuli are compared (Rosch, 1975). Moreover, different levels of abstraction are not equally informative. The level known as the 'basic level' of inclusion is generally more informative and consequently attended to more frequently than other levels. Categories at higher levels of abstraction tend to be characterized by relatively few attributes which tend to be very general, and consequently less informative, in nature. Conversely, categories at lower levels of abstraction possess relatively more numerous and more specific attributes; however, they tend to overlap. It is at the basic level of abstraction that categories are optimal in terms of their information content, since it is at this level that categories possess the maximum proportion of unique attributes relative to overlapping attributes, i.e. attributes shared by neighbouring categories. For this reason, the basic level is usually found at intermediate levels of abstraction and is said to possess 'high cue validity' relative to categories at higher and lower levels of abstraction (Rosch et al., 1976).

Drawing on this work from the cognitive sciences, Porac and his colleagues (e.g., Porac et al., 1987, 1989; Porac & Thomas, 1990; Porac & Rosa, 1996) have argued that managers' mental representations of competitors take the form of hierarchical taxonomies, and that attention is directed primarily towards intermediate, 'basic level' categories (see also Hodgkinson & Johnson, 1994). Researchers investigating the emergence of competitive structures from a sociocognitive perspective are also generally agreed that competitive groups are graded, as opposed to all-or-nothing, phenomena, with fuzzy boundaries and core and peripheral exemplars (see, e.g., Hodgkinson, Padmore & Tomes, 1991; Hodgkinson, Tomes & Padmore, 1996; Porac et al., 1987; Porac & Thomas, 1994; Reger & Huff, 1993; Lant & Baum, 1995; Peteraf & Shanley, 1997; Lant & Phelps, 1999). According to these researchers, the categorization of competitors in this way enables actors to simplify reality and hence take action within the constraints imposed by bounded rationality.

The Social Construction of Competitive Groups

It is as various basic-level cognitive categories defining the boundaries of competition come to be shared amongst rivals, through processes of social

Table 21.2 Outline summary of principal theoretical contributions to the socio-cognitive analysis of business competition

Key concept(s)	Principal contributor(s)	Theoretical origins	Key insight(s)
Competitor categorization	Porac, Thomas and Emme (1987) Hodgkinson and Johnson (1994) Porac and Thomas (1990, 1994)	Experimental psychology and cognitive anthropology	1. Due to fundamental information-processing limitations, individuals attend only to a limited subset of potential competitors and only consider a restricted range of strategic options 2. Competitor categorization schemes are formed on the basis of attribute comparisons and organized hierarchically
Competitive enactment	Porac, Thomas and Baden-Fuller (1989) Porac and Thomas (1990)	Social psychology of organizations and the sociology of knowledge	Discernible competitive structures emerge because over time strategists from rival firms develop highly similar (or 'shared') mental models of the competitive arena, due to the fact that they share similar technical and material problems and frequently exchange information in the conduct of their business transactions. This process of social exchange, in turn, leads to the development of a shared understanding – throughout the community of firms within the marketplace – of how to compete
Cognitive inertia	Porac and Thomas (1990) Reger and Palmer (1996) Hodgkinson (1997b)	Categorization theory Schema theory Population ecology	Once established, actors' mental representations of the competitive landscape are relatively difficult to change, due to the fact that new information is processed using extant categories. Consequently, there is a danger that major changes taking place within the business environment may go undetected until such time as the organization's capacity for successful adaptation has been seriously undermined. Left unchecked, cognitive inertia may ultimately render entire populations or subpopulations of firms extinct
The cognitive life-cycle of market domains	Levenhagen, Porac and Thomas (1993)	Various, including cognitive categorization theory, competitive enactment, population ecology, and institutional theory	1. A four-stage lifecycle (concept formation → concept championing → concept appropriation → institutionalization) underpins the social construction of market domains 2. 'Frame-making' and 'frame-breaking' entrepreneurs initiate the key processes of social construction

(Contd.)

Table 21.2 (*Contd.*)

Key concept(s)	Principal contributor(s)	Theoretical origins	Key insight(s)
Competitive sets and institutional isomorphism	Lant and Baum (1995)	Cognitive categorization theory, competitive enactment, and institutional theory	1. As argued by Porac et al. (1989), mutual enactment processes result in discernible groupings of competitors, i.e., 'competitive sets' (the cognitive analogue to strategic groups) 2. In turn, these shared cognitive categorization schemes of competitors act as a vital source of institutionalized behaviour among groups of rival firms, potentially giving rise to two forms of isomorphism: mimetic adoption and normative isomorphism
Relational modelling, vicarious learning, and social identification	Peteraf and Shanley (1997)	Competitor categorization theory, competitive enactment, social learning theory, and social identification theory	1. The accumulated experience gained through social learning (via a combination of direct and vicarious interorganizational interactions) enables organizations to reduce their transaction costs, by promoting continued exchange only with those firms found to be reliable interaction partners, predictable in their behaviours and providing tolerable levels of risk. In the long run, this tendency to look to the same group of firms on repeated occasions leads to the development of a relatively stable cognitive entity. 2. These processes of social learning are a necessary but insufficient condition for the emergence of strategic groups that have real and measurable effects, i.e., groups that will ultimately influence the conduct and performance of their individual members. In addition, social identification must occur; group members must not only perceive the fact that a group exists ('identification of the group'), but also identify with the group
Situated learning	Lant (1999) Lant and Phelps (1999)	Situated learning theory	Extant sociocognitive explanations for the emergence of knowledge and identity within cognitive communities represent an understated perspective, which underemphasizes the extent to which learning within and between competitive groups is embedded in a social milieu. Within this body of work, learning is viewed primarily as a vicarious process. In reality, however, the emergence and evolution of competitive groups is underpinned by a relatively complex, dynamic process. Ongoing interactions among the various players both central and peripheral to the group yield not only common and predictable patterns of behaviour, but also help to preserve variations in the structures, strategies, and beliefs within these groups

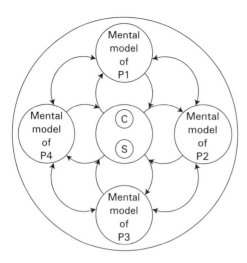

Figure 21.3   *Mutual enactment processes within an industrial sector. C = customers; S = suppliers; Pn = producers.(Source: J.F. Porac, H. Thomas, & C. Baden-Fuller [1989]. Competitive groups as cognitive communities: the case of Scottish knitwear manufacturers.* Journal of Management Studies, 26, 397–416. © Blackwell Publishers Limited. Reproduced by kind permission of the publisher.)

construction, that discernible competitive structures are hypothesized to emerge, by a number of researchers. Drawing on the work of Berger and Luckmann (1967) and Weick's (1979) observation that organizations often create their environments through collective sense-making processes, then act as if their cognitive constructions were true, Porac et al. (1989) have termed this process of social construction 'competitive enactment' (see also Porac & Rosa, 1996; Porac & Thomas, 1990; Weick, 1995). Porac and his associates contend that over time, individuals' beliefs about the identity of their competitors, suppliers, and customers become highly unified through mutual enactment processes, in which subjective interpretations of externally situated information are objectified via behaviour.

This argument is illustrated graphically in Figure 21.3. Each competitor is involved in an individual enactment process in which the mental model of its strategists is reciprocally intertwined with its strategic choices and the material conditions of the marketplace. Other parties involved in the same transactional network, however, are also enacting their beliefs, through activities within the marketplace. While the interpretations of customers, suppliers, and competitors are all involved in structuring the transactional network, it is the enactment processes of the latter which are particularly important, due to the fact that they serve to link firm-level and group-level competitive activities, through the creation of socially shared belief systems.

As summarized in Table 21.2, various strands of theory from a number of sources are broadly supportive of the notion of competitive enactment. They each offer complementary insights that extend this line of reasoning. The cognitive lifecycle conception explicated by Levenhagen et al. (1993), for example, highlights the importance of leadership as a major factor governing all elements of this social construction process, from initial concept creation and the development of category prototypes, through their wider adoption by groups of rivals within the marketplace, to the institutionalization of competitive practices and their eventual destruction by entrepreneurial agents actively seeking to overturn 'the rules of the game'.

While the lifecycle notion outlined by Levenhagen and his colleagues identifies a key role for business entrepreneurs as the engineers of new categories of competitor definition, the phenomenon known as 'cognitive inertia', highlights one of the potential difficulties confronting would-be innovators: they must also be able to successfully challenge the legitimacy of extant categories if their ideas are to ultimately gain credence within the wider marketplace. Cognitive inertia has been identified by a number of researchers as a major barrier to organizational learning and strategic renewal. As Porac and Thomas (1990) have observed, the literature abounds with anecdotal evidence suggesting that all too often strategists are unable to reconceptualize the identities of their organizations sufficiently quickly in the face of radically new forms of competition (see also Abrahamson & Fombrun, 1994; Barr & Huff, 1997; Barr, Stimpert & Huff, 1992; Huff, Huff & Thomas, 1992; Rindova & Fombrun, 1999; Senge, 1990).

The work of Lant and Baum (1995) adds additional, complementary insights into this social construction process, through a consideration of 'isomorphism', the tendency observed by institutional theorists (e.g., DiMaggio & Powell, 1983; Meyer & Rowan, 1977) for organizations to develop shared beliefs, structures, networks of relations, and practices over time. Like Porac and his colleagues, Lant and Baum contend that managers *enact* a structure of strategic groups, responding to, and creating, their competitive worlds in a manner consistent with their own cognitions. Lant and Baum have identified two mechanisms of isomorphism, each underpinned by categorization processes, which potentially may play a key role in the social construction of competitive groups and the institutionalization of competitive practices: (1) *mimetic isomorphism*, resulting from firms monitoring one another; and (2) *normative isomorphism*, arising from cues taken from various normative sources, such as the parent company (if the organization is part of a wider conglomerate), and agents in the institutional environment who act as transmitters of information, including, for example, higher education institutions and industry consultants. Lant and Baum have suggested that it is managers' conceptualizations of their strategic identities, embodied in their shared categorization schemes, that ultimately give rise to the development of competitive groups within industries and the existence of isomorphic practices within these groups:

> ... homogeneous firms, typically identified post hoc as strategic groups based on objective measures, may exhibit institutionalized behavior in their causal attributions and choices of strategies and practices, as a result of the development of shared cognitions about who are members of these strategic groups and which attributes distinguish members from non-members. (Lant & Baum, 1995: 36)

Each of these notions (competitive enactment, cognitive inertia, the cognitive lifecycle conception, and the processes of normative and mimetic adoption associated with institutional isomorphism) highlight the importance of direct and indirect interaction in the marketplace as bases for the emergence of homogeneous and stabilized cognitions, which in turn underpin the formation of competitive structures and substructures. In another highly complementary development, Peteraf and Shanley (1997) have introduced the notions of relational modelling and vicarious learning from social learning theory (Bandura, 1986; Wood & Bandura, 1989). In common with Porac and Thomas (1990) and Lant and Baum (1995), they have also drawn attention to the importance of managers' conceptions of identity in the social construction of competitive groups, borrowing concepts from social identification theory (Ashforth & Mael, 1989; Tajfel & Turner, 1985). The more recent work of Lant (1999) and Lant and Phelps (1999), however, drawing on the work of Wenger (1998), calls into question the adequacy of this portrayal of learning as a predominantly vicarious process, in which referent others are modelled or imitated, as exemplified Peteraf and Shanley's paper, but also implicit in much of the other recent work on the sociocognitive analysis of competitive structures.

The Situated Learning Perspective

As summarized in Table 21.2, the situated learning perspective draws attention to the fact that the ongoing interactions among actors within the marketplace do not merely result in common and predictable patterns of behaviour within strategic groups. Additionally, they help to preserve variations in structures, strategies and beliefs within these groups. According to this view, such variations are vital to the accomplishment of learning and change, thereby enhancing the longer-term survival capabilities of the wider population of organizations.

Building on this key insight, this new perspective challenges a fundamental premise of conventional strategic groups theory, the notion that mobility barriers serve as protective devices which preserve the long-term survival chances of established groups (Caves & Porter, 1977). According to Lant and Phelps (1999), strategic groups with high mobility barriers will actually have *lower* long-term survival chances, compared to groups with lower barriers, due to the fact that these barriers inhibit learning by preventing players with new beliefs and practices from entering the group. Over time, this will result in a lessening of variation in structures, strategies and beliefs, thus rendering the wider population of firms vulnerable to competency-destroying technological changes of the sort discussed by Tushman and Anderson (1990).

The situated learning perspective also calls into question the adequacy of the 'topographic' view of organizations portrayed within much of the extant body of work on the sociocognitive analysis of competition and indeed the field of organization studies more generally. Drawing on the work of Tsoukas (1992), Araujo (1998) and Palinscar (1998), Lant and Phelps (1999) challenge two assumptions in particular implicit within this view: (1) the assumption that knowledge is localized in individual minds or other anthropomorphized entities such as organizations; and (2) the assumption that organizations are relatively self-contained, bounded entities that learn through key individuals, such as top managers.

Empirical Studies of Competitor Cognition

Unfortunately, very few elements of this emerging body of sociocognitive theory have been empirically tested with an acceptable degree of rigour. The basic argument that individuals attend only to a limited subset of potential competitors and competitor categories has been well established empirically (see, e.g., Gripsrud & Gronhaug, 1985; Hodgkinson & Johnson, 1994; Johnson, Daniels & Asch, 1998; Porac & Thomas, 1994; Porac et al., 1987, 1989; Porac, Thomas, Wilson, Paton & Kanfer, 1995; Reger & Huff, 1993). Porac and his colleagues have also uncovered empirical evidence suggesting that business strategists regard their own firms as the prototypical exemplar of the category or categories in which they locate their major source(s) of competitive threat, i.e., the 'primary competitive group'. Porac and his colleagues argue that the manager's own business acts as the cognitive reference point against which they evaluate potential rivals on the basis of feature comparisons; the greater the perceived similarity between a strategist's own firm and a given rival, the greater the perceived competitive threat (Porac et al., 1987; Porac & Thomas, 1994). Beyond these basic observations, however, there is very little high-quality evidence to substantiate the claims of the various sociocognitive theorists, discussed above.

As with virtually any new line of inquiry, theorizing in this area has evolved largely on an inductive basis, using studies of particular industries and markets in order to illustrate the applicability of selected focal concepts. The basic features of competitive enactment, for example, were demonstrated empirically by means of a small scale, inductive study of the Scottish knitwear industry ($N = 17$ participants) conducted by Porac et al. (1989). This study, revealed an overwhelming tendency for managers from a number of rival firms to disregard as competitors those firms located outside the immediate vicinity of Scotland, despite the fact that Scottish knitwear producers account for a mere 3% of the total amount of knitted outerwear manufactured on a worldwide basis. The cognitive lifecycle conception developed by Levenhagen and his colleagues was also grounded contextually, by drawing on occasional examples 'provided from research conducted by the authors in the software development industry' (Levenhagen et al., 1993: 76).

Building on the notion of competitive enactment, competitor categorization theory and the arguments outlined earlier concerning institutional isomorphism, Lant and Baum (1995) drew on a study of $N = 43$ hotel managers in the Manhattan district of New York. Using a form of network analysis (Borgatti, Everett & Freeman, 1992) in conjunction with hierarchical cluster analysis, some 14 competitive groupings (i.e., 'competitive sets') were identified from a total of 167 hotels. As predicted, managers within each discernible group of hotels tended to regard one another as relevant competitors. Also as predicted, a number of significant differences emerged between the competitive groups in relation to the mean size, price, and location (street and avenue) of the hotels, indicating that the aggregation of the competitive sets elicited from the individual managers reveals relatively homogeneous groups of hotels. Like the aforementioned Scottish knitwear study, the findings of this study offer broad support for the general proposition that competitive structures may evolve through processes of social construction, involving competitive enactment. However, as the authors themselves readily acknowledge, due to limitations in the research design, this study contributes very little to understanding of the precise mechanisms through which such managerial perceptions converge over time, thereby giving rise to institutional isomorphism. Given that this study utilized a cross-sectional design, it was not possible to discern which of the various hypothesized forms of mimetic and normative isomorphism ultimately accounts for the observed pattern of findings.

As with the Scottish knitwear study, the findings of this research should be regarded as tentative rather than conclusive, opening the field to further lines of inquiry, with larger samples and greater controls. A larger-scale follow-up investigation of the Scottish knitwear industry reported by Porac et al. (1995) and a more recent study of mimetic adoption processes (Greve, 1998) illustrate two rather differing (but nonetheless complementary) ways in which this preliminary work might inform future research in this area.

Commencing with a series of field interviews of managing directors (MDs) ($N = 20$) as a basis for capturing the 'nomenclature' of the knitwear industry, Porac and his colleagues developed a structured questionnaire which was subsequently administered to a further sample of $N = 89$ MDs. (A panel of three industry experts was consulted in order to help verify and interpret the information gathered during the preliminary interviews, prior to constructing the questionnaire.) The questionnaire data were submitted to a network analysis, along similar lines to the Lant and Baum (1995) study. The findings suggested a six-category model of organizational forms which seemed to capture actors' common perceptions of competition within the industry, with several attributes (principally size, technology, product style, and geographic location) forming the underlying basis of this commonly perceived structure.

In a population ecology study of the spread of new radio formats in the USA, Greve (1998) modelled processes of innovation diffusion, using the technique of event history analysis (Tuma & Hannan, 1984), the study population being commercial radio stations. On the basis of his findings, Greve concluded that the major driver of the mimetic adoption of new market positions is managers' mental models, which in turn are informed by information access (the degree to which they are able to observe competitors by virtue of geographical proximity) and relevancy judgements (as measured by market size). According to Greve, differential access to information, coupled with variations in perceived relevance, has given rise to the emergence of new strategic groups within this industry, through selective mimetic adoption. These results, suggesting that managers distinguish markets using market size as a relevancy criterion for deciding which competitors' practices are worthy of imitation, represent the beginnings of a journey to discover how managers categorize and distinguish markets.

Ultimately, if social constructionist notions such as competitive enactment, cognitive inertia, institutional isomorphism, the related cognitive lifecycle conception, outlined above, are to be tested with an acceptable degree of rigour, large-scale longitudinal field studies are required, in order to track actors' mental representations over time. Thus far, however, only three studies have investigated actors' mental representations of competition using some form of longitudinal design (Grohaug & Falkenberg, 1989; Hodgkinson, 1997b; Reger & Palmer, 1996). Two of these studies (Hodgkinson's study of the UK residential estate agency industry and Reger and Palmer's study of the US financial services industry) provide evidence in support of cognitive inertia. Unfortunately, however, the latter study and the study by Gronhaug and Falkenberg suffer from serious methodological drawbacks.

The Reger and Palmer study of the U.S. financial services industry is in actual fact an amalgamation of three data sets, respectively gathered in 1981, 1986, and 1989 from different subsectors, each located in different geographical regions of the USA. This, and the fact that different researchers gathered the data on each occasion, using varying elicitation procedures, severely limits the inferences that can be drawn in respect of the findings. The Gronhaug and Falkenberg study, by contrast, is limited by virtue of the fact that the data were gathered retrospectively, using an extremely small sample (just seven participants from four organizations). The reliability and validity of subjective recall techniques in strategy research has been increasingly called into question over recent years and clearly should only be used in circumstances when no feasible alternative is possible (cf. Golden, 1992, 1997; Miller, Cardinal & Glick, 1997).

Hodgkinson's study is the only study to date, in this area, to have employed a truly prospective research design. In this study the participants were each required to identify 20 competing estate agency firms (including their own organization) in response to a series of standardized category titles (identified through documentary sources and pilot interviews). The participants assessed each firm in turn, using a series of 21 bipolar attribute-rating scales. A 'three-way scaling' (Arabie, Carroll & DeSarbo, 1987) analysis revealed a two-dimensional group space configuration ('quality' × 'market power') which meaningfully represented the aggregated data ($N = 206$ participants from $N = 58$ organizations) gathered at time 1. A follow-up investigation of a subsample of $N = 114$ of the original participants from $N = 41$ of the organizations concerned, some 12–18 months later, found that neither the group space configuration, nor the 'source weight' (Arabie et al., 1987) vectors, reflecting individual differences in the relative salience of the underlying dimensions of the group space configuration, differed significantly, despite a highly significant downturn in the domestic housing market from time 1 to time 2. Whilst this study is commendable for its incorporation of a prospective research design, unfortunately, the interval between the data-gathering exercises may have been too short for significant cognitive changes to have emerged. Clearly there is an urgent need for additional studies employing this type of design, over extended time periods, across a range of industries.

The notion that competitive groups are socially constructed implies a strong requirement for studies in which the mental representations of multiple informants, situated at differing vantage points within and between organizations in the same industrial sector, are assessed repeatedly over differing time periods. Such studies would enable researchers to explore the extent to which, under what circumstances, and over what time scale and with what effect, actors' mental representations of competition converge, diverge, stabilize, and change. Thus far, however, very few studies have sought to systematically compare and contrast actors' mental representations of competitive environments on a cross-sectional basis, let alone using longitudinal datasets.

Virtually all of the empirical evidence that has been gathered as a basis for developing and/or testing this emerging body of sociocognitive theory has relied on the use of single informants (typically the owner-manager, managing director, or CEO) from each participating organization, as exemplified by the Scottish knitwear (Porac et al., 1989, 1995) and Manhattan hotel industry (Lant & Baum, 1995) studies outlined above. These and a number of other researchers investigating strategic groups from a cognitive perspective (e.g., Dess & Davis, 1984; Fombrun & Zajac, 1987; Porac et al., 1987; Porac & Thomas, 1994; Reger & Huff, 1993) have implicitly or explicitly assumed away the significance of potential intra- and inter-organizational variations in cognition, treating such variations as a source of unwanted error variance, focusing instead on commonly reported perceptions and beliefs. This practice rests on the largely untested assumption that the views of those particular individuals investigated are actually representative of the wider organization as a whole (or at least the dominant coalition). Recently, however, a number of researchers have amassed findings that cast considerable doubt on the validity of this assumption and hence the adequacy of single informant designs as a basis for modelling competitive industry structures (see, e.g., Bowman & Ambrosini, 1997a, b; Bowman & Johnson, 1992; Calori, Johnson & Sarnin, 1992, 1994; Daniels, Johnson & de Chernatony, 1994; Hodgkinson & Johnson, 1994; Johnson et al., 1998). Unfortunately, however, the varying levels of cognitive homogeneity and diversity observed across these studies are confounded, by virtue of the wide range of cognitive mapping methods employed, coupled with the fact that they have been carried out in a diverse range of industries, thus severely limiting the interpretations which can be placed on the findings (for further details see Hodgkinson, 1997a, 2001).

Summary and Implications

As with the work on heuristics and biases in strategic decision making, and that exploring the interrelationships between top team composition, executive cognition and organizational outcomes, research into the sociocognitive underpinnings of competitive industry structures is still in its early infancy. In recent years a number of interrelated theoretical notions have been brought to bear on the sociocognitive analysis of business rivalry, in an effort to refine understanding of the ways in which actors create, legitimize, destroy, and re-create industries and markets over time. Unfortunately, however, as we have seen, there is a dearth of high-quality empirical evidence to substantiate the claims of theorists in respect of these key processes. The overwhelming majority of studies have utilized cross-sectional, single-informant designs, whereas longitudinal designs, involving multiple informants from large numbers of participating organizations, are ultimately required if this emerging body of sociocognitive theory is to be adequately scrutinized empirically. The situated learning perspective recently advanced by Lant (1999) and Lant and Phelps (1999) has further heightened the need for such investigations, by drawing attention to the importance of multilevel system interaction effects within and between organizations. When viewed from this perspective, it is clear that, as in the analysis of cognitive processes in top management teams, researchers have barely begun to scratch the surface in the quest to explore the antecedents and consequences of actors' mental representations.

CONCLUDING REMARKS

This chapter has presented an overview of theory and research into a number of cognitive processes in strategic management. Three streams of work in particular have been highlighted, in an attempt to convey something of the excitement captivating the community of scholars involved in the development of this emerging subfield: applications of behavioural decision theory and research to strategic decision making, the antecedents and consequences of strategic cognition amongst executive team members, and the sociocognitive analysis of competitive industry structures. In each case, a number of nontrivial methodological hurdles have been identified that need to be overcome if the psychology of strategic management is to progress beyond its present status, within the field of industrial, work and organizational psychology, as an emergent topic area. Arguably, the greatest challenge confronting researchers in this respect is the need to secure access to sufficiently large samples of individual participants and participating organizations

for statistically robust findings to be generated. As with virtually any newly developing line of inquiry, the overwhelming majority of studies used to support the development of theory in this area have been relatively small-scale, exploratory studies, characterised by poor or nonexistent controls, thereby rendering problematic the extent to which alternative explanations for key findings can be ruled out.

A partial solution to this problem in future work could involve the greater use of experimental techniques. As noted earlier in the section on heuristics and biases, despite the obvious advantages of the experimental method, this approach has been greatly underutilized in the field of strategic management. Two recently published papers by Clark and Montgomery (1999) and Kilduff, Angelmar and Mehra (2000) illustrate how use of the experimental method might be fruitfully extended beyond the study of heuristics and biases in strategic decision making in future work, both in order to further understanding of the sociocognitive processes underpinning the development of competitive structures in industries and markets, and as a basis for illuminating the nature and significance of cognitive processes in top management teams.

Clark and Montgomery (1999: study 2) employed MARKSTRAT2 (Larreche & Gatignon, 1990), a business game designed to simulate processes of competition, as part of a wider investigation into competitor categorization processes. The overall findings complement and add to various insights derived from previous studies into competitor categorization processes, reviewed earlier in this chapter, showing, for example, that managers may name too few competitors, that they should focus more on competitors as defined by customers (using demand-based as opposed to supply-based attributes), that they should be aware of perceptual asymmetries (e.g., the tendency for small firms to 'look up to' larger firms but not the converse), that they should periodically revisit how they identify competitors, and that they should identify potential competitors for tracking purposes.

More recently, Kilduff et al. (2000) have employed a variant of the MARKSTRAT simulation as a vehicle for examining: (1) the linkages between demographic and cognitive team diversity, and (2) the reciprocal effects of diversity and firm performance. The findings indicated that high-performing teams were marked by a tendency to preserve multiple interpretations of reality at the outset, with greater clarity emerging towards the end of the team's lifecycle. Whilst cognitive diversity in teams affected and was affected by changes in firm performance, contrary to the researchers' expectations – but by no means inconsistent with several other recent studies conducted outside the confines of the laboratory (e.g., Markoczy, 1997) – demographic diversity had no noticeable effects on the measures of cognitive diversity employed. There are, of course, a variety of possible explanations for this negative finding, not least the possibility that the particular simulation package (MARKSTRAT) and/or the particular measures of demographic and cognitive diversity employed may have been insensitive to the detection of such relationships (cf. the earlier discussion of demographic faultlines (Lau & Murnighan, 1998) and Pelled's (1996) intervening process theory). Nevertheless, these findings, together with those of the Clark and Montgomery study, demonstrate that, as in the case of heuristics and biases research, laboratory simulations provide a potentially useful basis for ensuring that findings obtained through less rigorous procedures, such as observational field studies and interviews, can be replicated under controlled conditions. Further work along these lines would greatly strengthen the empirical knowledge base underpinning all three streams of theory and research surveyed in this chapter.

A second major methodological challenge confronting strategic cognition researchers concerns the need to develop additional methods, beyond basic summated rating scales, which are suitable for the mass assessment of actors' mental representations of strategic issues and problems. With the notable exceptions of the technique devised by Markoczy and Goldberg (1995) for the systematic elicitation and comparison of causal maps, policy-capturing methods, such as that employed by Tyler and Steensma (1995, 1998) in their studies of technological alliances, and three-way scaling procedures, such as the one employed by Hodgkinson (1997b) in his study of competitor cognition in the UK residential estate agency industry, few of the techniques presently available for mapping strategic thought yield data in a form amenable to large-scale, multilevel hypothesis testing of the sort required to enable research within this topic area to progress to levels of maturity that would be comparable to those of the better-established subfields of industrial, work and organizational psychology. As noted by Hodgkinson (2001), all too often researchers have employed cognitive mapping procedures that have yet to be screened in terms of their basic psychometric efficacy and/or which yield data in a form unsuitable for the comparison of large numbers of maps on a systematic basis.

Ultimately, if the problems identified in this chapter are to be addressed on a satisfactory basis, researchers will need to collaborate with one another in large-scale, multidisciplinary teams, in some cases spanning several institutions. While this type of collaboration is undoubtedly a highly labour-intensive process in comparison with conventional approaches to the conduct and management of applied psychological research, the potential benefits must surely outweigh the considerable transaction costs involved, for, in the final

analysis, laboratory experiments, however well designed and executed, are no substitute for the gathering of large-scale, high-quality data sets from top-level executives *in situ*.

NOTES

1 For additional applications of the Markoczy–Goldberg procedure see Markoczy (1995).

2 Ordinarily, an $R^2 < 0.40$ is taken as the cutoff, respondents failing to generate individual models that exceed this minimum level of explained variance being thrown out on the grounds of unacceptably low reliability (Keats, 1991; Tyler & Steensma, 1995, 1998). The stepwise regression technique employed in policy capturing also provides a convenient basis for the assessment of cognitive complexity at the level of the individual participant, namely, the number of statistically significant predictors ($P < 0.05$) entered into their final model.

AUTHOR ACKNOWLEDGEMENT

Portions of this chapter have been adapted from Hodgkinson, G.P. (2001). The psychology of strategic management: diversity and cognition revisited. In C.L. Cooper and I.T. Robertson (Eds.), *International Review of Industrial and Organizational Psychology* – *Vol. 16*. (pp. 65–119). Chichester: Wiley. Copyright © John Wiley & Sons Ltd. Adapted by kind permission of the publisher.

REFERENCES

Abrahamson, E., & Fombrun, C.J. (1994). Macrocultures: Determinants and consequences. *Academy of Management Review, 19*, 728–755.

Arabie, P., Carroll, J.D., & DeSarbo, W.S. (1987). *Three-way scaling and clustering*. Sage University Paper Series on Quantitative Applications in the Social Sciences, 07-065. London: Sage.

Araujo, L. (1998). Knowing and learning as networking. *Management Learning, 29*, 317–336.

Argyris, C., & Schon, D.A. (1974). *Theory in practice: Increasing professional effectiveness*. San Francisco: Jossey-Bass.

Ashforth, B., & Mael, F. (1989). Social identity theory and the organization. *Academy of Management Review, 14*, 20–39.

Axelrod, R.M. (1976). The mathematics of cognitive maps. In R.M. Axelrod (Ed.), *Structure of decision: The cognitive maps of political elites* (pp. 343–348). Princeton NJ: Princeton University Press.

Bandura, A. (1986). *Social foundations of thought and action*. Englewood Cliffs, NJ: Prentice-Hall.

Bantel, K., & Jackson, S.E. (1989). Top management and innovation in banking. Does the composition of top teams make a difference? *Strategic Management Journal, 10*, 107–124.

Barnes, J.H. (1984). Cognitive biases and their impact on strategic planning. *Strategic Management Journal, 5*, 129–137.

Barr, P.S. (1998). Adapting to unfamiliar environmental events: A look at the evolution of interpretation and its role in strategic change. *Organization Science, 9*, 644–669.

Barr, P.S., & Huff, A.S. (1997). Seeing isn't believing: Understanding diversity in the timing of strategic response. *Journal of Management Studies, 34*, 337–370.

Barr, P.S., Stimpert, J.L., & Huff, A.S. (1992). Cognitive change, strategic action, and organizational renewal. *Strategic Management Journal, 13*, 15–36.

Bateman, T.S., & Zeithaml, C.P. (1989). The psychological context of strategic decisions: A model and convergent experimental findings. *Strategic Management Journal, 10*, 59–74.

Bazerman, M.H. (1998). *Judgment in managerial decision making* (4th ed.). New York: Wiley.

Berger, P.L., & Luckmann, T. (1967). *The social construction of reality*. Harmondsworth: Penguin.

Beyer, J., Chattopadhyay, P., George, E., Glick, W.H., ogilvie, d., & Pugliese, D. (1997). The selective perception of managers revisited. *Academy of Management Journal, 40*, 716–737.

Boone, C., & De Brabander, B. (1993). Generalized vs. specific locus of control expectancies of chief executive officers. *Strategic Management Journal, 14*, 619–625.

Boone, C., & De Brabander, B. (1997). Self-reports and CEO locus of control research: A note. *Organization Studies, 18*, 949–971.

Boone, C. De Brabander, B., & van Witteloostuijn, A. (1996). CEO locus of control and small firm performance: An integrative framework and empirical test. *Journal of Management Studies, 33*, 667–699.

Borgatti, S.P., Everett, M.G., & Freeman, L.C. (1992). *UCINET IV Version 1.0*. Columbia: Analytic Technologies.

Bowman, C., & Ambrosini, V. (1997a). Perceptions of strategic priorities, consensus and firm performance. *Journal of Management Studies, 34*, 241–258.

Bowman, C., & Ambrosini, V. (1997b). Using single respondents in strategy research. *British Journal of Management, 8*, 119–131.

Bowman, C., & Daniels, K. (1995). The influence of functional experience on perception of strategic priorities. *British Journal of Management, 6*, 157–167.

Bowman, C., & Johnson, G. (1992). Surfacing competitive strategies. *European Management Journal, 10*, 210–219.

Calori, R., Johnson, G., & Sarnin, P. (1992). French and British top managers' understanding of the structure and dynamics of their industries: A cognitive analysis and comparison. *British Journal of Management, 3*, 61–78.

Calori, R., Johnson, G., & Sarnin, P. (1994). CEOs' cognitive maps and the scope of the organization. *Strategic Management Journal, 15*, 437–457.

Cartwright, S., & Cooper, C.L. (1990). The impact of mergers and acquisitions on people at work: Existing research and issues. *British Journal of Management, 1*, 65–76.

Cartwright, S., & Cooper, C.L. (1993). The psychological impact of merger and acquisition on the individual: A study of building society managers. *Human Relations, 46*, 327–347.

Caves, R.E., & Porter, M.E. (1977). From entry barriers to mobility barriers: Conjectural decisions and contrived deterrence to new competition. *Quarterly Journal of Economics, 91*, 421–434.

Chattopadhyay, P., Glick, W.H., Miller, C.C., & Huber, G.P. (1999). Determinants of executive beliefs: Comparing functional conditioning and social influence. *Strategic Management Journal, 20*, 763–789.

Clark, B.H., & Montgomery, D.B. (1999). Managerial identification of competitors. *Journal of Marketing, 63*, 67–83.

Daboub, A.J., Rasheed, A.M.A., Priem, R.L., & Gray, D.A. (1995). Top management team characteristics and corporate illegal activity. *Academy of Management Review, 20*, 138–170.

Daniels, K., Johnson, G., & de Chernatony, L. (1994). Differences in managerial cognitions of competition. *British Journal of Management, 5*, S21–S29.

Das, T.K., & Teng, B.-S. (1999). Cognitive biases and strategic decision processes. *Journal of Management Studies, 36*, 757–778.

D'Avini, R.A. (1990). Top managerial prestige and organizational bankruptcy. *Organization Science, 1*, 121–142.

Dearborn, D.C., & Simon, H.A. (1958). Selective perception: A note on the departmental identification of executives. *Sociometry, 21*, 140–144.

Dess, G.G., & Davis, P.S. (1984). Porter's (1980) generic strategies as determinants of strategic group membership and organizational performance. *Academy of Management Journal, 27*, 467–488.

Diffenbach, J. (1982). Influence diagrams for complex strategic issues. *Strategic Management Journal, 3*, 133–146.

DiMaggio, P.J., & Powell, W.W. (1983). The iron cage revisited: Institutional isomorphism and collective rationality in organizational fields. *American Sociological Review, 48*, 147–160.

Duhaime, I.M., & Schwenk, C.R. (1985). Conjectures on cognitive simplification in acquisition and divestment decision making. *Academy of Management Review, 10*, 287–295.

Dutton, J.E., & Dukerich, J.M. (1991). Keeping an eye on the mirror: Image and identity in organizational adaptation. *Academy of Management Journal, 34*, 517–554.

Dutton, J.E., & Jackson, S.E. (1987). Categorizing strategic issues: Links to organizational action. *Academy of Management Review, 12*, 76–90.

Eden, C., & Ackermann, F. (1998). *Making strategy: The journey of strategic management*. London: Sage.

Eden, C., & Spender, J.-C. (Eds.) (1998). *Managerial and organizational cognition: Theory, methods and research*. London: Sage.

Finkelstein, S., & Hambrick, D.C. (1996). *Strategic leadership: Top executives and their effects on organizations.* St. Paul, MN: West.

Flood, P.C., Dromgoole, T., Carroll, S., & Gorman, L. (Eds.) (2000). *Managing strategy implementation.* Oxford: Blackwell.

Floyd, S.W., & Lane, P.J. (2000). Strategizing throughout the organization: Managing role conflict in strategic renewal. *Academy of Management Review, 25,* 154–177.

Fombrun, C.J., & Zajac, E.J. (1987). Structural and perceptual influences on intra-industry stratification. *Academy of Management Journal, 30,* 33–50.

Forbes, D.P., & Milliken, F.J. (1999). Cognition and corporate governance: Understanding boards of directors as strategic decision-making groups. *Academy of Management Review, 24,* 489–505.

Gioia, D.A., & Thomas, J.B. (1996). Identity, image, and issue interpretation: Sensemaking during strategic change in academia. *Administrative Science Quarterly, 41,* 370–403.

Golden, B. (1992). The past is past – or is it? The use of retrospective accounts as indicators of past strategy. *Academy of Management Journal, 35,* 848–860.

Golden, B.R. (1997). Further remarks on retrospective accounts in organizational and strategic management research. *Academy of Management Journal, 40,* 1243–1252.

Goodwin, P., & Wright, G. (1998). *Decision analysis for management judgment* (2nd ed.). Chichester: Wiley.

Grant, R.M. (1998). *Contemporary strategy analysis: Concepts, techniques, applications* (3rd ed.). Malden, MA: Blackwell.

Greenley, G. (1989). *Strategic management.* London: Prentice Hall.

Greve, H.R. (1998). Managerial cognition and the mimetic adoption of market positions: What you see is what you do. *Strategic Management Journal, 19,* 967–988.

Gripsrud, G., & Gronhaug, K. (1985). Structure and strategy in grocery retailing: A sociometric approach. *Journal of Industrial Economics, XXXIII,* 339–347.

Gronhaug, K., & Falkenberg, J.S. (1989). Exploring strategy perceptions in changing environments. *Journal of Management Studies, 26,* 349–359.

Haleblain, J., & Finkelstein, S. (1993). Top management team size, CEO dominance and firm performance: The moderating roles of environmental turbulence and discretion. *Academy of Management Journal, 36,* 844–863.

Hambrick, D.C., Cho, T.S., & Chen, M-J. (1996). The influence of top management team heterogeneity on firms' competitive moves. *Administrative Science Quarterly, 41,* 659–684.

Hambrick, D., & Mason, P. (1984). Upper echelons: The organization as a reflection of its top managers. *Academy of Management Review, 9,* 193–206.

Hitt, M.,A., Ireland, R.D., & Hoskisson, R.E. (1996). *Strategic management: Competitiveness and globalization* (2nd ed.). St Paul, MN: West.

Hitt, M.A., & Middlemist, R.D. (1979). A methodology to develop the criteria and criteria weightings for assessing subunit effectiveness in organizations. *Academy of Management Journal, 22,* 356–374.

Hitt, M.A., & Tyler, B.B. (1991). Strategic decision models: Integrating different perspectives. *Strategic Management Journal, 12,* 327–351.

Hodgkinson, G.P. (1992). Development and validation of the strategic locus of control scale. *Strategic Management Journal, 13,* 311–317.

Hodgkinson, G.P. (1993). Doubts about the conceptual and empirical status of context-free and firm-specific control expectancies: A reply to Boone and De Brabander. *Strategic Management Journal, 14,* 627–631.

Hodgkinson, G.P. (1997a). The cognitive analysis of competitive structures: A review and critique. *Human Relations, 50,* 625–654.

Hodgkinson, G.P. (1997b). Cognitive inertia in a turbulent market: The case of UK residential estate agents. *Journal of Management Studies, 34,* 921–945.

Hodgkinson, G.P. (2001). The psychology of strategic management: Diversity and cognition revisited. In C.L. Cooper, & I.T. Robertson (Eds.), *International Review of Industrial and Organizational Psychology* (Vol. 16, pp. 65–119). Chichester: Wiley.

Hodgkinson, G.P., Bown, N.J., Maule, A.J., Glaister, K.W., & Pearman, A.D. (1999). Breaking the frame: An analysis of strategic cognition and decision making under uncertainty. *Strategic Management Journal, 20,* 977–985.

Hodgkinson, G.P., & Johnson, G. (1994). Exploring the mental models of competitive strategists: The case for a processual approach. *Journal of Management Studies, 31,* 525–551.

Hodgkinson, G.P., & Maule, A.J. (in press). The individual in the strategy process: Insights from behavioural decision research and cognitive mapping. In A.S. Huff, & M. Jenkins (Eds.), *Mapping strategic knowledge.* London: Sage.

Hodgkinson, G.P., Padmore, J., & Tomes, A.E. (1991). Mapping consumers cognitive structures: A comparison of similarity trees with multidimensional scaling and cluster analysis. *European Journal of Marketing, 25*(7), 41–60.

Hodgkinson, G.P., & Thomas, A.B. (Eds.), (1997). Thinking in organizations. *Journal of Management Studies, 34* (special issue), 845–952.

Hodgkinson, G.P., Tomes, A.E., & Padmore, J. (1996). Using consumers perceptions for the cognitive analysis of corporate-level competitive structures. *Journal of Strategic Marketing, 4,* 1–22.

Hogan, E.A., & Overmyer-Day, L. (1994). The psychology of mergers and acquisitions. In C.L. Cooper, & I.T. Robertson (Eds.), *International review of industrial and organizational psychology* (Vol. 9, pp. 247–281) Chichester: Wiley.

Huff, A.S. (Ed.) (1990). *Mapping strategic thought.* Chichester: Wiley.

Huff, J.O., Huff, A.S., & Thomas, H. (1992). Strategic renewal and the interaction of cumulative stress and inertia. *Strategic Management Journal, 13,* 55–75.

Huff, A.S., & Jenkins, M. (Eds.) (in press). *Mapping strategic knowledge.* London: Sage.

Huff, A.S., & Schwenk, C.R. (1990). Bias and sensemaking in good times and bad. In A.S. Huff (Ed.), *Mapping strategic thought* (pp. 89–108). Chichester: Wiley.

Hunt, M.S. (1972). Competition in the major home appliance industry. Unpublished doctoral dissertation, University of Harvard, USA.

Jackson, S.E. (1992). Consequences of group composition for the interpersonal dynamics of strategic issue processing. *Advances in Strategic Management, 8,* 345–382.

Jackson, S.E., & Dutton, J.E. (1988). Discerning threats and opportunities. *Administrative Science Quarterly, 33,* 370–387.

Johnson, G. (1987). *Strategic change and the management process.* Oxford: Blackwell.

Johnson, G., & Scholes, K. (1999). *Exploring corporate strategy* (5th ed.). London: Prentice Hall Europe.

Johnson, P., Daniels, K., & Asch, R. (1998). Mental models of competition. In C. Eden, & J.-C. Spender (Eds.), *Managerial and organizational cognition: Theory, methods and research* (pp. 130–146). London: Sage.

Joreskog, K.G., & Sorbom, D. (1993). *LISREL 8: Structural equation modelling with the SIMPLIS command language.* Hillsdale, NJ: Lawrence Erlbaum.

Kahneman, D., Slovic, P., & Tversky, A. (Eds.) (1982). *Judgment under uncertainty: Heuristics and biases.* Cambridge, UK: Cambridge University Press.

Kahneman, D., & Tversky, A. (1979). Prospect theory: An analysis of decision under risk. *Econometrica, 47,* 263–291.

Kahneman D., & Tversky A. (1984). Choices, values and frames. *American Psychologist, 39,* 341–350.

Keats, B.W. (1991). An empirical investigation of strategic investment decision models. *Strategic Management Journal, 12,* 243–250.

Keck, S.L. (1997). Top management team structure: Differential effects by environmental context. *Organization Science, 8,* 143–156.

Keck, S.L., & Tushman, M.L. (1993). Environmental and organizational context and executive team structure. *Academy of Management Journal, 36,* 314–344.

Kilduff, M., Angelmar, R., & Mehra, A. (2000). Top management-team diversity and firm performance: Examining the role of cognitions. *Organization Science, 11,* 21–34.

Knight, D., Pearce, C.L., Smith, K.G., Olian, J.D., Sims, H.P., Smith, K.A., & Flood, P. (1999). Top management team diversity, group process, and strategic consensus. *Strategic Management Journal, 20,* 445–465.

Lakeoff, G. (1987). *Women, fire and dangerous things: What categories reveal about the mind.* Chicago, IL: University of Chicago Press.

Langley, A., Mintzberg, H., Pitcher, P., Posada, E., & Saint-Macary, J. (1995). Opening up decision making: The view from the black stool. *Organization Science, 6,* 260–279.

Lant, T.K. (1999). A situated learning perspective on the emergence of knowledge and identity in cognitive communities. *Advances in Management Cognition and Organizational Information Processing, 6,* 171–194.

Lant, T.K., & Baum, J.C. (1995). Cognitive sources of socially constructed competitive groups: Examples from the manhattan hotel industry. In W.R. Scott, & S. Christensen (Eds.), *The institutional construction of organizations: International and longitudinal studies.* Thousand Oaks, CA: Sage.

Lant, T.K., Milliken, F.J., & Batra, B. (1992). The role of managerial learning and interpretation in strategic persistence and reorientation: An empirical exploration. *Strategic Management Journal, 13,* 585–608.

Lant, T.K., & Phelps, C. (1999). Strategic groups: A situated learning perspective. *Advances in Strategic Management, 16,* 221–247.

Larreche, J.-C., & Gatignon, H. (1990). *MARKSTRAT2: Instructor's manual.* Redwood City, CA: The Scientific Press.

Lau, J., & Murnighan, J.K. (1998). Demographic diversity and faultlines: The compositional dynamics of organizational groups. *Academy of Management Review, 23,* 325–340.

Lawrence, B.S. (1997). The black box of organizational demography. *Organization Science, 8,* 1–22.

Levenhagen, M., Porac, J.F., & Thomas, H. (1993). Emergent industry leadership and the selling of technological visions: A social constructionist view. In J. Hendry, & G. Johnson with J. Newton (Eds.), *Strategic thinking: leadership and the management of change* (pp. 69–87). Chichester: Wiley.

Luffman, G., Sanderson, S., Lea, E., & Kenney, B. (1987). *Business policy: An analytical introduction.* Oxford: Blackwell.

Lyles, M.A., & Thomas, H. (1988). Strategic problem formulation: Biases and assumptions embedded in alternative decision-making models. *Journal of Management Studies, 25,* 131–145.

Markoczy, L. (1995). States and belief states. *International Journal of Human Resource Management, 6,* 249–270.

Markoczy, L. (1997). Measuring beliefs: Accept no substitutes. *Academy of Management Journal, 40,* 1228–1242.

Markoczy, L., & Goldberg, J. (1995). A method for eliciting and comparing causal maps. *Journal of Management, 21,* 305–333.

Maule, A.J. (1995). Framing elaborations and their effects on choice behavior: A comparison across problem isomorphs and subjects with different levels of expertise. In J.-P. Caverni, M. Bar-Hillel, F.H. Barron, & H. Jungermann (Eds.), *Contributions to decision research* (Vol. 1, pp. 281–300). Amsterdam: Elsevier.

McGee, J., & Thomas, H. (1986). Strategic groups: theory, research and taxonomy. *Strategic Management Journal, 7,* 141–160.

Meyer, J.W., & Rowan, B. (1977). Institutionalized organizations: Formal structure as myth and ceremony. *American Journal of Sociology, 83,* 340–363.

Miller, C.C., Burke, L.M., & Glick, W.H. (1998). Cognitive diversity among upper-echelon executives: implications for strategic decision processes. *Strategic Management Journal, 19,* 39–58.

Miller, C.C., Cardinal, L.B., & Glick, W.H. (1997). Retrospective reports in organizational research: A reexamination of recent evidence. *Academy of Management Journal, 40,* 189–204.

Miller, D. (1983). The correlates of entrepreneurship in three types of firms. *Management Science, 29,* 770–791.

Miller, D., Kets DeVries, M.F.R., & Toulouse, J.M. (1982). Top executive locus of control and its relationship to strategy-making, structure and environment. *Academy of Management Journal, 25,* 237–253.

Miller, D., & Toulouse, J.M. (1986). Chief executive personality and corporate strategy and structure. *Management Science, 32,* 1389–1409.

Milliken, F., & Martins, L. (1996). Searching for common threads: Understanding the multiple effects of diversity in organizational groups. *Academy of Management Review, 21,* 402–433.

Mintzberg, H. (1983). *Power in and around organizations.* Englewood Cliffs, N.J: Prentice-Hall.

Mintzberg, H., Ahlstrand, B., & Lampel, J. (1998). *Strategy safari: A guided tour through the wilds of strategic management.* London: Prentice-Hall.

Norburn, D., & Birley, S. (1988). The top management team and corporate performance. *Strategic Management Journal, 9,* 225–237.

Oster, S.M. (1990). *Modern competitive analysis.* Oxford: Oxford University Press.

Palinscar, A.S. (1998). Social constructivist perspectives on teaching and learning. *Annual Review of Psychology, 49,* 345–375.

Pelled, L.H. (1996). Demographic diversity, conflict, and work group outcomes: An intervening process theory. *Organization Science, 7,* 615–631.

Pelled, L.H., Eisenhardt, K.M., & Xin, K.R. (1999). Exploring the black box: An analysis of work group diversity, conflict and performance. *Administrative Science Quarterly, 44,* 1–28.

Peteraf, M., & Shanley, M. (1997). Getting to know you: A theory of strategic group identity. *Strategic Management Journal, 18* (Summer Special Issue), 165–186.

Pettigrew, A.M. (1973). *The politics of organizational decision making.* London: Tavistock.

Pettigrew, A.M. (1985). *The awakening giant: Continuity and change in imperial chemical industries.* Oxford: Blackwell.

Pettigrew, A.M. (1992). On studying managerial elites. *Strategic Management Journal, 13,* 163–182.

Pfeffer, J. (1983). Organizational demography. In B.M. Staw, & L.L. Cummings (Eds.), *Research in organizational behavior* (Vol. 5, pp. 299–357). Greenwich, CT: JAI Press.

Porac, J., & Rosa, A. (1996). Rivalry, industry models, and the cognitive embeddedness of the comparable firm. *Advances in Strategic Management, 13,* 363–388.

Porac, J.F., & Thomas, H. (Eds.) (1989). Managerial thinking in business environments. *Journal of Management Studies, 26* (Special Issue), 323–438.

Porac, J.F., & Thomas, H. (1990). Taxonomic mental models in competitor definition. *Academy of Management Review, 15,* 224–240.

Porac, J.F., & Thomas, H. (1994). Cognitive categorization and subjective rivalry among retailers in a small city. *Journal of Applied Psychology, 79,* 54–66.

Porac, J.F., Thomas, H., & Baden-Fuller, C. (1989). Competitive groups as cognitive communities: The case of Scottish knitwear manufacturers. *Journal of Management Studies, 26,* 397–416.

Porac, J.F., Thomas H., & Emme, B. (1987). Knowing the competition: The mental models of retailing strategists. In G. Johnson (Ed.), *Business strategy and retailing* (pp. 59–79). Chichester: Wiley.

Porac, J.F., Thomas, H., Wilson, F., Paton, D., & Kanfer, A. (1995). Rivalry and the industry model of Scottish knitwear producers. *Administrative Science Quarterly, 40,* 203–227.

Porter, M.E. (1980). *Competitive strategy: Techniques for analyzing industries and competitors.* New York: Free Press.

Reger, R.K., & Huff, A.S. (1993). Strategic groups: A cognitive perspective. *Strategic Management Journal, 14,* 103–124.

Reger, R.K., & Palmer, T.B. (1996). Managerial categorization of competitors: Using old maps to navigate new environments. *Organization Science, 7,* 22–39.

Rindova, V.P., & Fombrun, C.J. (1999). Constructing competitive advantage: The role of firm-constituent interactions. *Strategic Management Journal, 20,* 691–710.

Rosch, E. (1975). Cognitive reference points. *Cognitive Psychology, 7,* 532–547.

Rosch, E. (1978). Principles of categorization. In E. Rosch, & B.B. Lloyd (Eds.), *Cognition and categorization* (pp. 27–48). Hillsdale, NJ: Lawrence Erlbaum.

Rosch, E., Mervis, C.B., Gray, W.D., Johnson, D., & Boyes-Braem, P. (1976). Basic objects in natural categories. *Cognitive Psychology, 8,* 382–439.

Sambharya, R.B. (1996). Foreign experience of top management teams and international diversification strategies of US multinational corporations. *Strategic Management Journal, 17,* 739–746.

Schwenk, C.R. (1982). Why sacrifice rigor for relevance? A proposal for combining laboratory and field research in strategic management. *Strategic Management Journal, 3,* 213–225.

Schwenk, C.R. (1984). Cognitive simplification processes in strategic decision making. *Strategic Management Journal, 5,* 111–128.

Schwenk, C.R. (1988). The cognitive perspective on strategic decision making. *Journal of Management Studies, 25,* 41–55.

Schwenk, C.R. (1989). Linking cognitive, organizational and political factors in explaining strategic change. *Journal of Management Studies, 26,* 177–187.

Schwenk, C.R. (1995). Strategic decision making. *Journal of Management, 21,* 471–493.

Senge, P. (1990). *The fifth discipline: The art and practice of the learning organization.* New York: Doubleday.

Sieck, W., & Yates, J.F. (1997). Exposition effects on decision making: Choice and confidence in choice. *Organizational Behavior and Human Decision Processes, 70,* 207–219.

Simon, H.A. (1955). A behavioral model of rational choice. *Quarterly Journal of Economics, 69*, 99–118.

Simon, H.A. (1956). Rational choice and the structure of the environment. *Psychological Review, 63*, 129–138.

Simons, T., Pelled, L.H., & Smith, K.A. (1999). Making use of difference: Diversity, debate and decision comprehensiveness in top management teams. *Academy of Management Journal, 42*, 662–673.

Slovic, P., & Lichtenstein, S. (1971). Comparison of Baysian and regression approaches to the study of information processing in judgment. *Organizational Behaviour and Human Performance, 6*, 649–744.

Smith, K.G., Smith, K.A., Olian, J.D., Sims, H.P., O'Bannon, D.P., & Scully, J.A. (1994). Top management team demography and process: The role of social integration and communication. *Administrative Science Quarterly, 39*, 412–438.

Sparrow, P.R. (1994). The psychology of strategic management: Emerging themes of diversity and cognition. In C.L. Cooper, & I.T. Robertson (Eds.), *International review of industrial and organizational psychology* (Vol. 9. pp. 147–181). Chichester: Wiley.

Sparrow, P.R. (2000). Strategic management in a world turned upside down: The role of cognition, intuition and emotional intelligence. In P.C. Flood, T. Dromgoole, S. Carroll, & L. Gorman (Eds.), *Managing strategy implementation* (pp. 15–30). Oxford: Blackwell.

Starbuck, W.H., & Milliken, F.J. (1988). Executives perceptual filters: What they notice and how they make sense'. In D.C. Hambrick (Ed.), *The executive effect: concepts and methods for studying top managers.* (pp. 35–65). Greenwich, CT: JAI Press.

Sutcliffe, K.M. (1994). What executives notice: Accurate perceptions in top management teams. *Academy of Management Journal, 37*, 1360–1378.

Sutcliffe, K.M., & Huber, G.P. (1998). Firm and industry as determinants of executive perceptions of the environment. *Strategic Management Journal, 19*, 793–807.

Tajfel, H., & Turner, J.C. (1985). The social identity theory of intergroup behavior. In S. Worchel, & W.G. Austin (Eds.), *Psychology of intergroup relations* (2nd ed., pp. 7–24). Chicago, IL: Nelson-Hall.

Thomas, H., & Venkatraman, N. (1988). Research on strategic groups: Progress and prognosis. *Journal of Management Studies, 25*, 537–555.

Tsoukas, H. (1992). Ways of seeing: Topographic and network representations in organization theory. *Systems Practice, 5*, 441–456.

Tsui, A.S., & Gutek, B.A. (1999). *Demographic differences in organizations: Current research and future directions.* Lanham, Maryland: Lexington Books.

Tuma, N.B., & Hannan, M.T. (1984). *Social dynamics: Models and methods.* Orlando, FL: Academic Press.

Tushman, M.L., & Anderson, P. (1990). Technological discontinuities and dominant designs: A cyclical model of technological change. *Administrative Science Quarterly, 35*, 604–633.

Tversky, A., & Kahneman, D. (1974). Judgment under uncertainty: Heuristics and biases. *Science, 185*, 1124–1131.

Tversky, A., & Kahneman, D. (1981). The framing of decisions and the psychology of choice. *Science, 211*, 453–458.

Tyler, B.B., & Steensma, H.K. (1995). Evaluating technological collaborative opportunities: A cognitive modelling perspective. *Strategic Management Journal, 16* (Summer Special Issue), 43–70.

Tyler, B.B., & Steensma, H.K. (1998). The effects of executives' experiences and perceptions on their assessment of potential technological alliances. *Strategic Management Journal, 19*, 939–965.

Waller, M.J., Huber, G.P., & Glick, W.H. (1995). Functional background as a determinant of executives' selective perception. *Academy of Management Journal, 38*, 943–974.

Walsh, J.P. (1988). Selectivity and selective perception: An investigation of managers belief structures and information processing'. *Academy of Management Journal, 31*, 873–896.

Walsh, J.P. (1995). Managerial and organizational cognition: Notes from a trip down memory lane. *Organization Science, 6*, 280–321.

Walsh, J.P., & Fahay, L. (1986). The role of negotiated belief structures in strategy making. *Journal of Management, 12*, 325–338.

Weick, K.E. (1979). *The social psychology of organizing* (2nd ed.). Reading, M.A: Addison-Wesley.

Weick, K.E. (1995). *Sensemaking in organizations.* Thousand Oaks, CA: Sage.

Weick, K.E. (2001). *Making sense of the organization.* Oxford: Blackwell.

Wells, R.S., & Bantel, K.A. (2000). Competitive external pressures: Building top management teams to sustain competitive advantage in a changing world. In R.E. Quinn, R.M. O'Neill, & L. St. Clair (Eds.), *Pressing problems in modern organizations (that keep us up at night): Transforming agendas for research and practice* (pp. 175–196). New York: AMACOM.

Wenger, E. (1998). *Communities of practice.* Cambridge: Cambridge University Press.

Wiersema, M.F., & Bantel, K.A. (1992). Top team demography and corporate strategic change. *Academy of Management Journal, 35*, 91–121.

Williams, K.Y., & O'Reilly, C.A. (1998). Demography and diversity in organizations: A review of 40 years of research. In L.L. Cummings, & B.M. Staw (Eds.), *Research in organizational behavior* (Vol. 20, pp. 77–140). Greenwich, CT: JAI Press.

Williams, R.J., Barrett, J.D., & Brabston, M. (2000). Managers' business school education and military service: Possible links to corporate criminal activity. *Human Relations, 53*, 691–712.

Wood, R., & Bandura, A. (1989). Social cognitive theory of organizational management. *Academy of Management Review, 14*, 361–384.

Zajac, E.J., & Bazerman, M.H. (1991). Blindspots in industry and competitor analysis: Implications of interfirm (mis)perceptions for strategic decisions. *Academy of Management Review, 16*, 37–56.

Author Index to Volume 2

Subject Index to Volume 2

The Glaven Ports
People & Places

A photographic portrait of the Norfolk coastal villages
Blakeney, Cley, Morston and Wiveton

Liz Shand Kendall, Judith Paxton & John Warham

Dedication

To our families and friends in Norfolk.

First Published 2014

© Text and photographs copyright 2014 Liz Shand
Kendall, Judith Paxton and John Warham except those
on p90/91 by Hazel Denslow and p138 (middle, bottom)
by Ruth Boxall.

The rights of Liz Shand Kendall, Judith Paxton and John
Warham to be identified as the authors of this work
have been asserted in accordance with the Copyright,
Designs and Patents Act 1988.

ISBN 978-0-9553333-6-1

A catalogue record for this book is available from the
British Library.

Designed by Dick Malt

Published by Thornham Local History Society
Red Brick House
Hall Lane
Thornham
Norfolk PE36 6NB

Printed in Norfolk by Swallowtail Print
www.swallowtailprint.co.uk

Contents

Introduction

The Glaven Ports – People and Places, is the fourth in a series of books on the north Norfolk coast. The series started in 2009 in Thornham and moved, via The Burnhams, to Wells-next-the-Sea before arriving at Blakeney, Cley, Morston and Wiveton. This will probably be the final stopping place for this little series, which never expected to journey so far.

Once again, the book has emerged from the Julia Rafferty School of Photography where the authors studied digital photography under Julia's tutelage at Wells Learning Centre. We are grateful to Julia for the inspiration she has given us.

Two of the photographers on this project, Liz Shand Kendall and Judith Paxton, have both lived in Blakeney for many years and are, therefore, able to bring an intimacy to the book which only local knowledge can provide. They are both excellent photographers, indeed, Liz is an Associate Member of the Royal Photographic Society. Their photos provide the backbone of this book.

In common with other villages along the Norfolk coast, the Glaven Ports of Blakeney, Cley, Morston and Wiveton have seen fundamental changes to their economy over the centuries and, particularly, over the last fifty or sixty years, as the old agricultural industries have been replaced by tourism as the main source of income. The days when they were thriving ports servicing the prosperous woollen industry are long gone. Second-home owners and holiday makers are now as numerous as residents. However, in spite of the many changes which have taken place, the villages are still very much recognisable as they were when I first visited Cley as a young aspiring bird watcher back in 1956, and many of the places are the same, though their usage may have changed. The Bishop family is still looking after Cley Marshes for the NWT, and visits to see the seals at Blakeney Point are as popular as ever. Sadly, Nancy's Café, The Forge and the coastguard station are no more.

Blakeney

Blakeney, with a population of 800 or so, is the largest of the Glaven port villages, and is a popular tourist attraction, with pubs and hotels catering for all tastes. Sailing and crabbing in the harbour, seal trips to the Point and walks across the marshes and beaches provide year round activities with something for everyone.

The High Street

Though many of the High Street shops of yesteryear have
disappeared, a few still remain, and there is plenty of activity,
particularly during the summer months.

105 HIGH STREET

12

Blakeney Neighbourhood Housing Society

The idea of the Blakeney Neighbouhood Housing Society began in 1944, when Norah Clogstoun, shocked by the poor state of many dwellings in Blakeney, purchased a terrace of five cottages to improve the standard of housing for local people.

BNHS was founded two years later and the Society now has forty-three cottages, including seven in Cley and two in Wiveton. Twenty-one are listed buildings.

Privies were part of the first BNHS purchase of 'five cottages with gardens, five privies, outbuildings and common yard … together with the right to use the well on paying a proportionate part of the expense of keeping the said well and the going gears thereof in repair'.

Blakeney Guildhall

It is hard to imagine that Blakeney was a prosperous port in the fifteenth century – the third biggest in Norfolk when the Guildhall was built. English Heritage records the varied uses of the Guildhall over the centuries from its origins as a merchant's house, through to becoming home to the Guild of Fish Merchants in the reign of Henry VIII, to its use as a Coal Barn and, bizarrely, as a temporary mortuary for shipwrecked sailors in the First World War.

Joan Wade has opened and closed the Guildhall daily since 1962.

The Rising Tide from Blakeney High Street

9346

The Barometer

The Royal National Lifeboat Institution has a long tradition of helping to prevent accidents at sea by supplying barometers to coastal communities.

Blakeney's barometer was put up in new housing at the beginning of the 21st century by the Parish Council.

The Carnser

The Carnser is a popular, busy area throughout the summer and is host to a variety of activities, including the annual Lifeboat Service.

Carnser is an East Anglian dialect word for a causeway over a marsh.

REAL
CLOTTED
CREAM
TEAs
£3.90

FRESHLY
MADE
SANDWICHES
TO
TAKEAWAY
FROM
£2.80

ST. NICHOLAS' CHURCH HALL

PRESENTED TO THE
PARISH
BY THE BLAKENEY
WOMENS INSTITUTE
TO COMMEMORATE
THEIR
GOLDEN JUBILEE YEAR
1915-1965

BLAKENEY

The White Horse

For many years a popular watering hole at the bottom of the High Street, and once a Bullards of Norwich pub, the White Horse became part of the Adnams estate in 2011. Francis Guildea (*left*) is the current lease holder.

The Blakeney Hotel

The Blakeney Hotel was built in 1921 and has welcomed visitors to its perfect setting on the harbour ever since. This family-owned hotel has recently been refurbished and features a swimming pool and spa.

The King's Arms

The King's Arms probably dates from the Restoration period of the mid seventeenth century. Certainly, its royalist credentials are set out in the fine Royal Coat of Arms displayed on the outside wall.

The building may originally have been a row of fisherman's cottages. The initials on the roof are possibly those of the landlord at the time the pub was reroofed.

Lots of show-business photos hang on the walls depicting the former careers of the landlords Howard & Marjorie Davies, who featured in the Black & White Minstrel TV series. Howard died in 2010.

The King's Arms remains firmly a village local, despite Blakeney's ever-increasing number of visitors. An unusual sight these days – beer straight from a cask on the bar – in this case it is Woodeforde's *Revenge*.

Manor Hotel

The Manor House Hotel is a seventeenth-century building and an excellent base for exploring the coast. There is an attractive courtyard with converted flint barns providing accommodation. The mulberry tree in the garden is 400 years old.

The staff are (*left to right*) Louise Wilgress, Karen Hill, Sophie Hill, Aaron Hill, Julie Womack (Manageress) Gail Nadine-Ellis.

MULBERRY TREE
400 years old.
Please do not
climb on branches
or supports

Thank you

Above Di Garner and Jill Craske, centre, the cook and (*below*) Maureen Buckey, the Co-ordinator.

Eddie Ray, Treasurer of Glaven Caring, and Melody Beeley, at a garden open day at Kettle Hill in aid of the charity.

Glaven Caring

Glaven Caring is voluntary organisation which provides extra care and comfort, as well as medical and personal services, to the elderly and frail living in Blakeney and surrounding villages.

Left volunteer helpers Amanda Brownlow, Priscilla Hunt and Jan Hope

Methodist Church

The present Methodist Chapel was erected in 1812 and enlarged in the 1840s with a classroom added in 1903. The Rev Jenny Pathmarajah was ordained in 2013 and serves Blakeney, Holt and Wells.

St Peter's Catholic Church

Father Keith Tullock is the priest in charge, helped by a rota of priests from Walsingham. The west window is a depiction of Christ ascending above the marshes of Blakeney, complete with herons, oystercatchers and reed beds.

St Nicholas' Church

Standing high above the village, and with towers at both ends, St Nicholas' Church creates a fine impression on the approach to Blakeney.

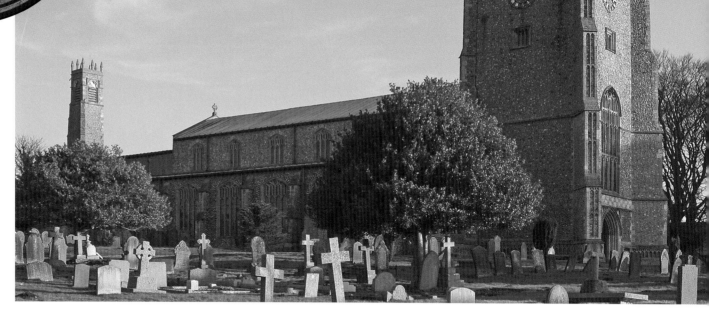

Simon Jenkins' book, *England's 1000 Best Churches*, characterises this medieval church as 'a community centre, market place and museum' – an apt description.

There is speculation as to the purpose of the lantern tower at the east end – the most common theory is that it held a beacon to act as a navigational aid to ships approaching the harbour.

Revd Libby Dady was appointed Rector in 2014.

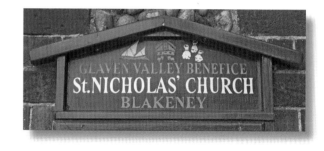

Hettie was Blakeney's lifeboat from 1873 to 1891. This model of *Hettie* was presented by the National Lifeboat Institution to George Firth, the Bradford cloth manufacturer who paid for the building of the lifeboat and its upkeep. The model was subsequently given to Blakeney Historical Society by Constance Firth, his grandaughter.

In the church, painted boards record the service of Blakeney's lifeboats.

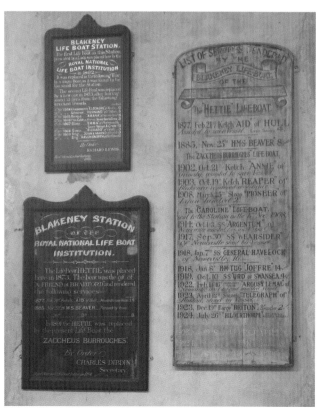

In August 2013 a Frazer-Nash car was squeezed into the church for the funeral of Joé Watts-Farmer, whose father, Archie Frazer-Nash, was one of the designers of the 1920s chain-driven car.

38

The kneelers were stitched between 1984-1989. The designs for this project were gleaned from many sources but they are all symbolic.

Nancy Murfitt was the leader, Polly Seed took over in 1988. Val Marchant was the designer.

The oak benches have a whole menagerie of animals climbing on the pew ends. More animals are found on the misericords in the chancel.

Derek Woodhouse has been sexton at Blakeney for thirty-five years.

Olympic torch relay

Bill Blackiston carrying the Olympic torch
in the round-Britain relay which led up to
the opening of the 2012 Games. Bill has
parachuted twice to raise money for the East
Anglian Air Ambulance amongst other fund-
raising events.

Jubilee Celebrations

The Queen's Diamond Jubilee in 2012 was celebrated
in style in Blakeney with events throughout the week,
including street parties for all ages in the High Street,
which was closed off for the occasion.

A Jubilee regatta flotilla of boats sailed down the cut into Agar creek as part of the celebrations.

There was a sandcastle building competition and the challenge of a greasy pole for the braver souls who were happy to get wet.

Gillying competition

Gillying, or crabbing, has been a popular pastime along the north Norfolk coast for generations. Blakeney has an annual competition with prizes for the winners.

The Fair

Grays' annual Fair takes place on the Carnser in August and has been running at least since the 1920s.

FUN FAIR
BLAKENEY QUAY

WEDNESDAY 8 AUGUST TO SATURDAY 11 AUGUST

Open: Weekdays 6pm
Saturday 2pm

WALTER F. LONG.

BURGH COTTAGE,
BLAKENEY.

CHURCH GARAGE,
BLAKENEY,
NORFOLK.

Blakeney has had another garage – Church garage stood where the Roman Catholic church is now but closed when Walter Long and Freddie Grand were called up in about 1940. Petrol was last 1s 4d a gallon in the 1930s.

Blakeney Garage

Blakeney Garage with owners Brian Daniels and David Chenery. Dave Buckey at the pumps.

Rachel Rafferty,
Manager

Spar Shop

Started in 1948 as the Hill Brothers, the Spar convenience store has been open in Blakeney for about seven years and employs over twenty staff in the summer season.

Postmistresses Eva Gambriel, Hazel Dawkins and Jess Tutt.

50

Claire Pepper

Blakeney Delicatessen

Blakeney Deli is situated on the High Street and is a family run business. The shop has a working kitchen that supplies bread, tarts, pastries and delicious sausage rolls amongst other dishes. The Deli also has a selection of wines and the menus change regularly with the seasons.

The Moorings

The Moorings restaurant is owned and run by Richard and Angela Long, who serve local fish in summer, game in the winter and fresh vegetables from Angela's garden.

THE MOORINGS
HIGH STREET · BLAKENEY · NORFOLK

SORRY...
NO DOGS OR
CROCODILES

Andy and Hilary Randell

The Randells' Crab shop is on New Road where Andy and Hilary sell crabs, lobsters, prawns and crabcakes in the summer, and mussels in the winter.

Blakeney Marine

Carl Bishop owns and runs Blakeney Marine. He sells, repairs and restores boats and, during the winter, prepares them for the summer season. Boats may be stored with him and he will take them out of the water at the end of the summer.

Hoi Larntan

St Ayles skiffs were begun in 2009 by a request from the Scottish Fisheries Museum in Anstruther, Fife, to Alec Jordan of Jordan Boats to build a boat to revive the regatta races that finished in the fifties. A design was chosen based on a Fair Isle skiff.

The Blakeney St Ayles skiff, *Hoi Larntan,* was built by local amateur boatbuilders and launched on the 25th May 2013. She was taken to the SkiffieWorlds Championship in Ullapool as the only English contender. A rowing club has been started in association with the Blakeney sailing club and another boat is being built, as well as two in Wells.

The Cockle fleet

Cockles are built by George Hewitt in Stiffkey. There is now a fleet of over 100 boats which sail in the harbour. The world championships are held annually in Blakeney.

FLOOD LEVEL
1976

FLOOD LEVEL
1897

WARNING
This area is liable
to unpredictable
tidal flooding

Harbour tours and trips to Blakeney Point are popular excursions and most visitors make the trip at least once. Many of the trips to the seals now leave from Morston.

Blakeney Point and the National Trust

Blakeney Point has been managed by the National Trust since 1912 and is the oldest nature reserve in Norfolk, part of one of the largest expanses of undeveloped coastal habitat in Europe.

The Lifeboat House was built in 1898 but was only in use for a few years before a build-up of shingle made launching the boat too difficult. It is used now as an information centre and accommodation for the NT warden during the summer. During 2012 and 2013 the building was entirely reclad, weather-proofed and insulated to protect it for the future. The old, rotten lookout tower was replaced and former features including the ramp and big doors were re-instated.

Below Coastal Ranger Ajay Tegala and the warden's living quarters.

The Point is a tourist highlight for visitors keen to see the colonies of grey and common seals. For bird watchers its attractions include the rare migratory species that turn up to rest and refuel in the sea bushes and scrub.

In summer there is a breeding colony of thousands of sandwich terns, with common and little terns in smaller numbers.

The easiest way to get to the Point is via the ferries out of Morston Quay, but perhaps a better way to appreciate the remote beauty of the place is to walk the three kilometres along the bank from Cley, although it can be hard work trekking over the shingle when the tide is in.

North Sea surge

On the night of Thursday, 5 December 2013 a combination of a spring tide, low pressure and a northerly gale caused a sea surge along the east coast of England as bad in places as the infamous 1953 floods.

In Blakeney the water was several feet high in quayside buildings. The bank by the Carnser was breached and Blakeney Freshes, the marshes towards Cley, were inundated.

Cley

It is hard to believe that, many years ago, Cley was a major port with a quayside running down past the mill. Its harbour long since silted up, the village is perhaps best known now as a gathering point for both birds and bird watchers, with activity centred on Norfolk Wildlife Trust's famous Cley Marsh.

Cley Mill

Built in the early nineteenth century and run by the Farthing family until 1875, Cley mill was sold in 1921 for £350 and converted into a holiday home. It came on the market again in 2006. This time the asking price was £1,500,000! Now a restaurant and B&B, it remains one of the most photographed buildings on the Norfolk coast and has adorned many book covers, calendars, chocolate boxes and tea towels over the years.

Cley Mill

The sluice near Cley Mill allows the Glaven to flow out towards the sea. It is closed when there is a risk of tidal flooding.

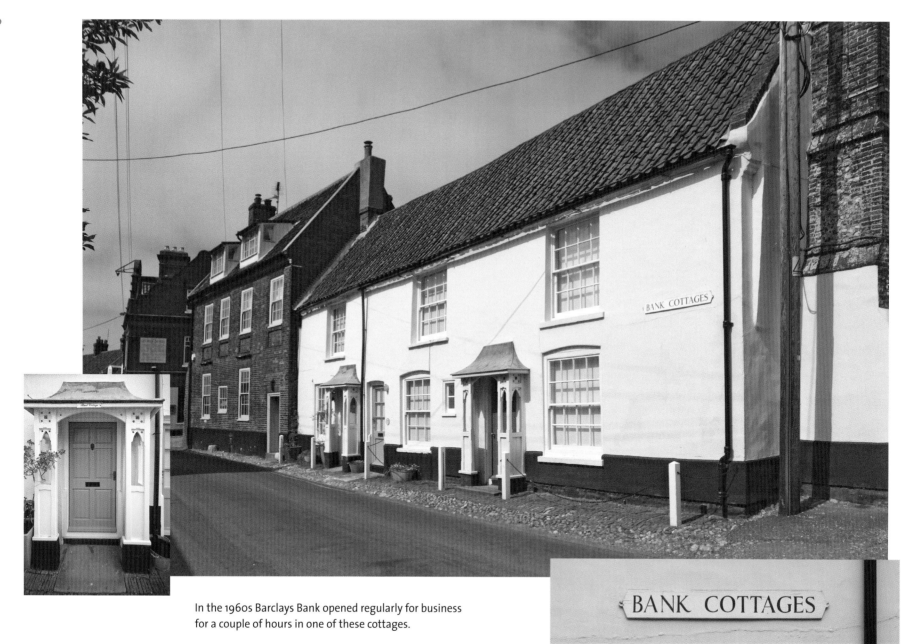

In the 1960s Barclays Bank opened regularly for business
for a couple of hours in one of these cottages.

BANK COTTAGES

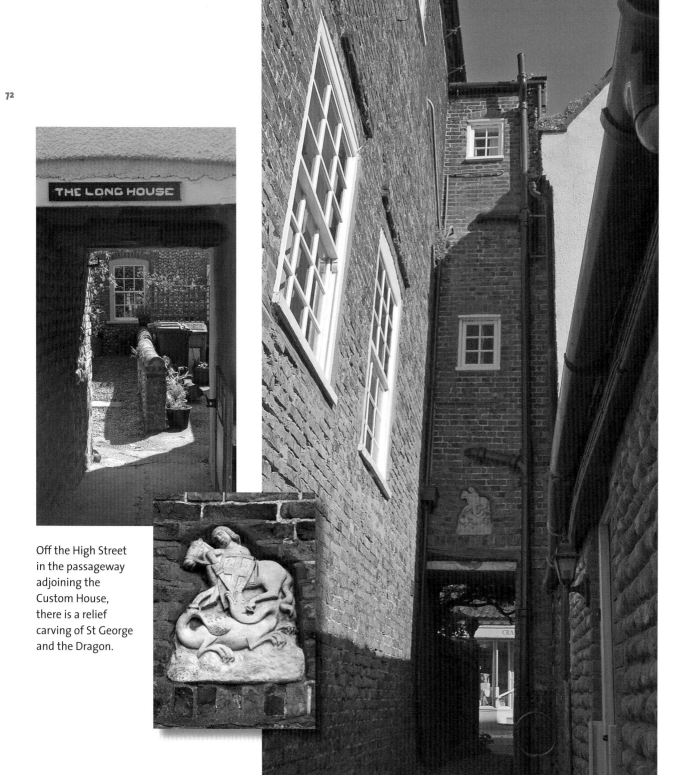

Off the High Street in the passageway adjoining the Custom House, there is a relief carving of St George and the Dragon.

Built about 1700, the Customs House is a three storey, red brick building and features a rectangular wooden panel above the front door showing Cley Mill, the Custom House and a boat being loaded. The business of the Customs House has been transferred to Wells.

St Margaret's and Beau Rivage. This terrace was a warehouse, presumably servicing the Mill, until it was converted into cottages in the early 1900s. The French connection is maintained on the row of cottages on the High Street called Maisons Bienvenues.

MAISONS
BIENVENUES

BRITISH SCHOOL

BRITISH SCHOOL

The British School was
built in 1860 at a cost
of £600 and once had
an attendance of 140
children.

Right These two
eighteenth-century
houses are situated on
The Fairstead which runs
above and parallel to the
High Street.

The twisting, narrow streets of a medieval port do not sit comfortably with the demands of the twenty-first century. They were clearly made for another age.

Picnic Fayre

Picnic Fayre was started by John Pryor in 1984 in the old forge. It is a wonderful stopping place for your picnic, with a wide choice of fresh food and a large range of top quality wines. Picnic Fayre is run by John and his wife Victoria, with Jane Goodwin.

Cley Smokehouse

Cley Smokehouse, owned by Glen Weston, is famous for its kippers and smoked prawns and has been producing smoked fish, shellfish and cured meats for over thirty years. Everything is smoked on the premises.

Made in Cley

The old village shop, with its beautifully preserved Regency fittings, has been home to Made in Cley since 1984. As well as a gallery there are workshops which include a pottery. The fired pots are loaded on to a wagon and travel to the gallery along tracks supplied by the Wells railway. Quay Proctor-Mears is the jeweller. Barbara Widdup and Mary Perry are two of the eight potters whose work is on sale.

83

Local painter Jane Hodgson signing copies of her book *Working North Norfolk – An Artists' Story* at the Pinkfoot Gallery.

Pinkfoot Gallery

Pinkfoot Gallery specialises in modern British nature art and shows a wide range of paintings and sculpture. Sarah Whittley also runs a publishing firm, Red Hare. [www.redharepublishing.co.uk]. Her partner in the gallery is artist Rachel Lockwood.

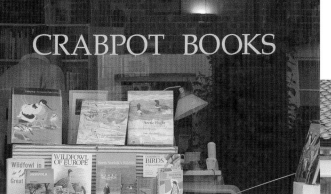

Crabpot Books

Crabpot bookshop on the High Street, run by Louise Abbot, is an excellent source of second-hand books, particularly bird books. It is also the domain of Marcia, the cat, who watches comings and goings with a very superior eye. Louise also runs another bookshop on Staithe Street in Wells.

This impressive window is the work of local artist, Tim Clarkson. He made it in 1987 whilst a student.

The George Hotel

Situated on a bend in the centre of the village is The George Hotel, formerly The George and Dragon. It has been a gathering point for bird watchers and naturalists for more than a century.

The copper fireplace, featuring the cross of St. George, was installed by previous landlord, Rodney Sewell in 1988.

The Bird Bible

Extracts from the famous Bird Bible held in the George Hotel. Birders visiting the George will find, displayed on a brass lectern in the bar, the famous Bible in which sightings of rare birds in the area have been recorded for thirty years and more. Best of all, it is crammed full of press cuttings and exquisite sketches from the pens of famous bird illustrators such as Richard Millington.

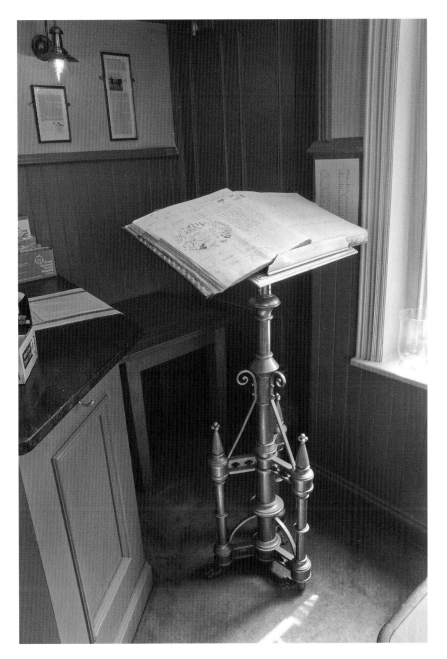

Together with the now closed Nancy's Café across the road, The George has long been a gathering place for birdwatchers from all over the country, paying pilgrimage to this East Coast Mecca where anything can, and does, turn up.

It was here that the Norfolk Naturalist's Trust, now the Norfolk Wildlife Trust, was established in 1926, immediately after the purchase of Cley Marsh.

Cley Visitor Centre

The Norfolk Wildlife Trust visitor centre was opened in 2007 and was designed with all the latest 'green' credentials, including solar panels, ground-source heating and a wind turbine to reduce its carbon footprint.

There are stunning views over the reserve. There are not many places where you can watch marsh harriers and avocets over a hot cup of coffee and a piece of cake!

A fund-raising campaign in 2013 has enabled the Trust to purchase Pope's Marsh, filling in the last piece in eight kilometres of coastal nature reserve from Blakeney to Salthouse.

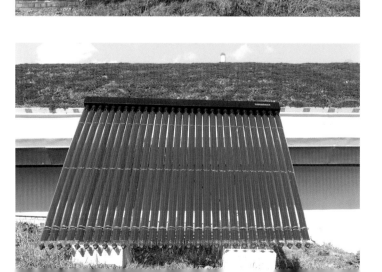

A fine panoramic view taken from one of the many hides on Cley Marsh. The famous mud 'scrapes' are a bountiful feeding area for waders, ducks and geese, throughout the year.

'There can scarcely be a serious bird watcher in the country who has not made the pilgrimage to Cley', wrote John Gooders in his book, *Where to Watch Birds*. These photos show some of the reasons why. The Reserve regularly records rare passage migrants as well as being a breeding ground for avocets, bearded tits, marsh harrier and bittern.

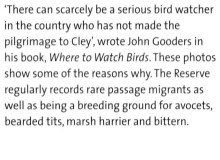

The Bishop Family

Pretty much synonymous with Cley Marsh, the Bishop family has provided the three wardens of the Reserve since it was established in 1926. Robert (*below left*) was the first warden, followed by Billy (*below*) and then Bernard, the current warden (*right*).

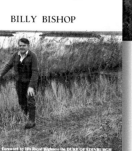

Cley Marsh
and its Birds

BILLY BISHOP

Foreword by His Royal Highness the DUKE OF EDINBURGH

An Anglia 'Survival' Book

Cley Marsh
and its Birds

Revised Edition
Billy and Bernard Bishop

'Bishop's Hide'

NORFOLK
WILDLIFE
TRUST

This hide was presented
to the Trust by
Lord Buxton
and was opened on December 2nd 1996
Built on the site of Irene Hide, destroyed
by floods in February 1996. It marks the
long association of the Bishop family
with Cley Marshes

NORFOLK ORNITHOLOGISTS ASSOCIATION

**WALSEY HILLS
RESERVE &
INFORMATION CENTRE**

**Guardian Spirit
of the East Bank**

A Celebration of the Life of R. A. Richardson

Moss Taylor

The East Bank

The East Bank epitomises Cley Marshes for generations of bird watchers. For those of an earlier generation, Richard Richardson symbolised the East Bank, where he cut a distinctive figure in his black leather jacket and beret, holding court to visitors.

Moss Taylor's excellent biography, *Guardian Spirit of the East Bank*, captures perfectly both this enigmatic character and a different era of bird watching.

Robert Gillmor

Robert Gillmor was a founder member of the Society
of Wildlife Artists and Chairman for many years.
He and his wife, Sue, have lived in Cley since 1978.
He is to current generations of birders and artists,
what Charles Tunnicliffe and Eric Ennion were to the
previous generation; an inspiration, with an instantly
recognizable style. Robert's illustrations have featured
on countless covers of the RSPB *Birds* Magazine and
dust covers of *The New Naturalist* series. As the title of
his popular book of linocuts says, he has been happily
'Cutting Away' up the lane in Cley for many years.

The Birds of Blakeney Point

Andy Stoddart and Steve Joyner

The Three Swallows

Sitting outside the Three Swallows on Newgate Green at Cley is one of the better ways of passing a summer afternoon. There are indeed swallows skimming over the grass, hawking for insects. Many years ago, there was a tethered goat chewing away on the Green, but little has changed from the view on the 1950s postcard opposite.

St. Margarets Church, Cley   9318

St Margaret's Church

Set on a gentle rise above the village green, St Margaret's would have overlooked the harbour which stretched across the valley to Wiveton and whose medieval traders and merchants financed the building of this magnificent church.

St Margaret's has some wonderful carved wooden pew ends and brass memorials, but also take care to look up, so as not to miss the carved figures high up in the nave.

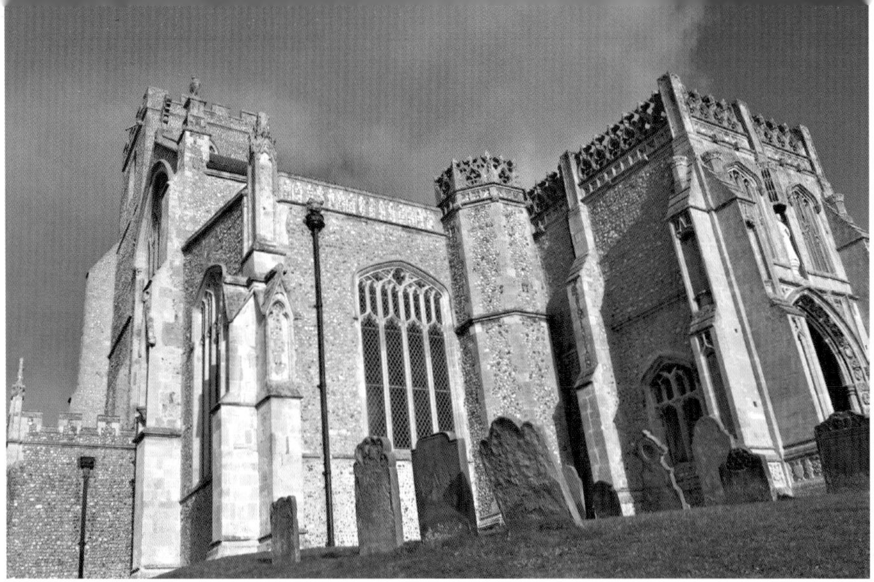

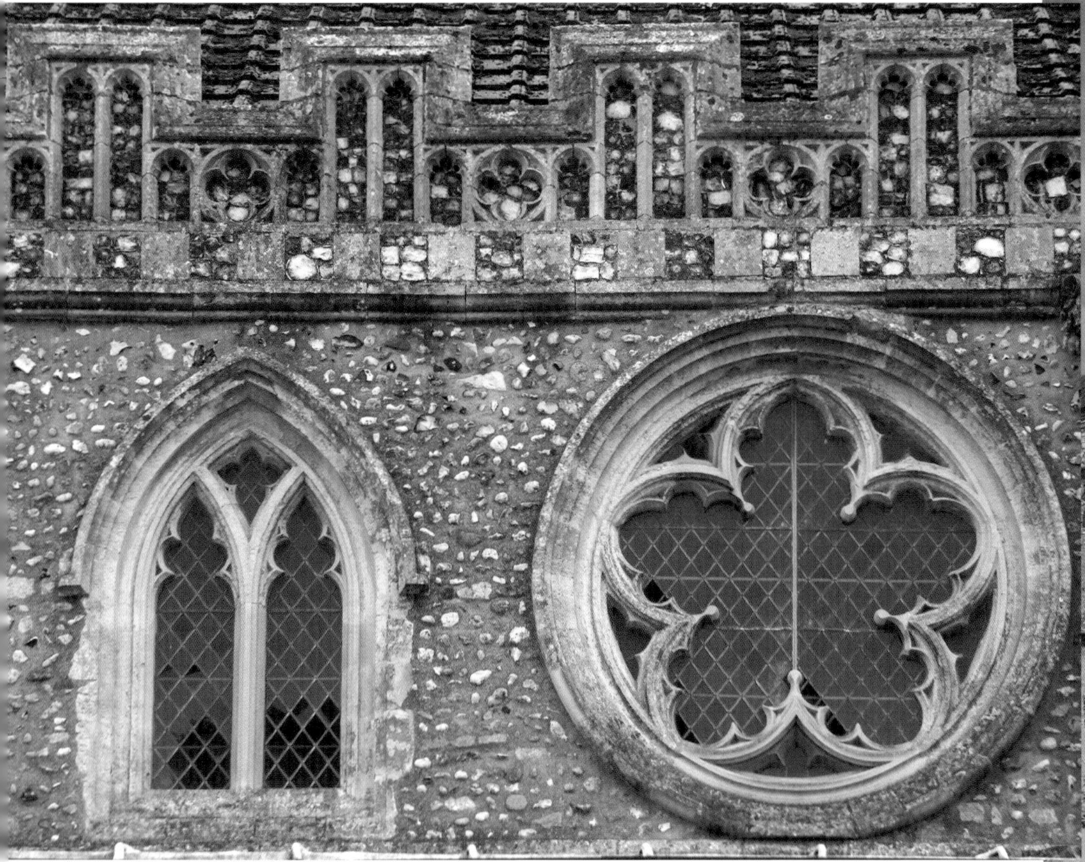

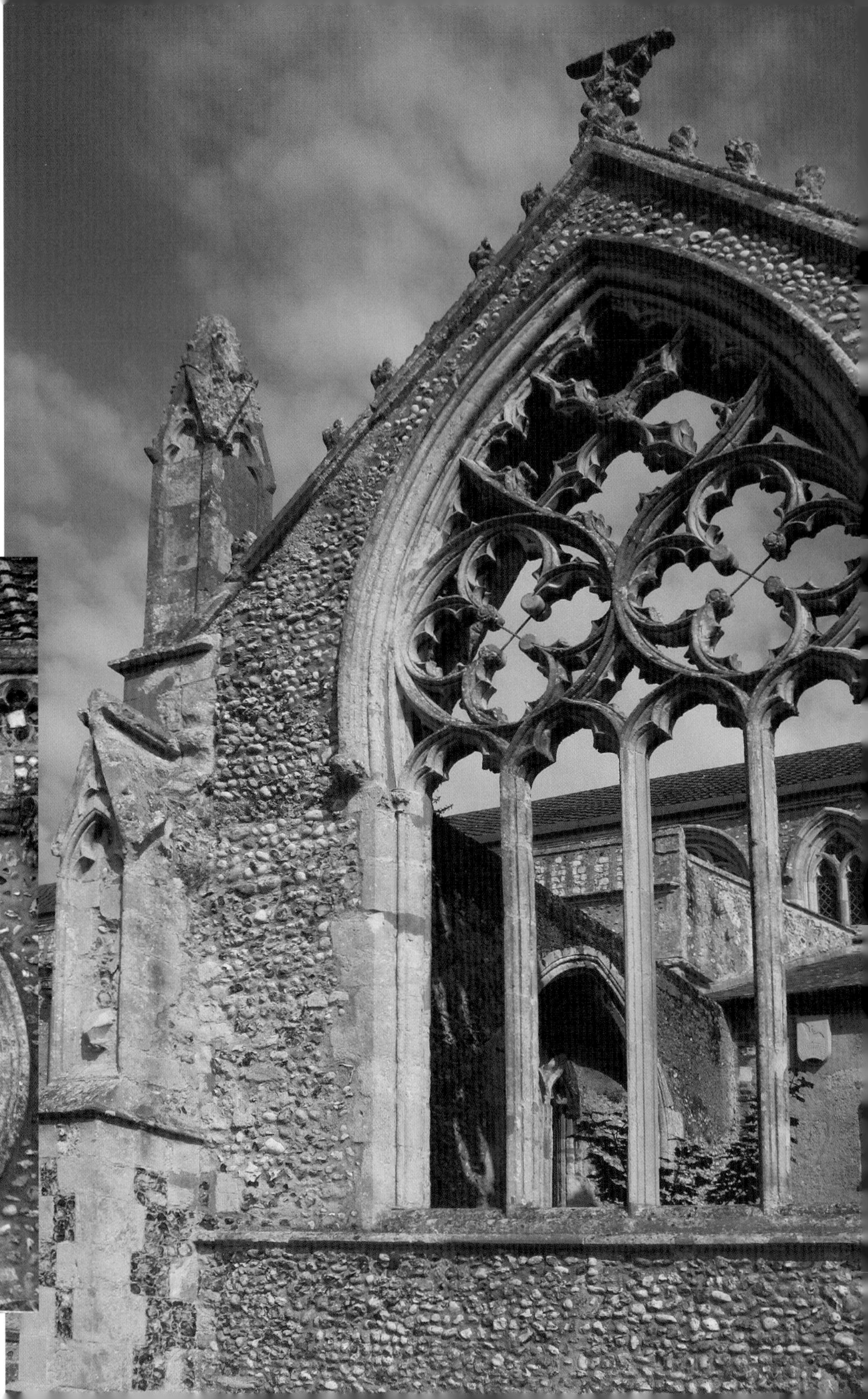

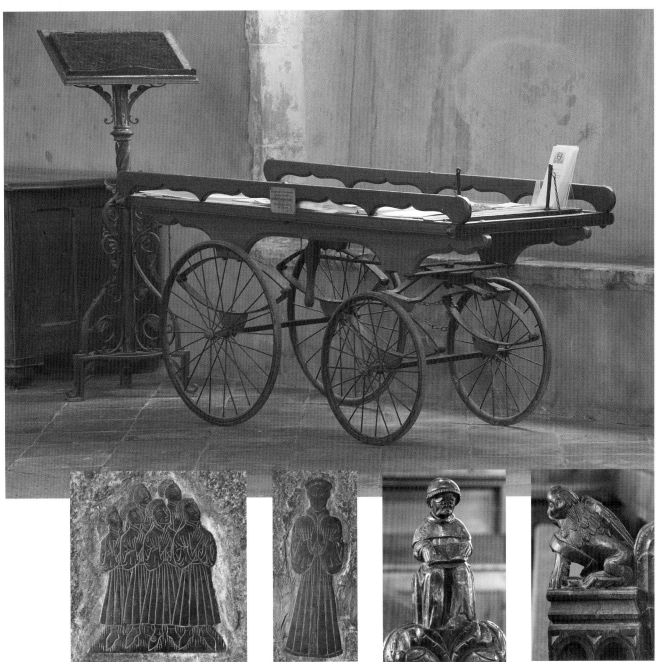

Cley is renowned as a hot-spot for producing rarities, as well as hundreds of twitchers, so the white-collared sparrow brought them out in force. This North American vagrant arrived in the garden of retired vicar, Richard Bending, in January 1998 and stayed for ten weeks. The collection box put out by the Cley Bird Club raised more than £6000 which was used to restore the west window in St. Margaret's Church. You may need your binoculars to locate the sparrow in the large window. The illustration is from a painting by local birdwatcher, Richard Millington.

IN
LOVING MEMORY OF
BLANCHE MARY
RANDALL
1893 – 1981
AND HER NEPHEW
ROLEY RANDALL
1907 · 1996

HENRY RUSSELL
BOYLE
1908 – 2002

Wilfrid Seymour
Andrews
MA(Oxon) PhD
1912-1994
Clerk in Holy Orders
Scholar and Schoolmaster
and Nell
née Letts
His beloved Wife
for 55 years
1916 - 2003

In
Fond Memory
of
FRIEDA ELLEN STARR
1904 – 1995
And
FLORENCE IVY STARR
1894 – 1972
Late of Commerce House
Cley
Village Shop
1906 ~ 1974

CHARLES
ALASTAIR HARDY
IVENS
(CARL)
1912-1993

✝
THOMAS
BIRD
Engineer & Sportsman
Dearly loved by his
family & friends
1901-1979

HOLD ON TO THE GOOD
CHRISTOPHER
MARCUS
PUGH-SMITH
30TH NOVEMBER 1988
TO 18TH MARCH 1989

PETER RAPKIN
WESTALL
1920 – 1970
PRIEST – DOCTOR

JACK
LINTOTT
1910 ~ 1991
Sportsman

I LOVE CLEY CHURCH
1918
Barbara
Davis
1998
IT REFRESHES ME DAILY

FELIX
SARA FELICITY
DEARDEN
Journalist
1955 - 1989

DEARLY LOVED HUSBAND FATHER AND GRANDFATHER
DAVID
CHALONER
· KEYS ·
12.2.1934 ~ 20.1.2009

✝
· LOVING WIFE · MOTHER & GRANDMOTHER · MVM ·
JANE
MARGARET
HUDSON
1930 -1998
NATURALIST · PAINTER · FRIEND TO ALL

IN LOVING MEMORY OF
DAVID
WEEDON
FEBRUARY 1927
JULY 2005
SUB-POST MASTER

Jean
Baker
14. 7. 1926
25. 4. 2011
A lass unparalleled

These memorials are some of the many set into the south wall of the churchyard.

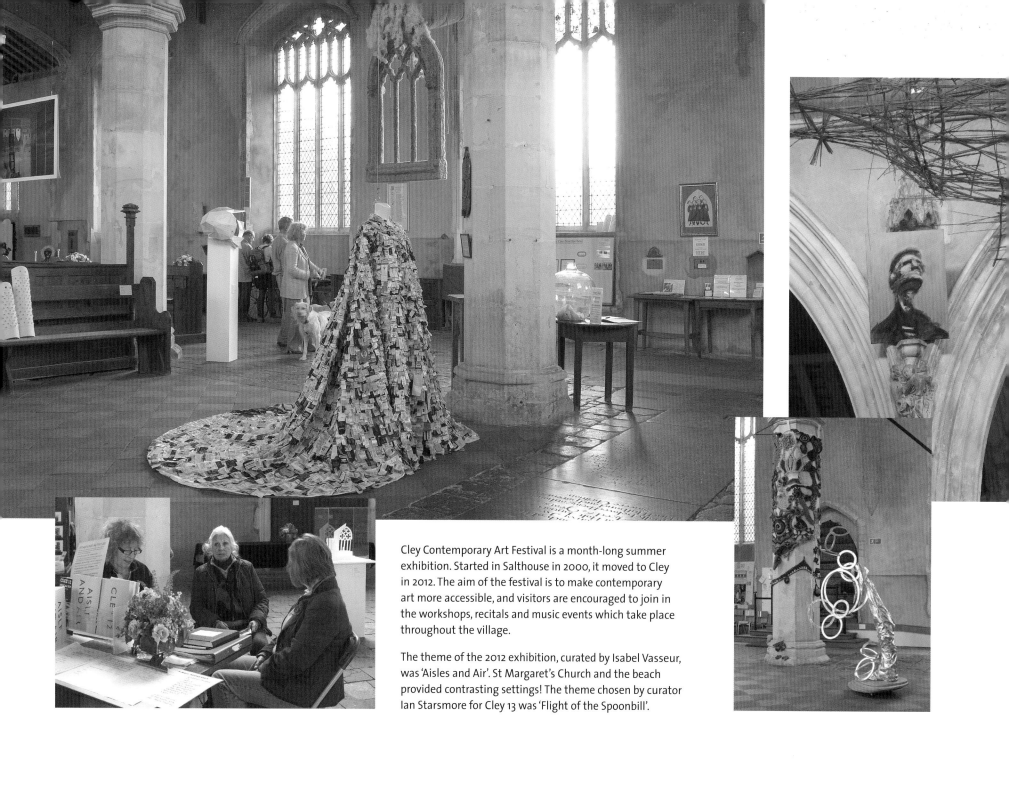

Cley Contemporary Art Festival is a month-long summer exhibition. Started in Salthouse in 2000, it moved to Cley in 2012. The aim of the festival is to make contemporary art more accessible, and visitors are encouraged to join in the workshops, recitals and music events which take place throughout the village.

The theme of the 2012 exhibition, curated by Isabel Vasseur, was 'Aisles and Air'. St Margaret's Church and the beach provided contrasting settings! The theme chosen by curator Ian Starsmore for Cley 13 was 'Flight of the Spoonbill'.

Cley's steeply sloped shingle bank is popular with sea anglers and hosts a few local fishing boats. The three kilometre walk westward is perhaps the best way to approach Blakeney Point and to appreciate its remote beauty.

The Watch House (*top right*), half way along the beach, features in Jack Higgins' novel, *The Eagle has Landed*. It was built about 1830 to help stop smuggling and has also been a weather station.

In 1930 it was bought by the National Trust and leased to the Girl Guides. By 1992 it had fallen into disrepair and the Watch House Trust was formed to make it habitable. It was then leased during the summer to visitors.

This metal object is a WWII coastal defence installation, an Allan Williams turret, which had a garrison of two or, if necessary three, men for whom there were folding seats inside.

Carl Greenacre and Henry Randell reed cutting. Done during the winter, it keeps the marshes in good condition and provides an income. Although the cutting is done by machine, tying and stacking are still done by hand.

Jane Hodgson is a local artist who specialises in portraying the traditional industries of the coast and the people who work in them.

The coast road follows the line of the shore as it
was before the marshes were reclaimed.

Morston

More than most of the villages which straddle the north Norfolk coastline, Morston seems to have been affected less by the currents of change. It would be easy to drive through the village and miss the track leading down to the harbour where the boats ply their trade to Blakeney Point, much as they have done since the 1940s.

Morston Hall

Morston Hall hotel is owned and run by Galton and Tracy Blackiston. Originally a country house dating from the 18th century, the hotel has an excellent cuisine with a Michelin Star and three red rosettes. It is set in a lovely garden and is only a short walk from Morston Quay.

The Anchor

The Anchor Inn dates back to the 1830s and for most of the last century was run by the Temple family. Since June 2011, it has been refurbished and is run by long time school friends Rowan Glennie and Harry Fowler.

The Anchor's connections with the Temple family go back to 1899. The booking office for Temple's seal trips is still in the front of the inn.

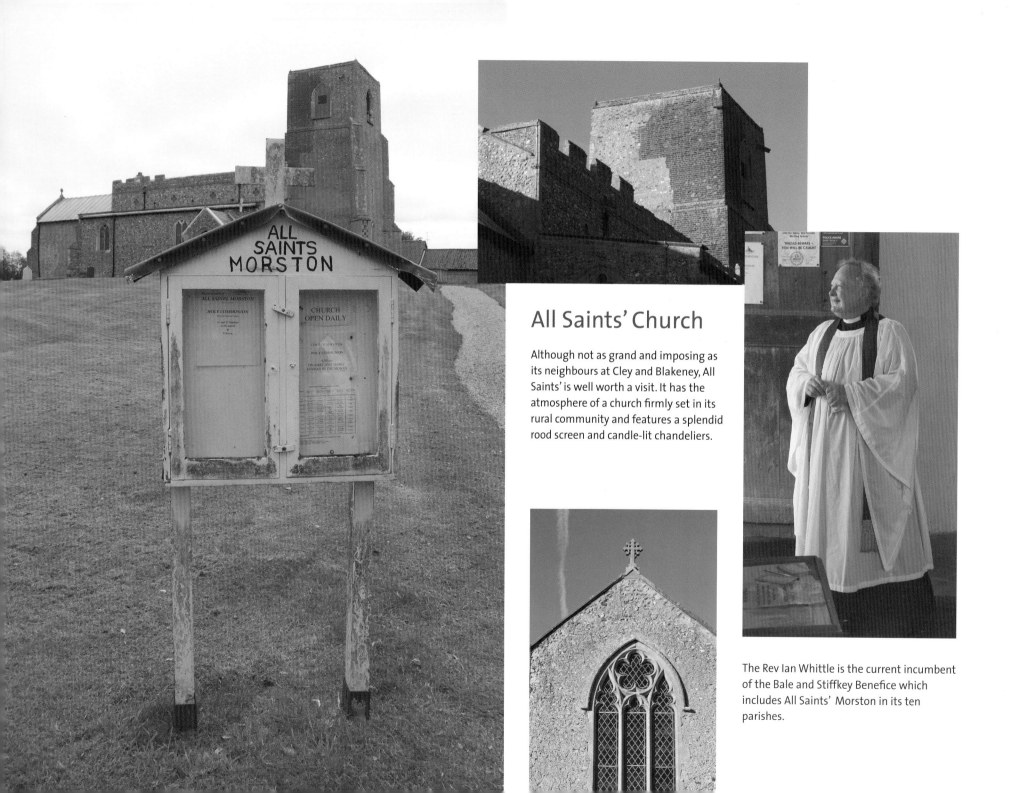

All Saints' Church

Although not as grand and imposing as its neighbours at Cley and Blakeney, All Saints' is well worth a visit. It has the atmosphere of a church firmly set in its rural community and features a splendid rood screen and candle-lit chandeliers.

The Rev Ian Whittle is the current incumbent of the Bale and Stiffkey Benefice which includes All Saints' Morston in its ten parishes.

The rood screen shows the four evangelists and four doctors of the early church. In an attempt to extirpate any vestiges of the 'Old Faith', Gregory's papal tiara and Augustine's cardinal's hat were scratched out by Protestant reformers.

Even in the twenty-first century there is no electricity in Morston church, only chandeliers, made by local artist Ned Hamond.

National Trust staff: Graham Baldock, Sally Chandler, Graham Lubbock, Marilyn Lubbock, Chris Everitt, Emily Chittenden, Ian Wolfe, John Sizer and Victoria Egan.

MORSTON CRAB STALL

www.hiddennorfolk.co.uk

Look here for Hidden Norfolks daily news

Sailing Times
Monday: 8-12
Tuesday: 9-1300
Weds 9.30-1330
Thurs: 10-1400

Gannets, Wimbrels migrating
Come + join us!

Contact No: 07776251158
for all enquiries 01362 668024

OYSTERS
FRESH CRAB
PEELED PRAWNS
SHELL-ON PRAWNS
PEELED SHRIMPS
COCKLES : WHELKS : MUSSELS
CRAYFISH : KING PRAWNS

SANDWICHES

Morston harbour

Seal trips, mussel, crab and lobster boats and fishermen as well as leisure sailors all use the quay in the tidal creek, keeping the harbour busy all year round.

The National Trust Information Centre has an observation tower with panoramic views over Blakeney Point National Nature Reserve.

Seal trips

The Bean, Temple and Bishop families have all been running boat trips out to Blakeney Point for over fifty years. More recently, Blakeney Point Seal Trips, run by Mike and Jo Girling have started plying the route.

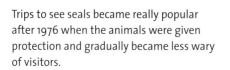

Trips to see seals became really popular after 1976 when the animals were given protection and gradually became less wary of visitors.

Both common and grey seals breed on the Point – common seals have their pups in the summer, grey seals in the winter. It is usually possible to see seals throughout the year. In recent years, numbers have peaked at about 500.

The bridges at Morston are now regularly maintained but, in the past, were sometimes very rickety structures. They were put up to give access to the harbour for fishermen.

Charlie Ward

The sign at Charlie Ward's gate is a leeboard from the sailing barge *Eliza Patience*, wrecked in Holkham Bay in 1903 during the 'great gale' of 11th September.

Juno was built by Charlie Ward, modelled on the shallow draught London barges which plied the east coast in the last century. She was launched in 2000 and can be chartered for coastal sailing.

Opposite: Juno at Blakeney

Norfolk etc

Norfolk etc is a family business run by James and Victoria Cowan. They teach sailing and power boating in Blakeney harbour with Tom Neall (*above left*).

146

Wiveton

Wiveton was a flourishing port with its own shipbuilding industry until reclamation of the land and silting up of the channel over centuries left the village over a mile from the coast.

Wiveton's stone bridge over the river Glaven is known locally as 'the bridge to nowhere'. It is a listed monument and may be the oldest bridge – it was built in the early fourteenth century – still open to commercial vehicles.

Wiveton Café and Farm Shop

With its bright Mediterranean colours, Wiveton Hall Café is a
popular stopping off place on the coast road. There is a large outside
seating area with views over farmland and marshes to the sea.

This is a working farm with hens and chickens running about. It is a great place to pick your own strawberries and raspberries in season.

Wiveton Hall

On the same site as Wiveton Farm and Café, the Hall is an imposing, flint-fronted merchant's house with Dutch gables, dating from the seventeenth century. A new wing was added in the Edwardian period and is now available for holiday rental.

Wiveton Bell

Parts of the Wiveton Bell date back to the fourteenth century, though it is now thoroughly modernised. The current owners are Berni Morritt and Sandy Butcher. Dean Horgan is the chef.

Charles Clark was landlord of the Bell in the 1990s. He loved cars and installed an E-type Jaguar engine in the fireplace with the exhaust going up the chimney so that the engine could be run. There was always something going on at the Bell, guest speakers, film shows and an annual Classic Car Rally which began in 1995. Charles was lost at sea in a boating accident in May 1998.

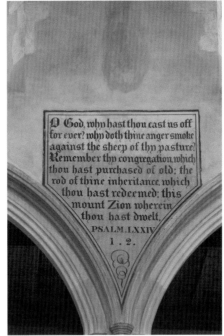

St Mary's Church

The nineteenth-century additions to the church are not to everybody's taste. The coloured turquoise and orange glass has been described as 'making you feel as though you are under water', while the biblical text pictured here is 'an awful inscription which needs to be whitewashed out'. We all have our own views it seems.

In 1779 the Rector of St Mary's achieved notoriety by being hanged at Tyburn for shooting dead his fiancée outside the Haymarket Theatre, London.

The Ralph Greneway Charity

In common with many villages, Wiveton has benefitted for more than 500 years from the legacy of one of its successful medieval merchants, Ralph Greneway. Greneway was born the son of a ship owner in the village and made his fortune as a merchant in London.

This plaque commemorates the legacy which provided for the poor and needy of the village in the first Elizabethan age. The current trustees ensure that the charity continues to meet the different needs of the second Elizabethan era.

162

Wiveton's bellringers are David Sidgwick, John Norman, Howard Rooke (Tower Captain), Sheila Rump, Theo Crowder and Robin Combe. The bells are rung for weddings in Wiveton and at Cley, when it is hoped that the wind will be blowing in the right direction so that they can be heard across the valley.

Tony Hoare
Reed panel maker

Tony Hoare works with reeds collected from Cley Marsh. It took him two years to perfect the skill of making the reed panels which are now his trademark.

Godfrey Sayers

Godfrey Sayers' art gallery is a landmark on the Carnser in Blakeney where his converted van has stood since 1975.

Godfrey grew up on the north Norfolk coast and was a longshore fisherman before taking up painting the famous coastal landscapes and skies.

The painting of Morston harbour, which can be seen in the church, shows how Morston might have looked when the Glaven ports were thriving.